A Review of the Events of 1986

The 1987 World Book Year Book

The Annual Supplement to The World Book Encyclopedia

World Book, Inc.

a Scott Fetzer company

Chicago London Sydney Toronto

Printed in the United States of America.
ISBN 0-7166-0487-6
ISSN 0084-1439
Library of Congress Catalog Card Number: 62-4818

Staff

Publisher
William H. Nault

Editor in Chief
Robert O. Zeleny

Editorial Staff
Executive Editor
A. Richard Harmet

Managing Editor
Wayne Wille

Associate Editor
Sara Dreyfuss

Senior Editors
David L. Dreier
Kevin J. Hawker
Mary A. Krier
Barbara A. Mayes
Jay Myers
Joan Stephenson
Rod Such

Contributing Editors
Gary A. Alt
Darlene R. Stille

Research Editor
Irene B. Keller

Index Editor
Claire Bolton

Statistical Editor
Tom Klonoski

Editorial Assistant
Ethel Matthews

Art Staff
Executive Art Director
William Hammond

Art Director
Roberta Dimmer

Senior Artist
Nikki Conner

Artists
Alice F. Dole
Alexandra Kalantzis
Melanie J. Lawson
Lucy Smith

Photography Director
John S. Marshall

Senior Photographs Editor
Sandra M. Ozanick

Photographs Editor
Barbara A. Bennett

Assistant Photographs Editor
Geralyn Swietek

Research Services
Director
Mary Norton

Researcher
David Shannon

Library Services
Mary Kayaian, Head
Susan O'Connell

Cartographic Services
H. George Stoll, Head
Wayne K. Pichler

Product Production
Executive Director
Peter Mollman

Director of Manufacturing
Joseph C. LaCount

Research and Development Manager
Henry Koval

Pre-Press Services
Jerry Stack, Director
Lori Frankel
Madelyn Krzak
Alfred J. Mozdzen
Barbara Podczerwinski

Proofreaders
Ann Dillon
Marguerite Hoye
Esther Johns
Daniel Marotta

Contents

8   The Year in Brief
An essay captures the spirit of 1986, and a month-by-month listing presents some of the year's significant events.

32   Special Reports
Seven articles—plus a special two-part feature—give in-depth treatment to wide-ranging subjects of current interest and importance.

34   The Age-Old Business of Espionage
by Douglas Lanphier Wheeler
Throughout history, nations have spied on one another, but never before on such a huge scale.

48   The New Look in Zoos by Eugene J. Walter, Jr.
Large, stunningly realistic new exhibits display animals as they have never been seen before in captivity.

64   Big Boom in Women's Sports by Martha J. Nelson
Women athletes are running and swimming faster, jumping farther, and competing in events once considered too difficult for females.

78   The U.S. Constitution: 200 Years of History
A special two-part feature marks the bicentennial celebration of this vital document in U.S. history.

    80   A More Perfect Union
    A colorful pictorial feature tells the story of the constitutional convention of 1787.
    86   The Constitution: Why It Has Endured by Stanley I. Kutler
    The U.S. Constitution is the oldest written constitution in the world, and it has achieved that status by being able to expand and develop to meet the changing needs of the United States.

100   Problems in the Parks by Philip Shabecoff
Air pollution, overcrowding, and development are tarnishing the splendor of United States national parks.

116   The Hazards of Teen-Age Drinking by John Camper
The number-one drug problem among young people in the United States is not cocaine or marijuana—it's alcohol.

130   New Life for Two Old Treasures by Walter Hays
Scientific restorations are rescuing the Sistine ceiling and *The Last Supper* from centuries of grime, humidity, vandalism, and previous destructive restoration attempts.

4

144 **Mexico: from Boom to Bust** by Susan Kaufman Purcell
Despite its vast oil resources, Mexico faces the worst economic crisis in its
history, intensified by political corruption and a growing population.

158 **A Year in Perspective**
THE YEAR BOOK casts a glance back 100 years at the events and the personalities
that made the year 1886 what it was.

172 **The Year on File**
A 50-question quiz—on pages 174 and 175—tests your knowledge of some of
the events of 1986, after which YEAR BOOK contributors report the year's major
happenings in alphabetically arranged articles, from "Advertising" to "Zoos."

528 **World Book Supplement**
Seven new or revised articles are reprinted from the 1987 edition of THE WORLD
BOOK ENCYCLOPEDIA: "AIDS," "Artificial Heart," "Cyclosporine," "Magellanic
Clouds," "Milky Way," "World War I," and "World War II."

581 **Dictionary Supplement**
Here is a listing of important words and definitions that are included in the 1987
edition of THE WORLD BOOK DICTIONARY.

585 **Index**
An 18-page cumulative index covers the contents of the 1985, 1986, and 1987
editions of THE YEAR BOOK.

A tear-out page of cross-reference tabs for insertion in THE WORLD
BOOK ENCYCLOPEDIA appears after page 16.

Contributors

Contributors not listed on these pages are members of THE WORLD BOOK YEAR BOOK editorial staff.

Adachi, Ken, B.A., M.A.; Literary Critic, *The Toronto Star.* [CANADIAN LITERATURE]

Alexiou, Arthur G., B.S.E.E., M.S.E.E.; Assistant Secretary, Intergovernmental Oceanographic Commission. [OCEAN]

Andrews, Peter J., B.A., M.S.; Free-Lance Writer; Biochemist. [CHEMISTRY]

Apseloff, Marilyn Fain, B.A., M.A.; Associate Professor, Kent State University. [LITERATURE FOR CHILDREN]

Barber, Peggy, B.A., M.L.S.; Associate Executive Director, American Library Association. [AMERICAN LIBRARY ASSOCIATION; LIBRARY]

Bednarski, P. J., Entertainment-Media Business Reporter, *Chicago Sun-Times.* [RADIO; TELEVISION]

Berman, Howard A., M.H.L.; Rabbi, Chicago Sinai Congregation. [JEWS AND JUDAISM]

Blackadar, Alfred K., A.B., Ph.D.; Professor Emeritus, The Pennsylvania State University. [WEATHER]

Bradsher, Henry S., A.B., B.J.; Foreign Affairs Analyst. [ASIA and Asian Country Articles]

Breslin, Paul, B.A., Ph.D.; Associate Professor of English, Northwestern University. [POETRY]

Brodsky, Arthur R., B.A., M.S.J.; Senior Editor, *Communications Daily.* [COMMUNICATIONS]

Brown, Kenneth, former Editor, *United Kingdom Press Gazette.* [EUROPE and Western European Country Articles]

Bruske, Edward H., Reporter, *The Washington Post.* [COURTS; CRIME]

Bukro, Casey, B.S.J., M.S.J.; Environment Writer, *Chicago Tribune.* [ENVIRONMENTAL POLLUTION]

Campbell, Robert, B.A., M.S., M. Arch.; Architect and Architecture Critic. [ARCHITECTURE]

Camper, John, B.A.; Reporter, *Chicago Tribune.* [Special Report: THE HAZARDS OF TEEN-AGE DRINKING]

Campion, Owen F., A.B.; Editor, *The Tennessee Register.* [ROMAN CATHOLIC CHURCH]

Cardinale, Diane P., B.A.; Assistant Communications Director, Toy Manufacturers of America. [TOYS AND GAMES]

Cawthorne, David M., Reporter, *The Journal of Commerce.* [Transportation Articles]

Coffman, Edward M., A.B.J., M.A., Ph.D.; Professor of History, University of Wisconsin. [WORLD BOOK SUPPLEMENT: WORLD WAR I]

Cooney, Jane, Executive Director, Canadian Library Association. [CANADIAN LIBRARY ASSOCIATION]

Cormier, Frank, B.S.J., M.S.J.; former White House Correspondent, Associated Press. [U.S. Government Articles]

Cormier, Margot, B.A., M.A.; Free-Lance Writer. [U.S. Government Articles]

Cromie, William J., B.S., M.S.; Executive Director, Council for Advancement of Science Writing. [SPACE EXPLORATION]

Cviic, Chris, B.A., B.S.; East European Specialist and Leader Writer, *The Economist.* [Eastern European Country Articles]

DeFrank, Thomas M., B.A., M.A.; Deputy Bureau Chief and White House Correspondent, *Newsweek* magazine. [ARMED FORCES]

Dent, Thomas H., Executive Director, The Cat Fanciers' Association, Inc. [CAT]

DiCesare, Annmaria B., A.B.; Director of Information Services, Magazine Publishers Association. [MAGAZINE]

Drotman, D. Peter, M.D., M.P.H.; Medical Epidemiologist, AIDS Program, Centers for Disease Control. [WORLD BOOK SUPPLEMENT: AIDS]

Duffy, Robert, Political Writer, *The Toronto Star.* [TORONTO]

Edmonds, Patricia L., B.A.; City-County Bureau, *Detroit Free Press.* [DETROIT]

Ellis, Barbara W., B.A., B.S.; Editor/Publications Director, *American Horticulturist.* [GARDENING]

Elsasser, Glen R., B.A., M.S.; Reporter, *Chicago Tribune.* [SUPREME COURT OF THE UNITED STATES]

Evans, Sandra, B.S.J.; Staff Writer, *The Washington Post.* [WASHINGTON, D.C.]

Farr, David M. L., M.A., D.Phil.; Professor of History, Carleton University, Ottawa. [CANADA; Canadian Province Articles; MULRONEY, M. BRIAN; SAUVÉ, JEANNE M.; TRUDEAU, PIERRE E.]

Feather, Leonard, B.Mus.; Author, *Encyclopedia of Jazz.* [POPULAR MUSIC (Close-Up)]

Fisher, Robert W., B.A., M.A.; Senior Economist, U.S. Bureau of Labor Statistics. [LABOR]

Fitzgerald, Mark, B.A.; Midwest Editor, *Editor & Publisher* magazine. [NEWSPAPER; PUBLISHING]

Francis, Henry G., B.S.; Executive Editor, American Contract Bridge League. [BRIDGE]

Gatty, Bob, President, Gatty Communications. [FOOD]

Goldner, Nancy, B.A.; Dance Critic, *The Philadelphia Inquirer.* [DANCING]

Goldstein, Jane, B.A.; Director of Publicity, Santa Anita Park. [HORSE RACING]

Gordon, Margaret T., B.S.J., M.S.J., Ph.D.; Director, Center for Urban Affairs and Policy Research, Northwestern University. [CITY]

Gould, William James, B.A.; Free-Lance Writer and Editor, England. [ENGLAND]

Graham, Jarlath J., B.A.; Director of External Relations, *Advertising Age.* [ADVERTISING]

Grigadean, Jerry, B.S., M.Mus., Ph.D.; Producer, Grigadean Productions. [POPULAR MUSIC]

Hannan, Patrick, B.A.; Producer/Presenter, British Broadcasting Corporation. [WALES]

Harakas, Stanley S., B.A., B.D., Th.D.; Professor, Holy Cross Greek Orthodox School of Theology. [EASTERN ORTHODOX CHURCHES]

Haverstock, Nathan A., A.B.; Affiliate Scholar, Oberlin College. [LATIN AMERICA and Latin-American Country Articles]

Hays, Walter, International Journalist, Rome. [Special Report: NEW LIFE FOR TWO OLD TREASURES]

Herreid, Clyde Freeman, II, A.B., M.Sc., Ph.D.; Professor of Biological Sciences, State University of New York at Buffalo. [ZOOLOGY]

Hester, Thomas R., B.A., Ph.D.; Professor of Anthropology and Director, Center for Archaeological Research, The University of Texas at San Antonio. [ARCHAEOLOGY (Close-Up)]

Higgins, James V., B.A.; Automotive Reporter, *The Detroit News.* [AUTOMOBILE]

Hillgren, Sonja, B.J., M.A.; Reporter, United Press International. [FARM AND FARMING]

Hunzeker, Jeanne M., D.S.W.; Associate Professor, Southern University at New Orleans. [CHILD WELFARE]

Jacobi, Peter P., B.S.J., M.S.J.; Professor of Journalism, Indiana University. [CLASSICAL MUSIC]

Johanson, Donald C., B.S., M.A., Ph.D.; Director, Institute of Human Origins. [ANTHROPOLOGY]

Joseph, Lou, B.A.; Senior Medical Writer, Hill and Knowlton, Inc. [DENTISTRY]

Kisor, Henry, B.A., M.S.J.; Book Editor, *Chicago Sun-Times.* [LITERATURE]

Knapp, Elaine Stuart, B.A.; Editor, Council of State Governments. [STATE GOVERNMENT]

Koenig, Louis W., B.A., M.A., Ph.D., L.H.D.; Professor of Government, New York University. [CIVIL RIGHTS]

Kolgraf, Ronald, B.A., M.A.; General Manager and Publisher, *Adweek* and *Computer & Electronics Marketing.* [MANUFACTURING]

Kuersten, Joan, B.A.; Editor/Writer, National PTA. [NATIONAL PTA]

Kutler, Stanley I., Ph.D.; E. Gordon Fox Professor of American Institutions, University of Wisconsin. [Special Report: THE CONSTITUTION: WHY IT HAS ENDURED]

Langdon, Robert, Visiting Fellow, Department of Pacific and SEAsian History, Australian National University. [PACIFIC ISLANDS]

Larsen, Paul A., P.E., B.S., Ch.E.; Member: American Philatelic Society; Collectors Club of Chicago; Fellow, Royal Philatelic Society, London; past President, British Caribbean Philatelic Study Group. [STAMP COLLECTING]

Lawrence, Al, A.B., M.A., M.Ed.; Associate Director, United States Chess Federation. [CHESS]

Lawrence, Richard, B.E.E.; Washington Correspondent, *The Journal of Commerce.* [INTERNATIONAL TRADE]

Levy, Emanuel, B.A.; Editor, *Insurance Advocate.* [INSURANCE]

Lewis, David C., M.D.; Professor of Medicine and Community Health, Brown University. [DRUG ABUSE]

Liebenow, Beverly B., B.S.; Author and Free-Lance Writer. [AFRICA and African Country Articles]

Liebenow, J. Gus, B.A., M.A., Ph.D.; Professor of Political Science/African Studies, Indiana University. [AFRICA and African Country Articles]

Litsky, Frank, B.S.; Sports Writer, *The New York Times.* [Sports Articles]

Maki, John M., B.A., M.A., Ph.D.; Professor Emeritus, University of Massachusetts. [JAPAN]

Mandile, Tony, Free-Lance Writer/ Photographer. [FISHING; HUNTING]

Maran, Stephen P., B.S., M.A., Ph.D.; Senior Staff Scientist, National Aeronautics and Space Administration-Goddard Space Flight Center. [ASTRONOMY]

Martin, Lee, Associate Editor/Columnist, Miller Magazines. [COIN COLLECTING]

Marty, Martin E., Ph.D.; Fairfax M. Cone Distinguished Service Professor, University of Chicago. [PROTESTANTISM; RELIGION]

Mather, Ian, M.A.; Defense Correspondent, *The Observer,* London. [GREAT BRITAIN; GREAT BRITAIN (Close-Up); IRELAND; NORTHERN IRELAND]

Maugh, Thomas H., II, Ph.D.; Science Writer, *Los Angeles Times.* [BIOCHEMISTRY]

McCarron, John F., B.S.J., M.S.J.; Urban Affairs Writer, *Chicago Tribune.* [CHICAGO]

McLaren, Christie, B.A.; Reporter, *The Globe and Mail,* Toronto. [Special Report Close-Up: CHALLENGES TO CANADA'S PARKS]

Medicine, Beatrice, Ph.D.; Director, Native Centre, and Professor of Anthropology, University of Calgary. [INDIAN, AMERICAN]

Merina, Victor, A.A., B.A., M.S.; Staff Writer, *Los Angeles Times.* [LOS ANGELES]

Millard, Patricia L., B.S.; Managing Editor, American Correctional Association. [PRISON]

Miller, J. D. B., M.Ec., M.A.; Professor of International Relations, Australian National University, Canberra. [AUSTRALIA]

Moores, Eldridge M., B.S., Ph.D.; Professor of Geology, University of California at Davis. [GEOLOGY]

Moritz, Owen, B.A.; Urban Affairs Editor, New York *Daily News.* [NEW YORK CITY]

Morris, Bernadine, B.A., M.A.; Fashion Critic, *The New York Times.* [FASHION]

Morris, Mark, M.A., Ph.D.; Professor of Astronomy, University of California at Los Angeles. [WORLD BOOK SUPPLEMENT: MAGELLANIC CLOUDS; MILKY WAY]

Nelson, Martha J., B.A.; Editor in Chief, *Women's Sports and Fitness* magazine. [Special Report: BIG BOOM IN WOMEN'S SPORTS]

Newcomb, Eldon H., A.B., A.M., Ph.D.; Chairman, Department of Botany, University of Wisconsin-Madison. [BOTANY]

Oatis, William N., former United Nations Correspondent, Associated Press. [UNITED NATIONS]

Pierce, William S., B.S., M.D.; Professor of Surgery; Chief, Division of Artificial Organs, College of Medicine, Pennsylvania State University. [WORLD BOOK SUPPLEMENT: ARTIFICIAL HEART]

Pollock, Steve, M.A.; Executive Editor, *Popular Photography.* [PHOTOGRAPHY]

Priestaf, Iris, B.A., M.A., Ph.D.; Water Resources Specialist, David Keith Todd Consulting Engineers. [WATER]

Purcell, Susan Kaufman, B.A., M.A., Ph.D.; Director, Latin American Program, Council on Foreign Relations, New York City. [Special Report: MEXICO: FROM BOOM TO BUST]

Raloff, Janet, B.S.J., M.S.J.; Policy/Technology Editor, *Science News.* [ENERGY SUPPLY (Close-Up)]

Reinken, Charles, B.B.A., M.A.; Associate Editor, *The Houston Post.* [HOUSTON]

Reitz, Bruce A., M.D.; Professor of Surgery, Johns Hopkins School of Medicine, Johns Hopkins University. [WORLD BOOK SUPPLEMENT: CYCLOSPORINE]

Robinson, Walter, B.A.; Contributing Editor, *Art in America* Magazine. [ART]

Rowse, Arthur E., I.A., M.B.A.; Associate Editor, Washington Letter, *U.S. News & World Report.* [CONSUMERISM; SAFETY]

Shabecoff, Philip, B.A., M.A.; Correspondent, Washington Bureau, *The New York Times.* [Special Report: PROBLEMS IN THE PARKS]

Shand, David A., B.C.A., B.Com.; Consultant, The Treasury, Wellington, New Zealand. [NEW ZEALAND]

Shapiro, Howard S., B.S.; Deputy New Jersey Editor, *The Philadelphia Inquirer.* [PHILADELPHIA]

Shearer, Warren W., B.A., M.A., Ph.D., J.D.; Partner, Thorpe & Shearer, Attorneys at Law; former Chairman, Department of Economics, Wabash College. [ECONOMICS]

Smith, R. Jeffrey, M.S.J.; National Security Correspondent, *The Washington Post.* [SPACE EXPLORATION (Close-Up)]

Spencer, William, A.B., A.M., Ph.D.; Writer; Former Professor of History, Florida State University. [MIDDLE EAST and Middle Eastern Country Articles; North Africa Country Articles]

Stasio, Marilyn, B.A., M.A.; Theater Critic, *New York Post.* [THEATER]

Stokesbury, James L., B.A., M.A., Ph.D.; Professor of History, Acadia University; Author, *Navy and Empire* and *A Short History of Air Power.* [WORLD BOOK SUPPLEMENT: WORLD WAR II]

Swanton, Donald W., B.S., M.S., Ph.D., M.B.A.; Chairman, Department of Finance, Roosevelt University. [BANK; STOCKS AND BONDS]

Taylor, Doreen, Free-Lance Journalist, Writer, and Broadcaster, Scotland. [SCOTLAND]

Thompson, Ida, A.B., M.S., Ph.D.; Free-Lance Science Writer. [PALEONTOLOGY]

Toch, Thomas, B.A.; Writer, Carnegie Foundation for the Advancement of Teaching. [EDUCATION]

Trotter, Robert J., B.S.; Senior Editor, *Psychology Today* magazine. [PSYCHOLOGY]

Tuchman, Janice Lyn, B.S., M.S.; Senior Editor, *Engineering News-Record.* [BUILDING AND CONSTRUCTION]

Vesley, Roberta, A.B., M.L.S.; Library Director, American Kennel Club. [DOG]

Voorhies, Barbara, B.S., Ph.D.; Professor and Chair, Department of Anthropology, University of California at Santa Barbara. [ARCHAEOLOGY]

Walter, Eugene J., Jr., B.A.; Editor in Chief, *Animal Kingdom* magazine, and Curator of Publications, New York Zoological Society. [CONSERVATION; ZOOS; Special Report: THE NEW LOOK IN ZOOS]

Weininger, Jean, A.B., M.S., Ph.D.; Research Fellow, University of California at Berkeley. [NUTRITION]

Wheeler, Douglas Lanphier, A.B., M.A., Ph.D.; Professor of History, University of New Hampshire. [Special Report: THE AGE-OLD BUSINESS OF ESPIONAGE]

Whitaker, Donald R., A.B.; Economist, National Marine Fisheries Service. [FISHING INDUSTRY]

White, Thomas O., B.S., Ph.D.; University Lecturer in Physics, Cambridge University, Cambridge, England. [PHYSICS]

Windeyer, Kendal, President, Windeyer Associates, Montreal, Canada. [MONTREAL]

Wolff, Howard, B.S.; Associate Managing Editor, *Electronics* magazine. [COMPUTER; ELECTRONICS]

Woods, Michael, B.S.; Science Editor, *The Toledo Blade.* [Energy, Mining, and Health Articles]

Wuntch, Philip, B.A.; Film Critic, *Dallas Morning News.* [MOTION PICTURES]

The Year
in Brief

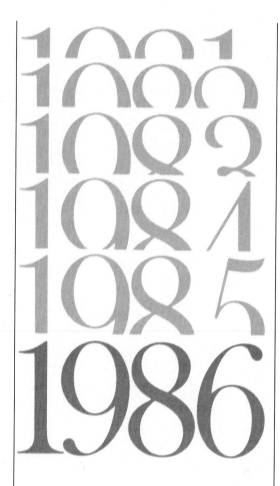

A short essay captures the spirit of 1986, and a month-by-month listing highlights some of the year's significant events.

See page 14.

The Year in Brief

A review of some of the major
trends and events that touched
many of our lives during 1986.

Political upheavals, terrorism, and high-technology disasters disturbed much of the world in 1986. Two of the upheavals took place on widely separated island nations. In Asia, the Philippines held a controversial presidential election in February that resulted in the declared winner fleeing the country, while the "loser" took over the government. In the Caribbean Sea, Haiti's President Jean-Claude Duvalier—who had ruled as a dictator since 1971—also fled the country in February, leaving a council of civilians and military officers in charge. Late in the year, controversy erupted in the United States after the disclosure that certain officials of President Ronald Reagan's Administration had been involved in secret arms dealings with Iran and that some of the money from the sales had been sent to U.S.-backed *contra* rebels seeking to overthrow Nicaragua's Marxist government.

Terrorism struck a number of countries in 1986. In France, for example, during one 10-day period in September, terrorists staged five bomb attacks in Paris. And in Sweden, a gunman shot and killed the country's Prime Minister Olof Palme in February.

One of the disasters that stunned the world was the explosion of the U.S. space shuttle *Challenger*, with the death of all seven crew members. And because of the rupture of a nuclear reactor at the Soviet Union's Chernobyl power station, radioactive substances were spewed into the air and spread throughout the world. Both of these were the worst such accidents in history, and—as it turned out— both could have been prevented.

The presidential election that took place in the Philippines on February 7 was probably the most dramatic political event of 1986. On the ballot were the incumbent, Ferdinand E. Marcos, who had been in power since 1965, and Corazon (Cory) Aquino, widow of an opposition leader who had been assassinated in 1983.

Opposite page: The United States space shuttle *Challenger* explodes on January 28, killing its crew of seven in the worst accident in the history of space flight.

11

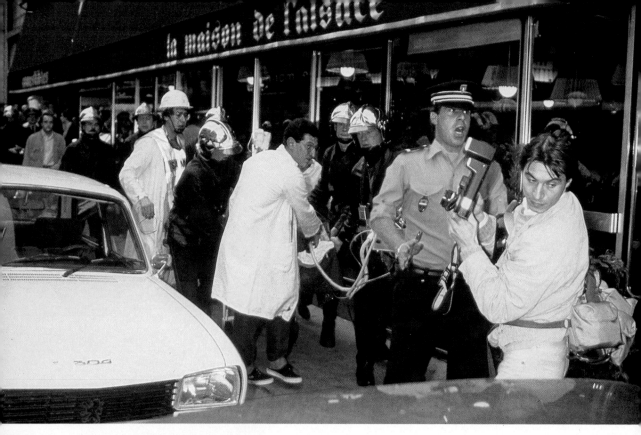

Terrorists hit Europe hard in 1986. French police, *top,* evacuate victims of a September wave of bombings in Paris. Flowers and a portrait, *above,* mark the place where an unknown assailant gunned down Sweden's Prime Minister Olof Palme on February 28.

The election was close, and each side accused the other of massive vote fraud. But U.S. Senator Richard G. Lugar (R., Ind.), cochairman of a U.S. delegation of election observers, said on February 13 that Marcos supporters had committed "the predominance of fraud." Marcos yielded to increasingly widespread public pressure and a military rebellion, stepping down on February 25 and fleeing to Hawaii. Aquino then took over the government as president.

As 1986 ended, the story of the secret United States arms sales to Iran was still unfolding. What was known for sure was that in 1981 President Reagan had put Iran on a list of nations prohibited from receiving U.S. arms because, he said, Iran supported terrorism. And Reagan said repeatedly that the United States would not negotiate with terrorists and would not pay ransom to secure the release of hostages.

Then, in November 1986, newspapers reported that the United States had been shipping arms to Iran since 1985 and that the shipments had apparently led to the release of three U.S. hostages held by terrorists in Lebanon. Reagan admitted that the shipments had been made and that he had authorized them. He denied that the talks leading to the shipments amounted to negotiating with terrorists, though he acknowledged that one of his aims was to motivate Iran "to use its influence in Lebanon to secure the release of all hostages held there." It later came out that some of the money from the arms sales was secretly funneled to the contras. Questions arose about the involvement of the U.S. Central Intelligence Agency, as well as Israel and Saudi Arabia.

In the wake of the disclosures, Reagan announced that his national security adviser, John M. Poindexter, had resigned, and that he had fired Oliver L. North, a staff member of the National Security Council. North had played a key role in the arms deal. Reagan named a three-man review board to investigate the entire matter.

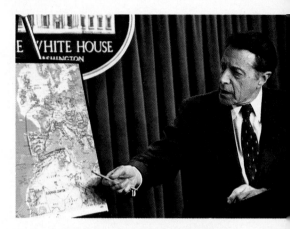

United States Secretary of Defense Caspar W. Weinberger shows the route taken by U.S. aircraft that bombed Libya on April 15 for its involvement in the terrorist bombing of a West Berlin nightclub 10 days earlier.

The revelations disturbed members of Congress. Key congressional leaders said they would investigate the negotiations with Iran and the diversion of the funds to the contras. Some said that the Administration apparently had violated some laws regarding sales of arms and requiring certain information to be divulged to Congress in a "timely" manner.

In other countries, reaction to the arms deal centered on what was viewed as U.S. inconsistency in dealing with terrorism. The United States had pursued a hard line earlier in 1986. In January, the United States broke nearly all economic connections with Libya because, according to President Reagan, Libya supported terrorism. And in April, the United States—citing Libyan involvement in a terrorist bombing in West Berlin, West Germany, earlier in the month—sent jet planes to bomb military and terrorist targets in two Libyan cities.

Terrorism seemed as widespread as ever in 1986. Great Britain took strong diplomatic measures against government-sponsored terrorism. An Israeli guard at London's Heathrow Airport discovered a bomb in a bag carried by a woman who was about to board an Israeli jet on April 17. Britain later said it had determined that Syria was involved in the Heathrow incident and broke diplomatic relations with Syria.

United States President Ronald Reagan and Soviet leader Mikhail S. Gorbachev meet in Reykjavík, Iceland, in October for a "preliminary" conference that nearly produces a breakthrough in arms control.

The Philippines advance toward full democracy, *above,* with the election of Corazon Aquino as their president in February. The struggle of South Africa's blacks for political equality continues as Winnie Mandela, *above right* (in red dress), wife of imprisoned activist Nelson Mandela, meets with Coretta Scott King, the widow of U.S. civil rights leader Martin Luther King, Jr.

France suffered heavily from terrorism in 1986. The five bomb attacks in Paris in September killed 10 people and injured more than 160 others. On September 24, France's Prime Minister Jacques Chirac said he had no proof that any nation had helped the terrorists. Doubts arose in some French citizens' minds, however, when it was learned that the day before Chirac's statement, a French cabinet minister had visited Syria for talks with the Syrian government. And on October 3, the French newspaper *Le Monde* reported that the head of France's secret service had also gone to Syria for talks. In November, because of apparent Syrian involvement in the Heathrow incident, the European Community (EC or Common Market) imposed sanctions on Syria—including a ban on arms sales and a reduction in diplomatic personnel.

Among the other incidents that helped make terrorism a major issue in 1986, five stood out. On February 28, Palme was assassinated. On April 2, a bomb exploded in a Trans World Airlines jet flying over Greece, killing four passengers. On September 5, terrorists shot passengers aboard a Pan American World Airways jet parked in Pakistan, killing 21 people. On September 6, terrorists killed 21 Jewish worshipers in a synagogue in Turkey. And in Paris on November 17, Georges Besse, president of France's state-owned automaker, Renault, was shot and killed.

In Reykjavík, Iceland, President Reagan met with Soviet leader Mikhail S. Gorbachev for two days in October. Reagan proposed a 50 per cent cut in long-range nuclear weapons during the first five

years of an agreement and a ban on all offensive ballistic missiles in a second five-year period. Reagan and Gorbachev also mentioned the elimination of all long-range cruise missiles and bombers.

The two leaders reached tentative agreement on a number of drastic cuts, but the talks broke down over the U.S. Strategic Defense Initiative (SDI or "Star Wars") research program aimed at developing a spacebased shield against missiles. Gorbachev insisted that research, testing, and development of SDI equipment be limited to the laboratory for the entire 10-year period of the proposed missile agreement. Reagan refused to restrict SDI work in this way.

The SDI dispute came at a time when the U.S. space program was in disarray following the *Challenger* disaster on January 28. The shuttle exploded about a minute after liftoff from Cape Canaveral, Fla. A presidential investigating commission headed by former Secretary of State William P. Rogers reported in June that the cause of the accident was a faulty seal in a booster rocket. The commission said that certain officials of the National Aeronautics and Space Administration (NASA) had not told top NASA managers that rocket seals were a continuing and increasing concern.

The Chernobyl explosion, which occurred on April 26, sent vast quantities of radioactive debris into the air. Winds eventually spread radioactive material from the reactor throughout the world. By year's end, at least 31 people had died as a result of the accident, and experts were disagreeing on just how catastrophic the accident finally would turn out to be. According to authoritative estimates,

High school students join the crackdown on *crack*—solid, smokable cocaine—as public concern about the danger of illegal drugs rises in the United States.

between 6,500 and 40,000 people in the western part of the Soviet Union alone would die of cancer in the next 30 years because of the Chernobyl explosion.

The cause of the explosion was a combination of human error and reactor design, according to the chief Soviet delegate at an international conference on the accident. The disaster prompted European countries to reconsider plans for nuclear power plants.

In 1986, the world was awash in one power source—oil—and the worldwide oversupply had triggered a dramatic plunge in oil prices. The decline was especially hard on petroleum-producing countries such as Venezuela, Nigeria, and Mexico, which depend on their exports of oil for income. But it helped such nations as Japan and Brazil, which import almost all the oil they use.

Brazil especially welcomed the oil-price plunge, because it helped President José Sarney deal successfully with runaway inflation. In 1985, Sarney had become the first civilian president of Brazil after 20 years of military dictatorship, and Sarney hoped that his success would give the Brazilian people confidence in civilian rule.

South Africa struggled much less successfully with an internal problem in 1986. South Africa excludes most of its population—the blacks—from representation in the national government by means of a policy known as *apartheid.* For several years, South Africa had been under pressure to end apartheid. The West stepped up the pressure in 1986. In September, the U.S. Congress passed a bill sharply limiting U.S. trade with South Africa. President Reagan vetoed the bill, but Congress overrode the veto. The EC in September enacted relatively mild sanctions against South Africa.

As South Africa struggled with the issue of political freedom, the United States celebrated the 100th birthday of a symbol of freedom—the Statue of Liberty—with a $30-million extravaganza held in New York City from July 3 to 6. On July 3, President Reagan pushed a button to illuminate the statue, which looked fresh after a $69.8-million restoration.

In June, Reagan announced a change in a body that makes some of the decisions regarding matters of freedom—the Supreme

Here are your

1987 YEAR BOOK
Cross-Reference Tabs

For insertion in your WORLD BOOK

Each year, THE WORLD BOOK YEAR BOOK adds a valuable dimension to your WORLD BOOK set. The Cross-Reference Tab System is designed especially to help youngsters and parents alike *link* THE YEAR BOOK's new and revised WORLD BOOK articles, its Special Reports, and its Close-Ups to the related WORLD BOOK articles they update.

How to Use These Tabs

First, remove this page from THE YEAR BOOK. The top Tab on this page is AIDS. Turn to the A volume of your WORLD BOOK and find the page with the AIDS article on it. Affix the AIDS Tab to that page. If your WORLD BOOK is an older set without an AIDS article in it, put the AIDS Tab in the A volume in its proper alphabetical sequence. For most older sets of WORLD BOOK, the AIDS Tab would go on the same page as the article about AIKEN, CONRAD POTTER.

Now do the same with the remaining Tabs, and your new YEAR BOOK will be linked to your WORLD BOOK set.

New Article
AIDS
1987 Year Book, p. 578

New Article
ARTIFICIAL HEART
1987 Year Book, p. 578

Special Report
CONSTITUTION OF THE U.S.
1987 Year Book, p. 78

New Article
CYCLOSPORINE
1987 Year Book, p. 579

Special Report
DA VINCI, LEONARDO
1987 Year Book, p. 130

Special Report
DRUG ABUSE
1987 Year Book, p. 116

Special Report
ESPIONAGE
1987 Year Book, p. 34

Year Book Close-Up
GOODMAN, BENNY
1987 Year on File (Popular Music)

New Article
MAGELLANIC CLOUDS
1987 Year Book, p. 579

Year Book Close-Up
MAYA
1987 Year on File (Archaeology)

Special Report
MEXICO
1987 Year Book, p. 144

Special Report
MICHELANGELO
1987 Year Book, p. 130

New Article
MILKY WAY
1987 Year Book, p. 579

Special Report
NATIONAL PARKS
1987 Year Book, p. 100

Year Book Close-Up
NUCLEAR ENERGY
1987 Year on File (Energy Supply)

Year Book Close-Up
SPACE SHUTTLE
1987 Year on File (Space Exploration)

Special Report
WOMAN
1987 Year Book, p. 64

New Article
WORLD WAR I
1987 Year Book, p. 530

New Article
WORLD WAR II
1987 Year Book, p. 546

Special Report
ZOO
1987 Year Book, p. 48

Court of the United States. The President said that Chief Justice Warren E. Burger would retire shortly, and he named Associate Justice William H. Rehnquist to succeed him. The President then named Antonin Scalia—a federal Appeals Court judge—to fill the vacant seat.

Rehnquist was a controversial choice for chief justice. His opponents questioned his candor and his record on civil rights and individual liberty. Rehnquist's supporters replied that he had served with distinction during his 14 years on the court, and the Senate confirmed him by a vote of 65 to 33. There were no doubts about Scalia, and the Senate confirmed him 98-0.

There were, however, growing doubts about the adequacy of U.S. narcotics laws in 1986. One reason was the recent emergence of strong medical evidence that cocaine is physically addictive. Another reason was the sudden appearance in late 1985 of *crack*—a solid, smokable cocaine that "hooks" the user almost immediately. And it had become obvious by 1986 that the United States efforts to cut the supply of drugs drastically were not working.

In July, Speaker of the House Thomas P. (Tip) O'Neill, Jr. (D., Mass.), urged congressional Democrats and Republicans to work together to de-

Natural and technological disaster strike in 1986. Dead cows in the African country of Cameroon, *bottom,* bear mute testimony to a release of volcanic gases that killed more than 1,700 people on August 21. After a nuclear reactor explosion in the Soviet Union on April 26, a Danish truckdriver, *below,* returns from Russia wearing clothing that shields him from radioactivity.

Vancouver, Canada, has reason to celebrate after its world's fair, Expo 86, *top,* draws 22 million people—about 50 per cent more than expected—from May to October. Argentine athletes celebrate, *above,* after winning the World Cup, soccer's world championship trophy, in Mexico City in June.

velop a comprehensive drug-control bill. In September, the President and first lady Nancy Reagan appeared together on a national television broadcast to launch a "national crusade" against illegal drugs. Nancy Reagan advised the young people in her audience, "When it comes to drugs and alcohol, just say 'no.' "

The day after the telecast, President Reagan signed an executive order requiring that federal employees with "sensitive" jobs be tested for the use of illegal drugs. And in October, Congress passed a drug bill backed by $1.7 billion in federal financing.

Other major bills passed by Congress included the most sweeping overhaul of the U.S. tax code in 40 years. The new tax law lowered maximum income-tax rates for individuals and corporations while repealing or cutting widely used deductions and credits.

A national election in November cut Republican congressional power considerably. The Democrats took over control of the Senate with 55 seats to 45 seats for the Republicans and picked up 5 seats in the House of Representatives.

The worst natural disaster of 1986 occurred in the African nation of Cameroon in August. Poison gases released from a lake in the center of a volcano killed more than 1,700 people.

Iran's war with Iraq and the struggle between the contras and government forces in Nicaragua seemed no closer to resolution in 1986 than they had been in 1985. Soviet troops remained locked in combat with Afghan rebels, and Vietnamese soldiers made little progress in routing Kampuchean rebels.

Nations came together peacefully in Vancouver, Canada, when 54 of them took part in the five-month-long Expo 86 world's fair. Fair planners had expected that about 14 million individuals would attend the fair—but 22 million showed up.

In June, Argentina won the World Cup—the world championship trophy of soccer. Led by the brilliant Diego Armando Maradona, Argentina defeated West Germany in an exciting finale played in Mexico City. World Cup excitement gave Mexico a brief distraction from its mounting troubles, and sports elsewhere provided some of the year's brightest moments.

Athletes from New England played for the championships of three U.S. professional sports—but came away with only one title. In January, they got the boot—or a swipe of a bear's paw—in football. In June, led by a Bird, they flew to the top in basketball. But in October, the team with the mitts met the Mets and went away muttering.

Also in 1986, some 5 million people held hands to reach almost across the United States. A woman named Weaver reached a distant planet—in a motion picture—and held her own against some aliens. A voyager that had been weaving through the heavens for many moons reached a distant planet too, and detected many previously unknown moons. And another *Voyager* made it all the way around our own planet without stopping for a refill at the fuel pump.

All things considered, affairs on our planet went along about as usual in 1986, with the good balancing the bad. Warfare, the Chernobyl and *Challenger* disasters, terrorism, and the U.S.-Iran-contra revelations were disturbing. But Aquino's progress in guiding her nation toward political liberty provided a shining example for countries still burdened by dictatorship, and the near-breakthrough at Reykjavík gave the world a glimmer of hope that the superpowers would lighten the burden of nuclear terror in 1987.

THE EDITORS

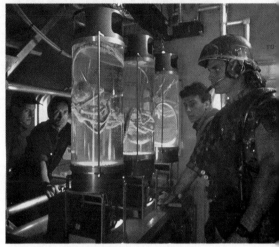

Jubilant New York Mets, *top,* whoop it up after defeating the Boston Red Sox in baseball's World Series in October. Apprehensive Earthmen, *above,* size up their opponents in the motion picture *Aliens,* a box-office smash released in July starring Sigourney Weaver.

For details about 1986:
The Year on File section—which begins on page 172—describes events of 1986 according to the country, field, or general subject area in which they occurred. The Chronology, which starts on page 20, lists events month by month.

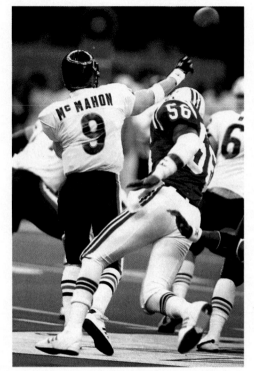

Jan. 26

Jan. 28

January

			1	2	3	4
5	6	7	8	9	10	11
12	13	14	15	16	17	18
19	20	21	22	23	24	25
26	27	28	29	30	31	

1   **United States President Ronald Reagan** and Soviet leader Mikhail S. Gorbachev deliver televised New Year's messages to each other's nation.

7   **Reagan severs** almost all U.S. economic ties with Libya, which he accuses of supporting international terrorist operations.
John R. Block announces his resignation as U.S. secretary of agriculture. On January 29, Reagan names Richard E. Lyng to succeed him.

9-24   **The British Cabinet** is rocked by two resignations because of a dispute over rival plans for rescuing the ailing Westland PLC helicopter company. Secretary of State for Defence Michael Heseltine resigns on January 9 and Secretary of State for Trade and Industry Leon Brittan on January 24.

16   **A New York State Supreme Court judge** dismisses attempted-murder and assault charges against Bernhard H. Goetz, who shot four youths who asked him for money on a New York City subway in 1984.

20   **France and Great Britain** announce plans to build a 31-mile (50-kilometer) rail tunnel, scheduled for completion in 1993, linking the two countries under the English Channel.
A military coup ousts Prime Minister Leabua Jonathan of Lesotho.
Martin Luther King, Jr., Day, honoring the American civil rights leader, is observed as a federal holiday for the first time.

22   **A judge in India** convicts three Sikhs of the 1984 assassination of Prime Minister Indira Gandhi and sentences them to death.

23   **Voters in Northern Ireland** reelect 14 of the 15 Protestant members of the British Parliament who resigned in November 1985 to protest an Anglo-Irish pact that gave Ireland a role in Northern Ireland's affairs.

24   **The *Voyager 2* spacecraft** makes its closest approach to the planet Uranus, coming within 50,679 miles (81,560 kilometers) of the planet's cloud tops.
Yemen (Aden) leader Ali Nasir Muhammad is overthrown by a rival Marxist faction after 11 days of bitter fighting.

24-26   **The National Resistance Army (NRA),** a rebel group, seizes control of Uganda. NRA leader Yoweri Museveni is sworn in as president on January 29.

26   **The Chicago Bears** win Super Bowl XX, defeating the New England Patriots 46-10.

28   **The space shuttle *Challenger*** explodes about 73 seconds after liftoff from Cape Canaveral, Fla., killing all seven crew members.
Angolan rebel leader Jonas Savimbi arrives in the United States on a 10-day visit in search of support for his rebel movement.

Feb. 1-10

Feb. 25

Feb. 25

February

						1
2	3	4	5	6	7	8
9	10	11	12	13	14	15
16	17	18	19	20	21	22
23	24	25	26	27	28	

1-10   **Pope John Paul II** visits 14 cities on a 10-day trip to India.

2   **Oscar Arias Sánchez,** a moderate, wins Costa Rica's presidential election. He takes office on May 8.

4   **The Canadian dollar** plunges to a record low of 69.13 U.S. cents.

6   **The Dow Jones Industrial Average** closes above 1,600 for the first time, ending the day at 1,600.69, and surpasses 1,700 on February 27, closing at 1,713.99.

7   **Haitian President Jean-Claude Duvalier** flees to France, leaving a military-civilian council to govern Haiti.

A presidential election in the Philippines pits President Ferdinand E. Marcos against Corazon Aquino, widow of an opposition political leader assassinated in 1983. The Philippine National Assembly declares Marcos the winner on February 15 despite widespread charges of fraud.

8   **Cyanide-tainted Tylenol** kills a Peekskill, N.Y., woman at a friend's home in Yonkers, N.Y. Investigators find a second bottle of contaminated Tylenol in nearby Bronxville, N.Y., on February 13.

11   **The Soviet Union** releases dissident Anatoly B. Shcharansky, who had been imprisoned for eight years as a spy, as part of an East-West exchange of prisoners in Berlin.

16   **Former Prime Minister Mário Soares,** a Socialist, is elected Portugal's first civilian president since 1926.

17-19   **Leaders** of about 40 French-speaking nations gather in Paris for the first summit of French-language nations in history.

22   **Two top-ranking Philippine military leaders** demand that Marcos resign.

24   **Eastern Airlines** agrees to be bought by the Texas Air Corporation, creating the largest airline in the United States.

25   **Marcos resigns,** ending a 20-year rule, and flees the Philippines. Aquino, shown above, assumes the presidency.

The 27th Communist Party Congress opens in Moscow, bringing together an estimated 5,000 delegates from more than 100 nations.

25-27   **Egyptian police** riot after hearing rumors that their tour of duty would be extended.

26   **Robert Penn Warren** is named the first official poet laureate of the United States.

27   **Jean Chrétien,** a popular leader of Canada's Liberal Party, resigns from the House of Commons.

28   **Prime Minister Olof Palme** of Sweden is assassinated by an unknown gunman on a street in Stockholm.

President José Sarney of Brazil orders wage-price controls and a new currency, the cruzado, to replace Brazil's cruzeiro.

March 13

March 19

March 31

March

						1
2	3	4	5	6	7	8
9	10	11	12	13	14	15
16	17	18	19	20	21	22
23	24	25	26	27	28	29
30	31					

2 **Queen Elizabeth II** of Great Britain signs an act dissolving the last constitutional links between Australia and Britain.

12 **Sweden's parliament** elects Ingvar Carlsson as prime minister to succeed Palme.

Spaniards vote to keep their country in the North Atlantic Treaty Organization.

13 **The European Space Agency probe *Giotto*** comes within 375 miles (600 kilometers) of Halley's Comet, shown above, the closest encounter ever between a spacecraft and a comet.

16 **Swiss voters** reject a motion to have their country join the United Nations.

A coalition of conservative parties wins a narrow victory over France's ruling Socialist Party in National Assembly elections. Conservative leader Jacques Chirac becomes prime minister on March 20, giving the nation a president and prime minister of opposing parties.

19 **Reagan and Canadian Prime Minister Brian Mulroney** endorse a U.S.-Canadian report calling acid rain a serious problem.

20 **The Dow Jones Industrial Average** closes above 1,800 for the first time, ending the day at 1,804.24.

21 **Henri Namphy,** the head of Haiti's ruling military council, fires three council members and declares himself president of the remaining three-person council.

SmithKline Beckman Corporation of Philadelphia recalls three nonprescription medicines after rat poison was found in capsules in Orlando, Fla., and Houston.

22 **Up to 1,500 Nicaraguan troops** enter Honduras to attack Nicaraguan rebel camps. Reagan authorizes $20 million in emergency military aid to Honduras on March 25 to help fight the incursion.

24 ***Out of Africa,*** a film about Danish author Isak Dinesen, wins seven Academy Awards, including best picture.

24-25 **U.S. Navy jets** sink at least two Libyan patrol boats, damage another, and attack two shoreline missile bases after Libya fires missiles at American planes in a dispute over Libya's claim to the Gulf of Sidra.

25 **Philippine President Aquino** abolishes the National Assembly and claims all legislative powers for herself until voters ratify a new constitution.

29 **An Italian court** finds insufficient evidence to convict three Bulgarians and three Turks accused of plotting to kill Pope John Paul II in 1981.

31 **The University of Louisville** wins the National Collegiate Athletic Association men's basketball championship, beating Duke University 72-69.

April 15

April 26

April 13

1-12   **Sudan** holds its first multiparty elections since 1968. Two centrist parties win the most votes and form a coalition government headed by Sadiq el Mahdi, who becomes prime minister on May 6.

2   **Alabama Governor George C. Wallace** announces his retirement from politics.
A bomb explodes aboard a Trans World Airlines jet over Greece, killing four passengers.

5   **A bomb explodes** in a West Berlin discothèque, killing a Turkish woman and two American servicemen.

6   **France** devalues its franc 3 per cent, while West Germany and the Netherlands boost their currencies by 3 per cent in a realignment of the European Monetary System.

8   **Film star Clint Eastwood** is elected mayor of Carmel-by-the-Sea, Calif.

10   **Pakistani opposition leader Benazir Bhutto,** who has spent most of the last nine years in self-imposed exile, returns to Pakistan.

13   **Golfer Jack Nicklaus** wins the Masters Tournament in Augusta, Ga., for a record sixth time.
Pope John Paul II visits a Rome synagogue, the first recorded trip by a pope to a Jewish temple.

15   **U.S. Air Force and Navy jets** bomb military and terrorist targets in Libya after evidence links Libya to the April 5 bombing in West Berlin.

18   **The South African government** announces that it will abolish most laws restricting the movement of blacks, including the pass laws that require blacks to carry identity books.
A Titan rocket bearing a secret military payload explodes seconds after liftoff at Vandenberg Air Force Base, California.

21   **Rob de Castella** of Australia wins the Boston Marathon in 2 hours 7 minutes 51 seconds, a course record.

25   **Prince Makhosetive Dlamini** of Swaziland, 18 years old, is crowned King Mswati III.

26   **The worst nuclear power disaster** in history occurs at the Chernobyl nuclear plant in the Soviet Union, near Kiev, killing at least 31 people and spewing radioactive debris across northern Europe.

29   **Reagan** arrives in Bali, Indonesia, for a meeting with Southeast Asian foreign ministers on May 1.
Japan's Emperor Hirohito, the world's longest reigning monarch, celebrates his 85th birthday and 60th year on the throne.

30   **Norway's government** collapses after Prime Minister Kaare Willoch loses a vote of confidence in parliament. Willoch resigns on May 2 and is succeeded on May 9 by Labor Party leader Gro Harlem Brundtland.

May 1

May 4-6

May 2

May 25

May

			1	2	3	
4	5	6	7	8	9	10
11	12	13	14	15	16	17
18	19	20	21	22	23	24
25	26	27	28	29	30	31

1 **A U.S.-Canadian expedition** reaches the North Pole by dog sled, the first group to do so since Robert E. Peary's 1909 expedition.
A U.S. federal jury in Tucson, Ariz., convicts 8 of 11 sanctuary movement activists charged with various offenses for smuggling Central American refugees into the United States.

2 **Expo 86,** a world's fair devoted to transportation, opens in Vancouver, Canada.

3 **Controllers destroy** an unmanned Delta rocket carrying a weather satellite after it tumbles wildly after liftoff from Cape Canaveral, Fla.

4 **Afghan President Babrak Karmal** resigns as head of Afghanistan's Communist party but retains the nation's presidency.

4-6 **An economic summit conference** in Tokyo is attended by leaders of Canada, France, Great Britain, Italy, Japan, the United States, and West Germany.

8 **Britain's ruling Conservative Party** suffers a stinging election defeat, losing hundreds of local council seats and one of two special

elections to fill empty parliamentary seats.

12 **Canadian Minister of Regional Industrial Expansion** Sinclair McKnight Stevens resigns due to conflict-of-interest charges.
A blizzard traps a group of student climbers on Mount Hood, Oregon. Two members of the party reach safety, and two are rescued on May 15, but nine students freeze to death.

13 **In a primary election,** Nebraska becomes the first state in history to nominate women for governor in both major parties.

16 **Former President Joaquín Balaguer,** a conservative, narrowly wins election as president of the Dominican Republic. He takes office on August 16.

19 **South Africa** attacks suspected black nationalist guerrilla bases in the capitals of Botswana, Zambia, and Zimbabwe.

21 **Jackie Presser,** who was indicted on May 16 on charges of embezzling union funds and racketeering, is elected president of the Teamsters Union.

22 **British Columbia Premier William Bennett** announces his decision to retire.

24 **The Montreal Canadiens** win professional hockey's Stanley Cup, defeating the Calgary Flames four games to one.

25 **More than 5 million volunteers** join hands nearly coast-to-coast in the Hands Across America benefit for the homeless.
Virgilio Barco Vargas of the Liberal Party is elected president of Colombia. He takes office on August 7.

27 **The United Nations (UN) General Assembly** opens a special session on the economic problems of Africa. It ends on June 1.

June 8

June 17

June 29

June

1	2	3	4	5	6	7
8	9	10	11	12	13	14
15	16	17	18	19	20	21
22	23	24	25	26	27	28
29	30					

1-27 **About 155,000 members** of the Communications Workers of America go on strike against the American Telephone and Telegraph Company.

4 **Former U.S. Navy intelligence analyst** Jonathan Jay Pollard pleads guilty to spying for Israel.

5 **A federal jury** in Baltimore convicts Ronald W. Pelton, a former employee of the National Security Agency, of selling defense secrets to the Soviet Union.

8 **Kurt Waldheim,** former UN secretary-general, is elected president of Austria despite being accused of Nazi war crimes.
The Boston Celtics win the National Basketball Association championship, beating the Houston Rockets four games to two.

9 **Austrian Chancellor Fred Sinowatz** resigns and is succeeded by Franz Vranitzky.
The Supreme Court of the United States strikes down the Reagan Administration's Baby Doe rules, which forced hospitals to treat severely handicapped infants.

12 **South Africa** declares a state of emergency and arrests more than 1,000 antiapartheid activists.

17 **Warren E. Burger** resigns as chief justice of the United States, and Reagan nominates Associate Justice William H. Rehnquist to succeed him and Appeals Court Judge Antonin Scalia to replace Rehnquist. The new justices are sworn in on September 26.

18 **The U.S. House of Representatives** passes economic penalties against South Africa that would require a near-total ban on trade and complete withdrawal of U.S. investment.

19 **A federal jury** in Los Angeles convicts Richard W. Miller, a former Federal Bureau of Investigation (FBI) agent, of espionage and bribery. He is sentenced to life in prison on July 14.

20 **The Bristol-Myers Company** ends the sale of all nonprescription capsules after two deaths in the Seattle area are linked to cyanide poisoning of Excedrin capsules.

25 **The U.S. House of Representatives** approves $100 million in humanitarian and military aid to Nicaraguan rebels.

26 **Irish voters** choose to keep a constitutional ban on divorce.

27 **The World Court** rules that the United States violates international law by supporting Nicaraguan rebels.

29 **Argentina** wins the World Cup soccer championship, beating West Germany 3 to 2.

30 **The U.S. Supreme Court** upholds a Georgia law banning private homosexual activity between adults.
Canadian Prime Minister Mulroney reorganizes his cabinet.

July 3

July 23

July

		1	2	3	4	5
6	7	8	9	10	11	12
13	14	15	16	17	18	19
20	21	22	23	24	25	26
27	28	29	30	31		

1   **The Dow Jones Industrial Average** closes above 1,900 for the first time, ending the day at 1,903.54.

1-7   **Pope John Paul II** visits Colombia.

1-21   **More than 15,000 Philadelphia city workers,** including clerks and trash collectors, strike in a wage dispute.

2   **The U.S. Supreme Court** upholds affirmative action as a remedy for past job discrimination.

3   **The renovated Statue of Liberty** is rededicated in New York City. The festivities include the largest fireworks display in U.S. history, shown above, on July 4.

5-6   **Martina Navratilova** and Boris Becker win Wimbledon singles tennis championships.

6   **Japan's ruling Liberal Democratic Party** wins the largest number of seats in its history in parliamentary elections.

7   **The U.S. Supreme Court** strikes down the automatic budget-cutting provision of the Gramm-Rudman Act.

16   **About 5,000 Detroit city workers** strike in a wage dispute that lasts until August 4.

17   **LTV Corporation,** the second largest U.S. steel producer, files for bankruptcy.

18   **Bolivia** and the United States begin joint raids on cocaine laboratories in the Bolivian jungle.

20   **Greg Norman** of Australia wins the British Open golf championship in Turnberry, Scotland.

22-23   **King Hassan II** of Morocco meets with Prime Minister Shimon Peres of Israel in Ifrane, Morocco.

23   **Great Britain's Prince Andrew** and Sarah Ferguson are married in Westminster Abbey in London.

     The U.S. Food and Drug Administration approves commercial production of the first genetically engineered vaccine for human use, a vaccine to prevent hepatitis B.

24   **A federal jury** in San Francisco convicts Jerry A. Whitworth, a retired Navy radioman, of spying for the Soviet Union as part of the Walker family spy ring. On August 28, he is sentenced to 365 years in prison and fined $410,000.

     The Commonwealth Games begin in Edinburgh, Scotland, with 32 of 58 nations boycotting to press Britain for economic sanctions against South Africa.

26   **Islamic extremists** in Lebanon release American hostage Lawrence M. Jenco, a Roman Catholic priest held since January 1985.

27   **Greg LeMond** becomes the first American to win the Tour de France bicycle race.

29   **The United States Football League** (USFL) wins an antitrust suit against the National Football League but gets only $1 in damages, which will be trebled under antitrust law.

Aug. 21

Aug. 14

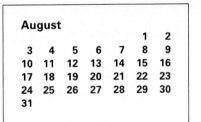

Aug. 31

August						
					1	2
3	4	5	6	7	8	9
10	11	12	13	14	15	16
17	18	19	20	21	22	23
24	25	26	27	28	29	30
31						

1   **USX Corporation** (formerly U.S. Steel Corporation) shuts its plants in a dispute with the United Steelworkers of America.

2-5   **Leaders** of Australia, the Bahamas, Canada, Great Britain, India, Zambia, and Zimbabwe meet in London to consider penalties against South Africa. All but Britain agree on stiff measures including bans on air travel and South African imports.

4   **The USFL** cancels its 1986 fall season.
The Organization of Petroleum Exporting Countries breaks a long deadlock and agrees to limit output to boost oil prices.

6   **William N. Vander Zalm** takes office as premier of British Columbia.
William J. Schroeder dies after living 620 days with an artificial heart, longer than any other person with the device.

7   **The Soviet Union** announces that it has granted asylum to Edward Lee Howard, a former employee of the Central Intelligence Agency (CIA) who disappeared in September 1985.

11   **Canadian fishing boats** rescue 155 Sri Lankan refugees found adrift in two lifeboats in the Atlantic Ocean off Newfoundland.

14   **Pakistani opposition leader Bhutto,** shown above addressing supporters before her arrest, is arrested and held in jail until September 8.

16   **Sudanese rebels** shoot down a civilian airliner near Malakal, Sudan, killing all 60 people aboard.

20   **Mail carrier Patrick H. Sherrill** shoots and kills 14 co-workers, then himself, in an Edmond, Okla., post office.

21   **Poisonous gas** from a volcanic lake kills more than 1,700 people in Cameroon.

22   **Pan American World Airways** (PanAm) agrees to pay $1.95 million for alleged federal safety violations, the largest fine paid in aviation history.

23   **The FBI** arrests Gennadi F. Zakharov, a Soviet employee of the UN, in New York City. He is charged on September 9 with spying.

24   **Frontier Airlines** stops operating because of financial problems and files for bankruptcy on August 28.

26   **South Korean President** Chun Doo Hwan shakes up his cabinet, replacing 10 ministers.

28   **Bolivia** declares a nationwide state of siege to quiet labor troubles.

30   **Soviet KGB police** arrest American reporter Nicholas S. Daniloff. He is charged on September 7 with spying.

31   **An Aeroméxico jetliner** and a small plane collide near Los Angeles, killing 82 people.
A Soviet freighter rams a liner and sinks it in the Black Sea near Novorossiysk, Soviet Union, causing 398 deaths.

Sept. 7

Sept. 8-17

Sept. 12

September

	1	2	3	4	5	6
7	8	9	10	11	12	13
14	15	16	17	18	19	20
21	22	23	24	25	26	27
28	29	30				

1-7 **The 101 member nations and organizations** of the nonaligned movement hold a summit conference in Harare, Zimbabwe.

2 **Three Dutch balloonists** set a record for the fastest Atlantic balloon crossing, 51 hours 14 minutes.

5 **Hijackers** fire at the passengers of a PanAm jet at the Karachi, Pakistan, airport, killing 21 people before being captured.

6 **Terrorists** spray machine-gun fire and throw grenades at a synagogue in Istanbul, Turkey, killing 21 Jewish worshipers.

7 **Desmond M. Tutu** is installed as Anglican archbishop of Cape Town, South Africa, becoming the first black to head the Anglican Church in that country.
Chilean President Augusto Pinochet Ugarte escapes an assassination attempt in which five of his bodyguards are killed.
Navratilova and Ivan Lendl win U.S. Open tennis championships.

8-17 **Paris** is rocked by five bombs in 10 days that kill 10 people and injure more than 160.

9 **Delta Air Lines** agrees to acquire Western Air Lines for about $860 million.

10 **Egypt and Israel** agree on international arbitration to resolve a dispute over Taba, a Red Sea beach area claimed by both, clearing the way for a summit on September 11–12 between Egyptian President Hosni Mubarak and Israeli Prime Minister Peres.

11 **The Dow Jones Industrial Average** plummets 86.61 points to 1,792.89, the biggest one-day loss ever.

12 **Accused spies** Daniloff of the United States—shown above—and Zakharov of the Soviet Union are freed from prisons in Moscow and New York City into the custody of their ambassadors.

15 **Philippine President Aquino** arrives in the United States on a nine-day visit, her first official visit to that country.
Austria's Chancellor Vranitzky says that his Socialist Party will end its coalition·with the smaller Freedom Party and calls an early election for November 23.
President Reagan orders drug testing for all federal employees in "sensitive" jobs.

16 **The 41st UN General Assembly** elects Foreign Minister Humayun Rashid Choudhury of Bangladesh as its president.

17 **The United States** orders the expulsion of 25 Soviet diplomats at the UN, who must leave by October 1.

21 **"Cagney & Lacey,"** a CBS series about two policewomen, wins four Emmy Awards, including the one for best drama series.

27 **Congress** approves the most sweeping changes in the federal tax system since the 1940's. Reagan signs the law October 22.

Oct. 11-12

Oct. 12-18

Oct. 27

October

			1	2	3	4
5	6	7	8	9	10	11
12	13	14	15	16	17	18
19	20	21	22	23	24	25
26	27	28	29	30	31	

2   **Congress** votes to override a veto by Reagan and impose tough economic penalties against South Africa, including bans on investment and many South African imports.

4-7   **Pope John Paul II** visits France.

5   **Nicaragua** shoots down a plane flying arms to anti-Sandinista rebels, killing three crew members and capturing Eugene Hasenfus, an American who says on October 9 that he was on a CIA mission. The United States denies any link to the plane.

6   **Gary Kasparov** of the Soviet Union clinches the world championship of chess over challenger Anatoly Karpov in Leningrad. By the end of the match on October 9, Kasparov has won 12½ points to 11½.

A Soviet nuclear submarine sinks in the Atlantic Ocean three days after being damaged by a fire and explosion in which at least three crew members died.

7   **Reagan** signs legislation establishing the rose as the national floral emblem of the United States.

9   **U.S. District Judge Harry E. Claiborne** becomes the first federal official to be impeached, convicted, and removed from office since 1936.

10   **An earthquake** rocks San Salvador, the capital of El Salvador, killing more than 1,200 people.

Israeli Prime Minister Peres resigns, as arranged under a 1984 power-sharing deal, and Deputy Prime Minister and Minister of Foreign Affairs Yitzhak Shamir becomes prime minister on October 20.

11-12   **Reagan and Gorbachev** hold a summit meeting in Reykjavík, Iceland.

12-18   **Queen Elizabeth II** becomes the first British monarch to visit China.

14   **Elie Wiesel,** a Romanian-born American author who has written about the sufferings of Jews, wins the 1986 Nobel Peace Prize.

17   **Reagan** signs a $9-billion, five-year Superfund toxic-waste cleanup bill.

19   **Mozambique's President Samora Moisés Machel** and 33 other people are killed in a plane crash in South Africa.

19-22   **The Soviet Union** expels five U.S. diplomats on October 19 and five more on October 22.

21   **The United States** expels 55 Soviet diplomats.

24   **Britain** breaks diplomatic ties with Syria because of "undisputed" evidence that Syria was involved in an attempt to blow up an Israeli airliner leaving London in April.

27   **The New York Mets** win the World Series, defeating the Boston Red Sox four games to three. New York City holds a victory parade, shown above, on October 28.

27   **Reagan** signs a major antidrug bill into law.

Nov. 1

Nov. 15

November						
						1
2	3	4	5	6	7	8
9	10	11	12	13	14	15
16	17	18	19	20	21	22
23	24	25	26	27	28	29
30						

1   **A fire** at a chemical warehouse near Basel, Switzerland, results in a major spill of toxic chemicals into the Rhine River, prompting protests, shown above.

2   **Sinn Féin,** the legal political wing of the outlawed Irish Republican Army, votes to end a boycott of the Irish Parliament that it began in 1922.
Islamic Jihad, a pro-Iranian Shiite Muslim group in Lebanon, frees David P. Jacobsen, an American hostage held since May 1985.

4   **The Democrats** gain control of the Senate in midterm elections, picking up 8 seats to establish a 55-45 majority.

6   **Reagan signs** into law a sweeping immigration reform act that prohibits hiring illegal aliens and offers legal status to many illegal aliens already in the United States.

9   **Montreal** voters elect Jean Doré as mayor.
Bangladesh lifts a state of martial law imposed in 1982.

13   **The National Conference of Catholic Bishops** approves a final policy statement

called a *pastoral letter* proposing greater government efforts to help the poor.

14   **Investor Ivan F. Boesky** agrees to pay a $50-million fine, the largest in history, and give up an additional $50 million in illegal profits he made by trading stock on inside information.

15   **A Nicaraguan court** sentences Hasenfus, shown above, to 30 years in prison for supplying arms to anti-Sandinista rebels.
Brazil's centrist ruling coalition wins a sweeping victory in congressional and gubernatorial elections.

17   **Assassins** in Paris kill Georges Besse, chairman of France's state-owned Renault automobile company. The terrorist group Direct Action claims responsibility.

17-23   **A six-day strike** at a Delco Electronics plant causes parts shortages that force the layoff of nearly 60,000 General Motors Corporation employees in the United States.

18   **Pope John Paul II** leaves on a 14-day, six-nation journey to Asia, the South Pacific, and Australia, his longest trip ever.

20   **Afghan President Karmal** resigns from all government and party posts.

23   **Philippine President Aquino** demands the resignations of her entire Cabinet and accepts that of Defense Minister Juan Ponce Enrile after the army foils a coup attempt.

24   **Austria's ruling Socialist Party** loses 10 seats in parliamentary elections but remains the strongest party.

25   **National Security Adviser** John M. Poindexter resigns because of a controversy over secret U.S. arms shipments to Iran and the funneling of Iranian money to Nicaraguan rebels.

Dec. 8

December

	1	2	3	4	5	6
7	8	9	10	11	12	13
14	15	16	17	18	19	20
21	22	23	24	25	26	27
28	29	30	31			

1   **Riots break out** in India after the killing of 22 Hindu bus passengers by Sikh terrorists on November 30.
The Dow Jones Industrial Average climbs to a record high of 1,955.57. The Standard & Poor's 500 Index also reaches a new high of 254.00.

2   **Reagan** names Frank C. Carlucci to replace Poindexter as national security adviser.

6   **A new Taiwanese opposition party,** the first allowed to compete, makes a strong showing in parliamentary elections.

7   **United States Army helicopters** carry Honduran soldiers into action against Nicaraguan troops reported to have entered Honduras in pursuit of Nicaraguan rebels.

8   **The French government** withdraws a university reform bill that triggered the worst student riots since 1968, shown above.
House Democrats choose Representative James C. Wright, Jr., of Texas to succeed retiring Thomas P. (Tip) O'Neill, Jr., of Massachusetts as Speaker of the House.

10   **A 60-day cease-fire** between the Philippine government and Communist rebels goes into effect.

12   **Nicaragua** arrests a U.S. citizen, Sam N. Hall, on suspicion of spying. The United States denies that it employs Hall, brother of Congressman Tony P. Hall (D., Ohio).
A Soviet jetliner crashes in East Berlin, killing 70 people, including 19 East German schoolchildren.

15   **Carnegie Hall,** New York City's famous concert hall, formally reopens after a $50-million, seven-month renovation.
Chemical New York Corporation and Texas Commerce Bancshares Incorporated announce that they will merge in a $1.19-billion deal, the biggest U.S. bank merger ever.

16   **Convicted spy** Ronald W. Pelton is sentenced to life in prison by a federal judge.

17   **Nicaragua** pardons and releases Hasenfus.
Three top Vietnamese leaders —Communist Party General Secretary Truong Chinh, Prime Minister Pham Van Dong, and Politburo member Le Duc Tho—resign their party posts.
British surgeons carry out the world's first triple transplant, replacing a patient's heart, lungs, and liver.

23   **The experimental *Voyager* aircraft** lands at Edwards Air Force Base, California, after a nine-day flight, becoming the first plane to fly nonstop around the world without refueling.

25   **An Iraqi jetliner** crashes in Saudi Arabia after an attempted hijacking, killing 67 people.

31   **A hotel fire,** which officials later attribute to arson, kills at least 96 people in San Juan, Puerto Rico.

Special Reports

1981
1982
1984
1985
1986

Seven articles and a two-part feature give special treatment to subjects of current importance and lasting interest.

34 **The Age-Old Business of Espionage**
by Douglas Lanphier Wheeler

48 **The New Look in Zoos**
by Eugene J. Walter, Jr.

64 **Big Boom in Women's Sports**
by Martha J. Nelson

78 **The U.S. Constitution: 200 Years of History**
A special two-part feature
    80 **A More Perfect Union**
    86 **The Constitution: Why It Has Endured**
        by Stanley I. Kutler

100 **Problems in the Parks**
by Philip Shabecoff

116 **The Hazards of Teen-Age Drinking**
by John Camper

130 **New Life for Two Old Treasures**
by Walter Hays

144 **Mexico: from Boom to Bust**
by Susan Kaufman Purcell

See page 159.

By Douglas Lanphier Wheeler

The Age-Old Business of Espionage

Throughout history, nations have spied on one another, but never before on such a huge scale.

Spying is older than war. The peoples of the ancient world regularly spied on one another, and the Egyptians raised this secret activity to a high art. The Bible contains some of the earliest historical references to spying. The Book of Joshua recounts that in about 1200 B.C., Joshua, the leader of the Israelites, sent two spies to the city of Jericho. Their objective was to acquire vital *intelligence* (secret information) about the city's defenses and the morale of its defenders. With the help of an inhabitant of the city, a woman named Rahab, the two spies succeeded in their perilous mission. The knowledge they obtained helped the Israelites capture Jericho.

Some nations have considered spying a distasteful business, but most have found it a necessary one. Today, spying is practiced on a global scale by all the major countries of the world. Spying sometimes becomes big news, as it did in 1985 and 1986, with the revelation that a number of citizens of the United States were selling secret government information to the Soviet Union and other foreign powers. Throughout 1986, one domestic spy after another was convicted and sentenced to prison. Most of these traitors were current or former employees of the various U.S. intelligence services, including the Central Intelligence Agency (CIA), the Federal Bureau of Investigation (FBI), the National Security Agency (NSA), and the Office of Naval Intelligence (ONI). Other convicted spies have included "private citizens" of the Soviet Union who had come to the United States supposedly to pursue business interests or scientific research, and Soviet secret agents posing as diplomats.

Those apprehended spies represented only the tip of a largely invisible iceberg. Worldwide in 1986, more than 1.3 million people were employed full-time in the intelligence services of more than 160 nations. Of that total, at least 800,000 worked for the intelligence services of the two major superpowers—600,000 of them for the Soviet Union and 200,000 for the United States. Other nations with sizable intelligence agencies included China, France, Great Britain, Israel, and the Soviet-bloc countries of Eastern Europe.

Of the 1.3 million full-time intelligence employees in 1986, only about 200,000 were actually working as spies, gathering secret information in foreign countries—an activity known as *espionage*. Much of the information acquired by intelligence agencies is obtained in other ways that are more like routine office work than spying. Many intelligence personnel, for instance, monitor electronic telecommunications to intercept secret messages, or read foreign publications in search of news or technical information that might be of value. But the dangerous business of espionage is an indispensable part of intelligence gathering.

The author:
Douglas Lanphier Wheeler is a professor of history at the University of New Hampshire in Durham.

Many spies work out of the embassies and consulates of their native countries. Knowledgeable observers estimate that at least one-third of the accredited diplomats representing the Soviet Union and its allied Communist states are active spies. More than 1,000 of these "diplomats," together with thousands of other Soviet and Communist-bloc spies, operate in the United States.

In an effort to thwart the activities of these intelligence agents, the FBI conducts *counterespionage* operations, often using specially recruited *double agents*—persons who pretend to cooperate with foreign spies, usually for money. (In a broader sense, a double agent is a person who works for the intelligence service of one country while actually feeding information from that service to an opposing nation. The most feared double agents are *moles*, persons who patiently climb the ranks of an intelligence service for the sole purpose of eventually betraying high-level secrets to the foreign power they secretly serve.) The FBI has complained that it cannot keep up with the task of counterespionage. The problem is one of numbers. The agency simply does not have the personnel to keep track of every suspected spy on American soil.

The United States built up a full-fledged intelligence system only recently, following its entry into World War II in late 1941. Although there had been small intelligence units in the Army and Navy during wartime since the Revolutionary War—George Washington was America's first chief of intelligence—there was no permanent military intelligence organization until the 1880's. Government intelligence operations expanded greatly during World War I, only to be reduced once hostilities had ended. The American people saw many potential dangers in the idea of having a permanent, peacetime intelligence service, and they opposed the establishment of one. That attitude soon changed.

In 1942, during World War II, the United States founded the Office of Strategic Services (OSS) for the dual purpose of gathering intelligence and disrupting enemy military operations. By the end of the war in 1945, the OSS had developed into a multifaceted intelligence service with more than 20,000 personnel. The OSS was disbanded in October of that year, but the Cold War, a period of great hostility between Communist and non-Communist nations, soon altered both the public's and the government's views on the necessity of establishing a peacetime intelligence service. A permanent intelligence organization, nearly everyone now agreed, was not only desirable but vital.

To meet that need, Congress in 1947 passed the National Security Act, which established the Central Intelligence Agency. The CIA was given a threefold mission: to gather and analyze intelligence about the intentions and military capabilities of other nations; to coordinate the intelligence-gathering operations of other U.S. agencies; and to carry out *covert* (secret) activities in other countries to support American foreign policy and defense goals.

The CIA's record in fulfilling its mission has been mixed. Like most intelligence services, it has had successes and failures. The agency has conducted many effective covert activities, such as supporting political parties and unions friendly to the United States to help them compete with Communists or other anti-American

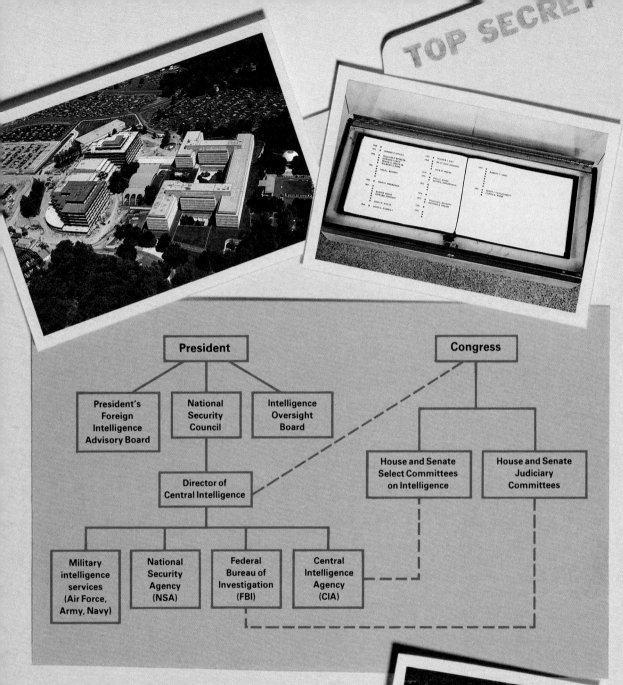

President

Congress

President's Foreign Intelligence Advisory Board

National Security Council

Intelligence Oversight Board

House and Senate Select Committees on Intelligence

House and Senate Judiciary Committees

Director of Central Intelligence

Military intelligence services (Air Force, Army, Navy)

National Security Agency (NSA)

Federal Bureau of Investigation (FBI)

Central Intelligence Agency (CIA)

Huge headquarters buildings in Langley, Va., *top,* and Fort Meade, Md., *right,* house the main offices of the Central Intelligence Agency (CIA) and the National Security Agency (NSA), respectively. The CIA's Book of Honor, *top right,* memorializes agents—some whose names remain secret—who died in the line of duty. The U.S. intelligence community is organized, *above,* within the executive branch of the government. The various agencies are under the director of central intelligence, who reports to the National Security Council (NSC). The NSC and two intelligence boards advise the President. Congress exerts secondary control over intelligence.

groups; spreading propaganda; and training and supplying foreign military groups. Its most noted successes have included providing assistance to democratic parties and labor unions in post-World War II France and Italy, which were threatened by growing Communist parties; aiding successful military coups in Guatemala and Iran in the mid-1950's; and acquiring a vital secret speech by Soviet leader Nikita S. Khrushchev in 1956.

Among the agency's bungles, none have been as spectacular or well-publicized as the ill-starred Bay of Pigs invasion of April 1961. The CIA-supported operation, an attempt by a militarily weak force of Cuban exiles to overthrow the Communist regime of Fidel Castro, fell apart on the beaches of Cuba.

The CIA's current director, William J. Casey, who was appointed by President Ronald Reagan in 1981, directs a staff of some 20,000 from the agency's main headquarters in Langley, Va., near Washington, D.C. The agency also maintains many foreign offices, called *stations*, a number of which are housed at American embassies.

Next to the FBI, whose role in the spy business is confined to domestic counterintelligence, the CIA is the best-known intelligence service. It is not, however, the largest. That distinction belongs to the even more secretive National Security Agency, founded in 1952. The NSA has more than 60,000 employees and operates some 2,000 electronic installations around the world. With its massive computer banks and huge dish antennas, the NSA carries out two primary missions: intercepting and interpreting the electronic transmissions of potentially hostile nations and groups, and protecting secret U.S. communications from foreign interception.

The U.S. intelligence system, which also includes several smaller agencies and the intelligence services of the individual branches of the armed forces, is contained almost wholly within the executive branch of the government. With the exception of the CIA, each of the agencies is part of a particular government department. The NSA, for example, is a branch of the Department of Defense, and the FBI is under the Justice Department. The head of the CIA coordinates the work of the various agencies and reports in turn to the National Security Council (NSC), a committee chaired by the President. The NSC advises the President on intelligence operations as well as on other matters affecting national security. Congress, through its *oversight* powers—the authority to review intelligence operations and budgets—exerts secondary control over intelligence.

Today, the United States intelligence services play an increasingly influential role in shaping government policy. The fulfillment of that role in our complex, technological world requires an extraordinarily diverse and well-educated work force. Intelligence personnel, who in times past were often ill-paid amateurs quickly recruited to meet wartime crisis needs, are now highly trained professionals. CIA employees, for example, include accountants, business manag-

Famous Spies of History

Through war and peace, spies have played an important role in Western history. Famous spies of the past 400 years include:

Christopher Marlowe (1564-1593). Famed English playwright; wrote *The Tragical History of Doctor Faustus* (about 1588) and other works. While a Cambridge University student, Marlowe spied on Roman Catholic conspirators in France for the government of Queen Elizabeth I.

Daniel Defoe (1660-1731). English journalist and author of *Robinson Crusoe* (1719). Sent by the English government on a spying mission to Scotland, where he passed himself off as Alexander Goldsmith, a writer gathering material for a novel.

The Chevalier d'Éon (1728-1810). French adventurer, diplomat, and spy who specialized in female impersonation. Went on many secret missions in England, France, and Russia for King Louis XV of France.

Nathan Hale (1755-1776). Patriot and spy during the Revolutionary War in America. While on a secret mission, was caught by the British and hanged. According to tradition, Hale's final words were "I only regret that I have but one life to lose for my country."

Elizabeth van Lew (1818-1900). Southern aristocrat whose hatred of slavery led her to aid the Union Army during the American Civil War. Organized a highly efficient spy network in the Richmond, Va., area.

Alfred Redl (1864-1913). High-ranking Austrian intelligence officer who for many years sold vital Austrian secrets to the Russians. His treachery added to international tensions in the years before World War I.

Sidney Reilly (1874-1925?). Russian-born secret agent who spied for Great Britain and other Western powers. Tried, in several missions, to undermine the Communist government in Russia, but was finally apprehended by the Soviet secret police and executed.

Mata Hari (1876-1917). Born Margaretha Gertrud Zelle in the Netherlands, she took the Indonesian name *Mata Hari* (*Eye of the Morning*) after divorcing her husband and becoming an exotic dancer and courtesan. Worked for both the French and German espionage networks during World War I, but was never an effective spy. Arrested by the French and executed by firing squad.

Louise de Bettignies (1880-1918). Courageous and highly decorated agent for British and French intelligence in World War I. Spied on the Germans under the name Alice Dubois.

Richard Sorge (1895-1944). Russian-born Communist spy of German descent. Posed as a German journalist in China and Japan in the 1930's and 1940's. After his apprehension and execution by the Japanese, he was declared a hero of the Soviet Union.

Christine Granville (1915-1952). Polish-born spy for British intelligence in World War II. Carried out many dangerous missions in Poland, Hungary, and France.

Harold (Kim) Philby (1912-   ). British double agent who, from 1940 to 1951, rose high in Great Britain's intelligence service while passing information to the Russians. Defected to the Soviet Union in 1963.

Oleg Penkovsky (1919-1963). High-ranking officer in Soviet army intelligence who became a "defector in place," staying in the Soviet Union and spying for Western intelligence services. His deception was discovered by the Soviets, and he was executed.

Stig Wennerstrom (1906-   ). Swedish air force colonel who spied for the Soviet Union in Sweden and the United States. Arrested by Swedish authorities in 1963 and sentenced to life in prison.   [D. L. W.]

Mata Hari, an exotic dancer before becoming a spy, died before a French firing squad in 1917. Daniel Defoe, author of *Robinson Crusoe* (1719), spied on the Scots for England. Harold (Kim) Philby fed British secrets to the Soviets and defected to Moscow in 1963.

ers, persons with advanced degrees in Soviet studies, pilots, ship captains, satellite technicians, language specialists, computer experts, and engineers. And of course, spies.

Like intelligence gathering in general, spying today relies heavily on technology. Much of that technology is developed by the agencies that use it. The CIA, for instance, has its own research and development division whose innovations have included the U-2, a high-altitude spy plane designed for aerial photography over foreign territory. The U-2 played a significant role in the Cuban missile crisis of 1962, when it obtained secret photographs of Soviet nuclear missiles being installed in Cuba. But the U-2's limited speed and altitude capabilities made it vulnerable to antiaircraft missiles. That vulnerability was forcibly demonstrated in 1960 when one of the planes, piloted by a CIA officer named Francis Gary Powers, was shot down over the Soviet Union. A new generation of swifter, higher-flying spy planes, including the SR-71 Blackbird, which can reach a speed of 2,000 miles (3,200 kilometers) per hour, replaced the U-2. The United States uses satellites as well as airplanes for high-altitude photography.

As important as these so-called spies in the sky are to intelligence gathering, airplanes and satellites will never replace the spy on the ground. In most cases, only the human spy can learn of the secret intentions and projects of adversary nations—the kinds of information most sought by intelligence services.

Spying, no matter which country it is done for, can be a hazardous and immoral occupation. The "tools of the trade" can include trickery, blackmail, bribery, and, when necessary, violence. Given the unpleasant realities of the job, psychologists have wondered what motivates people to choose espionage as a career. The experts have found no easy answers, but two common reasons seem to be patriotism or a strong belief in a particular ideology, such as Communism or democracy. Other individuals become spies, apparently, simply because they are attracted by the prospect of wielding secret authority and taking part in activities known only to a select few.

The personal motives of spies may vary, but their methods of op-

The CIA has had its successes and its failures. In 1961, during the Administration of President John F. Kennedy, *below,* news headlines trumpeted the failure of the Bay of Pigs invasion of Cuba. But in 1962, CIA aerial photos revealed that Soviet missiles were being installed in Cuba, *below left.*

Advanced technology is essential to modern intelligence work. The CIA operations center, *right,* receives reports from agents around the world. The tools used by spies include ultrasensitive night viewers and listening devices, *below.*

eration are similar the world over. A typical day at a foreign CIA station, perhaps in an East European capital, might begin with a thorough check for *bugs* (hidden listening devices). Eavesdropping on conversations is one of the oldest ways to obtain information. It is a technique that the agents at the station often employ themselves, using various kinds of tiny, ultrasensitive microphones, some of them disguised as fountain pens, cocktail olives, or other everyday objects. To find bugs that might have been secretly installed in the building—perhaps by an opposing spy pretending to be a maintenance worker—an electronics specialist, using sensitive instruments, must carefully examine walls, ceilings, and floors.

Other agents at the station might be involved with such tasks as recruiting spies from the local population, communicating with agents carrying out dangerous solitary missions, and keeping tabs on the known agents of rival intelligence services.

The recruitment of local spies and informants starts with a review of information compiled on various citizens who are thought to be pro-American. Likely prospects are approached in secret and offered money, and sometimes political asylum, for their help.

Communicating with spies in the field is a delicate task requiring "eyes in the back of one's head." If an exchange of information is observed by agents of an opposing service, it could mean exposure, or even death, for a spy who is operating alone. An agent from the CIA station might leave a message for such a spy in a newspaper on a park bench or a letter dropped in the hollow of a tree. Often, the real message will be contained in a *microdot,* a photograph reduced to the size of a dot and pasted on a page to look like a period.

In snooping on the activities of their adversaries, CIA agents use a variety of surveillance devices, such as concealed cameras and viewers that enhance night vision. To obtain a photograph of an

The SR-71 Blackbird, *above,* a plane designed for high-altitude photography, can reach speeds up to 2,000 miles (3,200 kilometers) per hour. Complex instruments at CIA headquarters, *left,* are used to analyze Soviet electronic signals.

individual, say a newly identified officer from an opposing intelligence service, an agent might sit for hours in a parked automobile equipped with a hidden long-range camera. While waiting for the foreign officer to emerge from a nearby building, the CIA agent may wonder, "Am I, too, being watched?" To the agent, every stranger is a potential spy, every dark window a possible vantage point for an unseen observer.

Such can be the life of a spy—secretive, paranoid, and always alert to the possibility of being outmaneuvered by the opposition. And the opposition can be formidable. More often than not, American agents find themselves locked in a battle of wits with the forces of the Soviet Union's Committee of State Security—the KGB.

With more than 500,000 employees, the KGB is the world's largest intelligence service. The KGB and the smaller GRU—the Soviet army-intelligence unit—work tirelessly to accomplish several aims: obtaining the government, military, and industrial secrets of Western nations; weakening the patriotism of those nations' citizens; and aiding revolutionary movements in the Third World.

The KGB cannot be compared to any Western intelligence service. It is unique in its size, its many functions, and the power and prestige it enjoys within the government. The KGB's duties include espionage and counterespionage, both at home and abroad, border protection, and the investigation of major crimes. In addition, the KGB serves as a political weapon, rooting out and suppressing opposition to the Communist Party's control of the state.

The KGB is descended from an organization called the Cheka, which was founded in late 1917 to battle adversaries of the newly established Communist regime. Within a few years, the Cheka extended its operations abroad to harass, and sometimes murder, Russian refugees and other "enemies of the revolution." The KGB, ac-

43

Spies of the Imagination

Although the first modern novel with a secret agent as the main character was American author James Fenimore Cooper's *The Spy* (1821), spies did not really enter popular culture until the 1900's. Literary authorities consider the first contemporary spy novel to be *The Riddle of the Sands* (1903) by Irish writer and nationalist Robert Erskine Childers. Since then, a multitude of novels, motion pictures, and television series have featured secret agents. The following are some of the best known of these fictional spies:

Sir Percy Blakeney. Blakeney, an English aristocrat, is better known as the Scarlet Pimpernel in the novel of the same name (1905), written by Hungarian-born author Baroness Orczy. Posing as an idle eccentric, Blakeney saves many French nobles from death during the French Revolution. The story has been retold a number of times on the stage, in film, and on television.

James Bond. This suave, sophisticated British agent, code name 007, is the world's most famous fictional spy. Bond is the creation of British author Ian Fleming who wrote a dozen James Bond novels, such as *Dr. No* and *Goldfinger*, between 1953 and 1964. Those and other Bond exploits were made into highly popular movies starring Sean Connery and, later, Roger Moore.

Richard Hannay. Hannay is the hero of three novels written between 1915 and 1924 by John Buchan of Great Britain, a member of Parliament, governor general of Canada, and writer. Hannay's battles with German, Russian, and Turkish spies were depicted in several movies, most notably Sir Alfred Hitchcock's 1935 adaptation of *The Thirty-Nine Steps*.

Matt Helm. American novelist Donald Hamilton created Helm as the U.S. answer to James Bond. Four of Hamilton's books were made into motion pictures in the 1960's, with singer-actor Dean Martin starring as Helm.

Mr. Moto. Master of disguise and fluent in several languages, I. M. Moto plunges into the thick of international intrigue in the Far East of the 1930's. Moto appeared in six novels by American writer John P. Marquand and was portrayed by Hungarian-born actor Peter Lorre in eight films.

Harry Palmer. British author Len Deighton's working-class hero is drawn reluctantly into the dark world of espionage. Through Palmer's eyes, we see spying as the dangerous, unromantic business that it really is. British actor Michael Caine played Palmer in three movies based on Deighton's books, including *The Ipcress File* (1962).

Maxwell Smart. Television actor Don Adams portrayed this bumbling unsecret agent in the TV series "Get Smart!" The popular program, which lasted from 1965 to 1970, was created by comedy writers Mel Brooks and Buck Henry. Assisted by Agent 99 (actress Barbara Feldon), Smart—against all odds—manages in each episode to best the forces of KAOS, the spy service of an unnamed enemy. Smart's famous line, "Would you believe . . . ?", was on everyone's lips in the late 1960's.

George Smiley. English author John le Carré (real name David Cornwell) wrote several novels about this disillusioned British intelligence agent. Like other spies in le Carré's books, Smiley is tired of his cloak-and-dagger life but doesn't know how to change it. In 1980, British actor Sir Alec Guinness played Smiley in a TV adaptation of le Carré's 1974 novel *Tinker, Tailor, Soldier, Spy*.

Napoleon Solo. Solo and his partner, Illya Kuryakin—played by actors Robert Vaughn and David McCallum, respectively—were the supercool agents of the hit TV show "The Man from U.N.C.L.E." The program originated in 1964 and ran until 1967. Solo and Kuryakin do battle with T.H.R.U.S.H., a fictitious Soviet spy service based on James Bond's Russian adversary, S.M.E.R.S.H.   [D. L. W.]

Sappy Maxwell Smart (Don Adams) and sophisticated James Bond (Sean Connery) are about as different as two spies can be.

cording to a number of reports in the world press, has continued that unsavory tradition, striking out against various defectors and dissidents from the Soviet Union and other Eastern-bloc countries. Several murders, carried out with deadly poisons and gases that are lethal in tiny amounts and leave almost no trace in the victim's body, have been linked to the KGB.

The KGB, like the CIA, has "won a few and lost a few," but some of its successes have stunned the West. In one of its greatest triumphs, the KGB from 1939 to 1946 stole atomic-bomb research secrets from the United States, Canada, and Great Britain. The KGB has also been successful at placing moles in several opposing intelligence services. Its most famous mole was British-born agent Harold (Kim) Philby, who from 1940 to 1951 rose to the top ranks of MI-6, Great Britain's Secret Intelligence Service.

Other Soviet operations have fallen flat. The KGB's *disinformation* schemes—the planting of false and potentially disruptive information—have had an especially high failure rate. In 1981, for instance, KGB agents forged a letter from President Reagan to King Juan Carlos I of Spain suggesting that the United States was forcing itself into Spanish affairs. The letter, intended to stir up trouble between Spain and the United States, was quickly exposed as a hoax.

Many KGB agents have also been exposed. Since 1971, when Great Britain expelled 107 Soviet spies posing as diplomats, more than 500 other Soviets using diplomatic posts as covers for spy work have been deported by Britain, the United States, and other countries. One of the largest expulsions occurred in September and October 1986, when the Reagan Administration ordered 80 Soviet diplomats to leave the United States.

The KGB's power and status within the Soviet political system is immense. KGB influence in government affairs reached a high point in 1982 when the spy service's chairman, Yuri V. Andropov, became general secretary of the Communist Party, the top Soviet political post. Under Andropov's successor at the KGB, Viktor M.

The headquarters of the Soviet spy service, the KGB—adorned temporarily with a portrait of V. I. Lenin, founder of the Soviet Union—looms over central Moscow, *below left.* The KGB's power was demonstrated in 1982 when its chairman, Yuri V. Andropov, *below,* became the top Soviet leader.

Chebrikov, the mammoth organization has grown even more powerful. Observers say the KGB, though presenting a more civilized image than it did in earlier decades, is cracking down with new fervor on dissent and corruption in Soviet society.

The free hand with which the KGB operates, both at home and abroad, points up the fundamental difference between dictatorships and democracies in the role played by intelligence agencies. Authoritarian systems, like those of the Soviet Union and its allies, lack the consent of the governed. The ruling elites of such systems, who consider themselves accountable to no one for their actions, must use force to maintain their privileged position. In their hands, intelligence services perform not only the legitimate function of safeguarding national security but also the more sinister one of keeping the populace in a state of obedience. Moreover, because authoritarian governments keep an iron grip on the flow of information, they have little trouble maintaining a high degree of secrecy.

The situation is much different in democracies, which abide by the rule of law and must operate their intelligence services within constitutional limits. Democratic governments are forced to find an acceptable balance between two contradictory necessities: the necessity for secrecy in matters relating to national security, on the one hand, and the need to protect constitutionally guaranteed freedoms, including the rights of inquiry and expression, on the other. Such a balance can be especially hard to achieve in peacetime, when there are relatively few government constraints on the citizenry or the news media. In a crisis requiring rapid decision-making and action, the "secrecy gap" between democracies and dictatorships can give an initial advantage to the latter.

Democracies, however, can also abuse power, including using intelligence organizations for improper purposes. In September 1985, for example, the government of France admitted that French intelligence agents in New Zealand were responsible for the sinking, two months earlier, of the *Rainbow Warrior*, a ship owned by the environmental group Greenpeace. The ship had been about to sail to an atoll in the South Pacific Ocean to protest French nuclear tests.

The intelligence agencies of the United States have experienced their own share of controversy. After the death of FBI Director J. Edgar Hoover in 1972, congressional investigators learned that the bureau had sometimes overstepped the law during the Hoover era. FBI agents, the investigators reported in 1975, had spied illegally on U.S. citizens, opened private mail, committed burglaries, and defamed persons whom Hoover considered threats to the nation.

Also in 1975, Congress and a presidential commission chaired by Vice President Nelson A. Rockefeller probed the activities of the CIA, and both found considerable evidence of wrongdoing. The CIA's principal misdeeds within the United States had been much the same as the FBI's: spying on Americans, opening their mail, and

The U.S. intelligence community has been rocked by scandals in recent years. In the 1970's, investigations showed that the CIA and FBI had spied on U.S. citizens. That upset was followed, in 1985, by the revelation that traitors had been selling American secrets to foreign powers. Jerry A. Whitworth, *above,* was part of a spy ring that sold Navy secrets to the Soviets.

carrying out illegal break-ins and buggings. The Rockefeller Commission balanced its criticisms with some positive notes, however. The panel concluded that "the great majority" of the CIA's activities during the previous 20 years had been within the law.

The revelations of the 1970's weakened the United States intelligence system, and it did not fully recover from the setback until the early 1980's. The restoration of public confidence in the FBI and CIA was largely the result of several congressional and executive-branch reform measures that brought those two agencies under tighter control. One of the most important actions was the establishment of a congressional intelligence oversight system in 1976 and 1977. Both houses of Congress formed permanent watchdog committees to monitor more closely the budgets and secret operations of the nation's intelligence services, particularly the CIA.

The U.S. intelligence community had no sooner returned to normal when it was rocked by new scandals—this time involving breaches of national security. In May 1985, John A. Walker, Jr., a retired Navy officer living in Norfolk, Va., was arrested by FBI agents and charged with spying for the Soviet Union. In succeeding weeks, Walker's son and brother and an associate in California, Jerry A. Whitworth, were also arrested. All later pleaded guilty or were convicted of selling vital Navy secrets to Soviet spies. The Walker case was thought to be one of the worst breaches of U.S. security since the loss of atomic secrets in the 1940's.

But the apprehension of the Walkers was only the beginning. In later months, a number of other Americans were also accused or convicted of selling classified government information to the Soviet Union and other foreign powers. They included two former agents of the CIA, Edward L. Howard and Larry Wu-Tai Chin.

By late 1986, the arrests had tapered off, but many government leaders feared that other shocks might be in store. They pointed to two disturbing facts: Virtually all of the Americans arrested for espionage in recent years have admitted they spied for one reason—money. And nearly 1 million citizens have access to top-secret information. How many of those people, government officials wondered, would put financial gain ahead of loyalty to the nation?

In the "spy wars" between competing powers, the stakes are nothing less than the survival of nations. All countries, whether authoritarian or democratic, feel a need to protect their military, political, and technological secrets while obtaining useful, accurate information about their adversaries. The citizens of an open society such as the United States may sometimes deplore government secrecy, but a certain amount of secretiveness cannot be avoided. Even George Washington, a firm believer in open government, realized that secrecy is frequently necessary when the nation is faced with enemies. In the hostile world we live in today, unfortunately, enemies—and their spies—have become a permanent fact of life.

By Eugene J. Walter, Jr.

The New Look in Zoos

Large, stunningly realistic new exhibits display animals as they have never been seen before.

The path winds around clusters of waterworn rock. You brush past dangling orchids and discover a mountain river cascading down a tumble of boulders into a series of pools. In the river and along its banks are dragonlike creatures—gharials, members of the crocodile family with long, extremely narrow snouts. One of these reptiles suddenly snaps its head sideways and clamps its needle-sharp teeth on a fish. High above the water, in the topmost branches of a dead tree, fruit bats roost. One fans itself, slowly stretching its wings their full 5 feet (1.5 meters).

Across the river stands a green wall of forest, decorated by a Thunbergia vine whose lavender blossoms string across the scene like Christmas-tree lights. A ghostly mist filters down through the dense vegetation. Through the shadows, humanlike figures seem to fly from branch to branch, vine to vine. They are gibbons, smallest and most agile of the apes. A harsh squawk registers the displeasure of a hornbill disturbed by the gibbons.

The path leads downward. After a few steps, you glance at a huge hollow log overhead. You stop suddenly—a long muscular python lies coiled inside the log, apparently ready to slither out and wrap itself around you. But it will not.

Contrary to all appearances, you are not in a rain forest in the foothills of an Asian mountain range. You are in JungleWorld, an exhibit that opened at the Bronx Zoo in New York City in June 1985, and the "hollow log" is part of a brilliantly designed display. Tinted glass, cleverly angled and lit to be almost invisible, restrains the reptile. In September 1986, the American Association of Zoological Parks and Aquariums (AAZPA) cited JungleWorld as the best exhibit of the year. Warren J. Iliff, director of Dallas Zoo and president of the AAZPA, describes the Bronx building as "undoubtedly the most ambitious, most successful zoo exhibit anywhere."

A variety of habitats

The 37,000-square-foot (3,400-square-meter) building that houses the rain forest also contains a volcanic island scrub forest, a large mangrove swamp, and a lowland rain forest—habitats that are home to such jungle denizens as proboscis monkeys, otters, silvered leaf monkeys, Malayan tapirs, crocodiles, and a variety of birds. Small galleries housing insects and other tiny creatures separate the large habitats.

The author:
Eugene J. Walter, Jr., is editor in chief of *Animal Kingdom* magazine and curator of publications at the New York Zoological Society in New York City.

William Conway, general director of the New York Zoological Society and the individual most responsible for the creation of JungleWorld, describes the arrangement as "choreographed," shifting from large galleries to small and back to large.

JungleWorld contains more than 20 species of large trees, some taller than 30 feet (9 meters); more than 30 orchid species and an even greater number of ferns; and 15 types of vines, including several grown from seeds collected in Java—an island in Indonesia. All this flora thrives under nearly 1 acre (0.4 hectare) of glass that forms most of the roof, 55 feet (17 meters) above the ground. Complementing the flora are 23 artificial trees up to 50 feet (15 meters) tall. And there are 17,000 square feet (1,600 square meters) of artificial limestone, sandstone, lava, and granite.

The artificial trees and rocks have stunningly realistic shapes, thanks to the use of space-age plastics that can be sculpted into natural forms. And the illusion builders paint these reproductions in amazing detail—in the case of trees, right down to artificial fungus on the "bark."

Special effects enhance the jungle illusion. Clouds billowing through treetops come from an agricultural atomizer—the kind of device that produces a mist to keep Florida citrus crops from freezing. Speakers hidden in trees, rocks, and shrubs at 65 locations broadcast eight-channel stereotapes of jungle noises, such as the sounds of crickets, cicadas, and other insects; frogs; and crabs popping from holes in swamp mud.

The reason for realism

JungleWorld and other new realistic exhibits are just the latest development in the long history of zoo curators' efforts to find better ways to display animals. Past efforts were concerned with making zoo animals more comfortable, but the emphasis gradually shifted. Today's exhibits are certainly comfortable, and they provide a rich environment that stimulates the animals mentally and physically. But the primary purpose of the realism is to enable a predominantly urban public to see how animals live in the wild. Zoo curators hope to give the public a sense of the wonder and beauty of wild animals and their natural habitats, and thus enlist the public's support for efforts to preserve wildlife and their habitats.

John Gwynne, the Bronx Zoo's curator of exhibition and graphic arts, refers to this use of realism as "environmental immersion"—putting people into the world of animals. This technique marks the greatest advance yet in the history of public zoos.

Today's realistic exhibits are a far cry from the first public zoo, which opened in London in 1828. The emphasis in London was on variety—exhibiting something of everything. There, and at later public zoos, animals occupied row after row of cages and corrals.

Yet in the early 1800's, certain visionaries advocated something similar to modern zoos. French zoologist the Comte de Lacépède, for example, describing his concept of the ideal zoo in 1801, said, "Two little artificial rivers cross the terrain. . . . Between the two sinuous little rivers an elevated path is used by the visitors. . . . The slopes are divided into several enclosures of irregular dimensions surrounded by fences which go down to the water and are hidden by vegetation."

No one built anything resembling Lacépède's concept until 1907, when German animal dealer Karl Hagenbeck and Swiss sculptor and designer Urs Eggenschwiller used moats to create an almost

Homes Away from Home

Exhibit designers use a variety of natural and artificial materials to construct realistic habitats for animals from all parts of the world.

Penguin Encounter at Sea World in San Diego, *above,* is a frigid duplicate of the rugged Antarctic coastline. Crushed ice substitutes for snow, and the "rocks" are reinforced concrete. A fiberglass replica of an ice shelf overlooks a pool of seawater.

The Mountain Habitat, *right,* at the Arizona-Sonora Desert Museum in Tucson is home to the American black bear (inset), a native of nearby mountains. All the trees in the scene are real, but the rocks are made of concrete.

Gorillas lounge in artificial trees in Tropic World, *left,* at Brookfield Zoo near Chicago. The trees, rocks, and riverbanks were built by spraying concrete onto steel frames. The bushes are steel, and the vines are epoxy-coated rope. Sand added to the epoxy discourages the animals from chewing the vines.

A dam at the Minnesota Zoo south of Minneapolis, *above,* looks as if it is the work of beavers, but it is actually a product of human hands. The structure is made of concrete, with a steel reinforcing wall. Real logs are built into the middle of the dam. The small trees are real—food for the beavers.

Unusual Points of View

The Minnesota Zoo goes to great lengths to enable visitors to see how large animals live in the wild in other parts of the world. Children in a room below ground level look up at a beluga whale, or white whale—an Arctic animal—swimming in a huge tank, *above*. Visitors in a monorail car, *below*, look down at a herd of Bactrian camels, which are native to Asia.

barless zoo in Stellingen, near Hamburg, in what is now West Germany. In this zoo's African scene, which still exists, visitors see a herd of gazelles and water birds such as flamingos, storks, and cranes. Just beyond these animals, large antelope and zebras graze. Farther away are lions, their natural predators; and, beyond the cats, an area of rocky, hilly land is inhabited by wild sheep and ibexes. Concealed moats separate the four animal groups from one another and from the spectators.

In 1918 and 1919, a German designer created moated bear dens at zoos in Denver and St. Louis. As early as the 1920's, several United States zoos built habitats for reptiles. By the 1930's, some zoos in the United States and Europe were creating habitats—and even modest jungles—for birds. The displays were not as elaborate as today's exhibits, but they were great improvements over rows of gloomy cages.

In 1928, Detroit hired Hagenbeck's company to design and direct the building of habitat exhibits, some with mixed groups of antelope, zebras, and ostriches. In St. Louis, at about the same time, designer John Wallace created a large complex of hoofed mammal exhibits with shelters and moats, modeled after granite formations in the area.

One of the most successful projects of this period opened in 1940 at the Bronx Zoo. There, antelope, ostriches, and other birds inhabit a handsome, rolling terrain landscaped with trees, grasses, and a water hole—to suggest an African *savanna* (grassland). Lions prowl the grassland and snooze on rocky outcroppings, but a camouflaged moat separates them from the antelope and ostriches.

Blocks, tiles, and bars

Unfortunately for the zoo world, modernistic art and architecture also began to flourish during these years and influenced zoo design. Artificial rock formations in zoos gradually became abstractions—concrete blocks with surfaces sculpted in unadorned planes. Moated exhibits were lined up in rows with no attempt to unify the exhibits. Bears, small mammals, and predators were often displayed in circular clusters so that each exhibit was merely a wedge-shaped enclosure behind a moat.

A tank 28 feet (8.5 meters) deep at Monterey Bay Aquarium in California harbors a forest of kelp—a giant seaweed found in cold waters throughout the world—and thousands of fish. The kelp, which must have moving water to grow, sways in waves created by machines.

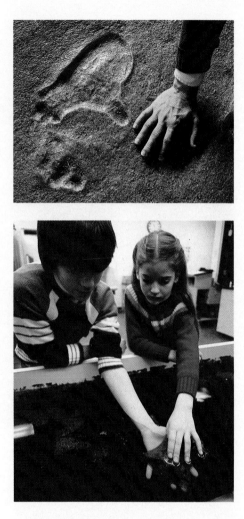

Modern zoos allow visitors to examine wild-life by the sense of touch as well as by sight. A man compares his hand with a gorilla print, *top,* built into a trail at Tropic World, an exhibit at Brookfield Zoo near Chicago. Children touch a live starfish, *above,* at Minnesota Zoo's Touch and Feel Zoo Lab.

But even if zoo officials had been inclined to experiment further with Karl Hagenbeck's model, they would have faced major technological limitations. Health concerns, for example, restricted the scope of mammal exhibits, particularly indoors. Mammals are extremely vulnerable to parasites and bacteria that live in soil and concrete. So, for decades, two of the most common materials used in mammal exhibits were ceramic tiles and steel bars—preformed units that could not be reshaped into natural designs.

Better medicine and better materials

After the end of World War II in 1945, two developments helped zoo designers move forward. The first was an improvement in the level of veterinary medicine practiced at zoos. More zoos hired full-time veterinarians, and the veterinarians were better trained and equipped to handle animal diseases. This development meant that zoo mammals no longer had to live in such sterile environments.

The second development was the introduction of colorfast and extremely strong plastics in which parasites and bacteria could not live, yet which were so flexible before hardening that they could be sculpted into finely detailed reproductions of trees, rocks, and other natural forms.

One of the foremost users of the new materials was zoologist Mervin W. Larson, who joined the staff at the Arizona-Sonora Desert Museum in Tucson, Ariz., in 1953. Larson experimented with fiberglass, epoxy, and other new substances to create small indoor exhibits for such creatures as ground squirrels, reptiles, and amphibians. As he developed his design and building skills, he applied them to larger exhibits. An outdoor display that opened in 1967 represents otters living in the Santa Cruz River Valley a century earlier. Visitors can view the acrobatic animals from a bridge across a pool at the base of a stream that trickles over an artificial rocky riverbank. Or, belowground, visitors can watch the otters through glass as the animals swim underwater or move about in their den.

In 1970, an even more impressive Larson-designed exhibit opened at the Arizona-Sonora Desert Museum. Realistic canyon scenes depicting foothills and dry streambeds are the habitat of small feline species native to the region, such as bobcats, jaguarundis, and ocelots. Visitors look at the cats from above and, through glass, at canyon-floor level.

Felines are difficult to display because most of them are small, secretive, and inactive during the day. The Brookfield Zoo near Chicago devised an indoor group of settings—called Predator Ecology—showing these animals as they behave in the wild at night. The opening display, completed in January 1975, represents a rocky desert canyon area on Algeria's Tassili Oua-n-Ahaggar plateau. Over the centuries, wind and water erosion there have carved natural grottoes in the massive rocks. In Brookfield's reproduction, visitors gaze out over a "starlit" desert scene populated by sand cats. The visitors then walk across a 30-foot (9-meter) bridge made of wood and rope—the type maintained for generations by people in the Himalaya. On one side of the bridge is a duplicate of the Hindu Kush mountains of Afghanistan at 15,000 feet (4,600 meters). Pallas cats, their ears sticking out at a peculiar angle, peer at the visitors from a craggy ledge. On the other side of the bridge, visitors peer into the Canadian Rockies at 7,000 feet (2,100 meters), the domain of lynxes. From there, they slip between rocky crags and cross a bridge that leads to a New World tropical forest at the level of lower tree branches—a location favored by small, spotted margays. Finally, another bridge leads through an Asian forest and across a rushing stream where fishing cats actually fish for their dinner.

Two imaginative exhibits enable children to experience the world much as animals do. A girl at Bronx Zoo's Children's Zoo, *top,* listens on a headset hidden inside a gigantic replica of the ears of a *fennec*—a small fox that lives in the Sahara and in the Syrian Desert. She hears what fennecs hear via a microphone mounted over a nearby fennec habitat. At Treehouse Zoo, an environmental display in Philadelphia, *above,* a child gets a hungry frog's view of a "fly."

Building rocks and trees

In producing these exhibits, the Brookfield designers relied heavily on epoxy for rocks and trees. To vary epoxy's color and texture in building rocks, the designers added pigments, sand, mica, and other minerals. Then they painted the rocks to create the illusion of shadows, stains, and *lichens* (certain combinations of fungi and algae).

Conway describes the basic structure of an artificial tree as a steel and wire-mesh frame like the skeleton of a fiberglass boat. Display builders blast the fiberglass coating with fine particles of sand, then cover it with epoxy. While the epoxy still has

Designers of habitats for zoo animals use conventional architectural techniques such as model building. For example, Brookfield Zoo's exhibit artist Raymond S. Robinson, *above* (at right), built an extremely detailed model to help zoo administrators visualize a proposed habitat for aardvarks. The actual habitat, *right,* opened in May 1986, complete with an underground aardvark den.

a puttylike consistency, artists sculpt in knotholes and other details and emboss the surface with bark ridges. Finally, they paint on the "lichens." Artificial vines are steel-cored nylon ropes covered with latex—sometimes epoxy—and paint.

In the late 1970's, landscape architects joined exhibit-making teams, adding another new dimension to modern zoo design. One architectural firm helped a zoo shatter an old myth. Designers had long assumed that naturalistic habitats for gorillas and other primates were out of the question because the great strength and curiosity of these animals make them extremely destructive. But Director David Hancocks of Seattle's Woodland Park Zoo—a typical old-fashioned zoological garden—and Johnpaul Jones, a partner in Jones & Jones, a local architectural and environmental-planning firm, proved that the assumption was incorrect. They constructed an 18,000-square-foot (1,700-square-meter) gorilla habitat that might have been airlifted from upland forests in west Africa.

The exhibit features a rippling, meadowlike clearing thick with tall grasses, a stream splashing over exposed boulders into a shallow pool, fallen trees, and, to the rear, dense forest. The only obvious barrier is glass on one side of a vine-covered rain shelter. To get to the exhibit, visitors follow a twisting path through thick growths of shrubs, trees, and grasses that obscure the outside world. The vegetation is not African but consists of look-alike plants that survive in Seattle's colder climate. The zoo's five gorillas thrive in the exhibit while doing minimal damage to the plants.

Woodland Park does an excellent job of creating the sense of wonder and beauty that zoo curators consider essential. Although no formal research was conducted when the gorilla jungle opened, Director Hancocks and two University of Washington graduate students—Michael Hutchins and Carolyn Crockett—kept notes on visitor reactions. "People tend to be quiet, even talking in whispers,"

The realistic appearance of Bronx Zoo's JungleWorld owes much to such exacting work as the painting of a detailed mural of a tropic scene, *above,* and the mounting of artificial fungus on the "bark" of a tree made of metal and plastic, *right.*

they wrote. "One rarely hears the typical jokes or ribald comments, and never expressions of pity. It is clear from unsolicited comments and letters that people genuinely enjoy the experience of this naturalistic habitat. . . . It is not unusual to hear people refer to the animals as 'beautiful.' "

In zoo exhibit design, one of the main tasks of landscape architects is to hide barriers that separate groups of animals from one another and from visitors. In Pittsburgh Zoo's African savanna exhibit designed by landscape architect Jon Charles Coe, for example, the animals' indoor quarters are hidden behind hilltops or banks of earth. And in an exhibit scheduled to open at Pittsburgh Zoo in 1987, underwater barriers will separate three groups of large mammals. Visitors will view all the animals from across a meandering creek. Elephants will frolic and relax on a sand bar formed by a U-shaped pond. On one side of the pond, giraffes will stroll across savanna. On the other, zebras and antelope will run about. A slope on the elephants' side will allow the elephants to walk down to the flat bottom of the pond. But an underwater wall forming the opposite edge of the pond will be vertical and too high for the elephants to climb. The elephants' splashing will send ripples of water toward visitors' feet, but the people will be too far away to be reached by the elephants' trunks.

In many of today's new zoo exhibits, electronic gadgetry and atmospheric touches add sensory impact to realistic scenery. The most common such features are "rainstorms" in bird and reptile displays. The basic ingredient is a sprinkler system—activated by a keeper or an automatic timer—with the sprinkler heads placed so that they water plants, not visitors. In many exhibits, the show begins when a timer closes louvers over skylights to darken the exhibit. Then tape recordings automatically set thunder to rumbling, and stroboscopic lights flash "lightning." Once the water starts to flow, sound and light build to a crescendo, and then diminish as the "rain" slackens and finally stops.

Wind and waves

An artificial storm adds realism to a simulated polar ice shelf at the main exhibit in Penguin Encounter, which opened at Sea World of San Diego in May 1983. The exhibit is home to six species of penguins—more than 300 of them—plus other birds that live near penguins in the wild. A saltwater pool, 7 feet (2.1 meters) deep, extends 40 feet (12 meters) under an icy overhang, and is chilled to about 45° F. (8° C). Air temperature is maintained at subfreezing level and, every day, two blowers blast in a "snowstorm" of 12,000 pounds (5,400 kilograms) of crushed ice.

At Washington Park Zoo in Portland, Ore., Jones & Jones revamped an ordinary penguin display into an award-winning exhibit in 1983. The designers reproduced a rocky island off the coast of Peru, and added a machine that triggers a large splash on one side of the island and a ripple elsewhere along the beach.

Similar machines shoot out powerful jets of water, creating waves in the Kelp Forest, an underwater display at the Monterey Bay Aquarium in California, which opened in 1984. The giant seaweed grows in a swaying aquatic jungle inside a tank measuring 65 feet (19 meters) long by 28 feet (8.5 meters) deep. The Kelp Forest harbors thousands of fish including flounder, halibut, striped bass, albacore, and garibaldi. The waves are not only pleasing to see but also essential to kelp growth.

The future holds the likelihood of other devices "to assault all the senses, to create a more powerful impact," according to Gwynne of the Bronx Zoo. Producing an impact on visitors' sense of smell will not be easy. Scent is one of the more difficult effects to manage because of the need to direct aromas and contain them within limited areas.

There are plenty of visual dazzlers to come, however. The technology is already available to manufacture clouds and rainbows, even in outdoor exhibits. And more optical illusions can be ex-

Like zoologists on a jungle trail, *top,* visitors at Brookfield Zoo's
Predator Ecology exhibit observe margays—small, spotted cats
native to Central and South America. The display's artificial
vegetation has an astonishingly natural appearance because its
designers paid close attention to such subtle details as bare
portions of ''tree'' branches, *above.*

Children gaze in awe at a polar bear, its shiny fur undulating gently in a saltwater pond at Point Defiance Zoo and Aquarium in Tacoma, Wash. The bear habitat depicts a coastal setting near Point Hope, Alaska, where polar bears live in the wild. The trees in the background are real, but the cliffs are made of concrete.

pected. To produce illusions of unlimited space, for example, Gwynne wants to experiment with *holograms*—three-dimensional images recorded by laser light on photographic plates or films.

Ironically, the naturalism that makes exhibits great sometimes makes it difficult to see animals. Gwynne voices the typical exhibitor's lament: "The public wants to see animals in gigantic, limitless space. Yet they also complain if the animal is not right up front."

Visitors also want to see animals *doing* something. But much of what many animals do in the wild involves hiding from other animals. So, to be realistic, many exhibits must contain places the public cannot see.

Strategies for coping with these dilemmas range from simple to complex. In primate exhibits such as those at Woodland Park, keepers scatter raisins, peanuts, and other treats through the tall grass, motivating the apes to forage as they would in the wild. Near a visitors' window at JungleWorld's "forest," there is a feeder in the form of a fallen tree killed by a strangler vine. A buzzer alerts the gibbons that treats are available at various points on the "tree."

In Bronx Zoo's Himalayan Highlands, heating coils in "rocks" attract snow leopards to locations where they are easily visible to human visitors. A habitat at Washington Park Zoo in Portland simulates a lush tropical setting for sun bears, which like to relax by draping themselves on tree branches where the limbs form a Y. To encourage this, Jones & Jones built heating pads into the branches of two large artificial trees.

Mental stimulation is particularly important to elephants and other intelligent species. Zoos have abandoned circuslike shows, but many of them display elephants "at work." An elephant habitat under development by Jones & Jones for Seattle's Woodland Park will look like a lumber camp, with a building for lumbering equipment, a cooking shack, and other facilities. At scheduled times, visitors will see elephants haul and stack logs.

Problems of space and money

There is virtually no limit to the imagination of zoo designers, but other limitations exist. One major limitation is space. Most zoos occupy less than 100 acres (40 hectares), usually a good deal less. Many zoos do not have enough space for more than one or two modest realistic exhibits, which occupy far more space than do cages and "tiled-bathroom" displays.

Another major limitation is money. Realistic habitats cost millions of dollars. To understand why, consider the snake's "log" that startles visitors at JungleWorld. That structure, a relatively small part of JungleWorld, is 3 feet (0.9 meter) in diameter and 35 feet (11 meters) long, and has 5 feet (1.5 meters) of stump. Built into it are a thermostatically controlled heating and air-conditioning system, a ventilation system, two drainage systems, neon lights, three doors, and two water systems. A steel I-beam holds the tinted, angled glass that creates the illusion, and the base of the log is stainless steel cable. Along the structure's exterior epoxy shell are "mushrooms," also made of epoxy. Pieces of broken log, covered with embossed epoxy, are scattered inside the hollow part of the structure. One of the pieces contains heating coils and is positioned to keep the python up front and clearly visible. Atop the structure are hidden planters that house real plants. Conway notes, "Only God can make a tree—inexpensively!"

But the men and women who are associated with these zoological institutions believe that the artificial habitats will be worth every penny if they motivate the viewing public to support efforts to preserve animal habitats in the wild. Two digital counters at the exit of JungleWorld convey a sense of the urgency of these efforts. One counter shows the amount of rain forest on Earth—an amount that is decreasing at the rate of 50 acres (20 hectares) every minute. The other registers Earth's human population, which is increasing by 125 people every minute and occupying more and more rain forest. On display near the counters is a quote from a Buddhist philosopher: "In the end, we will conserve only what we love. We will love only what we understand. We will understand only what we are taught."

By Martha J. Nelson

Big Boom in Women's Sports

Women are pursuing sports and fitness activities in
record numbers, and the top female athletes are
performing almost as well as their male counterparts.

About 100 superb athletes from all points of the globe are expected to take part in a grueling footrace at the 1988 Olympic Games in South Korea. The race will be a marathon—a 26-mile, 385-yard (42.2-kilometer) test of conditioning, tactics, and determination. The athletes will be women.

All the runners will suffer during the race, as the distance takes its toll on bone, muscle, connective tissue, and the sheer ability to find the energy and the will to keep putting one foot in front of the other. But almost certainly, all the women will recover from the contest quickly and will compete in many future marathons.

This last statement is so obviously true that it may not seem worth making in 1987. Yet, as recently as the 1970's, Olympic officials believed that the marathon distance was too long for women. Indeed, the first women's Olympic marathon took place only in 1984.

Even more extreme than the officials' outmoded belief about the marathon was an earlier view of women's "distance" running. Because several runners collapsed after finishing the women's 800-meter race in the 1928 Olympics, there was no women's Olympic footrace of more than 200 meters from 1932 through 1956.

The barrier keeping women out of middle-distance Olympic races fell in 1960 because women showed that they could handle the distances easily. By the time Joan Benoit (now Joan Benoit Samuelson) of the United States won the gold medal in the 1984 women's Olympic marathon, women had shown that they could handle any distance men could handle. In fact, Benoit's gold medal time of 2 hours 24 minutes 52 seconds was 8 seconds faster than the winning time in the 1956 *men's* Olympic marathon.

Benoit's victory symbolized the success of many champion women athletes who broke down barriers that kept them out of major competitions. But they were by no means alone. As the champions were chalking up success after success, millions of women who did not even think of themselves as athletes, let alone champions, were breaking down barriers of their own. In the United States by 1985, women made up 55.7 per cent of the new participants in tennis, 54.4 per cent in bicycling, and 50.2 per cent in softball, according to American Sports Data, a research firm in Hartsdale, N.Y.

The great strides taken by U.S. women in sports during the 1970's and 1980's owe much to the women's liberation movement, which led to parallel advances in business, politics, and a wide range of other activities previously dominated by men. Another major contributor has been the fitness movement. A growing recognition of the health benefits of aerobic exercise has made fitness activities and recreational sports tremendously popular with both sexes.

But the main drive behind the women's sports revolution in the United States has been Title IX of the federal Education Amendments of 1972 (formally set in motion when final regulations were issued in 1975). Title IX, designed to prohibit sex discrimination, reads: "No person in the United States shall, on the basis of sex, be excluded from participation in, be denied the benefits of, or be sub-

The author:
Martha J. Nelson is editor of *Women's Sports and Fitness* magazine.

jected to discrimination under any education program or activity receiving Federal financial assistance."

Almost all U.S. elementary schools, secondary schools, colleges, and universities received federal aid. So, as interpreted in the 1975 regulations, Title IX meant that sports programs for girls and women had to be equivalent to those for boys and men virtually throughout the U.S. education system.

Title IX promised vast changes because in 1972 sports programs for females fell far short of programs for males. The regulations gave institutions that did not comply with Title IX varying periods of time to make their programs equivalent. Schools that failed to meet deadlines faced a cutoff of federal funds.

Before its passage, Title IX had met with opposition on three counts. Some individuals believed that sports programs for females *should* fall short of those for males. Another objection was that Title IX would require schools to create coeducational physical education classes, which many believed were improper. And finally, there were fears that new collegiate programs for women would necessitate cutbacks in men's programs.

But equivalence was an idea whose time had come. And so, in the mid-1970's, with the threat of cutoffs looming over their budgets,

The boom in women's athletics has increased levels of participation in intercollegiate sports, but the growth has been uneven. In the mid-1980's, basketball, track and field, and softball continued to mushroom in popularity, but the other important sports already had seen their years of greatest growth.

Numbers of Women Participating in Intercollegiate Athletics*

	1966-1967	1971-1972	1976-1977	1981-1982	1986-1987
Selected sports					
Basketball	4,253	6,176	10,859	9,624	12,401
Field hockey	3,126	5,012	6,847	5,701	6,661
Gymnastics	579	1,855	2,722	2,063	2,245
Softball	1,366	3,185	6,310	7,465	10,375
Swimming	1,184	2,429	5,969	6,218	8,431
Tennis	1,361	3,071	7,127	6,599	8,560
Track and field	309	1,389	5,831	9,217	12,033
Volleyball	2,178	4,124	9,356	8,418	10,510
All sports	15,727	31,852	64,375	69,096	101,065
Number of institutions reporting	577	663	722	753	779

*Data for 1966 through 1982 are from reports of the National Collegiate Athletic Association. Figures for 1986-1987 are estimates made by the author.

Great Moments in the History of Women's Sports

1914 Theresa Weld Blanchard wins the first U.S. women's figure-skating title.

1938 Helen Wills Moody wins a record eighth Wimbledon tennis championship.

1950 Babe Didrikson, track star and golfer, is voted the greatest woman athlete of the first half of the 1900's.

1900   1914   1926   1938

1900 Charlotte Cooper of Great Britain becomes the first woman Olympic champ.

1926 Gertrude Ederle becomes the first woman to swim the English Channel.

1946 Patty Berg wins the first United States Women's Open golf tournament.

1952 Andrea Mead Lawrence captures two Olympic gold medals for skiing.

U.S. school administrators feverishly introduced women's sports programs.

The resulting change was dramatic. In 1972, only 5 per cent of high school athletes and 15 per cent of college athletes were female. Ten years later, those figures were 33 per cent and 30 per cent, respectively. The number of female high school athletes increased from 2¼ million to 7½ million; female college athletes, from 100,000 to more than 250,000.

Spending on women's sports also multiplied. Before Title IX, colleges spent 2 per cent of their $500-million budget for competitive sports on women. In 1982, the figure was 16 per cent. Before Title IX, there were virtually no athletic scholarships for women. By

1960 Wilma Rudolph sprints her way to three gold medals in the Olympic Games.

1974 Joan Joyce pitches the U.S. to the women's world softball title.

1984 Joan Benoit wins the first women's marathon race ever run in the Olympic Games.

1986 Martina Navratilova wins a record fifth consecutive Wimbledon title.

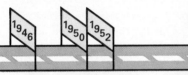

1946 1950 1952 1960 1964 1974 1979 1981 1984 1986

1964 Dawn Fraser of Australia wins her third Olympic 100-meter freestyle crown.

1979 Nancy Lieberman tops female college basketball ranks; later joins men's pro team.

1981 Beverly Francis of Australia bench-presses a record 150 kilograms (331 pounds).

1982, more than 20 per cent of such scholarships went to women.

In Canada, advances in women's sports paralleled the U.S. experience. The women's liberation and fitness movements helped to make sports and aerobic exercise popular with Canadian women. Canada did not pass legislation similar to Title IX in the 1970's, but most of the provinces gradually integrated sports for boys and girls through the seventh grade of elementary school.

Two recent measures committed Canada to equality in sports for girls and women of all ages. The Charter of Rights and Freedoms (Canada's bill of rights), which went into effect in April 1985, prohibits discrimination on the basis of sex. And the Women in Sport policy, announced in October 1986 by Fitness and Amateur Sport

Canada, an agency of the Department of National Health and Welfare, established equality in sport as a national goal.

The results of the boom in opportunity in the United States and Canada have meant that millions more girls and women are discovering the many pleasures that come from sports: the camaraderie of a team, the sense of achievement in a good performance, the feeling of physical power and fitness. Today's women are also experiencing the physical benefits of exercise—stronger muscles, better coordination, and greater flexibility. In addition, regular aerobic activity has a beneficial effect on cardiovascular health because of its demands on the heart and lungs.

Exercise can also aid women in the prevention of osteoporosis, a disease that often develops in middle-aged and older women. This disease—a "thinning" of the bones—can be partly counteracted by any weight-bearing exercise, such as jogging or walking. Exercise is also helpful in controlling the weight problems that are often associated with heart disease and diabetes. Finally, exercise not only relieves stress but also, at some levels, triggers the release into the blood of *endorphins*, tranquilizing substances produced by the brain and the pituitary gland, that promote a feeling of well-being.

Although women athletes have been boosted by Title IX and the fitness craze, women are certainly not new to sports. Wall paintings created by ancient Egyptian artists show women playing ball and performing gymnastic feats. Women in the early Greek city-state of Sparta maintained their own separate but equal version of the Olympics. Women in colonial North America competed in footraces; and by the late 1800's, women were active in a variety of other sports. In the 1890's, bicycling became popular in the United States and women joined the cycling crowd, thanks to the development of *bloomers*—long, loose trousers gathered around the ankles. These garments, considered radical at the time, enabled the wearer to straddle a two-wheeled bicycle. In another popular sport of the time, race walking, women not only participated in public races but sometimes even beat their male competitors. Nevertheless, the general public did not believe that women should pursue athletics vigorously. Most people thought that women were too delicate for strenuous athletics, and that extremely active exercise was unfeminine and therefore unsuitable for women.

Furthermore, public officials frowned on certain sports clothing worn by women. In the late 1800's, for example, some cities passed legislation outlawing bloomers. In 1907, Australian swimming champion Annette Kellerman was arrested for indecent exposure on a Boston beach while wearing a one-piece stretch suit. In 1912, U.S. all-around athlete Eleonora Randolph Sears was condemned in a public resolution for wearing "breeches" and riding a polo pony astride instead of sidesaddle.

Women athletes even had to perform in what was considered a

The boom in women's athletics has raised the level of competition in traditional women's sports such as gymnastics, *left,* and has introduced women to activities such as body building, *above,* once dominated by men.

feminine manner. In the 1914 U.S. national figure skating championships, for example, judges penalized the eventual champion, Theresa Weld Blanchard, for "unladylike" jumps and spins.

These incidents now sound comical, and so do the stories of changes in standards of acceptability. In 1927, for example, U.S. tennis champion Helen Wills made fashion history by appearing on the court without the long stockings that were considered proper.

Tennis was one of the few sports in which large numbers of women competed in the early 1900's, and it produced some great stars. Charlotte Cooper of Great Britain won five All-England (Wimbledon) championships from 1895 to 1908. (The annual Wimbledon tournament is the unofficial world championship for men's and women's singles and doubles.) In 1900, Cooper became the first female Olympic champion, winning in singles and mixed doubles. France's Suzanne Lenglen won six Wimbledon victories, the first in 1919; and Wills (who later played under her married name, Helen Wills Moody) captured a record eight singles titles at Wimbledon in the 1920's and 1930's.

Another outstanding athlete of the 1920's and 1930's was Norwegian figure skater Sonja Henie, who electrified crowds with breathtaking jumps, spins, and turns—which, by that time, were acceptable to judges. Henie won Olympic gold medals in 1928, 1932, and 1936.

In 1926, a U.S. swimmer, Gertrude C. Ederle, performed one of the most astonishing feats in the history of women's athletics, be-

World Records in the 400-Meter Freestyle Swim

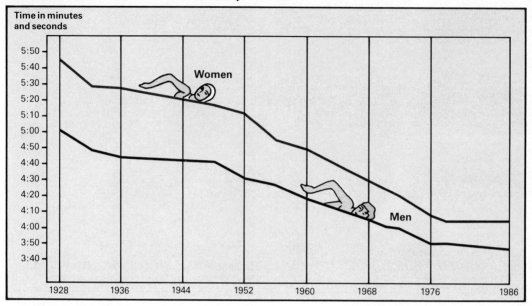

Time in minutes and seconds

The pattern of improvement in the 400-meter freestyle swim is typical of events in which strength is a major factor. Both men and women lowered their records dramatically over the years; and the women's record closed in on the men's standard, even breaking some recent records set by men.

coming the first woman to swim the English Channel. Her crossing came just three years after the first man swam the channel, and Ederle beat his time by more than two hours.

Two all-around sportswomen stood out in the early 1900's. The first was Eleonora Sears, who played tennis, squash, polo, and golf, and was also noted as a horsewoman, yachtswoman, flier, hunter, angler, shooter, canoeist, long-distance walker, and distance swimmer. The other was Babe Didrikson (later Babe Zaharias), also an American. This energetic, outspoken woman excelled in baseball, basketball, diving, lacrosse, and billiards, but was most honored for her outstanding golf and her achievements in track and field events. She won three medals—two golds and a silver—at the 1932 Olympics, then began a golf career that saw her win the U.S. Women's Open in 1948, 1950, and 1954. She was voted the greatest woman athlete of the first half of the 1900's in a 1950 Associated Press poll.

Didrikson's popularity opened the door for one of the most important developments in women's sports—professionalization. During the first half of the 1900's, almost all the brightest stars of women's sports were amateurs. Only rarely did a female athlete have an opportunity to earn a living in sports.

Near the end of Didrikson's remarkable career, women's golf tournaments—then amateur tournaments—became so popular that it seemed practical to set up a professional tour for women. The Ladies Professional Golf Association (LPGA) was founded in 1950 to manage the tour; and Didrikson and another excellent U.S. golfer, Patty Berg, turned pro. The popularity of Didrikson and Berg was largely responsible for the success of the professional tour.

The golf tour, in turn, helped to pave the way for the profession-alization of other women's sports—notably tennis and bowling.

Women's professional sports are still not as popular as men's pro sports. And in every professional sport, the total amount earned by female athletes each year is less than the total for male athletes. Nevertheless, millions of dollars are up for grabs in women's pro sports. Tennis is the most visible and lucrative of these sports, with some 300 players competing for more than $12 million in prize money. Golf is a close second, with 267 players in the LPGA's tour-nament division going after $10 million in 1986.

There are other women's professional sports, but they cannot match tennis and golf. The Ladies Pro Bowlers Tour, founded in 1979, offered prize money of $700,000 in 1986, and the Women's Professional Racquetball Association predicted that 1986-1987 would be its best year ever with $150,000 in prizes.

In 1979, the Women's Professional Basketball League was founded, with eight teams competing. The league folded after three seasons, but its failure did not mean the end of pro basketball for women. In 1986, the prospect of forming a new league seemed promising. And a National Women's Volleyball League was sched-uled to begin play in March 1987.

The lure of dollars available on pro tours and in professional

World Records for Men and Women*		
Event	Women	Men
Running		
100 meters	10.76 s.	9.93 s.
400 meters	47.60 s.	43.86 s.
1 mile	4 min. 16.71 s.	3 min. 46.32 s.
5,000 meters	14 min. 37.33 s.	13 min. 0.40 s.
10,000 meters	30 min. 13.74 s.	27 min. 13.81 s.
Marathon	2 hr. 21 min. 6 s.	2 hr. 7 min. 12 s.
Swimming		
100-meter freestyle	54.73 s.	48.74 s.
400-meter freestyle	4 min. 6.28 s.	3 min. 47.80 s.
1,500-meter freestyle	16 min. 4.49 s.	14 min. 54.76 s.
200-meter butterfly	2 min. 5.96 s.	1 min. 56.24 s.
200-meter backstroke	2 min. 8.60 s.	1 min. 58.14 s.
Jumping		
High jump		
meters	2.08	2.41
feet and inches	6—9¾	7—10¾
Long jump		
meters	7.45	8.90
feet and inches	24—5½	29—2½

*As of Nov. 15, 1986.

Male champions run and swim faster—and jump farther—than do female champions. There is no drastic dif-ference in performance, however, to indicate that any running or swimming event is too strenuous for women.

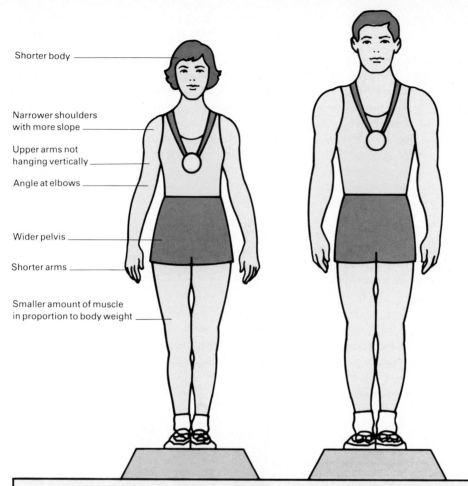

Shorter body

Narrower shoulders
with more slope

Upper arms not
hanging vertically

Angle at elbows

Wider pelvis

Shorter arms

Smaller amount of muscle
in proportion to body weight

How Physical Differences Between the Sexes Affect Athletic Performance

Physical difference	Consequence	Effect on performance
Female is shorter and smaller.	Lower center of gravity.	Advantage on balance beam. Disadvantage in high jump. Advantage in downhill skiing.
Female has wider pelvis, so thighs slant inward toward knees.	Legs swing inward to balance body. Body tends to sway from side to side more during running.	Less efficient movement is a disadvantage in running.
Female's arms are shorter.	Shorter levers for movement.	Disadvantage in hit-the-ball sports such as softball and tennis. Disadvantage in swimming. Ability to make body more compact by tucking in arms may be an advantage in floor exercises and diving.
Female's shoulders are narrower and more sloping. Upper arms do not hang vertically. Elbows are angled.	Shorter, more angular overhead reach.	Disadvantage in throwing overhand, but not in throwing underhand.
Female has smaller amount of muscle and larger amount of fat in proportion to body weight.	Female is not as strong for her weight.	Disadvantage in weight lifting.
	Female retains heat better.	Advantage in activities such as long-distance swimming where cold may be a factor.
	Female's feet may float higher in water.	May be an advantage in swimming.

leagues has led to another major development in women's athletics—specialization. Outstanding female athletes now specialize in one sport to virtually the same extent that male athletes do. Another powerful force for specialization is the chance to compete in the world's foremost amateur tournament—the Olympic Games. The opportunity to compete in the Olympics motivates young people to devote years of intense training to a single sport. (In many cases, of course, there is a professional payoff in the form of fees for product endorsements after the Olympic Games.)

As a result of specialization, recent U.S. sport heroines have been single-sport athletes. In golf, Mickey Wright was a dominant figure in the early years of the pro tour, winning four U.S. Women's Open championships from 1958 to 1964. A current superstar of the links is Pat Bradley, who made history on Aug. 17, 1986, by raising her season earnings to an LPGA record of $482,496.

In tennis, Billie Jean King is famous for winning 20 Wimbledon titles, more than any other woman, including six singles crowns captured from 1966 to 1975. King is known off the court for her efforts to gain equal prize money for women players. The best female player today is Czech-born Martina Navratilova, who stands virtually alone at the top in women's tennis. Navratilova dominates the women's game as no male rules the men's game, and her earnings reflect her superiority. From January through November 1986, Navratilova earned more than did the top man, Ivan Lendl of Czechoslovakia, and was expected to finish the year ahead of him.

In track and field, Wilma Rudolph is famous for winning three Olympic gold medals in 1960. A heroine of more recent vintage is Valerie Brisco-Hooks, a triple gold medalist at the 1984 Olympics.

In the Olympic Games and other international events, women from the United States, Canada, and other Western nations have faced keen competition, especially from government-supported athletes of the Soviet Union and other Eastern European countries; and, recently, from the surging Chinese athletes. The Chinese female volleyball team and divers have been particularly impressive.

Both the Soviet Union and China train their best athletes of both sexes intensively, but the Soviets pay less attention to fitness for the general public than the Chinese do. The Chinese have long been dedicated to daily exercise. Every morning, millions of Chinese perform ancient exercises called *t'ai chi ch'uan*, whose slow movements emphasize relaxation, balance, and breathing techniques.

Since the fitness movement took hold in the United States, millions of American men and women have become dedicated to daily exercise as well, but the U.S. style of exercise is much more vigorous than that of the Chinese. During the early 1970's, the running boom sent Americans into the streets. A few years later, aerobics and dance-exercise classes caught on.

Women are well represented in the U.S. fitness movement. To-

Since the fitness movement swept the United States and Canada, women in both countries have been pursuing various forms of regular exercise such as jogging, *above,* aerobic dancing, *above right,* and playing softball, *right.*

day, there are about 30 million U.S. runners, and about 15 million of them are women. About one-quarter of these women run at least 30 miles (48 kilometers) per week. An estimated 22.8 million people in the United States participate in aerobics classes or dance exercise. About 86 per cent of them are women. In addition, many American women exercise at home—women buy 68 per cent of all home exercise equipment.

While recreational athletes and fitness buffs are flooding roads, gyms, courts, and hillsides, women at the championship levels of sport continue to turn in astonishing performances. The marathon record, for example, has tumbled to 2 hours 21 minutes 6 seconds, some 4 minutes faster than Benoit's gold-medal time in the 1984 Olympics and the winning time in the 1956 men's Olympics.

And even more astonishing, women's running and swimming records are no longer far off *current* men's records. Both men's and women's times have been improving since the mid-1970's, but the gap between them has diminished. In 1975, the difference between the men's and women's world records in the 1,500- and 3,000-meter running races was nearly 15 per cent, and at longer distances the discrepancy was more than 20 per cent. Today, however, the women are only about 11 per cent slower than the men. And in the 100- through 400-meter sprints, women's records are as little as 8.4 per cent behind men's.

In swimming, women's times were about 11 per cent higher than men's in 1960, but the current women's records for the 400-, 800-, and 1,500-meter freestyle races are now only 7 to 8 per cent behind the men's.

Will women ever match or even surpass men's performances? In sports less reliant on strength, such as badminton, shooting, and sailing, women and men often compete as equals. In sports requiring power, strength, and speed, however—such as track and field or basketball—men's greater size and muscle mass probably will keep them ahead of women.

What has happened to the femininity issue? The sheer numbers of female participants in sports and fitness programs are forcing a change in attitude. Of 1,319 men and women responding to a 1983 survey sponsored by Miller Brewing Company, 84 per cent said that participation in sports does not diminish a woman's femininity.

With all these changes—new attitudes, skyrocketing participation, and an all-out assault on the record books—one would expect that there would be no stopping women's sports. A barrier that had been knocked down in the United States, however, may have been put back up. In 1984, the Supreme Court of the United States decided in *Grove City College v. Bell* that Title IX regulations govern only programs receiving federal funds directly. Virtually no athletic programs receive federal funds directly, so any legal enforcement of Title IX with respect to athletics will have to be based on further legislation.

How will the Supreme Court decision affect women's athletics in the meantime? In states that have shown a commitment to equal sports for women, there may be little change. Some 12 states have passed legislation requiring equivalence in the spirit of the original Title IX interpretation, and another 19 states have weaker equivalence provisions. But schools in the remaining 19 states that have no such legislation apparently are free to trim girls' and women's sports programs as they wish.

Experts agreed in 1986 that it was still too early to determine what the effects of the *Grove City* decision will be. But female athletes were hopeful, and their record supported their optimism. After all, women had once been told that they shouldn't wear bloomers, shouldn't jump on ice, and shouldn't run a marathon.

Childbearing does not slow down champion athletes for long. Olympic gold medal sprinter Evelyn Ashford, *top,* was as swift as ever in 1986 after giving birth in 1985. Sprinter Valerie Brisco-Hooks, *middle,* and distance runner Ingrid Kristiansen, *above,* set records within two years of becoming mothers.

We the People

insure domestic Tranquility, provide for the common Def
and our Posterity, do ordain and establish this Constitu

Articl

Section. 1. All legislative Powers herein granted shall
of Representatives.

Section. 2. The House of Representatives shall be compo
in each State shall have the Qualifications requisite for Electors of th

No Person shall be a Representative who shall not ha
and who shall not, when elected, be an Inhabitant of that State in

Representatives and direct Taxes shall be apportioned am
Numbers, which shall be determined by adding to the whole Num
not taxed, three fifths of all other Persons. The actual Enumer
and within every subsequent Term of ten Years, in such Mann
thirty thousand, but each State shall have at least one Repres
entitled to chuse three, Massachusetts eight, Rhode-Island an
eight, Delaware one, Maryland six, Virginia ten, North Car

When vacancies happen in the Representation from an
the House of Representatives shall chuse their Speak

Section. 3. The Senate of the United States shall be compose
Senator shall have one Vote.

Immediately after they shall be assembled in Consequ
of the Senators of the first Class shall be vacated at the Expirat
Class at the Expiration of the sixth Year, so that one third may be
Recess of the Legislature of any State, the Executive thereof may
such Vacancies.

No Person shall be a Senator who shall not have attain

The U.S. Constitution: 200 Years of History

In the following 20 pages, THE WORLD BOOK YEAR BOOK presents a special two-part article on the Constitution of the United States to mark the bicentennial celebration of this vital document in U.S. history. The first part—a pictorial representation of the constitutional convention of 1787—sets the stage for part two, an illuminating essay on why the U.S. Constitution has managed to survive as the oldest written constitution in the world.

A More Perfect Union

Creating a New Government

The Constitution of the United States, drafted in 1787, is the world's oldest written constitution. It replaced a series of laws called the Articles of Confederation, which the American Colonies had adopted during the Revolutionary War. The Articles gave the new states the chief powers of government. After the war, the states often acted independently. They lacked the unity needed to solve major national problems, and many Americans became convinced that the Articles had to be changed to ensure the nation's survival. The Constitutional Convention met in Philadelphia to consider revising the Articles. The result was an entirely new document—the Constitution of the United States —which established a new system of government. The Constitution gave the United States a strong central government and provided the world with an enduring symbol of democracy. This special unit examines the United States and Philadelphia in 1787 and the historic gathering that became known as the Grand Convention.

Part of Mass.

N.H.

Mass. • Boston

N.Y.

Conn. R.I.

New York City

Pa.

Philadelphia • N.J.

Baltimore

Md. Del.

United States Territory

Va.

Appalachian Mountains

N.C.

Mississippi River

S.C.

Ga.

• Charleston

The United States in 1787

The young nation controlled a vast area stretching from the Atlantic Ocean to the Mississippi River. Only about 4 million people lived in this rich and varied land. People of English ancestry made up about 65 per cent of the population. Americans of Scottish and German descent each formed about 5 per cent. Blacks, mostly slaves from Africa, made up most of the rest.

About 95 per cent of the people lived in small rural communities, most of which lay east of the Appalachian Mountains. Indians and small groups of pioneers occupied the western territory. Agriculture was the nation's chief activity, with at least 70 per cent of its workers farming the land. Approximately 5 per cent of the population lived in cities and towns, where they worked as merchants or in the trades.

Only five urban areas had over 10,000 people. Philadelphia, with a population of about 40,000, was the largest. The others, and their approximate populations, were New York City, 32,000; Boston, 18,000; Charleston, 15,000; and Baltimore, 13,000.

World Book map illustration by Mike Hagel. Other illustrations by Konrad Hack. Critically reviewed by Edwin Wolf 2nd, Librarian Emeritus of the Library Company of Philadelphia

The Grand Convention

Delegates from 12 states came together in Philadelphia for the Constitutional Convention. Rhode Island did not want the Articles of Confederation changed and so sent no delegates. The delegates included some of the most able men in U.S. history, such as George Washington, James Madison, and Benjamin Franklin. Of the 55 delegates who were present during at least part of the convention, 44 had served or were serving in the Congress under the Articles of Confederation. Eight had signed the Declaration of Independence.

The convention began on May 25, 1787. There were many debates, and several bitter disputes threatened to break up the convention. But the delegates worked hard to reach agreement. In time, they created a unique federal government. The central government, not the states, had the main powers. However, it was the first national government in which the chief powers were shared by three separate branches—an executive branch, a legislative branch, and a judicial branch. The Grand Convention ended on Sept. 17, 1787, after 39 delegates signed the Constitution.

The convention succeeded because the delegates were willing to compromise in order to achieve their goal of establishing a strong national government. This section describes four of the most important issues debated at the convention, lists all the men who attended, and shows some of the leading delegates.

Four Major Compromises

Issue: How should the states be represented in Congress? *Views*—Large states, such as Massachusetts and Virginia, wanted representation based on population. Small states, such as Connecticut and New Jersey, wanted each state to have an equal vote. *Compromise*—Congress would have two houses, a Senate in which each state got two votes and a House of Representatives in which representation was based on population. This solution, often called the Great Compromise, climaxed the most intense debate of the convention. The vote, on July 16, was 5 in favor (Connecticut, New Jersey, Delaware, Maryland, and North Carolina) and 4 against (Pennsylvania, Virginia, South Carolina, and Georgia). The Massachusetts delegation was evenly divided, New Hampshire's delegates had not yet arrived, New York's delegates had left, and Rhode Island was unrepresented.

Population of the States

State	Population*	State	Population*
1. Virginia	747,610	8. Connecticut	237,946
2. Massachusetts	475,327	9. New Jersey	184,139
3. Pennsylvania	434,373	10. New Hampshire	141,885
4. North Carolina	393,751	11. Georgia	82,548
5. New York	340,120	12. Rhode Island	68,825
6. Maryland	319,728	13. Delaware	59,096
7. South Carolina	249,073	*Census of 1790	

Issue: How should foreign trade be regulated? *Views*—The Northern States wanted the central government to regulate trade. The Southern States, whose prosperity depended on exports, feared that the central government would tax exports. They wanted the state governments to regulate foreign trade. *Compromise*—Congress would have the power to levy taxes on imports, but not on exports.

Issue: Should slaves be counted in determining the representation of each state in Congress? *Views*—The Southern States, where about 90 per cent of the slaves lived, wanted each slave counted. Northern States, which had few slaves, opposed counting the slaves. *Compromise*—Three-fifths of a state's slaves would be counted as part of its population.

Slaves in the United States

State	% of Population*	State	% of Population*
Massachusetts	0	Delaware	15.0
New Hampshire	.1	North Carolina	25.5
Pennsylvania	.9	Maryland	32.2
Connecticut	1.2	Georgia	35.5
Rhode Island	1.4	Virginia	39.1
New Jersey	6.2	South Carolina	43.0
New York	6.3	*Census of 1790	

Issue: Should Congress have the power to stop the slave trade? *Views*—The Northern States felt that there was no place for slavery in a free society. The Southern States, which benefited tremendously from the cheap supply of labor provided by the slaves, insisted on the continuation of the slave trade. *Compromise*—Congress could not limit the slave trade for 20 years, or until 1808.

Delegates to the Convention

Connecticut
Oliver Ellsworth
William S. Johnson*
Roger Sherman*

Delaware
Richard Bassett*
Gunning Bedford, Jr.*
Jacob Broom*
John Dickinson*
George Read*

Georgia
Abraham Baldwin*
William Few*

William Houstoun
William L. Pierce

Maryland
Daniel Carroll*
Daniel of St.
  Thomas Jenifer*
Luther Martin
James McHenry*
John F. Mercer

Massachusetts
Elbridge Gerry
Nathaniel Gorham*
Rufus King*

Caleb Strong

New Hampshire
Nicholas Gilman*
John Langdon*

New Jersey
David Brearley*
Jonathan Dayton*
William C. Houston
William Livingston*
William Paterson*

New York
Alexander Hamilton*

John Lansing, Jr.
Robert Yates

North Carolina
William Blount*
William R. Davie
Alexander Martin
Richard D. Spaight*
Hugh Williamson*

Pennsylvania
George Clymer*
Thomas FitzSimons*
Benjamin Franklin*
Jared Ingersoll*

Thomas Mifflin*
Gouverneur Morris*
Robert Morris*
James Wilson*

South Carolina
Pierce Butler*
Charles Pinckney*
Charles C. Pinckney*
John Rutledge*

Virginia
John Blair*
James Madison*
George Mason

James McClurg
Edmund Randolph
George Washington*
George Wythe

*Signed the Constitution

Philadelphia in 1787

Philadelphia was founded by the English Quaker William Penn in 1682. Penn's belief in freedom of religion helped attract many immigrants from Europe. The *City of Brotherly Love* became a growing center of commerce, culture, education, medicine, and science during the 1700's, and it served as the capital of the American Colonies during most of the Revolutionary War. In 1787, Philadelphia was the most advanced and exciting city in the United States. Visitors marveled at its paved streets, stately mansions, large banks, and fashionable stores. The city's many inns were lively social centers. Some quickly became unofficial meeting places for the distinguished delegates to the Constitutional Convention.

The Historical Society of Pennsylvania

Philadelphia Developed on the Delaware River, above. *The river, which flows into the Atlantic Ocean, helped make Philadelphia one of the chief ports and wealthiest cities in the country during the 1700's. The city was also a shipbuilding center.*

Benjamin Franklin, a leading citizen of Philadelphia, did much to help it become the country's most impressive city. He began programs to pave the streets and install street lights. A library he helped set up was the first in America to circulate books for a membership fee. He also helped establish the American Philosophical Society, the country's first scientific research organization.

The Pennsylvania Hospital *in Philadelphia,* above, *chartered in 1751, was America's first hospital.*

The State House *in Philadelphia,* below, *was the site of the Constitutional Convention. The Declaration of Independence was signed there in 1776, and the building is known today as Independence Hall. Its bell, rung to announce the adoption of the Declaration, became known as the Liberty Bell.*

The Signing of the Constitution

The Oldest Delegate at the Constitutional Convention was 81-year-old Benjamin Franklin of Pennsylvania. He had won fame throughout the world as a scientist, inventor, and statesman. Franklin was in poor health, and prisoners from the city jail often carried him to and from the meetings in a chair.

Franklin

"Father of the Constitution" *was the title given to James Madison of Virginia, probably the most influential delegate. He worked out the system of checks and balances in the power shared by the three federal branches. Madison became the fourth President of the United States.*

Madison

Wilson

James Wilson *of Pennsylvania argued forcefully for a strong central government. Probably only James Madison was more influential in the debates. Wilson later became an associate justice of the U.S. Supreme Court.*

The Most Famous Delegate *was George Washington of Virginia, commander of the Continental Army during the Revolutionary War in America. Washington served as president of the convention and brought much wisdom and dignity to its sessions. He made few speeches, but his skillful guidance kept the delegates working together in spite of some heated arguments. Washington later became the first President of the United States.*

Two Cousins from South Carolina *were leading spokesmen of the Southern States. They were Charles C. Pinckney and Charles Pinckney. Charles C. Pinckney later failed twice in bids for the presidency. Charles Pinckney became governor of South Carolina and a U.S. senator.*

C. Pinckney

C. C. Pinckney

Washington

Secrecy *was a key goal of the convention. The delegates felt that they could debate more effectively and work more efficiently if their actions were not subject to public review. Thus, they kept the windows draped in spite of the summer heat and stationed guards inside and outside each door.*

G. Morris

Rutledge

John Rutledge *of South Carolina had a leading role in convincing Northern delegates that the Southern States would withdraw from the United States if the Constitution prohibited slavery. He also worked to develop a strong central government. Rutledge later became an associate justice of the U.S. Supreme Court.*

Gorham

Nathaniel Gorham *of Massachusetts favored a strong central government and became an influential member of two key committees at the convention. He had served briefly as president of the Congress of the Confederation, which governed the United States from 1781 to 1789.*

"Author of the Constitution" *was the name given to Gouverneur Morris of Pennsylvania. Much of the credit for the Constitution's wording belongs to him. Morris was one of the most brilliant men of his time. He was also known for his wooden leg, resulting from an accident in his youth. Morris became a U.S. senator.*

By Stanley I. Kutler

The Constitution: Why It Has Endured

In September 1987, Americans will mark the bicentennial of the document that established a frame of government able to adapt to 200 years of change.

The United States is a young nation compared with many others, but it has the oldest surviving written constitution in the world. Few other nations have a framework of government that has lasted nearly so long. Of the 160 countries in the world that had constitutions in the early 1980's, 101 adopted their constitutions after 1970, and only 15 countries had constitutions that existed prior to World War II. Since the French Revolution (1789-1799), France has had several constitutions as its form of government has alternated between five republics and a few monarchies. China has adopted four different constitutions in the relatively brief period since the founding of its Communist government in 1949.

But on Sept. 17, 1987, the United States Constitution will have endured for 200 years. During 1987, people throughout the United States will celebrate the bicentennial of the Constitution in a variety of ways. The Commission on the Bicentennial of the United States Constitution—chaired by former Chief Justice of the United States Warren E. Burger—will act as a clearing house for information about local celebrations planned by many communities. More than 100 events will take place in Philadelphia, where the constitutional convention was held in 1787. Congress was scheduled to convene in special session in Philadelphia in July 1987 for the first time since the government moved from that city to Washington, D.C., in 1800. The high point of the yearlong observances was planned for Sept. 17, 1987, in Philadelphia. On that day, there will be a re-creation of the Grand Federal Procession that took place on July 4, 1788, to

Opposite page: Students view the original Constitution and Bill of Rights on display in the Exhibition Hall at the National Archives Building in Washington, D.C.

celebrate ratification of the Constitution. September 17 is the day that, 200 years earlier, 39 of the 55 delegates to the constitutional convention formally signed the Constitution.

The bicentennial observances will undoubtedly provide the occasion for many Americans to take stock and ask themselves how and why the Constitution has persisted for so long. "We must never forget that it is a *constitution* we are expounding. . . . intended to endure for ages to come, and consequently, to be adapted to the various *crises* of human affairs," wrote Chief Justice John Marshall with considerable foresight in 1819. This ability to "adapt" to crises is one of the principal reasons why the U.S. Constitution has endured when so many others have failed.

During its 200 years of existence, the Constitution has adjusted to and survived a variety of crises and historical changes. Among them were the Civil War (1861-1865); the transformation of a mainly agricultural country to an industrial giant in the early 1900's; the demands for woman suffrage during the same period; the Great Depression of the 1930's; the civil rights movement of the 1960's; and the growth of presidential power during the 1970's.

How were the framers of the Constitution able to draft a document that proved to be so adaptive? The answer lies in part in the fact that the Constitution itself was a product of history, its roots extending back centuries before the convention of 1787.

The framers of the Constitution drew on the history of ancient Greece and Rome and of the Middle Ages when they met in Philadelphia from May to September 1787. But what they knew best was the history of the previous three centuries, during which the principles of political freedom and self-government were formulated.

The framers had definite ideas on what good government should be. They believed in the concept of the *social contract*, the idea that people mutually agree to regulate and restrict their own rights in recognition of the rights of others. They believed that government should rest on the consent of the governed, and that governmental powers should be limited as much as possible so as not to interfere with the rights and privacy of the individual. They believed that if a government became tyrannical, the people had the right to rebel. Finally, they believed in the supremacy of law, that no one, including the President, could be above the law.

The author:

Stanley I. Kutler is the E. Gordon Fox Professor of American Institutions at the University of Wisconsin-Madison.

Forerunners of the Constitution

The present U.S. Constitution was preceded by several earlier state constitutions and one national constitution. When the colonists broke with Great Britain in 1776, they promptly adopted written state constitutions as the surest way to assert their rights and liberties. Establishing frameworks of government on the state level came naturally because the colonists still regarded themselves primarily as Virginians, New Yorkers, or Pennsylvanians—not as Americans.

When the Second Continental Congress resolved on July 4, 1776, to declare the united colonies "free and independent," it also voted to establish a framework of government for the new nation. In 1777, Congress adopted the Articles of Confederation. The Articles reflected the political experience of the colonists, who were reluctant to delegate too much power to a national government. As colonists, they had protested against the "distant central authority" in London; as new Americans, they distrusted central power.

The Articles of Confederation declared that the states retained their "sovereignty, freedom, and independence." Some scholars have suggested that the Articles failed because of an excessive emphasis on states' rights and powers. But *sovereignty* (supreme power) did not reside only in the states. Congress, representing the national government, could declare war, make peace, raise an army and navy, and resolve disputes between the states. The states were forbidden to make treaties with foreign powers, exchange ambassadors, interfere with national treaties, or make war—all things that only sovereign powers can do. In reality, under the Articles, powers were divided as Americans struggled to find a workable formula for *federalism* (the division of powers between a central government and local governments).

The Articles failed for a number of reasons. The document was inflexible, requiring unanimous consent of the states for amendments. Also, the national government lacked the power to enforce its will. The Articles required states to provide money to the national government, but when the states failed to do so, Congress had no ability to force them to pay up.

George Washington, James Madison, Alexander Hamilton, and other critics of the Articles also feared for the preservation of property rights. Many states had passed "stay laws," allowing poor farmers and others to postpone payment of their debts. When demands for such legislation failed in Massachusetts in 1786, Daniel Shays led the state's indebted farmers in a march on the federal arsenal and courthouse in Springfield. Critics of the Articles of Confederation demanded greater power for the national government to prevent this kind of "anarchy."

These and other flaws in the Articles led to a meeting in September 1786 in Annapolis, Md., to discuss proposals for changing the Articles. The Annapolis Convention resolved that Congress call a new meeting of the states to revise the Articles of Confederation. After some hesitation, Congress called for the states to send delegates to Philadelphia in May 1787.

The constitutional convention

The states dispatched their outstanding political thinkers to the Philadelphia convention. Virginia's delegation, for example, included Washington, perhaps the most prestigious man in the nation; Madison, an articulate, thoughtful student of political philosophy and government; George Mason, author of Virginia's bill of

The U.S. Constitution was only a few years old when the first controversy arose over how it was to be interpreted. The issue involved the creation of the First Bank of the United States, *right.* The protagonists were Secretary of State Thomas Jefferson, *below left,* who opposed the idea of a national bank, and Secretary of the Treasury Alexander Hamilton, *below right,* who favored it. Hamilton's position won, and the bank was founded in Philadelphia in 1791.

Engraving (about 1800) by an unknown artist; New York State Historical Association, Special Collection Library, Cooperstown, N.Y.

Frescoes (1860's) by Constantino Brumidi; President's Room, United States Capitol, Washington, D.C.

rights; and George Wythe, a prominent legal scholar and tutor to Thomas Jefferson and Marshall.

The delegates were committed to a republican form of government. But although they recognized the principle of majority rule, they also sought to protect the rights of minorities.

This concept of majority rule and minority rights guided the framers as they developed the Constitution's great principles. They established separate and independent powers for the executive, judicial, and legislative branches of government, providing a system of *checks and balances*—that is, limitations on the powers of each branch to prevent any one branch from growing too strong. And they created a national government with authority to enforce its decisions through its executive power and the federal courts.

The national government had power and authority, but the framers of the Constitution worked within the traditions of colonial and revolutionary history, and they carefully defined limitations on those powers. They corrected the inflexibility of the Articles by providing various means of amending the Constitution with the consent of three-fourths of the states—not requiring, as under the Articles, unanimous consent. Perhaps most important, the new Constitution clearly established the supremacy of the fundamental law and national power. "This Constitution, and the laws of the United States which shall be made in pursuance thereof," states Article VI, Section 2, "shall be the supreme law of the land. . . ."

Setting up the government

By June 1788, the necessary number of states had ratified the Constitution. The Electoral College unanimously elected Washington as President on Feb. 4, 1789, and the states overwhelmingly chose supporters of the Constitution to serve in the first Congress that launched the new government.

In September 1789, Congress submitted new amendments to the states, as the Constitution's supporters had promised during a number of state ratification contests. Those amendments—10 of which were ratified in 1791—are known as the Bill of Rights. They were crucial in strengthening individual liberties and rights and had the added value of offsetting much opposition to the Constitution.

The Constitution provided the framework required to solve the nation's problems during the late 1700's. But, inevitably, new problems emerged and ignited political sparks. How did the newly established constitutional system respond to these challenges?

The national-bank debate

The debate within the Washington Administration in 1791 over the creation of a national bank set the tone. This debate was noteworthy because it showed that although there was widespread agreement in support of the Constitution itself, differences existed over how the Constitution should be interpreted. To a certain extent, these differences over interpretation have persisted to this day.

Secretary of the Treasury Hamilton supported the creation of a national bank—a federal agency that would issue currency and perform other financial services for the government. Financial problems facing the early government had grown serious. Hamilton argued that a national bank funded by the federal government could handle payments on the national debt, make loans, and hold deposits, helping to solve the country's economic problems. Secretary of State Jefferson, however, opposed the idea, viewing government participation in the economy as harmful and a national bank as a

After the Sale (1853), an oil painting by Eyre Crowe; Chicago Historical Society

It was common for black families to be torn apart under slavery, the issue that dominated political life in the United States in the early to mid-1800's. The Constitution failed to provide a peaceful solution to the political dispute, and the Civil War began in 1861.

financial monopoly that could become too powerful and endanger American freedoms.

Each man cited the Constitution in support of his position. Hamilton contended that the government had certain *implied powers* under the Constitution, noting that Article I, Section 8, gave Congress the right to pass laws considered "necessary and proper" for carrying out the powers of the Constitution. Hamilton's position became known as the doctrine of *broad construction*, or broad interpretation, of the Constitution. Jefferson, however, argued that the Constitution had only *delegated powers* and that it did not give Congress the authority to establish a national bank. Jefferson's position became known as *strict construction*, or narrow interpretation, of the Constitution. Washington eventually agreed to the creation of the bank, supporting Hamilton's theory of implied powers.

The Hamilton-Jefferson debate demonstrated that the Constitution had quickly become the standard for resolving political controversies in the United States. The constitutionality of a particular law is still at the heart of our political discourse. Supreme Court Justice Robert Jackson observed in 1941 that disputes in other countries might call forth armies, but in the United States brought out only "battalions" of lawyers. With few exceptions, the Constitution has been the instrument for maintaining social and civil peace in our diverse society.

Although the Supreme Court of the United States was not involved in the debate over the national bank, it soon left no doubt that it was the ultimate authority on the interpretation of the Constitution. In 1803, Chief Justice Marshall's opinion in *Marbury v. Madison* asserted the Supreme Court's right "to say what the law is." Marshall's ruling established the court's power of *judicial review*—that is, its authority to declare laws unconstitutional.

Slavery and the Civil War

The next great test that challenged the constitutional system centered on the issue of slavery. Throughout much of the 1700's and early 1800's, the struggle over slavery between Northern and Southern states dominated political life. The clash was essentially economic. Southern plantation owners considered slave labor vital to their economy and way of life. The economy of the Northern states, on the other hand, was based on free labor.

The conflict came to a head over the question of whether slavery could be excluded from the Western territories—the area stretching west of the Mississippi River to California. Southerners contended that exclusion denied slaveholders the right to use their lawful property as they wished, thus violating the Fifth Amendment, which guarantees that no one can be "deprived of life, liberty, or property, without due process of law." Northerners insisted that Congress had the right to make "all needful rules and regulations" for the territories as written in Article IV, Section 3, of the Constitution. The stand-off on the territorial question reflected the hardening lines on the issue of slavery itself. In 1858, future President Abraham Lincoln warned that the nation could not long exist "half *slave* and half *free*." It must, he said, be "*all* one thing, or *all* the other."

The political stalemate eventually forced both sides to appeal to the Supreme Court for a constitutional settlement. "Scarcely any question arises in the United States that is not resolved, sooner or later, into a judicial question," the perceptive French observer Alexis de Tocqueville had written in 1835. But slavery was not resolved peacefully.

The Supreme Court's 1857 ruling in the Dred Scott Decision, fully sustaining Southern constitutional arguments, only hardened the competing positions further. The Supreme Court ruled that no blacks—either free or slave—could be U.S. citizens and that Congress could not outlaw slavery in the territories.

For once, the Constitution had failed to provide the framework for a peaceful resolution of a political dispute. Perhaps this time, the issue was too divisive. The dispute over slavery was, as Republican Senator William H. Seward of New York said, an "irrepressible conflict." And, in Lincoln's words, "the war came."

The Union victory in 1865 offered the occasion for constitutional change. Postwar amendments to the Constitution included the 13th Amendment (1865), which abolished slavery, and the 14th, which established national citizenship as primary and prohibited state governments from denying their citizens due process of law or the equal protection of the laws. The 14th Amendment (1868) fundamentally reshaped the nature of the union and, 100 years later, became the basis for asserting ideas of equality, ranging from the integration of public schools to the rights of criminal defendants.

The postwar amendments also enabled future generations to expand on their potential. Each amendment stated that Congress had the "power to enforce, by appropriate legislation, the provisions of this article." Nearly 100 years later, for example, Congress followed that section of the 15th Amendment (1870)—which says that a voter cannot be denied the ballot because of race—and enacted the Voting Rights Act of 1965, significantly altering what had been the states' exclusive control over voting rights.

The Constitution's ability to adapt to changing times was aided by amendments. The 19th Amendment—the result of years of protest by woman suffrage leaders, such as Susan B. Anthony, *right*—gave women the right to vote. It was ratified in 1920.

Oil painting (about 1900) by Carl Gutherz; Memphis Brooks Museum of Art

Forging the Shaft: A Welding Heat (1877), an oil painting by John Ferguson Weir;
The Metropolitan Museum of Art, New York City, Gift of Lyman G. Bloomingdale, 1901

Rapid industrial growth

The rapid industrialization of the United States in the late 1800's and early 1900's produced the next series of political controversies that tested the Constitution. These controversies revolved around questions concerning the responsibility of government to enforce fair economic competition, ensure safe and proper working conditions, and prevent corruption of the market place. Did the traditional powers of government extend to regulating the economy on a broad scale? Did the national government, with its power to regulate interstate commerce, have a role in such regulation? These were among the questions that faced the United States during this period. Once again, those on opposite sides of the issues cited the Constitution to justify their stand, either for government intervention or for little government regulation.

The issues of the day repeatedly made their way to the courts. "We are under a Constitution," Associate Justice—and later Chief Justice—Charles Evans Hughes said in 1907, "but the Constitution is what the judges say it is." Different judges interpreted the Constitution differently. Indeed, from the Civil War to 1937, the Supreme Court changed positions frequently. Sometimes, the court

The transformation of the United States into an industrial giant again tested the Constitution's ability to adapt to changing conditions. From the late 1800's until 1937, the Supreme Court of the United States changed positions frequently on whether it was constitutional for the government to help regulate the economy and workplace conditions.

supported government intervention, and sometimes it chose not to—for example, by ruling laws unconstitutional that restricted the hours of workers or the labor of children under 14.

In a 1905 case known as *Lochner v. New York*, the Supreme Court ruled that a New York state law enacted to protect the safety and health of workers in bakeries by limiting their workweek to 60 hours was unconstitutional. The court ruled that the state law violated the 14th Amendment to the Constitution by interfering with the "right of contract" between employer and employee. But in 1917, the court reversed itself and, in a case known as *Bunting v. Oregon*, ruled that an Oregon law limiting work hours was constitutional.

The Great Depression

The Great Depression of the 1930's brought into focus a number of constitutional questions regarding the government's role in the economy. President Franklin D. Roosevelt's New Deal program of relief, recovery, and reform measures confronted two competing streams of constitutional interpretation. These interpretations largely had their origins in the Hamilton-Jefferson debate over broad interpretation of the Constitution versus strict interpretation. The broad interpretation held that the government had the power to intervene in the economy because of its responsibility for ensuring the country's economic and social welfare. The strict, or narrow, interpretation insisted that the economy must operate without government interference. The strict interpretation was the majority view of the Supreme Court during the early years of the New Deal, when the court struck down many New Deal reforms.

The New Deal's political popularity and the harsh realities of the Great Depression, however, moved the Supreme Court to approve an expanded role for the federal government. "The Supreme Court follows the election returns," runs an old adage. Following Roosevelt's massive reelection triumph in 1936, the court shifted its position on government intervention from opposition to approval. For example, just a few months before the 1936 elections, the court ruled that a minimum-wage law in New York was unconstitutional. Then, in 1937, soon after the Roosevelt landslide, the court reversed itself by upholding a minimum-wage law.

The Constitution and the nation survived the Great Depression. But after 1937, other crises surfaced to test the Constitution's durability and strength. Constitutional debates since then have centered largely on the government's role in protecting civil rights and on the growing power of the presidency in a modern society.

The civil rights movement

In the 1950's and 1960's, the civil rights movement demanded equal treatment under the law for blacks and other minorities. Increasingly, the Supreme Court turned its attention to these issues and, in 1954, the court handed down its historic decision in *Brown v. Board of Education of Topeka*, outlawing the segregation of public schools. In this landmark decision, the high court signaled that the long-standing doctrine of "separate but equal" facilities for blacks and whites, which was originally upheld in 1896 in *Plessy v. Ferguson*, was no longer valid.

Racial minorities, women, and other disadvantaged groups maintained that the Constitution dictates the equality of all citizens. Those opposed to this view rested their case on appeals to liberty—that is, the liberty to conduct business or personal affairs free from outside interference as long as the action is not criminal.

The growth of presidential power

Finally, in the era since World War II, key constitutional issues have been raised concerning the power of the presidency. The larger U.S. role in world affairs and the expanded scope of national legislation have extended presidential power far beyond anything imagined when the Constitution was written in the late 1700's. This has raised the question of whether the executive branch of government has grown more powerful than the judicial and legislative

The Great Depression of the 1930's brought unemployment and despair, *below.* It also brought home the lesson that the Supreme Court's interpretation of the Constitution could be influenced by popular opinion. The court—at first hostile to the New Deal reforms of President Franklin D. Roosevelt—began ruling in favor of an expanded government role in the economy following Roosevelt's landslide reelection in 1936.

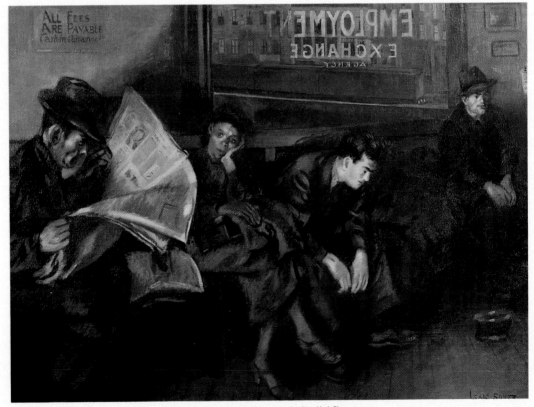

Employment Agency (1937), an oil painting by Isaac Soyer; Whitney Museum of American Art, New York City

branches, thereby violating the system of checks and balances fashioned by the framers of the Constitution.

Presidents in this era have often expressed a belief in broad, expansive powers for their office. President Harry S. Truman, for example, justified his seizure of the nation's steel mills to prevent a labor strike during the Korean War in the early 1950's. Truman cited his power as commander in chief under Article II, Section 2, of the Constitution. The Supreme Court ruled against President Truman's action, saying that only Congress had the right to authorize such a seizure.

In 1974, during the Watergate scandal, President Richard M. Nixon also expressed a belief in broad powers for the presidency. Nixon argued that "executive privilege" gave him the right to withhold potentially incriminating evidence from the courts. Presidents as far back as Washington had cited "executive privilege"—that is, constitutional powers belonging exclusively to the executive branch—to protect the privacy of their office. But the Supreme Court denied that Nixon had such a privilege in a criminal case. The court ruled that the powers of the executive were in conflict with the judiciary, and, in this case, judicial powers prevailed. Of course, Nixon's ultimate resignation was a result of demands from Congress. Congress also acted to uphold the Constitution and was prepared to impeach Nixon.

"Original intention"?

For 200 years, the true meaning of the Constitution has been a constant battleground. Different interests and groups have turned to the Constitution in support of their positions. The Supreme Court's role as "ultimate interpreter" of the Constitution, however, is largely beyond dispute at this time.

Attorney General Edwin Meese III has attacked as "bizarre" the Supreme Court's rulings on the separation of church and state over the last 25 years. He has called for a return to a "jurisprudence of original intention," implying that we can know with certainty how the framers would have ruled on modern-day controversies. But as Justice Sandra Day O'Connor has noted, we cannot easily turn to the 1700's for guidance on an issue such as prayer in public schools because public schools were almost nonexistent at that time. Chief Justice William H. Rehnquist remarked during his 1986 confirmation hearing that when the framers wrote Article I, Section 8, of the Constitution relating to commerce, there was no steamboat, no railroad, no airplane, no radio, and no television—all of which have since been regulated under that article.

"Original intention" lies obscured in the mists of history. Only the actual words of the Constitution can guide the courts. The Constitution's framers were men of great wisdom, but the American people are bound by the framers' work only as it commands their political respect and allegiance.

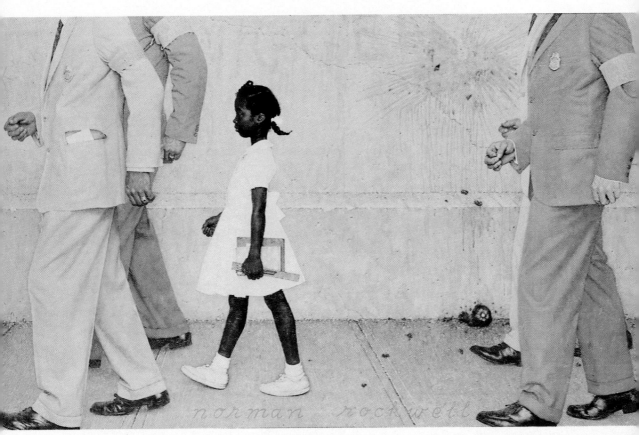

The Problem We All Live With (1964), an oil painting by Norman Rockwell; The Norman Rockwell Museum, Stockbridge, Mass., © 1964 Estate of Norman Rockwell, Reprinted by permission

The Constitution is largely the same in form as it was 200 years ago. But its scope and its application have changed—as has the nation. Nearly 70 years ago, Justice Oliver Wendell Holmes, Jr., eloquently described this phenomenon as a "living Constitution," meaning that our understanding of the Constitution has taken shape and changed as the nation has developed and changed.

We know what the framers wrote; we cannot know for certain what they were thinking when they wrote it or apply it literally in our own times. Yet their words have been adequate to maintain American institutions and society for 200 years. As the American people look to the future, they have every reason to believe that the Constitution will continue to serve the United States well.

Since World War II, constitutional debates have centered largely on the nature of civil rights and how the government should protect those rights. In 1954, the Supreme Court issued its historic decision in *Brown v. Board of Education of Topeka,* ruling that the segregation of public schools violated civil rights and was unconstitutional.

For further reading:

Bowen, Catherine Drinker. *Miracle at Philadelphia.* Little, Brown, 1986. Reprint of 1966 ed.

Hamilton, Alexander; Madison, James; and Jay, John. *The Federalist Papers.* New American Library, 1961.

Rossiter, Clinton L. *1787: The Grand Convention.* Macmillan, 1966.

By Philip Shabecoff

Problems in the Parks

Air pollution, overcrowding, and development are tarnishing the splendor of U.S. national parks.

The view from the rim of the Grand Canyon is world famous. Standing at the edge of this great gash in Earth's surface and looking out over the mesas and down the colorful layers of rock lining the canyon walls, one can see far through time as well as space. On some days, however, a visitor to the Grand Canyon can barely see to the other side of the canyon. Obscuring the majestic view is a veil of smog, some of it coming from coal-fired power plants as far away as Los Angeles, 400 miles (650 kilometers) to the southwest.

Air pollution is only one of a long list of problems threatening United States national parks, their wildlife, their ecology, and their beauty. A report called *State of the Parks* issued in 1980 by

Candlestick Tower stands out on a clear day in Utah's Canyonlands National Park but sometimes is veiled by smog from nearby power plants, *inset.*

the National Park Service, which manages the parks, listed 73 types of problems. Among them were air and water pollution, toxic wastes, overcrowding by visitors, mining and drilling activities on land adjoining the parks, and encroachment on parklands by urban development. A report issued in 1985 by the Conservation Foundation, an environmental group, found that the problems—especially overcrowding, encroaching development, and pollution—have steadily worsened.

The Park Service and such environmental groups as the Conservation Foundation and the Wilderness Society also warn that the broad array of problems threatening the parks will be difficult to solve. The needs of the parks often clash with other economic and social needs, such as the push to develop new sources of energy and the growing numbers of Americans who vacation in the parks. Seriously complicating the situation is a shortage of federal funds, the result of spending cuts aimed at reducing the U.S. budget deficit.

The pressures on the parks are making it even more difficult for the Park Service to balance its two primary, often conflicting goals. According to the legislation that established the service, it is required to "conserve the scenery and natural and historic objects in such a manner and such a means as will leave them unimpaired for future generations." At the same time, the agency is to run the parks for the "pleasuring" of its visitors.

Today, the United States national parks remain largely unspoiled—places of great beauty and wonder. With their dark forests, soaring mountains, rushing streams, and mysterious deserts, they can seem as timeless and indestructible as Earth itself. But park experts fear that unless the problems facing the parks are addressed soon, they could overwhelm these living memorials to an earlier, unspoiled age.

The United States has the world's biggest and perhaps best national park system. The system consists of 337 so-called *units*. But only 48 of these units are national parks. The rest include national historic sites, such as the birthplace of civil rights leader Martin Luther King, Jr., in Georgia, and the Knife River Indian Villages in North Dakota; national monuments, such as the Statue of Liberty in New York City; battlefields; seashores; riverways; and preserves. Every state except Delaware has at least one unit.

Park units range in size from the 9-million-acre (3.6-million-hectare) Wrangell-St. Elias National Park in Alaska—the largest national park, twice the size of Hawaii—to the 0.02 acre (0.008-hectare) memorial to Polish Revolutionary War hero Thaddeus Kosciuszko in Philadelphia—the smallest unit in the system. Altogether, the park system covers more than 124,000 square miles (321,000 square kilometers), an area larger than New Mexico or Poland. More than half of all national parkland is in Alaska.

Managing this vast domain is a daunting task. At first, the parks

The author:
Philip Shabecoff is a Washington, D.C.-based correspondent for *The New York Times.*

were run by the United States Cavalry, then by the Department of the Interior. In 1916, Congress established the National Park Service under the Department of the Interior to bring systematic management to the parks. The Park Service employs approximately 9,000 full-time workers and 9,000 part-time employees, most hired on a seasonal basis. They include administrators, rangers, scientists, maintenance workers, and police officers.

Preserving vast areas of public land for all Americans represented a sharp break with the land practices of the Old World, where land use and ownership were tightly controlled by governments and the upper classes. In fact, Yellowstone National Park in Idaho, Montana, and Wyoming, the first national park in the United States, was also the world's first national park.

The creation of Yellowstone National Park in 1872, however, did not start a rush to establish other parks. Yosemite National Park in California, the second U.S. park, wasn't established until 1890. The system continued to grow slowly into the 1900's, with nearly all the parks being created from public lands. Although the parklands were areas of great beauty, most were also lands unwanted by the railroads, mining companies, ranchers, and homesteaders who were given the first chance to buy federally owned property.

By the 1970's, the park system had nearly reached its current size. At that time, several new urban parks and dozens of cultural and historic sites were added to the system.

Expansion halted in 1981, after Ronald Reagan became President

Challenges to the Parks

A long list of problems, both internal and external, threaten United States national parks, their wildlife, ecology, and beauty.

A jammed campground at Yosemite National Park in California, *right,* is typical of the overcrowding facing many of the most popular parks. Some parks are in danger of being "loved to death" by crowds pouring through fragile natural areas. Air pollution—which spreads to the parks from power plants and factories that may be hundreds of miles away, *below* — obscures scenic views and damages wildlife.

Commercial development along the borders of parks, such as Yellowstone, *left,* can create nerve-racking traffic jams and clutter scenic vistas.

Exploring for energy supplies on lands surrounding the parks, such as blasting to locate oil deposits near Glacier National Park, *below,* as well as the drilling and mining that follow, can pollute parkland and disturb wildlife.

The need to find new sources of energy has increased mining and related activities on land adjoining the parks, which are often located near important sources of oil, gas, and minerals. For example, Arches National Park in Utah, *above,* with its strange wind-shaped arches and spires, is in an area rich in uranium. A plant for processing uranium sits just outside the park, *right.*

and appointed James G. Watt as secretary of the interior. Watt called the condition of the parks a "disgrace" and blamed the situation on the overexpansion of the park system. He established a four-year, $1-billion program to refurbish or replace deteriorating buildings, roads, bridges, sewer lines, and other structures in the parks. But he also declared a moratorium on land purchases for the park system. It officially lasted only about three months.

Since then, Congress has allocated about $100 million a year for parkland purchases, nearly all for private land within park boundaries. The Interior Department has spent only about half that amount, though expenditures rose somewhat in late 1985 and 1986.

Although conservationists have applauded the refurbishing program, they are highly critical of the slowdown in parkland purchases. And they criticize the government's failure to institute a program to restore the parks' natural resources, which they contend are woefully neglected. For example, they argue the government should spend more to monitor air and water quality in the parks. Heightening their concern is the surge in the number of tourists flocking to the parks. Lower gasoline prices and fear of terrorist attack abroad have made the parks especially appealing vacation spots.

In fact, overcrowding may present one of the greatest dangers to the most popular parks. Except for a few years in the 1970's when gasoline shortages and high gas prices reduced traffic on U.S. highways, the number of visitors to the national parks has risen steadily since World War II. According to the Park Service, park attendance was expected to reach 290 million in 1986, a 10 per cent jump over 1985 attendance.

An overwhelming percentage of visitor days—about 95 per cent— are concentrated in just one-third of the park units, mostly the urban parks and Yosemite, Grand Teton, Yellowstone, and the other "crown jewels" of the park system in the West. As a result, visitors arriving in these parks during the peak summer tourist season expecting to enjoy the splendors of the parks' waterfalls and mountains often encounter instead crowds, traffic jams, and air pollution.

On Memorial Day weekend in 1985, the Park Service for the first time restricted access to Yosemite, because overcrowding threatened what the agency called "the quality of the [visitors'] experience." In at least one of Yosemite's campgrounds, the earth has been packed so densely by thousands of visitors' feet that no tree, no bush, no blade of grass will grow there. The crowding is expected to grow even worse in the future, according to projections by the Park Service. The growth of the interstate highway system, more wealth, increasing leisure, and growing interest in outdoor recreation mean larger crowds pouring through the gates of the popular parks.

The increasing number of visitors has intensified the long-standing debate over whether the parks should be preserved in as natural a state as possible or managed chiefly for the enjoyment and use of

Challenges to Canada's Parks

In the early 1900's, James B. Harkin, the first superintendent of Canada's national park system, outlined his vision of the future. "The day will come when the population of Canada will be ten times as great as it is now," he wrote, "but the National Parks ensure that every Canadian, by right of citizenship, will still have free access to vast areas . . . in which the beauty of the landscape is protected from profanation, the natural wild animals, plants and forest preserved, and the peace and solitude of primeval nature retained."

More than 60 years later, Harkin's words hold true. Canada's population has swelled, but thanks to government foresight, Canadians enjoy access to a sparkling network of national parks stretching from the Atlantic Ocean to the Pacific, north to the Arctic Ocean, and beyond.

Yet, this network is incomplete. And both existing and future parks are threatened by overcrowding, disputes over natural resources, and other factors that, in the long run, may cloud Harkin's vision of unrestricted access to vast, unspoiled landscapes.

Canada's first national park—Banff—was created in Alberta in 1885. Since then, the government has created 32 national parks covering 71,500 square miles (185,000 square kilometers), 82 major national historic sites and parks, and 9 heritage canals. Canada's newest park, Ellesmere Island National Park north of the Arctic Circle near Greenland, was established in September 1986.

Parks Canada, an agency of the federal Department of the Environment, administers and protects Canada's parks. To do that, the agency in 1971 created a national parks "blueprint" that divides Canada into 48 major ecological zones. They include 39 terrestrial zones, such as prairie grassland and Pacific Coast mountains, and 9 marine zones, such as the West Isles in the Bay of Fundy. The goal of the blueprint, which became federal policy in 1979, is to establish a park representing each ecological region. Today, however, only half of the terrestrial zones have parks, and there are no marine parks at all.

Substantial barriers—both financial and political—stand in the way of completing the system. Among them are the hundreds of millions of dollars required to compensate provincial governments for giving up rights to the land and bitter land-use conflicts among environmentalists, loggers and miners, and Canada's native peoples—the Inuit. In addition, unresolved land claims by native people prevent the creation of new parks, particularly in the Arctic, without extensive discussions.

Obstacles like these prevented two proposed parks from becoming a reality in 1985 and 1986—Bruce Peninsula on Georgian Bay in Ontario, and the world-celebrated South Moresby wilderness area in British Columbia's Queen Charlotte Islands.

To address these problems, Canada's Environment Minister Thomas M. McMillan formed a national task force in April 1986 to

The appeal of Banff National Park in Alberta, *right,* and other popular Canadian parks has increased the demand for more tourist facilities.

recommend ways to speed up the protection of significant natural areas. The task force planned to investigate various methods of financing land acquisition for parks, including tax plans that would encourage corporate and individual donations to a preservation fund.

The task of creating new Canadian national parks is matched only by the challenge of solving problems in existing parks. Chief among these problems is the conflict between preservation and tourism. Since World War II, Canada's national parks have become increasingly popular with tourists. Many visitors, however, want no part of "roughing it" in the wilderness areas of the parks, preferring instead to travel by vehicle to the main tourist attractions and to stay in hotels or fully serviced campgrounds.

The resulting pressure to expand and develop tourist facilities has led to an enormous conflict between those who believe the primary purpose of national parks is preservation, and

those who believe the parks should serve people. Proposals for multimillion-dollar ski resorts, roads into remote areas, and cabins in the back country have stirred up furious fights.

Nowhere in Canada was this conflict more intense than in the four connected mountain parks—Yoho, Kootenay, Banff, and Jasper. After years of public planning sessions, Parks Canada in 1985 released a long-term plan that struck a compromise between increased development and wilderness protection.

Like parks in the United States, the most popular and scenic Canadian parks are being threatened by overcrowding. During peak periods, especially in the summer months, campers are often turned away from overflowing campgrounds. Overcrowding also has increased the clamor for more campgrounds and recreational and tourist facilities.

At present, Canada's official national parks policy favors protection over use. But Canada's federal government has been quietly reviewing this policy. As part of this process, in September 1985, Parks Canada invited more than 400 people from across Canada to the Canadian Assembly on National Parks and Protected Areas, a grass-roots conference in Banff. Held to celebrate Parks Canada's 100th anniversary, the meeting produced policy recommendations for the government and identified more than 500 significant areas in need of protection.

Other problems troubling the parks include financial restraints on park services and major industrial, commercial, or housing developments on the edges of the parks. Also continuing are disputes over whether the government should operate tourist services such as campgrounds and guide programs in the parks, or whether such services should be contracted out to private companies and operated for profit. In some Canadian national parks, notably Gros Morne in Newfoundland, wildlife poaching is a major problem. Nor has acid rain left Canada's parks untouched. One of the country's newest wilderness parks, Pukaskwa Park on Lake Superior, is receiving the worst of the acid rain showering northern Ontario. Studies in 1983 and 1984 found high levels of acidity in the soil and lakes in the park.

But so far, Canada has not been troubled by two of the major problems afflicting U.S. national parks. Canadian parks do not suffer from air pollution, and Canada's grizzly bears are not threatened, as they are in some U.S. parks such as Yellowstone, by territorial conflicts between people and wildlife. Christie McLaren

Christie McLaren is a reporter for The Globe and Mail *in Toronto.*

visitors. One of the central issues in this debate is economic development in the parks.

Most of the parks' hotels, restaurants, souvenir shops, dude ranches, and other tourist facilities are operated by private businesses called *concessionaires*. The Reagan Administration, which generally favors fewer restrictions on business and greater economic development on public lands, has encouraged the concessionaires to take a greater role in some traditional Park Service functions, such as managing campgrounds and providing guides for park visitors. Concessionaires and private developers have also won approval for more of their plans to build roads, parking lots, ski slopes, swimming pools, and other tourist attractions in the parks.

Officials of the Reagan Administration argue that such a policy increases the variety of recreational facilities available to park visitors. Not everyone, they point out, is interested in hiking and camping in the parks' remote areas. Park visitors who want to enjoy the scenery from their car or stay in a comfortable hotel with a good restaurant and a swimming pool should be able to do so. The Administration also contends that allowing private businesses to operate some park facilities saves money, a major consideration in a period of federal belt-tightening.

The new powers given to the concessionaires worry some Park Service officials and conservation groups, such as the Sierra Club and the National Parks and Conservation Association. They fear that the concessionaires' interest in profits will lessen the Park Service's commitment to conservation. They argue that too many tourist facilities in the parks clutter the landscape, destroy scenic vistas, and endanger wildlife, threatening the natural resources that make the parks attractive in the first place.

Although overcrowding and commercial development are serious problems, the Park Service has at least some control over them. Threats to the parks from outside their borders are another story. In its 1980 *State of the Parks* report, the Park Service reported that more than half of all threats to the parks came from sources outside park boundaries. Among the worst external problems listed were mining and drilling, air pollution, and industrial and residential development on adjoining lands.

For many years, the largely undeveloped national forests and private lands surrounding many parks served as buffer zones between the parks and civilization. The Arab oil embargoes of 1967 and 1973, however, sent energy companies scrambling to find new sources of coal, oil, and natural gas in the United States.

Public lands were—and are—likely places for exploration. Many parks are located in areas with rich deposits of coal or near the Overthrust Belt, a geologic formation in the Rocky Mountain region believed to contain huge stores of oil and natural gas. Since the embargoes, the Forest Service and the Bureau of Land Management, the federal agencies that manage the public lands adjoining the parks, have encouraged drilling and mining in these areas.

Problems arise because the parks are not isolated areas. They are closely linked to surrounding lands, sharing watersheds and animal habitats. As a result, activities outside park borders can seriously affect the environment and animals within. For example, pollution entering a *watershed* (the area drained by one river system) outside a park can contaminate streams and lakes within the park. Animals' migration routes and seasonal ranges often include both parkland and adjacent areas outside the park. In April 1986, a well to tap geothermal energy was dug just outside Yellowstone, despite geologists' warnings that the well could shut off or slow down some of the park's famous geysers and other geothermal features.

Air pollution may be one of the most serious and the least controllable external threats to the parks. The natural blue haze that gave the Great Smoky Mountains their name is now gray and consists largely of pollution. The Grand Canyon suffers from heavy air pollution for at least 100 days each year. Visitors who look east from one of Yosemite's ridges can see vivid images of snow-capped peaks through the clear, pristine air. But to the west, a thin line of haze smudges the view only a few miles away.

"That's smog from the San Joaquin Valley," a Yosemite natural resources specialist explains. "Forty years ago, you used to be able to see to the Pacific Ocean, 150 miles away. Now, you can't even see the Coast Range, which is closer."

Smog is one of the chief air pollutants damaging the parks. Much smog contains ozone, a gas created by the interaction of sunlight and exhaust fumes from automobiles and factories. According to the Park Service, ozone has damaged at least one-third of the ponderosa pines in Sequoia National Park in California and nearly two-thirds of the white pines in Acadia National Park in Maine.

Acid rain also takes a toll. Acid rain is precipitation with a high concentration of sulfuric and nitric acids. It develops from sulfur dioxide and nitrogen oxides emitted by power plants and other industries that burn fossil fuels. Acid rain pollutes the air and poisons lakes and rivers, killing plants and wildlife.

Thousands of U.S. lakes and rivers, including many in national parks, are being damaged by acid rain. The problem seems worst in the East, but acid rain also affects such Western parks as Zion National Park in Utah and Rocky Mountain National Park in Colorado.

Urban development, industrialization, and vacation-home building are also troublesome for the parks. In Florida, the diversion of water to supply Miami and other cities along the state's booming southeastern coast has dangerously reduced the flow of fresh water vital to the animals and plants in Everglades National Park. Development of the land around Yellowstone for ranches and vacation homes—as well as for oil and gas wells—destroys habitats used by

Easing Park Problems

Despite financial limitations, the U.S. Park Service has moved to deal with some of the problems facing the parks.

A park ranger monitors air quality in Bryce Canyon National Park in Utah, *right.* Measuring air pollution in the parks helps scientists determine the extent of environmental damage and provides information necessary to set pollution standards for industries and power plants near the park.

Hikers trek along a wilderness path at Isle Royale National Park in Michigan, *below.* Automobile traffic is banned from the more than 200 islands that make up the park—a federal game preserve with a large moose herd, timber wolves, and coyotes.

Visitors line up early at Yosemite, *left,* to reserve a campsite. To reduce overcrowding at the most popular parks, the Park Service limits the number of campers. A few parks, such as Yosemite and Denali in Alaska, *below,* provide public transportation to special points of interest.

Everglades National Park in Florida, though beset by pollution and low water levels, still enchants visitors with its exotic wildlife and lush jungle atmosphere. The preservation of Everglades and other U.S. parks represents a commitment to future generations.

the park's grizzly bears, elk, bison, and other wildlife. The animals, of course, do not read maps when hunting food and shelter, and often range outside park boundaries.

There is no shortage of suggestions about what to do about the problems facing the parks. Federal budget cuts, however, have discouraged any large, government-financed save-the-parks program. The Park Service's 1980 *State of the Parks* report concluded that the agency did not have the resources to deal effectively with the many problems facing the parks. Since then, the money and personnel available to the Park Service have dwindled. Once Secretary of the Interior Watt's face-lift program was completed in 1985, two years after Watt resigned, the Park Service budget was cut.

In March 1986, the park's budget was trimmed again, by $39 million, or 4.3 per cent. As a result, many parks were forced to prune staff, offer fewer guided tours, and reduce maintenance.

Congress increased the 1987 park's budget, however, by nearly 13 per cent, mainly by raising user fees. Supporters of the higher fees believe that the people who actually use the parks should pay more for their upkeep. But opponents argue that visiting the parks should not be an economic burden.

Despite its financial difficulties, the Park Service has taken steps to deal with some of its problems, particularly overcrowding. Several parks now require campers going into the back country to obtain permits. A few parks, including Yosemite and Denali in Alaska, offer public transportation to help ease traffic congestion. In some parks, such as Acadia, visitors can call private ticket companies to reserve a campsite instead of waiting in line.

Reducing air pollution in the parks may be one of the toughest problems to solve. Complicating the situation is the lack of detailed studies of the extent of air pollution in the parks and its effect on plants and wildlife. In fact, only slightly more than half of the national parks measure the level of air pollution within their boundaries. Federal law currently limits the amount of air pollution permitted in the parks and other wilderness areas, but conservationists argue that air-quality standards should be toughened and more strictly enforced.

Many conservationists believe that one of the best ways to protect the parks from external threats is to create buffer zones around the parks. In these zones, mining, drilling, grazing, development, and some types of recreation, such as hunting, would be strictly limited.

Such proposals are opposed by the energy, mining, and timber companies, developers, and others who operate in and around the parks. Many people living near the parks who depend on these businesses for jobs or who like to hunt in the national forests also oppose the plans.

In 1986, Park Service Director William Penn Mott, Jr., proposed a 12-point "Action Program" to protect the parks. The program would include conducting an inventory of natural and recreational resources in the parks, enlisting more public support for the parks, and promoting research on natural resources in the parks.

Conservationists welcomed Mott's plan, though they do not believe it is a cure-all for the ills of the park system. Many of Mott's proposals could be accomplished by changing park-management procedures. Others, such as research, would require additional funding—an unlikely event given the current financial climate.

Nevertheless, because the American people have demonstrated a deep and abiding love for the national parks, it is likely that the federal government will take steps to protect the parks. A survey conducted in 1986 for the President's Commission on Americans Outdoors found that 81 per cent of those polled strongly agree that the government should preserve natural areas for the use of future generations.

In his 1984 book, *This Land Is Your Land*, former Park Service official Bernard Shanks wrote, "National parks are more than wild laboratories or priceless historic and cultural sites; they are part of the power of our nation, as great a contributor to national strength as steel mills and armies."

For further reading:

Nikiforuk, Andrew, and others. "A Growing Threat to Canada's Parks." *Maclean's*, Sept. 16, 1985, pp. 48-49.
Shanks, Bernard. *This Land Is Your Land: The Struggle to Save America's Public Lands*. Sierra Club Bks., 1984.
Tilden, Freeman. *The National Parks*. Knopf, 1986.

By John Camper

The Hazards of Teen-Age Drinking

The number-one drug problem among young people in the United States is not cocaine or marijuana—it's alcohol.

"Have a beer," Jason said, thrusting a can in the direction of his friend Rod. Both boys were 15 years old.

"Nah, I'm allergic to it," said Rod.

"Whatsa matter? Afraid Mommy might find out?"

"No, but I've got an uncle who's an alcoholic," Rod lied, "so I try to lay off the stuff."

Jason frowned, "Oh, I didn't know. Well, have whatever you like."

Jason and Rod weren't at a teen-age party; they were in a high school classroom, practicing how to resist pressure to drink. Rod's lie about having an alcoholic relative was one of the suggested techniques for getting out of a difficult situation. Such exercises are being used in schools throughout the United States, from grade

school through high school, as educators and counselors search for new ways to battle teen-age drinking, a major social problem.

Alcoholic beverages cannot legally be sold to people under 18 in any state, and in most states the legal drinking age is 21. Twenty-three states have raised their legal age to 21 since 1984, spurred by a new law reducing federal highway funds to states that failed to make 21 the minimum drinking age by Oct. 1, 1986. Statistics show, however, that many young people begin to drink long before they reach the legal age. As a result, schools, youth organizations, and other groups are trying various methods to help combat alcohol abuse among teen-agers.

"We've tried scare tactics and they didn't seem to work," says Lynda Chott, coordinator of InTouch, a statewide drinking-prevention program in Illinois. "And we've tried providing information, hoping the students would make the right decisions, but that didn't seem to work either. They need to learn the skills to say no. Just giving them information, or scaring them, isn't enough."

The raw information on teen-age drinking is pretty scary—so scary, perhaps, that teen-agers simply tune it out. Alcohol is the number-one drug problem among young people in the United States. Two-thirds of high school seniors drink at least once a month, compared with one-fourth who smoke marijuana.

When a teen-ager who has been drinking gets behind the wheel of a car, teen drinking becomes everyone's problem. Automobile accidents are the number-one cause of death among American youth. They kill more young people than cancer and suicide combined. In 1985, car crashes killed almost 14,000 young people—6,063 aged 15 to 19 and 7,772 aged 20 to 24. Every 38 minutes, a young person dies on the road. And again, statistics show that half of the teen-agers involved in fatal accidents have been drinking.

Young drinkers do not cause all the highway deaths, of course, but they are responsible for more than their share. Any drinking driver is a menace on the road, but teen-aged drivers who have been drinking are especially dangerous because they are new at drinking as well as new at driving. According to the National Highway Traffic Safety Administration, people aged 16 to 21 made up 12 per cent of all licensed drivers in 1983 but caused 26 per cent of the fatal accidents where alcohol was involved.

Alcohol abuse causes other problems for teen-agers, according to psychiatrist William B. Hawthorne, Jr., of Harvard Medical School in Boston. Heavy-drinking teens, Hawthorne says, suffer from low self-esteem and depression, and have "shallow and empty" relationships with their friends.

Young drinkers' grades suffer, too, according to a landmark 1978 survey of 4,918 teen-agers by the Research Triangle Institute (RTI) in Research Triangle Park, N.C. The RTI is a nonprofit organization jointly owned by three North Carolina universities—Duke,

The author:
John Camper is a reporter for the *Chicago Tribune.*

More Than Their Share

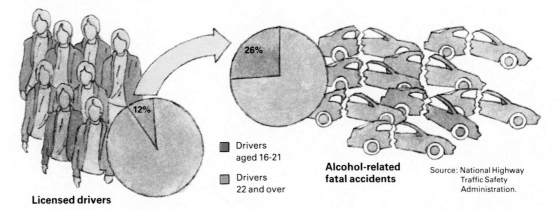

26%

12%

Drivers
aged 16-21

Drivers
22 and over

Licensed drivers

**Alcohol-related
fatal accidents**

Source: National Highway
Traffic Safety
Administration.

North Carolina State, and the University of North Carolina—that performs research under contracts from government and industry. The RTI study found that only 8 per cent of students who usually got A's and B's were heavy drinkers, compared with 25 per cent of students who usually got C's, D's, and F's. It was not clear, however, whether drinking caused low grades or whether poorer students just do more drinking.

It's a rare youngster who manages to get through high school without having a drink, according to data from the University of Michigan's Survey Research Center. In 1985, when the center asked 17,000 high school seniors whether they had ever used alcohol, 92 per cent said yes, and 56 per cent said they began drinking before entering high school.

This might not be too disturbing if it meant only an occasional beer on a hot day or a glass of wine at a family celebration. And for many young people, that's all it does mean. But 37 per cent of the seniors—45 per cent of the boys and 28 per cent of the girls—said they had consumed five or more drinks in a row on at least one occasion during the previous two weeks. And 30 per cent said that most or all of their friends get drunk at least once a week. The typical young problem drinker gets drunk mainly on weekends with friends, throwing down beer after beer.

Few of these heavy-drinking students, however, suffer from the disease called alcoholism, in which drinking alcoholic beverages becomes a compulsion. "The major 'drinking problem' among youth today is not alcoholism, nor problems associated with heavy drinking over a long period of time, but the negative consequences of intoxication," such as accidents or violence, says the National Institute on Alcohol Abuse and Alcoholism (NIAAA). "In youth, alcohol problems are more often associated with episodic or binge drinking than with either physical or psychological addiction to alcohol." Such alcohol addiction affects only about 3 per cent of adolescents.

Teen-aged drivers who have been drinking are especially dangerous because they are new at drinking as well as new at driving. Statistics show that people aged 16 to 21 make up about 12 per cent of the driving population but cause 26 per cent of the highway deaths in which alcohol is involved.

Nobody is quite sure why teen-agers drink so heavily when they drink, but there are many theories. "What they tell me is that they feel they're lucky to get alcohol and they're not sure when it will be available again, so they drink as much as they can while they can," says Harvard's Hawthorne, who runs a treatment center for young problem drinkers in Keene, N.H. "There's no sense of moderate social drinking among teen-agers as there is among adults. Teen-agers go to parties to get wasted."

Robert Anastas, founder of a youth organization called Students Against Driving Drunk (SADD), says he believes binge drinking is part of young people's desire for immediate gratification. "Kids want to live for today, and they don't want to worry about tomorrow," he explains. "They talk about the mess the world's in—political corruption and nuclear war—and they say, 'I'm going to take what's available right now.' I hear this all the time."

If young people seem unable to do "moderate social drinking," as Hawthorne says, a major reason may be the circumstances under which teen-agers drink. Because they face disapproval from parents, school authorities, and police, they tend to drink in secret, in a hurry, and without food—unlike adults, who usually drink in relaxed, comfortable surroundings and eat while they drink. Drinking fast on an empty stomach means that alcohol gets to the bloodstream faster. As a result, many teen-agers get dangerously drunk dangerously fast.

There is no simple explanation for why teen-agers start drinking. The NIAAA says they drink because their friends and parents drink, because teens consider drinking a sign of adulthood and a normal part of growing up, and because alcohol is easy to get. The institute says that teen-age rebelliousness, low self-esteem, and "involvement in other delinquent acts" also play a part.

The experts, as well as young people themselves, agree that peer pressure—the influence of friends and acquaintances—plays a major role. Economist J. Valley Rachal of the RTI says, "Prevalence, frequency, and level of drinking all vary directly with the number of friends who drink, the extent of friends' drinking, and the degree of consensus among friends approving drinking."

"Peer pressure is more of a factor among the younger kids, the 13- or 14-year-olds who are just switching into high school and want so badly to be accepted by older kids," says 17-year-old Kristin Kelly of Arlington Heights, Ill. Kelly, who is active in an antidrinking group called Operation Snowball, continues, "I think the older kids drink because they've got nothing else better to do. The boys call each other 'chicken' or 'not a real man' if they don't drink."

"The hardest to resist is not direct pressuring, but subtle and constant nudging: 'Aw, come on, everybody does it,' " says John Blood of Brooklyn Park, Minn., student leader of the federally sponsored National Conference for Youth on Drinking and Driving in 1983.

Peer pressure—the influence of friends and acquaintances—is a major cause of teen-age drinking, according to experts on alcohol abuse and young people themselves. Teen-agers fear that they will be left out, *opposite page,* if they do not drink.

Drugs Other Than Alcohol

Cocaine, the drug that ended the lives of two top athletes in June 1986, has been gaining popularity among high school students in the United States. And a downward trend in the use of other drugs since the late 1970's has come to a halt. Those were the disturbing findings, reported in July 1986, of an annual survey of 16,000 high school students conducted by the Institute for Social Research at the University of Michigan in Ann Arbor under a contract from the National Institute on Drug Abuse (NIDA).

The University of Michigan researchers collected the most recent data in mid-1985, about a year before cocaine caused the deaths of Len Bias, a University of Maryland basketball player who had just been drafted by the Boston Celtics, and Don Rogers, a professional football player for the Cleveland Browns. At the time of the survey, nevertheless, the Michigan researchers had expected that what they called "the growing publicity about the very real hazards of the drug" would result in a reduction of student use of cocaine.

On the contrary, the percentage of seniors who reported having used cocaine within 30 days before the survey rose from 5.8 in 1984 to 6.7 in 1985—the highest figure since the survey was first conducted in 1975. In that year, only 1.9 per cent reported having used the drug in the previous month.

Moreover, 17.3 per cent of the 1985 seniors reported having tried cocaine at least once, compared with 9 per cent in 1975. And 13.1 per cent of the students in 1985 said they had used the drug within the past year, compared with just 5.6 per cent 10 years ago.

Only 34 per cent of the 1985 students surveyed said they believe there is great risk in trying cocaine once or twice. Most teen-agers consider such experimentation to be safe, an opinion that puts them at odds with experts. "There is no 'safe' dose of cocaine," says Lewis R. Goldfrank, director of emergency medical services at New York City's Bellevue Hospital. "The risk of serious adverse effects is there every time they take the drug. They can die from just one episode." Bias, one of the dead athletes, was said to have used the drug only a few times.

Scientists believe that cocaine stimulates the release in the brain of chemicals that cause feelings of pleasure, confidence, and energy. It is "far more inherently health-threatening than heroin," according to a 1984 report published by NIDA and written by Roy A. Wise, a psychologist at Concordia University in Montreal, Canada. Wise noted that laboratory rats would rather take cocaine than eat, and that human beings who have unlimited access to the drug frequently engage in "compulsive and potentially lethal cocaine abuse."

A smokable form of cocaine called *crack* is much more potent and addictive than cocaine that is sniffed. When the University of Michigan survey was done, crack had not emerged as a significant problem and the researchers did not ask whether teen-agers smoked cocaine or inhaled it.

Cocaine still is less common among high school seniors than marijuana or amphetamines. Within the month before the 1985 survey, 25.7 per cent of the students had used marijuana and 6.8 per cent had used amphetamines. But those drugs are less popular than they once were. Use of marijuana peaked at

A teen-ager buys drugs.

37.1 per cent in 1978, and amphetamines were most prevalent—10.7 per cent—in 1982. Although 54.2 per cent of the teen-agers admitted in 1985 that they had tried marijuana at least once, only 4.9 per cent of the students reported smoking it daily, compared with 10.7 per cent in 1978.

Marijuana produces a dreamy, relaxed state in which many people find that their senses are heightened. The drug also has many of the same effects as alcohol, including impaired judgment and coordination, making driving under its influence dangerous. But researchers say additional dangers of smoking marijuana may not yet have been discovered. "The situation is like that following the popularization of cigarette smoking at the time of World War I," says psychiatrist William Pollin, former director of NIDA. "It required 50 years of research for the truly serious implications of cigarette smoking to become apparent."

Amphetamines or "uppers" increase physical and mental activity, decrease appetite, prevent sleep, and may overtax the heart. Withdrawal from amphetamines may cause prolonged sleeping, irritability, anxiety, and depression. Users who try to avoid these symptoms by taking more amphetamines find that they require progressively higher doses of the drug to achieve the same effect.

The other drugs studied in the University of Michigan survey were less popular but no less dangerous. Hallucinogens, including LSD and PCP, had been used within the previous 30 days by 4.2 per cent of the seniors in 1985. Hallucinogens can cause convulsions, violent behavior, and mental illness lasting from several days to several months. Inhalants, used by 2.9 per cent of the seniors within the previous month, can damage the nervous system, liver, kidneys, blood, and bone marrow. Sedatives, used by 2.4 per cent, and tranquilizers, used by 2.1 per cent, can cause death when taken in overdoses or in combination with alcohol. Heroin—used by 0.3 per cent—and other opiates, such as codeine and morphine—used by 2.3 per cent—are among the most dangerous and addictive drugs.

Perhaps the worst news in the 1985 survey, besides rising cocaine use, was the end of a five-year decline in student use of illicit drugs, defined as drugs other than alcohol that are not used for medical treatment. The percentage of seniors who had used an illicit drug within the previous year had risen from 45 per cent in 1975 to 54 per cent in 1978 and 1979, then declined each year until 1984, when it hit 45.8 per cent. In 1985, that figure rose to 46.3 per cent.

And the Michigan researchers point out that their overall figures on drug use are probably conservative. They surveyed only high school students, not dropouts, many of whom are heavy drug users.

"Clearly," the researchers commented, "this nation's high school students and other young adults still show a level of involvement with illicit drugs which is greater than can be found in any other industrialized nation in the world. Even by historical standards in this country, these rates still remain extremely high." [J. C.]

"Another reason kids drink," Blood adds, "is because they don't have a good self-image. This goes along with peer pressure—students feel they have to do something everybody else does to get acceptance."

Sandra Garcia, a 15-year-old high school junior from San Antonio, says students drink to be noticed and to appear more grown-up. "If you show up drunk at a party, people are going to look at you. And you hope they're going to say, 'Hey, he's so much older, he can go somewhere and get beer or wine coolers.' "

Parents bear some responsibility, too, researchers say. The RTI study showed that students' drinking habits tend to mirror those of their parents: 59 per cent of students who had at least one parent who drank were themselves moderate or heavy drinkers, compared with 29 per cent of students whose parents did not drink any alcoholic beverages.

Some students, on the other hand, seem to rebel against antidrinking parents. RTI economist Rachal says, "There is evidence that some of the heaviest drinking occurs among adolescents who perceive their parents as strongly disapproving." The NIAAA, in one of its reports, adds, "Parents who drink in a light or moderate fashion tend to rear offspring who also drink in a problem-free manner. . . . However since parents who abstain provide no role model for light or moderate drinking, they may find that their children tend to drink heavily."

If young people fail to recognize the dangers of alcohol, it's not because educators haven't tried to get the message across. The National Clearinghouse for Alcohol Information says 93 per cent of high schools in the United States offer classes on alcohol. Some schools begin teaching about drinking as early as elementary school. But students tend to resist these efforts, particularly if they're preachy or heavy-handed. Films of gruesome crack-ups and alcohol-ravaged livers have little effect on young people who believe it won't happen to them.

So some educational programs move away from the immediate problem of alcohol abuse and concentrate instead on what educators call *values clarification.* The theory is that if young people become better aware of their own values, they will develop the self-confidence and self-esteem to resist pressure to drink. These programs are designed to convince students that it's more adult to say no than to be pressured by friends into saying yes.

"Whatever will get them out of the situation is OK," says Deborah Orrick, executive director of the San Antonio Council on Alcoholism. "If the teen-ager wants to come back heavy, he might say, 'If you're really my friend, why are you offering me that?' or 'I can't believe you're doing that.' Some kids are uncomfortable being that strong, so for them we suggest 'I'm in training' or even 'I've got a hangover from last night.' The alcoholic-in-the-family line works pretty well, and as a last resort they can always say 'I've got to go to the bathroom' just to get away. Ideally," Orrick adds, "the refusal will come from strength of conviction: 'I don't believe in doing this. It's not right for me.' "

Some of the most successful programs mobilize peer pressure against irresponsible drinking, on the theory that teens who refuse to listen to adults may be willing to listen to other teens. "Our parents and the governmental system had their turn to warn us, but young people need to hear it from each other," 19-year-old Kevin Tunnell told the National Conference for Youth on Drinking and Driving in 1983.

Tunnell spoke from experience. A year earlier, he drank too much champagne at a New Year's Eve party and killed an 18-year-old girl in a head-on auto crash. A juvenile court judge found Tunnell guilty of manslaughter and ordered him to spend a year discussing his experience before groups of young people. "I sit up in bed all night long thinking how I killed somebody," Tunnell says.

Many antidrinking programs for teen-agers use role playing, in which young people practice saying no and learn how to resist pressure to drink.

John Blood, the student moderator of the conference, adds, "Many kids who give in to peer pressure are just waiting for some other kid to say, 'No, let's not do this.' To speak out against peer pressure, it only takes one kid in the group to say, 'I'm just like everybody else. I like to party, too. But let's set limits.' Or, 'I don't feel like drinking beer. Why don't we go out for a pizza instead?' "

State programs such as the Ohio Teen Institute, Operation Snowball in Illinois, and the Peer Resources Education Program in Wisconsin train young volunteers to help friends resist alcohol. One of the best-known national programs, SADD, combines alcohol education with a document called a Contract for Life designed to protect young drinkers from being killed on the highway.

Under the contract, teen-agers promise to call their parents for a ride home if they have been drinking or are with a driver who has been drinking. The parents agree to come and get their youngsters or to send a taxi, no questions asked, and to put off discussion of the incident until later.

Bob Anastas, a high-school teacher and hockey coach of Wayland, Mass., founded SADD in 1981 after two of his students were killed within four days in alcohol-related accidents. "I went to their wakes and saw their friends angry and frustrated and depressed," he recalls, "and I kept thinking to myself: 'They hate this. Why do they keep challenging death and losing?' "

Anastas admits that many parents were appalled when their children handed them a SADD contract. "They had no idea their kids were drinking," he says. "But we make it clear that the contract doesn't condone drinking. It just allows the kids to get home safely."

A SADD contract can also open new channels of communication between parents and children, Anastas says. "The parents can say, 'Hey, buddy, you drink. Let's talk about this.' "

A group called PRIDE—Parents' Resource Institute for Drug Education—believes mothers and fathers must take a more active role in combating teen-age alcohol abuse. Parents can do so by setting a proper example with their own drinking habits, by discussing the subject with their children, and by exercising more parental control when necessary.

According to the National Council on Alcoholism, parents may fail to recognize the dangers of drinking for their children because they are so relieved that the children aren't using other drugs. Parents may indicate approval of alcohol, directly or indirectly, just because it isn't cocaine or marijuana.

PRIDE and other parents' groups note that adolescent drinking often occurs in someone's home, and they believe it should be controlled there. In the RTI survey, 44 per cent of high school students said they often drank at teen-age parties unsupervised by adults—but presumably in someone's home—while 21 per cent often drank at teen-age parties with adults present. The National Clearinghouse for Alcohol Information reports, not surprisingly, that teen-agers drink more heavily when adults are absent.

In communities throughout the United States, parents have set up networks, often with the cooperation of schools and police, to warn one another when a teen-age drinking party is planned. Besides providing an early-warning system, it gives peer support to parents, says Howard Johnson, a youth officer in Hinsdale, Ill., a Chicago suburb that has such a system. "It gives parents a little more backbone," he explains. "They don't feel like they're alone when they tell their kids not to drink." Parental peer support also is evident in Greenwich, Conn., where more than 1,000 parents signed a pledge to supervise all teen-age parties in their homes and to refuse alcohol to anyone under the legal drinking age.

Some high schools have set up "chemical-free" prom nights and graduation parties in an effort to prevent the heavy drinking or drug taking that often accompanies such events. The schools hope to show that it's possible to have fun without getting drunk.

At the college level, a group called BACCHUS has 200 campus chapters that encourage students to use alcohol moderately if they use it at all. BACCHUS stands for Boost Alcohol Consciousness Concerning the Health of University Students and is also the name of the Roman god of wine. The organization's projects include a designated driver program, in which one student agrees to remain

To combat drinking at a teen-age party, parents should remain home during the party, supply plenty of food and soft drinks, and provide games and other activities for the guests.

sober for the evening, and free taxis for students with no safe way home from a party. BACCHUS chapters sponsor coffee houses and alcohol-free parties and urge fraternities and sororities to provide nonalcoholic beverages at their parties.

Many colleges, on their own, have begun to clamp down on student drinking. Some ban alcohol in public areas of dormitories or at parties where freshmen are present. Others employ campus security guards to check the age of student drinkers.

There's no agreement on whether underage people should ever be allowed to drink. Some experts say it is naive to expect that teens won't drink in light of statistics showing that the majority of young people do use alcohol. Anastas says, "There's no such thing as a responsible drinker who's a teen-ager, because it's against the law."

"There is no consensus as to whether or how teen-agers should be taught to drink or prepared to live in a drinking society," says Gail G. Milgram, director of education at the Center of Alcohol Studies at Rutgers University in New Brunswick, N.J. "Teen-agers need to be taught what constitutes social or light or responsible drinking—what's appropriate and what's inappropriate," Milgram declares. "Just talking about drinking with teen-agers doesn't mean we expect them to drink."

A teen-age drinking party, it should be remembered, would be illegal almost everywhere in the United States. In 1984, Congress passed, and President Ronald Reagan signed, a law requiring the states to raise their minimum drinking age to 21 by Oct. 1, 1986, or lose 5 per cent of some federal highway funds. After Oct. 1, 1987, the penalty rises to 10 per cent a year.

Reagan had previously opposed the law as unwarranted federal interference in state affairs, but he reversed himself following an intense lobbying campaign led by a group called Mothers Against

A youth group called Students Against Driving Drunk (SADD) uses an agreement called a Contract for Life, *above,* to protect teen-agers from being killed on the road. Under the contract, children agree to call their parents if they have been drinking or are with a driver who has been drinking. The parents promise to provide a safe ride home, with no questions asked until later. SADD members also take part in parades, *above right,* and other activities to publicize their program.

Drunk Driving (MADD), formerly Mothers Against Drunk Drivers. Candy Lightner of Fair Oaks, Calif., founded MADD in 1980 after her 13-year-old daughter, Cari, was killed by a drunken driver.

All but eight states—Colorado, Idaho, Louisiana, Montana, Ohio, South Dakota, Tennessee, and Wyoming—met the 1986 deadline. (Tennessee raised the legal drinking age to 21 for all except members of the armed services.) Many states reversed action they had taken only 10 or 15 years earlier. In the early 1970's, 23 states lowered their drinking age, partly in response to reduction of the voting age to 18 in 1971 and partly because of the Vietnam War. "If they're old enough to vote and to die for their country, they're old enough to drink," state legislators said. By 1976, people under the age of 21 could legally drink some form of alcohol in 38 states. The result was an increase of about 700 traffic deaths per year in the 18- to 20-year-old group, according to Allan F. Williams, vice president of research for the Insurance Institute for Highway Safety, a Washington, D.C., research group supported by the insurance industry.

Some states raised the drinking age back to 21 before the federal pressure was applied, and with noticeable results. According to the Transportation Systems Center in Cambridge, Mass.—an agency of the U.S. Department of Transportation—traffic fatalities dropped 9 to 14 per cent in states that raised the drinking age from 18 to 21. Highway deaths fell 6 to 9 per cent in states that raised the age from 19 to 21, and 3 to 5 per cent in states that raised it from 20 to 21.

But no one expected the new laws to solve the problem of underage drinking. In states with a minimum drinking age of 21, only 30 per cent of high school students said they were nondrinkers, according to the RTI survey, meaning that 70 per cent were breaking the law. In states with lower drinking ages, only 20 per cent of high school students said they did not drink.

Anastas believes the higher drinking age will merely reduce the "trickle-down effect" of teen-age liquor purchases. Instead of 18-year-olds buying beer for 15-year-olds, 21-year-olds will buy it for 18-year-olds. "I don't want parents ever to think that a higher minimum drinking age is going to solve the problem," he says.

The problem hasn't been solved by any means. There is evidence, however, that antidrinking programs coupled with growing nationwide concern over drunken driving by all age groups may be having some effect. The number of teen-agers who drink appears to have stabilized since the mid-1970's after rising rapidly for two decades, and there's some evidence of a slight decline in heavy drinking.

"I think there's been a change in attitude on the campuses away from drunkenness," says Gerardo Gonzalez, founder and president of BACCHUS. "It's part of the national trend against tolerating heavy drinking and drunk driving, along with the rising interest in personal fitness."

And even teen-agers who drink heavily may pass through that stage without developing a lasting drinking problem as adults. According to Harvard's Hawthorne, drinking appears to peak in the middle 20's for men and drop off sharply in the early 30's. For women, drinking peaks when they reach 45, but even at that age, heavy drinking is twice as common among men as among women.

But Hawthorne notes that heavy drinking has been associated, at all age levels, with higher mortality rates due to accidents, suicide, and violence. "Some of the heaviest drinkers may not be surviving beyond young adulthood," he says, "which could contribute to the impression that the prevalence of heavy drinking declines as a function of age." In other words, teen-agers may outgrow their heavy drinking—if they're lucky enough to outlive it.

For further information:

Here are the addresses of some groups concerned with teen-age drinking.

National Clearinghouse
  for Alcohol Information
P.O. Box 2345
Rockville, MD 20852

Students Against Driving Drunk
  (SADD)
P.O. Box 800
Marlboro, MA 01752

Mothers Against Drunk Driving
  (MADD)
669 Airport Freeway
Suite 310
Hurst, TX 76053

BACCHUS
124 Tigert Hall
University of Florida
Gainesville, FL 32611

PRIDE (National Parents'
  Resource Institute
  for Drug Education)
Suite 1002
100 Edgewood Avenue
Atlanta, GA 30303

National Council on Alcoholism
12 W. 21st Street
New York, NY 10010

By Walter Hays

New Life
for Two Old
Treasures

Scientific restorations are rescuing the Sistine ceiling
and *The Last Supper* from centuries of grime, humidity,
vandalism, and previous destructive restoration attempts.

On a broad platform high above the floor of the Sistine Chapel in the palace of the Vatican in Rome, three men labor to remove nearly five centuries of grime and dirt from the spectacular frescoes by Michelangelo that cover the ceiling and part of the walls. Screens of sacking material shield the restorers from the public view. But their long shadows, cast by the powerful lights needed to illuminate their delicate work, stretch across the ceiling, mingling with the Biblical figures depicted there.

About 300 miles (480 kilometers) north of Rome, in Milan, another renowned restorer toils at the Monastery of Santa Maria delle Grazie. Her task is the restoration of one of the world's most famous paintings, *The Last Supper* by Leonardo da Vinci.

The two multimillion-dollar restoration efforts, hailed as the most daring and spectacular currently in progress anywhere, were about half finished in 1986 after more than six years of painstaking labor. The work in the Sistine Chapel is targeted for completion in 1992, that of *The Last Supper* in about 1993. When the restorations are finished, these works will resemble their original splendor more closely than at any time since their creation.

Both restorations have revealed some surprises. The restorers have found the colors in Michelangelo's frescoes to be unexpectedly rich and vivid. *The Last Supper* restoration has recovered a delicacy of hand gestures and facial expressions in Jesus and His 12 apostles that had been lost in disastrous restoration attempts of the past. The modern restorers use scientifically advanced restoration methods backed up by steps to minimize additional environmental damage. Both efforts will benefit civilization for centuries to come.

Michelangelo's paintings in the Sistine Chapel are among the greatest masterpieces from an age of masterpieces. Yet he reluctantly agreed to paint the Sistine ceiling when Pope Julius II offered him the commission in 1508. Michelangelo considered anything but sculpture a forced deviation from his true vocation.

To cover the ceiling's huge expanse—an area 134 by 44 feet (41 by 13 meters)—Michelangelo created nine rectangular panels illustrating scenes from Genesis, the first book of the Bible. The scenes he portrayed, which include Adam and Eve's creation and their banishment from the Garden of Eden, God creating the universe, and the Flood, are depicted with great animation and power.

Michelangelo also created 14 *lunettes*—crescent-shaped paintings—above the windows flanking two sides of the chapel and on one wall. These paintings depict the Biblical ancestors of Christ. Michelangelo finished the ceiling with prophets, classical prophetic women called *sibyls*, nude youths, cherubs, and scenes from the Bible. Altogether, he painted 343 figures, a task that took 4½ years.

About 20 years after the ceiling was finished, Pope Clement VII asked Michelangelo to decorate the wall behind the chapel's altar. That magnificent painting, *The Last Judgment*, measures 60 feet (18 meters) high and 30 feet (9 meters) wide, and took seven years—from 1534 to 1541—to finish.

The author:
Walter Hays is an international journalist who lives in Rome.

A restorer cleans one of Michelangelo's frescoes on the Sistine ceiling, *left*, while standing on a movable bridge similar to the scaffolding Michelangelo used when painting the chapel. The bridge and a sketch by Michelangelo of himself at work on the ceiling, *above*, debunk the myth that the artist painted the Sistine ceiling while lying on his back. The sketch accompanies a sonnet by Michelangelo in his own handwriting about the project.

Michelangelo created *The Last Judgment* and the works on the Sistine ceiling using *fresco*, a technique in which the artist paints on a plastered surface while the plaster is still damp. As the plaster dries and hardens, the colors are sealed in.

For a long time, the thousands of tourists who troop through the Sistine Chapel each day have seen Michelangelo's frescoes "as through heavily smoked glass," as one past restorer put it. Dust from the air and smoke and soot from candles and oil lamps once used to light the chapel stuck to the paintings. Making the situation worse, previous restorers, perhaps as early as the late 1500's, applied thick layers of glue, made of animal materials. They used the glue to cover stains left on the frescoes by rain water seeping into the chapel and to brighten the colors of the paintings.

In fact, applying the glue was a remarkably bad idea. Between the time Michelangelo finished the ceiling and the time he painted *The Last Judgment*, the ceiling had already become soiled with smoke and soot. The glue only cemented the grime to the paintings and attracted even more dust and soot. In addition, the glue darkened with age, further obscuring the frescoes. By the end of the 1700's, the frescoes were so dull and dingy that most art scholars began to think of Michelangelo as a painter with little skill or interest in color.

A number of restorers tried over the years to remove the glue. Some tried to clean the frescoes with alcohol-based solvents or with crumbled bread wrapped in cloth and dipped in water. But, according to Gianluigi Colalucci, who heads the Vatican's restoration team,

The Sistine Chapel

Michelangelo's spectacular frescoes on the ceiling of the Sistine Chapel consist of nine panels illustrating scenes from Genesis, surrounded by scenes from the Bible and a variety of figures, including prophets and sibyls. Above the chapel's windows are 14 lunettes—crescent-shaped frescoes—depicting the Biblical ancestors of Christ. *The Last Judgment* covers the wall behind the chapel's altar.

Scenes from Genesis

Prophets, sibyls, and Bible scenes

Lunettes depicting the ancestors of Christ

The Last Judgment

"Using bread poultices to clean the painting is like using an eraser to remove dust and grease." Because these methods failed to clean the frescoes evenly—or even remove much of the glue—the restorers did considerable repainting.

According to Fabrizio Mancinelli, the Vatican art historian in charge of the restoration, it was essential to go ahead with the project now, otherwise Michelangelo's frescoes would have been damaged irreparably. Mancinelli explains that the animal glue expands and contracts with heat and cold, and when it cracks, it removes some of the paint—the way peeling cellophane tape from a magazine picture will lift off some of the color. In addition, restoration technology has advanced to the stage where projects such as this can be carried out nearly perfectly.

At first glance, the cleaning process seems simple enough. Colalucci and his colleagues apply a cleaning solvent to a patch of fresco about 1 to 2 feet square (900 to 1,800 square centimeters). They leave the solvent to work for about three minutes, depending on the thickness of the glue and dirt, then wipe it off with a sponge dipped in distilled water. The patch is then left to dry for about 24 hours. If necessary, the process is repeated.

In reality, however, the process is more complicated. The actual work on the frescoes is backed by a tremendous amount of historical and scientific research. Art historians studied Michelangelo's sketches and other records of his work to determine what was his and what was added later by restorers and artists. Scientists then analyzed the frescoes themselves to determine the thickness of the glue and the extent of the repainting. They also figured out how to cope with special problems, such as extensive water stains.

The solvent used by the restorers was developed during 10 years of testing by the Italian Central Institute of Restoration. Called AB57, the solvent consists of several cleaning solutions, a fungicide, and a gel that holds all the other ingredients together. The solvent does not damage the underlying color or leave a residue. It also cleans more thoroughly than solvents used in the past. Before tackling Michelangelo's frescoes, the restorers tested the solvent on another Sistine Chapel fresco by Domenico Ghirlandajo, a Florentine artist with whom Michelangelo studied painting.

The restorers are not repainting the frescoes. In a few places, they are using easily removable water color to hide cracks and stains. The restorers carefully document all such retouching for future art historians.

The $3-million restoration began in June 1980, financed by the Nippon Television Network Corporation of Japan. The restorers started with the lunettes, completing this phase of the job in 1984. They are now inching their way across the ceiling, hoping to finish these frescoes by 1988. Then from 1988 to 1992 they will tackle the huge and awesome *Last Judgment* fresco.

A thick layer of dirt and soot plus glue applied by previous restorers shroud a Sistine Chapel lunette depicting Jacob and his son Joseph, the husband of Christ's mother, Mary, *right.* The dinginess of this and other Sistine frescoes had led many scholars to think of Michelangelo as a painter with little interest or skill in color. But after cleaning, *below,* brilliant yellow, blue, and green blaze from the lunette.

While cleaning the ceiling frescoes, the restorers stand on an ingenious bridge, the design of which is based on the wooden scaffolding Michelangelo used when he painted the ceiling. The bridge consists of a flat platform with steps at the sides that allow the restorers to reach the curved parts of the ceiling where it meets the walls. The platform, which spans the width of the chapel, has wheels and moves along the length of the chapel on steel rails set into the same holes in the walls used for Michelangelo's scaffolding.

The bridge debunks the legend that Michelangelo painted the ceiling frescoes lying on his back. "Michelangelo painted the ceiling in the same position we use in restoring it—standing up," Colalucci said. "Of course, he may have lain on his back at times—as we do—to get a better look at what he was doing."

The restoration has provided the art world with a few surprises. The two most important revelations have enhanced Michelangelo's already lofty reputation as one of the greatest artists of all time.

According to Colalucci and Mancinelli, the frescoes are in a remarkable state of preservation under the dirt. "They might have been painted 50 years ago," Mancinelli said. The excellent condition of the frescoes testifies to Michelangelo's absolute mastery of fresco painting. In the past, many art scholars believed that because Michelangelo worked chiefly as a sculptor, he had little expertise in fresco painting. They also thought that Michelangelo ignored the preparatory steps involved in fresco painting, creating his figures and scenes practically freehand. In fact, just the opposite is true. According to the restorers, Michelangelo worked quickly, but he was also methodical and thorough in creating his frescoes.

From the huge number of preparatory sketches that have survived, the restorers know that Michelangelo spent months planning his figures and the colors he would use. He then drew full-sized outlines of the figures on thick paper. These outlines, called *cartone* in Italian, *cartoons* in English, were then fixed to the wall, which was covered with wet plaster. Like other fresco painters of his time, Michelangelo had numerous assistants who

An Old Art in a Modern Age

To create a fresco, an artist first sketches a full-sized drawing—called a cartoon—of the figures that will appear in the painting, *top*. The cartoon is then fixed to the wall, and the outlines of the figures are transferred to the wet plaster. The artist then paints in the figures, *above*, working quickly before the plaster dries. As the plaster hardens, the colors are sealed in.

applied the plaster to the wall. These helpers applied enough plaster for only one day's painting—covering an area of about 6 by 4 feet (1.8 by 1.2 meters).

The assistants punched holes in the cartoons along the lines of the figures and forced carbon powder into the holes, leaving an outline on the plaster. They then removed the cartoons, and Michelangelo painted his figures.

The restoration has also forced art scholars to revise their judgment about Michelangelo's mastery of color. "What has been revealed is a painting style of striking color, far from the Michelangelo of shadows imagined up to now," said Mancinelli. Under the grime, the restorers found bright yellows, vivid blues, lime-greens, reds, and violet. The change is obvious to anyone who stands in the Sistine Chapel and compares the spectacular color of the frescoes already cleaned with the dingy, plum-colored images not yet restored.

The Vatican has already taken steps to protect the newly restored frescoes. The candles and oil lamps that produced the soot and grime that coated the paintings have been banned from the chapel.

The restoration has not won universal applause, however. Some Italian artists and art scholars complain that the restorers are stripping the paintings of a dark glaze Michelangelo applied after the frescoes dried to deepen colors and create shadows. They argue that the restored frescoes are too brightly colored and have lost their subtlety.

The Vatican restorers, however, point out that extensive studies of all documents describing Michelangelo's fresco technique reveal no indication that he retouched his Sistine frescoes after they dried. And most art scholars believe the restorers' work is both accurate and careful. For the tourists who flock to the Sistine Chapel each day, there is no doubt. They are witnessing a modern resurrection.

Covered only by a tarpaulin, Leonardo da Vinci's *Last Supper* stands amid the rubble of the refectory after an Allied bomb damaged the monastery of Santa Maria delle Grazie in August 1943 during World War II. The painting remained exposed to the elements until the refectory was rebuilt nearly two years later.

The task of restoring *The Last Supper* is very different from that of cleaning Michelangelo's frescoes, which remained in good condition under the dirt. Humidity, mold, vandalism, smog, and destructive restoration attempts in the past have all taken their toll on *The Last Supper*, a painting described by its restorer as a "dying masterpiece." Much of the blame for the painting's sorry state, however, can be placed squarely on its creator, Leonardo da Vinci, who used an inappropriate technique to create the painting.

As the subject of the painting, Leonardo chose that supremely dramatic moment at the Last Supper when Jesus shocked His apostles by announcing, "Verily, verily, I say unto you, that one of you shall betray me" (John 13: 21). Lodovico Sforza, the Duke of Milan, commissioned the painting in 1494 as a gift to the monks of the Monastery of Santa Maria delle Grazie in Milan. Leonardo spent three years painting the mural—rather a long time—on the north wall of the monks' *refectory* (dining room), finishing in 1497. He took such a long time in part because the painting is so large—28 feet (8.5 meters) wide and 15½ feet (4.7 meters) high. In addition, Leonardo was working on other projects at the same time. But the main reason for the delay was that Leonardo was a perfectionist who took days or even weeks to polish an expression or gesture.

For that reason, he decided against using the fresco technique normally used for wall paintings. An artist using the fresco method must work quickly. Instead, Leonardo probably used *tempera*—color pigments mixed with egg yolk—and perhaps glue and chalk on a dry base. This method allowed him to work slowly, reworking his

The restored part of *The Last Supper* (at right), though more colorful and detailed than art scholars had believed, is still only a shadow of the painting's former glory. Humidity, vandalism, pollution, and disastrous restoration attempts of the past have taken their toll on one of the world's most famous works of art.

Close-up photographs of *The Last Supper* reveal the extent of damage. Layers of brown and gray paint, typical of the work of previous restorers, cover the original red and blue (arrows) Leonardo used for the apostle James's tunic and sleeve, *below.* Cracks in the painting's white base, *bottom* (greatly magnified)—the result of excess humidity and the expansion and contraction of the wall—caused Leonardo's paint (the yellow flecks) to flake and fall away.

figures and creating fine detail. Unfortunately, this method was not at all suitable for painting on the stone wall of the refectory.

Leonardo coated the refectory wall with a special base, which consisted of three layers. The base was supposed to make the surface of the wall smooth—which it did—and to bind the paint to the wall—which it did not. The dampness of the wall and temperature changes that caused the wall to expand and contract began to damage the painting almost immediately. The base began to crack, and the paint began to flake and drop from the wall. By 1566, only 69 years after Leonardo finished the mural, a visitor reported that "nothing was visible but a mass of blots."

In addition to the original flaw in Leonardo's technique, the mural suffered a catastrophic series of damaging incidents down through the centuries. In the mid-1600's, the monks of the monastery cut off part of the painting depicting Jesus' feet and those of two apostles to enlarge a doorway between the refectory and the kitchen. In the late 1700's, soldiers of the invading army of French leader Napoleon Bonaparte used the refectory as a stable and amused themselves by throwing stones at *The Last Supper.*

The most threatening incident, however, occurred in August 1943, during World War II, when an Allied bomb blew off the roof and east wall of the refectory. Fortunately, a double wall of sandbags and planks shielded the painting. But Leonardo's masterpiece remained exposed to the elements, protected only by a tarpaulin, until the roof and wall were rebuilt nearly two years later.

Some previous restorations had an equally disastrous effect. Restorers cleaned the mural with harsh solvents and even repainted areas where the painting was too badly decomposed to follow Leonardo's original line. Other restoration efforts in the 1900's, however, did halt some deterioration. Without them, the painting would be in even worse shape than it is.

The current restoration, the seventh recorded effort, began in 1980. Financed by Olivetti, an Italian office-machine manufacturer, the work is expected to cost nearly $1 million. This restoration is the most scientific and thorough to date. An eminent art historian and restorer, Pinin Brambilla Barcilon, heads the project.

Brambilla first spent months studying Leonardo's preparatory sketches for the mural, which are kept at Windsor Castle in England. Meanwhile, a team of scientists began analyzing the painting itself. They exposed samples of the paint to ultraviolet and infrared light to distinguish Leonardo's pigments from those of restorers. They also ran the samples through a *chromatograph,* a device that identifies the chemical makeup of a substance. This information helped scientists develop solvents that would loosen or remove the restorers' work without damaging Leonardo's color. The scientists also heated the wall with floodlights and photographed the mural with infrared film to find Leonardo's sketches underneath the paint.

In addition, the scientists performed numerous other tests to locate areas where Leonardo's original color had disappeared altogether and to identify the minerals in his pigments in order to determine the colors he used.

The actual restoration has been no less painstaking. Brambilla's basic tools are a double microscope, which magnifies the wall up to 40 times and shines an intense, coin-sized beam of light on her work area, and a *bistoury*, a surgical knife about the size of a nail file. Often, simply applying solvent cleans away surface grime and flakes of paint, varnish, and other materials applied by previous restorers. For stubborn particles, she uses the bistoury.

Much of her work involves repositioning flecks of color displaced during a restoration effort in 1924. At that time, a restorer injected glue behind the surface color of the painting and used hot metal rollers and rubber rollers to make the paint flecks stick to the wall. In the process, however, many flecks were moved from their original position. Brambilla is putting them back where they belong.

All this makes for painfully slow work. Seven years after she started the restoration, Brambilla, working from the right side of the painting as you look at it, is about half finished.

The emerging painting shows that the effort is clearly worthwhile. Although large patches of original color are gone forever—and there will be no attempt at repainting—many glorious details of Leonardo's work have been rediscovered.

"People are traumatized by the first impact of what they see—the

Peering through a double microscope that shines an intense light on *The Last Supper,* restorer Pinin Brambilla Barcilon painstakingly cleans the painting inch by inch, *top.* To scrape away surface grime and remove paint and other materials applied by previous restorers, Brambilla uses a surgical knife called a bistoury, *above.*

A "New" Matthew

The restoration of *The Last Supper* has corrected many alterations made by previous restorers. Before restoration, Matthew, *above* (at the left), appeared with a closed mouth and a beard. In the restored figure, *right,* Matthew's mouth is open in speech and his "beard" is seen to be the shadow of his head on Thaddaeus' shoulder, *above* (center).

difference from the way it was before," Brambilla said. "Look at the head of Thaddaeus," she said, pointing to the second apostle from the right as you look at the painting. This figure had been heavily repainted. "All you could see before was the outline, with dark brushstrokes. He had an enormous nose, an overlarge lip, and an eye depicted only with a diagonal brushstroke because the original eye was missing. But look at it now—the face has become slimmer, more spiritual, I would say. The eye is bigger, with the folds redis- covered. The lips and nose are smaller."

Simon, who sits next to Thaddaeus at the extreme right of the painting, has undergone an equally remarkable transformation. Be- fore the restoration, Simon, seen in profile, was beetle-browed, and had a fat neck, a small nose, and only a diagonal stroke for an eye. "But after the cleaning," Brambilla pointed out, "we see that Simon is turning toward Thaddaeus. You see the muscles in his neck as he turns. The head has acquired a serenity that was completely lacking before." Simon's tangled beard now appears as the original goatee, and he has regained his classic profile.

In the case of Matthew, third from the right, Brambilla discov- ered that his mouth is open, not closed as a previous restorer left it. In addition, what had seemed to be Matthew's beard turned out to be the shadow of his head on Thaddaeus' shoulder.

The discovery of previously unknown details is one of two major revelations of this restoration. In the restored part of the mural, one can see gold rims on the wine glasses, the reflection of the apostles' beautifully colored robes on the silver supper plates, and architec- tural details of the Renaissance-style dining room in which Leo- nardo set his dramatic scene. The other important revelation is the painting's vivid colors. Art historians had thought that Leonardo created his mural in dusky, shadowy tones.

To protect Leonardo's newly rejuvenated work, the restoration team plans to install a special carpet and air purifiers to absorb the dust tracked into the refectory by tourists. Dehumidifiers will re- move some of the moisture that plagues the room. The restorers ruled out installing large-scale air-conditioning and climate control systems because of space and aesthetic considerations.

When Brambilla has finished, *The Last Supper* will more accurately proclaim Leonardo's genius. The dying masterpiece, though only a shadow of its original glory, is coming back to life.

For further reading:

Angier, Natalie. "Last Chance for the 'Last Supper.'" *Discover*, May 1982.
Bertelli, Carlo. "Restoration Reveals the Last Supper." *National Geographic*, November 1983.
Pietrangeli, Carlo, and others. *The Sistine Chapel: The Art, the History, and the Restoration.* Harmony Books, 1986.

By Susan Kaufman Purcell

Mexico: from Boom to Bust

Despite its vast oil resources, Mexico faces the worst economic crisis in its history, intensified by political corruption and a growing population.

The eyes of the world were on Mexico in the spring of 1986 as that nation hosted the World Cup, the championship of the world's most popular sport—soccer. The Mexican government was eager for Mexico to put on its best appearance, hoping that the World Cup would stimulate tourism and give the economy a much-needed boost. Road crews filled potholes. Buildings and bridges gleamed with fresh paint. Netzahualcoyotl, a poor neighborhood on the outskirts of Mexico City and the site of one of the World Cup stadiums, got a face-lift as roads were paved, electricity installed, and slums cleared.

But the excitement generated by the event quickly faded. Mexico's team lost to West Germany in a quarterfinal game, and during one game, Mexicans booed the introduction of Mexican President Miguel de la Madrid Hurtado, using the opportunity to express their unhappiness with the mounting economic, political, and social

Polluted skies hover over Mexico City like a symbol of the economic troubles and other problems that hover over the entire country.

problems that Mexico faces today. The World Cup glitter proved to be only a temporary distraction.

Less than 15 years ago, the discovery of vast new petroleum deposits in the southern part of the country and in the Gulf of Mexico had seemed to promise nothing but prosperity. By 1974, estimates of the richness of the discovery ran as high as 20 billion barrels of oil, comparable to some Middle East countries. The government speeded up its spending on public works and industry, expecting the income from petroleum to help balance this spending.

Then, in the early 1980's, the oil bubble burst. World demand for petroleum declined. Mexico's oil income dropped sharply, the government became greatly indebted, and economic growth, which had reached 8 per cent in 1980, slowed. The resulting social tensions are threatening Mexico's political stability.

Mexico's troubled economic situation first became obvious in August 1982, when the government ran out of money to pay the interest on its debt to international lenders. The debt at that time totaled $82 billion. Since then, Mexico's economy has hardly grown at all, while its population of more than 76 million people continues to increase by 2.8 per cent annually.

The result of the nation's sluggish economic growth has been rising unemployment. In the aftermath of the 1982 crisis, a million people lost their jobs. By 1986, the unemployment rate hovered around 20 per cent. Adding to the problem, a million new people enter the labor force each year.

Immediate relief for the unemployment problem is not in sight. It is hard for the government to use its money to create jobs while Mexico owes more than $100 billion to foreign lenders. Just to pay the interest on the debt, Mexico must use almost all the money it earns from selling its petroleum abroad. In 1982, Mexico's oil revenues reached a high of $15.6 billion. Since then, a severe drop in oil prices—from $27 per barrel in January 1985 to about $14 per barrel in 1986—has drastically reduced Mexico's oil-export earnings. Mexico's oil receipts were expected to plummet to $6.5 billion by the end of 1986, leaving the government with even less money to spend and helping to raise its total debt to an estimated $102.5-billion in 1986.

The author:
Susan Kaufman Purcell is director of the Latin-American program of the Council on Foreign Relations in New York City.

What seems strange about Mexico's current economic plight is that the nation got into debt during the oil-boom days when it had millions of barrels of oil to sell abroad and oil prices were high. This apparent paradox was the result of bad luck, bad government, and rampant corruption.

Following the discovery of oil in southern Mexico, President José López Portillo, who governed Mexico from 1976 to 1982, decided to build up Mexico's oil industry quickly to finance a crash-development program. He hoped that his construction of ports, roads, industrial parks, steel mills, and factories for producing heavy ma-

Mexico at a Glance

Mexico's many resources include vast oil fields, *below.* In the early 1970's, new oil finds were made in the Bay of Campeche and near Villahermosa, making Mexico the world's fourth-largest oil country.

United States

Tijuana

Juárez

Baja California Norte

Sonora

Hermosillo

Chihuahua

Chihuahua

Coahuila

Baja California Sur

Saltillo • Monterrey

Durango

Nuevo León

Sinaloa

Durango

Zacatecas

Tamaulipas

Gulf of Mexico

Pacific Ocean

San Luis Potosí

Tampico

Nayarit

Aguascalientes

León

Guanajuato

Querétaro

Hidalgo

México

Mérida

Cancún

Yucatán

Cozumel

Guadalajara

Jalisco

Veracruz

Bay of Campeche

Quintana Roo

Manzanillo

Colima

Mexico City*

Michoacán

Cuernavaca

Veracruz

Tlaxcala

Puebla

Tabasco

Campeche

Morelos

Guerrero

Villahermosa

Belize

Acapulco

Oaxaca

Chiapas

Guatemala

Honduras

International boundary

State boundary

National capital

Other city or town

Oil field

0   300 Miles
0   300 Kilometers

*Mexico City is located in the Federal District.

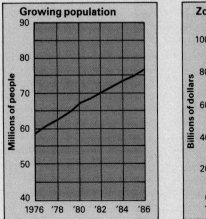

Monterrey

Guadalajara

Mexico City

Persons per sq. mile

More than 125

25 to 125

Fewer than 25

Mexico's mounting problems include a growing population, zooming foreign debt, and falling oil revenues. The growing population has made Mexico City the world's largest metropolitan area.

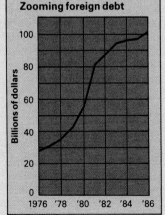

Growing population

Millions of people

90

80

70

60

50

40

1976 '78 '80 '82 '84 '86

Zooming foreign debt

Billions of dollars

100

80

60

40

20

0

1976 '78 '80 '82 '84 '86

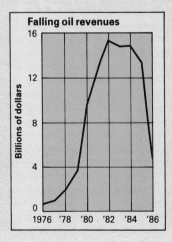

Falling oil revenues

Billions of dollars

16

12

8

4

0

1976 '78 '80 '82 '84 '86

Source: Wharton Econometric Forecasting; 1986 figures are estimates.

147

Mexico's status as a major oil supplier is the result of the discovery in the early 1970's of vast oil reserves near the southern city of Villahermosa, *right*. The modern oil rig there contrasts sharply with old methods of farming still in use in some areas of Mexico, *below*.

chinery would transform Mexico into a modern industrialized country by the time he left office.

The world did not cooperate. Oil prices and the demand for oil began to slide. Instead of adjusting his ambitious goals to this new reality, López Portillo borrowed money from foreign lenders to plug the gap between what Mexico was spending on its ambitious development plans and what it was earning from oil exports. López Portillo expected that the decline in oil prices would be temporary. He was wrong. By the time he left office, his overspending had pushed Mexico's traditionally low annual rate of inflation to an incredible 100 per cent.

Mexico's unhappy economic situation has been particularly hard for Mexicans to endure, given what came before. Most of the years under López Portillo were boom years. Mexicans of all classes went on a spending spree. Middle-class families bought waterfront condominiums in Texas and California and mountain condominiums near Colorado's ski resorts. Wages were so high that workers who had never earned enough to travel abroad were able to vacation in Europe and the United States. Television antennas multiplied across the rooftops of urban slums. Mexicans who had never owned a car could finally afford one, and those who already owned one car bought a second. Luxury residences sprung up throughout southern Mexico City. And the poor filled their modest dwellings with new possessions.

Then suddenly everything collapsed. Mexicans had to sell their condominiums abroad because they could no longer pay the mortgages. The second, and sometimes the first, car had to be sold. Many luxury buildings remained unfinished skeletons. And Mexicans began to "see Mexico first," as the declining value of the peso, the basic unit of Mexico's currency, made foreign travel too costly.

A period of economic decline is always a trying time. For Mexicans, it was especially unbearable after the spending sprees and wild hopes that oil had produced. They began to vent their anger and frustration at the government, which, in turn, meant the governing party—the Institutional Revolutionary Party (PRI). The PRI has been Mexico's dominant party since it was founded in 1929. It has never lost a presidential or gubernatorial election, but as a result of the crisis, the PRI has finally run into significant opposition in some areas of the country.

Unhappiness over the government's handling of the oil boom brought to the surface other long-standing weaknesses in Mexico's political system. These included complaints about government corruption and the unequal distribution of land and wealth. The roots of this dissatisfaction can be traced to the Mexican Revolution of 1910. The Mexican political system was created in the aftermath of the revolution, which was really two revolutions—a middle-class revolt and a peasant revolt. Both were aimed at overthrowing the dictatorship of Porfirio Díaz, who governed Mexico from 1876 until 1911, when he was finally forced to resign.

The peasant revolution, which produced such heroes as Pancho Villa and Emiliano Zapata, tried to improve the lot of Mexico's peasants by restoring their *ejidos* (farmland held in common by small communities). These communal lands had been unjustly taken from the peasants and made available to large landowners, both Mexican and foreign, who wished to modernize agricultural production and get rich at the same time. The slogans of the peasant revolution were "Land and Liberty" and "Social Justice."

The peasant revolution was fueled by economic grievances, but the middle-class revolt was primarily a political one. During the Díaz dictatorship, economic growth had produced a new middle class centered in the northern border states. This economic growth stemmed in great part from investments by United States businesses. The middle class's new economic power, however, was not matched by increased political power. Instead, the political system remained tightly controlled by Díaz, who killed, jailed, or exiled his political opponents and rigged his elections. The revolutionary slogan of the middle class was "Effective Suffrage and No Reelection." They wanted honest elections and a one-term presidency.

The 1910 revolution failed to uproot the authoritarian rule that Díaz had established. Instead, its ultimate result was to replace a single dictator with a single dominant political party. The Mexican Constitution of 1917 limited the president to one six-year term, so no one person could ever again monopolize power. But the new Constitution could not prevent the rise of a dominant political party with a powerful hold on the country's economy. By 1929, that party was the PRI and, like Díaz, it always won the presidency.

The Mexican Revolution was also supposed to have changed Mexico's social structure. Yet Mexico's peasants have profited least from the revolution. The revolution restored the collective use of some ejidos to the peasants, but many of these were on poor land in regions that received little rainfall. The best farmland remained in private hands—often the hands of government party politicians. In addition, government irrigation projects have benefited the large private landowners. The government has set up institutions to supply peasants with low-cost food, inexpensive credit, and agricultural equipment. But the number of peasants has continued to grow, while the land available for distribution to them has not.

Many Mexicans have moved north to the United States as illegal immigrants seeking jobs and a better life. Many others have moved from the countryside to the cities in search of work, particularly to Mexico City, the capital. Mexico City has become the world's largest metropolitan area with a population unofficially estimated at 18 million. Growing at a rate of 9 per cent per year, Mexico City's population may climb to 30 million by the year 2000. Once in Mexico

Poverty and wealth exist side by side in Mexico. Squatters live in ramshackle houses on the outskirts of Mexico City, *right*. Three businessmen stroll through a posh district of Mexico City, *below*.

Two of Mexico's most pressing problems—a mushrooming population and political corruption—are evident in the teeming streets of Mexico City, *above*, and at the city's Museum of Corruption, *right*. The museum was the multimillion-dollar home of former Mexico City Police Chief Arturo Durazo Moreno, who was indicted for tax evasion and went on trial in 1986.

City, the rural poor become part of the urban poor, settling in the vast slum areas that encircle the city, crowding their large families into one or two rooms. Those fortunate enough to find jobs frequently commute four hours a day because their homes are located far from their jobs, and traffic in congested Mexico City moves at an average 7 miles (11 kilometers) per hour. Exhaust fumes from that traffic are a major contributor to pollution in Mexico City, which ranks as one of the most polluted cities in the world.

The living standards of the peasants and urban poor contrast vividly with those of Mexico's middle class, which has been the true beneficiary of the Mexican Revolution. This class has grown rapidly. Many middle-class families live considerably better than their U.S. counterparts, with large houses, luxurious cars, and servants. As for the very rich, their extravagant life style has not changed since the revolution, though the source of their wealth has. Before the revolution, the rich derived their wealth from large rural landholdings called *haciendas*, which were broken up by the revolution's land-reform policies. Mexico's new upper class owes its fortune to manufacturing, commerce, and real estate.

Despite the revolution's quest for equality, Mexico has one of the most unequal distributions of income in all of Latin America. The gap between the rich and poor has steadily widened. When the oil boom began in the mid-1970's, for example, the wealthiest 10 per cent of the population earned 40 per cent of Mexico's total national income, according to a study by the World Bank, an agency of the

United Nations (UN). The poorest 20 per cent of the population received only about 3 per cent of the national income. In the past, Mexico was able to live with such inequality without disruptions to its stability, because its economy kept growing. For example, in the 1950's and 1960's, the gap between the rich and poor was large, but an economic growth rate of 6 to 8 per cent a year allowed everyone's standard of living to rise. People were confident that Mexico would grow out of its problems.

The current economic crisis has replaced such optimism with pessimism and deep anxiety. Mexico's political leaders believe that unless they can revive the economy, political unrest will grow, endangering not only the continued rule of the PRI but also the stability of the country. This realization has led to a number of economic and political reforms.

To restore economic growth, the Mexican government first had to stop spending more than it was earning. In 1983, Mexican President de la Madrid began to cut government spending. He ordered a reduction in the number of government employees, which had swelled from 740,000 in 1970 to 2.5 million in 1981, and held down their wage increases. He sold off or closed down more than half of the 1,150 state-owned companies that were costing the government too much money to subsidize, though most of these were small businesses. The government still subsidizes many large companies, except for a steel mill in Monterrey that employed about 11,000 people before it was closed.

The government not only had to spend less but also had to earn more. This involved lessening Mexico's dependence on oil exports—which accounted for as much as 75 per cent of its export earnings in 1983—and increasing Mexico's nonoil exports. But many of Mexico's export products were badly made compared with foreign goods and had to be improved. The government therefore allowed more foreign manufacturers into Mexico, forcing Mexican companies to improve their products and lower their costs if they wished to compete. De la Madrid also raised the prices the government charged for goods and services, including telephone calls, electricity, water, gasoline, transportation, and food.

Such policies made many Mexicans angry and unhappy. Some workers lost their jobs, either because of government cutbacks or because competition from abroad bankrupted their employers. Others saw their wages fall behind price increases due to inflation. Since 1982, the earning power of Mexican workers has declined by one-third. The middle class has been hit hard, too. Between 1982 and 1986, the average income for the middle class, after adjusting for inflation, declined 45 per cent. The poor, however, suffered the most because they had to spend more of their meager incomes on basic necessities.

To help restore Mexico's economic health and to give the PRI a political face-lift, de la Madrid launched a "moral renovation campaign." The campaign was aimed at eliminating, or at least curtailing, long-standing government corruption. Corruption became especially blatant during the oil-boom years when much more money was put into circulation.

One of the best-known examples of suspected corruption was the case of Mexico City Police Chief Arturo Durazo Moreno, who served during the term of López Portillo. His meager salary of $300 a month could hardly have allowed him to build two multimillion-dollar mansions—one in Mexico City and the other in the Pacific Coast resort town of Zihuatanejo. The $2.5-million mansion in Mexico City came complete with its own casino, heliport, race track, discothèque, and expensive imported furnishings. It has since been turned into a public Museum of Corruption, as part of de la Madrid's anticorruption campaign. Durazo was indicted for tax evasion and extortion in January 1984 and went on trial in 1986.

A different sort of corruption surfaced after the tragic earthquakes of September 1985, which took almost 10,000 lives and destroyed parts of Mexico City. Most of the buildings that collapsed during the quakes were public buildings constructed by companies under contract to the government. In many cases, it appeared that substandard construction was at fault—due to either corrupt or incompetent government inspectors.

The government's handling of earthquake relief measures also angered many Mexicans. Government soldiers and police officers

Political corruption surfaced in an unexpected way during the September 1985 earthquakes that struck Mexico City and took nearly 10,000 lives. Most of the structures that collapsed were public buildings, and it appeared that in some cases, substandard construction was at fault, though the buildings had passed government inspection.

The exclusive Las Hadas resort was built on the Pacific Coast in Manzanillo during the oil-boom years of the 1970's. Despite its failing economy, Mexico is still a major tourist haven, and the development of new resorts has been a bright spot in an otherwise bleak picture.

stood by while ordinary citizens helped direct the first efforts to rescue those trapped in the fallen buildings. By March 1986, some 38,000 people made homeless by the quakes still had not found new homes.

Despite de la Madrid's "moral renovation" campaign, discontent over his economic reforms has increased demands on the PRI for a more democratic political system. People want more control over their government.

Judging from the results of the governor's elections in Chihuahua and Sonora in 1985 and 1986, however, the PRI does not want the honest elections that a truly democratic system requires. The elections for governor in these northern border states had been hotly contested by the main opposition party—the conservative National Action Party (PAN). In the summer of 1985, PRI supporters worried about a possible PAN upset were caught stuffing and stealing ballot boxes during the election for governor of Sonora state. Then, in July 1986, during the election for governor of Chihuahua state, voters arriving as the polls opened at 8 A.M. found ballot boxes already crammed. PAN officials charged that the election was fraudulent, and they staged protest demonstrations.

Mexico has now entered a new phase of its crisis. After four years of hardship measures from 1983 to 1986, pressures have begun building on the government to relax its cutbacks on spending, even if doing so will increase inflation and undermine a genuine recovery. Some Mexicans want the government to pay only the interest, not the principal, on its foreign debt—or to *default* (fail to pay) entirely. Such steps, however, would undoubtedly harm confidence in Mexico and cause some foreign lenders to take punitive action.

To avoid pushing Mexico toward such extremes, the de la Madrid government during 1986 worked with the World Bank and the International Monetary Fund (IMF)—also a UN agency—as well as with the U.S. government and private commercial banks. The purpose of their collaboration was to get additional financial help so that Mexico could continue its reforms but ease the suffering of its people. In late September, Mexico reached agreement with the World Bank and the IMF on a new financial plan under which Mexico was to receive $12 billion in new loans. The agreement was expected to help prop up the ailing Mexican economy over the next 12 years.

As Mexico's northern neighbor, the United States has a particularly big stake in the success of Mexico's reform efforts. United States banks hold more than $35 billion of Mexico's debts. If Mexico defaulted on its foreign loans, it would cause serious damage to the U.S. banking system. Mexico is a big customer of U.S. businesses, buying more than $19 billion in goods from the United States each year. An economic downturn in Mexico, therefore, harms U.S. businesses that export to Mexico. Also, if Mexico's economy fails to grow, the number of Mexicans illegally entering the United States in search of work will increase. Of the estimated 2 million to 4 million illegal aliens living in the United States, about 50 per cent are believed to be Mexican. United States immigration officials believe that between 200,000 and 300,000 Mexicans illegally cross the United States border each year.

Despite its problems, Mexico has a rich culture and many educated and talented people. It still has vast oil reserves and other resources and shares a 2,000-mile (3,200-kilometer) border with the United States, the richest and biggest economic market in the world. Closer economic ties with that country could offer Mexico a vast outlet for its exports. Exactly how Mexico can solve its problems is still unclear, but what is clear is that Mexico stands at a political and economic crossroads. And no matter what road it takes to solve the worst economic crisis in its stormy history, Mexico will never be quite the same again.

For further reading:

McDowell, Bart. "Mexico City: An Alarming Giant." *National Geographic*, August 1984.

Paz, Octavio. *The Labyrinth of Solitude: Life and Thought in Mexico.* Grove Press, 1961.

Riding, Alan. *Distant Neighbors: A Portrait of the Mexicans.* Knopf, 1985.

A Year in Perspective

THE YEAR BOOK casts a backward glance at the furors, fancies, and follies of yesteryear. The coincidences of history that are revealed offer substantial proof that the physical world may continually change, but human nature—with all its inventiveness, amiability, and even perversity—remains fairly constant, for better or worse, throughout the years.

See page 166.

A Year
in Perspective

1886

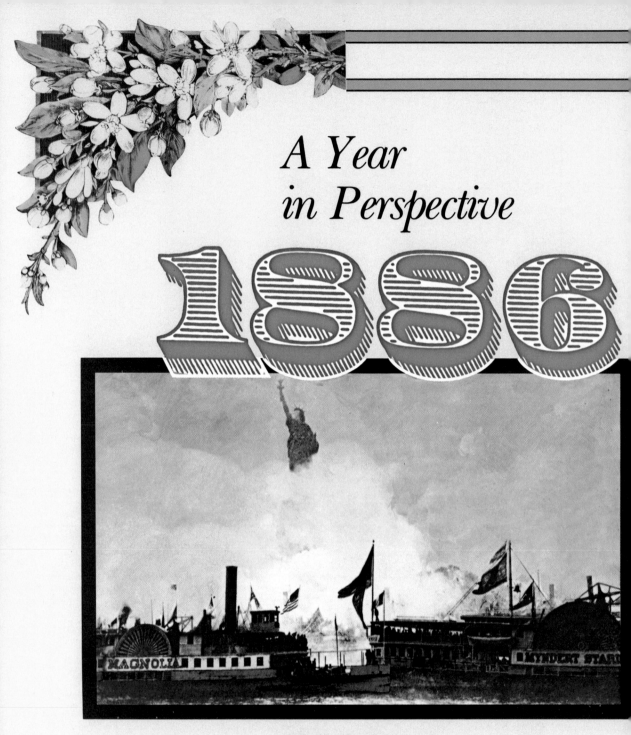

By Sara Dreyfuss

The Statue of Liberty was dedicated, Geronimo surrendered, and the Haymarket Riot increased antilabor feeling.

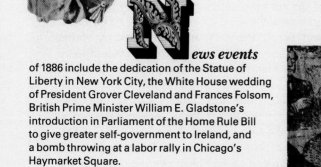

News events

of 1886 include the dedication of the Statue of Liberty in New York City, the White House wedding of President Grover Cleveland and Frances Folsom, British Prime Minister William E. Gladstone's introduction in Parliament of the Home Rule Bill to give greater self-government to Ireland, and a bomb throwing at a labor rally in Chicago's Haymarket Square.

Attention Workingmen!

GREAT

MASS-MEETING

TO-NIGHT, at 7.30 o'clock,

AT THE

HAYMARKET, Randolph St., Bet. Desplaines and Halsted.

Good Speakers will be present to denounce the latest atrocious act of the police, the shooting of our fellow-workmen yesterday afternoon.

Workingmen Arm Yourselves and Appear in Full Force!

THE EXECUTIVE COMMITTEE.

Achtung, Arbeiter!

Große

Maffen-Verfammlung

Heute Abend, 8 Uhr, auf dem

Heumarkt, Randolph-Straße, zwischen Desplaines- u. Halsted-Str.

Gute Redner werden den neuesten Schurkenstreich der Polizei, indem sie gestern Nachmittag unsere Brüder erschoß, geißeln.

Arbeiter, bewaffnet Euch und erscheint massenhaft!

Das Exekutiv-Comite.

Ships of every size and shape filled the water in New York Harbor. The huge statue loomed overhead, glistening with rain, its face covered with a giant red, white, and blue French flag.

It was Oct. 28, 1886, the day the Statue of Liberty—a gift from France to the United States—was to be dedicated. Schools and many businesses were closed for the day, and there had been a huge parade from Central Park to the harbor, where the majestic statue stood on an island. Spectators jammed the sidewalks, rooftops, and windows along the parade route despite a daylong cold drizzle. The U.S.S. *Despatch*, with President Grover Cleveland aboard, led a fleet of 300 ships that sailed past the monument.

At the dedication ceremony, Cleveland promised, "We will not forget that Liberty has here made her home; nor shall her chosen altar be neglected." When the statue's face was unveiled, a great cheer went up from the crowd of about a million people on shore and on boats. Cannons boomed. Boat whistles shrieked. "Liberty!" *The New York Times* exclaimed in its report on the ceremony. "A hundred Fourths of July broke loose to exalt her name." (A century later, the *Times* proclaimed "A Very Special Day" as an even greater celebration marked the statue's 100th anniversary and its reopening after 20 months of restoration work.)

The Statue of Liberty was not alone in having its beginning in 1886. New companies sprang up throughout the United States that year, including what are now the Coca-Cola Company, Avon Products Incorporated, and Sears, Roebuck and Company. A young Austrian physician named Sigmund Freud set up a private practice in Vienna. And the tuxedo made its debut at a country club dance in New York.

There were also endings in 1886. The famous Apache chief Geronimo surrendered to the United States Army, marking the beginning of the end of the Apache wars—and of the Apache way of life. Settlement of the West had brought the frontier era nearly to a close. Almost every American Indian had been pushed onto a reservation. Among the last holdouts were the Apache Indians of the Southwest, who had been fighting desperately since the 1860's to keep their freedom. The most notorious Apache leader was Geronimo, chief of the Chiricahua band, who had escaped from an Arizona reservation in 1885 and begun to terrorize white settlers in the area. About 5,000 soldiers chased Geronimo and his band of about 20 warriors and a similar number of women and children. Probably never before in U.S. military history had so many pursued so few. The Apaches' great endurance and knowledge of the countryside enabled them to avoid capture for a year and a half.

Finally, Geronimo agreed to meet Brigadier General Nelson A. Miles on Sept. 3, 1886, in Skeleton Canyon, Arizona. Geronimo dismounted from his horse, walked up to Miles, and shook his hand. "General Miles is your friend," an interpreter told Geronimo. The Apache chief replied, "I never saw him, but I have been in need of friends. Why has he not been with me?"

The author:
Sara Dreyfuss is Associate Editor of THE WORLD BOOK YEAR BOOK.

Miles promised that if the Apaches surrendered, they would be sent to Florida, where many of their families were already being held. On September 4, Geronimo said to Miles, "I will quit the warpath and live at peace hereafter."

The Army sent the Apaches to Fort Pickens, Florida, where malaria and other diseases killed many of them. Geronimo lived until 1909 and became a national celebrity. He appeared at the St. Louis World's Fair in 1904 and rode in President Theodore Roosevelt's inaugural parade in 1905.

By 1886, with the spread of Western settlement, many former frontier towns had developed into commercial and cultural centers. One such town was St. Paul, Minn., which started its annual Winter Carnival that year after a New York City newspaper described the community as "another Siberia, unfit for human habitation in winter." The centerpiece of the festival was an ice palace 106 feet (32 meters) high built of blocks cut from the frozen Mississippi River. *Frank Leslie's Illustrated Newspaper* called it "the most imposing and beautiful structure of the kind," and *Scientific American* said, "The architectural design is excellent, with square towers and round ones, and various arches, flying buttresses, and other features. . . . One can only regret that the labor has been expended on such fragile material."

Another frontier settlement that made news in 1886 was Gastown, a bustling young lumber town on the Pacific coast of Canada. Gastown got its original name from a saloonkeeper who was called Gassy Jack Deighton because he talked so much. Gastown was incorporated as the city of Vancouver on April 6, 1886. Less than nine weeks later, on June 13, a fire destroyed most of the city. Only two sawmills, a hotel, and a shack remained. Vancouver's people quickly rebuilt their community. Within a month, the energetic citizens of Vancouver had erected 14 hotels, 9 saloons, a church, and hundreds of stores and houses.

Another city struck by disaster in 1886 was Charleston, S.C. On August 31, an earthquake rocked Charleston, causing 92 deaths and more than $5 million in damage.

Other grim news in the United States involved labor disputes, which reached new depths of bitterness in 1886. There were twice as many strikes that year as in any previous year. Employers fought back by hiring strikebreakers and armed guards to crush the strikes.

The labor problem became so severe that President Cleveland, on April 22, 1886, delivered the first-ever message to Congress on the subject of labor. Cleveland proposed that the federal government set up a permanent board to hear the evidence in labor disputes and hand down decisions that would be binding on both sides. Nothing came of the President's proposal, though in 1887 Congress provided for voluntary arbitration of labor controversies in the railroad industry.

Labor's chief goal in 1886 was reduction of the workday from 10 hours to 8. On May 1, labor organizations called a nationwide strike in support of the eight-hour movement. More than 300,000 workers laid down their tools. In Chicago alone, over 40,000 went on strike, and an estimated 80,000 people marched arm in arm up Michigan Avenue singing labor songs.

Labor's leading federation, the Knights of Labor, fades from the scene after losing a railroad strike, *below,* in May 1886. A new group called the American Federation of Labor (AFL) is founded in December under the leadership of Samuel Gompers, shown working in the first AFL office, *bottom.*

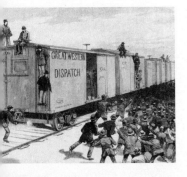

Two days later, a violent incident at the McCormick Harvesting Machine Company plant in Chicago set the stage for what became known as the Haymarket Riot. Workers at the plant had been on strike since February in protest against a pay cut and the firing of union members. Company president Cyrus H. McCormick, Jr., the son of the inventor of the reaping machine, had replaced the striking men with strikebreakers and kept his plant running. At the end of the shift on May 3, strikers gathered outside the plant and threw stones at the strikebreakers. Police fired into the crowd, killing at least two men.

Labor leaders called a meeting for the next night in Chicago's Haymarket Square "to denounce the latest atrocious act of the police, the shooting of our fellow-workmen." On the night of the meeting—May 4, 1886—a crowd of about 2,000 people gathered in Haymarket Square despite a threat of rain. The first speaker was August Spies, a German-born labor leader who delivered an angry blast urging that McCormick "be held responsible for the murder of our brothers." Next, a Chicago typesetter named Albert R. Parsons spoke calmly in support of the eight-hour workday.

The third speaker, a British-born wagon driver named Samuel Fielden, had just begun his remarks when rain started to fall and the crowd broke for cover. Only about 300 people remained in the audience when a column of 180 police officers arrived and tried to break up the meeting.

Suddenly, a deafening explosion echoed through the dark streets, and several police officers fell to the ground. Someone had thrown a bomb into their ranks. The police drew their guns and opened fire on the crowd, which scattered and ran. Eight police officers and two other people were killed.

In Business 100 Years

The birthplace of Sears, Roebuck and Company, a giant mail-order firm, was this railroad station in North Redwood, Minn., in 1886.

Many major companies in the United States trace their beginnings to 1886. Most were founded by young people who saw an opportunity and seized it or recognized a need and filled it. A 22-year-old railroad station agent named Richard W. Sears, for example, started on his way to fortune in North Redwood, Minn. Early in 1886, he accepted a shipment of pocket watches that had been refused by a local jeweler and sold the watches by mail. Sears moved to Chicago in 1887 and hired Alvah C. Roebuck to repair customers' watches. In 1893, the two men founded **Sears, Roebuck and Company**, now the world's largest retail firm.

A pharmacist in Atlanta, Ga., John Styth Pemberton, concocted **Coca-Cola** in May 1886. In a 30-gallon (110-liter) brass kettle in his backyard, Pemberton brewed a mixture of caffeine, fruit syrup, extracts of coca leaves and kola nuts, and secret ingredients. The first Coca-Cola, advertised as an "esteemed Brain Tonic and Intellectual Beverage," sold at pharmacies for 5 cents a glass. Today, Coke ranks as the world's largest-selling soft drink.

Few homes in 1886 had central heating. During cold weather, most people kept warm by wearing itchy woolen underwear, believing it was healthy to wear "wool next the skin." A young inventor in Minneapolis, Minn., named George D. Munsing developed a method of weaving silk and wool together to eliminate the itch. In 1886, Munsing and two partners founded the Northwestern Knitting Company—now a major apparel maker called **Munsingwear Incorporated**.

Homes and businesses were just beginning to use electricity. Scientists and inventors debated the advantages of the two types of electric current—*direct current* (DC), which flows in only one direction, and *alternating current* (AC), which regularly reverses direction. DC was safer to use in homes, but AC was easier to transmit. All the first power plants produced DC, but the great inventor George Westinghouse believed in AC. On Jan. 8, 1886, he founded Westinghouse Electrical & Manufacturing Company (now **Westinghouse Electric Corporation**) to market AC generators and transformers. AC became the standard form of electricity, and the Westinghouse company one of the largest electrical manufacturers.

William E. Upjohn, a country doctor in southwestern Michigan, made it easier to take medicine. At that time, most drugs came in powder form, which a doctor would give to the patient to choke down. The few pills available were so hard that they passed through the body without being absorbed. Working in his attic, Upjohn developed pills that dissolved easily in the stomach. In 1886, Upjohn and his three brothers founded the Upjohn Pill and Granule Company in Kalamazoo, Mich. The **Upjohn Company** became one of the world's largest drug makers.

Medical science was beginning to understand the need to protect wounds from germs. A businessman named Robert Wood Johnson had the idea of making ready-to-use surgical dressings in individual sterile packages. In 1886, Johnson and his two brothers established **Johnson & Johnson** in New Brunswick, N.J.—today the maker of Band-Aid bandages and other medical products.

A flooring salesman named Samuel C. Johnson bought a wood-flooring business in Racine, Wis., in 1886. Because customers kept asking him how to care for their floors, Johnson experimented with wax mixtures and developed Johnson's Prepared Paste Wax. It was the first successful product of the **Johnson Wax** company, a major manufacturer of household and personal care products.

David J. McConnell, a door-to-door book salesman in California, began giving free small bottles of perfume to customers who listened to his sales pitch. The perfume became so popular that in 1886 McConnell gave up books and began selling perfume instead. The firm he founded is now **Avon Products Incorporated**, the largest cosmetic company in the world. [S. D.]

Fashions

and fads of 1886 include—
clockwise from right—hats
trimmed with stuffed birds, which
caused the killing of millions of
songbirds; an exciting roller-
coaster ride at New York City's
Coney Island; velvet suits for boys
inspired by the 1886 novel *Little
Lord Fauntleroy;* and the heavily
ornamented architecture of the
Victorian style, exemplified by the
mansion of Eureka, Calif.,
lumberman William Carson,
completed in 1886.

The Haymarket Riot helped turn public opinion against labor. Many Americans blamed the violence on the labor movement in general, and a revolutionary wing called *anarchism* in particular. The anarchists proposed replacing government with small associations of workers that would own and operate all economic resources and handle all political affairs.

The police rounded up hundreds of known or suspected anarchists in the Chicago area after the Haymarket Riot. A grand jury eventually charged eight men—including Fielden, Parsons, and Spies—with murder. Five of the defendants were German-born.

Distrust of foreigners contributed to the public's reaction against the defendants. "The whole country rose in a cry of consternation and indignation at the crime of European anarchists upon American soil," *Harper's New Monthly Magazine* said. "It was perpetrated by the most worthless of men, who are pests everywhere, and whose presence in this country American generosity had tolerated."

The trial of the eight Haymarket defendants, which began on June 21, 1886, has gone down in history as a mockery of justice. The presiding judge, Joseph E. Gary, filled the jury with men who admitted they were prejudiced against the defendants—including a relative of one of the slain police officers. The prosecution offered no evidence linking any of the eight defendants with the bomb throwing.

On August 20, all eight Haymarket defendants were convicted of murder. All but one were condemned to death. *Leslie's Newspaper* said, "The verdict has everywhere been hailed with satisfaction by the friends of peace and order." One of the condemned men, a German-born labor leader named Louis Lingg, managed to cheat the hangman. Lingg killed himself the day before his scheduled execution by exploding a stick of dynamite in his mouth. Parsons, Spies, and two others went to the gallows on Nov. 11, 1887.

In 1893, Governor John P. Altgeld of Illinois pardoned the remaining three defendants. In a statement accompanying the pardon, Altgeld explained, "The jury which tried the case was a packed jury selected to convict. . . . [and] the trial judge was either so prejudiced against the defendants, or else so determined to win the applause of a certain class in the community, that he could not and did not grant a fair trial." The Haymarket Riot and trial had set the labor movement back, however. Opposition to labor unions increased, and many states passed laws restricting union activity.

The most powerful labor organization in 1886 was the Noble Order of the Knights of Labor. In 1885, the Knights had won an important strike against railroads owned by millionaire Jay Gould. In March 1886, the organization began a second strike against the Gould railway system. This time, however, Gould was determined to outlast the Knights. On May 4, 1886, the Knights called off the strike without winning any of their demands. Nearly all the strikers

isaster strikes two cities in 1886 —fire destroys most of Vancouver, Canada, *below,* in April, and an earthquake rocks Charleston, S.C., *bottom,* in August.

Births

of notable people in 1886 included:

Barth, Karl (1886-1968), Swiss-born Protestant theologian.

Ben-Gurion, David (1886-1973), Russian-born Israeli statesman who served as Israel's first prime minister.

Brooks, Van Wyck (1886-1963), American historian and literary critic.

Brown, Sir Arthur Whitten (1886-1948), British aviator who in 1919, with Sir John W. Alcock, made the first nonstop flight across the Atlantic Ocean.

Cobb, Ty (1886-1961), one of baseball's greatest all-around players.

Flanagan, Edward J. (1886-1948), Roman Catholic priest who founded Boys Town for underprivileged boys.

Jolson, Al (1886-1950), entertainer who starred in the first talking motion picture, *The Jazz Singer* (1927).

Kilmer, Joyce (1886-1918), American poet best known for his short poem "Trees."

Kokoschka, Oskar (1886-1980), Austrian expressionist painter.

Masaryk, Jan G. (1886-1948), Czechoslovak political leader.

Mies van der Rohe, Ludwig (1886-1969), German-born architect whose philosophy of design was summed up in his motto *Less Is More.*

Rivera, Diego (1886-1957), Mexican mural painter.

Sassoon, Siegfried (1886-1967), British poet who wrote dramatic poems in reaction to the horrors of World War I.

Stout, Rex (1886-1975), American writer who created the lazy but brilliant detective Nero Wolfe.

lost their jobs. After this failure, the Knights' influence and membership rapidly declined.

As the Knights of Labor faded from the scene, a new labor federation arose to take its place. In 1881, several labor leaders—including Samuel Gompers, an English-born cigar maker—had organized a group called the Federation of Organized Trades and Labor Unions of the United States and Canada. On Dec. 8, 1886, they reorganized the federation and changed its name to the American Federation of Labor (AFL). Gompers became the AFL's first president and held that office, with only one year's interruption, until his death in 1924. The AFL stressed shorter hours, higher pay, and other job demands instead of political issues. "Our labor movement," Gompers said, "has no system to crush . . . nothing to overturn." In 1955, the AFL merged with another labor federation to form the American Federation of Labor and Congress of Industrial Organizations (AFL-CIO).

While the United States wrestled with the labor problem, Great Britain's chief political controversy in 1886 involved Ireland. At that time, Ireland and Northern Ireland formed a single country that was united with Great Britain and ruled by it. Irish nationalists, including many Irish members of the British Parliament, had long struggled to win independence for Ireland. They found an ally in Liberal Party leader William E. Gladstone, who became prime minister for the third time in January 1886. Gladstone, known as the Grand Old Man, was 77 years old and probably the most respected leader in Britain. He decided to stake his political career on an effort to give the Irish more self-government.

The press in the United States praised Gladstone's Home Rule Bill, under which Ireland would have remained part of Britain but would have had its own parliament for domestic affairs. *Leslie's* called it "an heroic climax to a marvelous career."

Reaction in Britain to the Home Rule Bill was less favorable. *The Economist,* a London periodical, called it "a scheme which . . . will only strengthen and embitter the antagonism that exists." Gladstone's own Liberal Party was deeply split between those who favored home rule for Ireland and those who opposed it. The House of Commons defeated the bill on June 8, 1886. Gladstone dissolved Parliament and called elections, only to see his party suffer a major setback at the polls. He resigned in July 1886 and was succeeded by the leader of the Conservative Party, the Marquess of Salisbury.

In the United States, the year's most important legislation was the Presidential Succession Act of 1886. It was enacted on January 19 as a result of an unusual situation that occurred after the death of Vice President Thomas A. Hendricks. The law at that time stated that two congressional officers, the Speaker of the House and the president pro tempore of the Senate, were next in succession to the presidency after the Vice President. But both those offices were vacant when Hendricks died on Dec. 3, 1885, because the last Congress had adjourned in March and the new one would not convene and elect officers until December 7.

With no one in the line of succession, President Cleveland decided that it was too dangerous for him even to go to Hendricks' funeral in Indianapolis. "In the present peculiar and delicate situation," he explained, "I ought not to take even the remote chance of accident incident to travel." The Presidential Succession Act added the Cabinet officers to the line of succession, beginning with the secretary of state, and thus eliminated the danger that the nation might be left without a chief executive.

The chief executive made an important decision about his personal future, too. On May 28, 1886, President Cleveland, a 49-year-old bachelor, delighted the nation by announcing his engagement to 21-year-old Frances Folsom. The bride-to-be had been Cleveland's ward since her father, one of his law partners, died in 1875. Cleveland often visited the widow and her daughter. Rumors had circulated throughout the spring of 1886 that the President intended to marry, but as late as mid-May it was not known whether his fiancée was Frances or her mother.

The wedding took place on the evening of June 2, 1886, in the candlelit Blue Room of the White House. Florists had covered the walls with roses and pansies. A few minutes before 7 P.M., conductor John Philip Sousa lifted his white-gloved hand and the scarlet-coated Marine Band struck up a wedding march. The bride descended the great staircase in a gown of ivory satin with a 15-foot (4.6-meter) train. "Tall, graceful, blue-eyed and fair," *Leslie's* reported, "Miss Folsom looked an ideal American bride."

After a short Presbyterian ceremony, which Cleveland himself had revised and condensed, cannons in the Navy Yard boomed out a 21-gun salute and all the church bells in Washington rang. The newlyweds slipped away to a honeymoon cottage at Deer Park, a summer resort in western Maryland.

The bride began married life with many stylish new clothes, but her trousseau did not include a fashionable accessory that was becoming increasingly controversial—a hat trimmed with a stuffed bird. There were no laws at the time to prevent people from killing almost any bird they pleased. Fashionable species for decorating hats, *The Nation* said, included "linnets, bluebirds, orioles, woodpeckers, snowbirds, song-sparrows, indeed everything that has feathers and is not too large a load to be carried on one's head." An estimated 5 million birds were killed every year in the United States to trim women's hats, and bird lovers became concerned. In 1886, the American Ornithologists' Union formed a committee on bird protection, and local Audubon Societies throughout the country supported the crusade. The press joined in denouncing what *The Nation* called "a worse than barbarous fashion," and *Leslie's* declared,

Deaths
of notable people in 1886 included:

Adams, Charles F. (1807-1886), American diplomat, son of President John Quincy Adams.

Arthur, Chester A. (1829-1886), 21st President of the United States.

Buntline, Ned (Edward Z. C. Judson) (1823-1886), author of popular Western novels.

Caldecott, Randolph (1846-1886), British illustrator known for children's picture books.

Dickinson, Emily (1830-1886), American poet who lived in solitude and wrote lyrics about love, nature, and death.

Hancock, Winfield Scott (1824-1886), Union Army general in the Civil War and Democratic candidate for President in 1880.

Liszt, Franz (1811-1886), Hungarian pianist and composer who developed the rhapsody and symphonic poem as musical forms.

Logan, John A. (1826-1886), Union Army general during the Civil War.

Ludwig II (1845-1886), eccentric king of Bavaria who built lavish castles.

Noyes, John Humphrey (1811-1886), founder of the Oneida Community, an experimental cooperative society in Oneida, N.Y.

Poundmaker (1826-1886), Cree Indian chief who led an uprising against the Canadian government in 1885.

Ranke, Leopold von (1795-1886), German historian who developed the basic methods of research used by modern historians.

Richardson, Henry Hobson (1838-1886), one of the first American architects to include modern elements in his designs.

Tilden, Samuel J. (1814-1886), Democratic candidate for President in 1876.

reud's office in Vienna, Austria, where young Sigmund Freud began his private practice in the spring of 1886 specializing in nervous disorders, is the birthplace of psychotherapy.

"Every lover of nature, every lover of the beauty of birds, and every lover of the sweetness of their songs, should utter his protest against this massacre of the innocents." Soon many states passed strict bird protection laws, and public opposition to the use of birds as decorations led to the end of the practice.

Although bird-trimmed hats quickly passed away, a new fashion for men arrived to stay. In 1886, the proper formal dress for gentlemen was a swallow-tailed coat. So when tobacco heir Griswold Lorillard showed up at the autumn ball of the Tuxedo Park, N.Y., country club wearing a short black coat with satin lapels, he shocked high society. A society columnist sniffed, "Grizzly looked for all the world like a royal footman." But his coat, thereafter called a tuxedo, became standard formal evening wear.

A boys' fashion started in 1886 with the publication of *Little Lord Fauntleroy*, a novel by the English-born American author Frances Hodgson Burnett. Fauntleroy, the 7-year-old hero, was a model little gentleman who wore velvet suits and called his mother "Dearest." Thousands of parents dressed their little boys to look like Fauntleroy, whom the book described as "a graceful childish figure in a black velvet suit, with a lace collar, and with love-locks waving about the handsome, manly little face."

Other popular books published in 1886 included two novels by the Scottish author Robert Louis Stevenson—the adventure story *Kidnapped* and the horror tale *The Strange Case of Dr. Jekyll and Mr. Hyde*. Another 1886 novel that became a classic was *The Mayor of Casterbridge*, by the English author Thomas Hardy, which traces the spiritual and physical deterioration of a prominent man. The 1886 play *Rosmersholm* by the Norwegian dramatist Henrik Ibsen was a stark tragedy about two lovers who commit suicide together. *Beyond*

Good and Evil by the German philosopher Friedrich Nietzsche argued that human beings should reexamine moral values.

Some reexamination did begin in 1886, due to the pioneering work of two doctors. One was the 30-year-old Sigmund Freud, who in his new practice in Vienna specialized in nervous disorders, thus founding the science of psychotherapy. That same year, a German neurologist named Richard von Krafft-Ebing completed *Psychopathia sexualis*, a scientific study—in Latin—of sexual disorders. Freud and Krafft-Ebing opened the way to modern studies of sexuality and transformed thinking about the human mind and behavior.

A pioneering group of French artists called impressionists held their eighth exhibition of paintings in Paris in 1886. The impressionists, who included Claude Monet and Pierre Auguste Renoir, had revolutionized painting with their attempts to capture the everchanging light and color of nature. The 1886 show was the last in which the impressionists exhibited as a group. It included a masterpiece by Georges Seurat—*Sunday Afternoon on the Island of La Grande Jatte*, a huge canvas almost 7 by 10 feet (2.1 by 3.0 meters). Seurat's scientific studies of color had led him to develop a new technique called *pointillism*, in which the painter used thousands of tiny dots of pure color instead of brushstrokes. *La Grande Jatte* attracted several painters to Seurat's theories. As a group, they became known as neoimpressionists or postimpressionists.

Other events of 1886 included a new edition of *The World Almanac*, which was revived by Hungarian-born publisher Joseph Pulitzer after a 10-year lapse and has been published annually ever since. And the first issue of *The Sporting News* appeared on March 17, 1886, to chronicle the increasingly popular sport of baseball. *Scientific American* said, "Probably there has never been an out of door amusement which has taken the whole country so by storm as baseball playing has done this season."

The Chicago White Stockings won the National League title that season with a record of 90 wins and 34 losses, and the St. Louis Browns were champions of the American Association at 93-46. In a winner-take-all "world series," the underdog Browns then won 4 of 6 games from the Chicagoans. The White Stockings' owner was so angry that he sold the contract of his star outfielder-catcher, Michael J. (King) Kelly—who had led the league in batting with a .388 average—to Detroit for $10,000. The leading pitcher in 1886 was Detroit's Charles B. (Lady) Baldwin, who won 42 games while losing 13. (In 1986, only five major league pitchers managed to win as many as 20 games.) Thanks to such players as Baldwin and Kelly, baseball gained so many fans that *Lippincott's Monthly Magazine* said, "It stands unchallenged in its position as 'our national game.'"

Baseball, like the labor movement, the tuxedo, and the ideas of Sigmund Freud, had come to stay. And like many other events of 1886, they still affect our lives a century later.

The Year
on File

Contributors to THE WORLD BOOK YEAR BOOK report on the major developments of 1986. The contributors' names appear at the end of the articles they have written, and a complete roster of contributors, listing their professional affiliations and the articles they have written, is on pages 6 and 7.

A quiz on some events of 1986 as reported in various Year on File articles appears on pages 174 and 175.

Articles in this section are arranged alphabetically by subject matter. In most cases, the article titles are the same as those of the articles in THE WORLD BOOK ENCYCLOPEDIA that they update. The numerous cross-references (in **bold type**) guide the reader to a subject or information that may be in some other article or that may appear under an alternative title. "See" and "See also" cross-references appear within and at the end of articles to direct the reader to related information elsewhere in THE YEAR BOOK. "In WORLD BOOK, see" references point the reader to articles in the encyclopedia that provide background information to the year's events reported in THE YEAR BOOK.

See ''Space Exploration,'' page 472.

The Year
on File Quiz

THE YEAR BOOK presents a quiz on some events of 1986 as reported in various articles in the Year on File. Answers appear on page 527.

1. What city was the site of the Goodwill Games, a competition between American and Soviet athletes, in July?
2. Union organizer William J. Schroeder died in August but not before making medical history. What did he do?
3. Richard E. Lyng was nominated in January to succeed John R. Block in what United States Cabinet post?
4. Who is this Russian-born pianist, whose concert tour of the Soviet Union in April was his first return to his homeland since 1925?

5. In January, France and Great Britain announced plans for a construction project that will bring the two countries closer together. What will be built?
6. Where did deadly volcanic gas kill more than 1,700 people in August?
7. How did a death in Yonkers, N.Y., in February 1986 resemble seven deaths in the Chicago area in 1982?
8. What three-year-old professional sports league announced in August that it was canceling its 1986 season?
9. What famous financial indicator made history by breaking through both the 1,600 and the 1,700 mark in February, the 1,800 mark in March, and the 1,900 mark in July, only to drop below 1,800 in September?
10. What Latin-American country joined the United States in July in a military assault on cocaine traffickers?
11. What two superpowers expelled dozens of each other's diplomats in the fall of 1986?
12. In July, Greg LeMond became the first American to win the Tour de France, the world's major competition in what sport?

13. What motion picture won seven Academy Awards in March, including the Oscar for best picture?
14. What was Sarah Ferguson's title after she married Great Britain's Prince Andrew in July?
15. What motion-picture star was elected mayor of a California town in April?
16. What 100-year-old gift from France to the United States was rededicated in New York City in July?
17. Who, at the age of 46, won the Masters Tournament of golf in April for a record sixth time?
18. In what two major U.S. cities did municipal workers strike in July, disrupting trash collections and other services?
19. In April, the world's longest-reigning monarch celebrated his 85th birthday and his 60th year on the throne. Who was he?
20. In June, President Ronald Reagan nominated Associate Justice William H. Rehnquist to fill what high judicial office?
21. More than 5 million volunteers in the United States held hands in May for what charitable event?
22. The World Cup contest played in Mexico City in June was the world championship match of what professional sport?
23. What was the name of the experimental aircraft that in December completed the first nonstop, unrefueled flight around the world?
24. In June, Jonathan Jay Pollard, a former U.S. Navy intelligence analyst, pleaded guilty to charges of spying for what country considered a friend of the United States?
25. What caused France in September to announce that it would require visas from all foreign visitors except those from the European Community countries and Switzerland?
26. Why is this hay from Illinois being loaded into a railroad car in July?

27. A collection of more than 240 paintings and sketches of this woman, named Helga, sold in 1986 for several million dollars. Who was the artist?

28. Why did the World War II record of former UN Secretary-General Kurt Waldheim become an issue during his campaign for the presidency of Austria?

29. Match the locations on the left with the descriptions on the right.

    1. Gulf of Sidra   a. nuclear power plant that exploded in the Soviet Union

    2. Taba   b. site of an Iranian oil terminal bombed by Iraq

    3. Sirri Island   c. body of water claimed by Libya but considered international territory by most other countries

    4. Lake Nios   d. Red Sea resort area claimed by both Israel and Egypt

    5. Chernobyl   e. volcanic crater in Cameroon that released poisonous gas

30. What flower was designated the "national floral emblem" of the United States by a law enacted in October?

31. How did the United States retaliate against Libya after evidence linked Libya to the April 5 bombing of a West Berlin discothèque?

32. What nation's racial policies caused several countries in 1986 to enact economic *sanctions* (penalties) against it?

33. What four-time Democratic governor, who ran for President of the United States on a third-party ticket in 1968, announced his retirement from politics in April?

34. What European nation's voters decided in March to keep their country out of the UN?

35. What is the Line of Death?

36. What Scandinavian leader was assassinated in February while walking with his wife on a street in his capital city?

37. What party won control of the U.S. Senate in November's midterm election?

38. Two presidents fled their nations in February—one whose family had ruled in the Caribbean for 29 years and one who had ruled in the Pacific for 20 years. Who were they?

39. In January, President Ronald Reagan severed almost all U.S. economic ties with what Middle Eastern nation, which he accused of supporting international terrorism?

40. What black American leader was honored by a new federal holiday observed for the first time on Jan. 20, 1986?

41. Who is Nicholas S. Daniloff?

42. What landmark in Berlin had its 25th anniversary in August 1986?

43. What sweeping reform bill passed by Congress in September was expected to produce major changes in how Americans spend and save money?

44. Why did some people suggest that the U.S. Open tennis championship in September should be renamed the Czechoslovak Open?

45. What Latin-American leader escaped an assassination attempt in September that killed five of his bodyguards?

46. How did Nebraska voters know in May, six months before the election, that their next governor would be a woman?

47. What visitor from outer space made its closest approach to Earth in April and will not be seen again until the year 2061?

48. In June, Irish voters overwhelmingly voted to remain the only European country besides Malta prohibiting what civil-law procedure?

49. What labor union in May elected a president by an overwhelming margin who had been indicted five days earlier on charges of embezzling union funds and racketeering?

50. Where are these women marching to celebrate the 2,000th day of a "holy war" with a neighboring country?

ADVERTISING. The biggest news in the United States advertising industry in 1986 can be summed up in the word *merger,* and advertising agencies made most of the merger news. Agency mergers were closely related to previous mergers of large advertisers. The April 1986 purchase of Backer & Spielvogel, Incorporated, of New York City by Saatchi & Saatchi PLC of London, for example, put the combined agency in an excellent position to compete with other multinational agencies for the overseas advertising of General Foods Corporation, which had been taken over in 1985 by Philip Morris, Incorporated, a client of Backer & Spielvogel.

The Biggest Agency Merger in history occurred on April 25, 1986, when three agencies—Doyle Dane Bernbach Group Incorporated, Needham Harper Worldwide, and BBDO International Incorporated, all based in New York City—agreed to merge under the ownership of a new holding company, which later was named Omnicom Group. The company immediately became the biggest agency in the world, with billings of more than $5 billion and gross income of $736 million.

But an even larger merger occurred on May 12. Saatchi & Saatchi bought Ted Bates Worldwide of New York City, boosting its ad empire's billings to $7.6 billion.

The two giant mergers led to massive changes among United States advertisers. In several cases, a client changed agencies because a merger put the client with an agency that handled a competitor's advertising.

Many clients expressed dissatisfaction about the quality of service they could expect from the giant merged agencies. Among the dissatisfied clients were Procter & Gamble Company (P & G) and Colgate-Palmolive Company, both of which buy tremendous amounts of advertising.

Plaque Attack. In 1985, most U.S. adults did not know what plaque is. But, thanks to advertising, only someone who did not watch television or read newspapers or magazines was unlikely to know in 1986. Led by P & G with its Crest brand, toothpaste manufacturers in 1986 told consumers about plaque—and tartar—and what consumers should do about these substances. And one company, Minnetonka, Incorporated, of Minnetonka, Minn., brought out Check-Up, described as a plaque-fighting chewing gum.

(*Plaque* and *tartar* are substances deposited on the teeth. Bacteria and sugar in the mouth combine to form a film of plaque. Tartar, a hard substance, forms from a build-up of plaque.)

Cigarette Advertising. In 1986, congressional critics of cigarette advertising continued their ef-

Transamerica Corporation of San Francisco added a new dimension to print advertising with a pop-up insert in the Sept. 8, 1986, issue of *Time.*

fort to ban such advertising from all media. In March, the American Cancer Society joined the American Medical Association, the American Lung Association, and other groups calling for a total prohibition of cigarette ads. The federal government had already banned radio and television commercials for cigarettes, beginning in 1971. Congress conducted hearings on a complete ban in the fall of 1986, but political observers expected no legislative action until 1987.

Critics won an important part of their battle, however, when the government banned radio and TV commercials for chewing tobacco and snuff. The ban took effect on Aug. 28, 1986. This ban left cigars and pipe tobacco as the last tobacco products with access to radio and TV advertising.

Advertising Statistics. In December 1985, Robert J. Coen, senior vice president and director of forecasting for McCann Erickson, Incorporated, a New York City advertising agency, estimated that spending on advertising in the United States in 1986 would be 8 per cent higher than in 1985. But in late June, he lowered the estimated increase to 7.6 per cent. Part of the difference between the two estimates resulted from a slowdown in the buying of commercial time on television. The National Broadcasting Company hiked rates for early buys of commercials to be aired during the TV season beginning in the fall of 1986, but the American Broadcasting Companies and CBS Inc. cut rates for the first time.

All three networks had trouble selling TV commercial time for sports programs for the first time in their history. Rates for the 1986 National Football League season dropped at least 15 per cent from 1985.

Agencies. Worldwide gross income of U.S. advertising agencies rose 15.3 per cent in 1985 to $8.17 billion on $55.8 billion in billings, according to an annual survey conducted by *Advertising Age* magazine. This was less than the gain in percentage from 1983 to 1984, mainly because foreign business declined. For the sixth consecutive year, Young & Rubicam led all U.S. agencies in worldwide income in 1985 with a gross income of $536-million on billings of $3.58 billion. In second place was Ogilvy Group, with $481.1 million in gross income.

Advertisers. The top 100 advertisers in the United States spent $26.67 billion on advertising in 1985, up only 2.7 per cent from 1984, according to an annual report published by *Advertising Age*. P & G led the pack, spending $1.6 billion. Other top advertisers in 1985 were Philip Morris, Incorporated, in second place with $1.4 billion; RJR Nabisco Incorporated third with $1.09 billion; and Sears Roebuck & Company fourth with $800 million. Jarlath J. Graham

In WORLD BOOK, see ADVERTISING.

AFGHANISTAN. Najibullah—he uses only one name—became the leader of Afghanistan's ruling Communist party on May 4, 1986. He succeeded Babrak Karmal, whom the Soviet Union installed in power when it invaded Afghanistan in 1979. Karmal resigned from all government and party posts on Nov. 20, 1986. Haji Mohammad Chamkani became acting president on November 23.

Najib, as Najibullah was known, was made head of the secret police by the Soviets in 1980 and gained a reputation for brutality and efficiency. Foreign observers believed the Soviets had lost patience with Karmal's failure to build popular support for his regime or make it more efficient.

Government Affairs. Najib intensified a campaign begun under Karmal to try to broaden the regime with non-Communists. He announced on Sept. 22, 1986, the formation of a commission for national reconciliation. It was made clear, however, that the Communists would retain power, and only persons already cooperating with them responded to the new effort. On September 29, Najib claimed that nationwide elections for local governments that began in August 1985 had been completed, despite the regime's inability to exercise authority in most of the war-torn country.

The War. Scattered fighting continued between Soviet troops plus their desertion-weakened Afghan army auxiliaries and many separate groups of Afghan resistance fighters. On April 22, 1986, the Soviets announced the fall and destruction of a major guerrilla base at Jawar, southeast of Kabul, which guarded supply routes from nearby Pakistan. On August 18, one of the most successful resistance commanders, Ahmad Shah Masood of the Panjshir Valley, captured an Afghan army garrison at Farkhar. Throughout 1986, Soviet and Afghan forces fought with the resistance for control of two of Afghanistan's largest cities, Qandahar in the south and Herat in the west.

In Kabul, the capital, a car bomb narrowly missed injuring a visiting Soviet first deputy premier in October. Resistance rockets frequently hit near the Soviet Embassy.

The Soviet Union announced that in the second half of October it withdrew six regiments—about 8,000 troops—from Afghanistan. The United States labeled this a trick, saying the Soviet army still had some 120,000 troops in Afghanistan.

Peace Talks. The seventh and eighth rounds of indirect talks between Afghanistan and Pakistan on a war settlement were held in Geneva, Switzerland, during 1986 under United Nations (UN) auspices. Afghanistan asked Pakistan to halt aid to the guerrillas; Pakistan asked for a quick Soviet withdrawal. The talks were deadlocked, but the UN continued to seek a solution. Henry S. Bradsher

See also ASIA (Facts in Brief Table). In WORLD BOOK, see AFGHANISTAN.

AFRICA

After his coronation on April 25, King Mswati III
of Swaziland, at right—at 18, the world's youngest
monarch—appears before his subjects in Mbabane.

Increasingly violent opposition to the South African government's racial policies hastened efforts in 1986 to isolate South Africa from the rest of the world community. Elsewhere on the continent, famine continued to ease in most countries—the result of good rains and massive food donations from the West. Famine persisted, however, in six African nations—Angola, Botswana, Cape Verde, Ethiopia, Mozambique, and Sudan—while a new woe, locusts, afflicted many areas. Although conflicts between nations diminished in 1986, civil wars continued to plague Africa, and democracy remained an elusive goal for most Africans.

South Africa. Throughout the year, clashes erupted between police and blacks opposing the government's policy of enforced segregation—a policy known as *apartheid*. By the end of 1986, by some estimates, more than 4,000 people had been killed in the seemingly endless confrontations, which began in September 1984.

On June 12, 1986, four days before the 10th anniversary of 1976 riots in the black township of Soweto, near Johannesburg, the government declared a state of emergency to head off expected violent demonstrations. Although the June 16 anniversary passed quietly, the emergency decree remained in effect. During the remainder of the year, the government arrested an estimated 22,000 people—opposition leaders, labor unionists, educators, writers, and others—and banned or censored media coverage of many events.

Human Suffering. The rains, which returned to most parts of Africa in 1985, came again in 1986. Nevertheless, wars and repressive government policies in some countries, such as Ethiopia and Sudan, caused a growing flood of refugees and disruptions in agriculture. As a result, malnutrition and high infant mortality rates remained widespread problems. One improvement in health, however, was the reported progress in controlling *onchocerciasis* (river blindness), a parasite-caused disease that is widespread in West Africa.

The long-awaited rains were a mixed blessing. They caused farmlands to produce once again but also stimulated a massive hatching of locust and grasshopper eggs in 16 African countries. The Food and Agriculture Organization (FAO), an agency of the United Nations (UN), called the invasion of crop-devouring pests the worst in 60 years.

Disaster struck northwest Cameroon on the night of August 21, when poison gas was released from Lake Nios, a volcanic lake. More than 1,700 people were killed, many while they slept.

Ailing Economies. Many African nations struggled in 1986 with persistent economic crises caused, in large part, by declining export revenues and rising military expenditures. In May, the UN identified other key reasons for the continent's economic ills. These included a failure to stimulate and diversify agriculture; too-rapid industrialization; inefficient government-owned corporations; and rigid government control of the economy. By 1986, most African states had agreed to let the International Monetary Fund (IMF)—a UN agency that helps countries overcome economic problems—supervise their finances and development plans. Africa's foreign debt was estimated to exceed $170 billion in 1986.

Relations Between African Nations. In December, Mali and Burkina Faso (formerly Upper Volta) agreed to an equal partition of a mineral-rich area on their border. In 1985, the two countries went to war for five days over control of the area.

Nigeria reopened its borders with all of its neighbors except Chad in 1986. It had sealed the borders in 1984 to keep out alien workers and reduce smuggling. The border between Liberia and Sierra Leone, closed in 1985 because of the latter's role in a Liberian coup attempt, was also reopened in 1986.

In other actions during the year, Zaire and Zambia agreed to end disorders linked to a border dispute, and Ghana and Burkina Faso accepted a 10-year timetable for the establishment of a political union between them. But the year's most dramatic reconciliation occurred in January in Djibouti, where the leaders of Ethiopia and Somalia met for the first time since 1977, when Somalia tried to reassert its historic claim to the Ogaden region of Ethiopia.

A less promising development in 1986 was a stalemate in the 10-year armed struggle between Morocco and guerrillas of the Polisario Front over the independence of Western Sahara. The Polisario Front seeks to make Western Sahara an independent nation, the Sahara Arab Democratic Republic (SADR). Sixty-four countries, including a majority of those in Africa, recognize the SADR, and the Polisario Front rebels have received military support from Libya and Algeria.

Civil Wars. The task of African leaders who are striving to build cohesive nations is complicated by borders that encompass scores or hundreds of traditional societies that differ from one another in many ways. The Organization of African Unity—an association of 50 African nations—has sought to preserve those boundaries, which were established by the European colonial powers in the 1800's, but by so doing it has perpetuated rivalries among many cultural groups. Those rivalries often lead to civil war.

Sudan, for example, has been wracked since 1984 by the resumption of armed conflict between the people of the south, who are Christian or practitioners of local religions, and the people of the primarily Islamic north, who control the central government. The northerners have been attempting to divide the south and impose an Islamic code of justice on the entire country. By mid-1986, the Sudanese People's Liberation Army, the main rebel group, controlled most of the rural south and several key southern towns.

A similar ethnic split accounts for the civil war in Chad, which by 1986 had been going on for about 20 years. In February, France answered Chad's calls for military aid for the fourth time since 1968. Chad's President Hissein Habré is opposed by rebels loyal to former President Goukouni Weddeye, who suffered both military defeats and the defection of key officers in 1986.

In Ethiopia, a rebellion aimed at uniting the Ogaden region with Somalia reached a stalemate in 1986, but resistance movements in three other regions—Eritrea, Oromo, and Tigre—continued. The new Soviet-style Constitution approved by the Ethiopian government in September made no concessions to local rule.

179

Facts in Brief on African Political Units

Country	Population	Government	Monetary Unit*	Foreign Trade (million U.S. $) Exports†	Imports†
Algeria	23,516,000	President Chadli Bendjedid; Prime Minister Abdelhamid Brahimi	dinar (4.5 = $1)	12,600	10,000
Angola	9,220,000	President José Eduardo dos Santos	kwanza (29.9 = $1)	2,000	1,700
Benin	4,252,000	President Mathieu Kerekou	CFA franc (336.7 = $1)	173	225
Botswana	1,159,000	President Quett K. J. Masire	pula (1.8 = $1)	670	690
Burkina Faso (Upper Volta)	7,317,000	National Council of Revolution President Thomas Sankara	CFA franc (336.7 = $1)	110	230
Burundi	4,891,000	President Jean-Baptiste Bagaza	franc (101 = $1)	84	158
Cameroon	10,230,000	President Paul Biya	CFA franc (336.7 = $1)	855	1,101
Cape Verde	330,000	President Aristides Pereira; Prime Minister Pedro Pires	escudo (89.3 = $1)	1.6	68.1
Central African Republic	2,667,000	President & Prime Minister André-Dieudonné Kolingba	CFA franc (336.7 = $1)	115	140
Chad	5,257,000	President Hissein Habré	CFA franc (336.7 = $1)	113	114
Comoros	485,000	President Ahmed Abdallah Abderemane; Prime Minister Ali Mroudjae	CFA franc (336.7 = $1)	16	27
Congo	2,073,000	President Denis Sassou-Nguesso; Prime Minister Ange Edouard Poungui	CFA franc (336.7 = $1)	1,300	618
Djibouti	366,000	President Hassan Gouled Aptidon; Prime Minister Barkat Gourad Hamadou	franc (176.7 = $1)	88	200
Egypt	49,127,000	President Hosni Mubarak; Prime Minister Atef Sidqi	pound (1.43 = $1)	3,714	9,961
Equatorial Guinea	336,000	President Teodoro Obiang Nguema Mbasogo; Prime Minister Cristino Seriche Bioko	ekuele (336.7 = $1)	17	41
Ethiopia	42,108,000	Provisional Military Administrative Council & Council of Ministers Chairman Mengistu Haile-Mariam	birr (2 = $1)	403	906
Gabon	1,209,000	President Omar Bongo; Prime Minister Léon Mébiame	CFA franc (336.7 = $1)	2,000	900
Gambia	757,000	President Sir Dawda Kairaba Jawara	dalasi (7.6 = $1)	59	73
Ghana	13,450,000	Provisional National Defense Council Chairman Jerry John Rawlings	cedi (140.8 = $1)	857	669
Guinea	5,701,000	President and Prime Minister Lansana Conté	franc (285.7 = $1)	537	403
Guinea-Bissau	891,000	President João Bernardo Vieirà; Vice President Paulo Correia	peso (169.5 = $1)	9	57
Ivory Coast	10,475,000	President Félix Houphouët-Boigny	CFA franc (336.7 = $1)	3,500	1,600
Kenya	22,397,000	President Daniel T. arap Moi	shilling (14.3 = $1)	967	1,648
Lesotho	1,600,000	King Moshoeshoe II; Military Council Chairman Justinus M. Lekhanya	loti (2.3 = $1)	29	476
Liberia	2,334,000	President Samuel K. Doe	dollar (1 = $1)	432	366
Libya	4,030,000	Leader of the Revolution Muammar Muhammad al-Qadhafi; General People's Committee Chairman (Prime Minister) Mohamed el Zarouk Ragab	dinar (1 = $3.12)	10,929	5,368

*Exchange rates as of Dec. 1, 1986, or latest available data.   †Latest available data.

Country	Population	Government	Monetary Unit*	Foreign Trade (million U.S. $)	
				Exports†	Imports†
Madagascar	10,605,000	President Didier Ratsiraka; Prime Minister Désiré Rakotoarijaona	franc (742.4 = $1)	350	353
Malawi	7,500,000	President H. Kamuzu Banda	kwacha (2 = $1)	260	303
Mali	8,525,000	President Moussa Traoré; Prime Minister Mamadou Dembele	CFA franc (336.7 = $1)	146	233
Mauritania	2,007,000	President Maaouiya Ould Sidi Ahmed Taya	ouguiya (74.6 = $1)	275	215
Mauritius	1,058,000	Governor General Sir Veerasamy Ringadoo; Prime Minister Aneerood Jugnauth	rupee (12.9 = $1)	430	521
Morocco	23,557,000	King Hassan II; Prime Minister Azzedine Laraki	dirham (8.8 = $1)	2,182	3,814
Mozambique	14,907,000	President Joaquím Alberto Chissano	metical (40 = $1)	95	539
Namibia (South West Africa)	1,175,000	Administrator-General Louis Pienaar	rand (2.3 = $1)	no statistics available	
Niger	6,489,000	Supreme Military Council President Seyni Kountché; Prime Minister Hamid Algabid	CFA franc (336.7 = $1)	319	352
Nigeria	101,992,000	President Ibrahim Babangida	naira (1.9 = $1)	12,548	8,877
Rwanda	6,567,000	President Juvénal Habyarimana	franc (84.7 = $1)	148	205
São Tomé and Príncipe	101,000	President Manuel Pinto da Costa	dobra (47.7 = $1)	9	20
Senegal	6,888,000	President Abdou Diouf	CFA franc (336.7 = $1)	525	805
Seychelles	67,000	President France Albert René	rupee (7.6 = $1)	4.4	73
Sierra Leone	3,741,000	President Joseph S. Momoh	leone (25.8 = $1)	104	126
Somalia	5,732,000	President Mohamed Siad Barre	shilling (36 = $1)	107	561
South Africa	34,071,000	State President Pieter Willem Botha	rand (2.2 = $1)	16,523	11,469
Sudan	22,876,000	Supreme Council President Ahmed al Mirghani; Prime Minister Sadiq el Mahdi	pound (2.4 = $1)	374	771
Swaziland	691,000	King Mswati III; Prime Minister Sotsha Dlamini	emalangeni (2.3 = $1)	360	498
Tanzania	24,186,000	President Ali Hassan Mwinyi; Prime Minister Joseph Warioba	shilling (43.9 = $1)	284	1,028
Togo	2,208,000	President Gnassingbé Eyadéma	CFA franc (336.7 = $1)	202	390
Tunisia	7,412,000	President Habib Bourguiba; Prime Minister Rachid Sfar	dinar (1 = $1.17)	1,738	2,757
Uganda	15,691,000	President Yoweri Museveni; Prime Minister Samson Kisekka	shilling (1,408 = $1)	380	509
Zaire	32,328,000	President Mobutu Sese Seko	zaire (62.9 = $1)	1,846	1,102
Zambia	7,135,000	President Kenneth David Kaunda; Prime Minister Kebby Musokotwane	kwacha (6.3 = $1)	793	654
Zimbabwe	8,881,000	President Canaan Banana; Prime Minister Robert Gabriel Mugabe	dollar (1.7 = $1)	1,170	989

Refugees from the civil war in the Eritrea region of Ethiopia wait
for a ration of food at a relief camp in Sudan in March.

Ethnic and religious differences are also at the
root of conflicts in several other African countries.
A long-standing civil war in Angola, for example,
is due in part to the influence of *mestizos* (people
of mixed race) within the government. In Uganda,
a people called the Ganda or Baganda have been
seeking to restore the post of *Kabaka*, or king. And
in Nigeria, the government's decision to join the
Organization of the Islamic Conference, an association of 64 Islamic nations, aroused fears among
Nigeria's Christians and followers of traditional
religions.

Coups, Plots. Occasionally, as in Tanzania and
Sierra Leone in 1985, a new regime in Africa
comes to power through peaceful means. The military coup, however, remains the most common
mechanism for bringing about a change in leadership in Africa. January 1986 saw two coups. In
Uganda, the government of Military Council
Chairman Tito Okello Lutwa was driven from the
capital, Kampala, by the National Resistance
Army, led by Yoweri Museveni. Museveni proclaimed himself president and refused to set a
date for a return to civilian rule.

In Lesotho, the 20-year regime of Prime Minister Leabua Jonathan was toppled by rebel forces
under General Justinus M. Lekhanya, who had
the support of South Africa. Prior to the coup,
South Africa had imposed a blockade on Lesotho

because Jonathan provided sanctuary to South African black dissidents and supported economic
sanctions against South Africa. On January 27,
Lekhanya was sworn in as chairman of a Council
of Ministers.

During the year, abortive plots were uncovered
by the leaders of Burkina Faso, Equatorial Guinea,
Ghana, Guinea-Bissau, Mauritania, Nigeria, Seychelles, Sierra Leone, Togo, and Uganda. And in
Swaziland, ministers of the new king, 18-year-old
Mswati III—the world's youngest monarch—
reduced the power of the legislative council.

Democracy—the Elusive Dream. Many African
leaders continued to pay lip service to democratic
ideals in 1986, but their actions seldom matched
their words. In Liberia, for example, the January
inauguration of military leader Samuel K. Doe as
president was clouded by evidence of electoral
fraud and ruthless repression of dissent before
and after the October 1985 election.

A multiparty election in Sudan in April 1986
produced a two-party majority coalition under
Prime Minister Sadiq el Mahdi of the Islamic
Umma Party. But people in the southern areas of
Sudan, who are rebelling against the central government, were excluded from the voting. Those
Sudanese challenged the legality of the election
and the authority of the National People's Assembly to draft a new constitution.

In June, former President Julius K. Nyerere of Tanzania, a long-time advocate of the single-party system, criticized the concept. He decried the stifling of initiative and the inefficiency, complacency, and inflexibility of single-party governments. Despite his advice, Prime Minister Robert Gabriel Mugabe of Zimbabwe negotiated during much of 1986 with his main political rival, Joshua Nkomo, to consolidate their two parties. Mugabe also reaffirmed his goal of eliminating the legislative seats reserved for whites.

Following the model of other single-party states that permit a choice among legislative candidates within the party, Sierra Leone in May gave voters that option. The voters surprised the government by rejecting over half of the incumbents. Cameroon's dominant party gave voters a choice among local candidates in January but banned the major opposition party in July. And in Kenya, where voters frequently reject the incumbent legislators of the only legal party, the Kenya African National Union, President Daniel T. arap Moi in August eliminated the secret ballot. Somalia's President Mohamed Siad Barre and Togo's President Gnassingbé Eyadéma both overwhelmingly won reelection in uncontested elections in late December.

In 1985 and 1986, Amnesty International—a London-based human rights organization—and other groups charged that South Africa and many black African states were routinely arresting and torturing political and religious dissenters.

Foreign Relations. In addition to intervening militarily in Chad, France responded to a request from Togo in September for help in dealing with the attempted coup. With the aid of French troops and planes, the uprising was crushed.

The United States altered its role in southern Africa in 1986 by pledging $15 million in military aid to rebel forces in Angola and cutting economic aid to Zimbabwe. The latter action came in response to a diplomatic incident in Harare on July 4 during a visit by former President Jimmy Carter.

Israel strengthened its links with Africa during the year when Ivory Coast and Cameroon became the sixth and seventh African nations to reestablish diplomatic relations with Israel. At the quadrennial meeting of the nonaligned movement—a group of 101 Third World nations and organizations—held in September in Harare, delegates called for economic sanctions against South Africa and asked for help in solving the continent's economic crisis.   J. Gus Liebenow and Beverly B. Liebenow

See also the various African country articles. In WORLD BOOK, see AFRICA.

AGRICULTURE. See FARM AND FARMING.

AIR FORCE. See ARMED FORCES.

AIR POLLUTION. See ENVIRONMENTAL POLLUTION.

ALABAMA. See STATE GOVERNMENT.

ALASKA. See STATE GOVERNMENT.

ALBANIA. The most important political event in Albania in 1986 was the Ninth Congress of the ruling Communist party, which took place in Tiranë, the capital, from November 3 to 8. This was the first congress since the death in April 1985 of Enver Hoxha, who had ruled Albania since 1944. After Hoxha died, his chosen successor, Ramiz Alia, took over as leader of Albania. The party elected Alia first secretary (leader) of the party at the congress.

According to information published at the congress, Albania's *gross domestic product* (the value of all goods produced and services performed within the nation) grew by more than 16 per cent from 1981 to 1985. Industrial production grew by 26 per cent.

Alia, Prime Minister Adil Çarçani, and other speakers at the congress said that the oil industry and a number of other industries did not reach their targets. In agriculture, prolonged drought caused losses. But Alia blamed other shortfalls on organizational weakness, poor workmanship, and inefficiency. The party set a target of 35 to 37 per cent for growth in the gross domestic product from 1986 to 1990.

The East. Albania expanded its trade during the year with all the Communist countries of Eastern Europe, except the Soviet Union. Political relations with Eastern Europe remained cool, but Moscow and its allies continued to make friendly overtures toward Albania. Albania also increased its trade with China.

The West. Albania continued its steady warming of relations with the West. It established diplomatic relations with Spain in September. Sweden sent a diplomatic and economic mission to Albania in November.

Relations with Greece continued to improve. The general secretary of Greece's foreign ministry visited Albania in July. During the visit, Albania promised to grant greater freedom to its ethnic Greek minority, estimated at 200,000 by Greece and 45,000 by Albania.

Relations with Yugoslavia remained cool because of a continuing dispute about the status of ethnic Albanians living in Kosovo, a province of the Republic of Serbia, which is part of Yugoslavia. Many of these people want to upgrade Kosovo to a republic within Yugoslavia. At the party congress, Alia spoke of the "inquisition" to which Yugoslavia subjected ethnic Albanians in Kosovo.

In spite of the coolness between Albania and Yugoslavia, a railway line linking Shkodër, Albania, with Titograd, Yugoslavia, opened for freight traffic on September 1. The railway is the first link connecting Albania's entire rail system with that of the rest of Europe.   Chris Cviic

See also EUROPE (Facts in Brief Table). In WORLD BOOK, see ALBANIA.

ALBERTA. Severe recessions in the province's oil and agriculture industries in 1986 disturbed Premier Donald Getty's first full year in office as head of a Progressive Conservative (PC) government. Plunging oil prices in the early months of 1986 brought massive layoffs in the oil industry and a loss of more than half of the previously projected oil revenues. Also, depressed grain prices, drought, and a grasshopper plague hurt farmers.

On April 1, Energy and Natural Resources Minister John B. Zaozirny announced a $400-million program of tax credits to provide temporary relief for the oil industry. (All monetary amounts in this article are Canadian dollars with $1 = U.S. 72 cents as of Dec. 31, 1986.) Two days later, in opening the new legislative session, the Getty government announced a program of almost $2.5 billion to be spent on agricultural relief and higher education.

Election. On April 10, Getty called a general election to be held on May 8, with plans to expand the legislature from 79 to 83 seats. The governing PC's went into the contest holding 75 of the 79 seats in the legislature. The popularity that had kept the PC's in power since 1971 deserted them, however, and they lost 14 seats. Moreover, the PC's share of the popular vote dropped to 51 per cent from 62 per cent in the 1982 election.

The chief beneficiary of the PC's setback was the socialist New Democratic Party (NDP), which won 16 seats, 14 more than it held in the previous house. The Liberal Party—shut out of the legislature since 1967—took 4 seats, and the Representative Party won 2 seats.

Getty named a new cabinet on May 26, 1986, squeezing 10 newcomers into a smaller cabinet of 25. Most senior positions went to veteran PC's. Four women were among the appointees.

A New Budget on June 16 projected a deficit of $2.5 billion—the largest in the province's history—topping an earlier estimate of $2.13 billion. Falling revenues from oil and natural gas were the cause of the shortfall.

Accidents. Alberta was the scene of several tragic accidents in 1986. On February 8, a freight train slammed into a passenger train near Jasper in the Rocky Mountains, killing 26 people and piling tanker cars on some of the crushed coaches. Thirteen people died in early June when two search planes and the missing light aircraft they were seeking crashed in the rugged mountain country in southwestern Alberta. A derailment on June 14 on the world's largest indoor roller coaster, located at the West Edmonton Mall, killed 3 people and injured 17 others.　　David M. L. Farr

In WORLD BOOK, see ALBERTA.

Tragedy strikes the Calgary Stampede in Alberta in July, when three chuckwagons collide, killing five horses and injuring three riders.

ALGERIA. The government of President Chadli Bendjedid continued to steer a middle course in Arab and African affairs in 1986, concentrating its efforts on economic development. In January, Bendjedid met with Libyan leader Muammar Muhammad al-Qadhafi in Algeria to restore "fraternal relations" between their two countries. Relations had deteriorated after Libya signed a treaty of union with Morocco in 1984, and they worsened in 1985 when Algeria offered aid to Tunisia against a possible Libyan invasion.

Algeria strongly supported Libya in its confrontation with the United States in 1986. After American warplanes attacked targets in Libya on April 15, a special session of the ruling National Liberation Front (FLN) condemned the raid as a form of "state terrorism."

National Charter. A January 16 referendum approved by 98 per cent of the electorate made a number of revisions in the 1976 National Charter, which forms the basis for Algeria's development as a socialist state. The revisions, already approved by the Popular National Assembly, gave a larger role to private enterprise in national development and defined a plan of action for the next decade. The country will retain its socialist system, but in less rigidly Marxist terms.

In May, a new agricultural marketing system was introduced under the provisions of the revised charter. Private farmers' markets were allowed to operate in cities, and controls were set on profit margins to ensure farmers a fair income.

The Economy. The continued drop in revenues caused by low world oil prices caused Bendjedid to announce an austerity program in March. Among other measures, Algerians traveling abroad could henceforth draw travel allocations in foreign currency only in alternate years.

In August, the government devalued the dinar by 10 per cent and announced that foreign visitors would be required to exchange all their currency at Algerian banks. The budget, originally approved by the National Assembly in April, was revised downward in September by 14 per cent to 9.16 billion dinars (about $2 billion), and most large development projects were either postponed or eliminated.

Despite its difficulties, Algeria remained a favorable market for foreign loans and contracts because of its political stability. After Bendjedid made an official visit to Moscow in March, the Soviet Union granted Algeria a $350-million credit line. Under new contractual agreements, Algerian natural gas remained competitive on world markets despite its high price. During the year, Algeria signed natural gas agreements with Belgium, Brazil, France, and Spain.   William Spencer

See also AFRICA (Facts in Brief Table). In WORLD BOOK, see ALGERIA.

AMERICAN LIBRARY ASSOCIATION (ALA). The ALA broke all previous attendance records at its 105th annual conference, held in New York City from June 28 to July 3, 1986, and coinciding with the city's Liberty Week celebration. More than 16,200 participants crowded the new Jacob K. Javits Convention Center to participate in some 2,400 sessions on a wide range of topics.

Outgoing ALA President Beverly P. Lynch welcomed three special conference speakers. British author Anthony Burgess gave the keynote address, speaking out against censorship. William D. Carey, executive officer of the American Association for the Advancement of Science, spoke about public access to government information. Rosabeth Moss Kanter discussed the themes in her best-selling book *The Change Masters: Innovation for Productivity in the American Corporation* (1983).

Regina U. Minudri, director of the Berkeley (Calif.) Public Library, took office as the new ALA president. Margaret E. Chisholm, director of the Graduate School of Library and Information Science at the University of Washington in Seattle, became ALA vice president and president-elect.

Government Information Policy. "What our citizens don't know *can* hurt them," Lynch said in releasing a report by the Commission on Freedom and Equality of Access to Information, an ALA-sponsored panel of 18 experts in several fields. Summing up the commission's conclusions, Lynch said the public's right to know about concerns such as the locations of toxic waste sites, the development of new weapons, and the safety of new drug and food products is jeopardized by a government trend to restrict access to information.

Service Awards. World Book, Incorporated, awards two grants each year to advance the development of library services. The Intellectual Freedom Committee, an ALA group charged with furthering the association's views on First Amendment rights, received a 1986 grant for a workshop to coordinate efforts against censorship. The second award went to three ALA divisions—the American Association of School Librarians, the Association for Library Service to Children, and the Young Adult Services Division—and the University of Illinois Graduate School of Library and Information Science, for a children's-services project.

Children's Books. The 1986 Newbery Medal for the most distinguished contribution to American children's literature published in 1985 was awarded to Patricia MacLachlan, author of *Sarah, Plain and Tall.* Illustrator Chris Van Allsburg won the 1986 Caldecott Medal for the most distinguished American children's picture book for the illustrations in *The Polar Express.*   Peggy Barber

See also CANADIAN LIBRARY ASSOCIATION; LIBRARY; LITERATURE FOR CHILDREN. In WORLD BOOK, see AMERICAN LIBRARY ASSOCIATION.

ANDREW, PRINCE (1960-   ), is the second son of Queen Elizabeth II of Great Britain and the Duke of Edinburgh and is the fourth in line to the British throne. On July 23, 1986, he married Sarah Ferguson in Westminster Abbey in London. Before the wedding ceremony, Queen Elizabeth gave him the titles of Duke of York, Earl of Inverness, and Baron Killyleagh. The title Duke of York is traditionally given to a monarch's second son. Prince Andrew is a younger brother of Prince Charles, heir to the British throne. See FERGUSON, SARAH; GREAT BRITAIN (Close-Up).

Prince Andrew Albert Christian Edward was born on Feb. 19, 1960, in Buckingham Palace in London. He received his education at a number of schools, including Heatherdown Preparatory School in England and Gordonstoun School in Scotland.

Prince Andrew began a 12-year military career in 1979 when he joined the Royal Navy as a helicopter pilot. In 1980, he completed his training at the Britannia Royal Navy College in Dartmouth and a training course for Royal Marines officers.

From April to June 1982, Prince Andrew served as a helicopter pilot on the ship *Invincible* during the war between Britain and Argentina over the ownership of the Falkland Islands, a group of islands in the South Atlantic Ocean. He was promoted to lieutenant in February 1984.   Mary A. Krier

ANGOLA. The Marxist regime of President José Eduardo dos Santos continued to battle for its existence in 1986. In August, South African troops from Namibia penetrated 156 miles (251 kilometers) north of the Angola-Namibia border in an apparent attempt to capture the village of Cuito Cuanavale. In June, South African divers sank a Cuban ship and damaged two Soviet freighters in the port of Namibe.

Internally, dos Santos' party, the Popular Movement for the Liberation of Angola (MPLA), was challenged by three rivals, including its former ally, the National Union for the Total Independence of Angola (UNITA). UNITA, which is openly supported by South Africa, controlled large areas of eastern and southeastern Angola. UNITA leader Jonas Savimbi repeated demands that dos Santos share power with UNITA in a coalition government. Throughout most of the year, UNITA guerrillas conducted raids on military and civilian targets. Two other rebel groups challenged the MPLA in 1986—the Zaire-based National Front for the Liberation of Angola and the Front for the Liberation of the Cabinda Enclave. Cabinda is an oil-rich area north of the mouth of the Zaire River.

Savimbi Visits U.S. In late January, Savimbi traveled to the United States for a 10-day visit. He met with President Ronald Reagan, who agreed to send him $15 million worth of military aid, including Stinger antiaircraft missiles.

As a rebuff to Reagan's warm reception of Savimbi, the dos Santos government asked the United Nations to resume the major negotiating role in Southern Africa. Despite the fact that the United States had not given diplomatic recognition to the MPLA, Angola had previously accepted U.S. help in mediating conflicts in that part of the continent, though it rejected American insistence that the estimated 25,000 to 30,000 Cuban troops stationed in Angola be sent home. Dos Santos has argued that the Cuban forces are needed to defend against UNITA and South Africa.

Several nations, including Great Britain, Italy, and Sweden, criticized the Reagan Administration for its support of Savimbi. In May, dos Santos made a state visit to Moscow, where he was assured of increased military and economic aid.

Economic Stresses. The fall in global oil prices reduced Angola's income by one-third in 1986. The economic slowdown and the continuing armed conflict made it increasingly difficult for Angola to grow or import adequate amounts of food.   J. Gus Liebenow and Beverly B. Liebenow

See also AFRICA (Facts in Brief Table). In WORLD BOOK, see ANGOLA.

ANIMAL. See CAT; CONSERVATION; DOG; ZOOLOGY; ZOOS.

ANTHROPOLOGY. The discovery of a nearly complete 2.5-million-year-old *hominid* cranium in northern Kenya, reported in August 1986, has challenged theories about the structure of the human evolutionary tree. (Hominids include human beings and our closest human and prehuman ancestors.) The fossil cranium, known as WT 17000, was found in 1985 by anatomist Alan C. Walker of Johns Hopkins University in Baltimore. It was discovered west of Lake Turkana in an area where anthropologist Richard E. Leakey of the National Museums of Kenya and his associates have been working for several years.

WT 17000 possesses a unique combination of primitive characteristics and specialized features thought to have evolved later in hominid history. Its primitive features include an apelike projecting face—rather than the more vertical face found in human beings—an apelike joint between the jaw and cranium, and the shape of the ridges on the skull for the attachment of strong jaw and neck muscles. Its specialized characteristics include its large, rugged build, a dish-shaped face with huge cheekbones, and apparently small front teeth.

Walker and Leakey proposed that WT 17000 represents an early member of a ruggedly built hominid species called *Australopithecus boisei*. This species lived in East Africa and became extinct by about 1 million years ago.

The 2.5-million-year-old cranium of a rugged apelike creature found in Kenya has challenged theories about the development of early human ancestors.

Hominid Family Tree Revised. The WT 17000 cranium suggests alteration of the most generally accepted theory of hominid evolution, which was proposed in 1979 by anthropologists Donald C. Johanson of the Institute of Human Origins and Timothy D. White of the University of California, both in Berkeley. According to this theory, an apelike hominid species called *Australopithecus afarensis* that lived from 3 million to 4 million years ago was the ancestor of all later hominid species. The most well-known example of this species is "Lucy," a skeleton found in Ethiopia in 1974.

Johanson and White proposed that between 2 million and 3 million years ago, the hominid line split. One branch developed into *Homo habilis*, the first human species, and eventually into modern human beings. The other branch led to A. *africanus*, a smaller australopithecine, which gave rise to the more heavily built A. *robustus* and A. *boisei*.

Walker and Leakey argue that WT 17000's age and form indicate that it probably did not descend from A. *afarensis* either. Johanson and White, however, contend that WT 17000 does not challenge A. *afarensis'* position as the ancestor of all later hominids, because the fossil shares many more features with A. *afarensis* than it does with A. *boisei*. They propose that WT 17000 represents an intermediate form between the older, more primitive A. *afarensis* and the younger, more specialized A.

boisei. In fact, some researchers believe that WT 17000 may belong to a distinct species, called A. *aethiopicus*, that was proposed in 1967.

The discovery of WT 17000 has also stimulated some rethinking about the number of branches on the hominid evolutionary tree. The most popular theory suggests a three-branch tree with A. *afarensis* at the base. One branch gave rise to *Homo habilis* and modern human beings. Another led to A. *africanus*, then to A. *robustus*. The third included WT 17000 and, later, A. *boisei*. Some researchers suggest that WT 17000 may represent a common ancestor of both A. *boisei* and A. *robustus*.

Early Cannibalism. An analysis of Stone Age human bones found in a cave in southeastern France has provided rare evidence for cannibalism, according to a report by an international team of scientists published in July 1986.

Archaeological evidence indicated that the cave was used repeatedly as a temporary camp from 7,000 to 6,000 years ago. The researchers found that human bones in the cave—those of three adults, two children, and a person of undetermined age—were treated in exactly the same way as the animal bones found there. Both groups had *cut marks* (nicks and grooves made by stone tools), were split open so that marrow could be extracted, and were· apparently deposited deliberately in shallow pits on the cave floor. These findings led

Stone tools, found in Zaire and thought to be more than 2 million years old, are the first ancient tools found in that part of Africa.

the researchers to conclude that the human bones were strong evidence of cannibalism.

The scientists found the bones in clusters. Because each cluster appeared to consist of the bones from only a few individuals, the scientists concluded that each cluster resulted from a single incident of butchering. In addition, the presence in the cave of body parts with little food value led the researchers to suggest that the butchering took place in the cave.

Ancient Brains. An analysis of 8,000-year-old human brain tissue found in Florida has yielded the oldest known samples of human deoxyribonucleic acid (DNA), according to a report published in October 1986. DNA is the substance of which most genes are made.

A team of scientists headed by archaeologist Glen H. Doran of Florida State University in Tallahassee found the remarkably preserved brain tissue in skulls dug from a swampy pond called the Windover site, about 15 miles (24 kilometers) west of Cape Canaveral. The discovery of bones from at least 40 people at the pond indicates that the site was once a burial ground.

The scientists found DNA in five brains. They were attempting to clone the DNA for more detailed study.   Donald C. Johanson

See also ARCHAEOLOGY. In WORLD BOOK, see ANTHROPOLOGY; PREHISTORIC PEOPLE.

AQUINO, CORAZON (1933-   ), assumed the presidency of the Philippines on Feb. 25, 1986, after President Ferdinand E. Marcos resigned under pressure and fled abroad. Aquino had declared herself president on February 16, claiming victory in the turbulent February 7 election. She then mounted a nonviolent campaign to force Marcos from office.

Aquino was born Corazon Cojuangco on Jan. 25, 1933, in Manila to a wealthy and prominent family. In 1946, she moved with her family to the United States, where she attended high school. In 1953, she graduated from the College of Mount St. Vincent in New York City with a degree in French and mathematics.

Corazon returned to the Philippines to attend law school but dropped out in 1954 to marry Benigno S. Aquino, Jr., a journalist with political ambitions. As her husband rose rapidly in politics, Corazon devoted herself to raising the couple's son and four daughters.

The August 1983 assassination of Benigno Aquino, who was challenging Marcos' leadership, made Corazon Aquino the most popular symbol of opposition to the Marcos regime. A reluctant candidate for president, she entered the race only after a special court acquitted 26 men accused of her husband's murder.   Barbara A. Mayes

See also PHILIPPINES.

ARCHAEOLOGY. A rock shelter in a sandstone cliff in northeastern Brazil has provided evidence of the earliest known human presence in the Americas, according to a report by French scientists published in June 1986. In the lowest layer of sediment in the rock shelter, known as Boqueirao do Sitio da Pedra Furada, the scientists found charcoal apparently left from campfires. Using radiocarbon dating methods, the scientists dated the charcoal to approximately 32,000 years ago. The shelter appears to have been occupied from that time until about 6,000 years ago.

At a higher—more recent—level dated to 17,000 years ago, the scientists found a fragment of a *pictograph* (a picture used as a sign or symbol) that had fallen from one of the walls, which are covered with prehistoric paintings. This discovery suggests that cave art in the Americas is nearly as old as that in Europe and Africa.

Most archaeologists believe that people reached the Americas between 11,500 and 20,000 years ago, when a land bridge connected Siberia and Alaska. Recent discoveries of South American sites older than the oldest North American sites, however, have led some researchers to speculate that the first Americans may have arrived in South America after crossing the Pacific Ocean from Asia by boat and then spread northward.

Columbus' Landing. Christopher Columbus did not make his first landfall in the New World on San Salvador Island in the Bahamas as most historians believe, according to findings reported in October 1986. A team of archaeologists, historians, navigators, cartographers, and other experts who conducted a five-year investigation for the National Geographic Society in Washington, D.C., concluded that Columbus really landed 65 miles (105 kilometers) to the southeast on Samana Cay.

The 1986 findings were based chiefly on a new translation of Columbus' log for the voyage and on computer analyses of the ocean currents and wind factors that would have affected his course. Such analyses had never been done before. The experts also discovered that the actual length of the *sea league* (the Spanish unit of nautical measurement) was 2.82 nautical miles, not 3.18 nautical miles as previously thought. (A nautical mile equals 1.15 land miles or 1.85 kilometers.)

Scholars have argued over the site of Columbus' first landfall for centuries. Many scholars disputed the new findings.

Nazca Lines. The fascinating lines etched into the surface of the desert near Nazca on the southwest coast of Peru were part of a ritual involving water, planting, and worship, according to a report published in July 1986 by astronomer and

Israeli archaeologists and volunteers uncover the first intact fishing boat from the time of Christ, found in February near the Sea of Galilee.

Blood and Sacrifice: New Look at the Maya

Archaeological excavations and breakthroughs in deciphering ancient Maya writing, called *hieroglyphs*, during the past five years have changed scholars' beliefs about nearly every aspect of Maya life. In May 1986, the Kimbell Art Museum in Fort Worth, Tex., opened an exhibit of Maya art focusing on an aspect of Maya society most scholars had failed to recognize, despite abundant evidence.

A major theme of the exhibit, called "The Blood of Kings," was human sacrifice and bloodletting. The exhibit was organized by art historians Linda Schele of the University of Texas at Austin and Mary Ellen Miller of Yale University in New Haven, Conn., both experts in Maya hieroglyphs. The exhibit moved to the Cleveland Museum of Art in October 1986.

The Maya occupied a large area of Central America in what is now southern Mexico, all of Belize and Guatemala, and parts of Honduras

A Maya relief sculpture depicts a bloodletting rite in which the wife of a ruler pulls a thorn-lined rope through her tongue.

and El Salvador. Their civilization became increasingly complex between about 200 B.C. and A.D. 900.

For many years, scholars viewed the Maya as an artistic, intellectual, cultured people ruled by priests who devoted their time to astronomy and calendar-making. The Maya were thought to have been a chiefly rural society that practiced a primitive form of agriculture and entered their magnificent cities only for religious ceremonies. They were believed to be peaceful by nature, becoming warlike only when threatened by the militaristic Toltec people, their neighbors to the north.

Discoveries at Maya ruins and the decipherment of perhaps 80 per cent of Maya hieroglyphs have revealed a darker—but perhaps more realistic—view of the Maya. This, coupled with archaeological field work, shows that the Maya were sophisticated farmers who produced enough food to support a substantial urban population—at least 40 cities, some with perhaps 20,000 people each. And although the Maya achieved much in astronomy, mathematics, architecture, and art, they were also aggressive people who frequently waged war against rival cities, chiefly to acquire captives. Long before the Aztec engaged in human sacrifice, the Maya offered captives as part of their sacrifices to the gods and to revered ancestors.

Bloodletting was not confined to captives, however. Both Maya elite and commoners practiced ritual self-mutilation on a regular basis, using sting ray spines, flint or obsidian knives, and thorny ropes.

The importance of bloodletting in Maya society is shown over and over again in Maya hieroglyphs, paintings, and sculptures from various sites. For example, at Colha in Belize, archaeologists have excavated a cache dating from about A.D. 100 to 200 containing pottery vessels, sharks' teeth, and a large, needle-sharp flint blade stained with a dark substance. Analysis revealed that the substance was human blood, probably resulting from a bloodletting ritual. At the nearby site of Kichpanha, a grave of about the same age contained a bone carved with seven hieroglyphs, some of which relate to bloodletting. The bone may have been used as a bloodletting tool.

The Maya believed that blood nourished the gods and kept the universe in order. Indeed, the Maya believed that bloodletting by a king resurrected the gods and the king's ancestors. But for the most part, bloodletting served as a way to induce visions and communicate with the gods. Schele and Miller have stated, thus, in this new view of Maya ritual, "Blood was the mortar of Maya ceremonial life."

Thomas R. Hester

anthropologist Anthony F. Aveni of Colgate University in Hamilton, N.Y. The lines, which form geometric figures, zigzags, spirals, animals, plants, and straight lines, were constructed between A.D. 400 and 1000 by people who lived in the hills bordering the desert. The lines were made by clearing away the rocks that cover the surface of the desert and exposing the pinkish-colored sand beneath. The rocks were then stacked along the edges of the lines.

The patterns are so striking and unique that they have attracted a great deal of speculation about their function. One theory is that the lines were part of a giant calendar, marking the sun's position on the horizon at important times, such as when crops should be sown. Another, more fanciful, idea is that the lines served as runways for astronauts from outer space.

Aveni's study focused on the straight lines, the most common type of Nazca line. These lines form webs that connect centers, most of which are on hills bearing a rock cairn that may have been a marker.

Aveni recognized that these connecting lines resembled the system of pathways built by the ancient Inca. The Inca lines were unmarked except for eight or nine sacred places called *huacas*. In many cases, the huaca farthest from the central point of origin was located in an important place, such as at one of the underground water sources that fed the Inca irrigation system.

Aveni found that the Nazca lines seem to have served several purposes. Some seem to designate pathways that led to sacred places. Other lines appear to mark the sun's position on the horizon when water starts to flow in the area's rivers and underground canals, indicating that some lines functioned as part of an agricultural calendar. Aveni also found that many lines open into four-sided figures. In many cases, the *axis* of the figure—an imaginary line about which a figure seems to turn—follows a river or stream. Frequently, the figures point upstream.

Ancient Tools. The discovery in Africa of 300 stone tools believed to be more than 2 million years old was reported in February 1986 by a team of United States scientists. The quartzite tools, which were found in eastern Zaire, may be among the most ancient tools ever discovered. The oldest known tools were found in eastern Ethiopia and are estimated to be from 2.4 million to 2.6 million years old.

The tools in Zaire were found with animal bones and teeth, including those of pigs, elephants, antelope, and a three-toed ancestor of the horse. The remains suggest that the tools are about 2.3 million years old.   Barbara Voorhies

In WORLD BOOK, see ARCHAEOLOGY; COLUMBUS, CHRISTOPHER.

ARCHITECTURE. Many events around the world in 1986 honored the 100th anniversary of the birth of Ludwig Mies van der Rohe, one of the most influential architects of the 1900's. Centennial observances included a retrospective exhibition at the Museum of Modern Art (MOMA) in New York City from Feb. 10 to April 15, 1986. In Barcelona, Spain, a team of Spanish architects re-created a lost Mies masterpiece, the Barcelona Pavilion, on its original site. Mies designed the glass-and-marble-walled structure as the German Pavilion at the Barcelona international exposition of 1929. The pavilion was demolished after the fair, but architects have long considered it one of the century's most significant designs.

Notable New Buildings of 1986 included the headquarters of Lloyd's insurance company in London, which opened in November. British architect Richard Rogers designed the Lloyd's building in the high-tech style, employing air ducts, structural columns, and mechanical equipment as decorative elements.

Japanese architect Arata Isozaki created the Museum of Contemporary Art in Los Angeles, opened in December. The museum is a collection of skylit galleries under a vaulted pavilion.

The Jacob K. Javits Convention Center in New York City, which opened in April, resembles the great exhibition halls of the 1800's. The architects were I. M. Pei & Partners of New York City.

Competitions, in which a jury awards the architectural contract for a building to one of many architects who have submitted designs, continued to flourish. In the most important competition of 1986, the firm of Venturi, Rauch and Scott Brown of Philadelphia triumphed in January over five rivals with its design for an extension to the National Gallery of Art in London. The design had not been made public at year-end.

Barton Myers Associates of Toronto, Canada, won the Phoenix Civic Center competition, proposing a new city hall and tower for that Arizona city. A tentlike roof suspended over the complex will provide shade in summer. A design by the small firm of Woo & Williams of Cambridge, Mass., won over 39 competitors for the Olympic Village at the 1988 Summer Olympics in Seoul, South Korea. The Olympic Village will house some 22,000 athletes and journalists.

Television surveyed U.S. architecture in an eight-part series called "Pride of Place: Building the American Dream" hosted by New York City architect Robert A. M. Stern. The series appeared on the Public Broadcasting System from March to May 1986. Cameras followed Stern through some 100 American buildings as the architect gave his personal view of their history and design.

Exhibitions included a major show at MOMA from July 3 to October 21 called "Vienna 1900:

Structural columns dominate the atrium of the Lloyd's building in London, designed by British architect Richard Rogers, which opened in 1986.

Art, Architecture and Design." The exhibit helped revive interest in such turn-of-the-century architects as Josef Hoffmann and Adolf Loos of Austria. Other noteworthy exhibits included "The Architecture of Frank Gehry" at the Walker Art Center in Minneapolis, Minn., from September 21 to November 16 and "Louis Sullivan: The Function of Ornament" at the Chicago Historical Society from Sept. 5, 1986, to Jan. 4, 1987.

Controversies raged during 1986 over several architects' plans for new buildings in New York City. Among the controversial designs were proposed additions to two city museums. The Solomon R. Guggenheim Museum announced in October 1985 that a small new wing would be designed by Gwathmey Siegel & Associates of New York City. The Whitney Museum of American Art made public in May 1985 plans for a major addition and reconstruction to be done by Michael Graves of Princeton, N.J. Ever since these plans were announced, they had come under fire from critics who said the additions would ruin the older buildings. American architect Frank Lloyd Wright designed the Guggenheim in 1960, and Hungarian-born architect Marcel L. Breuer did the Whitney in 1966.

The proposed expansions were both unresolved at the end of 1986. Opponents of the Whitney addition had succeeded in getting the original build-

ing listed as a state landmark, which would hinder efforts to change it.

A November 1985 proposal by New York City developer Donald J. Trump underwent major changes in 1986. The original design for the project, called Television City, included a 150-story tower that would be the world's tallest building. Critics charged that the huge complex, designed by architect Helmut Jahn of Chicago, would overwhelm its surroundings. Trump then hired architect Alexander Cooper of New York City to create new plans, which included a 136-story tower—still the world's largest.

St. Bartholomew's Church, a Park Avenue landmark, lost another round in a long struggle with the New York City Landmarks Preservation Commission in February when the commission rejected the Episcopal church's third request for permission to build a new office tower on its land. The church claims that it needs the income from such a building to support its services to the poor. The church continued its fight by filing suit against the city in U.S. District Court.

In Miami Beach, Fla., a neighborhood of hotels built in the streamlined art deco style of the 1930's and 1940's was declared a historic district. The declaration was seen as a victory for architectural preservationists. Robert Campbell

In WORLD BOOK, see ARCHITECTURE.

ARGENTINA. Three members of the military junta that led Argentina into the 1982 Falkland Islands war with Great Britain were found guilty on May 16, 1986, of negligence in conducting the war. Argentina lost the war, and ever since, public opinion has demanded punishment for those deemed responsible.

The Supreme Military Council, Argentina's highest military tribunal, convicted the former junta members and handed down stiff sentences. General Leopoldo F. Galtieri, the president of Argentina at the time of the war and chief architect of the army assault on the Falklands, was sentenced to 12 years in prison. Admiral Jorge I. Anaya, the navy commander, received 14 years for the failure of the navy to support the army during its assault. Brigadier General Basilio Lami Dozo, chief of the air force, was given 8 years of imprisonment. All three officers were stripped of their military rank and privileges.

Also during 1986, military and civil courts were jammed with the trials of some 300 military officers facing 1,700 charges of homicide, illegal detention, and torture related to human rights violations against dissidents in the late 1970's, when the military ruled Argentina. An estimated 9,000 people disappeared during this period. In April 1986, Argentine President Raúl Alfonsín instructed the courts to hurry up the trials by dis-

City buses block traffic opposite the Government House in the Argentine capital of Buenos Aires as bus drivers demand wage hikes in February.

missing charges where evidence was deemed insufficient and where the officers being charged were following orders. Human-rights groups criticized this move as an effort to grant amnesty to some officers.

The Economy. Some Argentines reacted angrily as the nation's economy headed into tough times during 1986. The January visit of U.S. banker David Rockefeller, retired chairman of Chase Manhattan Bank, touched off the worst riots in Argentina since democracy was restored in 1983. Some political groups saw Rockefeller as a symbol of the austerity measures imposed on the Argentine economy by foreign creditors.

The bloom was off the tough economic reforms implemented by President Alfonsín in 1985. Known as the Austral Plan, the reforms had been credited with dramatically reducing inflation and paving the way for the restoration of economic stability. Argentines who had welcomed the reforms—which included the issuance of a new currency, the austral, to replace the peso—began expressing doubts in 1986.

Labor union leaders were bitter about wage controls, imposed under the reforms, that caused the wages of Argentine workers to fall behind the cost of living. Business owners were angry over price controls that made it difficult for them to make a profit. Opinions were divided over the wisdom of

the government's decision to sell to the private sector money-losing, state-owned enterprises that had mushroomed under military rule.

The uncertainties of the economy helped stimulate a continued flight of capital out of Argentina. Argentines have invested some $20 billion abroad in recent years, according to some estimates, owing to a lack of confidence in their own nation's economy.

To make matters worse, inflation showed a resurgence. The announcement of 6.8 per cent inflation in July touched off the resignation in August of Alfredo Concepción, chairman of the Central Bank and one of the architects of the Austral Plan.

Escape to the South. Some Argentines sought economic relief by settling in remote Tierra del Fuego—an island territory at the southernmost tip of South America. Foreign and domestic businesses there have taken advantage of a 1972 law that largely exempts the area from taxes and tariffs and have created the world's southernmost electronics industry. The town of Ushuaia on the island has doubled its population to 25,000 during the past 10 years, and the island itself has increased its population from 10,000 in 1970 to more than 60,000 in 1986.   Nathan A. Haverstock

See also LATIN AMERICA (Facts in Brief Table). In WORLD BOOK, see ARGENTINA.

ARIAS SÁNCHEZ, OSCAR (1941-   ), took office as president of Costa Rica on May 8, 1986, becoming the youngest president in the country's history at the age of 44. In his inaugural speech, Arias vowed to keep Costa Rica out of an armed conflict with its Central American neighbor Nicaragua, though he voiced his opposition to Nicaragua's Soviet-backed regime.

Arias was born on Sept. 13, 1941, an heir to one of Costa Rica's wealthiest families. He attended Boston University and also studied in England at the University of Exeter and the London School of Economics. He obtained a law degree in 1967 at the University of Costa Rica in San José.

During the 1970's, Arias wrote several books on political and economic conditions in Costa Rica and served in a number of government positions, including economic adviser to the president and minister of national planning. In 1975, he became head of the National Liberation Party, a liberal party. He was named the party's candidate for president in 1985 and was elected on Feb. 2, 1986, with 52 per cent of the vote.

Arias is married and has two children—a son, Oscar Felipe, and a daughter, Silvia Eugenia. His wife, Margarita, has a degree in chemistry from Vassar College in Poughkeepsie, N.Y.   Rod Such

ARIZONA. See STATE GOVERNMENT.

ARKANSAS. See STATE GOVERNMENT.

ARMED FORCES. United States warplanes conducted intensive bombing raids against Libyan
military targets in 1986. The first attacks were
launched on March 24, shortly after U.S. jets—
part of a naval task force conducting "freedom of
navigation" exercises in the Gulf of Sidra off the
Libyan coast—were attacked by Libyan surface-to-
air missiles. United States carrier aircraft sank at
least two Libyan patrol boats and bombed missile
batteries on the Libyan coast, as the United States
carried out its first combat operations since the
1983 invasion of Grenada.

Heavier attacks were launched on April 15, after U.S. intelligence reported that Libyan agents
were responsible for the April 5 bombing of a
West Berlin discothèque, killing two U.S. servicemen. In a joint attack, U.S. F-111 bombers from
bases in Great Britain joined jets from the aircraft
carriers *Coral Sea* and *America* in raids against military targets in two Libyan cities, Benghazi and the
capital city of Tripoli. One F-111 and its two crew
members were lost during the attack.

Arms Control Stalemate. The United States and
the Soviet Union engaged in an intensive series of
negotiations in 1986 in an attempt to reduce nuclear weapons, but the efforts were unsuccessful.
A summit meeting was held on October 11 and 12
in Reykjavík, Iceland, between President Ronald
Reagan and Communist Party General Secretary
Mikhail S. Gorbachev of the Soviet Union. The
leaders agreed in principle to limit intermediate-
range nuclear missiles in Europe and to make
drastic reductions in strategic missiles and bombers over the next 10 years. The landmark agreement collapsed, however, in a dispute over Reagan's Strategic Defense Initiative (SDI), a space-
based ballistic missile defense program popularly
known as "Star Wars." President Reagan offered
to delay activation of the SDI system for 10 years,
but he rejected Gorbachev's insistence that research and testing on the program be restricted to
the laboratory.

In the absence of an arms agreement, the
United States moved forward on the SDI program and other strategic weapons systems. The
Pentagon reported several successful tests of
experimental laser weapons and said that they
demonstrated the technological feasibility of the
SDI program. On December 22, the first 10 MX
land-based intercontinental ballistic missiles became operational. The Pentagon also reported
that testing continued on submarine-launched nuclear cruise missiles; a single-warhead mobile missile known as Midgetman; and ASAT (antisat-
ellite), a system designed to destroy enemy surveillance satellites in outer space. On October 15,

A Soviet nuclear-missile submarine, damaged by an on-board explosion and
fire, sinks in the Atlantic Ocean east of Bermuda before dawn on October 6.

Soldiers at a U.S. base near Mainz, West Germany, in May supervise
a few of the 900 white geese that the Army is training for guard duty.

however, Congress imposed a moratorium on ASAT testing until Sept. 30, 1987.

Contra Aid. The Reagan Administration's campaign to undermine the Marxist government in Nicaragua received a substantial boost on August 13 when the Senate approved $100 million in military and humanitarian assistance for the *contras*, rebels fighting to overthrow the government. The House of Representatives had approved an identical measure in June. The legislation also removed congressional restrictions that would prevent the Central Intelligence Agency (CIA) and other government agencies from becoming involved in the contra cause. Reagan authorized the aid in October.

Debate intensified, however, over the alleged involvement of U.S. government officials in efforts to provide assistance to the contras in 1985 and 1986. The Sandinistas charged that a U.S.-built cargo plane shot down over Nicaragua on October 5 was part of a CIA operation that was supplying contras with weapons. Two Americans were killed in the crash and the only survivor—Eugene Hasenfus of Marinette, Wis.—claimed that the CIA had supervised the flight. The Reagan Administration denied any connection to the incident. Controversy flared up late in November over the secret sale of U.S. weapons to Iran, with the funneling of at least some of the money from the sale

to the contras (see PRESIDENT OF THE UNITED STATES).

Conventional Weapons. On August 18, the Pentagon approved Army plans to develop an $11-billion air-defense system that would protect ground troops from enemy helicopter attacks. This system, called the Forward Area Air Defense program, will replace the Sergeant York antiaircraft gun system, which was canceled in 1985 due to poor performance. The Pentagon began limited production of nerve-gas bombs for the first time since the production of chemical weapons was halted in 1969. Congress, on Aug. 7, 1986, rejected an amendment designed to block production of such weapons.

Newspaper reports published in August disclosed that the United States Air Force had purchased 50 Stealth fighter planes and had hidden them in the Nevada desert. Flying only at night, the highly secret Stealth jet can reportedly evade enemy radar because of its revolutionary shape and other technological advancements. An Air Force jet that crashed in California on July 11 was revealed to have been a Stealth jet.

Defense Budget. On February 5, for the sixth consecutive year, the Reagan Administration submitted a record peacetime defense budget to Congress. The request was for the 1987 fiscal year, which began on Oct. 1, 1986. Reagan asked for

A "Darth Vader" helmet, tested by the U.S. Air Force in 1986, allows pilots to aim at targets simply by moving their heads.

position of vice chairman of the Joint Chiefs of Staff and gave more authority to field commanders over troops in combat situations.

Espionage. Jonathan Jay Pollard, a former U.S. Navy intelligence analyst, pleaded guilty on June 4 to selling government secrets to Israel. Four Israelis, who were named co-conspirators in the case, were not indicted. In a statement on June 6, the Israeli Embassy in the United States called the case "an unauthorized deviation from Israel's policy of not conducting any espionage activities in the United States."

Personnel Developments. Reagan signed a new law on July 2 that reforms the military retirement system. The law, which will eventually reduce annual military pension benefits by 18 per cent, went into effect July 11. It applies only to personnel who join the military after Aug. 1, 1986.

Command Changes. General Larry D. Welch, commander of the Strategic Air Command, was named Air Force chief of staff on June 30, succeeding retiring General Charles A. Gabriel. Admiral James D. Watkins retired as chief of naval operations on June 30 and was replaced by Admiral Carlisle A. H. Trost.   Thomas M. DeFrank

In the Special Reports section, see THE AGE-OLD BUSINESS OF ESPIONAGE. In WORLD BOOK, see the articles on the branches of the armed forces.

ARMY. See ARMED FORCES.

$311.6 billion for defense, an increase of $33.2 billion over fiscal 1986. Actual defense outlays in the proposed budget were $274.3 billion, a $19.9-billion increase over the previous year.

The single largest budget item was a $4.8-billion request for the SDI or Star Wars program. The Pentagon also requested $4.8 billion for Trident submarines and nuclear missiles, and $3.9 billion for F-16 jet fighters.

The budget request was not well received on Capitol Hill, where even long-time supporters of the Pentagon complained that the defense budget was excessive at a time when problems with federal budget deficits were growing. On October 15, Congress passed the defense appropriations bill after slashing more than $29 billion from Reagan's proposed budget. Federal spending was cut on several weapons systems and more than $1 billion was taken from the SDI request. Congress froze fiscal 1987 expenditures at the level of inflation for the second consecutive year.

Military Reform. The most sweeping reorganization of the U.S. military in 40 years was signed by Reagan on October 1. The legislation designated the chairman of the Joint Chiefs of Staff as the principal military adviser to the President, giving the chairman authority over the joint military staff and raising his maximum length of service from four to six years. The law also created a new

ART. Andrew Wyeth, a world-famous American realist painter whose best-known work is *Christina's World* (1948), became the center of attention in United States art circles in August 1986. Publisher Leonard Andrews announced that he had bought a series of 240 previously unknown paintings and drawings by Wyeth for an undisclosed sum, presumably many millions of dollars.

Mystery surrounded the identity of the solemn blond model portrayed in most of the 240 works. Wyeth had been painting the woman, at first identified only as Helga, in secret for 15 years. She turned out to be Helga Testorf, a long-time neighbor of Wyeth's in Chadds Ford, Pa. Some of the works were scheduled to be exhibited at the National Gallery of Art in Washington, D.C., from May to August 1987.

Cultural Exchange. The United States and the Soviet Union exchanged museum exhibitions in 1986 for the first time since 1979. A total of 41 paintings by Paul Cézanne, Paul Gauguin, Edouard Manet, Henri Matisse, Pablo Picasso, and Vincent Van Gogh came from Leningrad's State Hermitage Museum and Moscow's A. S. Pushkin State Museum of Fine Arts. The exhibition opened at the National Gallery of Art in May and June and also appeared at the Los Angeles County Museum of Art from June to August and the Metropolitan Museum of Art in New York City from

Braids is one of more than 240 previously unknown paintings and sketches by Andrew Wyeth that sold in 1986 for several million dollars.

August to October. In return, the National Gallery sent 41 impressionist and postimpressionist works from its own collection to tour Soviet museums.

French Painting in general received much attention from museums in the United States in 1986. A major exhibition of the art of François Boucher, a French court painter of the 1700's, appeared at the Metropolitan from February to May and at the Detroit Institute of Arts from May to August. A historical show re-creating the first eight impressionist exhibitions in Paris, held between 1874 and 1886, appeared at the National Gallery from January to April 1986 and traveled to the Fine Arts Museums of San Francisco from April to July.

From November 1986 to March 1987, the National Gallery showcased paintings from Matisse's underappreciated middle period in "Henri Matisse: The Early Years in Nice, 1916-1930," which focused on paintings made during those years. Van Gogh's last works, about 90 paintings and drawings made during the 14 months before his suicide in 1890, went on view at the Metropolitan from November 1986 to March 1987.

Centennials. Some 150 works by the Austrian expressionist painter Oskar Kokoschka appeared at the Solomon R. Guggenheim Museum in New York City from December 1986 to February 1987, coinciding with the 100th anniversary of Kokoschka's birth in 1886. "Diego Rivera: A Retrospec-

tive," the first U.S. retrospective of the Mexican muralist, also born in 1886, opened at the Detroit Institute of Arts from February to April 1986 and appeared at the Philadelphia Museum of Art from June to August. The show was scheduled to travel to Mexico City; Madrid, Spain; and West Berlin in late 1986 and 1987.

American Art. John Singer Sargent and Winslow Homer, two of the greatest American painters of the 1800's, received in-depth museum treatments in 1986. The Whitney Museum of American Art in New York City mounted the largest retrospective ever of Sargent, known for his perceptive portraits. The exhibition appeared at the Whitney from October 1986 to January 1987 and was due to open at the Art Institute of Chicago in February 1987. The National Gallery showed almost 100 water colors dating from 1873 to 1905 by Homer, a Maine realist noted for his paintings of the sea.

Contemporary Art in the United States was livelier than ever in 1986, with no single style predominating. Neo-expressionist painters Eric Fischl and David Salle, both in their 30's, had museum surveys of their bold, representational work. Salle's show appeared at the Institute of Contemporary Art in Philadelphia in 1986 and was due at the Whitney from January to March 1987.

The Mendel Art Gallery in Saskatoon, Canada, organized Fischl's retrospective in 1985. The ex-

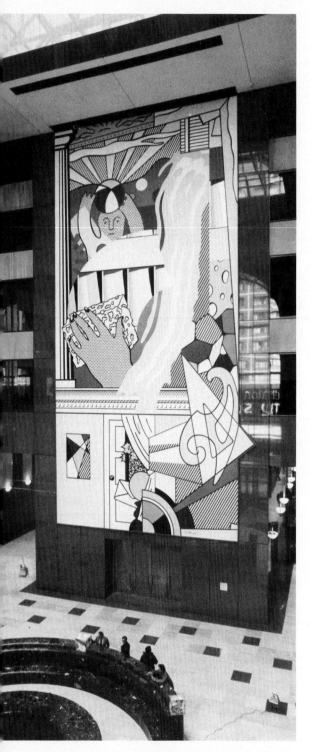

Roy Lichtenstein's *Mural with Blue Brushstroke*
nearly fills the atrium of New York City's new
Whitney Museum of American Art at Equitable Center.

hibition toured Canada and Europe before appearing in 1986 at the Museum of Contemporary Art in Chicago and the Whitney.

Modern abstraction was featured at the Museum of Modern Art (MOMA) in New York City in a 20-year retrospective of sculpture by Richard Serra. Serra's simple arrangements of huge steel plates exemplify minimal art, which reduces art to compositions of form, shape, or sometimes color.

The art world's newest movement, dubbed *neo-geo*, consisted of both abstract painting and realistic sculpture with elements derived equally from pop art, minimalism, and conceptual art. Art enthusiasts could see neo-geo in art galleries and in two group shows, one at the Institute of Contemporary Art in Boston and the other at the New Museum of Contemporary Art in New York City.

Cultural Cross Sections. Three New York City museum exhibitions in 1986 combined fine and applied arts to give a broad picture of distinct cultural periods. MOMA's "Vienna 1900: Art, Architecture and Design" from July to October surveyed the robust graphic design, painting, and architecture that emerged in Vienna, then capital of Austria-Hungary, at the turn of the century.

The Metropolitan presented "In Pursuit of Beauty: Americans and the Aesthetic Movement" from October 1986 to January 1987. The exhibition featured the exquisitely ornamented home furnishings of the first popular decorative arts movement in the United States, which arose about 1876. And the Brooklyn Museum's "The Machine Age in America, 1918-1941" from October 1986 to February 1987 charted the influence of modern art and machine design on the streamlined style of the era between World Wars I and II. The show was to travel to Pittsburgh, Pa.; Los Angeles; and Atlanta, Ga., in 1987.

The Museum Boom continued as several leading museums in 1986 inaugurated new facilities with ambitious exhibitions. The Los Angeles County Museum of Art opened its new Robert O. Anderson Building for art of this century. Hardy Holzman Pfeiffer Associates of New York City designed the 115,200-square-foot (10,700-square-meter) complex. The first exhibition was "The Spiritual in Art," a survey of abstract painting.

The Los Angeles Museum of Contemporary Art in December opened a new $23-million, 98,000-square-foot (9,100-square-meter) building designed by Japanese Post-Modernist architect Arata Isozaki. The museum inaugurated its new quarters with "Individuals: A Selected History of Contemporary Art, 1945-1986," works by 77 artists.

The American Craft Museum in October opened its new 18,500-square-foot (1,720-square-meter) museum in a midtown New York City skyscraper. Its first exhibition was "Craft Today: The Poetry of the Physical," a survey of contemporary

Visitors at the A. S. Pushkin State Museum of Fine Arts in Moscow view paintings in May loaned by the National Gallery of Art in Washington, D.C.

works by 286 artists including ceramics, textiles, woodworking, and other crafts. The show was scheduled to appear at the Craft Museum through March 1987, then go on tour to Denver; Laguna Beach, Calif.; Phoenix; Milwaukee; Louisville, Ky.; and Richmond, Va.

Important Museum Acquisitions in 1986 included the bequest to the Philadelphia Museum of Art of the celebrated private art collection of Henry P. McIlhenny, who had been its chairman of the board. McIlhenny's bequest had an estimated market value of $100 million.

The National Gallery of Art was exceptionally fortunate in 1986. It received 186 paintings from financier Paul Mellon and his wife, Rachel Mellon, the museum's long-time patrons. Robert E. and Jane B. Meyerhoff of Phoenix, Md., provided an undisclosed sum, estimated at more than $4 million, to buy "The Stations of the Cross," a set of 14 abstract-expressionist masterpieces by American painter Barnett Newman. The National Gallery also received 150 works and 16 sketchbooks worth about $2 million by the American modernist John Marin, from the artist's son.

The Pennsylvania Academy of the Fine Arts in Philadelphia purchased for an undisclosed sum a collection of 29 paintings and some 1,000 other items remaining in American realist painter Thomas Eakins' studio at the time of his death in 1916. The Smithsonian Institution in January bought the $7-million Persian art collection of French jeweler and art collector Henri Vever.

Auction Prices continued their climb in 1986. The boldly colored pop art painting *Out the Window* (1959) by American painter Jasper Johns sold for $3,630,000 in November 1986, a record for a work by a living artist. Manet's *La Rue Mosnier aux Paveurs* brought $11,088,000 at a London auction in December, the highest price ever for an impressionist painting. Also during the December London sales, a 1911 cubist painting by French artist Georges Braque sold for $9,504,000, a record for a work painted in this century; and a 1632 Rembrandt portrait of a young girl sold for $10,309,200, just below the Old Master record of $10,449,000 set in 1985.

A 1963 welded steel sculpture by the American abstract sculptor David Smith sold in May 1986 for $1,300,000, a record price for contemporary sculpture. The record auction price for furniture was set and reset in January 1986, when a carved mahogany Chippendale tea table, dating from 1760 to 1780, sold for $1,045,000, and a week later a lavishly embellished French rococo desk sold for $2,090,000. Walter Robinson

In the Special Reports section, see NEW LIFE FOR TWO OLD TREASURES. In WORLD BOOK, see ART AND THE ARTS; PAINTING; SCULPTURE.

ASIA

Democratic elections were held in several Asian countries during 1986, while others remained under one-person or one-party rule. In the Philippines, a controversial election led to a change of presidents. Regional cooperation flourished in South and Southeast Asia. Seemingly endless conflicts continued within several countries.

Elections. On February 7, the Philippines held Asia's first national elections of 1986. President Ferdinand E. Marcos called the elections in an effort to win a new endorsement from the voters after 20 years in office. His opponents united behind Corazon Aquino, widow of a leading opposition politician who had been murdered in 1983. Two top-ranking Philippine military leaders rejected Marcos' claim to have won the election and accused him of fraud and misconduct. With public backing, they forced Marcos to flee into exile, and Aquino assumed the presidency on February 25.

Nepal on May 12 held its second general election under a system that barred political parties. Voters chose 112 members for the 140-seat National Panchayat, a one-chamber legislature. King Birendra Bir Bikram Shah Dev named the remaining members. Young opponents of the non-party system defeated many veteran legislators, indicating widespread dissatisfaction with the government.

In Japan, the Liberal Democratic Party that had ruled since 1955 won its largest number of seats ever in parliamentary elections on July 6. In the more powerful lower house of parliament, the party won 300 seats. Four people who ran as independents later joined the party, giving it 304 seats, compared with 250 in the previous house. In the upper house, the party's seats rose from 131 to 142. The unexpectedly strong victory enabled Prime Minister Yasuhiro Nakasone to win from his party a one-year extension in office beyond his scheduled retirement in October. Nakasone had served four years, the traditional limit for prime ministers in Japan.

Thailand's Prime Minister Prem Tinsulanonda also won another term, to become that country's longest-serving civilian prime minister, as a result of parliamentary elections on July 27. Although he did not run for parliament, he was selected by a coalition of four parties to continue in office.

Crowds at the Malacañang Palace in Manila, the official residence of Philippine President Marcos, celebrate his overthrow in February.

Facts in Brief on Asian Countries

Country	Population	Government	Monetary Unit*	Foreign Trade (million U.S. $) Exports†	Imports†
Afghanistan	16,267,000	People's Democratic Party General Secretary Najibullah; Acting Revolutionary Council President Haji Mohammad Chamkani; Prime Minister Sultan Ali Keshtmand	afghani (50.5 = $1)	778	902
Australia	16,102,000	Governor General Sir Ninian Martin Stephen; Prime Minister Robert Hawke	dollar (1.5 = $1)	22,759	25,889
Bangladesh	106,651,000	President Hussain Muhammed Ershad; Prime Minister Mizanur Rahman Choudhury	taka (29.4 = $1)	811	2,300
Bhutan	1,476,000	King Jigme Singye Wangchuck	Indian rupee (13.1 = $1) & ngultrum (no data available)	15	69
Brunei	236,000	Sultan Sir Muda Hassanal Bolkiah	dollar (2.2 = $1)	3,260	701
Burma	38,919,000	President U San Yu; Prime Minister U Maung Maung Kha	kyat (7 = $1)	349	672
China	1,085,472,000	Communist Party General Secretary Hu Yaobang; Communist Party Deputy Chairman Deng Xiaoping; President Li Xiannian; Premier Zhao Ziyang	yuan (3.72 = $1)	27,327	42,526
India	789,805,000	President Zail Singh; Prime Minister Rajiv Gandhi	rupee (13.1 = $1)	7,915	14,608
Indonesia	170,288,000	President Suharto; Vice President Umar Wirahadikusumah	rupiah (1,650 = $1)	22,200	15,300
Iran	47,757,000	President Ali Khamenei; Prime Minister Hosein Musavi-Khamenei	rial (76.3 = $1)	13,185	11,256
Japan	121,150,000	Emperor Hirohito; Prime Minister Yasuhiro Nakasone	yen (162 = $1)	177,164	130,488
Kampuchea (Cambodia)	6,514,000	People's Revolutionary Party Secretary General & Council of State President Heng Samrin (Coalition government: President Prince Norodom Sihanouk; Vice President Khieu Samphan; Prime Minister Son Sann)	riel (4 = $1)	no statistics available	
Korea, North	21,012,000	President Kim Il-song; Premier Yi Kun-mo	won (1 = $1.06)	1,590	1,360
Korea, South	42,033,000	President Chun Doo Hwan; Prime Minister Shinyong Lho	won (866.5 = $1)	29,566	31,129
Laos	4,644,000	Acting President Phoumi Vongvichit; Prime Minister Kayson Phomvihan	kip (108 = $1)	36	98
Malaysia	16,260,000	Paramount Ruler Tunku Mahmood Iskandar Al-Haj Ibni Almarhum Sultan Ismail; Prime Minister Mahathir bin Mohamed	ringgit (2.6 = $1)	15,442	12,302
Maldives	187,000	President Maumoon Abdul Gayoom	rupee (7 = $1)	146	233
Mongolia	2,001,000	People's Great Khural Presidium Chairman Jambyn Batmonh; Council of Ministers Chairman Sodnom Dumaagiyn	tughrik (3.3 = $1)	540	822
Nepal	17,253,000	King Birendra Bir Bikram Shah Dev; Prime Minister Marich Man Singh Shrestha	rupee (20 = $1)	157	450
New Zealand	3,345,000	Governor General Sir Paul Reeves; Prime Minister David R. Lange	dollar (2.02 = $1)	5,721	5,992
Pakistan	106,425,000	President M. Zia-ul-Haq; Prime Minister Mohammed Khan Junejo	rupee (17.25 = $1)	2,739	5,890
Papua New Guinea	3,894,000	Governor General Sir Kingsford Dibela; Prime Minister Paias Wingti	kina (1.04 = $1)	840	906
Philippines	57,369,000	President Corazon Aquino; Vice President Salvador Laurel	peso (20 = $1)	4,607	5,459
Russia	283,620,000	Communist Party General Secretary Mikhail S. Gorbachev; Supreme Soviet Presidium Chairman Andrei A. Gromyko; Council of Ministers Chairman Nikolai I. Ryzhkov	ruble (1 = $1.09)	91,492	80,352
Singapore	2,637,000	President Wee Kim Wee; Prime Minister Lee Kuan Yew	dollar (2.2 = $1)	22,812	26,285
Sri Lanka	17,051,000	President J. R. Jayewardene; Prime Minister R. Premadasa	rupee (27 = $1)	1,333	1,947
Taiwan	19,943,000	President Chiang Ching-kuo; Prime Minister Yu Kuo-hwa	new Taiwan dollar (36.25 = $1)	30,400	21,600
Thailand	53,441,000	King Bhumibol Adulyadej; Prime Minister Prem Tinsulanonda	baht (25 = $1)	7,120	9,231
Vietnam	61,798,000	Communist Party General Secretary Nguyen Van Linh; Council of State Chairman Truong Chinh; Council of Ministers Chairman Pham Van Dong	dong (10.9 = $1)	763	1,823

*Exchange rates as of Dec. 1, 1986, or latest available data. †Latest available data.

Girls in Kathmandu present garlands to Queen Elizabeth II of Great Britain to welcome her on her four-day state visit to Nepal in February.

In Malaysia, Prime Minister Mahathir bin Mohamed led a coalition to a strong victory in parliamentary elections on August 2 and 3, ensuring his continued leadership. The returns showed increasing polarization between Mahathir's ethnic Malay supporters and ethnic Chinese opponents, raising prospects of future difficulties.

After violent and disputed parliamentary elections on May 7, Bangladesh held a presidential election on October 15. The party of self-proclaimed President Hussain Muhammad Ershad won 153 out of 300 parliamentary seats in the May voting. In October, Ershad's main opponents boycotted the contest, and he was elected overwhelmingly to the office he had already claimed.

Taiwan held legislative elections on December 6. On September 28, 130 opposition leaders had defied a ban on opposition parties by announcing the creation of the Democratic Progressive Party. In the elections, the ruling Kuomintang party retained control of the legislature, but its share of votes dropped from 73 per cent in the previous election to 66 per cent.

Other Leadership Changes. Two Asian Communist countries changed their leadership without elections during the year. Babrak Karmal, who had been installed as general secretary of the Afghan Communist party after the Soviet Union invaded Afghanistan in 1979, resigned from that office on May 4, 1986. Apparently, the Soviet advisers who controlled his regime had decided to remove him from office. Najibullah, the former head of Afghanistan's secret police, replaced Karmal. Le Duan, the general secretary of Vietnam's Communist party, died on July 10 and was succeeded by Truong Chinh. Chinh resigned his party post on December 17, along with Prime Minister Pham Van Dong—who remained prime minister—and Politburo member Le Duc Tho. Nguyen Van Linh succeeded Chinh as party leader.

Relations Between Asia's Largest Countries remained poor during 1986. The two nations largest in population—China and India—accused each other of border violations in the same part of the Himalaya where their 1962 border war had erupted. The two nations largest in area—the Soviet Union and China—exchanged their highest-level visitors since 1969 and increased trade, but failed to overcome deep-seated hostility.

Soviet Communist Party General Secretary Mikhail S. Gorbachev made a major speech on July 28 in Vladivostok, a Soviet city near the Chinese border, outlining a new Asian policy of regional cooperation. He proposed discussions with China on troop reductions along their mutual border. Gorbachev also announced that some Soviet troops would withdraw from Afghanistan. The U.S. government said, however, that the Soviet claim to have withdrawn 8,000 of its 120,000 troops from Afghanistan by October 31 was a sham.

Regional Cooperation. The new South Asian Association for Regional Cooperation, which had adopted a charter at a summit meeting in Dhaka, Bangladesh, on Dec. 8, 1985, held its second summit in Bangalore, India, on Nov. 16 and 17, 1986. Leaders of Bangladesh, Bhutan, India, Maldives, Nepal, Pakistan, and Sri Lanka ratified a decision of their foreign secretaries to establish the association's headquarters in Kathmandu, Nepal, with a Bangalee (a citizen of Bangladesh) as the first secretary-general. The group established committees to work for economic ties and other forms of cooperation, but it agreed to avoid discussing disputes between members.

The Association of Southeast Asian Nations (ASEAN)—Brunei, Indonesia, Malaysia, the Philippines, Singapore, and Thailand—continued to cooperate in seeking a solution to the conflict in Kampuchea, where three different groups are fighting a guerrilla war against a Vietnamese-backed regime. But Philippine President Aquino, as a new member of ASEAN leadership, criticized the organization for failing to do much about its original primary aim, to spur economic growth.

ASEAN efforts to reduce trade barriers between Southeast Asian countries were controversial. Indonesia, for example, feared that its small industries would be ruined if exposed to competition from more industrially advanced member countries such as Singapore and Malaysia.

Wars and Other Conflicts. The guerrilla war in Kampuchea, fought by both Communist and anti-Communist guerrilla armies opposing the Vietnamese-controlled government, showed no signs of ending. Vietnamese troops tried to block the Kampuchean border with Thailand, cutting off supplies for the guerrillas from China and Southeast Asia.

The foreign ministers of Vietnam, Kampuchea, and Laos held their 12th conference on January 23 and 24 in Vientiane, Laos, and their 13th on August 17 and 18 in Hanoi, Vietnam. Communiqués on both meetings called for settlement of the Kampuchean conflict on Communist terms.

The other major war in Asia, the effort by the Soviet Army and Afghan auxiliaries to defeat Afghan guerrilla resistance, continued without either side gaining a clear advantage. The United Nations persevered with efforts to mediate a settlement, but the talks were deadlocked.

Aside from border clashes between India and Pakistan on a glacier in the Karakoram Mountains, and clashes between Chinese and Vietnamese border forces, Asia's conflicts were internal. Separatist movements caused violence in Bangladesh, India, Indonesia, and Sri Lanka. Political and racial riots caused hundreds of deaths in Pakistan, and a Communist rebellion continued in the Philippines.

These conflicts drove more refugees from their countries and kept millions huddled in refugee camps. Afghanistan disclosed plans to relocate Afghan civilians from guerrilla areas, causing many people to flee to Pakistan, where some 3 million Afghan refugees were already living. Thousands of refugees from Kampuchea and Laos remained in Thailand hoping for permanent settlement abroad.

Economic Growth in Asia was slower in 1986 than in the early 1980's, largely as a result of low world prices for the agricultural products and other raw materials that are Asia's chief exports. Although such countries as Japan and South Korea benefited from the low price of imported oil, petroleum exporters such as Indonesia and Malaysia suffered. Thailand protested United States subsidies on rice exports that undercut its markets. Both Malaysia and Indonesia continued to be hurt by the low prices that prevailed for tin since a world tin-selling agreement collapsed in 1985.

Several Asian countries that had long been cool to foreign investors put out welcome mats in 1986. India, Indonesia, Malaysia, Thailand, and others made efforts to lure foreign capital. Henry S. Bradsher

See also the various Asian country articles. In WORLD BOOK, see ASIA.

ASTRONOMY. In 1986, astronomers received photographs from the first space probes to fly by the planet Uranus and Halley's Comet. They puzzled over a double quasar and wondered why galaxies seem to be located on giant bubbles in space.

Voyager at Uranus. The space probe *Voyager 2* swept by Uranus and its system of moons and rings, passing within 81,560 kilometers (50,679 miles) of the seventh planet from the sun on Jan. 24, 1986. *Voyager 2*'s cameras photographed the surfaces of Uranus and its 5 large moons—Miranda, Ariel, Umbriel, Titania, and Oberon. Astronomers knew little about Uranus prior to this mission, but data from *Voyager 2* added greatly to the storehouse of scientific knowledge. The spacecraft discovered 10 small moons, in addition to the 5 already known.

The large moons are strikingly different from one another. Oberon and Umbriel are pockmarked by large impact craters, but Titania has only a few large craters, and Ariel has just one. Each moon has many small craters. Tall cliffs rise on Titania and Ariel.

Miranda stood out as the most peculiar of the moons, according to a report by the *Voyager* imaging team. Miranda is a bizarre jumble of different land features. One area is dotted with small craters, while other regions—shaped like huge race tracks—are marked by dark bands, cliffs,

Halley's Comet streaks across the sky, making its closest approach to Earth in April 1986 before heading back to the outer reaches of the solar system.

ridges, and deep valleys. Another area consists of two sets of bright parallel lines—resembling *fault lines* (breaks in the surface crust)—that meet at a pronounced V-shaped angle.

Scientists put forward a number of theories to explain why Miranda has such unusual surface features. One theory was that Miranda may have had many collisions with *planetesimals*—asteroid-sized objects that astronomers believe collected some 4.6 billion years ago to form the planets and large moons of the solar system. Such collisions may have caused huge sections of Miranda to break off. Then, gravity would have caused most of the fragments to re-collect, re-forming the moon. This theory could explain Miranda's bizarre, jumbled terrain.

Halley's Comet. In March 1986, five automated spacecraft flew by Halley's Comet, obtaining the most detailed images ever of a comet. Among the scientific surprises revealed by the spacecraft was hot, black material on the surface of the comet's *nucleus* (core). The images confirmed a scientific theory that predicted the nucleus would resemble a "dirty snowball"—a mixture of ice, dust, and frozen gases. But the theory did not predict that the surface layer of the nucleus would be as hot or as dark as observations showed it to be.

Halley's Comet was last seen in 1910. In 1986, it made its closest approach to the sun in February

and to Earth in April, as it headed back to the outer reaches of the solar system. During 1985, the European Space Agency (ESA), Japan, and the Soviet Union launched spacecraft to intercept the comet during the week of March 6 to 13, 1986. With the ESA's *Giotto* spacecraft and the Soviet Union's *Vega 1* and *Vega 2* spacecraft, scientists obtained the first visual pictures of a comet's nucleus. The nucleus is too small for its size or shape to be seen with Earth-based telescopes.

The spacecraft cameras revealed that the nucleus is potato-shaped and larger than expected, about 16 kilometers (10 miles) long and 8 kilometers (5 miles) wide. Bright jets spew out gas and dust from certain spots on the surface as the nucleus rotates once every 53 hours. Whenever the sun shines on these spots, the jets of gas and dust spout from them like faithful geysers.

Vega 1 and *Vega 2* and *Giotto* made close-up photos that revealed the nucleus and jets, while instruments on Japan's spacecraft—*Sakigake* and *Suisei*—studied the cloud of hydrogen gas that surrounds the comet's atmosphere. Measurements of *infrared* (heat) radiation from the nucleus, made by *Vega 1*, revealed that the black surface has a temperature of about 77° C (170° F.), much hotter than the temperature at which ice will vaporize in the vacuum of space. Thus, scientists reasoned that the surface layer must be an insulating crust of

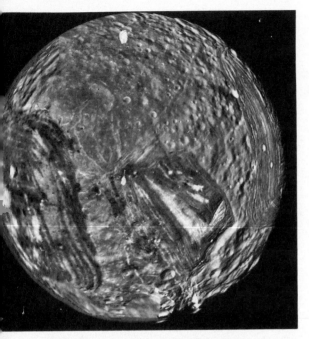

The mysterious moon Miranda reveals its odd geologic features in a photo taken during the *Voyager 2* spacecraft's probe of Uranus in January.

may be a *black hole*, an object so massive that not even light can escape its gravitational field. Consequently, it cannot be seen directly.

Other astronomers suggested that the unseen lens may be an even more unusual phenomenon, a *cosmic string*. Cosmic strings have never been observed, but their existence is predicted by some theories of particle physics and cosmology. Cosmic strings may be the primitive material that the universe was made of at the beginning of time. Some astronomers also theorize that cosmic strings may have caused matter to clump together, thus forming galaxies and clusters of galaxies.

Other astronomers challenged Turner's findings. They suggested that the two quasar images really represent two different quasars.

Giant Bubbles. In January, astronomers at the Harvard-Smithsonian Center for Astrophysics in Cambridge, Mass., announced the discovery of huge spherical structures, resembling "bubbles," in the universe. The astronomers surveyed 1,100 galaxies and, by mapping their positions, found that the galaxies appear to be on the surfaces of the "bubbles," whose interiors appear to be empty of matter that gives off light.   Stephen P. Maran

See also SPACE EXPLORATION. In the WORLD BOOK SUPPLEMENT section, see MAGELLANIC CLOUDS; MILKY WAY. In WORLD BOOK, see ASTRONOMY.

dark matter, possibly formed from rock dust, that covers the underlying ice.

A Matter of Gravity. In May, a team of astronomers led by Edwin L. Turner of Princeton University in New Jersey reported that faint images of two *quasars* (highly energetic objects at the centers of extremely distant galaxies) may actually show one quasar. Through powerful telescopes, astronomers can see two quasar images in the direction of the constellation Leo.

Turner and his research team proposed that there is actually only one quasar. The image of the single quasar, they reported, is split in two by the gravitational force of an object that lies between the quasar and Earth. This phenomenon is known as a *gravitational lens*. A gravitational lens is a massive object whose gravity bends the light rays from a more distant object, splitting the rays so that multiple images of the object are seen from Earth.

Astronomers had previously found several gravitational lenses. In this case, however, the two quasar images in Leo are about 20 times farther apart than has occurred with any other gravitational lens. To produce such wide image-splitting, the apparent gravitational lens in Leo must have a greater mass than any known object in the universe. But powerful telescopes reveal no huge object along the line of sight to the pair of quasars. This prompted speculation that the unseen lens

AUSTRALIA. The troubled economy, plagued by continued deficits in overseas trade, a depressed currency, and a stubbornly high rate of inflation, was Australia's dominant news story of 1986. Despite the economic bad news, the Labor Party government of Prime Minister Robert Hawke remained in place, and in state elections on February 8, voters returned to power the Liberal Party government of Tasmania and the Labor Party government of Western Australia.

The Economy. The economic bad news arose from the balance-of-payments deficit and unfavorable terms of foreign trade. Led by declines in the prices of grains and dairy goods, the real value of rural export products fell 20 to 25 per cent in the fiscal year ending in June 1986. Sugar, coal, and iron ore exports also suffered from low prices. The result—in spite of record quantities of wheat and coal exports—was a series of monthly balance-of-trade deficits and a mounting foreign debt.

The trade problems were not immediately reflected in the domestic economy. The Australian dollar, which began the year at $A1 = U.S. 68 cents, was left free to float against major currencies for the first time. Although it fell to just over U.S. 60 cents by midyear, it rebounded to U.S. 65 cents as of Dec. 31, 1986. Moreover, unemployment remained level at about 8.3 per cent for the fiscal year ending in June 1986.

Australian farmers protest U.S. subsidies for overseas wheat sales by shoveling wheat onto U.S. Embassy grounds in Canberra in August.

On the other hand, the inflation rate was slightly higher—roughly 8 per cent for fiscal 1986 compared with 6.7 per cent in 1985—and was two or three times that of Australia's main trading partners. Interest rates continued high, and the 1985-1986 federal budget deficit reached nearly $A825 million more than originally estimated. In addition, industrial production was depressed. Reacting to these economic indicators, Moody's Investors Services reduced the Australian government's credit rating on September 11 from AAA, the highest rating, to AA1, the second-best rating.

Even before the action by Moody's, the Labor government had taken steps to reassure foreign investors that Australia was determined to correct its trade problems and control its public spending. Prime Minister Hawke had told the nation on June 11 that there would be unpopular decisions, including budget restraint. This prediction was fulfilled on August 19, when Treasurer Paul Keating introduced a federal budget that reduced projected government spending and postponed promised cuts in income tax. The budget included reductions in federal grants to the states and a freeze on hiring of public-service employees.

The government blamed the export subsidy policies of the United States and the European Community (EC or Common Market) for much of the decline in value of Australia's rural exports. Min-

isterial and parliamentary delegations visited Washington, D.C., in late July to protest the effects of U.S. legislation that subsidized U.S. grain exports. Australia also sent representatives to the European Commission—the EC executive body—to protest EC export subsidies.

Foreign investment continued to be important to Australia, particularly since any drop in new capital imports would increase balance-of-payments difficulties. On July 28, Keating announced a relaxation of the guidelines for foreign investment, making it possible for foreigners to buy the whole of existing firms.

Australian investment in other countries—a long-term source of external income—continued to grow and diversify. It amounted to more than $A10 billion at the end of 1985, more than twice the overseas investment in mid-1983.

The opposition parties in Parliament attacked the Labor government's continued support of the national arbitration system, which makes binding decisions in wage disputes. These decisions often raise domestic industrial costs, according to opposition leaders, thereby fueling inflation and placing Australian-made goods at a competitive disadvantage both at home and abroad. Critics proposed that the system of compulsory arbitration be dismantled or that firms and industries be allowed to opt out of it.

Foreign Affairs. Aside from the issue of export subsidies, concerns over the ANZUS (*Australia, New Zealand,* and the *United States*) mutual defense treaty largely dominated foreign affairs in 1986. The ANZUS alliance, established in 1952, was affected by New Zealand's refusal to allow U.S. nuclear-armed or nuclear-powered ships to use its ports.

On August 11, the United States formally suspended its military obligations to New Zealand under the ANZUS pact. The Australian government supported the United States. At a meeting in San Francisco from August 25 to 27, the defense and foreign ministers of Australia and the United States agreed that access for Allied ships and aircraft was essential to the effectiveness of ANZUS, which thereafter operated as an alliance between only the two countries. Australia and New Zealand, however, retained military cooperation outside of ANZUS.

In other matters of international policy, the Australian government in August imposed economic sanctions against South Africa. This action followed the August meeting of the Commonwealth Heads of Government, during which Prime Minister Hawke was one of the most outspoken critics of the racial policies of South Africa.

Other Developments. On March 2, in Canberra, Queen Elizabeth II signed the Australia Act 1986, which abolished all remaining constitutional links between Australia and Great Britain except their sharing of the same constitutional monarch. The act had been passed by both the Australian and British parliaments. Although it made little difference to daily life or Australia's practical independence, it carried considerable symbolic significance. Previously, decisions rendered by certain Australian courts could be appealed to the Judicial Committee of the Privy Council in London, and the Australian states' access to the monarch was by way of the British government. The act ended these largely symbolic practices.

The unprecedented case of Justice Lionel K. Murphy, a judge on Australia's High Court (the country's highest judicial body), continued into 1986. Murphy had been convicted in 1985 of perverting the course of justice but had been granted a new trial later that year. The retrial acquitted him of the charge on April 28, 1986.

On May 8, however, the federal government introduced legislation to appoint three parliamentary commissioners—in practice, three retired judges—to consider Murphy's fitness to remain on the High Court. The commission began to investigate but canceled its inquiry when it became clear that Murphy had terminal cancer. He died on October 21. 　　　　　　　　　　　　J. D. B. Miller

See also ASIA (Facts in Brief Table). In WORLD BOOK, see AUSTRALIA.

AUSTRIA conducted three national elections in 1986. The first was a presidential vote held on May 4 after a stormy election campaign. In this election, former United Nations (UN) Secretary-General Kurt Waldheim outpolled all other candidates but failed to gain the majority necessary to win office. As a result, Austrians went to the polls for a runoff on June 8. Waldheim won.

In a parliamentary election held on November 23, the ruling Socialists lost 10 seats, leaving them with 80 of the 183 seats in parliament. The conservative People's Party lost 5 seats for a total of 76. The right wing Freedom Party advanced from 12 to 18 seats, and the environmentalist Greens Party won its first seats in parliament—9.

Waldheim's Election Campaign. On March 4, an article in *The New York Times* accused Waldheim of having joined a Nazi paramilitary organization, the storm troopers, in 1938. The article said also that, during World War II, Waldheim served in Greece as interpreter and ordnance officer in a German Army unit that shipped more than 46,000 Jews to death camps. Waldheim denied that he was ever a member of any Nazi organization and said that, when he was in the army, he was "unaware" of the roundup of Jews in Greece.

UN File Opened. Waldheim also denied that he knew about atrocities that the army unit committed against civilians during the war. On April 9, 1986, the UN gave Austria and Israel secret documents containing information about Waldheim's war record. After examining the documents, Austria's President Rudolph Kirschläger said that there was insufficient evidence of charges that Waldheim knew about the deportation of Jews to death camps. But, Kirschläger added, "knowledge of reprisal measures in warfare against the partisans [guerrillas] has to be taken for granted."

Chancellor Quits. In the June runoff, Waldheim—representing the People's Party—won 53.9 per cent of the vote to 46.1 per cent for his Socialist opponent, Kurt Steyrer. Steyrer's showing prompted Socialist Chancellor Fred Sinowatz to resign on June 9. Finance Minister Franz Vranitzky succeeded Sinowatz.

Coalition Collapses. The coalition government of the Socialists and the Freedom Party collapsed on September 15, after the Freedom Party elected Jörg Haider chairman. Haider had generated controversy in 1985, calling a Nazi war criminal "a soldier who had done his duty." After the Freedom Party elected Haider, Vranitzky said that the party's "liberal element had been shoved into the background." Vranitzky ended the coalition and called the election. At year-end, Vranitzky had not yet formed a coalition government with the People's Party. 　　　　　　　　　　　　Kenneth Brown

See also EUROPE (Facts in Brief Table); WALDHEIM, KURT. In WORLD BOOK, see AUSTRIA.

AUTOMOBILE. The United States automobile industry continued to hold its own in 1986, the fourth consecutive year of prosperity. Most economic conditions in the United States during the year favored automakers. An important change in international currency values weakened Japanese automakers' hold on the U.S. market. In addition, the inflation rate—as well as gasoline prices—stayed low, and gasoline supplies were stable.

Many auto industry executives and private economists felt that any sales decline in 1987 would be mild. They expected that changes in federal tax regulations in 1986 would enhance consumer buying power and that consumer confidence would remain high. Some economists predicted that 1987 car sales would decline less than 10 per cent and that 1988 sales would increase slightly.

U.S. Advantage. In 1986, the U.S. auto industry was the beneficiary of one of the most significant economic changes in its history—a sharp decline in the value of the U.S. dollar against the Japanese yen. In its impact on U.S. automakers, this event rivaled the overwhelming change in consumer preference in the United States to small cars that occurred in the early 1980's. But although this earlier change severely damaged the U.S. auto industry, the weakening of the U.S. dollar worked largely in its favor.

In September 1985, the finance ministers of the five leading industrial nations—France, Great Britain, Japan, West Germany, and the United States—decided to weaken the dollar to reduce the growing U.S. trade deficit. A major cause of this deficit was Japan's overwhelmingly favorable balance of automotive trade. At that time, the exchange rate was 240 yen to U.S. $1. The U.S. dollar was so strong against the Japanese yen that it made Japanese cars much cheaper to produce than U.S.-made cars. As the dollar weakened, the yen rose to 150 to U.S. $1 in 1986, increasing its strength by almost 40 per cent. At that level, the cost difference between U.S. and Japanese cars declined so significantly that Lee A. Iacocca, chairman of Chrysler Corporation, said that U.S. automakers no longer had valid excuses for failing to compete with Japan.

Tough Competition. This competitive market forced Japanese automakers to raise prices on their cars and trucks by 15 to 18 per cent. In spite of these large price increases, the strengthening yen hurt their profits. The Toyota Motor Corporation, for example, predicted that its profits would fall by two-thirds during fiscal 1987, which ends June 30, 1987.

Sales of Japanese cars in the United States leveled off during 1986. Earnings from those sales

Excel cars, the first South Korean car for the U.S. market, are loaded aboard ship for transport to the United States for their February introduction.

An American Motors Corporation salesman tries to entice customers with the ultimate in auto loans—interest-free financing—in September 1986.

were reduced as well, making it more difficult for Japanese automakers to continue their practice of sustaining losses elsewhere in the world while deriving almost all their earnings from the U.S. market. Some analysts predicted that Japanese car sales would continue to decline in 1987.

U.S. Automakers had good sales in 1986. Total car and truck sales, including imports, reached an estimated 15.8 million in 1986, up slightly from 15.7 million in 1985. Sales of domestic cars in 1986 were 8.21 million, compared with 8.20 million in 1985. Domestic truck sales were expected to reach 3.63 million, down from 1985 sales of 3.98 million. Overall, domestic automakers made profits in 1986. The combined earnings of General Motors Corporation (GM), Ford Motor Company, and Chrysler Corporation reached $5.89 billion for the first nine months of 1986.

Even though sales held steady during the year, U.S. automakers worried about a slowly weakening domestic market. On November 6, GM announced that it would close 11 assembly and parts-manufacturing plants in four states, and reduce production at several other plants. Troubled by excess production capacity for more than two years, GM said the shut-downs were necessary because of slower sales.

Financing-Rate War. GM also hoped that production cuts would help avoid the need for mas-

sive sales incentive campaigns, similar to the ones it mounted in 1986. The most notable of these was announced on August 28, when GM offered finance rates of 2.9 per cent on three-year car loans as well as cut-rate financing and cash rebate plans on all 1986 autos and small trucks. Ford and Chrysler were forced to follow suit, and profits suffered. American Motors Corporation, however, made the ultimate offer to potential car buyers. On September 3, the company announced interest-free financing on two-year loans.

New Models. The stars of the 1986 model year were the Ford Taurus and Mercury Sable cars from Ford, which won high praise from critics for styling, quality, and driving characteristics. The public also liked them, and by the end of the year, they were Ford's best-selling models. Public acceptance of two new GM car lines was slower, and by year's end, GM was forced to curtail production of its H-body Buick LeSabre and Oldsmobile Delta 88 models, and the E-body Cadillac Eldorado, Buick Riviera, and Oldsmobile Toronado. Chrysler created a new market segment in the truck business with the introduction of its Dakota mid-sized pickup.

Perhaps the most significant new model in 1986, however, was Hyundai Motor Company's Excel, the first South Korean car offered for sale in the United States. With prices starting around $5,000, the Excel quickly became a hot seller, paving the way for several other South Korean cars, which were scheduled to enter the U.S. market before 1990.

Japanese Venture. Two Japanese companies, Fuji Heavy Industries and Isuzu Motors, announced in December a $500-million joint venture to build a car-assembly plant in Indiana. With that announcement, all of the major Japanese automakers were represented in the United States, either with actual production plants in operation or with plants under construction.

Other News. In May 1986, Toyota Motor Corporation began construction of a new assembly plant in Georgetown, Ky. The new plant will produce approximately 200,000 Toyota Camry cars annually when it is completed in two years, according to Toyota executives.

The leading heavy-duty truck manufacturer in the United States changed its name in 1986. In February, International Harvester Company of Chicago became Navistar International Corporation. The company sold its old name, along with its farm equipment operations, to Tenneco Incorporated in 1985. The Navistar name, which was created by a computer, reflects a more progressive and dynamic image for the manufacturer, company officials said.   James V. Higgins

In WORLD BOOK, see AUTOMOBILE.

AUTOMOBILE RACING. Bobby Rahal and Dale Earnhardt of the United States and Alain Prost of France won major automobile-racing series championships in 1986. Rahal won the Championship Auto Racing Teams (CART) series for Indianapolis-type cars, Earnhardt the National Association for Stock Car Auto Racing's (NASCAR) Winston Cup series for late-model sedans, and Prost the international Formula One Grand Prix series for the World Drivers' Championship.

Indy Cars. The 17-race series ran from April to November. The 33-year-old Rahal of Dublin, Ohio, won six races, led in prize money ($1,488,049), and beat 24-year-old Michael Andretti of Nazareth, Pa., for the points title (179 to 171).

As always, the highlight of the series was the world's richest race, the $4,001,450 Indianapolis 500, on May 31. For laps 195 to 198 of the 200-lap race, a yellow caution flag forced the cars to drive slowly, with no passing. With two laps left, drivers got a green flag, and the 500-mile (800-kilometer) race became a 5-mile (8-kilometer) sprint among Rahal, Kevin Cogan of Redondo Beach, Calif., and Rick Mears of Bakersfield, Calif.

Rahal dived for the inside, got in front of Cogan, and beat him by 1.4 seconds. Mears finished third, four-tenths of a second behind Cogan, in the closest three-car finish in Indianapolis history. Rahal's average speed of 170.722 miles per hour

(mph) or 274.750 kilometers per hour (kph) broke the Indianapolis record.

NASCAR. The Winston Cup series comprised 29 races from February to November. Earnhardt of Kannapolis, N.C., led Darrell Waltrip of Franklin, Tenn., in earnings ($1,768,880 to $1,099,735) and points (4,468 to 4,180). Tim Richmond of Ashland, Ohio, won seven races, Earnhardt five, and Waltrip three. Geoff Bodine of Julian, N.C., in a Chevrolet Monte Carlo, won the richest race of the series, the $1,468,715 Daytona 500, on February 16 in Daytona Beach, Fla.

Formula One. The world championship was decided in 16 races from March to October in Europe, the United States, Canada, Mexico, Brazil, and Australia. Nigel Mansell of Great Britain, who drove a Williams-Honda, could have become the champion by finishing first, second, or third in the final race—the Australian Grand Prix on October 26 in Adelaide. Instead, a tire shredded, and his car went out of control and did not finish. Prost, in a McLaren-TAG-Porsche, won the race and his second consecutive world title.

Mansell won the Canadian Grand Prix on June 15 in Montreal, Que. Ayrton Senna of Brazil, in a Lotus-Renault, captured the Detroit Grand Prix on June 22. In all, Mansell won five races, Prost four, Brazil's Nelson Piquet four, and Senna two.

Other Races. At age 54, Don Garlits of Ocala, Fla., became the first to win the National Hot Rod Association's top-fuel championship for two consecutive years. On March 23, in Gainesville, Fla., he became the first drag racer to top 270 mph (435 kph), reaching 272.56 mph (438.64 kph).

In endurance racing, Jo Gartner, 32, of Austria won the 12 Hours of Sebring, Fla., on March 22. In the world's major endurance race, the 24 Hours of Le Mans from May 31 to June 1 in France, Gartner was killed in a one-car crash. The winning car, a Porsche, was driven alternately by Al Holbert of Warrington, Pa.; Derek Bell of Great Britain; and Hans Stuck of West Germany.

Safety. Race cars became faster and more dangerous. On May 1, in qualifying for NASCAR's Winston 500 in Talladega, Ala., Bill Elliott of Dawsonville, Ga., set a NASCAR one-lap record of 212.229 mph (341.549 kph). In the July 31 qualifying for CART's Michigan 500 in Brooklyn, Mich., Mears raced one lap in 223.401 mph (359.529 kph), a closed-course record for race cars, and he raised his record in November to 233.932 mph (376.477 kph) over the same track.

For 1987, CART ordered smaller and lower rear wings, thus reducing speeds in the turns. The International Auto Sports Federation decided to start phasing out Formula One turbocharged engines in 1987. By 1989, it planned to have only conventional 3.5-liter engines.   Frank Litsky

In WORLD BOOK, see AUTOMOBILE RACING

AVIATION. The big news in aviation in the United States in 1986 was a wave of airline mergers that eliminated most discount carriers and reduced the importance of discount fares to the industry. This prompted a round of fare increases in October.

In February, Texas Air Corporation agreed to acquire Eastern Airlines. The Department of Transportation (DOT) initially rejected the plan, saying it would reduce competition in the Northeast shuttle market, traditionally dominated by Eastern and New York Air, a Texas Air subsidiary. To alleviate the DOT's objections, Texas Air agreed to sell landing rights to Pan American World Airways (PanAm) to run a shuttle.

Also, Texas Air agreed on September 15 to take over financially troubled People Express Incorporated, the pioneering low-fare carrier. People's financial problems had been aggravated by the July bankruptcy of Frontier Airlines, which People Express had acquired in November 1985. Texas Air formally took over Eastern in late November 1986 and People Express a month later. The two acquisitions made Texas Air the largest airline company in the United States.

In February, Trans World Airlines (TWA) announced plans to acquire Ozark Airlines for $250 million, which would permit the two carriers to combine their bases in St. Louis, Mo. In addi-

tion, on July 31, the DOT approved the take-over of Republic Airlines by Northwest Airlines. Delta Air Lines agreed on September 9 to purchase Western Air Lines. Large carriers also continued to buy commuter airlines, which operate smaller planes between large cities and between medium-sized and small airports.

Labor. There were fewer labor disputes in the aviation industry in 1986 than in the previous year, though negotiating problems played a major role in the People Express decision to shut down its Frontier Airlines subsidiary and Eastern's acceptance of Texas Air's offer. People Express had agreed to sell Frontier to United, but the agreement fell apart when United's pilots could not reach an accord on how to handle wage differences between United and Frontier pilots. Also, the failure of Eastern's management to obtain substantial labor-cost concessions from some of its unions played a key role in the decision to accept Texas Air's offer.

Crashes and Air Safety. In April, the Federal Aviation Administration (FAA)—using a new reporting system—reported a record number of incidents in 1985 in which aircraft nearly collided in midair. The FAA said that a total of 777 such incidents were reported, 31.9 per cent more than in 1984. The number of reported near-collisions involving major commercial airlines rose to 35 from 20. But the agency said it was unreasonable to compare the 1985 figures with previous years, because fewer incidents go unreported under the new reporting system.

On March 31, a Mexicana Airlines Boeing 727 airliner crashed in a remote mountainous region of central Mexico, killing all 167 people aboard. The main cause of the crash was later found to be equipment failure. An August 31 midair collision between an Aeroméxico DC-9 and a small private plane killed 82 people and prompted the FAA to announce it will require a collision-avoidance system in commercial jets by 1989. The device, called the Traffic Alert Collision Avoidance System, warns pilots of approaching planes and instructs them to move up or down to avoid a collision.

The FAA and Eastern Airlines were involved in a bitter court fight in 1986 over $9.5 million in civil fines the agency sought for 78,000 alleged violations of aircraft maintenance and safety regulations by Eastern. Eastern refused to pay the fine, claiming that many of the charges involved the failure to keep proper maintenance records rather than actual maintenance problems.

On March 27, Continental Airlines paid a $402,000 fine for violations of FAA safety rules—the fourth largest ever collected by the FAA. The fine arose out of a two-year dispute in which the Air Line Pilots Association alleged that Continental failed to comply with pilot-training rules, and

Nick Hobart, *The Wall Street Journal*, permission, Cartoon Features Syndicate

"Folks, we're ready to begin boarding. We'll start with those passengers who paid more than $99 for the trip."

Crews paint over the Republic Airlines logo in August following Republic's take-over by Northwest Airlines, one of a wave of airline mergers in 1986.

that the FAA had been cooperating with the airline in covering up the violations. The FAA said the violations involved the crew-training program, inadequate record keeping, and faulty maintenance. And on August 22, PanAm agreed to pay $1.95 million for alleged federal safety violations, the largest fine paid in aviation history.

Several studies during the year indicated that there may be safety problems ahead for the airline industry. The U.S. General Accounting Office (GAO), a congressional investigative arm, reported in March that the nation's 12,500 air-traffic controllers may be "stretched too thin," and that a reduction in flights similar to the cutback imposed during the 1981 air-traffic controllers' strike may be needed. And in May, the GAO told Congress that the FAA "cannot say with assurance that airlines are complying with government safety regulations." Although GAO officials said they were not saying that flying was unsafe, and though they conceded that the FAA had been taking some corrective actions, they charged that serious short-term problems remained.

On April 29, the National Transportation Safety Board echoed concern about near-collisions and safety problems on airport runways. The board made recommendations to the FAA for reducing these hazards, particularly stressing improved training for flight controllers.

International Aviation Agreements. The first U.S. commercial flight to the Soviet Union since 1978 arrived in Moscow on April 29, 1986. PanAm quit flying to Moscow in 1978 because of financial losses. But a new aviation agreement between the United States and Moscow was expected to ensure a profitable operation.

An emergency air-control link, aimed at preventing another aviation disaster similar to the shooting down of a Korean Air Lines plane by the Soviet Union in 1983, began operating in August 1986. The system enables the Soviet Union to get in touch with the United States if an airliner strays off a North Pacific route toward Soviet territory.

Aircraft Sales. In August, the Boeing Company received a $2.3-billion order from British Airways for 16 of its new 747-400 jumbo jetliners. The 747-400 model carries 418 passengers and has a greater range—8,000 miles (13,000 kilometers) without refueling—than earlier models. British Airways also had an option to buy 12 more planes—bringing the possible total value of the contract to $4.1 billion, which would be the largest order for commercial aircraft in history. In March, Boeing had received an order for the 747-400 model from Singapore Airlines that could total as much as $3.3 billion.   David M. Cawthorne

See also TRANSPORTATION. In WORLD BOOK, see AVIATION.

AWARDS AND PRIZES presented in 1986 included:

Arts Awards

ACADEMY OF MOTION PICTURE ARTS AND SCIENCES. "Oscar" Awards: Best Picture, *Out of Africa.* **Best Actor,** William Hurt, *Kiss of the Spider Woman.* **Best Actress,** Geraldine Page, *The Trip to Bountiful.* **Best Supporting Actor,** Don Ameche, *Cocoon.* **Best Supporting Actress,** Anjelica Huston, *Prizzi's Honor.* **Best Director,** Sydney Pollack, *Out of Africa.* **Best Original Screenplay,** William Kelley, Pamela Wallace, and Earl W. Wallace, *Witness.* **Best Screenplay Adaptation,** Kurt Luedtke, *Out of Africa.* **Best Cinematography,** David Watkin, *Out of Africa.* **Best Original Score,** John Barry, *Out of Africa.* **Best Original Song,** Lionel Richie, "Say You, Say Me." **Best Foreign-Language Film,** *The Official Story* (Argentina). See HURT, WILLIAM; PAGE, GERALDINE.

AMERICAN ACADEMY AND INSTITUTE OF ARTS AND LETTERS. Gold Medal in Drama, American playwright Sidney Kingsley. **Gold Medal in Graphic Art,** American painter and sculptor Jasper Johns.

AMERICAN DANCE FESTIVAL. Samuel H. Scripps-American Dance Festival Award, Katherine Dunham, American dancer and choreographer.

AMERICAN MUSIC AWARDS. Pop/Rock Awards: Female Vocalist, Tina Turner. **Male Vocalist,** Bruce Springsteen. **Duo or Group,** Chicago. **Single,** "The Power of Love," Huey Lewis and the News. **Album,** *Born in the U.S.A.,* Bruce Springsteen. **Female Video Artist,** Pat Benatar. **Male Video Artist,** Bruce Springsteen. **Video Duo or Group,** Wham! **Video Single,** "The Power of Love," Huey Lewis and the News.

Soul Music/Rhythm and Blues Awards: Female Vocalist, Aretha Franklin. **Male Vocalist,** Stevie Wonder. **Duo or Group,** Kool & the Gang. **Single,** "You Give Good Love," Whitney Houston. **Album,** *Emergency,* Kool & the Gang. **Female Video Artist,** Aretha Franklin. **Male Video Artist,** Stevie Wonder. **Video Duo or Group,** The Pointer Sisters. **Video Single,** "Saving All My Love for You," Whitney Houston.

Country Music Awards: Female Vocalist, Crystal Gayle. **Male Vocalist,** Willie Nelson. **Duo or Group,** Alabama. **Single,** "Forgiving You Is Easy," Willie Nelson. **Album,** *40 Hour Week,* Alabama. **Female Video Artist,** Crystal Gayle. **Male Video Artist,** Hank Williams, Jr. **Video Duo or Group,** Highwayman (Willie Nelson, Johnny Cash, Kris Kristofferson, and Waylon Jennings). **Video Single,** "Highwayman," Willie Nelson, Johnny Cash, Kris Kristofferson, and Waylon Jennings.

CANNES INTERNATIONAL FILM FESTIVAL. Golden Palm Grand Prize, *The Mission* (Great Britain). **Best Actor,** Michel Blanc, *Tenue de Soirée* (France) and Bob Hoskins, *Mona Lisa* (Great Britain). **Best Actress,** Barbara Sukowa, *Rosa Luxemburg* (West Germany) and Fernanda Torres, *Speak to Me of Love* (Brazil). **Best Director,** Martin Scorsese, *After Hours* (United States). **Special Jury Prize,** *The Sacrifice* (Sweden). **Jury Prize,** *Thérèse* (France). **Special Jury Prize,** *The Sacrifice* (Sweden).

HYATT FOUNDATION. Pritzker Architecture Prize, Gottfried Böhm, West Germany.

JOHN F. KENNEDY CENTER FOR THE PERFORMING ARTS. Honors, actress Lucille Ball; singer Ray Charles; Canadian-born actor Hume Cronyn; violinist Yehudi Menuhin; British-born actress Jessica Tandy; British-born choreographer Antony Tudor.

MACDOWELL COLONY. Edward MacDowell Medal, photographer Lee Friedlander.

NATIONAL ACADEMY OF RECORDING ARTS AND SCIENCES. Grammy Awards: Record of the Year, "We Are the World," USA for Africa. **Album of the Year,** *No Jacket Required,* Phil Collins. **Song of the Year,** "We Are the World," Michael Jackson and Lionel Richie, songwriters. **Best New Artist,** Sade. **Music Video, Short Form,** "We Are the World," USA for Africa. **Music Video Long Form,** *The Heart of Rock 'n' Roll,* Huey Lewis and the News.

Pop Awards: Pop Vocal Performance, Female, "Saving All My Love for You," Whitney Houston. **Pop Vocal Performance, Male,** *No Jacket Required,* Phil Collins. **Pop Vocal Performance by a Duo or Group,** "We Are the World," USA for Africa. **Pop Instrumental Performance,** "Miami Vice Theme," Jan Hammer.

Rock Awards: Rock Vocal Performance, Female, "One of the Living," Tina Turner. **Rock Vocal Performance, Male,** "The Boys of Summer," Don Henley. **Rock Vocal Performance by a Duo or Group,** "Money for Nothing," Dire Straits. **Rock Instrumental Performance,** "Escape," Jeff Beck.

Rhythm and Blues Awards: Rhythm and Blues Vocal Performance, Female, "Freeway of Love," Aretha Franklin. **Rhythm and Blues Vocal Performance, Male,** *In Square Circle,* Stevie Wonder. **Rhythm and Blues Vocal Performance by a Duo or Group,** "Nightshift," The Commodores. **Rhythm and Blues Instrumental Performance,** "Musician," Ernie Watts. **Rhythm and Blues Song,** "Freeway of Love," Narada Michael Walden and Jeffrey Cohen, songwriters.

Country Awards: Country Vocal Performance, Female, "I Don't Know Why You Don't Want Me," Rosanne Cash. **Country Vocal Performance, Male,** "Lost in the Fifties Tonight (In the Still of the Night)," Ronnie Milsap. **Country Vocal Performance by a Duo or Group,** *Why Not Me,* The Judds. **Country Instrumental Performance,** "Cosmic Square Dance," Chet Atkins and Mark Knopfler. **Country Song,** "Highwayman," Jimmy L. Webb, songwriter.

Jazz Awards: Jazz Fusion Performance, Vocal or Instrumental, *Straight to the Heart,* David Sanborn. **Jazz Vocal Performance, Female,** *Cleo at Carnegie (The 10th Anniversary Concert),* Cleo Laine. **Jazz Vocal Performance, Male,** "Another Night in Tunisia," Jon Hendricks and Bobby McFerrin. **Jazz Vocal Performance by a Duo or Group,** *Vocalese,* Manhattan Transfer. **Jazz Instrumental Performance, Solo,** *Black Codes (from the Underground),* Wynton Marsalis. **Jazz Instrumental Performance, Group,** *Black Codes (from the Underground),* Wynton Marsalis Group. **Jazz Instrumental Performance, Big Band,** *The Cotton Club,* John Barry and Bob Wilber.

Classical Awards: Classical Album, *Berlioz: Requiem,* Robert Shaw, conductor. **Classical Orchestra Recording,** *Fauré: Pelléas et Melisande,* Robert Shaw, conductor. **Opera Recording,** *Schönberg: Moses und Aron,* Sir Georg Solti, conductor. **Choral Performance,** *Berlioz: Requiem,* Robert Shaw, conductor.

NATIONAL ACADEMY OF TELEVISION ARTS AND SCIENCES. Emmy Awards: Comedy Series, "The Golden Girls." **Lead Actor in a Comedy Series,** Michael J. Fox, "Family Ties." **Lead Actress in a Comedy Series,** Betty White, "The Golden Girls." **Supporting Actor in a Comedy Series,** John Larroquette, "Night Court." **Supporting Actress in a Comedy Series,** Rhea Perlman, "Cheers." **Drama Series,** "Cagney & Lacey." **Lead Actor in a Drama Series,** William Daniels, "St. Elsewhere." **Lead Actress in a Drama Series,** Sharon Gless, "Cagney & Lacey." **Supporting Actor in a Drama Series,** John Karlen, "Cagney & Lacey." **Supporting Actress in a Drama Series,** Bonnie Bartlett, "St. Elsewhere." **Drama or Comedy Special,** *Love Is Never Silent.* **Miniseries,** "Peter the Great." **Variety, Music, or Comedy Program,** *The Kennedy Center Honors: A Celebration of the Performing Arts.* **Lead Actor in a Miniseries or Special,** Dustin Hoffman, *Death of a Salesman.* **Lead Actress in a Miniseries or Special,** Marlo Thomas, *Nobody's Child.* **Supporting Actor in a Miniseries or Special,** John Malkovich, *Death of a Salesman.* **Supporting Actress in a Miniseries or Special,** Colleen Dewhurst, *Between Two Women.*

Whoopi Goldberg shoulders a welcome burden, the Grammy Award for best comedy recording that she won for her album *Whoopi Goldberg* in February.

NATIONAL SOCIETY OF FILM CRITICS AWARDS. Best Film, *Blue Velvet.* **Best Actor,** Bob Hoskins, *Mona Lisa.* **Best Actress,** Chloe Webb, *Sid & Nancy.* **Best Supporting Actor,** Dennis Hopper, *Blue Velvet.* **Best Supporting Actress,** Dianne Wiest, *Hannah and Her Sisters.* **Best Director,** David Lynch, *Blue Velvet.* **Best Screenplay,** Hanif Kureishi, *My Beautiful Laundrette.*

NEW YORK DRAMA CRITICS CIRCLE AWARDS. Best New Play, *A Lie of the Mind,* Sam Shepard. **Best New Foreign Play,** *Benefactors,* Michael Frayn. **Special Citation,** *The Search for Signs of Intelligent Life in the Universe,* Lily Tomlin and Jane Wagner.

NEW YORK FILM CRITICS CIRCLE AWARDS. Best Film, *Hannah and Her Sisters.* **Best Actor,** Bob Hoskins, *Mona Lisa.* **Best Actress,** Sissy Spacek, *Crimes of the Heart.* **Best Supporting Actor,** Daniel Day Lewis, *A Room with a View.* **Best Supporting Actress,** Dianne Wiest, *Hannah and Her Sisters.* **Best Director,** Woody Allen, *Hannah and Her Sisters.* **Best Screenplay,** Hanif Kureishi, *My Beautiful Laundrette.* **Best Cinematography,** Tony Pierce-Roberts, *A Room with a View.* **Best Foreign-Language Film,** *The Decline of the American Empire* (Canada).

ANTOINETTE PERRY (TONY) AWARDS. Drama Awards: Best Play, *I'm Not Rappaport.* **Leading Actor,** Judd Hirsch, *I'm Not Rappaport.* **Leading Actress,** Lily Tomlin, *The Search for Signs of Intelligent Life in the Universe.* **Featured Actor,** John Mahoney, *The House of Blue Leaves.* **Featured Actress,** Swoosie Kurtz, *The House of Blue Leaves.* **Direction,** Jerry Zaks, *The House of Blue Leaves.*

Musical Awards: Best Musical, *The Mystery of Edwin Drood.* **Leading Actor,** George Rose, *The Mystery of Edwin Drood.* **Leading Actress,** Bernadette Peters, *Song & Dance.* **Featured Actor,** Michael Rupert, *Sweet Charity.* **Featured Actress,** Bebe Neuwirth, *Sweet Charity.* **Direction,** Wilford Leach, *The Mystery of Edwin Drood.* **Book for a Musical,** Rupert Holmes, *The Mystery of Edwin Drood.* **Score for a Mu-** sical, Rupert Holmes, *The Mystery of Edwin Drood.* **Choreography,** Bob Fosse, *Big Deal.*

Best Reproduction of a Play or Musical, *Sweet Charity.*

UNITED STATES GOVERNMENT. National Medal of Arts, opera singer Marian Anderson; film director Frank Capra; composer Aaron Copland; painter Willem de Kooning; Dominique de Menil, Houston art collector; choreographer Agnes de Mille; Exxon Corporation, which supports the "Great Performances" television series; Seymour H. Knox, founder of the Albright Knox Gallery, Buffalo, N.Y.; actress Eva Le Gallienne; folk-music scholar Alan Lomax; social critic Lewis Mumford; writer Eudora Welty.

Journalism Awards

AMERICAN SOCIETY OF MAGAZINE EDITORS. National Magazine Awards. See MAGAZINE.

LONG ISLAND UNIVERSITY. George Polk Memorial Awards: National Reporting, Diana Griego and Louis Kilzer, *The Denver Post,* for a series showing that statistics about missing children were exaggerated. **Metropolitan Reporting,** Jimmy Breslin, New York City *Daily News,* for columns about alleged police torture. **Local Reporting,** Stan Jones, Fairbanks, Alaska, *Daily News-Miner,* for articles on questionable leasing practices by the state of Alaska. **Foreign Reporting,** Alan Cowell, *The New York Times,* for reports from South Africa. **International Reporting,** Pete Carey, Katherine Ellison, and Lewis M. Simons, *The* (San Jose) *Mercury News,* for articles documenting the transfer of wealth from the Philippines by then-President Ferdinand E. Marcos. **Political Reporting,** Frank Greve, Knight-Ridder Newspapers, for a report tracing the development of President Ronald Reagan's Strategic Defense Initiative, a proposed space-based missile defense system commonly known as "Star Wars." **Business Reporting,** The Spotlight/Business team of *The*

Boston Globe, for articles linking the Bank of Boston to money laundering for the Mafia. **Medical Reporting,** Lawrence K. Altman, *The New York Times,* for reports from Africa on acquired immune deficiency syndrome (AIDS). **Criticism,** Arthur C. Danto, *The Nation,* for art criticism. **Network Television Reporting,** Ted Koppel and Richard N. Kaplan, ABC News "Nightline," for a series of broadcasts from South Africa. **Local Television Reporting,** Vic Lee, Craig Franklin, and Brian McTigue, KRON-TV, San Francisco, for the series "Clean Rooms, Dirty Secrets." **Radio Reporting,** Peter Laufer, NBC Radio News, for "Nightmare Abroad." **Career Award,** George Tames, photographer, *The New York Times.*

THE SOCIETY OF PROFESSIONAL JOURNALISTS, SIGMA DELTA CHI. Sigma Delta Chi Distinguished Service Awards, Newspaper Awards: **General Reporting, Circulation More than 100,000,** Jim Stewart, Cox Newspapers, for a series about an inept heart surgeon at a naval hospital; **General Reporting, Circulation Less than 100,000,** Art Geiselman, *Albuquerque* (N. Mex.) *Journal,* for a series about irregularities in the awarding of state disaster-relief contracts; **Editorial Writing,** Henry B. Bryan, *Dallas Times Herald,* for editorials about hazards in construction work and about mentally retarded inmates of state prisons; **Washington Correspondence,** James O'Shea and Nicholas M. Horrock, *Chicago Tribune,* for articles about fraud and waste in the Pentagon; **Foreign Correspondence,** Robert J. Rosenthal, *The Philadelphia Inquirer,* for reports from South Africa; **News Photography,** Jay Dickman, *Dallas Times Herald,* for photographs of the November 1985 volcanic eruption in Colombia; **Editorial Cartooning,** Doug Marlette, *The Charlotte* (N.C.) *Observer,* for a cartoon critical of the Moral Majority's stance on sex education, birth control, and abortion; **Public Service**

Academy Awards in 1986 went to actor William Hurt for *Kiss of the Spider Woman,* and actress Geraldine Page for *The Trip to Bountiful.*

in Newspaper Journalism, Circulation More than 100,000, *Detroit Free Press* for articles about the early release of convicts from Michigan prisons to relieve overcrowding; **Public Service in Newspaper Journalism, Circulation Less than 100,000,** The (Tucson) *Arizona Daily Star* for a series about contaminated water in Tucson.

Magazine Awards: Magazine Reporting, Mark Singer, *The New Yorker,* for a series examining the failure of the Penn Square Bank in Oklahoma City, Okla.; **Public Service in Magazine Journalism,** *Tropic,* the Sunday magazine of *The Miami* (Fla.) *Herald,* for an article about problems in Miami's juvenile court system.

Radio Awards: Radio Reporting, Tony Hanson, Richard Maloney, and Larry Litwin, KYW-AM, Philadelphia, for reports about the police siege and bombing of the MOVE compound in Philadelphia in May 1985; **Public Service in Radio Journalism,** KGO-AM, San Francisco, for a series about problems in nursing homes; **Editorializing on Radio,** Nicholas DeLuca and Joan Margalith, KCBS-AM, San Francisco, for editorials criticizing area hospitals for refusing to treat a stabbing victim who was unemployed and uninsured.

Television Awards: Television Reporting, WFAA-TV, Dallas, for coverage of an airplane crash near Dallas in August 1985; **Public Service in Television Journalism, Stations in the Top 50 Markets,** KPRC-TV, Houston, for a documentary about problems in a Houston nursing home; **Public Service in Television Journalism, Stations in All Other Markets,** KTUL-TV, Tulsa, Okla., for a series about misuse of funds by a charitable foundation; **Editorializing on Television,** Phil Johnson, WWL-TV, New Orleans, for comments on a point-shaving scandal involving a Tulane University basketball team.

Research About Journalism: Leonard W. Levy, *Emergence of a Free Press.*

UNIVERSITY OF GEORGIA. George Foster Peabody Broadcasting Awards, WHAS Radio, Louisville, Ky., for a documentary about the homeless; *Liberation Remembered,* an independently produced program marking the 40th anniversary of the freeing of prisoners from Nazi concentration camps; CBS News for a program about German composer Johann Sebastian Bach; *Breakdown and Back,* an independently produced documentary about mental illness; WGBH Radio, Boston, for overall programming; WCCO-TV, Minneapolis, Minn., for exposing abuses in the home health care industry in Minnesota; "The MacNeil/Lehrer NewsHour" for a program about racial segregation in South Africa; National Broadcasting Company (NBC) News for programs marking the 10th anniversary of the United States withdrawal from Vietnam; CBS News for *Whose America Is It?,* a report about the newest wave of immigrants to the United States; CBS Entertainment and Dave Bell Productions for *Do You Remember Love?,* a drama about Alzheimer's disease; WBZ-TV, Boston, for *Tender Places,* a drama about divorce as seen through the eyes of a child; NBC Television for *An Early Frost,* a drama about AIDS; KGO-TV, San Francisco, for *The American West: Steinbeck Country;* Spinning Reels and Home Box Office for "Braingames," an animated series for children; WSMV-TV, Nashville, Tenn., for a program examining the integrity and moral standards of a U.S. congressman; *The Final Chapter?,* a documentary about nuclear destruction; "Frontline" for its four-part series about the crisis in Central America; The Harvey Milk Project, Incorporated, and WNET/13 for *The Times of Harvey Milk,* a documentary about a gay-rights leader; WBBM-TV, Chicago, for *Armed and Dangerous,* an investigation of security guards in the Chicago area; KDKA-TV, Pittsburgh, Pa., for a program about organ transplants; KDTV-TV, San Francisco, for its reports of the earthquakes in Mexico City in September 1985; Columbia University Graduate School of Journalism for its seminars on media and society; Central Independent Television and WETA-TV, Washington, D.C., for a program about the emotional and sexual lives of the disabled; Lincoln Center for the Performing Arts, New York City, for "Live from Lincoln Center"; Bob Geldof and Live Aid for helping relieve hunger throughout the world; Lawrence Fraiberg for his contributions to broadcasting; Johnny Carson for "The Tonight Show Starring Johnny Carson."

Literature Awards

ACADEMY OF AMERICAN POETS. Lamont Poetry Selection, *The Minute Hand,* Jane Shore. **Harold Morton Landon Award for Translation,** *The Storm and Other Things* by Eugenio Montale, translated by William Arrowsmith. **Walt Whitman Award,** *Fragments from the Fire,* Chris Llewellyn.

AMERICAN LIBRARY ASSOCIATION. Newbery Medal, *Sarah, Plain and Tall,* Patricia MacLachlan. **Caldecott Medal,** *The Polar Express,* Chris Van Allsburg.

ASSOCIATION OF AMERICAN PUBLISHERS. American Book Awards: Fiction, *World's Fair,* E. L. Doctorow. **Nonfiction,** *Arctic Dreams,* Barry Lopez.

CANADA COUNCIL. Governor General's Literary Awards, English-Language: Fiction, *The Handmaid's Tale,* Margaret Atwood. **Poetry,** *Waiting for Saskatchewan,* Fred Wah. **Drama,** *Criminals in Love,* George F. Walker. **Nonfiction,** *The Regenerators: Social Criticism in Late Victorian English Canada,* Ramsay Cook.

French-Language: Fiction, *Lucie ou un midi en novembre,* Fernand Ouellette. **Poetry,** *Action Writing,* André Roy. **Drama,** *Duo pour voix obstinées,* Maryse Pelletier. **Nonfiction,** *La littérature contre elle-même,* François Ricard.

CANADIAN LIBRARY ASSOCIATION. Book of the Year for Children Award, *Julie,* Cora Taylor. **Amelia Frances Howard-Gibbon Illustrator's Award,** *Zoom Away,* Ken Nutt.

COLUMBIA UNIVERSITY. Bancroft Prizes in American History, *Crabgrass Frontier: The Suburbanization of the United States,* Kenneth T. Jackson; *Labor of Love, Labor of Sorrow: Black Women, Work, and the Family from Slavery to the Present,* Jacqueline Jones.

INGERSOLL FOUNDATION. Ingersoll Prizes: T. S. Eliot Award for Creative Writing, V. S. Naipaul, Trinidad-born novelist. **Richard M. Weaver Award for Scholarly Letters,** Andrew Lytle, former editor of the *Sewanee Review.*

NATIONAL BOOK CRITICS CIRCLE. National Book Critics Circle Awards, Fiction, *The Accidental Tourist,* Anne Tyler. **General Nonfiction,** *Common Ground: A Turbulent Decade in the Lives of Three American Families,* J. Anthony Lukas. **Biography/Autobiography,** *Henry James: A Life,* Leon Edel. **Poetry,** *The Triumph of Achilles,* Louise Gluck. **Criticism,** *Habitations of the Word,* William H. Gass.

PEN AMERICAN CENTER. Faulkner Award, *The Old Forest and Other Stories,* Peter Taylor.

RITZ PARIS HEMINGWAY AWARD. *The Lover,* Marguérite Duras.

UNIVERSITY OF OKLAHOMA. Neustadt International Prize for Literature, Swiss author Max Frisch.

Nobel Prizes. See NOBEL PRIZES.

Public Service Awards

AMERICAN INSTITUTE FOR PUBLIC SERVICE. Thomas Jefferson Awards, Ruby Ferrell Callaway, cofounder of an Atlanta, Ga., organization for alcohol and drug education; Therese Dozier, Columbia, S.C., high-school teacher; Robert Hughes, founder of the Coalition for the Homeless; Eugene Lang, chief executive officer of REFAC Technology Development Corporation, for his gifts to colleges and scholarship funds; H. Ross Perot, chairman, Electronic Data Systems, for his campaigns to fight drug abuse and improve education in Texas; Fannie Royston, Pittsburgh, Pa., for her aid to impoverished people in that city; U.S. Secretary of State George P. Shultz; Philip Viall, New Bedford, Mass., for providing electronic communications equipment to the disabled; Sonya and Tanya Witt, West Palm Beach, Fla., high school students who collected clothing, medicine, and other aid for impoverished areas in Latin America.

FOUR FREEDOMS FOUNDATION. Four Freedoms Medal, Sandro Pertini, former president of Italy, for his "lifelong struggle against totalitarianism." **Freedom of Speech Medal,** *El País,* Madrid daily newspaper, for sustaining democracy in Spain. **Freedom of Worship Medal,** Bernard Cardinal Alfrink, former head of the Roman Catholic Church in the Netherlands. **Freedom from Want Medal,** F. Bradford Morse, director of the United Nations Development Program. **Freedom from Fear Medal,** Prime Minister Olof Palme of Sweden (posthumous), in honor of his work for disarmament.

MARTIN LUTHER KING, JR., CENTER FOR NONVIOLENT SOCIAL CHANGE. Martin Luther King, Jr., Peace Prize, Desmond M. Tutu, South African civil rights leader and Anglican bishop.

NATIONAL ASSOCIATION FOR THE ADVANCEMENT OF COLORED PEOPLE (NAACP). Spingarn Medal, Benjamin L. Hooks, executive director of the NAACP.

TEMPLETON FOUNDATION. Templeton Prize for Progress in Religion, James I. McCord, founder of the Center for Theological Inquiry, Princeton, N.J.

UNITED STATES GOVERNMENT. Medal of Liberty, Irving Berlin, Russian-born songwriter; Franklin R. Chang-Diaz, Costa Rican-born astronaut; Kenneth B. Clark, Jamaican-born psychologist; Hannah Holborn Gray, German-born president of the University of Chicago; Bob Hope, British-born entertainer; Henry A. Kissinger, German-born former secretary of state; I. M. Pei, Chinese-born architect; Itzhak Perlman, Israeli-born violinist; James B. Reston, Scottish-born journalist; Albert B. Sabin, Polish-born developer of oral polio vaccine; An Wang, Chinese-born computer executive; Elie Wiesel, Romanian-born author.

Presidential Medal of Freedom, Walter H. Annenberg, former U.S. ambassador to Great Britain; Earl H. "Red" Blaik, former football coach; Senator Barry Goldwater (R., Ariz.); actress Helen Hayes; Russian-born pianist Vladimir Horowitz; General Matthew B. Ridgway, former U.S. Army chief of staff; journalist Vermont Royster; Albert B. Sabin, Polish-born developer of oral polio vaccine.

Pulitzer Prizes

JOURNALISM. Public Service, *The Denver Post* for a series showing that statistics about missing children were exaggerated. **General News Reporting,** Edna Buchanan, *The Miami* (Fla.) *Herald,* for police reporting. **Investigative News Reporting,** Jeffrey A. Marx and Michael M. York, *The Lexington* (Ky.) *Herald-Leader,* for articles revealing payoffs to University of Kentucky basketball players. **Explanatory Journalism,** *The New York Times* for a series on President Reagan's proposed space-based missile defense system, commonly known as "Star Wars." **Specialized Reporting,** Andrew Schneider and Mary Pat Flaherty, Pittsburgh, Pa., *Press,* for articles about the scientific and ethical questions involved in organ transplants. **National Reporting,** Craig Flournoy and George Rodrigue, *The Dallas Morning News,* for their investigation of racial discrimination in subsidized housing; and Arthur Howe, *The Philadelphia Inquirer,* for reporting problems in the processing of tax returns by the Internal Revenue Service. **International Reporting,** Lewis M. Simons, Pete Carey, and Katherine Ellison, *The* (San Jose) *Mercury News,* for articles documenting large-scale transfer of wealth out of the Philippines by then-President Ferdinand E. Marcos.

British-born comedian Bob Hope becomes one of 12 naturalized Americans to receive the Medal of Liberty during Liberty Weekend in New York City in July.

Feature Writing, John Camp, *St. Paul* (Minn.) *Pioneer Press & Dispatch,* for a series about a farm family struggling to maintain their way of life. **Commentary,** Jimmy Breslin, New York City *Daily News,* for his columns. **Criticism,** Donal Henahan, *The New York Times,* for music criticism. **Editorial Writing,** Jack Fuller, *Chicago Tribune,* for editorials on constitutional issues. **Editorial Cartooning,** Jules Feiffer, *The Village Voice.* **Spot News Photography,** Michel duCille and Carol Guzy, *The Miami Herald,* for photographs of the November 1985 volcanic eruption in Colombia. **Feature Photography,** Tom Gralish, *The Philadelphia Inquirer,* for photographs of homeless people.

LETTERS. **Biography,** *Louise Bogan: A Portrait,* Elizabeth Frank. **Fiction,** *Lonesome Dove,* Larry McMurtry. **General Nonfiction,** *Move Your Shadow: South Africa, Black and White.* Joseph Lelyveld; and *Common Ground: A Turbulent Decade in the Lives of Three American Families,* J. Anthony Lukas. **History,** . . . *the Heavens and the Earth: A Political History of the Space Age,* Walter A. McDougall. **Poetry,** *The Flying Change,* Henry Taylor.

MUSIC. **Music Award,** Wind Quintet No. 4, George Perle.

Science and Technology Awards

COLUMBIA UNIVERSITY. Louisa Gross Horwitz Prize, Erwin Neher and Bert Sakmann, Max Planck Institute for Biophysical Chemistry, Göttingen, West Germany.

ALBERT AND MARY LASKER FOUNDATION. Albert Lasker Basic Medical Research Award, Stanley Cohen, Vanderbilt University School of Medicine; Rita Levi-Montalcini, Institute of Cell Biology, Rome. **Albert Lasker Clinical Medical Research Award,** Myron Essex, Harvard School of Public Health; Robert C. Gallo, National Cancer Institute, Bethesda, Md.; Luc Montagnier, Pasteur Institute, Paris. **Public Service Award,** Ma Haide, Ministry of Public Health, Beijing (Peking), China.

ROYAL SOCIETY OF CANADA. Bancroft Award, Derek York, University of Toronto. **Thomas W. Eadie Medal,** W. H. Gauvin, Noranda Mines Limited. **Flavelle Medal,** G. H. N. Towers, University of British Columbia. **Jason A. Hannah Medal,** Wilfred G. Bigelow, University of Toronto. **McLaughlin Medal,** André Barbeau, University of Montreal. **Rutherford Medal in Chemistry,** David Griller, National Research Council. **Rutherford Medal in Physics,** W. J. L. Buyers, Atomic Energy of Canada Limited. **Tyrrell Medal,** John W. Holmes, Canadian Institute of International Relations.

UNITED STATES GOVERNMENT. National Medal of Science, Solomon J. Buchsbaum, Bell Laboratories; Stanley Cohen, Vanderbilt University School of Medicine; Horace R. Crane, University of Michigan; Herman Feshbach, Massachusetts Institute of Technology; Harry B. Gray, California Institute of Technology; Donald A. Henderson, Johns Hopkins University; Robert Hofstadter, Stanford University; Peter D. Lax, New York University; Yuan Tseh Lee, University of California at Berkeley; Hans W. Liepmann, California Institute of Technology; Tung Yen Lin, University of California at Berkeley; Carl S. Marvel, University of Arizona; Vernon B. Mountcastle, Johns Hopkins University; Bernard M. Oliver, Hewlett-Packard Company; George E. Palade, Yale University; Herbert A. Simon, Carnegie-Mellon University; Joan Argetsinger Steitz, Yale University; Frank H. Westheimer, Harvard University; Chen Ning Yang, State University of New York at Stony Brook; Antoni Zygmund, University of Chicago.

UNIVERSITY OF SOUTHERN CALIFORNIA. John and Alice Tyler Ecology-Energy Prize, Swiss chemist Werner Stumm; Swiss-born Canadian ecologist Richard A. Vollenweider.

Sara Dreyfuss

AZCONA DEL HOYO, JOSÉ (1927-   ), became president of Honduras on Jan. 27, 1986, succeeding Roberto Suazo Córdova. The peaceful transfer of power marked the first time in more than 50 years that one elected civilian president succeeded another in that country, which has been torn by frequent military coups. See HONDURAS.

Azcona's inauguration came one day after his 59th birthday. He was born on Jan. 26, 1927, in La Ceiba, a coastal town where his Spanish immigrant parents had an import business. Azcona was educated at the National Autonomous University of Honduras in Tegucigalpa, the capital, obtaining a civil engineering degree.

Azcona continued his studies in Mexico and the United States, where he developed an interest in public housing and urban planning. From 1973 to 1982, he was general manager of the Honduran Federation of Housing Cooperatives Limited.

Azcona became active in politics in the early 1960's. In 1977, he became a leader in the Liberal Party. In 1982, he was elected a representative to the National Assembly.

Azcona is married to Miriam Bocock Selva, and the couple have a daughter and two sons. Azcona enjoys relaxing with books, movies, and table tennis.   Rod Such

BAHAMAS. See LATIN AMERICA.

BAHRAIN. See MIDDLE EAST.

BALAGUER, JOAQUÍN (1907-   ), president of the Dominican Republic from 1960 to 1962 and from 1966 to 1978, was again elected to the presidency of that Caribbean nation in May 1986. Balaguer, a remarkably durable politician in a politically volatile country, narrowly defeated Jacobo Majluta Azar, the president of the Senate, and Juan Bosch, like Balaguer a former president. Balaguer began his term on Aug. 16, 1986.

Balaguer was born on Sept. 1, 1907, in Santiago de Los Caballeros. In addition to being a politician, Balaguer is a poet, lawyer, economist, historian, and author of many books. He earned a law degree from the University of Santo Domingo in 1929, and—while a diplomat in Paris—a degree of doctor of law at the Sorbonne.

Balaguer rose in the government during the 30-year dictatorship of General Rafael Leonidas Trujillo Molina. After Trujillo was assassinated in 1961, a period of great political upheaval ensued. Balaguer emerged as a dominant figure in Dominican politics.

Balaguer's age and state of health were an issue during the 1986 election. Afflicted with glaucoma for more than 20 years, he is now blind. Aides said that the 79-year-old Balaguer would form a council of outstanding Dominicans to help him govern the country.   Joan Stephenson

BALLET. See DANCING.

BANGLADESH. Hussain Muhammed Ershad was elected president of Bangladesh on Oct. 15, 1986. He had headed the nation as martial law administrator since 1982 and self-proclaimed president since 1983. The official election results gave him 21.8 million votes. Ershad's nearest competitor, a religious leader, received only 1.5 million votes. The major opposition parties boycotted the election and complained of vote fraud.

Ershad was sworn in on Oct. 23, 1986, as Bangladesh's third elected president. On November 10, he ended martial law and restored the Constitution, which had been suspended since 1982. On Dec. 1, 1986, he appointed A. K. M. Nurul Islam as vice president.

Ershad had retired from the army on August 31, turning over his power base as chief of army staff to Lieutenant General M. Atiqur Rahman. In September, Ershad formally joined the Jatiya Party, which made him its presidential candidate. Despite the election boycotts, 11 other candidates ran against Ershad.

Parliamentary Elections were held on May 7. Opponents of Ershad's army-based government charged that elections held under martial law would be rigged. Ershad's Jatiya Party won 153 of the 300 parliamentary seats contested. The opposition Awami League won 76 seats.

Voting was marred by widespread intimidation and vote fraud. Some 20 people were killed in election violence, and ballot boxes were stolen.

Ershad swore in Mizanur Rahman Choudhury as prime minister on July 9, and the next day the first parliamentary session in four years opened. There were protests, however, and more than 30 people were injured during demonstrations. More violence surrounded special elections in August, which progovernment candidates won to fill eight vacancies in parliament.

Regional Violence. In southeastern Bangladesh, hundreds of people were killed during 1986 in scattered clashes between people of the area and government soldiers. The area residents, mostly Buddhists of the Chakma tribe, charged that the government was taking their land to give to Bengali Muslims from other parts of the country. In one of the worst incidents, on April 29, Chakma guerrillas attacked Bangladesh army camps and Bengali immigrant settlements. Some 130 settlers were killed. The army in reprisal reportedly killed 53 area residents.

Food Production reached a record 16.3 million metric tons (17.9 million short tons), and industrial output grew 10 per cent in the fiscal year that ended June 30. Despite its high population density, Bangladesh was producing more than 80 per cent of its normal food needs.   Henry S. Bradsher

See also ASIA (Facts in Brief Table). In WORLD BOOK, see BANGLADESH.

BANK

BANK. In 1986, the big news in banking was a series of nonevents, based on a list of dire predictions that failed to materialize. There was no wave of international defaults to send any big banks into failure, and though the Federal Deposit Insurance Corporation (FDIC) paid out a record $2.8 billion in claims to depositors of failed banks, its reserves were not exhausted.

The year also marked the end of Regulation Q of the Federal Reserve System (Fed). Regulation Q, which since 1934 kept ceilings on the rate of interest banks may pay on deposits, was repealed on April 1, 1986, but the expected rise in interest rates did not take place.

The merger of Chemical New York Corporation of New York City and Texas Commerce Bancshares, Incorporated, of Houston was announced on December 15. It was the largest U.S. bank merger ever.

Money. The money supply increased faster in 1986 than in 1985. Although economic growth slowed, inflation turned to deflation as prices fell during the first three months of 1986.

M1, a basic measure of the money supply, consists of money the public has available to spend, such as currency, checking accounts, and NOW and Super NOW accounts. M1 began 1986 at $629 billion, remained flat through January and

A blind woman reads the instructions for New York City's first braille automatic teller, which was installed by Chemical Bank in January.

February, and then rose steadily at a rate of 18 per cent through August before slowing in September and October. By the end of December, M1 stood at $741 billion, showing a growth rate of 18 per cent. This was much higher than the Fed's target range of 3 to 8 per cent.

M2, the money that the public saves, including M1, savings accounts, certificates of deposit (CD's), money market mutual funds (MMF's), and money market deposit accounts, opened the year at $2.58 trillion and rose about 9 per cent to finish at about $2.80 trillion. This growth was within the Fed's target range of 6 to 9 per cent.

The Fed's target ranges for the growth rates of M1 and M2 are intended to keep inflation in check. If the money supplies—M1 and M2—grow much faster than the gross national product (GNP), which is the value of all goods and services produced during a year, the prices of those goods and services usually rise. In 1986, however, the GNP grew at a rate of only 2.7 per cent, slower than M1 or M2.

The Consumer Price Index (CPI)—a measure of the average level of all retail prices—fell 1.9 per cent annually during the first three months of 1986. It finished the year only 1.1 per cent higher than it began.

Prices rose much slower than money in 1986 for two reasons. First, there was a dramatic fall in oil prices in the first quarter of 1986. The spot price for odd lots of oil fell from $31 per barrel to below $10 per barrel. As a result, the cost of energy and crude materials, such as coal, also dropped.

Second, *M1 velocity*—the average number of times an M1 dollar is spent to produce GNP—slowed during the year. In 1980, the velocity was 7.0, which means that the average M1 dollar turned around seven times during 1980 to finance GNP. Velocity had been rising steadily since 1970, but it began to fall in 1981 and was down to 6.3 in 1986.

The reason for this fall was a change in the type of money included in M1. Before the Depository Institutions Deregulation and Monetary Control Act of 1980 allowed Super NOW's—accounts paying high interest rates—currency and checking accounts included in M1 paid little or no interest and were considered "money to spend." Super NOW's, however, have made people either more willing to save their M1 dollars or willing to spend these dollars more slowly. Slower spending puts less upward pressure on prices, so that even though M1 rose much faster than the GNP in 1986, inflation remained low.

Interest Rates. Short-term interest rates in the United States fell in 1986. The three-month Treasury-bill (T-bill) rate, which began the year at 7.0 per cent, fell to 5.8 per cent in the third week of April. In the first week of June, it peaked at 6.4

per cent and then fell steadily, finishing the year at 5.65 per cent.

Three-month CD rates are usually a little higher than T-bill rates. CD rates began 1986 at 7.9 per cent, fell steadily to 6.4 per cent in the third week of April, and rose to 6.9 per cent in early June. By the first week of September, the rates were falling, finishing the year at 6.05 per cent.

The prime rate used to be the interest rate banks charged their best corporate customers for short-term loans, but in 1986 more floating-rate home-equity and consumer loans were pegged to it. Because the prime rate is more of an advertising tool than a rate determined by the demands of the market place, it changes more slowly than other short-term rates. The prime rate began 1986 at 9.5 per cent and ended the year at 7.5 per cent.

Bank Regulation. An era ended on April 1, 1986, when Regulation Q of the Fed was repealed. Regulation Q, set up by Congress in 1934 to avoid a repetition of the bank failures that occurred during the Great Depression, gave the Fed the power to put ceilings on the interest rates banks pay to attract deposits. In the late 1970's, inflation had raised the market rates on MMF's high enough to drain deposits from banks and savings and loan associations. To remedy this situation, the Fed lifted ceilings on savings accounts from 5¼ to 5½ per cent and removed ceilings from some kinds of CD's. The Deregulation Act of 1980 required an end to all ceilings on interest rates by 1986.

By the beginning of 1986, the only deposits still subject to Regulation Q were passbook savings and NOW accounts. Many economists thought that removing the ceilings would set off a quick increase in both the interest rates paid on checking accounts and the dollar total of those accounts.

Interest rates on NOW accounts, however, did not rise as expected after April 1 because rates on other short-term assets were falling at the time. Falling rates on other alternatives made checking accounts more attractive even at 5½ per cent interest. Total funds in checking accounts rose 29 per cent between April and June and were still rising at 20 per cent in September, when T-bill and even some MMF rates were below 5½ per cent. Banks even began to lower NOW account rates to 5¼ and 5 per cent by the end of the year.

Banks and International Debt. Another event that did not materialize in 1986 was the collapse of at least one large bank as a result of international defaults. Debt owed by developing countries continued to rise. Brazil and Mexico each owed more than $100 billion, and together Brazil, Mexico, and Argentina owed more than three times their annual exports. Even so, most debts were renegotiated, and banks held on.   Donald W. Swanton

In WORLD BOOK, see BANK.

BARCO VARGAS, VIRGILIO (1921-   ), was elected president of Colombia on May 25, 1986. With 58 per cent of the vote, he ran up the largest margin in a presidential contest in Colombia's history. Barco was inaugurated on August 7, succeeding Belisario Betancur. See COLOMBIA.

Born to a wealthy family in the town of Cúcuta on Sept. 17, 1921, Barco has had an active political and diplomatic career. He received his higher education in the United States, obtaining a degree in civil engineering in 1943 from the Massachusetts Institute of Technology (M.I.T.) in Cambridge and a master's degree in 1952 in the social sciences from Boston University. He also studied economics at M.I.T. from 1951 to 1954.

Barco served as Colombia's ambassador to Great Britain in 1961 and 1962 and to the United States from 1977 to 1980. He also represented Colombia and several other Latin-American countries as an executive director of the World Bank, an agency of the United Nations, from 1966 to 1969.

Barco became a national political figure in 1966—known for his public works projects as the mayor of Bogotá, the capital of Colombia. He had served in Colombia's Senate as a member of the Liberal Party since 1958.

In 1950, Barco married an American, Carolina Isackson, and the couple have four grown children—three daughters and a son.   Rod Such

BASEBALL. The New York Mets capped a superb 1986 season by defeating the Boston Red Sox in seven games to win the World Series. The World Series and the league championship play-offs were exciting, with dramatic come-from-behind victories in the late innings.

Fan interest in baseball was high during the regular season. The 26 major league teams attracted 47,500,347 spectators, a record. For the first time, every team exceeded 1 million in attendance.

The Mets, managed by Davey Johnson, had strong pitching, good hitting, and speed. They had outstanding players in catcher Gary Carter, first baseman Keith Hernandez, and outfielder Darryl Strawberry.

The Mets' regular-season record of 108-54 was the best in the National League in 11 years. They led the National League's Eastern Division from April 23 on and won it by 21½ games, their first division championship in 13 years.

The Houston Astros took the National League Western Division lead on July 22 and led from then on. They clinched their first division title in six years on September 25 when pitcher Mike Scott threw a no-hit game against the San Francisco Giants, 2-0.

In the American League, Boston finished 5½ games ahead in the Eastern Division, and the California Angels finished 5 games ahead in the

Western Division. It was an astounding turnabout for Boston, which had finished fifth in 1985.

National League Play-Off. The Mets' big problem in the play-off was Houston's Scott. He won the first game, 1-0, on five-hit pitching and the fourth game, 3-1, on three-hit pitching.

In the fifth game, the Mets seemed in trouble when pitcher Nolan Ryan held them to two hits and struck out 12 in 9 innings. But the Mets won the game, 2-1, in 12 innings and took a 3-2 lead in the 4-of-7-game series.

Then came the longest postseason game in major league history. With Houston leading 3-0 and only three outs from victory, the Mets tied the game in the top of the 9th inning. In the 14th, the Mets took the lead, 4-3, and in the bottom of the inning, the Astros were only two outs from elimination until outfielder Billy Hatcher hit a home run. Then in the 16th, the Mets scored three runs and took a 7-4 lead. In the bottom of the 16th, the Astros scored twice. They had the tying and winning runs on base, but outfielder Kevin Bass struck out for the final out.

The Mets won the game, 7-6, and the pennant, 4 games to 2. Scott was voted the Most Valuable Player of the play-off.

American League Play-Off. The Red Sox did well all season with the help of outstanding pitching by Roger Clemens. But in the play-off, they fell behind the Angels, 3 games to 1, and in the fifth game, they were one strike from elimination.

The Red Sox took a 2-1 lead into the sixth inning of that game. But then Angels infielder Bobby Grich hit a towering fly ball to left-center field. Center fielder Dave Henderson appeared to make a spectacular leaping catch, but the ball hit the heel of his glove, getting an extra bounce over the wall for a home run, and the Angels took a 3-2 lead. The Angels scored twice more and led 5-2 going into the ninth. The Sox rallied for two runs but were down to their last strike with the tying run on base and Henderson at bat. He drilled a home run over the left field fence, and the Sox took a 6-5 lead in the top of the ninth. It didn't end there. The Angels rallied and tied it in the ninth, but the Red Sox won, 7-6, in 11 innings.

The Red Sox won the sixth game, 10-4. They won the seventh and deciding game, 8-1, depriving Gene Mauch of the Angels of his first pennant in 25 years as a major league manager. Marty Barrett, the Red Sox second baseman, was voted the play-off's Most Valuable Player.

World Series. The Mets had not won a World Series in 17 years. The Red Sox had not played in a World Series in 11 years or won one since 1918.

In this World Series, held from October 18 to

Final Standings in Major League Baseball

American League

Eastern Division	W.	L.	Pct.	G.B.
Boston Red Sox	95	66	.590	
New York Yankees	90	72	.556	5½
Detroit Tigers	87	75	.537	8½
Toronto Blue Jays	86	76	.531	9½
Cleveland Indians	84	78	.519	11½
Milwaukee Brewers	77	84	.478	18
Baltimore Orioles	73	89	.451	22½
Western Division				
California Angels	92	70	.568	
Texas Rangers	87	75	.537	5
Kansas City Royals	76	86	.469	16
Oakland Athletics	76	86	.469	16
Chicago White Sox	72	90	.444	20
Minnesota Twins	71	91	.438	21
Seattle Mariners	67	95	.414	25

Offensive Leaders

Batting Average—Wade Boggs, Boston	.357
Runs Scored—Rickey Henderson, New York	130
Home Runs—Jesse Barfield, Toronto	40
Runs Batted In—Joe Carter, Cleveland	121
Hits—Don Mattingly, New York	238
Stolen Bases—Rickey Henderson, New York	87

Leading Pitchers

Games Won—Roger Clemens, Boston	24
Win Average—Roger Clemens, Boston (24-4)	.857
Earned Run Average (162 or more innings)—Roger Clemens, Boston	2.48
Strikeouts—Mark Langston, Seattle	245
Saves—Dave Righetti, New York	46

Awards*

Most Valuable Player—Roger Clemens, Boston
Cy Young—Roger Clemens, Boston
Rookie of the Year—Jose Canseco, Oakland
Manager of the Year—John McNamara, Boston

National League

Eastern Division	W.	L.	Pct.	G.B.
New York Mets	108	54	.667	
Philadelphia Phillies	86	75	.534	21½
St. Louis Cardinals	79	82	.491	28½
Montreal Expos	78	83	.484	29½
Chicago Cubs	70	90	.438	37
Pittsburgh Pirates	64	98	.395	44
Western Division				
Houston Astros	96	66	.593	
Cincinnati Reds	86	76	.531	10
San Francisco Giants	82	79	.509	13½
San Diego Padres	74	89	.457	22
Los Angeles Dodgers	73	88	.453	22½
Atlanta Braves	72	89	.447	23½

Offensive Leaders

Batting Average—Tim Raines, Montreal	.334
Runs Scored—Tony Gwynn, San Diego, and Von Hayes, Philadelphia (tie)	107
Home Runs—Mike Schmidt, Philadelphia	37
Runs Batted In—Mike Schmidt, Philadelphia	119
Hits—Tony Gwynn, San Diego	211
Stolen Bases—Vince Coleman, St. Louis	107

Leading Pitchers

Games Won—Fernando Valenzuela, Los Angeles	21
Win Average—Bob Ojeda, New York (18-5)	.783
Earned Run Average (162 or more innings)—Mike Scott, Houston	2.22
Strikeouts—Mike Scott, Houston	306
Saves—Todd Worrell, St. Louis	36

Awards*

Most Valuable Player—Mike Schmidt, Philadelphia
Cy Young—Mike Scott, Houston
Rookie of the Year—Todd Worrell, St. Louis
Manager of the Year—Hal Lanier, Houston

*Selected by Baseball Writers Association of America.

27, the Red Sox won the opener, 1-0, as pitcher Bruce Hurst held the Mets to four hits over eight innings. Infielder Tim Teufel's error allowed the lone Red Sox run. The Red Sox won the second game, 9-3, with 18 hits off Dwight Gooden and three relievers.

That gave the Red Sox a 2-0 lead, with the next three games in Boston. The Mets, however, won the third game, 7-1, as Bob Ojeda allowed five hits in seven innings, and the fourth game, 6-2, as Ron Darling pitched a four-hit shut-out for seven innings. The Red Sox took the fifth game, 4-2, when Hurst outpitched Gooden.

In the sixth game, the Red Sox scored two runs in the top of the 10th inning on a home run by Henderson and a run-scoring single by Barrett. Twice the Sox came within one strike of winning the World Series in the bottom of the 10th. With two outs and the bases empty, the Shea Stadium electronic message board momentarily flashed the words, "Congratulations Boston Red Sox."

But then the Mets rallied. With the bases loaded, a wild pitch by reliever Bob Stanley scored the tying run. And when first baseman Bill Buckner allowed Mookie Wilson's grounder to go through his legs, the Mets scored the winning run in a 6-5 game.

The Mets won the seventh game, 8-5, and the World Series. Ray Knight, the veteran third baseman, was the Most Valuable Player in the World Series. Two months later, Knight left the Mets when they could not agree on a new contract.

The Stars. In the American League, first baseman Don Mattingly of the New York Yankees finished first in hits (238), doubles (53), and slugging average (.573); second in batting (.352); and third in runs scored (117) and runs batted in (113). Red Sox third baseman Wade Boggs, with a .357 average, won his third batting title in four years.

In the National League, third baseman Mike Schmidt of the Philadelphia Phillies led in home runs (37), runs batted in (119), and slugging average (.547). Schmidt was named the regular season's Most Valuable Player in the National League.

Among National League pitchers, Houston's Scott, with a won-lost record of 18-10, led major league pitchers in earned-run average (2.22), strikeouts (306), and innings pitched (275⅓). Scott received the Cy Young Award in the National League. Fernando Valenzuela (21-11) of the Los Angeles Dodgers ranked first in victories (21) and complete games (20) and second in strikeouts (242) and innings pitched (269⅓). In the All-Star Game on July 15 in Houston, which the American League won, 3-2, Valenzuela equaled Carl Hubbell's 1934 All-Star record by striking out five consecutive batters.

Among American League pitchers, Clemens

Mets third baseman Ray Knight drives a home run to give his team the lead in the final game of the World Series in October, which the Mets won.

(24-4) was first in victories (24), first in earned-run average (2.48), and second in strikeouts (238). On April 29, in a 3-1 victory over the Seattle Mariners in Boston, he set a major league record of 20 strikeouts in one game. Clemens received the Cy Young Award and Most Valuable Player Award in the American League.

First baseman Rod Carew of the Angels, who won seven American League batting titles from 1969 to 1978, retired in 1986 at age 40. At 41, Steve Carlton, the only pitcher to win four Cy Young Awards, was released by Philadelphia during the season, signed and released by San Francisco, and signed by the Chicago White Sox. On August 4, Carlton recorded his 4,000th career strikeout to become only the second player in baseball history to reach that figure. (The first was Nolan Ryan.)

Hall of Fame. First baseman Willie McCovey, second baseman Bobby Doerr, and catcher Ernie Lombardi were elected to the National Baseball Hall of Fame in Cooperstown, N.Y. McCovey hit most of his 521 home runs as a San Francisco Giant from 1959 to 1980. The Committee on Veterans elected Doerr, who played from 1937 to 1951 for the Red Sox, and Lombardi, who played from 1931 to 1947 for four National League clubs.   Frank Litsky

In WORLD BOOK, see BASEBALL.

BASKETBALL. The Boston Celtics, the best team in the National Basketball Association (NBA) during the 1985-1986 regular season, were the best in the play-offs, too, and won the league championship. The University of Louisville in Kentucky, ranked seventh at the end of the season, won the National Collegiate Athletic Association (NCAA) men's tournament. The undefeated University of Texas became the women's college champion.

Professional. The NBA's 23 teams played 82 games each from October 1985 to April 1986. Attendance rose 6.7 per cent to 11,214,888, a record, and television ratings—indicating audience size for national telecasts—increased 11 per cent.

On the court, the best regular-season records belonged to the Celtics (67-15) and the defending champion Los Angeles Lakers (62-20). The division winners were the Lakers by 22 games, the Celtics by 13, the Milwaukee Bucks by 7, and the Houston Rockets by 4.

Sixteen teams advanced to the play-offs. The major surprise came in the Western Conference finals, where the Rockets upset the Lakers, 4 games to 1. The Rockets won the final game in Los Angeles on a twisting, off-balance jump shot by Ralph Sampson, their 7-foot 4-inch (223-centimeter) center.

Meanwhile, the Celtics advanced to the championship finals by eliminating the Chicago Bulls by 3 games to 0; the Atlanta Hawks, 4-1; and Milwaukee, 4-0. Then the Celtics defeated Houston, 4 games to 2, for their 16th NBA championship in 30 years. With their victory in the final game on June 8, the Celtics extended their winning streak on their home court to 41 games and finished the season with a 50-1 record at home.

Honors. Larry Bird, the Celtics' forward, was Most Valuable Player in the play-offs. He led the Celtics' offense, and his double-teaming and triple-teaming was a key to the Celtics' defense.

Bird also was voted the Most Valuable Player during the regular season. Then, he ranked first in the league in free-throw percentage (.896), fourth in scoring average (25.8 points per game), fourth in 3-point field-goal percentage (.423), seventh in rebounding (9.8 per game), and ninth in steals (2.02 per game).

In balloting by 78 writers for the regular season's Most Valuable Player award, Bird received 73 votes for first place and 5 for second. The remaining 5 first-place votes went to Dominique Wilkins, the Atlanta forward. Wilkins won the regular-season scoring championship, averaging 30.33 points per game; Adrian Dantley of the Utah Jazz averaged 29.83 and Alex English of the Denver Nuggets, 29.80.

The all-star team consisted of Bird and Wilkins at forward, Kareem Abdul-Jabbar of the Lakers at center, and Earvin (Magic) Johnson of the Lak-

National Basketball Association Standings

Eastern Conference

Atlantic Division	W.	L.	Pct.	G.B.
Boston Celtics	67	15	.817	
Philadelphia 76ers	54	28	.659	13
New Jersey Nets	39	43	.476	28
Washington Bullets	39	43	.476	28
New York Knicks	23	59	.280	44

Central Division				
Milwaukee Bucks	57	25	.695	
Atlanta Hawks	50	32	.610	7
Detroit Pistons	46	36	.561	11
Chicago Bulls	30	52	.366	27
Cleveland Cavaliers	29	53	.354	28
Indiana Pacers	26	56	.317	31

Western Conference

Midwest Division				
Houston Rockets	51	31	.622	
Denver Nuggets	47	35	.573	4
Dallas Mavericks	44	38	.537	7
Utah Jazz	42	40	.512	9
Sacramento Kings	37	45	.451	14
San Antonio Spurs	35	47	.427	16

Pacific Division				
Los Angeles Lakers	62	20	.756	
Portland Trail Blazers	40	42	.488	22
Los Angeles Clippers	32	50	.390	30
Phoenix Suns	32	50	.390	30
Seattle SuperSonics	31	51	.378	31
Golden State Warriors	30	52	.366	32

Individual Leaders

Scoring	G.	F.G.	F.T.	Pts.	Avg.
Dominique Wilkins, Atlanta	78	888	577	2,366	30.3
Adrian Dantley, Utah	76	818	630	2,267	29.8
Alex English, Denver	81	951	511	2,414	29.8
Larry Bird, Boston	82	796	441	2,115	25.8
Purvis Short, Golden State	64	633	351	1,632	25.5
Kiki Vandeweghe, Portland	79	719	523	1,962	24.8
Moses Malone, Philadelphia	74	571	617	1,759	23.8

Rebounding	G.	Tot.	Avg.
Bill Laimbeer, Detroit	82	1,075	13.1
Charles Barkley, Philadelphia	80	1,026	12.8
Buck Williams, New Jersey	82	986	12.0
Moses Malone, Philadelphia	74	872	11.8

ers and Isiah Thomas of the Detroit Pistons at guard. The 39-year-old Abdul-Jabbar, already the league's career scoring leader, in 1986 became the leader in longevity (17 years), games (1,328), and minutes played (51,002).

Drafts. The Rookie of the Year was Patrick Ewing, the New York Knicks' center from Georgetown University. In his first year in the NBA, Ewing averaged 20.0 points and 9.0 rebounds per game, though he missed 32 games due to injuries.

The NBA draft on June 17 was highlighted by heavy trading. The Philadelphia 76ers recast their front line in deals with the Washington Bullets and the Cleveland Cavaliers. The 76ers traded away all-star center Moses Malone and acquired center Jeff Ruland and forwards Cliff Robinson and Roy Hinson.

As part of those deals, the 76ers sent the overall first choice in the draft to Cleveland. The Cavaliers used it to pick Brad Daugherty, a center from the University of North Carolina. The Celtics, choosing next, took Len Bias, a forward from the University of Maryland. On June 19, the 22-year-old Bias died of cocaine intoxication. In October, Charles (Lefty) Driesell resigned under pressure after 17 years as Maryland's coach.

College. In the preseason polls of the Associated Press (AP) panel of sportswriters and broadcasters and the United Press International (UPI) board of coaches, the favorites were Georgia Tech and Michigan. Louisville and Duke ranked lower in the top 10.

When the regular season ended, the AP ranked Duke first with a 32-2 won-lost record, Kansas (31-3) second, Kentucky (29-3) third, St. John's of New York (30-4) fourth, Michigan (27-4) fifth, Georgia Tech (25-6) sixth, and Louisville (26-7) seventh. The UPI rankings were almost identical.

The first four teams in the final polls became the four top-seeded teams for the NCAA's 64-team, three-week tournament. Duke had won its last 16 games, and Kansas had won its last 11.

St. John's was the first of the four favorites to be eliminated from the tournament, falling to Auburn, 81-65, in the second round of the West regional competition in Long Beach, Calif. Kentucky was beaten by Louisiana State, 59-57, in the Southeast regional final in Atlanta, Ga.

Duke, Kansas, Louisiana State, and Louisville advanced to the national semifinals on March 29 in Dallas. There, Duke eliminated Kansas, 71-67, and Louisville won over Louisiana State, 88-77.

The March 31 final in Dallas between Louisville and Duke was close. In the last minute, Pervis Ellison, Louisville's freshman center, retrieved a missed shot and scored. Seconds later, after he was fouled making a defensive rebound, he converted two free throws.

Ellison's strong finish ensured Louisville's 72-69 victory. He was the game leader with 25 points and 11 rebounds, and he became the first freshman since Arnie Ferrin of Utah in 1944 to be voted the tournament's Most Valuable Player.

Honors. Walter Berry, the St. John's center, was the general choice as College Player of the Year. Others named to major all-American teams were Bias of Maryland and Kenny Walker of Kentucky at forward, David Robinson of Navy at center, and Johnny Dawkins of Duke, Scott Skiles of Michigan State, and Steve Alford of Indiana at guard. In various polls, Eddie Sutton of Kentucky, Dick Versace of Bradley, and Denny Crum of Louisville were selected as Coach of the Year.

The 1985-1986 College Basketball Season

College Tournament Champions

NCAA (Men) Division I: Louisville
    Division II: Sacred Heart College (Connecticut)
    Division III: Potsdam State (New York)

NCAA (Women) Division I: Texas
    Division II: California State Polytechnic
    Division III: Salem State (Massachusetts)

NAIA (Men): David Lipscomb College (Tennessee)
    (Women): Francis Marion College (South Carolina)

NIT: Ohio State

Junior College (Men): San Jacinto (Texas)
    (Women): Odessa (Texas)

College Champions

Conference	School
Atlantic Coast	Duke*
Atlantic Ten	St. Joseph's*
Big East	St. John's*
Big Eight	Kansas*
Big Sky	Northern Arizona (regular season) Montana State (conference tournament)
Big South	Baptist*
Big Ten	Michigan
Colonial Athletic	Navy*
East Coast	Drexel*
Eastern College Athletic-North Atlantic	Northeastern*
Eastern College Athletic-Metro	Fairleigh Dickinson (regular season) Marist (conference tournament)
Gulf Star	Sam Houston State
Ivy League	Brown
Metro	Louisville*
Metro Atlantic	Fairfield*
Mid-American	Miami (Ohio) (regular season) Ball State (conference tournament)
Mid-Continent	Cleveland State*
Mid-Eastern	North Carolina A & T*
Midwestern City	Xavier*
Missouri Valley	Bradley (regular season) Tulsa (conference tournament)
Ohio Valley	Akron*
Pacific Coast Athletic	Nevada-Las Vegas*
Pacific Ten	Arizona
Southeastern	Kentucky*
Southern	Tennessee-Chattanooga (regular season) Davidson (conference tournament)
Southland	Northeast Louisiana*
Southwest	Texas A&M—Texas Christian—Texas (tie; regular season) Texas Tech (conference tournament)
Southwestern Athletic	Southern (regular season) Mississippi Valley (conference tournament)
Sun Belt	Old Dominion (regular season) Jacksonville (conference tournament)
Trans America Athletic	Arkansas-Little Rock*
West Coast Athletic	Pepperdine
Western Athletic	Texas-El Paso—Utah—Wyoming (tie; regular season) Texas-El Paso (conference tournament)

*Regular season and conference tournament champions.

In the 1984-1985 season, 19 college basketball conferences used a 45-second clock on an experimental basis. For the 1985-1986 season, the NCAA made the 45-second clock mandatory for all regular-season and tournament games. The rule required a team to shoot within 45 seconds of gaining possession of the ball or surrender the ball. The idea was to prevent teams from maintaining possession indefinitely, especially when they were protecting leads near the end of a game. Many observers of the game believed that such stalling tactics made college basketball less exciting than pro basketball, which has a shot clock.

Women. After the regular season, a poll of 62 coaches ranked Texas first nationally, Georgia second, Southern California third, Louisiana Tech fourth, and Western Kentucky fifth. In the final of the NCAA's 40-team tournament, Texas defeated Southern California, 97-81, on March 30 in Lexington, Ky.

Texas finished the season with a 34-0 record. In previous years, only Louisiana Tech, Delta State, and Immaculata had undefeated seasons.

Texas provided the Player of the Year in Kamie Ethridge, its point guard, and the Coach of the Year in Jody Conradt. Cheryl Miller, Southern California's star, was voted an all-American for the fourth consecutive year.   Frank Litsky

In WORLD BOOK, see BASKETBALL.

BELGIUM. Labor problems followed a May 1986 bid by Prime Minister Wilfried A. E. Martens' center-right government to reduce public spending by 10 per cent in 1987. Government employees, including teachers, railroad and other transportation workers, and communications personnel, struck in early and mid-May to protest cuts they suspected were coming. On May 21, the government announced budget cuts of $4.5 million, affecting education, defense, health, and transportation. Belgium's largest bank estimated that the cuts would cause between 27,000 and 61,000 workers to lose their jobs.

The government also planned to cut welfare expenditures by $10.5 million and to sell some state-owned businesses, including the agency that operates ferryboats that cross the English Channel. On May 22, government employees struck again.

Back to Work. Support for the strikes was patchy because many workers were afraid of losing their jobs. The unemployment rate was already 12.2 per cent. By the end of May, most workers had returned to their jobs.

Demonstrations and marches continued to embarrass the government, however. Martens, a member of the Christian Social Party of the Dutch-speaking Flemings, faced opposition from the Christian Social Party of the French-speaking Walloons.

Martens based his hope that Parliament would approve the cuts on Christian Social labor unions' opposition to strikes. These unions saw strikes as a political weapon to bring down the government.

Language Crisis. Martens' government almost collapsed in the fall, after José Happart, a French-speaking rural mayor, refused to take a mandatory test of his knowledge of Dutch. Belgium's highest court dismissed Happart, but his village council reappointed him. The resulting dispute split the Christian Social Party along linguistic lines. Martens offered a compromise to settle the dispute, but the French-speaking branch of the party rejected the deal.

On October 14, Prime Minister Martens offered his resignation to King Baudouin I, but the king refused to accept it. Martens announced on October 17 that a commission would seek a long-term solution to the crisis.

Ex-Leader Convicted. On June 25, a panel of judges in Brussels convicted former Prime Minister Paul Vanden Boeynants of tax fraud and forgery, and sentenced him to a suspended term of three years in prison.   Kenneth Brown

See also EUROPE (Facts in Brief Table). In WORLD BOOK, see BELGIUM.

BELIZE. See LATIN AMERICA.

BENIN. See AFRICA.

BHUTAN. See ASIA.

BIOCHEMISTRY. A protein produced by cancer cells that enables the cells to migrate from one site in the body to another—a process known as *metastasis*—was discovered in 1986 by scientists at the National Institutes of Health (NIH) in Bethesda, Md. The NIH researchers reported in May that the protein, called *autocrine motility factor* (AMF), stimulated cancer cells in the laboratory to squeeze through small pores in a filter, which normal cells would have been unable to do. The presence of the protein in a cancer patient's blood might mean that the patient's tumor is spreading to another part of the body. The NIH scientists said it may be possible to keep cancer cells from producing AMF, thereby preventing metastasis.

In October, researchers in the Boston area announced discovery of the first known gene that blocks the development of cancer. The scientists, at Massachusetts Eye and Ear Infirmary in Boston and Massachusetts Institute of Technology in Cambridge, found that inherited defects in the gene permit the development of rare forms of eye or bone cancer. Scientists hope to identify the biochemical signal sent by the normal gene to block cancer and use that signal to prevent other forms of cancer.

Genetics and Obesity. Heredity is a more important factor than eating habits in the development of obesity, according to a January report by a re-

Researchers at Massachusetts General Hospital in Boston display a container
of genetically engineered cells used to produce a protein that may fight cancer.

search team at the University of Pennsylvania in
Philadelphia. The investigators studied 540 adoptees in Denmark and found a strong relationship
between the adult weight of the adopted children
and the weight of their biological parents. Between the adoptees and their adoptive parents, on
the other hand, there was no such correlation. But
the researchers said the children of obese parents
are not doomed to becoming fat—they just have
to diet and exercise more than other people.

Fertility-Regulating Protein. The discovery of a
protein that helps regulate fertility in mammals
was reported in June by researchers at the Salk
Institute for Biological Studies in La Jolla, Calif.
The protein spurs the secretion of *follicle-stimulating hormone,* a substance that plays a key role in
causing egg cells to mature. The newly found protein has a structure that is similar to that of another protein, isolated at Salk in 1985, that
suppresses the secretion of follicle-stimulating
hormone. The new protein is expected to be useful in treating certain types of infertility.

Bone-Growth Factor. California scientists announced in March that they had found a previously unknown protein that stimulates bone
healing. The researchers, at the University of
California at San Francisco, said the protein,
called *osteogenic growth factor,* is at least the sixth
such substance that has been discovered. During

the year, scientists began testing two of the other
known growth factors in attempts to speed the
healing of large bone defects resulting from injuries, infections, or other causes.

Genetic Engineering. The first release of a genetically engineered microorganism into the environment occurred in October 1985 but was not revealed publicly until April 1986. In October 1985,
veterinarians in the Midwest began injecting baby
pigs with a genetically engineered vaccine designed to combat pseudorabies, an often-fatal viral
disease that costs the pork industry as much as
$60 million a year.

The vaccine contains an altered form of the virus, which infects the vaccinated animal and protects it from infection by the normal pseudorabies
virus. The engineered virus does not cause disease
or spread to other livestock. The Biologics Corporation of Omaha, Nebr., received approval
from the United States Department of Agriculture
in January to market the vaccine. That approval,
however, was not announced until April 3, when
Jeremy Rifkin, an outspoken opponent of biotechnology, revealed it.

In May, botanists at Agracetus, a genetic-engi-
neering company in Middleton, Wis., planted 200
genetically altered tobacco seedlings in an open
field near Middleton. The seedlings, the first engineered plants to be introduced into the environ-

227

ment, had been given a gene from yeast that blocked infection of the plants by a bacterium.

During the summer, scientists at Calgene, Incorporated, of Davis, Calif., planted a field in northern California with tobacco plants that had been given a gene, taken from *Salmonella* bacteria, that provides resistance to the herbicide glyphosate. If crop plants could be made resistant to herbicides, farmers could use the poisons to control weeds without damaging crops.

New Products. The U.S. Food and Drug Administration (FDA) approved two new genetically engineered products for human use in 1986, bringing the total number of approved products to four. The first two were human insulin, approved in 1982, and human growth hormone, approved in 1985.

In June, Schering-Plough Corporation of Madison, N.J., and Hoffman-La Roche Incorporated of Nutley, N.J., each received FDA approval to market a protein called alpha-interferon for use against a form of *leukemia*, cancer of the white blood cells. In July, Merck Sharp & Dohme of West Point, Pa., received FDA approval to market a genetically engineered vaccine against the liver disease hepatitis B.   Thomas H. Maugh II

In WORLD BOOK, see BIOCHEMISTRY.

BIOLOGY. See BIOCHEMISTRY; BOTANY; PALEONTOLOGY; ZOOLOGY.

Dodge Morgan of Cape Elizabeth, Me., waves in triumph in April after sailing around the world nonstop and by himself in a record 150 days.

BOATING. Preliminary competition for the America's Cup, the most cherished prize in yachting, began in October 1986 and was scheduled to run until January 1987. The winner among the 13 challengers was scheduled to meet one of six Australian defense candidates in the cup finals starting on Jan. 31, 1987.

For their defense of the cup, the Australians selected Fremantle, a small town near Perth on the Indian Ocean, as the site of the competition. Fremantle was also the site of the separate trials to determine the challenger and the defender.

Of the 13 challenging yachts, six came from the United States, two from both Italy and France, and one each from Canada, Great Britain, and New Zealand. The favorites among the challengers were the American yachts *America II*, sponsored by the New York Yacht Club and skippered by John Kolius of Houston, and *Stars and Stripes*, sponsored by the San Diego Yacht Club and sailed by Dennis Conner of San Diego.

America II, however, was eliminated in the second round of the challengers' trials. The four yachts that advanced to the semifinals were *Stars and Stripes* and *USA* of the United States, *French Kiss* of France, and *New Zealand* of that country.

The competition was held in sloops of the 12-Meter class. The term *12-Meter* does not refer to the length of the yachts, which was about 70

feet (21 meters), but to a complex formula incorporating length, sail area, and hull measurements.

The winds and waves at Newport, R.I., where Australia won the cup in 1983, were usually modest. But at Fremantle, there were brisk winds up to 30 knots and steep and choppy waves. Each of the challengers spent up to $15 million designing, building, and outfitting their yachts to adapt to the conditions at Fremantle.

Distance Yachting. Dodge Morgan of Cape Elizabeth, Me., set a solo record by sailing around the world nonstop in 150 days, landing in Hamilton, Bermuda, on April 11. The Swiss yacht *UBS Switzerland* finished first in the Whitbread round-the-world race, arriving in Portsmouth, England, on May 9 after 117 days, a race record.

Powerboats. In the last race of the 11-race season, *Miss Budweiser*, driven by Jim Kropfeld of Cincinnati, Ohio, barely won the United States national series title for unlimited hydroplanes, the fastest type of powerboat. *Miss Budweiser* finished the season with 8,500 points to 8,469 for *Miller American*, driven by Chip Hanauer of Seattle. The superboat competition in the national offshore series was dominated by two boats named *Popeye's/Diet Coke*, both driven by Al Copeland or his son—Al., Jr.—of Metairie, La.   Frank Litsky

In WORLD BOOK, see BOATING; SAILING.

BOLIVIA. United States troops landed at Santa Cruz, Bolivia, on July 14, 1986, to assist Bolivian authorities in their war against drug traffickers. On July 18, U.S. and Bolivian forces conducted the first of a series of joint raids on cocaine laboratories located in Bolivian jungles. The U.S. forces included six Army Black Hawk helicopters, armed with M-60 machine guns, and more than 160 U.S. military personnel. The last U.S. troops left Bolivia on November 15.

The Administration of President Ronald Reagan provided the assistance in accordance with a national security directive that authorizes the use of U.S. military forces to aid foreign governments in curtailing the drug trade. The drug trade poses a threat to U.S. security because of its links with international terrorism. Official U.S. sources estimate that Bolivia produces more than 35,000 short tons (32,000 metric tons) of coca leaf annually, much of which is processed into cocaine and smuggled into the United States.

Bolivian President Víctor Paz Estenssoro requested U.S. help partly because of the growing influence of drug traffickers on the Bolivian political scene. Drug traffickers reportedly were financing and corrupting candidates for local and national offices. The president was also motivated by an increase of drug abuse among young Bolivians, and the way that illegal drug profits have undermined legitimate businesses in Bolivia.

Paz Estensssoro's action was also prompted by a U.S. move in June to withhold $7.2 million in economic aid to Bolivia because of its lack of progress in wiping out the drug trade. The drug trade brings about $600 million annually into Bolivia.

Economic Measures. During his first year in office in 1985-1986, Paz Estenssoro cut back bloated work forces at government-run mines, laying off 7,000 workers out of a mining force of 20,000. By the end of 1986, he was expected to cut an additional 8,000 mining jobs. By Paz Estenssoro's calculation, Bolivian mines were producing tin for $10 a pound (0.45 kilogram), though it sold on world markets for only $2.48 a pound.

In August, Bolivian authorities pleaded with creditor nations for more aid to help make up anticipated shortfalls in earnings caused by low prices for Bolivia's mineral exports and expected losses resulting from the crackdown on drugs. "If we don't find a solution to the unemployment problem and find funds to relocate miners, we could see develop in Bolivia a leftist guerrilla movement," warned Gonzalo Sánchez de Lozada Bustamante, the minister of planning and coordination. Nathan A. Haverstock

See also LATIN AMERICA (Facts in Brief Table). In WORLD BOOK, see BOLIVIA.

BOOKS. See CANADIAN LITERATURE; LITERATURE; LITERATURE FOR CHILDREN; POETRY; PUBLISHING.

BOTANY. Meeting in Washington, D.C., in September 1986, some of the leading botanists and conservationists in the United States called for worldwide action to slow the accelerating mass extinction of plant and animal species caused by the destruction of tropical rain forests. Among the keynote speakers at the meeting, called by the National Academy of Sciences and the Smithsonian Institution, were Paul R. Ehrlich, professor of biology at Stanford University in California, and Edward O. Wilson, professor of science at Harvard University in Cambridge, Mass.

Tropical Rain Forests cover about 3 million square miles (7.8 million square kilometers) in a broad belt around the equator. These forests, which receive 100 inches (250 centimeters) or more of rain a year, occupy only 7 per cent of Earth's land surface but have served as "hothouses" for the development of millions of forms of plant and animal life.

Scientists estimate that there are 5 million to 30 million species of plants and animals on Earth, of which no more than 1.7 million have been scientifically classified. Most of the unknown species inhabit the tropical rain forests and represent a vast and irreplaceable storehouse of genetic diversity. At present, more than 70,000 acres (28,000 hectares) of rain forest are being cleared each day to make way for farms and pastureland. If that rate of destruction continues, scientists estimate, between 25 to 50 per cent of all existing species of plants and animals will become extinct within the next 30 years.

At the conference, F. William Burley, senior associate of the World Resources Institute, a private Washington, D.C.-based research center, urged support for a global plan to save the tropical forests. Sponsored by the institute and the United Nations, the plan proposes specific conservation strategies for each of the 56 nations engaged in extensive clearing of forests.

Plant Life in the Fast Lane. The development of several new plant varieties that complete their life cycles in the extremely short period of four to five weeks was reported in June 1986 by botanists Paul H. Williams and Curtis B. Hill of the University of Wisconsin at Madison. All but one of the fast-growing plants are in the mustard genus *Brassica.* Williams spent several years developing the rapid-cycling brassicas in order to speed up research on *crucifers,* a plant family that also includes radishes, cauliflower, and cabbage.

The researchers predicted that the new plants will be of great use in the teaching of botany. In addition to developing quickly, the plants require minimal care and thrive indoors under fluorescent lighting. Eldon H. Newcomb

In WORLD BOOK, see BOTANY.

BOTSWANA. See AFRICA.

BOWLING. In 1985, Walter Ray Williams, Jr., won his fourth world championship in horseshoe pitching. In 1986, he became the dominating player on the Professional Bowlers Association of America (PBA) tour.

The 26-year-old Williams of Stockton, Calif., won tournaments in Peoria, Ill., in March; Baltimore in April; and Edmond, Okla., in July. In a six-week stretch of tournaments in February and March, he successively finished fifth, ninth, out of the money, third, first, and second.

Steve Cook of Roseville, Calif., won four tournaments—in Venice, Fla., in February; Windsor Locks, Conn., in April; Las Vegas, Nev., in June; and Austin, Tex., in July. The leading money earners on the PBA tour were Williams with $145,550; Marshall Holman of Medford, Ore., with $122,510; and Cook with $115,290.

U.S. Open. Cook's first victory of the year came February 9 to 15 in the $200,000 United States Open in Venice, Fla. In the one-game final, he defeated Frank Ellenburg of Mesa, Ariz., 245-211, rolling seven strikes in his last eight balls.

Tom Crites of Tampa, Fla., won the $235,000 PBA national championship held from March 23 to 29 in Toledo, Ohio. In the final, he beat Mike Aulby of Indianapolis, 190-184.

All tour winners from the previous 12 months qualified for the $250,000 Firestone Tournament of Champions April 21 to 26 in Akron, Ohio. Holman beat Mark Baker of Garden Grove, Calif., 233-211, in the final. The first prize of $50,000 put Holman over $1 million in career earnings.

The 1985-1986 all-America team, selected by *Bowlers Journal*, consisted of Williams, Cook, Holman, Aulby, and Baker. The women's team comprised Patty Costello of Scranton, Pa.; Cindy Coburn of Buffalo, N.Y.; Lorrie Nichols of Algonquin, Ill.; Aleta Sill of Detroit; and Lisa Wagner of Palmetto, Fla.

The PBA tour paid prize money of $6.5 million, mostly for 35 major tournaments. The women competed for smaller purses in 15 tournaments on the Ladies Pro Bowlers Tour (LPBT).

Women. Jeanne Solon of Solon, Ohio, and Wagner won three tournaments each. Sill led in earnings ($36,212), and Nikki Gianulias of Vallejo, Calif., had the highest average (213.87, a tour record). The women's U.S. Open, held from March 30 to April 5, in Topeka, Kans., was won by an amateur, 18-year-old Wendy Macpherson of San Diego. She beat Wagner, 265-179, in the final, and four months later, she turned professional.

Tish Johnson of Downey, Calif., set a tour six-game record of 1,550 pins in a tournament in August in Liverpool, N.Y. Johnson rolled games of 236, 221, 247, 267, 289, and 290, to achieve an average of 258.   Frank Litsky

In WORLD BOOK, see BOWLING.

BOXING. The major boxing developments of 1986 were mainly preliminaries to two major fights scheduled to take place in 1987. One of those 1987 attractions would be a bout between Marvelous Marvin Hagler and Sugar Ray Leonard for Hagler's undisputed world middleweight championship. The other 1987 attraction would be a heavyweight title fight recognized by all the major governing bodies in boxing. An eight-bout series begun in 1986 set the stage for the title fight.

Hagler, from Brockton, Mass., has held the middleweight title since 1980. In his only 1986 defense, he knocked out John (the Beast) Mugabi of Uganda on March 10 in Las Vegas, Nev. Hagler's original schedule called for a defense against either Thomas Hearns of Detroit or Donald Curry of Fort Worth, Tex. The Hearns bout fell through. Curry was eliminated when he was upset in a bout on September 27 in Atlantic City, N.J.

Hagler instead found an unexpected challenger in Leonard of Potomac, Md. Leonard, a former welterweight champion, had retired in 1984. He said he would come out of retirement only to fight Hagler, and the two fighters signed contracts that guaranteed Hagler $12 million and Leonard $11 million for the bout.

Heavyweights. The three major governing bodies recognized different heavyweight champions. Early in 1986, the World Boxing Council (WBC) recognized Pinklon Thomas of Newark, N.J., and later Trevor Berbick of Jamaica. The World Boxing Association (WBA) recognized Tony Tubbs of Cincinnati, Ohio, and then Tim Witherspoon of Philadelphia. Michael Spinks of St. Louis, Mo., was recognized by the International Boxing Federation (IBF).

With promoters Don King and Butch Lewis, Home Box Office (HBO), the pay-cable television network, worked out a series of fights that would lead to an undisputed heavyweight champion. From March to December 1986, in the first fights of the series, Berbick outpointed Thomas to become WBC champion. Spinks outpointed Larry Holmes of Easton, Pa., and later stopped Steffen Tangstad of Norway to remain IBF champion. Witherspoon stopped Frank Bruno of Great Britain in 11 rounds but then lost the WBA title to James (Bonecrusher) Smith of Magnolia, N.C., in December. Berbick lost the WBC title to Mike Tyson of Catskill, N.Y., in November.

Tyson, at 20 the youngest heavyweight champion ever, was scheduled to fight Smith in early 1987. Promoter Lewis, however, matched Spinks and Gerry Cooney of Huntington, N.Y., for a 1987 title fight. HBO went to court to try to prevent that fight and preserve its series.   Frank Litsky

In WORLD BOOK, see BOXING.

BOY SCOUTS. See YOUTH ORGANIZATIONS.

BOYS CLUBS. See YOUTH ORGANIZATIONS.

World Champion Boxers

World Boxing Association

Division	Champion	Country	Date won
Heavyweight	Tony Tubbs	U.S.A.	1985
	Tim Witherspoon	U.S.A.	Jan. '86
	James Smith	U.S.A.	Dec. '86
Junior heavyweight	Dwight Muhammad Qawi	U.S.A.	1985
	Evander Holyfield	U.S.A.	July '86
Light heavyweight	Marvin Johnson	U.S.A.	Feb. '86
Middleweight	Marvelous Marvin Hagler	U.S.A.	1980
Junior middleweight	Mike McCallum	Jamaica	1984
Welterweight	Donald Curry	U.S.A.	1983
	Lloyd Honeyghan	Great Britain	Sept. '86
	Vacant		Dec. '86
Junior welterweight	Ubaldo Sacco	Argentina	1985
	Patrizio Oliva	Italy	March '86
Lightweight	Livingstone Bramble	U.S. Virgin Islands	1984
	Edwin Rosario	Puerto Rico	Sept. '86
Junior lightweight	Wilfredo Gómez	Puerto Rico	1985
	Alfredo Layne	Panama	May '86
	Brian Mitchell	South Africa	Sept. '86
Featherweight	Barry McGuigan	N. Ireland	1985
	Steve Cruz	U.S.A.	June '86
Junior featherweight	Victor Callejas	Puerto Rico	1984
Bantamweight	Richard Sandoval	U.S.A.	1984
	Gaby Canizales	U.S.A.	March '86
	Bernardo Pinango	Venezuela	June '86
Junior bantamweight	Khaosai Galaxy	Thailand	1984
Flyweight	Santos Laciar	Argentina	1982
	Hilario Zapata	Panama	April '86
Junior flyweight	Yoo Myong-Woo	South Korea	1985

World Boxing Council

Division	Champion	Country	Date won
Heavyweight	Pinklon Thomas	U.S.A.	1984
	Trevor Berbick	Jamaica	March '86
	Mike Tyson	U.S.A.	Nov. '86
Cruiserweight	Bernard Benton	U.S.A.	1985
	Carlos DeLeon	Puerto Rico	March '86
Light heavyweight	J. B. Williamson	U.S.A.	1985
	Dennis Andries	Great Britain	April '86
Middleweight	Marvelous Marvin Hagler	U.S.A.	1980
Super welterweight	Thomas Hearns	U.S.A.	1982
	Vacant		Nov. '86
	Duane Thomas	U.S.A.	Dec. '86
Welterweight	Donald Curry	U.S.A.	1985
	Lloyd Honeyghan	Great Britain	Sept. '86
Super lightweight	Lonnie Smith	U.S.A.	1985
	Rene Arredondo	Mexico	May '86
	Tsuyoshi Hamada	Japan	July '86
Lightweight	Hector Camacho	Puerto Rico	1985
Super featherweight	Julio Cesar Chavez	Mexico	1984
Featherweight	Azumah Nelson	Ghana	1984
Super bantamweight	Lupe Pintor	Mexico	1985
	Samart Payakaroon	Thailand	Jan. '86
Bantamweight	Miguel Lora	Colombia	1985
Super flyweight	Jiro Watanabe	Japan	1984
	Gilberto Roman	Mexico	April '86
Flyweight	Sot Chitalada	Thailand	1984
Light flyweight	Jung-Koo Chang	South Korea	1983

BRAZIL. President José Sarney's centrist coalition won a sweeping victory ín national elections on Nov. 15, 1986. The elections were the first in Brazil since the return of civilian government in 1985 ended 21 years of military rule. The coalition, made up of the Brazilian Democratic Movement Party and the Liberal Front Party, won all 23 state governorships and nearly two-thirds of the seats in the National Congress.

Trade with North America. Brazil girded itself during 1986 to fight for economic markets long monopolized by the industrialized nations of the Northern Hemisphere. In one of many signs of its growing economic health, Brazil began to export small station wagons and compact cars to the United States and Canada in late 1986. The vehicles were produced by Brazilian companies operated by Volkswagen, General Motors Corporation, Ford Motor Company, and Fiat. Brazil is the world's 10th largest automaker.

Trade discussions were a chief topic when President Sarney met with President Ronald Reagan in Washington, D.C., in early September. The talks came at a time when the United States government was threatening retaliation for Brazil's protectionist trade policies, particularly its exclusion of U.S. computer firms. Brazil prohibits the import of many products because similar goods are made in Brazil.

Sarney defended his country's trade barriers, noting that Brazil's $12.5-billion trade surplus in 1985 was essential to paying off its foreign debt. He also explained that the ban on U.S. computer imports was necessary for Brazil to develop its own computer industry and avoid being swamped by foreign competition.

Trade with Argentina. In July, Brazil and its chief trade rival Argentina signed a series of agreements that revived hopes for a Latin-American common market. Under the agreements signed in Buenos Aires, Argentina's capital, on July 29, the two South American nations agreed to work together to develop their biotechnology, energy, and agricultural industries and to double the existing amount of trade with each other. They also agreed to participate in a joint venture for a hydroelectric installation on the Brazil-Argentine border and to provide equipment for a steel mill under construction in Iraq.

Energy Woes. Following the nuclear power plant accident at Chernobyl in the Soviet Union in April, many Brazilians had second thoughts about their country's rush to build nuclear power plants. Two plants that were being built with West German technology experienced severe cost overruns, and Brazil's first operational nuclear power plant—Angra I—earned the nickname *vagalume* (lightning bug) because of its tendency to turn on and off.

Brazil's President José Sarney acknowledges applause before addressing a joint session of the United States Congress on September 11.

Brazilians had second thoughts, too, about a massive program to substitute sugar-based alcohol for gasoline made from oil as fuel for vehicles. Continued low prices for oil made sugar-based fuels more expensive.

Religious Matters. To put an end to divisions between conservatives and progressives within Brazil's Roman Catholic Church, Pope John Paul II in March called Brazil's bishops to Rome for discussions. The pope reportedly told the bishops he wanted them to end their squabbling and to purify their ranks of priests who have become social and political activists.

Brazil lost one of its most beloved practitioners of a native religion known as *candomblé*—a mixture of African spiritualism and Catholicism—when Maria da Conceição Nazaré died on August 13 in Salvador. She was known to an adoring Brazilian public as *Mae Menininha* (little girl-mother).

Death of a Scientist. At the public's insistence, President Sarney arranged for the treatment in January of Brazilian naturalist Augusto Ruschi by an Indian *shaman* (medicine man). Before a national television audience, the shaman supposedly extracted a toad poison that Ruschi believed had caused his liver ailment. Ruschi's health improved briefly, but he died on June 3.　　Nathan A. Haverstock

See also LATIN AMERICA (Facts in Brief Table). In WORLD BOOK, see BRAZIL.

BRIDGE. The United States won every event at the Seventh World Bridge Championships held in Bal Harbour, Fla., from Sept. 13 to 27, 1986. The winner of the Rosenblum Teams championship was the team consisting of Kit Woolsey of Kensington, Calif.; Robert Lipsitz of Annandale, Va.; Peter Boyd of Falls Church, Va.; Ed Manfield of Arlington, Va.; and Neil Silverman of Fort Lauderdale, Fla. Jeff Meckstroth of Columbus, Ohio, and Eric Rodwell of West Lafayette, Ind., won the Open Pairs competition. Amalya L. Kearse and Jacqui Mitchell, both of New York City, became Women's Pairs champions. Winners in the Mixed Pairs division were Pamela Wittes and Jon Wittes of Los Alamitos, Calif.

Nearly 70,000 pairs competed at more than 1,000 sites in 80 countries in the first-ever World Simultaneous Pairs on June 14. All competitors had the same 24 computer-chosen hands to play, and play began in all countries simultaneously. The victors were Francis Frainais and Jann Bouteille, both of Paris. Organizer José Damiani of Paris was named Bridge Man of the Year.

The American Contract Bridge League's Summer Championships in Toronto, Canada, from July 18 to 27, was the largest bridge tournament in history. During the course of the competition, there were 21,075 tables in play.　　Henry G. Francis

In WORLD BOOK, see BRIDGE.

BRITISH COLUMBIA. Leadership of the governing Social Credit (Socred) party changed hands during 1986. On May 22, William R. Bennett, premier of the province since 1975, unexpectedly announced his retirement. William N. Vander Zalm, a 52-year-old millionaire horticulturist, was sworn in as the province's 27th premier on August 6.

Strikes. The new premier's first test was a threatened strike by the 34,000 members of the British Columbia Government Employees' Union. Bennett, faced with the same challenge in early July, forced the union to back down by threatening the would-be strikers with back-to-work legislation. In his first month in office, Vander Zalm won a tentative contract.

Vander Zalm was less successful with a forest industry strike, which began on July 27 and lasted 4½ months. Forestry is the largest industry in British Columbia, and the economic impact was great. The strike, involving 21,000 workers, arose out of the union's desire to restrain lumber companies from contracting out work to independents. The contracting-out issue was referred to a royal commission, which was to report by March 1988. The settlement also called for a wage increase and pension-plan improvements.

Election. Vander Zalm moved swiftly to call a general election for October 22. He campaigned vigorously, showing a pleasant openness and ex-

Retiring British Columbia Premier William R. Bennett, right, raises the hand of William N. Vander Zalm, the new premier-elect, in July.

pressing moderate views on social questions. The opposition parties criticized his campaign as all style and no substance. But the voters responded to it, and the Socred party won a decisive victory.

Logging Dispute. Logging resumed on Lyell Island, off the Pacific Coast, where a confrontation in late 1985 had resulted in the local Haida Indians setting up a blockade to keep logging crews off the island. A government-appointed committee later approved logging on four small islands, including Lyell Island, which is in the South Moresby group of the Queen Charlotte Islands. The committee also recommended that most of the environmentally sensitive South Moresby region be turned into a national or provincial park.

Expo 86, the Vancouver world's fair devoted to the theme of transportation, closed its doors on October 13 after 5½ months of operation. Fifty-four nations participated in the exposition, which was opened by Prince Charles of Great Britain on May 2. More than 22 million visitors crowded the site, encouraged by good weather—130 of the 172 days of Expo 86 were dry. The organizers of the fair had originally predicted 13.7 million visitors. Despite the high attendance, a deficit of $311 million (Canadian dollars; $1 = U.S. 72 cents as of Dec. 31, 1986) was projected.   David M. L. Farr

See also VANDER ZALM, WILLIAM N. In WORLD BOOK, see BRITISH COLUMBIA.

BRUNDTLAND, GRO HARLEM (1939-   ), became prime minister of Norway for the second time on May 9, 1986, heading a Labor Party *minority government* (one whose party holds fewer than half the seats in parliament). She succeeded Kaare Willoch, a Conservative, who resigned after the Storting (parliament) rejected his proposal to hike gasoline taxes.

In Brundtland's inaugural statement on May 13, she said, "The government's first and most pressing task will be to address the great challenges facing the Norwegian economy." Among the challenges were a balance-of-payments deficit and the plummeting price of oil. See NORWAY.

The new prime minister was born on April 20, 1939. She obtained a medical degree from the University of Oslo in 1963 and a master's degree from Harvard School of Public Health in Boston in 1965. In 1974, she accepted her first political post—minister of environment. Brundtland was elected vice chairman of the Labor Party in 1975 and became a member of the Storting in 1979.

In February 1981, Brundtland became Norway's first woman prime minister. But parliamentary elections in September 1981 swept Willoch into office.

The prime minister and her husband, Arne O. Brundtland, have four children.   Jay Myers

BRUNEI. See ASIA.

BUILDING AND CONSTRUCTION. The value of new construction erected in the United States in 1986 was expected to total almost $360 billion, the U.S. Department of Commerce reported in June. Of that figure—up $18 billion from 1985 and $47-billion from 1984—$290 billion represented private construction, and the remainder was government-sponsored construction.

Government construction grew by $8 billion over 1985 despite a slight overall decline in federal spending for building projects. The growth occurred because state and local governments shouldered more of the financing for improvements to the nation's *infrastructure*—public works, such as roads and bridges. Federal spending was down by 3.3 per cent in the first six months of 1986, but state and municipal spending was up by 8.3 per cent. The largest expenditures were for highways, schools, military construction, and water-supply facilities.

Government Projects. Federal, state, and local governments awarded some $16 billion in new contracts for transportation projects in the first eight months of 1986. That total included almost $12 billion for highways and $3.5 billion for bridges and tunnels. Another $7 billion in contracts was granted for the construction of educational buildings.

The most publicized federal building program

The Sunshine Skyway, the world's longest concrete-roadway cable-stayed bridge, nears completion near St. Petersburg, Fla., in July.

of 1986, an upgrading of security at U.S. embassies around the world, got underway late in the year. The project was authorized by the Omnibus Diplomatic Security and Antiterrorism Act of 1986, signed by President Ronald Reagan in August. The bill authorized $2.1 billion over five years to make U.S. embassies more resistant to attack. New embassy designs include extra-heavy frameworks, reinforced concrete walls, and fewer windows. Buildings will be set back at least 100 feet (30 meters) behind walls. In cases where such improvements are too difficult to make, the embassies will be relocated.

Private Construction. Office-building construction took a nose dive in 1986, with new contract awards down almost 20 per cent from 1985. Contracts for manufacturing plants were down by a similar percentage. The private building market was buoyed, however, by a surge in contracts for stores, shopping centers, and restaurants—up by more than 20 per cent.

One of the most spectacular buildings completed in the United States in 1986 was the Allied Bank Tower in Dallas, the first of twin 60-story towers in a complex called Fountain Place. The design, created by American architect Henry N. Cobb, resembles a giant rocket. The tower required innovative engineering and complex construction methods. Of the 19,500 short tons (17,700 metric tons) of fabricated steel in the building, 10,000 short tons (9,100 metric tons) went into the first five floors. Powerful cranes were required to move the steel pieces into place.

Older Structures Rehabilitated. High office vacancy rates in many U.S. cities depressed rents and discouraged developers from erecting new office buildings. As rents fell, numerous companies decided to relocate to get a more favorable lease. With fewer new buildings going up, however, companies often opted to move into older buildings. When a company moves, it usually redecorates—and often completely renovates—its new quarters. Thus, the slowdown in office construction acted as a spur to the rehabilitation of many older buildings.

The rehabilitation trend was not confined to office buildings. For example, Carnegie Hall in New York City, one of the world's foremost symphony halls, underwent a painstaking $50-million restoration that was completed in December.

Housing Sales, Construction. The sale of new homes soared in March to the highest recorded level in U.S. history, the Department of Commerce reported in April. The Commerce Department said new homes sold in March at an annual rate of 903,000 units. That pace was 24.4 per cent higher than February's rate and the highest rate since the government started publishing monthly home-sales statistics in 1963. The buying surge, which flattened out later in 1986 after consumer demand had been satisfied, was attributed to lower mortgage rates. Fixed mortgage rates in March averaged 9.9 per cent, their lowest level since 1978.

The construction of new housing picked up considerably in 1986. As of October 1, single-family homes were being built at a pace that would bring the total to 1.2 million units by year's end—13.2 per cent more than the 1985 total. Multifamily housing starts posted a much more modest increase. During the first nine months of 1986, multifamily housing was being built at a 676,000-unit annual rate, up 1.0 per cent from 1985.

Channel Tunnel. The governments of France and Great Britain announced jointly in January 1986 that they had agreed to construct a 31-mile (50-kilometer) electric-railway tunnel under the English Channel to link the two countries. The $3.7-billion project, which is expected to be completed by 1993, will be carried out by a group of 5 banks and 10 construction companies. Both governments had wanted automobile as well as train tunnels, but engineers said that a breakthrough in ventilation technology would be required before a safe tunnel for gasoline-burning vehicles could be built.

The railway tunnel will actually be three parallel tunnels—twin rail tunnels separated by a service and ventilation tunnel. A similar set of rail tunnels, linking the Japanese islands of Honshu and Hokkaido, neared completion in late 1986.

Big Dams. Construction of the Guri Dam in Venezuela, one of the largest and most powerful dams ever built, drew to a close in 1986. The 10,000-megawatt, $5.2-billion project on the Caroni River in Venezuela's Bolívar state had been under construction since 1963.

Two and a half years into the construction, Turkey's giant Atatürk Dam on the Euphrates River was apparently on schedule in 1986. The dam is a key part of a $4-billion plan to return the region of the Tigris and Euphrates rivers to cultivation and produce 2,400 megawatts of power for industrial development. The dam will be the fifth largest in the world when it is completed in 1990.

Cable-Stayed Bridges. Two of the world's longest *cable-stayed bridges*—bridges on which the cables supporting the roadway are anchored to steel or concrete towers—were completed in 1986. The world's longest steel-roadway cable-stayed bridge was built near Vancouver, Canada. The six-lane bridge's main span extends 1,526 feet (465 meters).

The world's longest concrete-roadway cable-stayed span, Sunshine Skyway near St. Petersburg, Fla., was also finished in 1986. The main span is 1,200 feet (366 meters) long. Janice Lyn Tuchman

In WORLD BOOK, see BRIDGE; BUILDING; CONSTRUCTION; DAM; TUNNEL.

BULGARIA. Bulgaria's Communist Party reelected Todor Zhivkov as its leader at its congress in April 1986. Zhivkov has been party leader since 1954 and head of state since 1962.

Zhivkov told the 1986 congress that Bulgaria needed greater "responsibility, order, and discipline" in the economy and needed to improve its technology. He also promised to crack down on incompetence and waste. Political observers interpreted Zhivkov's speech to mean that he would follow the lead of Soviet leader Mikhail S. Gorbachev in initiating domestic reforms. At the congress, Soviet Council of Ministers Chairman Nikolai I. Ryzhkov praised the Bulgarian Communist Party and Zhivkov. Gorbachev and other Soviet leaders had criticized Bulgaria in 1985.

On March 21, 1986, Georgi Atanasov replaced Georgi Stanchev Filipov as prime minister. Filipov became a Central Committee secretary.

Consolidations. In January, Bulgaria created a single agency for agriculture to replace ministries and other bodies that had been responsible for agriculture. It also created three powerful councils—one each for economics; science, education, and culture; and social affairs. The councils replaced eight ministries.

Production. In the first nine months of 1986, industrial output grew by 5.4 per cent, compared with the first nine months of 1985. Industrial productivity climbed 7.2 per cent, but there were shortfalls in electrical power, steel, and other industries. On November 17, the Politburo—the policymaking body of the Communist Party—called for tightened restrictions on the production, sale, and consumption of alcohol.

Relations with Turkey remained strained, but Bulgaria's Foreign Minister Petur Mladenov met his Turkish counterpart, Vahit Halefoglu, in Vienna, Austria, in November for what were described as "constructive, businesslike talks." An Amnesty International report published in April had accused Bulgaria of "massive oppression" of its minority of ethnic Turks. Greece's Prime Minister Andreas Papandreou visited Bulgaria in September. He and Atanasov signed a declaration of friendship and cooperation.

Suspect Freed. On March 29, a court in Rome, Italy, acquitted Sergei I. Antonov, a Bulgarian airline official accused of complicity in the attempt to assassinate Pope John Paul II in May 1981. The ruling indicated that the court did not have enough evidence to convict Antonov. He returned to Bulgaria on April 1. Chris Cviic

See also EUROPE (Facts in Brief Table). In WORLD BOOK, see BULGARIA.

BURKINA FASO. See AFRICA.

BURMA. See ASIA.

BURUNDI. See AFRICA.

BUS. See TRANSIT; TRANSPORTATION.

BUSH, GEORGE H. W. (1924-   ), 43rd Vice President of the United States, divided his time in 1986 between his unofficial campaign for the 1988 Republican presidential nomination and his duties as a far-ranging emissary for President Ronald Reagan. Bush won the largest share of precinct delegates elected by Michigan Republicans on August 5—the first contest to have a direct bearing on the 1988 Republican presidential race. A Gallup Poll in May 1986 indicated Bush was the Republican candidate most favored by voters.

On April 1, as Bush prepared for a visit to Saudi Arabia, he said, "It is essential that we talk about stability" in world oil prices. The Reagan Administration promptly distanced itself from Bush's remark, saying it had no intention of interfering with oil price movements. The trip also took Bush to Bahrain, Oman, and North Yemen. In late July, the Vice President returned to the Middle East, visiting Israel, Jordan, and Egypt.

On May 15, a common and highly curable form of skin cancer was removed from Bush's left cheek. The 1986 income tax return filed by Bush and his wife, Barbara, revealed that they paid $31,039 in federal tax on income of $165,821 in 1985.   Frank Cormier and Margot Cormier

In WORLD BOOK, see BUSH, GEORGE H. W.

BUSINESS. See BANK; ECONOMICS; LABOR; MANUFACTURING.

CABINET, UNITED STATES. Two major changes occurred in President Ronald Reagan's Cabinet in 1986. Secretary of Agriculture John R. Block resigned in February and was succeeded by Richard E. Lyng, a former deputy secretary in the Department of Agriculture (see LYNG, RICHARD EDMUND). In November, Vice Admiral John M. Poindexter, Reagan's national security adviser, resigned as a controversy erupted over the sale of arms to Iran. Reagan named Frank C. Carlucci, a former deputy director of the Central Intelligence Agency, to succeed Poindexter. See PRESIDENT OF THE UNITED STATES.

During the year, an "influence peddling" controversy erupted over the lobbying activities of former top Reagan aide Michael K. Deaver, who left the Administration in 1985 and founded a public relations firm.

A report on May 12 by the General Accounting Office concluded that the former aide had apparently violated federal conflict-of-interest laws. Later in the month, a three-judge panel of the U.S. Court of Appeals appointed a special counsel to investigate Deaver.   David L. Dreier

In WORLD BOOK, see CABINET.

CALIFORNIA. See LOS ANGELES; STATE GOV'T.

CAMBODIA. See KAMPUCHEA.

CAMEROON. See AFRICA.

CAMP FIRE. See YOUTH ORGANIZATIONS.

CANADA

Canada's Progressive Conservative Party administration, led by Prime Minister Brian Mulroney, reached the midpoint of its first term in 1986. Under Canadian electoral law, Mulroney must call an election by September 1989, five years after taking office. Although the party swept into office with an enormous majority in September 1984, its popularity had fallen since coming to power. Popular support for its major rival, the Liberal Party, had risen meanwhile.

Midterm Accomplishments, Goals.

The Progressive Conservatives (PC's) could point to a number of solid accomplishments. They had resolved in 1985 a dispute with the energy-rich Western provinces of Alberta, British Columbia, and Saskatchewan over oil and gas pricing and taxing. In foreign policy, the PC's had earned broad support. Since 1984, Canada's economy had grown at an annual rate of about 4 per cent after adjusting for inflation. Unemployment, inflation, and interest rates had all dropped. The PC's had restrained federal spending and halted the rise in the deficit.

In 1986, Mulroney marked out three principal objectives for the remainder of his first term. One goal was to negotiate a free-trade agreement with

Expo 86, a world's fair held in Vancouver, B.C., attracted more than 22 million visitors during its 5½-month run from May 2 to Oct. 13, 1986.

the United States, so that trade between the two nations would be unrestricted by tariffs or other barriers. A second aim was to reach an agreement with Quebec that would permit the province to sign Canada's 1982 constitution. Quebec was the only province to refuse to sign. A third objective was to reform Canada's taxation system.

Cabinet Changes.

Mulroney shuffled his cabinet on June 30 to place key ministers in each of the three areas of intended action. To supervise trade

237

The Ministry of Canada*
In order of precedence

Martin Brian Mulroney, prime minister

George Harris Hees, minister of veterans affairs

Charles Joseph Clark, secretary of state for external affairs

Flora Isabel MacDonald, minister of communications

John Carnell Crosbie, minister of transport

Roch La Salle, minister of state

Donald Frank Mazankowski, deputy prime minister, president of the Queen's Privy Council for Canada, and government House leader

Elmer MacIntosh MacKay, minister of national revenue

Jake Epp, minister of national health and welfare

John Wise, minister of agriculture

Ramon John Hnatyshyn, minister of justice and attorney general of Canada

David Edward Crombie, secretary of state and minister responsible for multiculturalism

Robert R. de Cotret, president of the Treasury Board

Henry Perrin Beatty, minister of national defence

Michael Holcombe Wilson, minister of finance

Harvie Andre, minister of consumer and corporate affairs

Otto John Jelinek, minister of state (fitness and amateur sport)

Thomas Edward Siddon, minister of fisheries and oceans

Charles James Mayer, minister of state (Canadian Wheat Board)

William Hunter McKnight, minister of Indian affairs and northern development

Thomas Michael McMillan, minister of the environment

Patricia Carney, minister for international trade

André Bissonnette, minister of state (transport)

Benoît Bouchard, minister of employment and immigration

Michel Côté, minister of regional industrial expansion

James Francis Kelleher, solicitor general of Canada

Marcel Masse, minister of energy, mines and resources

Barbara Jean McDougall, minister of state (privatization) and minister responsible for the status of women

Gerald S. Merrithew, minister of state (forestry and mines)

Monique Vézina, minister of supply and services

Steward McInnes, minister of public works

Frank Oberle, minister of state for science and technology

Lowell Murray, leader of the government in the Senate and minister of state (federal-provincial relations)

Paul Wyatt Dick, associate minister of national defence

Pierre Cadieux, minister of labour

Jean Charest, minister of state (youth)

Thomas Hockin, minister of state (finance)

Monique Landry, minister for external relations

Bernard Valcourt, minister of state (small businesses and tourism)

Gerry Weiner, minister of state (immigration)

*As of Dec. 31, 1986.

Premiers of Canadian Provinces

Province	Premier
Alberta	Donald Getty
British Columbia	William N. Vander Zalm
Manitoba	Howard Pawley
New Brunswick	Richard B. Hatfield
Newfoundland	Brian Peckford
Nova Scotia	John Buchanan
Ontario	David Peterson
Prince Edward Island	Joseph A. Ghiz
Quebec	Robert Bourassa
Saskatchewan	Grant Devine

Commissioners of Territories

Northwest Territories	John H. Parker
Yukon Territory	J. Kenneth McKinnon

relations with the United States, he transferred Patricia Carney, who had been a successful minister of energy, mines, and resources, to minister of international trade. Mulroney designated Lowell Murray, a member of the Senate, to be minister of state for federal-provincial relations, with special responsibility to gain Quebec's approval of the constitution. The prime minister directed Michael Holcombe Wilson, minister of finance, to carry out changes in the tax system.

Erik H. Nielsen gave up his post as deputy prime minister and minister of national defense in the June 30 shuffle. Many members of the opposition and the press found Nielsen's manner abrasive, and he had not helped the government's standing in the House of Commons. Mulroney appointed Donald Frank Mazankowski, a respected legislator from Alberta, to the post of deputy prime minister. Marcel Masse, who had left the cabinet briefly in 1985 until he was cleared of charges of campaign-spending irregularities, received the important energy portfolio.

Another veteran, Minister of Regional Industrial Expansion Sinclair McKnight Stevens, left the cabinet on May 12, 1986. Stevens resigned to face conflict-of-interest charges arising from his personal business holdings.

Opposition Parties. A Quebec member left the Progressive Conservative Party in May to sit as an independent, leaving the PC with 209 of the 282 seats in the House of Commons. Against that majority, the opposition parties mustered only 69 seats—40 Liberals and 29 members of the socialist New Democratic Party (NDP). There were 2 independents and 2 vacancies in the House.

The Liberals suffered a blow when one of their most popular members, Quebec lawyer Jean Chrétien, resigned his House seat on February 27. Chrétien had unsuccessfully challenged John N. Turner for leadership of the Liberal Party in 1984, though opinion polls showed Chrétien as more popular than Turner throughout Canada. On Nov. 30, 1986, however, a Liberal Party national convention strongly endorsed Turner's continued leadership of the party.

The Liberals won a special election on September 29 to fill Chrétien's seat in the St.-Maurice district of Quebec. The PC's retained another vacant seat, in Alberta, in an election on the same day. The main surprise of the September elections was a strong showing by the NDP, traditionally weak in the two provinces.

Legislation passed by Parliament in 1986 included a no-fault divorce bill and a new act governing the treatment of young offenders in the criminal justice system. New arrangements slowed the rate of growth in federal support payments to the provinces for health and higher education. Parliament also placed a cap on yearly inflation increases in family allowance payments, which provide financial assistance to needy families.

Quebec's Conditions for accepting the 1982 constitution were spelled out on May 9, 1986, by the new Liberal government of Quebec Prime Minister Robert Bourassa, who assumed office in December 1985. The province's terms were listed as:

■ Recognition, in the constitution, of Quebec as a "distinct society" within Canada.

■ More authority for Quebec in controlling immigration within its territory.

■ The right to veto constitutional amendments.

■ Participation in the selection of Supreme Court judges.

■ Limitations on federal spending power.

The premiers of Canada's other nine provinces considered Quebec's terms at their 27th annual meeting in Edmonton, Alta., on Aug. 11 and 12, 1986. Bourassa refined his definition of a veto at the meeting. He proposed that the consent of seven provinces with at least 75 per cent of the country's population be required to approve a constitutional amendment. (The 1982 constitution says that amendments require the approval of seven provinces with at least 50 per cent of the people.) Because Quebec has about 26 per cent of Canada's population, the proposed formula would, in effect, give Quebec the power to veto an amendment. The other provinces seemed prepared to consider Quebec's terms.

The conference of premiers showed more interest in such economic issues as unemployment and regional development. With only one dissenter, Manitoba's Premier Howard Pawley, the premiers endorsed the Mulroney government's free-trade negotiations with the United States.

The Economy continued the recovery begun in 1982, though it grew at a slower pace in 1986 than in 1985. The gross national product, after adjusting for inflation and seasonal fluctuations, was estimated to be $485 billion. (Unless otherwise indicated, all monetary amounts in this article are Canadian dollars with $1 = U.S. 72 cents as of Dec. 31, 1986.)

Over the first six months of the year, Canada recorded a significant trade surplus, though it was lower than in 1985. Sluggish economic conditions in the United States and low prices for petroleum and wheat, two of Canada's major exports, hurt Canada's export income.

Unemployment dropped slightly from 1985, the seasonally adjusted rate standing at 9.4 per cent in October 1986. Mild inflation continued. The Consumer Price Index, the most commonly used measure of inflation, rose slightly to 4.4 per cent in October over a 12-month period.

The Canadian dollar leveled off at about U.S. 72 cents in October after it had fallen in February to its lowest point in history, U.S. 69.13 cents.

Canada, Provinces, and Territories Population Estimates

	1985	1986
Alberta	2,348,800	2,389,500
British Columbia	2,892,500	2,905,900
Manitoba	1,069,600	1,078,600
New Brunswick	719,200	721,100
Newfoundland	580,400	580,200
Northwest Territories	50,900	50,900
Nova Scotia	880,700	883,800
Ontario	9,066,200	9,181,900
Prince Edward Island	127,100	128,100
Quebec	6,580,700	6,627,200
Saskatchewan	1,019,500	1,021,000
Yukon Territory	22,800	22,900
Canada	**25,358,400**	**25,591,100**

City and Metropolitan Population Estimates

	Metropolitan Area June 1, 1985, estimate	City 1981 Census
Toronto	3,202,400	599,217
Montreal	2,878,200	980,354
Vancouver	1,348,600	414,281
Ottawa-Hull	769,900	
Ottawa		295,163
Hull		56,225
Edmonton	683,600	532,246
Calgary	625,600	592,743
Winnipeg	612,100	564,473
Quebec	593,500	166,474
Hamilton	559,700	306,434
St. Catharines-Niagara	309,400	
St. Catharines		124,018
Niagara Falls		17,010
Kitchener	303,400	139,734
London	292,700	254,280
Halifax	290,600	114,594
Windsor	249,800	192,083
Victoria	245,100	64,379
Regina	174,800	162,613
Oshawa	172,800	117,519
Saskatoon	170,100	154,210
St. John's	160,700	83,770
Sudbury	147,600	91,829
Chicoutimi-Jonquière	139,400	
Chicoutimi		60,064
Jonquière		60,354
Thunder Bay	123,500	112,486
Saint John	116,800	80,521
Trois-Rivières	114,300	50,466

The Budget. Finance Minister Wilson presented his second budget—for the fiscal year beginning April 1, 1986—on February 26. The budget called for stiff new taxes—a 3 per cent surtax on personal and corporate income taxes; a 1 percentage-point increase in the sales tax, with a partial rebate for low-income earners; and higher taxes on tobacco and alcoholic beverages. Wilson estimated the new taxes would raise about $1.5 billion, boosting revenue to $87.3 billion. He projected expenditures for the year at $116.8 billion, producing a deficit of $29.5 billion.

Wilson's forecasts proved to be optimistic. In February, he predicted economic growth of 3.7 per cent for the year, a figure that he had revised

Federal Spending in Canada

Estimated Budget for Fiscal 1986-1987*

Transfer payments:	Millions of dollars†
To other levels of government:	
Health insurance	6,805
Post-secondary education	2,380
Fiscal transfer payments	5,768
Canada Assistance Plan	4,059
Other	1,866
To persons:	
Old age security	9,510
Guaranteed income supplement	3,566
Spouse's allowance	605
Government's contribution to unemployment insurance	2,880
Family allowances	2,531
Other	1,536
Subsidies:	
Petroleum incentive payments	950
Western Grain Transportation Act	706
Agriculture Stabilization Act	359
Western Grain Stabilization Act	96
Petroleum compensation	10
Other	210
Other transfer payments:	
Foreign aid	2,044
Regional industrial expansion	819
Indians and Inuit	1,096
Job creation projects of employment and immigration	1,719
Other	2,226
Public debt charges	27,000
Payments to Crown corporations:	
Canada Mortgage and Housing Corporation	1,582
Canadian Broadcasting Corporation	870
VIA Rail Canada Inc.	500
Canada Post Corporation	121
Atomic Energy of Canada Ltd.	216
Other	958
Operating and capital expenditures:	
National defense	9,955
Other departments and agencies	14,065
Total	**107,008**

*April 1, 1986, to March 31, 1987.
†Canadian dollars; $1 = U.S. 72 cents as of Dec. 1, 1986.

Spending Since 1981

Billions of dollars

Fiscal year: 1981-'82, '82-'83, '83-'84, '84-'85, '85-'86, '86-'87

Source: Treasury Board of Canada.

downward by September to 3.1 per cent. Wilson also assumed oil prices of U.S. $22.50 a barrel, but by the second half of the year they had dropped to U.S. $14.00 a barrel. These developments forced the finance minister to offer a revised economic statement on September 18. He said that the federal deficit would swell to $32 billion because of unfavorable economic conditions.

Free Trade and its opposite, called *protectionism,* figured prominently in relations between the United States and Canada during 1986. The two nations are each other's largest trading partner.

Negotiations for a free-trade agreement, endorsed by U.S. President Ronald Reagan and Prime Minister Mulroney, followed a close vote in the U.S. Senate Finance Committee in April. Reagan had asked the committee to approve a "fast-track" procedure that would give Congress authority to approve or reject a trade treaty in its entirety, but not to amend it. On April 23, a resolution blocking the fast-track procedure lost by a tie vote, 10-10. (Disapproval resolutions are not carried on a tie vote.) Canada had warned that it would withdraw its offer to negotiate a free-trade pact if the resolution were approved.

Shingles and Shakes. The free-trade talks began in May and continued throughout the summer, meeting in alternate months in the two national capitals, Ottawa, Ont., and Washington, D.C. The negotiations faced a rising tide of protectionist sentiment in the U.S. Congress and got off to a rocky start. On May 22, the day the talks began, the United States imposed a 35 per cent tariff for 2½ years on shakes and shingles made of Canadian red cedar (called *redwood* in the United States). It was estimated that Canadian exports of *shakes* (rough shingles) and shingles, used for roofing and siding on houses, had captured 73 per cent of the United States market. The tariff was designed to block Canadian exports from the U.S. market, boosting sales by U.S. producers.

The shakes-and-shingles case aroused Canadian public opinion against protectionist U.S. trade policies. Mulroney, who had worked to cultivate a good relationship with Reagan, felt personally betrayed. He called the U.S. action "bizarre" and sent a letter of protest to the White House.

The mood of Canada left the Mulroney government no course but to retaliate. On June 2, Canada reimposed tariffs that had been suspended for seven years on certain types of United States books, periodicals, and computer parts. The Mulroney government refused to show its displeasure by abandoning the free-trade talks, however.

Softwood Lumber. The United States proposed another tariff as a result of a Department of Commerce ruling on October 16. It concerned Canadian exports of softwood lumber (pine, spruce, and fir). Helped by the decline of the Canadian dollar against U.S. currency, these exports had captured about one-third of the U.S. market.

United States lumber producers asked the Commerce Department to impose a 27 per cent duty. They claimed, as they had done three years before, that *stumpage fees* (the fees charged for the right to cut standing timber) on government-owned land in Canada were so low as to constitute a subsidy. In 1983, the lumber producers had lost this argument, but in 1986 they were successful. The Commerce Department imposed a 15 per cent duty in a preliminary ruling, subject to a final judgment in December.

The Canadian reaction to the new duty was indignant. Minister of International Trade Carney called it "deplorable, artificial, and contrived." But on November 21, after a conference with the provinces, Carney said that Canada would negotiate with the United States. On December 30, the two nations reached a compromise. Canada imposed a 15 per cent tax on softwood lumber exports to the United States, which dropped its duty.

Corn. Meanwhile, trade tensions increased again on November 7, when Canada slapped a stiff duty on U.S. corn imports. In response to complaints from Canadian farmers, Canada's Department of National Revenue ruled that the U.S. farm bill enacted in 1985 unfairly subsidized corn producers. The department imposed a duty of U.S. $1.05 per bushel on corn.

Mulroney and Reagan met in Washington, D.C., on March 18 and 19, 1986. They discussed a joint U.S.-Canadian report on acid rain pollution prepared following the March 1985 "Shamrock Summit" in Quebec City, Que. The report called on the two countries to join forces in a $6.9-billion (about U.S. $5-billion) research and development program over five years to explore ways to burn coal more cleanly. Reagan endorsed the report, the firmest step he has taken toward admitting that acid rain is a serious problem.

The two leaders also signed an agreement extending for another five years the North American Aerospace Defense Command (NORAD), a joint air-defense system. In addition, Canada agreed to cooperate in a United States project to put a space station in permanent orbit by 1990.

South Africa occupied much of Canada's diplomatic effort in 1986. Archbishop Edward W. Scott of the Anglican (Episcopalian) Church of Canada participated in a Commonwealth committee of "eminent persons" asked to open a dialogue with the South African government on its policy of *apartheid* (racial segregation). Canada belongs to the Commonwealth, a group of nations that includes Great Britain and its former colonies.

The Commonwealth committee went to South Africa in March and met there with imprisoned black leader Nelson Mandela. But the committee failed to move South Africa in its racial policies. Later, the group recommended economic *sanctions* (penalties) as a means of persuading South Africa to institute political change.

Mulroney tried to persuade Britain's Prime Minister Margaret Thatcher to adopt sanctions in a meeting at Mirabel Airport near Montreal, Que., on July 13. But the two leaders failed to agree. Mulroney then went to a Commonwealth "mini-summit" conference determined to make a last attempt to achieve agreement on the subject. Leaders of Australia, the Bahamas, Britain, Canada, India, Zambia, and Zimbabwe met in London from August 2 to 5 to consider action against South Africa. All but Britain agreed on stiff sanctions including bans on air travel and South African imports. Thatcher agreed to only some of the measures proposed by the conference.

Facts in Brief: Population: 26,198,000. Government: Governor General Jeanne M. Sauvé; Prime Minister M. Brian Mulroney. Monetary unit: the Canadian dollar. Value of foreign trade (in U.S. dollars): exports, $90,635,000,000; and imports, $81,056,000,000. David M. L. Farr

See also the Canadian provinces articles: CANADIAN LIBRARY ASSOCIATION (CLA); CANADIAN LITERATURE; GHIZ, JOSEPH A.; MULRONEY, M. BRIAN; SAUVÉ, JEANNE M.; TRUDEAU, PIERRE E.; VANDER ZALM, WILLIAM N.

CANADIAN LIBRARY ASSOCIATION (CLA) in February 1986 sent a brief to the Canadian government regarding proposed copyright legislation expected to take effect in 1987. The items covered in the brief included a CLA recommendation that there be no copyright on works produced by the government.

The CLA also produced seminars to help libraries assess their compliance with copyright law to ensure that any photocopying does not violate the rights of authors and publishers.

The CLA during 1986 also expressed concern about cutbacks in the number of federal government libraries and protested a 10 per cent tariff on imported English-language books. The Canadian government imposed the book tariff in June to retaliate against a United States tariff on cedar shakes and shingles imported from Canada. See CANADA.

The annual CLA meeting was held jointly with the Association pour l'avancement des sciences et des techniques de la documentation in Quebec City, Que., from June 19 to 24. Outgoing president Beth Miller was succeeded by Ken Jensen of the Regina (Sask.) Public Library. Jane Cooney, formerly of the Bank Marketing Association in Chicago, was appointed CLA executive director in October 1986. Jane Cooney

In WORLD BOOK, see CANADIAN LIBRARY ASSN.

CANADIAN LITERATURE. Canadian authors welcomed the formal establishment in 1986 of the Public Lending Right Commission to oversee the spending of an annual $3-million fund (Canadian dollars; $ 1 = U.S. 72 cents on Dec. 31, 1986) allocated by the federal government to pay writers for the use of their works in libraries. Canada was the 12th country to inaugurate such a plan. The year was also commendable for the number of excellent books published in all categories.

Fiction. The outstanding work of Canadian fiction in 1986, in the opinion of many critics, was Alice Munro's *The Progress of Love*, a short-story collection that again demonstrated her gift for inventing ordinary characters and placing them in significant situations that touch the heart and mind. Scott Symons' novel *Helmet of Flesh* was another publishing event. The result of 10 years of work, the novel—thought to be autobiographical—depicted the sexual and intellectual adventures of a Canadian in Morocco.

Three excellent novels were based on real-life characters. Heather Robertson's *Lily* featured Canada's former Prime Minister W. L. Mackenzie King; Josef Skvorecky's *Dvorak in Love* depicted Czechoslovak composer Antonín Dvořák; and Andreas Schroeder's *Dust-Ship Glory* portrayed a prairie farmer who built an oceangoing ship during

Alice Munro, a leading practitioner of the short story, received critical acclaim for her new collection, *The Progress of Love*, in 1986.

the Great Depression of the 1930's. Perhaps the best first novel of 1986 was Wayne Johnston's *The Story of Bobby O'Malley*, an account of a boy struggling to free himself from restraints of his narrow Newfoundland community.

Among the many fine short-story collections were Alistair MacLeod's *As Birds Bring Forth the Sun and Other Stories*, Brian Fawcett's *The Secret Journal of Alexander Mackenzie*, Janice Kulyk Keefer's *The Paris-Napoli Express*, Margo Livesay's *Learning from the Heart*, and John Metcalf's *Adult Entertainment*.

Biographies and Memoirs. Phyllis Grosskurth's *Melanie Klein* was a sympathetic and exhaustively researched biography of the Vienna-born psychoanalyst and pioneer in the field of child analysis. Patricia Morley's *Kurelek* examined the deeply troubled life of the popular Canadian painter William Kurelek. Muriel Miller's *Bliss Carman* and John Coldwell Adams' *Sir Charles God Damn: The Life of Sir Charles G. D. Roberts* shed new light on the careers of two famous and influential Canadian poets. *Escape from the Glue Factory*, a memoir by Joe Rosenblatt, explained how his childhood in the Jewish district of Toronto, Ont., led to his work as an important contemporary poet.

Two books that provoked lively controversy were Roger Bowen's *Innocence Is Not Enough* and James Barros' *No Sense of Evil*, biographies of Herbert Norman, the distinguished scholar and Canada's ambassador to Egypt. Norman committed suicide in 1957, following the revival of Communist espionage charges against him by a United States Senate committee. Bowen vindicated Norman's integrity, but Barros attempted to show that the case against Norman was substantially accurate. Lynne Gordon's *Working Without a Net*, a memoir by a Toronto broadcaster, also dealt with her U.S. experience in the 1950's when her then-husband, radio and television entertainer John Henry Faulk, was accused as a Communist.

Politics and History. Pierre Berton's *Vimy* and Daniel Dancocks' *Legacy of Valour* recalled the sacrifices made by Canadian soldiers on the battlefields of World War I (1914-1918). Barry Broadfoot contributed *The Immigrant Years*, which examined the immigration of Europeans to Canada between 1945 and 1967.

Many of the other books in this category—mainly reminiscences of political careers—had a more contemporary flavor. Among them were René Lévesque's *Memoirs*, Sheila Copps's *Nobody's Baby*, Senator Keith Davey's *The Rainmaker*, Roy MacLaren's *Honourable Mentions*, and J. W. Pickersgill's *The Way Back*.

Poetry. Margaret Atwood's *Selected Poems* included work from 1976 to 1986, and two other major poets, Alfred Purdy and Miriam Waddington, each had a remarkably accomplished life's work published in their *Collected Poems*. Other new collections included work by Robert Bringhurst, Don Domanski, Robert Finch, Gary Geddes, Marty Gervais, Don Cole, Mary di Michele, Irving Layton, Joy Kogasa, and Raymond Souster.

Essays and Criticism. Stephen Vizinczey, a strongly opinionated novelist and critic, wrote *Truth and Lies in Literature*, a collection of essays and book reviews. Mavis Gallant, a fine story writer and novelist, contributed *Paris Notebooks*. This collection, rich in insight and elegance of language, touched on such topics as the 1968 student riots in France, in which Gallant was both a bemused observer and an irritated participant.

Among other essay collections were *The Bumper Book*, edited by John Metcalf, which attempted to demolish the reputations of many Canadian writers; novelist Jane Rule's *A Hot-Eyed Moderate*, which reflected her literary and feminist preoccupations; and Clark Blaise's *Resident Alien*, an account of his development as a writer born in North Dakota of Canadian parents.

Business and Finance. Diane Francis' *Controlling Interest* told how 32 powerful family dynasties operate in Canada. Peter Foster's *The Master Builders* looked at the Reichmann business empire, and *Breaking the Banks*, by Arthur Johnson, explored the failure in Canada of certain banking interests.

Art and Photography. David Burnett's *Harold Town* was an important portfolio of work by the major Canadian painter. Ken Tolmie's book of paintings and photographs, *A Rural Life*, attractively showcased views of life in the Annapolis Valley of Nova Scotia. Doris Shadbolt's *Bill Reid* featured 200 illustrations by Reid, a Haida Indian artist. Brian Milne produced a book of photographs, *Trans-Canada Country*.

Awards. The Governor General's Literary Awards for books published in 1985 went to Margaret Atwood for *The Handmaid's Tale* (English fiction); Fred Wah for *Waiting for Saskatchewan* (English poetry); Ramsay Cook for *The Regenerators* (English nonfiction); George F. Walker for *Criminals in Love* (English drama); Fernand Ouellette for *Lucie ou un midi en novembre* (French fiction); André Roy for *Action Writing* (French fiction); François Ricard for *La littérature contre elle-même* (French nonfiction); and Maryse Pelletier for *Duo pour voix obstinées* (French drama).

Yvonne M. Klein won the Canada Council Translation Prize for her English translation of Jovette Marchessault's *Lesbian Triptych*, and Michelle Robinson won for her French translation of Rudy Wiebe's *The Scorched-Wood People*. Joey Slinger received the Stephen Leacock Memorial Award for humor for his collection of newspaper columns, *No Axe Too Small to Grind*.   Ken Adachi

In WORLD BOOK, see CANADIAN LITERATURE.

CAPE VERDE. See AFRICA.

CARLSSON, INGVAR (1934-   ), became prime minister of Sweden on March 12, 1986, succeeding Olof Palme, who was assassinated on February 28. On March 13, Carlsson announced that his government would follow policies advocated by Palme. See SWEDEN.

Carlsson was born on Nov. 9, 1934, in Borås, a textile center in southwestern Sweden. In 1958, he received a degree in political science and economics at the University of Lund. From 1958 until 1960, he was an assistant to Prime Minister Tage Erlander.

In 1964, Carlsson was elected to the Riksdag (parliament). Erlander appointed him undersecretary of state in 1967. When Palme became prime minister in 1969, Carlsson succeeded Palme as minister of education and cultural affairs. Carlsson became minister of housing and physical planning in 1973.

Carlsson was chairman of the Stockholm County branch of the Social Democratic Party from 1971 until 1974. He joined the party's executive committee in 1972. The Social Democrats lost a general election in 1976 but returned to power in 1982, with Carlsson assuming the post of deputy prime minister. He became minister for the environment in 1985.

The new prime minister and his wife, Ingrid, have two daughters.   Jay Myers

CARTER, JAMES EARL, JR. (1924-   ), the 39th President of the United States, was joined by President Ronald Reagan on Oct. 1, 1986, for the dedication of the Carter Presidential Center in Atlanta, Ga. In his remarks, Reagan spoke glowingly of Carter's "passion and intellect and commitment" as President.

In March, Carter accused Reagan of "habitually" taking all the credit for programs to build up the nation's military capabilities. Reagan subsequently praised Carter's defense record.

An angered Carter walked out of a Fourth of July reception at the United States Embassy in Harare, Zimbabwe. Carter—along with his wife, Rosalynn; their daughter, Amy; and the acting U.S. ambassador—walked out on a speech, read on behalf of Zimbabwe's foreign minister by the minister of culture, attacking U.S. policy toward South Africa. Carter called the speech "an insult to my country and to me personally."

Amy Carter, 19, a student at Brown University in Providence, R.I., was arrested on November 24 at the University of Massachusetts in Amherst. She was among 59 people arrested for occupying a building to protest campus recruitment by the Central Intelligence Agency. It was the second time in 1986 that Carter's daughter had been arrested at a sit-in.   Frank Cormier and Margot Cormier

In WORLD BOOK, see CARTER, JAMES EARL, JR.

CAT. Figures released in 1986 by the Market Research Corporation of America (MRCA) indicated that cats were kept as pets in 26 million U.S. households. The MRCA estimated that the number of pet cats rose to 56 million in 1985, an increase of 11 per cent over the 1984 total. The cat is now the most popular pet in the United States.

The Cat Fanciers' Association, Incorporated, the world's largest pedigreed cat registry, said that 60,000 cats were registered in 1986. Persians continued to lead in popularity, followed by the Siamese, Abyssinian, Maine Coon, and Burmese. The American Curl became a registered breed in 1986.

The 1986 National Best Cat was Grand Champion Rambo's Rocky Mountain Sunrise, a red-and-white Persian male bred by Jim and Anne Rambo and Judy Phillips and owned by the Rambos, Phillips, and Ashley Reynolds, all of Atlanta, Ga. A copper-eyed, white Persian male named Grand Champion Windborne Guardian Angel won the title of National Best Kitten. Guardian Angel was bred by Vicki Dickerson and owned by Dickerson and Barbara and Clifford Farrell of Phoenix. Grand Premier Abyko Boomer, a ruddy Abyssinian neuter, was the 1986 Best Altered Cat and was bred by Suzie Kidder of Costa Mesa, Calif. The owners were Kidder, Audrey Hayes, and Berdeen Pigarsh of North Bergen, N.J.   Thomas H. Dent

In WORLD BOOK, see CAT.

CENSUS. On Jan. 1, 1987, the population of the United States was about 242.1 million, 2.2 million more than a year earlier. During 1985, the population increased by 1.6 million to 239.1 million, according to the U.S. Bureau of the Census. Because older age groups make up a larger proportion of the population, the death total in 1985—2,083,000 deaths—set a new record. The black population grew by 1.5 per cent in 1985 to 29.2 million, more than double the 0.7 per cent growth rate of the white population.

Fertility Rate. Census Bureau figures released in August 1986 revealed that the total fertility rate, an estimate of the number of children born to 1,000 women during their lifetimes, was 1,837 in 1985, compared with a peak rate of 3,760 in 1957. A rate of 2,100 is considered a replacement level—providing for replacement of 1,000 mothers and 1,000 fathers, with the 100 extra accounting for children who die. Thus, in 1985, for the 13th consecutive year, Americans did not bear children at a rate sufficient to replace themselves. Population growth has continued largely because Americans born during the baby boom that followed World War II have reached prime child-bearing age.

Farm Populations. The Census Bureau reported a 7 per cent drop in the farm population in 1985—a figure that reflects the economic difficulties endured by many farm families in the 1980's. According to the report, the farm population dropped from 5.7 million to 5.3 million. The report said 2.2 per cent of all Americans lived on farms in 1985, with 49 per cent of all farm residents living in the Midwest.

Income. In August 1986, the Census Bureau reported that the South, traditionally the region of the country with the lowest income levels, climbed past the Midwest in average after-tax household income in 1984. The national average was $21,564, with the West highest at $23,038, followed by the Northeast ($22,001), the South ($20,951), and the Midwest ($20,865). In a study published in July 1986, the bureau reported the median *net worth*—assets such as ownership of savings and housing, minus debts—of white households was $39,135 in 1984. The figure for Hispanic households was $4,913, and for black households, $3,397.

Illegal Aliens. In 1986, the Census Bureau began estimating the number of illegal aliens in the United States. The inclusion of these figures in population estimates resulted in sizable population increases for California, Florida, Illinois, New York, and Texas.   Frank Cormier and Margot Cormier

See also POPULATION. In WORLD BOOK, see CENSUS.

CENTRAL AFRICAN REPUBLIC. See AFRICA.

CEREZO, VINICIO (1942-   ), became president of Guatemala on Jan. 14, 1986. The candidate of the Christian Democratic Party, he was elected in December 1985 with 68 per cent of the vote.

Marco Vinicio Cerezo Arévalo was born on Dec. 26, 1942, in Guatemala City. His father was a member of the Guatemalan Supreme Court. In 1968, Cerezo obtained a law degree from the University of San Carlos in Guatemala City and became a leader of the Christian Democratic Party. He served in Guatemala's Congress from 1974 to 1978.

Cerezo has survived three assassination attempts during his political career. In the first attack, in February 1981, snipers opened fire on him and his bodyguards in Guatemala City. Two people were killed, but Cerezo was unhurt. Later that year, Cerezo sent his wife and four children to live abroad. Two other attempts then were made on his life. In the second attempt, uniformed police officers stormed a hotel where Cerezo was staying in Guatemala City. The third attack was a bazooka assault on the house where he was living. Cerezo was elected to Congress again in 1982, but he was prevented from taking office by a military coup.

Cerezo married Raquel Blandón, who is also a lawyer, in 1965. The couple have three sons and a daughter.   Rod Such

CHAD. See AFRICA.

CHEMISTRY. Jeffrey R. Aldrich, an *entomologist* (insect specialist), revealed in September 1986 that he had used an artificial chemical mixture to assemble a powerful army of helpful bugs. Aldrich and his colleagues at the United States Department of Agriculture laboratory in Beltsville, Md., made the first artificial sex attractant that works on the spined soldier bug, an insect that eats other insects. The attractant is made up of three simple chemicals that the spined soldier bug produces naturally and that are both easy and inexpensive to make in the laboratory.

Spraying the attractant on crop plants lures an "army" of spined soldier bugs to the plants, where the bugs eat insects that otherwise would harm the plants. Using predator insects to eat pests may reduce farmers' need for chemical pest killers, cutting both costs and the burden of poisonous chemicals on the environment.

Chemicals that attract pests have been known for years—they are used, for example, in so-called bug bags that trap Japanese beetles. But pest attractants eventually become ineffective. They work against the pests, so the pests adapt themselves to ignore the chemicals.

By contrast, the predator attractant should become more effective because it will benefit predators. The attractant will not only draw the spined soldier bugs to sites of pest infestation where food is readily available but also draw them away from areas designated for spraying with chemical pest killers that could harm them. Spined soldier bugs that are strongly attracted will multiply especially well, making the attractant more effective with each succeeding generation.

The first use of the attractant is expected to be in home gardening. The scientists have used it to draw "bug armies" to broccoli, tomatoes, cabbages, and beans.

Memory Drug. Experimental psychologist Victor J. DeNoble of Ayerst Research, Incorporated, in Princeton, N.J., announced in April 1986 that he and his colleagues had used a new drug, called *vinpocetine*, to speed up the rate at which rats learn by about 40 per cent. The scientists also found that, although oxygen deprivation and certain chemicals disrupt the memories of rats that are not treated with vinpocetine, treated rats retain their memories.

Other research on the drug has shown that it truly enhances memory. It does not simply increase alertness, as do caffeine and other stimulants. Scientists do not know how the new drug works, but they suspect that it makes brain cells use sugars and other nutrients more efficiently.

Ayerst plans to ask the United States Food and Drug Administration for permission to use vinpocetine on human beings. The first people in the United States to benefit from the drug probably will be *multi-infarct dementia* patients—individuals who suffer mental disorders because of a cutoff of blood to many small areas of the brain.

Communications Breakthrough. A plastic crystal announced in April may correct a hitch in *fiberoptic systems*—communications systems in which telephone conversations and data travel as flashes of laser light through hair-thin strands of glass. The systems' *switchers*—electronic devices that sort out the flashes that belong to the various conversations and data transmissions—operate more slowly than do the lasers. If the switchers were faster, fiberoptic systems could handle more information.

Scientists at GTE Laboratories, Incorporated, in Waltham, Mass., announced the development of a plastic crystal that could become the first ultrafast light-activated switcher. Polymer physicist Mrinal K. Thakur reported that the new crystals might enable fiberoptic systems to handle 1,000 times more telephone calls than at present. The crystal also might enable computers to communicate with one another more rapidly and more economically by fiberoptics.

Thakur and his colleagues developed a new technique called *shear growth* to make the crystals. First, they put melted or dissolved crystals of plastics called *polydiacetylenes* under high pressure and gave them a sideways push—a *shear force*. The molecules aligned themselves to form *thin films* (structures about as thin as a contact lens) that had fewer defects than any other thin-film plastic crystal ever produced.

The new crystals turn on and off in response to light signals faster than any other material. Prototype optical switchers made from the crystals may be demonstrated in about two years.

Barnacles at Bay. In May 1986, researchers at Duke University's Marine Laboratory in Beaufort, N.C., said they had found a nonpolluting compound that may stop barnacles from fouling ships, oil rigs, and other structures having underwater surfaces. The current way to keep barnacles from attaching themselves to underwater surfaces is to coat the surfaces with paints containing poisonous metals such as tin and copper. Such paints also kill harmless organisms, however.

According to marine zoologist John C. Costlow, the sea pansy, a common soft coral, produces a compound that prevents barnacles from attaching themselves to underwater surfaces. Costlow and his colleagues extracted the compound from sea pansies, then sent it for identification to chemists Kenneth L. Rinehart and Paul A. Keifer at the University of Illinois in Urbana-Champaign. Chemists hope to develop artificial, long-lasting versions of the compound that can be used to make antibarnacle paints that will not kill harmless creatures.   Peter J. Andrews

In WORLD BOOK, see CHEMISTRY.

CHESS. World chess champion Gary Kasparov of the Soviet Union held on to his title, narrowly defeating countryman Anatoly Karpov on Oct. 9, 1986. At the end of the 24-game match, which was held in London and in Leningrad, Kasparov had won 5 games, Karpov had won 4, and 15 games had been drawn.

Kasparov is to face his next challenger in a championship match in 1987. He will play the winner of a match between Karpov and Andrei Sokolov, a young Soviet player. Neither match had been scheduled by the end of 1986.

In the women's world championship battle, Maya Chiburdanidze kept her title in October when she defeated Elena Akhmilovskaya in a match played in Sofia, Bulgaria, and Borzhomi, Soviet Union, near Tbilisi. Both women are from the Soviet Union.

Olympiad. A Soviet team took the gold medal at the biennial Chess Olympiad held in Dubayy, United Arab Emirates, from November 19 to December 2. Great Britain won the silver medal, and the United States team won the bronze medal.

U.S. Champs. Yasser Seirawan of Seattle won the U.S. championship title on November 5 in Estes Park, Colo. Lev Alburt and Joel Benjamin, both of New York City, tied for second place. All three men qualified for a series of play-offs that will culminate in the world championship match of 1989. Inna Izrailov of New York City won the U.S. women's championship.

Other Tournaments. In the second annual match between the United States and Great Britain, in May in London, U.S. champion Alburt defeated British champion Jon Speelman.

Other winners during the year included Nick de Firmian of San Francisco, who won the 1,500-player World Open in Philadelphia in July, and Larry Christiansen of Pasadena, Calif., who won the U.S. Open in Somerset, N.J. Jan Smejkal of Yugoslavia won the New York Open in New York City in April.

Younger Players. John Litvinchuk, 19, of New York City won the U.S. Junior Invitational Championship. Fifteen-year-old Vivik Rao of Pittsburgh, Pa., took the title of U.S. Junior Open champion.

More than 1,600 young U.S. chess players competed in national team chess championships in 1986. Cherry River Elementary School of Ridgewood, W. Va., won the elementary school team chess championship. Teams from Hostermann Junior High of Brooklyn Park, Minn., and Pulaski Junior High of Pulaski, Va., became cochampions for the eighth grade and below. University High of Tucson, Ariz., took the championship for the ninth grade and below, as well as the title of high school chess champion.   Al Lawrence

In WORLD BOOK, see CHESS.

CHICAGO. Democratic Mayor Harold Washington finally wrested control of the City Council from his Democratic opponents in 1986 with the April 29 victory of his ally, Luis V. Gutierrez, in a hotly contested special election for alderman of the 26th Ward. Gutierrez' victory, plus wins by pro-Washington candidates in other wards, created a 25 to 25 split in the council with the mayor having the deciding vote.

The new alignment permitted Washington, elected the city's first black mayor in 1983, to cast several tie-breaking votes. In May 1986, for instance, the council approved the mayor's long-stalled appointments to the governing board of the Chicago Park District. Retired architect Walter A. Netsch was named parks president, which led to the resignation of Parks Superintendent Edmund Kelly, a leader of the mayor's opposition.

Scandals. One unknown in the mayor's bid for reelection in 1987 was the eventual impact of a bribery scandal that surfaced during the final weeks of 1985 and dogged Washington throughout 1986. The scandal involved a professional "con man" named Michael Raymond who was hired by the Federal Bureau of Investigation (FBI) to pose as a free-spending contractor in search of city business. On November 21, federal prosecutors announced bribery indictments against seven local political figures, including two City Council members aligned with the mayor. It remained to be seen at year's end whether the indictments would lead to convictions or cause serious political damage to Mayor Washington.

Meanwhile, the federal courts in Chicago continued to try Cook County judges indicted in the FBI's Operation Greylord probe of corruption in the Cook County Circuit Court. On May 21, former Judge Reginald J. Holzer was sentenced to 18 years in prison, and on July 30 former Judge John Reynolds received a 10-year sentence. They were the fifth and sixth judges convicted in the Greylord investigation.

Budget and Taxes. In November, the City Council approved a $2.4-billion municipal budget for 1987, though council members complained about an $80-million property-tax increase needed to balance the 1986 budget. To win votes for the property tax, Washington promised to reduce it with proceeds from a new tax on motor fuels.

Schools. For the first time in five years, Chicago's public schools opened in September without a teachers' strike or the threat of one. After seeing a new state "report card" on schools, city education officials were glad children would not miss any days in class. The evaluation showed that students in all but 2 of the city's 64 high schools scored below average on college entrance exams and that most elementary students had reading and math scores below the state average.

Illinois Governor James R. Thompson (in bow of boat) surveys flooded areas of Chicago's northwest suburbs in September after heavy rains.

Economy, Construction. Chicago continued to lose manufacturing jobs in 1986, but steady growth in service and financial industries fueled a downtown construction boom. The value of downtown buildings completed during 1986 was estimated at $1.4 billion. After five years of false starts, the city on October 1 sold a key block of its North Loop urban-renewal district for $12 million to a developer who agreed to build an office tower and hotel on the site. In addition to new construction, many older buildings in the city were restored. Among them was the landmark Chicago Theatre, which reopened under new ownership on September 10 for stage performances.

Organized Crime. The battered bodies of reputed Chicago mob boss Anthony Spilotro and his brother Michael Spilotro were found buried in an Indiana cornfield on June 23. The two were apparently murdered in an underworld feud.

Sports. The city was seized with "Bear Mania" in 1986 after the Chicago Bears won the National Football League championship, their first championship since 1963. On Dec. 5, 1986, the Illinois state legislature approved measures providing for a new stadium to be built for the Chicago White Sox baseball team and a new race track to replace the fire-damaged Arlington Park in suburban Arlington Heights.   John F. McCarron

See also CITY. In WORLD BOOK, see CHICAGO.

CHILD WELFARE. On April 7, 1986, President Ronald Reagan signed a law designed to help children make the transition from foster care to independent living. The law, an amendment to the Social Security Act, entitles individual states to $45 million in fiscal years 1987 and 1988 to be used for a variety of foster-care services. Those services include helping foster-care children get a high school diploma or vocational training; providing training in daily living skills, such as budgeting and apartment maintenance; and offering individual and group counseling.

Cocaine Babies. The number of infants in the United States born with traces of cocaine in their body increased dramatically in 1986. At Martin Luther King, Jr., General Hospital in Los Angeles, for example, physicians reported that they saw 180 cocaine-affected newborns by May 1986, compared with just 10 in all of 1984. While still in the womb, such babies absorb the drug from their cocaine-user mothers.

Although doctors are certain that the number of cocaine-affected babies is rising throughout the United States, they have been unable to determine exactly how many there are. Many mothers do not tell their physician about their addiction to cocaine.

Cocaine-affected babies can suffer many health problems. Some show no apparent symptoms at all, but others are born with symptoms of drug withdrawal. They may be screaming one moment and sleeping the next. Cocaine-affected newborns also suffer a high incidence of strokes and respiratory problems, and they may experience additional serious effects over the long term.

Youth Suicide. From 1950 to 1986 in the United States, the rate of suicide for persons aged 15 to 24 tripled, while rates for other age groups remained comparatively stable. About 6,000 young people now kill themselves each year, and another 250,000 attempt to do so. Suicide has become the third-leading cause of death for Americans from 15 to 24 years old.

In April 1986, Congressmen Gary L. Ackerman (D., N.Y.) and Tom Lantos (D., Calif.) introduced the Youth Suicide Prevention Act in the U.S. House of Representatives. The act would make about $10 million available each year for local programs to counter youth suicide and increase community awareness of the problem. The bill did not make it through Congress in 1986, but Ackerman and Lantos said they planned to reintroduce it in the new Congress in 1987. Jeanne M. Hunzeker

In the Special Reports section, see THE HAZARDS OF TEEN-AGE DRINKING. In WORLD BOOK, see CHILD WELFARE.

CHILDREN'S BOOKS. See LITERATURE FOR CHILDREN.

CHILE. Chile's 70-year-old President Augusto Pinochet Ugarte was slightly wounded on Sept. 7, 1986, in an assassination attempt in which 5 of his bodyguards were killed and 11 wounded. The attack occurred in the Maipo canyon, 18 miles (29 kilometers) southeast of Santiago, the capital, when the president's motorcade came under heavy fire by attackers who fired rockets and automatic rifles and lobbed grenades. Left wing guerrillas were believed responsible.

Pinochet survived by throwing himself on the floor of his Mercedes-Benz automobile to protect his 10-year-old grandson. He suffered a minor wound to his left hand.

U.S. Pressures. The attack put an end—at least temporarily—to pressures from the United States government for a relaxation of repressive controls in place in Chile since a military coup in 1973. Earlier in 1986, the United States had been encouraging opponents to the Pinochet regime. The U.S. Department of State released politically sensational information in March indicating that more than 500 Chileans had been kidnapped in 1985 alone by unknown individuals, presumed to be acting on Chilean government orders.

On July 2, Rodrigo Rojas de Negri, a 19-year-old photographer—a resident of Washington, D.C., who was born in Chile—was set on fire by men in Chilean military uniforms, according to

eyewitnesses, while participating in antigovernment demonstrations in Chile. He died from his burns on July 6.

State of Siege. Hours after the September assassination attempt, Pinochet imposed a 90-day state of siege, which allowed his government to tap telephones, open mail, and hold prisoners at secret locations. The measure also suspended constitutional guarantees, banned public gatherings, and provided for censorship of the press.

Using their new powers, government authorities cracked down on dissidents. Three French priests, working in urban ghettos, were arrested and later expelled from the country on September 11. Six opposition magazines were shut down indefinitely. Two foreign news agencies—Reuters of Great Britain and ANSA of Italy—were also closed down. José Carrasco Tapia, the 38-year-old foreign editor of the respected weekly magazine *Análisis*, was found dead, shot many times in the head, after being seized by men who were believed to be plainclothes security officers.

The government lifted the state of siege on December 5 except in Santiago and four other cities. On December 31, Pinochet announced that the state of siege would end in the remaining areas on Jan. 6, 1987. Nathan A. Haverstock

See also LATIN AMERICA (Facts in Brief Table). In WORLD BOOK, see CHILE.

CHINA during 1986 continued its slow movement away from the system of political and economic beliefs developed in the Soviet Union and adapted for China by Mao Zedong (Mao Tse-tung in the traditional Wade-Giles spelling), China's leader from 1949 to 1976. Instead, China headed toward an unprecedented new leadership system for a Communist country.

Economic Growth Top Priority. The Central Committee of the Chinese Communist Party met in Beijing (Peking) on Sept. 28, 1986, and adopted a policy statement entitled *Resolution on the Guiding Principles of Building a Socialist Society with an Advanced Culture and Ideology*. Mao had made class struggle the "key link"—the top priority—in his policy, considering economic development and other practical goals secondary in importance to creating a classless society. The result—particularly during the Cultural Revolution of 1966-1976, the period of most vigorous pursuit of Mao's vision of social equality—has been widespread disruption. The Cultural Revolution shattered China's educational system and set back the nation's economic growth.

Under the guidance of Mao's successor, Deng Xiaoping (Teng Hsiao-p'ing), the 1986 resolution said the party would "take economic development as the key link." The party thus supported Deng's emphasis on improved living standards and eco-

A Chinese boy presents flowers to Queen Elizabeth II, the first British monarch to visit China, in Beijing (Peking) on October 12.

nomic modernization, even though some people got richer than others in the process, creating class differences that Mao had tried to eliminate. The resolution said that taking class struggle as the key link had been "a serious miscalculation." The Central Committee went on to say that the chief conflict in Chinese society was "between the ever-growing material and cultural needs of the people and the country's backward production," not between social or economic classes.

Cultural Freedom. The party warned in its resolution that China faced "stagnation and backwardness" if it failed "to accept elements of advanced science and culture from abroad." In setting policies and making plans, the resolution said, there must be "democratic centralism," the Communist term for control by party leaders. But on academic or artistic matters, the resolution promised "creative writing, freedom of discussion, and freedom of criticism and counter-criticism." These forms of expression had long been politically dangerous.

Drive Against Corruption. The party called for "a high standard of Communist ethics" and said its officials should oppose "bureaucratism, cheating, and abuse of power for selfish purposes." This was part of a major campaign against corruption, which had grown as government control over the economy relaxed and more opportunities for private profit appeared.

A conference of 8,000 senior party, government, and army officials in January sought to eliminate those guilty of corruption and favoritism to family members. Party General Secretary Hu Yaobang warned that "laws must be followed and enforced strictly, and all lawbreakers must be punished."

At the time of the conference, almost 70,000 party and government officials were known to have been involved in illegal activities, but few had been jailed. The Communist Party newspaper *People's Daily* said on January 9 that enforcing anticorruption laws had so far been "just empty talk" and a better job would require officials to "hack through difficulties." The conference set up a new anticorruption team headed by Vice Premier Qiao Shi, a member of the Communist Party's Politburo, China's top policymaking body.

Three men, two of whom were sons of former senior officials, were paraded in public and then executed by gunshot in Shanghai on February 19 for unspecified crimes, reportedly including rape. They were the first children of high officials to be openly executed. *People's Daily* said a few such children "consider themselves privileged and flout the law and discipline," thinking "the law should bend before them."

Hu Yaobang said in a speech for the 65th anniversary of the party, on July 1, that some members placed personal interests above party welfare and violated laws to make personal gains. "Vulgarity, more than political principle, reigns," he said.

New Five-Year Plan. The National People's Congress, China's parliament—which is completely controlled by the Communist Party—approved on April 12 the seventh Five-Year Plan for economic development, for 1986-1990. Premier Zhao Ziyang presented the plan, which called for slower industrial growth than occurred during the previous five years, down from an average 12 per cent to 7.5 per cent. This slowdown was intended to combat inflation, which had reached 12 per cent in 1985. Slower growth would also allow China to reduce its imports, helping the country shrink its trade deficit and hold on to its dwindling reserves of foreign currency.

Agricultural output, which had risen at an annual average of 8.1 per cent from 1981 through 1985, would increase by 4 per cent. The annual increase in people's income was to be cut approximately in half, to 7 per cent for agricultural workers and 4 per cent for those in industry.

The new plan incorporated major changes, moving away from the Soviet system of centrally directed economic operations that China had installed in the 1950's. "Except for a few special government departments and industries," the plan said, "no ministries, provinces, or autonomous regions will exercise direct control over enterprises. City government functions must be separated from those of enterprises so that manufacturers, wholesalers, and retailers have full authority for their own management and full responsibility for their own profits and losses."

The new plan extended to industry the partial relaxation of price controls applied to agriculture in 1978. Instead of the government rationing electricity, its price would be set by supply and demand. Airlines and postal services would fix their own prices, within limits. But Chinese authorities hesitated to overhaul the system of pricing raw materials and some other essential industrial goods and services.

Resistance to Economic Reforms continued despite the official policy decisions. One party leader, Hu Qili, warned that it probably would take "10 years or even longer" to transform the economic system. A national symposium said taxes on bonuses for good work discouraged initiative. And a Beijing newspaper warned that a headlong plunge into modernization along Western lines could mean "a colonization without colonizers."

Labor Changes. On October 1, China revised Mao's system of permanent employment at state-owned enterprises, known as "the iron rice bowl" because it provided a guaranteed income to those hired. Although the 67 million workers already employed by the state kept their guaranteed jobs, new workers would receive a contract for a certain term subject to renewal if both parties agreed. The government also extended the grounds for firing to include wasting materials, arrogance toward customers, and other offenses.

Efforts to Attract Foreign Investment faltered. In the first half of 1986, the investment rate fell 20 per cent from the rate in the first half of 1985 because foreigners had become discouraged by high costs, small returns, and management problems. China devalued its unit of currency, the yuan, by 15.8 per cent against the U.S. dollar on July 5, 1986, making China's exports cheaper in an effort to increase foreign sales.

Student Unrest. A clash between foreign and Chinese students at Tianjin (Tientsin) University on the night of May 24-25 led to charges by African students of Chinese racism. The 1,600 Africans studying in China, mainly on Chinese scholarships, reported similar incidents at other schools. Chinese students reportedly resented the favored treatment given to foreigners. A representative of the State Education Commission denied that there was racial tension.

Some 38,000 Chinese went to Western universities to study between 1978, when Deng began sending students abroad, and 1986. By 1986, only 15,000 had returned, and authorities were con-

A crowd gathers at the entrance to China's first securities market, which began selling stocks and bonds in Shenyang in August.

cerned about a "brain drain." Officials conceded that 70 per cent of those who returned could not utilize their new expertise because of "a shortage of facilities and suitable work assignments."

In December, students seeking more freedom of speech and greater voice in the selection of officials held marches and rallies in at least a dozen cities, including Shanghai and Beijing. The protests continued at year's end.

Foreign Relations. China improved ties with some Soviet-bloc countries. Soviet First Deputy Premier Ivan V. Arkhipov visited Beijing in August for economic talks. In October in Beijing, Soviet Deputy Foreign Minister Igor A. Rogachev discussed establishing more normal relations. China's Foreign Minister Wu Xueqian agreed with his Soviet counterpart, Eduard A. Shevardnadze, that in February 1987 the two countries would resume talks on their border dispute. The talks had been suspended since 1979.

Poland's President Wojciech Jaruzelski met top Chinese leaders on an unofficial working visit to Beijing that began on Sept. 28, 1986. East Germany's leader Erich Honecker arrived in China on October 21 for a state visit that Hu Yaobang said marked the start of a new stage in relations.

United States Secretary of Defense Caspar W. Weinberger visited China from October 7 to 11. His trip produced an agreement that three U.S. naval vessels would call at Chinese ports. The ships visited Qingdao (Tsingtao) from November 5 to 11, the first U.S. Navy call in China since 1949. The ships had been scheduled to come in 1985, but the port call was canceled when Washington refused to say whether the ships would carry nuclear weapons. China did not publicly raise the issue before the 1986 visit.

Space and Technology. Weinberger visited Chinese facilities in Sichuan (Szechwan) province for launching artificial satellites. With both the U.S. and European space programs temporarily suspended because of major rocket failures, China sought a foothold in the launch business. The Chinese announced on May 12 that they had won orders from an American company to put two communications satellites into orbit before December 1987. China offered lower prices than U.S. or European competitors. See SPACE EXPLORATION.

After intense debate, the U.S. Senate had in November 1985 approved a nuclear trade agreement with China in hope that American companies would get some of China's expected $6-billion expenditure on nuclear power plants. On Sept. 23, 1986, China signed contracts in Beijing for British and French help in building a nuclear power plant at Daya Bay, 40 miles (64 kilometers) northeast of Hong Kong.   Henry S. Bradsher

See also ASIA (Facts in Brief Table). In WORLD BOOK, see CHINA.

CHIRAC, JACQUES (1932-   ), became prime minister of France for the second time on March 20, 1986, after allied parties of the political center and right narrowly defeated the ruling Socialists and their allies in national elections. Chirac, mayor of Paris and leader of a party named Rally for the Republic, succeeded Laurent Fabius, a Socialist. Chirac continued to serve as mayor of Paris. See FRANCE.

Jacques René Chirac was born in Paris on Nov. 29, 1932. He graduated from the Institute of Political Science in that city, then served as a military officer during Algeria's war for independence. After his tour of duty, he returned to Paris and attended the National School of Administration.

In 1967, Chirac was elected to Parliament and named secretary of state for social affairs in charge of employment. He held several other cabinet posts between 1968 and 1974.

Chirac was prime minister from May 1974 until August 1976, when he resigned because of disagreements with President Valéry Giscard d'Estaing. Chirac was elected mayor of Paris in 1977 and reelected in 1983.

The new prime minister and his wife, Bernadette, have two daughters.   Jay Myers

CHURCHES. See EASTERN ORTHODOX CHURCHES; JEWS AND JUDAISM; PROTESTANTISM; RELIGION; ROMAN CATHOLIC CHURCH.

CITY. By the end of 1986, there was nearly unanimous consensus among government officials, urban affairs experts, and city-policy critics alike that there had been some improvement in the economies of many cities throughout the United States. They also agreed, however, that people living in poverty had not benefited from the improvement and that their living conditions had actually worsened. Many officials and experts concluded that the issue of persistent poverty, with all of its ramifications, especially in the inner cities, was the most important problem facing the United States.

Local Economies. A report issued in December by the National Urban Policy Committee of the National Academy of Sciences (NAS) noted that the economic health of many cities had improved—188 of 204 U.S. metropolitan areas showed increases in jobs since 1982, and 198 showed decreases in unemployment rates. Joblessness rose, however, in cities dependent on the manufacture of steel and textiles, on oil and gas production, on mining, or on agriculture. Many workers who lost jobs in declining industries could not get work in new service and information-based industries, which increasingly located in the suburbs. Furthermore, in many cities, there were reportedly many "discouraged workers" who had not looked for work in more than six months and were therefore not counted among the unemployed.

50 Largest Cities in the United States

Rank	City	Population*	Per cent change in population since 1980	Mayor†
1.	New York City	7,164,742	+1.3	Edward I. Koch (D, 1/90)
2.	Los Angeles	3,096,721	+4.3	Thomas Bradley (N, 6/89)
3.	Chicago	2,992,472	−0.4	Harold Washington (D, 4/87)
4.	Houston	1,705,697	+6.9	Kathryn J. Whitmire (NP, 1/88)
5.	Philadelphia	1,646,713	−2.5	W. Wilson Goode (D, 1/88)
6.	Detroit	1,088,973	−9.5	Coleman A. Young (D, 1/90)
7.	Dallas	974,234	+7.7	A. Starke Taylor (NP, 5/87)
8.	San Diego	960,452	+9.7	Maureen F. O'Connor (D, 1/89)
9.	Phoenix	853,266	+8.0	Terry Goddard (D, 12/87)
10.	San Antonio	842,779	+7.2	Henry G. Cisneros (D, 4/87)
11.	Baltimore	763,570	−2.9	Clarence H. Burns (D, 12/87)
12.	San Francisco	712,753	+5.0	Dianne Feinstein (NP, 1/88)
13.	Indianapolis	710,280	+1.4	William H. Hudnut III (R, 12/87)
14.	San Jose	686,178	+9.0	Thomas McEnery (D, 12/90)
15.	Memphis	648,399	+0.3	Dick Hackett (I, 12/87)
16.	Washington, D.C.	622,823	−2.4	Marion S. Barry, Jr. (D, 1/91)
17.	Milwaukee	620,811	−2.4	Henry W. Maier (D, 4/88)
18.	Jacksonville	577,971	+6.8	Jake M. Godbold (D, 7/87)
19.	Boston	570,719	+1.4	Raymond L. Flynn (D, 1/88)
20.	Columbus, Ohio	566,114	+0.2	Dana G. Rinehart (R, 1/88)
21.	New Orleans	559,101	+0.2	Sidney J. Barthelemy (D, 5/90)
22.	Cleveland	546,543	−4.7	George V. Voinovich (R, 11/89)
23.	Denver	504,588	+2.4	Federico Peña (D, 6/87)
24.	Seattle	488,474	−1.1	Charles Royer (NP, 1/90)
25.	El Paso	463,809	+9.1	Jonathan W. Rogers (NP, 4/87)
26.	Nashville	462,450	+1.5	Richard H. Fulton (D, 9/87)
27.	Oklahoma City	443,172	+9.7	Andy Coats (D, 4/87)
28.	Kansas City, Mo.	443,075	−1.0	Richard L. Berkley (NP, 4/87)
29.	St. Louis	429,296	−5.2	Vincent L. Schoemehl, Jr. (D, 4/89)
30.	Atlanta	426,090	+0.3	Andrew J. Young, Jr. (D, 1/90)
31.	Fort Worth	414,562	+7.6	Bob Bolen (NP, 4/87)
32.	Pittsburgh	402,583	−5.0	Richard S. Caliguiri (D, 1/90)
33.	Austin	397,001	+14.8	Frank Cooksey (NP, 5/87)
34.	Honolulu	385,489	+5.6	Frank Fasi (R, 1/89)
35.	Long Beach	378,752	+4.8	Ernie Kell (D, 7/88)
36.	Tulsa	374,535	+3.8	Dick Crawford (R, 5/88)
37.	Miami	372,634	+7.4	Xavier L. Suarez (NP, 11/87)
38.	Cincinnati	370,481	−3.9	Charles J. Luken (D, 11/87)
39.	Portland, Ore.	365,861	−0.6	J. E. Clark (NP, 11/88)
40.	Tucson	365,422	+8.4	Lewis C. Murphy (R, 12/87)
41.	Minneapolis	358,335	−3.4	Donald M. Fraser (D, 1/90)
42.	Oakland	351,898	+3.7	Lionel J. Wilson (D, 7/89)
43.	Albuquerque	350,575	+5.5	Ken Schultz (NP, 12/89)
44.	Toledo	343,939	−3.0	Donna Owens (R, 12/87)
45.	Buffalo	338,982	−5.3	James D. Griffin (D, 12/89)
46.	Omaha	332,237	+1.4	Michael Boyle (NP, 6/89)
47.	Charlotte	330,838	+4.9	Harvey B. Gantt (D, 11/87)
48.	Newark	314,387	−4.5	Sharpe James (D, 7/90)
49.	Virginia Beach	308,664	+17.7	Robert G. Jones (D, 6/88)
50.	Sacramento	304,131	+10.3	Anne Rudin (NP, 12/87)

*1984 estimates (source: U.S. Bureau of the Census except for Honolulu, which is a YEAR BOOK estimate).
†The letters in parentheses represent the mayor's party, with D meaning Democrat, R Republican, I independent, and NP nonpartisan. The date is when the term of office ends (source: National League of Cities).

General revenue‡	Total debt outstanding‡	Unemployment rate§	Cost of living index#	Per capita income	Sales tax rate††
$20,724,633,000	$12,127,073,000	7.1%	142.9	$15,076	8.25%
2,117,867,000	3,372,291,000	8.1	115.7	14,526	6.5
2,037,519,000	1,506,108,000	7.2	119.7 est.	14,655	8
1,070,057,000	2,273,200,000	10.7	102.1	14,517	6.125
2,671,326,000	2,294,981,000	5.3	118.0	13,746	6
1,264,871,000	911,886,000	8.7	109.5 est.	13,943	4
580,822,000	807,308,000	5.9	110.8	15,861	7.25
600,694,000	817,544,000	5.7	116.8	13,474	6
604,702,000	1,002,953,000	5.6	109.1	13,199	6
311,833,000	1,857,246,000	7.5	98.5	11,540	6.75
1,458,924,000	999,930,000	4.7	105.7	13,563	5
1,573,391,000	1,250,883,000	5.2	126.2 est.	19,592	6.5
531,352,000	421,831,000	5.1	97.6	12,997	5
385,171,000	381,337,000	6.4	111.7	17,577	6
669,085,000	655,913,000	6.8	101.2	11,575	7.75
2,576,276,000	2,119,578,000	3.6	121.9 est.	17,724	6
432,251,000	481,428,000	6.1	116.4 est.	14,184	5
360,103,000	1,087,105,000	6.2	103.6 est.	12,168	5
1,021,763,000	574,633,000	3.3	123.0 est.	15,932	5
327,489,000	769,272,000	5.8	103.3	12,609	6
544,596,000	752,985,000	10.5	98.7	12,389	9
396,611,000	407,320,000	7.5	101.7	14,216	6.5
675,745,000	645,578,000	6.1	103.5	15,783	6.6
437,985,000	636,761,000	6.5	107.8	14,787	7.9
190,560,000	326,824,000	12.3	98.6	8,745	6.25
507,472,000	862,324,000	5.2	100.4 est.	12,125	7.75
296,724,000	393,815,000	7.1	97.5	13,201	5.25
397,546,000	343,697,000	4.6	105.2 est.	13,821	5.225
462,864,000	379,560,000	7.1	96.0	13,991	6
458,355,000	1,042,670,000	4.9	107.5	13,848	4
215,600,000	453,119,000	7.0	105.3 est.	14,138	6.5
282,552,000	372,071,000	7.4	96.1	12,680	6
274,710,000	1,175,435,000	5.8	106.1	13,483	7.25
430,405,000	249,809,000	4.3	149.8 est.	13,709	4
388,473,000	341,051,000	8.1	115.0 est.	14,526	6
295,285,000	982,006,000	8.9	103.7 est.	12,962	6.25
216,511,000	216,161,000	7.5	107.4 est.	13,249	5
323,919,000	183,653,000	6.4	102.2	12,905	5.5
250,603,000	508,177,000	8.1	108.5	13,247	0
232,844,000	521,596,000	5.8	104.3	11,626	7
484,663,000	1,302,475,000	4.1	113.7 est.	15,189	6
354,440,000	553,470,000	6.4	114.5 est.	16,365	6.5
311,306,000	773,633,000	6.6	103.0	12,305	5.375
192,170,000	194,297,000	9.2	102.3	12,629	6
494,819,000	263,155,000	7.3	97.8	12,626	7
174,124,000	170,536,000	5.2	95.6	13,156	6
198,493,000	259,900,000	4.8	99.0	12,430	4.5
270,493,000	153,080,000	6.1	124.4	16,274	6
313,451,000	272,806,000	4.5	103.2 est.	12,177	4.5
170,450,000	55,567,000	6.5	110.1	12,831	6

‡Figures are for 1983-1984 fiscal year (source: U.S. Bureau of the Census).
§July 1986 figures for metropolitan areas (source: U.S. Bureau of Labor Statistics).
#The higher the number, the higher the cost of living. Entries marked *est.* are YEAR BOOK estimates. Based on a survey done in spring 1986 (source: American Chamber of Commerce Researchers Assocation).
††Total sales tax rate, including state, county, city, school district, and special district taxes (source: Tax Foundation, Inc.).

50 Largest Cities in the World

Rank	City	Population
1.	Shanghai	11,859,748
2.	Mexico City	9,373,353
3.	Beijing (Peking)	9,230,687
4.	Seoul, South Korea	8,364,379
5.	Tokyo	8,349,209
6.	Moscow	8,275,000
7.	Bombay, India	8,227,332
8.	Tianjin (Tientsin), China	7,764,141
9.	New York City	7,164,742
10.	São Paulo, Brazil	7,033,529
11.	London	6,608,598
12.	Jakarta, Indonesia	6,503,449
13.	Cairo, Egypt	6,133,000
14.	Hong Kong	5,826,000
15.	Teheran, Iran	5,734,199
16.	Karachi, Pakistan	5,208,170
17.	Bangkok, Thailand	5,153,902
18.	Rio de Janeiro, Brazil	5,093,232
19.	Delhi, India	4,884,234
20.	Leningrad, Soviet Union	4,295,000
21.	Santiago, Chile	4,225,299
22.	Lima, Peru	4,164,597
23.	Bogotá, Colombia	4,055,909
24.	Shenyang (Shen-yang), China	3,944,240
25.	Ho Chi Minh City, Vietnam	3,419,978
26.	Calcutta, India	3,305,006
27.	Wuhan (Wu-han), China	3,287,720
28.	Madras, India	3,276,622
29.	Madrid, Spain	3,188,297
30.	Guangzhou (Canton), China	3,181,510
31.	Pusan, South Korea	3,159,766
32.	Los Angeles	3,096,721
33.	Berlin (East and West), East and West Germany	3,038,689
34.	Chicago	2,992,472
35.	Baghdad, Iraq	2,969,000
36.	Lahore, Pakistan	2,952,689
37.	Buenos Aires, Argentina	2,908,001
38.	Sydney, Australia	2,874,415
39.	Rome	2,830,569
40.	Yokohama, Japan	2,773,822
41.	Chongqing (Ch'ung-ch'ing), China	2,673,170
42.	Osaka, Japan	2,648,158
43.	Pyongyang, North Korea	2,639,448
44.	Melbourne, Australia	2,578,527
45.	Hanoi, Vietnam	2,570,905
46.	Istanbul, Turkey	2,547,364
47.	Harbin, China	2,519,120
48.	Chengdu (Ch'eng-tu), China	2,499,000
49.	Bangalore, India	2,476,355
50.	Kinshasa, Zaire	2,443,876

Sources: 1984 Bureau of the Census estimates for cities of the United States; censuses and estimates from governments for cities of other countries.

Profile of Poverty. The NAS report and the President's National Urban Policy Report 1986, published by the U.S. Department of Housing and Urban Development (HUD), indicated that increasing numbers of those who live in persistent poverty are members of female-headed households, blacks, Hispanics, and young people. The latest available statistics indicated that 33.7 million Americans, 14.4 per cent of the population, were living below the poverty level in 1984. Among blacks, the poverty percentage was 33.8 per cent; among female-headed households, 34 per cent. The HUD report stated that in 1984, 3.7 million families received Aid to Families with Dependent Children (AFDC) payments averaging $338 per month; 21.5 million people received Medicaid services averaging $1,569 annually; and 19.9 million people were eligible for food stamps, a four-year low. Many local officials reported that the decrease in the number of people eligible for food stamps was a result of making the eligibility requirements more stringent.

Hardship Study. A study called *Hardship and Support Systems in Chicago*, released in October, surveyed the impact that cuts in federal programs had on individuals and families. It also examined the ability of community institutions and agencies to provide needed support services. The report was compiled by researchers at Northwestern University, the University of Illinois, the University of Chicago, and Loyola University, all in the Chicago area.

The researchers measured "hardship" in terms of hunger, access to adequate housing, and ability to obtain needed medical and dental care. They found that in 1983, 1 in every 4 families in Chicago suffered hardship in at least one of these areas. By 1985, the hardship ratio had increased to 1 in 3 families. Furthermore, blacks were twice as likely as whites to suffer hardships.

In examining where people and families in need look for help, the researchers found that people turn first to relatives and friends. The study also found that community organizations and churches were increasingly overburdened with needs of the poor, while at the same time many of the poor were unaware of social service agencies or did not want to go to such institutions for help.

Workfare Programs in several cities and states were attempting to help those on welfare enter the economic mainstream through job training. Programs such as Project ET (*E*ducation and *T*raining) in Massachusetts, Project Chance in Illinois, and Project GAIN (*G*reater *A*venues to *In*dependence) in California offered a range of services to AFDC mothers. The programs reportedly had considerable success in getting AFDC mothers off welfare in Boston, Chicago, and Los Angeles.

Another workfare program, Project Self-Sufficiency, was sponsored by HUD and operated in 100 cities. About 10,000 AFDC mothers participated in 1986. They received housing vouchers as well as job training, counseling, child care, and job placement services.

Poverty Budgets. Policy analysts used cost data from these workfare training programs to construct what they called the "poverty budget" for New York City and Chicago. The analysts concluded in December that the federal and state governments were spending an average of $28,000 a year on behalf of a welfare family of four. This was far above the poverty line—even above the median income—in New York City and Chicago. The analysts also claimed that of $120 billion spent in 1985 by the federal government to combat poverty, only $19 billion ever made it into the pockets of the poor. The bulk of the money—$101 billion—went to people providing services to the poor, such as job counselors, health educators, and caseworkers. The analysts suggested that it would be better to give the money directly to the poor.

Homelessness. In October, officials reported record numbers of homeless people seeking aid in U.S. cities. There was also a dramatic shift in the characteristics of the homeless. More of them were women, children, and younger men, according to Ruth Schecter, director of the Housing Information Center in Kansas City, Mo.

Estimates of the number of homeless varied widely. New York City officials estimated they had 10,000 homeless single people and 5,500 homeless families. An additional 35,000 families were living "doubled up" illegally with friends and relatives in apartments owned by the New York City Housing Authority. Between 45,000 and 200,000 potentially homeless families lived in overcrowded private apartments. In Chicago, estimates of the homeless ranged from 9,000 to 22,000 people; in Newark, N.J., from 4,000 to 7,000 people. Other estimates showed that Atlanta, Ga., had 5,000; Philadelphia, 13,000; and Los Angeles, 40,000 homeless people.

The estimates also varied from time to time. Many of the homeless were able to find shelter, but only for short periods, while others moved to warmer cities in fall and winter.

Facing cuts in federal aid—as were all the states—the state governments of California, Connecticut, Kentucky, Massachusetts, New Jersey, and New York had to provide additional assistance for the homeless. The Council of State Governments reported in March that the states' initiatives to help the homeless had been fueled by the belief of most state officials that federal cutbacks would continue for some time. They also believed that city governments did not have the resources to fill the gap left by the federal budget cuts. The

Actor Clint Eastwood meets with reporters in Carmel-by-the-Sea, Calif., in April after being elected mayor of the town by a landslide.

federal revenue-sharing program, established in 1972, came to an end in October 1986.

"Slumbusters." A local group of architects and business owners calling themselves "slumbusters" began planning a new shopping center in 1986 in a blighted area of Chicago called North Lawndale. North Lawndale had been featured in a series of *Chicago Tribune* articles in late 1985, highlighting the problems of the inner city poor. In 1986, the newspaper won the Robert F. Kennedy Award for its reports. The slumbusters did a financial study of the North Lawndale area and found that the 58,000 people living in the neighborhood have access to $152 million, much of it in food stamps, housing subsidies, and other forms of welfare.

Other new approaches to neighborhood revitalization included the "Oasis Technique" developed in Fort Lauderdale, Fla. It focused on developing "oases" of safe, decent housing in areas of urban blight. Along with *urban homesteading* (reuse of abandoned property), the establishment of oases has helped to stabilize neighborhoods and reverse decline in several cities.

Population Gains or at least population stability were reported by the U.S. Bureau of the Census in April for several of the nation's largest metropolitan areas—New York City, Chicago, San Francisco-Oakland, and Indianapolis. This reversed a trend toward declining urban populations that began in the 1970's. The San Francisco-Oakland area became the fourth largest U.S. metropolitan area in 1986, surpassing Philadelphia.

Crime Rates dropped by 1.9 per cent during 1985, according to a federal report released in October 1986. But crime rates for the first half of 1986 were up over those of 1985 for all types of crimes in all regions of the United States and in all sizes of cities and towns. The Federal Bureau of Investigation's Crime Index total for major crimes was up 8 per cent. Aggravated assault was up 14 per cent, robbery and motor vehicle theft were up 11 per cent, murder and burglary were up 8 per cent, larceny was up 6 per cent, and rape was up 2 per cent over the 1985 rates.

In cities with more than a million inhabitants, crime was up 4 per cent over 1985; in cities with populations between 250,000 and 1 million, crime was up 11 to 12 per cent. Cities with populations of 10,000 to 250,000 and suburbs showed crime increases of 8 to 9 per cent.

Increases by region ranged from 4 per cent in the Midwest and 5 per cent in the Northeast and the West to 13 per cent in the South. Other studies showed that fear of crime, which has increased more than 350 per cent since 1974, has continued its upward climb.   Margaret T. Gordon

See also ELECTIONS and articles on individual cities. In WORLD BOOK, see CITY.

CIVIL RIGHTS. Oppressive regimes that violated the civil rights of their citizens were toppled or threatened in several Asian and Latin-American nations in 1986. In the United States, issues involving drug testing and victims of acquired immune deficiency syndrome (AIDS) were added to the traditional civil rights concerns.

Amnesty International, a worldwide human rights organization based in London, in its annual report issued in October called for increased pressure on the governments of Comoros, Iraq, South Africa, the Soviet Union, and other nations that the group said tortured political prisoners. The U.S. Congress in October passed limited economic sanctions against South Africa to protest that government's policy of separating blacks and whites.

The regime of President Ferdinand E. Marcos of the Philippines was toppled by Corazon Aquino and her supporters in February. Marcos fled into exile, and Aquino became president.

In South Korea, dissident politicians, members of the clergy, and students demanded a constitutional revision to permit direct presidential elections. The Korean Institute for Human Rights and the North American Coalition for Human Rights, both based near Washington, D.C., reported the arrest of more than 1,500 activists and an average of 10 students in South Korea daily. The human rights groups reported instances of

government-sanctioned torture of labor leaders, student activists, and publishers.

Latin America was the scene of both setbacks and progress in civil rights in 1986. Chile experienced a general strike on July 2 and 3, when opposition groups demanded an end to the military dictatorship of President Augusto Pinochet Ugarte and a return to democracy. In retaliation, the government shut down radio stations and a news agency and arrested journalists. Pinochet ignored U.S. urgings to modify his regime. On March 14, the United Nations passed a resolution expressing concern about Chile's human rights violations.

In El Salvador, the government of President José Napoleón Duarte, under U.S. pressure, greatly reduced physical torture, government-sanctioned killings by death squads, and disappearances of civilians. By August, human rights investigators and church officials estimated that politically motivated killings had fallen from about 800 a month in 1985 to fewer than 30 in 1986.

The government of Nicaragua warred against the press and broadcasters. In January, it shut down the Roman Catholic radio station in Managua, the capital, and in June closed down *La Prensa,* Nicaragua's only independent newspaper.

In Haiti, the 29-year-old dictatorship of the Duvalier family collapsed when President Jean-Claude Duvalier fled to France on February 7 aboard a U.S. Air Force jet.

Affirmative Action. In two separate decisions on July 2, the Supreme Court of the United States upheld the use of affirmative action programs in the workplace when less drastic measures did not overcome past discrimination. The court also ruled that the hiring goals of affirmative action plans may benefit members of minority groups who are not personally victims of discrimination.

The Administration of President Ronald Reagan had opposed these plans and their goals of hiring women and minority-group members. The Administration contended that job preferences for minority-group members at the expense of white male employees should be extended only to those who have personally suffered from discrimination. The Department of Justice in 1985 had filed suits challenging 51 affirmative action plans as violating civil rights laws. The Justice Department disclosed on August 12, however, that it would not continue its challenge of those plans.

Set-Aside Program. The staff of the U.S. Commission on Civil Rights in April presented a draft report that recommended a one-year suspension of federal programs that "set aside" contracts for businesses owned by blacks, other minorities, or women. This touched off a controversy among commission members, five of whom are considered to be conservative and three liberal. The conservatives, including Commission Chairman Clarence M. Pendleton, Jr., saw the set-aside programs as giving unfair preference to minorities. They also regarded the programs as costly, ineffective, and prone to fraud. The liberal commission members said the draft report reflected a "pattern of misuse of taxpayers' funds in furthering a pre-set ideological agenda."

The Reagan Administration issued a statement in support of minority set-aside contracts, and on April 11 the Civil Rights Commission voted, 5 to 3, to have its staff rewrite the controversial draft proposal. But it refused to reject the report.

New Holiday. A new federal holiday observed for the first time on January 20 honored civil rights leader Martin Luther King, Jr.

Comparable Pay. A landmark dispute between the state of Washington and state employees involving the complex issue of comparable pay was resolved on April 11. The settlement resulted in an average salary increase of 4 per cent for about 35,000 employees and annual increments that will total $482 million by 1992. The state agreed to eliminate wage differentials between low-paying jobs usually performed by women and minorities and higher-paying jobs usually filled by white males when the low-paying jobs require comparable skill, effort, and responsibility. Under a procedure worked out by the state and the American Federation of State, County and Municipal Employees, numerical values are assigned to reflect each job's level of skill, effort, responsibility, and working conditions. Jobs whose numbers total the same amount will be given the same pay scales.

Women and Law. A 23-member task force established in 1984 by the chief judge of New York state reported on April 20, 1986, that bias against women is so pervasive in the state court system that "they are often denied equal justice." The study also concluded that women lawyers are treated patronizingly by male judges and attorneys. It found that the credibility of female witnesses was sometimes discounted because some judges viewed women as emotional and untrustworthy. Among other consequences of sexual bias, the task force reported, was the misunderstanding by some judges of the nature of family violence and their predisposition to blame its women and children victims. Still other judges did not take seriously enough the efforts of women to obtain and enforce child-support awards, the report said.

In the 1986 elections, women made striking gains as candidates for statewide offices. The National Women's Political Caucus estimated in May that nearly 20 women were running for governorships, and 2 were elected in November. In Nebraska, both major parties nominated women for that post: Helen Boosalis, a Democrat and former mayor of Lincoln, and Kay A. Orr, a Republican and state treasurer. Orr won the election. The

Soviet dissident Anatoly B. Shcharansky, center, imprisoned in Russia for eight years, crosses into West Germany in a February prisoner exchange.

other woman governor elected was incumbent Democrat Madeleine M. Kunin of Vermont.

Drug Testing became a major civil liberties issue in 1986 as mandatory testing to identify employees who use illegal drugs spread rapidly. Labor unions launched legal challenges to have the tests declared unconstitutional.

AIDS Victims. A referendum was held in California in November on whether to quarantine people with AIDS. The measure was defeated by a margin of 2 to 1.

In June, the Department of Justice ruled that a person with AIDS could be fired or otherwise discriminated against if the discrimination was based on fears of spreading the disease, but an employer could not fire an AIDS victim because of an erroneous assumption that the illness would prevent the employee from doing the job. The ruling was part of an opinion that AIDS is not a handicap.

Nevertheless, on August 8, the federal government cited an employer for illegally discriminating against a person with AIDS when it accused the Charlotte Memorial Hospital and Medical Center in North Carolina of dismissing an AIDS victim from his job as a nurse and refusing to consider him for other employment. Louis W. Koenig

See also COURTS; SUPREME COURT OF THE UNITED STATES. In WORLD BOOK, see CIVIL RIGHTS.

CLASSICAL MUSIC. A trip by an 81-year-old musician may not have been the most significant musical event of 1986, but it was the most noted. The eminent Russian-born pianist Vladimir Horowitz returned to his homeland in April, 61 years after he left to build his renowned career. The Soviet government did not officially recognize the Horowitz visit, but people in Moscow and Leningrad knew he was coming. A single notice in front of each city's concert hall caused devotees to scramble for tickets.

The Horowitz trip was only one result of a renewal in United States-Soviet cultural relations. Also during 1986, the U.S.S.R. State Symphony Orchestra and the Kirov Ballet toured the United States. An unusual twist to the cultural exchanges was provided by an opera company from Surry, Me., a town of 900. The town underwrote the company's journey—a $180,000 venture—to Tbilisi and Leningrad in the Soviet Union in November to perform the most classic of Russian operas, Modest Mussorgsky's *Boris Godunov*.

Tour Halted. In May, New York City's Metropolitan Opera completed its spring travels with performances in Minneapolis, Minn. This tour was the Met's last, said the management, thus ending a century-old tradition. Sending forth such a vast array of talents had become too expensive.

Halls New and Renewed. The refurbished Carnegie Hall in New York City reopened in December with a gala concert. In September, the Orange County Performing Arts Center opened in Costa Mesa, Calif.

New also in 1986 was a Spoleto Festival in Melbourne, Australia, celebrating music, art, and drama, like the similarly named annual festivals in Spoleto, Italy, and Charleston, S.C. The Great Woods Center for the Performing Arts opened in Mansfield, Mass.

Sold-out houses greeted the new Los Angeles Music Center Opera, which opened its premiere season in October.

Survival and Demise. The San Diego Symphony Orchestra managed to hold on after declaring bankruptcy in late February. It was saved by a community campaign that collected $2 million in just two weeks. Not so lucky was New York City's Light Opera of Manhattan, which ceased performing after 19 seasons because of financial problems.

Anniversaries. The San Francisco Symphony Orchestra celebrated its 75th anniversary; the Israel Philharmonic Orchestra, its 50th; and the American Guild of Musical Artists, the union that represents opera performers and musicians, its 50th. The Houston Grand Opera and the Santa Fe (N. Mex.) Opera both marked their 30th year.

Pianist Vladimir Horowitz waves to a cheering audience in Moscow in April after concluding his first formal concert in his native Russia since leaving in 1925.

American composer and music critic Virgil Thomson marked his 90th birthday; and Italian-American composer Gian Carlo Menotti, his 75th. Menotti did not pause to celebrate. He worked, instead, to prepare his newest opera, *Goya*, introduced by the Washington Opera in November.

Conductors. Several cities welcomed new conductors. Dutch conductor Edo de Waart took over the Minnesota Orchestra; Russian-born conductor Maxim Shostakovich, the New Orleans Philharmonic Symphony; Spanish conductor Jesús Lopez-Cobos, the Cincinnati (Ohio) Symphony Orchestra; and French pianist and conductor Philippe Entremont, the Denver Symphony Orchestra.

Opera Premieres. New works that enriched the realm of opera in 1986, in addition to *Goya*, included: Volker David Kirchner's *Belshazzar* in Munich, West Germany, and *Chinchilla* by Myron Fink in Binghamton, N.Y., in January; Richard Meale's *Voss* in Adelaide, Australia, and Thomas Pasatieri's *Three Sisters* in Columbus, Ohio, in March; Hans-Jürgen von Bose's *The Sorrows of the Young Werther* in Schwetzingen, West Germany, Raymond Pannell's *As Long As a Child Remembers* in Little Rock, Ark., and John Adams' *Nixon in China* in Washington, D.C., in April; *The Mask of Orpheus* by Harrison Birtwistle in London in May; and *Stephen Climax* by Hans Zender in Frankfurt, West Germany, and William Neil's *The Guilt of Lilian Sloan* by Chicago Lyric Opera's Center for American Artists in Evanston, Ill., in June.

Other opera premieres in 1986 included Aribert Reimann's *Troades* in Munich and Lee Hoiby's *The Tempest* by the Des Moines Metro Opera in Indianola, Iowa, in July; Krzysztof Penderecki's *The Black Mask* at Austria's Salzburg Festival in August; Otto Ketting's *Ithaka* in Amsterdam, the Netherlands, in September; and Robert Sierra's *Mensajero de Plata* in Puerto Rico, in October.

Considerable attention was given to two September introductions. The first was the official premiere of Anthony Davis' *X (The Life and Times of Malcolm X)* by the New York City Opera, a work that received a staged trial performance in Philadelphia in 1984. The other was *Queenie Pie*, which composer Duke Ellington called his "street opera." It was produced by the American Music Theater Festival in Philadelphia.

Symphony Premieres. Orchestras were busy introducing new works, too. Premieres included Ezra Laderman's *Pentimento* (Albany, N.Y.); Marga Richter's *Landscapes of the Mind* (Atlanta, Ga.); Dominick Argento's *Le Tombeau d'Edgar Poe* (Baltimore); *Drala* by Peter Lieberson (Boston); Lukas Foss's Renaissance Concerto for Flute and Orchestra (Buffalo, N.Y.); Frank Proto's *Dialogue for Synclavier and Orchestra* (Cincinnati); Antal Dorati's *Querela Pacis* (Detroit); Tobias Picker's Symphony Number Two (Houston); Alan Hovhaness' Symphony Number 60 (Knoxville, Tenn.); Valentin Silvestrov's *Postludium* (Las Vegas, Nev.); and John Adams' *The Chairman Dances, Fox Trot for Orchestra* (Milwaukee).

Also, Steven Stucky's *Dreamwaltzes*, Ivan Eröd's *Minnesota Sinfonietta*, and Stanislaw Skrowaczewski's Concerto for Orchestra (Minnesota); Deborah Drattell's *The Tell-Tale Heart* and Rene Staar's *Just an Accident?* (New Orleans); *Athanor* by Jacob Druckman, *Fantasia on an Ostinato* by John Corigliano, *On Freedom's Ground* by William Schuman, and *Kegrops* by Iannis Xenakis (New York City); Richard Wernick's Violin Concerto (Philadelphia); Morton Gould's *Classical Variations on Colonial Themes* (Pittsburgh, Pa.); Joseph Schwantner's *A Sudden Rainbow*; Argento's Capriccio for Clarinet and Orchestra, and Steve Reich's *Three Movements for Orchestra* (St. Louis, Mo.); *The Golden Dance* by Charles Wuorinen (San Francisco); and *Beren and Luthien* by Glenn Buhr (Toronto, Canada).

Miscellany. In April, the director of the Mozart Institute in Salzburg, Austria, opened a piano bench and discovered a 35-page score of *The Meow That Saved the Kingdom*, believed to be the work of Wolfgang Amadeus Mozart. Included in the score is a notation that real cats are to meow throughout the work. Peter P. Jacobi

In WORLD BOOK, see CLASSICAL MUSIC; OPERA.

CLOTHING. See FASHION.

COAL. United States President Ronald Reagan on March 19, 1986, announced his support for a five-year program in which the U.S. government and American industry would spend $5 billion on developing the technology to burn coal more cleanly. Reagan's endorsement of the so-called Clean Coal Technology program came during a meeting in Washington, D.C., with Canada's Prime Minister Brian Mulroney.

Mulroney had urged Reagan to support the program as part of an effort to reduce the amount of sulfur dioxide, nitrogen oxides, and other pollutants released into the air chiefly by coal-burning factories and power plants. The pollutants are involved in the formation of acid rain, which has damaged forests and lakes in Canada and the northeastern United States.

The program was the result of a joint United States-Canadian report on acid rain issued on January 8, which concluded that a substantial amount of acid rain falling in Canada comes from the United States. In the past, Reagan had insisted that more research was needed before any action could be taken to curb acid rain.

The Clean Coal Technology program includes research on technology that removes pollutants from coal before it is burned, captures pollutants during burning, and converts coal to a clean-burning gas similar to natural gas. On July 28, the U.S.

Department of Energy announced the recipients of $360 million in government aid for clean coal research projects. The companies must pay at least 50 per cent of the cost of each project.

Coal Consumption, Production. The National Coal Association (NCA) predicted on June 29 in its annual forecast that U.S. coal production would increase slightly during 1986. The NCA, the major association of coal producers, estimated that the United States would produce 894 million short tons (811 million metric tons) of coal, an increase of about 1 per cent from the 1985 level of 886 million short tons (804 million metric tons). The association forecast that consumption would total 898 million short tons (815 million metric tons), about 1.4 per cent below the 1985 record of 911 million short tons (826 million metric tons). Exports were expected to total about 85 million short tons (77 million metric tons), a decrease of about 8.6 per cent from the 93 million short tons (84 million metric tons) sold to other countries in 1985. NCA officials blamed the decline in exports on increased competition from other coal-exporting countries.

The NCA's long-range projections indicated that U.S. coal production and consumption would increase by about 2 per cent per year through the year 2000. By then, the United States would be producing and consuming more than 1 billion short tons (907 million metric tons) of coal annually. But the group predicted that continued sluggish world demand would limit U.S. exports of coal to about 102 million short tons (93 million metric tons) per year by 2000—well below the record 110 million short tons (100 million metric tons) exported in 1981.

Coal Leasing Plan. On Feb. 26, 1986, Secretary of the Interior Donald P. Hodel announced that a program for leasing federal land to private companies for coal mining would resume in late 1987. The program was suspended in 1984 after complaints that Secretary of the Interior James G. Watt, who resigned in 1983, was not obtaining fair market value for the coal. The new program sets forth procedures for accurately appraising the value of the coal and for determining the demand.

Welsh Closing. A 200-year-old tradition of coal mining in the Rhondda Valley in southern Wales ended on June 30, 1986, with the closing of the area's last coal mine. The valley once was one of the world's most famous coal-mining regions, employing about 40,000 miners at the peak of production in 1913. But officials of the state-owned coal industry said that mining no longer was economical in the area, with most of the remaining coal in deep, difficult-to-reach seams.   Michael Woods

See also ENERGY SUPPLY; ENVIRONMENTAL POLLUTION; MINING; WALES. In WORLD BOOK, see COAL.

COIN COLLECTING. United States commemorative coins honoring the Statue of Liberty and Ellis Island sold briskly in 1986. As of mid-October, sales of the coins totaled $253 million, of which $67-million went to the Statue of Liberty-Ellis Island Foundation. The foundation is using the funds to help pay for the now-completed restoration of the statue and the renovation of the former immigration facilities on the island, both of which are located in New York Harbor. Three kinds of coins were minted: a copper-nickel half dollar, priced at $7.50; a silver dollar, selling for $24; and a $5 gold piece, which went for $175.

Auction Prices varied considerably in 1986. A few rarities brought higher prices than their owners had paid for them, but many valuable coins were sold at a loss. In June, a scarce 1804 silver dollar, purchased for $400,000 in 1980, went for $170,000 at an auction in New York City.

Among the larger sales was a July auction in Chicago at which 2,000 lots were sold for a total of $8.2 million. Notable coins sold included an 1870 U.S. half dime minted in San Francisco, which went for $253,000, and a matte-proof 1912 U.S. $20 gold piece designed by Augustus Saint-Gaudens, a famous American sculptor, which sold for $36,300. At a New York City auction in May, a set of five 1915 Panama-Pacific International Ex-

United States gold coins, with face values of $5 to $50—but actually priced much higher—were offered for sale in October by the U.S. Mint.

position gold coins minted in San Francisco sold for $70,000 in their original copper frame.

Coin Grading. The *grading* (assessment of condition) of coins is a controversial subject with collectors because a coin's grade, together with its rarity, determines its value. Thus, collectors had a mixed reaction in 1986 when the American Numismatic Association (ANA) refined its system of grading uncirculated coins. Previously, the ANA grading system used five numbers between 60 and 70, with 60 being slightly flawed and 70 perfect. The new method uses 11 numbers—the consecutive digits from 60 through 70. This more exact grading scheme raises the possibility that many coins, when offered for sale, will be slightly downgraded from their previous rating.

U.S. Gold Coins. On October 20, the Department of the Treasury began selling American Eagle gold coins, the first gold coins minted by the U.S. government since 1933. The coins were issued in four weights, ranging from 1 troy ounce (31 grams) to 1/10 troy ounce (3.1 grams), and carried face values of $50, $25, $10, and $5. The actual prices of the coins were much higher and were based on the fluctuating price of gold.

Gold, Silver Prices were fairly steady during the year, with gold ranging from $300 to $450 per troy ounce and silver selling for $5 to $6.   Lee Martin

In WORLD BOOK, see COIN COLLECTING.

COLOMBIA. The Liberal Party of Colombia returned to power on Aug. 7, 1986, when Virgilio Barco Vargas took office as Colombia's president. The 64-year-old Barco pledged that his administration would continue efforts begun by his predecessor, Belisario Betancur of the Conservative Party, to work for a negotiated peace in Central America, where rebels are fighting the Nicaraguan government. Betancur was a leader of the Contadora Group, a coalition of four Latin-American nations trying to mediate a settlement.

The new president said his government would continue to seek peace with Colombia's own leftist rebels. Barco said he welcomed the presence in Congress of members of the Patriotic Union, one of four guerrilla groups that halted armed action to participate in the political process.

But efforts for a peaceful reconciliation appeared to be undercut when unknown assassins killed four members of the Patriotic Union at three different locations the weekend of August 30 to September 1. All were killed by motorcyclists who threw bombs, then sped off to escape.

By October, high officials of Colombia's armed forces declared that leftist guerrillas were stepping up their recruitment and were seeking to form a single unified rebel command. An air of crisis seemed to hover over the administration of Barco. Critics questioned his decision to end a 28-year-

old tradition of appointing supporters of both major political parties to the president's administration. Instead, Barco formed a government entirely made up of supporters from his own Liberal Party. The tradition, begun in 1958, helped put an end to fighting between the two major parties that had left 200,000 people dead.

Drug Trade. Barco spurned suggestions that Colombia, like Bolivia, should seek the help of United States troops in stopping the mushrooming production of illegal drugs. The illicit drug trade is a main source of financing for leftist guerrillas and has led to the corruption of state and municipal governments. Colombia has not been successful in curtailing the flow of cocaine to the United States, according to U.S. officials.

Colombia's principal drug dealers have offered to invest their huge profits in legitimate businesses in Colombia if the authorities agree to block extradition to the United States, where many of the drug traffickers face criminal charges. The drug dealers reportedly increased their offer in 1986 by pledging to pay off Colombia's foreign debt of $13-billion.   Nathan A. Haverstock

See also BARCO VARGAS, VIRGILIO; LATIN AMERICA (Facts in Brief Table). In WORLD BOOK, see COLOMBIA.

COLORADO. See STATE GOVERNMENT.

COMMON MARKET. See EUROPE.

COMMUNICATIONS. The American Telephone and Telegraph Company (AT&T) continued to dominate the intercity long-distance telephone business in the United States in 1986, despite challenges from an old competitor—MCI Communications Corporation—and a new one—US Sprint Communications Company. Much of the power in the industry remained in the hands of the seven so-called regional holding companies (RHC's), the telephone companies formed when AT&T broke up on Jan. 1, 1984.

On Feb. 28, 1986, the Pacific Telesis Group, the RHC that owns the Bell telephone companies in California and Nevada, completed the first step in a $435-million purchase of Communications Industries, Incorporated, a Texas firm that makes telephone equipment and provides cellular-telephone and paging services. On April 22, Nynex Corporation, the RHC for New York and New England, purchased retail computer stores owned by International Business Machines Corporation.

Southwestern Bell Corporation announced the biggest deal of all on June 30—a $1.65-billion purchase of the cellular-telephone and paging businesses of Metromedia Incorporated. The price was later cut to $1.2 billion.

Mergers. On July 1, GTE Corporation merged its Sprint long-distance operation with US Telecom, owned by United Telecommunications, In-

Telephone workers picket American Telephone and Telegraph Company (AT&T) in June. Some 155,000 workers struck AT&T for 26 days.

ruled that District Judge Harold H. Greene had erred by forbidding RHC's to provide cellular and paging service outside the areas served by their telephone companies.

The Cable-TV Industry was jolted at 12:30 A.M. on April 27, when a man calling himself "Captain Midnight" jammed the Home Box Office (HBO) satellite transmission of the movie *The Falcon and the Snowman*. The jammer, John R. MacDougall, turned himself in. On August 7, the FCC approved a plan requiring cable operators to carry certain types of programs and to offer subscribers switches that would enable the subscriber to receive signals over cable or through the air.

Satellites. The communications satellite business suffered two severe blows in 1986. The explosion of the U.S. space shuttle *Challenger* on January 28 grounded the shuttle fleet—a major means of launching satellites—for at least two years.

On May 30, an Ariane 2 owned by Arianespace, Western Europe's satellite-launching company, blew up with a communications satellite aboard shortly after take-off from Kourou Space Center in French Guiana. Arianespace canceled the remainder of the Ariane launching schedule pending an investigation.   Arthur R. Brodsky

See also SPACE EXPLORATION; TELEVISION. In WORLD BOOK, see COMMUNICATION.

COMOROS. See AFRICA.

corporated, to form US Sprint. The new business held about 4 per cent of the long-distance market, compared with about 9 per cent for MCI, AT&T's largest competitor. And on September 29, Continental Telecom, Incorporated, announced a $2.5-billion merger with Communications Satellite Corporation (COMSAT).

AT&T Leads. About 75 per cent of all consumers who chose long-distance companies by ballot in 1986 selected AT&T. That company also held on to an estimated 80 per cent of the overall long-distance market. During 1986, AT&T lowered long-distance rates by more than 12 per cent. The competitors also slashed their prices.

Strike. James E. Olson took over as chief executive officer of AT&T on June 1. That also happened to be the day that 155,000 members of the Communications Workers of America union walked off their jobs in the first strike since the 1984 breakup. The strike ended on June 27, 1986.

Court Decisions played a larger than usual role in the telecommunications industry in 1986. On May 27, the Supreme Court of the United States ruled that the Federal Communications Commission (FCC) could not set depreciation rates for telephone equipment used within only one state. On August 15, the U.S. Court of Appeals for the District of Columbia overturned a portion of the rules governing the breakup of AT&T. The court

COMPUTER sales in the United States were weak in 1986, but the computer industry made striking advances in technology and product development. Industry executives followed a strategy that had worked before in high-technology areas: Generate a wave of new products—in this case, more powerful, less expensive, and easier-to-use computers—in the hope that the products will reach previously unattainable markets. Manufacturers had high hopes that this strategy would turn the sales picture around as early as 1987.

Innovation was most notable in three major areas: computer *architecture* (design), computer graphics, and scientific computing. Perhaps the most significant changes were those in architecture, from the largest computer to the smallest.

Two Major Trends in computer architecture continued—the use of *scalable systems*, consisting of equipment that can be built up in stages; and the linking together of many small computers to produce one large computer that provides *parallel processing*, the simultaneous manipulation of data by some or all of the small computers. A conventional computer processes data one operation at a time, or *in series*. Parallel processing is much faster than serial processing.

The main reason for the development of scalable systems is that people who buy computers—other than small personal computers—prefer to avoid the expense of replacing a great deal of equipment when they need more computing power. And one reason for the popularity of parallel-processing systems is that they are easy to expand. By the end of 1986, more than 40 companies were manufacturing parallel-processing systems.

More Bits. A long-awaited development in *microprocessors* occurred in 1986—the introduction of the *32-bit chip*. A microprocessor is a virtually complete computer on a single piece of material, usually a chip of silicon about the size of a fingernail. A 32-bit chip can process 32 *bits* of information simultaneously. (A bit is a 0 or 1 in the binary numeration system that computers use.)

The new chips are much faster than the 8- and 16-bit microprocessors that preceded them. A typical 16-bit chip can carry out 500,000 to 1 million instructions per second. The 32-bit chip can handle 2 million to 3 million instructions.

More Tasks. Industry observers expected computer makers to use the new chips in parallel-processing machines and in high-performance *engineering work stations*—desk-top computers for product design, engineering, and manufacturing. As soon as the first 32-bit work station was announced, it became apparent that the new chips have the "muscle" to solve many kinds of problems that are beyond the capacity of 8- and 16-bit machines—problems in manufacturing, robotics, and machine-tool control, for example.

To do such advanced processing, designers will need sophisticated work stations. And computer experts and business executives organized a raft of companies in 1986 to manufacture them.

Supercomputers. Leading the way in the development of *supercomputers*—the fastest computers—was Cray Research Incorporated of Minneapolis, Minn. Cray, already the world leader in the production of these giant machines, continued to work on three advanced supercomputers in 1986. The first to arrive will probably be the Y-MP. Cray expects this computer, with eight processors hooked up in parallel, to perform 3 billion *floating-point operations* per second. (A floating-point operation is a calculation in which the location of the decimal point may vary from number to number.) With a main memory of up to 500 million 64-bit words, the Y-MP will cost nearly $20 million.

Scientific Computing continued to be the brightest spot in the industry. The leading products in this field were *minisupercomputers*, machines that do not have quite the speed and memory capacity of supercomputers, but which cost less than $1 million. These machines "crunch numbers" well enough to handle a wide range of scientific applications such as predicting the weather and calculating rates of chemical reactions. Sales of minisupercomputers in 1986 were more than 30 per cent

An experimental desk-top computer made by International Business Machines Corporation displays sentences that are dictated to it.

higher than in 1985. The technical trends in both supers and minisupers followed those of their smaller cousins, with parallel processing playing a major role.

Storage. All computers need a permanent place to store information. In 1986, the magnetic disk, in both hard and flexible styles, continued to be the most common storage device. Other popular devices included magnetic tape, videotape, microfilm, and the *optical disk*, on which a laser records data. (A laser also "reads" information recorded on an optical disk.)

Optical disks, which have the potential to replace magnetic disks as the most common storage devices, began to move into commercial production in 1986. There are three basic types of optical disk: read-only, on which the user cannot write; write-once; and erasable-rewritable. The most common is a read-only disk known as a CD-ROM (*Compact Disk Read-Only Memory*). The basic technology of CD-ROM's did not change in 1986, but there was a change in their size. Manufacturers began to produce them in the same size—5.25 inches (13.3 centimeters) in diameter—as the most common magnetic disks that are used for mass data storage. Howard Wolff

See also ELECTRONICS. In WORLD BOOK, see COMPUTER.

CONGO. See AFRICA.

CONGRESS OF THE UNITED STATES. Before adjourning for the year on Oct. 18, 1986, Congress overcame its seeming paralysis and surprised even itself by achieving one of the most productive legislative sessions in recent history.

Little had been expected of the election-year Congress because it planned to adjourn early for campaigning. Moreover, the Administration of President Ronald Reagan had applied concerted pressure on the lawmakers for only one major domestic policy initiative—a sweeping overhaul of the United States income tax code. As it turned out, the Senate and House of Representatives extended their session by two weeks and, in a final burst of activity, passed a series of major bills that exceeded nearly everyone's expectations.

The politically divided Congress often took a cue from Reagan on domestic policy but approached many of his foreign-policy and national-security goals with skepticism or opposition. Reflecting on the give-and-take nature of the session, Senate Democratic Leader Robert C. Byrd of West Virginia declared, "I believe the 99th Congress will be remembered as a Congress that made the system of checks and balances work."

Arms-Sale Investigations. Senator Byrd's observation on checks and balances took on new meaning late in the year. In December, Congress began looking into revelations that officials of the Administration had secretly sold arms to Iran and diverted profits from the transactions to *contra* rebels fighting the Marxist government of Nicaragua. The inquiries were expected to pick up steam in 1987 with the appointment of special investigating committees in both the House and Senate. See PRESIDENT OF THE UNITED STATES.

Summary of Legislation. Congress not only rewrote the income tax code but also overhauled immigration policy after six years of effort, strengthened environmental protections, and passed a major antidrug program. In other important actions, the lawmakers revamped a costly water-projects program, eliminated mandatory retirement at age 70 for most Americans, and imposed stiff constraints on both defense and domestic spending in an effort to curb federal deficits of more than $200 billion a year.

Among other legislation, Congress continued the 16-cents-a-pack cigarette tax; voted to advance daylight-saving time by three weeks to the first Sunday of April; eased gun controls but banned armor-piercing "cop killer" bullets; made part-time college students eligible for student loans; boosted veterans' compensation by 1.5 per cent; voted to reduce future military pensions; and designated the rose as the national flower.

In the summer, before learning of the Administration's secret arms deals, Congress authorized $100 million in military and humanitarian aid for the contras of Nicaragua. But it defied the President by imposing *sanctions* (penalties) on the white-dominated government of South Africa, voting to override his veto. It also revamped the top military command system, a scheme for which Reagan showed scant enthusiasm.

The President prevailed in heading off major protectionist trade legislation as the House on August 6 failed by eight votes to override his veto of a bill that would have reduced imports of textiles, clothing, shoes, and copper. The vote of 276 to 149 was short of the needed two-thirds majority.

Tax Reform. The year's foremost accomplishment was the enactment of the landmark Tax Reform Act of 1986, which had been given up for dead several times during its two-year journey through Congress. An early version of the Tax Reform Act barely got through the House in 1985 and, for a time, seemed doomed in the Senate. But a bold redrafting under the leadership of Senator Bob Packwood (R., Ore.), chairman of the Finance Committee, won broad support for the most sweeping changes in the U.S. income tax code in more than 40 years. Sharing major credit with Packwood were Reagan and two Democrats, Representative Dan Rostenkowski of Illinois, chairman of the House Ways and Means Committee, and Senator Bill Bradley of New Jersey.

The new law, signed by Reagan on October 22, coupled a dramatic reduction in individual and corporate income tax rates with a curtailment of many deductions, tax shelters, and special-interest tax breaks. Starting on Jan. 1, 1988, there will be just two income tax rates for individuals—15 per cent and 28 per cent, plus a surcharge creating a third rate of 33 per cent for certain high-income taxpayers. A transitional system of five tax rates, ranging from 11 per cent to 38.5 per cent, will be in effect in 1987. Under the old tax structure, the top rate for individuals was 50 per cent.

Many corporations will also benefit under the new law, which lowers the top corporate tax rate from 46 per cent to 34 per cent. But the law will also require a number of major companies that have paid little or no taxes to begin paying them. That change is expected to boost corporate tax payments by $120 billion over five years, exactly offsetting cuts in individual payments.

Immigration Bill. The enactment of legislation reforming U.S. immigration policies was an even bigger surprise than the tax bill. Final passage came just three weeks after a procedural vote in the House seemingly doomed such legislation for the third straight year. The House passed the bill, 238 to 173, on Oct. 15, 1986, and the Senate gave it final approval two days later, 63 to 24. Reagan signed the bill into law on November 6.

A principal feature of the measure is a provision offering amnesty to millions of illegal aliens who

Members of the United States Senate

The Senate of the first session of the 100th Congress consisted of 55 Democrats and 45 Republicans when it convened in January 1987. Senators shown starting their term in 1987 were elected for the first time in the Nov. 4, 1986, elections. Others shown ending their current terms in 1993 were reelected to the Senate in the 1986 balloting. The second date in each listing shows when the term of a previously elected senator expires.

State	Term	State	Term	State	Term
Alabama		**Louisiana**		**Ohio**	
Howell T. Heflin, D.	1979–1991	J. Bennett Johnston, Jr., D.	1972–1991	John H. Glenn, Jr., D.	1975–1993
Richard C. Shelby, D.	1987–1993	John B. Breaux, D.	1987–1993	Howard M. Metzenbaum, D.	1977–1989
Alaska		**Maine**		**Oklahoma**	
Theodore F. Stevens, R.	1968–1991	William S. Cohen, R.	1979–1991	David L. Boren, D.	1979–1991
Frank H. Murkowski, R.	1981–1993	George J. Mitchell, D.	1980–1989	Don Nickles, R.	1981–1993
Arizona		**Maryland**		**Oregon**	
Dennis DeConcini, D.	1977–1989	Paul S. Sarbanes, D.	1977–1989	Mark O. Hatfield, R.	1967–1991
John McCain III, R.	1987–1993	Barbara A. Mikulski, D.	1987–1993	Bob Packwood, R.	1969–1993
Arkansas		**Massachusetts**		**Pennsylvania**	
Dale Bumpers, D.	1975–1993	Edward M. Kennedy, D.	1962–1989	John Heinz, R.	1977–1989
David H. Pryor, D.	1979–1991	John F. Kerry, D.	1985–1991	Arlen Specter, R.	1981–1993
California		**Michigan**		**Rhode Island**	
Alan Cranston, D.	1969–1993	Donald W. Riegle, Jr., D.	1977–1989	Claiborne Pell, D.	1961–1991
Pete Wilson, R.	1983–1989	Carl Levin, D.	1979–1991	John H. Chafee, R.	1977–1989
Colorado		**Minnesota**		**South Carolina**	
William L. Armstrong, R.	1979–1991	David F. Durenberger, R.	1978–1989	Strom Thurmond, R.	1956–1991
Timothy E. Wirth, D.	1987–1993	Rudy Boschwitz, R.	1979–1991	Ernest F. Hollings, D.	1966–1993
Connecticut		**Mississippi**		**South Dakota**	
Lowell P. Weicker, Jr., R.	1971–1989	John C. Stennis, D.	1947–1989	Larry Pressler, R.	1979–1991
Christopher J. Dodd, D.	1981–1993	Thad Cochran, R.	1979–1991	Thomas A. Daschle, D.	1987–1993
Delaware		**Missouri**		**Tennessee**	
William V. Roth, Jr., R.	1971–1989	John C. Danforth, R.	1977–1989	James Sasser, D.	1977–1989
Joseph R. Biden, Jr., D.	1973–1991	Christopher S. (Kit) Bond, R.	1987–1993	Albert A. Gore, Jr., D.	1985–1991
Florida		**Montana**		**Texas**	
Lawton Chiles, D.	1971–1989	John Melcher, D.	1977–1989	Lloyd M. Bentsen, D.	1971–1989
Bob Graham, D.	1987–1993	Max Baucus, D.	1979–1991	Phil Gramm, R.	1985–1991
Georgia		**Nebraska**		**Utah**	
Sam Nunn, D.	1972–1991	Edward Zorinsky, D.	1977–1989	Edwin Jacob Garn, R.	1975–1993
Wyche Fowler, Jr., D.	1987–1993	J. James Exon, D.	1979–1991	Orrin G. Hatch, R.	1977–1989
Hawaii		**Nevada**		**Vermont**	
Daniel K. Inouye, D.	1963–1993	Chic Hecht, R.	1983–1989	Robert T. Stafford, R.	1971–1989
Spark M. Matsunaga, D.	1977–1989	Harry M. Reid, D.	1987–1993	Patrick J. Leahy, D.	1975–1993
Idaho		**New Hampshire**		**Virginia**	
James A. McClure, R.	1973–1991	Gordon J. Humphrey, R.	1979–1991	John W. Warner, R.	1979–1991
Steven D. Symms, R.	1981–1993	Warren B. Rudman, R.	1981–1993	Paul S. Trible, Jr., R.	1983–1989
Illinois		**New Jersey**		**Washington**	
Alan J. Dixon, D.	1981–1993	Bill Bradley, D.	1979–1991	Daniel J. Evans, R.	1983–1989
Paul Simon, D.	1985–1991	Frank R. Lautenberg, D.	1983–1989	Brock Adams, D.	1987–1993
Indiana		**New Mexico**		**West Virginia**	
Richard G. Lugar, R.	1977–1989	Pete V. Domenici, R.	1973–1991	Robert C. Byrd, D.	1959–1989
J. Danforth Quayle, R.	1981–1993	Jeff Bingaman, D.	1983–1989	John D. Rockefeller IV, D.	1985–1991
Iowa		**New York**		**Wisconsin**	
Charles E. Grassley, R.	1981–1993	Daniel P. Moynihan, D.	1977–1989	Willian Proxmire, D.	1957–1989
Tom Harkin, D.	1985–1991	Alfonse M. D'Amato, R.	1981–1993	Robert W. Kasten, Jr., R.	1981–1993
Kansas		**North Carolina**		**Wyoming**	
Robert J. Dole, R.	1969–1993	Jesse A. Helms, R.	1973–1991	Malcolm Wallop, R.	1977–1989
Nancy Landon Kassebaum, R.	1979–1991	Terry Sanford, D.	1987–1993	Alan K. Simpson, R.	1979–1991
Kentucky		**North Dakota**			
Wendell H. Ford, D.	1975–1993	Quentin N. Burdick, D.	1960–1989		
Mitch McConnell, R.	1985–1991	Kent Conrad, D.	1987–1993		

Members of the United States House of Representatives

The House of Representatives of the first session of the 100th Congress consisted of 258 Democrats and 177 Republicans (not including representatives from American Samoa, the District of Columbia, Guam, Puerto Rico, and the Virgin Islands) when it convened in January 1987, compared with 253 Democrats and 182 Republicans when the second session of the 99th Congress convened. This table shows congressional district, legislator, and party affiliation. Asterisk (*) denotes those who served in the 99th Congress; dagger (†) denotes "at large."

Alabama
1. H. L. Callahan, R.*
2. William L. Dickinson, R.*
3. Bill Nichols, D.*
4. Tom Bevill, D.*
5. Ronnie G. Flippo, D.*
6. Ben Erdreich, D.*
7. Claude Harris, D.

Alaska
†Donald E. Young, R.*

Arizona
1. John J. Rhodes III, R.
2. Morris K. Udall, D.*
3. Bob Stump, R.*
4. Jon Kyl, R.
5. Jim Kolbe, R.*

Arkansas
1. Bill Alexander, D.*
2. Tommy Robinson, D.*
3. John P. Hammerschmidt, R.*
4. Beryl F. Anthony, Jr., D.*

California
1. Douglas H. Bosco, D.*
2. Wally Herger, R.
3. Robert T. Matsui, D.*
4. Vic Fazio, D.*
5. Sala Burton, D.*
6. Barbara Boxer, D.*
7. George Miller, D.*
8. Ronald V. Dellums, D.*
9. Fortney H. (Pete) Stark, D.*
10. Don Edwards, D.*
11. Tom Lantos, D.*
12. Ernest L. Konnyu, R.
13. Norman Y. Mineta, D.*
14. Norman D. Shumway, R.*
15. Tony Coelho, D.*
16. Leon E. Panetta, D.*
17. Charles Pashayan, Jr., R.*
18. Richard H. Lehman, D.*
19. Robert J. Lagomarsino, R.*
20. William M. Thomas, R.*
21. Elton Gallegly, R.
22. Carlos J. Moorhead, R.*
23. Anthony C. Beilenson, D.*
24. Henry A. Waxman, D.*
25. Edward R. Roybal, D.*
26. Howard L. Berman, D.*
27. Mel Levine, D.*
28. Julian C. Dixon, D.*
29. Augustus F. (Gus) Hawkins, D.*
30. Matthew G. Martinez, D.*
31. Mervyn M. Dymally, D.*
32. Glenn M. Anderson, D.*
33. David Dreier, R.*
34. Esteban E. Torres, D.*
35. Jerry Lewis, R.*
36. George E. Brown, Jr., D.*
37. Alfred A. McCandless, R.*
38. Robert K. Dornan, R.*
39. William E. Dannemeyer, R.*
40. Robert E. Badham, R.*
41. William D. Lowery, R.*
42. Daniel E. Lungren, R.*
43. Ronald C. Packard, R.*
44. Jim Bates, D.*
45. Duncan L. Hunter, R.*

Colorado
1. Patricia Schroeder, D.*
2. David Skaggs, D.
3. Ben Nighthorse Campbell, D.
4. Hank Brown, R.*
5. Joel Hefley, R.
6. Daniel Schaefer, R.*

Connecticut
1. Barbara B. Kennelly, D.*
2. Samuel Gejdenson, D.*
3. Bruce A. Morrison, D.*
4. Stewart B. McKinney, R.*
5. John G. Rowland, R.*
6. Nancy L. Johnson, R.*

Delaware
†Thomas R. Carper, D.*

Florida
1. Earl Hutto, D.*
2. Bill Grant, D.
3. Charles E. Bennett, D.*
4. Bill Chappell, Jr., D.*
5. Bill McCollum, R.*
6. Kenneth H. (Buddy) MacKay, D.*
7. Sam M. Gibbons, D.*
8. C. W. Bill Young, R.*
9. Michael Bilirakis, R.*
10. Andy Ireland, R.*
11. Bill Nelson, D.*
12. Thomas F. Lewis, R.*
13. Connie Mack III, R.*
14. Daniel A. Mica, D.*
15. E. Clay Shaw, Jr., R.*
16. Lawrence J. Smith, D.*
17. William Lehman, D.*
18. Claude D. Pepper, D.*
19. Dante B. Fascell, D.*

Georgia
1. Lindsay Thomas, D.*
2. Charles F. Hatcher, D.*
3. Richard B. Ray, D.*
4. Pat Swindall, R.*
5. John Lewis, D.
6. Newt Gingrich, R.*
7. George Darden, D.*
8. J. Roy Rowland, D.*
9. Edgar L. Jenkins, D.*
10. Doug Barnard, Jr., D.*

Hawaii
1. Patricia Saiki, R.
2. Daniel K. Akaka, D.*

Idaho
1. Larry Craig, R.*
2. Richard Stallings, D.*

Illinois
1. Charles A. Hayes, D.*
2. Gus Savage, D.*
3. Marty Russo, D.*
4. Jack Davis, R.
5. William O. Lipinski, D.*
6. Henry J. Hyde, R.*
7. Cardiss Collins, D.*
8. Dan Rostenkowski, D.*
9. Sidney R. Yates, D.*
10. John Edward Porter, R.*
11. Frank Annunzio, D.*
12. Philip M. Crane, R.*
13. Harris W. Fawell, R.*
14. J. Dennis Hastert, R.
15. Edward R. Madigan, R.*
16. Lynn M. Martin, R.*
17. Lane A. Evans, D.*
18. Robert H. Michel, R.*
19. Terry L. Bruce, D.*
20. Richard J. Durbin, D.*
21. Melvin Price, D.*
22. Kenneth J. Gray, D.*

Indiana
1. Peter J. Visclosky, D.*
2. Philip R. Sharp, D.*
3. John Patrick Hiler, R.*
4. Dan R. Coats, R.*
5. James Jontz, D.
6. Danny L. Burton, R.*
7. John T. Myers, R.*
8. Frank McCloskey, D.*
9. Lee H. Hamilton, D.*
10. Andrew Jacobs, Jr., D.*

Iowa
1. Jim Leach, R.*
2. Thomas J. Tauke, R.*
3. David R. Nagle, D.
4. Neal Smith, D.*
5. Jim Ross Lightfoot, R.*
6. Fred Grandy, R.

Kansas
1. Pat Roberts, R.*
2. James C. Slattery, D.*
3. Jan Meyers, R.*
4. Dan Glickman, D.*
5. Bob Whittaker, R.*

Kentucky
1. Carroll Hubbard, Jr., D.*
2. William H. Natcher, D.*
3. Romano L. Mazzoli, D.*
4. Jim Bunning, R.
5. Harold (Hal) Rogers, R.*
6. Larry J. Hopkins, R.*
7. Carl C. (Chris) Perkins, D.*

Louisiana
1. Robert L. Livingston, R.*
2. Corinne C. (Lindy) Boggs, D.*
3. W. J. (Billy) Tauzin, D.*
4. Charles Roemer, D.*
5. Thomas J. (Jerry) Huckaby, D.*
6. Richard Hugh Baker, R.
7. James A. (Jimmy) Hayes, D.
8. Clyde C. Holloway, R.

Maine
1. Joseph D. Brennan, D.
2. Olympia J. Snowe, R.*

Maryland
1. Roy P. Dyson, D.*
2. Helen Delich Bentley, R.*
3. Benjamin L. Cardin, D.
4. Thomas McMillen, D.
5. Steny H. Hoyer, D.*
6. Beverly B. Byron, D.*
7. Kweisi Mfume, D.
8. Constance A. Morella, R.

Massachusetts
1. Silvio O. Conte, R.*
2. Edward P. Boland, D.*
3. Joseph D. Early, D.*
4. Barney Frank, D.*
5. Chester G. Atkins, D.*
6. Nicholas Mavroules, D.*
7. Edward J. Markey, D.*
8. Joseph P. Kennedy II, D.
9. John Joseph Moakley, D.*
10. Gerry E. Studds, D.*
11. Brian J. Donnelly, D.*

Michigan
1. John Conyers, Jr., D.*
2. Carl D. Pursell, R.*
3. Howard E. Wolpe, D.*
4. Fred Upton, R.
5. Paul B. Henry, R.*
6. Bob Carr, D.*
7. Dale E. Kildee, D.*
8. Bob Traxler, D.*
9. Guy Vander Jagt, R.*
10. Bill Schuette, R.*
11. Robert W. Davis, R.*
12. David E. Bonior, D.*
13. George W. Crockett, Jr., D.*
14. Dennis M. Hertel, D.*
15. William D. Ford, D.*
16. John D. Dingell, D.*
17. Sander M. Levin, D.*
18. William S. Broomfield, R.*

Minnesota
1. Timothy J. Penny, D.*
2. Vin Weber, R.*
3. Bill Frenzel, R.*
4. Bruce F. Vento, D.*
5. Martin O. Sabo, D.*
6. Gerry Sikorski, D.*
7. Arlan Stangeland, R.*
8. James L. Oberstar, D.*

Mississippi
1. Jamie L. Whitten, D.*
2. Mike Espy, D.
3. G. V. (Sonny) Montgomery, D.*
4. Wayne Dowdy, D.*
5. Trent Lott, R.*

Missouri
1. William L. (Bill) Clay, D.*
2. Jack Buechner, R.
3. Richard A. Gephardt, D.*
4. Ike Skelton, D.*
5. Alan D. Wheat, D.*
6. E. Thomas Coleman, R.*
7. Gene Taylor, R.*
8. Bill Emerson, R.*
9. Harold L. Volkmer, D.*

Montana
1. Pat Williams, D.*
2. Ron Marlenee, R.*

Nebraska
1. Doug Bereuter, R.*
2. Hal Daub, R.*
3. Virginia Smith, R.*

Nevada
1. James H. Bilbray, D.
2. Barbara F. Vucanovich, R.*

New Hampshire
1. Robert C. Smith, R.*
2. Judd Gregg, R.*

New Jersey
1. James J. Florio, D.*
2. William J. Hughes, D.*
3. James J. Howard, D.*
4. Christopher H. Smith, R.*
5. Marge Roukema, R.*
6. Bernard J. Dwyer, D.*
7. Matthew J. Rinaldo, R.*
8. Robert A. Roe, D.*
9. Robert G. Torricelli, D.*
10. Peter W. Rodino, Jr., D.*
11. Dean A. Gallo, R.*
12. Jim Courter, R.*
13. H. James Saxton, R.*
14. Frank J. Guarini, D.*

New Mexico
1. Manuel Lujan, Jr., R.*
2. Joe Skeen, R.*
3. William B. Richardson, D.*

New York
1. George J. Hochbrueckner, D.
2. Thomas J. Downey, D.*
3. Robert J. Mrazek, D.*
4. Norman F. Lent, R.*
5. Raymond J. McGrath, R.*
6. Floyd H. Flake, D.
7. Gary L. Ackerman, D.*
8. James H. Scheuer, D.*
9. Thomas J. Manton, D.*
10. Charles E. Schumer, D.*
11. Edolphus Towns, D.*
12. Major R. Owens, D.*
13. Stephen J. Solarz, D.*

14. Guy V. Molinari, R.*
15. Bill Green, R.*
16. Charles B. Rangel, D.*
17. Ted Weiss, D.*
18. Robert Garcia, D.*
19. Mario Biaggi, D.*
20. Joseph D. DioGuardi, R.*
21. Hamilton Fish, Jr., R.*
22. Benjamin A. Gilman, R.*
23. Samuel S. Stratton, D.*
24. Gerald B. Solomon, R.*
25. Sherwood L. Boehlert, R.*
26. David O'B. Martin, R.*
27. George C. Wortley, R.*
28. Matthew F. McHugh, D.*
29. Frank Horton, R.*
30. Louise M. Slaughter, D.*
31. Jack F. Kemp, R.*
32. John J. LaFalce, D.*
33. Henry J. Nowak, D.*
34. Amory Houghton, Jr., R.

North Carolina
1. Walter B. Jones, D.*
2. Tim Valentine, D.*
3. Martin Lancaster, D.
4. David E. Price, D.
5. Stephen L. Neal, D.*
6. Howard Coble, R.
7. Charlie Rose, D.*
8. W. G. (Bill) Hefner, D.*
9. J. Alex McMillan III, R.*
10. Cass Ballenger, R.
11. James McClure Clarke, D.

North Dakota
†Byron L. Dorgan, D.*

Ohio
1. Thomas A. Luken, D.*
2. Willis D. Gradison, Jr., R.*
3. Tony P. Hall, D.*
4. Michael G. Oxley, R.*
5. Delbert L. Latta, R.*
6. Bob McEwen, R.*
7. Michael DeWine, R.*
8. Donald E. Lukens, R.
9. Marcy Kaptur, D.*
10. Clarence E. Miller, R.*
11. Dennis E. Eckart, D.*
12. John R. Kasich, R.*
13. Donald J. Pease, D.*
14. Thomas C. Sawyer, D.
15. Chalmers P. Wylie, R.*
16. Ralph Regula, R.*
17. James Traficant, Jr., D.*
18. Douglas Applegate, D.*
19. Edward F. Feighan, D.*
20. Mary Rose Oakar, D.*
21. Louis Stokes, D.*

Oklahoma
1. James M. Inhofe, R.
2. Mike Synar, D.*
3. Wesley W. Watkins, D.*
4. Dave McCurdy, D.*
5. Mickey Edwards, R.*
6. Glenn English, D.*

Oregon
1. Les AuCoin, D.*
2. Robert F. Smith, R.*

3. Ron Wyden, D.*
4. Peter A. DeFazio, D.
5. Denny Smith, R.*

Pennsylvania
1. Thomas M. Foglietta, D.*
2. William H. (Bill) Gray III, D.*
3. Robert A. Borski, Jr., D.*
4. Joseph P. Kolter, D.*
5. Richard T. Schulze, R.*
6. Gus Yatron, D.*
7. W. Curtis Weldon, R.
8. Peter H. Kostmayer, D.*
9. E. G. (Bud) Shuster, R.*
10. Joseph M. McDade, R.*
11. Paul E. Kanjorski, D.*
12. John P. Murtha, D.*
13. Lawrence Coughlin, R.*
14. William J. Coyne, D.*
15. Don Ritter, R.*
16. Robert S. Walker, R.*
17. George W. Gekas, R.*
18. Doug Walgren, D.*
19. William F. Goodling, R.*
20. Joseph M. Gaydos, D.*
21. Thomas J. Ridge, R.*
22. Austin J. Murphy, D.*
23. William F. Clinger, Jr., R.*

Rhode Island
1. Fernand J. St Germain, D.*
2. Claudine Schneider, R.*

South Carolina
1. Arthur Ravenel, Jr., R.
2. Floyd Spence, R.*
3. Butler Derrick, D.*
4. Liz J. Patterson, D.
5. John McK. Spratt, D.*
6. Robert M. (Robin) Tallon, D.*

South Dakota
†Tim Johnson, D.

Tennessee
1. James H. Quillen, R.*
2. John J. Duncan, R.*
3. Marilyn Lloyd, D.*
4. James H. Cooper, D.*
5. William H. Boner, D.*
6. Bart Gordon, D.*
7. Donald K. Sundquist, R.*
8. Ed Jones, D.*
9. Harold E. Ford, D.*

Texas
1. Jim Chapman, D.*
2. Charles Wilson, D.*
3. Steve Bartlett, R.*
4. Ralph M. Hall, D.*
5. John W. Bryant, D.*
6. Joe Barton, R.*
7. Bill Archer, R.*
8. Jack Fields, R.*
9. Jack Brooks, D.*
10. J. J. (Jake) Pickle, D.*
11. J. Marvin Leath, D.*
12. James C. Wright, Jr., D.*
13. Beau Boulter, R.*
14. Mac Sweeney, R.*
15. Eligio (Kika) de la Garza, D.*
16. Ronald Coleman, D.*
17. Charles W. Stenholm, D.*

18. Mickey Leland, D.*
19. Larry Combest, R.*
20. Henry B. Gonzalez, D.*
21. Lamar Smith, R.
22. Tom DeLay, R.*
23. Albert G. Bustamante, D.*
24. Martin Frost, D.*
25. Michael A. Andrews, D.*
26. Richard Armey, R.*
27. Solomon P. Ortiz, D.*

Utah
1. James V. Hansen, R.*
2. Wayne Owens, D.
3. Howard C. Nielson, R.*

Vermont
†James M. Jeffords, R.*

Virginia
1. Herbert H. Bateman, R.*
2. Owen B. Pickett, D.
3. Thomas J. (Tom) Bliley, Jr., R.*
4. Norman Sisisky, D.*
5. Dan Daniel, D.*
6. James R. Olin, D.*
7. D. French Slaughter, R.*
8. Stanford E. (Stan) Parris, R.*
9. Frederick C. Boucher, D.*
10. Frank R. Wolf, R.*

Washington
1. John Miller, R.*
2. Al Swift, D.*
3. Don Bonker, D.*
4. Sid Morrison, R.*
5. Thomas S. Foley, D.*
6. Norman D. Dicks, D.*
7. Mike Lowry, D.*
8. Rod Chandler, R.*

West Virginia
1. Alan B. Mollohan, D.*
2. Harley O. Staggers, Jr., D.*
3. Robert E. Wise, Jr., D.*
4. Nick J. Rahall II, D.*

Wisconsin
1. Les Aspin, D.*
2. Robert W. Kastenmeier, D.*
3. Steven Gunderson, R.*
4. Gerald D. Kleczka, D.*
5. Jim Moody, D.*
6. Thomas E. Petri, R.*
7. David R. Obey, D.*
8. Toby Roth, R.*
9. F. James Sensenbrenner, Jr., R.*

Wyoming
†Dick Cheney, R.*

Nonvoting Representatives
American Samoa
Fofo I. F. Sunia, D.*

District of Columbia
Walter E. Fauntroy, D.*

Guam
Ben Blaz, R.*

Puerto Rico
Jaime B. Fuster, D.

Virgin Islands
Ron de Lugo, D.*

William H. Rehnquist testifies in July at Senate Judiciary Committee hearings on his nomination as U.S. chief justice. He was confirmed in September.

have resided continuously in the United States since before Jan. 1, 1982. Those immigrants will be eligible for temporary-resident status and, after 18 months, may apply to become permanent-resident aliens. After another five years, they will be eligible to apply for citizenship. The law also provides for penalties for employers who knowingly hire illegal aliens.

Antidrug Legislation. Congress approved only one major initiative calling for new spending, and it did so with Reagan's blessing. On October 17, acting in a bipartisan campaign-season stampede to do something about a problem that many Americans thought was getting out of hand, the lawmakers approved a $1.7-billion bill to combat drug abuse. The House passed the legislation 378 to 16, after eliminating a provision allowing the death penalty for some drug offenses, and the Senate acted by voice vote.

The bill provides almost $500 million for increased efforts by the Coast Guard, Customs Service, and Drug Enforcement Administration to keep drugs out of the country; $200 million for state-administered programs to combat drug use in schools; $42 million for the treatment of drug and alcohol abusers; and $322.5 million for the purchase of surveillance aircraft and radar systems. Penalties for illicit drug manufacturing were increased, and money *laundering*—financial

transactions designed to make illegally acquired sums appear legitimate—was made subject to a $500,000 fine and up to 20 years in prison. Reagan signed the bill on October 27.

The Environment. After two years of complex bargaining, Congress voted to extend for five years the Superfund toxic waste cleanup program authorized in 1980. The House approved the $9-billion measure 386 to 27 on October 8, a week after the Senate passed it 88 to 8. Reagan wanted to veto the bill on the grounds that it would be financed by taxes of which he disapproved. But lopsided congressional approval and preelection pressure from governors and Republican lawmakers persuaded him to reluctantly give it his signature on October 17.

A second major environmental bill, a renewal of the Water Quality Act, did not fare as well. The measure would have provided $18 billion over eight years to build or improve thousands of municipal sewage-treatment plants and clean up the nation's waterways. Although both houses of Congress gave the legislation unanimous approval in mid-October, Reagan vetoed the bill on November 6, saying it was too costly and too dependent on federal grants.

On October 17, the day before adjournment, Congress passed a $16-billion water-projects bill. The measure, which became law on November 17, was noteworthy because it called for building some 270 new dams, ports, and other waterway projects under new cost-sharing provisions aimed at curbing federal spending.

The final piece of legislation approved by Congress was a health bill backed by drug makers, medical organizations, and child-advocacy groups. One provision would allow the sale overseas of drugs made in the United States but not yet approved for domestic sale—a measure to keep U.S. drug manufacturers from moving their operations to other countries. The bill also created a no-fault compensation program for the estimated 60 to 70 children harmed each year by vaccines. Drug companies had been abandoning the production of vaccines because of liability suits and insurance costs. Reagan signed the bill on November 14.

Reducing the Deficit. Nothing Congress did in 1986 required as much time and debate as its efforts to comply with the so-called Gramm-Rudman Act. That measure, passed in 1985, fixed annual targets for reducing federal budget deficits and called for a balanced budget by 1991. The deficit ceiling for the 1987 fiscal year, which began on Oct. 1, 1986, was $144 billion.

Although the Supreme Court ruled in July that certain of the law's provisions providing for automatic spending cuts were unconstitutional, Congress managed to get within striking distance of the 1987 target. In doing so, however, it resorted to a variety of accounting dodges and gimmicks that created more the illusion than the reality of compliance. But the lawmakers did succeed in clamping a lid on federal spending that was relaxed only for the antidrug program. Federal spending hikes were limited roughly to the inflation rate—the smallest increase in 20 years.

Squabbling over the budget prevented Congress from acting on an array of individual appropriations bills, so on October 17 it approved a 1,200-page, $576-billion catchall spending bill for fiscal 1987. Reagan signed the legislation, the largest appropriations bill ever enacted, the next day.

The measure limited defense spending to $290-billion, up $3.5 billion or 1.3 per cent—the smallest increase in military spending since Reagan took office in 1981. Funds for Reagan's Strategic Defense Initiative missile defense system, popularly known as "Star Wars," were slashed to $3.5 billion from a requested $5.3 billion. Foreign aid was cut 10 per cent, and funds for most domestic programs were frozen or changed only slightly.

Congress once again found it necessary to boost the national debt limit, the accumulated total that the federal government is allowed to borrow. The lawmakers raised the limit by $189 billion to $2.3-trillion—a level 133 per cent higher than the national debt during Reagan's first year in office.

Tributes, Appointments. As the session wound down, members of both parties bade farewell to retiring Speaker of the House Thomas P. (Tip) O'Neill, Jr. (D., Mass.), and the Senate lavished tributes on two of its retirees, Republican Barry Goldwater of Arizona and Democrat Russell B. Long of Louisiana. Later, both houses selected new leaders. On November 20, Senate Democrats chose Byrd as majority leader, and Senate Republicans elected Robert J. Dole of Kansas as minority leader. On December 8, Representative James C. Wright, Jr. (D., Tex.) was chosen Speaker of the House.

Other 1986 Actions. On October 9, the Senate overwhelmingly convicted Harry E. Claiborne, chief U.S. District Court judge for Nevada, on three of four articles of impeachment. The conviction removed Claiborne from the judgeship he had refused to vacate despite serving a two-year prison sentence for tax evasion.

The Senate voted 67 to 21 on February 27 to permit live television and radio coverage of its sessions on an experimental basis from June 1 to July 15. The House had permitted coverage since 1979. On July 29, the Senate voted 78 to 21 to continue the broadcasts beyond the experimental period.　　　　Frank Cormier and Margot Cormier

See also UNITED STATES, GOVERMENT OF THE. In WORLD BOOK, see CONGRESS OF THE UNITED STATES.

CONNECTICUT. See STATE GOVERNMENT.

CONSERVATION. Most United States citizens in 1986 were concerned about preserving the nation's natural environment and wildlife, shorelines, and habitats, according to a study prepared for the President's Commission on Americans Outdoors in February. The survey found that 81 per cent of those interviewed "strongly agree" that the government should preserve natural areas for the use of future generations, and a large majority indicated their willingness to pay the taxes necessary to accomplish this goal. On November 18, the commission proposed a multibillion-dollar fund to acquire, develop, and protect open spaces. Some key officials of President Ronald Reagan's Administration opposed the program, mainly because of its cost and the fact that it would place more land under government control.

National Parks. Vacationers made approximately 400 million visits to the national parks during 1986. By the end of April, attendance at Grand Canyon National Park in Arizona was up 23 per cent from the same period in 1985, and other Western parks experienced similar tourist booms. But popularity also created problems. In May, for example, Park Service officials expressed concern over the growing crime rate in the national parks. In the Special Reports section, see PROBLEMS IN THE PARKS.

Development Battles. The U.S. Forest Service found itself repeatedly at odds with conservationists during 1986. In April, environmental groups fought vainly in the Oregon courts to save Millennium Grove, a 56-acre (23-hectare) stand of giant Douglas fir trees in the Willamette National Forest near Portland. The trees, 700 to 1,000 years old, had been sold by the Forest Service in 1983 to Willamette Industries. After the court ruling, the company declined an offer of substitute lumber and cut down the trees.

The Forest Service was also at the center of a conflict over the preservation of Tongass National Forest, a 25,860-square-mile (66,980-square-kilometer) preserve that covers most of Alaska's southeast coast. On April 28, the Wilderness Society accused the Forest Service of furthering the destruction of this unspoiled area by selling its timber to lumber companies at a loss to taxpayers of $50 million a year. The society's report charged that the Forest Service recovered only 7 cents on every dollar it spent to build roads and promote logging in the area. Tongass, one of the world's few remaining temperate-zone rain forests, is a vital habitat for numerous animals, including the largest concentration of bald eagles and grizzly bears on the North American continent.

After several years of geologic studies, energy companies determined in 1986 that huge oil and gas deposits lie in the Arctic National Wildlife Refuge on the northeast coast of Alaska. To prevent oil companies from moving into the refuge, Trustees for Alaska, an environmental group, successfully sued in a federal court to halt energy exploration until the U.S. Fish and Wildlife Service (FWS) completed an environmental impact study. The 1.5-million-acre (606,000-hectare) refuge is home to North America's largest herd of migratory caribou, as well as musk oxen, wolves, lynx, polar bears, and, in warm weather, large flocks of nesting waterfowl.

On November 25, the FWS released a draft report recommending that all of the coastal plain within the refuge be opened for oil and gas development. The proposal, however, requires congressional approval, and there appeared to be strong backing in Congress for turning the entire area into a protected wilderness.

Wildlife. By early 1986, an epidemic of canine distemper in Wyoming had reduced the only known population of black-footed ferrets to 6 animals. State fish and game officials captured them in the hope of launching a captive-breeding program to save the species from extinction. In August, researchers located and trapped 14 more. Despite this addition, biologists agreed that hope is slim for this member of the weasel family unless other populations are found.

On November 12, four pairs of captive-bred red wolves were placed in holding pens at the Alligator River National Wildlife Refuge on the North Carolina coast, the first step toward their anticipated release into the 120,000-acre (48,600-hectare) refuge in 1987. The cinnamon-colored canine once ranged throughout the Southeast, but the species was declared extinct in the wild by the 1970's, a victim of habitat destruction and predator-control programs. Only about 75 red wolves still exist in zoos and federal research centers in the United States.

In August, international conservation officials meeting in Geneva, Switzerland, stated that the continued survival of whales was in jeopardy because several nations were circumventing the moratorium on commercial whaling put into effect in 1986. Iceland, Norway, and South Korea announced their intent to continue hunting whales for "scientific purposes."

The international convention regulating whaling allows species to be hunted for research purposes, provided the resulting whale meat is used primarily for local consumption. Iceland announced plans to kill up to 120 whales a year, which would produce approximately 4,000 short tons (3,600 metric tons) of meat. Fifty-one per cent of the meat would be consumed by the local population. But conservationists noted that this would be an increase of 1,800 short tons (1,600 metric tons)—almost twice as much whale meat as is normally consumed—and charged that the meat

would actually be used as feed on commercial mink farms.

Pollution Issues. On March 19, President Reagan and Prime Minister Brian Mulroney of Canada reached an accord on fighting acid rain, which has destroyed much aquatic life and vegetation in both countries. The agreement endorsed a five-year, $5-billion program to develop and study new methods of burning coal, a major source of acid rain. Environmental groups responded negatively to the agreement and called for implementation of present technology and increased legislation—rather than more research—to correct the problem.

In mid-August, algae erupted across more than 100 square miles (260 square kilometers) of Lake Okeechobee, a key element in south Florida's water network and a critical factor in the survival of the Everglades. The problem was caused by nutrient-rich runoff from nearby dairy farms and municipalities. The state announced a $200-million project to clean up the lake.

On October 10, the House and Senate agreed to renew the Clean Water Act of 1972, which had expired at the end of 1981. President Reagan, however, vetoed the bill on Nov. 6, 1986, saying it was too expensive.   Eugene J. Walter, Jr.

See also ENVIRONMENTAL POLLUTION; WATER; ZOOLOGY. In WORLD BOOK, see CONSERVATION.

CONSTITUTION OF THE UNITED STATES. On
March 25, 1986, the United States Senate defeated a constitutional amendment requiring balanced federal budgets. The vote was 66 to 34—one vote short of the necessary two-thirds majority. The amendment would have prohibited Congress from passing a deficit budget unless the nation was at war or two-thirds of each house approved a deficit. A similar amendment won Senate approval in 1982 but lost in the House of Representatives.

In 1985, Congress passed the so-called Gramm-Rudman law requiring a balanced budget by 1991 and large spending cuts in each fiscal year until then. But on July 7, 1986, the Supreme Court of the United States struck down a key provision of the law. The court ruled, 7 to 2, that a mechanism for making automatic spending cuts, activated if the budget ceiling for any given year were exceeded, violated the Constitution.

Many advocates of reduced federal spending have hoped that the states would call for a constitutional convention to write a balanced-budget amendment. Although 32 of the required 34 states have passed resolutions calling for a convention, no state has done so since 1983. Kentucky and Virginia rejected the idea in 1986. David L. Dreier

In the Special Reports section, see THE U.S. CONSTITUTION: 200 YEARS OF HISTORY. In WORLD BOOK, see CONSTITUTION OF THE UNITED STATES.

CONSUMERISM. Living costs in the United States were again a bright spot on the consumer horizon in 1986. For the first six months of the year, the Consumer Price Index (CPI), the measurement of changes in the cost of goods and services, actually dropped. The decrease of 0.2 per cent was the first in more than 30 years, according to the United States Office of Consumer Affairs.

June was the turning point, however, and the CPI began edging upward in the second half of the year. By year-end, prices for consumer goods and services were up 1.1 per cent for the year but were still substantially below the 3.8 per cent recorded for the entire year of 1985. Energy prices appeared to be rising again as well, after dropping more than 20 per cent in the first half of 1986. Although gasoline prices rose 2.5 per cent in September, they still stood at 1979 levels.

Food Prices also moved up in the fall, increasing 0.4 per cent in September and 0.3 per cent in October. These increases were due, in large part, to price rises for beef, pork, fresh fruits and vegetables, and dairy products. Prices of dairy products rose in some areas as much as 10 per cent in one two-week period in October. The increases were blamed on 1986's drought, which affected milk production, and on new government restrictions, which reduced the surplus of other dairy goods.

By fall, price hikes also occurred in the airline industry. The end of bargain air fares appeared to be near as numerous mergers during the year left the industry with almost the same number of large airlines as before deregulation. In October, the major carriers began raising regular fares and dropping discount deals.

Lower Phone Bills. At least one important consumer service, however, headed toward lower prices in 1986. American Telephone and Telegraph Company (AT&T), which services three-fourths of all long-distance telephone customers in the United States, announced in October that it would lower its rates beginning Jan. 1, 1987. Consumers were expected to save a total of approximately $1 billion a year. AT&T's main competitors, MCI Communications Corporation and US Sprint Communications Company, said they would also lower rates. Local telephone companies laid the groundwork for these rate reductions by lowering their connection charges to long-distance carriers.

Consumer Credit. Interest rates dropped further in 1986, particularly for new car buyers, thanks to a financing-rate war that broke out in late summer. The war began on August 28, when General Motors Corporation announced a 2.9 per cent interest rate on three-year car loans and cash rebates up to $1,000 on all 1986 autos and small trucks. The rate was immediately matched by the Ford Motor Company, which offered rebates up to

Boxes of capsule drugs are removed from store shelves in Houston on March 20 after authorities found evidence of tampering.

$1,000 on selected models, and by the Chrysler Corporation, which dropped its finance charge to 2.4 per cent on two-year loans. On September 3, the American Motors Corporation carried the one-upmanship to the ultimate extreme with zero per cent financing on two-year loans. The low finance charges lured car buyers, and automobile sales boomed in early fall, leaving many car lots empty.

Other loan rates also fell to low levels. Terms for home-equity loans tumbled during the year as banks and other financial institutions fought to offer consumer loans at beginning rates as low as 6.5 per cent. After the first few months, most deals were pegged to 1.5 percentage points above the prime rate, which hovered around 7.5 per cent for much of 1986.

The average interest rate on most credit cards, on the other hand, continued to stay between 18 and 21 per cent. A few savings-and-loan companies dropped their credit-card rates to 14 per cent, but this did not spark widespread rate cuts.

Home buyers, however, managed to wield some influence on mortgage rates. People with adjustable-rate loans pressured lenders to lock in the low market rate into fixed-rate mortgages. As a result, the proportion of fixed-rate loans to total loans soared above 60 per cent during the summer, compared with only 25 per cent in 1984.

Legislative Developments. In early November, United States President Ronald Reagan vetoed a law passed by Congress in October that would have required the government to set energy-efficiency standards for major home appliances. Administration officials had refused to take action on the issue for six years, preferring to let individual states set standards. The result was a hodgepodge of legislation that forced appliance manufacturers and consumer representatives to seek federal standards. After vetoing the law, Reagan said that he would direct the U.S. Department of Energy to establish the standards.

Congress passed a number of other laws affecting consumers in 1986, particularly the sweeping tax revision signed by President Reagan on October 22 (see TAXATION). The new tax law no longer allows taxpayers to deduct state sales taxes and interest on consumer debt, except for mortgage payments on residential property. (The consumer-debt interest deduction will be phased out.) Lower tax rates in both upper and lower income brackets, however, will give many people more money to spend. On October 17, President Reagan signed legislation that extends the Superfund bill over the next five years. The bill provides funds to clean up toxic-waste dumps.

Lemon Law. In August, Michigan became the 41st state in the United States to have an automobile "lemon" law in effect. This legislation requires car manufacturers—under certain conditions—to replace a defective new car or refund the purchase price. In most states, a car is eligible if a major repair has been attempted four times unsuccessfully, or if the vehicle has been in the repair shop at least 30 days during the year.

Irradiation OK. The U.S. Food and Drug Administration (FDA) on April 16 gave final approval to the irradiation of fruits and vegetables. Irradiation is a process that preserves food by killing insects and microbes with low levels of radioactive energy. With the FDA approval, irradiation could replace traditional processes of preserving food. Few food companies, however, were willing to be among the first to offer irradiated food items, because many believe that consumers might not be ready to eat such food.

Oil Violations. Many people on low incomes in the United States are likely to benefit indirectly from a court decision in August involving major oil companies. Consolidating 42 cases brought to court by the Department of Energy, a federal court in Wichita, Kans., ordered Exxon Corporation and other petroleum companies to pay $728-million in penalties to energy-assistance programs for price violations that occurred during the oil crisis of 1973-1981. Arthur E. Rowse

See also AVIATION; ENVIRONMENTAL POLLUTION. In WORLD BOOK, see CONSUMERISM.

COSBY, BILL (1937-   ), starred in the top-rated television show of the 1985-1986 season, "The Cosby Show," a warm-hearted, humorous portrayal of family life.

Cosby was born in Philadelphia on July 12, 1937. He grew up there and later immortalized his boyhood friends and experiences in his comedy routines. He dropped out of high school after the 10th grade to join the United States Navy but earned a high school diploma through a correspondence course.

After Cosby left the Navy in 1960, he attended Temple University in Philadelphia on an athletics scholarship. He soon discovered his talent for comedy and left college to perform in nightclubs. Cosby's big break came in 1965 in the television series "I Spy," in which he became the first black man to co-star with a white on television.

Cosby has been described as a one-man multimedia phenomenon, with several books, including the best-selling *Fatherhood* (1986), 22 record albums, 10 films, and scores of nightclub appearances. He also has a long-standing interest in education and received a doctor's degree in education from the University of Massachusetts in 1977.

Cosby married Camille Hanks on Jan. 25, 1964. They have five children. Joan Stephenson

COSTA RICA. See ARIAS SÁNCHEZ, OSCAR; LATIN AMERICA.

COURTS. A ruling by the International Court of Justice at The Hague, in the Netherlands, ordering the United States to cease its military involvement in Nicaragua fizzled in 1986. United States officials rejected the court's findings and then vetoed a resolution in the United Nations (UN) that would have required compliance with the ruling.

On June 27, the court—the judicial arm of the UN, often called the World Court—decided in favor of Nicaragua's Sandinista government in a suit protesting U.S. support for anti-Sandinista rebels called *contras*. The court said the United States was violating international law by aiding the contras.

On July 29, Nicaragua's President Daniel Ortega addressed the 15-member UN Security Council, urging it to support a resolution endorsing the World Court decision. The vote in the Council on July 31 was 11 to 1 in favor of the resolution, with 3 nations—France, Great Britain, and Thailand—abstaining. By UN rules, however, the lone vote by the United States against the resolution was enough to kill it.

Reagan Puts His Stamp on Courts. President Ronald Reagan broadened his influence on the federal judiciary, including the Supreme Court of the United States, in 1986. After Chief Justice of the United States Warren E. Burger announced in June that he was retiring from the court, Reagan named Associate Justice William H. Rehnquist,

Cages at the rear of a courtroom in Palermo, Italy, hold about 100 of the 474 defendants in a Mafia trial that began in February.

whose conservative views generally match those of the President, as Burger's successor. Reagan then nominated a second conservative jurist, Antonin Scalia, a judge on the U.S. Court of Appeals for the District of Columbia, to take the seat vacated by Rehnquist. Both men were sworn in on September 26. See REHNQUIST, WILLIAM HUBBS; SCALIA, ANTONIN.

Reagan's appointments to the Supreme Court and other federal courts in 1986 fueled a continuing debate among politicians and scholars on the question of whether U.S. judges should adhere to strict interpretations of the Constitution or use their positions to advance particular moral and social positions. Some critics charged that the President's judicial appointments were based more on the candidates' political views than on their legal expertise.

Judges Face Personal Trials. More difficult problems faced some already seated judges. In October, U.S. District Court Judge Harry E. Claiborne of Las Vegas, Nev., became the first federal judge in 50 years to be removed from office by Congress. Claiborne was convicted in 1984 of failing to report nearly $107,000 in income and sentenced to two years in prison. But he refused to resign his life-tenured judgeship and continued to collect his $78,700 salary, claiming he had been the victim of incompetent accountants. After being

impeached by the House of Representatives in July, Claiborne was convicted by the Senate on October 9 on three of the four articles of impeachment.

During the year, U.S. District Court Judge Alcee L. Hastings of Miami, Fla., attempted to block his possible removal from the bench on charges that he accepted a bribe from racketeers in return for reducing their prison sentences. In 1983, he was found not guilty of these charges, but in 1986 a federal judicial panel concluded that Hastings was guilty of the crime and had obstructed justice in his trial. The panel's report, issued in August, could lead to Hastings' impeachment by Congress.

In February, Walter L. Nixon, Jr., chief judge of Mississippi's southern U.S. district, was convicted of perjury. He thus became the second federal judge ever convicted of a crime while sitting on the bench (Claiborne was the first). The jury found that Nixon lied to a grand jury about his handling of a marijuana smuggling case in which he had been suspected of accepting a bribe. Nixon was sentenced to two concurrent five-year prison sentences.

In California, Rose Elizabeth Bird, chief justice of the state's Supreme Court, was removed from office in the November 4 general election. Bird had been the target of conservative groups, who charged that she was opposed to capital punishment. Bird's critics pointed out that she had never

273

voted to affirm a death-penalty verdict during more than eight years on the court.

Crackdown on the Mafia. Prosecutors in the United States and Italy went after the Mafia with a vengeance in 1986. Three major trials held the public's attention, and one U.S. prosecuting attorney vowed—perhaps with undue optimism—that "the Mafia will be crushed."

In New York City on November 19, eight alleged leaders of organized crime, representing four of New York's five Mafia "families," were convicted in a Manhattan courtroom for various underworld activities. In Brooklyn, meanwhile, John Gotti, the reputed head of the most powerful crime family, was being tried with six associates on racketeering charges.

The biggest proceeding was in Palermo, Italy, where 474 defendants were on trial for crimes ranging from automobile theft to murder. That trial was being held in a specially constructed courthouse guarded by more than 2,000 police officers. United States and Italian authorities cooperated in bringing the many defendants in both countries to trial.

Spy Trials. Several Americans accused of spying for the Soviet Union were convicted in 1986. In June, a federal jury in Los Angeles found Richard W. Miller, a former agent of the Federal Bureau of Investigation, guilty of passing classified government information to a female Soviet spy in return for money and sexual favors. He was sentenced in July to life in prison.

Ronald W. Pelton, a former employee of the National Security Agency, was also found guilty in June of spying for the Soviets. In December, he received a 30-year prison sentence.

At a trial in San Francisco, former Navy radioman Jerry A. Whitworth was convicted in July of participating in a spy ring that sold U.S. military secrets to the Soviet Union. He later received a 365-year prison sentence. The other known members of the spy ring—Arthur, John, and Michael Walker—have also been sentenced to prison. In the Special Reports section, see THE AGE-OLD BUSINESS OF ESPIONAGE.

Texaco v. Pennzoil. The courts in 1986 wrestled with the legal complexities involved in a battle between oil giants Texaco Incorporated and the Pennzoil Company. In 1985, a Texas jury made an unprecedented award of $11.1 billion to Pennzoil in a lawsuit against Texaco. The jury found that Texaco had improperly interfered with an agreement Pennzoil had made to buy 42 per cent of another oil company. Texaco appealed the jury award to a Texas appeals court but was ordered to post a $12-billion bond while the appeal was in progress.   Edward H. Bruske

See also CRIME; SUPREME COURT OF THE UNITED STATES. In WORLD BOOK, see COURT; LAW.

CRIME. White-collar crimes set new records in the United States in 1986. The U.S. Securities and Exchange Commission (SEC) brought its largest case ever against an investment banker and received its largest settlement in history from another convicted investor.

Stepping up its activities against illegal insider stock trading—the buying and selling of stocks based on confidential or inside information—paid off for the SEC. On June 5, Dennis B. Levine pleaded guilty to federal charges of securities fraud and tax evasion. Following a government investigation into the trading of more than 50 stocks between 1980 and 1985, the SEC charged that Levine had made at least $12.6 million in profits from stock transactions based on confidential inside information. Levine, a 33-year-old executive with Drexel Burnham Lambert Incorporated, was accused of using advance knowledge of corporate take-overs to buy stocks before their prices soared. Other investors were implicated after Levine agreed to cooperate with the government.

On February 26, eight foreign investors agreed to return $7.8 million in profits following an SEC investigation into insider trading of the Santa Fe International Corporation of Alhambra, Calif., an oil-drilling contractor. According to the SEC, Santa Fe stocks were traded while the firm was involved in a merger with a foreign petroleum company. At that time, the settlement was the largest ever for the SEC.

The record was shattered on November 15, when investor Ivan F. Boesky agreed to pay a $50-million fine and give up an additional $50 million in illegal profits he made trading on inside information. The SEC said Boesky's companies made the profits by trading on take-over stocks on the basis of information provided by Levine.

Donovan on Trial. Former U.S. Secretary of Labor Raymond J. Donovan, the first Cabinet official ever to be indicted while still in office, went on trial in New York City on September 30. Donovan and eight other men were charged with stealing $7.4 million from funds earmarked for a New York City Transit Authority subway project while Donovan was executive vice president of a New Jersey construction firm. Donovan and his associates were accused of steering the money to a company that allegedly had connections with organized crime.

Mass Slaying. A disgruntled mail carrier shocked the city of Edmond, Okla., on August 20 when he walked into the U.S. post office there and shot 20 of his co-workers, killing 14 people, before taking his own life. The mass slaying was one of the worst single shooting sprees in U.S. history.

Only days before the murders, post office supervisors told the assailant, Patrick H. Sherrill, 44, that he would have to improve his work if he

Two men—wearing Ronald Reagan and Jimmy Carter masks—hold up a bank in Mount Washington, Ky., in August. They were suspects in other robberies.

wanted to keep his job. Police who searched his house after the killings found several pistols.

Tragic Jewelry Robbery. On June 23, a swank Beverly Hills jewelry store became a scene of carnage when Steven Livaditis, a convicted burglar, took three hostages following an apparent robbery attempt. Livaditis held police at bay for more than 13½ hours before he attempted to escape from the Van Cleef & Arpels store on Rodeo Drive. All three hostages were killed. Two were found inside the store, lying facedown on the floor, one stabbed and the other shot. The third was shot to death when Livaditis reportedly used him as a shield from police gunfire during his attempt to flee.

Organized Crime. On February 10, 474 men, members of the Sicilian Mafia, went on trial in Palermo, Italy, in the largest trial in Italian history. The Mafia is a secret criminal organization that originated in southern Italy and spread to the United States and other countries.

The 8,607-page indictment accused the defendants of a variety of serious crimes, including political assassinations and at least 90 murders. The trial, being held in a special courtroom equipped with 30 cages for the defendants, was expected to continue for more than a year. The trial will not wipe out the Mafia in Sicily, but Italian law-enforcement officers said they hope it will weaken the organization.

In the United States, the President's Commission on Organized Crime issued its final report on April 1. The report estimated that the annual revenue of organized crime in the United States is somewhere between $41.6 billion and $106 billion. In 1986 alone, organized crime was expected to reap profits of $75 billion, costing the government an estimated $6.5 billion in lost tax revenues, the report said.

Although the Mafia continued to be the most dominant crime organization in the United States, the study found that motorcycle gangs, Asian crime rings, and secret crime societies in prisons are growing. The study strongly suggested that states increase their attack on organized crime by using electronic surveillance and witness immunity. Nine commission members, however, criticized the study for not adequately assessing the government's response to the problem.

Crime Statistics. During the first six months of 1986, the number of violent crimes in the United States rose 8 per cent, according to a report released by the Federal Bureau of Investigation (FBI) on October 14. The increase was the largest in six years. Some criminologists attributed the jump to a greater willingness of victims to report crimes rather than a major increase in actual crimes.

Two reports on 1985 crime rates issued in 1986

came to different conclusions. In July, the FBI reported that the number of major crimes in 1985 rose 4.6 per cent over 1984. The Bureau of Justice Statistics, however, in its National Crime Survey issued in October, found that the number of violent crimes in the United States in 1985 dropped 1.9 per cent from 1984 to the lowest level in 13 years. Some experts attributed the discrepancy to the different methods used to gather the statistics. The FBI report is based on the number of crimes reported to law-enforcement officials. The Bureau of Justice Statistics report, on the other hand, is a survey of households around the United States. FBI figures are higher, criminologists said, because more people chose to report crimes in 1985.

Drug Abuse. Growing use of *crack*, a smokable form of cocaine, fueled concern over drug abuse in the United States in 1986 and prompted a flurry of antidrug activity in Congress.

The death of college basketball star Len Bias on June 19 brought home the tragic outcome of cocaine use. Bias, 22, a student at the University of Maryland at College Park, died of a cocaine overdose two days after he was drafted to play basketball with the Boston Celtics. His death touched off an intense investigation that led to criminal charges against two other college basketball players and a friend, who were accused of supplying Bias with the cocaine that killed him.

In an attempt to curb the nation's drug problem, Reagan signed into law on October 27 legislation that will funnel $1.7 billion into drug-abuse enforcement and treatment programs. The bill also increased the penalties for many drug crimes.

Pornography. A Department of Justice Commission on Pornography released a controversial report on July 9. The report found that some forms of pornography probably lead to sexual violence. It urged state and local governments to seek federal assistance in cracking down on the production and distribution of pornographic materials.

The commission members who developed the report came under attack from critics who charged that they lacked objectivity. The American Civil Liberties Union complained that one recommendation—that citizen groups monitor newsstands and television programs for sexually explicit material and express their opposition by picketing and boycotts—was so severe that "they risk returning America to the sexual dark ages." Several scientists whose work was cited in the report charged that their research had been misrepresented. Attorney General Edwin Meese III defended the commission but declined to predict whether any of its recommendations would be implemented.   Edward H. Bruske

In the Special Reports section, see THE AGE-OLD BUSINESS OF ESPIONAGE. In WORLD BOOK, see CRIME.

CUBA. Tense relations continued between Cuba and the United States in 1986. Although Cuba's President Fidel Castro released a number of political prisoners during the year, the United States government took a hard line against Cuba's support for Third World revolutions.

On August 22, U.S. President Ronald Reagan tightened trade embargoes against Cuba. He also signed a proclamation that would prevent Cuban citizens from immigrating to the United States through Third World countries. United States officials alleged that Cuban authorities were extorting exorbitant fees to allow people to travel to other countries to obtain U.S. visas.

Prisoners Freed. On September 15, Castro released 67 political prisoners who had been held in Cuban jails for 10 to 20 years. When they arrived in Miami, Fla., they were greeted joyously by their families. The Reagan Administration had considered barring the former prisoners from the United States as a way to pressure Castro into honoring a 1984 U.S.-Cuba immigration agreement. See IMMIGRATION.

Two other political prisoners were released during the year. On June 8, Castro freed Colonel Ricardo Montero Duque, who had helped lead the Bay of Pigs invasion in 1961. The invasion, secretly supported by the U.S. government, was an

President Castro, at a Communist Party Congress in Havana in February, warns that Cuba can no longer tolerate lazy and incompetent workers.

attempt by Cuban exiles to overthrow Castro's government. On October 18, Ramón Conte Hernandez, another prisoner taken during the invasion, was also freed.

Life in Cuban Prisons was movingly portrayed in *Against All Hope* (1986). The author, Armando Valladares, was 23 years old in 1960 when he was sentenced to 22 years in prison for criticizing the Castro regime.

Economic Doldrums. Attempts to strengthen Cuba's economy were plagued by bureaucracy and mismanagement in 1986. Wages were low, and factories shut down frequently when raw materials did not arrive on time from the Soviet Union and other Soviet-controlled countries. The economy was further burdened by huge military outlays.

During a speech at a Communist Party conference in Havana on February 4, Castro called Cuba's progress since 1981 "mediocre and insufficient." Among the problems he identified were low exports and inadequate sugar production.

North Korea Visit. On his trip back from the Congress of the Communist Party of the Soviet Union, Castro stopped off in North Korea from March 8 to 11. He expressed his appreciation for North Korea's support. Nathan A. Haverstock

See also LATIN AMERICA (Facts in Brief Table). In WORLD BOOK, see CUBA.

CYPRUS. See MIDDLE EAST.

CZECHOSLOVAKIA in 1986 remained politically and economically the most hard-line Communist state in Soviet-dominated Eastern Europe. This fact was evident in March, when Czechoslovakia's Communist Party held its congress—a national meeting that takes place every five years. At the congress, the party reelected virtually its entire leadership, including Gustáv Husák, party leader since 1969 and head of state since 1975.

For the first time since 1948, the Soviet Communist Party leader did not attend a Czechoslovak congress. Political observers viewed the absence of Soviet leader Mikhail S. Gorbachev as an indication of Gorbachev's displeasure with Czechoslovakia for resisting his urgings to adopt major economic reforms. Speaking at the congress, Husák called for decentralizing the economy, but he did not use the word "reform."

Foreign Relations. Czechoslovakia remained cool toward Communist states such as Hungary that were incorporating certain features of free enterprise into their economies. Furthermore, official Czechoslovak publications attacked Hungary for holding a conference on Christian-Marxist relations in October, though official Soviet representatives attended the meeting.

Martina Returns. In July, Czechoslovakia made a small conciliatory gesture toward tennis star Martina Navratilova, who was born in Czechoslovakia, defected to the United States in 1975, and became a United States citizen in 1981. Czechoslovak authorities allowed Navratilova to visit Czechoslovakia for the first time since her defection. Led by Navratilova, a U.S. team won a tennis tournament played in Prague, the capital. Czechoslovak media provided the scores of Navratilova's matches but otherwise did not mention her.

Church and State. The government continued to crack down on Roman Catholic activists throughout 1986, but a number of the sentences imposed by courts were relatively mild. In July, a record number of people—more than 100,000—turned up for the annual pilgrimage of Catholic worshipers to Levoča, in the Slovak Socialist Republic.

Production. Industrial output grew by 3.2 per cent in the first half of 1986, compared with the first half of 1985. Labor productivity was 2.6 per cent higher. Imports increased by 4.0 per cent; exports, by 0.6 per cent. Exports to non-Communist countries grew by 10.6 per cent, and imports from them were up 26.5 per cent.

Czechoslovak farmers harvested 10.9 million metric tons (12.0 million short tons) of grain in 1986, off 7 per cent from the 1985 harvest, and well below the target of 11.4 million metric tons (12.6 million short tons). Chris Cviic

See also EUROPE (Facts in Brief Table). In WORLD BOOK, see CZECHOSLOVAKIA.

DANCING. Although rising costs have cut into international touring, the United States in 1986 saw an unusually large number of companies from around the world. The trend of commissioning dances from modern-dance and post-modern choreographers for U.S. ballet companies' repertories continued.

Kirov Tour. The most newsworthy event in dance in the United States was undoubtedly a visit from the Soviet Union's famed Kirov Ballet. In the early 1900's, the troupe spawned such great artists as Vaslav Nijinsky, Anna Pavlova, and George Balanchine. More recently, it was the training ground for Rudolf Nureyev, Natalia Makarova, and Mikhail Baryshnikov, all of whom later defected to the West.

Originally, the Kirov was to have performed only at Expo 86, a world's fair in Vancouver, Canada. But a cultural exchange agreement signed by the United States and the Soviet Union in November 1985 enabled the Kirov to tour the United States as well—its first visit since 1964. The company's repertory consisted of a mixed bill of old ballets from the late 1800's, the Kirov's heyday; *Swan Lake*; and the full-length modern ballet *The Knight in the Tiger's Skin* by Kirov Artistic Director Oleg Vinogradov, performed only in Canada.

French Ballet. Like the Soviet Union, France has a long ballet tradition in the Paris Opera Ballet,

Members of the Soviet Union's Kirov Ballet leap across the stage in
Swan Lake during the troupe's first tour of North America since 1964.

the oldest company in the world. After two canceled visits, the troupe finally made it to the United States for the first time since 1948, appearing at the Metropolitan Opera House in New York City and at the John F. Kennedy Center for the Performing Arts in Washington, D.C.

Under the direction of Nureyev, the repertory was dominated by his stagings of classics. His version of *Swan Lake* drastically altered the traditional story. Odette, the Swan Queen, appeared to the prince in a dream, which took place in a ballroom rather than at the traditional lakeside. The minor role of the tutor became central, played at most performances by Nureyev himself.

Most critics deplored the prominence Nureyev provided for himself. Yet reports that under his leadership the Paris Opera Ballet dancers had become revitalized proved true.

British Ballet. Yet a third bastion of national style, Great Britain's Sadler's Wells Ballet, toured the United States in 1986. The company performed a mixed bill of contemporary work and the ballet that is considered synonymous with English dance achievement, *The Sleeping Beauty*. Many enjoyed the quiet radiance of the troupe but agreed that the ensemble's strength did not compensate for the lack of an outstanding ballerina.

Chinese Versatility. A visit by the Central Ballet of China was considered a major curiosity because

China's experience with classical ballet began only in the 1950's and has suffered from political turmoil. The troupe opened on March 4 at the Brooklyn Academy of Music in New York City and toured 11 cities. Most critics were amazed that the troupe, which was virtually disbanded during the Cultural Revolution—a period of political upheaval from 1966 to 1976—was as capable in ballets from the West as in works based on Chinese themes.

Avant-Garde Ballet. As established troupes grow older—the young-in-image Joffrey Ballet celebrated its 30th anniversary in 1986—and as proliferating regional companies expand their seasons, the need for novelty programming becomes more pressing. As a result, many artistic directors look to avant-garde choreographers to infuse the ballet repertory with new perspectives. Robert Joffrey, the leading trendsetter, in 1986 commissioned works from Laura Dean and Mark Morris for the Joffrey Ballet. Dean's *Force Field*, set to a score by Steve Reich, premiered on February 26 in Iowa City, Iowa, and showed Dean's increasing use of ballet technique while maintaining her own minimalist approach to structure. Morris, who once danced with Dean's group, premiered his new work, *Esteemed Guests*, at the City Center Theater in New York City on October 29.

The most heralded new productions by American Ballet Theatre (ABT) came from the avant-garde. On February 18, in San Francisco, the ABT premiered David Gordon's *Murder*, a parody, with Baryshnikov in the starring role. The fashionable painter David Salle collaborated with choreographer Karole Armitage in *The Mollino Room*, first seen on April 10 at the Kennedy Center. Although it was generally felt that Salle's large and ever-changing sets overpowered the dancing, Armitage's talent as a choreographer was evident.

Classical Tradition. The New York City Ballet was the one major institution to produce new work solely in the classical style, by Jerome Robbins, Peter Martins, and Jean-Pierre Bonnefoux. For three weeks in October, the company toured the West Coast for the first time since 1974.

Dance Fusion. In small and regional troupes, the great impetus for cross-fertilization between ballet and modern dance came from the National Choreography Project, funded by the National Endowment for the Arts, Exxon Corporation, and the Rockefeller Foundation for a total of $250,000. Grants for 1986-1987 were awarded to Ballet Metropolitan in Ohio for a work by David Parsons; the Boston Ballet and Jim Self; the Dallas Metropolitan Ballet and Susan Marshall; the Eliot Feld Ballet (New York City) and Carolyn Carlson; the Joffrey Ballet (New York City) and Mark Mor-

ris; the José Limón Dance Company (New York City) and Meredith Monk; the Oakland (Calif.) Ballet and Brenda Way; and the Washington Ballet and Manuel Alum.

Revival. The most intriguing repertory of 1986 came from the past. To celebrate her 60th anniversary as a choreographer, Martha Graham revived several solos dating from her days as a dancer with the Denishawn dance company in the 1920's. This retrospective included *Incense*, a 1906 dance by Ruth St. Denis, whom Graham acknowledges as the great influence in her life, and *Tanagra*, a 1926 example of Graham's own early choreography. A group work by Graham, *Heretic*, from 1929, amazed the public with its austere yet powerfully conceived social message.

Deaths. Several notable figures in dance died in 1986. Lucia Chase, a cofounder of the ABT who guided the group to international stature, died on January 9. Danish-born dancer Erik Bruhn, who died on April 1, became a model of classicism to American audiences through his appearances with the ABT. The National Ballet of Canada, which Bruhn was directing at the time of his death, had just scored a triumph with Glen Tetley's *Alice*, set to the Pulitzer Prize-winning score by David Del Tredici.   Nancy Goldner

In WORLD BOOK, see BALLET; DANCING.

The dancers of choreographer Mark Morris' company perform his *Soap-Powders and Detergents,* an inventive and light-hearted look at washday.

DEATHS of notable people in 1986 included those listed below. Those listed were Americans unless otherwise indicated. An asterisk (*) indicates the person is the subject of a biography in THE WORLD BOOK ENCYCLOPEDIA.

Adams, Pepper (1930-Sept. 10), jazz saxophonist.

*Adams, Sherman (1899-Oct. 27), Republican governor of New Hampshire from 1949 to 1953 and chief of staff for President Dwight D. Eisenhower from 1953 to 1958.

Addabo, Joseph P. (1925-April 10), Democratic congressman from New York since 1961.

Aherne, Brian (1902-Feb. 10), British-born actor who starred in more than 35 films.

Agnew, Sir Geoffrey (1908-Nov. 22), leading British art dealer.

Alda, Robert (Alfonso D'Abruzzo) (1914-May 3), actor who starred on Broadway in *Guys and Dolls* (1950) and in numerous films including *Rhapsody in Blue* (1945). He was the father of actor Alan Alda.

Alessandri Rodríguez, Jorge (1896-Aug. 31), president of Chile from 1958 to 1964.

Almond, J. Lindsay, Jr. (1898-April 14), Democratic congressman from Virginia from 1945 to 1948 and governor of that state from 1958 to 1962.

Andrews, V. C. (Virginia Cleo Andrews) (1935?-Dec. 19), author of *Flowers in the Attic* (1979).

Arlen, Harold (Hyman Arluck) (1905-April 23), composer of some 500 songs, including "Blues in the Night," "Stormy Weather," and "Over the Rainbow."

Cary Grant, suave
leading man

Harold Macmillan,
British prime minister

Hyman G. Rickover,
U.S. naval officer

Georgia O'Keeffe, painter
of desert landscapes

Armstrong, Herbert W. (1892-Jan. 16), radio evangelist and founder of the fundamentalist Worldwide Church of God.

Arnaz, Desi (Desiderio Alberto Arnaz y de Acha III) (1917-Dec. 2), Cuban-born entertainer who played Ricky Ricardo on television's "I Love Lucy."

Arnow, Harriette Simpson (1908-March 22), novelist who wrote *The Dollmaker* (1954).

Baddeley, Hermione (1908-Aug. 19), British actress who played the housekeeper on television's "Maude" during the 1970's.

Baldwin, Raymond E. (1893-Oct. 4), Republican governor of Connecticut from 1939 to 1941 and again from 1943 to 1946 and senator from that state from 1946 to 1949.

Bascomb, Paul (1910-Nov. 25), jazz saxophonist.

Bauer, Eddie (1899-April 18), founder of the sporting goods company that bears his name and original designer of the quilted goose-down jacket.

Bayar, Celal (1882-Aug. 22), president of Turkey from 1950 to 1960.

*Beauvoir, Simone de (1908-April 14), French writer and feminist whose books included the best-selling *The Second Sex* (1949) and *Memoirs of a Dutiful Daughter* (1958).

Bennett, Donald Clifford Tyndall (1910-Sept. 14), Australian-born British aviator who, at the age of 33, became the youngest air vice marshal in the history of the Royal Air Force.

Bernardi, Herschel (1923-May 10), actor who starred on stage in *Fiddler on the Roof*, which he joined in 1965, and in *Zorba* (1968).

Besse, Georges (1927-Nov. 17), French automobile executive.

Bestall, Alfred (1892-Jan. 15), British cartoonist who illustrated the Rupert Bear stories in London's *Daily Express*.

Bias, Len (1964?-June 19), all-American basketball player at the University of Maryland.

Bingham, Jonathan B. (1914-July 3), Democratic congressman from New York from 1965 to 1982.

Boothby, Lord (Robert John Graham Boothby) (1900-July 16), Scottish member of the House of Commons from 1924 to 1958, when he became a life peer.

*Borges, Jorge Luis (1899-June 14), Argentine short-story writer, poet, and essayist.

Bowles, Chester B. (1901-May 25), Democratic governor of Connecticut from 1949 to 1951 and congressman from that state from 1959 to 1961.

Braine, John (1922-Oct. 28), British novelist who wrote *Room at the Top* (1957).

Brennan, Michael (1896-Oct. 24), chief of staff of the Irish Army from 1931 to 1940.

Bricker, John W. (1893-March 22), Republican governor of Ohio from 1939 to 1945 and senator from that state from 1947 to 1959.

Brown, Harrison S. (1917-Dec. 8), geochemist, editor in chief of the *Bulletin of the Atomic Scientists*, and long-time member of THE YEAR BOOK Board of Editors.

*Bruhn, Erik (1928-April 1), Danish ballet dancer who served as artistic director of the National Ballet of Canada since 1983.

Bubbles, John (John William Sublett) (1902-May 18), dancer who invented rhythm tap-dancing.

Caesar, Adolph (1933?-March 6), actor best known as Sergeant Waters in *A Soldier's Play* (1981) on stage and in *A Soldier's Story* (1984) on film.

*Cagney, James (1899-March 30), jaunty film star who set the standard for gangster roles in *The Public Enemy* (1931).

Canfield, Cass (1897-March 27), leading editor and publisher with Harper & Row.

Canning, Victor (1911-Feb. 21), British thriller writer.

Cash, Norm (1934-Oct. 12), first baseman for the Detroit Tigers from 1960 to 1974.

Chase, Lucia (1907-Jan. 9), ballet dancer who helped found the American Ballet Theatre in 1940.

Chenoweth, J. Edgar (1897-Jan. 2), Republican congressman from Colorado from 1941 to 1949 and again from 1951 to 1965.

Christiansen, Jack (1928-June 29), defensive back with the Detroit Lions in the 1950's and member of the National Professional Football Hall of Fame.

*****Ciardi, John** (1916-March 30), poet noted for his 1954 translation of Dante's *Inferno.*

Clancy, King (Francis M. Clancy) (1903-Nov. 10), Canadian hockey star of the 1920's and 1930's; member of the Hockey Hall of Fame.

*****Coatsworth, Elizabeth** (1893-Aug. 31), author of children's books who won the Newbery Medal in 1931 for *The Cat Who Went to Heaven.*

Cohen, Myron (1902?-March 10), Polish-born stand-up comic who specialized in Yiddish-accented jokes.

Cohn, Roy M. (1927-Aug. 2), lawyer who aided Senator Joseph R. McCarthy (R., Wis.) in his investigations of alleged Communist influence in the U.S. government in the 1950's.

Colonna, Jerry (1904-Nov. 21), comedian whose trademarks were his saucer eyes, walrus mustache, and bellowing voice.

Cooper, Lady Diana (Diana, Viscountess Norwich) (1892-June 16), leader of British high society in the 1920's and 1930's.

Cousins, Frank (1904-June 11), British labor leader; head of the Transport and General Workers' Union from 1956 to 1964 and 1966 to 1969.

Crawford, Broderick (1911-April 26), actor who starred in the television series "Highway Patrol."

Crawford, Cheryl (1902-Oct. 7), producer of such Broadway hits as *Brigadoon* (1948) and *Sweet Bird of Youth* (1959).

Crothers, Scatman (Benjamin Sherman Crothers) (1910-Nov. 22), musician, singer, and character actor.

Crowley, Jim (1903?-Jan. 15), football halfback, one of the famed Four Horsemen who led the University of Notre Dame to an undefeated season in 1924.

Crumpacker, Shepard J., Jr. (1917-Oct. 14), Republican congressman from Indiana from 1951 to 1957.

Da Silva, Howard (Harold Silverblatt) (1909-Feb. 16), actor whose 55-year career included the starring role in *1776* (1969) on Broadway.

Dalton, John N. (1931-July 30), Republican governor of Virginia from 1978 to 1982.

Dassault, Marcel (Marcel Bloch) (1892-April 18), French aviation designer who created the Mirage jet fighter.

Davis, Eddie "Lockjaw" (1921-Nov. 3), jazz saxophonist.

Dickerson, Earl B. (1891-Sept. 1), lawyer, insurance executive, and civil rights leader.

Dillon, James M. (1902-Feb. 10), Irish politician; leader of the Fine Gael Party from 1959 to 1965.

Dionne, Elzire (1909?-Nov. 22), Canadian farm wife who gave birth to the Dionne quintuplets, five identical girls, in 1934.

Doisy, Edward A., Sr. (1893-Oct. 23), biochemist who received the 1943 Nobel Prize in physiology or medicine for synthesizing vitamin K.

Dolgun, Alexander M. (1926-Aug. 26), U.S. Embassy clerk held in Soviet prisons from 1948 to 1956 who described his experience in *Alexander Dolgun's Story: An American in the Gulag* (1975).

Dorsey, Lee (1926-Dec. 1), rhythm and blues singer and songwriter best known for his 1966 hit "Working in a Coal Mine."

Douglas, Thomas C. (1904-Feb. 24), Scottish-born Canadian socialist, premier of Saskatchewan from 1944 to 1961.

Duchess of Windsor, widow
of former British king

Jacques Plante,
Canadian goalie

Henry Moore,
British abstract sculptor

James O. Eastland,
Democratic senator

East, John P. (1931-June 30), Republican senator from North Carolina since 1981.

*****Eastland, James O.** (1904-Feb. 19), Democratic senator from Mississippi in 1941 and from 1943 to 1979.

Ellis, Perry (1940-May 30), fashion designer known for his sportswear.

Ellsworth, M. Harris (1899-Feb. 7), Republican congressman from Oregon from 1943 to 1957.

Erickson, Leif (William Wycliff Anderson) (1911-Jan. 29), actor best known for his role in the TV series "High Chaparral" from 1967 to 1971.

Everett, Thomas H. (1903?-Sept. 26), British-born horticulturist; author of the *New York Botanical Garden Illustrated Encyclopedia of Horticulture* (1982).

Farr, Tommy (1915?-March 1), British heavyweight boxing champion who in 1937 became the first fighter to go the 15-round distance with world heavyweight champion Joe Louis.

Finch, Cliff (Charles C. Finch) (1927?-April 22), Democratic governor of Mississippi from 1976 to 1980.

Flesch, Rudolf F. (1911-Oct. 5), Austrian-born expert on literacy and clear English writing who wrote *Why Johnny Can't Read* (1955).

Gabel, Martin (1912-May 22), actor and long-time panelist on the TV game show "What's My Line?"

Garcia, Mike (Edward Miguel Garcia) (1923-Jan. 13), pitcher for the Cleveland Indians in the 1950's.

*****Genet, Jean** (1910-April 15), French playwright whose works included *The Maids* (1947) and *The Balcony* (1956).

Gillmore, Margalo (1897-June 30), British-born actress

who appeared on Broadway in *The Women* (1936) and *Life with Father* (1949).

Gilmore, Virginia (Sherman Virginia Poole) (1919-March 28), actress who played in such films as *Western Union* (1941) and *Pride of the Yankees* (1942).

Glubb, Sir John Bagot (1897-March 17), British Army general known as Glubb Pasha who commanded the Arab Legion, Jordan's elite fighting force.

*****Goodman, Benny** (1909-June 13), legendary jazz clarinetist and bandleader. See POPULAR MUSIC (Close-Up).

Gore, Wilbert L. (1912?-July 26), inventor of Gore-Tex waterproof fabric.

*****Grant, Cary (Alexander Archibald Leach)** (1904-Nov. 29), British-born motion-picture actor famous for his good looks and casual sophistication.

Greenberg, Hank (1911-Sept. 4), first baseman for the Detroit Tigers in the 1930's and 1940's; member of the National Baseball Hall of Fame.

Grotberg, John E. (1925-Nov. 15), Republican congressman from Illinois since 1985.

Haas, Ernst (1921-Sept. 12), Austrian-born photojournalist and pioneer in abstract color photography.

Halleck, Charles A. (1900-March 3), Republican congressman from Indiana from 1935 to 1969.

Halop, Florence (1923-July 15), actress who played the bailiff on TV's "Night Court."

*****Harriman, W. Averell** (1891-July 26), diplomat and adviser who served four Democratic Presidents.

Harris, Sydney J. (1917-Dec. 7), British-born syndicated newspaper columnist.

Haughton, Billy (1923-July 15), leading harness-racing driver.

Hayden, Sterling (Sterling Relyea Walter) (1916-May 23), actor whose films included *The Asphalt Jungle* (1950) and *Dr. Strangelove* (1964).

Haydon, Murray P. (1926-June 19), factory worker; the world's third artificial-heart recipient.

Hayes, Arthur H. (1904-April 14), president of CBS Radio from 1955 to 1967.

Headlam-Morley, Agnes (1902-Feb. 21?), British historian who in 1948 became the first woman professor at Oxford University.

Heidt, Horace (1901-Dec. 1), bandleader.

Helpmann, Sir Robert (1909-Sept. 28), Australian ballet dancer and choreographer.

*****Herbert, Frank** (1920-Feb. 11), science-fiction writer best known for his novel *Dune* (1965).

*****Hobson, Laura Z.** (1900-Feb. 28), author whose novels included *Gentleman's Agreement* (1947) and *Consenting Adult* (1975).

Hubbard, L. Ron (1911-Jan. 24), science-fiction writer and founder of the Church of Scientology.

Hyman, Flo (Flora Hyman) (1954?-Jan. 24), volleyball player who led the U.S. women's team to a silver medal to the 1984 Summer Olympics.

Hynek, J. Allen (1910-April 27), astronomer who served as consultant to the U.S. Air Force on unidentified flying objects (UFO's).

*****Isherwood, Christopher** (1904-Jan. 4), British-born writer whose book *Goodbye to Berlin* (1939) became the 1951 play and 1955 film *I Am a Camera* and the 1966 musical and 1972 film *Cabaret*.

Isley, O'Kelly (1937-March 31), rhythm-and-blues singer with the Isley Brothers.

Izumi, Shigechiyo (1866-Feb. 21), Japanese laborer said to be the world's oldest man.

Jacuzzi, Candido (1903?-Oct. 7), Italian-born inventor of the whirlpool bath that bears his name.

Jameson, Storm (1891-Sept. 30), British novelist.

Jamieson, Donald C. (1921-Nov. 19), Canadian Liberal Party leader who held several cabinet posts.

Jarvis, Gregory B. (1944-Jan. 28), aeronautic engineer; payload specialist on the *Challenger* space shuttle, which exploded moments after liftoff.

Jarvis, Howard A. (1902-Aug. 12), leader of California's tax-reduction movement.

Javits, Jacob K. (1904-March 7), liberal Republican senator from New York from 1947 to 1954 and from 1957 to 1981.

Joliat, Aurel (1901-June 2), Canadian hockey star; left wing with the Montreal Canadiens from 1922 to 1938; member of the Hockey Hall of Fame.

Jolly, Hugh R. (1918-March 4), British pediatrician and author of best-selling books on child care.

Jones, Thad (1923-Aug. 20), jazz trumpeter and cornetist.

Jónsson, Emil (1902-Nov. 30), prime minister of Iceland in 1958 and 1959.

Kaldor, Lord (Nicholas Kaldor) (1908-Sept. 30), Hungarian-born British economist, adviser to Labour governments in the 1960's and 1970's.

Kantorovich, Leonid V. (1912-April 7), Russian-born economist who shared the 1975 Nobel Prize in economics.

Kay, Beatrice (Hannah Beatrice Kuper) (1907-Nov. 8), singer who revived many 1890's songs.

*****Kekkonen, Urho Kaleva** (1900-Aug. 31), president of Finland from 1956 to 1981.

Kent, Corita (1918-Sept. 18), artist who designed the U.S. Postal Service's "Love" stamp.

Knight, Ted (Tadeus W. Konopka) (1923-Aug. 26), actor best-known as the anchorman Ted Baxter on TV's "The Mary Tyler Moore Show" in the 1970's.

Donna Reed, film and TV actress

Jacob K. Javits, Republican senator

Olof Palme, prime minister of Sweden

Teddy Wilson, jazz pianist

Killed in the *Challenger* explosion in January were, left to right, crew members Ellison S. Onizuka, Michael J. Smith, Christa McAuliffe, Dick Scobee, Gregory B. Jarvis, Judith A. Resnik, and Ronald E. McNair.

Kraft, Joseph (1924-Jan. 10), journalist whose columns on political affairs appeared in some 200 newspapers.

Krishnamurti, Jiddu (1895-Feb. 17), Indian-born religious philosopher.

Lancaster, Sir Osbert (1908-July 27), cartoonist for London's *Daily Express* from 1939 to 1981.

Lanchester, Elsa (1902-Dec. 26), British-born stage and screen actress.

Landgrebe, Earl F. (1916-June 29), Republican congressman from Indiana from 1969 to 1975.

Lartigue, Jacques-Henri (1894-Sept. 12), French photographer.

Layne, Bobby (1926-Dec. 1), quarterback for the Detriot Lions from 1950 to 1958; member of the National Professional Football Hall of Fame.

Le Duan (1908-July 10), general secretary of Vietnam's Communist Party.

Lee, Russell (1903-Aug. 28), photographer famous for documenting the Great Depression of the 1930's.

Lerner, Alan Jay (1918-June 14), lyricist who collaborated with composer Frederick Loewe on such hit musicals as *My Fair Lady* (1956) and *Camelot* (1960).

Libby, Leona Marshall (1919-Nov. 10), nuclear physicist, the only woman on the Manhattan Project, which developed the atom bomb.

Lipmann, Fritz A. (1899-July 24), German-born biochemist who shared the 1953 Nobel Prize in physiology or medicine for his research into how cells convert food into energy.

Liu Bocheng (Liu Po-ch'eng) (1892-Oct. 7), a leader of China's Communist revolution.

Loewy, Raymond F. (1893-July 14), French-born industrial designer known as "the father of streamlining."

Lovett, Robert A. (1895-May 7), U.S. secretary of defense from 1951 to 1953.

Lund, Mary (1945?-Oct. 14), first woman recipient of an artificial heart.

Lyons, Ted (1900-July 25), pitcher for the Chicago White Sox from 1923 to 1946 and member of the National Baseball Hall of Fame.

*****MacDonald, John D.** (1916-Dec. 28), mystery writer, creator of private eye Travis McGee.

Machel, Samora Moisés (1933-Oct. 19), president of Mozambique since 1975.

MacLysaght, Edward A. (1887-March 3?), Irish historian and authority on heraldry.

*****Macmillan, Harold (Lord Stockton)** (1894-Dec. 29), prime minister of Great Britain from 1957 to 1963.

MacRae, Gordon (1921-Jan. 24), singer and actor whose films included *Oklahoma!* (1955) and *Carousel* (1956).

*****Malamud, Bernard** (1914-March 18), writer whose books included *The Assistant* (1957) and *The Fixer* (1966).

Malone, Dumas (1892-Dec. 27), historian; authority on Thomas Jefferson.

Manuel, Richard (1946?-March 4), Canadian-born pianist and singer with the rock group The Band.

Markham, Beryl (1902-Aug. 3), British-born pilot who in 1936 became the first person to fly solo across the Atlantic Ocean from east to west.

Maybray-King, Lord (Horace Maybray King) (1901-Sept. 3), first Labour Party Speaker of Great Britain's House of Commons, serving from 1965 to 1970.

McAuliffe, Christa (Sharon Christa McAuliffe) (1948-Jan. 28), high-school teacher and citizen observer on the space shuttle *Challenger*.

McKenna, Siobhan (1923-Nov. 16), Irish actress acclaimed for her Broadway performance as Joan of Arc in *Saint Joan* (1956).

McNair, Ronald E. (1950-Jan. 28), physicist and mission specialist on the *Challenger*.

Milland, Ray (Reginald Truscott-Jones) (1907-March 10), Welsh-born actor who won an Oscar in 1945 for his performance in *The Lost Weekend*.

Miller, Merle (1919-June 10), author of *Plain Speaking: An Oral Biography of Harry S. Truman* (1974).

Minnelli, Vincente (1910-July 25), film director who won an Academy Award in 1958 for directing *Gigi*. He was the father of actress Liza Minnelli.

***Molotov, Vyacheslav M.** (1890-Nov. 8), foreign minister of the Soviet Union from 1939 to 1949 and from 1953 to 1956. His name was given to the *Molotov cocktail*, a homemade fire bomb.

Moore, Daniel K. (1906-Sept. 7), Democratic governor of North Carolina from 1965 to 1969.

***Moore, Henry** (1898-Aug. 31), British sculptor known for his huge reclining figures of wood or stone.

Moult, Ted (1926?-Sept. 3), English farmer who became a panelist on numerous British quiz shows.

***Mulliken, Robert S.** (1896-Oct. 31), chemist who won the 1966 Nobel Prize for chemistry for his theory of how atoms combine to form a molecule.

Multer, Abraham J. (1900-Nov. 4), Democratic congressman from New York from 1947 to 1967.

Murphy, Lionel K. (1922-Oct. 21), judge of the High Court of Australia since 1975.

***Myrdal, Alva Reimer** (1902-Feb. 1), Swedish diplomat and sociologist, co-winner of the 1982 Nobel Peace Prize.

Nakian, Reuben (1897-Dec. 4), abstract sculptor.

Neagle, Dame Anna (1904-June 3), British stage and film actress.

Nichols, Dandy (Daisy Waters) (1907-Feb. 6), British television actress who starred in the long-running comedy series "Till Death Us Do Part."

Nolen, William A. (1928-Dec. 20), physician who wrote such books as *The Making of a Surgeon* (1970) and *Surgeon's Book of Hope* (1980).

O'Brien, George M. (1917-July 17), Republican congressman from Illinois since 1973.

O'Connor, Martin J. (1900-Nov. 28), Roman Catholic archbishop.

***O'Keeffe, Georgia** (1887-March 6), painter whose best-known subjects included animal skulls, flowers, and desert landscapes.

Onizuka, Ellison S. (1946-Jan. 28), aerospace engineer; mission specialist on the *Challenger*.

Palme, Olof (1927-Feb. 28), prime minister of Sweden since 1982.

Palmer, Lilli (Lillie Marie Peiser) (1914-Jan. 27), German-born actress who starred in the film *Body and Soul* (1947).

Paris, Jerry (1925-April 1), actor and director on "The Dick Van Dyke Show" in the 1960's. He played Jerry the dentist, Van Dyke's next-door neighbor.

Pears, Sir Peter (1910-April 3), British tenor noted for his roles in such operas as *Death in Venice* and *Peter Grimes*.

Pellegrino, Michele Cardinal (1903-Oct. 10), Italian clergyman; Roman Catholic archbishop of Turin from 1965 to 1977.

Perkins, Marlin (1905-June 14), zoologist who hosted TV's "Wild Kingdom" from 1963 to 1985.

Phoenix, Pat (1923-Sept. 17), Irish-born actress who played Elsie Tanner in the long-running British soap opera "Coronation Street."

Pigeon, Louis-Philippe (1905-Feb. 23), judge of the Supreme Court of Canada from 1967 to 1980.

Plante, Jacques (1929-Feb. 26), Canadian who was one of the greatest goaltenders in National Hockey League history.

Pollard, Fritz (1894-May 11), coach of the Hammond, Ind., Pros in the 1920's, the only black head coach of a National Football League team.

Preminger, Otto L. (1906-April 23), Austrian-born film producer and director of such films as *Laura* (1944), *Anatomy of a Murder* (1959), and *Exodus* (1960).

Pritzker, Abram N. (1896-Feb. 8), founder of the Hyatt hotel chain.

Rainwater, L. James (1917-May 31), physicist who shared the 1975 Nobel Prize for physics for his work in analyzing the structure of atomic nuclei.

Reed, Donna (Donna Belle Mullenger) (1921-Jan. 14), actress who starred in TV's "The Donna Reed Show" in the 1950's and 1960's and won an Oscar in 1953 for her performance in *From Here to Eternity*.

Resnik, Judith A. (1949-Jan. 28), electrical engineer; mission specialist on the *Challenger*.

Richards, Sir Gordon (1904-Nov. 10), first British jockey to be knighted.

***Rickover, Hyman George** (1900-July 8), Polish-born admiral responsible for the development of the U.S. Navy's nuclear submarine fleet.

Ritz, Harry (1908-March 29), youngest and last survivor of the Ritz Brothers comedy team.

Rogers, Don (1963?-June 27), defensive back for football's Cleveland Browns.

Rous, Sir Stanley (1895-July 18), secretary of Great Britain's Football Association from 1934 to 1961 who rewrote many soccer rules.

Rubbra, Edmund (1901-Feb. 13), British composer of instrumental and choral music.

Rudenko, Ludmila (1904-March 2), Russian-born chess player who became the first women's world chess champion, holding the title from 1950 to 1953.

James Cagney,
jaunty film star

Kate Smith, singer
of "God Bless America"

Bill Veeck, owner
of baseball teams

Otto L. Preminger,
Austrian-born filmmaker

Ruffing, Red (1904-Feb. 17), pitcher for the New York Yankees in the 1930's and 1940's; member of the National Baseball Hall of Fame.

Russell, Dora (1894-May 31), British feminist and peace activist; divorced wife of philosopher Bertrand Russell.

Santmyer, Helen Hooven (1895-Feb. 21), author of the best-selling ". . . *And Ladies of the Club*" (1982).

Saunders, Allen (1899-Jan. 28), cartoonist who created the "Mary Worth" and "Steve Roper" comic strips.

Schroeder, William J. (1932?-Aug. 6), retired government worker who lived 620 days with an artificial heart, longer than any other person with the device.

Scobee, Dick (Francis R. Scobee) (1939-Jan. 28), mission commander on the *Challenger*.

Seifert, Jaroslav (1901-Jan. 10), Czechoslovak poet who won the 1984 Nobel Prize for literature.

*Semenov, Nikolai N. (1896-Sept. 25), Russian chemist who shared the 1956 Nobel Prize in chemistry for his exploration of chemical chain reactions.

Shinwell, Lord (Emanuel Shinwell) (1884-May 8), British Labour Party leader.

Siemens, Hermann von (1885-Oct. 13), German industrialist who headed the Siemens company, West Germany's largest electronics firm.

Six, Robert F. (1907-Oct. 6), founder of Continental Airlines.

Smith, Al (Albert Schmidt) (1902-Nov. 24), cartoonist who drew "Mutt and Jeff" since 1932.

Smith, Kate (1909-June 17), singer best known for her stirring rendition of "God Bless America."

Smith, Michael J. (1945-Jan. 28), pilot of the *Challenger*.

Sonneborn, Rudolf G. (1898-June 1), leader of the Zionist movement in the United States.

Stevenson, Robert (1905-April 30), British-born film director best known for *Old Yeller* (1958) and *Mary Poppins* (1965).

Sweet, Blanche (1896-Sept. 6), stage and screen star of silent-film days.

Szent-Györgyi, Albert (1893-Oct. 22), Hungarian-born physiologist who discovered vitamin C and received the Nobel Prize in physiology or medicine in 1937.

Tarkovsky, Andrei (1932-Dec. 29), Russian film director.

*Taussig, Helen Brooke (1898-May 20), physician who helped develop the surgical procedure to correct the heart defect of "blue babies."

Tenzing Norgay (1914-May 9), Nepalese Sherpa mountaineer who in 1953, with Sir Edmund Hillary, became the first to climb Mount Everest.

Terry, Sonny (Saunders Terrill) (1911-March 11), blues singer and harmonica player who provided music for the film *The Color Purple* (1985).

Tucker, Forrest (1915?-Oct. 25), stage, film, and television actor who played Sergeant O'Rourke in TV's "F Troop" in the 1960's.

Ullman, Al (1914-Oct. 11), Democratic congressman from Oregon from 1957 to 1981; chairman of House Ways and Means Committee from 1975 to 1981.

Vallee, Rudy (Hubert Prior Vallee) (1901-July 3), popular crooner in the 1920's and 1930's.

Van Wagoner, Murray D. (1898-June 12), Democratic governor of Michigan in 1941 and 1942.

Van Zandt, James E. (1898-Jan. 6), Republican congressman from Pennsylvania from 1939 to 1943 and from 1947 to 1963.

Veeck, Bill (1914-Jan. 2), former owner of three major-league baseball teams—the Cleveland Indians, St. Louis Browns, and Chicago White Sox.

Wallace, Sippie (Beulah Thomas Wallace) (1898-Nov. 1), blues singer and songwriter.

Wallis, Hal B. (1899-Oct. 5), motion-picture producer.

Waring, Eddie (1910?-Oct. 28), British Broadcasting Corporation (BBC) sports commentator.

Marlin Perkins, host of TV's "Wild Kingdom"

Hank Greenberg, baseball great

Simone de Beauvoir, French writer and feminist

W. Averell Harriman, veteran diplomat

Wheldon, Sir Huw (1916-March 14), managing director of the BBC from 1968 to 1975.

White, Theodore H. (1915-May 15), journalist best known for *The Making of the President 1960* (1961) and a series of similar books about the presidential campaigns of 1964, 1968, and 1972.

Williams, William B. (1923-Aug. 3), disk jockey on New York City's WNEW-AM radio since the mid-1940's.

Wilson, Teddy (1912-July 31), jazz pianist who played with Louis Armstrong and Benny Goodman.

Windsor, Duchess of (Wallis Warfield Simpson) (1896-April 24), widow of the Duke of Windsor, once King Edward VIII of Great Britain, who abdicated the throne in 1936 to marry her.

Winston, Henry (1911-Dec. 12), chairman of the Communist Party of the U.S.A.

Wynn, Keenan (1916-Oct. 14), actor who played supporting roles in more than 200 films; son of comedian Ed Wynn.

Yamasaki, Minoru (1912-Feb. 6), architect who designed the World Trade Center in New York City.

Ye Jianying (Yeh Chien-ying) (1899-Oct. 22), a leader of China's Communist revolution.

Young, Stuart (1934-Aug. 29), British broadcasting executive; chairman of the BBC since 1983.

Zorin, Valerian A. (1902-Jan. 14), Russian diplomat, the Soviet Union's delegate to the United Nations from 1960 to 1962.　　　　　　　　　　　　　　　Sara Dreyfuss

DELAWARE. See STATE GOVERNMENT.

Senators George J. Mitchell (D., Me.), left, and Robert C. Byrd (D., W. Va.) in November celebrate the Democrats' new 55-45 Senate majority.

DEMOCRATIC PARTY leaders hailed their party's recapture of the United States Senate in the 1986 midterm elections as evidence that Republican hopes of an enduring political realignment were without foundation. Ever since President Ronald Reagan's 1980 landslide reelection victory, the Republican Party (GOP) had talked about a national realignment of voters that would make the GOP the majority party. But even before the November 4 balloting, Democratic National Committee (DNC) Chairman Paul G. Kirk, Jr., said, "Realignment is a myth, and 1986 will bury it."

Actually, the results of the November 4 election suggested that neither party can claim national dominance. The Democrats were the big winners by virtue of seizing Senate control by a surprising 55 to 45 margin, reversing a 53 to 47 preelection GOP edge. And they padded their 2 to 1 advantage in the number of state legislatures they controlled, picking up more than 150 additional seats. But Republicans gained eight governorships and lost only five seats in the House of Representatives—far fewer than normal for the party holding the White House in the middle of a President's second term in office.

Governorships. Although most Democrats emphasized party advances, others pointed out that a net loss of eight governorships could not be taken lightly. Former Governor Charles S. Robb of Vir-

ginia, head of the Democratic Leadership Council, a conservative offshoot of the DNC, said the gubernatorial defeats—especially in Florida and Texas—were "a real dose of cold water" for the party.

In Texas, Democratic Governor Mark White was beaten by William P. Clements. In Florida, Mayor Bob Martinez of Tampa, a former Democrat, was elected the first Hispanic governor of that state. In Alabama, four-time Democratic Governor George C. Wallace, who had run for President on a third-party ticket in 1968, announced his retirement from politics in April 1986. In November, Guy Hunt was elected the state's first Republican governor in more than 100 years. Other states in which Democrats lost governorships were Arizona, Kansas, Maine, Nebraska, New Mexico, Oklahoma, South Carolina, and Wisconsin. Democrats won three governorships from the GOP—in Oregon, Pennsylvania, and Tennessee.

Changes in Senate. No incumbent Democratic senator lost, but seven incumbent Republicans lost. Representative Richard C. Shelby won over Jeremiah Denton in Alabama; former Governor Bob Graham over Paula Hawkins in Florida; former Governor Terry Sanford over James T. Broyhill in North Carolina; Representative Wyche Fowler, Jr., over Mack Mattingly in Georgia; Representative Thomas A. Daschle over James

Abdnor in South Dakota; state Tax Commissioner Kent Conrad over Mark N. Andrews in North Dakota; and former Representative Brock Adams over Slade Gorton in Washington. Other new Democratic senators, winning open seats, were Representative Barbara A. Mikulski of Maryland and Representative Harry M. Reid of Nevada.

New Democratic Strength in the Senate, coupled with long-standing Democratic control of the House, heightened prospects for favorable congressional action in 1987 on *protectionist* trade legislation. Such legislation, opposed by Reagan, would impose high tariffs and other barriers to limit imports, thus protecting domestic industries from foreign competition. Democratic majorities in both houses also increased chances that Congress would further curtail funding for the President's Strategic Defense Initiative, the so-called Star Wars antimissile system.

The Democratic National Committee held an unusually harmonious meeting on March 8 at which it adopted its 1988 presidential nomination rules. For the first time in 16 years at a DNC meeting, delegates avoided a squabble over a major midterm rules overhaul. The DNC lowered to 15 per cent, from 20 per cent, the percentage of the total vote a presidential candidate must receive in district primaries or caucuses to claim a share of 1988 national convention delegates. Blacks had favored eliminating the threshold but were turned down in a voice vote. A later proposal by former Atlanta, Ga., Mayor Maynard Jackson for a 10 per cent threshold was also defeated, 178 to 92.

The lower threshold was expected to help Jesse L. Jackson, a black civil rights leader from Illinois, should he, as expected, run again for the Democratic nomination. On April 17 in Washington, D.C., Jackson announced the formation of the National Rainbow Coalition, an organization that he said would become a permanent "progressive force" within the Democratic Party.

Right Wing Gains. The Democratic Party in Illinois was dealt a major blow on March 18 when voters in the state primary election nominated followers of ultraconservative activist Lyndon H. LaRouche, Jr., of Virginia as the party's candidates for lieutenant governor and secretary of state. The winners, unknowns who barely campaigned, upset the hand-picked choices of the Democratic candidate for governor, Adlai E. Stevenson III. Stevenson campaigned as an independent after refusing to run on the same ticket as the LaRouche followers, but he lost to incumbent Republican Governor James R. Thompson.

LaRouche supporters were reported to be active in a number of states, including New York, Michigan, and Ohio.   Frank Cormier and Margot Cormier

See also ELECTIONS; REPUBLICAN PARTY. In WORLD BOOK, see DEMOCRATIC PARTY.

DENMARK put its membership in the European Community (EC or Common Market) to a *referendum*, or direct vote of the people, on Feb. 27, 1986, to resolve a crisis centering on EC procedures. The EC had been debating revisions known as the *Luxembourg reforms*, designed to streamline decision-making within the EC. All 12 member countries had to approve the reforms for them to take effect.

Political forces within Denmark feared that the reforms would enable the EC to overrule Denmark's right to stop imports of certain products, and so Denmark had not approved the reforms. The center-right minority government of Conservative Prime Minister Poul Schlüter favored the reforms; but the opposition parties, led by the Social Democrats, were against them.

Unofficial Veto. On January 21, the Folketing (parliament) voted, 80 to 75, to reject the reforms. One member of the Folketing abstained from voting, and 23 members were absent during the vote. Schlüter decided immediately to put the issue to a referendum. The referendum did not bind the Folketing officially. Nevertheless, it amounted to a vote on Denmark's future membership in the EC.

On February 27, Danish voters approved the Luxembourg reforms, 56.2 to 43.8 per cent. Of Denmark's 3.8 million voters, 74.8 per cent cast ballots in the referendum. Political observers said the margin of approval showed that Danes remained highly suspicious about Common Market membership.

More Austerity. Schlüter presented on March 14 his government's third *austerity package* (a set of proposals to cut consumer demand) in 12 months. This package, intended to cut demand by $1.3-million, included higher taxes on energy, wine, liquor, ale, tobacco, and candies.

Trade Ban. The Folketing voted on May 30 to ban all trade between Denmark and South Africa to protest South Africa's policy of *apartheid*, or racial separation. The ban passed, 76 votes to 5, with 63 abstentions. The vote also set a 30-month deadline for the termination of contracts for trade between the two countries.

Inflation Fears. Denmark must avoid an increase in its inflation rate and excessive consumer demand, according to an April 1986 report by the Organization for Economic Cooperation and Development (OECD), an association of 24 nations, including Denmark. The OECD criticized Denmark for allowing its *balance-of-payments deficit* to rise, but noted favorably that government spending had decreased sharply. (A balance-of-payments deficit results when a country pays more money to foreign nations than it receives from them.)   Kenneth Brown

See also EUROPE (Facts in Brief Table). In WORLD BOOK, see DENMARK.

DENTISTRY

DENTISTRY. After a decade of research, biochemist J. Herbert Waite of the University of Connecticut in Farmington reported in June 1986 that he had unlocked the secret of a natural glue that creates a strong bond in water. This characteristic would make the glue ideal for a variety of dental treatments, such as holding fillings in place and repairing broken teeth. Waite and his colleagues were able to reproduce the natural "superglue" in their laboratory after identifying a key protein and hardening agent that makes it so effective.

The glue is a sticky substance provided by the sea mussel, a type of shellfish. The glue's ability to form a strong bond in wet environments makes it more effective than the most powerful manufactured glues on the market.

Fighting Tooth Decay. Researchers at the American Dental Association's (ADA) Paffenbarger Research Center in Gaithersburg, Md., reported in May 1986 that they have developed a *fluoride treatment* that is more effective in preventing cavities. Fluoride treatments replace minerals lost from tooth enamel in a process called *remineralization*. This process repairs early decay before cavities develop. Saliva eventually dissolves the remineralized areas, and the treatment must be repeated.

This new treatment uses a calcium phosphate solution to convert small areas of the tooth's enamel into *dicalcium phosphate dihydrate*, a natural mineral that allows the tooth to absorb more fluoride. This mineral also creates a stronger bond between the fluoride and the tooth that is more resistant to saliva. In addition, the solution is more effective than traditional fluoride treatment because it changes fluoride into *fluorapatite*, a fluoride-containing mineral that is less likely to be dissolved by saliva, according to the ADA researchers. They are seeking the approval of the U.S. Food and Drug Administration to test the treatment on human volunteers.

Jaw Implants. Scientists at the National Institute of Dental Research in Bethesda, Md., reported in July 1986 that they have developed a technique to help jaw-surgery patients heal more comfortably. In the technique, called *rigid fixation*, the surgeon places titanium-mesh plates and screws into a broken jawbone during surgery. These plates and screws, which remain in the jawbone permanently, anchor the jaw in place so that it heals properly.

The jaw implant eliminates the need to wire a patient's teeth together for six to eight weeks after surgery while the jaw is healing—a technique that restricts the patient's ability to speak and eat. The implant procedure allows patients to open their mouths five days after surgery. Lou Joseph

In WORLD BOOK, see DENTISTRY.

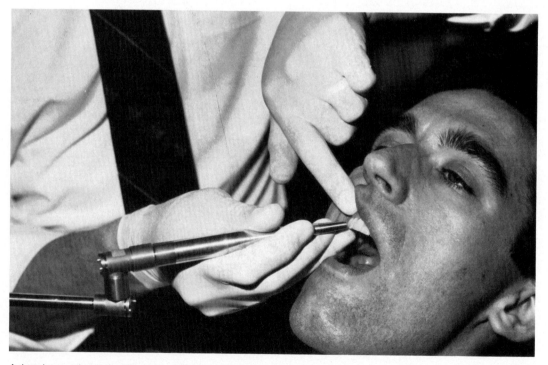

A dental researcher at the University of Alberta in Canada shows how a laser drill, tested on animals in 1986, may someday be used on human patients.

DETROIT in 1986 weathered a 19-day municipal-workers' strike, pressed ahead with several major urban redevelopment plans, and enjoyed improved fiscal health. But spiraling crime plagued the city, and sales slipped in the automobile industry, the dominant segment of Detroit's economy.

City Government. On January 10, Mayor Coleman A. Young was inaugurated for a fourth term. Young, who was first elected in 1973, is Detroit's longest-serving mayor.

The city chalked up a more than $55-million surplus for the 1985-1986 fiscal year, the largest in Detroit history. Young said priorities in the 1986-1987 budget would be to hire more police officers, renovate aging municipal buildings, and raise city workers' pay.

Strike. Contracts for 17,500 city workers expired on June 30, and workers demanded pay increases of 26 per cent over three years. When that demand was refused by city officials, Detroit's largest municipal-workers' union, the 7,000-member American Federation of State, County and Municipal Employees, called a strike for July 16.

Police and fire fighters did not join the strike, but as many as 5,000 other city workers did, including trash collectors and bus drivers. The work stoppage idled bus service for 200,000 riders and left trash uncollected. After 19 days, the workers ended the walkout—the longest municipal strike in Detroit history—by approving a three-year contract that gave them 8 per cent raises and up to $1,500 in bonuses.

Auto Industry. Despite drastic autumn reductions in automobile-loan interest rates by all major United States carmakers, domestic auto sales dipped to 8.06 million in the 1986 model year, from 8.4 million the previous model year.

City officials announced in October that a soon-to-be-built Chrysler Corporation truck assembly plant would be the center of a planned $2-billion development on Detroit's east side. The "new town in town" will include residential and commercial buildings as well as the Chrysler plant. Plant construction is to begin in January 1987, financed in part by city bonds and state and federal grants, and loans.

Development Projects. The city moved to complete its People Mover, a 2.9-mile (4.7-kilometer) elevated train that will loop around the city's downtown area. After its October 1985 take-over of the system from a regional transit authority, the city promised that the line would begin carrying riders in August 1987.

City officials continued to support the redevelopment of areas along the Detroit River. In addition to encouraging private development projects along the waterway, the city is constructing new riverfront parks and expanding the Cobo Hall convention center. City officials were also consid-

Amid uncollected trash, municipal workers in Detroit picket for higher pay in July during the second week of a 19-day strike.

ering two other possible projects in 1986: an aquarium, and a new baseball park to replace 74-year-old Tiger Stadium by the year 2000.

Street Crime. Detroit ranked among the top cities in the United States in serious crimes in 1986. Between January and October, five police officers were killed on duty—more than in the previous six years combined. During the same 10-month period, more people under the age of 21 were shot or killed—a total of 868—than in all of 1985.

Detroit's City Council and community leaders proposed a number of crime-control measures, including a freeze on the sale of handguns and mandatory jail sentences for people carrying guns illegally. But Young blocked the measures, saying they would not work.

Newspapers Join Operations. On April 14, publishing executives in Detroit announced that the city's two daily newspapers, the *Detroit Free Press* and *The Detroit News*, would merge all of their operations except their news departments. Officials of the Gannett Company, Incorporated, owner of the *News*, and Knight-Ridder Newspapers, Incorporated, which owns the *Free Press*, said the action was being taken to stem severe losses at both papers and prevent the financial failure of the *Free Press*.   Patricia L. Edmonds

See also CITY. In WORLD BOOK, see DETROIT.

DISASTERS. The worst nuclear power disaster in history occurred on April 26, 1986, at the Chernobyl nuclear power plant near Kiev in the Soviet Union. An explosion and fire at the plant caused a partial meltdown of the radioactive fuel in the reactor's core, spewing deadly radioactive debris across northern Europe. Two people died fighting the fire, and at least 29 other people died of radiation sickness before year's end. Soviet officials estimated that the Chernobyl accident might eventually cause more than 6,500 cancer deaths in the Soviet Union. Other nuclear-energy experts said that as many as 40,000 fatal cancers might develop over the next 70 years as a result of the disaster. See ENERGY SUPPLY (Close-Up).

One of the worst natural disasters of 1986 happened in Cameroon, in western Africa, on August 21. Lake Nios, the crater of an old volcano, released poisonous gas—probably carbon dioxide. The gas killed more than 1,700 people.

Disasters that resulted in 30 or more deaths in 1986 included the following:

Aircraft Crashes
Jan. 18—Near Santa Elena, Guatemala. A jetliner carrying tourists to the Maya ruins at Tikal, Guatemala, crashed on its approach to Santa Elena airport, killing all 95 people aboard in the worst air crash in Guatemala's history.

March 27—Bangui, Central African Republic. A French fighter jet crashed into a schoolhouse, killing 35 people.

March 30—Pemba, Mozambique. A Mozambican air force plane crashed and burst into flames on take-off, causing 49 deaths.

March 31—Near San Miguel el Alto, Mexico. A Mexicana Airlines jetliner plowed into a mountain, killing all 167 people aboard in the worst air crash in Mexican history.

May 1—Ilopango, El Salvador. A Salvadoran air force plane caught fire just after take-off and slammed into a hill, killing all 33 soldiers and 4 crew members aboard.

Aug. 14—Northeastern Honduras. A Honduran military plane crashed in the jungle, causing 52 deaths.

Aug. 31—Cerritos, Calif., near Los Angeles. An Aeroméxico jetliner and a single-engine plane collided in midair. The crash killed all 67 people aboard the two planes and 15 people on the ground.

Oct. 19—Near Komatipoort, eastern South Africa. The personal plane of Mozambique President Samora Moisés Machel slammed into a mountain, killing Machel and 33 other passengers.

Nov. 2—Near Zahedan, Iran. An Iranian military transport plane crashed into a mountain near the Afghan border, killing all 103 people aboard.

Nov. 6—Near the Shetland Islands. A helicopter carrying workers from an offshore oil rig crashed in the North Sea, killing 45 people in the worst helicopter disaster in history.

Dec. 12—East Berlin, East Germany. A Soviet jetliner crashed in heavy fog approaching East Berlin's Schönefeld airport, killing 70 people, including 19 East German schoolchildren.

Bus and Truck Crashes
Jan. 17—Western India. A bus skidded off a turn and hurtled down a mountain, killing at least 49 people.

March 29—Near Irapuato, Mexico. A train hit a truck at a railroad crossing, killing 30 people in the truck.

Early May—Mandi Bahauddin, Pakistan. More than 45 people died after a bus plunged from a high bridge into a river.

May 12—Northeastern Transkei. After its gears and brakes failed on a steep hill, a bus rolled backward and overturned, killing 30 passengers.

May 13—Near Engcobo, Transkei. A bus carrying 176 schoolchildren overturned, killing 31, in Transkei's second bus disaster in two days.

July 25—Near Harer, Ethiopia. Forty people died after a bus hurtled into a ravine.

Aug. 3—Eastern Bihar state, India. A bus plunged into a flooding river, drowning 70 passengers.

Aug. 10—Near Benin City, Nigeria. Two buses collided, causing 72 fatalities.

Early October—Northern India. Sixty-eight people died after a bus plunged off a bridge over the Ganges River.

Oct. 20—Karachi, Pakistan. A train slammed into two buses at a crossing, killing at least 35 bus passengers.

Dec. 20—Near Simla, India. A bus fell into a gorge, and 47 people were killed.

Earthquake
Oct. 10—San Salvador, El Salvador. An earthquake killed more than 1,200 people.

Explosions and Fires
Jan. 23—New Delhi, India. A smoky fire, probably caused by an electrical short circuit, swept through a hotel and killed 37 people.

April 20—Dhaka, Bangladesh. Thirty-two people died in a fire at a refugee camp on the outskirts of Dhaka.

April 26—Chernobyl, Soviet Union, near Kiev. An explosion and fire at a nuclear power plant killed at least 31 people.

Early May—Yunnan province, China. Forest fires left 80 people dead.

Floods
April 20—Kantalai, Sri Lanka, near Trincomalee. An earthen dam at a reservoir burst, flooding dozens of villages and killing as many as 100 people.

July and early August—Northern and eastern India. More than 200 people died in monsoon floods.

Early August—Northeastern China. Floods killed at least 74 people.

Hurricanes, Tornadoes, and Other Storms
April 1—Bangladesh. A fierce storm swept across much of Bangladesh, leaving 20 known dead and more than 200 other people missing and feared dead.

April 14—Central Bangladesh. A storm of giant hailstones killed at least 92 people.

May 19—Solomon Islands. Typhoon Namu left more than 1,000 people dead.

May 20—Sichuan (Szechwan) province, China. A hailstorm killed more than 100 people.

July 9-11—Philippines and China. Typhoon Peggy left 199 people dead in the Philippines and 210 in China.

Aug. 22-Sept. 5—Southeast Asia. Typhoon Wayne left 63 people dead in Taiwan, 36 in the Philippines, and nearly 400 in Vietnam.

Mine Disasters
Sept. 16—Near Bethal, South Africa. Welders at the Kinross gold mine accidentally ignited a fire that killed at least 177 miners in South Africa's worst gold-mine disaster.

Early October—Serra Pelada, Brazil. At least 50 prospectors died after a wall collapsed at a gold field.

Dec. 24—Near Donetsk, Soviet Union. A methane gas explosion in a coal mine killed dozens of miners.

Dead cattle are sprawled on the ground near Lake Nios, Cameroon, where poisonous gas released by the lake killed more than 1,700 people in August.

Shipwrecks

Mid-January—Off Sibutu Island, Philippines. Fifty people were missing and feared drowned after a cargo ship sank in rough seas.

April 11—Shanxi (Shansi) province, China. A large wave capsized an overloaded ferry in the Huang Ho (Yellow River), leaving 129 people missing or dead.

April 20—Munshiganj, Bangladesh. A ferry hit by a sudden storm sank in the Dhaleswari River, drowning at least 300 and perhaps as many as 500 passengers.

April 24—Off Leyte Island, Philippines. A cargo and passenger ship sank, leaving more than 170 people dead or missing.

May 25—Near Bhola, Bangladesh. A double-decked ferry capsized during a storm and sank in the Meghna River, drowning at least 600 passengers in Bangladesh's worst river disaster ever.

Aug. 5—Northern Bangladesh. At least 30 people drowned after their boat capsized on the Padma River.

Aug. 31—Near Novorossiysk, Soviet Union. A Soviet freighter rammed a cruise liner in the Black Sea, sinking the liner and causing 398 deaths.

Sept. 7—Off Port Harcourt, Nigeria. Two Nigerian passenger ships collided in mid-ocean, and at least 100 people were drowned.

Sept. 13—Near Barisal, Bangladesh. At least 60 people were feared drowned after the sinking of a ferry on the Arial Khan River.

Oct. 9—Near Narail, Bangladesh. More than 200 people died after a ferry capsized in the Kajla River.

Nov. 11—Off Île de la Gonâve, Haiti. A ferry boat sank, and as many as 200 people drowned.

Train Wrecks

Late January—Near Durban, South Africa. Thirty-nine people died in the collision of two passenger trains.

Feb. 17—Near Limache, Chile. Two trains collided head-on, killing at least 58 people in the worst rail disaster in Chile's history.

Aug. 6—Near Dhanbad, India. A passenger train smashed into some abandoned freight cars, killing at least 52 people.

Other Disasters

Early January—Northern India. A cold wave and series of winter storms caused more than 220 deaths, including at least 72 in the state of Bihar.

Early January—Guangxi (Kwangsi) autonomous region, China. A partially completed dam caved in, killing 48 construction workers.

March 9—Near Huánuco, Peru. An avalanche buried parts of three villages, leaving 13 people known dead and about 50 others missing and feared dead.

March 15—Singapore. A six-story hotel collapsed, killing 33 people.

April 14—Hardwar, India, near Delhi. Hindu pilgrims rushing to bathe in the sacred Ganges River during a major religious festival trampled at least 48 people to death.

May 25—Taichi Gorge, Taiwan. A landslide at a scenic gorge killed 39 sightseers.

June 21—Southern Colombia. Up to 200 people died after a huge slide of mud and rocks crashed across a mountain highway.

Aug. 21—Lake Nios, Cameroon, near Nkambe. The lake, the crater of an old volcano, released poisonous gas that killed more than 1,700 people.

Nov. 9—Ayodhya, India. At least 32 and perhaps more than 50 people were trampled to death in a stampede that began after a barrier rope gave way at a Hindu temple.　　　　　　　　　　　　　　Sara Dreyfuss

DJIBOUTI. See AFRICA.

DOG. Judge Ann Wanner of Largo, Fla., selected Champion Marjetta National Acclaim, a pointer, as best-in-show at the Westminster Kennel Club's 110th annual show held in February at Madison Square Garden in New York City. The champion is owned by Michael Zollo of Bernardsville, N.J., and Isabel Robson of Glenmoore, Pa.

The American Kennel Club (AKC) registered 1,089,149 dogs from among 129 breeds during 1985. Cocker spaniels headed the list, followed by poodles, Labrador retrievers, German shepherds, golden retrievers, Doberman pinschers, beagles, chow chows, miniature schnauzers, and Shetland sheepdogs.

In September, the Dog Museum of America announced that it would move from New York City to St. Louis, Mo., in 1987. A new museum building will be constructed as part of a 1,000-acre (400-hectare) development.

In 1986, the AKC began to administer the *stud book* (published breeding records) and to regulate events for the nine varieties of coonhounds registered by the American Coon Hunter's Association (ACHA). There will be no crossover between ACHA and AKC registration. Roberta Vesley

In WORLD BOOK, see DOG.

DOMINICAN REPUBLIC. See BALAGUER, JOAQUÍN; LATIN AMERICA.

DROUGHT. See WATER; WEATHER.

DRUG ABUSE. Public concern about drug abuse in the United States intensified in 1986 with the availability of a new, inexpensive, and highly addictive form of cocaine called *crack* or *rock*, and the cocaine-related deaths of two star athletes—University of Maryland basketball star Len Bias and Cleveland Browns defensive back Don Rogers. Such concern prompted President Ronald Reagan and first lady Nancy Reagan to appear on national television on September 14 to launch a crusade against drug abuse.

The next day, Reagan announced a plan for combating drug abuse, which included increased spending on drug education, treatment programs, and enforcement. The President said he would support legislation increasing penalties for drug trafficking.

Drug Testing. Reagan also called for a controversial program of mandatory drug testing of government employees in sensitive positions. In December 1986, Northwestern University in Evanston, Ill., reported that a study of 230 businesses showed that one-third of the firms required routine drug screening of all applicants. Opponents of mandatory drug testing were challenging the practice in the courts, saying the practice violates the rights of those tested.

Cocaine Use remained high, though use of other illicit drugs has declined since 1981, accord-

President Ronald Reagan and his wife, Nancy, prepare to launch a national crusade against drug abuse from the White House in September.

ing to two surveys reported in 1986. About 23 million people in the United States have used cocaine at least once. Researchers said that 17.3 per cent of a group of high school seniors studied had tried cocaine and that 6.7 per cent had used it within the month before they were surveyed.

On July 10, government health authorities issued a public warning about cocaine's toxic effects, stressing that a single dose could be fatal. Deaths due to cocaine use have tripled since 1981.

Other Drugs. Marijuana use has decreased in the general population, but its use remains significant among young people. Researchers reported that 25.7 per cent of the senior students used marijuana in the month before they were surveyed, with 4.9 per cent smoking marijuana daily. By their mid-20's, approximately 80 per cent of today's young adults have used an illicit drug, and more than 50 per cent have used an illicit drug other than—or in addition to—marijuana.

Of all forms of drug abuse, addiction to alcohol and cigarette smoking continued to cause the greatest disability and the highest cost to society. Although studies revealed that the number of regular users of alcohol and cigarettes declined in 1985, overall use remained high. David C. Lewis

In the Special Reports section, see THE HAZARDS OF TEEN-AGE DRINKING. In WORLD BOOK, see DRUG ABUSE.

DRUGS. Recombivax HB, the first human vaccine produced with genetic engineering, or recombinant DNA technology, was approved by the United States Food and Drug Administration (FDA) on July 23, 1986. The new vaccine protects against hepatitis B, a disease that can lead to cirrhosis of the liver and liver cancer.

Unlike the existing hepatitis B vaccine, which is made from the blood plasma of people who carry the hepatitis virus, Recombivax HB is produced from genetically altered yeast cells. Many people have refused the blood-derived vaccine in fear of contracting acquired immune deficiency syndrome (AIDS), which can be transmitted through blood products. FDA Commissioner Frank E. Young predicted that the new laboratory-made vaccine would ease such fears and help to prevent many of the 200,000 cases of hepatitis B that occur annually in the United States.

AIDS Research. The National Institutes of Health (NIH) in Bethesda, Md., on June 30 awarded $100 million in contracts for research on five drugs that have the potential to combat AIDS. The NIH gave the contracts to 14 medical centers in the United States. The centers will also try to develop medications that can prevent AIDS from developing in people who have been infected with the AIDS virus but do not have symptoms of the disease.

The drugs selected for initial testing are HPA-23, ribavirin, foscarnet, alpha-interferon, and azidothymidine (AZT). On September 19, U.S. health officials said that AZT had shown such promise in early experiments that it would be made available to a larger number of AIDS patients. They pointed out, however, that although AZT appeared to extend the life of some AIDS patients, it did not cure them of the disease.

Hope for Alzheimer's. On November 13, researchers at the University of California at Los Angeles reported that an experimental drug called tetrahydroaminoacridine (THA) significantly improved the memories of 16 of 17 people suffering from Alzheimer's disease. Alzheimer's is a brain disorder that results in progressive memory loss and the inability to function. Because there is currently no treatment for the disease, the researchers and the FDA said they would move quickly to launch a major clinical test of THA by the end of the year.

Tranquilizer Treatment. The FDA approved a tranquilizer on October 1 that relieves anxiety without causing drowsiness and without interfering with a person's ability to drive or work. The Bristol-Myers Company of New York City will sell the drug, buspirone hydrochloride, under the trade name BuSpar.

Medical researchers at the Addiction Research Foundation in Toronto, Canada, on October 1 re-

A technician monitors production of Recombivax HB, the first genetically engineered vaccine approved for human use by the U.S. FDA.

ported that definite withdrawal symptoms occur after long-term use of Valium and similar tranquilizers. The symptoms include temporary numbness in the hands, blurred vision, muscle aches, and other minor problems. The researchers said that physicians should be aware that patients may become physically dependent on these tranquilizers.

Easing Psoriasis. The FDA on October 7 approved a medication for treating the most severe and disfiguring form of psoriasis, a skin disease. The drug, etretinate, is for people who have skin lesions so severe that they are unable to work or even tolerate clothing on their skin. The FDA cautioned that etretinate may cause serious birth defects if taken by pregnant women or by women who may become pregnant several years after using it. Hoffman-La Roche Incorporated of Nutley, N.J., will sell the drug under the name Tegison.

Anticancer Drugs. The National Cancer Institute (NCI) on March 24 urged physicians in the United States to be more aggressive in using *chemotherapeutic drugs*, medications used to treat cancer. The NCI, located in Bethesda, estimated that 9,000 cancer patients die each year because of inadequate use of chemotherapy. The agency charged that some physicians, concerned about adverse side effects and possible malpractice suits, prescribe insufficient doses of anticancer drugs.

EASTERN ORTHODOX CHURCHES

Fewer Capsules. Drug companies were forced to halt the sale of a number of nonprescription capsule products following a rash of product tamperings similar to the Tylenol poisonings that killed seven people in 1982. The 1986 episodes, which killed three people, began on February 8 when a Peekskill, N.Y., woman died at a friend's home in Yonkers, N.Y., after taking a Tylenol capsule that had been laced with cyanide.

The poisoning prompted Johnson & Johnson of New Brunswick, N.J., maker of Tylenol, to announce on February 17 that it would discontinue production of all over-the-counter capsule medications. Bristol-Myers quit selling its nonprescription capsule products on June 20, after the deaths of two people in Auburn, Wash., on June 5 and June 11. Both victims took capsules of Bristol-Myers' Extra-Strength Excedrin that had been contaminated with cyanide. On March 21, the SmithKline Beckman Corporation of Philadelphia recalled its Contac cold capsules, Dietac weight-control capsules, and Teldrin allergy capsules after minute quantities of rat poison were found in some of the products. All three drug companies reintroduced their capsule products as *caplets*, tablets shaped like capsules. Michael Woods

See also DRUG ABUSE; MEDICINE. In the WORLD BOOK SUPPLEMENT section, see CYCLOSPORINE. In WORLD BOOK, see DRUG.

Archbishop Vitaly is installed as Metropolitan of the Russian Orthodox Church Outside Russia in New York City on January 9.

EASTERN ORTHODOX CHURCHES. A number of Orthodox churches responded in 1986 to the statement on baptism, the Eucharist, and ministry issued in 1983 by the World Council of Churches, an organization of Eastern Orthodox and Protestant churches. Overall, the responding churches—the patriarchates of Alexandria, Moscow, Bucharest, and Sofia; the Church of Finland; and the Orthodox Theological Society in the United States—gave the statement a warm reception.

Disagreement continued, however, over the portion of the statement dealing with ministry. The document states that bishops, *presbyters* (priests), and deacons are essential to the Christian church. Although this statement is not strong enough for some Orthodox churches, it has caused concern for Protestant churches that do not have a priesthood.

Church Union. In September, the Antiochian Orthodox Archdiocese in Englewood, N.J., agreed in principle to accept members of the Evangelical Orthodox Church (EOC) of Isla Vista, Calif., near Santa Barbara, into its archdiocese. The EOC is composed primarily of former Protestants who accept the traditions of the Orthodox church. The group had been seeking the acceptance of an Orthodox church for several years.

Orthodox Outreach. The Orthodox Church continued to increase its involvement in contemporary social issues. Patriarch Demetrios of Constantinople, Turkey, focused on the theme of world peace in his New Year's message ushering in 1986. Following an April visit to South America, Archbishop Iakovos, primate of the Greek Orthodox Archdiocese of North and South America, called for support of the peace proposal of the Contadora group, four nations seeking to restore peace to Central America.

New Leader. Archbishop Vitaly of Montreal and Canada, 76, was elected to succeed Metropolitan Philaret of the Russian Orthodox Church Outside Russia on January 9. Metropolitan Philaret died on Nov. 21, 1985.

Three Prominent Leaders of the Eastern Orthodox Churches died in 1986. Patriarch Nicholas VI, 72, of the patriarchate of Alexandria in Egypt, died on July 5. On July 31, Patriarch Justin of Romania, 76, died after a brief illness. He was elected the fourth Patriarch of Romania in 1977 and was active in ecumenical activities. On Nov. 16, 1986, Metropolitan Theoktistos was elected to succeed him. Funeral services were conducted on August 25 in Athens, Greece, for Nikos Nissiotis, 61, a professor at the University of Athens School of Theology, who was killed in an automobile accident. Stanley Samuel Harakas

In WORLD BOOK, see EASTERN ORTHODOX CHURCHES.

ECONOMICS. In November 1986, the United States economy moved into the fifth year of its current expansion—the third longest expansion period since World War II ended in 1945. The length of the current expansion has been exceeded only four times in the more than 100 years that the business cycle has been more or less accurately measured. At the end of 1986, there were signs that growth would continue through much, if not all, of 1987. Few economists were willing to forecast when the growth would come to an end.

The gross national product (GNP)—the total value of all goods and services produced—rose to $4.215 trillion, as measured by 1986 prices. This was nearly 5 per cent higher than the total for 1985 and, after correcting for inflation, represented a 2.7 per cent increase in real growth, just about the same rate that the economy had grown in 1985. Consumer prices rose by only 1.1 per cent in 1986, and prices actually dropped for three consecutive months beginning in February, the first such decline in more than 20 years.

Total civilian employment, including agricultural workers and the self-employed, rose to 110 million at the end of the year. Total nonagricultural employment, excluding the self-employed, was more than 100 million at year-end, the first time this figure had ever been reached.

The success of the U.S. economy can best be appreciated by noting that since 1979, more than 10 million jobs have been created. The industrialized nations of Western Europe have suffered a net decline in employment during the same period.

Unemployment. On the bleaker side, unemployment in the United States continued throughout 1986 to hover around 7 per cent. Blacks and other minority groups and teen-agers continued to suffer significantly higher rates of joblessness than did adult whites. The median length of unemployment was a little more than 7 weeks, but 1 out of 6 unemployed people were out of work for 27 weeks or more. This pulled up the average duration of unemployment to almost 15 weeks.

Wages. Average hourly and weekly earnings grew by less than 3 per cent as many labor contracts, especially in hard-pressed industries such as steel, called for cuts in pay in return for promises of job security and retraining for displaced workers. The lower rate of inflation, however, meant that real weekly earnings—the actual buying power of those earnings after adjusting for inflation—rose in 1986 after declining by 1.4 per cent in 1985.

Stock Market. Stock prices rose briskly until September 1986, when all the major indices set record highs. Stock prices then dropped but re-

The leaders of major industrial nations take a stroll in a palace garden during their annual economic summit conference, held in May in Tokyo.

Selected Key U.S. Economic Indicators

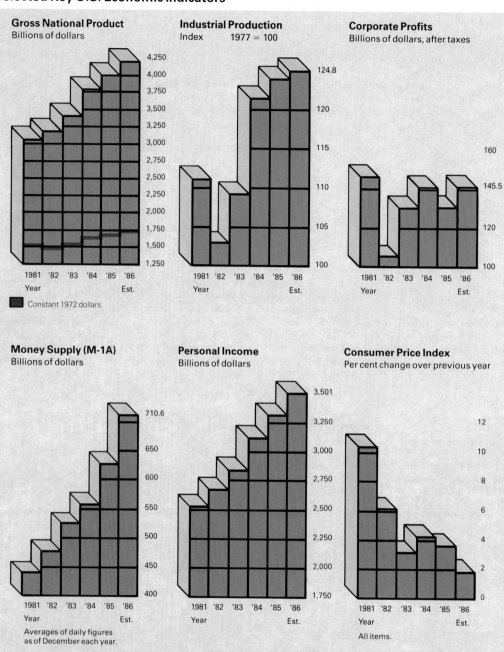

Gross National Product
Billions of dollars

4,250
4,000
3,750
3,500
3,250
3,000
2,750
2,500
2,250
2,000
1,750
1,500
1,250

1981 '82 '83 '84 '85 '86
Year   Est.

■ Constant 1972 dollars.

Industrial Production
Index   1977 = 100

124.8
120
115
110
105
100

1981 '82 '83 '84 '85 '86
Year   Est.

Corporate Profits
Billions of dollars, after taxes

160
145.5
120
100

1981 '82 '83 '84 '85 '86
Year   Est.

Money Supply (M-1A)
Billions of dollars

710.6
650
600
550
500
450
400

1981 '82 '83 '84 '85 '86
Year   Est.

Averages of daily figures
as of December each year.

Personal Income
Billions of dollars

3,501
3,250
3,000
2,750
2,500
2,250
2,000
1,750

1981 '82 '83 '84 '85 '86
Year   Est.

Consumer Price Index
Per cent change over previous year

12
10
8
6
4
2
0

1981 '82 '83 '84 '85 '86
Year   Est.

All items.

The most comprehensive measure of the nation's total output of goods and services is the gross national product (GNP). The GNP represents the dollar value in current prices of all goods and services plus the estimated value of certain other outputs, such as the rental value of owner-occupied dwellings. Industrial production is a monthly measure of the physical output of manufacturing, mining, and utility industries. Corporate profits are quarterly profit samplings from major industries. Money supply (M-1A) measures the total amount of money in the economy in currency and checking account deposits. Personal income is current income received by people (including nonprofit institutions and private trust funds) before taxes. The consumer price index (CPI) is a measure of changes in the prices of selected goods and services consumed by urban families and individuals.

All 1986 figures are *Year Book* estimates based on data from The Conference Board.

covered in early December and surpassed their previous highs. At year-end, the 30-stock Dow Jones Industrial Average stood at 1,895.95. The more representative New York Stock Exchange Index stood at 138.58, and Standard & Poor's 500 Index was 242.17. These levels were approximately 15 to 20 per cent above those of 1985 and reflected investors' confidence that corporate profits would advance significantly in 1987, along with the general growth of the U.S. economy. This was all the more surprising because many experts had expected that investors would sell stocks at year-end to take advantage of a preferential tax rate that disappears under the Tax Reform Act of 1986, taking effect in 1987.

Profits. Corporate profits rose slightly from their 1985 levels but were still below the total reached in 1980. Undistributed profits, for example, fell from $97 billion in 1980 to approximately $50 billion in 1986. Consumers continued to spend at a healthy rate, but their savings—as a percentage of their disposable income—continued to fall, reaching only 4.0 per cent compared with 7.5 per cent in 1981 and 5.1 per cent in 1985. This rate of spending unquestionably contributed to the growth of the economy in 1986, but the low savings level also served to check the decline in interest rates, which remained at historically high levels.

Threatening Problems. The most threatening problems facing the U.S. economy as 1986 drew to a close were also those most likely to persist in 1987. They included a massive balance-of-trade deficit of more than $160 billion, the inability of Congress to reduce the fiscal 1986 federal deficit of $220.7 billion, and the failure of long-term interest rates to fall as they had in 1984 and 1985. These were all complicated by the enormous debt problems of some developing countries—particularly those in Latin America, and especially Argentina, Brazil, and Mexico. All these problems are interrelated and offer no immediate prospect for solution.

Trade Imbalance. The United States unfavorable trade balance—the excess of imports over exports—has been building for several years. In 1977, the excess was a little over $3 billion per month, a state of affairs that continued roughly unchanged until 1983. Then, it jumped to just under $6 billion per month and rose in 1984 to more than $10 billion per month and in 1985 to more than $12 billion per month.

Some of this tremendous increase was due to the high value of the U.S. dollar in relation to the currency of other countries, which made it more expensive for those countries to buy goods made in the United States. More important, however, the high value of the dollar made foreign exports unusual bargains in the United States. The relatively low price of small Japanese-made automobiles, for example, was largely attributed to the dollar's high value.

By the end of 1986, however, the dollar had fallen nearly 35 per cent in value since early 1985, thus removing much of the advantage built up over the years. There were signs that the lower value of the dollar will in time serve to increase U.S. exports and limit imports. That process, however, takes time, because markets once lost are not quickly regained. Furthermore, firms in other countries that have found the United States a rich market have reduced their profit margins rather than raise prices and risk losing their share of the U.S. market.

Another factor contributing to the trade imbalance has been the relatively slow growth in U.S. productivity compared with the rest of the world. This may be attributed to the fact that the savings level as a percentage of GNP is much lower in the United States than in other industrialized nations. As a result, *capital investment*—that is, investment in new factories, tools, supplies, and equipment, which is considered a principal spur to increased productivity—has lagged in the United States.

Protectionism. The massive trade deficit—combined with the loss of jobs in certain manufacturing and other industries—has tremendously increased protectionist pressure in Congress—that is, demands for high tariffs and other trade barriers to protect U.S. industries from foreign competition. Protectionist measures could result in a disastrous repetition of the crisis that occurred in the 1930's when high tariffs in the United States helped to prolong a worldwide depression.

The other side of the coin, however, is that the massive outflow of U.S. dollars has been accompanied by a substantial increase in foreign investment in the United States. Total foreign investment has risen from under $40 billion in 1979 to $127 billion in 1985 and an estimated $160 billion in 1986. Much of this money has gone to the purchase of U.S. government securities, such as Treasury bills and bonds, and has thus helped to finance the federal deficit. As a result, interest rates in the United States have been held to a level lower than they would otherwise be.

Federal Deficit. The federal deficit for the fiscal year ending on Sept. 30, 1986, was $220.7 billion compared with $212.3 billion in fiscal 1985. The deficit was estimated at $166 billion for fiscal 1987, approximately $20 billion above the target set by Congress. Thus, Congress was expected to be faced again with the task of reducing government expenditures or raising taxes if efforts to reduce the deficit were to succeed.

The biggest chunk in the federal budget are the expenditures for health, Medicare, welfare, and social security payments, which totaled more than $425 billion in fiscal 1986, compared with $273-

"Now here's *my* idea for a 'fair' tax—tax the rich, provide assistance for the poor, and leave the rest of us alone."

billion for national defense. Interest payments as a proportion of the federal budget continue to rise as the national debt increases because of the continuing deficit. An increasing proportion of these interest payments are due to foreigners who have invested large sums in U.S. government securities. This outflow adds to the pressure to increase U.S. exports in order to prevent a further deterioration of the balance-of-payments picture.

Foreign Debt. Problems among the indebted Latin-American countries vary, but the one common thread is that most of the large debtors are finding it difficult, if not impossible, to pay the interest on their foreign debts. These debts were contracted at a time when economic conditions were quite different. For example, Mexico—among the largest of the debtors—received substantial loans for internal development at a time when oil prices were high and Mexico's vast oil reserves seemed to promise lenders substantial security for repayment. With the collapse of oil prices, plus internal problems, Mexico's ability to repay was severely limited. In the Special Reports section, see MEXICO: FROM BOOM TO BUST.

Most of these loans were made in U.S. dollars and have to be repaid in U.S. dollars. But, for most of the Latin-American debtors, declining exports, falling monetary reserves, and a heavy demand for imports have greatly reduced the

amount of foreign exchange available to pay interest on the debts. This has caused fears that some countries may *default* (fail to pay) on their loans. Some rescheduling and additional loans from the International Monetary Fund (IMF)—an agency of the United Nations—have averted an immediate crisis, but the pressure remains great.

The problem is complicated by a substantial decline in U.S. investment abroad since 1981 and 1982, when a large number of bank loans were made to then apparently secure Latin-American nations. In 1981, the outflow of U.S. dollars exceeded $110 billion, and rose to $120 billion in 1982.

In 1985, that outflow had dropped to $32 billion, and a much smaller proportion went to those large debtor nations because banks were reluctant to continue loaning money to them. If any of these large debtor nations did default, however, it would cut off their access to international capital markets; slow—if not stop—further development; and probably threaten the existence of civilian governments in countries such as Argentina and Brazil where years of military rule only recently ended.

A further complication directly affecting the United States was that many of its largest banks have made loans to one or more of these nations or to private enterprises within them. The total amount of these loans nearly equals the total capital of the lending banks.

A default would force the U.S. banks to write these loans off their books and would require massive amounts of new capital for the banks. Otherwise, the entire U.S. banking system might be threatened. For these reasons, international efforts were made in 1986 to provide temporary relief for the debtor nations and to restructure these debts to avoid such a write-off. Most observers believe that there is no immediate danger of default. Political instability in much of Latin America is, however, of concern. See LATIN AMERICA.

In the absence of any violent economic shocks from abroad, the United States economy was expected to continue its mild expansion throughout most of 1987. Inflation should remain low, at least by the standards set a few years ago, with the rate probably increasing to between 3 and 4 per cent as the lower-valued dollar affects import prices more strongly than in earlier years. Unemployment was expected to continue to fall slightly. To sum up, the year 1986 saw a solid, if not spectacular, economic performance, and 1987 promised more of the same.   Warren W. Shearer

See also INTERNATIONAL TRADE; MANUFACTURING; STOCKS AND BONDS; and individual country articles. In WORLD BOOK, see ECONOMICS.

ECUADOR. See LATIN AMERICA.

EDUCATION. The teaching profession in the United States was the subject of two influential reports prepared in 1986. In April, education deans from 40 leading universities presented *Tomorrow's Teachers*, a study of the profession that called for prospective teachers to earn a bachelor's degree in the subjects they plan to teach rather than in undergraduate education programs, as is now required by virtually all states. The report also proposed that teachers be classified according to their ability, with the most skillful teachers being given greater responsibilities and higher salaries.

Carnegie Report. In mid-May, the Carnegie Forum on Education and the Economy released its report on the teaching profession. The Forum was established in 1985 by the prestigious Carnegie Corporation of New York as a 10-year, $10-million project to promote school reform. The report, *A Nation Prepared: Teachers for the 21st Century*, called for teachers to be licensed by a national standards board. The report recommended creating positions for "lead teachers," who would play a major role in the organization and leadership of schools and receive higher salaries.

Among other changes, the study also called for eliminating undergraduate education degrees, tying educators' salaries to students' academic performance, recruiting minority graduates for teaching careers, and easing the bureaucratic restraints

under which most teachers work. In September, the Carnegie Forum announced the appointment of a 33-member panel to plan the creation of a national standards board to certify teachers.

The two largest and most influential teachers unions—the 1.7-million-member National Education Association (NEA) and the 600,000-member American Federation of Teachers (AFT)—responded differently to the Forum's recommendations. At its annual meeting in Louisville, Ky., in early July, the NEA, headed by Mary H. Futrell, tentatively endorsed a national teacher certification board but did not consider other proposals of the Carnegie Forum. On the other hand, at its national convention in Chicago, the AFT, led by union president Albert Shanker, endorsed the Carnegie report as "the most important contribution to the continuing public discussion of education reform."

The Florida Legislature voted in June to end the state's two-year-old master-teacher program, which had been burdened by administrative difficulties. The program—which was established to make teaching a more attractive profession—awarded bonuses to the top 3 per cent of the state's teachers, judged on the basis of competency tests and classroom visits.

The Florida lawmakers voted to create a similar career achievement program. The plan will provide a permanent three-step career path for teachers, using years of experience, education, and a series of evaluations as the criteria for promotion. Higher salaries will also accompany promotions. The new program, to be introduced during the 1987-1988 school year, had the endorsement of Florida's teachers unions, Governor Bob Graham, and a consortium of business leaders.

Competency Tests. Despite widespread controversy, more teachers were required to prove their academic skills during 1986. On March 10, Texas became the second state—after Arkansas in 1985—to evaluate the competency of its public-school teachers. Of more than 202,000 teachers tested on their knowledge of grammar and diction and their reading comprehension, 6,579—about 3 per cent—failed the test.

The examination, which had been mandated as part of a sweeping reform bill passed by the Texas legislature in 1984, followed bitter statewide debates and unsuccessful legal challenges by the Texas State Teachers Association. By September 1986, the state had granted 23 school systems exemptions to a state law requiring the dismissal of teachers who fail the exam twice.

Funding and Enrollments. Total enrollment in U.S. elementary and secondary schools rose for the second year in a row. The number of students in public and private schools reached 45.3 million at the beginning of the 1986-1987 school year, an

299

Teachers picket a San Antonio school in March to protest a test of basic
reading, writing, and math skills they must pass to keep state certification.

increase of 62,000 from 1985-1986. But college enrollment for the same period declined—by approximately 80,000 students—to 12,164,000. The nation's total education bill was estimated at $278.8 billion in 1986-1987, a one-year increase of $15.4 billion. Spending at the elementary and secondary levels was estimated at $170 billion.

School Reform. At its annual meeting in August, the National Governors Association presented a detailed plan for restructuring the U.S. public school system. The report, *Time for Results: The Governors' 1991 Report on Education,* called for state legislation that will permit families to select the public schools their children will attend as a way to generate competition in the educational market place. The report also recommended that schools remain open year-round and that states be allowed to take over school systems deemed "academically bankrupt."

The report was prepared under the direction of Governor Lamar Alexander of Tennessee. In October, the Carnegie Corporation announced a grant of $890,000 to the National Governors Association to assist state governments in implementing the report's recommendations.

As the school year began in early September, U.S. Secretary of Education William J. Bennett scrutinized elementary education in *First Lessons: A Report on Elementary Education in America.* Although Bennett found no serious faults with the quality of grade-school education, he recommended that history, geography, and civics replace social studies in the curriculum, and that *phonics*—a system of matching letters to sounds—be used to teach reading. He also proposed that elementary school principals be drawn from business and other fields.

The education of preschool children became a national issue in 1986. In September, the New York City public school system opened its first prekindergarten classes in a plan to offer school programs to all of the city's 4-year-olds by 1989. School districts in Illinois, Missouri, and South Carolina also started similar programs. The major issues in the debate were how primary-grade teachers would adjust their instructional methods to meet the preschoolers' needs and whether 4-year-olds would benefit from early academic training.

Secretary Bennett helped to spark national controversy on a sensitive subject when, in April, he criticized the dispensing of birth-control information and contraceptives at school health clinics. The practice, he said, amounted to an "abdication of moral authority" and encouraged students who "do not have sexual intimacy on their minds to have it on their minds."

According to the Center for Population Options

in Washington, D. C., there were 71 school-based clinics in the United States and 80 others in the planning stages at the end of 1986. A Johns Hopkins University study released in October said that the pregnancy rate dropped by 30 per cent among students at schools with clinics, and girls in schools with clinics were no more sexually active than girls in schools without clinics.

Combating Drugs. The death on June 19 of University of Maryland basketball star Len Bias of cocaine intoxication focused educators' attention on student drug use. At the beginning of the 1986-1987 academic year, schools and colleges throughout the United States introduced drug-testing programs for athletes and other students involved in extracurricular activities. On September 30, many of the 913,000 students in New York City took part in a citywide teach-in on *crack*, a new and potent form of cocaine.

On September 14, President Ronald Reagan and his wife, Nancy, made a televised appeal for a "national crusade" against drug abuse. In October, the President signed a $1.7-billion antidrug law that includes $200 million for drug-abuse prevention programs in the nation's schools.

Academics Versus Athletics. In January, the National Collegiate Athletic Association (NCAA), the governing body of college sports, voted to delay for two years the full implementation of minimum academic standards for college athletes. The standards are designed to ensure that freshmen at the 284 Division I colleges and universities—schools with the most competitive sports programs—meet certain educational requirements before they are allowed to participate in intercollegiate athletics. By 1988, incoming freshmen athletes at these schools must earn a 2.0 grade-point average (with 4.0 as the highest possible) in an 11-course core curriculum in high school and attain a combined score of 700 out of a possible 1,600 on the Scholastic Aptitude Test.

"Troubled" Colleges. In November, the Carnegie Foundation for the Advancement of Teaching questioned the priorities of the nation's colleges and universities when it presented the results of a three-year study entitled *College: The Undergraduate Experience in America.* The report described the four-year college as a "troubled institution" that emphasized career preparation rather than a broad education. Colleges, the report said, lacked commitment to good teaching and creativity in the classroom, and were confused about how to instill shared values and a sense of civic obligation in their students.

To remedy these problems, the report recommended introducing a senior thesis as a graduation requirement, rewarding professors for excellence in teaching, and requiring all college students to perform community service. The study

also suggested that nationwide, standardized college entrance examinations should be less important in the admission process.

Other Developments. On January 28, Christa McAuliffe, a Concord, N.H., social studies teacher, died with the six other crew members of the space shuttle *Challenger* when the craft exploded seconds after its launch from Cape Canaveral, Fla. McAuliffe made the highly publicized flight as the first private citizen observer to ride the shuttle and the inaugural member of the National Aeronautics and Space Administration's "Teacher in Space Program." See SPACE EXPLORATION (Close-Up).

In October, seven Christian conservative families in Tennessee won the legal right to exempt their children from reading classes that used texts they considered objectionable and "antireligious." Citing the First Amendment provision of the free exercise of religion, a federal district judge ruled on the families' behalf. The judge's decision applied only to their children and only to reading classes. In Alabama, Christian conservatives petitioned in federal court to have textbooks they found offensive removed from the public schools in Mobile. Final testimony in the case concluded in October, and the judge's ruling was pending at year-end.   Thomas Toch

In WORLD BOOK, see EDUCATION.

EGYPT. The worst outbreak of political violence since the 1981 assassination of President Anwar el-Sadat erupted on Feb. 25, 1986, in Cairo. As many as 17,000 draftees assigned to the paramilitary police force rioted after hearing false reports that their three-year term of service, required by law, would be extended to four years. The draftees were joined by hundreds of civilians.

The rioters were brought under control by the army on February 27, but only after they had ransacked, looted, and burned hotels, nightclubs, and shops catering to foreigners, causing millions of dollars in damage. Casualties were also heavy, with 107 killed and more than 700 injured.

The riots shook Egyptian and international confidence in the regime of President Hosni Mubarak. Mubarak responded swiftly to the riots with a purge of government security officials, including the minister of the interior. About 1,300 of the conscripts were held for trial, and 10 per cent of the 300,000-member police force were dismissed outright. By December, 546 of the draftees had been released. Another riot in Asyut in central Egypt in April prompted the People's Assembly, Egypt's legislature, to extend the 1981 state of emergency for another two years.

Fundamentalism. The growing influence of Islamic fundamentalists in Egyptian life posed a more serious long-term threat to the Mubarak government. In July, fundamentalists burned video rental stores and liquor stores in Cairo. In December, 4 army officers and 29 civilians were arrested after Egypt exposed a plot by a group of Islamic extremists to overthrow Mubarak.

İsraeli Relations. Mubarak met with Israel's Prime Minister Shimon Peres on September 11 and 12 in Egypt, the first meeting between leaders of the two countries since 1981. The two leaders agreed to international arbitration to settle their long-running dispute over Taba, a tiny Israeli-held beach resort in the Sinai Peninsula.

The Economy. Economic problems continued to be a major concern for the government. Revenues from oil and tourism and tolls from the Suez Canal fell sharply. Money sent home by Egyptians working abroad in Arab oil-producing states was also down. The 1986 budget, approved by the Assembly in May, forecast a deficit of $4 billion. In August, the government introduced an economic reform package intended to satisfy Egypt's creditors and thus improve the country's ability to arrange new loans.

On November 9, Mubarak dismissed Prime Minister Ali Lofty for failing to aid Egypt's troubled economy. Mubarak appointed Atef Sidqi, an economist, to replace him. William Spencer

See also MIDDLE EAST (Facts in Brief Table). In WORLD BOOK, see EGYPT.

ELECTIONS. The Democratic Party claimed control of the United States Senate by a surprisingly wide margin in midterm elections on Nov. 4, 1986. But Republicans made a strong showing in gubernatorial races and virtually held their own in contests for the House of Representatives. Democrats scored gains in state legislatures, picking up more than 150 additional legislative seats and adding to their 2 to 1 edge in the number of legislatures controlled.

Most Senate campaigns hinged on local issues, and many were marked by negative, even nasty, television advertising aimed at blackening the reputation of opponents. The absence of national issues may have contributed to the lowest voter turnout in an off-year national election since 1942, when World War II disrupted voting habits. The nonpartisan Committee for the Study of the American Electorate calculated that only 37.3 per cent of eligible voters went to the polls.

President Ronald Reagan traveled almost 25,000 miles (40,000 kilometers) in a strenuous but largely futile campaign on behalf of Republican Party (GOP) candidates in 22 states.

Senate. Gaining 8 Senate seats, Democrats claimed a 55 to 45 edge over Republicans, who had controlled the Senate by a 53 to 47 margin. Seven Republican senators were defeated, but no incumbent Democrat lost. The ousted Republicans

and their victorious opponents were Senators Jeremiah Denton, beaten by Representative Richard C. Shelby in Alabama; Paula Hawkins, topped by former Governor Bob Graham in Florida; Mack Mattingly, defeated by Representative Wyche Fowler, Jr., in Georgia; James T. Broyhill, losing to former Governor Terry Sanford in North Carolina; Mark N. Andrews, beaten by state Tax Commissioner Kent Conrad in North Dakota; James Abdnor, defeated by Representative Thomas A. Daschle in South Dakota; and Slade Gorton, topped by former Representative Brock Adams in Washington.

Democrats also won two Senate seats that had been held by retiring Republicans. In Maryland, Representative Barbara A. Mikulski took the seat vacated by Charles McC. Mathias, Jr.; and in Nevada, Representative Harry M. Reid won the seat of Paul Laxalt. In Missouri, the seat of retiring Democratic Senator Thomas F. Eagleton was taken by former Republican Governor Christopher S. (Kit) Bond.

House. It was a banner year for incumbents in the House of Representatives. Only 1 sitting Democrat and 5 incumbent Republicans were defeated. In 43 House races not involving incumbents, Democrats won 22 and Republicans 21. Altogether, the Democrats gained 5 House seats, padding their margin to 258 to 177. The preelection division was 253 Democrats, 180 Republicans, and 2 vacancies. Blacks won 22 House seats, adding 2 to their total.

Two noteworthy Democratic victories occurred in Boston and Atlanta, Ga. In Boston, Joseph P. Kennedy II, 34, eldest son of the late Senator Robert F. Kennedy, won the seat vacated by retiring Speaker of the House Thomas P. (Tip) O'Neill, Jr., also a Democrat. The same seat had once been held by his uncle, Congressman—later President—John F. Kennedy. In Atlanta, John Lewis won an easy victory in his bid for the House. On September 2, Lewis had scored a stunning upset over Julian Bond, a fellow black civil rights leader, in a bitter runoff to represent most of Atlanta in Congress.

Governorships. Republicans gained 8 governorships but still trailed Democrats 26 to 24 in that department. Prior to the election, the GOP had lagged 34 to 16. Republican William P. Clements reclaimed the Texas governorship from Democrat Mark White, who had defeated him four years earlier. The only other losing incumbent was Democrat Anthony S. Earl of Wisconsin, defeated by state legislator Tommy G. Thompson. Tampa Mayor Bob Martinez, a former Democrat, was elected the first Hispanic governor of Florida. Guy Hunt, an Amway Corporation distributor, was chosen the first Republican governor of Alabama in 112 years. Altogether, Democrats won three

Winners in the November elections include, *clockwise from above,* Democrat Joseph P. Kennedy II of Massachusetts, who shakes a supporter's hand after gaining the congressional seat of retiring Democratic Speaker of the House Thomas P. (Tip) O'Neill, Jr.; Fred Grandy, formerly an actor on the TV series "The Love Boat," elected a Republican U.S. representative from Iowa; Democratic Congresswoman Barbara A. Mikulski of Maryland, winner of the Senate seat vacated by Republican Charles McC. Mathias, Jr., who did not seek reelection; and Guy Hunt, looking thoughtful as he meets the press after being elected the first Republican governor of Alabama in 112 years.

governorships from the GOP—in Oregon, Pennsylvania, and Tennessee. Republicans took 11 governor's chairs that had been held by Democrats—in Alabama, Arizona, Florida, Kansas, Maine, Nebraska, New Mexico, Oklahoma, South Carolina, Texas, and Wisconsin. In Nebraska, state Treasurer Kay A. Orr became the first Republican woman ever elected to a governorship.

Earlier Elections. Kenneth A. Gibson, who became the first black to head a major Northeastern city when he was elected mayor of Newark, N.J., in 1970, was defeated on May 13 in his bid for an unprecedented fifth term. He was upset by City Council member Sharpe James, also a black. In New Orleans, City Councilman Sidney J. Barthe-

lemy, a black, was elected on March 1 to succeed Ernest N. Dutch Morial, the city's first black mayor, who was prohibited by city law from running for a third consecutive term.

In Chicago, Harold Washington, elected in 1983 as the city's first black mayor, finally won control of the City Council when two allies won an April 29 runoff election. But perhaps as much attention was paid to the April 8 victory of actor Clint Eastwood, who ousted the mayor of Carmel-by-the-Sea, Calif. Frank Cormier and Margot Cormier

See also CONGRESS OF THE UNITED STATES; DEMOCRATIC PARTY; REPUBLICAN PARTY; STATE GOVERNMENT. In WORLD BOOK, see ELECTION.

ELECTRIC POWER. See ENERGY SUPPLY.

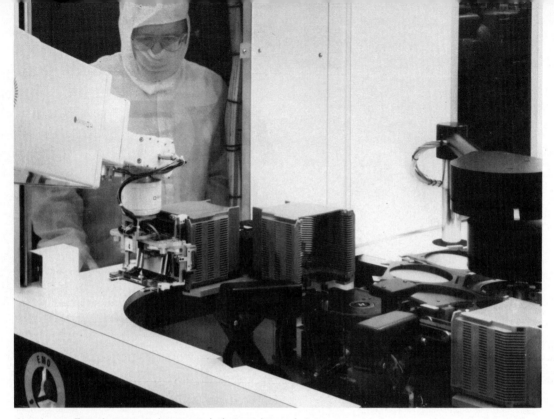

A worker at a Texas Instruments, Incorporated, plant watches a robot manufacture electronic chips that will hold 1 million bits of data.

ELECTRONICS. The electronics industry, still in the grip of a recession in 1986, did what it does best in hard times—develop and market new products and technologies. The emphasis on the new had a profound impact on the *semiconductor chip*, a piece of material—usually silicon—containing complete electronic circuits. A typical chip is about the size of a fingernail and contains many thousands of circuits.

In 1986, the next generation of a major type of *memory* (information-storage) chip began to gain ground about two years earlier than expected. This device is called a *dynamic random access memory* (*DRAM*) chip due to its reprogrammability and because it will lose its memory unless it gets an occasional jolt of electricity. Chip manufacturers measure generations in terms of the number of *bits*—0's and 1's of the binary numeration system—of information a chip can hold. Chips known as *256-kilobit* (*256K*) *DRAM's*—each capable of holding 262,144 bits—hit the market heavily in 1984, and were expected to give way to the *1-megabit* (*1-Mb*, or 1-million-bit) DRAM in 1988. As predicted, at the beginning of 1986, only three or four chip makers were circulating samples of about half a dozen 1-megabit DRAM's among potential customers—computer manufacturers. By the end of the year, however, at least six suppliers were ready to produce large quantities of such chips.

Even More Memory. Semiconductor companies also began to tool up for the 4-Mb DRAM, the probable successor to the 1-Mb DRAM. Industry observers expected the move to the 4-Mb device to be slower than the jump to the 1-Mb chip because it costs several million dollars to set up production facilities for each succeeding generation.

Thinner Lines. Chip makers in 1986 extended manufacturing technology to a new limit in producing the static RAM, which differs from the DRAM by not requiring electrical pulses to keep from losing its memory. Today's chips can hold so much data because the individual electronic components built into them are extremely small and the lines connecting the components are incredibly thin. In 1985, commercially available static RAM's had lines as thin as about 2 *microns* (a micron is one-millionth of a meter). In 1986, at least two static RAM chips with lines of just 1.25 to 1.50 microns thick appeared on the market.

Consumer Electronics also gained from new technology in 1986. Digital electronics moved into position to dominate audio and video equipment, enticing consumers with such products as videocassette recorders that provide special features including freeze-frame, slow playback, and picture search.　　　　　　　　　　　　Howard Wolff

See also COMPUTER. In WORLD BOOK, see ELECTRONICS.

EL SALVADOR. An earthquake rocked San Salvador, El Salvador's capital, on Oct. 10, 1986, destroying almost all the city's hospitals and thousands of houses. Doctors set up emergency tent facilities, and the world watched via television the pitiful spectacle of rescuers searching in the rubble for the living and the dead.

The Quake, which left more than 1,200 people dead and tens of thousands homeless, was followed by more than 900 aftershocks. It was one of a long-series of earthquakes that have devastated heavily populated cities along the so-called Median Trough, a fault that extends through Central America.

In the immediate aftermath of the quake, rebels fighting the Salvadoran government declared a truce. The ability of the government to care for quake victims soon became a prime test of the effectiveness of President José Napoleón Duarte's administration. Some critics charged that poor neighborhoods devastated by the quake were neglected by government relief efforts. To show support for a country now as ravaged by nature as by civil war, United States Secretary of State George P. Shultz toured San Salvador on October 16 and pledged $50 million in emergency aid.

Civil War. Early in 1986, the government's efforts to put down a seven-year-old rebellion appeared to be going well, with the United States supplying $1 million a day in economic and military aid. Salvadoran forces undertook a sustained offensive in January to clear out guerrillas from Guazapá Volcano near San Salvador. From positions on the hillsides of the volcano, guerrillas had menaced vital roads and communications.

At the insistence of U.S. officials, Salvadoran government forces staged well-orchestrated efforts in 1986 to win the hearts and minds of the Salvadoran people. To attract local townspeople to propaganda films, government forces hired mariachi bands and scantily clad dancers. With funding from U.S. churches, Protestant evangelists in El Salvador mounted a campaign using church-owned radio stations to persuade people to identify with the government in the battle against Marxist guerrillas.

The Economy, though still battered by conflict, was somewhat bolstered by a drought in Brazil that affected the Brazilian coffee crop. The drought boosted El Salvador's earnings from coffee, which brings in more than half of El Salvador's export revenue.   Nathan A. Haverstock

See also LATIN AMERICA (Facts in Brief Table). In WORLD BOOK, see EL SALVADOR.

EMPLOYMENT. See ECONOMICS; LABOR.

ENDANGERED SPECIES. See CONSERVATION.

Troops watch over the ruins of a building in San Salvador, capital of El Salvador, following an earthquake in October that killed some 1,200 people.

ENERGY SUPPLY

The worst accident in the history of nuclear power occurred on April 26, 1986, near Kiev in the Soviet Union. The Chernobyl nuclear power station exploded and burned, spewing radioactive particles into the atmosphere. At least 31 people died either in the accident or from radiation sickness. See Close-Up.

Nuclear Power Growth. Despite increased concern about the safety of nuclear power plants following the Chernobyl disaster, nuclear power generated a growing proportion of the world's electricity in 1986. On September 25, the United States Department of Energy (DOE) reported that the 98 operable nuclear power plants in the United States generated 5 per cent more electricity during the first half of 1986 than during the same period in 1985. In addition, the 310 nuclear plants operating in non-Communist countries generated 10 per cent more electricity during the first half of 1986 than during the same period in 1985.

Energy Plan. A new national energy plan, issued by the DOE on March 26, called for the complete elimination of federal price controls on natural gas and for greater efforts to encourage exploration for new domestic sources of natural gas and oil on federal lands and offshore areas. The DOE promised government support for scientific efforts to find new ways of burning coal—the most abundant U.S. energy source—with less pollution.

In an effort to encourage the growth of nuclear power, the plan proposed streamlining the licensing process for new nuclear power plants, developing safe ways of disposing of nuclear waste, and easing export barriers for nuclear power plant components.

Synfuels Shut-Down. The United States ambitious attempt to become self-sufficient in energy through development of a domestic synthetic fuels industry ended on April 18, when the U.S. Synthetic Fuels Corporation officially went out of existence. The corporation was created by Congress in 1980 to develop the technology for converting coal and other abundant domestic energy resources into gas and other fuels. But declining oil prices led Congress to declare the effort too costly and to eliminate funding for the corporation.

In July 1986, a U.S. District Court in North Dakota transferred legal ownership of the Great Plains coal gasification plant, the only full-scale synthetic fuels plant in the United States, to the

DOE. The five energy companies that developed the plant, located near Beulah, N. Dak., defaulted on $1.5 billion in federal loans to build and operate the plant and abandoned the project in 1985. The DOE continued to operate the plant, which converts low-grade coal into synthetic gas.

NRC Fine. The U.S. Nuclear Regulatory Commission (NRC) on Oct. 15, 1986, announced a $310,000 fine against Sequoyah Fuels Corporation in Gore, Okla., a subsidiary of the Kerr-McGee Corporation. The NRC cited the plant, a uranium-processing facility, for safety violations that led to the death of a worker on January 4.

Diablo Canyon Decision. The owners of the Diablo Canyon nuclear power plant near San Luis Obispo, Calif., on October 20 won an 18-year fight to operate the plant. The Supreme Court of the United States refused to hear a challenge to a ruling by a lower court upholding NRC approval of the plant's license. Environmentalists had argued that the NRC should not have licensed the plant, which lies near an earthquake fault, without requiring preparation of an emergency evacuation plan in case an earthquake and a nuclear accident occurred at the same time.

Daylight-Saving Time. President Ronald Reagan on July 8 signed into law a bill intended to save energy by extending daylight-saving time. Under the law, which takes effect in 1987, Americans will set their clocks one hour ahead on the first Sunday of April, rather than on the last. Supporters of the legislation said that the extra hours of afternoon daylight will conserve electricity. Opponents charged that the savings would be small and that the law will increase the risk of accidents for schoolchildren and farmers, who will be forced to start their day before sunrise.

Energy Outlook. A new report on the United States energy outlook during the 1990's predicted on March 5, 1986, that energy consumption would increase by about 10 per cent by 1995. The report, prepared by the DOE, said that U.S. petroleum production would decline from about 11 million barrels per day (bpd) in 1985 to less than 9 million bpd in 1995. In contrast, demand is expected to increase from 15.7 million bpd to about 16.4 million bpd. Falling production and rising demand are expected to result in higher oil imports, with imports accounting for about half of all oil consumed in the United States by 1995, compared with 40 per cent in 1986.

United States natural gas production is expected to remain steady until 1990 and then decline slightly. The DOE predicted that, as a result, natural gas imports from Canada would rise. According to the DOE, demand for electricity will increase by about 2.7 per cent per year—faster than that for any other form of energy. The DOE said that the production of electricity from coal and

Explosion at Chernobyl

At about 1:23 A.M. on April 26, 1986, a hydrogen explosion ripped apart a nuclear reactor at the Soviet Union's Chernobyl power station in Pripyat, about 70 miles (110 kilometers) north of Kiev, initiating the worst nuclear accident in history. The explosion blew the roof off the plant building and ignited more than 30 fires. It also lofted radioactive debris—including extremely radioactive nuclear fuel—into the environment.

Within 48 hours of the explosion, more than 200 medical teams had been airlifted to the plant site, where they examined some 1,000 people. The teams sent the 299 most severely injured victims to Moscow hospitals.

Most of the world did not learn of the accident until April 28, when researchers in Sweden detected radiation over a nuclear power station there. At first, they suspected that the radiation was coming from one of the reactors at the Swedish station. But it soon became clear that air blowing from the Soviet Union was carrying radioactive debris into Sweden.

Before long, fallout from Chernobyl was raining down throughout Europe. Radiation in the air reached 100,000 times the normal amount in Poland and 10,000 times normal in Scotland. Fallout contaminated farm vegetables and the forage of cows and sheep. Many European nations destroyed foods with radiation levels that appeared unsafe.

Masked workers hose down a contaminated area in an effort to control radioactivity at the crippled Chernobyl power station.

The Soviets worked for about two weeks to cool the reactor enough so that they could begin to clean up the plant. To help absorb heat that was lofting radioactive materials skyward, they dropped about 5,000 short tons (4,500 metric tons) of sand, clay, lead, and other materials onto the flaming debris. They also dug tunnels under the reactor and pumped liquid nitrogen through the tunnels to remove heat. The measures proved effective, but not before about 3.5 per cent of the radioactive material in the reactor had escaped.

Details of the accident emerged in late August at a conference of the International Atomic Energy Agency in Vienna, Austria. There, the Soviets reported numerous errors made by the reactor operators. According to the Soviets, workers who were testing a *turbine-generator*—an electric generator that runs on steam supplied by the reactor—lost control of the reactor. A sudden, large surge in reactor power set in motion a chain of events that led to the hydrogen explosion.

The report also acknowledged that other Soviet plants designed like the Chernobyl station have numerous safety flaws. One of the most serious flaws is that these plants have no *reactor vessel*—a steel enclosure built to contain radioactive materials that otherwise might escape during an accident. Most Western reactors have such vessels.

By year-end, the accident had claimed the lives of at least 31 Soviets—mainly fire fighters and plant workers. But the final death toll was expected to climb much higher. Calculations based on figures supplied by the Soviets suggested that, in the next 30 years, radioactivity from Chernobyl may cause 6,500 to 40,000 deaths due to cancer in the western part of the Soviet Union.

The accident has not changed the Soviet Union's plan to develop nuclear power. In several other European countries, however, the Chernobyl disaster prompted moves to reevaluate reactor safety or even the very need for nuclear power.

The nuclear industry in the United States considered its plants relatively safe from the degree of failure seen at Chernobyl. Nevertheless, by the fall of 1986, U.S. nuclear experts already had begun to talk of developing more reliable and quicker-acting safeguards for reactors.

The accident may rekindle interest in the development of an *inherently safe* nuclear reactor, one that could essentially shut itself down without the aid of human operators. Researchers in the United States, Sweden, and West Germany have been experimenting with such reactors for several years.   Janet Raloff

nuclear power will ensure ample supplies, and that the cost of electricity—unlike other forms of energy—is expected to decline.

Coal production is expected to increase by about 2 per cent per year, with only slight increases in price. Coal will continue to be the major energy source exported by the United States, with exports reaching 100 million short tons (91 million metric tons) per year by 1995, the DOE said.

Canadian Sale. Canada on Feb. 14, 1986, announced the largest export sale of hydroelectric power in that nation's history. Manitoba Hydro, a provincial utility, agreed to sell about $2 billion worth of electricity from 1993 to 1996 to the Upper Mississippi Power Group and Northern States Power Company, consortiums of U.S. utilities.

Waste Storage Sites. The DOE announced on May 28, 1986, that sites in Nevada, Texas, and Washington had been selected as candidates for the United States first permanent disposal site for spent nuclear fuel and other highly radioactive wastes. The candidate sites were Deaf Smith County, Texas; Yucca Mountain in Nevada; and the Hanford Nuclear Reservation in Washington. Each site will undergo studies before the DOE selects a site by the 1994 deadline imposed by law.

Midland Conversion. Consumers Power Company of Jackson, Mich., and the Dow Chemical Company in September signed an agreement in principle to convert the mothballed Midland nuclear power plant in Michigan to a gas-fired facility. Construction on the $4.1-billion facility began in 1967 and was about 85 per cent completed when work was halted in 1984.

Dow, originally a partner in the project, withdrew when costs escalated. The two firms then filed $520 million in lawsuits against each other. Under the new agreement, Consumers and Dow were to end the litigation and invest an additional $560 million to convert the plant into a facility that will burn natural gas to produce both steam and electricity.

Hotter Than the Sun. On Aug. 7, 1986, the DOE announced "a major milestone" in efforts to develop fusion energy. The DOE said that an experimental fusion reactor at Princeton University's Plasma Physics Laboratory in New Jersey had achieved a temperature of 200 million degrees Celsius, roughly 400 million degrees Fahrenheit. The temperature, 10 times hotter than that at the center of the sun, was the highest ever recorded in a laboratory and was within the range necessary for a fusion reaction to occur. Unlike a fission reaction—which powers all existing nuclear reactors—a fusion reaction does not produce radioactive waste. Michael Woods

See also COAL; PETROLEUM AND GAS. In WORLD BOOK, see ENERGY SUPPLY.

ENGINEERING. See BUILDING AND CONSTRUCTION.

ENGLAND. On Feb. 5, 1986, less than three months before a disaster at the Chernobyl nuclear plant in the Soviet Union, a faulty pump caused a radiation leak at Sellafield in Cumbria, Great Britain's main nuclear waste disposal plant. This was the first of two leaks at Sellafield—a second leak was reported on February 18. As a result of the leaks, British Nuclear Fuels, the government-owned company that runs Sellafield, announced that it would give certain nongovernment inspectors more access to the plant and would publicize any future radiation leaks.

The question of where to dump nuclear waste also caused concern in 1986. Four English villages were selected as test dumping sites for nuclear waste: Bradwell in the county of Essex, Fulbeck in the county of Lincolnshire, Elstow in the county of Bedfordshire, and South Killingholme in the county of Humberside. Drilling at the sites was held up because of local protests.

The Royal Year. On March 31, a fire at Hampton Court in London destroyed two floors of the south wing and damaged several Renaissance art treasures. In other respects, it was a good year for the royal family. Queen Elizabeth II of Great Britain celebrated her 60th birthday on April 21. The highlight of the day came when 6,000 daffodil-waving children sang her a birthday song.

On July 23, Prince Andrew, the second son of Queen Elizabeth, married Sarah Ferguson. See GREAT BRITAIN (Close-Up).

Queen Elizabeth made a successful tour of China in October. The tour was the first by a reigning British monarch.

Boy George Arrested. On July 12, London police arrested singing star Boy George and charged him with heroin possession. The arrest came two days after he announced his addiction to heroin. Boy George was convicted and fined 250 pounds (about $375) for his offense, a light sentence that angered many members of Parliament.

Deaths. Pat Phoenix, 62, the Irish-born actress who starred in the television soap opera "Coronation Street," died of lung cancer on September 17. Police Constable Philip Olds, 34—shot and paralyzed in a 1980 robbery—died on Oct. 1, 1986. His efforts to walk again encouraged many handicapped people. The year ended with the death on December 29 of Harold Macmillan, Earl of Stockton. Macmillan, 92, was Britain's prime minister from January 1957 until October 1963.

Hippies Reemerge. The word *hippies* returned to English newspaper headlines in May when a convoy of 300 people, mostly unemployed and driving decrepit vehicles, camped illegally in the field of a Somerset farmer. The convoy was evicted under a court order and later broken up by police. On June 20, some 200 hippies were arrested by police near the ancient monument of Stonehenge when they tried to hold an illegal summer solstice festival.

Sports. England's soccer team was eliminated in the first round of the 1986 World Cup when it lost to Argentina on June 22 in Mexico. On September 27, London welterweight boxer Lloyd Honeyghan, 26, beat United States champion Donald Curry to win the undisputed world title.

The year did not go well for England's national cricket team. Having lost every match in their winter Test series against the West Indies, they also lost the summer series at home against India and New Zealand.

In April, the Somerset team's star Ian Botham was suspended for two months because of his use of illegal drugs and his disrespect toward the Test and County Cricket Board. Botham still managed to take his 356th Test wicket by the end of August, however, setting a new world record.

For the first time in 11 years, Cambridge University beat Oxford University on March 29 in the 132nd Boat Race on the River Thames. On June 29, recording millionaire Richard Branson, 36, broke the record for the fastest transatlantic crossing aboard his powerboat *Virgin Atlantic Challenger II*. He completed the trip in 3 days 8 hours 40 minutes.   William James Gould

See also GREAT BRITAIN. In WORLD BOOK, see ENGLAND.

ENVIRONMENTAL POLLUTION. The worst release of radioactive material from a nuclear power plant occurred on April 26, 1986, at the town of Pripyat, near Kiev, in the Soviet Union. An explosion and fire at the Chernobyl reactor at Pripyat released a cloud of radioactive debris that contaminated large sections of the world. The accident killed at least 31 people by year-end and forced the evacuation of almost 100,000 residents. More than 200 people suffered radiation sickness. By some estimates, the accident could cause an additional 6,500 to 40,000 cancer deaths by 2016, mostly in and around the Soviet Union.

Unsafe levels of fallout were detected in areas of Eastern Europe, a region with about 120 million people. Worldwide, the atmosphere was contaminated with radioactivity, some of which fell to Earth in rain. The first Chernobyl fallout was detected in the United States on May 5, but the U.S. Environmental Protection Agency (EPA) reported radioactivity levels were far below those that would cause concern.

By October, thousands of reindeer that normally provide a livelihood for many Lapp people in the Arctic areas of Sweden and Norway had to be slaughtered because of radioactive contamination. Elsewhere in Western Europe, farmers suffered millions of dollars worth of crop losses. Fish in some places were unfit to eat. The Chernobyl

accident resulted in major reappraisals of reactor safety and nuclear-emergency planning around the world. See ENERGY SUPPLY (Close-Up).

Rhine River Spill. Western Europe faced a major ecological disaster in November after a warehouse fire in Basel, Switzerland, released poisonous chemicals into the Rhine River. Swiss officials estimated that 10 to 30 short tons (9 to 27 metric tons) of chemicals, including dyes, insecticides, and mercury, were spilled into the river.

France, West Germany, the Netherlands, and Switzerland closed all drinking-water plants along the Rhine and banned fishing. They also closed locks and sluices in an attempt to prevent polluted water from entering the Rhine's tributaries. Government officials and ecologists feared that most life in the river would be destroyed and that it would take years for the Rhine to recover from the disaster.

Radon Hazards. Indoor pollution by the naturally occurring radioactive gas radon was a cause for increased concern during the year. On August 14, the EPA set a health guideline for safe levels of radon gas in homes—4 picocuries (a unit for measuring radioactivity) per liter (61 cubic inches) of air. Readings of hundreds of picocuries have been found in some homes. The EPA estimated that the levels in 8 million U.S. residences exceed the limit. The agency planned to test 20,000 homes nationwide to determine the average level of radon as well as locate "hot spots" of high radon production.

Radon—a tasteless, odorless, colorless gas—is produced by natural radium decay in soil and rock around the world. Trapped in airtight, energy-efficient homes, it could be responsible for 5,000 to 20,000 lung cancer deaths annually in the United States, according to public health experts.

Radon also contaminates drinking water. The EPA in September said it planned to propose rules on permissible amounts of radioactivity in drinking water. Some experts think radioactive water might cause as many as 730 U.S. cancer deaths a year. Current drinking-water rules cover only radium and artificially made radioactive materials, not naturally occurring radon.

Superfund Returns. A $9-billion Superfund program for cleaning up toxic waste dumps was adopted by Congress and signed into law by President Ronald Reagan on October 17. The measure was hailed as a major environmental breakthrough after months of uncertainty over the fate of the program.

Leaks from hazardous waste dumps are among the top environmental concerns in the United States. Superfund, originally adopted in 1980 and funded at $1.6 billion, expired on Sept. 30, 1985. Only weeks before passage of the new Superfund program, EPA Administrator Lee M. Thomas

Where Polluted Rain Falls

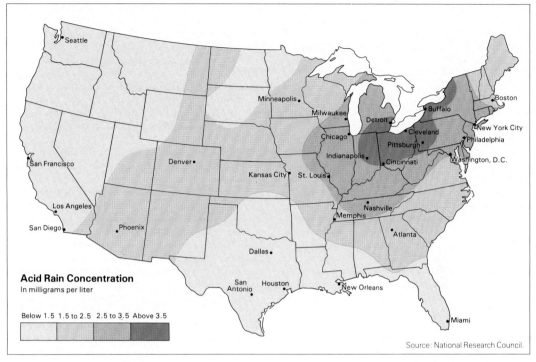

Acid Rain Concentration
In milligrams per liter

Below 1.5   1.5 to 2.5   2.5 to 3.5   Above 3.5

Source: National Research Council.

warned members of Congress that he would soon be forced to terminate Superfund activities and lay off 1,500 EPA workers because the program was running out of money.

The Reagan Administration had recommended that no more than $5.3 billion be authorized for the toxic waste fund. But, facing congressional override of a veto, Reagan signed the bill.

The EPA has identified 888 sites that endanger public health and the environment and require Superfund attention. Since 1981, the EPA has conducted 780 emergency cleanup actions and completed cleanup operations at 13 hazardous waste dumps.

The new Superfund program greatly expands the scope of cleanup efforts. Under the new law, the EPA must clean up at least 375 sites over the next five years. The law also contains so-called "community-right-to-know" provisions requiring chemical companies to inform local governments and residents about potentially dangerous chemicals at nearby chemical plants. The companies are expected to report spills or routine emissions of chemicals that could cause health hazards.

Clean Water Issues. Congress on May 21, 1986, passed changes in the 1974 Safe Drinking Water Act giving the EPA three years to set maximum levels for 83 hazardous contaminants found in drinking water. Reagan signed the measure on

June 19, 1986. More than 700 drinking-water contaminants are known, and by 1986 the EPA had set maximum acceptable levels for 22. The law also called for creation of a program to guard against chemical pollution of underground water.

On October 16, Congress passed amendments to the 1972 Clean Water Act authorizing $18 billion in federal grants to states for building sewage- and wastewater-treatment plants. Reagan vetoed the measure on Nov. 6, 1986.

Pesticides and Herbicides. The General Accounting Office (GAO), the investigative arm of Congress, in April issued a report saying that most of the 50,000 pesticide products registered for use in the United States have not been fully tested for health effects. In 1972, Congress had given the EPA four years in which to reevaluate all older pesticides. The GAO said that as of March 31, 1986, the EPA had still not completed a final reassessment of any of the 600 active pesticide ingredients on the market. Preliminary assessments had been made on 124 ingredients.

On October 2, the EPA proposed limited restrictions on alachlor, the most widely used agricultural herbicide in the United States. The new rules are intended to protect farmworkers by requiring those who apply the weedkiller to be certified as competent to handle the chemical. The pesticide must be labeled as a potential health hazard. The agency took no steps to limit how much of the herbicide may be used or where, despite evidence that residues on food and in drinking water might cause cancer.

On October 7, the EPA issued an emergency order banning the use of dinoseb, a widely used herbicide that had been linked to birth defects and sterility.

Asbestos Cleanup. A phase-out of the use of asbestos over the next 10 years was proposed by the EPA on January 23. The phase-out would cost about $2 billion. Once called a "miracle fiber" and widely used in building materials such as insulation and tile, asbestos is believed responsible for 3,300 to 12,000 U.S. cancer deaths a year. About 65,000 people in the United States suffer from *asbestosis*, a scarring of the lungs that impairs breathing and eventually causes death. The EPA calculates that the asbestos phase-out would avoid 1,900 cancer deaths over the next 15 years.

A law was passed by Congress and signed by Reagan in October requiring the EPA to toughen its program for removing asbestos products from an estimated 35,000 schools attended by 15 million students.   Casey Bukro

See also CONSERVATION; WATER. In the Special Reports section, see PROBLEMS IN THE PARKS. In WORLD BOOK, see ENVIRONMENTAL POLLUTION.

EQUATORIAL GUINEA. See AFRICA.

ETHIOPIA. Drought and famine eased in most areas of Ethiopia in 1986 except for the Hārargē region in the east. Refugees from several parts of Ethiopia nonetheless continued to strain United Nations (UN) relief efforts in Sudan and Somalia.

Critics of the Marxist regime of Lieutenant Colonel Mengistu Haile-Mariam charged that the famine was due more to government policies than to the environment. Relief supplies of grain were allegedly denied to the northern rebel strongholds in Shoa and Gemu Gofa provinces, were bartered for Soviet arms, and were used to lure into refugee camps many of the 600,000 northerners who were then forcibly relocated in the south. Roughly 100,000 people died in the forced move, which was part of a larger, long-term resettlement of 30 million peasants into villages. Although the Mengistu government insisted that the new area was more fertile and less densely populated, it was more subject to malaria and other diseases. In addition, the relocation further disrupted the planting, harvesting, and marketing of crops.

Socialist Transformation. Another apparent reason for the large-scale resettlements was the government's program of *villagization*—the replacement of individual landholding with collective and state-run farms. Villagization is part of Mengistu's plan for firmly establishing Marxist socialism in Ethiopia. The villagization program also helped

the ruling Workers' Party of Ethiopia tighten its control over the populace.

In September, Ethiopia's leaders approved a new Soviet-style constitution that emphasized the key role of the Workers' Party in a highly centralized state. The government rejected demands by Ethiopia's many ethnic and religious minorities for greater freedom. Foreign Minister Goshu Wolde, protesting the regime's totalitarianism, announced his resignation in October. Goshu was only the latest of several high-ranking officials to resign in 1986.

Foreign Relations. The Soviet Union continued to supply military and economic assistance to the Ethiopian government, including logistical support for 25,000 Cuban troops stationed in Ethiopia. The Cubans, in 1985 and 1986, participated in an unsuccessful military offensive against rebels in the regions of Tigre and Eritrea.

In January, for the first time since 1977—when Somalia invaded Ethiopia in an effort to reclaim the Ogaden area as part of the Somali nation—the two countries started peace talks. Mengistu also negotiated with Sudan in midyear to end support for exiled dissidents in each other's countries. Ethiopia's relations with the United States remained strained.   J. Gus Liebenow and Beverly B. Liebenow

See also AFRICA (Facts in Brief Table). In WORLD BOOK, see ETHIOPIA.

EUROPE. Three events dominated European affairs in 1986. The first was the United States air attack on Libya on April 15. The United States struck Libya because of what the U.S. called "irrefutable proof" of Libya's involvement in international terrorism.

The attack had two adverse effects in Europe. Many political figures in Great Britain and other European countries condemned British Prime Minister Margaret Thatcher for having allowed U.S. aircraft to take off from bases in Great Britain to strike Libya. And the attack cost Europe millions of dollars in tourist business because many U.S. residents who feared reprisals by Libya canceled vacation trips to Europe.

The second dominant event was a nuclear disaster at the Soviet Union's Chernobyl power station near Kiev. On April 26, a nuclear reactor at the station exploded, spewing radioactive debris into the air. By year-end, the accident had killed at least 31 people in the Soviet Union. In addition, radioactive substances carried by winds contaminated crops and livestock in many other European countries.

The third event was the struggle of leaders of the 12-nation European Community (EC or Common Market)—meeting in The Hague, the Netherlands, on June 26 and 27—to agree on *sanctions* (penalties) against South Africa. The proposed

West Berliners protest at the Berlin Wall in August to mark the 25th anniversary of the beginning of construction on the wall.

sanctions were intended to express the EC's disapproval of South Africa's policy of *apartheid* (racial segregation). Most EC nations wanted to impose strong sanctions, but Great Britain, Portugal, and West Germany held out for negotiations with South Africa. (The other nine EC nations are Belgium, Denmark, France, Greece, Ireland, Italy, Luxembourg, the Netherlands, and Spain.)

Libya Raid. The first U.S. move against Libya was nonviolent. On January 7, the United States imposed economic sanctions against Libya because of what U.S. President Ronald Reagan called Libya's support of international terrorism. The EC did not follow suit, but it did agree on January 28 not to export military equipment to "countries clearly implicated in supporting terrorism."

The EC's attitude toward Libya hardened after two terrorist bombings in April. On April 2, a bomb exploded in a Trans World Airlines jet approaching Athens, Greece, killing four passengers. On April 5, a bomb exploded in a crowded nightclub in West Berlin, West Germany, killing three people, including two U.S. servicemen, and injuring more than 200. Reagan said he had evidence linking Libya with these bombings and ordered the air strike on Libya.

The raid disturbed many European governments. The Netherlands, which held the presidency of the EC's executive branch, the Council of Ministers, called the U.S. action "a slap in the face" for Europe.

European diplomats worried that the raid would split the North Atlantic Treaty Organization (NATO), because NATO's southern states—Greece, Spain, and Italy—feared Arab reprisals against U.S. bases and other facilities on their soil. (The members of NATO are Canada, Iceland, Norway, Turkey, and the United States, plus all the EC nations except Ireland.) On April 21, EC foreign ministers decided to reduce the number of Libyan diplomats in Europe and to confine them to capital cities.

Tourism Hit. The flow of U.S. tourists to Europe dropped sharply soon after the raid. On August 3, France and Greece reported a decrease of 60 per cent from 1985; Italy, 45 per cent; Spain, 40 per cent; and Denmark, 30 per cent. But the royal wedding of Great Britain's Prince Andrew and Sarah Ferguson on July 23 boosted tourism from the United States. Britain lost only 30 per cent of its expected American visitors.

After the Chernobyl Disaster, Scandinavian governments advised their citizens not to drink or use rain water, and outlawed cattle-grazing in many areas. They also feared that between 10,000 and 30,000 reindeer—on which Lapps depend for their livelihood—would have to be destroyed. Authorities as far away as Italy and Britain banned

313

Facts in Brief on European Countries

Country	Population	Government	Monetary Unit*	Foreign Trade (million U.S. $) Exports†	Imports†
Albania	3,181,000	Communist Party First Secretary and People's Assembly Presidium Chairman Ramiz Alia; Prime Minister Adil Çarçani	lek (7.1 = $1)	290	280
Andorra	43,000	The bishop of Urgel, Spain, and the president of France	French franc & Spanish peseta	no statistics available	
Austria	7,487,000	President Kurt Waldheim; Chancellor Franz Vranitzky	schilling (13.8 = $1)	17,239	20,986
Belgium	9,884,000	King Baudouin I; Prime Minister Wilfried A. E. Martens	franc (41 = $1)	53,669 (includes Luxembourg)	56,147
Bulgaria	9,293,000	Communist Party General Secretary & State Council Chairman Todor Zhivkov; Prime Minister Georgi Atanasov	lev (1 = $1.08)	12,200	12,000
Czechoslovakia	15,772,000	Communist Party General Secretary & President Gustáv Husák; Prime Minister Lubomir Strougal	koruna (5.7 = $1)	17,398	17,585
Denmark	5,142,000	Queen Margrethe II; Prime Minister Poul Schlüter	krone (7.4 = $1)	17,081	18,246
Finland	4,900,000	President Mauno Koivisto; Prime Minister Kalevi Sorsa	markka (4.9 = $1)	13,631	13,241
France	55,182,000	President François Mitterrand; Prime Minister Jacques Chirac	franc (6.4 = $1)	101,674	108,341
Germany, East	16,616,000	Communist Party Secretary General & State Council Chairman Erich Honecker; Prime Minister Willi Stoph	mark (3.43 = $1)	25,180	22,970
Germany, West	60,920,000	President Richard von Weizsäcker; Chancellor Helmut Kohl	Deutsche mark (1.97 = $1)	183,912	158,489
Great Britain	56,616,000	Queen Elizabeth II; Prime Minister Margaret Thatcher	pound (1 = $1.44)	101,248	108,957
Greece	10,042,000	President Christos Sartzetakis; Prime Minister Andreas Papandreou	drachma (136.6 = $1)	4,539	10,134
Hungary	10,810,000	Communist Party First Secretary János Kádár; President Pál Losonczi; Prime Minister György Lázár	forint (46.7 = $1)	8,538	8,224
Iceland	246,000	President Vigdis Finnbogadottir; Prime Minister Steingrimur Hermannsson	krona (40.6 = $1)	743	844
Ireland	3,675,000	President Patrick J. Hillery; Prime Minister Garret FitzGerald	pound (punt) (1 = $1.39)	10,357	10,018
Italy	57,128,000	President Francesco Cossiga; Prime Minister Bettino Craxi	lira (1,365 = $1)	79,024	91,123
Liechtenstein	28,000	Prince Franz Josef II; Prime Minister Hans Brunhart	Swiss franc	no statistics available	
Luxembourg	368,000	Grand Duke Jean; Prime Minister Jacques Santer	franc (42.7 = $1)	53,669	56,147
Malta	387,000	President Agatha Barbara; Prime Minister Karmenu Mifsud Bonnici	lira (1 = $2.64)	394	718
Monaco	29,000	Prince Rainier III	French franc	no statistics available	
Netherlands	14,600,000	Queen Beatrix; Prime Minister Ruud Lubbers	guilder (2.22 = $1)	68,257	65,197
Norway	4,167,000	King Olav V; Prime Minister Gro Harlem Brundtland	krone (7.49 = $1)	19,858	15,557
Poland	38,173,000	Communist Party First Secretary & President Wojciech Jaruzelski; Council of Ministers Chairman Zbigniew Messner	zloty (196 = $1)	17,448	16,197
Portugal	10,207,000	President Mário Soares; Prime Minister Aníbal Cavaço Silva	escudo (146 = $1)	5,685	7,652
Romania	23,396,000	Communist Party General Secretary & President Nicolae Ceauşescu; Prime Minister Constantin Dăscălescu	leu (4.3 = $1)	12,600	10,300
Russia	283,620,000	Communist Party General Secretary Mikhail S. Gorbachev; Supreme Soviet Presidium Chairman Andrei A. Gromyko; Council of Ministers Chairman Nikolai I. Ryzhkov	ruble (1 = $1.09)	91,492	80,352
San Marino	24,000	2 captains regent appointed by Grand Council every 6 months	Italian lira	no statistics available	
Spain	39,629,000	King Juan Carlos I; President Felipe González Márquez	peseta (133 = $1)	24,247	29,963
Sweden	8,340,000	King Carl XVI Gustaf; Prime Minister Ingvar Carlsson	krona (6.9 = $1)	30,457	28,522
Switzerland	6,347,000	President Alphons Egli	franc (1.64 = $1)	27,450	30,702
Turkey	52,340,000	President Kenan Evren; Prime Minister Turgut Ozal	lira (747 = $1)	7,958	11,035
Yugoslavia	23,503,000	President of the Presidency Sinan Hasani; Federal Executive Council President Branko Mikulić	dinar (433 = $1)	10,700	12,207

*Exchange rates as of Dec. 1, 1986, or latest available data. †Latest available data.

sales of some foods and livestock contaminated by radiation. Norway warned its citizens not to eat freshwater fish and said on June 17 that radioactivity had affected reindeer, cattle, deer, elk, and even bears. The EC banned all East European food, then later replaced the ban with a system of monitoring food imports.

Compensation Sought. The European Parliament—the EC's legislature—called on May 15 for an international conference to establish nuclear safety rules. Parliament also criticized Moscow's "underhanded attempts to conceal its responsibility" for the disaster and demanded that the Soviets pay its EC neighbors for damage to their crops and livestock.

Some European nations shelved plans for nuclear power plants. Austria decided to ship a new $525-million nuclear reactor near Vienna to China; the Netherlands halted plans for two $1.5-billion reactors; and Belgium delayed plans for its eighth reactor.

Antiapartheid Sanctions. In September 1985, the EC had imposed sanctions against South Africa, including bans on the sale of oil and military equipment to South Africa. At a June 26, 1986, meeting in The Hague, the EC leaders agreed to postpone a decision on further sanctions for three months. During this time, Britain's Foreign Secretary Sir Geoffrey Howe was to make a final try to start a dialogue with South Africa's State President Pieter Willem Botha. The measure of Howe's success would be Botha's willingness to free political prisoners, lift the ban on certain black political parties, and initiate talks with black leaders.

The EC leaders agreed that if Howe's mission failed, they would consider a ban on new investments in South Africa and on the importing of South African coal, iron, steel, and gold coins. There was angry reaction in the capitals of most of the EC's member countries, most of it directed at Thatcher.

Howe's mission was a total failure. Botha told him to "leave South Africa to the South Africans." On September 16, the EC agreed on the new sanctions, except for the coal ban.

Commonwealth Crisis. The sanctions issue isolated Great Britain from its partners in the Commonwealth—countries that formerly were part of the British Empire. Commonwealth leaders met in London from August 2 to 5 to discuss the imposition of sanctions against South Africa. Thatcher did not want to impose strong sanctions, but the others did. The leaders avoided an irreparable split by "agreeing to disagree" over the scale and timing of new sanctions.

Sanctions Against Syria. On November 10, the EC enacted sanctions against Syria at the urging of Great Britain, which blamed Syria for a terrorist incident at London's Heathrow Airport on

April 17. An Israeli guard at the airport discovered a bomb in a bag carried by a woman who was about to board an Israeli passenger jet. Great Britain said that Syrian military intelligence officers were behind the attempt to smuggle the bomb aboard the jet and broke diplomatic relations with Syria on October 24.

The November 10 sanctions included a ban on new arms deals with Syria, an end to high-level diplomatic contacts with Syria, a review of the activities of Syrian diplomats, and heightened surveillance of Syria's national airline. Greece refused to sign an EC statement blaming Syria for the airport incident.

Rhine Disaster. On November 1, a fire at a chemical warehouse near Basel, Switzerland, released an estimated 30 short tons (27 metric tons) of toxic chemicals into the Rhine River. Shortly thereafter, fish and eels in the river began to die by the hundreds of thousands. Poisons also killed plants and tiny animals that are the basis of the Rhine ecosystem. Switzerland offered to pay its neighbors along the Rhine—France, West Germany, and the Netherlands—for damage caused by the disaster.

U.S.-Iran Deal. A revelation about U.S. relations with Iran upset Western European leaders in late 1986. In November, President Reagan reported that the United States had been selling arms to Iran since 1985 and that profits from the sales had been channeled to *contra* rebels fighting the government of Nicaragua. The sales violated stated U.S. policy concerning trade with Iran, and the donation of profits to the contras may have violated U.S. law. See PRESIDENT OF THE UNITED STATES.

Budget Crisis. Great Britain caused a crisis on March 17 by obtaining an injunction in the European Court of Justice—the judicial branch of the EC—blocking extra spending that the EC had approved as part of the 1986 budget. The extra money would have met the cost of Spain's and Portugal's entry into the EC on Jan. 1, 1986, and other commitments. Great Britain would have had to provide $105 million of the extra money. On July 3, the Court of Justice ruled that the EC budget was illegal. The EC approved a new budget on July 10.

Food Surpluses. The EC's agriculture ministers attempted to decrease its stock of surplus food and wine during 1986. The EC sold 100,000 metric tons (110,000 short tons) of butter to the Soviet Union at about 10 per cent of the cost of storing the butter. Another 150,000 metric tons (165,000 short tons) of butter were fed to cattle. In July, it was reported that 11,000 metric tons (12,100 short tons) of beef were going into storage each week.

Snow Kills Troops. NATO called off military maneuvers in Norway on March 6, after a snow-

Speaking in April, King Juan Carlos I of Spain becomes the first foreign monarch to address a joint session of Great Britain's Parliament.

troleum Exporting Countries (OPEC) arranged cuts in oil production to force up world oil prices. Great Britain is not in OPEC; nevertheless, the OPEC action boosted the price of oil pumped from British wells in the North Sea from $10.90 per barrel to $15.

Trade Dispute. The EC quarreled with the United States over trade restrictions. The United States said that the terms under which Spain and Portugal joined the EC discriminated unfairly against the export of U.S. products, particularly grain, to those two countries. The United States threatened to retaliate against the EC by restricting the importing of EC products. On April 9, the EC issued a list of American products that it would restrict if the United States took measures against EC exports. The EC and the United States averted a trade war on July 2, reaching a six-month agreement on agricultural exports.

Trade friction increased again in December, when the United States threatened to retaliate for high EC tariffs on U.S. grain. Unless a settlement was reached in January 1987, the United States planned to impose stiff tariffs on some European foods and alcoholic beverages.   Kenneth Brown

See also the various European country articles. In WORLD BOOK, see EUROPE.

EXPLOSION. See DISASTERS; ENERGY SUPPLY (Close-Up).

slide in northern Norway killed 13 Norwegian soldiers. The maneuvers were to have involved 20,000 troops from eight countries.

Revaluation. On April 6, EC finance ministers changed the relative value of the currencies of several EC nations. They decreased the value of the French franc by 6 per cent relative to the West German Deutsche mark and by an average of 4.7 per cent against all other currencies of the European Monetary System (EMS)—a program that eight nations established in 1979 to stabilize their exchange rates. (All the EC members except Britain, Greece, Portugal, and Spain are in the EMS.)

The ministers increased the value of the Deutsche mark by 3 per cent, the Dutch guilder by 3 per cent, the Belgian and Luxembourg francs by 1 per cent, and the Danish krone by 1 per cent. (When a nation increases the value of its currency relative to that of another nation's currency, the exports of the revaluing nation become more expensive in the other nation.)

Oil Slump. Oil prices fell sharply throughout the world in early 1986. Because Great Britain exports a great deal of oil, the price plunge hurt the British economy and therefore decreased the value of Britain's currency, the pound. On July 14, the oil price fell to below $9 per barrel, and the value of the pound dropped to U.S. $1.4830.

On August 4, the 13-nation Organization of Pe-

FARM AND FARMING. Record drought in the South, torrential autumn rains in the Midwest, and fewer acres planted resulted in a smaller harvest in the United States in 1986. Nevertheless, production greatly exceeded domestic and foreign demand. Grain bins bulged as exports tumbled for the fifth consecutive year because foreign customers and competitors harvested larger crops. At the same time, the United States imported more products such as coffee and vegetables. For three months of 1986, farm imports surpassed exports for the first time since 1959.

Farm income lost in the market place was replaced by a record $25.8 billion in government income and price supports for fiscal year 1986, which ended on Sept. 30, 1986. Farmers continued to lose their farms, however, in the most difficult economic period for U.S. agriculture since the Great Depression of the 1930's.

U.S. Production. The 1986 harvest of corn—the largest U.S. crop, which is used mostly for livestock feed, sweeteners, and industrial products—was 7 per cent smaller than the record 1985 harvest. Nevertheless, it was the third largest crop ever, with farmers harvesting a record national average of 119.3 bushels per acre (0.4 hectare).

Wheat production was down 14 per cent, the smallest crop since 1978. Grain sorghum was down 19 per cent; soybeans, 4 per cent; cotton, 27

per cent; peanuts, 16 per cent; and rice, 4 per cent. Beef production rose 2 per cent; pork fell 5 per cent; and poultry rose 5.8 per cent.

Crop surpluses were so large as the 1986 harvest began that the United States still had a year's supply of wheat and an eight-month supply of corn in storage. Surplus crops were piled on the ground and on river barges.

Crop Acreage. Surpluses mounted, despite a five-year decline in crop acreage encouraged by government programs that require farmers to idle land to qualify for subsidies. Farmers planted 356 million acres (144 million hectares) in 1986, 18 million acres (7 million hectares) less than in 1985 and 8 per cent less than a 1981 peak of 387 million acres (157 million hectares).

A new soil-conservation program paid farmers to grow trees or grass instead of crops on land in danger of erosion from wind or water. In 1986, farmers took 9 million acres (3.6 million hectares) out of production. The program aims to idle five times that much land.

Drought and Flood. Southern states suffered their worst drought in the more than 100 years for which weather records have been kept. Because the South produces a relatively small percentage of key crops, the national impact of the drought was limited. But livestock feed supplies were so scarce in midsummer that farmers from 41 states shipped an estimated 600,000 short tons (540,000 metric tons) of hay to the South by airplane, train, and truck. Heavy rains and floods in the Midwest in the fall slowed harvesting and damaged some crops.

World Production. Despite a smaller U.S. crop, world wheat production rose 4 per cent in 1986, a record. Corn production declined by less than 1 per cent. Production of coarse grains, which include corn, was down 1 per cent. Rice production was down slightly. Soybean production rose 3 per cent to set a record. Global beef production fell slightly. Pork output rose 1 per cent and poultry, 4 per cent, both setting records.

Farm Crisis. Thousands of U.S. farmers lost their farms in 1986 as the farm crisis that began in 1980 continued. In August 1986, the U.S. Department of Agriculture (USDA) estimated that about 220,000 farms went bankrupt between 1981 and 1986, reducing the number of U.S. farms from 2.43 million to 2.21 million. The USDA said 53,670 farms were lost in 1985 and 60,310 in 1986, accelerating the pace of a 50-year decline in the number of American farms.

Farmers who lost their farms were victims of high interest rates of the 1980's combined with a sluggish demand for crops and livestock, heavy farming expenses, and a decline in the value of land used as collateral for debts accumulated during the agricultural expansion of the 1970's.

Agricultural Statistics, 1986
World Crop Production
(million units)

Crop	Units	1985-1986*	1986-1987*†	% U.S. 1986-1987
Coarse grains‡	Metric tons	844	837	30
Corn	Metric tons	481	474	44
Wheat	Metric tons	500	522	11
Rice (rough)	Metric tons	470	467	1
Barley	Metric tons	177	184	7
Soybeans	Metric tons	96	99	56
Cotton	Bales§	79	70	14
Coffee	Bags#	96.4	83	0.04
Sugar (centrifugal)	Metric tons	98.1	100.1	6

*Crop year. †Preliminary.
‡Corn, barley, sorghum, rye, oats, millet, and mixed grains.
§480 pounds (217.7 kilograms) net.
#132.3 pounds (60 kilograms).

Output of Major U.S. Crops
(millions of bushels)

Crop	1985-1986*	1986-1987*†
Corn	8,865	8,223
Sorghum	1,113	900
Wheat	2,425	2,077
Soybeans	2,099	2,009
Rice (rough)‡	136	131
Potatoes‡	407	352
Cotton§	13.4	9.78
Tobacco#	1,511	1,190

*Crop year. †Preliminary.
‡1 million hundredweight (45.4 million kilograms).
§1 million bales (480 million pounds) (217.4 million kilograms).
#1 million pounds (454,000 kilograms).

U.S. Production of Animal Products
(millions of pounds)

	1985-1986*	1986-1987*†
Beef	23,728	24,187
Pork	14,807	14,048
Total red meat‡	39,408	39,089
Eggs§	5,688	5,704
Turkey	2,942	3,311
Total milk#	1,405	1,463
Broilers	13,762	14,366

*Crop year. †Preliminary.
‡Beef, pork, veal, lamb, and mutton.
§1 million dozens.
#100 millions of pounds (45.4 million kilograms).

In April 1986, the USDA estimated that the average value of an acre of U.S. farmland had fallen by 29 per cent between 1981 and 1986, to $596. But the decline was more drastic in the hardest-hit states. The value of farmland fell by 59 per cent in Iowa and 55 per cent in Minnesota and Nebraska.

Credit Woes. In January 1986, the General Accounting Office, the investigative arm of Congress, estimated that half of the $28 billion in farm loans made by the Farmers Home Administration, an agency of the USDA, was in danger of default. In February, the agency began notifying 65,000 farmers who had fallen behind in debt repayments that they must arrange new financing or

An Illinois farmer loads hay for shipment to drought-stricken farms in the Southeast in July, one of many such donations in the summer of 1986.

face foreclosure. The action followed a decision in December 1985 to lift a two-year moratorium on farm foreclosures in an effort to collect $5.8 billion in delinquent loans.

In March 1986, to help banks ride out the farm crisis, federal banking regulators agreed to ease the amount of capital that banks, another source of credit to farmers, must have.

The Farm Credit System, a federally supervised farmer-owned network of banks, reported a loss of $2.7 billion in 1985, a record annual loss for any U.S. financial institution. In October 1986, Congress approved a law allowing the system's banks to extend the period for writing off losses.

Also in October, Congress passed a special bankruptcy law to give farmers a chance to stretch out or reduce payments to creditors and still remain in business. The law was patterned after bankruptcy provisions for farmers instituted during the Great Depression.

Agriculture Secretary. John R. Block, an Illinois farmer who had served as secretary of agriculture since 1981, resigned in February 1986. Richard E. Lyng, who was deputy secretary during the first four years of Block's tenure, became the 22nd secretary of agriculture in March. Lyng was the first secretary of agriculture from California, the nation's largest agricultural state. See LYNG, RICHARD E.

Imports, Exports. The 1985 farm law, which established U.S. agricultural programs for the next five years, had lowered the floor on price supports—thus lowering prices—to make U.S. farm products more competitive abroad. The law was most successful in raising rice and cotton sales, but its impact on other crops was disappointing. During 1986, the overall value of U.S. farm exports continued to fall in the face of tough international trade competition.

Agricultural imports surpassed exports in May, June, and July, creating the first U.S. farm-trade deficit since 1959, except for an artificial deficit during a 1971 dockworkers' strike.

When all farm exports and imports for fiscal year 1986 were added up, the U.S. farm trade surplus totaled $5.4 billion. It was the smallest surplus since a $2-billion surplus in 1972, at the start of the 1970's farm export boom. The USDA said agricultural exports in fiscal 1986 were $26.3 billion, down 40 per cent from a 1981 record of $43.8 billion. Imports rose to $20.9 billion in fiscal 1986, up 35 per cent from 1982.

Export Subsidies. A 1985 program to sell U.S. farm crops to selected countries at prices below market value had only limited results in 1986. An offer to sell subsidized wheat to the Soviet Union failed altogether. In fiscal year 1986, the Soviets bought 6.8 million metric tons (7.5 million short tons) of U.S. corn. But they bought only 152,500 metric tons (168,000 short tons) of U.S. wheat, refusing to buy the 4 million metric tons (4.4 million short tons) of wheat specified in a five-year U.S.-Soviet grain agreement in effect since 1983.

In August, President Ronald Reagan, at Lyng's urging, offered to sell the Soviets the 4 million metric tons of wheat for about $15 a ton less than its price on the U.S. market. The offer angered Australia, Canada, and other grain exporters that do not subsidize exports. In the end, the Soviets ignored the offer and bought a smaller amount of French wheat with a larger subsidy. The Soviets in 1986 needed fewer imports after harvesting a grain crop of 210 million metric tons (231 million short tons), the country's second largest crop ever after several years of disappointing harvests.

Trade Tensions flared in March after Spain and Portugal entered the European Community (EC or Common Market). After the EC placed quotas and tariffs on grain and soybeans imported by those two countries, most of which was coming from the United States, Reagan announced a plan to restrict an equal amount of EC farm products entering the United States. A temporary pact kept trade flowing, but the Europeans bought less grain and soybeans than the pact specified. In December, Reagan said he would impose 200 per cent duties on about $400 million in EC products, unless a settlement was reached in January 1987, to compensate for export losses.

In November 1986, Canada charged that U.S. farm programs established by the 1985 farm law had artificially lowered U.S. export prices. Canada imposed a duty equal to the alleged subsidy on imports of U.S. corn. It was the first such duty ever levied by Canada and the first ever levied against the United States.

Genetic Science. In January 1986, the USDA approved the limited sale of the first genetically engineered product for commercial agricultural use. The product is a virus developed as a vaccine against *pseudorabies*, a swine disease. (*Genetic engineering* is the insertion of genes from one organism into the genetic material of another.)

In March, the Environmental Protection Agency (EPA) fined Advanced Genetic Sciences, a California firm, for releasing genetically engineered bacteria into the air without permission. The bacteria were designed to prevent frost from forming on plants. In May, however, the EPA approved plans for a similar outdoor test with antifrost bacteria at the University of California at Berkeley. Also in May, scientists began the first outdoor test of genetically engineered tobacco plants resistant to *crown gall*, a bacterial disease.   Sonja Hillgren

See also FOOD. In WORLD BOOK, see AGRICULTURE; FARM AND FARMING.

FARM MACHINERY. See MANUFACTURING.

FASHION. The long and full wool coat emerged in the fall of 1986 as everybody's favorite fashion. It became the unifying link in a still-fragmented fashion picture where, increasingly, anything goes. The big coat, ending somewhere between lower calf and ankle, could cover long flaring skirts, skinny knee-baring skirts, or trousers. In addition, the big coat was comfortable over bulky sweaters, shirts, blouses, and jackets, all components of the dominant fashion look. The choices, in fact, were so varied that some women yearned for the recent past, when decisions on what to wear were easier.

Fresh Looks. The search was on in all the fashion capitals of the world for new designers who could bring a fresh touch to the way women dressed. In London, the most promising new designer was Alistair Duncan Blair, whose first collection was acclaimed for its stylish, tailored look.

Romeo Gigli was the new name in Milan. Trained as an architect, he brought a quiet, old-fashioned, and romantic charm to sweaters and skirts.

Also working in Italy was Zack Carr, a former assistant to American designer Calvin Klein. Carr turned out spare, minimalist designs for a Turin-based concern named Gruppo Finanziario Tessile. The company manufactures ready-to-wear clothing for Italian designers Giorgio Armani and Val-

The big coat of 1986, as interpreted by French designer Emanuel Ungaro, is long and loose, with a dramatic collar and flared hem.

entino, and for French designer Emanuel Ungaro, and wanted an American designer to appeal to the United States market.

In Paris, Christian Lacroix, who designs for Jean Patou, created excitement with his odd mixture of crinolines, bustles, and 1960's patchwork effects. He was credited with bringing a new liveliness to *couture* (made-to-order clothes).

Enthusiastically heralded in New York City was Marc Jacobs, 23, who was considered the most promising up-and-coming designer by some experts. With fanciful designs that ran from battle jackets in printed satin to princess dresses with petticoats, he revealed an expert control of fabrics and shapes as well as a rare sense of whimsy.

Luxury Sportswear. New York City sportswear designers were widely praised for their contemporary approach to fashion. They upgraded their clothes by using luxury fabrics such as cashmere and alpaca rather than by adding unnecessary frills and furbelows.

Among the leading names in this group were Calvin Klein, Ralph Lauren, and Donna Karan. Perry Ellis, a leading member of the sportswear hierarchy, died on May 30 at the age of 46, but his company continued operations.

Fabulous Furs. A high spot in the fashion business was the popularity of furs. The fur industry has recorded sales increases for the past 15 years. Mink is still the favorite, accounting for 50 to 75 per cent of the fur business. The growth is due, in part, to the increasing number of women who buy their own furs, industry sources say. As they move into better-paying professions and managerial positions, women are able and willing to buy mink and the other more expensive furs.

Awards. When the Coty American Fashion Critics' Awards, a fixture of the fashion scene since 1943, passed into history in 1984, the Council of Fashion Designers of America stepped in to fill the gap. The council, a group of creative people in the fashion business, organized an awards ceremony in New York City on Jan. 19, 1986. Actress Katharine Hepburn was honored for her distinctive style. Karan was cited "outstanding designer of the year," and Liz Claiborne, Norma Kamali, and Geoffrey Beene received awards for their contributions to American fashion.

There was a retrospective of the avant-garde styles of Rudi Gernreich, best known for his topless bathing suit of 1964. Ray-Ban sunglasses, made by Bausch & Lomb Incorporated of Rochester, N.Y., were honored as one of the most popular accessories of 1986. Bausch & Lomb began manufacturing Ray-Ban sunglasses in 1938. Robert Lee Morris received an award for his jewelry, and "Miami Vice," the TV show, was honored for its colorful use of men's clothes.   Bernadine Morris

In WORLD BOOK, see CLOTHING; FASHION; FUR.

FERGUSON, SARAH (1959-   ), married Prince Andrew, the second son of Queen Elizabeth II of Great Britain, on July 23, 1986. The wedding took place in Westminster Abbey in London before hundreds of invited guests and millions of television viewers around the world. See ANDREW, PRINCE; GREAT BRITAIN (Close-Up).

As the wife of Prince Andrew, Duke of York and fourth in line to the British throne, she is the Princess Andrew and the Duchess of York. Her most popular "title," however, is "Fergie," a nickname adopted by the press and the public.

Sarah Margaret Ferguson was born on Oct. 15, 1959, in London. She was educated at two local boarding schools and attended a secretarial college in London. At the time of her engagement to Prince Andrew on March 19, 1986, she ran the London office of a publishing company.

Her parents, divorced for more than 10 years, are Major Ronald Ferguson, deputy chairman of the Guards Polo Club and polo manager for the Prince of Wales, and Susan Barrantes, now married to Argentine polo player Hector Barrantes. The Princess Andrew has an older sister, Jane; a younger half-brother, Andrew; and two younger half-sisters, Alice and Eliza. She is a distant relative to Queen Elizabeth—her father's mother is a cousin of Princess Alice of Gloucester, an aunt by marriage to the queen.   Mary A. Krier

FINLAND. A series of strikes that began in March 1986 and lasted until the end of June threatened Finland's economy. On March 13, SAK, a federation of labor unions, struck all major factories in Finland, forcing them to close. This was the nation's first big strike since 1971.

The SAK strike, called because wage negotiations were failing, ended 58 hours after it began. Workers accepted a 2.4 per cent pay hike for 1986 and a 2.6 per cent raise for 1987.

On March 18, 1986, a walkout by 42,000 civil servants halted trains, disrupted air traffic, and closed post offices. The strike lasted only two days but was renewed "indefinitely" on April 2. Workers demanded a 6 per cent pay increase plus $160 per month. In mid-April, a mediator said the situation was "hopeless."

Airport Reopens. Nonunion workers restored some air traffic, but the cutoff of rail traffic threatened trade between Finland and the Soviet Union. Trains carry about 80 per cent of goods transported between the two countries.

On April 18, with the strike still raging, President Mauno Koivisto returned by air from a visit to Yugoslavia. He landed at Helsinki airport, prompting union leaders to accuse him of strikebreaking.

On April 22, 1,200 electricians struck Finland's two nuclear power plants and other power-generating facilities. The public employees' strike ended on May 18, but the electricians' stoppage continued until July 1.

White-Collar Anger. A new phenomenon—white-collar militancy—caused much of the disruption. Past wage agreements have favored blue-collar workers. Teachers, nurses, pharmacists, and other professionals say their pay has fallen far below that of skilled carpenters, metalworkers, and typographers.

Nuclear Fears. Finland evacuated its citizens from the Kiev area in the Soviet Union after disaster struck the Chernobyl nuclear power station on April 26. A special airplane carried 100 construction workers and 50 tourists back to Finland. See ENERGY SUPPLY (Close-Up); RUSSIA.

The Chernobyl disaster led to a political crisis. In Finland's parliament, the populist Finnish Rural Party submitted a motion to dismantle the nation's four nuclear reactors by the year 2000. Prime Minister Kalevi Sorsa said the government would resign if motions on the nuclear power issue were not withdrawn. A resignation would have triggered national elections. The Rural Party did not feel strong enough to face national elections and so withdrew its motion.   Kenneth Brown

See also EUROPE (Facts in Brief Table). In WORLD BOOK, see FINLAND.

FIRE. See DISASTERS.

FISHING. The first National Fishing Week was proclaimed in the United States in 1986. On May 8, President Ronald Reagan issued a proclamation dedicating June 2 to 8 to the sport of fishing.

White Sharks. On August 6, fisherman Donnie Braddick caught a 16-foot 9-inch (510.5-centimeter) white shark off Long Island, New York. According to the International Game Fish Association (IGFA), the shark was the largest fish ever taken on a rod and reel. Using 150-pound (68-kilogram) nylon line, Braddick subdued the shark in two hours. He was fishing with the famous shark hunter Frank Mundus.

At 3,427 pounds (1,554 kilograms), Braddick's shark was 763 pounds (346 kilograms) heavier than the current 2,664-pound (1,208-kilogram) record, a white shark caught off Australia in 1959. There was some question about whether the IGFA would recognize the fish as a world record because Braddick's line exceeded the 130-pound (59-kilogram) maximum allowable strength.

Eight days after Braddick's catch, Tommy Lizza, his family, and several friends harpooned a 2,602-pound (1,180-kilogram) white shark off Long Island, New York. Lizza said he first had hooked the shark on a conventional rod and reel, but after the shark spit out the hook, he decided to harpoon it.

Prizewinners. Charles Reed of Broken Bow, Okla., won the first-place prize of $50,000 in the

Donnie Braddick sits on the 3,427-pound (1,554-kg) white shark, largest fish ever caught with a rod and reel, that he took off Long Island, New York.

16th annual Bass Anglers Sportsman Society Masters Classic. The tournament was held in August on Chicamauga and Nickajack lakes on the Tennessee River near Chattanooga. Reed caught three limits of seven fish each, totaling 23 pounds 9 ounces (10.7 kilograms). Danny Correia of Marlboro, Me., received the $12,000 second-place prize.

With a 33.61-pound (15.25-kilogram) catch, Rickey Clunn of Montgomery, Tex., in July became the first two-time champion of the annual $300,000 U.S. Open tournament on Lake Mead near Las Vegas, Nev. Clunn is bass tournament fishing's top money winner. The $17,000 second-place prize went to John Murray of Phoenix.

On November 14 and 15, at Lake Havasu on the Colorado River in Arizona, Joseph Yates of Barling, Ark., won the $100,000 first prize in the Red Man All American Bass Championship with a total catch of 24 pounds 1 ounce (10.9 kilograms). Larry Golden received the $15,000 second-place prize.

In October, June McMannus of Baton Rouge, La., won $18,500 in the 10th annual Bass N' Gal Classic at Sam Rayburn Reservoir near Jasper, Tex. Her winning total weighed 17 pounds 7 ounces (7.9 kilograms). Linda Buie of Scottsboro, Ala., was runner-up.   Tony Mandile

In WORLD BOOK, see FISHING.

FISHING INDUSTRY. In October 1986, the United States agreed for the first time to pay for fishing rights for U.S. tuna fleets operating in certain areas of the Pacific Ocean. The agreement will funnel $60 million in fees and developmental aid to the 16 island nations in the region over the next five years.

The accord ended a two-year dispute over payment, which had prompted several of the Pacific nations to negotiate fishing agreements with the Soviet Union. The Administration of President Ronald Reagan was reportedly eager to end the dispute and solidify friendly relations with the Pacific nations, in order to counter Soviet military, diplomatic, and economic activities in the area. Edward E. Wolfe, deputy assistant secretary of state for oceans and fisheries affairs, said the settlement paved the way for a formal treaty to be signed in December. See PACIFIC ISLANDS.

The United States Fish Catch in 1985 totaled 6.3 billion pounds (2.86 billion kilograms) of fish and shellfish, valued at more than $2.3 billion. Landings fell slightly from the 1984 total of 6.4 billion pounds (2.90 billion kilograms), worth about $2.4-billion. Flounder and tuna harvests fell, but were generally offset by strong catches of clams, Alaskan pollack, shrimp, and salmon. Americans ate a record amount of seafood in 1985, 14.5 pounds (6.6 kilograms) per capita.

World Fish Catch. According to preliminary data from the Food and Agriculture Organization of the United Nations, the 1985 world catch of fish and shellfish was 84.0 million metric tons (92.6 million short tons), about 1 million metric tons (1.1 million short tons) more than the catch of 1984. Japan was again the leading producer, but its catch dropped from 12.0 million metric tons (13.2 million short tons) in 1984 to 11.5 million metric tons (12.7 million short tons) in 1985.

U.S.-Japanese Agreement. Japanese seafood companies in January agreed to significantly increase their purchases of pollack caught and processed in the United States. The most immediate beneficiaries of the industry-to-industry agreement will likely be U.S. fishing crews who sell their catch directly to Japanese factory vessels.

Tuna Industry Investigation. At the request of United States Trade Representative Clayton K. Yeutter, the nation's top trade negotiator, the International Trade Commission (ITC) will conduct an extensive investigation into the state of the tuna industry. Yeutter acted on behalf of the owners of several U.S. fishing vessels, who contend that large quantities of imported canned tuna have seriously damaged their industry. Donald R. Whitaker

In WORLD BOOK, see FISHING INDUSTRY.

FLOOD. See DISASTERS.

FLORIDA. See STATE GOVERNMENT.

FLOWER. See GARDENING.

FOOD. The United States food industry had a generally good year in 1986. The combination of plentiful harvests of major crops and a low inflation rate produced a modest 2.3 per cent increase in food prices. Food prices rose slightly more than the Consumer Price Index—the most widely used measure of inflation—which showed only a 1.1 per cent price gain for the items in the index. Nevertheless, American consumers spent only 16.5 per cent of disposable income—income left after taxes—on food, one of the world's lowest rates.

New farm policies, which called for higher government payments on crops, helped ease the financial problems of some American farmers. Farmers with a lighter debt load fared relatively well, though those with heavy debts continued to be squeezed out.

Although the percentage of malnourished people worldwide declined in 1986, between 400 million and 500 million people remained significantly underfed. Poor distribution channels, lack of management, and inadequate financial resources in the developing world—rather than a lack of supplies—were to blame. Severe famine in parts of Africa was relieved by an end to drought conditions and improved crop output. The number of countries with exceptional food shortages fell to 11—mostly in Africa and Asia—compared with 20 countries in 1985.

Agriculture. United States crop production failed to reach 1985's banner levels, but in most cases this was the result of an 8 per cent decrease in the number of acres planted. A drought in the East and Southeast hurt production of some crops grown in those regions. But weather conditions in the Midwest were favorable, so that supplies of all crops remained plentiful. Livestock inventories continued to decline as producers slaughtered their animals, and a lack of available credit kept many producers from rebuilding their herds.

Eating Out continued to be a popular American pastime in 1986, accounting for more than 40 per cent of the total spent on food. Sales for all eating and drinking establishments rose to nearly $180-billion, a 6.6 per cent increase over 1985. Menu prices rose by 3.9 per cent. Fast-food eateries continued to outpace other eating establishments, with an 8.7 per cent increase in sales over 1985.

Grocery Store Sales increased just 5 per cent, for a real growth rate of 3.6 per cent. The rate of growth was slightly up from 1985's growth rate, ending a five-year downward trend.

Newly built supermarkets were generally larger, typically about 40,000 square feet (3,700 square meters). Remodeling was a common trend in grocery stores, as operators sought to offer customers a wider variety of goods and services in more attractive surroundings. Supermarkets continued to woo the two-paycheck family by featuring salad

West Berlin trash collectors dump vegetables contaminated by radiation from an explosion in April at the Chernobyl nuclear plant in the Soviet Union.

bars; stocking a wide variety of fruits, vegetables, and ethnic foods; and expanding delicatessen selections to include more prepared foods. Many stores promoted the concept of "one-stop shopping," by featuring automated teller machines and by stocking more general merchandise, health and beauty aids, and even rental videocassettes.

Consumption. Health-conscious Americans continued to eat less red meat, consume more poultry and fish, and count their calories—the latter reflected in the increasing popularity of such items as low-fat milk and lower-calorie frozen dinners. Brand-name products continued to sell well, and price often took second place to convenience and ease of preparation.

Labeling. Throughout 1986, the U.S. Food and Drug Administration (FDA) indicated its intent to allow some health claims on food labels, reversing a long-standing policy that forbade food manufacturers from using a disease-prevention claim on their labels. The FDA, consumer groups, and industry struggled to develop practical guidelines to ensure that labels contain accurate information that does not mislead the consumer.

Some manufacturers have responded to consumer interest in more healthful, less fattening products by labeling their products as "lite" or "lean." In March 1986, to lessen the possibility of the public being misled by such claims, the U.S.

Department of Agriculture revised its standards and its labeling guidelines for meat and poultry. The actual amount of the component in the product must now be disclosed. "Lean" and "low fat" products may contain no more than 10 per cent fat, and "extra lean" no more than 5 per cent. "Lite" products must reduce by 25 per cent the amount of fat routinely found in the product.

The Lite Food Labeling Act—a bill that proposes to restrict the use of the word *light* to products containing 33 per cent fewer calories, 50 per cent less fat, or 75 per cent less sodium than a company's standard counterpart—was pending in three congressional committees when Congress adjourned in 1986. The bill was expected to get a hearing after the new Congress convened early in 1987.

Tampering. In 1986, the FDA reported more than 2,000 complaints of tampering—up from 128 complaints in 1985—most of which proved groundless. Several well-publicized cases of tampering and contaminated products impelled food industry trade associations to work with their members and with the government to find better ways to report tampering complaints, to disseminate accurate information, and to speed the recall of suspect products.   Bob Gatty

See also FARM AND FARMING; NUTRITION. In WORLD BOOK, see FOOD; FOOD SUPPLY.

FOOTBALL

FOOTBALL. The biggest winners in football in the United States in 1986 were the New York Giants and the Denver Broncos among the 28 professional teams in the National Football League (NFL) and Pennsylvania State University among the 105 colleges with major football programs. The biggest loser was the United States Football League (USFL), which sought $1.69 billion in damages in an antitrust suit against the NFL but was awarded damages of only $1, trebled to $3. The outcome put the USFL virtually out of business.

USFL. In 1983, the USFL began playing as a springtime league with limited payrolls. Although league officials said the USFL would not compete with the NFL for players and ticket buyers, it started competing. Franchises were created and dissolved, and the league's losses during the four years of its existence totaled an estimated $150 million to $200 million.

In 1985, the USFL club owners voted to abandon spring football in 1986 and play instead in the fall. The American Broadcasting Companies (ABC), however, which had been televising USFL games in the spring, said it would not show them in the fall, when it would be televising NFL and college games. CBS Inc. also televised NFL and college games in the fall, and the National Broadcasting Company (NBC) showed NFL games. Not one of the major television networks was interested in televising USFL games in the fall.

When the USFL could not negotiate a contract with the major networks, it sued the NFL. The federal trial in New York City lasted from May 12 to July 29. The jury of five women and one man found the NFL guilty of having monopoly power "to control prices or exclude competition." But the jury also found that the NFL had not tried to keep the USFL off the three networks and thus awarded the USFL only token damages.

On August 4, the USFL voted not to play its 1986 season. It released its players, and such stars as running backs Herschel Walker and Kelvin Bryant and quarterback Jim Kelly signed multi-million-dollar contracts with NFL teams.

Meanwhile, the USFL sought to have the jury's verdict overruled. On October 2, Judge Peter K. Leisure, who had presided at the trial, denied the USFL's motion for a new trial. He rejected the USFL's request to force the NFL to abandon one television network.

NFL Season. The NFL also thrived outside the courtroom. The attendance total of 13,582,141 for 224 regular-season games and the per-game average of 60,635 were the second highest since the league originated in 1920 as the American Professional Football Association. It was renamed the National Football League in 1922.

The Chicago Bears, who won Super Bowl XX in

Heisman Trophy winner Vinny Testaverde of the University of Miami in Florida lofts a pass during a game against Florida State.

January 1986, kept winning during the 1986 regular season despite the loss of Buddy Ryan, the innovative coach who had created their mighty defense, and Jim McMahon, the quarterback who geared their offense. Ryan left after Super Bowl XX to become head coach of the Philadelphia Eagles. McMahon played only six games and underwent surgery because of an injured right shoulder that threatened his career. In midseason, the Bears signed Doug Flutie, who had played in the USFL, and near season's end he became their starting quarterback.

The division champions were the Giants (14-2), the Bears (14-2), and the San Francisco 49ers (10-5-1) in the National Conference and the Cleveland Browns (12-4), the Broncos (11-5), and the New England Patriots (11-5) in the American Conference. The six division winners advanced to the play-offs with four wild-card teams—the Washington Redskins (12-4), the Los Angeles Rams (10-6), the New York Jets (10-6), and the Kansas City Chiefs (10-6).

During the regular season, the leading passers were Tommy Kramer of the Minnesota Vikings in the National Conference and Dan Marino of the Miami Dolphins in the American Conference. The leading rushers were running backs Eric Dickerson of the Rams with 1,821 yards (1,665 meters), Joe Morris of the Giants with 1,516 yards (1,386

National Football League Final Standings

American Conference

Eastern Division
	W.	L.	T.	Pct.
New England Patriots	11	5	0	.688
New York Jets	10	6	0	.625
Miami Dolphins	8	8	0	.500
Buffalo Bills	4	12	0	.250
Indianapolis Colts	3	13	0	.188

Central Division
	W.	L.	T.	Pct.
Cleveland Browns	12	4	0	.750
Cincinnati Bengals	10	6	0	.625
Pittsburgh Steelers	6	10	0	.375
Houston Oilers	5	11	0	.313

Western Division
	W.	L.	T.	Pct.
Denver Broncos	11	5	0	.688
Kansas City Chiefs	10	6	0	.625
Seattle Seahawks	10	6	0	.625
Los Angeles Raiders	8	8	0	.500
San Diego Chargers	4	12	0	.250

Individual Statistics

Leading Scorers, Touchdowns
	TDs.	Rush	Rec.	Ret.	Pts.
Sammy Winder, Denver	14	9	5	0	84
Curt Warner, Seattle	13	13	0	0	78
Lorenzo Hampton, Miami	12	9	3	0	72
Wesley Walker, N.Y. Jets	12	0	12	0	72
Mark Duper, Miami	11	0	11	0	66
Stephone Paige, Kansas City	11	0	11	0	66
Mark Clayton, Miami	10	0	10	0	60
Cris Collinsworth, Cincinnati	10	0	10	0	60
Kevin Mack, Cleveland	10	10	0	0	60
Stanley Morgan, New England	10	0	10	0	60

Leading Scorers, Kicking
	PAT	FG	Longest	Pts.
Tony Franklin, New England	44-45	32-41	49	140
Norm Johnson, Seattle	42-42	22-35	54	108
Rich Karlis, Denver	44-45	20-28	51	104
Jim Breech, Cincinnati	50-51	17-32	51	101
Nick Lowery, Kansas City	43-43	19-26	47	100
Chris Bahr, L.A. Raiders	36-36	21-28	52	99
Gary Anderson, Pittsburgh	32-32	21-32	45	95
Fuad Reveiz, Miami	52-55	14-22	52	94
Tony Zendejas, Houston	28-29	22-27	51	94
Pat Leahy, N.Y. Jets	44-44	16-19	50	92

Leading Quarterbacks
	Att.	Comp.	Yds.	TDs.	Int.
Dan Marino, Miami	623	378	4,746	44	23
Dave Krieg, Seattle	375	225	2,921	21	11
Tony Eason, New England	448	276	3,328	19	10
Boomer Esiason, Cincinnati	469	273	3,959	24	17
Ken O'Brien, N.Y. Jets	482	300	3,690	25	20
Bernie Kosar, Cleveland	531	310	3,854	17	10
Jim Kelly, Buffalo	480	285	3,593	22	17
Jim Plunkett, L.A. Raiders	252	133	1,986	14	9
John Elway, Denver	504	280	3,485	19	13
Dan Fouts, San Diego	430	252	3,031	16	22

Leading Receivers
	No. Caught	Total Yds.	Avg. Gain	TDs.
Todd Christensen, L.A. Raiders	95	1,153	12.1	8
Al Toon, N.Y. Jets	85	1,176	13.8	8
Stanley Morgan, New England	84	1,491	17.8	10
Gary Anderson, San Diego	80	871	10.9	8
Tony Collins, New England	77	684	8.9	5
Matt Bouza, Indianapolis	71	830	11.7	5
Steve Largent, Seattle	70	1,070	15.3	9
Mickey Shuler, N.Y. Jets	69	675	9.8	4
Mark Duper, Miami	67	1,313	19.6	11
Bill Brooks, Indianapolis	65	1,131	17.4	8

Leading Rushers
	No.	Yds.	Avg.	TDs.
Curt Warner, Seattle	319	1,481	4.6	13
James Brooks, Cincinnati	205	1,087	5.3	5
Earnest Jackson, Pittsburgh	216	910	4.2	5
Walter Abercrombie, Pittsburgh	214	877	4.1	6
Freeman McNeil, N.Y. Jets	214	856	4.0	5
Lorenzo Hampton, Miami	186	830	4.5	9
Sammy Winder, Denver	240	789	3.3	9
Marcus Allen, L.A. Raiders	208	759	3.6	5
Kevin Mack, Cleveland	174	665	3.8	10
Mike Rozier, Houston	199	662	3.3	4

Leading Punters
	No.	Yds.	Avg.	Longest
Rohn Stark, Indianapolis	76	3,342	45.2	63
Reggie Roby, Miami	56	2,476	44.2	73
Rich Camarillo, New England	89	3,746	42.1	64
Ralf Mojsiejenko, San Diego	72	3,026	42.0	62
Jeff Gossett, Cleveland	83	3,423	41.2	61

National Conference

Eastern Division
	W.	L.	T.	Pct.
New York Giants	14	2	0	.875
Washington Redskins	12	4	0	.750
Dallas Cowboys	7	9	0	.438
Philadelphia Eagles	5	10	1	.344
St. Louis Cardinals	4	11	1	.281

Central Division
	W.	L.	T.	Pct.
Chicago Bears	14	2	0	.875
Minnesota Vikings	9	7	0	.563
Detroit Lions	5	11	0	.313
Green Bay Packers	4	12	0	.250
Tampa Bay Buccaneers	2	14	0	.125

Western Division
	W.	L.	T.	Pct.
San Francisco 49ers	10	5	1	.656
Los Angeles Rams	10	6	0	.625
Atlanta Falcons	7	8	1	.469
New Orleans Saints	7	9	0	.438

Individual Statistics

Leading Scorers, Touchdowns
	TDs.	Rush	Rec.	Ret.	Pts.
George Rogers, Washington	18	18	0	0	108
Jerry Rice, San Francisco	16	1	15	0	96
Joe Morris, N.Y. Giants	15	14	1	0	90
Herschel Walker, Dallas	14	12	2	0	84
Eric Dickerson, L.A. Rams	11	11	0	0	66
Walter Payton, Chicago	11	8	3	0	66
James Jones, Detroit	9	8	1	0	54
Mike Quick, Philadelphia	9	0	9	0	54
Gerald Riggs, Atlanta	9	9	0	0	54
Rueben Mayes, New Orleans	8	8	0	0	48

Leading Scorers, Kicking
	PAT	FG	Longest	Pts.
Kevin Butler, Chicago	36-37	28-41	52	120
Ray Wersching, San Francisco	41-42	25-35	50	116
Chuck Nelson, Minnesota	44-47	22-28	53	110
Morten Andersen, New Orleans	30-30	26-30	53	108
Raul Allegre, N.Y. Giants	33-33	24-32	46	105
Rafael Septien, Dallas	43-43	15-21	50	88
Paul McFadden, Philadelphia	26-27	20-31	50	86
Mike Lansford, L.A. Rams	34-35	17-24	50	85
Ed Murray, Detroit	31-32	18-25	52	85
Al Del Greco, Green Bay	29-29	17-27	50	80

Leading Quarterbacks
	Att.	Comp.	Yds.	TDs.	Int.
Tommy Kramer, Minnesota	372	208	3,000	24	10
Joe Montana, San Francisco	307	191	2,236	8	9
Eric Hipple, Detroit	305	192	1,919	9	11
Phil Simms, N.Y. Giants	468	259	3,487	21	22
Neil Lomax, St. Louis	421	240	2,583	13	12
Jay Schroeder, Washington	541	276	4,109	22	22
Dave Archer, Atlanta	294	150	2,007	10	9
Ron Jaworski, Philadelphia	245	128	1,405	8	6
Steve Pelluer, Dallas	378	215	2,727	8	17
Randy Wright, Green Bay	492	263	3,247	17	23

Leading Receivers
	No. Caught	Total Yds.	Avg. Gain	TDs.
Jerry Rice, San Francisco	86	1,570	18.3	15
Roger Craig, San Francisco	81	624	7.7	0
J. T. Smith, St. Louis	80	1,014	12.7	6
Herschel Walker, Dallas	76	837	11.0	2
Gary Clark, Washington	74	1,265	17.1	7
Art Monk, Washington	73	1,068	14.6	4
Mark Bavaro, N.Y. Giants	66	1,001	15.2	4
James Lofton, Green Bay	64	840	13.1	4
Charlie Brown, Atlanta	63	918	14.6	4
Dwight Clark, San Francisco	61	794	13.0	2

Leading Rushers
	No.	Yds.	Avg.	TDs.
Eric Dickerson, L.A. Rams	404	1,821	4.5	11
Joe Morris, N.Y. Giants	341	1,516	4.4	14
Rueben Mayes, New Orleans	286	1,353	4.7	8
Walter Payton, Chicago	321	1,333	4.2	8
Gerald Riggs, Atlanta	343	1,327	3.9	9
George Rogers, Washington	303	1,203	4.0	18
James Jones, Detroit	252	903	3.6	8
Roger Craig, San Francisco	204	830	4.1	7
Stump Mitchell, St. Louis	174	800	4.6	5
Darrin Nelson, Minnesota	191	793	4.2	4

Leading Punters
	No.	Yds.	Avg.	Longest
Sean Landeta, N.Y. Giants	79	3,539	44.8	61
Rick Donnelly, Atlanta	78	3,421	43.9	71
Steve Cox, Washington	75	3,271	43.6	58
Brian Hansen, New Orleans	81	3,456	42.7	66
John Teltschik, Philadelphia	108	4,493	41.6	62
Max Runager, San Francisco	83	3,450	41.6	62

The 1986 College Football Season

1986 College Conference Champions

Conference	School
Atlantic Coast	Clemson
Big Eight	Oklahoma
Big Sky	Nevada-Reno
Big Ten	Michigan—Ohio State (tie)
Ivy League	Pennsylvania
Mid-American	Miami (Ohio)
Ohio Valley	Eastern Kentucky—Murray State (tie)
Pacific Coast	San Jose State
Pacific Ten	Arizona State
Southeastern	Louisiana State
Southland	Arkansas State
Southwest	Texas A & M
Southwestern	Jackson State
Western Athletic	San Diego State
Yankee	Connecticut—Delaware—Massachusetts (tie)

Major Bowl Games

Bowl	Winner	Loser
All-American	Florida State 27	Indiana 13
Aloha	Arizona 30	North Carolina 21
Amos Alonzo Stagg (Div. III)	Augustana (Ill.) 31	Salisbury State (Md.) 3
Bluebonnet	Baylor 21	Colorado 9
Blue-Gray	Blue 31	Gray 7
California	San Jose State 37	Miami (Ohio) 7
Cotton	Ohio State 28	Texas A & M 12
Fiesta	Penn State 14	Miami (Fla.) 10
Florida Citrus	Auburn 16	Southern California 7
Freedom	UCLA 31	Brigham Young 10
Gator	Clemson 27	Stanford 21
Hall of Fame	Boston College 27	Georgia 24
Holiday	Iowa 39	San Diego State 38
Hula	West 16	East 14
Independence	Mississippi 20	Texas Tech 17
Liberty	Tennessee 21	Minnesota 14
Orange	Oklahoma 42	Arkansas 8
Palm (Div. II)	North Dakota State 27	South Dakota 7
Peach	Virginia Tech 25	North Carolina State 24
Rose	Arizona State 22	Michigan 15
Senior	North 42	South 38
Sugar	Nebraska 30	Louisiana State 15
Sun	Alabama 28	Washington 6
NCAA Div. I-AA	Georgia Southern 48	Arkansas State 21
NAIA Div. I	Carson-Newman (Tenn.) 17	Cameron (Okla.) 0
NAIA Div. II	Linfield (Ore.) 17	Baker (Kans.) 0

All-American Team (as picked by AP)

Offense

Tight end—Keith Jackson, Oklahoma
Wide receivers—Tim Brown, Notre Dame; Cris Carter, Ohio State
Tackles—Harris Barton, North Carolina; Danny Villa, Arizona State
Guards—Jeff Bregel, Southern California; Mark Hutson, Oklahoma
Center—Ben Tamburello, Auburn
Quarterback—Vinny Testaverde, Miami (Fla.)
Running backs—Brent Fullwood, Auburn; Paul Palmer, Temple
Place kicker—Jeff Jaeger, Washington

Defense

Ends-outside linebackers—Cornelius Bennett, Alabama; Shane Conlan, Penn State
Tackles—Jerome Brown, Miami (Fla.); Al Noga, Hawaii
Nose guard—Danny Noonan, Nebraska
Inside linebackers—Brian Bosworth, Oklahoma; Chris Spielman, Ohio State
Backs—Bennie Blades, Miami (Fla.); Thomas Everett, Baylor; Mark Moore, Oklahoma State; Rod Woodson, Purdue
Punter—Barry Helton, Colorado

Player Awards

Heisman Trophy (best player)—Vinny Testaverde, Miami (Fla.)
Lombardi Award (best lineman)—Cornelius Bennett, Alabama
Outland Award (best interior lineman)—Jason Buck, Brigham Young

meters) and Curt Warner of the Seattle Seahawks with 1,481 yards (1,354 meters).

Play-Offs. The play-offs started on December 28. In the National Conference, Washington defeated the Rams, 19-7, in the wild-card game by forcing six turnovers. In the next round, the Giants routed San Francisco, 49-3, with a mighty defense, and Washington upset Chicago, 27-13, by forcing four turnovers. In the conference championship game on Jan. 11, 1987, the Giants' brilliant defense shut down Washington, 17-0, as their offense took advantage of strong winds and scored early in the game.

In the American Conference, the Jets, after losing their last five regular-season games, replaced quarterback Ken O'Brien with Pat Ryan and won the wild-card game from Kansas City, 35-15. The next week, the Jets led Cleveland by 10 points with less than four minutes remaining, but Cleveland won in overtime, 23-20, on Mark Moseley's 27-yard (25-meter) field goal. Denver advanced with a 22-17 victory over New England behind a resurrected running game. In the conference championship game, Denver beat Cleveland in another 23-20 overtime contest. Denver quarterback John Elway led the Broncos on a dramatic 98-yard (90-meter) scoring drive in the final minutes of regulation time to tie the game. Then, in overtime, Denver won on a field goal by Rich Karlis.

That set the Giants against Denver in Super Bowl XXI on Jan. 25, 1987, in the Rose Bowl in Pasadena, Calif. The Giants won, 39-20. Giant quarterback Phil Simms was named Most Valuable Player, completing 22 of 25 passes.

Instant Replay. After years of discussion, the NFL introduced a one-year experiment of limited videotape replay of certain plays. The replay system had problems, but many were resolved.

The replays were limited to plays involving goal lines, end lines, and possession or touching of the ball. The replays were called for by the referee or by a replay official who sat in a sectioned-off part of the stands, but were used only after the field officials had ruled on the play.

The replay official watched monitors of replays available to the television audience and notified the officials on the field of his findings. He could uphold the field officials' ruling, reverse it, or decide that the replays were not totally conclusive and therefore the original decision would stand.

Other Pro Developments. On July 7, NFL Commissioner Pete Rozelle announced a drug-testing program that called for three tests a year and a lifetime ban for three-time violators. Arbitrator Richard Kasher, however, ruled on October 27 that the program could not be implemented because it violated the collective-bargaining agreement between the owners and the players.

That agreement expired after the 1986 season,

and a drug program was anticipated in the next agreement. Those negotiations were expected to be concluded in 1987 after new television contracts were negotiated. In 1986, the final year of the NFL's $2.1-billion, five-year television contracts with the three major networks, ratings dropped 5 per cent at ABC, 4 per cent at CBS, and 2 per cent at NBC.

The National Professional Football Hall of Fame in Canton, Ohio, inducted five retired players in 1986—quarterback Fran Tarkenton, running backs Paul Hornung and Doak Walker, linebacker Willie Lanier, and defensive back Ken Houston.

Canada. In the nine-team Canadian Football League, the Hamilton Tiger-Cats (9-8-1) had the poorest record of the six teams that qualified for the play-offs. In the Grey Cup championship game on November 30 in Vancouver, B.C., however, Hamilton combined 10 turnovers and 13 sacks to upset the Edmonton Eskimos, 39-15.

College. When the regular season ended, the best records among major colleges belonged to Miami of Florida (11-0), Penn State (11-0), Michigan (11-1), Oklahoma (10-1), and Arizona State (9-1-1). In the separate polls of the Associated Press and United Press International, Miami ranked first and Penn State second.

Three post-season bowls free of conference commitments—the Fiesta in Tempe, Ariz.; the Florida Citrus in Orlando; and the Gator in Jacksonville, Fla.—tried to match Miami and Penn State in a game for the unofficial national championship. The Fiesta Bowl succeeded by moving its New Year's Day afternoon game to prime time on NBC on January 2 and by raising each team's $1.2-million payment to $2.4 million.

Miami was led by quarterback Vinny Testaverde, a runaway winner in the Heisman Trophy voting as the nation's outstanding college player. But in the Fiesta Bowl, Penn State intercepted Testaverde's passes five times. Penn State won the game, 14-10, and almost universal recognition as the national champion.

The National Collegiate Athletic Association, the major governing body of college sports, instituted drug testing before and after major bowl games and tested 720 players from 20 universities. Although none tested positive for cocaine or heroin, 11 players tested positive for anabolic steroids and were banned from the bowl games. *Steroids* are synthetic male hormones that help build muscle but can cause liver damage, cancer, and circulatory and reproductive problems. Among the players who tested positive were two all-Americans—linebacker Brian Bosworth of Oklahoma and offensive guard Jeff Bregel of Southern California. Frank Litsky

In WORLD BOOK, see FOOTBALL.

FORD, GERALD RUDOLPH (1913-   ), the 38th President of the United States, joined President Ronald Reagan in March for a St. Patrick's Day salute to Speaker of the House Thomas P. (Tip) O'Neill, Jr. (D., Mass.), who had announced his intention to retire at the end of 1986. Ford and Reagan spoke at a Washington, D.C., dinner attended by Ireland's Prime Minister Garret FitzGerald. Former President Ford once served as Republican leader of the House when O'Neill was Speaker and the two men, long friends, have appeared together annually in celebrity golf tournaments. The dinner raised money for a scholarship fund benefiting O'Neill's alma mater, Boston College.

In September, Ford hosted a two-day symposium on "Humor and the Presidency" at the Gerald R. Ford Museum in Grand Rapids, Mich. Participants included humorists Art Buchwald and Mark Russell; comedian Chevy Chase; and editorial cartoonists Paul Conrad and Jeff MacNelly.

Besides appearing in occasional golf tournaments, Ford remained active on the boards of several major corporations. His spokesman, Robert Barrett, reported that Ford has helped raise more than $310 million for charitable and political causes since 1977. Frank Cormier and Margot Cormier

In WORLD BOOK, see FORD, GERALD R.

FOUR-H CLUBS. See YOUTH ORGANIZATIONS.

Former President Ford pretends to trip comedian Chevy Chase at the Humor and the Presidency Symposium in Grand Rapids, Mich., in September.

Investigators examine rubble in Paris after a bomb
blasted a department store during a wave
of terrorist attacks in that city in September.

FRANCE. A narrow right wing victory in a national
election on March 16, 1986, led to an unprecedented power-sharing arrangement known in
France as *cohabitation*. For the first time since the
founding of the Fifth Republic in 1958, France's
president and prime minister were members of
opposing parties. On the left was François Mitterrand, who was elected the first Socialist president
of the Fifth Republic in 1981. On the right was the
mayor of Paris, Jacques Chirac, of the conservative
Rally for the Republic (RPR) party, whom Mitterrand invited to become prime minister on March
18, 1986. Chirac accepted the post on March 20,
succeeding Laurent Fabius, a Socialist.

Right Wing Alliance. The right wing alliance of
the RPR and the center-right Union for French
Democracy (UDF) party had to rely on the support of deputies from various moderate-right tickets for their majority in the National Assembly,
the more powerful of the two houses of Parliament. On their own, the two rightist parties won
only 277 of the 577 seats in the Assembly, and
some deputies feared that they would have to seek
the support of the far-right National Front (NF),
which made a good showing in the elections.

With 9.8 per cent of the vote, the NF entered
the Assembly for the first time in the party's 14
years of existence. By winning 35 seats, the NF became one of the five major political parties in
France, along with the Socialists, the RPR, the
UDF, and the Communists.

First Clash. Chirac's first skirmish with Mitterrand came a week after Chirac became prime minister. Chirac introduced two bills to allow the government to implement certain economic reforms
and to alter election procedures without parliamentary approval. According to the French Constitution, however, the government would have to
obtain Mitterrand's approval of individual government decrees. Mitterrand, who opposed the reforms and the election changes, worked out a
compromise. He said he would not sign decrees
that he believed violated workers' rights but
agreed to go along with decrees to sell certain
publicly owned businesses.

Second Clash. President and prime minister
clashed again on April 9 when Mitterrand said he
would not sign decrees to sell off companies or institutions taken over by the government before the
Socialists came to power in 1981. Chirac wanted to
sell off more than 50 state-owned companies.

On April 22, Chirac presented a bill that would
enable the government to sell off publicly owned
businesses by decree. He used a parliamentary
maneuver called the *guillotine rule* to gain passage
of the bill in mid-May.

Terrorist Bombs shook Paris five times from
September 8 to 17. The bombs killed 10 people
and wounded more than 160. On September 14,

France tightened visa requirements to make it easier to keep track of the movements of foreign visitors, some of whom might be terrorists.

On November 17, unknown assailants in Paris shot and killed Georges Besse, chairman of the state-owned Renault automobile company. The French terrorist group Direct Action claimed responsibility.

France Apologized to New Zealand on July 23 for the July 1985 sinking of the *Rainbow Warrior* in Auckland Harbor, N.Z. French agents sank the ship, which was owned by Greenpeace, an environmental organization opposed to French nuclear-weapons tests in the Pacific Ocean.

Other Developments. On Dec. 8, 1986, the French government dropped a university reform bill that had triggered the worst student riots since 1968. On Dec. 18, 1986, about 20,000 railroad engineers and other workers went on strike to protest a new salary system that emphasized merit over seniority. The strike, which crippled rail service, continued at year-end.   Kenneth Brown

See also CHIRAC, JACQUES; EUROPE (Facts in Brief Table). In WORLD BOOK, see FRANCE.

FUTURE FARMERS OF AMERICA (FFA). See YOUTH ORGANIZATIONS.

GABON. See AFRICA.

GAMBIA. See AFRICA.

GAMES. See TOYS AND GAMES.

A rare Andean plant blooms early—in just 28 years instead of taking the usual century or more to flower—in Berkeley, Calif., in September.

GARDENING. In October 1986, President Ronald Reagan signed a congressional resolution designating the rose as the national "floral emblem" of the United States. The resolution stated that the rose "stands for love, peace, friendship, courage, loyalty and devotion." The legislation did not select a specific species or cultivated variety for the official emblem. Species roses, hybrid tea roses, historic "old roses," and miniature roses will all be eligible for use as the national flower.

The resolution ended a long-standing debate over selection of the U.S. floral emblem. Individuals and groups had lobbied for the day lily, marigold, sunflower, and yucca.

Some people argued that the rose is an inappropriate choice because it is not exclusively native to the United States. Although several individual species of rose are U.S. natives, the roses grown in the nation's gardens today are descended from species from all over the world. But Charles A. Huckins, executive director of the American Horticultural Society, said that the rose symbolizes the diversity of the American people.

Living Legacy Project. On Sept. 17, 1986, the Commission on the Bicentennial of the United States Constitution launched the "Plant a Living Legacy" project to encourage gardeners throughout the United States to plant trees, create new parks and gardens, or restore historic gardens in celebration of the bicentennial of the signing of the Constitution on Sept. 17, 1787.

Trees are the only "witnesses" to the signing of the Constitution still living today, and the project expressed the hope that "living legacy" plantings will survive to witness the Constitution's tercentenary and serve as living reminders of the value and importance of the Constitution.

National Gardening Week Declared. In 1986, Congress declared the week of April 13 to 19 to be National Gardening Week. Each year, activities during this week will serve to recognize the contribution that gardeners have made to the quality of life in the United States.

Resistant Elms Released. The National Arboretum in Washington, D.C., released two new cultivated varieties of American elm (*Ulmus americana*) that are resistant to Dutch elm disease, an infection that has devastated elm trees throughout the United States. The disease is caused by a fungus carried by the European bark beetle and the American bark beetle. Both of the elm varieties—'Homestead' and 'Pioneer'—were inoculated with the fungus that causes the disease, and cuttings taken from the parent plants show promise of survival.   Barbara W. Ellis

In WORLD BOOK, see GARDENING; ROSE.

GAS AND GASOLINE. See ENERGY SUPPLY; PETROLEUM AND GAS.

GEOLOGY. A cloud of toxic gas released by Lake Nios in the central African country of Cameroon on Aug. 21, 1986, killed more than 1,700 people. Shortly after the accident, the United States Agency for International Development dispatched a team of scientists to investigate the cause of the tragedy. Their preliminary findings indicated that the gas consisted almost exclusively of carbon dioxide released from water at the bottom of the lake. High levels of carbon dioxide can cause asphyxiation.

The scientists believe that underlying Lake Nios is a *diatreme*—a pipelike vent in the rock formed by the eruption of gas and of cooled and broken volcanic rock from deep within Earth's interior. They think that carbon dioxide leaked slowly from Earth's interior through the diatreme into the water. Eventually, the gas-rich lake water became saturated with carbon dioxide. Some unknown event, such as a landslide, minor earthquake, or surface water disturbance, caused the lake water to bubble up and release the dissolved gas. The poisonous gas drifted over villages near the lake, killing nearly everyone who came in contact with it.

Jagged Core. The molten core of Earth is not a smooth ball but instead has a rugged landscape with valleys six times deeper than the Grand Canyon and mountains taller than Mount Everest, ac-cording to findings reported in December 1986. The discovery was made by an international team of scientists.

The findings were based on maps made with a procedure called *seismic tomography*, which uses vibrations produced by earthquakes to create cross-sectional images of Earth's interior. The maps revealed valleys 1,800 miles (2,900 kilometers) below Europe and Mexico and mountains beneath eastern Australia and the northeast Pacific Ocean. There, a mountain 6 miles (10 kilometers) high rises under the Gulf of Alaska.

The researchers suggested that the core's peaks and valleys are created by the rise and fall of currents of partly molten rock in the *mantle*—the layer of Earth between the central core and the outer crust. The scientists also theorized that the peaks and valleys may explain the five-millisecond variation in daylength that occurs every 10 years. This jerkiness in the Earth's rotation may result from the movement of the mantle's molten rock against the jagged core.

Unemployment. Economic events buffeted the field of geology in 1986. The sharp drop in oil prices led to massive layoffs among geologists working in petroleum research and exploration and to less money for research in industry and at universities. In September, the 43,000-member American Association of Petroleum Geologists reported that 25 per cent of its active members were unemployed, the highest jobless rate since the 1930's.

Venuslike Earth. Earth's terrain 2.5 billion years ago may have been similar to that of today's Venus, according to speculation published in October 1986 by geologist Eldridge M. Moores of the University of California at Davis. Moores based his ideas on radar images of Venus that seem to indicate the presence of *folded mountains* (mountains formed when the Earth's crust folds), similar to the Appalachian Mountains on Earth. The surface of Venus, however, is much more uniform than that of Earth, which has a thinner ocean crust and thicker continental crust.

Moores suggested that from 1 billion to 2.5 billion years ago, Earth's crust may also have been more uniform, with a thicker oceanic crust. If so, ocean basins would have been shallower and most of the continents would have been covered with water.

According to Moores, this could explain several geologic puzzles, such as the presence of thick layers of ocean sediment over large parts of ancient continental areas. Scientists have found no evidence of the geologic upheavals that would have been necessary to move these sediments from the ocean bottom.   Eldridge M. Moores

In WORLD BOOK, see GEOLOGY.

GEORGIA. See STATE GOVERNMENT.

Smoke billows from a new island, created by an undersea volcano in the Pacific Ocean, about 800 miles (1,300 kilometers) south of Tokyo, in January.

GERMANY, EAST. The East German Communist Party reelected Secretary General Erich Honecker to another five-year term at its party congress, held in East Berlin from April 17 to 21, 1986. Honecker's reelection meant that he also would serve for another five years as head of government.

Flood of Refugees. East Germany drew protests from West Germany for sending thousands of Third World refugees into West Berlin in 1986. The refugees came from such countries as Iran, Pakistan, Ghana, Lebanon, and Sri Lanka.

West Germany had adopted a liberal policy on political asylum after World War II ended in 1945 and claimed in 1986 that East Germany was taking improper advantage of this policy. The flow of refugees reached 66,814 by August, placing a tremendous burden on West German cities where the refugees eventually settled.

East Germany recruited refugees by purchasing advertisements in Third World newspapers. The ads offered cheap fares to East Berlin. Refugees arriving in East Berlin received passes allowing them to go to the Berlin Wall, which divides East Berlin from West Berlin. They then entered West Berlin.

East Germany Gained from this refugee traffic in two ways. First, East Germany received payments for the fares in *hard currency*, money that is freely exchanged in international markets. (Eastern bloc currencies such as Russia's ruble or East Germany's mark are not freely exchanged.)

Second, the traffic put pressure on the West to introduce immigration checks and restrictions that would support East Germany's claims that the Berlin Wall is its national border and that East Berlin is the capital of East Germany. For all practical purposes, East Berlin is indeed the capital of East Germany. But according to agreements reached by victorious powers in World War II—France, Great Britain, the Soviet Union, and the United States—no part of Berlin has ever been integrated completely into either East Germany or West Germany. On September 18, West Germany announced that East Germany had promised to stop the flood of refugees on October 1.

Passport Rule. On May 22, East Germany announced that foreign diplomats would have to show their passports before entering East Berlin. Previously, East Germany had demanded only identity cards. Western governments protested, arguing that East Germany was trying to force the West into recognizing the Berlin Wall as an international boundary. On June 8, East Germany dropped the passport requirement.   Kenneth Brown

See also EUROPE (Facts in Brief Table). In WORLD BOOK, see BERLIN; GERMANY.

East Germany's leader Erich Honecker, right, joins Soviet chief Gorbachev in a clenched-fist salute at the East German Communist Party Congress in April.

GERMANY, WEST, faced a flood of Third World refugees from East Berlin in 1986. West German officials feared the number of such refugees entering the country would reach 100,000 by year-end. The government said that East Germany was taking improper advantage of West Germany's refugee policy. West Germany gives an unrestricted right of entry to any foreign citizen claiming political asylum. The refugees came from Libya, Iran, Turkey, Ghana, Sri Lanka, and other countries. See GERMANY, EAST.

New Rules. To stem the tide, West Germany's Chancellor Helmut Kohl announced on August 27 that citizens of certain Third World countries would need visas to enter West Germany. Airlines that failed to check passengers for visas would have to pay for illegal passengers' return journeys and face fines of $1,000 per illegal passenger.

Kohl Cleared. On February 17, a prosecutor in Koblenz decided to investigate charges that Kohl lied to a parliamentary committee of the state of Rhineland-Palatinate in 1985. The committee had been investigating alleged illegal campaign contributions made through tax-exempt foundations.

On March 11, 1986, a state prosecutor in Bonn announced an investigation into charges that in 1984 Kohl lied to a federal committee investigating a much bigger case involving undeclared polit-

ical donations. Otto Schily, a member of the environmentalist and antinuclear Green Party, said Kohl had concealed the receipt of $22,000 from the giant Flick group of companies for the Christian Democratic Union.

In May 1986, the two prosecutors halted their investigations, citing insufficient evidence. Kohl accused his opponents of misusing "the organs of justice for political goals."

Terrorist Blast. On April 5, a terrorist bomb exploded in a crowded discothèque in West Berlin, killing three people, including two United States soldiers, and injuring more than 200. The La Belle disco was popular with U.S. troops stationed in the city. The United States blamed Libya for the attack and on April 9, West Germany expelled two Libyan diplomats. Bonn said that clues pointed to Libyan involvement in the attack.

Nuclear Protests. A nuclear disaster that occurred in the Soviet Union on April 26 had political repercussions in West Germany. The disaster occurred when operators at the Soviets' Chernobyl nuclear power station lost control of a reactor. The reactor exploded, and winds spread radioactive particles throughout the world.

West German environmentalists, led by the Green Party, protested and demonstrated against the use of nuclear power in West Germany. On

West German police confront demonstrators during a May protest against
the construction of a nuclear waste reprocessing plant in eastern Bavaria.

May 19, the Greens demanded an immediate shutdown of all West Germany's nuclear power plants. On May 25, the Free Democratic Party, a partner in the coalition that governs West Germany, called for a review of nuclear policy. And on the same day, West Germany's President Richard von Weizsäcker criticized the government's plan to build more nuclear plants.

Kohl promised safety checks at all nuclear plants and on June 3 created a ministry of the environment, nature conservation, and reactor safety. But protests continued throughout the summer. See ENERGY SUPPLY (Close-Up).

Wall Anniversary. On August 13, West Germany marked the 25th anniversary of the start of construction on the Berlin Wall, which separates West from East Berlin. West Germans laid wreaths along the wall in memory of individuals who were killed while trying to get into West Berlin.

Falling Prices. Consumer prices fell in West Germany for the first time in 27 years, resulting in an inflation rate of zero for 1986. The government still feared inflation, however. On September 9, Finance Minister Gerhard Stoltenberg had said that, because of this fear, the government would not meet U.S. and French requests to stimulate consumer demand.   Kenneth Brown

See also EUROPE (Facts in Brief Table). In WORLD BOOK, see GERMANY.

GHANA. Good rains, together with the government's economic recovery program, made Ghana again self-sufficient in rice, palm oil, yams, and cassava in 1986. The nation's foreign-trade deficit was eased by larger exports of cacao and timber and the increased mining of bauxite, gold, diamonds, and manganese. Nevertheless, Ghana continued to face an economic crisis and was forced to seek a loan from the International Monetary Fund (IMF), an agency of the United Nations. As a result of IMF-required austerity measures, as well as a government crackdown on corruption and tax evasion, the inflation rate dropped and shortages in many consumer items eased.

Rebel plots against the regime of Ghana's leader, Jerry John Rawlings, were uncovered during the year in the United States, Brazil, and Togo. Although army and local chiefs still supported Rawlings, many citizens protested the government's belt-tightening policies and alleged human-rights violations.

Rawlings strengthened Ghana's links with the Soviet Union, Libya, and Nicaragua in 1986— even though most economic aid to Ghana is provided by Western Europe and the United States. Ghana also improved its relations with its African neighbors.   J. Gus Liebenow and Beverly B. Liebenow

See also AFRICA (Facts in Brief Table). In WORLD BOOK, see GHANA.

GHIZ, JOSEPH A. (1945-   ), leader of the Liberal Party of Prince Edward Island, was elected premier on April 21, 1986. His decisive victory ousted Progressive Conservative leader James M. Lee, 49, who had been premier since 1981. See PRINCE EDWARD ISLAND.

Ghiz's campaign centered on the depressed state of the farm economy and a commitment to family values and community. In one of his first moves as premier, he established new ministries for tourism and fisheries. He also combined community and cultural affairs into one ministry.

Ghiz was born in Charlottetown, P.E.I., on Jan. 27, 1945. He graduated from Dalhousie University in Halifax, N.S., in 1966 and earned a law degree from Harvard Law School in Cambridge, Mass., in 1969.

In 1970, he became crown prosecutor for Queens County, Prince Edward Island. From 1972 to 1979, he served as federal narcotics drug prosecutor.

In 1981, Ghiz left the law firm of Scales, Ghiz, Jenkins & McQuaid in Charlottetown to set up private practice in that city, and became leader of the Liberal Party.

In 1972, Ghiz married Rose Ellen McGowan. They have two children.   Mary A. Krier

GIRL SCOUTS. See YOUTH ORGANIZATIONS.
GIRLS CLUBS. See YOUTH ORGANIZATIONS.

GOLF. Greg Norman of Australia and Bob Tway and Pat Bradley of the United States became the golfers of the year in 1986. The 31-year-old Norman and the 27-year-old Tway dominated the men's tour, and the 35-year-old Bradley dominated the women's. They broke earnings records, and they played their best golf in the Grand Slam tournaments.

In the four Grand Slam tournaments, 46-year-old Jack Nicklaus became the oldest winner of the Masters (see NICKLAUS, JACK). Raymond Floyd, 43, became the oldest winner of the United States Open. The other Grand Slam winners were Norman in the British Open and Tway in the Professional Golfers' Association (PGA) championship.

Norman was at his best in those major tournaments. He led after the third round of the Masters; the second and third rounds of the United States Open; the second, third, and final rounds of the British Open; and the first, second, and third rounds of the PGA. Norman finished second in the Masters and the PGA and 12th in the United States Open. He won two tournaments in the United States, three in Europe, and three in Australia. He led the American tour in earnings with $653,296, and overall he won $1.8 million.

Grand Slam. The Masters, played from April 10 to 13 in Augusta, Ga., provided Nicklaus with his 6th Masters victory and his 20th Grand Slam title,

Jack Nicklaus watches as his birdie putt rolls toward the 17th hole at the Masters in April. Nicklaus won it a record sixth time—at age 46.

both records. The win surprised many because he had in recent years spent more time designing golf courses than playing on them.

In the Masters, he was 4 strokes out of first place with four holes to play. He made an eagle and two birdies on those four holes, giving him a 65 for the day and 279 for the 72 holes.

Tom Kite, needing an 8-foot (2.4-meter) putt on the last hole to tie Nicklaus, barely missed it. Norman, after four straight birdies, needed a par on the 18th to tie Nicklaus. But Norman hit his approach shot into the crowd and took a bogey 5. He and Kite each finished a shot behind Nicklaus.

In the United States Open, held from June 12 to 15 in Southampton, N.Y., Floyd's 279 beat Lanny Wadkins and Chip Beck by 2 strokes. In the British Open, held from July 17 to 20 in Turnberry, Scotland, Norman's 280 provided a 5-stroke victory over Gordon Brand of England. In the PGA championship, from August 7 to 11 in Toledo, Ohio, Tway sank a 25-foot (7.6-meter) bunker shot on the last hole for a birdie and a 276. A disheartened Norman then took a bogey and finished 2 strokes behind Tway.

PGA Tour. The 43 tournaments on the PGA Tour paid record prize money of more than $25-million plus a $2-million bonus pool. Tway won four tournaments, more than anyone else.

LPGA Tour. The Ladies Professional Golf Association (LPGA) staged 36 tournaments with record prize money of $10.1 million. Bradley won five tournaments. She led in prize money with $492,021 and became the first woman to reach $2 million in career earnings.

Bradley won three of the four Grand Slam tournaments. She took the Nabisco Dinah Shore by 2 strokes in April in Rancho Mirage, Calif. Her 15-foot (4.6-meter) birdie putt on the last hole of the LPGA championship tournament, played from May 29 to June 1 in Kings Island, Ohio, gave her a 1-stroke victory. In the Du Maurier Classic, held from July 24 to 27 in Woodbridge, Canada, she was 9 strokes behind after two rounds. Then she shot a 67 and a 66, tying Ayako Okamoto of Japan. Bradley then won on the first play-off hole.

The only Grand Slam tournament that eluded Bradley was the United States Open, held from July 10 to 14 in Kettering, Ohio. Bradley tied for fifth place. Jane Geddes and Sally Little tied for first, and Geddes' 71 beat Little by 2 strokes in an 18-hole play-off.

Seniors. On the PGA Seniors tour for golfers 50 and older, Bruce Crampton of Australia led in tournament victories (seven) and earnings ($454,299). Dale Douglass won the United States Open, Gary Player won the PGA Seniors championship, and Chi Chi Rodriguez won the Tournament Players Championship. Frank Litsky

In WORLD BOOK, see GOLF.

GREAT BRITAIN. As 1986 began, the Conservative Party government of Prime Minister Margaret Thatcher was already engulfed in a major political crisis that forced the resignation of two of her Cabinet ministers in January and weakened her chances for reelection. The crisis was over the unlikely subject of helicopters.

In late 1985, Westland PLC, Britain's only helicopter manufacturer, was on the verge of bankruptcy. Although the company manufactured helicopters used by Britain's military forces, Thatcher refused to give financial aid to Westland. Instead, the government called in financier Sir John Cuckney to put together a plan to save the company. Acting as Westland's chairman, Cuckney turned to a United States helicopter manufacturer, Sikorsky Aircraft, a division of United Technologies Corporation in Hartford, Conn., which was willing to invest in the British company in cooperation with Fiat S.p.A. of Italy.

The American-backed deal, however, was opposed by Michael Heseltine, Britain's secretary of state for defense. Heseltine, a believer in European collaboration in defense manufacturing, began a furious campaign to stop the Sikorsky deal. He put together a rival deal involving five helicopter companies—one each from West Germany, France, and Italy; and two British companies, British Aerospace PLC and the General Electric Company of Britain.

This arrangement did not please Thatcher or Cuckney, who were convinced that the Sikorsky deal had the better chance of success. Thatcher and Leon Brittan, secretary of trade and industry, began working behind the scenes to prevent Heseltine's campaign from succeeding. On January 9, when Thatcher announced in a Cabinet meeting that all public statements on Westland would have to be cleared with her office, Heseltine rose dramatically from his chair, stalked out of the Cabinet room, and resigned. With Heseltine's departure, the Sikorsky deal moved forward. On February 12, Westland shareholders finally approved the Sikorsky-Fiat package.

The Westland crisis had a significant negative impact on Thatcher's political standing. At the height of the controversy, the House of Commons discovered that on January 6 the government leaked a confidential letter to the press from Solicitor General Sir Patrick Mayhew, the government's chief lawyer, to Heseltine. The letter accused Heseltine of inaccuracies in a letter he had written to *The* (London) *Times* on the Westland deal. The leaked letter damaged Heseltine's position, and Thatcher ordered an inquiry into how the letter was released.

Thousands of children carrying daffodils wish Queen Elizabeth II of Great Britain happy 60th birthday outside Buckingham Palace on April 21.

A Princely Wedding for Andrew and Sarah

On July 23, 1986, Sarah Margaret Ferguson, a vivacious redhead who answers to the nickname of Fergie, married Prince Andrew, second son of Queen Elizabeth II and fourth in line of succession to the British throne. It was a fairy-tale wedding that captured the hearts of millions of people around the world. It was also a defiant statement to the world by Great Britain that despite the British government's support for the United States bombing of Libya in April 1986, London was a safe place to visit.

The authorities took no chances, however. Security forces were out in strength on the wedding day. Specially trained dogs sniffed for explosives that might have been placed in sewers beneath the procession route. Potential bomb sites, such as mailboxes and manholes, were sealed shut. Some 2,000 uniformed police officers and 1,600 service personnel were on duty, including armed police disguised as royal coachmen and footmen.

Sarah Ferguson and Prince Andrew, the Duchess and Duke of York, wave to well-wishers after their wedding in London on July 23.

In the end, everything went smoothly, and the pomp and pageantry unfolded without a hitch. Some 500,000 people lined the royal procession route. Five state coaches drawn by impeccably groomed gray horses and escorted by the Household Cavalry in scarlet uniforms and gleaming breastplates clattered through the gates of Buckingham Palace. Andrew, a lieutenant in the Royal Navy, wore a blue naval uniform. He rode to Westminster Abbey with his younger brother, Edward, the best man. Just before the ceremony, Buckingham Palace announced that Queen Elizabeth had given Andrew the title of Duke of York, an honor traditionally bestowed on the second son of the sovereign. The title was last held by the queen's father, King George VI.

At 11:28 A.M., Sarah stepped from the glass coach traditionally used by royal brides at the west door of historic Westminster Abbey, and the watching world was able to see her wedding dress for the first time. Created by Linda Cierach, a Polish-born British designer, the dress was made of ivory satin with a fitted bodice and puffed medieval-style sleeves. It was embroidered with patterns of bees and thistles from the bride's newly created coat of arms, and the 17½-foot (5-meter) train shimmered with anchors, hearts, and waves that were etched in beadwork.

Sarah looked relaxed and radiant as she walked up the aisle past the approximately 1,800 guests, who included British Prime Minister Margaret Thatcher, first lady of the United States Nancy Reagan, and members of 17 foreign royal families. The couple were married by Robert A. K. Runcie, archbishop of Canterbury. Sarah had said that she would use the word ace (Andrew's initials) as a way of remembering the order of Andrew's four given names—Andrew Albert Christian Edward. Nevertheless, she stumbled briefly over the name *Christian* during the exchange of vows. Unlike Diana, Princess of Wales—who married Andrew's older brother, Prince Charles, in 1981—Sarah affirmed her willingness to obey her husband, according to the rites of the Church of England. She explained "someone is going to have to make the decisions." Andrew then slipped onto her finger a wedding ring made of 22-carat Welsh gold.

After a triumphal ride in an open carriage back to Buckingham Palace, the happy couple appeared on the balcony. There, Andrew gave Sarah a kiss, to the delight of the cheering crowd. After a wedding breakfast, the Duke and Duchess of York flew to the Azores—a group of islands off the coast of Portugal—to begin their honeymoon cruise aboard the royal yacht *Britannia*.   Ian Mather

Leaders of the Commonwealth meet with British Prime Minister Margaret Thatcher, right, in London on August 4 to discuss South Africa.

Trade Secretary Brittan admitted that he had authorized the leak, and he resigned on January 24 despite Thatcher's efforts to persuade him to stay. Many political observers, including the House of Commons Select Committee on Defence, found it difficult to believe that Thatcher did not know at the time she set up the inquiry that it had been her own trade secretary who had authorized the leak and that her press secretary, Bernard Ingham, was also involved.

Libyan Raid. Thatcher's personal popularity and the Conservative Party's reelection chances received a further blow when she agreed to let the United States use U.S. F-111 bombers based in Britain for a raid against Libya on April 15. The reaction in Britain to the raid was hostile. Many Britons, especially those who lived near U.S. bases, felt they had been placed in the front line against terrorism and feared reprisals from Libya.

Hard Line Against Terrorism. Britain took a firm step against terrorism after the October 24 conviction of Nezar Hindawi, a Jordanian who hid a sophisticated bomb in the baggage of his pregnant Irish girlfriend just before she boarded an El Al flight from London to Tel Aviv, Israel. The bomb, timed to explode in midair, would have killed 375 people if an airport security guard had not spotted it. Hindawi was sentenced to 45 years in prison. Evidence showing the Syrian government's involvement in the bombing attempt was considered so overwhelming that Britain broke off diplomatic relations with Syria on October 24.

Britain's Labour Party. During the year, the opposition Labour Party used Thatcher's misfortunes to move ahead in the opinion polls. Labour Party leader Neil G. Kinnock presented a new moderate image to voters. The Labour Party substituted gray for the traditional red color in its campaign materials and adopted the rose as its symbol. It also dropped most of its traditional radical demands, including the nationalization of key industries.

Kinnock also had some success against members of the Militant Tendency, an extreme left wing group that had become influential within the Labour Party. At its annual conference on September 29, Labour Party members approved the expulsion of eight Militant leaders who had taken over the Labour Party in Liverpool.

Disagreement with the United States over the Labour Party's defense program grew in 1986. The party reaffirmed that a Labour government would order all U.S. nuclear weapons out of Britain and would scrap Britain's aging Polaris nuclear-missile submarines and cancel plans to replace them with submarines carrying Trident missiles. In December, however, the party hinted that it might relax its firm stand if it came to power.

Big Bang. To reestablish London as a leading financial center, the government abolished all restrictions and regulations governing the Stock Exchange on October 27. The move, dubbed "Big Bang," allowed foreigners to become members. It also merged the functions of *stockjobbers*, members of the exchange who deal with other exchange members, with those of *stockbrokers*, who act as agents for investors. Minimum commissions were abolished, opening up competition. Foreign financial institutions, particularly in the United States and Japan, quickly moved in, signaling another step toward a unified world financial market.

Economy. The British government continued its austere economic policies in 1986. The inflation rate held steady at about 3 per cent, wages rose about 7 per cent, and unemployment dropped for the first time in 10 years. Critics claimed that the improved unemployment figures did not reflect an actual drop in joblessness. Under a new policy, long-term unemployed who failed to appear for government interviews were dropped from the unemployment rolls.

"Chunnel" Go-Ahead. Prime Minister Thatcher and French President François Mitterrand met at the northern French city of Lille on January 20 to announce the approval of a tunnel under the English Channel. The 31-mile (50-kilometer) link between England and France will consist of two separate rail tunnels. An Anglo-French consortium, the Channel Tunnel Group Limited, won the contract to build the "chunnel," which is expected to be completed in 1993. Cross-channel ferry companies and environmental groups announced that they would fight the plan.

Labor. For once, Britain did not live up to its reputation as a strike-prone nation. The only major industrial dispute in 1986 began on January 24 when three print unions, which had successfully resisted the introduction of labor-saving technology for many years, went out on strike. On January 26, Rupert Murdoch, owner of four national newspapers, including *The Times* and *The Sunday Times*, moved his printing operation from Fleet Street to a new computerized plant in Wapping, another area of London. Murdoch fired 5,500 workers who had gone on strike to protest the new facility. The unions began a massive campaign to force Murdoch to close the Wapping plant, and there were frequent clashes between police and demonstrators. Several attempts at negotiating a settlement failed.

Archer Resigns. Best-selling novelist Jeffrey Archer, deputy chairman of the Conservative Party, announced on October 26 that he was resigning from the post after press reports revealed that he had arranged to pay a prostitute to leave Britain. Archer denied any relationship with the woman and said he had offered her the money to avoid harmful publicity. He was resigning, he said, because of a "lack of judgment."

The Royal Year. Queen Elizabeth celebrated her 60th birthday on April 21. In the afternoon, 6,000 daffodil-waving children visited Buckingham Palace and sang her a special birthday song. The day was capped with a special gala in her honor at Covent Garden.

The royal event of the year, however, was the wedding of Prince Andrew, the second son of Queen Elizabeth and Prince Philip, to Sarah Ferguson on July 23. The ceremony took place at Westminster Abbey (see Close-Up).

In October, Queen Elizabeth toured China, the first such visit by a reigning British monarch. The visit was important for business and international relations.

Sports. England's soccer team lost to Argentina in the quarterfinal round of the 1986 World Cup on June 22 in Mexico (see SOCCER). On September 27, London welterweight boxer Lloyd Honeyghan, 26, beat welterweight champion Donald Curry of the United States to win the world title. On March 29, Cambridge University beat Oxford in the 132nd University Boat Race on the River Thames for the first time in 11 years.   Ian Mather

See also ANDREW, PRINCE; ENGLAND; FERGUSON, SARAH; IRELAND; NORTHERN IRELAND; SCOTLAND; WALES. In WORLD BOOK, see GREAT BRITAIN.

GREECE. Relations with the United States became strained in the spring of 1986 after Greece criticized the United States for bombing what the U.S. called "terrorist-related targets" in Libya on April 15. Greece called for an emergency meeting of European foreign ministers to consider the "abnormal and dangerous" situation. In addition, Foreign Minister Karolos Papoulias criticized Great Britain and France for failing to inform Greece that they knew of the U.S. raid in advance.

No Sanctions. Greece rejected an April 21 decision by its fellow members of the European Community (EC or Common Market) to impose sanctions against Libya. Greece refused to impose sanctions until it had what it considered conclusive evidence of a link between Libya and international terrorism. Robert V. Keeley, U.S. ambassador to Greece, told Prime Minister Andreas Papandreou that the United States was displeased with Greece's attitude toward Libya. Keeley hinted that friction over the Libyan issue might jeopardize relations with the United States at a time when the future of U.S. military bases in Greece was not settled. In July, Greece fell into line with the EC, cutting the size of Libya's diplomatic mission in Athens by one-third.

Quarrel with Turkey. On March 21, Greece rejected a proposed dialogue with Turkey to end disputes that have disrupted North Atlantic

Treaty Organization (NATO) planning. Both nations are members of this organization, but they have refused to cooperate in NATO military exercises in the eastern Mediterranean Sea.

In August 1986, Greece took action to block the normalization of relations between the EC and Turkey. Turkey had become an EC *associate*—entitled to special trading rights with EC nations—in 1964. But the EC suspended that agreement in 1980 after army officers took control of Turkey. In June 1986, the EC granted special aid to Turkey to mark the end of the suspension. But in August, Greece asked the Court of Justice, the EC's supreme court, to cancel the aid.

Economic Woes. In January, the EC granted Greece an emergency loan of $1.5 billion to support the government's austerity program, imposed in 1985 to curb inflation and cut imports. Austerity measures included a wage freeze and restrictions on imports.   Kenneth Brown

See also EUROPE (Facts in Brief Table). In WORLD BOOK, see EUROPEAN COMMUNITY; GREECE.

GRENADA. See LATIN AMERICA; WEST INDIES.

GUATEMALA. See LATIN AMERICA.

GUINEA. See AFRICA.

GUINEA-BISSAU. See AFRICA.

GUYANA. See LATIN AMERICA.

HAITI. Haitians took to the streets in wild jubilation on Feb. 7, 1986, to celebrate the end of a father-son dictatorship that had lasted 29 years. That day, President Jean-Claude Duvalier flew into exile in France, following months of street protests and strikes. A state of siege proclaimed by Duvalier on January 31 had been unable to silence the protests, which were sparked by political repression and bad economic conditions.

Baby Doc, as he was called to distinguish him from his father—Haitian dictator François (Papa Doc) Duvalier, who died in 1971—turned over the government to a joint military-civilian council before fleeing. The new provisional government was headed by the armed forces chief of staff, 54-year-old Lieutenant General Henri Namphy. He was assigned the task of returning the country to democracy. That proved to be a tall order. Haiti emerged from dictatorship as the poorest country in the Western Hemisphere.

Haitians' Hopes for a quick reversal in their fortunes were not to be realized. Half of the country's labor force was unemployed. Life expectancy was just 53 years—a third less than in some of Haiti's Caribbean neighbors. Illiteracy was so widespread that 4 out of 5 Haitians could not read or write any language, and 9 out of 10 could not read or write French, the official language.

Haiti's President Jean-Claude Duvalier and his wife, Michele, drive to the airport in February, fleeing Haiti for exile in France.

HANDICAPPED

Haitians vented their anger at hated officials of past Duvalier administrations. Riots broke out when Haitians learned that the government had allowed the former chief of police of Port-au-Prince, Colonel Albert Pierre, to leave the country.

In reaction, the provisional government announced on February 27 that it would forbid the departure of those popularly believed to have participated in Duvalier-era crimes. Earlier that month, the government had announced the abolition of the hated Tontons Macoutes, the secret security police who reportedly tortured and killed thousands of Haitians. On July 16, Luc Desyr, chief of security under both François and Jean-Claude Duvalier, was convicted of murder and torture and sentenced to death.

New Constitution. The turnout was low when Haitians voted on October 19 to select 41 people to write a new constitution. The planned constitution was part of a process that called for a gradual transition to democracy with Haitians electing a new president in November 1987. Some critics blamed the low voter turnout on inadequate publicity for the election. Others said that Haitians stayed away from the polls to protest the failure of the provisional government to meet basic economic needs. Nathan A. Haverstock

See also LATIN AMERICA (Facts in Brief Table). In WORLD BOOK, see HAITI.

Canadian Rick Hansen wheels across the Great Wall of China in May during his world tour to raise money for spinal research and wheelchair sports.

HANDICAPPED. Government regulations requiring hospitals to treat newborn infants with severe handicaps were struck down by the Supreme Court of the United States on June 9, 1986. The so-called Baby Doe regulations also gave federal investigators access to hospital records and facilities. The court said that the federal Baby Doe regulations were unjustified, because there was no evidence that any hospital had discriminated against handicapped newborns by refusing treatment. Federal law does not require hospitals to treat handicapped infants without parental consent, according to the 1986 ruling.

Airline Exemption. The Supreme Court also ruled in June that commercial airlines are exempt from a 1973 federal law barring discrimination against the handicapped. The law prohibits discrimination in any program or activity that receives federal funds.

A federal appeals court had ruled that airlines were covered by the law because air-traffic controllers are paid by the government and airlines use airports that receive federal grants. Advocates for the rights of the handicapped had argued that coverage under the law was necessary to eliminate requirements by some airlines that make air travel difficult for handicapped people. For example, some airlines require handicapped passengers to travel with an attendant. The court ruled, however, that the 1973 law applies only to airlines that receive direct aid from the federal government—a small number of air carriers.

AIDS as Handicap. Federal laws forbidding discrimination against the handicapped provide only limited protection for victims of acquired immune deficiency syndrome (AIDS), according to a ruling by the U.S. Department of Justice in June 1986. The ruling distinguished between the disabling effects of AIDS and the ability of AIDS victims to communicate the disease to others. As a result, an employer may fire employees with AIDS—and employees who have been exposed to the virus but show no symptoms of the disease—if the employer is acting solely out of fear that the employee will spread the disease.

Employers may take such action even if their fear of contagion is unreasonable, according to the ruling. An employer may not discriminate against employees with AIDS simply on the assumption that the disease will prevent the employee from doing the job.

Many states rejected the Justice Department's ruling. They declared that AIDS victims are entitled to the same civil rights protection as other handicapped people. Barbara A. Mayes

In WORLD BOOK, see HANDICAPPED.
HARNESS RACING. See HORSE RACING.
HAWAII. See STATE GOVERNMENT.

HEALTH AND DISEASE. The United States Department of Health and Human Services (HHS) predicted on June 12, 1986, that the number of cases of acquired immune deficiency syndrome (AIDS) in the United States will reach "staggering" proportions by 1991. HHS estimated that AIDS cases and deaths will grow tenfold during the period. AIDS is a viral disease that cripples the body's disease-fighting immune system, making victims vulnerable to lethal infections and rare forms of cancer. By early December 1986, the United States Centers for Disease Control (CDC) in Atlanta, Ga., had reported more than 28,000 cases of AIDS and almost 16,000 deaths since 1981.

The HHS projections were based on reports from a panel of AIDS specialists who met from June 4 to 6 in Berkeley Springs, W. Va., to review national objectives in battling the disease. HHS estimated that 270,000 Americans will develop AIDS by the end of 1991. Of these, 179,000 will have died. In 1991 alone, AIDS will kill 54,000 Americans, causing more deaths than automobile accidents did in 1982. HHS predicted that costs of caring for AIDS patients will reach $8 billion to $16 billion annually by 1991.

The officials foresaw no scientific breakthrough in the next five years that might halt the AIDS epidemic or cure the disease. They explained that because most of the people who will develop AIDS by 1991 already have the virus, a vaccine would be of little help to them.

HHS said that AIDS will continue to strike primarily homosexual and bisexual men, who will account for 70 per cent of AIDS cases. Approximately 25 per cent of the victims will be intravenous drug abusers who use contaminated needles. CDC officials, however, predicted more frequent AIDS transmission among heterosexual men and women who are intravenous drug abusers. AIDS will also spread more and more outside of New York City and San Francisco, which account for 41 per cent of all cases at present.

The World Health Organization (WHO), an agency of the United Nations, expressed concern about the growing number of AIDS cases in other parts of the world. On June 23, 1986, WHO estimated that 5 million to 10 million people around the world have been infected with the AIDS virus.

Chemical Cancer. A study conducted by the National Cancer Institute in Bethesda, Md., and the University of Kansas Medical Center in Kansas City concluded on August 29 that agricultural workers exposed to *herbicides* (poisonous chemicals used to kill weeds) face an increased risk of lymphatic cancer. The study found that farmers exposed to herbicides for 20 or more days per year are six times more likely to develop cancer than other farmers.

The risk was especially great for workers exposed

AIDS: Reported U.S. Cases and Deaths*

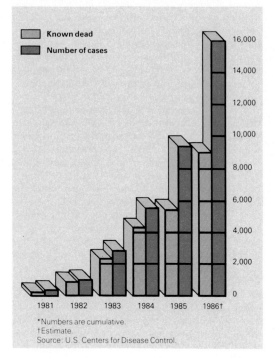

Known dead
Number of cases

16,000
14,000
12,000
10,000
8,000
6,000
4,000
2,000
0

1981 1982 1983 1984 1985 1986†

*Numbers are cumulative.
†Estimate.
Source: U.S. Centers for Disease Control.

to a chemical called 2,4-D, which is found in many herbicides. The study said farmers could reduce the risk by wearing masks, gloves, and other protective clothing when handling herbicides.

On September 17, scientists at Barnert Memorial Medical Center in Paterson, N.J., verified for the first time that Vietnam War veterans exposed to Agent Orange—a weedkiller used to defoliate trees and kill crop plants during the war—still have high levels of dioxin in their blood and body fat. Dioxin, a component of Agent Orange, is a highly poisonous substance. Some Vietnam veterans believe it is responsible for cancer and other health problems, such as birth defects and nerve and skin disorders.

No Pill Peril. Millions of women who take birth control pills received reassurance on August 14 when the CDC released the results of a cancer study described as the largest and most comprehensive ever conducted. The study presented conclusive evidence that long-term use of the pill does not increase a woman's risk of breast cancer, even among women with a family history of the disease. The study included approximately 9,400 women between the ages of 20 and 54.

Sulfites Banned. On July 8, the United States Food and Drug Administration (FDA) banned the use of sulfite food preservatives on raw fruits and vegetables. The FDA had proposed such a ban in

1985 after reports of severe allergic reactions and deaths among people sensitive to sulfites. The ban applied to sulfite compounds used to preserve the color of fresh fruits and vegetables served in restaurant and supermarket salad bars.

Cold Clue. Scientists at Purdue University in West Lafayette, Ind., on Sept. 12, 1986, reported progress in understanding how viruses that cause the common cold and other diseases spread and reproduce. Working with two experimental drugs, the researchers found they could interrupt the process by which viruses reproduce. The drugs may eventually be tested as cold preventives.

Infant Deaths. Finland had the lowest infant mortality rate in the world in 1982, according to data released on Sept. 17, 1986, by the Population Reference Bureau of Washington, D.C. The infant mortality rate, an indicator of a country's health status, is the number of deaths among infants under 12 months old for every 1,000 live births. Finland's infant mortality rate was 6.0, followed by Japan with 6.6 and Sweden with 6.8. Canada's rate of 9.1 put it in 9th place. With a rate of 11.5, the United States was 17th.   Michael Woods

See also MEDICINE; MENTAL ILLNESS; NUTRITION; PSYCHOLOGY; PUBLIC HEALTH. In the WORLD BOOK SUPPLEMENT section, see AIDS.

HOBBIES. See COIN COLLECTING; STAMP COLLECTING; TOYS AND GAMES.

HOCKEY. The National Hockey League (NHL) enjoyed a prosperous 1985-1986 season. Gate receipts and television income for the 21 teams exceeded $200 million, a record. Arenas were filled to 85 per cent of capacity. And the Stanley Cup play-offs produced one surprise after another, ending in victory for the Montreal Canadiens.

Regular Season. Each team played 80 games from October 1985 to April 1986, with the 16 leaders advancing to the play-offs. The division winners were the Edmonton Oilers with 119 points, the Philadelphia Flyers with 110, the Quebec Nordiques with 92, and the Chicago Black Hawks with 86.

Wayne Gretzky, Edmonton's celebrated center, led the league with 163 assists and 215 points, breaking his NHL single-season records of 135 assists and 212 points. Jari Kurri, Gretzky's linemate, led in goals with 68. Play-off records were broken by Gretzky's 103rd assist and Mike Bossy's 83rd goal. Bossy played for the New York Islanders.

Gretzky won the Hart Trophy as the regular season's Most Valuable Player for a record seventh straight year. He won the Ross Trophy as scoring champion for the sixth straight year.

Play-Offs. Three division winners were eliminated in the first round—Philadelphia by the New York Rangers, Quebec by the Hartford Whalers,

National Hockey League Standings

Prince of Wales Conference

Charles F. Adams Division	W.	L.	T.	Pts.
Quebec Nordiques	43	31	6	92
Montreal Canadiens	40	33	7	87
Boston Bruins	37	31	12	86
Hartford Whalers	40	36	4	84
Buffalo Sabres	37	37	6	80

Lester Patrick Division				
Philadelphia Flyers	53	23	4	110
Washington Capitals	50	23	7	107
New York Islanders	39	29	12	90
New York Rangers	36	38	6	78
Pittsburgh Penguins	34	38	8	76
New Jersey Devils	28	49	3	59

Clarence Campbell Conference

James Norris Division				
Chicago Black Hawks	39	33	8	86
Minnesota North Stars	38	33	9	85
St. Louis Blues	37	34	9	83
Toronto Maple Leafs	25	48	7	57
Detroit Red Wings	17	57	6	40

Conn Smythe Division				
Edmonton Oilers	56	17	7	119
Calgary Flames	40	31	9	89
Winnipeg Jets	26	47	7	59
Vancouver Canucks	23	44	13	59
Los Angeles Kings	23	49	8	54

Scoring Leaders	Games	Goals	Assists	Pts.
Wayne Gretzky, Edmonton	80	52	163	215
Mario Lemieux, Pittsburgh	79	48	93	141
Paul Coffey, Edmonton	79	48	90	138
Jari Kurri, Edmonton	78	68	63	131
Mike Bossy, New York Islanders	80	61	62	123
Peter Stastny, Quebec	76	41	81	122
Denis Savard, Chicago	80	47	69	116
Mats Naslund, Montreal	80	43	67	110
Dale Hawerchuk, Winnipeg	80	46	59	105
Neal Broten, Minnesota	80	29	76	105
Michel Goulet, Quebec	75	53	51	104

Leading Goalies (25 or more games)	Games	Goals against	Avg.
Bob Froese, Philadelphia	51	116	2.55
Al Jensen, Washington	44	129	3.18
Kelly Hrudey, New York Islanders	45	137	3.21
Clint Malarchuk, Quebec	46	142	3.21

Awards

Calder Trophy (best rookie)—Gary Suter, Calgary
Hart Trophy (most valuable player)—Wayne Gretzky, Edmonton
Lady Byng Trophy (sportsmanship)—Mike Bossy, New York Islanders
Masterton Trophy (perseverance, dedication to hockey)—Charlie Simmer, Boston
Norris Trophy (best defenseman)—Paul Coffey, Edmonton
Ross Trophy (leading scorer)—Wayne Gretzky, Edmonton
Selke Trophy (best defensive forward)—Troy Murray, Chicago
Smythe Trophy (most valuable player in Stanley Cup)—Patrick Roy, Montreal
Vezina Trophy (most valuable goalie)—John Vanbiesbrouck, New York Rangers

The Calgary Flames' Lanny McDonald tries to slip the puck past Montreal
Canadiens goalie Patrick Roy during the Stanley Cup finals in May.

and Chicago by the Toronto Maple Leafs. In the
second round, Edmonton, favored to win its third
straight Stanley Cup, was eliminated in the seventh and final game by the Calgary Flames.

The play-off finals between Montreal and Calgary were the first between two Canadian teams
since 1967. Calgary had a strong offense but a
weak defense. Montreal was a good defensive
team with a rookie coach in Jean Perron and eight
rookie players. Among those rookies were goalie
Patrick Roy and forward Claude Lemieux, who
both emerged as play-off stars.

The play-off finals ran from May 16 to 24. After
Calgary had won the first game, Montreal took the
next four for a 4-1 victory in games. The Stanley
Cup was Montreal's 23rd.

Roy, who humorously revealed that he talked to
the goal posts before games, won the Conn
Smythe Trophy as the Most Valuable Player in the
play-offs. His play-off record showed a goals-
against average of 1.92. Lemieux scored 10 play-
off goals, including 4 game winners.

World. The Soviet Union won its 20th world
championship on April 28 in Moscow. It swept its
seven games in the round-robin preliminaries and
the three games in the medal round. Canada was
third. The United States, using both professional
and college players, was sixth.   Frank Litsky

In WORLD BOOK, see HOCKEY.

HONDURAS. José Azcona del Hoyo, a 59-year-old
engineer, was sworn in as Honduras' president on
Jan. 27, 1986 (see AZCONA DEL HOYO, JOSÉ).
Throughout 1986, Azcona carefully avoided discussing what former Foreign Minister Edgardo
Paz Bárnica characterized as the "Lebanonization"
of Honduras—a reference to Honduras' central
position in strife-torn Central America. But Hondurans on all levels of society expressed growing
fears about their country's use as a military base
for United States and Nicaraguan rebel forces
seeking to overthrow the regime in Nicaragua.

In 1986, the United States began construction
of an airfield in Honduras, near the village of Mocorón and the Nicaraguan border—the sixth airfield built since 1983. Large-scale U.S. military
maneuvers also took place during 1986. One exercise involved 4,400 U.S. troops over a two-
month period. Another involved 2,000 U.S. troops
in March in an exercise apparently aimed at preparing for a possible invasion of Nicaragua at
some time in the future. By mid-1986, 40,000 U.S.
troops had participated in military maneuvers in
Honduras since those maneuvers began in 1983.

Despite an economic boom fueled by U.S. military spending, the Honduran government announced on Aug. 22, 1986, that it would not permit the United States to use its territory to train
Nicaraguan rebels. The announcement followed

Newly elected Honduran President José Azcona del Hoyo waves to supporters as he rides in a motorcade to his inauguration in January.

HORSE RACING. The third annual Breeders' Cup at Santa Anita Park in Arcadia, Calif., on Nov. 1, 1986, focused attention on two possible Horse of the Year candidates. They were Lady's Secret, the 4-year-old daughter of Secretariat, who won 10 of 15 races in 1986, and Manila, a 3-year-old colt with 8 wins in 10 starts, most on the turf.

Lady's Secret won the $1-million Breeders' Cup Distaff, and Manila captured the $2-million Turf, in which Dancing Brave—the favorite and the champion of Europe—was fourth. Lady's Secret was trained by D. Wayne Lukas, who for a second straight year won two Breeders' Cup races and surpassed his own earnings record, going over $11.1 million. His other winner was Capote in the Juvenile.

None of the Triple Crown winners competed in the Breeders' Cup. Ferdinand won the Kentucky Derby at Churchill Downs in Louisville, Ky., on May 3 to give renowned 73-year-old trainer Charles Whittingham his first victory in that classic and 54-year-old jockey Willie Shoemaker his fourth.

Snow Chief, who in 1985 earned more money than any 2 year-old Thoroughbred in history, was favored to win the Kentucky Derby but finished 11th. Snow Chief bounced back, however, and won the Preakness at Pimlico in Baltimore on May

the approval by the U.S. Congress on June 25 of $100 million in new funding for the rebels. This funding and the dismissal in July of the U.S. ambassador to Honduras, John A. Ferch, was interpreted by Hondurans as preparation for a stepped-up U.S. military presence in their country. Ferch reportedly had been relieved for not giving enthusiastic backing to the Nicaraguan rebel effort.

Military Revolt. Conflict within the Honduras military establishment nearly erupted in violence on September 26 when Colonel Thomas Saíd Speer—who lost his bid to become chief of the Honduran armed forces—returned to his headquarters and mobilized his armored cavalry division. General Humberto Regalado Hernández—who held the position as armed forces chief that Speer had sought—reportedly surrounded Speer's forces with artillery and antitank guns.

The tense situation was defused on September 27 after Speer was persuaded to surrender his command in return for a post as military attaché to a Honduran embassy in South America. The incident reflected divisions among Honduran officers over the U.S. role in their country. Many officers feared that their country was being dragged into a war with Nicaragua.   Nathan A. Haverstock

See also LATIN AMERICA (Facts in Brief Table). In WORLD BOOK, see HONDURAS.

Major Horse Races of 1986

Race	Winner	Value to Winner
Belmont Stakes	Danzig Connection	$338,640
Breeders' Cup Juvenile	Capote	450,000
Breeders' Cup Juvenile Fillies	Brave Raj	450,000
Breeders' Cup Sprint	Smile	450,000
Breeders' Cup Mile	Last Tycoon	450,000
Breeders' Cup Distaff	Lady's Secret	450,000
Breeders' Cup Turf	Manila	900,000
Breeders' Cup Classic	Skywalker	1,350,000
Breeders' Cup Steeplechase	Census	125,000
Budweiser-Arlington Million	Estrapade	600,000
Budweiser Irish Derby	Shahrastani	409,077
Ever Ready Derby (England)	Shahrastani	359,890
Grand National Steeplechase (England)	West Tip	83,590
Kentucky Derby	Ferdinand	609,400
Preakness	Snow Chief	411,900
Prix de l'Arc de Triomphe (France)	Dancing Brave	610,400
Rothmans International Stakes (Canada)	Southjet	303,480

Major U.S. Harness Races of 1986

Race	Winner	Value to Winner
Cane Pace	Barberry Spur	$108,552
Hambletonian	Nuclear Kosmos	586,041
Little Brown Jug	Barberry Spur	150,841
Meadowlands Pace	Laughs	512,750
Roosevelt International	Habib	125,000
Woodrow Wilson Pace	Cullin Hanover	780,750

Jockey Willie Shoemaker at age 54 wins his fourth Kentucky Derby as he guides Ferdinand to victory in the 112th running of the race in May.

17. Danzig Connection won the Belmont Stakes at Belmont Park in Elmont, N.Y., on June 7, providing trainer W. C. (Woody) Stephens with his fifth consecutive Belmont victory.

John Henry, the 11-year-old gelding who retired in July 1985, returned to training in May 1986 but in mid-August suffered a ligament injury and was re-retired.

Flatterer became the first horse in United States steeplechasing to carry 176 pounds (80 kilograms) to victory when he won the National Hunt Cup at Malvern, Pa., on May 17. The 7-year-old gelding, champion jumper from 1983 to 1986, was too lame to compete in the first Breeders' Cup Steeplechase at Fair Hill, Md. Census won the race.

Harness Racing. Billy Haughton, 62, died on July 15 of head injuries incurred in a spill at Yonkers (N.Y.) Raceway on July 5. The driver-trainer won more than 4,900 races.

Jate Lobell won the Kentucky Pacing Derby at Louisville Downs, Ky., on September 6. Forrest Skipper won the Breeders' Crown Aged Horse Pace at Los Alamitos, Calif., in October.

Quarter Horse Racing. Ronas Ryon earned $1.3-million in the $2.5-million All-American Futurity at Ruidoso Downs, N. Mex., on September 1, outrunning favorite Lil Bit Shiney.   Jane Goldstein

In WORLD BOOK, see HARNESS RACING; HORSE RACING.

HOSPITAL. A comprehensive three-year study conducted by the Institute of Medicine concluded on June 4, 1986, that for-profit hospitals in the United States provide care comparable to that available at nonprofit hospitals, but that costs at for-profit institutions tend to be higher. The institute is an agency of the National Academy of Sciences in Washington, D.C.

The study was conducted because an increasing number of hospitals are being operated as profit-making enterprises by large, investor-owned corporate chains. It found that for-profit hospitals provide high-quality care and do not skimp on services to increase profits. Medical costs, however, were higher in for-profit hospitals, ranging from only slightly higher for elderly and disabled people covered by the federal Medicare program to 24 per cent higher for patients covered by private health insurance.

Baby Doe Overruled. The Supreme Court of the United States on June 9 declared unconstitutional a controversial government rule that required hospitals to feed and treat severely handicapped infants. The regulation, widely known as the "Baby Doe" rule, said that denying treatment to such infants was a form of discrimination against the handicapped. The court found no evidence that any hospital ever had withheld care because of such discrimination and said that hospitals usually withhold care at the request of the parents of such infants. The court concluded that there was no justification for the Baby Doe regulation.

AIDS Hospital. The first hospital in the United States specializing in the treatment of acquired immune deficiency syndrome (AIDS) opened on September 2 in Houston. The 150-bed Institute for Immunological Disorders was organized by American Medical International, Incorporated, a private health-care firm; the M. D. Anderson Hospital and Tumor Institute; and the University of Texas, all in Houston. The hospital will also conduct research on AIDS, a viral disease that attacks the body's immune system, making victims vulnerable to lethal infections and cancer.

Canadian Strike. On July 7, physicians in Ontario, Canada, ended a 25-day strike that curtailed elective surgery and other treatment in hospitals thoughout the province. The strike was called to protest a new law forbidding physicians from charging fees higher than those established by the provincial health-insurance plan. The Ontario Medical Association, which represents about 17,000 physicians, vowed that physicians would continue to strike in hospitals throughout Ontario on a rotating basis. Michael Woods

In WORLD BOOK, see HOSPITAL.

HOUSING. See BUILDING AND CONSTRUCTION.

HOUSTON. After faltering for more than a year, Houston's economy worsened sharply in 1986, primarily because of a continued decline in worldwide petroleum prices. By midyear, home foreclosures had become common. In June, Houston officials scrapped a $5-million federally funded plan to build low-income housing and announced that the money would instead be used to buy foreclosed houses, which will be rented to the poor. In May, Houston's unemployment rate hit a record 10.7 per cent.

The economic picture had some bright spots, however. For instance, on October 2, Grumman Corporation said it would move part of its civilian space systems division to Houston, a move that could add as many as 2,000 jobs to the local economy. On October 21, a nonprofit corporation announced plans to build a $40-million visitors' center at the Lyndon B. Johnson Space Center. And on November 11, Continental Airlines unveiled plans to expand its Houston operations, which was expected to bring in about 1,000 jobs.

Budget Troubles. On June 26, the Houston City Council cut city employees' pay by 3 per cent, and in July and August Mayor Kathryn J. Whitmire laid off more than 400 city workers. On October 29, the council approved a $1.27-billion budget that included increases of 7 per cent in property

A computer-controlled display of lights, lasers, and fireworks sets Houston's skyline ablaze on April 5 to celebrate the city's 150th birthday.

taxes and 20 per cent in water and sewer rates.

Education. On July 3, the Houston Independent School District, the city's largest, named Joan Raymond as its new superintendent. Raymond, who had been school superintendent in Yonkers, N.Y., succeeded Billy R. Reagan, who retired after 12 years in the office. Two weeks later, the district froze the salaries of all school personnel for the 1986-1987 school year.

Several former University of Houston (UH) football stars claimed in March that, while students at the university, they were paid thousands of dollars by UH coaches—a violation of National Collegiate Athletic Association (NCAA) rules. The former players also said they were given passing grades for courses in which they did little work. A UH report in August admitted that the university had been deficient in educating athletes.

Labor. City garbage workers staged a three-day strike in August to protest the layoff of 159 employees and a lengthening of collection routes. Mayor Whitmire declared the walkout illegal and fired 91 workers for their involvement. The mayor rehired 84 of the discharged employees on August 29. On April 21, dockworkers in Houston and nearby ports accepted a three-year cut in their wages and benefits, the first such cut in their history.

***Challenger* Disaster.** The January 28 explosion of the U.S. space shuttle *Challenger* and the death of its seven crew members were a personal loss for many Houstonians. The control of shuttle flights is the chief function of the Johnson Space Center, and five of the *Challenger* crew members were Houston-area residents.

On June 30, in an action unrelated to the *Challenger* disaster, James C. Fletcher, head of the National Aeronautics and Space Administration (NASA), announced plans to transfer most of the agency's space station program out of Houston. But when Houston-area members of Congress protested the plan and threatened to block NASA's budget, Fletcher canceled the order.

Crime. At midyear, police department statistics showed that major crime in Houston had increased 13.7 per cent over 1985. Police attributed the rise in part to the state of the local economy. Almost 95 per cent of the crimes reported in 1986 involved money or property.

Professional Sports. Athletics provided an emotional lift to recession-weary Houstonians in 1986. The Houston Rockets won the National Basketball Association's (NBA) Western Conference title. On June 8, however, they lost the overall NBA title to the Boston Celtics. Baseball's Houston Astros had a similar story. They won the National League Western Division title but lost the race for the pennant to the New York Mets.   Charles Reinken

See also CITY. In WORLD BOOK, see HOUSTON.

HUNGARY during 1986 maintained its efforts to reform its economy and raise the standard of living. But the nation experienced growing economic and financial difficulties. Hungary's net foreign debt rose by $2.4 billion, from $5 billion in 1985 to $7.4 billion by the second half of 1986.

Industry and Agriculture. Industrial output during the first nine months of 1986 increased 1 per cent over the level of the first nine months of 1985. This fell short, however, of the 2.7 per cent increase projected for the entire year.

Agricultural output was higher in 1986 than in 1985. Nevertheless, Hungary's agricultural exports suffered losses because the produce was contaminated by radioactive fallout from an explosion and fire at the Chernobyl nuclear power plant in the Soviet Union in April. The European Community (EC or Common Market) placed a temporary ban on agricultural imports from East European nations, including Hungary. See ENERGY SUPPLY (Close-Up).

Search for Solutions. The Communist Party Central Committee met in November to consider the economic situation but failed to come up with any new measures, apparently because of disagreements over future policies. On December 1, the government imposed a wage freeze until April 1987. Hungary's unit of currency, the forint, was devalued in September by 7.47 per cent against the U.S. dollar.

Hungary's first bankruptcy law went into force on September 1. It allows creditors, unpaid suppliers, and others to whom money is owed to start bankruptcy proceedings against insolvent or delinquent companies—the first such law in a Communist nation.

Coal Miners' Dispute. There were mounting problems in Hungary's coal industry during 1986. Miners were generally dissatisfied with poor working conditions in the coal mines. Then the government on July 17 announced it was closing some coal mines and moving from a five-day to a six-day workweek in others. This triggered a mass resignation of more than 700 miners in the Borsod and Tatabanya mines.

Soviet Relations. In August, Hungary signed an agreement with the Soviet Union for Soviet construction of two new reactors at the Paks nuclear plant, 60 miles (100 kilometers) south of Budapest. Hungary has four reactors already in operation or about to be completed.

Soviet Communist Party General Secretary Mikhail S. Gorbachev made a two-day visit to Hungary in June. Following the visit, the Soviet press was less critical of Hungary and its economic policies.

Cardinal Laszlo Lekai, head of Hungary's Roman Catholic Church, died on June 30.   Chris Cviic

See also EUROPE (Facts in Brief Table). In WORLD BOOK, see HUNGARY.

HUNTING. California in 1986 moved to allow hunting of Nelson's bighorn sheep, a subspecies of desert bighorn sheep, for the first time since 1873. A bill permitting hunting of the sheep was passed in August 1986 by the California state legislature.

Both the California Wildlife Federation and the state Society for the Conservation of Bighorn Sheep strongly supported the bill, which limits the annual harvest to no more than 15 per cent of the estimated 4,800 bighorn sheep in the state. The legislation included a "sunset" clause requiring officials to review the program after five years. Only 12 to 15 permits will be issued for the first hunt, scheduled for 1987, in the Old Dad Mountains and Kelso Peak areas.

Lead-Shot Issue. On Feb. 14, 1986, the National Wildlife Federation (NWF) filed suit in a federal court in Sacramento, Calif., to force a nationwide ban on the use of lead shot. The organization claimed that lead shot poison waterfowl, which eat the spent shot, and eagles, which eat other birds fatally wounded by lead shot.

There was no action on the suit, however, because the U.S. Department of the Interior's Fish and Wildlife Service in June announced its own anti-lead-shot proposal. The agency planned to phase in nationwide use of nontoxic steel shot by autumn 1991.

Assistant Interior Secretary William P. Horn stated, "This is a constructive occasion in resource conservation history. The Department of the Interior is fully committed to solving this lengthy controversy over lead poisoning in waterfowl."

As a result, federal District Judge Edward J. Garcia dismissed the NWF suit, ruling it premature because of the new plan. The NWF did not appeal Garcia's decision. "Judge Garcia's ruling is a major step toward our goal of protecting the nation's endangered bald eagles as well as our waterfowl, both of which have been threatened by lead poisoning from toxic shot," said Jay D. Hair, executive vice president of the NWF. The cooperative effort between the NWF and the Department of Interior ended more than a decade of debate over the lead-shot issue.

Big Game Records. In June, the Boone and Crockett Club, the record-keeping organization for North American big game, officially recognized five new world-record trophies at the club's 19th Annual Big Game Awards program in Las Vegas, Nev. The new records, taken during the 1983 to 1985 scoring period, included: a pronghorn taken in Arizona; a barren-ground caribou taken in the Northwest Territories; a Sitka deer (a subspecies of mule deer) taken in Alaska; an elk taken in Oregon; and a grizzly bear taken in British Columbia.   Tony Mandile

In WORLD BOOK, see HUNTING.

HURT, WILLIAM (1950-   ), won the Academy of Motion Picture Arts and Sciences Award for best actor on March 24, 1986. The award honored his performance in *Kiss of the Spider Woman* as an imprisoned homosexual with a rich fantasy life who learns commitment and courage.

Hurt was born on March 20, 1950, in Washington, D.C. He spent most of his childhood in the South Pacific, where his father, an official of the United States Department of State, was posted.

Hurt earned a bachelor's degree from Tufts University in Medford, Mass., in 1972. Originally a theology student, he discovered greater satisfaction in acting in college stage productions and spent his senior year studying theater in England. After graduation, he entered the acting program at the Juilliard School in New York City.

Hurt made his New York City acting debut in *Henry V* in 1976. He was cast in his first leading role in 1977 in the premiere of *My Life*, for which he won an Obie Award. His other stage credits include roles in *The Fifth of July* (1981) and *Hurlyburly* (1984).

Hurt made his film debut in *Altered States* (1980). He has also appeared in *Eyewitness* (1981), *Body Heat* (1981), *The Big Chill* (1983), *Gorky Park* (1983), and *Children of a Lesser God* (1986).

Divorced from actress Mary Beth Hurt, he has a son by dancer Sandra Jennings.   Barbara A. Mayes

ICE SKATING. Americans enjoyed a highly successful year on the ice during 1986. Debi Thomas of San Jose, Calif., and Brian Boitano of Sunnyvale, Calif., the 1986 U.S. singles figure-skating champions, unexpectedly won the singles titles in the world figure-skating championships. Bonnie Blair of Champaign, Ill., won the world speed-skating short-track championship for women.

Figure Skating. In the world championships held from March 17 to 23 in Geneva, Switzerland, Katarina Witt of East Germany was favored to win her third consecutive women's title. Thomas, an 18-year-old Stanford freshman, was given little chance of winning. Witt fell during her short program, however, and dropped to fourth place. Thomas then needed a first or second placing in the concluding long program to become the first black to win the world singles title.

Witt skated superbly in the long program and received two perfect scores of 6.0. But Thomas improvised a triple jump-double jump combination during her long program, finishing second to Witt to win the world championship.

In the men's competition, the 22-year-old Boitano began the long program trailing defending champion Aleksandr Fadeev of the Soviet Union, Jozef Sabovcik of Czechoslovakia, and Brian Orser of Orillia, Canada. Although Boitano and Orser eventually finished with identical overall scores,

Debi Thomas of San Jose, Calif., spins in style
to become the first black ever to win a title
in the world figure-skating championships, in March.

Boitano won the championship because six of the nine judges had given him higher scores than Orser in the long program.

Natalya Bestemianova and Andrei Bukin of the Soviet Union won their second straight ice dance title. Sergei Grinkov and 14-year-old Ekatarina Gordeeva of the Soviet Union won the pairs title.

Speed Skating. Although Karin Enke Kania of East Germany dominated women's speed-skating competition, winning the world overall and sprint titles, Blair took many honors. In the world short-course championships held in Chamonix-Mont-Blanc, France, from April 4 to 6, she won three of the four races en route to the title. At the world sprint championships in Karuisawa, Japan, held on February 22 and 23, she finished third. At the world overall championships held on February 8 and 9 at The Hague, the Netherlands, Blair won the 500-meter race.

The men's overall world champion was Hein Vergeer of the Netherlands. Igor Dhelezovski of the Soviet Union took the sprint title, and Tatsuyoshi Ishihara of Japan won the short-course championship.   Frank Litsky

See also THOMAS, DEBI. In WORLD BOOK, see ICE SKATING.

ICELAND. See EUROPE.

IDAHO. See STATE GOVERNMENT.

ILLINOIS. See CHICAGO; STATE GOVERNMENT.

IMMIGRATION. After more than a decade of failed attempts and controversy, Congress passed a major overhaul of United States immigration laws in 1986. In October, just three weeks after a procedural vote in the House of Representatives had seemingly doomed the legislation once again, the measure was revived and enacted when Senate and House conferees agreed to compromises on the most controversial provisions. The House passed the bill, 238 to 173, on October 15, and the Senate followed suit two days later by a vote of 63 to 24. President Ronald Reagan signed the legislation into law on November 6.

Law Grants Amnesty. Many of the new law's provisions were scheduled to take effect in May 1987. Chief among them was amnesty for illegal aliens who have resided continuously in the United States since before Jan. 1, 1982. Those aliens would be given temporary-resident status and, after 18 months, could apply to become permanent residents eligible for citizenship in another five years. The law also provided civil and criminal penalties for employers who knowingly hire illegal aliens.

Congress provided for the regular entry of temporary agricultural workers. Almost all such workers would come, as in the past, from Mexico. In response to concerns that the legislation would lead to discrimination against Hispanics who are full-time U.S. residents, the new law provides for a special office in the Department of Justice. The office will prosecute cases of job discrimination against aliens with legal status in the United States.

Cuban Prisoner Release. Sixty-seven Cubans who had been political prisoners in Cuba were flown from Havana, Cuba, to Miami, Fla., along with 37 of their relatives, on Sept. 15, 1986. The Reagan Administration decided to admit the Cubans after debating how to pressure Cuba to honor a 1984 agreement aimed at restoring normal immigration between the United States and Cuba.

That dispute, still unresolved at the end of 1986, had strained the Reagan Administration's ties with Miami's heavily Republican Cuban community. Reagan announced on August 22 that long-term political prisoners in Cuba would be admitted to the United States. He added that almost all other immigration from Cuba would be barred and that United States visas would no longer be granted to Cubans seeking to enter the United States from other countries. Because United States visas were not issued in Cuba, that action closed the one avenue of immigration open to most Cubans. President Reagan allowed exceptions only for immediate family relations of Cubans living in the United States or for long-term political prisoners in Cuba.   Frank Cormier and Margot Cormier

In WORLD BOOK, see IMMIGRATION.

INCOME TAX. See TAXATION.

INDIA was disturbed by internal strife during 1986, and the country made slow economic progress while many of its people suffered hunger and poverty. The worst violence continued to arise from a militant minority of the Sikh religious community. They demanded the creation of a sovereign Sikh nation in Punjab state to be named Khalistan.

Sikh Militants during the year conducted a campaign of terror against Hindus living in the Punjab, where Sikhs make up a majority of the population. On April 29, 1986, five Sikh militants announced the creation of Khalistan and called for international recognition. They made their announcement from the holiest Sikh shrine, the Golden Temple in Amritsar, which they had occupied for three months. In 1984, the Indian Army had cleared the temple of extremists in a battle that took at least 646 lives.

This time, Indian security forces stormed the temple and dislodged the militants without casualties. Nevertheless, there were strong protests against the raid and several killings in reprisal.

On August 10, Sikh terrorists killed retired General Arun S. Vaidya, who led the 1984 attack on the Golden Temple. Then, on October 2, a man reported to be a Sikh tried to assassinate Prime Minister Rajiv Gandhi.

Hindu faithful partake in a ritual cleansing in the Ganges River at Hardwar, India, during a religious festival in April.

There were also retaliations against Sikh terrorism. Incidents on July 25 and November 30 in the Punjab, in which terrorists selected Hindus from passengers on buses and killed them, led to anti-Sikh rioting in New Delhi. Sikhs were killed in both outbreaks of rioting. Indian observers said the terrorists were succeeding in driving Hindus from the Punjab and provoking an anti-Sikh backlash elsewhere that would force Sikhs to move to the Punjab. On January 22, three Sikhs were convicted of assassinating Prime Minister Indira Gandhi in 1984.

Other Conflicts broke out in various parts of India. Strife between Hindus and Muslims in Gujarat state in July killed some 65 people. At least 40 people were killed in conflicts surrounding demands by migrants from Nepal, known as Gurkhas, for a separate state in part of West Bengal. Dozens of people died in clashes over whether Konkani or Marathi would be the official language of the former Portuguese possession of Goa.

In eastern India, which had been torn by separatist conflicts since the 1950's, the Mizo National Front on June 30, 1986, signed a peace agreement with the government.

Opposition to Rajiv Gandhi and his personal domination of Indian politics increased during 1986. Pressure from worried leaders of his Congress Party forced Gandhi to partially rescind a February increase in prices for food, coal, and fertilizer. A 24-hour general strike was staged on February 26 to protest the price increases.

On April 22, the party's ranking leader under Gandhi, Kamlapati Tripathi, complained in a letter that Gandhi and the "so-called operators" around him were inept in handling party affairs. This reflected widespread discontent by party officials at their lack of political influence. Under pressure from Gandhi, Tripathi and the other top Congress Party leaders resigned on November 12, clearing the way for a reorganization of the party.

On October 22, Gandhi made a sweeping reshuffle of his cabinet ministers to stifle political dissent. It was the eighth cabinet reshuffle since he took office in 1984. He added two new posts, increasing his cabinet from 56 to 58 members.

Foreign Relations with India's two largest neighbors—Pakistan and China—remained tense. Occasional shooting occurred between Indian and Pakistani troops on the disputed Siachen Glacier in the remote Karakoram Mountains. At the eastern end of India's northern border, India and China accused each other of military encroachment across a vaguely defined border.

Because of its foreign troubles, India continued to build up its armed strength. The Indian government decided to buy a second aircraft carrier from Great Britain, ordered MIG-29 jet fighters from the Soviet Union, and decided to buy jet engines from the United States for an Indian-built fighter.

United States Defense Secretary Caspar W. Weinberger met with Gandhi in New Delhi on October 11 and discussed possible joint production of weapons. Soviet leader Mikhail S. Gorbachev visited India from November 25 to 29 to reinforce close Soviet-Indian relations.

Some Economic Progress was reflected in rising supplies of grain in a nation that once had to depend on imported food. The distribution system, however, primarily benefited city workers, while the 39 per cent of Indians living below the official poverty line were mostly in rural areas.

The foreign trade deficit rose 50 per cent from early 1985 to early 1986. Although Gandhi had relaxed licensing restrictions on Indian business in 1985, the measures failed to generate enough export goods to equal increased imports.

In September, the Indian government filed suit against the U.S. firm of Union Carbide Corporation on behalf of the victims of a 1984 chemical leak at the company's Bhopal pesticide plant. Union Carbide filed a countersuit against the Indian government in November, holding it partly responsible for the disaster.   Henry S. Bradsher

See also Asia (Facts in Brief Table). In World Book, see India.

INDIAN, AMERICAN. The United States Department of the Interior reported in December 1986 that the economic status of Indians living on reservations was poor and was expected to worsen. The report said that poverty and high levels of unemployment had been aggravated by diminishing federal spending on social problems.

Navajo Relocation. Federal relocation of more than 10,000 Navajo Indians from disputed tribal lands in Arizona met resistance in 1986 and failed to meet the July 6 deadline ordered by Congress. The relocation—the federal government's attempt to settle a century-old land dispute between the Navajo and Hopi Indians—involved the redivision of about 1.8 million acres (730,000 hectares) used jointly by the two tribes.

Health Concerns. In May, a U.S. government study revealed that significant gains in the health of American Indians had been made during the last 30 years. But the report also said that despite these improvements, Indians continue to have higher rates of illness and disease and to die younger than other U.S. citizens.

Drug and alcohol abuse continued to be a devastating problem in Indian communities in 1986. American and Canadian Indians—including experts from NECHI of Edmonton, Canada, the only native-controlled alcohol-treatment center in

Navajo supporters tear down a barbed-wire fence in Arizona on July 7 to protest a 1974 settlement that awarded land to the Hopi Indians.

351

INDIANA

North America—participated in the first International Conference on Drug Addiction, held in New York City in June 1986. (*Nechi* is a Cree Indian term meaning *the people*.)

Indians in Canada continued to dispute a 1985 ruling by Canada's Parliament concerning native status. The ruling had struck down the 114-year-old Indian Act that denied native status to native women who married non-Indians, and to natives who engaged in certain activities, such as registering to vote or working outside a reserve. Indians who lose native status are denied the right to live on reserves, participate in tribal affairs, or receive certain government benefits. In 1986, the Sawridge Band in northern Alberta lobbied against reinstating women who had lost native status.

In 1986, the Lubicon Lake Cree Band of Alberta asked museums to refuse to lend native artifacts for an exhibit at the 1988 Olympic Games. The Cree said the action was intended to protest development by multinational oil companies that threatened their traditional way of life.

The trend toward more self-government by the bands continued in 1986. Some bands assumed the administration of social services, and community controlled schools emerged among the Stoney Band in Alberta and other groups.   Beatrice Medicine

In WORLD BOOK, see INDIAN, AMERICAN.

INDIANA. See STATE GOVERNMENT.

INDONESIA was plagued in 1986 by economic problems caused by a drop in world oil and gas prices. The two commodities provide 60 to 70 per cent of Indonesia's foreign earnings and 55 per cent of the government's tax revenues.

The government devalued Indonesia's currency, the rupiah, by 31 per cent against the U.S. dollar on September 12. The devaluation was intended to encourage exports and discourage imports in order to reduce the problems caused by low oil prices. Announcing the devaluation, Finance Minister Radius Prawiro said oil and natural gas export revenues were expected to fall 47 per cent during the fiscal year that began April 1. World prices for some of Indonesia's other major exports—tin, rubber, and palm oil—were also down. Prospects were good for coffee, timber, and tourism, however.

Relations with Australia were temporarily disrupted after a Sydney newspaper on April 10 published allegations of corruption by the family of Indonesia's President Suharto. The article said the Suharto family had amassed as much as $3 billion through corrupt business dealings during Suharto's 20-year rule. Indonesia reacted by restricting Australian journalists. The government deported two Australian reporters who tried to accompany President Ronald Reagan of the United States on his visit to Indonesia, beginning April 29.

Indonesians parade an effigy of a warrior during the funeral in April of 90-year-old King Pemecutan, the last king of the Indonesian island of Bali.

Domestic Critics of the government focused on waste and inefficiency, as well as on the lack of any system of checks and balances under the vaguely defined presidency. As the nation prepared for elections in 1987, most of this criticism came from the Group of 50, which included some formerly important officials. One of them, Hartono R. Dharsono, a retired army lieutenant general who had been secretary-general of the Association of Southeast Asian Nations, was sentenced in January to 10 years in prison on charges of subversion. In May, his sentence was reduced to 7 years.

Scattered Fighting against Indonesian control continued in two areas. In East Timor, a former Portuguese colony that Indonesia seized in 1975, the two main independence movements announced in late March 1986 that they had united to continue their guerrilla struggle. Opposition to Suharto also flared occasionally in Irian Jaya (the western half of New Guinea, ruled by Indonesia).

The defense ministry announced on August 30 that it had ordered F-16 jet fighters from the United States. It chose the plane over a French fighter because Singapore and Thailand also planned to buy the F-16. The three countries are neighbors and could have such economies as joint F-16 maintenance agreements.   Henry S. Bradsher

See also ASIA (Facts in Brief Table). In WORLD BOOK, see INDONESIA.

INSURANCE. Predictions by insurance executives that property and casualty companies in the United States would show growth proved accurate in 1986. By year-end, the insurance industry reported an estimated consolidated net after-tax income of $11.5 billion, which was a significant increase over the $1.9 billion earned in 1985. This gain included operating earnings totaling $4.5 billion, compared with a loss of $5.6 billion for 1985.

Sean Mooney, senior vice president and economist for the Insurance Information Institute, stated that 1986 was the first full year of improving overall financial results since 1978. Although a portion of this profit was derived from record gains in the stock and bond portfolios of the insurance companies, an important factor was a reduction in underwriting losses and an increase in earned premiums. For 1986, there was an underwriting loss of $17 billion, which was 10.3 per cent of the $164.7 billion in earned premiums. For 1985, the underwriting loss was $25 billion, expressed as 18.8 per cent of an earned premium of only $132.7 billion.

These gains, however, were made amid a raging controversy concerning the tactics employed by insurance firms. During 1986, the word *crisis* aptly described the situation of many businesses in the United States—as well as government agencies—that were unable to obtain or renew their insurance. Many of the firms and agencies that did obtain insurance paid high rates—sometimes more than twice as much as they had paid in 1985.

Peter Lardner, who completed his term as head of the American Insurance Association in November, said that insurance prices "must reflect the cost pressures exerted by society." He explained that the increases in premiums and the underwriting decisions to avoid certain risks had been "critical to the economic equilibrium of the insurance business." Lardner predicted that the industry "will pay a price for years to come through legislative or regulatory restrictions." But, he said, "survival has been at stake."

In fact, during 1984, 1985, and 1986, 58 insurance companies failed, compared with 39 from 1975 to 1980. There were 21 failures in 1986 alone. These bankrupt insurance companies underwrote property insurance, medical malpractice, and other liability policies.

"Conspiracy" Charged. Ralph Nader and Robert Hunter of the National Insurance Consumers Organization had charged in August 1985 that insurance companies conspired to create the insurance "crisis" to gain legislative support for their campaign to change laws relating to civil justice—the right of victims to sue for damages. In early 1986, the U.S. Department of Justice found no substance to the charges of Nader and Hunter.

Meanwhile, an insurance industry campaign seeking laws to limit recovery of damages came before most state legislatures and Congress during the year. The insurance industry argued that the *tort* system—the right of a victim to sue the one responsible for injury—was running rampant and was a direct cause of the liability crisis.

The campaign proved successful in 1986, as state legislatures enacted more tort, insurance, and regulatory reform measures than in any previous year. These reforms included ceilings on the amount of compensation a victim may receive for other than actual out-of-pocket costs; reduction of compensation based on money received from other sources, such as health insurance; and limits on fees lawyers may charge plaintiffs in cases involving bodily injury or property damage.

In Other News, President Ronald Reagan in October signed legislation permitting groups of similar businesses to create their own insurance company. Under the new law, such a company can be organized in one state but operate throughout the United States. Insurance coverage is not limited to product liability as under the previous law but can cover other risks as well.

Insured property damage from 26 catastrophes during 1986 came to $871.5 million, a drop of 69 per cent from $2.82 billion in 1985.   Emanuel Levy

In World Book, see Insurance.

INTERNATIONAL TRADE. The world economy grew by less than 3 per cent in 1986, despite lower interest rates and falling oil prices. It was the second year in a row of decline in the world's economic growth rate. Growth rates among major industrial nations were remarkably similar—about 2.5 per cent.

In the developing nations of Africa, Asia, Latin America, and the Middle East, economic growth averaged less than 3 per cent, down from 4 per cent in 1984-1985. The economies of oil-exporting nations were particularly hard hit. Oil exports averaged about $15 a barrel, a drop of almost 50 per cent from 1985 levels.

Most nations continued to reduce inflation, which averaged about 3.2 per cent in the industrial nations. Inflation in the developing nations, though much higher, generally moderated during the year, averaging less than 30 per cent.

Foreign Debt. By the end of 1986, the United States was by far the world's largest debtor nation, with a foreign debt of approximately $200 billion. The foreign debt of the developing nations rose to about $1 trillion by the end of 1986. The benefits of lower interest rates on their debt were more than offset by declines in their export revenues. There was little, if any, rise in their foreign aid, and commercial banks made fewer loans to highly indebted nations.

Money traders on the Tokyo foreign exchange market frantically make deals on January 27 as the U.S. dollar falls to its lowest rate against the yen since 1979.

Mexico, however, was a major exception to this trend. Largely because of the U.S. government's urging, an aid package of up to $12 billion was arranged for Mexico. The aid came from commercial banks and two agencies of the United Nations—the International Monetary Fund (IMF) and the World Bank. The banks also reduced the interest rate and extended the repayment period on Mexico's outstanding debt. See MEXICO.

Longer-range programs to help the developing nations were put in place. Some World Bank nations on December 15 pledged a $12.4-billion increase in funds for its International Development Association to aid developing nations. The IMF on March·7 began lending to the 60 poorest developing countries from a $3.1-billion fund.

Trade Imbalances. Unprecedented trade and payments imbalances among the major industrial nations were a growing concern. The United States incurred a record deficit estimated at $140 billion in its *international payments* (transactions in merchandise, services, trade, and corporate fund transfers). Japan and West Germany posted a combined surplus exceeding $110 billion.

The value of the U.S. dollar fell about 30 per cent against other major currencies during the year. Ironically, this tended to increase the U.S. deficit, partly because foreign imports became more expensive.

United States Treasury Secretary James A. Baker III and Federal Reserve Board Chairman Paul A. Volcker spent much of 1986 urging Japan and West Germany to spur their economies. United States officials aimed to restore a better payments balance by increasing those countries' buying power for U.S. and other exports.

On October 31, Japan agreed to reduce the interest rate charged to financial institutions to 3 per cent, its lowest ever. Japan also committed itself to greater domestic spending and lower income taxes to help boost its economy. West Germany, however, resisted any action to stimulate its economy, claiming it was growing fast enough.

International Cooperation. The leaders of seven major industrial nations—Canada, France, Great Britain, Italy, Japan, the United States, and West Germany—met at an economic summit in Tokyo from May 4 to 6. The leaders agreed to cooperate more closely on economic policy. They instructed their finance ministers to conduct a joint review of each country's economic objectives and forecasts at least once a year and to discuss policy corrections.

On September 20, trade ministers from 74 nations, meeting at Punta del Este, Uruguay, agreed to launch negotiations for liberalizing world trade and halting the trend toward *protectionism*—the use of high tariffs and other trade barriers to protect domestic industries from foreign competition.

The negotiations began on October 31 in Geneva, Switzerland.

Trade Restrictions. On August 1, the United States and some 50 other nations announced a five-year extension of controls on textile and apparel exports from developing nations.

The United States concluded new accords with Hong Kong, Japan, South Korea, and Taiwan during the year. Those countries, four of the leading textile exporters, individually agreed to reduce the rate of increase of their shipments to the United States.

On August 6, the U.S. House of Representatives upheld President Ronald Reagan's veto of a bill that would have imposed stricter import quotas on textiles, apparel, and footwear.

As a protest against South Africa's racial policies, Congress on October 2 overrode Reagan's veto and imposed a partial trade embargo, prohibiting imports of South African coal, uranium, iron and steel, textiles, and food products.

Trade Disputes between the United States and Canada overshadowed talks aimed at establishing a free trade pact between the two countries. The United States imposed a higher tariff on Canadian cedar shakes and shingles in May. Canada in June retaliated with increased tariffs on U.S. computer chips, publications, and other goods. In November, Canada put a stiff duty on U.S. corn imports. In December, the two nations reached an agreement on softwood lumber. The United States dropped a proposed 15 per cent duty, and Canada enacted a 15 per cent export tax.

The European Community (EC or Common Market) complained that the United States and Japan had entered into a price-fixing agreement in July after Japan agreed to raise its computer-chip prices as of September 1.

The United States and the EC in July settled—in some cases only tentatively—trade disputes involving tariffs on citrus fruits, pasta, and grain. The EC also agreed, as of March 1, to broaden its control of steel exports to the United States to include specialty and semifinished steel. In December, the United States threatened to retaliate for high EC tariffs on U.S. grain. Unless a settlement was reached in January 1987, the United States would impose stiff tariffs on European cheeses, other foods, and alcoholic beverages.

Top Officials of both the World Bank and the IMF announced their resignations during 1986. On July 1, Barber B. Conable, Jr., a former U.S. congressman, succeeded A. W. Clausen as president of the World Bank. Jacques de Larosière de Champfeu resigned as IMF managing director as of Jan. 15, 1987.   Richard Lawrence

See also ECONOMICS. In WORLD BOOK, see INTERNATIONAL TRADE.

IOWA. See STATE GOVERNMENT.

IRAN. Divisions and rivalries among factions within the regime of Ayatollah Ruhollah Khomeini broke into the open in 1986, creating a more serious threat to Iran's internal stability than the danger from any organized opposition.

Disagreements arose mainly from two groups. One group advocated Iran's reintegration into the international community and reconciliation with outside powers—notably the United States—to resolve pressing economic problems. This group also argued for less control of the government by religious leaders. They were opposed by the "hard-liners," who rejected all compromises with foreign powers and insisted on rigid Islamic orthodoxy and state control of the economy.

The first group, led by Prime Minister Hosein Musavi-Khamenei, brought Iran into direct contact with the United States in 1986 in an unexpected manner. He was involved in secret arms shipments to Iran by the United States, which reportedly hoped to secure the release of American hostages in Lebanon and increase American influence in Iran. See PRESIDENT OF THE U.S.

Arrests. Evidence of the deep internal divisions in Iran included the October arrests of relatives and associates of Ayatollah Hussein Ali Montazeri, Khomeini's designated successor. They were accused of various crimes, including treason. But the main reason for their arrest was their creation of an independent foreign policy through the Global Islamic Movement, the organization created to spread Iran's Islamic revolution abroad after the 1979 overthrow of Shah Mohammad Reza Pahlavi. The Global Islamic Movement was seen by Musavi-Khamenei and his associates as undercutting the government's efforts toward reconciliation with other countries.

French Deportations. The last organized movement opposed to the government was weakened in June 1986, when France deported Massoud Rajavi, head of the Mujahedin-e Khalq (People's Crusaders), to Iraq. About 1,000 of Rajavi's supporters reportedly had left earlier.

Kurdistan Control. In August, the government completed the pacification of Kurdistan province along the Iraqi border. Kurdish leaders had maintained internal autonomy there since 1980.

Political Dissent. The regime's strong internal position early in 1986 encouraged officials to permit some political dissent. In May, a new organization called the Association for the Defense of Freedom and Sovereignty of the Iranian Nation was allowed to hold a public meeting. In September, Khomeini announced an amnesty for all political prisoners except those still considered a danger to society.

Yet the Islamization of Iranian society along the principles of *sharia* (Islamic law) continued. In the summer, the government disbanded motorcycle

Women in traditional Muslim dress and carrying weapons parade in Teheran, Iran, on March 14 to mark the 2,000th day of the Iran-Iraq war.

gangs that had been enforcing public dress and behavior codes, particularly for women. But security forces took over the enforcement process.

War with Iraq. Iranian commandos captured the abandoned Iraqi oil port of Fao and the Fao Peninsula, near the mouth of the Shatt al Arab River, in February and held them despite furious Iraqi counterattacks. Iranian forces also captured the border town of Mehran and several strategic peaks along the northern front. But in late December, Iran suffered casualties estimated in the tens of thousands during an unsuccessful offensive at the Shatt al Arab River.

The Iranian navy also imposed a blockade on the Persian Gulf early in 1986, as its gunboats began halting and searching Iraq-bound ships. A U.S. freighter was stopped in January.

The Economy. Iraqi air raids and a world oil glut cut Iran's oil production to 1.3 million barrels per day (bpd) during 1986, well below the country's quota of 2.3 million bpd, established by the Organization of Petroleum Exporting Countries (OPEC). In September, the government ordered a $12-billion cut in imports, causing severe shortages in basic commodities and the shut-down of factories unable to obtain parts manufactured abroad.
William Spencer

See also IRAQ; MIDDLE EAST (Facts in Brief Table). In WORLD BOOK, see IRAN.

IRAQ. The six-year-long war with Iran seemed as endless as ever in 1986. Iraq lost some ground in February when Iranian forces captured the strategic Fao Peninsula—site of the former Persian Gulf oil port of Fao.

But as the Iraqis have done since the Iran-Iraq border war began in 1980, Iraqi forces regrouped to contain the Iranian thrust into their territory. Iraqi losses were heavy, with more than 9,000 reported killed, bringing total casualties in the war to nearly 250,000.

In May, Iraq mounted a counteroffensive elsewhere along the front and seized briefly the Iranian border town of Mehran, about 100 miles (160 kilometers) east of Baghdad, Iraq. Thereafter, the ground war settled into a stalemate.

Iraq Changed Tactics during the year, stressing air raids to take full advantage of its air superiority. The main Iranian oil export terminal on Kharg Island in the Persian Gulf was bombed many times, though never put completely out of commission. In August, Iraqi jets attacked Sirri Island, 350 miles (560 kilometers) southeast of Kharg. Because Sirri was thought to be out of Iraqi range, Iran had developed it to replace Kharg as Iran's main oil port. Other Iraqi raids hit the Iranian heartland, damaging factories, oil refineries, and other key targets in Teheran and other cities.

Despite the war's economic and human cost, often with the deaths of three or four *shahids* (martyrs) to a family, most Iraqis seemed to support it. Iran's failure to launch more massive ground attacks contributed to optimism that Iraq could contain its enemy. In October, some 100,000 university students called up in June for military service in expectation of an invasion were allowed to return to their studies.

Political Scene. President Saddam Hussein remained in full control. In July, he convened the first meeting of the Baath Party Regional Command, the party's governing body, since 1982. Its membership was enlarged, though the ruling Revolutionary Command Council (RCC), Iraq's central policymaking organization, remained unchanged. One new RCC policy decision was to allow air force commanders greater freedom of action in selection of targets and war strategy.

Arab Relations. Some Arab states backed the Iraqi war effort, and others did not. In May, Kuwait and Saudi Arabia began supplying 300,000 barrels per day (bpd) of oil to Iraqi customers from the Neutral Zone, which they administer jointly. Egypt continued to provide arms to Iraq, and the Arab League made strenuous efforts to heal the breach between the rival Baathist regimes of Syria and Iraq in order to present a common Arab front against Iran.

Foreign-Debt Woes. Occupation of the Fao Peninsula compounded Iraq's foreign creditor problems. In July—six months behind schedule because of a cash shortage—Iraq paid $295 million owed to Indian contractors for development projects. Iraq resolved a similar problem with Turkey in March. Iraq agreed to pay half of its $1.2-billion debt to Turkish contractors by means of oil sales, with another 10 per cent paid in cash, and the balance deferred. Fortunately for Iraq, its military debts of $9 billion to industrialized countries were covered by export credits—credit extended by the governments of those countries to buyers of their exports—and thus subject to lenient repayment terms.

The Economy. Economic development was hampered by war costs averaging $600 million per month, lowered oil revenues, and reduced production. Oil production during the year averaged 2 million bpd, about 50 per cent of capacity. Oil revenues of $8 billion were also half the amount expected, and a freeze was put on all new industrial projects.

In July, three new dams went into operation, including the huge Soviet-built Qadisiya Dam on the Euphrates River. The dams are key components in long-range plans for flood control and energy production. William Spencer

See also IRAN; MIDDLE EAST (Facts in Brief Table). In WORLD BOOK, see IRAQ.

IRELAND. The unpopular Labour Party and Fine Gael (Gaelic People) minority coalition, headed by Prime Minister Garret FitzGerald, narrowly averted defeat on a vote of confidence in Parliament on Oct. 23, 1986. A *vote of confidence* is usually called when Parliament votes on a bill introduced by the government. If FitzGerald had received a vote of no confidence, he and his Cabinet would have been forced to resign and a general election would have been held immediately. On December 19, FitzGerald survived another close vote in Parliament when a motion calling for early elections lost by one vote.

In opinion polls, the opposition party—Fianna Fáil (Soldiers of Destiny)—led by 18 per cent and had been consistently ahead for two years. The coalition seemed destined to lose the upcoming general election, which must be held in 1987.

Part of FitzGerald's trouble stemmed from the country's economic woes. Although inflation dropped to about 3 per cent, the country headed for its largest deficit ever. During 1986, Ireland's unemployment rate reached 17 per cent, highest in the European Community (EC or Common Market), and interest rates soared to 17 per cent.

No Divorce. Prime Minister FitzGerald's credibility was also damaged by a *referendum* (direct vote of the people) on legalizing divorce, which he ordered to go before voters on June 26. The Irish voters rejected by a majority vote of 63 per cent a proposed amendment to the Constitution that would have permitted divorce. The stunning defeat was attributed to an astute opposition campaign by the Roman Catholic Church and to the unpopularity of FitzGerald's government. Ireland and Malta are the only two countries in Western Europe where divorce is illegal.

Boycott Ends. On November 2, Sinn Féin, the political wing of the outlawed Irish Republican Army, voted to end a boycott of Parliament it began in 1922. Sinn Féin members elected to Parliament will no longer refuse to take their seats.

Terrorism. On Feb. 24, 1986, Ireland signed the European Convention on the Suppression of Terrorism, which was expected to smooth the *extradition* (handing over) of terrorist offenders between Great Britain and Ireland.

On March 22, a Dublin court freed Evelyn Glenholmes, who had been arrested by the Irish police at the request of the British police. Glenholmes was wanted for questioning about a series of bombings in 1981 and a 1984 assassination attempt on British Prime Minister Margaret Thatcher. An Irish judge found technical faults in the wording of the extradition warrants sent from London and released Glenholmes. Ian Mather

See also NORTHERN IRELAND. In WORLD BOOK, see IRELAND.

IRON AND STEEL. See STEEL INDUSTRY.

357

ISRAEL. Prime Minister Shimon Peres swapped jobs with Foreign Minister Yitzhak Shamir, leader of the opposition Likud bloc, on Oct. 20, 1986. Peres had completed his 25-month term under the power-sharing agreement that was reached between his Labor Party and Likud after Labor failed to win a clear majority in the 1984 elections for the Knesset (parliament). The agreement called for Shamir to take the post of prime minister until elections in 1988.

Governmental Crises. Peres faced a number of governmental crises during 1986. In May, several no-confidence motions were introduced in the Knesset after the government was accused of covering up the fatal beatings in 1984 of two Palestinian bus hijackers by agents of Shin Bet, Israel's intelligence and security agency. If the no-confidence motions had passed, Peres and his Cabinet would have been expected to resign, but the motions were defeated.

Attorney General Yitzhak Zamir, who had spearheaded the investigation, was dismissed in June, as Peres declared the issue would endanger national security if Shin Bet's methods and personnel were exposed to public knowledge. Subsequently, the head of Shin Bet, Avraham Shalom, resigned. President Chaim Herzog, taking the same position as Peres, issued grants of immunity from prosecution for those implicated in the affair. In August, the Supreme Court upheld the presidential amnesties.

Although Labor did not gain significantly in popular support during Peres' term in office, the prime minister proved to be the most popular leader in recent Israeli history. Polls in May and July indicated that 76 per cent of the voters approved of his policies, compared with 4 per cent when he took office.

Foreign Affairs. Peres' most important successes were in foreign policy. In May, Margaret Thatcher visited Israel, the first visit to the country by a British prime minister.

In July, Peres met in Morocco with King Hassan II, the first such high-level direct Arab-Israeli negotiations since Egyptian President Anwar Sadat's historic "journey to Jerusalem" in 1977. Although the two leaders made no significant breakthroughs in the stalled Arab-Israeli peace process, the 10-point position paper they issued jointly after the meeting underscored agreement in principle on a peaceful solution to the Palestinian problem.

Peres also improved relations with Egypt. In September, he met with Egyptian President Hosni Mubarak in Alexandria, Egypt, in the first Israeli-Egyptian summit meeting since 1981. The two leaders agreed to submit the border dispute over

Outgoing Prime Minister Shimon Peres, left, shakes hands with successor Yitzhak Shamir in October during a transfer of power arranged in 1984.

Taba, a small beachfront area in the Sinai Peninsula currently held by Israel, to international arbitration.

Israeli delegates met with Soviet diplomats in Helsinki, Finland, on August 18—the first official contact between the two countries since 1967. A Soviet representative said the 90-minute talks produced no agreement—the issues were said to include the Soviet restrictions on the emigration of Soviet Jews and the persecution of Jews for Zionist activities—and that no further talks were planned.

The Lebanon Problem. The return of Palestine Liberation Organization (PLO) guerrillas to Beirut and southern Lebanon resulted in a revival of rocket and missile attacks on northern Israeli towns. In March, two Israeli soldiers were kidnapped by Lebanese militiamen. Israeli military units crossed the border in pursuit, and two Israelis were killed, the first casualties since the 1985 withdrawal from Lebanon. Thereafter, Israeli forces avoided ground contact in favor of air raids on Palestinian targets in Lebanon.

The West Bank. No new Israeli settlements were started on the Israeli-occupied West Bank, but the program to appoint moderate Palestinian mayors for West Bank towns ran into difficulties. On March 2, the Israeli-appointed mayor of Nablus, Zafer el-Masri, was murdered by gunmen of the Popular Front for the Liberation of Palestine. Israel had planned to appoint four mayors of West Bank towns, of whom Masri was the first. After the killing, other moderate West Bank leaders withdrew their names from consideration. On September 28, however, Israel appointed Arab mayors for three towns previously controlled by Israeli officials.

One encouraging development for the West Bank population was growing Israeli-Jordanian cooperation. The three new Arab mayors were considered to be pro-Jordanian. And Israel in September allowed Jordan to reopen a branch of the Cairo-Amman Bank in Nablus. The bank is the first Arab bank to operate on the West Bank since Israel's occupation began in 1967. In June, Jordan's King Hussein I proposed a $1.3-billion, five-year development plan for the West Bank, with funding to come from foreign aid channeled through the reopened bank in Nablus.

The Economy. In January, the government introduced a new currency, called the New Israeli Shekel, worth 1,000 old shekels, or about 67 cents. The budget, approved by the Knesset on January 20, set expenditures at $26.5 billion, 4 per cent below 1985. With inflation down to about 2 per cent per month, it appeared that the austerity program Peres began when he took office was working. William Spencer

See also MIDDLE EAST (Facts in Brief Table). In WORLD BOOK, see ISRAEL.

ITALY. The five-party coalition government of Socialist Prime Minister Bettino Craxi collapsed on June 27, 1986, one day after losing a key vote in the Chamber of Deputies, one of the two houses of Parliament. The Chamber of Deputies defeated a government proposal dealing with local government finance by a vote of 293 to 266, with 70 members of coalition parties voting against the proposal.

On July 10, President Francesco Cossiga asked Foreign Minister Giulio Andreotti to form a government. Andreotti, a Christian Democrat, had served five terms as prime minister, most recently in 1979 for 11 days.

The formation process deteriorated into a trial of strength between the Socialists and the Christian Democrats—the largest party in the coalition—over who should be prime minister in a revived coalition. The Christian Democrats said they would agree to having Craxi stay on until the end of 1986. Andreotti failed to form a government, and President Cossiga asked Craxi to try again.

Confidence Vote. Craxi relaunched his coalition government on August 5, and on August 6 sought a vote of confidence in the Senate, the other house of Parliament. He told the Senate that the country demanded the "political stability" he had achieved since becoming prime minister in August 1983. His administration had been in power longer than any other Italian government since World War II ended in 1945.

Craxi won the vote of confidence, 181 to 114, and announced that he would relinquish his post in early 1987, allowing a Christian Democrat to become prime minister. On August 8, the Chamber of Deputies also gave him a vote of confidence, 352 to 227.

Wine Scandal. In March and April, 20 people died after drinking adulterated Italian wine. The wine contained dangerous amounts of methyl alcohol, which normally is present in extremely small quantities. (*Ethyl* alcohol is the main alcohol in alcoholic beverages. *Methyl* alcohol, used as a fuel and as antifreeze, is a poison.) The higher alcoholic content, which buyers assumed was ethyl alcohol, increased the wine's market value.

On April 11, the United States banned imports of Italian wine that had not been certified as being free of contamination. On April 16, the Italian government charged two wholesale wine traders with murder and seven others with manslaughter.

Fighting Terrorists. On March 12, Craxi and Great Britain's Prime Minister Margaret Thatcher held a summit conference in Florence, Italy, to deal with terrorism. The meeting led to the signing of the first extradition treaty between the two countries in more than a century.

On April 15, Craxi criticized the United States bombing of Libya as "risking provoking explosive reactions of fanaticism." Nevertheless, on April 26, Italy told Libya to cut the staff of its diplomatic mission in Rome by 10 and curb the activities of those who remained.

Firm Stand. Italy had taken a firm stance against terrorists in January, when Interior Minister Oscar Luigi Scalfaro toured European capitals to urge closer cooperation in the fight against terrorism. Scalfaro's proposal to set up a permanent antiterrorist organization had received a lukewarm reception earlier. But terrorist attacks at airports in Rome and Vienna, Austria, in December 1985 added impetus to his efforts.

High Unemployment. In June, the 24-nation Organization for Economic Cooperation and Development (OECD) said that Italy's main economic problems were inflation and a high and growing rate of unemployment, especially among women and young people. But the OECD said that lower oil prices and a depreciating U.S. dollar would help Italy to increase its growth rate. The OECD expected inflation to dip sharply from 7.5 per cent in 1986 to 3.5 per cent in 1987 but said that the unemployment rate was unlikely to decrease from the 1986 level of 11 per cent.   Kenneth Brown

See also EUROPE (Facts in Brief Table). In WORLD BOOK, see ITALY.

IVORY COAST. See AFRICA.

JAMAICA. See LATIN AMERICA.

JAPAN. Prime Minister Yasuhiro Nakasone and his Liberal Democratic Party (LDP)—a conservative party despite its name—won an impressive victory in parliamentary elections on July 6, 1986. In the House of Representatives, the more powerful of the two houses of Japan's Diet (parliament), the LDP won 300 of the 512 seats. Four people who had run as independents then joined the LDP, giving it a total of 304, an increase of 54. In the House of Councilors, where half of the 252 seats were at stake, the party won 72 seats for a total of 142, 11 more than before the election.

The largest opposition party, the Japan Socialist Party (JSP), got 86 seats, down from 111. Results for the other parties were: Komeito (Clean Government Party) 57, down from 59; Japan Communist Party 27, unchanged; Democratic Socialist Party 26, down from 37; New Liberal Club 6, down from 8; and Social Democratic Federation 4, up from 3. Independents won 2 seats, down from 5.

As a result of the JSP's election defeat, the party in September elected a new leader, Takako Doi. She was the first woman to head a major Japanese political party. Doi promised to try to make the Socialist Party competitive with the LDP.

Nakasone Reelected. Under party rules, an LDP prime minister can serve only two terms as party president, a requirement for election as prime minister. Nakasone's second term as party president was scheduled to end in October 1986. As a result of the resounding election victory, however, the LDP voted in September to have him serve an additional year as party president.

As is customary, Nakasone appointed a new Cabinet in July following the election. In September, new Education Minister Masayuki Fujio was forced to resign. Fujio had made a series of undiplomatic comments defending the long history of Japanese aggression against both Korea and China. Nakasone issued a public apology for the remarks of his minister on a trip to Seoul, South Korea, to attend the opening of the Asian Games.

Nakasone soon had more apologies to make. Two leading Japanese newspapers reported on September 23 that the prime minister had made insulting remarks at an LDP meeting about the intellectual levels of blacks, Puerto Ricans, and Mexicans in the United States. Nakasone issued a public apology to the United States and later apologized to his own people, saying that he would strive for "self-discipline to recover the honor of the Japanese people."

The Mighty Yen. The value of the yen against the dollar rose from about 240 yen to U.S. $1 in the fall of 1985, when finance ministers of five leading economic powers agreed that the value of the dollar should be reduced, to about 155 yen to $1 in the fall of 1986. Raising the value of the yen, and thus lowering the value of the dollar, would make U.S. goods cheaper for Japan to buy and Japanese products more expensive for Americans to buy. Thus—in theory—it would reduce the unfavorable U.S. balance of trade with Japan.

The higher yen did not produce the hoped-for result. Japan announced a record $41.73-billion surplus from its U.S. trade in 1985. The United States, which calculates the figure somewhat differently, estimated that the unfavorable balance was $49.7 billion.

The higher yen did, however, have far-reaching, largely unexpected results. It caused the failure of many small Japanese firms specializing in export items, and it reduced profits for large corporations producing for the U.S. market. Japan's unemployment climbed to a record 3 per cent, in part because of shrinking exports.

In the first quarter of 1986, Japan's gross national product (GNP)—the value of goods and services produced—declined 0.5 per cent, the first quarterly drop since 1975. The government predicted a 4 per cent increase in the GNP for the fiscal year ending in March 1987. Private economic forecasters predicted a rise of only about 2 per cent.

Although the stronger yen had reduced the profits of Japan's export trade, it contributed to a spectacular increase in Japan's influence in the

Election officials count ballots from Japan's parliamentary election in July, in which the ruling party won the largest number of seats in its history.

world financial market. In 1986, Japan became the world's largest lending nation, supplanting Great Britain. International financial transactions in yen rose in 1986 to a daily average of about $65 billion, ahead of about $45 billion in West German marks and $42 billion in British pounds.

On December 30, the Cabinet approved a budget for the fiscal year beginning April 1, 1987, that for the first time boosted military spending above 1 per cent of the GNP. Japan had observed the self-imposed 1 per cent limit since 1979.

Tokyo Summit. Japan from May 4 to 6, 1986, hosted the 12th economic summit conference of the leaders of seven major industrialized democracies—Canada, France, Great Britain, Italy, Japan, the United States, and West Germany—and representatives of the European Community (EC or Common Market). The conferees announced the creation of the Group of Seven, consisting of the seven nations' finance ministers, to work together between summits on common problems.

On May 4, during welcoming ceremonies for the summit, leftist extremists fired crude homemade rockets at the Akasaka Palace, where the summit would take place. No rockets actually landed on the palace, and there were no injuries.

Better Soviet Relations. Japan's Foreign Minister Shintaro Abe and Soviet Foreign Minister Eduard A. Shevardnadze met in Tokyo from January 15 to 19 in the first visit to Japan by a high-level Soviet official in 10 years. The two signed a trade agreement covering the shipment of goods, the handling of trade disputes, and other matters. They also agreed to a two-year extension of a cultural agreement providing for exchanges of performers, publications, and films.

In addition, Abe and Shevardnadze exchanged invitations for Prime Minister Nakasone to visit the Soviet Union and Soviet leader Mikhail S. Gorbachev to visit Japan. The two nations also agreed to resume negotiations suspended in 1976 on a treaty of peace that would formally end World War II hostilities between the two countries.

Shevardnadze's visit brought no progress on Japan's demand that the Soviet Union return four of the Kuril Islands northeast of Hokkaido, Japan. The Soviets have occupied the four islands since the end of World War II in 1945, but Japan claims them. In August 1986, the Soviet Union permitted a group of elderly Japanese to visit family graves on the disputed islands.

South Africa Friction. Abe's successor, Foreign Minister Tadashi Kuranari, on September 4 denounced South Africa's restrictive racial policies to that country's foreign minister, Roelof F. Botha. Botha was in Tokyo on a five-day unofficial visit. Kuranari also criticized South African raids into neighboring countries and demanded the freeing of Nelson Mandela, a black leader imprisoned in South Africa.

Kuranari warned Botha that Japan would impose new *sanctions* (economic penalties) if South Africa did not quickly change its policy of *apartheid* (racial segregation). When the sanctions were announced on September 19, however, they were mild. Japan banned iron and steel imports from South Africa, suspended tourist visas for South African citizens, and advised Japanese travelers against visiting South Africa. Already in effect were bans on Japanese investments in South Africa and on imports of South African gold coins.

The Prince and Princess of Wales visited Japan from May 8 to 13, the first visit to Japan by members of the British royal family. On May 12, Prince Charles addressed the Diet. The Japanese people gave the royal couple an enthusiastic welcome. A crowd estimated at 100,000 turned out to greet them in Tokyo on May 11.

Emperor Hirohito celebrated his 85th birthday on April 29. A special ceremony in Tokyo commemorated the 60th year of his reign, the longest in Japanese history and longer than that of any other living monarch. The government in November issued a special gold coin in celebration of the emperor's reign. Demand for the coin was expected to be high. 　　　　　　　John M. Maki

See also ASIA (Facts in Brief Table). In WORLD BOOK, see JAPAN.

JEWS AND JUDAISM

JEWS AND JUDAISM. The ongoing struggle to end the repression of the approximately 2½ million Jews in the Soviet Union reached a high point in 1986. On February 11, religious activist Anatoly B. Shcharansky was released after spending eight years in Soviet prisons and labor camps. Shcharansky, a physicist, had led a movement to open up emigration for Soviet Jews and had worked to develop Jewish religious and cultural life in the Soviet Union. The Soviet government imprisoned him in 1979 on charges of treason.

Shcharansky's wife, Avital, who was separated from her husband in 1974 when he was denied an exit visa to accompany her to Israel, led international efforts to secure her husband's release. After he walked to freedom across a bridge between East Germany and West Berlin, Shcharansky flew to Jerusalem, Israel, to be reunited with his wife. Following his release, Shcharansky continued to speak out for Soviet Jews who wish to emigrate and for the civil rights of all oppressed people.

The Soviet Union in 1986, however, continued to severely restrict the number of Jews allowed to emigrate. An estimated 400,000 Jews have applied for exit visas within the past few years. Jewish and Christian groups in the United States encouraged U.S. President Ronald Reagan in 1986 to discuss the problems of Soviet Jews and other dissidents in his summit discussions with Communist Party General Secretary Mikhail S. Gorbachev of the Soviet Union.

Terrorism. Terrorist acts against Jewish individuals and institutions escalated in 1986 in Israel and other countries. Extremist Arab groups, most associated with the Palestine Liberation Organization—a political group that seeks to establish a Palestinian state for Arabs—have claimed responsibility for most of the attacks.

The most serious incident occurred on September 6, when two Arab gunmen attacked the Neve Shalom Synagogue in Istanbul, Turkey, with machine guns and grenades as worshipers gathered for the Sabbath morning service. The gunmen killed 21 people before setting fire to the synagogue. Religious and national leaders condemned the murders.

Debate Continued over Israel's Law of Return, which grants citizenship to any Jew who chooses to settle in Israel. Because this law also applies to converts, Orthodox leaders have tried to restrict this right to Jews converted by Orthodox rabbis. Reform and Conservative Jews have opposed this policy.

In an important decision, Israel's Supreme Court ruled in December that Jewish converts who have not been converted by an Orthodox rabbi are entitled to full citizenship as Jews in Israel. The decision involved Shoshana Miller, a convert who served as a Reform cantor in the United States.

During a January visit to West Germany, Israel's Prime Minister Peres visits a memorial to Jews murdered in the Nazi Bergen-Belsen concentration camp.

After Miller immigrated to Israel, Orthodox authorities questioned her Jewish status.

Historic Visit. On April 13, Pope John Paul II visited Rome's Great Synagogue, the first known visit by a pope to a synagogue. Chief Rabbi Elio Toaff welcomed the pope with an embrace and called the visit "a gesture destined to go down in history . . . a true turning point in the policy of the [Roman Catholic] Church." In a special ceremony of prayer and friendship, the pope spoke of the deep spiritual ties that bind together Jews, "our elder brothers," and Christians. He discussed the Roman Catholic Church's role in centuries of Jewish persecution and forcefully condemned anti-Semitism "at any time and by anyone."

Jewish Writer and philosopher Elie Wiesel was awarded the 1986 Nobel Peace Prize on October 14. Wiesel, born in Romania and now a naturalized citizen of the United States, is a survivor of two Nazi concentration camps. He has devoted his life to keeping alive the memory of the 6 million Jews murdered by Nazis during World War II. Wiesel has also been a spokesman for oppressed people, including Soviet Jews and black South Africans. He is the recipient of numerous literary awards. The Nobel Prize Committee honored Wiesel as "a spiritual guide in a time of violence and hatred."   Howard A. Berman

In WORLD BOOK, see JEWS; JUDAISM.

King Hussein I of Jordan takes U.S. Vice President George Bush for a cruise off Jordan's coast after meetings in August.

JORDAN. King Hussein I announced in February 1986 that Jordan would no longer cooperate with the Palestine Liberation Organization (PLO) in pursuing a Middle East peace settlement, thereby canceling a year-old agreement with PLO leader Yasir Arafat. That agreement had called for a joint Jordanian-PLO delegation in peace talks with Israel. The break with the PLO was underscored in July, when Hussein ordered 25 PLO offices in Jordan closed.

Hussein blamed the split on Arafat's refusal to accept United Nations Security Council Resolutions 242 and 338 as the basis for negotiations. These resolutions call for the evacuation of Israeli troops from occupied Arab lands in exchange for peace and Arab recognition of Israel. Arafat has long opposed the resolutions because they do not guarantee the creation of a Palestinian state.

West Bank Plan. In the wake of the Jordanian-PLO split, the king announced in June a five-year development program for the West Bank—the Israeli-occupied territory west of the Jordan River that is home to some 586,000 Palestinians. The plan would channel economic development funds of $150 million to $240 million annually to the West Bank.

Jordan hoped to obtain funds for the plan from other Arab countries and from the United States, Western Europe, and Japan. According to ana-

lysts, the plan was intended to prevent an influx of West Bank Palestinians into Jordan and to present Jordan—or Palestinian leaders acceptable to Jordan—as an alternative to the PLO.

Relations with Syria, which had been severed in 1971, were restored to full diplomatic status in April 1986. This followed a December 1985 meeting between Hussein and Syrian President Hafiz al-Assad, the first meeting between leaders of the two countries since 1979.

New Electoral Law. The two-house National Assembly, Jordan's legislature, approved in May 1986 a new law that increased the number of seats in the elected lower house from 60 to 142. The new law guaranteed 11 seats for West Bank Palestinian refugees and 71 for Jordanians. The law also lowered the voting age from 20 to 19.

The Economy. Despite spending about 30 per cent of its 1986 budget on defense, Jordan continued to prosper economically. In February, the Cabinet approved the so-called 1986-1990 Five-Year Plan, an economic strategy calling for investments of $10 billion in the Jordanian economy. Funding would come from foreign aid, phosphate exports, and wages sent home by Jordanians working abroad.   William Spencer

See also MIDDLE EAST (Facts in Brief Table). In WORLD BOOK, see JORDAN.

JUDAISM. See JEWS AND JUDAISM.

KAMPUCHEA. Fighting for control of Kampuchea (formerly called Cambodia) continued in 1986. A three-party coalition of Communists and non-Communists opposing Kampuchea's Vietnamese-backed government met in Beijing (Peking), China, on March 17 and proposed a settlement.

The Peace Proposal was made by leaders of the coalition—Prince Norodom Sihanouk, the country's former chief of state; former Prime Minister Son Sann, head of the Khmer People's National Liberation Front; and Khieu Samphan, head of the Communist Khmer Rouge. The proposal called for negotiations with Vietnam on a withdrawal of Vietnamese troops and a cease-fire supervised by the United Nations (UN). The U.S. Embassy in Thailand in June estimated there were 140,000 Vietnamese troops in Kampuchea.

The coalition parties wanted to share governing power four ways with the present regime until free elections could be held, supervised by UN observers. But Vietnamese officials on March 19 rejected the proposal, which they said would restore the Khmer Rouge to power. The Khmer Rouge had conducted a reign of terror, killing thousands of people, when it ruled Kampuchea from 1975 until its overthrow by Vietnam in early 1979.

The Resistance. The Khmer Rouge in 1986 continued to provide the main guerrilla resistance to

Vietnamese Army control of Kampuchea. Khmer Rouge troops staged ambushes and surprise attacks throughout the country.

There was some cooperation between the three coalition partners in guerrilla actions. On March 28, Sihanouk's troops reportedly guarded the flanks of Khmer Rouge forces during an attack on Kampuchea's second-largest city, Battambang. But there were also reports of clashes between the Khmer Rouge and other coalition troops.

Son Sann struggled to maintain control of his National Liberation Front. The front's army commander and other dissident officers tried to take over from him in January. Neither side, however, was strong enough to establish absolute control.

The Kampuchean Government tried to build up its own army so that it would not have to depend on the Vietnamese. But desertions were high, and the army reportedly numbered only 40,000 troops.

Refugees reported in October that it was becoming more difficult to flee to Thailand because the Vietnamese forces were sealing the border with earthworks, fences, and land mines. Henry S. Bradsher

See also ASIA (Facts in Brief Table); VIETNAM. In WORLD BOOK, see CAMBODIA or KAMPUCHEA.

KANSAS. See STATE GOVERNMENT.

KENTUCKY. See STATE GOVERNMENT.

Refugees take to the road once again after their refugee camp on the Thai-Kampuchean border comes under shelling by Kampuchean rebels in May.

KENYA, which may have had the highest population growth rate in world history in the late 1970's—4.1 per cent—posted a 3.8 per cent population increase in 1986. The modest, but important, decline in the growth rate was apparently due to the family-planning program of President Daniel T. arap Moi. The program has been resisted by many people on cultural or religious grounds, but in May the government warned those opponents against causing any disruptions.

Kenya's economy received a boost in 1986 from good rainfall and increases in world prices and demand for Kenya's products. In midyear, Moi introduced a new investment code for businesses in Kenya. It specifies that the majority of a new company's stock must be held by Kenyans.

In January, Moi charged that the leaders of government development projects and businesses were inefficient and corrupt. Responding to women's demands for better career opportunities, he appointed women to head 20 such enterprises.

Moi introduced a controversial plan in August aimed at countering the tendency of voters to reject incumbents of the Kenya African National Union, the only legal political party. Voters must now stand in public next to their preferred candidates.   J. Gus Liebenow and Beverly B. Liebenow

See also AFRICA (Facts in Brief Table). In WORLD BOOK, see KENYA.

KOREA, NORTH. Communist North Korea strengthened its relations with the Soviet Union in 1986. The Soviet foreign minister visited North Korea in January, the first such visit since 1968. During his four-day visit, Eduard A. Shevardnadze emphasized "complete consensus" on foreign affairs with President Kim Il-song's government. Kim, in turn, visited the Soviet Union from October 22 to 26.

Kim and Cuba's President Fidel Castro signed a friendship treaty in Pyongyang, North Korea, on March 11. Chinese President Li Xiannian visited Pyongyang from October 3 to 6.

During 1986, North Korea looked for support from its Communist allies in its efforts to share in hosting the 1988 Olympic Games, scheduled to be held in Seoul, South Korea. The International Olympic Committee offered to hold four minor events in Pyongyang, but further negotiations ended when the North rejected this offer.

South Korea reported in mid-November that Kim had been assassinated. The South Korean government said that North Korean loudspeakers at the border had repeatedly broadcast the news from November 16 to 18, when Kim appeared in public. Each side then accused the other of spreading false rumors.   Henry S. Bradsher

See also ASIA (Facts in Brief Table); KOREA, SOUTH. In WORLD BOOK, see KOREA.

KOREA, SOUTH. Disagreements over possible constitutional changes and South Korea's political future created turmoil throughout 1986. Economic growth was steady, however, as South Korea entered new export markets. Cheaper oil imports contributed to the strong economic growth. South Korea began exporting cars to the United States and Canada, and increased its exports of personal computers.

Direct-Vote Drive. The New Korea Democratic Party (NKDP), the main opposition to President Chun Doo Hwan's Democratic Justice Party (DJP), on February 12 launched an effort to collect 10 million signatures on a petition asking for a constitutional amendment to allow direct election of the president in 1988. The NKDP wanted to end the electoral college system, in which 5,200 people are elected to choose the president. Chun, an army general, in January had promised not to run again in 1988. But the NKDP feared that the electoral system would enable Chun to arrange for another general to succeed him.

Claiming that a 1963 law made petitions like that of the NKDP illegal, the government immediately put the two main opposition leaders, Kim Dae Jung and Kim Young Sam, and 78 National Assembly members under house arrest. Chun on Feb. 24, 1986, released those arrested and offered to let the constitution be amended in 1989—after a new president had taken office. The NKDP rejected this offer.

Rallies and Riots. On March 9, 1986, the head of the Roman Catholic Church in Korea said constitutional reform was needed. Major Protestant churches also called for democratic reforms.

The NKDP then resumed its signature drive. It began staging rallies in South Korean cities, attracting large crowds. At Inchon on May 3, a rally turned into a six-hour riot, with about 10,000 dissidents shouting slogans against Chun and against the United States, which had troops stationed in South Korea to protect it from North Korea.

There were several student demonstrations during the year. On May 20, a university student burned himself to death, and on October 31, riot police arrested 1,000 student demonstrators.

Constitutional Debates. Meanwhile, Chun said in May that he would allow a constitutional amendment if the two political sides could agree. National Assembly members began to discuss proposed constitutional changes in June and set up a 45-member committee to examine the issue in July. But the committee was soon deadlocked between DJP insistence on indirect presidential elections and NKDP demands for direct voting. On September 30, NKDP leaders began a boycott of the committee.

The situation deteriorated further on October 17, when 1,000 police officers stormed the National Assembly and arrested an NKDP member for making an antigovernment statement. To protest the arrest, the NKDP staged a sit-in at the National Assembly.

The government mobilized a record number of police—some 70,000—in Seoul on November 29 to prevent an opposition rally. NKDP leaders said later they might have to resort to more militant action in their "fight to overthrow this regime."

A Bomb Exploded at Seoul's international airport on September 14. It killed 5 people and wounded more than 30 others. Police blamed North Korea and accused it of trying to discourage attendance at the Asian Games, which began in Seoul on September 20.

Foreign Relations. On November 17, the South Korean government reported that North Korean President Kim Il-song had been shot and killed. But Kim appeared in public on November 18. See KOREA, NORTH.

The U.S. Department of State issued statements during 1986 criticizing human rights violations in South Korea. During a visit to Seoul on May 7 and 8, however, U.S. Secretary of State George P. Shultz praised Chun for "moving fast" on political evolution.   Henry S. Bradsher

See also ASIA (Facts in Brief Table). In WORLD BOOK, see KOREA.

KUWAIT. See MIDDLE EAST.

LABOR. The job picture continued to be generally bright in the United States during 1986. About 2 million more people were employed in 1986 than in 1985. More than 10 million jobs had been created between December 1982, the close of the devastating 1981-1982 recession, and December 1986. And the unemployment rate had by April returned to its prerecession level of 7 per cent.

Wage increases for the 12-month period ending in September 1986, as measured by the U.S. Bureau of Labor Statistics Employment Cost Index, averaged 3.1 per cent for private workers. Wages and benefits together rose 3.2 per cent. Wage increases for workers covered by collective bargaining agreements in the first nine months of 1986 averaged 1.9 per cent.

The relative importance of cost-of-living adjustments in bargaining declined because inflation in 1986 continued to be low at 1.1 per cent. The trend toward substituting lump-sum payments for permanent wage increases continued. In some cases, management tried to reduce hourly wage and benefit costs. Two-tiered pay systems, which permit payment of lower wages to new employees, continued to make gains, affecting 11 per cent of jobs under major contracts by the end of 1985.

Unions, meanwhile, strove to balance the need to maintain pay and benefits against the need to preserve jobs in industries that have never recov-

ered from the onslaught of imports and the 1981-1982 recession. But the influence of unions continued to decline. Statistics released in 1986 revealed that the proportion of U.S. private sector workers in unions fell from 18.8 per cent in 1984 to 18.0 per cent in 1985. Major new collective-bargaining pacts negotiated in the first nine months of 1986 covered 1.8 million workers.

Cold Steel. Faced with a weakened U.S. steel industry, 550 local United Steelworkers of America (USWA) presidents met in January and changed their bargaining procedures. They agreed that local presidents would no longer approve contracts; instead, this would be done by the memberships of the local unions. Industrywide bargaining would be replaced by individual company and local union negotiations.

In agreements reached later during the year, many local unions accepted cuts in pay and benefits in exchange for job security. At LTV Steel Corporation, the USWA local on March 15 agreed to a cut in wages of $1.14 per hour and benefit reductions. At Bethlehem Steel Corporation, the workers in June agreed to pay and benefit cuts that reduced wages by $1.96 per hour over 37 months. At Inland Steel Company, the USWA on June 20 agreed to a 40-cent-per-hour wage cut, a wage freeze, and no cost-of-living adjustments.

Changes in the United States Labor Force

	1985	1986
Total labor force	**117,167,000**	**119,547,000**
Armed forces	1,706,000	1,706,000
Civilian labor force	115,461,000	117,841,000
Total employment	108,856,000	111,307,000
Unemployment	8,311,000	8,240,000
Unemployment rate	7.1%	7.0%
Change in real earnings of production and nonsupervisory workers (private nonfarm sector)*	−1.1%	+1.3%
Change in output per employee hour (private nonfarm sector)†	+0.5%	+0.3%

*Constant (1977) dollars, 1985 change from December 1984 to December 1985; 1986 change from November 1985 to November 1986 (preliminary data).
†Annual rate for 1985; for 1986, change is from third quarter 1985 to third quarter 1986 (preliminary data).
Source: U.S. Bureau of Labor Statistics.

Teamsters President Jackie Presser rides a Roman chariot at the union's convention in May, days after being indicted on charges of embezzling union funds.

On April 9, the National Steel Corporation and the USWA reached agreement on a 39-month contract that reduced benefits and cut hourly wages 99 cents over the life of the agreement. The contract did, however, provide for guaranteed lump-sum payments each year equal to 50 cents for each hour worked—even if the company was not profitable. If the company did make a profit, the lump sums could go as high as $1.75 for each hour worked. The agreement, approved in late April, guaranteed employment unless the plant closed, the company declared bankruptcy, or the union and management agreed that the company was in dire financial straits.

In other cases, union locals refused pay and benefit reductions, and strikes occurred. On February 16, 13,000 members of the USWA struck four major can companies after local leaders rejected an offer of a year-end bonus instead of a wage increase. The strike ended on March 5, when workers settled for better benefits in place of a wage hike.

USX Corporation, the largest steel producer in the United States, shut down its plants on August 1 after failing to reach an agreement with the USWA. USX called the dispute a strike, but the union, which had offered to extend the existing contract, called it a lockout. By the end of 1986, no settlement was in sight. The strike had become

the longest in the history of the steel industry, surpassing a 116-day strike in 1959.

Aluminum and Copper. The USWA and the Aluminum, Brick, and Glass Workers International Union approved a new contract in July with the Aluminum Company of America. Wages will be frozen over the three-year contract, and the benefit package will be cut by about 4 per cent. The settlement ended a strike that began in early June after contracts expired on May 31. Similar terms were reached between the unions and Reynolds Metals Company.

Continuing a tradition of coalition bargaining, 14 unions together reached agreements with two major copper-mining companies, Magma Copper Company and Pinto Valley Copper Company, in late June. Because employment in the industry was down by more than 80 per cent, the workers accepted pay cuts of more than $2.80 an hour and benefit reductions. The unions in negotiations with a third copper producer—Kennecott Corporation—on July 7 agreed to pay and benefit cuts of more than 20 per cent.

Telecommunications. The Communications Workers of America (CWA) and American Telephone and Telegraph Company (AT&T) tried to work out a new settlement by May 31. But there was a breakdown in talks, and 155,000 union members struck AT&T on June 1. An agreement was reached on June 17 that would raise wages and benefits 10.2 per cent over three years. The CWA remained on strike until June 27 because of local disagreements.

The CWA also bargained with the seven regional telephone companies. In August, strikes were called against NYNEX (serving New York and New England) and U.S. West (serving parts of the Midwest and West) before agreements were reached. The NYNEX settlement called for wage increases of 2.5 per cent in the first year and 1 per cent in the second and third years of the contract.

Petroleum Pacts. In mid-January, the Oil, Chemical and Atomic Workers International Union accepted a two-year contract offer from Amoco Oil Company. This settlement became the pattern for the industry. It called for a $1,000 bonus when the union members ratified the pact, a 2 per cent wage increase in January 1987, and about 28 cents more per hour in 1988.

Longshoring. On October 1, the International Longshoremen's Association (ILA) struck Atlantic Ocean ports along the Northeast coast of the United States in a dispute over management's proposal of a two-tiered pay system with cuts for some work crews. On October 3, the union and the dock companies agreed to extend the expired contract for 45 days while bargaining continued. But in mid-October, they compromised on wages of $17 an hour for the first two years, rising to $18 an hour in the third year of the contract. Employees unloading cargo that is not containerized, however, would receive $16 an hour.

East and Gulf coast union negotiators had split, however, from their Northeastern counterparts in early May over issues involving lower-paid nonunion workers. The Southern union locals did not strike but agreed on pay cuts of $3 to $5 an hour, a reduction in paid holidays from 16 to 10 days, and cuts in crew size. Leaders of the ILA then tightened bargaining rules in Northern ports, prohibiting locals from negotiating agreements without approval of the international union.

Dockworkers in New Orleans staged a week-long strike in mid-October in a dispute involving overtime pay policies.

"Comparable Worth." The settlement of a landmark lawsuit involving the state of Washington and the Washington State Federation of Employees was approved by a federal court on April 11. The settlement provided pay adjustments over seven years to raise wages of employees in female-dominated occupations to match those of employees in comparable, but male-dominated, jobs. The worth of a job would be determined by assigning points to such requirements as skill and education.

Striking members of the United Food and Commercial Workers union shout at a trucker leaving the Hormel meat-packing plant in Austin, Minn., in January.

The total settlement was valued at $482 million. See CIVIL RIGHTS.

Other Disputes and Settlements. A strike at Delco Electronics in Kokomo, Ind., from November 17 to 23 created an auto-parts shortage that led to the layoff of nearly 60,000 General Motors Corporation workers.

On March 5, almost two years after their previous pact expired, the Brotherhood of Railway, Airline and Steamship Clerks, Freight Handlers, Express and Station Employees ratified a four-year national agreement. Its terms were retroactive to July 1, 1984. The pact included increases of 6.57 per cent over the four years.

The Distillery, Wine and Allied Workers International Union struck 12 California wineries beginning on August 18. Members of the Winery Employers Association used management employees and temporary help to press the grapes. In retaliation, the striking union called for a wine boycott. But on October 2, the workers accepted a contract with wage and benefit cuts.

The United Automobile Workers and Caterpillar Incorporated, a farm-machinery manufacturer, agreed on a 28-month pact on July 4 that freezes pay but continues cost-of-living adjustments and increases pension benefits.

A bitter, yearlong strike against the George A. Hormel & Company plants in Minnesota ended with new labor contracts in September. National leaders of the United Food and Commercial Workers International Union took over a renegade local for conducting a strike at the Hormel plant in Austin, Minn.

Drug Testing. On September 15, U.S. President Ronald Reagan signed an executive order authorizing random drug testing of federal employees in all "sensitive" jobs, and testing of other federal employees suspected of drug use. But on September 18, an appeals court ruled against the testing of U.S. customs workers, and this decision threatened the drug-testing program.

In January, the Supreme Court of the United States allowed the Reagan Administration to put into immediate effect nationwide regulations requiring drug and alcohol testing of railroad employees involved in rail accidents.

Union Scandal. A federal grand jury in Cleveland on May 16 indicted Teamsters Union President Jackie Presser and two local union officials on charges of embezzling more than $700,000 from two local Cleveland unions. The head of the Cleveland Federal Bureau of Investigation's (FBI) organized crime squad was also indicted for lying about Presser's relation with the FBI. On May 21, Presser was overwhelmingly reelected as Teamsters president for five years.   Robert W. Fisher

See also ECONOMICS. In WORLD BOOK, see LABOR FORCE; LABOR MOVEMENT.

LAOS. A joint session of the Supreme People's Assembly and the Council of Ministers in Vientiane named Phoumi Vongvichit as acting president of Laos on Oct. 29, 1986. He replaced President Souphanouvong, hospitalized since October 21.

Souphanouvong is known as the "Red Prince" because he was born into the old Laotian royal family but became a founder of the country's Communist organization, the Lao People's Revolutionary Party (LPRP). He was a leader of the Communist guerrilla forces—known as the Pathet Lao—that came to power in 1975 after more than 20 years of fighting against governments led by his half-brother Souvanna Phouma.

Phoumi had long served as a deputy to Souphanouvong, and both were members of the Politburo of the LPRP, which controls Laos. Before assuming the presidency—a primarily ceremonial office—Phoumi had also served as a deputy prime minister. Both men ranked in importance behind Prime Minister Kayson Phomvihan, who was the party general secretary, and Deputy Prime Minister Nouhak Phoumsavan.

Party Congress. From Nov. 13 to 15, 1986, the LPRP held in Vientiane its fourth *congress* (meeting) since the Pathet Lao gained control in 1975. The congress endorsed recent economic reforms and reelected Kayson as general secretary, but Nouhak was dropped from the party secretariat. Kayson said many party members remained "narrow-minded and selfish," and he called for a purge of some members.

New Five-Year Plan. The congress also approved details of Laos' Second Five-Year Plan for economic development—for 1986 through 1990. The First Five-Year Plan had achieved an annual growth rate of about 6 per cent, but both the trade deficit and foreign debt had grown. The Second Five-Year Plan called for a 5 per cent annual growth rate that would ensure adequate food, reduced nonfood imports, and an improved balance of payments.

At an economic aid conference in Geneva, Switzerland, during April, the Laotian government looked for $290 million in foreign aid during its Second Five-Year Plan. Laos sought some of this aid from Western nations. Although some 70 per cent of economic aid for the First Five-Year Plan came from Communist countries, the Soviet Union and other Marxist governments stiffened their terms for assistance during 1986.

Foreign Relations. A dispute that began in 1984 with Thailand over three border villages continued to disrupt relations between the two countries in 1986. On October 5, Laos accused China of "trying in every way to destroy and undermine our young regime."   Henry S. Bradsher

See also ASIA (Facts in Brief Table). In WORLD BOOK, see LAOS.

LATIN AMERICA. More than 400 million Latin Americans struggled with the problems of over-population and recession during 1986. Those who were born during the mid-1960's baby boom, when Latin-American women gave birth to an average of six children each, compared with four in 1986, were especially hard hit by the consequences of that population explosion.

The consequences included crowded cities, un-employment rates comparable to those in the United States during the Great Depression of the 1930's, and social discontent approaching the flashpoint in half a dozen countries.

"Not since the Great Depression of the 1930's has Latin America suffered such economic damage," declared Miguel Urrutia of Colombia, chief author of a hard-hitting report released on September 7 by the Inter-American Development Bank (IDB). The report noted that Latin America's recession was "lengthening dangerously." Debts were piling up, the IDB said, with 23 Latin-American countries accounting for nearly two-thirds of the $1 trillion owed by Third World nations to foreign creditors. Latin America has paid nearly $100 billion in interest alone—not including principal—on its debt in the 1980's.

The IDB report noted that the area's output of goods and services increased only 3.9 per cent be-tween 1980 and 1985, while its population increased by 12.7 per cent. This translated into an 8 per cent drop in per capita output and a drop in annual per capita earnings from $1,933 in 1980 to $1,782 in 1985.

The effect of the recession was not evenly distributed. Fourteen countries suffered a decline in the standard of living of more than 10 per cent while seven other countries—Argentina, Bolivia, El Salvador, Guatemala, Guyana, Uruguay, and Venezuela—experienced a decline of more than 15 per cent.

Uneasy Military. Latin America's military leaders were nervous as they read about trials of military officers in Argentina accused of human rights violations and other misconduct. The three top officers who led Argentina into a losing war with Great Britain over the Falkland Islands in 1982 were given jail sentences ranging from 8 to 14 years and stripped of rank and privilege. Among them was former President Leopoldo F. Galtieri.

Before relinquishing their power to civilians, generals in Brazil, El Salvador, Guatemala, and Uruguay had demanded pledges that they would not be subjected to Argentine-style trials. In Uruguay, a brief declaration by 19 retired generals in October 1986, expressing opposition to a proposed human rights law, stirred fears of a coup.

Military police guard the offices of the Central Elections Board in Santo Domingo, Dominican Republic, during the presidential election in May.

Facts in Brief on Latin American Political Units

Country	Population	Government	Monetary Unit*	Foreign Trade (million U.S. $) Exports†	Imports†
Antigua and Barbuda	82,000	Governor General Sir Wilfred Ebenezer Jacobs; Prime Minister Vere C. Bird	dollar (2.7 = $1)	41	147
Argentina	31,500,000	President Raúl Alfonsín	austral (1 = $1)	8,396	3,814
Bahamas	241,000	Governor General Sir Gerald C. Cash; Prime Minister Lynden O. Pindling	dollar (1 = $1)	2,300	3,000
Barbados	270,000	Governor General Sir Hugh Springer; Prime Minister Errol Walton Barrow	dollar (2 = $1)	390	656
Belize	168,000	Governor General Minita Gordon; Prime Minister Manuel Esquivel	dollar (2 = $1)	93	126
Bolivia	6,730,000	President Víctor Paz Estenssoro	peso (2,000,000 = $1)	730	477
Brazil	141,459,000	President José Sarney	cruzado (14.1 = $1)	25,639	14,346
Chile	12,421,000	President Augusto Pinochet Ugarte	peso (199 = $1)	3,797	2,743
Colombia	29,943,000	President Virgilio Barco Vargas	peso (216 = $1)	3,500	4,500
Costa Rica	2,645,000	President Oscar Arias Sánchez	colón (57.8 = $1)	956	1,101
Cuba	10,214,000	President Fidel Castro	peso (1 = $1.07)	6,200	8,100
Dominica	74,000	President Clarence Seignoret; Prime Minister Mary Eugenia Charles	dollar (2.7 = $1)	26	57
Dominican Republic	6,531,000	President Joaquín Balaguer	peso (3 = $1)	735	1,487
Ecuador	9,983,000	President León Febres-Cordero	sucre (145 = $1)	2,600	1,600
El Salvador	5,906,000	President José Napoleón Duarte	colón (2.5 = $1)	676	961
Grenada	118,000	Governor General Sir Paul Godwin Scoon; Prime Minister Herbert Blaize	dollar (2.7 = $1)	19	56
Guatemala	8,895,000	President Vinicio Cerezo	quetzal (1 = $1)	1,100	1,300
Guyana	989,000	President Hugh Desmond Hoyte; Prime Minister Hamilton Green	dollar (4.3 = $1)	212	222
Haiti	5,552,000	National Council President Henri Namphy	gourde (5 = $1)	168	284
Honduras	4,657,000	President José Azcona del Hoyo	lempira (2 = $1)	675	705
Jamaica	2,392,000	Governor General Sir Florizel Glasspole; Prime Minister Edward Seaga	dollar (5.5 = $1)	549	1,124
Mexico	76,300,000	President Miguel de la Madrid Hurtado	peso (871 = $1)	22,108	13,459
Nicaragua	3,502,000	President Daniel Ortega	córdoba (833 = $1)	320	850
Panama	2,274,000	President Eric Arturo Delvalle	balboa (1 = $1)	419	1,340
Paraguay	3,897,000	President Alfredo Stroessner	guaraní (317 = $1)	361	649
Peru	20,727,000	President Alan García Pérez; Prime Minister Luis Alva Castro	inti (14.5 = $1)	2,966	1,835
Puerto Rico	3,197,000	Governor Rafael Hernández Colón	U.S. $	10,543	10,112
St. Christopher and Nevis	44,000	Governor General Clement Arrindell; Prime Minister Kennedy Alphonse Simmonds	dollar (2.7 = $1)	31	47
St. Lucia	125,000	Governor General Sir Allen Montgomery Lewis; Prime Minister John Compton	dollar (2.7 = $1)	50	107
St. Vincent and the Grenadines	128,000	Governor General Joseph Lambert Eustace; Prime Minister James Mitchell	dollar (2.7 = $1)	42	71
Suriname	391,000	Commander of the National Army Desire D. Bouterse; Acting President L. F. Ramdat-Misier; Prime Minister Pretapp Radhakisun	guilder (1.8 = $1)	356	346
Trinidad and Tobago	1,221,000	President Ellis Emmanuel Innocent Clarke; Prime Minister A. N. R. Robinson	dollar (2.3 = $1)	2,204	1,533
Uruguay	2,972,000	President Julio María Sanguinetti	peso (175 = $1)	925	732
Venezuela	18,408,000	President Jaime Lusinchi	bolívar (23 = $1)	12,272	8,178

*Exchange rates as of Dec. 1, 1986, or latest available data.   †Latest available data.

Nicaraguan soldiers man a machine-gun nest near the Honduran border in March during fighting with rebel forces known as *contras*.

During the year, the U.S. Central Intelligence Agency added to military anxieties by charging that General Manuel Antonio Noriega, commander of the Panama Defense Force (formerly the National Guard), had rigged the 1984 presidential elections in Panama.

In two countries, differences within the military nearly led to shooting. In Honduras, troops led by rivals for the top post within the high command were actually positioned to attack one another in September. Behind the incident was the fear of many Honduran officers that their army was being dragged into a war with Nicaragua that it could not win. To help relieve their fears, the United States supplied Honduras with advanced jet fighters. In Ecuador, General Frank Vargas Pazos, the former armed forces chief of staff, staged a revolt from an air base 150 miles (240 kilometers) from Quito, the capital, on March 7. The incident could have had serious repercussions, but it was defused by March 14.

In Peru, tempers ran high among military officers when the government began to slash military spending. Bolivian officers were unhappy when their government invited U.S. troops to provide support for the war against drug traffickers.

Expanded Role for U.S. Military. The U.S. military expanded its operations in Latin America in 1986 and acquired new responsibilities. On April

8, a White House national security directive authorized the use of U.S. military forces to combat the illegal drug trade, which has been linked to international terrorism. On orders from President Ronald Reagan, U.S. military units were provided to the Bahamas and to Bolivia to assist local authorities in raids on cocaine laboratories located in remote areas.

The U.S. military presence in Honduras became more prominent as the U.S. Senate in August approved $100 million in additional aid for rebels known as *contras* fighting the Marxist regime in Nicaragua. Some 2,000 U.S. military personnel have been assigned to the Palmerola air base near Tegucigalpa, the capital of Honduras. The air base is the headquarters of U.S. military operations in Central America.

The United States also made available advanced model jet fighters to the Honduran air force, despite protests by Latin-American nations seeking a negotiated settlement of the Central American conflict. United States officials previously had declared that the introduction of jet fighters into Nicaragua by the Soviet Union would trigger U.S. armed retaliation. The U.S. support for the contra effort, however, came under a cloud in late 1986 with revelations about the diversion of funds to the contras from secret arms sales to Iran (see PRESIDENT OF THE UNITED STATES).

A Pentagon proposal to put the U.S. military in charge of patrolling the U.S.-Mexican border to stop the flow of illegal aliens was sidetracked by Secretary of Defense Caspar W. Weinberger, who called the idea "ridiculous." But plans for the U.S. military to train the Haitian army and the contra rebels moved ahead. The contras were to be trained on U.S. soil, after several Central American nations refused to allow such training in their territories.

Economic Proposals. During 1986, there were some ingenious new proposals for relieving Latin America's debt woes. A 12-year financial plan to aid Mexico, involving close collaboration between private and international lenders, provided unprecedented long-term support for a troubled economy. Several Latin-American countries worked out "debt swaps," whereby foreign investors buy foreign debt in return for discounted national currencies that can be used to invest in the country.

To defuse a rising tide of *protectionism* (the use of tariffs and other trade barriers to protect domestic industries from foreign competition), the trade ministers of 74 nations met at Punta del Este, Uruguay, in September as members of the General Agreement on Tariffs and Trade. Their final declaration addressed Latin-American concerns, including the need to reduce government subsidies that hurt Latin America's earnings from its agricultural exports.

Old Leaders. For political leadership, some countries turned to aging politicians whose economic and political programs seemed to have worked in the past. On August 16, 78-year-old Joaquín Balaguer, blind from glaucoma, was again inaugurated as president of the Dominican Republic. His previous presidential term ended in 1978 (see BALAGUER, JOAQUÍN). In Bolivia, another former president who was reelected for the fourth time in 1985, 79-year-old Víctor Paz Estenssoro, confounded his critics during 1986 with the vigor of his efforts to manage an unmanageable economy.

U.S. Immigration Bill. On October 17, the U.S. Congress approved the Immigration Reform and Control Act of 1986. The law was a far-reaching measure to control the flow of new immigrants into the United States and to enable some of those living in the United States illegally to become legal residents and eventually apply for citizenship. The law subjects U.S. employers who knowingly hire illegal aliens to civil penalties ranging from $250 to $10,000 for each illegal alien they hire. Repeat offenders are criminally liable for fines up to $3,000 and six months imprisonment for a "pattern or practice" of violation.

The bill provides legal status for aliens who entered the United States illegally before Jan. 1, 1982, and who have resided in the United States continuously since that date. Under the new law, the federal government will set aside $1 billion annually for four years to reimburse state governments for public assistance, health care, and education provided for illegal aliens who are acquiring legal status as U.S. citizens.

Argentina: Sadness and Joy. June brought both bad and good news to Argentina. Jorge Luis Borges, 86, an acclaimed short-story writer, died on June 14 while visiting Geneva, Switzerland. Many of his 20 volumes of essays and stories are as popular in the United States and elsewhere in the world as in his native Argentina. Borges was considered by some critics to be Latin America's greatest modern writer.

The mourning was cut short by outbursts of delirious joy on the streets of the capital, Buenos Aires, on June 29, when Argentines celebrated the World Cup victory of their soccer team over West Germany at Mexico City's Aztec Stadium. The win gave Argentina possession of soccer's coveted World Cup until 1990.

Early Americans. In June, French scientists reported finding signs of human habitation in rock shelters of northeast Brazil indicating that people lived there 32,000 years ago. Previously, most archaeologists believed that people first settled in the Americas between 11,500 and 20,000 years ago, arriving first in North America by crossing a land bridge between Siberia and Alaska. An American anthropologist working in Chile had found similar evidence of early human occupation in South America in 1981. Both findings were supported by radiocarbon dating. Some scientists have suggested that the earliest Americans arrived first in South America by boat from Asia and then spread northward.

Oil Spill. The Smithsonian Institution in Washington, D.C., announced on April 27 that the rupture of an oil-storage tank in the Caribbean Sea off Panama had sent tens of thousands of barrels of crude oil into the water. The oil spilled from a Texaco-owned refinery 3 miles (5 kilometers) east of Galeta Island. It contaminated much of a large coral reef where the Smithsonian maintains a marine laboratory, and it destroyed thousands of marine organisms.

Latin-American Culture. Latin-American dance and music enjoyed increasing popularity in the United States. *Tango Argentino*, a program of tango music and dancing that opened to widespread acclaim in New York City in 1985, toured many North American cities in 1986, again to great enthusiasm. The new interest in Latin-American culture extended to food. In trendsetting cities, such as New York City, several chic restaurants began specializing in Caribbean delicacies. These include barbecued shrimp wrapped in banana leaves, Jamaican curried goat, and Barbados-style codfish stew with tomatoes and onions.

Two rising new stars of Latin-American music received a big assist in 1986 from the U.S. government. The duo—Tatiana Palacios, 17, of Mexico and Johnny Lozada Correa, 18, of Puerto Rico—had won acclaim for popular songs with lyrics that promoted a healthy, go-slow route in romantic entanglements. The U.S. Agency for International Development invested $300,000 to record and promote their song "When We're Together," which advises boys and girls to refrain from premarital sex.

Adventure. During 1986, people again sought to satisfy their craving for adventure in Latin America. A team of hardy souls navigated the 4,000 miles (6,400 kilometers) of the Amazon River by kayak. While en route, the explorers were briefly held captive by armed leftist guerrillas and also had to make their peace with cocaine traffickers who controlled some of the territory through which they passed.   Nathan A. Haverstock

See also articles on the various Latin-American countries. In the Special Reports section, see MEX-ICO: FROM BOOM TO BUST. In WORLD BOOK, see LATIN AMERICA and articles on the individual countries.

LAW. See CIVIL RIGHTS; COURTS; CRIME; SUPREME COURT OF THE UNITED STATES.

LEBANON. In January 1986, fighting broke out between Maronite Christian factions, dashing hopes that the Syrian-sponsored unity pact signed by Lebanon's warring factions on Dec. 28, 1985, would ease the suffering of the Lebanese people. A large segment of the Christian community, including Lebanon's President Amine Gemayel and his supporters, had opposed the agreement, which they thought would weaken the dominant Maronites' position in Lebanon and turn the country into a Syrian protectorate. In a series of battles, Maronite opponents overthrew Elie Hobeika, a supporter of the unity pact and commander of the principal Maronite militia, the Lebanese Forces. He was succeeded by his chief rival, Samir Geagea.

The conflict between Christian factions, the worst in five years, killed 200 people and injured 600. When talks with Syria's President Hafiz al-Assad in January failed to win Gemayel's support for the agreement, Lebanon reverted to its all-too-familiar pattern of sectarian strife.

PLO Return. A new complication emerged with the return of the Palestine Liberation Organization (PLO). PLO guerrillas had been filtering back into Lebanon since the Israeli withdrawal from the country in 1985, and the number returning increased after PLO offices in Jordan were closed in July 1986. The PLO established bases in refugee

Syrian-backed Shiite Muslim militiamen fire rocket-propelled grenades at Palestinian positions inside a battered refugee camp in Beirut in April.

camps around Sidon and Beirut, and guerrillas resumed their hit-and-run attacks against Israel.

The PLO return ignited hostility with other Lebanese factions, notably the Amal (Hope), the largest Shiite Muslim militia. In July, the PLO seized several strategic mountain villages near Sidon from Amal. In retaliation, Amal and Sunni Muslim militias surrounded the refugee camps, until mediation by Iranian Revolutionary guards stationed nearby brought a cease-fire.

Peril to Foreigners. Life in Lebanon for foreigners continued to be dangerous. Following the United States raid on Libya in April, a librarian from the American University of Beirut and two Britons were murdered by their kidnappers, allegedly in retaliation. But Lawrence Martin Jenco, an American Roman Catholic priest, was released from 19 months captivity by Islamic Jihad (Holy War) guerrillas on July 2. Another American hostage, David P. Jacobsen, director of American University Hospital in Beirut, was released on November 2 after being held since May 1985. In September and October, however, three other Americans were kidnapped. At the end of 1986, these men and three other Americans, as well as French and British nationals, remained in captivity.

Attack on Peacekeepers. Foreign military observer forces in Lebanon came under attack in August and September. Units of the United Nations Interim Force in Lebanon (UNIFIL), assigned in 1978 to monitor the border between Lebanon and Israel, clashed with Shiite militias.

Earlier, in April, the small French contingent remaining from the multinational peacekeeping force sent to Lebanon in 1982, shortly after the Israeli invasion, left the country. The contingent was evacuated after a member—the ninth victim of the fighting—was killed by a sniper.

Educational Loss. The political crisis threatened to destroy Lebanon's educational system, once the best in the Arab world. In May, the 120-year-old American University of Beirut closed briefly as its faculty went on strike to protest kidnappings of staff members and attacks on students. More than 40 elementary and secondary schools closed, and those remaining open held classes in 2½-hour shifts. Most villages provided no education at all because of a shortage of teachers.

Syrian Intervention. In late June, another Syrian-sponsored security plan went into effect in Beirut. This one was enforced by 200 Syrian elite commandos, who were stationed in Muslim West Beirut to back up the Lebanese Army. But the cease-fire held only where the Syrians could control the militias. In late July, a spate of car bombings caused nearly 1,000 casualties, mainly innocent bystanders in markets or on the street.

Peace Plan. Under such negative circumstances, it was surprising that a serious effort to reconcile

the warring Lebanese factions could ever be initiated by the Lebanese themselves. But in September, the impossible began to happen. Lebanon's Muslim Prime Minister Rashid Karami met with senior Christian leaders and then with his entire Cabinet on September 2.

Karami announced a cease-fire and an agreement among leaders to write a new National Charter that would confirm Lebanon's independence and its Arab character. The proposed charter would also provide for equal representation of Christians and Muslims and protection of minority rights. But there was no guarantee that adoption of a new charter would be followed by genuine reconciliation or lead to recovery for the country's battered economy.

Bloody combat between Christian factions broke out again in late September, and a Sunni religious leader, an outspoken advocate of Christian-Muslim cooperation, was assassinated in early October.

Palestinian-Shiite Strife. In late September, savage fighting erupted between Palestinian guerrillas and Shiite militias and Shiite units of the Lebanese Army in Palestinian areas of Lebanon. The fighting, which continued through December, left about 550 dead and 2,000 wounded. William Spencer

See also MIDDLE EAST (Facts in Brief Table). In WORLD BOOK, see LEBANON.

LESOTHO. See AFRICA.

LIBERIA. On Jan. 6, 1986, Samuel K. Doe, who had headed a military government in Liberia since coming to power in a 1980 coup, was sworn in as president under a new Constitution. Citizens and outside observers rejected the results of the 1985 election, in which Doe's party limited competition and counted the ballots in secret. Also criticized was Doe's reaction to an attempted coup on Nov. 12, 1985. Doe ordered the arrest of opposition leaders and journalists, trials of civilians by military courts, and a ban on public meetings.

Doe's plans for a single-party system were resisted by leaders of four opposition parties, who formed a Grand Coalition in March and called for new elections. Hoping to avoid conflict, Doe called for national unity and tried to win his foes over to his side. But that approach failed, so in August, Doe imprisoned the coalition's leaders. He later released them in response to worldwide criticism.

The economy worsened in 1986, in large part because of a decline in world demand for Liberia's iron ore and rubber. The nation was afflicted with food and gas shortages and mounting inflation. After defaulting on international loan payments, the regime sought foreign supervision in collecting revenues and managing government spending. J. Gus Liebenow and Beverly B. Liebenow

See also AFRICA (Facts in Brief Table). In WORLD BOOK, see LIBERIA.

LIBRARY. One of the largest library fires in United States history blazed through the Los Angeles Central Public Library for almost six hours on April 29, 1986. The fire, which the fire department believes was set by an arsonist, caused $22-million in damages. See LOS ANGELES.

Playboy **Restored.** A federal judge ruled in September that Librarian of Congress Daniel J. Boorstin's 1985 decision to stop producing and distributing a braille edition of *Playboy* magazine was unconstitutional. Boorstin took the action after Congress cut the library's budget by exactly the amount needed to produce the braille edition.

Coalition Formed. On July 29, 1986, representatives of 20 national organizations led by the American Library Association (ALA) formed the Coalition on Government Information to fight actions taken by the Administration of President Ronald Reagan that the coalition said would restrict access to government information. Such actions included a proposal to sell the National Technical Information Service, a clearing house for information resulting chiefly from government-sponsored research, to private industry.

Literacy. The Coalition for Literacy, a group of 11 organizations founded by the ALA, reported that a three-year campaign, launched in late 1984, to increase public awareness of adult functional illiteracy and to recruit volunteer tutors was succeeding. A person who is functionally illiterate cannot read and write well enough to function in society. The coalition said the number of Americans aware of the problem rose from 21.4 per cent to 30 per cent during the campaign's first year.

Technology. During 1986, more libraries rolled away their old card catalogs and introduced computerized catalog and circulation systems. Often, the transition provided an occasion for celebration. In Cleveland, the Cuyahoga County Public Library's card catalog was given a gala retirement party to honor its 62 years of dedicated service. As part of the celebration of its new computerized catalog system, the Health Sciences Library at the University of Maryland in Baltimore launched 500 helium-filled balloons, to which catalog cards stamped "genuine artifact from the Health Sciences Library" were attached.

Library Buildings. In May, the New York City Public Library celebrated the 75th anniversary of the neoclassical building that houses the central library. The festivities also marked the completion of a large part of the library's 10-year, $77-million renovation project. During National Library Week in April, the Orlando (Fla.) Public Library dedicated a new 290,000-square-foot (27,000-square-meter) library.   Peggy Barber

See also AMERICAN LIBRARY ASSOCIATION; CANADIAN LIBRARY ASSOCIATION. In WORLD BOOK, see LIBRARY.

LIBYA. A "war of nerves" between the regime of Leader of the Revolution Muammar Muhammad al-Qadhafi and the United States over the issue of alleged Libyan support for international terrorism reached a flash point in 1986. On April 15, 33 U.S. warplanes from bases in England and from aircraft carriers in the Mediterranean Sea struck military targets in Tripoli and Benghazi, Libya. President Ronald Reagan said he ordered the attack because the United States had obtained "solid evidence" that Libya was behind the bombing of a West Berlin dance club on April 5, in which two American soldiers were killed.

Striking at night, the U.S. planes bombed the El Azziziya barracks in Tripoli—Qadhafi's headquarters—as well as port installations and army bases said to be centers of terrorist training. The bombs caused extensive damage to residential districts adjacent to the targets. Among the alleged casualties were Qadhafi's adopted daughter, reportedly killed in the El Azziziya attack, and two sons, who were seriously wounded.

The attack was the second major confrontation during the year between the United States and Libya. In March, American warships crossed the so-called Line of Death that Qadhafi had proclaimed as the boundary of Libyan territorial waters in the Gulf of Sidra. On March 24, Libyan missiles were fired at U.S. jets over the gulf. In retaliation, the jets sank at least two Libyan patrol boats and damaged missile sites at Surt, on the coast.

Qadhafi Keeps Power. The Reagan Administration had expected that the April raid might fuel a growing dissatisfaction in Libya with Qadhafi and his policies, thereby leading to his overthrow. But Qadhafi in defeat became a rallying point for Libyan patriotism, and the hoped-for uprising did not materialize.

In August, Qadhafi emerged from a self-imposed isolation. On August 31, he led a patriotic rally, and on September 1, the 17th anniversary of the coup that brought him to power, he reviewed a large military parade.

In response to the U.S.-Libyan conflict, Libyan authorities stamped out the last vestiges of Western influence in the nation. In March, Libyan universities closed down their English- and French-language departments, and foreign-language textbooks and Western musical instruments were burned in a mass public ceremony in Tripoli. In April, the teaching of English was banned in Libyan schools, to be replaced by Russian.

Political Reorganization. The General People's Congress (GPC), Libya's only legislative body, held its 11th session in March. Because of economic pressures due to declining oil revenues, as well as the need for better management and centralization of authority, the GPC made some organizational changes. The congress abolished a large

Workers dig in the rubble of a building damaged during a U.S. bombing raid on Libya in April in retaliation for alleged Libyan-sponsored terrorism.

number of *secretariats* (government departments) and combined others. An 11-member General People's Committee (cabinet) was named to run the government.

The Economy. In January, the Reagan Administration froze Libyan assets in U.S. banks, ordered a total trade embargo with Libya, and told Americans living and working in Libya to leave. Those measures, however, had little effect on the Libyan economy. But with oil revenues down to $8 billion a year, the government faced a serious shortage of cash, and foreign debts piled up. Italy—Libya's major creditor—agreed in September to buy Libyan oil at below-market prices to recover $800 million owed to Italian firms. And in October, Libya sold its 15 per cent stake in Fiat S.p.A., an Italian automobile company, to raise $3 billion.

The only development project unaffected by the fiscal squeeze was the Great Man-Made River, a huge irrigation project. In August, a pipe factory opened at Brega to supply concrete pipe for the project, which will carry underground water by pipeline from the Sahara northward to coastal agricultural areas. The costs of the project are met through an annual tax of one month's salary on the labor force. William Spencer

See also AFRICA (Facts in Brief Table). In WORLD BOOK, see LIBYA.

LIECHTENSTEIN. See EUROPE.

LITERATURE. Fiction from other countries during 1986 overwhelmed the output of United States writers in quality, if not quantity. While most American novelists dealt with shallow issues and exotic language, foreign authors wrestled with cosmic questions—and many honored the idea of telling a story with appeal for a broad audience.

Latin-American writers were a case in point. The Brazilian Rubem Fonseca used such techniques of popular fiction as melodrama and suspense in *High Art* for an elegant and subtle detective novel. Argentine writer Omar Rivabella wrote *Requiem for a Woman's Soul,* an eloquent novel based on the testimony of victims of torture by military regimes in his country. Augusto Roa Bastos' *I the Supreme* was a powerful historical novel based on the life of a Paraguayan dictator of the 1800's. Peruvian writer Mario Vargas Llosa produced an apocalyptic novel of guerrilla warfare, *The Real Life of Alejandro Mayta.*

Italian writers also provided vigorous novels of wide appeal, including Primo Levi's *The Monkey's Wrench*—a lively and affirmative novel that explored how work can save humanity—and Leonardo Sciascia's *Sicilian Uncles,* a detective story that was a hybrid of the popular and the literary novel.

English-Speaking Countries produced much excellent fiction in 1986. Notable among the British

Stephen King, whose horror novel *It* shot to the top of the best-seller list in 1986, works in his home office in Bangor, Me.

offerings were John le Carré's brilliant *A Perfect Spy*, which transcended the espionage formula, and John Mortimer's *Paradise Postponed*, an amusing variation on the Victorian-Edwardian novel, set in post-World War II Britain. Great Britain also contributed Rachel Billington's *The Garish Day*, a compelling comic novel about an inept diplomat; William Trevor's *The News from Ireland and Other Stories*, a masterly collection of short stories; Peter Dickinson's *Tefuga*, a novel about colonialism in Nigeria; A. N. Wilson's *Gentlemen in England*, a novel of manners set in 1880; and Iris Murdoch's *The Good Apprentice*, a philosophical novel and social comedy.

Ruth Prawer Jhabvala, born in Poland, reared in England, and married to an Indian, offered *Out of India*, a collection of short stories notable for their cool observations. The Indian writer Amitav Ghosh's first novel, *The Circle of Reason*, was an extravagant tale of life in an East Bengal village.

From South Africa came a number of novels about that nation's political struggles, including Lynn Freed's *Home Ground*, Dalene Matthee's *Fiela's Child*, and Lewis Nkosi's *Mating Birds*. Australia's Nobel laureate Patrick White wrote *Memoirs of Many in One by Alex Xenophon Demirjian Gray*, a comic exploration of the nature of art. Elizabeth Jolley, an English immigrant to Australia, produced two exuberant novels, *The Well* and *Woman*

in a Lampshade. Thomas Keneally's *A Family Madness* told the story of an Australian immigrant family with a Nazi history. Canada contributed Margaret Atwood's collection *Bluebeard's Egg & Other Stories* and Alice Munro's *The Progress of Love*.

Fiction from the United States. Few U.S. novelists managed to produce major works in 1986. Among those who did, however, were Peter Taylor, whose *A Summons to Memphis* was an elegant exploration of the leisurely rituals of the Southern upper-middle class; John Updike, who mixed theology and computer science in *Roger's Version;* Jimmy Breslin, who deftly described working-class life in *Table Money;* Reynolds Price, who produced a passionate generational saga of the South, *Kate Vaiden;* Robert Stone, whose *Children of Light* was a scorching portrait of the film industry; and Louise Erdrich, whose luminous *The Beet Queen* was an eventful novel of a girl's arrival and maturity in a small North Dakota town.

Several younger Americans turned out important first novels. David Leavitt's *The Lost Language of Cranes* dealt with a homosexual's revelation of his secret to his family. Daphne Merkin's *Enchantment* told of growing up under the heel of a brave but difficult mother. Sherley Anne Williams' *Dessa Rose* told a powerful story of two women—one white and one black—in the antebellum South. Sue Miller's *The Good Mother* explored the risks and responsibilities of love and motherhood. Susan Minot's *Monkeys* was a family novel of affections and loyalties, set during the cultural upheavals of the 1960's and early 1970's.

Ernest Hemingway's *The Garden of Eden*, a posthumous novel edited from a mass of manuscript, also appeared in 1986. The work, which dealt with a *ménage à trois* (in this instance, a household composed of a married couple and the lover of both of them), showed a surprisingly compassionate side of its author.

Essays. Polish writer Adam Michnik's *Letters from Prison & Other Essays* was a stunning collection of articles about growing up in a Communist society that is struggling to reform. *The Fifties* was the fourth collection of critic Edmund Wilson's notebooks and diaries, ably edited by Leon Edel. *Going to the Territory* gathered novelist Ralph Ellison's essays and occasional pieces. One of the year's most entertaining book of essays was Oliver Sacks's *The Man Who Mistook His Wife for a Hat*, a collection of tales about neurological patients.

Biography and Autobiography. The year's big surprise among political biographies was *Eisenhower: At War 1943-1945*, the first volume of David Eisenhower's life of his grandfather, Dwight D. Eisenhower. This work ably and thoroughly underscored the general's brilliance as a politician in handling the conflicting claims and goals of Allied military commanders during World War II. Another able biography by a presidential descendant was *Bess W. Truman*, Margaret Truman's touching life of her mother, the wife of President Harry S. Truman.

Among literary biographies, Richard Lingeman's *Theodore Dreiser: At the Gates of the City 1871-1907* examined the early life of the great novelist. William Wright's *Lillian Hellman* was a fascinating examination of the talented playwright who, Wright contended, could also be an appalling liar.

A. M. Sperber's *Murrow* was a compelling portrait of Edward R. Murrow, the eminent CBS News broadcaster of the 1940's and 1950's. *Red* was Ira Berkow's fascinating biography of Walter W. (Red) Smith, a sportswriter whose stylish prose was admired by two generations of journalists.

John Maynard Keynes: Hopes Betrayed 1883-1920, the first volume of Robert Skidelsky's magisterial multivolume biography, began what promised to be a major reassessment of the great economist. Also notable were *Shackleton*, Roland Huntford's superb life of the Antarctic adventurer Ernest Shackleton, and Richard Wrightman Fox's *Reinhold Niebuhr*, which explored the life of the most influential Protestant theologian of this century.

The Fabulous Lunts, by Jared Brown, was a well-researched study of actors Alfred Lunt and Lynn Fontanne that ably echoed a lost age of the theater. *John Singer Sargent* was Stanley Olson's thoughtful biography of a leading American painter of the late 1800's. Jonathan Brown's *Velazquez* closely observed the life of Diego Velázquez, a Spanish painter of the 1600's.

Politics and the arts were backdrops for many autobiographies in 1986. The year's most controversial autobiography was David A. Stockman's *The Triumph of Politics*. Stockman, President Ronald Reagan's former budget director, drew a devastating portrait of incompetence and deceit in the White House. Gail Lumet Buckley's *The Hornes* told of a black American middle-class family that included the author's mother, singer Lena Horne. *Dancing on My Grave* by ballerina Gelsey Kirkland and Greg Lawrence related a scandalous story of drugs and sex in the ballet world.

History. In 1986, there was much to choose from in this perennially fruitful genre. *The Wise Men*, by Walter Isaacson and Evan Thomas, explored the lives and work of six Americans who forged the United States post-World War II foreign policy. Robert Conquest's *The Harvest of Sorrow* explored Soviet dictator Joseph Stalin's brutal collectivization of the agriculture of the Ukraine between 1929 and 1933. Michael E. Beschloss's *Mayday* recalled the shooting down of an American spy plane in 1960 over the Soviet Union.

The Holocaust of World War II, in which 6 million Jews died, continued to grip historians' imaginations. Robert Jay Lifton's *The Nazi Doctors*, one

French writer Marguérite Duras receives the Ritz Paris Hemingway Award in April for her autobiographical novel *L'Amant* (*The Lover*).

of the most original such studies in years, asked how physicians who were dedicated to healing could turn into monstrous experimenters and executioners in the Nazi death camps. Martin Gilbert's *The Holocaust* told the story of the Nazi concentration camps from the point of view of the victims. From Poland came two studies, Malgorzata Niezabitowska's *Remnants: The Last Jews of Poland*, a study of the 4,000 to 5,000 Jews now remaining in that country; and Hanna Krall's *Shielding the Flame*, a series of conversations with Marek Edelman, last surviving leader of the Warsaw ghetto uprising of 1943.

Contemporary Affairs. The year was notable for diversity and richness in this category. *Reckless Disregard* by Renata Adler ably explored the complex issues of two celebrated 1985 libel cases, that of Israeli General Ariel Sharon against *Time* magazine and U.S. General William C. Westmoreland against CBS Inc. "*The Target Is Destroyed*" was the thoughtful and convincing result of Seymour Hersh's two-year investigation into the shooting down of Korean Air Lines Flight 007, killing all 269 people aboard, over the Soviet Union in 1983.

The novelist A. G. Mojtabai dissected the national conscience in *Blessed Assurance*, a study of Amarillo, Tex.—home to a large number of religious fundamentalists and an assembly plant for U.S. nuclear bombs. In *Cities on a Hill*, Frances

FitzGerald studied the attempts of four groups—San Francisco homosexuals, the fundamentalist church of broadcaster-evangelist Jerry Falwell, the cult of the Rajneeshpuram commune in Oregon, and the Florida retirement town of Sun City—to establish themselves as functioning communities.

Seweryn Bialer's *The Soviet Paradox*, which predicted that the Soviet Union's foreign expansionism would continue even as its internal troubles grew worse, was hailed as brilliant. John Ranelagh's *The Agency* was a scholarly analysis of the "rise and decline" of the Central Intelligence Agency (CIA), and Peter Maas's *Manhunt* explored how CIA agent Edwin Wilson grew rich illegally by selling terrorist weapons to Libya.

Business. The year's most notable book in this increasingly important category was David Halberstam's immense and ambitious *The Reckoning*, which assessed the postwar economic history of the United States and Japan. Others were Moira Johnston's *Takeover*, a discussion of corporate take-overs; John A. Garraty's *The Great Depression*, which found similarities between the economic problems of the 1980's and those of the late 1920's; and two books on the Coca-Cola Company's attempt to change the soft drink's flavor—Thomas Oliver's *The Real Coke, The Real Story*, and Roger Enrico and Jesse Kornbluth's *The Other Guy Blinked: How Pepsi Won the Cola Wars*.

Science, Social Science, and Natural History. Among the prominent books in this genre were Jane Goodall's *The Chimpanzees of Gombe*, a fascinating distillation of the author's 26 years of research; John McPhee's *Rising from the Plains*, an exploration of Wyoming geology; Barry Lopez' *Arctic Dreams*, an elegant tribute to the Canadian Arctic and its living things; and Robert Coles's *The Moral Life of Children* and *The Political Life of Children*, which investigated the development of political and moral consciousness in children.

Best Sellers of the year in hard-cover included *Prince of Tides* by Pat Conroy; *It* by Stephen King; *His Way* by Kitty Kelley; *James Herriot's Dog Stories* by Herriot; *Callanetics* by Callan Pinckney; *Fit for Life* by Harvey and Marilyn Diamond; *Red Storm Rising* by Tom Clancy; *Wanderlust* by Danielle Steel; *Through a Glass Darkly* by Karleen Koen; and *You're Only Old Once!* by Dr. Seuss.

Among top-selling paperbacks of 1986 were *Secrets* by Steel, *The Hunt for Red October* by Clancy; *Women Who Love Too Much* by Robin Norwood; *Dancing in the Light* by Shirley MacLaine; *The Bachman Books* by King; *Contact* by Carl Sagan; *The Far Side Gallery* by Gary Larson; and *The Road Less Traveled* by M. Scott Peck.   Henry Kisor

See also AWARDS AND PRIZES (Literature Awards); CANADIAN LITERATURE; LITERATURE FOR CHILDREN; POETRY; PUBLISHING. In WORLD BOOK, see LITERATURE.

LITERATURE FOR CHILDREN. Books for preschoolers were especially abundant in 1986, and a great variety of picture books were available. Many fantasy, realism, and informational books were published. Some outstanding books of 1986 were:

Picture Books

Half a Moon and One Whole Star, by Crescent Dragonwagon, illustrated by Jerry Pinkney (Macmillan). A lullaby reveals nighttime activities and daytime expectations as Susan goes to sleep. Beautiful color illustrations. Ages 3 to 6.

The Magic Horse, retold by Sally Scott (Greenwillow Bks.). Jewel-toned paintings grace this Arabian Nights tale of a magic ebony horse and the fascinating adventures surrounding it. Ages 5 to 9.

A Lion in the Night, by Pamela Allen (Putnam). When a lion steals a baby, the chase begins—and ends with a surprise. Ages 3 to 7.

Night in the Country, by Cynthia Rylant, illustrated by Mary Szilagyi (Bradbury Press). Quietly descriptive of night sights and sounds, the text is illuminated with color drawings. Ages 3 to 6.

Demi's Count the Animals 1 2 3, by Demi (Grosset & Dunlap). Vibrantly colored animals cavort across double pages as the rhymed text explains what they are. Numbers and rhymes go up to 20, but a page of 100 animals appears for counting. Ages 3 to 7.

White Dynamite and Curly Kid, by Bill Martin, Jr., and John Archambault, illustrated by Ted Rand (Holt, Rinehart & Winston). A son's fear for—and pride in—his bull-riding dad come vividly to life in this story poem and dramatic full-color illustrations. Ages 4 to 8.

Amanda & April, by Bonnie Pryor, illustrated by Diane de Groat (Morrow). Amanda "takes care of" her little sister April on their way to a birthday party, with funny consequences. Ages 4 to 7.

Shapes, Shapes, Shapes, by Tana Hoban (Greenwillow Bks.). The reader is challenged to find various shapes in everyday scenes. Ages 4 to 8.

Willie and the Big World: An Adventure with Numbers, by Sven Nordqvist (Morrow). An imaginative, zanily illustrated tale of Willie's adventures as he searches for the big world. Ages 4 to 8.

Pecos Bill, retold by Steven Kellogg (Morrow). Another hilariously told and exuberantly illustrated tall tale by Kellogg. Ages 5 and up.

Suleiman the Elephant, by Margret Rettich, translated by Elizabeth D. Crawford (Lothrop, Lee & Shepard Bks.). Prince Max's journey from Spain with his bride and an elephant causes quite a commotion. Ages 7 to 10.

Paddy to the Rescue, by John S. Goodall (Atheneum Pubs.). Paddy pursues and captures a burglar in this wordless, full-color book. All ages.

Brave Little Pete of Geranium Street, by Rose and Samuel Lagercrantz, adapted from Swedish by

The Polar Express, written and illustrated by Chris Van Allsburg, won the 1986 Caldecott Medal for children's picture books.

Jack Prelutsky, illustrated by Eva Eriksson (Greenwillow Bks.). The saga of Pete, his family, and his problems with two bullies is delightfully illustrated and told in verse. Ages 5 to 9.

Doctor Change, by Joanna Cole, illustrated by Donald Carrick (Morrow). Tom, trapped by the magical Dr. Change, learns the spells he needs to gain his freedom. Expressive illustrations capture an eerie mood. Ages 7 to 10.

Piggybook, by Anthony Browne (Knopf). When Mrs. Piggott leaves, fed up with her husband and son's behavior, they realize how much she means to them. Ages 5 and up.

A Regular Rolling Noah, by George Ella Lyon, illustrated by Stephen Gammell (Bradbury Press). Fine, expressive water colors and a rhythmical text depict a boy's train travels with farm animals. Ages 4 to 8.

Very Last First Time, by Jan Andrews, illustrated by Ian Wallace (Atheneum Pubs.). A young Eskimo girl searches for mussels alone under the ice for the first time. Striking paintings capture the eeriness of the underwater world. Ages 5 to 9.

Not So Fast Songololo, by Niki Daly (Atheneum Pubs.). Warm relationships and colors highlight the tale of Malusi's shopping trip with his grandmother. Ages 4 to 7.

The Dallas Titans Get Ready for Bed, by Karla Kuskin, illustrated by Marc Simont (Harper & Row).

An amusing and informative look at what goes on in the locker room after a professional football game. Ages 8 and up.

Five Minutes' Peace, by Jill Murphy (Putnam). Mrs. Large, an elephant, tries unsuccessfully to spend a quiet few minutes in the tub away from her children. Comical illustrations. Ages 1 to 5.

I'm in Charge of Celebrations, by Byrd Baylor, illustrated by Peter Parnall (Scribner). A girl describes her special days in lilting prose. Ages 8 and up.

Kite Flier, by Dennis Haseley, illustrated by David Wiesner (Four Winds Press). A father creates kites for his son and learns that a time comes to let go. Dramatic water colors. Ages 8 and up.

Benjamin Rabbit and the Fire Chief, by Irene Keller, illustrated by Dick Keller (Ideals). Benjamin Rabbit's entertaining adventure teaches young children about fire prevention. Ages 3 to 8.

Poetry and Songs

Brats, by X. J. Kennedy, illustrated by James Watts (Atheneum Pubs.). Hilarious verses are about bratty children who get their just deserts. Ages 8 and up.

Fresh Paint, by Eve Merriam, illustrated by David Frampton (Macmillan). Imaginative poems about familiar subjects are nicely illustrated. Ages 5 and up.

Patricia MacLachlan's *Sarah, Plain and Tall*—
a tale of a mail-order bride and her new
family—won the 1986 Newbery Medal.

Street Talk, by Ann Turner, illustrated by Catherine Stock (Houghton Mifflin). The city in all its facets is dramatically presented in verse and fine woodcuts. Ages 7 and up.

Sea Songs, by Myra Cohn Livingston, illustrated by Leonard Everett Fisher (Holiday House). Images and moods of the sea are portrayed in the poem and in rich paintings. Ages 5 and up.

Once: A Lullaby, by bp Nichol, illustrated by Anita Lobel (Greenwillow Bks.). Repetitious verses are made magical by the full-color illustrations. Music is included. Ages 1 to 4.

Fantasy

Oaf, by Julia Cunningham, illustrated by Peter Sis (Greenwillow Bks.). Three unusual magical gifts help Oaf and his animal friends face hardships. Ages 8 to 11.

The Spring of Butterflies and Other Chinese Folktales, by He Liyi, edited by Neil Philip, illustrated by Pan Aiqing and Li Zhao (Lothrop, Lee & Shepard Bks.). This collection of traditional, often amusing, Chinese tales is beautifully illustrated. Ages 10 and up.

Outside the Gates, by Molly Gloss (Atheneum Pubs.). Vren, a village outcast, is taken in by Rusch. After the spellbinder—a kind of sorcerer—ensnares Rusch, Vren tries to find his friend and save him. Ages 12 and up.

The Ice Bear, by Betty Levin (Greenwillow Bks.). Wat, an apprentice, risks his life when he, the girl Kaila, and a polar bear cub attempt to reach Kaila's homeland. Ages 12 and up.

Henry's Quest, by Graham Oakley (Atheneum Pubs.) Henry, a shepherd, goes in search of gasoline to win the princess's hand in this satirical, futuristic tale. Ages 10 and up.

The Woman Who Loved Reindeer, by Meredith Ann Pierce (Atlantic Monthly Press). Caribou raises a demon reindeer's child who later becomes her lover and helps her lead others to a new, safe land. Ages 12 and up.

Fiction

The Whipping Boy, by Sid Fleischman, illustrated by Peter Sis (Greenwillow Bks.). When Prince Brat runs away, Jemmy, his whipping boy, must go with him. Plenty of action and mood-capturing illustrations. Ages 7 to 11.

Sentries, by Gary Paulsen (Bradbury Press). The lives of various people change until the biggest change of all occurs—the bomb. An unusual, fascinating book. Ages 12 and up.

I Wear the Morning Star, by Jamake Highwater (Harper & Row). Sitko Ghost Horse, an American Indian, suffers brutalities and anguish trying to discover who and what he is. Ages 12 and up.

Trouble Half-Way, by Jan Mark (Atheneum Pubs.). Amy, shy with her stepfather, goes with him in his truck, and a warm relationship develops. Ages 10 to 13.

Third Girl from the Left, by Ann Turner (Macmillan). A Maine girl, 18, becomes a mail-order bride and journeys to Montana. Three weeks later, her husband is killed, leaving her with many decisions to make. Ages 12 and up.

What's the Matter with Herbie Jones?, by Suzy Kline, illustrated by Richard Williams (Putnam). Herbie has only a passing interest in Annabelle, but Annabelle's interest in Herbie persists. Ages 7 to 11.

Holding Me Here, by Pam Conrad (Harper & Row). Robin, upset over her parents' divorce, tries to reunite their boarder, Mary, and her family—with painful results. Ages 12 and up.

Elliott & Win, by Carolyn Meyer (Atheneum Pubs.). Elliott, a lover of opera, wild flowers, and cooking, acts as "big brother" to fatherless Win, 14, who learns about values and people. Ages 12 and up.

Bad Man Ballad, by Scott R. Sanders (Bradbury Press). When Ely finds massive human tracks in Ohio in 1813, he and a citified lawyer hunt the giant to make him face murder charges. Ages 12 and up.

More Stories Julian Tells, by Ann Cameron, illustrated by Ann Strugnell (Knopf). Five delightful stories about Julian, brother Huey, and friend

Gloria often include Julian's dad with his fine sense of humor. Ages 7 to 11.

Animals, People, Places, and Projects

The Great Wall of China, by Leonard Everett Fisher (Macmillan). The building of the wall, its purpose, and its history are simply told, with dramatic black-and-white art. Ages 7 to 9.

Make Way for Sam Houston, by Jean Fritz, illustrated by Elise Primavera (Putnam). The good and bad sides of Houston's character are interestingly revealed. Index, notes, a bibliography, and a map are included. Ages 10 and up.

Living in Two Worlds, by Maxine B. Rosenberg, illustrated by George Ancona (Lothrop, Lee & Shepard Bks.). Text and photographs explore the benefits and problems of biracial families. All ages.

Clem, the Story of a Raven, by Jennifer Owings Dewey (Dodd, Mead). A fascinating, humorous description of a raven's antics as he is reared from baby to adult by a human couple that also has an owl, other creatures, and an infant. Ages 10 and up.

So Far from the Bamboo Grove, by Yoko Kawashima Watkins (Lothrop, Lee & Shepard Bks.). As World War II is ending, a Japanese family flees through Korea to Japan. Ages 11 and up.

The Sun and *The Stars*, by Seymour Simon (Morrow). Both books have clear, informative texts and superlative photographs. Ages 10 and up.

Giant Pandas, by Kay McDearmon (Dodd, Mead). The animals are interestingly described in text and beautifully photographed. Index. Ages 7 to 10.

Children of the Maya, by Brent Ashabranner, photographs by Paul Conklin (Dodd, Mead). The tragic treatment of this ancient people in Guatemala and their attempts to create new lives in Florida are movingly described. Ages 10 and up.

Guess Again: More Weird & Wacky Inventions, by Jim Murphy (Bradbury Press). Clues are given to help the reader guess what the inventions are. Five inventors are featured. Ages 10 and up.

Up Goes the Skyscraper! by Gail Gibbons (Four Winds Press). A complex process is simply explained and clearly demonstrated. Ages 4 to 8.

Awards in 1986 included:

The Newbery Medal for "the most distinguished contribution to American literature for children" was awarded to Patricia MacLachlan for *Sarah, Plain and Tall*. The Caldecott Medal for "the most distinguished American picture book for children" went to Chris Van Allsburg for *Polar Express*. The Mildred L. Batchelder Award cited Creative Education for its publication of *Rose Blanche* by Roberto Innocenti.   Marilyn Fain Apseloff

In World Book, see Caldecott Medal; Literature for Children; Newbery Medal.

LOS ANGELES. Two fires, believed set by arsonists, swept through the Los Angeles Central Public Library in 1986 destroying hundreds of thousands of books, documents, and artwork at the downtown landmark. The first, and most severe, fire occurred on April 29. The blaze caused $22 million in damage as it raged through book stacks for almost six hours. Library officials estimated that at least 360,000 of the library's 2 million volumes were destroyed.

Security at the 60-year-old library intensified after that fire, but on September 3 another fire broke out in the reading room of the library's art and music department. About 25,000 volumes were lost in the second fire, which caused another $2 million in damage.

No injuries were reported in either blaze. The Los Angeles Fire Department concluded that both fires were set by arsonists. By year-end, no arrests had been made.

Metro Rail Subway. On September 29, city and state officials held an elaborate groundbreaking ceremony at the Civic Center to launch construction of the first 4.4 miles (7.1 kilometers) of the Metro Rail subway project. The rail line, which will run for 18.6 miles (29.9 kilometers) from downtown Los Angeles to the San Fernando Valley, is expected to usher in a new transportation era in Los Angeles County. The Southern California Rapid Transit District hopes to have the initial leg of the subway in operation by 1992.

Redistricting. The Los Angeles City Council voted on September 12 to override Mayor Thomas Bradley's veto of a redistricting plan that established new geographic boundaries for the city's 15 council districts. The plan was the last of three proposals approved by the City Council in two months in response to a lawsuit filed in 1985 by the U.S. Department of Justice. The Justice Department accused Los Angeles of splitting up Hispanic neighborhoods and diluting their political strength in violation of the federal Voting Rights Act of 1965. The adopted plan created a Hispanic-majority council district west of downtown Los Angeles and provided for an election in the new district in 1987.

Limiting Growth. In a *referendum* (direct vote) in November, Los Angeles residents approved a law to curb the city's growth. The law limits construction of new office towers, shopping centers, and other commercial buildings, cutting by 50 per cent the amount of floor space of such buildings that can be built in the future. The measure exempts downtown Los Angeles and a few other established business districts.

Street Scene. The future of the Los Angeles Street Scene, an annual cultural festival, was in doubt after violence marred the 1986 event. The Street Scene attracted 1 million visitors on Sep-

A rubble-strewn gash through a Cerritos, Calif., neighborhood marks the path of an Aeroméxico DC-9 that crashed on August 31 after a collision with a small plane.

tember 20 and 21 to a program of music, entertainment, and ethnic food displays. But by the time the festivities were over, 1 person had been killed and at least 40 people had been injured.

The incidents began on September 20. Fighting erupted after a band that was scheduled to appear did not perform. The next day, a man was shot in the back at another band performance and later died.

Bradley called for an end to the eight-year-old event, but City Council members favored tougher restrictions to control Street Scene crowds. The council hoped to save what has become the city's largest and most diversified festival.

Budgets. The Los Angeles County Board of Supervisors adopted a $7.1-billion budget on July 16 that gave high priority to law enforcement and fire prevention. The budget also included $6.1-million for the county's probation and children's services departments to develop programs for mentally disturbed children.

On May 23, the Los Angeles City Council approved a $2.36-billion budget that included funds for 100 additional police officers, a new crime laboratory, and police computer systems.   Victor Merina

See also CITY. In WORLD BOOK, see LOS ANGELES.

LOUISIANA. See STATE GOVERNMENT.
LUXEMBOURG. See EUROPE.

LYNG, RICHARD EDMUND (1918-   ), was sworn in as United States secretary of agriculture on March 6, 1986. He succeeded John R. Block, who resigned in February.

Lyng was born on June 29, 1918, in San Francisco. After attending public schools in Modesto, Calif., he attended the University of Notre Dame in Indiana, graduating in 1940. During World War II, Lyng spent 2½ years in the South Pacific with the U.S. Army. He took part in the battles of Guadalcanal and Bougainville.

From 1949 to 1967, Lyng was president of a family-owned bean and seed company in Modesto. In 1967, Ronald Reagan, the newly elected governor of California, named Lyng the state's director of agriculture. Two years later, Lyng became assistant U.S. secretary of agriculture, and from 1973 to 1979 he served as president of the American Meat Institute, a national association of meat processors based in Washington, D.C.

When Reagan became President of the United States in 1981, he appointed Lyng deputy U.S. secretary of agriculture. In 1985, Lyng and an associate, William Lesher, formed an agricultural consulting firm, Lyng and Lesher, Incorporated.

Lyng is married to the former Bethyl Ball. The couple have two daughters and four grandchildren.   David L. Dreier

MADAGASCAR. See AFRICA.

MAGAZINE advertising revenues in the United States increased in 1986 by about 4 per cent over 1985, reaching a record $5.1 billion. The number of advertising pages remained flat, however, numbering about 150,000 for the year.

The combined circulation per issue of all consumer magazines surveyed by the Audit Bureau of Circulations (ABC) in the United States climbed to a record high of 325.3 million during the first six months of 1986, up 1.2 per cent over the same period in 1985. The ABC is an independent organization that issues circulation figures, verified by auditors, for magazines and other publications.

An annual survey conducted by the Magazine Publishers Association (MPA) and Price Waterhouse indicated that U.S. magazines were less profitable in 1985 than in 1984. The magazines showed a pretax operating profit of 9.7 per cent in 1985, compared with 11.3 per cent in 1984.

According to a survey conducted in the spring of 1986 by Mediamark Research, Incorporated, 94 per cent of all U.S. adults read magazines, and these people read 10 different issues per month. The survey indicated that the average magazine reader is 37.8 years old, has at least a high school education, is married, lives in a household of three or more people, and has a household income of $33,594, 12 per cent above the U.S. average.

Awards. The MPA named Gilbert Maurer, president of Hearst Corporation's Magazine Division, as the 1986 recipient of the Henry Johnson Fisher Award, the industry's most prestigious honor. The American Society of Magazine Editors presented its National Magazine Awards in April. Among the winning publications were *Farm Journal* for personal service, *Popular Mechanics* for special interests, *Rolling Stone* for reporting, *Science 85* for public interest, *Time* for design, *Vogue* for photography, *The Georgia Review* for fiction, *The Sciences* for essays and criticism, and *IEEE Spectrum* for single-topic issue.

In the category of general excellence, which is presented in four groups according to circulation size, the winners were *New England Monthly* (less than 100,000); *3-2-1 Contact* (100,000 to 400,000); *Discover* (400,000 to 1,000,000); and *Money* (more than 1 million).

New Magazines about children and parenting rolled off the presses in 1986. A joint partnership of Time Incorporated and publisher Robin Wolaner introduced a monthly magazine called *Parenting* in December. Fathers, Incorporated, introduced *Fathers* nationwide around Father's Day—June 15. And in August, Taxi Publishing Incorporated began to publish *Child*, a bimonthly aimed at affluent parents.

The 50th anniversary issue of *Life*, right, recalls some of the momentous events that occurred since the magazine's first issue, left, appeared on Nov. 23, 1936.

Esquire Magazine Group, Incorporated, introduced *New York Woman* in September. The company broke up in December, selling *New York Woman* to American Express Publishing Corporation and *Esquire* magazine to the Hearst Corporation.

Changes. Meredith Corporation, publisher of *Better Homes and Gardens* and other magazines, purchased *Ladies' Home Journal* from Family Media, Incorporated, for a reported $92 million in January. Also in January, Forbes, Incorporated, publishers of the business magazine *Forbes*, purchased *American Heritage* from a group of investors for more than $8 million. In November, Time Incorporated announced that it had formed a joint venture with Working Woman Incorporated that would buy *McCall's, Baby!*, and other women's magazines from McCall Publishing.

Three science magazines changed hands in 1986. In June, Time paid the American Association for the Advancement of Science $6 million for *Science 86*. In July, Time paid Hearst Corporation about $2 million for *Science Digest*. Both *Science 86* and *Science Digest* ceased publication. Also in July, a West German company, Verlagsgruppe Georg von Holtzbrinck, bought *Scientific American* from Scientific American Incorporated for $52.6-million.   Annmaria B. DiCesare

See also PUBLISHING. In WORLD BOOK, see MAGAZINE.

MAHDI, SADIQ EL (1936-   ), in May 1986 became prime minister of Sudan for the second time, almost 20 years after his first elevation to that post. Mahdi, the leader of the moderate Umma Party, immediately set to work trying to arrange a peace with the Sudanese People's Liberation Army, which has been waging a guerrilla war against the Muslim-dominated central government for several years. See SUDAN.

Mahdi is the great-grandson of the Muslim leader Muhammad Ahmed, who in 1881 proclaimed himself *al-Mahdi* (the guide) and wrested control of Sudan from Egypt. Mahdi was born on Dec. 25, 1936, in Omdurman, Sudan. He was educated at Oxford University in England, where he earned bachelor's and master's degrees in economics and political science.

In 1964, Mahdi became chairman of the Muslim Umma Party, and the following year he was elected to Sudan's parliament. He was appointed prime minister in July 1966 but was forced out of office 10 months later by an opposition coalition.

Mahdi said in 1986 that his government would not align itself with any major world power. Mahdi's moderate stance in politics made him the preferred candidate of the United States in the 1986 election.   David L. Dreier

MAINE. See STATE GOVERNMENT.

MALAWI. See AFRICA.

MALAYSIA. Parliamentary elections on Aug. 2 and 3, 1986, gave Malaysia's Prime Minister Mahathir bin Mohamed a strong new endorsement by voters. The 13-party National Front coalition won 148 of parliament's 177 seats. Of the 148 seats, Mahathir's United Malays National Organization (UMNO) won 83.

The results, however, caused political observers to worry about worsening racial divisions between the Malay majority and Chinese minority. The main opposition party, the Democratic Action Party (DAP), drew Chinese support away from the coalition's Malaysian Chinese Association. In general, Muslim Malays backed, and ethnic Chinese opposed, the Mahathir government.

Deputy Prime Minister Musa Hitam, the UMNO's long-time deputy president, resigned as of March 16 from both government and party jobs after a quarrel with Mahathir. In the August elections, however, Musa and his supporters won large majorities. So he remained a rival and possible successor to Mahathir.

Drug Executions. Two Australians who had been arrested in 1983 for dealing in heroin and thus violating Malaysia's Dangerous Drugs Act were executed on July 7. The tough antidrug law makes the death penalty mandatory for anyone caught with more than 15 grams (0.53 ounce) of heroin,

Seated before a portrait of himself, Malaysia's Prime Minister Mahathir bin Mohamed names his new Cabinet after his party's victory in August.

on the assumption that such a person is a dealer. The Australians were the first non-Asians executed under the law. By the end of 1986, Malaysia had executed at least 40 people, mainly Southeast Asians, for drug offenses since 1975.

Economic Growth Slowed to almost zero in 1986. This forced Mahathir to suspend the government's New Economic Policy in May and revise foreign investment rules in October. The New Economic Policy was adopted in 1970 to increase Malays' holdings in corporations from 1 per cent in 1969 to 30 per cent by 1990. The combined Chinese and Indian ethnic groups' holdings were to fall to 40 per cent. Foreign investment in any venture was limited to 30 per cent.

The economic slowdown was caused by several factors, including the reluctance of foreign companies to invest in Malaysia and the drop in world prices for such exports as oil, tin, and palm oil. Under the new rules, companies that export at least 50 per cent of their output may be 100 per cent foreign-owned, and ownership restrictions were lifted on companies employing 350 or more ethnic Malays.   Henry S. Bradsher

See also ASIA (Facts in Brief Table). In WORLD BOOK, see MALAYSIA.

MALDIVES. See ASIA.

MALI. See AFRICA.

MALTA. See EUROPE.

MANDELA, WINNIE (1936?-   ), is one of South Africa's most prominent antiapartheid leaders. On July 7, 1986, the South African government formally lifted restrictions on her personal freedom in effect since 1977. Winnie Mandela is the wife of imprisoned black nationalist leader Nelson Mandela. See SOUTH AFRICA.

Nomzamo Winifred Madikizela was born in Transkei, a so-called black homeland in southeastern South Africa. In 1955, she graduated from Jan Hofmeyr Social Centre in Johannesburg, becoming South Africa's first black medical social worker. In 1957, shortly after meeting Nelson Mandela, a leader of the African National Congress (ANC), she joined the ANC's Women's League. She and Mandela were married in 1958.

Since 1964, when Nelson Mandela was sentenced to life imprisonment on charges of treason and sabotage, Winnie Mandela has served as her husband's spokesperson. She has organized numerous soup kitchens and medical clinics. For most of that time, she has been *banned*, a legal status that involves restrictions on personal movement and public speaking. Over the years, she has been jailed repeatedly. After her home was burned in August 1985, Mandela broke her ban, appearing at political events.

Winnie and Nelson Mandela have two daughters and four grandchildren.   Barbara A. Mayes

MANITOBA went to the polls on March 18, 1986, and the election was the closest in Manitoba's history. Premier Howard Pawley, 51, led the New Democratic Party (NDP) to a second victory over the Progressive Conservative (PC) Party. The NDP entered the election with 32 seats in the 57-seat legislature, and emerged with only 30 members. The PC's gained 4 seats, for a total of 26 members, and the Liberals won the remaining seat.

The bitter controversy over the issue of restoring language rights in government and education to the 60,000 Manitobans whose native language is French—a measure sponsored by the Pawley government—did not appear to be a factor in the election. On the other hand, the PC's were hurt by fears that federal spending in Manitoba would be reduced by a cost-cutting federal government.

In August, the Pawley government ordered an investigation of the Manitoba Telephone System's (MTS) operation to deliver telecommunications equipment to Saudi Arabia. A consultant's report confirmed allegations of mismanagement, bribery, and kickbacks, and on November 21, five senior officials of MTS resigned or were fired. Alvin Mackling resigned as the minister responsible for MTS, but remained in the cabinet as minister of labor and corporate affairs.   David M. L. Farr

In WORLD BOOK, see MANITOBA.

Manitoba Premier Howard Pawley and his family wave to supporters in Winnipeg in March, after his party's victory at the polls.

MANUFACTURING

MANUFACTURING. The short-term outlook for manufacturing in the United States continued to be sluggish in 1986. "The industrial sector never really got out of low gear," reported *Business Week* magazine. But with the positive impact of high technology on U.S. factories, and with a dollar that had a lower value abroad in 1986, the extended outlook for U.S. manufacturing was promising.

"While total manufacturing output was weak in 1986, manufacturing productivity continued to improve far more rapidly than industry in general," said Alexander B. Trowbridge, president of the National Association of Manufacturers. Trowbridge said the improvement "is due to efforts of manufacturing firms to sharply cut costs and increase efficiency in order to better compete in world markets."

The cheaper dollar made U.S. products less costly overseas and increased the price of imports to the United States. Imports have hurt U.S. manufacturers, accounting for 21 per cent of total U.S. sales of manufactured products in 1985—twice the percentage that prevailed during the 1970's.

In 1986, manufacturers continued to cut costs, close marginal plants, lay off workers, and invest in new technologies that made their operations more efficient. Manufacturing performance in 1986 varied by sector. The overall U.S. trend was away from basic metals, such as steel and metal fabrication, and toward the manufacturing of office and printing equipment and computer software. Manufacturing for the defense, aerospace, automobile, and construction industries was strong in 1986. Nonelectrical machinery, farm machinery, mining equipment, and basic metals sales were flat.

Productivity. For the first time in recent memory, U.S. manufacturers were "lean and mean" in 1986. In other words, to compete with imports, U.S. manufacturers began to cut labor and other costs.

Manufacturing productivity increased 4.2 per cent during the summer of 1986, while the rest of the economy grew at a rate of only 0.2 per cent. Manufacturers increased output at an annual rate of 3.4 per cent in the summer months, while reducing hours worked by 1 per cent and cutting per-unit labor costs by 1.5 per cent.

Employment. Growth in employment remained concentrated in service industries. Although 58,000 factory jobs were created in October and November 1986, there were still 96,000 fewer factory jobs than there were in November 1985. The biggest employment gains were in business and health services, finance, insurance, real estate,

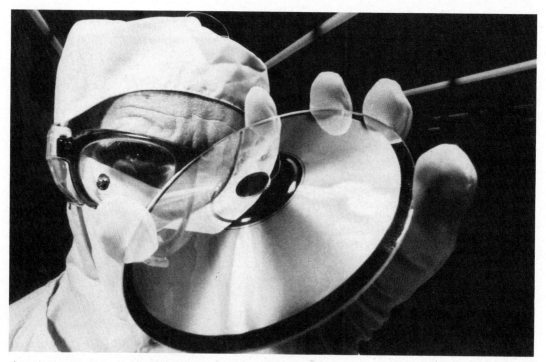

A production superintendent for 3M in Menomonie, Wis., holds an optical disk used with desktop computers that holds data equal to 275,000 printed pages.

transportation, printing, publishing, rubber, and plastics. In fact, 9 out of 10 new jobs created in the next 10 years are expected to be in the service industries.

Manufacturing employment as a per cent of total employment continued to decline in 1986. In 1962, manufacturing industries employed 26 per cent of the work force, and the service sector provided jobs for 59 per cent. In 1986, manufacturing employed 20 per cent, and the service industry employed 70 per cent.

Manufacturing Inventories fell 0.3 per cent in September to $588.4 billion. Factories were not exactly churning out goods. Overall operating rates were 79.4 per cent of capacity, more like the rate that occurs during a recession than an expansion. But again, the picture was uneven.

Factories that produced *durable goods* (goods expected to last at least three years) operated at 75.9 per cent of capacity, while plants producing nondurable goods operated at a more brisk capacity of 84.7 per cent. This was not surprising because sales of nondurables, such as food, textiles, chemicals, paper, and clothing, performed much better than the durable goods industry in 1986.

Factory Orders plummeted 3.5 per cent in October, just after things began looking rosier in September. This was the sharpest drop since May 1980, a recession year when factory orders declined 4.5 per cent. Orders for manufactured goods totaled $192.3 billion in October 1986, $7.1-billion below September's level. September orders had increased 3.4 per cent. New orders rebounded in November to $200.4 billion, an increase of 4.1 per cent, led by a surge in military orders.

Capital Investment—that is, investment by companies in new factories, tools, supplies, and equipment, an important indicator of the country's economic health—fell 2.5 per cent in 1986, according to the U.S. Department of Commerce. This represented the biggest drop since 1982 and the first decline since 1983. In more expansive times, capital investment rose 15.8 per cent in 1984 and 8.7 per cent in 1985.

Overall, $346.5 billion was spent in 1986 on capital commitments. Capital investment accounts for approximately 10 per cent of the gross national product (GNP)—the value of all goods and services produced.

One of the biggest reasons for the decline in capital investment was the collapse in oil prices, which forced oil companies to cut back. Oil usually accounts for 7 to 10 per cent of all capital investment. One economic analyst noted the trickle-down effect that occurs when oil companies reduce drilling; postpone purchases of computers, steel pipes, compressors, and other equipment; and suspend construction of buildings and plat-

Northrop Corporation employees work on the center fuselage of a Boeing 747 jet as the company gets ready in March to deliver its 650th such fuselage.

forms. For example, the Mobil Corporation, which spent $3.5 billion in 1985, was expected to spend $4.1 billion in 1986, but its actual capital investment in 1986 was $3 billion. The Exxon Corporation, which spent $8.2 billion in 1985, spent approximately $6 billion in 1986.

The computer industry, which makes large sales to companies that are expanding and modernizing, was particularly hard hit in 1986. Even industry giant International Business Machines Corporation reported lower earnings for the year—an unprecedented happening.

Machine Tools. The economically depressed machine-tool industry saw orders jump 30 per cent in October to $176 million. After seasonal adjustment, however, the order level was at its lowest in 3½ years, a decline of 23.4 per cent from October 1985.

Competition from other countries was responsible for the decline. Imports accounted for 43 per cent of the $4.3-billion U.S. market. The shrinking dollar helped U.S. producers only marginally in their efforts to secure overseas business.

One good sign for the industry was the announcement in December 1986 of agreements with Japan and Taiwan. Both nations voluntarily agreed to reduce their exports of certain machine tools to the United States to 1981 levels for five years.

Research and Development (R & D) spending in 1986 totaled $118.6 billion, according to Battelle Columbus Laboratories, an independent research concern, and the National Science Foundation. The figure represented an increase of 9 per cent over the 1985 figure of $108.8 billion. The federal government's R & D expenditures totaled $55.3-billion in 1986, up 8.5 per cent, and industry accounted for $59.3 billion, a rise of 9.4 per cent. Colleges and universities spent $2.5 billion.

Factory Automation. Sales of factory automation systems doubled to $18.1 billion from 1980 to 1985 and were expected to double again by 1990. Sales of robots amounted to $442.7 million in 1985. Robots were being used in factories to weld, paint, assemble, and perform tasks too monotonous or dangerous for human workers. Half of the 20,000 robots in use in the United States in 1986 were in the automobile industry.

Analysts feel automation could be the key to making U.S. industry more competitive abroad. The technology eliminates the advantage of lower labor costs in other countries by reducing the amount of labor needed and the amount of material wasted. The United States currently has one of the highest labor costs in the world.

Sales of microcomputers to manufacturing concerns were also increasing, by 36 per cent annually, aided by lower prices and improved performance. Another rapid-growth area was "machine vision," which incorporates video cameras that give machines "eyes" and computers that provide "brains." Products made by automated processes can be made for less money and with more accuracy and safety than before.

The General Motors Corporation (GM) currently uses more than 500 machine-vision systems and plans to use more than 40,000. GM and others have started their own machine-vision ventures or backed smaller companies involved in the field. Sales of machine-vision systems were $275 million in 1985 and were expected to grow to $1 billion by 1990.

Another important new word in factory automation circles was manufacturing automation protocol (MAP), a set of rules and standards for electronic communication in the factory. GM and Boeing Computer Services, among others, are spearheading this drive to enable various machines and computers from all departments in a manufacturing facility to "talk" to one another. Currently, most vendors have unique, totally incompatible formats.   Ronald Kolgraf

In WORLD BOOK, see MANUFACTURING.

MARINE CORPS, U.S. See ARMED FORCES.

MARYLAND. See STATE GOVERNMENT.

MASSACHUSETTS. See STATE GOVERNMENT.

MAURITANIA. See AFRICA.

MAURITIUS. See AFRICA.

MEDICINE. The United States Food and Drug Administration (FDA) on June 4, 1986, approved the first commercial use of a drug manufactured with genetic engineering technology. The medication is alpha-interferon, a protein produced by the body to fight infections. Scientists are able to make large quantities of this substance by using recombinant DNA technology, in which the gene that codes for the protein is transplanted into harmless bacteria. The bacteria then manufacture the protein, just as the human body does.

The FDA approved the sale of two preparations of synthetic interferon: Roferon-A, developed by Hoffmann-La Roche Incorporated of Nutley, N.J., and Intron-A, developed by Schering-Plough Corporation of Madison, N.J. Both preparations will be used to treat hairy cell leukemia, a rare blood cancer for which there is no other effective medication. The FDA predicted that the approval of these drugs would mark the beginning of a new era in the use of genetically engineered medications to treat cancer and other diseases.

Genetic Key. After six years of research, scientists at the Harvard Medical School in Boston reported on October 16 that they had discovered the gene that causes Duchenne dystrophy, the most common form of muscular dystrophy. Muscular dystrophy is an inherited disease that causes the muscles to become weak and waste away.

Before this discovery, scientists knew nothing about the disease except that it was caused by a malfunctioning gene. The Muscular Dystrophy Association in New York City, which funds research on the disease, called the finding a breakthrough. The next step, according to the scientists, is to identify the protein produced by the gene and what failure in protein production causes the disease.

Implanted Insulin Pump. On November 10, F. Jackson Piotrow, 55, became the first recipient of an implanted insulin pump. The small, battery-powered pump, called the Programmable Implantable Medication System, is designed to control the blood sugar of a person with diabetes by releasing insulin at a steady rate, similar to the way the pancreas releases insulin into the bloodstream of a nondiabetic person.

Physicians at Johns Hopkins University in Baltimore, who implanted the pump just below the skin covering Piotrow's abdominal cavity, called the pump a significant advance in treating diabetes. Not only is it an improvement over insulin shots, they said, but also it is more convenient than other insulin pumps, which are worn on a belt outside the body. The pump will be tested for the next two years.

Reducing Cancer. The National Cancer Institute (NCI) in Bethesda, Md., on October 28 said that the number of cancer deaths in the United States could be reduced by one half by the year 2000 through better use of existing medical knowledge. Cancer specialist Vincent T. DeVita, Jr., director of the NCI, announced a new cancer-control program involving more aggressive application of existing knowledge about the prevention, early detection, and treatment of cancer. He called for new efforts to reduce cigarette smoking; encourage the public to eat more fiber and less fat; expand the use of annual tests for breast, cervical, and other cancers; and increase the use of advanced cancer-treatment techniques.

Radical Leukemia Treatment. Medical researchers on July 17 reported success with a complex, experimental treatment for patients with terminal leukemia. The new technique, developed at Johns Hopkins University, has the potential for extending the life of terminal leukemia patients, and carries a 50 per cent chance of curing the disease, according to the researchers. The treatment involves the surgical removal of some bone marrow from the patient, followed by massive chemotherapy that kills all of the patient's remaining bone marrow. The extracted bone marrow is treated to remove the cancer cells and implanted back into the patient. The marrow then has a chance to regenerate and resume normal production of blood cells.

Frozen Embryos. A new treatment for infertility resulted in the birth of a baby boy to a California woman on June 6. It was the first baby in the United States born from an embryo that had been preserved through freezing and then implanted into a woman's uterus.

Transplant Debate. William J. Schroeder, the longest-living recipient of a permanent artificial heart, died on August 6 after suffering multiple strokes. Schroeder, 54, had lived for 620 days with the Jarvik-7 mechanical heart. Shortly after the device was implanted on Nov. 25, 1984, he experienced a series of strokes, infections, and other complications that left him partially paralyzed, unable to speak, and mentally impaired. Surgeon William C. DeVries of Humana Hospital Audubon in Louisville, Ky., who implanted the mechanical heart, hailed Schroeder as a medical pioneer.

Schroeder's death renewed debate over whether a mechanical heart should be used as a permanent replacement for a damaged human heart. Some physicians argued that the mechanical heart should be used only on a temporary basis with patients suffering from terminal heart disease who are awaiting a human heart transplant.

Baby Jesse, a 16-day-old infant who received a heart transplant on June 10, 1986, focused attention on procedures used to select recipients of organ transplants. At first, physicians at Loma Linda University Medical Center in Loma Linda, Calif., refused to give Baby Jesse a transplant. They felt

A lab worker prepares Roferon-A, one of two brands of interferon approved by the FDA on June 4 for use against a rare form of leukemia.

that his young, unmarried parents could not provide the necessary stable home environment and long-term medical care he would need.

The doctors agreed to perform the operation, however, after the baby's grandparents took custody of the baby and a heart donor was found while the parents made an appeal on a television talk show on June 10. On June 12, the parents of another infant who had waited longer and was in more critical need of a transplant called for a more equitable system of allocating donor organs and one less dependent on publicity.

Organ Network. On September 30, the United States Department of Health and Human Services (HHS) announced the establishment of a national network for matching donors and recipients in organ transplants. The computerized system will be operated by the United Network for Organ Sharing of Richmond, Va., an agency that was organized in 1984 to match donors and recipients for kidney transplants.

Transplant Payment. In a major policy change, HHS announced on June 27, 1986, that the Medicare program will begin paying for a limited number of heart transplants. Medicare provides health care for approximately 30 million elderly and disabled people in the United States. Otis R. Bowen, HHS secretary, said the program will pay for up to 143 transplants per year. Officials said that a single transplant can cost more than $100,000. Medicare will not pay for drugs that transplant patients must take to suppress the body's rejection of a transplanted organ.

Preventing Blood Clots. A panel of medical authorities concluded on March 27 that many of the 50,000 to 100,000 annual deaths in the United States from blood clots in the lungs could be prevented through wider use of medications and other measures. The panel, sponsored by the National Institutes of Health in Bethesda, said that blood clots, which most commonly form in veins in the legs and sometimes lodge in the lungs, represent a major health problem. Known medically as *deep vein thrombosis*, such clots are responsible for 600,000 hospitalizations each year. To prevent these clots, panel members recommended small doses of *heparin*, a drug that prevents the clotting of blood; *dextran*, which helps to dissolve clots; and special stockings or boots that compress leg veins and reduce the risk of clot formation.

Fetal Monitoring. On September 4, researchers at the University of Texas Southwestern Medical School in Dallas reported that though routine use of electronic fetal monitoring leads to a small increase in Caesarean deliveries, it does not improve the health of babies. The finding was based on a study of 35,000 births. Electronic monitoring during labor provides a continuous record of the unborn infant's heartbeat and the mother's contractions, giving physicians and nurses early warning if the infant is in physical distress. The researchers verified that fetal monitoring is valuable in deliveries where the infant's life is threatened.

Fetal monitoring was first used in high risk deliveries, but today it is used in at least 7 out of every 10 deliveries. The researchers found that routine use of fetal monitoring has almost no medical advantages.

Shattering Stones. A U.S. government evaluation concluded on May 23 that a nonsurgical treatment for kidney stones is safer, cheaper, and more effective than the traditional surgical procedure. The new treatment—*extracorporeal shock-wave lithotripsy* or ESWL—uses high-frequency sound waves to shatter kidney stones into fragments that can be passed out of the body through the urinary system. The study said shock-wave technology may be useful in other diseases, including the nonsurgical treatment of gallstones.

Costs Rise Slowly. HHS reported on July 29, 1986, that Americans spent $425 billion for medical care in 1985. Nevertheless, the rate of increase—8.9 per cent over 1984—was the smallest increase since 1965.   Michael Woods

See also DRUGS; HEALTH AND DISEASE; PUBLIC HEALTH. In the WORLD BOOK SUPPLEMENT section, see AIDS; ARTIFICIAL HEART; CYCLOSPORINE. In WORLD BOOK, see MEDICINE.

MENTAL ILLNESS. Citing the difficulty in curing mental illness and its enormous economic impact on society in the United States, a national commission on May 5, 1986, recommended intensifying efforts to prevent mental and emotional disorders.

The Commission on the Prevention of Mental-Emotional Disabilities, organized by the National Mental Health Association in Alexandria, Va., estimated that at least 19 per cent of all adults in the United States suffer from some form of emotional illness. Although only 1 of every 5 victims obtains professional help, treatment costs still exceed $24-billion per year. Yet, according to the commission, science has "barely made a dent" in curing emotional disorders.

The study found that additional research on prevention and greater efforts at providing preventive services offer the only realistic hope of controlling these disorders. The commission said that it is already possible to prevent some mental illnesses and made a number of recommendations for mental health professionals, physicians, teachers, employers, and others who could play key roles in prevention. These measures include educating employers about the mental health aspects of work and training teachers and school administrators to recognize and help troubled students.

Hypnosis Abuse. On August 24, the American Psychological Association (APA), based in Washington, D.C., acted to curtail the growing use of hypnosis by police, who use it in the questioning of witnesses, victims, and suspects in criminal cases. An estimated 5,000 to 10,000 police officers in the United States have had some training in the use of hypnosis to "refresh" the memories of people under interrogation. The APA said that such use of hypnosis has resulted in numerous abuses. For example, during hypnosis, police officers can unknowingly suggest what victims or witnesses saw or experienced. The hypnotized person may accept the suggestion and become convinced that it is true. The APA recommended that hypnosis be taught only to health professionals.

Death Row Disorders. Researchers reported evidence on July 7 that many prison inmates awaiting execution suffer from severe—but unrecognized—psychiatric or neurological disorders. The American Psychiatric Association, which published the study, said the findings had important implications in criminal cases that involve the death penalty.

In 1976, the Supreme Court of the United States ruled that the death penalty is constitutional if imposed during a separate sentencing in which information on mitigating circumstances, which might lead to a less severe sentence, is presented to the jury. Psychiatrist Dorothy Otnow Lewis of New York University in New York City, who headed the research team, said that evidence of mental disease would qualify as being a mitigating circumstance.

Lewis believes that such disorders frequently go unrecognized because murderers and their attorneys fail to request the necessary examinations. She noted that murderers typically do not consider themselves mentally sick or impaired, and have no idea that certain injuries, accidents, or symptoms might have affected their judgment or self-control.

Medication Decision. New York state's Court of Appeals on June 10 ruled that patients involuntarily committed to psychiatric institutions cannot be forced to take antipsychotic medication without a court order. The decision was expected to make it easier for patients to refuse medication. The court ruled that mental illness often affects only certain areas of a patient's ability to function normally, leaving other areas unimpaired. Thus, many mental patients retain the capacity to make competent decisions about medication. The court said that physicians and hospitals can force patients to take medication only after a court has found such patients incompetent to make decisions about their own treatment, or if the patients pose a danger to themselves or to others.   Michael Woods

See also PSYCHOLOGY. In WORLD BOOK, see HYPNOTISM; MENTAL ILLNESS.

MEXICO made its peace with foreign bankers at meetings in September 1986 with the World Bank and International Monetary Fund (IMF)—both agencies of the United Nations—in Washington, D.C. Under a new arrangement, Mexico was to receive $12 billion in new loans while agreeing to a long-term austerity program.

The bailout was expected to raise Mexico's total foreign debt to more than $100 billion, the second largest in the developing world, after Brazil. The agreement was seen as crucial to prop up the battered Mexican economy over the next 12 years.

Mexico's economic bind was caused by continuing declines in earnings from petroleum exports, by political corruption, and by mismanagement of government-run enterprises. Many government businesses had become unprofitable due to uncontrolled *featherbedding* (the creation of unnecessary jobs) or to depressed markets for their products. A typical casualty was the failure of the Lázaro Cárdenas Steel Complex near Lázaro Cárdenas—once hailed as a symbol of Mexico's drive to become an industrial power. During 1986, a governmental commission concluded that it would cost Mexico $2.1 billion to moth-ball the plant, or $1.4 billion to shut it down completely.

Austerity Measures. President Miguel de la Madrid Hurtado imposed new hardships on work-

In a demonstration in Mexico City in September, residents protest the lack of government aid to people still homeless because of the 1985 earthquakes.

ing-class Mexicans on August 8, when his administration raised the price of gasoline by 48 per cent. With this boost, Mexico's national oil company, Petróleos Mexicanos, estimated that it would be able to supply half of governmental revenues.

Mexicans grumbled at mounting inflation, which was 105.7 per cent in 1986, the worst one-year inflation rate in Mexico's history. The previous record was 98.8 per cent in 1982. The already much devalued peso lost 30 per cent of its value in trading in June.

Political Repercussions. On May 31, President de la Madrid was booed by crowds attending the opening of the World Cup soccer matches in Mexico City. This unprecedented show of public displeasure with an incumbent president was repeated in September when de la Madrid appeared at the annual independence ceremonies in the Zócalo, the main governmental square in Mexico City. Mexicans have traditionally shown great respect for their president.

State Elections. Following the election for governor in the state of Chihuahua on July 6, the conservative National Action Party (PAN) charged widespread fraud on the part of Mexico's long-dominant Institutional Revolutionary Party (PRI). PAN supporters demonstrated throughout the summer, alleging numerous election irregularities, such as stuffed ballot boxes and expulsions of poll watchers. They said these actions denied their candidate victory.

Roman Catholic bishops in Chihuahua closed the city's Catholic churches for one day on Sunday, July 20, to protest the election. The protest was unusual because Mexico's Catholic clergy have long been silent on domestic political issues.

U.S. Relations. During 1986, corruption within the PRI was openly criticized by officials within the Administration of United States President Ronald Reagan, including John Gavin, who retired as U.S. ambassador to Mexico in April, and high-level drug-enforcement officials. United States officials linked some state governors and Mexican police officials to drug trafficking. Tempers flared in August when a U.S. narcotics agent, Victor Cortez, Jr., was tortured while he was being detained by Jalisco state police.

President Reagan sought to smooth relations with Mexico by inviting de la Madrid for a visit in August. The drug issue was a major focus of talks, and on August 14, the Reagan Administration announced plans to spend at least $266 million to stop drug smuggling into the United States at the Mexican border. Nathan A. Haverstock

In the Special Reports section, see MEXICO: FROM BOOM TO BUST. See also LATIN AMERICA (Facts in Brief Table). In WORLD BOOK, see MEXICO.

MICHIGAN. See DETROIT; STATE GOVERNMENT.

MIDDLE EAST. Revelations that the United States had secretly provided arms to Iran—apparently in return for Iranian help in obtaining the release of American hostages held by pro-Iranian groups in Lebanon—created a major foreign policy problem in the United States in November 1986. But it was a problem of more relevance to U.S. domestic politics than to the relationships between Middle Eastern countries. See PRESIDENT OF THE U.S.

Relationships within the region, already scarred by the inability—or unwillingness—of outside powers to set a high priority on resolving the region's conflicts, were further damaged by the spread of uncontrolled terrorism. Firm U.S. support for Israel not only alienated moderate Arab states but also encouraged destabilizing efforts by radical Arab groups opposed to their governments' friendly relationships with the United States. In addition, the global oil glut and resulting drop in oil prices sharply reduced revenues in Arab oil-producing states, threatening to end the boom that had brought high employment and high economic expectations to the region.

Terrorism took a variety of forms during 1986. It was no longer necessarily a case of embittered Palestinians attempting to dramatize their cause through well-publicized hijackings or hostage-taking, though such incidents continued to occur. Muslim terrorists massacred Jewish worshipers at a synagogue in Istanbul, Turkey, in September, and launched a grenade attack on Israeli soldiers and their families at the Wailing Wall in Jerusalem in October. Although the root of the problem was still the unresolved Palestinian-Israeli conflict, terrorist groups and, occasionally, governments increasingly used the lawless climate of the region for their own purposes.

State Sponsorship. In general, the United States and its European allies considered Libya, Syria, and Iran the primary state sponsors of terrorism. But the United States took direct action against only Libya. On April 15, U.S. planes bombed bases and installations in Libya allegedly used for terrorist training. The targets included the headquarters of Libyan leader Muammar Muhammad al-Qadhafi. The United States claimed the action was necessary to demonstrate to Qadhafi that involvement in terrorist actions would automatically invite reprisals. The United States had accused Libya of being behind the April 5 bombing of a West Berlin, West Germany, discothèque, in which two American soldiers were killed.

Revelations in October that the Administration of President Ronald Reagan had engaged in a campaign to spread false information about Qadhafi weakened U.S allegations about Libyan actions, however. In November, the United Nations General Assembly voted overwhelmingly to censure the United States for the raid.

The Strife-Torn Middle East

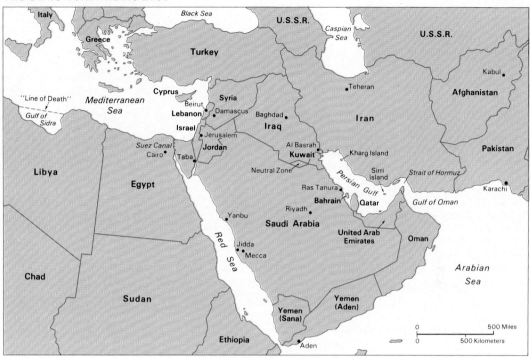

The European Response to terrorism was directed mainly at Syria. In October, a London court convicted Nezar Hindawi, a Jordanian-born Palestinian, of attempting to blow up an Israel-bound El Al airliner with a smuggled bomb. The British prosecutor produced evidence that Syria had financed and sponsored the plot. Britain broke diplomatic relations with Syria and urged its partners in the European Community (EC or Common Market) to adopt stiff *sanctions* (penalties) against that country. The United States and Canada withdrew their ambassadors to Syria but did not break relations.

In November, the EC imposed the sanctions on Syria requested by Britain. They included a ban on arms sales, a reduction in Syrian diplomatic missions, and the suspension of visits by high officials. Greece qualified its support for the sanctions by refusing to blame Syria for Hindawi's actions.

A spate of bombings in Paris and other French cities in September spurred the French government into adopting strict security measures, including requiring visas for all foreign visitors except those from EC countries and Switzerland. The attacks were intended to force the French government to free Georges Ibrahim Abdallah, leader of the secret Lebanese Armed Revolutionary Faction, who was imprisoned on terrorism charges.

Hostages Freed. Two American hostages held in Lebanon were released in 1986. Lawrence Martin Jenco, a Roman Catholic priest, was freed in July, and David P. Jacobsen, an administrator at the American University of Beirut, was released in November. Both allegedly were released as a result of Iran's intervention with the hostages' pro-Iranian Shiite captors following U.S. arms shipments to Iran. Three French hostages were also released in November and December.

But in September and October, three more Americans, all long-time residents of Lebanon who had converted to Islam, were abducted. Following the United States raid on Libya in April, three hostages—two Britons and one American, American University of Beirut librarian Peter Kilburn—were murdered.

French Departure. In this atmosphere of uncontrolled violence, not only the lives of foreigners but also the presence of stabilizing influences from abroad were increasingly affected. The American University of Beirut was closed in May. The French observer force remaining from the multinational peacekeeping force sent to Beirut after the 1982 Israeli invasion was withdrawn in April. And in November, the French units of the United Nations Interim Force in Lebanon went home.

***Achille Lauro* Convictions.** On July 10, 1986, an Italian court convicted 11 Palestinians on charges

Facts in Brief on Middle Eastern Countries

Country	Population	Government	Monetary Unit*	Exports†	Foreign Trade (million U.S. $) Imports†
Bahrain	465,000	Amir Isa bin Sulman Al-Khalifa; Prime Minister Khalifa bin Sulman Al-Khalifa	dinar (1 = $2.65)	2,815	3,159
Cyprus	681,000	President Spyros Kyprianou (Turkish Republic of Northern Cyprus: Acting President Rauf R. Denktaş)	pound (1 = $1.93)	483	1,195
Egypt	49,127,000	President Hosni Mubarak; Prime Minister Atef Sidqi	pound (1.43 = $1)	3,714	9,961
Iran	47,757,000	President Ali Khamenei; Prime Minister Hosein Musavi-Khamenei	rial (76.3 = $1)	13,185	11,256
Iraq	16,750,000	President Saddam Hussein	dinar (1 = $3.23)	11,700	11,500
Israel	4,131,000	President Chaim Herzog; Prime Minister Yitzhak Shamir	shekel (1.48 = $1)	6,256	10,154
Jordan	3,795,000	King Hussein I; Prime Minister Zaid Rifai	dinar (1 = $2.90)	789	2,733
Kuwait	1,948,000	Amir Jabir al Ahmad al Sabah; Prime Minister & Crown Prince Saad Al Abdullah Al Sabah	dinar (1 = $3.41)	11,300	7,400
Lebanon	2,762,000	President Amine Gemayel; Prime Minister Rashid Karami	pound (63 = $1)	482	2,203
Oman	1,312,000	Sultan Qaboos bin Said	rial (1 = $2.61)	4,500	2,700
Qatar	322,000	Amir & Prime Minister Khalifa bin Hamad Al Thani	riyal (3.62 = $1)	4,500	1,000
Saudi Arabia	12,112,000	King & Prime Minister Fahd ibn Abd al-Aziz Al Saud	riyal (3.75 = $1)	40,000	35,000
Sudan	22,876,000	Supreme Council President Ahmed al Mirghani; Prime Minister Sadiq el Mahdi	pound (2.4 = $1)	374	771
Syria	11,415,000	President Hafiz al-Assad; Prime Minister Abd al Ra'uf al-Kassem	pound (3.9 = $1)	1,900	4,100
Turkey	52,340,000	President Kenan Evren; Prime Minister Turgut Ozal	lira (747 = $1)	7,958	11,035
United Arab Emirates	1,417,000	President Zayid bin Sultan Al Nahayyan; Prime Minister Rashid ibn Said al Maktum	dirham (3.67 = $1)	14,254	7,590
Yemen (Aden)	2,250,000	Supreme People's Council Presidium Chairman Haydar Abu Bakr al-Attas; Council of Ministers Chairman Yasin Sa'id Nu'man	dinar (1 = $2.91)	40	768
Yemen (Sana)	6,891,000	President Ali Abdallah Salih; Prime Minister Abdel Aziz Abdel Ghani	rial (10.2 = $1)	9	1,400

*Exchange rates as of Dec. 1, 1986, or latest available data.   †Latest available data.

arising from the October 1985 hijacking of the cruise ship *Achille Lauro*. Leon Klinghoffer, an American passenger on the ship, was murdered by the terrorists.

Arab-Israeli Conflict. There was little tangible progress in 1986 toward resolution of the differences between the Arab states and Israel. The forward motion that occurred proceeded from efforts originating within the region. In September, Israel and Egypt agreed to submit their territorial dispute over Taba, a small Israeli-held area in the Sinai Peninsula, to international arbitration. The meeting of Israel's Prime Minister Shimon Peres and King Hassan II of Morocco in Morocco in July, though underlining the gulf between Arab and Israeli views on Palestinian rights to a homeland, was an encouraging sign.

The break between King Hussein I of Jordan and Palestine Liberation Organization (PLO) Chairman Yasir Arafat in February led to greater Israeli-Jordanian cooperation in the administration of the West Bank. The Jerusalem branch of the Cairo-Amman Bank of Jordan, closed since the 1967 Six-Day War, reopened in September. It will serve as the conduit for funds raised from outside sources for an ambitious Five-Year Plan for West Bank development announced by Hussein in June.

Iran-Iraq War Intensifies. Iranian forces seized the nearly abandoned Iraq oil port of Fao in February and moved rapidly northwest to occupy the adjacent peninsula. The drive brought them within artillery range of the vital Basra-Baghdad highway. Iranian successes on the northern front brought them to within 70 miles (110 kilometers) of Baghdad, Iraq's capital. But Iraq's air superiority held the Iranians at bay thereafter.

Iraqi raids on Iran's export terminals at Kharg Island and on newer terminals, such as Sirri and Larak islands, thought to be beyond Iraqi range, slashed Iranian oil exports. Other Iraqi raids deep into Iran during the summer damaged a steel mill at Isfahan and other industrial targets.

Iran's success at Fao was followed by a massive build-up of Iranian ground forces along the border. The government ordered a total mobilization of able-bodied men aged 18 to 28 and announced an imminent "final offensive" to win the war. But the offensive had not begun by year-end.

In August, Iran rejected a cease-fire offer from the Iraqi regime. But in October, the speaker of Iran's Majlis (parliament) said that Iran would accept the replacement of Iraqi President Saddam Hussein's regime by any other Iraqi government, even one allied with the "satanic" United States, as a precondition for peace talks. It was the first concession made by Iran since the start of the war in 1980.

Economic Slowdown. The global oil glut, low oil prices, and declining oil revenues affected both the oil-producing and the non-oil-producing states of the Middle East. Some oil-rich states adopted deficit budgets, while others canceled or postponed large-scale development projects. Such non-oil-producing states as Turkey and Morocco were also affected by the drop in money sent home by citizens working abroad in oil-producing countries.

Members of the Organization of Petroleum Exporting Countries (OPEC) struggled for most of 1986 to find a formula for restoring price and production levels. The October dismissal of Saudi Oil Minister Sheik Ahmed Zaki Yamani enhanced OPEC unity. In 1986, Yamani had fought for increased production and price cuts to force high-cost, non-OPEC oil producers to follow the cartel's lead, a strategy many OPEC members had opposed. See PETROLEUM AND GAS.

Two major Middle East projects were not affected by the downturn, however. Work continued on Libya's Great Man-Made River and Iraq's Bekme Dam, both vital to agriculture.

PLO Loses Ground. PLO Chairman Arafat faced continued erosion of his support base with Arab governments, despite his popularity among West Bank Palestinians. In July, King Hussein of Jor-

Smoke blankets Aden, the capital of Yemen (Aden), in January during fighting between rival Marxist factions for control of the government.

A Libyan patrol boat, hit by a U.S. missile, burns in the Gulf of Sidra
off Libya in March during a dispute over Libya's claim to the gulf.

dan cemented his February break with Arafat by
closing PLO offices in Jordan. Hussein charged
Arafat and the PLO generally with a lack of realism in refusing to accept the existence of Israel.

Other blows to Arafat were the September appointments by Israeli authorities, with Jordanian
approval, of mayors for three West Bank towns,
and Hussein's Five-Year Plan for the West Bank.
The plan would by-pass the PLO entirely.

In October, Arafat transferred his headquarters
from Tunis, Tunisia, where it had been moved after the 1982 Israeli invasion of Lebanon, to remote Sana, capital of Yemen (Sana). Arafat presumably believed he would be safe there from
Israeli raids, such as the 1985 attack that leveled
buildings in Tunis and caused numerous Tunisian
casualties.

But the durable PLO leader held on. In October
1986, after a PLO military command meeting in
Baghdad, Arafat announced a new strategy of attacking only targets inside Israel and Israeli-occupied areas. The new strategy was marked by the
grenade attack at the Wailing Wall in Jerusalem in
October, the murder of an Israeli seminary student in November, and a renewal in artillery attacks from across the Lebanese border.

Political Changes. A bloody coup overthrew Ali
Nasir Muhammad, the Marxist leader of Yemen
(Aden), in January. Muhammad's overthrow re-

sulted primarily from traditional tribal and family
rivalries. He had, however, been criticized by
tribal rivals for promoting closer links with non-
Marxist Arab neighbors, such as Saudi Arabia and
Oman, to obtain badly needed funds.

A new government, the fifth since independence in 1967, took office headed by Haydar Abu
Bakr al-Attas, the former minister of construction.
Casualties were heavy, with 10,000 killed and
Aden, the capital, nearly destroyed. Muhammad
and several thousand supporters took refuge in
neighboring Yemen (Sana).

In July, Amir Jabir al Ahmad al Sabah of Kuwait suspended the 50-member National Assembly
for the second time. He said the action was necessary because Assembly members had interfered in
foreign affairs.

Sudan. Parliamentary democracy fared better in
Sudan, where civilian rule was restored after 17
years. Elections for a new National People's Assembly were held in April. The election was not
entirely representative since the non-Muslim
southern provinces did not participate. Most of
southern Sudan is controlled by the rebel Sudanese People's Liberation Army, which opposes
dominance by the Muslim north.   William Spencer

See also articles on the various Middle Eastern
countries. In WORLD BOOK, see MIDDLE EAST and
individual Middle Eastern country articles.

MINING. The worst gold-mining disaster in South Africa's history killed 177 miners on Sept. 16, 1986. The accident occurred in the big Kinross gold mine, located 60 miles (100 kilometers) east of Johannesburg, when welders ignited cables and pipes sheeted with plastic in a underground shaft. Officials said that polyurethane foam used to line the mine tunnel caught fire, apparently producing a toxic gas that asphyxiated the miners.

The National Union of Mineworkers, the largest black labor union in South Africa, charged that mine owners ignored safety procedures. Miners organized protests to draw attention to safety conditions. A work stoppage was held on October 1, a national day of mourning for the dead miners.

Copper Contracts. The United States avoided a nationwide copper-mining strike on June 30, when unions and mining companies agreed on terms for new labor contracts. The settlements reflected the U.S. copper industry's troubled economic condition and struggle to compete with foreign producers. At Kennecott Corporation in Cleveland, for example, a group of 14 unions agreed to pay and benefit cuts totaling $3.22 per hour. As part of the settlement, Kennecott agreed to reopen its Bingham Canyon mine in Utah, the largest copper mine in the United States, which closed in 1985.

Uranium Risk? On Sept. 30, 1986, the U.S. Forest Service approved the development of a uranium mine in the Kaibab National Forest located just south of the Grand Canyon in Arizona. The approval came despite opposition from conservationists and the Havasupai Indians, who obtain drinking water from a creek that runs through the mine site. Energy Fuels Nuclear, Incorporated, of Denver will operate the mine.

Coal Leasing Resumes. The United States Department of the Interior on February 26 announced that it would resume leasing federal lands for coal mining. The coal-mine leasing program was suspended in 1983, following charges that James G. Watt, former secretary of the interior, had allowed leases to be sold at unrealistically low prices. Interior Secretary Donald P. Hodel said the new leasing program would include safeguards to ensure an accurate appraisal of the value of each lease.

Platinum Prices Rise. Concern over possible disruptions in the supply of platinum due to civil unrest in South Africa led to steep increases in the price of the metal during August and September. Prices reached about $550 per troy ounce (31 grams) in August, more than twice the 1985 level, and jumped to about $663 per troy ounce on September 2, a record high. Authorities predicted

Miners wait outside the Kinross gold mine in South Africa in September for word of survivors, after an underground fire killed at least 177 workers.

that platinum prices could rise to $1,000 per troy ounce within the next few years.

New Discovery. On September 30, Australia announced the discovery of huge deposits of platinum and other precious metals in Kakadu National Park in the country's Northern Territory. Gareth Evans, minister of energy and resources, said the deposit contained more than 1 million troy ounces (31 million grams) of platinum; 2.65 million troy ounces (82.4 million grams) of gold; 475,000 troy ounces (14.8 million grams) of silver; and 410,000 troy ounces (12.8 million grams) of palladium. Controversy flared, however, on whether to permit mining in the park, a popular tourist attraction.

Tin Crisis. A continued decline in world prices for tin forced Great Britain to take emergency action on August 8 to sustain operations at the two remaining tin mines in Cornwall, a county in southwestern England. Paul Channon, British secretary of state for trade and industry, said the government would provide $37 million in aid to the mines.   Michael Woods

In WORLD BOOK, see MINING.

MINNESOTA. See STATE GOVERNMENT.

MISSISSIPPI. See STATE GOVERNMENT.

MISSOURI. See STATE GOVERNMENT.

MONGOLIA. See ASIA.

MONTANA. See STATE GOVERNMENT.

Choked with emotion, Jean Drapeau, mayor of Montreal for 29 years, weeps as he announces on June 27 his retirement from office.

MONTREAL saw the end of an era in 1986 as Jean Drapeau, 70, the city's mayor for 29 years, stepped down. Drapeau had held the post since 1954, with one four-year interruption.

Bitter Mayoral Campaign. Drapeau's handpicked successor to lead the Civic Party he formed in 1960 was Claude Dupras, 54, a consulting engineer. Opposing Dupras was a 41-year-old labor lawyer, Jean Doré, leader of the Montreal Citizen's Movement (MCM), a generally left of center municipal party.

One of the harshest political battles in Montreal's history followed, with Dupras publicly branding Doré as a socialist and a separatist, and Doré pointing to the heavy burden of debt left by the Drapeau administration for building 1976 Olympic Games facilities, and accusing Drapeau of a generally autocratic administration. As the campaign became increasingly bitter, Drapeau himself entered the fray, warning the electorate that Doré's election would lead to a socialist era and threaten the financial community. But Doré received the public backing of Phillip O'Brian, the former head of the city's Chamber of Commerce, and other business leaders.

The Election, held on Nov. 9, 1986, resulted in an almost complete sweep for Doré's MCM, which won 52 of the City Council's 55 seats. Only 1 seat went to a member of Drapeau's Civic Party, who

represented a working-class district long loyal to Drapeau. Two seats were taken by independents, 1 of them by Nick Auf der Maur, a colorful author, columnist, and broadcaster.

New Administration. A week after the election, Doré was sworn into office and immediately installed an entirely new administration—balanced along the linguistic and racial lines of the population. His new team included English-speaking Councilor Michael Fainstat as chairman of the powerful Executive Committee; another English-speaking member, John Gardiner, as head of city planning; and three women in the inner circle of municipal administration.

Doré's first act as mayor was to negotiate a freeze on transit fares with the provincial government of Quebec. Under the agreement, the province of Quebec pays $157 million (Canadian dollars; $1 = U.S. 72 cents as of Dec. 31, 1986) of the $479-million cost of running the bus and subway system. Passengers pay about 45 per cent of the cost, and the Montreal Urban Community Council, an agency created by the Quebec legislature in 1969, pays the balance. By persuading the province to increase its share for 1987, Doré was able to keep the cost of traveling anywhere within the city under $1.

Doré urged the provincial government to strictly enforce laws that forbid the use of English in most public signs in Montreal. He also called on Canada's federal government to close Mirabel Airport, about 35 miles (56 kilometers) north of the city, and combine all air traffic at Dorval Airport, 12 miles (19 kilometers) from the city center.

Budget. Doré presented a record budget of $1.44 billion—an increase of 7.4 per cent over 1985—which will cause the taxes of a single-family dwelling to increase by about 6.6 per cent. Doré's administration eliminated a $60-per-dwelling water tax, however, making up the difference in revenue with increased parking and traffic fines.

Building Boom. Aside from the election, the dominant story in Montreal in 1986 was a building boom that was transforming the city's skyline. The value of construction starts in the Montreal metropolitan area in the first 10 months of 1986 rose to an unprecedented $1.2 billion, 28 per cent above the same period in 1985. The major factor in the boom was the construction of office towers, which increased 108 per cent during the period, to $396 million.

Unfortunately, the building boom failed to make a dent in unemployment in the city because of declines in manufacturing and transportation. The unemployment rate in Montreal for 1986 remained slightly below 12 per cent.   Kendal Windeyer

See also CANADA; QUEBEC. In WORLD BOOK, see MONTREAL.

King Hassan II of Morocco rides in a procession in Marrakech in March during festivities celebrating the 25th anniversary of his reign.

MOROCCO. King Hassan II incurred the wrath of much of the Arab world in 1986 by inviting Israel's Prime Minister Shimon Peres to meet him in July for talks in Ifrane in the Middle Atlas Mountains. Earlier, Hassan had marked his quarter-century of rule with a speech in which he quoted a verse from the Koran, the sacred book of Islam: "Hold fast to that which has been revealed to you for you are on the right path." Although the king's "revelation" produced no breakthrough in the stalled Arab-Israeli peace process, it underscored his skill at taking bold initiatives often contrary to the main body of Arab leadership.

The Hassan-Peres Talks caused a predictable reaction among Arab leaders. Only Egypt approved of the meeting. Syria and Libya issued a joint statement accusing Hassan of "an act of treason," and Syria broke diplomatic relations with Morocco. In August, the king abolished the treaty of union that he signed with Libya in 1984. On his orders, Morocco's borders were closed, and the army went on full alert. But the diplomatic crisis did not lead to military action.

The War in Western Sahara, however, entered its second decade with no solution in sight. Moroccan representatives held indirect talks in April and May with members of the Polisario Front guerrillas, who are fighting for independence from Morocco. The talks, conducted under the auspices of the United Nations (UN) and the Organization of African Unity, ended inconclusively after the Polisario Front accused Morocco of blocking the peace process. The Moroccan Army remained in control militarily behind a 900-mile (1,400-kilometer) fortified defense line from the Algerian border to Dakhla, near Mauritania. But most African states continued to recognize the Polisario Front as sovereign in Western Sahara.

The Economy. The costs of the Saharan war, declining world prices for phosphates, and a huge fuel import bill continued to hold down Morocco's economic development. In February, the government made a late payment of $85 million on its rescheduled $550-million debt to foreign banks. But disagreement among Morocco's leaders over the nation's economic goals caused the International Monetary Fund (IMF), an agency of the UN, to freeze payments on a $172-million loan granted in 1985 to bail out the economy. IMF officials said that Morocco was not serious about implementing a needed budget-tightening program.

On the plus side, the African Development Bank, an organization funded by 50 African states, lent Morocco $65 million in June for an agricultural credit bank. The loan was the bank's largest to any African country.   William Spencer

See also AFRICA (Facts in Brief Table). In WORLD BOOK, see MOROCCO.

MOTION PICTURES

The year 1986 was unexciting in the world of motion pictures. No major movie trends were set, and—in the opinion of most critics—no artistic peaks were reached. Among 1986 releases, there was the usual mix of surprise hits and unexpected disappointments. Excitement was provided chiefly by a lively controversy over the use of a process called *colorization*, which adds color to black-and-white films by computer.

Colorization was used in 1986 on such classic films as *The Maltese Falcon* (1941), *Yankee Doodle Dandy* (1942), and *It's a Wonderful Life* (1946). The copyrights had run out on all of the motion pictures treated, or else they had been purchased by broadcasting executive Ted Turner.

Turner and other supporters of the method claim that colorizing old movies is the only way to get young viewers to watch them. Opponents, particularly among film scholars and the filmmaking community itself, believe that a director's original vision should be honored. Black-and-white films, they say, were conceived, designed, and photographed as black-and-white films.

The American Film Institute and the Directors Guild of America, both influential organizations in the motion-picture industry, officially went on record in 1986 as opposing colorization. At a national board meeting on October 18, the Directors Guild voted unanimously to "use its full resources to stop the coloring of black-and-white films." The board referred to colorization as "cultural butchery" and a "mutilation of history."

Such renowned filmmakers as Woody Allen, Frank Capra, John Huston, and Fred Zinnemann condemned computer coloring of vintage films. Huston, enraged over the colorization of *The Maltese Falcon*, which he directed, urged the public in November to boycott products advertised on television showings of colorized films.

Welles Film Found. If colorization was bleak news for film scholars, their spirits were raised by the discovery, announced in August, of a long-lost film by the revered American director Orson Welles. When Welles died on Oct. 10, 1985, he left behind an uncut, unfinished film, a 1942 semidocumentary about Brazil called *It's All True*. Fred Chandler, director of technical services at Paramount Pictures Corporation and a long-time Welles buff, found the nearly 20 hours of footage among 300 film cans in Paramount's stock-footage vault in 1984. The footage is expected to be shown at film festivals during 1987.

The Wonder from Down Under. *"Crocodile" Dundee*, a lightweight but enjoyable film featuring Australian television celebrity Paul Hogan in his first starring role, became the highest grossing film in Australian history soon after its April opening in that country. It arrived in the United States in September and surprised the American motion-picture industry by becoming the first autumn release to gross $100 million in the United States alone. Like many blockbusters, *"Crocodile" Dundee* attracted a crossover audience, one that included older as well as younger viewers.

Other Hits. Another major hit was *Top Gun*, a trendy-looking but empty drama about fighter pilots vaguely fashioned after *An Officer and a Gentleman* (1982) but without the earlier film's punch. Critics dismissed *Top Gun*, with its startling camera angles and all-too-vivid rock score, as a feature-length music video—which may have been the secret of the film's commercial success. Another factor, undoubtedly, was the presence of the popular young actor Tom Cruise in the starring role.

Later in 1986, Cruise took on a more challenging dramatic role as a talented young pool player tutored by Paul Newman in *The Color of Money*, directed by Martin Scorsese. The film, a sequel to the 1961 classic *The Hustler*—in which Newman also starred—provided the veteran actor with one of his best roles. Newman responded with a rich, seasoned performance that confirmed his status as one of the best-liked American stars.

Crimes of the Heart presented a faithful adaptation of Beth Henley's drama about three frustrated Mississippi sisters, which won a Pulitzer Prize in 1981. Some critics praised the film version for its intelligent opening up of a stage play as well as for the performances of its distinguished cast. Stars Diane Keaton, Jessica Lange, and Sissy Spacek found the universality of the characters beneath the darkly comic situations of the plot.

Among other warmly received films of 1986 were three unusually successful sequels. *Star Trek IV: The Voyage Home* was critically and commercially the most rewarding of the four movies so far based on the 1960's television series "Star Trek." Gross box-office receipts for *The Karate Kid Part II* actually surpassed those of its popular 1984 predecessor. *Aliens*, a sequel to the 1979 science-fiction thriller *Alien*, delivered an engrossing performance by star Sigourney Weaver.

Stand by Me, based on an atypical, nostalgic tale by horror writer Stephen King, was a surprise hit. The film, a coming-of-age story of four outcast boys, was movingly directed by Rob Reiner, previously best known as "Meathead" on TV's "All in the Family." Comedian Rodney Dangerfield had a

A huge insectlike creature grapples with star Sigourney Weaver in *Aliens,* a popular 1986 sequel to the 1979 science-fiction thriller *Alien.*

Kathleen Turner is crowned queen of the reunion before a fainting spell transports her back 25 years to her high school days in *Peggy Sue Got Married.*

box-office smash with *Back to School.* Director John Hughes continued his sympathetic treatment of teen-age anxieties in *Ferris Bueller's Day Off.*

Children of a Lesser God, based on Mark Medoff's 1980 play, told a sensitive if sentimental love story with William Hurt as a teacher of the deaf. Critics endorsed the film, but audiences resisted it. Critics also had high praise for *Platoon,* written and directed by Oliver Stone, which many reviewers called the best film yet about the Vietnam War.

Successes by Old Pros. The Walt Disney Company, which since the 1970's had been relying primarily on reissues from its catalog of classics, made a strong impact on the 1986 movie scene with three hits from its Touchstone Pictures division. Besides the poolroom drama *The Color of Money,* Touchstone had two other hits with *Down and Out in Beverly Hills* and *Ruthless People.* Both films starred singer Bette Midler.

Ironically, a non-Disney film, *An American Tail,* won acclaim for its animation in the classic Disney style. The film, released by Universal City Studios, Incorporated, told a touching story of an immigrant mouse lost amid the chaos of New York City in the 1880's. Its animators were Don Bluth, John Pomeroy, and Gary Goldman, all of whom had resigned from Disney in 1979.

Francis Coppola made a critical comeback with *Peggy Sue Got Married,* starring Kathleen Turner.

But the time-travel drama, in which Turner gets a chance to relive her senior year in high school, was less popular with audiences than with critics.

Woody Allen had the most successful film of his career with *Hannah and Her Sisters.* It captured the rich variety of contemporary Manhattan life and kindled fresh appreciation for Mia Farrow, Barbara Hershey, and Dianne Wiest as the sisters.

Disappointments in 1986 included several well-intentioned films. Peter Weir's screen adaptation of Paul Theroux's 1982 novel *The Mosquito Coast* received mixed notices. Star Harrison Ford, cast against type as an egomaniacal dreamer and inventor, won praise for his unorthodox portrayal.

Mike Nichols' version of Nora Ephron's 1983 best seller *Heartburn,* the thinly disguised story of her marriage with reporter Carl Bernstein, was one of 1986's most eagerly awaited films. The screenplay, however, strung together too many short, jokey episodes, and stars Meryl Streep and Jack Nicholson delivered actorish performances.

Roland Joffe's *The Mission,* about the efforts of Roman Catholic priests to right the wrongs of colonial South America, won a good deal of praise, particularly for the acting of stars Jeremy Irons and Robert De Niro. But *The Mission* also had detractors who felt it was stilted and smug.

Cobra surprised its financial backers by being a big hit in Europe and a major disappointment in the United States. Featuring Sylvester Stallone as a Los Angeles cop investigating a series of grisly murders, the film's performance at the box office was a letdown following the public's enthusiastic response to Stallone's Rocky and Rambo movies.

British Films continued their artistic renaissance. Director James Ivory's tasteful and elegant adaptation of *A Room with a View*, a 1908 novel by British writer E. M. Forster, became a giant international art film hit. The gentle and humorous story, about the repercussions that occur after a beautiful and proper young Englishwoman is impetuously kissed by a young man, struck a universal chord. Maggie Smith won special praise for her performance as the strait-laced aunt of the heroine, played by Helena Bonham Carter.

Mona Lisa, with its searing view of the seamy side of London and its touching performance by Bob Hoskins as a sentimental ex-convict, also found favor with art house patrons.

International News. *Hannah and Her Sisters* became a big hit in Europe, as did *Out of Africa*, a 1985 release that won seven Academy Awards, including best picture, in 1986. *The Name of the Rose*, in which Sean Connery played a monk attempting to unravel several murders in a monastery in the 1300's, won a following in Europe but not in the United States. Bertrand Blier's comic *Ménage*, which surprised viewers by presenting the burly French movie idol Gérard Depardieu as a bisexual, won public support and critical approval.

In May 1986, the South African government agreed to open white-only motion-picture theaters to viewers of other races. South Africa has approximately 460 movie theaters, of which about one-fourth were reserved for whites only.

Movie Review Programs on television continued to multiply. Veteran reviewers Roger Ebert and Gene Siskel left "At the Movies" to become co-hosts of a similar show called "Siskel & Ebert & the Movies." Long-time columnist Rex Reed and relative newcomer Bill Harris signed on as their replacements in "At the Movies." Meanwhile, Jeffrey Lyons and Michael Medved continued to co-host "Sneak Previews," the original Ebert-Siskel show. To further complicate matters, the *New York Post* in October began to run Ebert's film reviews in place of Reed's.

Deaths. The deaths of two Hollywood legends—James Cagney on March 30 and Cary Grant on November 29—served as reminders of the dwindling ranks of Hollywood's pretelevision stars. Other deaths included those of actor Ray Milland and actress Donna Reed; directors Vincente Minnelli and Otto L. Preminger; and producer Hal B. Wallis.   Philip Wuntch

See also AWARDS AND PRIZES (Arts Awards); HURT, WILLIAM; PAGE, GERALDINE. In WORLD BOOK, see MOTION PICTURE.

Paul Hogan plays an Australian crocodile poacher who visits New York City in *"Crocodile" Dundee*, which conquered U.S. box offices in the fall.

MOZAMBIQUE. President Samora Moisés Machel of Mozambique was killed on Oct. 19, 1986, when a plane carrying him home from Zambia crashed in South Africa. At least 33 other people aboard the Soviet-piloted jet were also killed. South Africa immediately launched an investigation of the crash.

Machel's death led to a power struggle within the Marxist Front for the Liberation of Mozambique (Frelimo), the nation's only political party. On November 3, Frelimo's Central Committee elected Joaquím Alberto Chissano, the government's foreign minister since 1975, as president.

An estimated 4 million Mozambicans were at risk of starving in 1986 because of a famine caused largely by the Mozambique National Resistance (MNR), a rebel group that is trying to overthrow the government. MNR forces devastated crops and forced thousands of farmers in the provinces of Zambezia and Niassa to flee their farms. The MNR, which controls much of the north, destroyed major rail, pipeline, and communications links and threatened the capital, Maputo.

During the year, Mozambique government leaders continued to charge that South Africa was violating a 1984 treaty by which it pledged not to support the MNR. J. Gus Liebenow and Beverly B. Liebenow

See also AFRICA (Facts in Brief Table). In WORLD BOOK, see MOZAMBIQUE.

MULRONEY, M. BRIAN (1939-   ), reached the midpoint of his first term as prime minister of Canada in 1986. A poll published on September 2 revealed that Mulroney's personal popularity had fallen since he led the Progressive Conservative (PC) Party to an overwhelming victory in the general election of September 1984.

The Mulroney government acknowledged the public's dissatisfaction but stressed the accomplishments of its two years in power. Improvements in the economy included lower unemployment, inflation, and interest rates. The government had also made significant reforms in such areas as social legislation and divorce law.

Mulroney began to tackle some important challenges as he moved into the second half of his first term, including free-trade negotiations with the United States and working out terms that would persuade Quebec to endorse the federal constitution it had rejected in 1982. Reforming Canada's tax system was another major goal. Mulroney's progress in these areas was expected to help determine whether he and the PC Party would regain public favor. David M. L. Farr

See also CANADA. In WORLD BOOK, see MULRONEY, MARTIN BRIAN.

MUSIC, CLASSICAL. See CLASSICAL MUSIC.
MUSIC, POPULAR. See POPULAR MUSIC.
NAMIBIA. See AFRICA.

NATIONAL PTA. In October 1986, the National PTA premiered a yearlong campaign in the United States to "Celebrate Our Public Schools." The program's subtitle, "School Is What WE Make It," emphasized that the quality of education depends on the combined efforts of parents and teachers. Discussing the campaign, which ties in with the PTA's 90th birthday in February 1987, National PTA President Ann Kahn said, "Let us pledge to continue to help schools improve so that every child in this country has access to an education and a productive life."

In November 1986, the National PTA debuted Child Safety and Protection Month. PTA's throughout the United States and at American military bases in Europe conducted projects based on the theme "Build a Safer World for Children and Youth."

In 1986, the PTA, in cooperation with the March of Dimes Birth Defects Foundation, sent PTA's throughout the United States an information packet to help them sponsor programs on parenting skills. Joan Kuersten

In WORLD BOOK, see NATIONAL CONGRESS OF PARENTS AND TEACHERS; PARENT-TEACHER ORGANIZATIONS.
NAVY. See ARMED FORCES.
NEBRASKA. See STATE GOVERNMENT.
NEPAL. See ASIA.

NETHERLANDS. Prime Minister Ruud Lubbers won a decisive victory in national elections on May 21, 1986. His centrist Christian Democrat Party won 34.6 per cent of the vote to increase its representation in the 150-seat Second Chamber of the States-General (parliament) from 45 seats to 54. But the main partner in Lubbers' coalition government, the right wing Liberals, dropped from 36 seats to 27.

The opposition Labor Party gained 5 seats for a total of 52. Nevertheless, the election was a bitter blow to Labor. Its leader, Joop den Uyl, had hopes of becoming prime minister a second time.

Voters swung away from the small parties, cutting their 16 seats to 8. The Communists lost all 3 of their seats after having been represented in the Second Chamber since 1922.

Coalition Continues. Lubbers had made it clear before the election that if he and the Liberals maintained a majority in the Second Chamber, he would continue his coalition. But negotiations with the Liberals lasted until the summer. The negotiations centered on budget cuts and other measures intended to boost the economy. The Christian Democrats favored less severe measures than did the Liberals. A new coalition government finally took office on July 14.

Missiles Go-Ahead. On February 28, the Second Chamber approved the installation of 48 United

Queen Beatrix and Prince Claus of the Netherlands, wearing traditional Indian wreaths, arrive in New Delhi, India, for a visit in January.

States nuclear cruise missiles in the Netherlands by the end of 1988. Six left wing Christian Democrats voted with the Labor opposition against the ratification of a treaty with the United States to install the missiles.

The Second Chamber rejected an opposition call for a national referendum on the issue. But Foreign Minister Hans van den Broek said he would continue to strive for the removal of all nuclear missiles from both Western and Eastern Europe. The Labor Party threatened to review the decision if it won the election.

Advice to Police. Leen van der Linden, chairman of the Dutch Police Union, caused a storm on January 14 when he advised union members to "pack up and run" in case of terrorist attack. The international police organization Interpol had warned the Netherlands to expect terrorist attacks to be made on Jewish or Israeli targets. Van der Linden claimed that the Dutch police were not well enough trained or well enough equipped to fight terrorists.

The government, planning a major protection effort for a visit by Israel's Prime Minister Shimon Peres five days later, refuted van der Linden's claim. Peres' visit was without incident. Kenneth Brown

See also EUROPE (Facts in Brief Table). In WORLD BOOK, see NETHERLANDS.
NEVADA. See STATE GOVERNMENT.

NEW BRUNSWICK. Speculation about whether the province's premier, Richard B. Hatfield, would resign or face reelection continued to intrigue New Brunswick politicians and voters in 1986. The 55-year-old Hatfield, Canada's longest-serving provincial premier and leader of a Progressive Conservative (PC) administration since 1970, had been in political hot water since he was acquitted of a charge of marijuana possession in 1985. Voter disapproval was registered in a Feb. 10, 1986, special election in Edmundston in northwestern New Brunswick to fill a vacant seat in the provincial legislature. After having held the seat for 15 years, the PC's lost it decisively to a Liberal.

In June, when a long-awaited report on the status of English and French in the province was released, Hatfield approved of the report's appeal for linguistic fairness but rejected its recommendation that the scope of official bilingualism be broadened. He decided that the report's proposal that French-speaking people be given a larger role in the public service was too controversial to be carried out at that time. David M. L. Farr

See also CANADA. In WORLD BOOK, see NEW BRUNSWICK.
NEW HAMPSHIRE. See STATE GOVERNMENT.
NEW JERSEY. See STATE GOVERNMENT.
NEW MEXICO. See STATE GOVERNMENT.
NEW YORK. See NEW YORK CITY; STATE GOV'T.

NEW YORK CITY

NEW YORK CITY government in 1986 was shaken by its worst scandals in half a century. A series of disclosures of bribery and fraud began in January, when federal and local investigators alleged there was widespread corruption in the awarding of private collection contracts by the city's Parking Violations Bureau (PVB).

Queens Borough President Donald R. Manes, who was accused of accepting bribes from collection companies, resigned his post on February 11, then committed suicide on March 13. Geoffrey G. Lindenauer, a deputy director of the PVB, pleaded guilty to bribery charges and turned state's evidence in exchange for immunity. Several others, including Bronx Democratic Party leader Stanley M. Friedman, were indicted in April. On November 25, a jury convicted Friedman and three other former officials of racketeering, bribery, and fraud.

Real estate developer John A. Zaccaro, husband of 1984 Democratic vice presidential candidate Geraldine A. Ferraro, was charged on October 9 with attempted extortion. The indictment charged that Zaccaro, along with Manes, had asked for a $1-million bribe from a cable television company in exchange for a contract in Queens. Zaccaro pleaded innocent, and Ferraro accused the prosecutor of being politically motivated.

Other Crimes. Rudolph W. Giuliani, U.S. attorney for the Southern District of New York, who personally prosecuted the Friedman case, chalked up another conviction in November. He and his assistants won convictions of three top bosses and five lieutenants representing four of New York City's five so-called crime families. See COURTS.

A report released in August showed that in the first five months of 1986 there was an 8.4 per cent rise in major crimes in New York City over the same period in 1985. Murders were up 29.8 per cent overall, and up 82.5 per cent in certain high-crime areas of Manhattan. Police speculated that as many as 63 per cent of the murders were drug related. Robberies increased almost 16 per cent.

A New Convention Center named for former U.S. Senator Jacob K. Javits (R., N.Y.) opened in April. The man for whom the $486-million facility was named had died on March 7. In its first six months of operation, the Javits Center drew 1 million conventioneers and tourists.

On April 25, the owners of Madison Square Garden announced plans to demolish it and build twin office towers. A new Madison Square Garden would be constructed two blocks west.

And to the delight of New York ice skaters, the Wollman Memorial Rink in Central Park resumed operating in November for the first time since 1980. The outdoor rink, the largest in North America, had been rebuilt in 3½ months by real estate developer Donald J. Trump.

Runners surge past the Jacob K. Javits Convention Center in New York City in March at the start of a race heralding the center's April opening.

In autumn 1986, demolition began on an adult-entertainment theater on Broadway to make way for a 46-story hotel. This was heralded as continuing the revitalization of Times Square.

Mayor Edward I. Koch was sworn in on January 1 for a third four-year term. He pledged to tackle the city's tough budget problems in the face of massive losses in federal aid. On June 28, the City Council approved a $21.5-billion budget.

Statue of Liberty. An estimated 10 million tourists visited New York City for the dedication of the refurbished Statue of Liberty on the July 4 weekend. See Close-Up.

In contrast, the 100th birthday of the statue was marked by a quiet ceremony on October 28. About 1,500 people attended the official birthday party.

Traffic in New York City rose to record levels in 1986, prompting authorities to consider a number of drastic solutions to curb the volume. An average of 750,000 cars poured into midtown and lower Manhattan each business day.

As a result, traffic authorities announced that emergency plans may be implemented in 1987. They included a ban on single-occupant cars or a fee of $10 a day for motorists entering the central business district.   Owen Moritz

See also CITY. In WORLD BOOK, see NEW YORK CITY.

Lady Liberty's Birthday Bash

The rockets' red glare and bombs bursting in the air around the Statue of Liberty on July 4, 1986, gave proof in the night that Americans know how to throw a party. To celebrate the 100th birthday of Lady Liberty, Americans mounted a four-day, $30-million extravaganza in New York City that seemed to be equal parts patriotic fervor and show-biz razzmatazz. Never mind that the statue's real birthday wasn't until October 28. The Fourth of July was the perfect time to pay tribute to this most American symbol.

Liberty Weekend kicked off on July 3 with the unveiling of the statue, which had undergone a $69.8-million restoration. Beginning in 1983, craftworkers replaced the statue's corroded iron framework, fashioned a new torch,

Fireworks—part of the largest display in U.S. history—shower the Statue of Liberty in a dazzling 100th birthday celebration.

installed new elevators, and fitted the crown with new stairs and windows.

At the opening ceremonies, President Ronald Reagan played host to France's President François Mitterrand, whose country gave the United States the statue in 1886. After the speeches, the music, and the presentation of awards, Reagan pushed a button that sent a laser beam across the harbor to Liberty Island, where the statue stands. The beam triggered lights that illuminated the statue in stages and finally lit her upraised torch. Later that evening, 25,000 new citizens, including 200 on Ellis Island, the old immigrant entry station, were sworn in.

During Liberty Weekend, 50 blocks of lower Manhattan were closed to traffic for Harbor Festival '86, the largest street fair in U.S. history. Millions of people sampled ethnic delicacies and old-fashioned American hot dogs, visited sailing ships and naval vessels from around the world, and partied on the more than 30,000 pleasure boats that crammed the harbor.

Other events included barge and blimp races, a swimming-biking-running race from the statue to the Liberty Bell in Philadelphia more than 100 miles (160 kilometers) away, and a concert in Central Park. On a more serious note, a conference pondered "Liberty: The Next 100 Years." Across the United States, people watched the festivities on television.

On July 4, 2 million people jammed the shores of New York Harbor to watch the greatest fireworks display in U.S. history. Forty thousand projectiles were launched from 32 barges during a dazzling 28-minute light show.

On July 5, first lady Nancy Reagan cut a red, white, and blue ribbon to officially open the Statue of Liberty, closed to visitors since June 23, 1985. She then read a poem by Brad Travis, a fourth-grader from Bastrop, La. It said:

> Oh, Lady Liberty, teach me to see
> Where I need to go and what to be.
> Let me be like you,
> Tall and proud and free.

The weekend's grand finale was a three-hour spectacular at Giants Stadium in New Jersey. It featured a cast of 6,000, including an 800-member chorus and 75 Elvis Presley imitators. The spectacle took place on a 20-tiered motorized stage—the largest outdoor stage ever constructed—with fountains and a 12-story waterfall.

Not everyone was enthusiastic about the festivities. Some complained that the hoopla was tasteless and that it trivialized the real meaning of liberty. Some said that the United States has yet to fulfill liberty's promise for all her citizens. But most Americans rejoiced, enjoying the opportunity to celebrate a beloved symbol and, simply, to have a grand time.   Barbara A. Mayes

NEW ZEALAND. The Labour Party government headed by Prime Minister David R. Lange pressed ahead in 1986 with its conservative economic policies and its antinuclear foreign policy.

Economy. The government's economic policies of cutting public spending and curbing union wage demands led to some successes in 1986. Inflation fell in the first quarter of the year to an annual rate of approximately 10 per cent, compared with 17 per cent a year earlier. Interest rates also registered a decline from the record levels of the previous 12 months but still remained high. On the negative side, agriculture remained depressed, as farmers suffered the impact of low export prices, high interest rates, and the loss of agricultural subsidies.

The 1986-1987 budget presented in July provided for a 10.8 per cent increase in expenditures and a 14.9 per cent increase in revenue, with an estimated deficit of $2.5 billion New Zealand dollars ($NZ1 = U.S. 53 cents as of Dec. 31, 1986). The budget also provided for a major restructuring of $NZ7.2 billion in debts stemming from several major energy and heavy industrial projects that were underwritten by the previous New Zealand government.

A major change in the tax system occurred on October 1 with the introduction of a 10 per cent sales tax on all goods and services. This new tax was accompanied by significant reductions in personal income tax.

The government continued its radical economic restructuring of the public sector in 1986. Postal services, telecommunications, electric utilities, and forestry operations were transferred to new public business corporations and required to operate on a self-supporting basis.

Foreign Affairs. Relations with the United States remained strained over the government's policy of banning nuclear-armed or nuclear-powered ships from New Zealand ports. The United States formally suspended its military obligations to New Zealand under the ANZUS (*Australia, New Zealand, United States*) mutual defense treaty on August 11. New Zealand and Australia retained military ties outside the ANZUS pact.

The dispute with France over the 1985 bombing of the Greenpeace environmental group's ship *Rainbow Warrior* in Auckland Harbor by French agents was settled in July 1986. Under the settlement, New Zealand transferred to French custody two French agents who had been sentenced to 10 years in prison for their role in the bombing. France agreed to hold the agents for three years on a remote South Pacific island. In return, France formally apologized to New Zealand and paid $NZ13 million in compensation. David A. Shand

See also ASIA (Facts in Brief Table). In WORLD BOOK, see NEW ZEALAND.

NEWFOUNDLAND. Premier Brian Peckford's Progressive Conservative administration faced a bitter strike by public employees on two occasions in 1986. On March 3, some 600 highway maintenance workers left their jobs—defying a court injunction restricting strikes by essential workers—and demanded wage parity with other government employees. Later that month, nearly 3,500 public servants joined the strike.

The employees agreed to return to work on April 6 but walked out again on September 3, claiming that the government had not lived up to pledges made in discussions. Newfoundland's four largest religious denominations proposed that an independent monitoring commission be created to work with the parties to settle the dispute. The plan was accepted, and the strikers returned to their jobs on September 29.

The province's inshore fisheries continued to decline during 1986. Cod stocks were down significantly, and fishing crews' incomes fell by 50 per cent. The fishing industry union charged that shore fishing was being destroyed by large offshore trawlers and foreign ships, and demanded better management of the volume and types of fish that could be taken. On September 28, the federal government announced that a study of cod stocks would be undertaken. David M. L. Farr

In WORLD BOOK, see NEWFOUNDLAND.

NEWSMAKERS OF 1986 included the following:

It Made His Day. Motion-picture star Clint Eastwood, 56, was elected mayor of Carmel-by-the-Sea, Calif., in April, in an election that drew hundreds of news reporters and thousands of tourists to the scenic coastal town. Eastwood defeated incumbent mayor Charlotte Townsend, a retired librarian, who had blocked his attempt in 1985 to construct an office building in the town, which is noted for its quaint cottages and art galleries. During the campaign, the actor cast himself as a battler against bureaucracy, similar to some of his film roles. Asked if his election was the beginning of a political career like that of President Ronald Reagan, another actor turned politician, Eastwood replied, "This is where it stops."

Hail and Farewell to Halley's. "Like a headlight in a London fog," commented one observer. "A spot of spilled milk," said another. "A dull, smudgy, little old anticlimax," remarked still another. "That's it?" cried a woman standing on a hilltop near Cusco, Peru. "That's all there is? I came 4,000 miles to see this crummy little fuzzball?" It, of course, was Halley's Comet, and tens of thousands of people flocked to remote sites in the Southern Hemisphere to get the best possible view of this newsmaker as it passed closest to Earth in April. Some 18,000 people journeyed to isolated Alice Springs in Australia's rugged outback, where the view was touted as ideal. Although data from five spacecraft that monitored Halley's Comet proved a bonanza to scientists (see ASTRONOMY), the view from the ground was less than spectacular. "I just about cried," said a Los Angeles woman who spent $3,500 to see the comet from Alice Springs, only to find it comparable to what she had seen in the United States.

An American in Paris. His name sounded French, but Greg LeMond, 25, who lives near Sacramento, Calif., was definitely an American—the first American, in fact, to win the Tour de France. Regarded as the most prestigious bicycle race in the world, the Tour had been won by a European every year since it began in 1903. LeMond breezed past the finish line on the Champs Élysées in Paris on July 27. He beat his closest rival and teammate Bernard Hinault of France, who had won the Tour five times previously, by 3 minutes and 10 seconds. LeMond's time for the 2,500-mile (4,000-kilometer) race, which courses through the Alps and the Pyrenees, was 110 hours 35 minutes 19 seconds.

Some Like It Wilder. Billy Wilder, 80, who had the rare ability as a motion-picture director and writer to create both profound drama and hilarious comedy, received the American Film Institute's 14th Life Achievement Award in March. During his long career, Wilder won two and shared three Academy Awards. His work ranged from the drama of an alcoholic in *The Lost Weekend* (1945) to the seriocomic *The Apartment* (1960) to the farcical *Some Like It Hot* (1959) and the romantic *Sabrina* (1954).

Youth on Youth. Cyrille de Vignemont, 15, became the youngest ministerial aide in the French government in April when he was appointed special consultant to the Ministry of Civil Service and Planning. De Vignemont will advise the French government on the views of young people. He first caught the public eye at the age of 13 when he developed a computer program and sold it to Apple Computer Incorporated. As a minor, De Vignemont cannot earn a salary, but he was reportedly doing well from the sales of his computer program and was quite protective of his money—"my parents better not touch it."

A Mouthful. Jon Pennington, 14, of Mechanicsburg, Pa., won the 1986 National Spelling Bee in May by correctly spelling *odontalgia,* which means *toothache.* Second place went to Kenneth Larson, 13, of North Miami Beach, Fla.

Bureaucratic Roadblock in Space. A Florida company that offers "burials" in outer space was charged in March with operating an unlicensed cemetery. The Florida State Comptroller's office said the company, Celestis Group Incorporated, was in violation of a state law that requires a cemetery to have a paved road leading from a public

TV newswoman Maria Shriver, daughter of Sargent and Eunice Shriver, poses with actor Arnold Schwarzenegger after their wedding in April.

Recasting the Man of Steel

In 1985, they tried to change Coke. In 1986, they changed Superman—that strange visitor from another planet who came to Earth with powers and abilities far beyond those of mortal men.

DC Comics Incorporated, Superman's publisher, changed the comic-book hero because he was fighting a losing battle at the newsstand. In the 1950's, eight different comic books featured Superman, and some of them sold more than 1 million copies every month. In early 1986, however, the number of books was down to three; and, according to some estimates, the most popular sold only about 300,000 copies per month.

What went wrong? Announcing the change, DC's president, Jenette Kahn, noted, "The Man of Steel has a bit of rust on him."

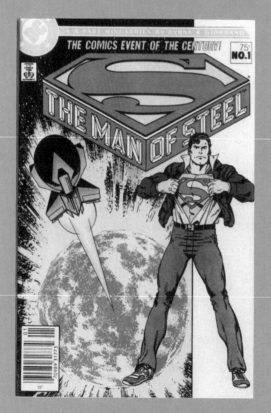

A new Superman introduces himself to the planet Earth in the first of six special comic books that were published in 1986.

Superman first appeared in a comic book in 1938. Forty-eight years of publishing had generated a vast amount of "plot baggage," including alternate Earths and other fantastic worlds; various forms of *kryptonite*, the only substance that could harm Superman; and numerous complications in the history of the Man of Steel.

In addition, Superman had accomplished some unbelievably stupendous feats, even for a being with powers far beyond those of mortal men. For example, he had traveled into the past by flying faster than the speed of light.

Superman also may have suffered from a lack of personal charm. As Superman, he fought evil in a businesslike manner. Disguised as newspaper reporter Clark Kent, he was mild-mannered to the point of apparent timidity.

DC shed all the "baggage" to make the Man of Steel's universe more familiar—it became *our* universe—and adjusted his powers and personality to make him less fantastic as Superman and more engaging as Kent. The publisher, in effect, started Superman all over again in 1986. DC suspended the three comic books that featured Superman and published a six-issue biweekly series retelling the legend of the Man of Steel's origin and early years. DC then resumed publication of three Superman comic books.

The Superman that emerged from the biweekly series was not so powerful as the old Superman had been, and the new Clark Kent was not so mild as his predecessor. The new Kent is a likable young man—courteous, but not meek; intelligent, but fully capable of making little mistakes; and open about his feelings, with a desire to be accepted as a human being.

In a major change, the Superman-Kent character no longer has a "split personality," with Superman as the real person and Kent as a disguise displaying an artificial personality. The real person is now Kent, and Superman is Kent in disguise.

DC also adjusted the personality of the female lead in the Superman drama—Kent's newspaper colleague, reporter Lois Lane. She is now a hard-driving reporter who respects Kent and considers him a serious professional rival. In the previous comic books, Kent—to borrow a phrase from comedian Rodney Dangerfield—"didn't get no respect" from Lane.

And respect is what the change was all about. DC wanted comic-book readers to respect Superman-Clark Kent as a modern, likable character who behaves in an admirable and believable way in a contemporary setting. By recasting the Man of Steel, DC Comics hoped to see a turnaround in the never-ending battle at the newsstand—and faster than a speeding bullet, if possible.

Jay Myers

highway. The Celestis Group offers to place the cremated remains of deceased people in permanent orbit around Earth for $3,900, or "burial" in deep space for $4,600. Access is achieved by a rocket launching, rather than a public highway.

Shipwrecked but What the Heck. Boatswain Leslie McNish said she proposed to first mate John (Sugar) Flanagan while they spent 4½ days together in a life raft after being shipwrecked in May. The two were crew members on the schooner *Pride of Baltimore*, which sank during a storm in the Atlantic Ocean. The most perilous moment came soon after the shipwreck, as they struggled to inflate their raft in fierce winds and rough seas. "I turned to Sugar," McNish related, "and I said, 'If we ever get out of this, we're going to get married.'" Flanagan replied, "Sure. What the heck." In August, the couple, who had known each other since 1982, were married.

Record-Breaking Elm Tree. Since the 1800's, Kansas has boasted the biggest American elm tree in the United States—the 99-foot-tall (30-meter) Louis Vieux, named for the pioneer who owned it. But in 1986, Louis Vieux's recordholding status was toppled by a 125-foot (38-meter) elm in Virginia, according to the American Forestry Association. The association keeps a record of the largest living specimens of some 650 species of trees in the United States. The height, circumference, and spread of the trees' branches are considered in determining the champions.

Voyager's Voyage. The experimental aircraft *Voyager* landed at Edwards Air Force Base in California on December 23, completing the first unrefueled nonstop flight around the world. Pilots Richard G. Rutan, 48, and Jeana Yeager, 34, completed the 9-day 3-minute 44-second flight despite turbulent winds and confinement to a cockpit the size of a telephone booth.

Shcharansky Wins Freedom. Soviet human rights activist Anatoly B. Shcharansky, 38, walked across the Glienicke Bridge and into West Berlin in February and became a free man. Shcharansky was released as part of an East-West prisoner exchange after human rights groups had campaigned for his freedom for eight years. Shcharansky had pressed for the right of Jews to emigrate from the Soviet Union. Known as a leading dissident, he was arrested in 1978 and charged with being a spy for the U.S. Central Intelligence Agency, a charge that he denied. Soon after his release, Shcharansky was reunited with his wife, Avital, whom he had not seen for 12 years.

Rite of Passage. Prince Makhosetive Dlamini, 18, of Swaziland became the world's youngest monarch in April when he assumed the throne as King Mswati III in a secret tribal rite. The teenaged king, who had been attending a boarding school in England, assumed the royal throne ear-

Voyager, piloted by Richard Rutan and Jeana Yeager, lands in California in December after making the first nonstop global unrefueled flight.

lier than had been expected because of unrest in Swaziland. The prince was to have become the reigning monarch on his 21st birthday. King Mswati succeeded his father, King Sobhuza II, who died in 1982.

Retired, but Not Retiring. Rear Admiral Grace Murray Hopper retired from the Navy at age 79 in August. She was the Navy's oldest officer on active duty. During her illustrious career, Hopper was a pioneer in the development of computers. She worked on the first large-scale computer and helped develop the computer language known as COBOL. Despite her retirement, Hopper planned to remain active by lecturing and keeping up with her field. "The day I stop learning is the day I die," she said.

It's a Small World, After All. They started from different places, on different days, and though their uncoordinated routes traversed hundreds of thousands of square miles of Arctic wilderness, they ran into each other. The odds of such an incredible coincidence were estimated at a million to one, but then their feats were incredible, too.

A party of six explorers, led by Will R. Steger, 41, and Paul Schurke, 30, both of Ely, Minn., encountered French explorer Jean-Louis Étienne on April 8 as Étienne was attempting to be the first to make it to the North Pole on his own power. The Steger-Schurke team was attempting to reach the

Having a Good Time for a Good Cause

In the United States, people are often urged to join hands in support of a cause, but in 1986 they were asked to do so literally. And so, on Memorial Day weekend—the afternoon of Sunday, May 25—they did. More than 5 million Americans of all ages linked hands to form a human chain across the United States. There were many sizable gaps in the chain, but Hands Across America was one of the biggest mass-participation events in history nevertheless. Even President Ronald Reagan and his wife, Nancy, took part, as did a host of celebrities.

By the time Hands Across America came together, a new word—*megaevent*—had been coined to describe the mammoth happenings that were occurring with increasing frequency in the United States and Europe. Megaevents ranged from rock concerts to athletic competitions to the human chain of Memorial Day weekend. Besides their sheer size, however, these extravaganzas shared a more basic element—charity. The avowed purpose of each enterprise was to benefit some needy group—the homeless, destitute farmers, or, most frequently, African famine victims.

It was the plight of the starving masses of

Singer Kenny Rogers (wearing cap) joins hands with other Hands Across America participants at the Texas-New Mexico border on May 25.

Ethiopia and other drought-stricken African nations that led to the megaevent craze. The first stirrings came in late 1984 when a group of British musicians, assembled by Irish rock star Bob Geldof, formed a musical group called Band Aid to raise money for famine relief.

Inspired by Band Aid, 46 rock and pop singers in the United States joined forces in January 1985 under the name USA for Africa to record the song "We Are the World." Together, Band Aid and USA for Africa raised more than $60 million for famine sufferers.

It appeared the public was ready to donate to a good cause, especially if it got something—an album, a T-shirt, or just a few hours of diversion—in return. Examining the possibilities, Geldof hit on the idea of staging a benefit rock concert to raise even more money for hungry Africans. But what a rock concert! Live Aid was the largest one-day event in music history. For 17 hours on July 13, 1985, more than 60 bands, featuring many of the top names in the rock world, performed at stadiums in London and Philadelphia. The transatlantic show was broadcast live on radio and television to more than 1½ billion people in 152 countries. Live Aid raised some $60 million for famine victims.

If Africans could be helped, why not needy groups in the United States—hard-pressed farmers and the urban poor, to name just two. By the end of 1985, organizers in the United States had staged Farm Aid—a 14-hour televised concert in Champaign, Ill.—and were planning several other events to benefit the homeless, hungry, and drug-addicted. Hands Across America, Comic Relief, The Concert That Counts—seemingly every week, promoters heralded a new megaevent.

But already, skeptics were raising questions about the new trend. Were megaevents animated solely by the spirit of giving, or was self-promotion an equally important element? The doubters pointed out that bands, celebrities, and record companies received millions of dollars worth of free advertising and public relations from their participation in megaevents.

And there was another question: Was anyone really being helped? In some cases, megaevents failed to raise the amount of money that organizers had hoped for. Hands Across America, for example, fell $30 million short of its $50-million goal. Even when goals were reached, the social problems being addressed dwarfed the sums of money donated to ease them. The contributions would help, of course, but many observers felt that it would take more than rock concerts to solve society's serious problems. A desperately ill patient, they said, cannot be restored to health with a Band-Aid.   David L. Dreier

A U.S.-Canadian expedition trudges over the frozen Arctic Ocean on its way to becoming, in May, the first group to reach the North Pole by dog sled since 1909.

pole by dog sled and without outside navigational aid for the first time since Robert E. Peary did it in 1909. Both succeeded.

The Steger-Schurke team also included Ann Bancroft, 30, who became the first woman to walk to the North Pole; Brent Boddy, 31; Geoff Carroll, 35; and Richard Weber, 26. All six—two others were unable to complete the journey—reached the pole on May 1 after 56 days. Étienne reached the pole, traveling by skis and pulling a sled, on May 11 after a journey that began on March 9.

Chip off the Old Disk. Pop singer Whitney Houston, 23, was not exactly unfamiliar with the music scene when she won two American Music Awards in January and a Grammy as best pop female vocalist in February. She comes from a musical family. Her mother is Cissy Houston, a gospel singer and backup vocalist to Aretha Franklin and other artists. Whitney's musical family also includes first cousin Dionne Warwick. "Blues"-blooded Whitney emerged in 1986 as a leading pop singer with four singles in the top five and a *platinum* (million-seller) debut album, *Whitney Houston.* Among her top songs were "Saving All My Love for You" and "Greatest Love of All."

Broker's Return on Investment. Texas broker Roy Whetstine turned a $10 investment into a $2.28-million fortune. Whetstine was not a stockbroker speculating on a new company, however,

but a gemstone broker who spotted what turned out to be the world's largest star sapphire at a rock and gemstone show in Tucson, Ariz., in February. The amateur rock collector who sold the sapphire came down from his original $15 price because the lavender gray stone with a hint of cornflower blue was not "as pretty as the others" he had on display in a Tupperware dish. Whetstine had immediately recognized the potato-sized stone as a sapphire and later learned that it weighed 1,905 carats (381 grams) in the rough—the largest ever.

Two Weddings in 1986 drew the Kennedy family and a flock of other celebrities to Cape Cod, Massachusetts. The brides were Maria Shriver, a television newswoman, and Caroline Bouvier Kennedy, a law student—cousins who took turns serving as each other's bridal attendant.

Shriver, 30, the daughter of Eunice Kennedy Shriver and former Peace Corps director Sargent Shriver, married Austrian-born actor Arnold Schwarzenegger, 38, in April. The reception was held at the Kennedy family's summer home in Hyannis, Mass.

Kennedy, 28, the daughter of Jacqueline Kennedy Onassis and President John F. Kennedy, married Edwin A. Schlossberg, 42, the son of a textile manufacturer, in July. The church was decorated with flowers and trees native to Cape Cod. Behind the altar were bay trees, delphinium, white

Three Dutch balloonists lift off from St. John's, Canada, in August. The trio went on to set a record for an Atlantic balloon crossing, 51 hours 14 minutes.

summer lilies, cornflowers, oak leaves, and Queen Anne's lace. The bride was given away by her uncle, Senator Edward M. Kennedy (D., Mass.).

Used Car Goes for $6.5 Million. Jerry J. Moore, 58, of Houston, in June paid the highest price on record for an automobile—$6.5 million for a 1931 Bugatti Royale. The French-made, black-and-yellow oversized coupe is one of only six in the world. That rarity made for some tense bidding during an auction in Reno, Nev. Moore, a shopping-center developer, was locked in a bidding war with William Lyon, chairman of a West Coast airline, until Moore topped Lyon's offer of $6.45-million. Moore later disclosed that he was prepared to go as high as $10 million for the Bugatti Royale because he said he wanted to be "the only kid on the block that has one."

Life in the Trees. In the spring of 1986, a bizarre scene took place in New York City's Central Park. Patrol officers from the city's Parks Department surrounded a beech tree as Bob Redman, 22, descended from his five-room, split-level house in the top branches. For the Parks Department, it was the completion of an eight-year investigation. For Redman, it was his 13th tree house, the previous 12 having been torn down by the Parks Department as they pursued Central Park's elusive tree dweller. After explaining that he liked to live in trees for the "solitude it gave him," Redman of-

fered to help the park officials dismantle his rugged and well-built creation. When park officials saw Redman scamper nimbly up the tree, they decided not to arrest him. Instead, they offered him a job—as a tree pruner.

Back in the U.S.A. Svetlana Alliluyeva, 60, daughter of Soviet dictator Joseph Stalin, returned to her former home in Spring Green, Wis., in April, after abandoning the Soviet Union for the second time. "I will never go back to Russia," Alliluyeva told *The Washington Post*. Alliluyeva originally defected from the Soviet Union in 1967. She spent 17 years in the West, mostly in the United States, where she obtained citizenship. She returned to the Soviet Union in 1984, saying she wished to be near her children from previous marriages. On her return, Alliluyeva said, "I know that the people who care for me are in America."

Bicycle Crashes Speed Barrier. In 1984, E. I. du Pont de Nemours & Company offered a prize of $18,000 to the first person to drive a human-powered vehicle at least 65 miles (105 kilometers) per hour on level ground and without the aid of a strong wind or another vehicle. In May 1986, Fred Markham, 29, of Aptos, Calif., claimed the prize money. Markham's bicycle, enclosed in a streamlined, aerodynamic shell and pedaled from a lying-down position, broke the speed barrier during a run at Big Sand Flat, California. Rod Such

NEWSPAPER. The wave of purchases, mergers, and fold-ups that struck the United States newspaper industry in 1985 continued in full force in 1986, fueling concern that the traditional competition of the U.S. press was being weakened. The wave hit two old-time newspaper families. On January 9, a long feud between brother and sister led the Bingham family to announce that it would sell *The* (Louisville, Ky.) *Courier-Journal* and *The Louisville Times*, newspapers that had been in the family since 1918. In mid-May, Gannett Company, the largest U.S. newspaper chain, bought the papers for about $300 million. On May 28, the Times Mirror Company bought the family-owned A. S. Abell Company, publisher of *The* (Baltimore) *Sun* and *The Evening Sun*, for $600 million.

In St. Louis, Mo., a dispute among the descendants of newspaper pioneer Joseph Pulitzer almost led to the sale of the *St. Louis Post-Dispatch*. On February 19, Detroit builder A. Alfred Taubman offered $500 million for the Pulitzer family company that publishes the paper. He later increased his bid to $650 million. After a court fight, however, Taubman ended the take-over attempt in late September.

Other Sales. On June 26, the Times Mirror Company agreed to sell its faltering *Dallas Times Herald* to a group headed by 34-year-old William

Dean Singleton for $110 million. On July 2, investors led by *Chicago Sun-Times* publisher Robert E. Page bought that newspaper from News America Holdings, Incorporated, for $145 million. News America is owned by Australian-born newspaper magnate Rupert Murdoch. On October 27, Knight-Ridder Newspapers, Incorporated, announced a preliminary agreement to buy State-Record Company of Columbia, S.C., publisher of six daily newspapers and two weeklies in South Carolina and Mississippi.

Joint Operation. Two huge newspaper chains agreed in April to operate their competing newspapers in Detroit under a joint operating agreement. Under this arrangement, Knight-Ridder's *Detroit Free Press* and Gannett's *Detroit News* would share profits and equipment such as printing presses and delivery trucks, but their news staffs would continue to compete.

Down to One. Baltimore and St. Louis became one-newspaper cities in 1986. *The* (Baltimore) *News-American*, established in 1773, published its last issue on May 27, 1986, and the *St. Louis Globe-Democrat* ceased publication on October 29. The *Globe-Democrat* had suspended publication on Dec. 6, 1985, and restarted on Jan. 27, 1986, after a change of ownership.   Mark Fitzgerald

See also AWARDS AND PRIZES (Journalism Awards). In WORLD BOOK, see NEWSPAPER.

Copies of the last issue of the 213-year-old Baltimore *News-American* leave the loading dock on May 27, 1986.

NICARAGUA. Uncertainty arose in late 1986 over the fate of the four-year-old war waged against the Sandinista regime in Nicaragua by rebels known as *contras*. On November 25, officials of the Administration of United States President Ronald Reagan disclosed that profits from U.S. arms sales to Iran were secretly diverted to the contras in an apparent violation of a U.S. congressional ban. Contra officials denied any direct knowledge of the secret funding, which totaled between $10 million and $30 million.

The disclosure threatened to erode future funding for the contras, who have relied on the United States for military aid. "We may now be seen as nothing more than the pet project of a lame-duck President," a contra official said. See PRESIDENT OF THE UNITED STATES.

Ironically, the U.S. Congress voted to renew military aid for the contras months earlier when the Senate approved President Reagan's request for $100 million, of which $70 million was earmarked for military purposes. Military aid had been suspended following the disclosure in 1984 that the U.S. Central Intelligence Agency (CIA) had mined Nicaraguan harbors. Congress had also voted to prohibit the CIA from providing direct military assistance to the contras. The 1986 legislation removed this restriction when it became law on October 18.

Eugene Hasenfus, right, a U.S. citizen on trial in Nicaragua in November, looks at weapons he is charged with supplying to contra rebels.

Hasenfus Case. Evidence that this congressional ban on CIA assistance may have been violated before the new law took effect surfaced in October. On October 5, a C-123K cargo plane carrying supplies to contra forces was shot down in southern Nicaragua. Two U.S. citizens died in the crash, though a third, Eugene Hasenfus, 45, of Marinette, Wis., a former Marine Corps parachute rigger, survived. At a news conference on October 9 in Managua, Nicaragua's capital, Hasenfus said that the supply flight was under the direct supervision of CIA agents operating out of El Salvador. On November 15, Hasenfus was convicted by the Anti-Somocista People's Tribunal—a political court—and sentenced to 30 years in prison. Reagan Administration officials denied any connection with the supply flight. On December 17, Nicaragua pardoned and released Hasenfus.

To Counter the Contras, Nicaragua maintained a military force estimated at 63,000, including reserves and militia, nearly twice as many as any of its Central American neighbors. Since conscription began in 1984, more than 7,000 Nicaraguans had completed two years of training and indoctrination and returned to civilian life. While in the service, many of these young people attended schools in Cuba, Eastern Europe, or the Soviet Union. On leaving the service, many obtained important jobs in government and business.

Economic Woes. Nicaragua's economy in 1986 continued to show the strains of large outlays for defense, which absorbed more than 25 per cent of the national budget. The Ministry of Trade reported that the country's cumulative trade deficit since Sandinista rule began in 1981 amounted to $2.7 billion. Nicaragua's foreign debt stood at $5.3 billion.

Nicaraguan private enterprise was increasingly wary of government promises to maintain a mixed economy. For example, when the Sandinistas came to power, Nicaragua had seven slaughterhouses in operation, and beef exports had tripled during the previous decade. By 1986, four slaughterhouses had closed, and the three remaining plants were state-owned and operating below capacity. Nicaraguan ranchers drove their animals across the borders to neighboring countries to sell them for 10 times more than they could receive under government-decreed prices in Nicaragua.

Since coming to power, the Sandinistas had by the end of 1986 put just three new factories into operation—a packaging plant, a milk-processing plant, and a sugar refinery, which produces sugar at more than double the world price. With little capital available for equipment, production in Nicaragua is often primitive, relying on unskilled workers, including children.   Nathan A. Haverstock

See also LATIN AMERICA (Facts in Brief Table). In WORLD BOOK, see NICARAGUA.

NICKLAUS, JACK (1940-   ), shot a four-round 279 to win an unprecedented sixth Masters golf tournament on April 13, 1986, at the Augusta National Golf Club in Georgia. Going into the final round of play, Nicklaus was 4 strokes behind third-round leader Greg Norman of Australia. But in an exciting 18-hole climax, he shot a 65 to capture the tournament by 1 stroke. At the age of 46, he was the oldest man ever to win a Masters.

Jack William Nicklaus was born in Columbus, Ohio, on Jan. 21, 1940. He began playing golf at the age of 10. While attending Ohio State University in Columbus, he won two U.S. Amateur titles, in 1959 and 1961. Playing as a professional in 1962, Nicklaus won his first U.S. Open. He won this event again in 1967, 1972, and 1980. He won the British Open in 1966, 1970, and 1978; the Professional Golfers' Association (PGA) tournament in 1963, 1965, 1966, 1972, and 1975; and the Masters tournament in 1963, 1965, 1966, 1972, and 1975. His 18 major professional tournament victories are a record, as are his more than $4.7 million in career earnings.

Nicklaus is nicknamed the "Golden Bear" for his blond hair and large, stocky frame. He and his wife, Barbara, have five children.   Kevin J. Hawker

See also GOLF. In WORLD BOOK, see NICKLAUS, JACK.

NIGER. See AFRICA.

NIGERIA. Debate on Nigeria's return to civilian rule, which the military government has promised will occur by October 1990, began in March 1986. Educators, lawyers, journalists, market vendors, and other citizens gave their views on provisions to be included in the future constitution.

Also in March, the government executed 10 military officers for taking part in an abortive coup in December 1985. Later in 1986, President Ibrahim Babangida, who seized power in an August 1985 coup, ended uncertainty about the fate of 1,017 civilian officials whom his government and the previous military government had accused of corruption. Former President Shehu Shagari was released in July but restricted to his home state and banned from national politics for life. Other officials were given reduced sentences and ordered to limit their political involvement. The leader whom Babangida deposed in 1985, Muhammadu Buhari, was apparently still under arrest in 1986.

Student Unrest. Police action in quelling a riot in May at Ahmadu Bello University in Zaria led to the death of 19 students. Demonstrations on other campuses to protest the deaths resulted in the temporary closing of nine universities.

Religious Conflict. In February, Babangida announced that Nigeria had joined the Organization of the Islamic Conference (OIC), an international body that promotes unity among Islamic countries. Babangida's action brought protests from many of Nigeria's Christians and practitioners of local religions, who together make up about 50 per cent of the population. The OIC decision followed earlier demands by Muslims, who predominate in the north, to increase Islamic influence throughout the country. To reassure citizens who feared that Nigeria was on the verge of becoming an officially Islamic nation, Babangida set up a commission to study OIC membership.

Economic Recovery. Declining world oil prices and a mounting trade deficit thwarted the hoped-for recovery of Nigeria's economy in 1986. At midyear, the Babangida regime introduced a number of austerity measures, including the elimination of gasoline subsidies and the creation of a revised foreign exchange system aimed at reducing the outflow of capital. Foreign creditors permitted Nigeria to reschedule interest payments on its $12-billion foreign debt.

Foreign Relations. In a move to strengthen regional economic cooperation, Nigeria reopened borders with all its neighbors except Chad. The borders were closed in 1984 to curb smuggling and illegal immigration. Diplomatic links with Great Britain, broken in 1984, were reestablished.   J. Gus Liebenow and Beverly B. Liebenow

See also AFRICA (Facts in Brief Table). In WORLD BOOK, see NIGERIA.

NIXON, RICHARD MILHOUS (1913-   ), 37th President of the United States, continued a low-key political comeback as "elder statesman" in 1986. In April, he addressed a San Francisco convention of North American newspaper publishers, and in July he met in Moscow with Soviet leader Mikhail S. Gorbachev. In his remarks at the San Francisco meeting, Nixon strongly endorsed U.S. support for rebel forces opposing the Soviet-backed government of Nicaragua. He said a rebel defeat would likely lead to Marxist guerrilla uprisings in other Central American nations and in Mexico.

On March 5, former Secretary of the Treasury William E. Simon, president of the Nixon Presidential Archives Foundation, said about $20 million had been raised to build a Nixon presidential library in San Clemente, Calif. Simon said construction was expected to begin in 1988, though an additional $5 million would be needed to complete the project.

Nixon was hospitalized briefly in January. Stopping at a Miami, Fla., hospital for a checkup after vacationing in the Bahamas, he was found to have influenza and was admitted for treatment.

Nixon's daughter Julie Eisenhower wrote a biography of her mother, Patricia Nixon, in 1986. The book, *Pat Nixon: The Untold Story,* was published in November.   Frank Cormier and Margot Cormier

In WORLD BOOK, see NIXON, RICHARD M.

NOBEL PRIZES

NOBEL PRIZES in peace, literature, economics, and the sciences were awarded in 1986 by the Norwegian Storting (parliament) in Oslo and by the Royal Academy of Science, the Caroline Institute, and the Swedish Academy of Literature, which are in Stockholm, Sweden.

The Peace Prize was awarded to Elie Wiesel, 58, a Jewish writer born in Romania who survived Nazi concentration camps during World War II to become a voice for those who perished at the hands of the Nazis. The Nobel committee lauded Wiesel, a naturalized United States citizen and author of 30 books, as a spiritual leader and a messenger to humankind, whose "message is one of peace, atonement, and human dignity."

In 1944, Wiesel and his family were sent to Auschwitz and Buchenwald—two Nazi death camps—where his parents and his younger sister died. In 1958, *La Nuit* (*Night*), Wiesel's account of Auschwitz and how the ordeal turned his life into "one long night," was published.

The Literature Prize was given to Wole Soyinka, 52, a Nigerian poet, playwright, and novelist who has championed the freedom of black Africans. Soyinka, the son of a schoolteacher and a businesswoman, and a member of the Yoruba ethnic group, was educated in Nigeria and England. He is the first African to win the literature prize.

Elie Wiesel enjoys a celebratory moment with his wife and son in New York City in October after learning he had won the Nobel Peace Prize.

Much of Soyinka's published work—about 20 volumes, all in English—deals with the myths and culture of the Yoruba people. Two of Soyinka's plays, *Death and the King's Horseman* and *A Dance of the Forests*, were singled out for special praise by the Nobel committee.

The Chemistry Prize was shared by three scientists—two United States citizens and a Canadian. The winners were Dudley R. Herschbach, 54, of Harvard University in Cambridge, Mass.; Yuan T. Lee, 49, of the University of California at Berkeley; and John C. Polanyi, 57, of the University of Toronto, Canada. They were honored for developing theories and experimental tools in the 1950's and 1960's to determine what happens between atoms—particularly the flow of energy around atoms—during a chemical reaction.

Herschbach invented a procedure called the *crossed molecular beam technique*, in which beams of molecules are fired at supersonic speeds in a vacuum chamber. As the molecules collide and recombine, the recombined molecules are analyzed for clues about the changes that occur during chemical reaction.

Lee, who was born in Taiwan, joined Herschbach's laboratory team in the 1960's. He further developed the crossed beam method, greatly expanding the technique.

Polanyi, born in Germany of Hungarian parents, discovered that tiny bursts of infrared light emitted during a chemical reaction—a process called *chemiluminescence*—could provide clues to how atoms changed during the reaction.

The Economics Prize went to James McGill Buchanan, 67, of George Mason University in Fairfax, Va., for his work applying economic principles to political problems. He is one of the leading proponents of the controversial "public choice theory," which proposes that politicians and governments, like consumers, choose policies based on self-interest.

The Physics Prize went to three pioneers in microscope design. Half of the prize was awarded to Ernst Ruska, 79, of the Fritz Haber Institute in West Berlin, West Germany. The other half was shared by Gerd Binnig, 39, of West Germany, and Heinrich Rohrer, 53, of Switzerland, both at the IBM Research Laboratory in Zurich, Switzerland.

Ruska was recognized for his invention of the electron microscope in 1931, which permitted scientists to peer at viruses and other previously invisible objects for the first time. Rohrer and Binnig were honored for their 1981 invention of the *scanning tunneling microscope*, which made it possible to map the surface structures—showing individual atoms—of various substances.

The Physiology or Medicine Prize was shared by two scientists—Rita Levi-Montalcini, 77, of the Institute of Cell Biology in Rome, who holds both

United States and Italian citizenship, and Stanley Cohen, 63, of Vanderbilt University of Tennessee. The Nobel committee said that the discoveries of the two scientists concerning natural substances that influence the growth of cells and the orderly development of tissues "opened new fields of widespread importance to basic science."

Levi-Montalcini was cited for her 1952 discovery of *nerve growth factor*, a protein that stimulates the growth of nerve cells. Cohen—who worked with Levi-Montalcini on early research on nerve growth factor—later discovered *epidermal growth factor*, a substance important in regulating the growth of many kinds of cells.

1985 Winners. The winners of Nobel Prizes in 1985 were the International Physicians for the Prevention of Nuclear War for peace, novelist Claude Simon of France for literature, Herbert A. Hauptman and Jerome Karle of the United States for chemistry, Italian-born Franco Modigliani of the United States for economics, Klaus von Klitzing of West Germany for physics, and Michael S. Brown and Joseph L. Goldstein of the United States for physiology or medicine.   Joan Stephenson

In WORLD BOOK, see NOBEL PRIZES.

NORTH ATLANTIC TREATY ORGANIZATION (NATO). See EUROPE.

NORTH CAROLINA. See STATE GOVERNMENT.

NORTH DAKOTA. See STATE GOVERNMENT.

NORTHERN IRELAND. Members of the two Protestant unionist parties in 1986 launched a campaign of protest, some of it violent, in an effort to destroy the Anglo-Irish Agreement. The agreement, which was signed by Great Britain and the Republic of Ireland in November 1985, gives the Republic of Ireland a voice in the affairs of Northern Ireland. The unionists want Northern Ireland to remain united with Great Britain, and oppose efforts to merge Northern Ireland with Ireland because they do not want to be a Protestant minority in a Roman Catholic nation.

The Protestant parties, the Official Unionist Party and the Democratic Unionist Party, formed a coalition to campaign against the agreement. Fifteen unionist members of the British Parliament (MP's) resigned their seats in November 1985 to protest the agreement and force an election on Jan. 23, 1986, that would stand as an unofficial vote on the pact. The voters reelected 14 of the 15 MP's who resigned, but the total vote for the unionists was much lower than they had hoped.

Agreement Protest. A one-day general strike, organized by unionists on March 3, degenerated into widespread violence. Tom King, secretary of state for Northern Ireland, denounced the unionist leaders for failing to control "the hoodlum element" during the protest. Unionist leaders threatened to withdraw from politics. A number of unionist-controlled local councils, including Belfast, suspended council business, forcing the British government to appoint its own commissioners to keep local services running.

Later in the year, the two unionist parties ordered all of their 330 councilors to resign their seats on November 15, the first anniversary of the signing of the Anglo-Irish Agreement. In the face of unionist opposition, British government ministers insisted that the British and Irish governments would continue to press ahead with implementing the agreement.

Death Threats. Roman Catholic workers in largely Protestant factories found themselves the victims of threats and discrimination in 1986. This prompted Harrison J. Goldin, comptroller of New York City, to call on the British government and Short Brothers, a Northern Ireland aircraft manufacturer, to take action against the Short People's Loyalist Council, which had issued the threats. New York City controls $250 million worth of investment in Northern Ireland by U.S. corporations. Death threats were issued, too, by the outlawed Irish Republican Army (IRA) against companies that provided services to Northern Ireland's police or to the British army in Northern Ireland.   Ian Mather

See also IRELAND. In WORLD BOOK, see NORTHERN IRELAND.

NORTHWEST TERRITORIES. Canada's North was dealt a staggering economic blow with the announcement on Aug. 25, 1986, that Gulf Canada Corporation would suspend its oil-drilling operations in the Beaufort Sea. Only weeks before, the company had disclosed plans to exploit a massive oil reservoir 75 kilometers (47 miles) north of the Arctic coastline. Plunging oil prices, high production costs, and economic uncertainty—combined with the federal government's refusal to extend grants for frontier oil exploration—ruined prospects for the project. Gulf stated that 750 jobs would be lost.

Earlier in 1986, Esso Resources Canada Limited and Dome Petroleum Limited revealed that their exploration efforts would also soon end, eliminating jobs for another 1,000 oil workers. Panarctic Oils Limited also canceled its exploration project in the Arctic islands.

Mary Simon, an Inuit (Eskimo) woman from Fort-Chimo in the Ungava Peninsula, was elected president of the Inuit Circumpolar Conference—the pan-Arctic Inuit movement—at its meeting in Alaska on August 3. Simon, who is the daughter of a white merchant and a non-English-speaking Inuit mother, will represent 115,000 Inuit people in Greenland, Canada, and Alaska.   David M. L. Farr

See also CANADA. In WORLD BOOK, see NORTHWEST TERRITORIES.

NORWAY. Prime Minister Kaare Willoch resigned on May 2, 1986, two days after losing a key vote in the Storting (parliament) on a proposal to hike gasoline taxes. Willoch lost by only 1 vote, 79 to 78. Willoch's center-right coalition had held on in the general election of September 1985 by the same margin—one seat.

New Leader. Gro Harlem Brundtland, the Labor Party leader, announced her decision to form a government on May 2, 1986. Brundtland had served briefly as Norway's first woman prime minister in 1981.

Brundtland took office on May 9, 1986, presenting a Cabinet of 8 women and 10 men. She faced a period of political difficulty because the Labor Party did not have a majority in the Storting. By law, Norway cannot hold another national election until 1989. See BRUNDTLAND, GRO HARLEM.

Early Devaluation. On May 11, 1986, the government announced a 12 per cent devaluation of the krone, Norway's currency. The devaluation made Norwegian goods cheaper in other countries. Brundtland said Norway's economy was out of control because of a collapse in oil prices. Norway is a major oil exporter, pumping tremendous amounts of petroleum from wells in the North Sea.

Oil and Gas. A strike in April removed 1 million barrels of oil per day from world output. After the strike ended, oil prospects worsened because of the plummeting price. By the end of August, 90 drilling rigs had been taken out of operation. On September 10, Norway announced that it would cut oil production to help boost world oil prices. On June 2, Norway closed a $60-billion deal to sell gas to Belgium, France, the Netherlands, and West Germany for 27 years, beginning in 1993.

Acid Rain. Great Britain's Prime Minister Margaret Thatcher faced demonstrations and riots when she visited Norway on Sept. 11 and 12, 1986. Thatcher announced a plan to spend $900-million in 10 years to curb the emission of sulfur dioxide from three coal-fired power stations in Britain. Norway has claimed that the emissions cause acid rain in Norway. Brundtland's attitude toward Thatcher was cool on the acid rain issue and on Britain's refusal to enact stiff sanctions against South Africa because of that country's policy of *apartheid* (racial separation).

Nationwide Lockouts put 100,000 people—about 10 per cent of Norway's labor force—out of work on April 8. The lockouts affected the metal, building and construction, hotel and restaurant, and chemical industries. A settlement on April 16 cut the average workweek from 40 hours to 37½ hours and hiked wages by about 40 cents per hour, beginning in 1987. Kenneth Brown

See also EUROPE (Facts in Brief Table). In WORLD BOOK, see NORWAY.

NOVA SCOTIA. Premier John Buchanan and his Progressive Conservative administration faced a barrage of opposition party criticism in 1986, much of it related to the conduct of one of Buchanan's close colleagues, former Culture Minister W. J. (Billy Joe) MacLean. Pleading guilty to charges of submitting forged documents on his expense account, MacLean was sentenced on October 3 to one day in jail and fined $6,000. On October 30, the legislature met in a special one-day session to expel MacLean.

The government's morale was also depressed by the announcement in September that Shell Canada Resources Limited would cease its oil exploration in the area, closing its Halifax shore base and withdrawing its last drilling rig from the Scotia Shelf. Shell's drill results had been marginal, revealing only small reserves of oil, and falling oil prices made it uneconomical to bring the gas reserves ashore.

A rich bed of fossils from a crucial turning point in biological history 200 million years ago was discovered on the north shore of the Minas Basin, an arm of the Bay of Fundy. The site contains thousands of fossil bones that may throw light on the theory of the mass extinction of dinosaurs through meteorite impact. David M. L. Farr

In WORLD BOOK, see NOVA SCOTIA.

NUCLEAR ENERGY. See ENERGY SUPPLY.

NUTRITION. The results of a 10-year study reported on Jan. 16, 1986, in *The New England Journal of Medicine* strongly suggest that heart disease prevention should begin in childhood. Researchers at the Louisiana State University Medical Center in New Orleans examined the heart and coronary arteries of people between the ages of 3 and 26 who died in Bogalusa, La. The most common causes of death were accidents, homicides, or suicides. The researchers evaluated the extent of *atherosclerosis*—a disease in which fatty deposits thicken and harden the walls of the arteries—and compared it with factors in the person's life style that may have caused or worsened the disease.

The researchers found evidence that high blood pressure and elevated blood cholesterol, particularly cholesterol carried in *low-density lipoproteins*, play an important role in the early development of atherosclerosis.

Obesity and Genetics. Albert J. Stunkard, an obesity researcher from the University of Pennsylvania in Philadelphia, and colleagues in Houston and in Copenhagen, Denmark, reported in *The New England Journal of Medicine* in January that genetic influences strongly determine a person's weight. Their study of 540 Danish adoptees found that a person's weight as an adult is similar to the weight of the person's biological parents and not to the weight of the adoptive parents. This conclu-

HERMAN®

© 1986 Universal Press Syndicate

4/25

Drawing by Jim Unger;
© Universal Press Syndicate

"You're not getting enough calcium."

sion, however, does not mean that obesity is determined only by genes. Family environment does have some effect, the researchers noted.

Weight Reduction. Overweight people with high blood pressure can greatly reduce the risk of dying from cardiovascular disease by reducing their weight, according to a February report by researchers from the University of New South Wales in Sydney, Australia. Overweight people with high blood pressure can suffer from a problem in which the left *ventricle* (chamber of the heart) becomes enlarged. Losing weight can decrease the size and thickness of the left ventricle, the researchers found, suggesting that heart damage caused by obesity can be reversed by weight loss. The moderate weight reduction seen in the study was also more effective in lowering blood pressure than was an antihypertensive drug.

Beneficial Fats. Research published in 1986 indicated that certain fats may be more beneficial than was previously thought. On March 20, Scott M. Grundy, a biochemist at the Veterans Administration Medical Center and the University of Texas Health Science Center, both in Dallas, reported that a diet rich in *oleic acid,* a monounsaturated fatty acid present in olive oil, actually reduced blood cholesterol levels more effectively than did a low-fat diet.

Low-fat diets have been recommended to keep

cholesterol levels down. But after following 11 patients with high cholesterol levels for 12 weeks on different diets, Grundy found that a diet rich in monounsaturated fatty acids might be an effective alternative as long as weight is controlled. The findings also may explain why people in Greece, Italy, and other areas where the traditional diet is high in olive oil tend to have low levels of blood cholesterol and a low incidence of heart disease.

The benefits of another fat—omega-3 fatty acids—also made headlines in 1986. On April 10, a study reported by researchers at Vanderbilt University in Nashville found that omega-3 fatty acids, a type of polyunsaturated fatty acid found in fish oils, wheat germ, soybeans, and other foods, may help prevent heart disease. Other research programs and clinical trials are underway worldwide to determine the role of these fatty acids in heart disease, cancer, and blood clotting.

Despite the possible benefits of a diet rich in monounsaturated and omega-3 fatty acids, medical experts warned consumers that further study is needed to determine the health risks of ingesting an excess amount of these oils. Of particular concern is the possibility of vitamin A and vitamin D poisoning if large quantities of fish oil or fish liver oil are taken. Jean Weininger

See also FOOD. In WORLD BOOK, see DIET; FAT; FOOD; NUTRITION.

OCEAN. In the spring of 1986, scientists drilled the first samples of zero-age rock from an ocean ridge. The drilling was part of the Ocean Drilling Program, a 10-year scientific research project that began in January 1985. Scientists on board the drill ship *JOIDES Resolution* returned to deepen a hole drilled in the winter of 1985-1986 on the crest of the Mid-Atlantic Ridge, about 1,200 miles (1,900 kilometers) southeast of Bermuda.

What is called *zero-age rock* can be up to 100,000 years old—a short period in geologic time. It is *lava rock*, formed when *magma* (molten rock) from deep within Earth flows up into cracks in the ridge crest, then cools and hardens. (Magma that reaches Earth's surface is known as *lava*.)

Zero-Age Rock is difficult to drill for two reasons. First, like certain older lava rock, it is extremely hard. And second, it has not existed long enough to become covered by a sedimentary layer. In ordinary ocean drilling, operators depend upon the thick sedimentary layer to keep the flexible drill pipe stable.

When the researchers on the *Resolution* drilled the original hole, they used a huge steel box to stabilize the drill. The box, called a *guide base*, has a funnel-shaped hole that guides the drill. The base is square, measures 18 feet (5.5 meters) on a side, and weighs 20 short tons (18 metric tons). The scientists lowered the base to the summit of a volcano on the ridge, 2 miles (3.2 kilometers) below the surface, then locked it into place with 50 short tons (45 metric tons) of cement.

On their return voyage in the spring, the researchers used a satellite navigation system to guide them to the exact location of the guide base. A television camera mounted on the end of the 10,000-foot (3,000-meter) drill pipe helped them to reinsert the drill bit into the hole. Scientists were eager to obtain samples of deep zero-age rocks to gain a better understanding of how magma originates and of the origin, nature, and evolution of new oceanic crust.

At a nearby site, scientists on board the deep-sea submersible *Alvin* located an area without sediment and without a lava cover. The absence of a lava cover made it relatively easy to drill out samples of the more crystalline rocks geologists believe are under all lava rocks that make up the highest layer of crust under the oceans.

Atlantic Geysers. On another spring expedition using *Alvin*, scientists explored the Mid-Atlantic Ridge in an area approximately 1,800 miles (2,900 kilometers) east of Miami, Fla. There, nearly 13,000 feet (4,000 meters) down, they made the first direct observations of hot geysers similar to those found previously in the Pacific Ocean.

The scientists saw swarms of a previously unknown variety of shrimp—tiny, blind animals that seemed to be feeding voraciously at the edge of the 660° F. (350° C) geysers. The researchers also discovered a six-sided creature about the size of a silver dollar. This animal may be a living representation of a species previously seen only as a fossil, 70 million to 350 million years old.

***Titanic* Photos.** In July, researchers headed by Robert D. Ballard of Woods Hole Oceanographic Institution in Massachusetts descended in the *Alvin* to the wreckage of the British luxury liner *Titanic*. In 1912, this huge vessel struck an iceberg about 500 miles (800 kilometers) off the coast of Newfoundland and sank in 12,500 feet (3,800 meters) of water. The exact location of the wreckage was unknown until Ballard discovered it in September 1985. At that time, Ballard viewed the wreckage through television cameras mounted on a remote-control submarine. No one had seen the wreckage directly until the July 1986 descent of the *Alvin*.

Ballard said there was no large gash in the ship's hull, contrary to what most analysts had expected. Instead, the collision apparently buckled plates in the riveted hull, allowing water to flood the ship. Ballard and his colleagues returned with 57,000 photographs and 140 videotapes.   Arthur G. Alexiou

In WORLD BOOK, see OCEAN.

OHIO. See STATE GOVERNMENT.

OKLAHOMA. See STATE GOVERNMENT.

OLD AGE. See SOCIAL SECURITY.

OLYMPIC GAMES. The International Olympic Committee (IOC), meeting in Lausanne, Switzerland, during October 1986, established a new schedule for the Olympic Games, chose sites for the 1992 games, and made new rulings concerning professional participation and eligibility.

The IOC voted to alternate the Summer Olympics and the Winter Olympics every two years, beginning in 1994. The new schedule will take effect after the 1992 Olympics, calling for Winter Games in 1994 and every four years thereafter, while the Summer Games will follow the present four-year schedule. The IOC devised the new schedule to focus more attention on the Winter Games, thereby generating more television coverage and more lucrative revenues.

With 85 of its 89 members casting secret ballots, the IOC chose the sites for the 1992 Olympics. Albertville, France, near Annecy, will host the 1992 Winter Games, and the Summer Games will be held in Barcelona, Spain.

Pros to Play. The IOC also adopted new eligibility rules that will allow amateur sports federations to admit professional athletes starting in 1988. In addition to ice hockey and soccer, professionals became eligible to compete in Olympic equestrian events and track and field competitions.

The United States Olympic Committee opposed an Olympics fully open to professionals but approved of professionals competing in Olympic sports in which they were not professionals. The International Federation of Association Football, soccer's world governing body, decided to follow its 1984 eligibility procedure, which allowed professionals to participate in the Olympics unless they had played World Cup matches for European or South American teams. The International Ice Hockey Federation also voted to allow professional participation in the Olympics.

North Korea continued its campaign in 1986 to host half of the 1988 Summer Games, which will be held in Seoul, South Korea, but the IOC and South Korea rejected the idea. The IOC proposed a compromise, allowing North Korea to stage four Olympic events—archery, cycling, soccer, and table tennis—but this overture was rejected. North Korea then threatened an Olympic boycott by Soviet-bloc nations.

Other Developments. On March 26, the National Broadcasting Company (NBC) signed an exclusive contract for United States radio, television, and cable broadcasting rights to the 1988 Olympic Games in Seoul. NBC agreed to pay $300 million to the IOC and the Seoul Olympic Organizing Committee for the rights.   Frank Litsky

In WORLD BOOK, see OLYMPIC GAMES.

OMAN. See MIDDLE EAST.

ONTARIO. The new Liberal government of Ontario, in office since June 26, 1985, experienced a tumultuous first year in power. As a minority government, the Liberals depended on the support of the New Democratic Party (NDP) to keep the Progressive Conservative (PC) Party in check.

A special election on April 17, 1986, to fill an empty seat in the provincial legislature in the Toronto district of York East confirmed the Liberals' popularity by electing a Liberal for the first time in 81 years. The Liberals gained additional support on October 6 when an NDP member from a northern district defected to the Liberal Party—a move that gave the Liberals 50 seats in the 125-seat legislature, with 51 for the PC and 24 for the NDP. The Liberal government's political triumphs were tempered by political embarrassment in June, however, when two cabinet ministers resigned over conflict-of-interest charges.

Catholic School Funding. The government's major legislation was a measure to extend public funding to all grades of Roman Catholic high schools, through grade 13. Previously, public support had been available only to grade 10. The bill was passed on June 23, after the Court of Appeal ruled on February 18 that giving public money to denominational schools did not violate Canada's Charter of Rights and Freedoms.

During his October visit to China, Ontario Premier David Peterson rubs a bronze lion's nose for good luck in Beijing's (Peking's) Forbidden City.

Doctors' Strike. Ontario physicians went on strike on June 12 to protest legislation before the provincial government that prohibited extra-billing—charging higher fees than the rates set by the provincial medical plan. Ontario had been penalized financially under a federal law, the 1984 Canada Health Act, for tolerating the practice. Despite vigorous opposition by the 17,000-member Ontario Medical Association, the legislature passed the measure banning extra-billing on June 20. Many physicians and hospitals continued to withhold services. On July 7—having lost public support during the 25-day strike—the doctors ended the walkout and decided to take their case to the courts.

Auto Plants. General Motors Corporation announced in March it would spend $2 billion (Canadian dollars; $1 = U.S. 72 cents as of Dec. 31, 1986) to redesign two assembly plants in Oshawa to produce a new generation of medium-sized cars. General Motors also stated that it would build, in partnership with the Suzuki Motor Company Limited of Japan, a $500-million manufacturing plant at Ingersoll.   David M. L. Farr

See also TORONTO. In WORLD BOOK, see ONTARIO.

OPERA. See CLASSICAL MUSIC.

OREGON. See STATE GOVERNMENT.

PACIFIC ISLANDS. The United States and the Soviet Union showed increased interest in the South Pacific in 1986. On October 20, the United States reached an agreement with Pacific island nations on fishing rights. The United States agreed to pay $60 million over five years for tuna-fishing rights in the 200-nautical-mile (370-kilometer) economic zones of the South Pacific Forum Fisheries Agency, an organization of 16 countries.

The agreement ended several years of often bitter wrangling between the South Pacific nations and the United States. Between 1982 and 1984, islanders seized two U.S. tuna boats when they pursued skipjack tuna into their territorial waters. In 1985, the island country of Kiribati signed a $1.5-million agreement that allowed Soviet boats to catch tuna in its waters for a year. When the Soviet Union suggested similar arrangements to other South Pacific nations, the United States offered deals to pay the islanders as well. The October 1986 agreement came a few days after the Soviets' Kiribati deal expired. Kiribati rejected Soviet efforts to renew their agreement on cheaper terms. At year's end, however, an agreement giving the Soviet Union fishing and airline landing rights in Vanuatu seemed likely.

Palau Snag. United States plans to terminate its 40-year administration of the United Nations

Children sit in the ruins of their village church in Honiara, the Solomon Islands, after Typhoon Namu struck the islands in May.

Facts in Brief on Pacific Island Countries

Country	Population	Government	Monetary Unit*	Exports†	Foreign Trade (million U.S. $) Imports†
Australia	16,102,000	Governor General Sir Ninian Martin Stephen; Prime Minister Robert Hawke	dollar (1.5 = $1)	22,759	25,889
Fiji	706,000	Governor General Sir Penaia Ganilau; Prime Minister Sir Kamisese Mara	dollar (1.1 = $1)	236	472
Kiribati	64,000	President Ieremia Tabai	Australian dollar	·1.5	15
Nauru	8,000	President Hammer DeRoburt	Australian dollar	93	11
New Zealand	3,345,000	Governor General Sir Paul Reeves; Prime Minister David R. Lange	dollar (2.02 = $1)	5,721	5,992
Papua New Guinea	3,894,000	Governor General Sir Kingsford Dibela; Prime Minister Paias Wingti	kina (1.04 = $1)	840	906
Solomon Islands	301,000	Governor General Sir Baddeley Devesi; Prime Minister Ezekiel Alebua	dollar (1.44 = $1)	94	79
Tonga	102,000	King Taufa'ahau Tupou IV; Prime Minister Prince Fatafehi Tu'ipelehake	pa'anga (1.47 = $1)	7	29
Tuvalu	8,000	Governor General Sir Fiatau Penitala Teo; Prime Minister Tomasi Puapua	Australian dollar	0.3	2.8
Vanuatu	141,000	President Ati George Sokomanu; Prime Minister Walter H. Lini	vatu (100 = $1)	44	66
Western Samoa	166,000	Head of State Malietoa Tanumafili II; Prime Minister Va'ai Kolone	tala (2.21 = $1)	20	57

*Exchange rates as of Dec. 1, 1986, or latest available data. †Latest available data.

(UN) Trust Territory of the Pacific Islands—which consists of Palau, the Marshall Islands, the Federated States of Micronesia, and the Northern Mariana Islands—were foiled in Palau. On January 14, President Ronald Reagan signed Compacts of Free Association, which granted limited self-government in "free association" with the United States to the Marshall Islands and Federated States of Micronesia.

Meanwhile, U.S. officials and the Palau government signed a revised treaty that provided self-government for Palau but permitted U.S. nuclear military sites there. Palau's Constitution, however, bans nuclear materials on Palau's 343 islands. A referendum was held on the treaty on February 21. Only 72 per cent of the country's voters approved it, 3 per cent short of the three-quarters majority vote needed to override the constitutional ban. Despite this, Palau's President Lazarus Salii proclaimed the treaty approved. But on September 17, a special Palau appeals court upheld the February vote. In a December 2 referendum, only 66 per cent of the voters approved the treaty, according to preliminary results.

The UN Trusteeship Council overwhelmingly approved termination of the U.S. trusteeship of the entire territory on May 28, though the Soviet Union voted against it. On November 3, U.S. administration ceased in the Marshall Islands and in the Federated States of Micronesia, and the Northern Marianas officially became a U.S. commonwealth, largely self-governing but receiving assistance from the U.S. government.

Gold Rush. Gold prospecting on a scale unprecedented in this century took place in an arc of islands stretching from Palau and Papua New Guinea to the Solomon Islands and Vanuatu to Fiji and New Zealand. The rush began in 1985 when spectacular gold discoveries were made on the Lihir and Tabar islands off New Ireland in Papua New Guinea. The Lihir deposit is estimated to contain approximately $4 billion in gold.

An Australian prospecting company, Placer Pacific Proprietary, made news in October when it was disclosed that Papua New Guinea's Deputy Prime Minister and Finance Minister, Sir Julius Chan, and his People's Progress Party had made huge sums of money trading Placer shares that were financed by bank loans. The disclosure was a hot political issue for the rest of the year.

UN Action. Despite strong French objections, the UN General Assembly on December 2 voted 89-24, with 34 abstentions, to support moves for independence for New Caledonia. The resolution classified New Caledonia as a French colony, whereas France claims it is part of France. The Assembly's resolution also affirmed "the inalienable right of the people of New Caledonia to self-determination and independence." Australia, New Zealand, and the 11 other South Pacific Forum nations had voted at a Forum meeting in Suva, Fiji, in August to ask the UN to take up the issue. Technically, the resolution requires France to make reports on New Caledonia to the UN and to allow missions to visit there. France said it would ignore the resolution.

Other Developments. On May 19, Typhoon Namu struck the Solomon Islands with unparalleled fury. More than 1,000 people were killed and approximately one-third of the country's 301,000 inhabitants were left homeless. Property damage was estimated at more than $60 million.

On December 2, Sir Peter Kenilorea was replaced as the Solomons' prime minister because he accepted French aid to repair his typhoon-damaged home village on Malaita Island. Ezekiel Alebua succeeded him.

On September 3, Ricardo J. Bordallo, governor of Guam—a territory of the United States—was indicted on a number of federal charges, including bribery, extortion, and conspiracy to obstruct justice. The charges did not hurt his political chances, however. On September 6, Bordallo won Guam's Democratic gubernatorial primary election.   Robert Langdon

In WORLD BOOK, see PACIFIC ISLANDS; PACIFIC ISLANDS, TRUST TERRITORY OF THE.

PAGE, GERALDINE (1924-   ), won the Academy of Motion Picture Arts and Sciences Award for best actress on March 24, 1986. She was honored for her performance as an elderly widow determined to make a final visit to her family home in *The Trip to Bountiful.* Page had been nominated for an Oscar seven times before.

Page was born in Kirksville, Mo., on Nov. 22, 1924. After studying at the Goodman School of Drama in Chicago, she acted in summer and winter stock in the Midwest. Her performance in a revival of Tennessee Williams' play *Summer and Smoke* in 1952 in New York City won her the first of many theater awards.

Page won her first Academy Award nomination—for best actress—for her role in *Hondo* (1953). She also won nominations for best actress for *Summer and Smoke* (1961), *Sweet Bird of Youth* (1962), and *Interiors* (1978). She was nominated as best supporting actress for *You're a Big Boy Now* (1967), *Pete 'n' Tillie* (1972), and *The Pope of Greenwich Village* (1984).

Page made her television debut in 1946. Her TV credits include *A Christmas Memory* (1966) and *A Thanksgiving Visitor* (1969), both of which earned her Emmy Awards.

Page married actor Rip Torn in 1963. They have a daughter and twin sons.   Barbara A. Mayes

PAINTING. See ART.

PAKISTAN. Party politics resumed in 1986, following President M. Zia-ul-Haq's decree that ended martial law on Dec. 30, 1985. Political parties had been banned since 1979.

Prime Minister Mohammed Khan Junejo on January 18 revived the Pakistan Muslim League, the party credited with the creation of Pakistan in 1947. A majority of members of parliament, who had been elected in 1985 on a nonparty basis, joined the League.

The speaker of parliament, Fakhar Imam, was voted out of office on May 26 after League members accused him of favoring independent members. He organized 20 independents into an opposition bloc.

Benazir Bhutto, 33-year-old daughter of former Prime Minister Zulfikar Ali Bhutto, returned to Pakistan from exile on April 10. Her father had been executed in 1979 by Zia's government. A crowd estimated at between 500,000 and 1 million people welcomed her at the city of Lahore. She continued to attract large crowds during a nationwide tour to rally opposition to Zia. Bhutto called for new elections, four years ahead of schedule.

Bhutto sought to rebuild her father's Pakistan People's Party (PPP). She and other leaders of the Movement for the Restoration of Democracy, an alliance of opposition parties, planned for rallies

Benazir Bhutto, a leader of Pakistan's political opposition, addresses a crowd of 80,000 people in Rawalpindi during a campaign rally in April.

The discovery in Texas of 225-million-year-old fossil bones of what may be the oldest known bird, called *Protoavis* (inset), was reported in August.

on August 14, the anniversary of Pakistan's independence. At least 26 people were killed in the resulting political violence. Bhutto and about 2,000 other Movement leaders were arrested, but all were released by September 8.

Arab Terrorists seized a Pan American World Airways airliner carrying 398 passengers at Karachi airport on September 5. The pilots managed to escape from the plane. An accidental light failure aboard the craft some 15 hours later caused the four hijackers to panic and begin shooting. They killed 21 people and wounded at least 100 before Pakistani commandos captured them.

Cabinet Shrunk. Junejo disbanded his 33-member Cabinet on December 20, after a week of ethnic riots in Karachi in which at least 180 people were killed. Two days later, a new 16-member Cabinet—drawn entirely from the old one—was sworn in.

Foreign Affairs. Junejo visited Washington, D.C., in July and received assurances of continued U.S. support for Pakistan. The United States promised $4.2 billion in military and economic aid from 1987 to 1992. United States Secretary of Defense Caspar W. Weinberger met with Zia in Pakistan in October to discuss weapons needed to protect Pakistan against attacks from Soviet-occupied Afghanistan.   Henry S. Bradsher

See also ASIA (Facts in Brief Table). In WORLD BOOK, see PAKISTAN.

PALEONTOLOGY. The discovery of what may be the largest animal fossil find in North America was reported in January 1986 by scientists at the Lamont-Doherty Geological Observatory in Palisades, N.Y., and Harvard University in Cambridge, Mass. The scientists found thousands of bones of dinosaurs, crocodiles, lizards, sharks, and other animals in 200-million-year-old rocks in Nova Scotia, Canada. Among the most important are 12 skulls and jaws of mammallike reptiles, which may help solve problems in understanding the evolution of mammals from reptiles.

The Oldest Known Bird fossils were reported in August. Two fossils in rocks dated at 225 million years old were described by paleontologist Sankar Chatterjee of Texas Tech University in Lubbock. The fossils, named *Protoavis* by Chatterjee, were found 50 miles (80 kilometers) southeast of Lubbock. They are 75 million years older than *Archaeopteryx*, previously the oldest known bird.

Paleontologists had considered *Archaeopteryx* a link between reptiles and modern birds. But the new-found fossil bird, in spite of being much older and having dinosaurlike legs and tail, is closer to modern birds in anatomy than is *Archaeopteryx*. Chatterjee thinks *Archaeopteryx* must have been a dead-end branch on the tree of bird evolution and that *Protoavis* was closer to the main evolutionary line from reptiles to modern birds.

Mass Extinctions. Debate continued about possible causes of mass extinctions. Most paleontologists accept that at least once, at the end of the Cretaceous Period—65 million years ago—an asteroid or comet collided with Earth. At that time, there was a mass extinction of plants and animals, including the dinosaurs. The main evidence for the impact is the presence of the rare element iridium—which can come from comets and asteroids—in 65-million-year-old sediments.

But not all paleontologists think the impact was a major cause of the extinctions. Four paleontologists led by Robert E. Sloan of the University of Minnesota in Minneapolis reported in May they had found the teeth of seven dinosaur species 1.3 meters (4.3 feet) above the iridium layer in a rock formation in Montana. The scientists believe this shows that some dinosaur species survived the asteroid or comet impact, to become extinct during the following 40,000 years.

Periods of Extinctions were the subject of several papers published in 1986. The main theory holds that mass extinctions occur on an average of every 26 million years. Some scientists have suggested periodic comet showers as the cause.

But two planetary scientists at the University of California in Los Angeles in June reported that iridium deposits were not rich enough to have come from comet showers. They measured the concentration of iridium in a core of deep-sea sediments deposited from 33 million to 67 million years ago. They found that the increase in iridium at the time of mass extinctions about 37 million and 65 million years ago was much less than they predicted would come from a comet shower.

Reversals of Earth's magnetic field, which could affect climate, might account for periodic extinctions, according to physical scientist Richard B. Stothers of the Goddard Institute for Space Studies in New York City. In a July report, Stothers suggested that impacts of asteroids or comets could trigger magnetic field reversals, which occur about every 30 million years.

A Major Debate between paleontologists and advocates of scientific creationism came to an end in June when both sides agreed that a set of footprints along a river southwest of Fort Worth, Tex., are not those of human beings but were made by dinosaurs. Scientific creationists, who believe that the world began through an act of creation perhaps only thousands of years ago, had pointed to the "human tracks" as evidence that human beings and dinosaurs existed together. But Glen T. Kuban, an amateur dinosaur expert, found faint impressions of dinosaur toes, proving the tracks were not human.   Ida Thompson

In WORLD BOOK, see PALEONTOLOGY.

PANAMA. See LATIN AMERICA.

PAPUA NEW GUINEA. See ASIA; PACIFIC ISLANDS.

PARAGUAY. Between March and May 1986, street demonstrations reappeared in Paraguay for the first time in more than 30 years as opposition political forces began challenging the dictatorial rule of 74-year-old President Alfredo Stroessner. But when the protests gave signs of getting out of hand, the government resorted to its usual repressive measures.

Police broke up rallies in Caraguatay on March 28 and in San José de los Arroyos on April 13, using whips, chains, and machetes. On April 18, workers at a state-run hospital in Asunción, the capital—who were demanding higher wages—were dispersed with fire hoses and nightsticks. About 4,000 doctors and hospital workers protesting in Asunción on April 24 were treated similarly, as were university students who supported the doctors. On April 29, a mob of Stroessner supporters attacked Radio Nanduti, an independent station. When the raid failed to silence the station's criticism of the Stroessner regime, the government jammed the station's frequency. Supporters of the station turned up their radios, broadcasting only static on the jammed frequency, to create a din of protest.   Nathan A. Haverstock

See also LATIN AMERICA (Facts in Brief Table). In WORLD BOOK, see PARAGUAY.

PENNSYLVANIA. See PHILADELPHIA; STATE GOVERNMENT.

PERU. Peru's President Alan García Pérez continued to defy the international financial community during 1986 by withholding payments on Peru's foreign debt. In Peru, he was credited with some success in slashing inflation, promoting a modest rise in the wages of Peruvian workers, and addressing the problems of Peru's long-neglected Indian population. By mid-1986, public opinion polls gave García a 70 per cent approval rating.

Military Disgruntled. High-ranking members of Peru's armed forces, however, blamed García for failing to end a six-year-old leftist rebellion that has cost 8,000 lives. Disgruntled officers cited his decision to reduce military outlays as a contributing factor. They disliked the reduction of Mirage fighters on order from France from 26 to 12 and the cancellation of a $240-million contract to renovate the navy's flagship.

Military officers were also irked at García's decision to put civilians in charge of the war against drugs, which had previously been under military supervision. One reason for the shift was that the military had reportedly become deeply corrupted by drug trafficking.

Prison Riots. The leftist rebellion suffered a series of setbacks during 1986. On June 19, Peruvian authorities brutally put down two prison riots begun by imprisoned guerrillas belonging to the group Sendero Luminoso (Shining Path). Army troops stormed the Lurigancho prison on the outskirts of Lima, the capital, where Shining Path guerrillas fell before withering fire as they sang revolutionary songs.

Meanwhile, guerrillas being held at El Frontón, a rocky barren island prison off Lima's port of Callao, staged what appeared to be a coordinated uprising. They battled government troops and naval forces for nearly 24 hours with four captured rifles, explosives, and homemade bows and arrows before surrendering. In all, some 260 prisoners were killed. About 100 of them were summarily executed after they had surrendered. García ordered arrests and trials of the prison guards responsible for the executions.

The riots broke out while the government was preparing to host a meeting in Lima of the Socialist International—the world's Socialist and Social Democratic parties. The government charged that the riots were an attempt to mar its image during the meeting.

Peruvian army patrols reported killing 39 Shining Path guerrillas in the week ending October 25. Among those reportedly killed was Claudio Bellido Huaytalla, a high-ranking member of the rebel movement.   Nathan A. Haverstock

See also LATIN AMERICA (Facts in Brief Table). In WORLD BOOK, see PERU.

PET. See CAT; DOG.

PETROLEUM AND GAS. The Organization of Petroleum Exporting Countries (OPEC) agreed on Aug. 4, 1986, to reduce production in an effort to bolster world oil prices, which had plunged to their lowest level since 1973. The members of the 13-nation oil cartel had failed to reach agreement on new production quotas during three earlier meetings in 1986.

With world petroleum production exceeding demand by as much as 50 million barrels per month, prices fell by more than 50 per cent during the first half of 1986. The United States Department of Energy (DOE) said that the price of a barrel of Saudi light crude, the oil used as a bench mark for establishing prices, fell from $28 on January 1 to less than $13 by July. Prices for other grades of oil fell below $10. OPEC ministers feared oil prices would fall further to $5.

The ministers, meeting in Geneva, Switzerland, unanimously agreed to temporary cuts in production from the prevailing level of roughly 20.5 million barrels per day (bpd) to 16.8 million bpd.

On October 22, OPEC ministers ended another meeting—their longest in the cartel's 26-year history—with an agreement to extend production controls through the end of 1986. The new agreement, reached after 17 days of debate, increased the cartel's total production limit to 17 million bpd for November and December.

"Petunia," the oil well on the lawn of the state Capitol in Oklahoma City, Okla., went dry in January, after yielding 1.5 million barrels of oil since 1942.

On December 20, all OPEC nations except Iraq agreed to cut oil production by 7 per cent and raise the price of oil to $18 a barrel. The agreement appeared to reduce OPEC oil production by 1 million bpd to roughly 16 million. Although Iraq refused to sign the pact because of a dispute over Iran's production quota, it agreed to "cooperate" in the effort to cut production.

Economic Problems. Declining oil prices created severe economic problems for OPEC members and other oil-producing countries. Saudi Arabia, for example, was forced to devalue its currency, the riyal, on June 1, 1986. In what was believed to be the largest devaluation in that country's history, the riyal's value against the United States dollar fell by 2.7 per cent.

Low prices caused a number of problems in the U.S. petroleum industry and raised concern about the industry's ability to produce enough oil in the future. Many oil firms closed wells, cut back production, laid off workers, and sharply reduced efforts to discover new deposits of oil and natural gas.

Exploration Low. Oil & Gas Journal, an industry publication, reported on July 28 that exploration for new oil wells in the United States had fallen to the lowest level since before World War II. The magazine predicted that the United States would have increased difficulty in the future in meeting domestic petroleum needs and would grow even more dependent on foreign oil. By June 1986, exploration for new sources of natural gas had declined to the lowest level since nationwide records were first kept in 1941.

The National Petroleum Council, an advisory council to the secretary of energy, on Oct. 17, 1986, said that depressed conditions in the U.S. petroleum industry would have a serious long-term effect on national security and economic stability. The council said that low oil prices were increasing U.S. vulnerability to possible future world oil shortages and embargoes.

The group, noting that oil companies had slashed spending on exploration for new sources of crude oil and natural gas, warned that reserves were declining. The council also predicted serious threats to the production capacity of the industry.

Consumer Gain. United States consumers benefited from the decline in petroleum prices, however. On July 4, at the peak of the summer driving season, nationwide gasoline prices fell to their lowest level since 1979. The Lundberg Survey, which monitors gasoline prices, reported on July 2, 1986, that U.S. gas prices averaged less than 96 cents per gallon (3.8 liters), 15 cents less than the January average.

Demand Forecast. The DOE predicted on August 8 that U.S. demand for crude oil would average 16.2 million bpd during 1987, with about 5.3 million barrels coming from imports. Natural gas demand was forecast at 16.7 trillion cubic feet (473 billion cubic meters).

The DOE on September 8 reported that U.S. reserves of natural gas declined in 1985 for the fourth straight year. Reserves stood at 193.4 trillion cubic feet (5.5 trillion cubic meters), the lowest level since the DOE first began issuing estimates of reserves in 1976. New discoveries of natural gas declined by 64 per cent to 999 billion cubic feet (28.3 billion cubic meters), also the lowest level since 1976.

Domestic crude oil reserves, in contrast, remained fairly stable, at 24.8 billion barrels. The figure represented a decline of only 0.1 per cent—about 30 million barrels—from 1984. But discoveries of new oil deposits fell sharply. New oil strikes added only 84 million barrels to U.S. reserves, compared with 242 million barrels added in 1984.

European Forecast. The Economic Commission for Europe (ECE), one of five regional economic commissions set up by the United Nations, on April 10, 1986, estimated that U.S. domestic oil reserves could be exhausted by 1993 if production continued at the present rate and no major new oil fields were discovered. According to the ECE, the Soviet Union would run out of domestic oil by the late 1990's. The commission estimated that Saudi Arabia's reserves, the largest in the world, would last for about 100 years. Iran has reserves sufficient to maintain production for about 60 years; Libya, for 50 years; and Mexico, for 40 years.

Libyan Withdrawal. United States oil companies ended all operations in Libya on June 30, meeting a deadline set by President Ronald Reagan on Jan. 7, 1986. Reagan had severed economic ties with Libya as punishment for that country's involvement in terrorism. But he gave the oil firms additional time to close down operations and arrange for the sale of their Libyan assets.

Gas for Soviets. The government of Iran on August 25 announced that it would resume shipments of natural gas to the Soviet Union. During the 1970's, Iran supplied the Soviets with about 350 billion cubic feet (9.9 billion cubic meters) of natural gas per year. But the revolutionaries who overthrew Shah Mohammad Reza Pahlavi in 1979 abruptly halted exports to the Soviet Union. Iran said it would begin with relatively small shipments, gradually increasing to the former level by 1990.

Gulf War. The long war between Iran and Iraq continued to exact a heavy toll on petroleum shipments through the Persian Gulf. Iraq on Oct. 6, 1986, conducted an air strike on Iran's main oil-exporting terminal on Kharg Island. The Iraqis claimed that the raid virtually eliminated Iran's ability to ship oil through the terminal. On August

12, Iraq had partially destroyed a secondary Iranian oil terminal on Sirri Island, near the mouth of the Persian Gulf. On October 11, Iran announced that a team of commandos had destroyed Iraq's main northern oil-refining and storage center at Kirkuk on October 10. Iraq denied that the center had been damaged.

New Source of Gas? Sweden's State Power Board on July 1 began drilling a $20-million well intended to test a controversial theory about the origin of natural gas. The theory maintains that gas does not originate from the decay of organic matter, as most scientists believe, but is a by-product left over from the formation of Earth. The new theory, developed by astrophysicist Thomas Gold of Cornell University in Ithaca, N.Y., implies that huge reserves of natural gas exist in areas not previously thought to contain the gas.

The new well is located about 150 miles (240 kilometers) northwest of Stockholm in the Siljan Ring, a crater formed by the impact of an asteroid 360 million years ago. The area has long puzzled geologists because studies indicate that gas is present. The rocks in the crater, however, do not contain deposits of ancient organic matter. Verification of the theory could revolutionize the exploration for gas and ensure virtually limitless new sources of gas.   Michael Woods

In WORLD BOOK, see GAS; PETROLEUM.

PHILADELPHIA. Displaced families from a west Philadelphia neighborhood that was destroyed by fire in 1985 when the city bombed the home of a radical group moved into new houses on the same site in the spring and summer of 1986. The row houses were built by the city at a cost of $138,000 each. The rebuilding project was plagued by cost overruns, construction delays, and the dismissal of the original contractor, Ernest A. Edwards, Jr. Philadelphia Mayor W. Wilson Goode removed Edwards in February for failing to complete the project by Christmas 1985.

Investigations. A special commission appointed by the mayor to probe the bombing incident concluded its work in 1986. The panel took testimony from city officials, fire fighters, police, and others about the bombing, which occurred on May 13, 1985, as police tried to evict members of a radical group called MOVE from a row house. The explosion and resulting fire left six adults and five children in the MOVE house dead. The commission's 70-page report, released on March 6, 1986, called for a grand jury to investigate the deaths of the children and severely criticized the mayor and his top aides for the bombing.

The Federal Bureau of Investigation in 1986 began its own probe of the events of May 13 to determine whether the city violated the civil rights of the MOVE group. In addition, a special inves-

A service station owner in Villa Park, Ill., lowers the price of gasoline in February to reflect plummeting world oil prices.

Children walk past tons of garbage piling up on a Philadelphia street during a three-week strike by two city workers unions in July.

tigating grand jury was formed at the request of Philadelphia District Attorney Ronald D. Castille to examine the MOVE incident. Both investigations continued at year's end.

In another investigation, 9 Philadelphia police officers and 18 other people were indicted in October on charges relating to the operation of illegal lotteries in the city. The police officers were accused of taking bribes to protect the lottery operators from arrest. Meanwhile, a continuing five-year federal investigation of corruption in the police department had resulted in the conviction of 31 former police officers by the fall of 1986.

Other Indictments. A number of city union leaders and officials were also indicted in 1986. A federal grand jury on October 23 indicted two city judges for taking bribes from the roofers union and 13 former and current members of the union for using intimidation tactics. The jury also brought indictments against a retired court aide, two local lawyers, and three alleged mobsters for crimes related to the union's activities.

On October 28, federal indictments charged City Councilman Leland M. Beloff with trying to extort $1 million from a local developer and with 14 counts of election fraud. Also indicted were the councilman's top aide, a reputed organized-crime figure, Beloff's wife, and two officials from the local Democratic Party.

On November 3, a state grand jury in New Jersey indicted 18 reputed mob figures, including Nicodemo (Little Nicky) Scarfo, allegedly the head of the Philadelphia-area crime family. Those indicted were charged with a variety of criminal activities.

City Workers Strike. More than 15,000 city workers in two municipal unions walked off their jobs on July 1 in a dispute over wages and benefits. As contract negotiations dragged on, garbage piled up on Philadelphia streets. All city workers returned to their jobs on July 21 without a contract after a judge found the sanitation division in contempt of court for refusing an order to resume duties. The next day, the city announced a tentative settlement for blue-collar workers, members of the larger of the two unions. The white-collar workers union had ratified a pact on July 12, but many of its members had remained on strike in support of the other union. Both unions won pay raises of about 10 per cent over two years.

Construction in Progress. Throughout the metropolitan area in 1986, new buildings were rising and roads were being repaired. The most ambitious project—and the cause of frequent traffic snarls—was the $175-million reconstruction of the Schuylkill Expressway linking numerous suburbs to the downtown area. Howard S. Shapiro

See also CITY. In WORLD BOOK, see PHILADELPHIA.

PHILIPPINES. Corazon Aquino became president of the Philippines on Feb. 25, 1986, and former President Ferdinand E. Marcos fled to Hawaii.

The ouster of Marcos followed a disputed election. Marcos had called an election for February 7 because of complaints about economic problems, official corruption, and human rights abuses. In addition, there was a growing threat from Communist guerrillas. Marcos, who had been president since 1965, sought a new mandate.

Marcos' opponents united behind "Cory" Aquino, the widow of Benigno S. Aquino, Jr., an opposition leader who was murdered in 1983. She blamed Marcos for the murder. Her running mate was Salvador Laurel. See AQUINO, CORAZON.

The Election Campaign was marked by violence, and more than 40 people were killed on election day. Aquino's supporters charged large-scale fraud and intimidation. They said that voter lists disappeared, ballots were stolen, and Marcos supporters cast multiple votes. Thirty computer operators compiling results for the government said the count was being manipulated and quit their jobs. On February 15, the National Assembly, in which Marcos' party held three-quarters of the seats, proclaimed him winner of the election.

Aquino claimed that she had won. On February 16, she called for nonviolent strikes and boycotts to force Marcos from office.

Military Role. Defense Minister Juan Ponce Enrile and the deputy chief of staff, Lieutenant General Fidel V. Ramos, threw their support behind Aquino. They occupied the Defense Ministry on February 22 and called on Marcos to resign, saying they would no longer accept his authority because of the election fraud and past misconduct.

Meanwhile, General Fabian C. Ver, the armed forces chief of staff and a relative of Marcos, began organizing an attack on soldiers supporting Enrile. Crowds of civilians, however, turned out to support Enrile's rebels and obstruct any attack. Some 20 people, mostly soldiers, died in scattered fighting over the next few days.

The United States threatened to cut off military aid if violence persisted. It also called for "a peaceful transition"—thus signifying that U.S. support for Marcos had been withdrawn.

Aquino Takes Over. In a chaotic situation on February 25, Aquino held a makeshift ceremony during which she was inaugurated as president at 10:45 A.M. At noon, Marcos was inaugurated for another term. But Marcos was under siege from crowds in the streets and under pressure from the United States to resign. He accepted a U.S. offer of asylum, and U.S. helicopters took him from his palace at 9:05 P.M. to Hawaii. He was accompanied by his family, Ver, and other close associates.

Aquino charged that much of the Philippines' $27.5-billion foreign debt had gone into foreign acquisitions by Marcos' family and friends. Marcos denied this, but documents showed that he had huge holdings abroad.

Amid popular celebrations and the looting of Marcos' palace, Aquino assumed control. Laurel became vice president, prime minister, and foreign minister. The post of prime minister was eliminated on March 25, when Aquino proclaimed a provisional constitution that abolished the Marcos-dominated National Assembly and enabled her to govern by decree.

New Constitution. A commission to write a new constitution was named by Aquino on May 25. The commission presented a draft constitution to Aquino on October 15. It restored the presidential system of government that Marcos had abolished under martial law in 1972 and limited a president to a single six-year term.

The draft called for a legislature consisting of a 24-member Senate and a 250-member lower house. The legislature would have the power to revoke any presidential proclamation of martial law. The draft also established a strong human rights commission, banned private armies, and sought to ensure an independent judiciary.

A national vote on the draft constitution was

In her first major public appearance after taking power, Philippine President Corazon Aquino waves to supporters at a Manila rally in March.

planned for Feb. 2, 1987. It would also be a vote on Aquino's remaining as president for six years. Elections for the new legislature and for local officials were scheduled for May 11, 1987.

Aquino's Problems. Marcos criticized the Aquino government from exile. Marcos supporters in Manila held demonstrations against Aquino that sometimes turned violent.

Arturo M. Tolentino, who had run for vice president with Marcos in February, claimed he was legally the vice president. On July 6, Tolentino took an oath of office as acting president. Supported by 400 troops, Tolentino then barricaded himself in a Manila hotel and appealed for backing from Enrile. Enrile refused and moved against the rebels. The coup attempt collapsed, and Tolentino and some 40 others were charged with rebellion.

Aquino sought support from foreign powers. United States Secretary of State George P. Shultz expressed U.S. backing for Aquino's government during a visit to Manila in May. Aquino then visited the United States from September 15 to 24 and received strong U.S. presidential, congressional, and popular support. In October, the International Monetary Fund approved $519 million in loans to aid the Philippine economy. In November, Aquino made a four-day visit to Japan to seek stronger economic ties.

Attempted Coup. On November 13, the day she returned, a leftist labor leader was found murdered. There was widespread suspicion that Enrile's supporters were behind the killing. Thousands of Filipinos marched in protest, and the nation's largest labor union called a general strike.

On November 23, Aquino fired Enrile and named a retired general, Rafael M. Ileto, as defense minister. Aquino acted after a reported coup attempt by Enrile's army supporters, which Ramos was credited with blocking. Aquino began making other Cabinet changes under army pressure to oust people considered leftist or corrupt.

Dealing with Rebels. Aquino's efforts to make peace with Communist guerrillas of the New People's Army were controversial. Some Philippine soldiers distrusted the Communists and therefore opposed negotiations. On the other side, hundreds of guerrillas were killed by their Communist comrades for wanting talks. Despite this, the government and the guerrillas agreed to a 60-day cease-fire that began on December 10. During the cease-fire, the two sides were to hold talks on ending the 17-year-old Communist rebellion.

Ramos said that from 1979 to 1985, 16,250 people had been killed in the rebellion. In the nine months of Aquino's presidency before the cease-fire, about 2,200 had died.   Henry S. Bradsher

See also ASIA (Facts in Brief Table). In WORLD BOOK, see PHILIPPINES.

PHOTOGRAPHY. Several companies introduced new 35-millimeter (mm) cameras in 1986 that combined the flexibility of a single-lens reflex (SLR) camera with a compact 35's ease of operation. The Olympus OM-77 AF, introduced in July, is an SLR with completely automatic operation, including autofocusing (AF) and a built-in electronic flash. It accepts a full range of interchangeable lenses and accessories but does not offer the manual exposure control common to most SLR's. Nikon's N2020 AF, introduced in February, is the first autofocusing SLR that accepts standard manual-focusing lenses as well as AF lenses.

In March, the Minolta Camera Company unveiled the Maxxum 5000 SLR, a streamlined and easier-to-operate version of the Maxxum 7000. A more elaborate autofocusing SLR, the Yashica 230 AF, was shown at the biennial *photokina* trade show in September in Cologne, West Germany. The 230 AF was quickly withdrawn from the market, however—reportedly because of patent-infringement charges. The dispute was later settled, and the camera was expected to be offered for sale early in 1987.

While SLR's were getting easier to use, "point-and-shoot" compact 35-mm models were becoming more versatile. The Pentax IQZoom is the first camera of this type with a zoom lens. At the touch of a button, the user can vary the lens focal length continuously over a range of 35 to 70 mm. The camera's viewfinder and flash unit adjust to match the angle of view of the lens.

Several other compact 35's offered to buyers in 1986 provide a choice of two focal lengths—generally a moderately wide-angle view and a semi-telephoto setting. The most elaborate model of this type is the Canon Sure Shot Tele, introduced in August, which also has a soft-focus lens and multiple-exposure capability.

Still-Video Cameras, which use magnetic disks rather than film to record images, were shown by many companies during the year. The Canon Still Video System (SVS), introduced in May, was the first to reach the market. The Canon RC-701 camera, which looks like a large 35-mm SLR, records images on a 47-mm (1.85-inch) diameter floppy disk, similar to those used in personal computers. Up to 50 images can be recorded on a disk, which is then placed in a playback unit for immediate display on any TV set. Other components of the system include a full-color printer and a device to transmit or receive electronic images over telephone lines.

Minolta took a different approach to electronic photography by demonstrating a still-video back, the SVB-90, for the Maxxum 7000 and 9000 35-mm cameras. The attachment, shown at *photokina*, replaces the standard film back and utilizes a 47-mm disk to hold up to 50 still-video images.

A throwaway camera—a film package with built-in lens and shutter—was introduced to Japanese consumers in July by the Fuji Photo Film Company.

Instant Photography. In March, the Polaroid Corporation introduced a new instant-picture system called the Spectra. Compared with the earlier Polaroid SX-70 system, Spectra produces prints with better color and a more pleasing balance between flash and natural light. Spectra prints are rectangular in format, rather than square, thus allowing either horizontal or vertical composition.

Color Film. Conventional color films continued to get faster in 1986. The most sensitive film available to consumers was Konica SR-V 3200 color-negative film, introduced at *photokina*. Prints made from the new film, which has a speed of ISO 3,200, had surprisingly fine grain and rich color.

Deaths. Ralph Steiner, 87, an American photographer and filmmaker, died on July 13. Steiner was noted for his magazine photography and documentary films. Russell Lee, 83, an American photographer famous for documenting Midwestern Dust Bowl conditions in the 1930's, died on August 28. Jacques-Henri Lartigue of France, one of the greatest photographers of the early 1900's, died on September 12 at the age of 92. His fascinating images of pre-World War I France overshadowed the rest of his career as a photographer, painter, and writer. Ernst Haas, 65, an Austrian-born photojournalist and master of abstract color photography, died on September 12.   Steve Pollock

In WORLD BOOK, see CAMERA; PHOTOGRAPHY.

PHYSICS. The theoretical physicist who won the Nobel Prize for Physics in 1967 for his work on nuclear reactions in the sun may have helped to solve a fundamental problem involving these reactions in 1986. The physicist, German-born Hans A. Bethe of Cornell University in Ithaca, N.Y., and the University of California at Santa Barbara, attempted in 1986 to explain certain experimental results that have puzzled physicists since the late 1960's.

The results have come from the detection and counting of *electron-neutrinos*, subatomic particles produced in vast amounts during nuclear reactions deep inside the sun. These particles rarely interact with other kinds of particles, so all but a tiny fraction of the electron-neutrinos streak to the solar surface and shoot out into space. Tremendous numbers of them reach Earth.

Underground Activities. In 1967, physicists built a huge instrument on Earth—actually, *inside* Earth—to detect and count electron-neutrinos that come from the sun. The main part of the instrument is a gigantic tank holding 678 short tons (615 metric tons) of dry-cleaning fluid, which happens to be an excellent detector of electron-neutrinos that have a certain level of energy. These particles react with the fluid extremely rarely, but often enough for scientific purposes.

Unfortunately, certain cosmic rays also react

with the fluid in a way that resembles the electron-neutrino reactions. To minimize the number of these cosmic-ray reactions, physicists shielded the tank from cosmic rays by building it nearly 1 mile (1.6 kilometers) underground in a South Dakota gold mine.

Particle Shortage. Since the instrument went into operation, scientists have observed only about one-third the number of electron-neutrinos predicted by well-understood theories of nuclear reactions taking place in the sun. Physicists strongly suspect that their theories are correct and that nuclear reactions within the sun do produce the number of electron-neutrinos predicted. They now believe that another phenomenon then takes over, converting electron-neutrinos into other particles. According to theories of electron-neutrinos and other subatomic particles, a specific percentage of electron-neutrinos turn into similar particles called *muon-neutrinos* as they travel through matter and relatively empty space.

The South Dakota instrument cannot detect muon-neutrinos, so the electron-neutrino shortage—the difference between the number of electron-neutrinos predicted and the number actually detected at the tank—should be equal to the number of muon-neutrinos produced by electron-neutrino conversion. The shortage has turned out to be much larger than the muon-neutrino production, however, and this is the problem that Bethe may have helped to solve.

Breakthrough. In late 1985, two Soviet physicists achieved a theoretical breakthrough that led to Bethe's work. S. P. Mikheyev and A. Y. Smirnov of the Institute of Nuclear Research at the Academy of Sciences of the U.S.S.R. in Moscow showed how the rate at which electron-neutrinos turn into muon-neutrinos could become much higher than previously thought as electron-neutrinos travel from the sun's core to its surface. In fact, they said, conversion could occur frequently enough to account for the electron-neutrino shortage.

Bethe supported the view of the Soviet physicists. In March 1986, he published a mathematically simpler method for reaching essentially the same conclusions as the Soviet scientists.

Detector Needed. The three scientists could not prove experimentally that their theory was correct, however, because not all the equipment necessary for the proof existed in 1986. To prove the theory, physicists must detect electron-neutrinos that have an energy level other than the level to which the South Dakota instrument is sensitive. The physicists need another instrument—one that is sensitive to another energy level. No such instrument existed in 1986, but the Soviet Union was building one, and France, Italy, and West Germany planned to construct another.   Thomas O. White

In WORLD BOOK, see NEUTRINO; PHYSICS.

POETRY. Several well-known poets issued collections or selected editions of their work in 1986. Derek Walcott's *Collected Poems 1948-1984* traces the West Indian-born poet's love-hate relationship with the Caribbean and his development of a style that combines island dialects with the echoes of English literary tradition. Philip Booth's *Relations: Selected Poems 1950-1985* evokes the landscape and daily life of Maine in appropriately spare, understated language. David Ignatow, as much an urban poet as Booth is a rural one, supplemented his *Poems, 1934-1969* with his *New & Collected Poems, 1970-1985*.

Robert Bly, known for his strange, dreamlike images and outspokenly political poems of the late 1960's and early 1970's, brought out *Selected Poems*. Elizabeth Jennings, whose religious themes and finely wrought, impersonal lyrics are remarkably independent of current literary fashions, gathered her work from 1953 to 1985 in a volume of *Collected Poems*. And Gary Snyder, in his *Left Out in the Rain*, took the unusual step of gathering poems not included in his previous books.

Traditional Forms. Perhaps the most publicized book of poetry in 1986 was Vikram Seth's *The Golden Gate*, a novel in the form of a sequence of sonnets, modeled after Russian poet Alexander Pushkin's *Eugene Onegin* (1825-1832). Although

Robert Penn Warren shows his delight in Fairfield, Conn., after being named the first poet laureate of the United States in February.

Seth's book was praised for its stylistic brilliance, some reviewers found the characters and the California social setting too stereotypical. Other new books by younger poets returning to traditional forms included *Daily Horoscope* by Dana Gioia, *What Women Know, What Men Believe* by Wyatt Prunty, and Timothy Steele's *Sapphics Against Anger and Other Poems.*

Autobiographical Sequences that also explore history and politics from a feminist point of view characterized Adrienne Rich's *Your Native Land, Your Life,* her first volume of poetry since a 1984 collection, *The Fact of a Doorframe.* Other new books by well-known poets included Donald Hall's *The Happy Man,* which was autobiographical in a more personal and nostalgic vein and recalled Hall's rural childhood. Robert Creeley's *Memory Gardens,* which had a clipped, incisive style, recalled his poetry of the 1950's. Raymond Carver, perhaps best known for his short fiction, completed *Ultramarine,* his second volume of poems.

Other Books of interest included Allen Grossman's *The Bright Nails Scattered on the Ground,* Mary Oliver's *Dream Work,* J. D. McClatchy's *Stars Principal,* Reginald Gibbons' *Saints,* Ralph Angel's *Anxious Latitudes,* Anne Winters' *The Key to the City,* and Henri Cole's *The Marble Queen.* Paul Breslin

See also WARREN, ROBERT PENN. In WORLD BOOK, see POETRY.

POLAND. The Polish United Workers' Party, Poland's Communist Party, reelected Wojciech Jaruzelski as its leader at its 1986 party congress, which ran from June 29 to July 3. Jaruzelski had come to power in 1981, during a crisis brought about by the rise of the independent labor union Solidarity. Jaruzelski's government declared martial law in 1981 and cracked down on Solidarity. In 1982, the regime formally outlawed Solidarity.

Speaking at the 1986 congress, Jaruzelski stressed Poland's need for innovation and modernization. Soviet leader Mikhail S. Gorbachev, who attended the congress, praised Jaruzelski's remarks.

Jaruzelski Consolidates. The representatives at the congress also elected a new Politburo—the party's policymaking body—and a new Central Committee, which runs the party between congresses. The previous congress had taken place in 1981, and Jaruzelski had consolidated his power a great deal since then. His power was evident in the makeup of the new Politburo. The party dismissed 7 of the 13 members of that body and added 9 new members—all considered by Western analysts to be loyal to Jaruzelski.

Solidarity Leader Emerges. On May 3, 1986, police captured Solidarity leader Zbigniew Bujak, who had been hiding since 1981. But on Sept. 12, 1986, the government released Bujak as part of an amnesty program. Between July 24 and September 15, the government released all 225 political prisoners it said it was holding, except for people who had been sentenced for spying, terrorism, and betrayal of state secrets.

On September 30, Solidarity openly set up a leadership council. The government proclaimed the council illegal but did not move against it.

The Roman Catholic Church in Poland welcomed the release of the political prisoners, but its relations with the regime remained cool. On September 2, the church announced that it was canceling a project for channeling international aid to private Polish farmers. The church blamed the government for the failure of the project.

Advisers Named. On December 7, the government announced the formation of a 56-member government advisory commission. Among the advisers were several individuals who had criticized government policy, including prominent Roman Catholic intellectuals. Only about one-third of the advisers were members of the Communist Party.

Jaruzelski called the commission "a historic experiment." None of Solidarity's leaders were included in the commission. Lech Walesa, former chairman of Solidarity and the winner of the 1983 Nobel Peace Prize, commented, "I don't see how it can work without input from experts in the Solidarity movement."

Finance. In May, Poland joined the International Monetary Fund (IMF)—a United Nations agency that helps countries with large international debts. At the end of June 1986, Poland's international debt was $31.3 billion, about $2 billion more than at the end of 1985.

Poland devalued its currency, the zloty, by 17.6 per cent against the United States dollar on September 1. The devaluation was the eighth in five years. In October 1981, U.S. $1 was worth 33.7 zlotys. On Dec. 1, 1986, U.S. $1 was worth 196 zlotys.

Production. Industrial output increased by 4.7 per cent in the first nine months of 1986, compared with the same period in 1985. Exports to the West declined by 3.6 per cent, while those to the East rose by 9 per cent. Inflation was running at an annual rate of 19 per cent.

Foreign Relations. Jaruzelski visited Mongolia, North Korea, and China at the end of September. He was the first East European leader to visit China since relations between China and the Soviet Union deteriorated in the early 1960's. Nikolai I. Ryzhkov, chairman of the Soviet Union's Council of Ministers, visited Poland in October 1986 and signed an agreement on long-term cooperation. Chris Cviic

See also EUROPE (Facts in Brief Table). In WORLD BOOK, see POLAND.

POLLUTION. See ENVIRONMENTAL POLLUTION.

POPULAR MUSIC. The United States popular music industry had a mixed year in 1986. Cassette and album sales dropped. Artistically, however, critics regarded much of the new music as high in quality, with especially good work by many female and black musicians. There also was a revival of interest in jazz and in classic rock.

The total number of records, compact disks (CD's), audiocassettes, and eight-track tapes sold in the first half of 1986 dropped about 6.9 per cent from the same period in 1985. A drastic decline in album sales, the result of growing consumer preference for audiocassettes and CD's, prompted some music experts to forecast a time when many titles would no longer be available on the traditional, black vinyl record.

Humanitarian Efforts by many musicians continued in 1986. Amnesty International—a London-based human-rights organization—was supported by U2, Sting, Peter Gabriel, and others in a Conspiracy of Hope tour in June. On July 4, in Manor, Tex., Farm Aid II, organized by Willie Nelson to show support for American farmers, raised $500,000 in telephone pledges during the show and $800,000 in ticket sales. The Concert That Counts, held on April 26 in Los Angeles to raise money to combat drug abuse, featured Madonna, Mr. Mister, Aretha Franklin, and many

others. Some artists gave concerts and wrote songs about the dangers of *crack*—a smokable form of cocaine. See NEWSMAKERS OF 1986 (Close-Up).

Women made popular music history in 1986 when six female vocalists had number-one albums on *Billboard* magazine's top pop albums chart—Barbra Streisand, Sade, Whitney Houston, Janet Jackson, Patti LaBelle, and Madonna—toppling the 1974 record of four female chart-toppers. The album *Whitney Houston* was number one for 14 weeks and sold more than 7 million copies in the United States, as well as more than 3 million in other countries. Madonna's *True Blue* was number one in the United States, Canada, Great Britain, West Germany, and Italy, and "The Virgin Tour" topped the music video chart for over two months. In the growing field of gospel music, Amy Grant won a Grammy for best female gospel vocal for the fourth year in a row.

Black Artists continued the trend toward broader acceptance by pop audiences. In September, Lionel Richie's *Dancing on the Ceiling* became the fifth number-one pop album by a black in 1986—following top pop albums by Sade, Houston, Jackson, and LaBelle—marking a record number for top pop albums by black artists in a single year.

Major record labels intensified their recording

The Everly Brothers, left and center, are inducted into the new Rock and Roll Hall of Fame in January in New York City as Neil Young looks on.

The Once and Future King

Benny Goodman, the jazz clarinetist and band-leader known as the King of Swing, died on June 13, 1986. Goodman led a groundbreaking orchestra during the swing era, the period from about 1935 to 1945 when a smooth, danceable type of jazz called *swing* dominated popular music. He delighted listeners with his rhythmic renditions of such hits as "King Porter Stomp" and "Sing Sing Sing."

Goodman's death was followed on July 31, 1986, by that of pianist Teddy Wilson, the last surviving member of the 1936 Benny Goodman Trio. Their passing seemed to mean that the swing era was gone forever. The trio's drummer, Gene Krupa, had died in 1973.

The King of Swing was first and foremost an extraordinarily gifted musician whose mastery of the clarinet made it the dominant horn of the swing years. Goodman was one of the first jazz musicians to double as a classical performer. In 1938, the Goodman band gave the first jazz concert ever presented at Carnegie Hall in New York City. That same year, Goodman recorded classical music with the Budapest String Quartet. He also commissioned and recorded works by Hungarian composer Béla Bartók, German composer Paul Hindemith, and others.

No less significant was Goodman's role as a pioneer in integrating black and white musicians. He introduced the great black singer Billie Holiday on a 1933 recording. In 1936, he hired Wilson as part of the Benny Goodman Trio. Later that year, he added vibraphonist Lionel Hampton, expanding the trio to a quartet. Wilson and Hampton were both black, making Goodman's band the first top group to put black and white musicians together on stage.

Benjamin David Goodman was born in Chicago on May 30, 1909. His father made a meager living as a tailor. The family had 12 children. The Kehelah Jacob Synagogue lent musical instruments to Benny and his brothers, who played in the synagogue's youth band.

Private lessons followed. Benny made his first public appearance at the age of 12. Shortly before Goodman's 16th birthday, he went to California to join one of the best jazz bands of the time, led by drummer Ben Pollack.

After leaving Pollack in 1929, Goodman became a busy free-lance studio musician in New York City. He led his own band on a 1934 radio series that aired at midnight on the East Coast and so drew most of its audience from the West Coast, where it began at 9 P.M. During the winter of 1934-1935, Goodman took his band on a cross-country tour, drawing larger audiences the farther west he went. By the time he arrived in California, his radio reputation brought him sellout crowds. The successful tour made the Goodman band famous and established swing as the dominant popular music of the time.

Goodman's clarinet solos, warm and subtle on ballads, spirited and exciting at faster tempos, provided the main ingredient for the band's success. Many of the group's greatest hits resulted from swinging arrangements of both standard jazz tunes and conventional popular songs by Fletcher Henderson, Edgar M. Sampson, and other gifted arrangers.

Many members of Goodman's band went on to form their own successful groups. Besides Wilson, Krupa, and Hampton, they included the trumpeters Bunny Berigan, Harry James, and Cootie Williams.

Goodman recorded the sound track for a biographical motion picture, *The Benny Goodman Story* (1956), with comedian Steve Allen playing the title role. In 1962, Goodman took a band to the Soviet Union as part of a cultural exchange program.

Although some jazz historians feel that the King of Swing title should have belonged to pianists Duke Ellington or Count Basie, Goodman's contribution as an artist has never been questioned. He continued playing until shortly before his death. The King of Swing may be gone, but he left a musical legacy that will long endure.   Leonard Feather

Benny Goodman, known as the King of Swing, became famous both as a bandleader and for his spirited, subtle jazz clarinet solos.

Whitney Houston, whose flexible, pop-gospel voice launched a best-selling debut album, thrilled concert crowds in 1986.

and promoting of rap music, a kind of rhythmic talking set to a musical beat. Top rap-music performers included the Fat Boys, Whodini, and Run-D.M.C., whose *Raising Hell* was the first *platinum* (million-selling) rap album. Timex Social Club's "Rumors" became the first rap single to crack the top 10 in *Billboard*'s singles chart since Blondie's "Rapture" in 1981.

Jazz flourished in 1986, with every major American record company actively recording jazz for the first time since the late 1960's. This resurgence of interest in jazz, also reflected by increased radio play, was stimulated by the rise in popularity of jazz-influenced "new age," or "meditative" music; the maturing musical tastes of the huge post-World War II generation; and jazz in such pop acts as Sade and Sting.

Guitarist Stanley Jordan's *Magic Touch* was the best-selling jazz album for a record 49 weeks. Another manifestation of the flowering of interest in jazz was the appearance of a full-length jazz film, *Round Midnight*, starring saxophonist Dexter Gordon and a band led by pianist Herbie Hancock.

Rock Music's veteran artists had an outstanding year. In February, *Rolling Stone* magazine announced that Bruce Springsteen was voted artist of the year in its annual readers' poll, and his "My Hometown" became the seventh top-10 single from his 1984 album, *Born in the U.S.A.*—tying Mi-

chael Jackson's record of seven from *Thriller*. In November 1986, fans lined up to purchase the newly released five-record set, *Bruce Springsteen & the E Street Band Live 1975-85*. The album sold a record 1 million units its first day in the stores.

The Rolling Stones' "Harlem Shuffle" became their 22nd top-10 single—more than 21 years after their first top single, "Time Is on My Side"—the longest top-10 span of any group. "Sledgehammer," a single from Peter Gabriel's critically acclaimed album *So*, became the first song by a veteran rock star to top *Billboard*'s dance/disco chart since David Bowie's "Let's Dance" in 1983. Many critics admired Paul Simon's *Graceland* album, recorded mostly in South Africa with black musicians and South African pop styles. Other popular rock albums featured Billy Joel, Huey Lewis and the News, Paul McCartney, Talking Heads, and Van Halen.

Rock History came alive in 1986, as many performers, record producers, and advertisers drew on the vitality and emotional impact of music of the 1960's and 1970's to enliven products and memories of the 1980's. The first annual Rock and Roll Hall of Fame induction dinner was held on January 23 at the Waldorf-Astoria Hotel in New York City. Many influential figures in rock and roll were honored, including James Brown and Jerry Lee Lewis. Artists Robert Johnson and Jimmie Rodgers were honored posthumously.

The Monkees had five albums on the charts due to extensive rebroadcasting of their old television shows on MTV and a 120-date tour by three of the original Monkees. Other indications of interest in the past were a six-part TV series, "Motown on Showtime," a line of Elvis Presley cosmetics called "Love Me Tender," release of MTV's Closet Classics—vintage videos of artists of the past—for home video, and an increasing reliance by radio stations on oldies or "classic cuts."

Country Music record sales—which had dipped in 1985—rose in 1986, partly spurred by interest in new artists, such as Randy Travis, the Judds, the Forester Sisters, Kathy Mattea, and George Strait, whose album *#7* was a big hit. With *Greatest Hits*, Alabama became the first country act to earn eight consecutive platinum albums, and *Alabama's Greatest Video Hits* was the first country video to go platinum. Other big-selling country albums were Willie Nelson's *The Promiseland*, Travis' *Storms of Life*, and Hank Williams, Jr.'s *Montana Cafe*.

Music Video sales and rentals for home viewing rose in 1986, though the number of video clips produced declined as major labels cut their video budgets. The Norwegian group a-ha won seven categories in the Third MTV Video Music Awards on September 5 for "Take On Me" and "The Sun Always Shines on TV." Dire Straits won best video for "Money for Nothing."

Charges of Bribery in the recording industry were made on the February 24 broadcast of "The NBC Nightly News." The report, which said that many independent promoters hired by record companies bribed disk jockeys to give their records radio airtime—a practice known as *payola*—prompted a Senate investigation. The resulting shakeup caused major record companies to stop hiring independent promoters.

Offensive Lyrics. The drive to require record companies to label records that contain lyrics offensive to some people—started in 1985 by the National PTA and a Washington, D.C.-based group called Parents' Music Resource Center—continued to have an effect in 1986. Wal-Mart Stores Incorporated and other retailers pulled questionable albums from their shelves. On June 12, Wal-Mart also decided not to sell rock and pop music publications in any of the chain's stores.

Deaths in 1986 included songwriters Harold Arlen and Alan Jay Lerner; bandleaders Benny Goodman (see Close-Up) and Teddy Wilson; singers Kate Smith and Rudy Vallee; and rockers Phil Lynot of Thin Lizzy, O'Kelly Isley of the Isley Brothers, Bobby Nunn of the Coasters, and Richard Manuel of The Band. Jerry M. Grigadean

See also AWARDS AND PRIZES (Arts Awards). In WORLD BOOK, see COUNTRY MUSIC; JAZZ; POPULAR MUSIC; ROCK MUSIC.

POPULATION. The population of the world reached the milestone 5-billion mark during 1986. Since 1950, global population has about doubled. In the next 35 to 40 years, world population will increase by 3 billion more, according to projections by the United Nations.

Growth Rates and Projections. In the industrialized nations, a pronounced decline in birth rates has lowered population growth to about 0.6 per cent per year. Population in the developing nations, however, is increasing at approximately 2 per cent annually. If this rate remains constant, population of the Third World will double by the year 2020. By that time, according to growth estimates from the Population Reference Bureau in Washington, D.C., about 83 per cent of the world's population will be living in Africa, Asia, and Latin America.

Life Expectancy showed little appreciable change in most countries of the world during 1986, though the disparity between industrialized and developing nations remained great. Life expectancy at birth was nearly 75 years for people living in Australia, Canada, Great Britain, and the United States. Life expectancies in central and southern Africa were slightly more than half that long. People living in Burundi or Niger had a life expectancy of only 41 years. Kevin J. Hawker

In WORLD BOOK, see POPULATION.

PORTUGAL. Mário Soares, a Socialist, won a hard-fought presidential election on Feb. 16, 1986, defeating the candidate of the "united Portuguese right," Christian Democrat Diogo Freitas do Amaral, by 51 per cent to 49 per cent. Soares succeeded another Socialist, António dos Santos Ramalho Eanes, who was required by law to step down. Soares had quit as prime minister in November 1985, after his coalition government of Socialists and Social Democrats broke up.

The February 1986 election was a runoff, held because no candidate received more than half the vote in balloting conducted on January 26. Freitas finished first in January, winning about 47 per cent of the vote to 25 per cent for Soares and 21 per cent for Francisco Salgado Zenha, who had strong Communist support. Maria de Lourdes Pintasilgo, another left wing candidate, finished a distant fourth with 7.6 per cent.

Before the February vote, Prime Minister Aníbal Cavaço Silva, a Freitas supporter, warned that the election of Soares threatened Portugal's stability and business success. On February 21, however, Cavaço Silva and Soares said they were determined to work in harmony. Soares promised to support Cavaço Silva's right-of-center minority government as long as it had the confidence of Parliament.

Terrorist Murder. A left wing terrorist group, the Popular Forces of April 25 (FP25), killed Gaspar Castelo Branco, head of Portugal's prison system, on the eve of the runoff. FP25 timed the murder to have the maximum impact on voters.

Anniversary. On May 8, Portugal and Great Britain celebrated the 600th anniversary of the Treaty of Windsor, signed by King John I of Portugal and England's King Richard II. The treaty bound the two countries in "perpetual and real league" for six centuries. Soares and Cavaço Silva attended ceremonies marking the occasion in London.

Labor Laws. Cavaço Silva threatened to call new elections if he failed to get his proposed legislation on labor, agricultural reform, internal security, and government news media through Parliament. The main point of disagreement was Cavaço Silva's proposal to modify labor laws to permit short-term contracts and to allow private employers to dismiss workers. On June 20, the government lost a vote on labor reform in Parliament. Soares did not follow through on his threat, however.

Economic Recovery. Falling oil prices helped Portugal's economy to recover from a decade of mounting deficits, high unemployment, and increasing foreign debt. The drop in oil prices enabled Portugal to save money at a rate of about $1 billion per year. Kenneth Brown

See also EUROPE (Facts in Brief Table). In WORLD BOOK, see PORTUGAL.

POSTAL SERVICE, UNITED STATES. For the U.S. Postal Service, 1986 was the most trying period in its 15-year history as an independent agency. There were three postmasters general during the year, and the vice chairman of the Postal Service's Board of Governors pleaded guilty to bribery charges.

Carlin Ousted. On January 6, the Board of Governors fired Postmaster General Paul N. Carlin, who had occupied the position for just one year. The board charged that Carlin had moved too slowly in making personnel cuts and improving the Postal Service's productivity. The Postal Service work force grew from 702,000 to 740,000 in the fiscal year that ended on Sept. 30, 1985. In the same period, a deficit of $251.5 million replaced a surplus of $117 million—the agency's first loss in four years. To replace Carlin on an interim basis, the Board of Governors hired Albert V. Casey, former chairman of AMR Corporation.

On March 24, Casey announced the elimination of one of four layers of Postal Service management. Casey established 74 divisions, whose managers were to report directly to five regional postmasters general. Casey's action eliminated 42 district offices.

Voss Pleads Guilty. On May 30, Peter E. Voss, vice chairman of the Board of Governors, pleaded guilty to defrauding the government as part of a kickback scheme. He was sentenced in October to a four-year term in prison. An appointee of President Ronald Reagan, Voss had been co-chairman of Reagan's 1980 presidential campaign in Ohio. On June 27, 1986, Carlin sued the Board of Governors—unsuccessfully—for reinstatement, claiming he was fired for trying to stymie Voss's efforts to influence granting of Postal Service contracts.

The Year's Third Postmaster General, Preston R. Tisch, took office on August 15. Tisch had been president of Loews Corporation, a New York City-based company with holdings in tobacco, hotels, and theaters. He and his brother Laurence, as the guiding lights of Loews, had amassed a family fortune estimated at $1.6 billion.

Subsidized Mail Rates for schools, libraries, churches, and other nonprofit mailers were raised twice in 1986. Increases of 23 to 41 per cent took effect on January 1, and increases of 14 to 20 per cent were approved by the Board of Governors on March 4. The increases were imposed to make up for cuts in the Postal Service budget.

New Postal Vehicles. In April, the Board of Governors approved a $1.1-billion contract with the Grumman Corporation of Bethpage, N.Y., to build 99,150 mail-delivery vans. It was the largest single purchase of vehicles in the history of the Postal Service.　　　Frank Cormier and Margot Cormier

In WORLD BOOK, see POST OFFICE; POSTAL SERVICE, UNITED STATES.

PRESIDENT OF THE UNITED STATES Ronald Reagan was rocked by the backlash of a major foreign-policy controversy in 1986 as he neared the end of his sixth year in office. On November 25, Reagan announced that two of his key national security aides were leaving the White House following a bombshell disclosure that profits from secret arms sales to Iran had been diverted to finance *contra* rebels fighting the government of Nicaragua.

The contra-aid revelations came amid sharp debate over a Reagan initiative to curry favor with moderate Iranians through secret arms sales. Those weapons shipments coincided closely with the release of three American hostages kidnapped by pro-Iranian Muslim extremists in Lebanon. Polls indicated most Americans were skeptical of Reagan's claim that there had been no arms-for-hostages swap. And there was bipartisan criticism of the President's approval of such arms deals even as he was urging allies not to sell weapons to Iran.

Downed Cargo Plane. The Reagan Administration's efforts to finance the Nicaraguan rebels pending Congress's approval of such support first attracted notice on October 5, when an American-owned C-123K cargo plane loaded with weapons bound for the contras was shot down over Nicaragua. Three crewmen were killed and one American, Eugene Hasenfus, was captured, tried, and sentenced to 30 years in a Nicaraguan prison. Hasenfus was pardoned and freed on December 17.

Reagan denied any U.S. government connection with the ill-fated flight, but it was apparently just one of a series of such flights that may have been financed by the Iranian arms sales. The financial transactions by which money was diverted to the contras were reportedly masterminded from offices of the National Security Council (NSC)—a body that advises the President on matters of intelligence, foreign policy, and defense—in the White House basement.

Ironically, the financing scandal threatened to overturn Reagan's biggest foreign-policy triumph of the year in Congress—a June 25 decision by the House of Representatives to reverse itself and approve, 221 to 209, his request for $100 million in military and other aid to the contras. In March, the House had rejected the request, 222 to 210. The Senate passed the aid package on August 13 by a 53 to 47 margin. But after the financing scandal broke, many members of Congress, including some Republicans, predicted that no further aid for the contras would be approved in 1987.

Eighteen Months of Secret Contacts between the Reagan Administration and Iranians came to light after a Beirut, Lebanon, magazine reported on November 3 that Robert C. McFarlane, a former

President Reagan and Soviet leader Mikhail S. Gorbachev emerge glumly from talks in Reykjavík, Iceland, on October 12 after failing to reach a nuclear arms agreement.

chief of Reagan's NSC staff, had traveled to Teheran, Iran, the previous month to meet with an Iranian faction. Hojatolislam Hashemi Rafsanjani, speaker of the Iranian parliament, confirmed McFarlane's visit the next day. Within hours, new reports detailed a series of U.S.-sanctioned arms shipments to Iran, which had been at war with Iraq for six years. The timing of the weapons shipments had coincided closely with the release, over a 14-month period, of three Americans held hostage in Lebanon by pro-Iranian extremists. During the same period, three more Americans were kidnapped in Beirut.

Because the United States had denounced Iran as a sponsor of terrorism, vowed never to negotiate with terrorists, and energetically urged other nations to block all weapons sales to that country, word of the arms shipments provoked a rapidly escalating controversy. And because the Administration had deliberately withheld information about the operation from Congress, many lawmakers claimed that Reagan had violated a law requiring congressional notification of such developments in "timely fashion"—a claim Reagan rejected. The clamor mounted as it became known that the maneuvering had also been kept secret from most top military and diplomatic officials.

An Embattled Reagan addressed the nation on November 13 to defend his "secret diplomatic initiative" and deny that the United States had made a "ransom payment" to Iran to obtain freedom for hostages. He said he had approved small, covert shipments of defensive arms to gain "access and influence" with Iranian moderates, end the Iran-Iraq war, and stem terrorism. At one of his infrequent televised news conferences, on November 19, the President insisted: ". . . I don't think a mistake was made. It was a high-risk gamble . . . that I believe the circumstances warranted, and I don't see that it has been a fiasco or a great failure of any kind." But he said he would make no further arms deals with Iran.

Then came Reagan's November 25 announcement that his national security adviser, Vice Admiral John M. Poindexter, had resigned and that a key NSC deputy, Marine Lieutenant Colonel Oliver L. North, had been fired. Looking grim, Reagan told reporters "I was not fully informed" about "one of the activities undertaken" in connection with the Iran arms sales. Attorney General Edwin Meese III then disclosed that $10 million to $30 million in profits from weapons sold to Iran had been deposited in Swiss bank accounts and "made available to the forces in Central America"—the contras—at a time when Congress had barred military aid to the rebels. Meese said North was the only person in the government with "precise knowledge" of the money transfers.

PRESIDENT OF THE UNITED STATES

Congress Scoffs. Members of Congress from both parties scoffed at the idea that North had carried out the contra financing scheme without authority from higher-ranking officials. "I don't think Ripley [of *Ripley's Believe It or Not*] would believe that," said Senate Republican leader Robert J. Dole of Kansas. A CBS-*New York Times* poll conducted on November 30 showed that 59 per cent of those questioned thought Reagan knew about the money dealings. The President's approval rating dropped more than 20 points in two months to 46 per cent of those polled; disapproval rose to 45 per cent.

As 1986 ended, an independent counsel and Congress were investigating the scandal, and a Reagan-appointed Special Review Board was studying the NSC structure. The President appointed Frank C. Carlucci, a former deputy secretary of defense and former deputy director of the Central Intelligence Agency, to succeed Poindexter as head of the NSC staff.

Iceland Meeting. The arms controversy was just one of a series of setbacks and embarrassments that Reagan experienced in 1986. A hastily arranged summit meeting in Reykjavík, Iceland, with Soviet leader Mikhail S. Gorbachev on October 11 and 12 collapsed amid confusing claims of near-agreement on nuclear arms control.

The two leaders, by their own accounts, came close to agreeing on sweeping arms-control proposals during their discussions, but they deadlocked on the key issue of restricting the planned U.S. space-based missile defense system known as the Strategic Defense Initiative (SDI) or "Star Wars." Gorbachev said Reagan's insistence on putting SDI into operation "frustrated and scuttled" an opportunity for dramatic accords.

One proposal raised by Reagan was a missile-free Europe—an idea he embraced without consulting European allies or the Joint Chiefs of Staff, his top military advisers. The allies complained that the removal of American missiles from Europe might leave them vulnerable to massive Soviet-bloc conventional forces. Reagan backed away from the idea in November after meeting at Camp David in Maryland with British Prime Minister Margaret Thatcher.

The Daniloff Incident. Reagan's conduct of foreign affairs was also called into question in September as a result of his Administration's handling of a diplomatic incident between the United States and the Soviet Union. On August 30, an American journalist, Nicholas S. Daniloff, was arrested in Moscow and charged—falsely, by most accounts—with being a spy. Daniloff's seizure was apparently in retaliation for the earlier arrest on spy charges

Dancers greet President Reagan and Nancy Reagan—flanked by Indonesia's
President Suharto and his wife—as they arrive in Bali for an April visit.

of a Soviet citizen, Gennadi F. Zakharov, working at the United Nations.

Daniloff was freed on September 29 after the United States agreed to let Zakharov return home. Soviet officials also allowed dissident Yuri Orlov and his wife to leave the Soviet Union on October 5. Although Reagan insisted that the episode was not a trade, his critics thought otherwise.

Reagan's Congressional Scorecard. Besides persuading Congress to authorize military aid to the contras, Reagan prevailed in winning approval for the production of a new generation of nerve gas weapons. The President also narrowly salvaged a reduced, $250-million arms sale to Saudi Arabia.

Reagan was dealt his biggest foreign-policy defeat in Congress when the Senate voted 78 to 21 on October 2 to override his veto of a measure imposing new economic *sanctions* (penalties) against South Africa's white-dominated minority government. The imposition of sanctions marked the first instance in which Congress voted to override a Reagan veto on a major foreign-policy issue.

Attacks on Libya. Tension between the United States and Libya mounted in early 1986 as Reagan assumed an increasingly muscular stance against Libyan leader Muammar Muhammad al-Qadhafi as a reputed sponsor of international terrorism. On January 7, Reagan imposed economic sanctions against Libya and ordered all Americans to leave that country. He acted because of reported Libyan support for terrorist attacks 11 days earlier at airports in Rome and in Vienna, Austria, that claimed the lives of five Americans.

On March 23, a large U.S. Navy task force began a "freedom of navigation" exercise in the Gulf of Sidra, claimed by Libya as its territorial waters. The next day, Libya fired antiaircraft missiles at American jets flying over the gulf. The warplanes struck back by attacking a mainland missile installation and sinking at least two Libyan patrol boats. There were no American casualties.

Two U.S. servicemen were killed by the April 5 terror bombing of a West Berlin discothèque. Asserting that he had conclusive evidence that the bombing had been executed under the direct orders of Qadhafi's regime, Reagan ordered air strikes on April 15 against targets in Libya.

On October 2, *The Washington* (D.C.) *Post* reported that Reagan had approved a secret plan to harass Qadhafi through a campaign of lies that found their way into the *Post*, *The Wall Street Journal*, and other news outlets. In October, State Department spokesman Bernard Kalb resigned in protest. Frank Cormier and Margot Cormier

See also CABINET, UNITED STATES; CONGRESS OF THE UNITED STATES; REAGAN, RONALD WILSON; UNITED STATES, GOVERNMENT OF THE. In WORLD BOOK, see PRESIDENT OF THE UNITED STATES.

PRINCE EDWARD ISLAND. Canada's smallest province returned to the Liberal Party fold on April 21, 1986, after seven years of Progressive Conservative (PC) rule. Joseph A. Ghiz led the Liberals to power and was chosen premier.

James M. Lee, premier since 1981, lost his own seat. In addition, the Liberals captured 21 seats in the island's legislature to the 11 taken by the PC's. About 80 per cent of the island's 86,805 eligible voters cast ballots. Some commentators said Lee was insensitive to women's issues, and they saw this as a reason for his party's loss of seats in the capital city of Charlottetown, where the shift of seats may have cost him the election.

Both Ghiz and Lee stressed employment and economic issues in their campaigns. Lee also campaigned on a pledge to bring a radar plant to be built by Litton Systems Canada Limited to the province. But the promise gained a mixed reaction. Some residents were concerned about introducing a military-equipment manufacturer into the island's traditional agricultural society, and others worried about financial burdens that might arise from inducements granted to Litton. Ghiz was noncommittal about the project before the election, and his government failed to work out an agreement with Litton. David M. L. Farr

See also CANADA; GHIZ, JOSEPH A. In WORLD BOOK, see PRINCE EDWARD ISLAND.

PRISON crowding continued to be a severe problem in the United States in 1986. From 1980 to 1985, the nation's prison population had grown by almost 174,000, or 53 per cent. Most state prison systems and the federal system had been filled beyond their capacity. During 1985, 19 states had reported the early release of 18,617 prisoners because of crowding. The Bureau of Justice Statistics, a unit of the U.S. Department of Justice, reported that the number of inmates housed in state and federal prisons grew by more than 5 per cent during the first six months of 1986 to a record 528,945 inmates.

The crowding problem has been brought to the attention of the courts. In most cases, the courts have found that the states were operating prisons under conditions that violated the Eighth Amendment to the United States Constitution, which forbids "cruel and unusual punishments." Correctional agencies or individual prisons operated under federal court orders in 37 states in 1986. Prison administrators continued to seek alternatives to imprisonment, including intensive supervision by probation and parole officers, the use of house arrest, and increased use of minimum-security work camps.

Women Behind Bars. On June 30, 1986, about 4.8 per cent of all prisoners were women. This was up from 4.2 per cent in 1981. There were 19 sentenced women in prison per 100,000 U.S. females on June 30, 1986, compared with 411 sentenced male prisoners per 100,000 males.

Beds. States added about 165,000 prison beds between 1978 and 1985, an increase of almost two-thirds. The number of inmates, however, increased by 188,000, leaving a shortfall of 23,000 beds. Federal and state correctional systems planned to spend more than $3 billion for 59,000 new beds in fiscal year 1986.

Death Penalty. In December 1986, 1,838 prisoners in 33 states awaited execution, an increase of about 13 per cent in one year. Eighteen prisoners were executed in 1986. On June 26, the Supreme Court of the United States ruled that it is unconstitutional to execute prisoners who have become insane while on death row and that states must provide such prisoners a fair opportunity to provide evidence of insanity.

Other Decisions. On March 4, 1986, the U.S. Supreme Court ruled that being shot by guards during a prison disturbance is not cruel and unusual punishment in violation of the Eighth Amendment. On June 19, the court upheld a Pennsylvania law requiring a minimum sentence of five years' imprisonment for possession of a firearm while committing certain crimes.   Patricia L. Millard

In WORLD BOOK, see PRISON.

PRIZES. See AWARDS AND PRIZES; NOBEL PRIZES.

PROTESTANTISM. The enthronement of Desmond M. Tutu, winner of the 1984 Nobel Peace Prize, as the first black Anglican archbishop of Cape Town, South Africa, on Sept. 7, 1986, focused the eyes of the Protestant world on the struggle against *apartheid*, South Africa's policy of racial segregation. Some 200 million television viewers around the world watched the ceremony at St. George's Cathedral in Cape Town.

Many of the Protestant leaders present were allies in the antiapartheid struggle, including Allan Boesak, chaplain of the University of the Western Cape in Bellville, South Africa, and president of the World Alliance of Reformed Churches. Boesak frequently traveled to Europe and the United States to seek support for antiapartheid efforts. Many Protestant ministers—both white and black—were among those detained by the South African government as part of emergency measures enacted in June to suppress dissent.

Criticism of the Right. Protestantism made news in Latin America as Roman Catholics voiced concern about the dramatic growth of Pentecostal, evangelical, fundamentalist, and other Protestant movements among Catholic populations. The reform-minded Catholic Liberation Theologians criticized conservative Protestant leadership for attracting people who supported right wing regimes, such as that in Chile.

The Catholic bishops, on the other hand, whose spokesman was Luis Eduardo Castano, ecumenical officer of the Latin American Bishops' Conference, were alarmed at what they considered "sheep stealing" by evangelizers. Some of these bishops, however, used this competition to spur their own followers to be more active in the Catholic Church.

Baptist Friction. The June 10 meeting of the Southern Baptist Convention (SBC), in Atlanta, Ga., was marked by an increase in disunity. For more than a decade, the Baptist convention has been torn apart by an ever-growing fundamentalist faction, which charges that not all of the denomination's seminary professors or managerial staffs follow a sufficiently conservative doctrine. Many in the fundamentalist faction have reduced the controversy to a battle over the *inerrancy* (freedom from error) of the Bible.

The SBC moderates, less organized and lacking charismatic leaders like those who have headed the convention in the 1980's, have seen their representation on church boards decline each year.

New Lutheran Church. The disunity evident at the Southern Baptist Convention was not present at the August meetings of three Lutheran groups. On August 8, the American Lutheran Church, the Lutheran Church in America (LCA), and the Association of Evangelical Lutheran Churches, meeting in Minneapolis, Minn., Milwaukee, and Chicago, respectively, voted simultaneously to merge into a new group called the Evangelical Lutheran Church in America. The new church, scheduled to come into being on Jan. 1, 1988, will be the fourth largest Protestant denomination in the United States. The merger will give the three groups a larger voice in Washington, D.C., on social issues, and church leaders hoped it would attract Hispanics and other ethnic groups to the church.

Throughout the negotiations, the three groups were united in doctrine, but controversies arose over the relative power of congregations and bishops and the quota system of racial and gender representation at conventions. There was also conflict over the location of the church's new headquarters. After much maneuvering, the three groups decided on Chicago.

Episcopal Election. On January 11, Edmond Lee Browning, 56, former bishop of Hawaii, was consecrated as presiding bishop of the Episcopal Church. He will serve a 12-year term. Browning is regarded as a strong leader who preaches that the church must show concern for the social order. He is expected to provide a morale boost for the Episcopal Church, which, along with other mainstream Protestant groups, has seen a loss in membership in the 1980's.

In other Episcopal news, Robert A. K. Runcie,

Dean Kenneth Cyril Gram, left, blesses Desmond M. Tutu during Tutu's enthrone-ment as Anglican archbishop of Cape Town, South Africa, on September 7.

the archbishop of Canterbury, joined Bishop James W. Crumley of the LCA in approving an Episcopal-Lutheran joint communion rite at the LCA convention in Milwaukee in August.

Former Hostage Elected. The Presbyterian Church (U.S.A.), at its June 11 convention in Minneapolis, elected Benjamin M. Weir as moderator of the church, its highest elected office. Weir is a missionary who had been a hostage of Shiite Muslims in Lebanon from May 1984 to September 1985.

This denomination, whose northern and southern branches merged in 1983, also debated where to locate its new headquarters. A decision was expected to be reached in January 1987.

Ethnic Potential. With the U.S. Hispanic population expected to grow from 23 million to 40 million in the next 20 years, many Protestant leaders have begun to assess the strength of ethnic minorities in their churches. In the Assemblies of God, a Pentecostal group, ethnic membership grew 48 per cent in 10 years, while the SBC saw a 70 per cent increase. The SBC has 4,600 non-English-speaking congregations, in which sermons are preached in 87 languages. The American Baptist Churches in the U.S.A. has had a 43 per cent increase in ethnic membership.

South African Stance. The issue of apartheid in South Africa became a part of Protestant church life as churches and their agencies, particularly pension boards, debated whether to *divest* (sell) their holdings in companies that did business with South Africa. Debates over divestment and support of United States sanctions against South Africa were also a hot topic at Protestant conventions in 1986.

Smuggling Refugees. Another controversial issue centered on whether churches should be used as sanctuaries for people fleeing from El Salvador and Guatemala, claiming that their lives would be jeopardized if they returned to their homes. On May 1, a Tucson, Ariz., court convicted 8 of 11 defendants for conspiracy to smuggle Salvadorans and Guatemalans out of their countries. Among the convicted was John M. Fife, a Presbyterian minister who helped to create a movement that gives church sanctuary to aliens from Central America. The courts found the activists guilty of breaking immigration and conspiracy laws.

An important side issue that surfaced during the trial was the federal government's use of paid informers to infiltrate church activities. The ALC, the Presbyterian Church (U.S.A.), and four of their local churches filed suit against the United States government in protest of such infiltration.

School Battle. In late October, a federal judge ruled in favor of Christian fundamentalists who had charged that officials of a Tennessee school had violated students' religious freedoms when they expelled them for refusing to read "anti-Christian" books. Christian fundamentalists expected the debate over evolution to become a hot topic in 1987, with a Louisiana law that requires the teaching of "scientific creationism" scheduled to come before the Supreme Court of the United States.

Presidential Potential. A much publicized development in Protestantism in the United States was an increase in political involvement among evangelicals, often described as the New Christian Right. The prime newsmaker was television evangelist Marion G. (Pat) Robertson. Robertson built up the Christian Broadcasting Network, which takes in more than $300 million annually. In this enterprise, he became a spokesperson for conservative causes, serving as a voice for people who feel that their positions, including opposition to abortion and support of school prayer, have not received sufficient publicity.

On September 17, Robertson announced to 200,000 followers on closed-circuit TV that he would become a candidate for the Republican presidential nomination in 1988 if 3 million Americans signed petitions supporting him. Martin E. Marty

See also RELIGION. In WORLD BOOK, see PROTESTANTISM and articles on Protestant denominations.

PSYCHOLOGY. A 1986 book by psychologist Robert J. Sternberg of Yale University in New Haven, Conn., proposed a new theory of intelligence that could change the way psychologists and educators measure intellectual ability. Sternberg's book, *Intelligence Applied,* uses the symbol of a *triarchy* (a government ruled by three people) to represent the three aspects of intelligence that he says every person has in varying degrees: *componential, experiential,* and *contextual.* Sternberg called this the triarchic theory of intelligence.

Sternberg Explained these different aspects of intelligence by describing the intellectual ability of three imaginary graduate students—Alice, Barbara, and Celia. Alice is extremely smart, according to conventional theories of intelligence and intelligence quotient (IQ) tests. This type of intelligence involves the *components* or parts of the thinking process that are used in test-taking and analytical thinking. Unfortunately, people like Alice do not always do well in graduate school because they rely too much on their test-taking ability and not enough on the other two aspects of intelligence, Sternberg said.

Barbara represents experiential thinking. Barbara does not earn high grades and does not do exceptionally well on typical IQ tests. She is, however, extremely creative, develops good ideas, and conducts exceptional research projects. She can combine distinctly different experiences in creative and insightful ways.

Celia represents contextual intelligence. She is neither exceptionally creative nor gifted as a test-taker, but she has what Sternberg called "street-smarts," practical knowledge of people and the world. Celia knows how to play the game of life. She can adapt to the environment or shape it to fit her needs so that she comes out on top in almost any context or environment.

Every person has varying degrees of these three aspects of intelligence, said Sternberg. To reach their maximum potential, people should take the thought processes used in componential or "Alice" intelligence, apply them to their knowledge of experiences or "Barbara" intelligence, and use them both to adapt to and shape their environment, as in contextual or "Celia" intelligence.

Sternberg expects that his theory will have an important impact on how psychologists and educators test intelligence. He is developing a new test of mental abilities based on this triarchic theory. Sternberg is also designing a training program that will help people make the most of their intellectual strengths and improve their intellectual weaknesses.

Drugs Versus Therapy. A long-standing argument over the best type of treatment for depression, a mental disorder characterized by deep feelings of sadness and worthlessness, was partially settled in 1986. In May, the National Institute of Mental Health in Rockville, Md., released the results of a study comparing the effectiveness of psychotherapy with a commonly used antidepressant drug, *imipramine.* Both were found effective.

Depression, one of the most common forms of psychological disturbance, strikes as many as 10 million to 14 million people in the United States every year. Two popular treatments for depression are psychotherapy and drugs. Supporters of psychotherapy claim that it gives patients the self-understanding and social skills necessary to ward off future bouts of depression, besides relieving symptoms. Supporters of drug therapy say that antidepressant drugs correct the brain chemical imbalances that accompany—and may even cause—depression. The research was conducted at the University of Pittsburgh in Bradford, Pa.; George Washington University in Washington, D.C.; and the University of Oklahoma in Oklahoma City. The study included 239 moderately to severely depressed patients who received either psychotherapy or drug therapy. Each type of therapy eliminated serious symptoms in 50 to 60 per cent of patients who remained in treatment for 16 weeks. Robert J. Trotter

See also MENTAL ILLNESS. In the Special Reports section, see THE HAZARDS OF TEEN-AGE DRINKING. In WORLD BOOK, see PSYCHOLOGY.

PUBLIC HEALTH. On March 13, 1986, officials of the U.S. Public Health Service and one of its agencies, the Centers for Disease Control (CDC) in Atlanta, Ga., recommended that Americans who run the risk of contracting acquired immune deficiency syndrome (AIDS) undergo periodic blood tests to determine whether they have been infected with the AIDS virus. The officials cited growing evidence that AIDS is spread largely by infected people who have not yet developed symptoms of the disease.

Donald R. Hopkins, deputy director of the CDC, recommended the blood tests for homosexual and bisexual men, past and present intravenous drug abusers, male and female prostitutes, sexual partners of AIDS victims, people born in Haiti or Central African countries where AIDS occurs, and other high-risk groups. He said that the blood tests could reduce the spread of AIDS because a positive test result would make infected people aware that they carry the virus and could infect their sexual partners.

They Know Better, But. The United States Public Health Service reported on May 14 that many Americans do not follow good health practices, despite widespread public knowledge about the benefits of a healthy life style. A survey of more than 21,000 people conducted by the agency, part of the Department of Health and Human Services, found that most Americans are aware that cigarette smoking, high blood cholesterol, and high blood pressure increase the risk of heart disease. Most people also recognize the dangers of driving after drinking, the benefits of seat belts, the need for regular exercise, and the importance of breast self-examination and other health and safety measures.

The study found, however, that approximately 30 per cent of the adults surveyed still smoke cigarettes; more than 10 per cent sometimes drive after excessive drinking; only 30 per cent wear seat belts regularly; and less than 50 per cent exercise regularly. Of the women surveyed, only 30 per cent follow recommendations for breast self-examination.

Smokeless Dangers. Surgeon General of the United States C. Everett Koop released a report on March 25 that warned about the health hazards of chewing tobacco and snuff—two forms of smokeless tobacco. Koop expressed concern about the growing use of smokeless tobacco in the United States, especially among teen-aged boys and young men.

Approximately 12 million Americans use chewing tobacco and snuff. Many people begin using smokeless tobacco after they quit smoking cigarettes, believing it is less of a health threat. But chewing tobacco and snuff are not safe substitutes for cigarettes, according to Koop. They can cause

Soldiers at Fort Belvoir, Virginia, puff away in special smoking areas after the U.S. Army began an antismoking program on July 7.

oral cancer as well as a number of other mouth diseases. On October 24, the Federal Trade Commission issued regulations requiring health warnings on packages of snuff and chewing tobacco, beginning on Feb. 27, 1987.

Army's War on Smoking. The U.S. Army launched an antismoking program on July 7, 1986, that bans smoking in all Army vehicles and aircraft, and restricts it to certain designated areas within all Army buildings. Army Secretary John O. Marsh, Jr., said the new policy was necessary because studies have found that smoking reduces combat readiness by impairing physical fitness and by increasing illness, absenteeism, and premature death.

Radon Warning. The U.S. Environmental Protection Agency (EPA) on August 14 advised members of the 1 out of every 8 households in states that have high levels of radon to avoid smoking indoors. Radon is a colorless, odorless, radioactive gas produced by the radioactive decay of radium, which is found in soil. If the gas seeps into homes that are well-insulated or have poor ventilation, it can build up. The EPA said that smoking cigarettes in the presence of radon can substantially increase the risk of lung cancer.   Michael Woods

See also HEALTH AND DISEASE; MEDICINE. In the WORLD BOOK SUPPLEMENT section, see AIDS. In WORLD BOOK, see PUBLIC HEALTH; SMOKING.

PUBLISHING. Book publishers were increasingly preoccupied with government actions during 1986. A big problem for United States publishers was foreign governments that turn a blind eye to *copyright piracy*, the unauthorized reprinting of books. In early March, the Association of American Publishers told Congress that copyright piracy in 10 nations cheated American authors and publishers of $400 million each year. Publishers rejoiced on July 21 when South Korea bowed to U.S. government pressure and said it would enact laws protecting copyrights on U.S. works.

On June 2, Canada announced that it would impose a 10 per cent import duty on certain U.S. books and periodicals sold in Canada. Canada imposed the duty to retaliate for a 35 per cent tariff that the United States had imposed on certain Canadian wood products.

Teen-Agers Buy. A Gallup Poll of U.S. teenagers, released on July 25, found that young people buy books at almost the same rate as adults. The survey showed that about 1 teen-ager in 5 bought a book in the preceding week. Teen-agers read nearly twice as much fiction as nonfiction, the poll found. Boys strongly prefer action and adventure stories and history, and girls read more romance novels and health and diet books.

Light Reading. In a year when true spy stories were big news, spy and adventure novels dominated fiction best-seller lists. *The Bourne Supremacy* by Robert Ludlum, *Lie Down with Lions* by Ken Follett, and *A Perfect Spy* by John le Carré were all top sellers.

Publishers obviously expected the trend to continue. On January 10, a furious auction for the hard-cover rights to *Whirlwind*, James Clavell's adventure set in Iran after the fall of the shah, was won by William Morrow & Company and Avon Books with a record bid of $5 million. The two most successful nonfiction books of 1986 were warm-hearted works: *Fatherhood*, by television star Bill Cosby, and *You're Only Old Once!*, a book about old age by Dr. Seuss, popular author of *The Cat in the Hat* (1957) and other children's classics.

Acquisitions. After three generations of family ownership, Doubleday & Company, founded in 1897, was sold in 1986 to Bertelsmann A.G., the West German communications giant. The $475-million sale did not include the New York Mets baseball team, owned by Doubleday.

Penguin Publishing Company of London announced on September 30 that it had agreed to buy New American Library and its hard-cover publishing affiliate, E. P. Dutton, for an undisclosed sum. On October 14, Time Incorporated said that it would buy textbook publisher Scott, Foresman & Company from SFN Companies in a deal valued at $520 million. Mark Fitzgerald

In WORLD BOOK, see PUBLISHING.

PUERTO RICO. A fire in the Dupont Plaza Hotel in San Juan on Dec. 31, 1986, killed 96 people. The fire began when an arsonist ignited furniture wrapped in plastic. On Jan. 13, 1987, police arrested a hotel maintenance man and charged him with 96 counts of murder.

Shortly after midnight on October 28, two bombs exploded near U.S. military installations on the island of Puerto Rico. Three radical groups claimed responsibility for the bombing. The most well-known is Los Macheteros (The Machete Wielders), a group seeking Puerto Rico's independence from the United States.

Cuban Tensions. A high unemployment rate escalated tensions between native-born Puerto Ricans and the country's Cuban community. Approximately 23,000 Cubans have settled in Puerto Rico. They have become prominent business leaders and—on the average—earn an income twice as high as most native-born Puerto Ricans, according to a study published in 1986 by Julio Antonio Muriente Perez, foreign affairs editor of *Claridad*, a weekly Puerto Rican newspaper. Their conservative, anti-Communist political stance has made them influential in the country's major political parties. Nathan A. Haverstock

See also LATIN AMERICA (Facts in Brief Table). In WORLD BOOK, see PUERTO RICO.

PULITZER PRIZES. See AWARDS AND PRIZES.

QUEBEC. In his second term as prime minister of Quebec, Robert Bourassa moved in 1986 to erase some of the policies associated with the separatist administration of the Parti Québécois (PQ) and Prime Minister René Lévesque. The PQ and Lévesque had worked to make Quebec an independent French-speaking nation. Bourassa, a Liberal who is committed to Canadian unity, asked three of his colleagues to chair committees that would prepare policy recommendations.

The reports, released in July, recommended a decrease in state ownership of business enterprises, fewer restrictions on economic activity, and a leaner government structure. The reports also proposed dissolving a score of government agencies created by the former PQ government. The studies pointed toward a Quebec that would more closely resemble other Canadian provinces, moving away from the PQ's aim that Quebec should constitute a distinct society in North America. At year-end, Bourassa had taken no action.

Amnesty for Students. A measure granting amnesty to children illegally enrolled in English-language schools passed on June 19 at the end of the legislative session. Under the province's 1977 language law, attendance in English-language schools was restricted to children whose parents had been educated in English in Quebec. Children of Greek, Italian, and Portuguese immigrants who desired an English-language education defied the law, however. About 1,500 such pupils were allowed to continue their education in English.

Language Law. The new government declined to prosecute owners of businesses displaying bilingual signs—in French and English—in Montreal, in violation of the 1977 law requiring signs to be in French only. Pierre Marc Johnson—the PQ leader who served briefly as prime minister in 1985—declared that Montreal would lose its French character unless the law was enforced. On Dec. 22, 1986, the Quebec Court of Appeal struck down the law, but it remained in force for 90 days while the province decided whether to appeal to the Supreme Court of Canada.

The Provincial Budget—with spending projected at $28.4 billion (Canadian dollars; $1 = U.S. 72 cents as of Dec. 31, 1986)—was presented on May 1 by Gerard D. Lévesque, minister of finance. The budget called for new taxes on retirement savings, home heating bills, and business.

In addition, the government planned to establish a force of "welfare police" to identify welfare recipients who abused the system. The additional revenues were expected to reduce the province's deficit from $3.15 billion in the current year to $2.89 billion in 1986-1987.   David M. L. Farr

See also CANADA; MONTREAL. In WORLD BOOK, see QUEBEC.

RADIO. A proposed merger of two of radio's biggest—and oldest—broadcasters was abandoned near the end of 1986. The National Broadcasting Company (NBC), which owned eight radio stations, sought a merger with Westinghouse Broadcasting Company, owner of 13 radio stations. But in December, Westinghouse withdrew from the arrangement. NBC then said it would investigate selling its radio stations and radio network to other prospective buyers.

Since 1978, the Federal Communications Commission (FCC)—which regulates radio and television stations—has allowed broadcasters to simultaneously own and operate radio and television stations in the same city. But the FCC also ruled that when dual broadcasting facilities are sold, the new owners must sell either the radio or television station in that market. Because NBC's former parent, RCA Corporation, was acquired by General Electric Company earlier in 1986, its dual ownership waiver was no longer valid in New York City, Chicago, and Washington, D.C.—cities where NBC operates both radio and television stations. The NBC-Westinghouse merger would have been arranged to circumvent the FCC rules.

The American Broadcasting Companies (ABC), purchased by Capital Cities Communications Incorporated in 1985, also faced the problem of disposing of radio stations in cities where ABC also operated TV stations. Late in 1986, Capital Cities/ABC executives said they planned to petition the FCC to exempt them from the ruling.

Radio Programming. Radio remained a local medium in the United States during 1986, with thousands of stations programming music, news, and other entertainment based on the needs of the communities they served and the competition in their market. Continuing a long trend, FM radio stations drew a larger audience than AM stations. Rock music was FM's most prevalent format, while in most cities, AM stations dominated in news, sports, and information programming. Some AM stations continued to broadcast in stereo during 1986, but—as in the past—there was no consensus among broadcasters to establish a standard AM stereo broadcasting system.

Risqué Radio. Some radio stations in major U.S. cities presented "shock radio," an increasingly popular format in which disk jockeys discussed sexually oriented topics and used frank—some would say shocking—language during their programs. In November, the FCC asked a New York City station, WXRK-FM, to respond to complaints that one of its disk jockeys consistently used obscene language on the program. The FCC sent similar requests to other stations.   P. J. Bednarski

See also POPULAR MUSIC. In WORLD BOOK, see RADIO.

RAILROAD. Railroad companies in the United States suffered a drop in earnings in 1986. Railroads earned about $435 million in the first half of 1986, down substantially from $1.034 billion in the first half of 1985. Rail traffic for the first 39 weeks of the year totaled 659.4 billion ton-miles, compared with 659.6 billion ton-miles for the same period in 1985. On National Railroad Passenger Corporation (Amtrak) trains, ridership was up about 3.8 per cent from 1985.

Railroad Sales and Mergers. In October, Congress passed legislation permitting the government to sell Consolidated Rail Corporation (Conrail) through a public stock offering. The sale, which was expected to be completed in 1987, will generate at least $1.7 billion in revenues.

On July 24, the Interstate Commerce Commission (ICC)—a federal agency that regulates commercial transportation across state lines—rejected the proposed merger of the Atchison, Topeka & Santa Fe and the Southern Pacific (SP) railroads into a single 25,000-mile (40,000-kilometer) system that would cover much of the Midwest and Southwest. The ICC said that the reduction in competition resulting from the merger would outweigh its benefits to the Santa Fe and SP.

The ruling, which marked the first time since 1968 that a major rail merger was rejected by the ICC, shocked the railroad industry.

A historic locomotive, built in 1883 and headed for the steam railway museum in Tottenham, Canada, gets an inspection in Toronto in June 1986.

The Santa Fe Southern Pacific Corporation—a holding company that runs the Santa Fe railroad directly and the SP through a separate trust—asked the ICC to reconsider its decision. The company started to negotiate operating agreements with other railroad systems in an effort to meet some of the objections raised by the agency.

Labor Issues. On September 30, President Ronald Reagan signed legislation imposing a solution to a 2½-year-old labor dispute between the Brotherhood of Maintenance of Way Employees—a railroad workers' union—and Guilford Transportation Industries. Guilford had lost almost $11-million in the first seven months of 1986, primarily due to a 73-day-old strike by workers on Guilford's Maine Central Railroad.

On October 6, the Supreme Court of the United States announced it would decide whether unions have the right to extend strikes to railroads not involved in a labor dispute. The court's decision will help determine if the industry continues to negotiate labor contracts on an industrywide rather than an individual basis.

Regulations. Coal and electric power companies were just one vote shy of getting Congress to restrict railroads' power to raise freight rates. The companies vowed to pursue the issue with Congress again in 1987.   David M. Cawthorne

In WORLD BOOK, see RAILROAD.

REAGAN, RONALD WILSON (1911-   ), 40th President of the United States and, at 75, the oldest chief executive in U.S. history, had only minor health problems in 1986. In 1985, he had undergone major surgery for intestinal cancer. In 1986, he twice had minor surgery at the Naval Medical Command Center in Bethesda, Md., for the removal of noncancerous intestinal growths. He also had a tiny patch of skin removed from the right side of his face in January. The facial tissue was benign.

On August 8, Reagan returned to the naval hospital for tests of his urinary tract. White House physician T. Burton Smith, a urologist, said the examination showed "no abnormalities or evidence of tumor or any other disease." In December, however, the White House announced that Reagan would undergo surgery for an enlarged prostate gland in January 1987.

Reagan's Top Staff was caught up in turmoil in November, when it was disclosed that officials of Reagan's Administration had made secret sales of arms to Iran and that some of the money had been funneled to rebels fighting the Nicaraguan government. See PRESIDENT OF THE UNITED STATES.

Reagan's chief speechwriter, Bentley T. Elliott, resigned in June after months of reported friction with Reagan's chief of staff, Donald T. Regan, and

Celebrating his 75th birthday in February, Reagan gets a kiss from his wife,
Nancy, as Cabinet members George Shultz, left, and Caspar Weinberger look on.

joined the staff of Congressman Jack Kemp (R., N.Y.). Margaret Noonan, a deputy speechwriter, also resigned after she was not selected to succeed Elliott.

M. B. Oglesby, Jr., Reagan's chief lobbyist as director of the White House Office of Legislative Affairs, resigned in February after two years in the post. He was succeeded by William L. Ball III, who had directed congressional relations for the Department of State. In March, Fred F. Fielding resigned as White House counsel, a job he had held since 1981, to enter private practice. Succeeding him as the President's legal adviser was Peter J. Wallison, a Washington, D.C., lawyer who had been counsel to Nelson A. Rockefeller when he was Vice President in the 1970's.

Nancy Reagan's Staff had a succession of chiefs in 1986. James S. Rosebush resigned in January to open a public relations firm, and his successor, Lee L. Verstandig, left after 24 days on the job to join the consulting firm of Michael K. Deaver, a former key Reagan aide. On February 22, the first lady named as her fifth chief of staff Jack L. Courtemanche, a long-time Reagan loyalist.

In August, the White House disclosed an unusual staff problem. Nancy Reagan's personal maid of five years, Anita S. Castelo, was placed on leave with pay after being charged with aiding and abetting an attempt to illegallly export arms. Cas-

telo subsequently was cleared of knowing involvement in the attempted export of 35,000 rounds of ammunition to Paraguay, where she was born. Castelo, a naturalized American, returned to work.

First Family Activities. Nancy Reagan remained active throughout the year in her long-standing antidrug campaign and traveled extensively. On March 20, an Air Force transport jet that was to carry her home from a drug abuse conference in Atlanta, Ga., slipped off a runway as it prepared to take off. No one was injured. In May, she broke off from her husband's trip to an economic summit in Japan to make good-will visits of her own to Malaysia and Thailand. In July, the first lady and Random House Incorporated agreed to a contract for her memoirs after she leaves the White House.

Patti Davis, the Reagans' daughter, published a highly autobiographical novel, *Home Front*, in February. Her parents reportedly were not pleased.

In February, the Reagans' son Ron was named a contributing editor of *Playboy* magazine. Maureen Reagan, the President's oldest daughter, was scheduled to become cochairman of the Republican National Committee on Jan. 1, 1987.

On April 11, 1986, the White House reported that the Reagans paid $122,703 in 1985 federal income taxes. They claimed charitable deductions of $23,298.   Frank Cormier and Margot Cormier

In WORLD BOOK, see REAGAN, RONALD WILSON.

REHNQUIST, WILLIAM HUBBS (1924-   ), was sworn in as chief justice of the United States on Sept. 26, 1986. Rehnquist, an associate justice since 1972, succeeded Warren E. Burger, who resigned to direct the 200th anniversary celebration of the U.S. Constitution in 1987. Many liberals opposed the appointment of Rehnquist to the top post at the Supreme Court, arguing that he was too conservative.

Rehnquist was born on Oct. 1, 1924, in Milwaukee. After serving in the U.S. Army Air Forces from 1943 to 1946, Rehnquist attended Stanford University in California and Harvard University in Cambridge, Mass. He returned to Stanford to earn a law degree with highest honors in 1952.

From 1953 to 1969, Rehnquist had a private law practice in Phoenix. In 1969, he was named an assistant U.S. attorney general in Washington, D.C., and in 1971 President Richard M. Nixon named him to the Supreme Court.

Throughout much of Rehnquist's public career, critics have charged that he has shown too little concern for minority groups or civil liberties. Those charges were repeated at his 1986 confirmation hearings, where his defenders said he had served on the bench with distinction.

Rehnquist is married to the former Natalie Cornell. They have three children.   David L. Dreier

In WORLD BOOK, see REHNQUIST, WILLIAM H.

RELIGION. At the invitation of Pope John Paul II, leaders of 12 religious groups met in Assisi, Italy, on Oct. 27, 1986, to participate in a "World Day of Prayer for Peace." Governments and guerrillas involved in 11 wars around the world honored the pope's plea for a day of peace, but conflict continued in Afghanistan, Lebanon, Mozambique, and Northern Ireland. The governments of 60 countries supported the pope's peace effort.

The religions represented in Assisi included African *animism* (the worship of nature spirits); native American; the Bahá'í faith; Buddhism; Christianity; Hinduism; Islam; Jainism (a religion similar to Buddhism); Judaism; Shinto (a religion from Japan); Sikhism; and Zoroastrianism (a religion based on the teachings of the Persian prophet Zoroaster). Among the 155 religious leaders present were the Dalai Lama, the exiled Tibetan Buddhist leader; Robert A. K. Runcie, archbishop of Canterbury and head of the Anglican Communion; Metropolitan Filaret, archbishop of Kiev and Galicia of the Russian Orthodox Church; and Muneyoshi Tokugawa, president of the Shinto Shrine Association of Tokyo. The leaders spent the day fasting, meditating, and praying.

Presidential Potential. One of the most heated debates of 1986 centered on the desire of Protestant fundamentalists and conservative evangelicals to nominate their own candidate in the 1988 U.S. presidential election. Religious broadcaster Marion G. (Pat) Robertson made news on September 17 when he announced that he would run in the next presidential election if 3 million Americans signed petitions supporting him.

Robertson, head of the Christian Broadcasting Network, made the announcement on his own national television show. His move delighted the New Christian Right but alarmed some Republican camps that had been trying to attract fundamentalists.

Robertson's platform differed little from President Ronald Reagan's. He advocated drug-free schools, a balanced budget, and a strong stand against Communism. Some of his opinions have been controversial, however. He has suggested that born-again Christians know best how to govern and that they represent a chosen people in the United States.

Religion and Public Education. United States Secretary of Education William J. Bennett criticized Robertson for implying that Christians have a monopoly on civic virtue, but Bennett challenged Americans to recognize the role of religion, particularly the shared Jewish and Christian tradition, in national life. Without recognizing and preserving this tradition, the United States would become morally adrift, he argued.

Pope John Paul II becomes the first pope in history to visit a Jewish temple when he meets with rabbis in a Rome synagogue on April 13.

U.S. Membership Reported for Religious Groups with 150,000 or More Members*

African Methodist Episcopal Church	2,210,000
African Methodist Episcopal Zion Church	1,202,229
American Baptist Association	225,000
American Baptist Churches in the U.S.A.	1,559,683
American Lutheran Church	2,332,316
Antiochian Orthodox Christian Archdiocese of North America	280,000
Armenian Apostolic Church of America	225,000
Armenian Church of America, Diocese of the	450,000
Assemblies of God	2,082,878
Baptist Bible Fellowship, International	1,405,900
Baptist Missionary Association of America	227,720
Christian and Missionary Alliance	227,846
Christian Church (Disciples of Christ)	1,116,326
Christian Churches and Churches of Christ	1,051,469
Christian Methodist Episcopal Church	718,922
Christian Reformed Church in North America	219,988
Church of God (Anderson, Ind.)	185,593
Church of God (Cleveland, Tenn.)	505,775
Church of God in Christ	3,709,661
Church of God in Christ, International	200,000
Church of Jesus Christ of Latter-day Saints	3,860,000
Church of the Brethren	159,184
Church of the Nazarene	522,082
Churches of Christ	1,604,000
Conservative Baptist Association of America	225,000
Episcopal Church	2,739,422
Free Will Baptists	217,838
General Association of Regular Baptist Churches	300,834
Greek Orthodox Archdiocese of North and South America	1,950,000
International Church of the Foursquare Gospel	177,787
International Council of Community Churches	200,000
Jehovah's Witnesses	730,441
Jews	5,834,635
Lutheran Church in America	2,898,202
Lutheran Church-Missouri Synod	2,638,164
National Baptist Convention of America	2,668,799
National Baptist Convention, U.S.A., Inc.	5,500,000
National Primitive Baptist Convention	250,000
Orthodox Church in America	1,000,000
Polish National Catholic Church of America	282,411
Presbyterian Church in America	179,696
Presbyterian Church (U.S.A)	3,048,235
Progressive National Baptist Convention, Inc.	521,692
Reformed Church in America	342,275
Reorganized Church of Jesus Christ of Latter Day Saints	192,082
Roman Catholic Church	52,654,908
Salvation Army	427,825
Seventh-day Adventists	651,954
Southern Baptist Convention	14,477,364
Unitarian Universalist Association	171,838
United Church of Christ	1,683,777
United Methodist Church	9,266,853
United Pentecostal Church, International	500,000
Wisconsin Evangelical Lutheran Synod	415,389

*A majority of the figures are for the years 1985 and 1986.
Source: National Council of the Churches of Christ in the U.S.A., *Yearbook of American and Canadian Churches* for 1987.

A study by New York University psychologist Paul C. Vitz that was released in June supported Bennett's views. Vitz, a Roman Catholic, studied 60 textbooks and found religion slighted or absent, even from historical accounts where it played an integral role. Religious conservatives as well as liberal groups chastised textbook publishers in the United States for producing religious and historical illiterates.

Many conservatives said the Biblical tradition of Jews and Christians should be implicitly taught as the truth about life. They saw exclusion of religion to be part of a "secular humanist" conspiracy. Liberal critics attributed the absence of religious references to the publishers' fear of alienating some markets if they include religious references.

Christian fundamentalists won a battle in late October when a federal judge ruled that officials of a Tennessee school had violated students' religious freedoms when they expelled them for refusing to read "anti-Christian" books. The debate over the teaching of evolution was expected to heat up in 1987, with a Louisiana law that requires the teaching of "scientific creationism" scheduled to come before the Supreme Court of the United States.   Martin E. Marty

See also EASTERN ORTHODOX CHURCHES; JEWS AND JUDAISM; PROTESTANTISM; ROMAN CATHOLIC CHURCH. In WORLD BOOK, see RELIGION.

REPUBLICAN PARTY (GOP) fortunes sagged in the midterm elections of Nov. 4, 1986, as Democrats seized control of the United States Senate by a surprisingly large margin of 55 to 45. The GOP had held a preelection edge of 53 to 47 in the Senate and had controlled that body since 1981. Republican candidates held their own in most races for the House of Representatives, losing just 5 seats to give the Democrats a 258 to 177 margin.

The GOP scored its biggest success in gubernatorial races, picking up a net gain of eight governorships, notably in such Sunbelt states as Texas, Florida, and Alabama. But Republicans suffered losses in state legislature contests, where Democrats had already enjoyed a 2 to 1 edge in the number of legislatures controlled.

President Ronald Reagan, who waged an energetic personal campaign in 22 states, with disappointing results, held a postelection "pep rally" for aides and vowed to "complete the revolution that we have so well begun." Barred by the 22nd Amendment to the Constitution from seeking a third term in 1988, he said, "For two more years, my friends, let us make history together."

Lyn Nofziger, a former key Reagan aide, said, "My own hope is that the [Senate] Democrats could well overplay their hand" by attacking the President. By doing so, Nofziger said, the Democrats would "make issues for us in 1988." But as

Former governor of Delaware Pierre S. du Pont IV announces his candidacy for the 1988 Republican presidential nomination in September.

the White House became embroiled in a controversy concerning the secret sale of military weapons to Iran and the funneling of Iranian money to Nicaraguan rebels, it appeared that the Democrats might have plenty to attack. See PRESIDENT OF THE UNITED STATES.

Senate Races resulted in defeat for seven incumbent Republicans, while no sitting Democrat lost. The losers were Senators Jeremiah Denton of Alabama, Paula Hawkins of Florida, Mack Mattingly of Georgia, James T. Broyhill of North Carolina, Mark N. Andrews of North Dakota, James Abdnor of South Dakota, and Slade Gorton of Washington. The GOP also lost the seats of two retiring senators—Charles McC. Mathias, Jr., of Maryland and Paul Laxalt of Nevada—while their opponents lost only one open seat, that of Thomas F. Eagleton of Missouri, who retired.

The Republican upset in the Senate may have harmed the barely concealed presidential aspirations of two prominent Republicans—Senators Robert J. Dole of Kansas and Laxalt of Nevada. Dole had to swap his position of Senate majority leader for the less prestigious and less visible post of minority leader. And many political observers believed that Laxalt, Reagan's closest friend in the Senate, lost any hopes he had for the presidency when the candidate he picked to succeed him in the Senate lost to a Democrat.

Gubernatorial Races. Republicans were most heartened by their gain of eight governorships. Although the GOP still trailed in governorships, 26 to 24, the previous margin had been 34 to 16. Republican William P. Clements reclaimed the Texas governorship from Democrat Mark White, who had defeated him four years earlier. The only other losing incumbent was Democrat Anthony S. Earl of Wisconsin, defeated by state legislator Tommy G. Thompson.

Tampa Mayor Bob Martinez, a former Democrat, became the first Hispanic governor of Florida. Guy Hunt, an Amway Corporation distributor, became the first Republican governor of Alabama in 112 years. While losing only three governorships to the Democrats—in Oregon, Pennsylvania, and Tennessee—Republicans took 11 that had been held by Democrats, in Alabama, Arizona, Florida, Kansas, Maine, Nebraska, New Mexico, Oklahoma, South Carolina, Texas, and Wisconsin. In Nebraska, State Treasurer Kay A. Orr became the first Republican woman ever elected to a governorship.

Republican National Committee. Maureen Reagan, the President's eldest daughter, had no opposition in her bid to succeed the retiring Betty G. Heitman as cochairman of the Republican National Committee (RNC). Although several women had been expected to vie for the post, none did so after the President told RNC Chairman Frank J. Fahrenkopf, Jr., in September that he wanted his daughter to take over the position.

Convention Delegates. The first steps in the process of naming delegates to the 1988 Republican National Convention that will nominate a candidate to succeed Reagan were taken by Michigan Republicans on August 5. Vice President George H. W. Bush, an unannounced candidate, spent nearly $1 million in Michigan and was later acknowledged as the front-runner. Trailing Bush were Representative Jack Kemp of New York and Marion G. (Pat) Robertson, a TV evangelist who sought to mobilize fundamentalist Christians.

On September 16, Pierre S. du Pont IV, former governor of Delaware, became the first Republican to formally announce his candidacy for the 1988 presidential nomination. A day later, Robertson appeared on closed circuit TV to tell 216 gatherings across the United States that he would seek the nomination if, within one year, 3 million voters signed petitions "telling me that they will pray, that they will work, that they will give toward my election. . . ." Frank Cormier and Margot Cormier

See also DEMOCRATIC PARTY; ELECTIONS. In WORLD BOOK, see REPUBLICAN PARTY.

RHODE ISLAND. See STATE GOVERNMENT.

RHODESIA. See ZIMBABWE.

ROADS. See TRANSPORTATION.

ROMAN CATHOLIC CHURCH. The relation of traditional Roman Catholic beliefs to modern times and experiences held the attention of Roman Catholics in 1986. On August 18, the Vatican revoked the right of an American theologian to teach Roman Catholic morality. Charles E. Curran, a Catholic priest from Rochester, N.Y., who taught moral theology for 20 years at the Catholic University of America in Washington, D.C., was censured for his public stance on moral issues that went against traditional Catholic teachings.

On March 11, Curran revealed that the Vatican had ordered him to retract his statements on the morality of artificial birth control, abortion, euthanasia, masturbation, premarital sex, homosexuality, and divorce. The order had come from Joseph Cardinal Ratzinger on Sept. 17, 1985. Cardinal Ratzinger heads the Vatican's Sacred Congregation for the Doctrine of the Faith. According to the Vatican, it had been reviewing Curran's untraditional views for several years.

In his March 1986 statement, Curran said that his conflict with the Vatican was over the *infallibility* (absolute freedom from error) of certain Catholic teachings and whether a Catholic theologian could, at times, publicly disagree with the church in matters admitted to be noninfallible church teaching. He insisted that theologians have the right to state opposing views on the moral issues

cited in the cardinal's letter because Catholic teachings on those issues are not considered infallible by the church. The Vatican's position, however, was that theologians should honor all church statements—even those that are not expressed as infallible.

On April 25, Curran responded by letter to Cardinal Ratzinger, saying that he could not change his position for "reasons of conscience" and that he believed that his dissent was legitimate. The Vatican responded in August by withdrawing Curran's credentials to teach as a Catholic theologian. Curran then announced that he would appeal the decision through university channels.

The Vatican Also Took Action against an American archbishop, Raymond G. Hunthausen of Seattle. On September 4, the Vatican announced that it was withdrawing authority from Archbishop Hunthausen in several areas following an investigation from 1983 to 1985 of his activities. The announcement gave Auxiliary Bishop Donald Wuerl responsibility for those areas, which include the liturgy, the Seattle archdiocese's court to resolve disputed marriages, and moral issues. Some Catholics had criticized Archbishop Hunthausen for his liberal positions on birth control, homosexuality, and nuclear arms.

The action against Archbishop Hunthausen captured the attention of the media for weeks in late summer and early fall and generated protest from some Roman Catholics in the United States. In an unusual move, the Vatican's representative in the United States, Archbishop Pio Laghi, responded to the controversy by publishing on October 27 a chronology of the events that led to the Vatican's decision. Archbishop Hunthausen stated that he did not have a similar recollection of the events or a clear understanding of the meaning behind the Vatican's action.

The issue was addressed at the annual meeting of the National Conference of Catholic Bishops in Washington, D.C., in November. The bishops met in closed sessions for five hours to consider Hunthausen's request that they intercede on his behalf with the Vatican. The archbishop distributed a 21-page document outlining his position.

On November 12, Bishop James W. Malone of Youngstown, Ohio, president of the conference, released a statement saying that though the bishops would offer assistance to any party in the dispute, they "unreservedly reaffirmed their unity with and loyalty to" the pope.

At a press conference held after the meeting on November 14, Archbishop Hunthausen reiterated that he had never deviated from church policy in his administration and that he failed to understand the reasons behind the Vatican's action. He requested that his authority in the Seattle archdiocese be fully restored.

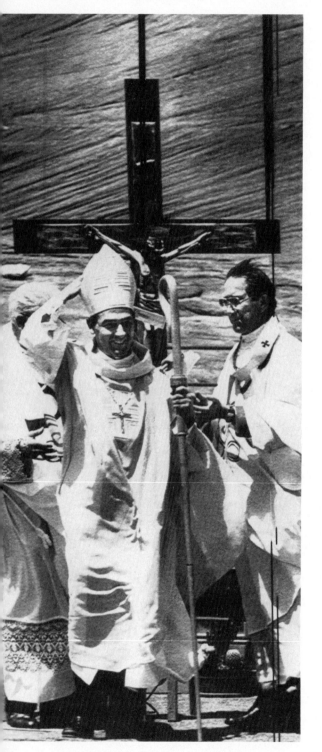

Donald E. Pelotte, the first American Indian to become a Roman Catholic bishop, smiles after his consecration in Gallup, N. Mex., in May.

Liberation Theology. Pope John Paul II addressed another theological controversy on March 13, 1986, when he told a group of Brazilian bishops in Rome that a set of beliefs called *liberation theology* is a necessary part of the church's social thought but that it must be "purified of elements which can water it down." Proponents of liberation theology believe that it is the church's mission to fight poverty and social injustice.

Since its development by priests working in Latin America, liberation theology has at times taken on some Marxist overtones. The pope specifically rejected the Marxist view that class struggle is inevitable and that violence is an appropriate way to correct social abuse.

On April 12, the Vatican released a letter from the pope telling the Brazilian bishops that "you and I are convinced that liberation theology is not only opportune but useful and necessary." He asked, however, that liberation theology be developed "correctly," taking into consideration the theologies of other periods.

The Vatican Issued two documents in the spring that also addressed the issue of liberation theology and the political and social role of the church. On April 5, the Vatican published a 59-page document that called for Catholics to work for the liberation of politically, socially, and economically oppressed people through the Christian values of love, justice, and peace.

On May 30, Pope John Paul II issued the fifth *encyclical* or message of his papacy, a 141-page document on the Holy Spirit, the mystical Third Person of the Christian Trinity. The encyclical said that Catholics should work to renew the world socially, economically, and politically, as well as take note of injustice and liberation. According to the pope, the message was an effort to heal "the break between the Gospel and culture."

Silence Lifted. The Vatican, on March 30, ended the year of silence it imposed on Leonardo Boff, a Franciscan friar and prominent Brazilian theologian. Boff, who had written and spoken extensively on liberation theology, was instructed on May 9, 1985, not to teach or publish for a year.

Debt Dilemma. Pope John Paul II and Catholic bishops in the United States expressed concern over Third World debts and poverty. During his visit to Colombia from July 1 to 7, 1986, the pope appealed for all nations to settle the Third World's massive debt to industrialized nations.

A month earlier, Catholic bishops in the United States expressed similar misgivings about the Third World's debts in the third draft of their proposed policy statement, called a *pastoral letter*, on the economy, published on June 3. The draft stated that the debts—many of them owed to U.S. banks—represent a "moral scandal" that "oppresses large numbers of people."

In the draft, the bishops also recommended that public policies give greater support to the family unit and to education that can help people realize their economic potential. The document emphasized that economic rights are fundamental human rights in the same way as civil and political rights, stating that those rights are essential to human beings and are not bestowed by societies.

During their November meeting, the bishops added some amendments to the third draft. The bishops accepted the final text on November 13. The 115-page document, titled *Economic Justice for All: Catholic Social Teaching and the U.S. Economy*, called for some Third World debts to be canceled and other debts to be restructured. The letter asserted that U.S. policy should support a "preferential option for the poor" in making foreign loans and giving aid. The document also denounced pay discrimination against women and called for a revision of the U.S. welfare system that would extend benefits to more of the poor.

Papal Visits. Pope John Paul II visited 14 cities on a 10-day trip to India from February 1 to 10 and toured Colombia from July 1 to 7. The pope's longest trip began on November 18, however, when he started a 14-day tour of Australia, Asia, and South Pacific islands. Owen F. Campion

In WORLD BOOK, see ROMAN CATHOLIC CHURCH.

ROMANIA. Romania's economic crisis deepened in 1986, but the crisis posed no threat to the regime of Communist Party General Secretary and President Nicolae Ceauşescu.

Ceauşescu's government continued its harsh austerity policy, which resulted in worsening shortages of food—particularly meat—and consumer goods. On August 23, Ceauşescu announced a "New Agricultural Revolution" that would end all shortages, but he gave few details.

A Financial Crisis hit Romania in 1986 despite progress in reducing its debt. By the end of 1985, Romania had reduced its foreign debt to $6.6-billion from a high of $10.2 billion at the end of 1981. But in May 1986, Romania was unable to make payments of $300 million to banks in Austria and the United States. In July, Romania had to reschedule $880 million in payments. Meanwhile, hard-currency reserves—its holdings of U.S. dollars, Japanese yen, and other widely accepted foreign currency—fell to $200 million.

The financial crisis was caused by a combination of factors, including insolvency of some of Romania's Middle Eastern trading partners, a decrease in Western tourists, and contamination of crops by radioactive fallout following a nuclear accident at the Soviet Chernobyl plant in April.

Foreign Relations. On May 16, Romania signed an agreement on economic cooperation with the Soviet Union until the year 2000. It was the last member of the Council for Mutual Economic Assistance—COMECON, the Soviet trading bloc—to do so. In return for more Soviet oil and raw materials, Romania promised to increase its stake in Soviet projects for the exploitation of natural resources. Soviet Foreign Minister Eduard A. Shevardnadze visited Bucharest in October.

There were also exchanges between Romanian and Western officials. General Vasile Milea, Romania's defense minister, visited Washington, D.C., in October, the first Warsaw Pact defense minister to do so. Greek Prime Minister Andreas Papandreou visited Bucharest in September to discuss a Balkan nuclear-free zone.

In June, U.S. President Ronald Reagan extended for one year Romania's most-favored-nation trading status, committing the United States to use its lowest tariff rates on all Romanian products. Some members of the U.S. Congress opposed this move because of Romania's poor record on human rights.

In May, Romania announced that it was extending its territorial waters in the Black Sea from a previous 12-nautical-mile (22-kilometer) limit to 200 nautical miles (370 kilometers). Chris Cviic

See also EUROPE (Facts in Brief Table). In WORLD BOOK, see ROMANIA.

ROWING. See SPORTS.

RUSSIA in 1986 continued to be preoccupied with its relationship with the United States, but the Soviets also tried to improve relations with China. At home, the government maintained its drive for greater efficiency and continued to fire corrupt and inefficient officials. The country's economic performance improved, but a nuclear accident at the Chernobyl power plant near Kiev damaged Soviet prestige.

Superpower Dialogue. Soviet leader Mikhail S. Gorbachev and United States President Ronald Reagan held talks at Reykjavík, Iceland, on October 11 and 12. The two leaders came close to settling arms-control issues that have divided the Soviets from the West for many years.

Gorbachev and Reagan reached tentative agreements in several areas. On long-range nuclear weapons, the Soviets accepted a U.S. proposal for a 50 per cent cut. The Russians offered to withdraw all their medium-range missiles from Eastern Europe in return for the withdrawal of all U.S. medium-range missiles from Western Europe. The two sides did not reach a tentative agreement on short-range missiles, but the Soviets dropped their demand for a nuclear test ban.

The talks broke down over a disagreement on the Strategic Defense Initiative (SDI or "Star Wars"), the U.S. research program aimed at establishing a space-based shield against missiles. Reagan rejected Gorbachev's demand that SDI work be confined to laboratory research for 10 years. Despite the failure to reach agreement at Reykjavík, the Soviet Union and the United States continued their arms-control dialogue in Geneva, Switzerland.

A Spy Affair almost prevented the Reykjavík meeting from taking place. On August 23, the U.S. Federal Bureau of Investigation arrested Gennadi F. Zakharov, a Soviet physicist employed by the United Nations in New York City, as he was buying highly classified U.S. documents. The United States charged Zakharov with espionage. On August 30, the Soviets arrested an American, Nicholas S. Daniloff, Moscow correspondent for *U.S. News & World Report* magazine, after a Soviet acquaintance handed him an envelope containing maps. Moscow charged Daniloff with espionage on September 7.

After hard bargaining, including talks between Soviet Foreign Minister Eduard A. Shevardnadze and U.S. Secretary of State George P. Shultz, the Soviets freed Daniloff on September 29, and the United States released Zakharov on September 30. The Soviets also released several Soviet dissidents, including physicist Yuri F. Orlov, who was active in the human-rights movement in the Soviet Union. The Daniloff affair set off a series of ex-pulsions involving a number of Soviet diplomats in the United States and U.S. diplomats in the Soviet Union.

Chernobyl. On April 26, a nuclear reactor at the Chernobyl power station exploded, spewing radioactive debris into the air. The outside world knew nothing of the explosion until two days later, when unusually high levels of radioactivity were reported in Sweden and Finland. The Soviet government confirmed that an accident had occurred, and then revealed its location. The government asked various Western institutions for help in putting out a fire at the reactor and for medical assistance.

Gorbachev spoke about the accident on Soviet television for the first time on May 14, 18 days after it occurred. On July 19, the Politburo—the Communist Party's policymaking body—said that human error caused the accident. See ENERGY SUPPLY (Close-Up).

At a special session of the International Atomic Energy Agency in Vienna, Austria, at the end of August, the Soviet delegate said that most Soviet reactors of the type that exploded had been closed temporarily for inspections and modifications. In November, Moscow announced that the Soviet Union faced an energy shortage because of safety measures taken at nuclear power stations after the

A Moscow graveyard is the final resting place for some of the 31 people killed by the disaster at the Chernobyl nuclear power station on April 26.

accident, and because a drought had crippled the hydroelectric industry.

Official Visits. Gorbachev attended the East German Communist Party Congress (meeting) in April and Poland's Communist Party Congress in June. Also in June, Gorbachev attended a meeting of leaders of the nations in the Warsaw Pact—the Communist bloc's military alliance.

China Overture. In a speech in Vladivostok, a Soviet city near the Chinese border, on July 28, Gorbachev called for a warming of relations between China and the Soviet Union. He offered China several inducements, including hints that the Soviet Union would withdraw troops from Mongolia, Afghanistan, and the Soviet border with China; border adjustments in the area of the Amur River, which forms a boundary between China and Russia; and an invitation to take part in joint space exploration.

Talks with Israel. Soviet and Israeli representatives met in Helsinki, Finland, on August 18, in the first official diplomatic contact between their nations since 1967. The main purpose of the meeting was to discuss the reestablishment of formal ties—though not full diplomatic relations.

The meeting lasted only 90 minutes. It ended abruptly after the Israelis brought up the matter of Soviet restrictions on the emigration of Jewish citizens of the Soviet Union.

Domestic Policy. Gorbachev showed that he was firmly in control at the Communist Party Congress in Moscow from February 25 to March 6, 1986. The party holds a congress at least every five years. Delegates at these meetings conduct routine party business, including the approval of individuals whom party leaders have appointed to various organizations.

One of the most important organizations is the Communist Party Central Committee, which handles the party's work between congresses. The makeup of the Central Committee approved at the 1986 congress was a measure of the speed with which Gorbachev consolidated his power after becoming party leader in March 1985. Of the 307 members approved in 1986, 125 were Gorbachev appointees.

The 1986 congress ushered in a new phase of increased openness in public life. In early 1986, Soviet newspapers discussed drug addiction for the first time. The government hiked the price of vodka by 25 per cent on July 31 as part of its campaign against drunkenness.

Anti-Russian Rioting. On December 17 and 18, students rioted in Alma-Alta, capital of the Kazakh Soviet Socialist Republic, a Soviet "state." A leadership change in the republic's Communist Party prompted the rioting. An ethnic Russian, Gennadi V. Kolbin, replaced an ethnic Kazakh, Dinmukhamed A. Kunayev, as party chief.

Soviet dissident physicist Andrei D. Sakharov returns to Moscow on December 23 after almost seven years of exile in the city of Gorki.

Molotov Dies. Vyacheslav M. Molotov, the last surviving member of the original Soviet leadership, died on November 8 at the age of 96. He was one of the leaders of the Bolshevik (now Communist) Party when it seized power in Russia in 1917. Molotov served as premier—head of government—from 1930 to 1941, and as foreign minister from 1939 to 1949 and from 1953 to 1956.

Sakharov Exile Ends. In mid-December, the Soviets terminated the exile of Andrei D. Sakharov, a physicist who won the 1975 Nobel Peace Prize for his efforts to promote human rights and world peace. His criticisms of the Soviet government led to his banishment in 1980 to the Soviet industrial city of Gorki, which is closed to foreigners. Sakharov returned to Moscow on Dec. 23, 1986.

The Economy grew moderately in 1986, but foreign trade fell sharply. National income grew by 4.3 per cent in the first nine months of 1986, compared with the same period in 1985. Industrial output rose by 5.2 per cent. Foreign-trade volume dropped by 9 per cent, reflecting the fall in world oil prices.

The 1986 Soviet grain harvest was 210 million metric tons (231 million short tons), the best since 1978.   Chris Cviic

See also EUROPE (Facts in Brief Table). In WORLD BOOK, see RUSSIA.

RWANDA. See AFRICA.

SAFETY

SAFETY. Transportation accidents again made headlines in the United States in 1986. Although the number of fatalities caused by large airline crashes dropped substantially from 1985's record level, a crash near Los Angeles on August 31 rekindled public concern over whether air traffic was adequately controlled. The spectacular midair collision of an Aeroméxico jetliner and a small plane over the Los Angeles suburb of Cerritos killed 82 people.

An intensive probe revealed that the private plane had entered the airspace of the jetliner without a *transponder*—a radar device that would have automatically notified air controllers at Los Angeles Airport of the plane's location.

Belts and Airbags. The campaign for mandatory seat-belt laws in the United States moved forward in 1986. Ten states passed the legislation during the year, but two states repealed their seat-belt laws, bringing the total to 24 states and the District of Columbia. In the fall, car makers in the United States began installing airbags—plastic bags that inflate in front of passengers during a collision to prevent them from being thrown forward—in 10 per cent of their 1987 models in compliance with federal rules. All cars except convertibles must have airbags or seat belts installed at the factory beginning in September 1989.

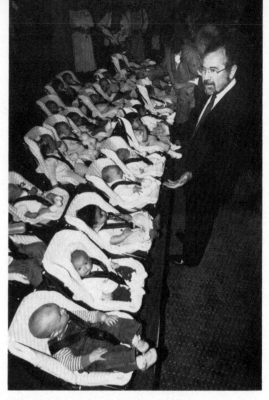

Thirty babies try out some of the car seats that Speedy Muffler King outlets in Canada lent to customers free of charge in 1986.

Accidental Deaths in the United States

	1984-1985*		1985-1986*	
	Number	Rate†	Number	Rate†
Motor Vehicle	46,100	19.4	46,500	19.4
Home	19,700	8.3	20,200	8.4
Public	18,100	7.6	19,400	8.1
Work	11,400	4.8	11,700	4.9
Total‡	**91,000**	**38.4**	**93,500**	**39.0**

*For 12-month period ending June 30.
†Deaths per 100,000 U.S. population.
‡The total does not equal the sum of the four classes because *Motor Vehicle* includes some deaths also included in *Work* and *Home.*

Source: National Safety Council estimates.

In November, however, the United States National Highway Traffic Safety Administration (NHTSA) announced that it may give car manufacturers until 1993 to install such devices. The proposed extension, filed by the Ford Motor Company of Dearborn, Mich., received criticism from Congress and the Center for Auto Safety.

Car Defects. United States government investigations into alleged auto defects created new controversy in 1986. On June 10, the General Accounting Office (GAO) said it could find no evidence that a 1980 agreement between the NHTSA and Ford had prevented accidents linked to possible transmission failures in Ford cars. The 1980 accord required Ford to warn drivers that the cars might shift suddenly from park to reverse. Consumer representatives had sought a recall of Ford cars made between 1970 and 1979, claiming that the defect had caused at least 100 deaths. The GAO urged the NHTSA to reopen the matter.

On August 15, the NHTSA ended an eight-year investigation of approximately 60 million automatic-transmission vehicles made by the General Motors Corporation of Detroit, Mich., between 1973 and 1978. Owners reported that the vehicles suddenly accelerated when shifting from park to drive or reverse, often resulting in an accident. The NHTSA said it was not able to identify any defect that could explain the 761 accidents and 31 deaths. Also in August, the NHTSA announced that it was investigating similar complaints involving 300,000 Audis imported by Volkswagen of America Incorporated of Warren, Mich., between 1978 and 1986.

Less Asbestos. On June 13, the 1.3 million workers who have jobs that expose them to asbestos won new protection from the United States Occupational Safety and Health Administration (OSHA) in Washington, D.C. During the manufacturing of building insulation, textiles, and other products that contain asbestos, asbestos fibers are released into the air and can cause a number of lung diseases. OSHA reduced the maximum exposure to asbestos from 2 fibers per cubic centimeter (0.06 cubic inch) of airspace over an eight-hour day to 0.2 fiber.

Chemical Hazards. The Food and Drug Administration in Washington, D.C., ended 25 years of debate over the safety of certain food, drug, and cosmetic dyes in June when it gave permanent approval to five dyes. The approval included four dyes some scientists said caused cancer: Orange 17 and Red 8, 9, and 19. Arthur E. Rowse

In the Special Reports section, see THE HAZARDS OF TEEN-AGE DRINKING. In WORLD BOOK, see SAFETY.

SAILING. See BOATING.

SASKATCHEWAN. Premier Grant Devine led his Progressive Conservative (PC) government to victory in a general election on October 20. The PC's won 38 of the legislature's 64 seats, well short of the 55 seats they won when first voted into office in 1982. The New Democratic Party won 25 seats, and 1 Liberal was elected, the first since 1978. The PC's won solidly in the agricultural areas of the province—regions badly hurt in the 1980's by drought, grasshoppers, and declining prices—helped by a federal announcement on October 7 that a $1-billion fund (Canadian dollars; $1 = U.S. 72 cents on Dec. 31, 1986) would be set up to aid hard-pressed grain farmers.

The PC government sponsored a measure creating a pension plan for homemakers and the self-employed, the first in Canada. Individuals would contribute up to $3,000 a year to the fund, with the government matching the amount. The government also announced a 10-year mortgage protection program, stabilizing mortgage interest at 9.75 per cent. The plan continued one created earlier by the PC's at a time of high interest rates.

The government reported a $389-million deficit on a $3.7-billion provincial budget submitted on March 26. Tax increases were imposed on corporations and tobacco products, allowing for more spending on farming and health care. David M. L. Farr

In WORLD BOOK, see SASKATCHEWAN.

SAUDI ARABIA. The government of King Fahd ibn Abd al-Aziz Al Saud was bedeviled during 1986 by two long-standing problems—falling oil revenues and the reluctance of the United States Congress to approve arms sales to the kingdom.

The Economy. Falling oil revenues forced dramatic shifts in the government's oil-production policies, culminating in the ouster of Sheik Ahmed Zaki Yamani as Saudi Arabia's oil minister on October 30. The charismatic Yamani, who had served in the post for 24 years, was replaced by Minister of Planning Hisham Nazer.

Since 1983, the Saudis had significantly cut their oil output in an effort to offset a worldwide oversupply of oil and thereby prop up the prices set by the Organization of Petroleum Exporting Countries (OPEC). Abandoning this policy in early 1986, the Saudis increased their production and sent oil prices into a steep plunge, from $28 a barrel in January to less than $13 a barrel by July. The intent was to drive the price so low that high-cost, non-OPEC producers would be forced to follow the oil cartel's lead in production and pricing. This strategy brought the Saudis into conflict with various OPEC members and was apparently rejected with the dismissal of Yamani.

Declining oil revenues seriously affected economic development. In March, Fahd postponed

Vice President George Bush cuts a ribbon at ceremonies opening a new U.S. Embassy compound in Riyadh, Saudi Arabia, in April.

the 1986 budget, citing the global oil crisis. The budget was finally passed in late December. A freeze was imposed in March on all new projects. On June 1, the Saudis devalued their currency by 2.7 per cent against the U.S. dollar. Because oil is purchased with dollars on the world market, the devaluation had the effect of increasing Saudi revenues from oil exports.

Arms Sales. In May, the U.S. Congress voted overwhelmingly to block President Ronald Reagan's proposed $354-million arms sale to Saudi Arabia. The sale included Sidewinder air-to-air and Harpoon air-to-sea missiles, as well as Stinger shoulder-fired surface-to-air missiles, which many members of Congress feared might fall into terrorists' hands. After dropping the Stingers from the package, Reagan vetoed the congressional action. The Senate upheld the President's veto on June 5 by one vote, clearing the way for delivery of a missile package valued at $265 million.

Saudi defense capabilities were improved with deliveries in February of British Tornado fighter-bombers ordered under a 1985 contract. And on June 30, the Saudis took delivery of the first of five AWACS (Airborne Warning and Control System) reconnaissance aircraft ordered from the United States in 1981. William Spencer

See also MIDDLE EAST (Facts in Brief Table). In WORLD BOOK, see SAUDI ARABIA.

SAUVÉ, JEANNE M. (1922-), undertook many official duties during 1986 as Canada's governor general, representing the country's head of state, Queen Elizabeth II. Among the more important of these functions was the reading of the Speech from the Throne at the opening of Canada's Parliament on October 1, which outlined the policy goals of the second half of Prime Minister Brian Mulroney's term in office. Sauvé's other duties included the receiving of foreign ambassadors and distinguished foreign leaders, and the presentation of awards such as the Order of Canada and the Order of Military Merit.

Although the governor general normally resides at Rideau Hall in Ottawa, Ont., Sauvé spent part of the year at her official residence, the Citadel, in Quebec City. She also traveled widely throughout Canada in 1986 and visited the provinces and territories for special events.

In March, the governor general paid a six-day official visit to Italy, accompanied by Minister for International Trade James F. Kelleher. The visit gave the Canadian group an opportunity to discuss Canada's relations with Italy. Sauvé met with Italian officials and with Pope John Paul II and visited the graves in Agira, Sicily, of Canadians who died in World War II. David M. L. Farr

See also CANADA. In WORLD BOOK, see CANADA, GOVERNMENT OF.

SCALIA, ANTONIN (1936-), became an associate justice of the Supreme Court of the United States on Sept. 26, 1986. Scalia, pronounced *skuh LEE yuh*, had been a judge on the U.S. Court of Appeals in Washington, D.C., since 1982. He took the Supreme Court seat vacated by William H. Rehnquist, who succeeded Warren E. Burger as chief justice. Scalia is the first person of Italian descent to serve on the Supreme Court. See REHNQUIST, WILLIAM H.; SUPREME COURT OF THE UNITED STATES.

Scalia was born on March 11, 1936, in Trenton, N.J. He graduated first in his class at Georgetown University in Washington, D.C., in 1957 and earned a law degree at Harvard University in Cambridge, Mass., in 1960.

From 1960 to 1967, Scalia practiced law in Cleveland, leaving to accept a teaching position at the University of Virginia Law School in Charlottesville. From 1974 to 1977, he was an assistant attorney general in the Administration of President Richard M. Nixon.

Scalia returned to teaching in 1977 at the University of Chicago. His outspoken conservatism attracted the attention of President Ronald Reagan, who named him to the Court of Appeals in 1982.

Scalia and his wife, the former Maureen McCarthy, have nine children. David L. Dreier

SCHOOL. See EDUCATION.

SCOTLAND. Arthur Guinness & Sons PLC, a British brewery and publishing firm, agreed on April 18, 1986, to acquire Distillers Company, one of Scotland's largest firms. Distillers makes Scotch whisky under the Johnnie Walker and Dewar's labels. The $4-billion Distillers merger ended a long take-over battle between Guinness and the Argyll Group PLC, a British supermarket chain. In December, the British government said it planned to investigate Guinness's take-over of Distillers. The investigation would be part of an inquiry into alleged *insider stock trading* (the buying and selling of stocks based on confidential information) at Guinness.

Oil Industry. A fall in crude oil prices, which began in January and continued throughout the year, had an adverse effect on the city of Aberdeen and on the Shetland Islands, off the north coast of Scotland in the Atlantic Ocean.

The National Union of Seamen reported a 40 per cent reduction in the use of oil-drilling and supply ships, resulting in unemployment for 700 workers. In August, another 700 workers were laid off at Britoil headquarters in Glasgow. The North Sea oil industry received some relief in August when the Organization of Petroleum Exporting Countries decided to limit oil production.

Unemployment. Despite the downturn in oil prices, the unemployment rate in Scotland's oil-producing areas remained the lowest in the country. Aberdeen's unemployment rate during the year was 8.3 per cent; the rate for the Shetland Islands was 6.4 per cent. In October, Scotland's average unemployment rate was 14.3 per cent.

Chernobyl Impact. As a result of the Chernobyl nuclear accident in the Soviet Union in April, the Scottish government banned the slaughter of sheep in western Scotland in June. The ban affected 1.4 million lambs, 17 per cent of all Scottish sheep. By October, 17,000 lambs were still under the ban.

A study of the effects of nuclear power plants on health drew protest against the construction of a proposed nuclear waste plant at Dounereay. The study, published by the Scottish Office as part of a public inquiry into the proposed plant, said that the incidence of leukemia and other diseases among children who lived near nuclear power plants "merited further investigation."

In June, the South of Scotland Electricity Board held an open day at the controversial Torness nuclear power station in East Lothian. The nuclear power plant, which began operation at the end of the year, had been beset with protests and demonstrations during its planning and construction. The Scottish branch of the National Union of Mineworkers claimed that the power generated by the Torness plant will weaken the demand for coal and eliminate 3,000 coal-mining jobs.

Scotland witnessed one of its largest antinuclear weapons demonstrations on October 5 when 45,000 people formed a human chain across the central region of Scotland from Glasgow to Grangemouth. The event was called "Arms Around Scotland."

Games Boycott. Scotland's major international event in 1986 was the Commonwealth Games, which were held in Edinburgh from July 24 to August 2. The games are an amateur sports competition for countries that have lived under British law. The competition was marred when 32 of the 58 participating countries boycotted the games in protest over Great Britain's opposition to economic sanctions against South Africa.

Cultural Honor. In October, Scotland's largest city, Glasgow, was nominated for the title of European City of Culture for 1990. The nomination is one result of the city's rejuvenation project. Under the slogan "Glasgow's Miles Better," the project promoted the city as an artistic center. Glasgow is the headquarters of the Scottish Opera, the Scottish Ballet, and the Scottish National Orchestra.   Doreen Taylor

See also GREAT BRITAIN. In WORLD BOOK, see SCOTLAND.

SCULPTURE. See ART.

SENEGAL. See AFRICA.

SEYCHELLES. See AFRICA.

SHIP AND SHIPPING. Overcapacity continued to take its toll on shipping lines and shipbuilders during 1986. The surplus of cargo space drove shipping rates downward and caused orders for new merchant vessels to remain at low levels.

Shipping. Some U.S. shipping companies posted huge losses during the first six months of 1986. United States Lines, Incorporated, owned by McClean Industries, lost $150 million and was forced to reduce service and file for bankruptcy. Sea-Land Corporation lost $59 million.

Rate conferences—groups of ocean carriers permitted to meet and set shipping rates—acted to stem the rate declines. The major conference of transpacific carriers was able to increase rates by as much as 15 per cent on freight hauled by its member carriers beginning April 15. This action came after the members voted to negotiate contracts with shippers on a conference-wide, rather than individual, basis. The move gave the conference more leverage with major customers.

A number of Asian shipping companies also experienced financial difficulties, including Hong Kong-based Wah Kwong & Company Limited and the Tung group. Both companies were hard hit by bankruptcies of some of their major charter operators and by defaults on lease agreements.

CSX Corporation's purchase of Sea-Land was the major financial story of 1986. CSX, a transportation and natural resources company that owns the Chessie Systems, Incorporated, and the Seaboard Coast Line railroad, agreed to pay $742 million for Sea-Land in a friendly take-over. Sea-Land calls at all major U.S. ports and operates a fleet of 56 container vessels. The Interstate Commerce Commission—the federal agency that regulates railroads—was expected to issue a final decision on the transaction in early 1987.

Shipbuilding remained depressed throughout the world due to the lack of orders for merchant ships. American shipyards continued to depend on U.S. Navy orders for their survival. In Europe, government-owned British Shipbuilders announced in May that it would release about 3,500 workers by year's end. A leading West German shipbuilder, Harmstorf A.G., said in July that it was placing its three shipyards in receivership.

In Japan, which accounts for nearly 50 per cent of the world's shipbuilding, three small shipbuilders filed for bankruptcy and several other firms sustained large losses. The Japanese industry has been hurt not only by the worldwide scarcity of orders, but also by the strength of the Japanese yen against other currencies.   David M. Cawthorne

In WORLD BOOK, see SHIP.

SHOOTING. See HUNTING; SPORTS.

SIERRA LEONE. See AFRICA.

SINGAPORE. See ASIA.

SKATING. See HOCKEY; ICE SKATING; SPORTS.

SKIING. Marc Girardelli of Luxembourg and Maria Walliser of Switzerland won the overall World Cup Alpine skiing titles in 1986. Girardelli took top honors for the second consecutive year, with 294 points to 284 for second-place Pirmin Zurbriggen of Switzerland. Zurbriggen lost an opportunity to win the title when he finished third in the last race of the season, a slalom event held in Bromont, Canada, on March 21, 1986.

In Women's Competition, Walliser scored 287 points, 45 more than second-place finisher Erika Hess of Switzerland. Pam Fletcher of Acton, Mass., was the highest placed American, finishing 23rd with 66 points. Fletcher started the season on the U.S. ski team's training squad. But she was later selected to ski the World Cup tour and won the season's final downhill event on March 15 in Vail, Colo. The next day, while leading in the Vail super giant slalom, she hooked a ski tip on a gate and injured an ankle. The mishap forced her to miss the last four races of the season.

Injuries also disrupted competition for other U.S. women skiers. Debbie Armstrong of Seattle, Wash., the 1984 Olympic giant slalom champion, tore knee ligaments in January 1986 and did not ski for the remainder of the season. Diann Roffe of Williamson, N.Y., the 1985 world giant slalom champion, missed half of the season due to injury.

Maria Walliser of Switzerland got caught on a gate during a World Cup giant slalom event in March but went on to win the overall Alpine skiing title.

Controversy Occurred during the World Cup tour. On March 9 at Aspen, Colo., world-class skiers seized control of an event from officials and organizers. When race officials refused to cancel the men's giant slalom event despite a course softened by rain, 40 European skiers blockaded the course. Organizers and officials relented, and the race was canceled.

Changes Proposed. Swiss journalist Serge Lang, who cofounded the World Cup circuit, said interest in the event had diminished because of too many races and too many competitors. As a change, the World Cup season had begun with two downhill competitions in Argentina in August 1985. The main part of the season then ran its normal schedule from December to March throughout Europe, the United States, Canada, and Japan. There were 38 events for men and 33 events for women. Lang proposed that there be instead a maximum of 13 World Cup races each for men and women, with a limit of 120 skiers competing on the circuit. Lang also suggested a schedule of only weekend races.

Nordic. In ski jumping, Matti Nykanen of Finland won the season-long World Cup competition. Andreas Felder of Austria won the world championship in ski flying on March 10 in Bad Mitterndorf, Austria. Frank Litsky

In WORLD BOOK, see SKIING.

SOCCER. The best soccer player in the world in 1986 was 25-year-old Diego Armando Maradona. The stocky but swift Maradona led Argentina to victory in the World Cup competition, the world's largest and most widely watched sports event, which is held every four years.

The World Cup competition ended a 110-nation tournament that began in May 1984. After 312 preliminary games, 22 nations qualified for the actual cup games held from May 31 to June 29 in nine Mexican cities. Two other teams qualified automatically—Italy as the defending World Cup champion and Mexico as the host nation.

Mexico became the host in 1983 when Colombia bowed out because of financial problems. The competition provided a brief respite for the Mexican people, burdened by falling oil prices, a vast foreign debt, and high inflation. (In the Special Reports section, see MEXICO: FROM BOOM TO BUST.)

Bookmakers in London made Brazil the favorite, followed by Argentina, Uruguay, and Mexico. In the first round of the competition, the 24 teams played in six round-robin groups of 4 teams each. Sixteen teams—the first two in each group plus the four teams with the next-best records—advanced to the second round.

Canada, making its first trip to a World Cup tournament, was shut out in all three first-round games and eliminated. The United States had been eliminated in 1985 in qualifying play.

From the second round on, the competition was direct elimination. In the second round, Italy was beaten by France, 2-0, and all the Eastern European nations—the Soviet Union, Poland, and Bulgaria—were eliminated. In the quarterfinals, France defeated Brazil on penalty kicks, 5-4.

Maradona's brilliance became evident in the quarterfinals when his two goals gave Argentina a 2-1 victory over England. On his astounding second goal, he took the ball near midfield, dribbled 55 yards (50 meters), eluded up to seven defenders, and scored. Within days, a plaque at the stadium commemorated the goal.

In the semifinals on June 25, West Germany defeated France, 2-0, and Argentina eliminated Belgium, 2-0. Maradona scored both goals against Belgium, slipping past four defenders on the second goal.

The final on June 29 in Mexico City matched Argentina's explosive offense against West Germany's rugged defense. The prize was the World Cup, a 14-inch (36-centimeter), 18-karat gold statuette that weighs a little more than 10 pounds (4.5 kilograms).

Argentina won the final, 3-2, but it was not easy. Argentina took a 2-0 lead, then allowed West Germany to score in the 74th and 81st minutes of the 90-minute game. In the 84th minute, Maradona's pass led to the winning goal by Jorge Luis Burruchaga. Although Maradona was often double-teamed and did not score, he was involved in Argentina's three goals.

U.S. Indoor. From October 1985 to April 1986, the 12 teams of the Major Indoor Soccer League played 48 games each. The San Diego Sockers and the Cleveland Force won the division titles. On May 26, San Diego won its second consecutive league championship by defeating the Minnesota Strikers, 5-3, in San Diego in the seventh and decisive game of the play-off finals.

The Pittsburgh Spirit and the Dallas Sidekicks were losing money, and, after the season, they disbanded. The remaining club owners tried to avoid the financial problems that in 1985 led to the demise of the North American Soccer League.

European. In the major competitions, Steaua Bucharest of Romania won the European Champions Cup, Dynamo Kiev of the Soviet Union won the European Cup Winners' Cup, and Real Madrid of Spain won the Union of European Football Associations Cup.

Liverpool defeated Everton, 3-1, for the English Football Association Cup. Aberdeen won the Scottish Cup, and Oxford United won the Milk Cup. Celtic won the Scottish League Championship. Wrexham won the Welsh Cup.   Frank Litsky

In WORLD BOOK, see SOCCER.

Argentina's José Luis Brown leaps over soccer star Diego Maradona to score in his team's World Cup victory over West Germany in June.

SOCIAL SECURITY. Trustees of the United States social security system reported on March 31, 1986, that the system was strong financially and that both the Old-Age and Survivors Insurance Trust Fund and the Disability Insurance Trust Fund would be able to pay benefits well into the next century. But the trustees predicted that the Hospital Insurance Trust Fund, which finances Medicare health benefits for the aged, would be bankrupt by 1996, two years sooner than had been projected a year earlier. During 1986, the system paid out $202 billion in old-age and disability benefits and $76 billion in Medicare benefits.

Old-age and disability funds were expected to accumulate reserves sufficient to pay benefits through the middle of the next century based on moderate financial projections. Even projecting the worst scenario, the trustees said that the benefits fund would be solvent until the year 2025.

Also in March, President Ronald Reagan nominated Dorcas R. Hardy as commissioner of the Social Security Administration, a post held by an acting commissioner since 1983. The Senate confirmed Hardy's nomination in June.

Payroll Deductions. Effective on Jan. 1, 1987, earnings subject to social security payroll taxes were to increase to $43,800, up from $42,000 in 1986 in line with an increase in average wages during 1986. The maximum per-worker tax was to rise to $3,131 from $3,003 in 1986.

Benefit Boost. Also to take effect on Jan. 1, 1987, was a 1.3 per cent increase in social security benefits—a cost-of-living adjustment (COLA). For a time, it appeared that COLA increases in benefits would not be paid in 1987 to 37 million social security recipients because of a decline in inflation. But the Reagan Administration announced in May that it would not oppose congressional efforts to mandate COLA increases even if the Consumer Price Index rose in 1986 by less than the 3 per cent required by law to initiate increases.

Benefits had been increased each year since the COLA provision became law in 1972. The Social Security Administration estimates that benefit payments rise by $2 billion for each percentage point of inflation. Over the long term, social security finances were expected to strengthen because of the 1987 COLA. A budget official noted that in years when no COLA is paid, the government cannot increase Medicare premiums or raise the earnings subject to social security taxes.

Disability Reviews. In January 1986, the Social Security Administration resumed periodic reviews of disability-benefit recipients for eligibility. The reviews had been halted in 1984 while procedures were revised following complaints about arbitrary and unfair rulings.   Frank Cormier and Margot Cormier

In WORLD BOOK, see SOCIAL SECURITY.

SOMALIA. See AFRICA.

SOUTH AFRICA in 1986 continued to suffer the escalating violence that began in September 1984. By some estimates, more than 4,000 people, nearly all of them blacks, had been killed by year's end. The hostility of the black majority to the government's policy of *apartheid* (racial separation) led on June 12 to a reimposition of the declared state of emergency, which had been lifted in March. The government of State President Pieter Willem Botha had anticipated violent demonstrations on June 16, the 10th anniversary of 1976 riots in the black township of Soweto, near Johannesburg.

Throughout 1986, scattered violence erupted in black townships near Cape Town, Durban, Johannesburg, Port Elizabeth, and other major cities. Although most of the clashes were between blacks and the police, some confrontations were provoked by bands of government-supported blacks known as *vigilantes,* who have tried to thwart the growing influence of young *comrades,* members of the banned African National Congress (ANC), the principal black dissident group.

The comrades have directed much of their violence against black police officers, municipal officials, and other blacks accused of cooperating with the government. The comrades executed many of those suspected collaborators, often by "necklacing" them—setting fire to a gasoline filled automobile tire draped around the neck of the victim. They also spearheaded a nationwide boycott of black schools.

In the last half of the year, an estimated 22,000 opposition political leaders, members of the clergy, labor unionists, and students of all races were detained under the state of emergency. The government rigidly censored media coverage of violence and dealt harshly with labor strikes, work stoppages, and boycotts. The government also continued to deny freedom to imprisoned ANC leader Nelson Mandela unless he renounced the ANC's use of violence. See MANDELA, WINNIE.

The Status of Apartheid. Botha promised in January that apartheid would be dismantled, but the government made little effort to carry out that pledge. South African citizenship, which Botha had vowed would be extended to all of the nation's blacks, was limited to the 1.75 million residents of the urban black townships. The abolition in 1985 of the ban on marriages between blacks and whites was not followed by reforms permitting an interracial couple to live together. A promise in April to drop the *pass laws,* regulations that restrict blacks' freedom of movement, was undermined in July by the introduction of identity cards similar to the former passes.

Sanctions. The move by many nations to economically isolate the South African government gained momentum in 1986. By year's end, economic *sanctions* (penalties) had been voted by the

South African activist Winnie Mandela, center, heads to court to challenge a government "ban" she says prevents her from living in her only home.

Organization of African Unity, the Commonwealth (Great Britain and its former colonies), the European Community (EC or Common Market), the United States, and other countries. In the United States, Congress in October overrode President Ronald Reagan's veto and imposed a number of sanctions, including bans on air links with South Africa, new business investments in that country, and the importation of several South African products.

Many corporations also abandoned South Africa in 1986, including General Motors Corporation and the Eastman Kodak Company. In November, Barclay's Bank of Great Britain closed more than 400 branch banks in South Africa. More than 11,000 whites, many with professional skills, emigrated during the year. Although sanctions cause many blacks to lose their jobs, the campaign for sanctions was supported by many black leaders, including Desmond M. Tutu, the first black archbishop of South Africa's Anglican Church.

Relations with Neighbors. Strife continued in South-African controlled Namibia. As in previous years, South Africa asserted that it would not grant independence to Namibia as long as some 25,000 to 30,000 Cuban troops continued to be stationed in neighboring Angola.

South Africa stepped up its military operations against Namibian rebels in Angola in 1986. South Africa also supported Angolan guerrillas trying to topple the government of Angola.

In January, a South African blockade of landlocked Lesotho was a major factor in the overthrow of Prime Minister Leabua Jonathan by rebel forces. Jonathan had displeased South Africa by providing sanctuary to ANC refugees and joining the call for sanctions.

Despite signing a peace treaty with Mozambique in 1984, South Africa continued to support the rebel forces of the Mozambique National Resistance. South Africa was suspected of sabotaging a plane carrying Mozambique's President Samora Moisés Machel, which crashed just inside the South African border on October 19, killing Machel and at least 33 other people. South Africa denied any involvement with the crash.

South Africa retaliated against Mozambique in 1986 for its support of economic sanctions. At midyear, the South African government began deporting Mozambican laborers and obstructing Mozambique's trade and transport links with Zambia and Zimbabwe. J. Gus Liebenow and Beverly B. Liebenow

See also AFRICA (Facts in Brief Table). In WORLD BOOK, see SOUTH AFRICA.

SOUTH AMERICA. See LATIN AMERICA and articles on Latin-American countries.

SOUTH CAROLINA. See STATE GOVERNMENT.

SOUTH DAKOTA. See STATE GOVERNMENT.

The space shuttle *Challenger* explodes shortly
after liftoff from Cape Canaveral, Fla., on
January 28, killing the crew of seven.

SPACE EXPLORATION. Tragedy and failure
thwarted the United States space program in
1986. An explosion that killed seven crew members grounded the space shuttle fleet, and the failure of several types of booster rockets curtailed
the launching of other spacecraft and satellites.

After seven delays, the National Aeronautics
and Space Administration (NASA) launched the
space shuttle *Columbia* on January 12. The crew of
seven put into orbit the most powerful communications satellite to date, *RCA Satcom*. Problems with
scientific instruments and a crowded flight schedule brought the mission to an end on January 18,
one day sooner than planned.

This was the first of 15 shuttle missions scheduled for 1986. The second mission, on January 28,
ended in tragedy when the shuttle *Challenger* exploded, killing six astronauts and teacher Christa
McAuliffe. The explosion occurred about 74 seconds after liftoff from Cape Canaveral, Fla. NASA
grounded the other three shuttles in the fleet until
it could determine and correct the cause of the
disaster. See Close-Up.

Failures and Delays. On April 18, the U.S. Air
Force attempted to launch a military reconnaissance satellite from Vandenberg Air Force Base in
California, but the Titan booster rocket exploded
five seconds after liftoff. Investigators blamed the
explosion on a gap in rubber insulation inside the
steel rocket casing. The gap allowed hot gases to
erode the casing.

On May 3, NASA attempted to launch a
weather satellite aboard a Delta rocket, a booster
that had performed successfully on 43 consecutive
flights. Seventy-one seconds after liftoff from
Cape Canaveral, the rocket's main engine shut
down. Controllers destroyed the rocket to prevent
a crash landing in a populated area. The accident
grounded Delta rockets until September 5, when a
Delta orbited two satellites for use in research on
the space-based defense system called the Strategic
Defense Initiative or "Star Wars."

Failures of three smaller boosters further crippled the U.S. space program. A Nike-Orion
rocket, launched from NASA's White Sands Test
Facility in New Mexico on April 25, failed on a
suborbital flight. On August 23, an Aries rocket
carrying X-ray detectors aloft from White Sands
had to be destroyed after it malfunctioned. And
on August 28, controllers blew up an unarmed
Minuteman 3 missile on a test flight between Vandenberg Air Force Base and Kwajalein Atoll in the
Marshall Islands in the Pacific Ocean.

Safety reviews of scheduled missions jeopardized future launches of the shuttle. In June,
NASA officials halted the development of a Centaur upper-stage rocket as a means of launching
spacecraft from the shuttle. NASA ruled that the
Centaur's liquid hydrogen and oxygen fuels made

The Soviet cosmonaut training center near Moscow displays a model of the new space station *Mir*. The actual station went into orbit in February.

the rocket too hazardous. This decision will delay planned launches of probes to Jupiter and the polar regions of the sun as well as a number of secret military payloads.

U.S. Successes. The news was not all bad. A U.S. spacecraft made the first close encounter with the planet Uranus on January 24. *Voyager 2* swooped within 50,679 miles (81,560 kilometers) of Uranus, 1.8 billion miles (2.9 billion kilometers) from Earth, and sent back photographs and scientific data about the planet's atmosphere, rings, and 15 moons.

Closer to home, an Atlas rocket orbited the *NOAA 10* weather satellite on September 17 in the first successful launch of a civilian satellite since the *Challenger* accident. *NOAA 10* transmits weather information, and it can receive emergency radio signals transmitted by people who are in distress in remote areas on Earth.

Halley's Comet. The U.S. *Pioneer* spacecraft orbiting Venus made measurements of Halley's Comet as the comet flew by Venus in February. The *International Cometary Explorer,* another U.S. craft, also collected data on the comet's long tail, and U.S. scientists analyzed data from other nations' space probes.

In March, two Soviet spacecraft, two from Japan, and one launched by the European Space Agency (ESA) flew close to Halley's Comet. ESA's

Giotto probe passed about 375 miles (600 kilometers) from the comet's core on March 13. This was so close that rock and dust from the comet damaged the spacecraft. Data from *Giotto* and the two Soviet probes, *Vega 1* and *2,* revealed that the nucleus of the comet is a dark, potato-shaped mass of ice and dust estimated to be 10 miles (16 kilometers) long and 5 miles (8 kilometers) wide.

Soviet Gains. The Soviet Union pressed toward its goal of establishing a permanently manned space station. On February 20, the Soviets launched a new station named *Mir.* On March 13, cosmonauts Leonid D. Kizim and Vladimir Solovyov lifted off in a *Soyuz T-15* spacecraft, and two days later, they docked at *Mir.* In May, the two flew from *Mir* to *Salyut 7,* a Soviet station that has been in orbit since 1982. The 1,875-mile (3,000-kilometer) trip took 28 hours, and the cosmonauts docked at *Salyut* on May 6, 1986. After 50 days and two spacewalks, Kizim and Solovyov flew the *Soyuz T-15* back to *Mir* on June 25 and 26. The cosmonauts returned to Earth on July 16.

Ariane. On February 21, an ESA Ariane-1 rocket sent a French and a Swedish satellite into orbit from Kourou Space Center in French Guiana. On the next day, the French satellite, *SPOT-1,* began to transmit extremely detailed photographs of Earth's surface to receiving stations in Europe.

NASA in the Wake of *Challenger*

On Jan. 28, 1986—about 73 seconds after liftoff from the John F. Kennedy Space Center at Cape Canaveral, Florida—the U.S. space shuttle *Challenger* was destroyed in an explosion that took the lives of all seven crew members. The plans of the National Aeronautics and Space Administration (NASA) for routine space flights also went up in smoke.

The most serious U.S. accident since the deaths of three astronauts in 1967, the explosion grounded the space shuttle fleet for at least two years. It also jeopardized the long-standing public consensus that has favored vigorous space exploration.

The financial and planning implications were staggering for a program accustomed to a relatively tight budget and a furious pace. A new shuttle orbiter to replace *Challenger* was expected to cost at least $2.4 billion. In addition, corrections of defects in the design of booster

The space shuttle *Challenger* lifts off from Cape Canaveral on January 28, just moments before the explosion that killed all seven crew members.

rockets for the remaining three shuttle orbiters were expected to cost hundreds of millions of dollars.

Launches of some military, commercial, and scientific satellites were delayed by up to three years. These included satellites designed to survey planets, such as Venus and Jupiter, and those that relay communications and photograph Earth's surface.

An official investigation of the *Challenger* disaster—completed in June by a 12-member commission appointed by President Ronald Reagan—found that the direct cause of the accident was a defective rubber seal on one of *Challenger*'s two booster rockets. Unusually cool temperatures at the launch site in Cape Canaveral affected the seal's performance so that hot gases escaped from a joint in the rocket and ignited the fuel in the shuttle's huge external tank, creating the catastrophic explosion.

The commission said that the defect went unnoticed because of persistently short-sighted and negligent decision-making by NASA officials and shuttle contractors. Both NASA and Morton Thiokol, Incorporated, the booster manufacturer, had ample warning of the effects of cool temperatures on rubber seals and should have corrected the defect long before the accident, the commission said.

The commission concluded that the error was due in part to political and economic pressures to maintain frequent shuttle launches and in part to poor internal NASA communications. Poor communications blocked the transmission of warnings by more than a dozen Morton Thiokol engineers to senior NASA officials in the hours before the launch.

By the end of 1986, a dozen or so senior officials at NASA and Morton Thiokol had resigned. And a variety of reforms were implemented by the space agency, including the creation of new safety officers and internal communications channels. But many of the financial and schedule pressures that beset NASA before the accident only worsened in its aftermath. Some agency engineers remained concerned that NASA would again cut corners as the February 1988 target date for the next space shuttle launch nears.

One of the most significant results of the accident was a decision by the government to remove most commercial satellites from the shuttle flights and to concentrate instead on military payloads and scientific experiments. That decision will likely be a shot in the arm for commercial launch firms such as Arianespace Incorporated, operated by the European Space Agency, and for China, which is anxious to improve its space launch capabilities.   R. Jeffrey Smith

On March 29, a more powerful Ariane-3 rocket launched a communications satellite for the United States and one for Brazil. On May 30, however, an Ariane-2 rocket with an international communications satellite aboard had to be destroyed a few minutes after liftoff, following failure of the rocket's third stage. The ESA then canceled the remaining Ariane launches scheduled for 1986, pending official investigation of the engine failure.

China and Japan. With United States and European launch vehicles unavailable, attention turned toward China's space program. On February 1, the Chinese had used a Long March 3 booster to launch a communications satellite. (China had not orbited a satellite since 1984.) This launch, together with the failure of the shuttle and the Ariane, prompted a private U.S. firm, Teresat, Incorporated, of Houston to sign an agreement with China for the launching of two communications satellites.

Japan demonstrated its ability to develop advanced rocket systems, launching its new H-1 booster on August 13. The rocket placed in orbit a small communications satellite and an 1,800-pound (820-kilogram) satellite that measures long distances on Earth.   William J. Cromie

In WORLD BOOK, see COMMUNICATIONS SATELLITE; SPACE TRAVEL.

Spain's President Felipe González Márquez asks for a ''sí'' in a March referendum, in which voters chose to keep Spain in NATO.

SPAIN. The Socialist Workers' Party (PSOE) of President Felipe González Márquez won national elections on June 22, 1986, capturing 184 of the 350 seats in the Chamber of Deputies, the lower house of the Cortes (parliament). Finishing second with 105 seats was the right wing Popular Coalition—a union of the Popular Alliance, Christian Democrat, and Liberal parties. In third place with 19 seats was the Democratic and Social Center, led by former President Adolfo Suárez González. The election result led to a split between the Christian Democrats and the rest of the right wing opposition, leading many observers to believe that the PSOE would rule for a long time.

NATO Referendum. President González had scheduled the elections four months earlier than necessary, apparently to take advantage of the political momentum he had gained in a March 12 *referendum* (direct vote of the people). In that referendum, Spanish voters elected to keep their country in the North Atlantic Treaty Organization (NATO). The referendum was nonbinding, but González had agreed to abide by its results.

Spain had joined NATO in May 1982 over the objections of left wing organizations, including the PSOE. But the PSOE eventually backed NATO membership for Spain.

In the balloting, 52.5 per cent of those voting favored remaining in NATO, 39.8 per cent op-

posed membership, and the remainder cast blank or invalid ballots. Voter turnout was 59.8 per cent.

The ballots listed three conditions that would limit Spain's participation in NATO: a continuation of the ban on nuclear weapons in Spain; keeping Spain's armed forces outside NATO's command structure; and a cut in the number of United States troops stationed on Spanish soil.

NATO's Secretary General Lord Carrington of Great Britain said the result of the referendum meant that a major European country now could play its full part in NATO and the European Community (EC or Common Market). Spain and Portugal had joined the EC on Jan. 1, 1986.

Terrorist Bombs. Terrorists from the military wing of a separatist group, the Basque Homeland and Liberty Organization (ETA), continued to attack military personnel and seaside resorts. Vice Admiral Cristóbal Colón de Carvajal y Maroto died in a grenade attack on his car in Madrid on February 6, and assassins shot two army officers in that city on June 17. Ten Civil Guard trainees died after a remote-controlled car bomb blasted their bus in Madrid on July 14. On July 21, an attack on the defense ministry in Madrid wounded nine people. Seaside bombing harassed vacationers, but killed no one.   Kenneth Brown

See also EUROPE (Facts in Brief Table). In WORLD BOOK, see SPAIN.

SPORTS. The use of illegal drugs continued to have a big impact on sports in 1986. The problem was dramatized by the cocaine-related deaths in June, eight days apart, of college basketball star Len Bias and professional football stand-out Don Rogers.

The 22-year-old Bias, an all-America player at the University of Maryland in College Park, died on June 19 shortly after the Boston Celtics had made him the second choice in the National Basketball Association (NBA) draft. The 23-year-old Rogers, a starting safety for the Cleveland Browns of the National Football League (NFL), died on June 27, a day before he was to be married.

Programs to control the use of drugs among athletes varied from sport to sport. In July, NFL Commissioner Pete Rozelle instituted a plan that called for random drug testing of players to uncover drug use. But Rozelle withdrew the plan after the NFL Players Association filed a grievance and insisted the matter was subject to collective bargaining. The dispute went to an arbitrator, who upheld the players in October. Similar objections prevented baseball officials from instituting a drug-testing program for major league players.

The Men's International Professional Tennis Council introduced drug testing at the Wimbledon tennis championships in July in England. The National Collegiate Athletic Association in January authorized testing at its 78 championship events for men and women and at the major-college football bowl games.

Goodwill Games. This 16-day, 18-sport, Olympic-type competition was staged for the first time from July 5 to 20 in Moscow. Although it attracted 3,500 athletes from about 70 nations, it was essentially a United States-Soviet battle. The Soviet Union led the United States in gold medals (118 to 42) and total medals (241 to 142). The games were conceived by Ted Turner, the owner of the Turner Broadcasting Systems of Atlanta, Ga., and were sponsored by Turner and the Soviet government.

Commonwealth Games. A political boycott hurt this 10-sport competition for members of the Commonwealth—Great Britain and other nations and political units that once were British colonies—held from July 24 to August 2 in Edinburgh, Scotland. Of the 58 teams expected to compete, 32 withdrew. They were protesting the refusal of British Prime Minister Margaret Thatcher to impose economic *sanctions* (penalties) on South Africa because of that nation's *apartheid* policy of racial separation.

The Sullivan Award. Joan Benoit Samuelson, 28, of Freeport, Me., the United States leading female marathon runner, won the Amateur Athletic Union's James E. Sullivan Award as the nation's outstanding amateur athlete of 1985.

Among the Winners in 1986 were the following:

Cycling. Greg LeMond of Reno, Nev., in July became the first American to win the Tour de France, the world's most prestigious bicycle race (see NEWSMAKERS OF 1986). In cycling's world championships, held from August 27 to September 7 in Colorado Springs, Colo., riders from the United States won 5 of the 48 medals.

Diving. Greg Louganis, 26, of Boca Raton, Fla., retained his springboard and platform titles in the world championships held from August 15 to 23 in Madrid, Spain. Chinese divers won 7 of the 12 world-championship medals, including the golds in women's springboard (Gao Min) and platform (Chen Lin).

Fencing. In the world championships, held from July 25 to August 3, in Sofia, Bulgaria, the individual winners were Andrea Borella of Italy in men's foil, Anja Fichtel of West Germany in women's foil, Sergei Mindirgassov of the Soviet Union in sabre, and Philippe Riboud of France in epee.

Gymnastics. The Soviet Union dominated the World Cup competition, held from August 30 to September 1 in Beijing (Peking). The Soviets won 11 gold, 4 silver, and 5 bronze medals. China was next with 4 gold and 3 bronze. The United States won no medals. Yuri Korolev of the Soviet Union and Li Ning of China tied for the men's all-around title, while Elena Shushunova of the Soviet Union took the women's title.

Marathon. For the first time in its 90-year history, the Boston Marathon on April 21 offered prize and appearance money. Rob de Castella of Australia was the men's winner in 2 hours 7 minutes 51 seconds, a course record and the third fastest time in history for the distance. He earned $235,000, plus contingency money from his sponsors. Ingrid Kristiansen of Norway, the women's winner in 2 hours 24 minutes 55 seconds, earned at least $140,000.

Rowing. Because funds were short, four men from the Penn Athletic Club of Philadelphia had to buy their own uniforms. Then they won the fours without coxswain title in the world championships held from August 16 to 24 in Nottingham, England. American women won the lightweight fours without coxswain and the double sculls. The University of Wisconsin men won the United States college championship.

Wrestling. The Soviet Union won six gold medals, two silver, and one bronze in the world freestyle championships held from October 19 to 22 in Budapest, Hungary. The United States was next with one gold, three silver, and three bronze in the 10 weight classes.

Other Champions

Archery, world field champions: men, Goran Bjerendal, Sweden; women, Carita Jussila, Finland.

Badminton, world team champions: Thomas Cup (men), China; Uber Cup (women), China.

Biathlon, world champions: men's 10-kilometer and 20-kilometer, Valeri Medvedtzev, Soviet Union; women's 10-kilometer, Eva Korpela, Sweden; women's 20-kilometer, Birk Anders, East Germany.

Billiards, world pocket champions: men, Nick Varner, Owensboro, Ky.; women, Loree Jon Ogonowski Jones, Hillsboro, N.J.

Bobsledding, world champions: two-man, Wolfgang Hoppe, East Germany; four-man, Erich Schaerer, Switzerland.

Canoeing, world 500-meter and 1,000-meter kayak champion: Jeremy West, Great Britain.

Casting, U.S. all-around champion: Steve Rajeff, Poulsbo, Wash.

Court tennis, U.S. open champion: Chris Ronaldson, Great Britain.

Croquet, U.S. champion: Reid Fleming, Vancouver, Canada.

Cross-Country, world champions: men, John Ngugi, Kenya; women, Zola Budd, Great Britain.

Curling, world champions: men, Ed Lukowich, Calgary, Canada; women, Marilyn Darte, St. Catharines, Canada.

Darts, world champion: Bobby George, Great Britain.

Equestrian, world champions: jumping, Gail Greenough, Edmonton, Canada; dressage, Anne Greth-Jensen, Denmark; three-day, Virginia Holgate Leng, Great Britain.

Field Hockey, world champions: men, Australia; women, the Netherlands.

Frisbee, U.S. open overall champions: men, Scott Zimmerman, Arcadia, Calif.; women, Anni Kreml, San Diego.

Handball, U.S. four-wall champions: men, Naty Alvarado, Hesperia, Calif.; women, Peanut Motal, Martinez, Calif.

Hang Gliding, U.S. world class champion: Mark Newland, Australia.

Horseshoe Pitching, world champions: men, Mark Seibold, Huntington, Ind.; women, Phyllis Negaard, St. Joseph, Minn.

Iceboating, U.S. DN Class champion: Jan Gougeon, Bay City, Mich.

Judo, U.S. open champions: men, Damon Keeve, San Francisco; women, Corrinne Shigemoto, San Jose.

Lacrosse, world champions: men, United States; women, Australia. U.S. college: North Carolina.

Lawn Bowling, national open champions: men, Orville Artist, Walnut Creek, Calif.; women, Ann Barber, Los Angeles.

Luge, world champions: men, Gerald Pilz, Austria; women, Irmgard Lanthaler, Italy.

Modern Pentathlon, world champion: Anatoly Starostin, Soviet Union, or Massulo Carlo, Italy (disputed).

Motorcycle Racing, world 500-cc champion: Eddie Lawson, Ontario, Calif.

Paddle Tennis, U.S. champions: men, Mark Rifenbark, Los Angeles; women, Kathy May Paben, Santa Monica, Calif.

Parachute Jumping, world women's combined champion: Terry Vares, Fort Bragg, N.C.

Platform Tennis, U.S. doubles champions: Hank Irvine, Short Hills, N.J., and Greg Moore, Morristown, N.J.

Polo, World Cup champion: White Birch Farm, Greenwich, Conn.

Racquetball, U.S. champions: DP men's nationals, Bret Hartnett, Las Vegas, Nev.; Ektelon men's nationals, Marty Hogan, San Diego; DP and Ektelon women's nationals, Lynn Adams, Costa Mesa, Calif.

Racquets, U.S. Open champion, William Boone, Great Britain.

Rhythmic Gymnastics, U.S. all-around champion: Marina Kunyavsky, Los Angeles.

Rodeo, U.S. all-around champion: Lewis Feild, Elk Ridge, Utah.

Roller Hockey, world champion: Italy.

Roller-Skating, world freestyle champions: men, Scott Cohen, North Brunswick, N.J.; women, Chiara Sartoni, Italy; U.S. freestyle champions: men, Scott Cohen; women, Jennifer Leck, Millbury, Ohio; men's 5,000-meter speed: Dante Muse, Des Moines, Iowa.

Rugby, U.S. college champion: California.

Sambo, U.S. unlimited champion: Craig Pittman, Quantico, Va.

Shooting, world champions: free rifle (three position and kneeling), Glenn Dubis, Fort Benning, Ga.; skeet, Matt Dryke, Fort Benning, Ga.

Skateboarding, Transworld champion: Tony Hawk, Oceanside, Calif.

Sled Dog Racing, Alpo International champion: Gary Edinger, Keenan, Wis.

Greg LeMond of the United States leads the pack down the Champs Élysées in Paris on the last stage of the Tour de France, which he won in July.

Snowmobile Racing, world champion: Jacques Villeneuve, St. Cuthbert, Canada.

Softball, world women's champion: Hi-Ho Brakettes, Stratford, Conn.; U.S. fast-pitch champions: men, Pay 'n Pak, Bellevue, Wash.; women, Southern California Invasion, Los Angeles.

Squash Racquets, North American men's champion: Mark Talbott, Marblehead, Mass.; U.S. women's champion, Alicia McConnell, New York City.

Squash Tennis, U.S. champion: Pedro Bacallao, Miami, Fla.

Surfing, world champion: Tommy Curren, Carpinteria, Calif.

Synchronized Swimming, world champion: Carolyn Waldo, Beaconsfield, Canada.

Table Tennis, U.S. open champions: men, Teng Yi, China; women, Xu Wanhua, China.

Tae Kwon Do, World Cup heavyweight champion: Myung Sik Yoo, South Korea.

Team Handball, world champion: Yugoslavia.

Triathlon, U.S. series champions: men, Scott Molina, Boulder, Colo.; women, Kirsten Hanssen, Denmark.

Volleyball, world champions: men, United States; women, China.

Water Polo, world champions: men, Yugoslavia; women, Australia.

Water-Skiing, U.S. overall champions: men, Carl Roberge, Orlando, Fla.; women, Deena Brush, West Sacramento, Calif.

Weight Lifting, world super heavyweight champion: Antonio Krustev, Bulgaria.   Frank Litsky

See also articles on the various sports. In the Special Reports section, see BIG BOOM IN WOMEN'S SPORTS. In WORLD BOOK, see articles on the various sports.

SRI LANKA. Violence continued throughout 1986 as militants of Sri Lanka's Tamil Hindu minority continued to demand a separate state—which they call Tamil Eelam—in the northern and eastern sections of the island nation.

Guerrilla Activity. Up to 300 people were killed in early May when the Liberation Tigers of Tamil Eelam, the country's most powerful separatist group, clashed with the Tamil Eelam Liberation Organization, a rival faction. Although both groups seek to establish an independent Tamil state, they have disagreed over tactics—both military and political—to achieve their goal.

Terrorist activity spread to Colombo, the nation's capital, on May 3. A bomb destroyed an AirLanka jetliner minutes before take-off from the city's international airport. The blast killed 17 passengers. On May 8, 12 people died after an explosion at the central telegraph office in the city's business district. Government officials blamed both explosions on the Liberation Tigers. Tamil militants accused the army of killing innocent villagers in retaliation for the guerrilla attacks.

Political Accommodation. Although the government, which is dominated by the Sinhalese Buddhist majority, resisted any partition of the country, President J. R. Jayewardene sought a compromise that would give some self-govern- ment to Tamil areas. On June 25, he proposed a plan to establish elected councils with extensive legal authority in each of the country's provinces.

The opposition Sri Lanka Freedom Party voted on July 14 to reject Jayewardene's plan and boycott further negotiations, apparently in a bid to win support from Sinhalese who did not want to compromise. At the same time, the Liberation Tigers pressured the moderate Tamil United Liberation Front, the political group negotiating with the government, to press for the consolidation of the northern and eastern provinces. The government rejected this demand.

Mysterious Seafarers. In August, Canadian fishing boats rescued 155 Sri Lankans found adrift off the Newfoundland coast. The castaways identified themselves as Tamils who had sailed to Canada by way of Madras, India, seeking political asylum. They claimed that, after a month-long Atlantic crossing, they were set adrift in lifeboats and spent five days on the open sea. Canadian officials determined, however, that the refugees sailed from Hamburg, West Germany, and were the victims of an international scheme to exploit people seeking asylum in North America. The Tamils received work permits and were allowed to remain in Canada for at least a year.   Henry S. Bradsher

See also ASIA (Facts in Brief Table). In WORLD BOOK, see SRI LANKA.

Where Tamils Want Their Own State

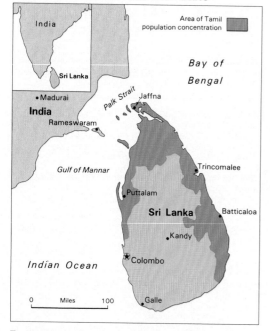

Tamil Hindus, a minority in most of Sri Lanka, are agitating for an independent state they call Tamil Eelam in predominantly Tamil sections.

STAMP COLLECTING. In August 1986, the United States Postal Service discontinued the use of postage-due stamps on mail carrying insufficient postage. The stamps had been produced since 1879 in varying denominations. The last such stamp, with a 17-cent value, was issued in June 1985. Post office clerks now affix regular postage stamps or a postage-meter stamp to mail in exchange for postage due.

Most Popular Stamps. In the 1986 *Linn's Stamp News* popularity poll of 1985 issues, collectors named the U.S. American Horses commemorative block of four as their favorite issue and as the previous year's best commemorative design. The 33-cent international airmail China Clipper postal card was voted the best postal-stationery design.

AMERIPEX '86, the first international stamp exhibition in the United States in a decade, was held at Chicago's O'Hare Exposition Center from May 22 to June 1. About 164,000 people, including almost 11,000 youth-activities participants, crowded the mammoth exhibition hall, making AMERIPEX '86 the largest stamp show ever held in the United States.

In the youth section of the show, national winners in the Postal Service's Youth Exhibiting Stamps (YES) competition showed their collections. YES was a nationwide program in which young people were invited to enter their stamp

A "miniblock" of stamps depicting the first nine Presidents of the United States was part of a series of Presidents stamps issued in May.

collections in competition. The six finalists and their parents received expenses-paid trips to AMERIPEX.

Special exhibits at the show included private collections lent by Queen Elizabeth II of Great Britain and by Prince Rainier III of Monaco. Rarities on display included the only known copy of the world's most valuable stamp—the 1856 British Guiana one-penny black on magenta, which sold for $850,000 in 1980. Other rarities included five of the six known blocks of 1918 U.S. 24-cent airmail inverted-center stamps.

A single copy of the 1918 inverted-center airmail stamp sold for $82,500 at an AMERIPEX auction. Also at the show, a buyer paid $5,500 for a 1979 U.S. Americana 50-cent stamp with an invert error. The stamp pictures a candleholder with a lighted candle, but the yellow candle and the circular red glow around it are printed upside down. In a later auction, another copy of the Americana stamp sold for $17,600. In the biggest sale of the year, one of two known copies of the 1867 U.S. 1-cent blue Benjamin Franklin stamp with a Z grill—a wafflelike pattern impressed into the paper to increase the penetration of canceling ink—sold at a November auction in Los Angeles for $418,000, a record for that stamp.

New U.S. Stamps. The Postal Service issued a block of four commemorative stamps honoring

STATE GOVERNMENT

Arctic explorers on May 28. The stamps depict Adolphus W. Greely, a U.S. Army officer who explored Arctic regions in the late 1800's; Elisha Kent Kane, an American physician who was one of the pioneers of Arctic exploration in the mid-1800's; American explorer Robert E. Peary and his associate Matthew A. Henson, who in 1909 became the first persons to reach the North Pole; and Canadian explorer Vilhjalmur Stefansson, who adopted Eskimo ways and traveled through vast areas of northern Canada.

On May 22, four nine-stamp sheets of the U.S. Presidents, the first smaller-sized sheets issued in the United States, were released at a first-day ceremony at AMERIPEX. One stamp shows the White House, and 35 depict the Presidents, from George Washington to Lyndon B. Johnson (living Presidents may not be pictured on stamps or coins). During AMERIPEX, a printing error—an omitted border inscription—was discovered on five sheets.

On July 4 in New York City, Postmaster General Albert V. Casey introduced the 22-cent Statue of Liberty stamp honoring the centennial of the statue's dedication. In Paris on the same day, a 2.2-franc stamp of similar design was issued by France, commemorating France's gift of the statue to the United States in 1884.   Paul A. Larsen

In WORLD BOOK, see STAMP COLLECTING.

STATE GOVERNMENT. The economic situation faced by state legislatures varied widely in 1986. Many states in the Northeast and Middle Atlantic regions and on the West Coast had thriving economies. These states were able to pass savings along to taxpayers in the form of tax cuts and were able to spend more money on government programs.

In sharp contrast, parts of the Midwest, South, and Southwest were hit by hard times. Former oil-boom states, such as Oklahoma, Texas, and Alaska, were devastated by a plunge in oil prices in the spring. Midwestern farm states, such as North Dakota and South Dakota, and some states in the South and West, which are heavily dependent on timber and textile industries, were also hard-hit.

Depressed economies forced 18 states to cut their budgets during fiscal 1986 (which for most states ended on June 30), a record for a nonrecession year. Budget-cutting continued in 1986 as states attempted to prevent deficits by the end of fiscal 1987. Three states—Colorado, Louisiana, and South Carolina—ended fiscal 1986 in debt. Because of poor economies, Alaska, Montana, Nevada, Oregon, and Wyoming actually spent less in fiscal 1986 than they did in fiscal 1985.

Taxes. Some states predicted financial relief from the Tax Reform Act of 1986, which President Ronald Reagan signed into law October 22.

Selected Statistics on State Governments

State	Resident population*	Governor†	Legislature† House (D)	House (R)	Senate (D)	Senate (R)	State tax revenue‡	Tax revenue per capita‡	Public school expenditures per pupil§
Alabama	4,021,000	Guy Hunt (R)	89	16	30	5	$ 2,924,000,000	$ 727	$ 2,000
Alaska	521,000	Steve Cowper (D)	24	16	8	12	1,886,000,000	3,619	5,900
Arizona	3,187,000	Evan Mecham (R)	24	36	11	19	2,945,000,000	924	2,500
Arkansas	2,359,000	Bill Clinton (D)	91	9	31	4	1,745,000,000	740	2,200
California	26,365,000	George Deukmejian (R)	44	36	24	15#	28,952,000,000	1,098	2,900
Colorado	3,231,000	Roy Romer (D)	25	40	10	25	2,284,000,000	707	3,000
Connecticut	3,174,000	William A. O'Neill (D)	92	59	25	11	3,498,000,000	1,102	3,600
Delaware	622,000	Michael Castle (R)	19	22	13	8	816,000,000	1,312	3,000
Florida	11,366,000	Bob Martinez (R)	75	45	25	15	7,883,000,000	694	2,700
Georgia	5,976,000	Joe Frank Harris (D)	153	27	46	10	4,525,000,000	757	2,100
Hawaii	1,054,000	John Waihee (D)	40	11	20	5	1,363,000,000	1,293	2,800
Idaho	1,005,000	Cecil D. Andrus (D)	20	64	16	26	733,000,000	729	2,200
Illinois	11,535,000	James R. Thompson (R)	67	51	31	28	9,228,000,000	800	2,700
Indiana	5,499,000	Robert D. Orr (R)	48	52	20	30	4,336,000,000	789	2,500
Iowa	2,884,000	Terry E. Branstad (R)	59	41	30	20	2,307,000,000	800	2,900
Kansas	2,450,000	Mike Hayden (R)	51	74	16	24	1,915,000,000	782	3,200
Kentucky	3,726,000	Martha Layne Collins (D)	73	27	29	9	3,013,000,000	809	2,300
Louisiana	4,481,000	Edwin W. Edwards (D)	83	22	34	5	3,856,000,000	860	2,300
Maine	1,164,000	John R. McKernan, Jr. (R)	86	65	20	15	1,005,000,000	864	2,700
Maryland	4,392,000	William Donald Schaefer (D)	124	17	43	4	4,322,000,000	984	3,100
Massachusetts	5,822,000	Michael S. Dukakis (D)	126	33#	32	8	6,621,000,000	1,137	3,200
Michigan	9,088,000	James J. Blanchard (D)	64	46	18	20	8,684,000,000	956	3,000
Minnesota	4,193,000	Rudy Perpich (DFL)	83	51	47	20	5,228,000,000	1,241	3,100
Mississippi	2,613,000	Bill Allain (D)	115	7	47	4#	1,812,000,000	693	1,800
Missouri	5,029,000	John Ashcroft (R)	111	52	21	13	3,352,000,000	666	2,300
Montana	826,000	Ted Schwinden (D)	49	51	25	25	641,000,000	776	3,600
Nebraska	1,606,000	Kay A. Orr (R)	(unicameral) 49 non-partisan				1,040,000,000	648	2,600
Nevada	936,000	Richard H. Bryan (D)	29	13	9	12	941,000,000	1,005	2,800
New Hampshire	998,000	John H. Sununu (R)	133	267	8	16	434,000,000	435	2,400
New Jersey	7,562,000	Thomas H. Kean (R)	30	49	23	17	7,719,000,000	1,021	3,800
New Mexico	1,450,000	Garrey E. Carruthers (R)	47	23	21	21	1,439,000,000	993	3,200
New York	17,783,000	Mario M. Cuomo (D)	94	56	26	35	20,702,000,000	1,164	3,800
North Carolina	6,255,000	James G. Martin (R)	82	38	42	8	5,198,000,000	831	2,300
North Dakota	685,000	George A. Sinner (D)	45	61	27	26	692,000,000	1,011	3,000
Ohio	10,744,000	Richard F. Celeste (D)	60	39	15	18	8,652,000,000	805	2,600
Oklahoma	3,301,000	Henry Bellmon (R)	70	31	31	17	2,982,000,000	903	3,200
Oregon	2,687,000	Neil Goldschmidt (D)	34	26	18	12	1,983,000,000	738	3,700
Pennsylvania	11,853,000	Robert P. Casey (D)	103	100	26	24	10,162,000,000	857	3,200
Rhode Island	968,000	Edward D. DiPrete (R)	80	20	38	12	862,000,000	891	3,000
South Carolina	3,347,000	Carroll A. Campbell, Jr. (R)	92	32 *	37	9	2,732,000,000	816	1,600
South Dakota	708,000	George S. Mickelson (R)	22	48	11	24	355,000,000	502	1,900
Tennessee	4,762,000	Ned R. McWherter (D)	61	38	23	10	2,998,000,000	630	1,500
Texas	16,370,000	William P. Clements (R)	94	56	24	7	11,541,000,000	705	2,100
Utah	1,645,000	Norman H. Bangerter (R)	27	48	8	21	1,324,000,000	805	1,600
Vermont	535,000	Madeleine M. Kunin (D)	75	75	19	11	459,000,000	857	3,200
Virginia	5,706,000	Gerald L. Baliles (D)	65	33**	31	9	4,469,000,000	783	2,700
Washington	4,409,000	Booth Gardner (D)	61	37	25	24	4,586,000,000	1,040	3,200
West Virginia	1,936,000	Arch A. Moore, Jr. (R)	78	22	27	7	1,856,000,000	958	2,500
Wisconsin	4,775,000	Tommy G. Thompson (R)	54	45	20	13	5,066,000,000	1,061	3,000
Wyoming	509,000	Mike Sullivan (D)	20	44	11	19	806,000,000	1,584	5,400

*1985 estimates (source: U.S. Bureau of the Census).
†1986 election results (source: state officials).
‡1985 figures (source: U.S. Bureau of the Census).
§1983-1984 per pupil in average daily attendance (source: National Center for Education Statistics).
#One independent.
**Two independents.

480

The act increases the level of income the federal government can tax. Because some state income taxes are based on this federal taxable income, state tax revenue was expected to rise in approximately 25 states.

Seventeen states raised consumer or personal income taxes in 1986, but six other states cut taxes—Connecticut, Delaware, Massachusetts, Michigan, Pennsylvania, and Vermont. Five states—Idaho, Kansas, Nebraska, New Mexico, and Texas—raised sales taxes.

It became more expensive to drive a car or smoke in some areas in 1986 as seven states hiked motor-fuel taxes and five states raised the sales tax on cigarettes. Five other states coupled crackdowns on tax evaders with limited amnesty programs allowing delinquents time to pay up. Despite its economic woes, Alaska announced in September that the state would pay each citizen $556.26 in December from the state savings account built on oil revenues.

State lotteries became more popular as one way to raise state revenues. In November elections, voters in Florida, Idaho, Kansas, Montana, and South Dakota joined 22 other states that have legal lottery games. A lottery proposal in North Dakota, however, lost at the polls. Florida residents voted down for the second time a referendum to legalize casino gambling. In Louisiana, state legislators did not pick up Governor Edwin W. Edwards' idea of using casino gambling to help solve the state's budget crisis.

Insurance. One of the single most important issues facing state legislatures in 1986 concerned liability insurance—insurance that protects businesses and people against financial losses if their actions result in bodily or property injury to others. In the 1980's, the cost of liability insurance has skyrocketed, preventing many state governments, local businesses, and professionals from buying or affording insurance protection against lawsuits.

In response to claims by insurance companies that exceedingly large court awards were to blame for much of the problem, more than 40 states enacted reforms affecting insurance regulations in 1986. The new laws put a ceiling on the total amount of damages that can be awarded to victims for "pain and suffering." They also limit the amount of damages towns and cities have to pay to victims who are unable to collect damages from others who may have caused the injury.

Liability issues were on the ballots in three states in November. California and Montana voters approved limits on awards. Arizona voters rejected such limits. West Virginia aroused the displeasure of the insurance industry when it legislated regulatory reforms. The state was forced to modify its insurance-reform law after medical-malpractice

A sign goes into storage in July after Nevada decides to retain the federally mandated speed limit of 55 miles (89 kilometers) per hour.

insurance companies threatened to cancel thousands of policies in the state in protest.

Encouraging Business. States continued to appropriate funds to spur economic development. The Kentucky legislature cleared the way for the Toyota Motor Corporation to begin building its first independent U.S. automobile-assembly plant, in Georgetown, Ky., by approving tax incentives. West Virginia began offering tax credits to out-of-state businesses that move to the state. In addition to traditional tax breaks, six states lowered top-bracket personal-income-tax rates as a way to attract new corporations.

Other states concentrated on building or sprucing up state roads to attract business. Tennessee and Virginia raised gasoline taxes to pay for new roads, and Georgia invested $100 million in roads to stimulate economic growth. New York and West Virginia joined 28 other states in authorizing enterprise zones to encourage companies to bring new growth to declining areas.

Public Safety. Despite losing part of their federal highway aid, Colorado, Idaho, Louisiana, Montana, Ohio, South Dakota, Tennessee, and Wyoming still allowed people 18 to 20 years old to drink alcoholic beverages. Six more states raised the legal drinking age to 21 during the year, however. In the Special Reports section, see THE HAZARDS OF TEEN-AGE DRINKING.

The number of states that passed mandatory seat-belt laws rose to 26, plus the District of Columbia, in 1986 as 10 more states approved the measure. Voters in Massachusetts and Nebraska, however, voted in the November election to repeal state seat-belt laws.

A debate heated up in some states over the nation's 55 miles per hour (mph), about 89 kilometers per hour (kph), speed limit. For the first time since the speed limit was enacted in 1974, the U.S. Department of Transportation (DOT) in May announced that it would withhold federal highway funds from states—Arizona and Vermont—for not adequately enforcing the 55 mph speed limit. By the end of the year, however, the DOT had not taken action on its decision. Some Western states pressed for an increase in the national speed limit, and Nevada briefly raised its limit in July as part of a court challenge.

The dangers of toxic waste and nuclear waste were major state concerns in 1986. New York and New Jersey voters approved bonds to finance hazardous-waste cleanup, and California voted to protect drinking water from toxic chemicals.

The Chernobyl nuclear power plant accident in April in the Soviet Union added to state concerns over nuclear safety and waste storage. Nevada, Texas, and Washington challenged the federal government's proposed selection of one site in each state for nuclear-waste storage. On September 20, Governor Michael S. Dukakis of Massachusetts rejected emergency evacuation plans for the Seabrook nuclear power plant in New Hampshire in an effort to delay—and possibly block—the plant's federal licensing. The plant is located on the New Hampshire coast only 2 miles (3 kilometers) from the Massachusetts border.

Education. On August 23, state governors issued a major report on school reforms that could trigger educational changes in 1987 legislative sessions. In an effort to upgrade teacher competency while preventing future teacher shortages, Delaware accepted college graduates with degrees in fields other than education as teachers. Most states spent more money on higher education in 1986 than they did in 1985.

Other Measures. Kentucky made history on Jan. 6, 1986, when it established the first private prison in the United States. On March 19, however, Pennsylvania legislators passed a bill forbidding privately operated prisons in the state until after it examines the issue in 1987.

In March 1986, New Mexico became the first state to formally declare itself a "state of sanctuary" for Central American refugees. In November, California approved a proposition to make English the official state language. Elaine Stuart Knapp

See also ELECTIONS. In WORLD BOOK, see STATE GOVERNMENT and articles on the individual states.

STEEL INDUSTRY. The United States steel industry continued to face hard times in 1986. Beset by aging plants and costly employee wage and benefit obligations, U.S. steelmakers struggled against competition from cheap imported steel. Adding to the industry's woes, aluminum, plastics, and ceramics continued to replace steel in the manufacture of automobiles and other products.

The American Iron and Steel Institute (AISI), a steel industry association based in Washington, D.C., reported that domestic steel production declined slightly during the first half of 1986. American mills produced 44.97 million short tons (40.80 metric tons) of raw steel, compared with 45.11 million short tons (40.92 metric tons) during the same period in 1985.

Employment also continued a long downward trend. On Aug. 11, 1986, the AISI announced that the average number of U.S. steelmaking jobs had declined to 186,000 during June. This represented the lowest level since 1933, when the AISI began publishing employment statistics.

The AISI estimated that U.S. steel companies had lost $7.4 billion between 1982 and 1985. In an annual report issued on June 11, 1986, the institute said that American steel companies had shut down 700 steel-manufacturing and related facilities since 1974, including 72 complete plants.

Problems extended beyond the United States. In September, the International Iron and Steel Institute in Brussels, Belgium, reported a worldwide decline in steel production. Production during the first eight months of 1986 in non-Communist countries declined 3.2 per cent from the same period a year earlier.

New Name, Old Problems. In a move that reflected the declining fortunes of the American steel industry, the United States Steel Corporation, the nation's largest steel producer, on July 8 dropped the "Steel" from its name. As part of an overall corporate restructuring, the firm changed its name to USX Corporation.

Under the restructuring, USX functions as a holding company that oversees the operations of four independent units, one of which, USS, consists of the steel and iron ore business. The other units are Marathon Oil Company; Texas Oil and Gas Corporation; and U.S. Diversified Group, which consists of chemical, engineering, real estate, and other interests. Industry analysts saw the restructuring as a move to make the company's unprofitable steelmaking operation carry its own economic weight.

More than 45,000 members of the United Steelworkers of America struck USX on August 1 when the union refused a company request for concessions on wages and benefits. USX asked workers to accept wage and benefit cuts of $2 to $3 per hour, matching contract settlements the

A flag with U.S. Steel's new name—USX, reflecting the company's diversification outside the steel industry—is raised at its headquarters in July.

union had made with other major steel companies. The union argued, however, that USX was in better financial condition than its competitors.

On November 25, the strike became the longest in the history of the U.S. steel industry, surpassing a 116-day strike in 1959. The union claimed the work stoppage was not a strike but a lockout, in which USX would not permit the employees to work. At year's end, the strike continued.

LTV Woes. Heavy business losses due to cheap imported steel, reduced demand, and other factors forced LTV Corporation, the second largest U.S. steel producer, to file for bankruptcy on July 17. The firm continued to operate while working out a plan to pay off its creditors.

As part of the bankruptcy action, LTV decided to terminate the health and life insurance benefits of about 76,000 retirees. Officials of the steelworkers union, maintaining that the decision violated their contract, called a strike July 25 by about 4,400 workers at the Indiana Harbor Works in East Chicago, Ind., one of LTV's most modern and profitable mills. The company argued that under bankruptcy laws it could not pay the retirees' benefits without court approval. The strike ended on July 30, when a U.S. bankruptcy judge ruled that LTV could—over the objections of its creditors—pay the disputed benefits.   Michael Woods

In WORLD BOOK, see IRON AND STEEL.

STOCKS AND BONDS. Despite several scares, 1986 was a good year for the United States stock market. The Standard & Poor's 500 Index (S&P 500), which tracks 500 stocks representing about 90 per cent of the dollar volume on the New York Stock Exchange, hit its low of 203.5 for 1986 on January 22. It then began a sustained rise through the end of June, setting new highs nearly every month. In mid-September, the S&P 500 fell briefly below 230 before a sustained climb brought it to the year's high of 254.00 on December 2. It finished the year at 242.17 for a total rise of 15 per cent.

The Dow Jones Industrial Average (the Dow) fluctuated widely during 1986. The Dow covers 30 stocks traded on the New York Stock Exchange. It began the year at 1,545, fell to the 1986 low of 1,502.3 on January 22, and rose sharply, passing 1,800 for the first time on March 20.

The Dow rose to a new high of 1,919.7 on September 4 before plunging a record 86.6 points on September 11. It recovered to set a new record of 1,955.57 on December 2 and finished the year at 1,895.95.

Other World Markets. The year was a good one for investors around the world. Australian shareholders saw their stocks rise an average of 34.6 per cent. Japanese stocks rose 35.2 per cent; British shares rose an average 12.3 per cent, and Spanish shares, an average of 85.9 per cent.

STOCKS AND BONDS

The Bouncing Dow

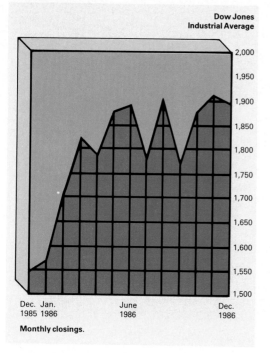

Dow Jones Industrial Average

Dec. Jan.   June   Dec.
1985 1986   1986   1986

Monthly closings.

The tightly controlled London Stock Exchange was deregulated on October 27 and opened up to new competition and technology. Fixed commissions were abolished, and traditional face-to-face trading on the exchange floor was quickly being replaced by computer and telephone transactions.

Arbitrage (the buying and selling of the same stock in different places at the same time) became a household word in 1986 after its effects sent the Dow plummeting in September and its manipulations led to the biggest insider-trading scandal in history. Arbitrage trading controlled by computer programs was at least partly responsible for the Dow's spectacular rises and falls. The deals involved using futures or options on stock indexes traded against the underlying stocks. Increasingly, computers were used to make buy and sell decisions. On September 11, computer-inspired "program trades" pushed the Dow down 86.6 points the day before futures and options contracts expired.

Insider Trading. Another kind of arbitrage, known as *risk arbitrage*, was behind the insider-trading scandal. Risk arbitrage consists of buying the stocks of firms rumored to be the targets of take-over bids by another company. A take-over bid is usually more than 15 per cent above the current market price of the target company's stock. Buying stock at the lower market price can lead to

a quick profit when the offer is finally made.

Ivan F. Boesky, a professional arbitrager, was an expert in knowing which firms were going to be take-over targets. But in November, the Securities and Exchange Commission revealed the secret of his success. Boesky pleaded guilty to violating insider-trading laws by planting an accomplice in the New York City investment banking firm of Drexel Burnham Lambert Incorporated. The accomplice told Boesky when Drexel's customers were preparing take-over offers. On November 14, Boesky agreed to pay a $50-million fine and restore another $50 million in illegal profits from take-over deals—the biggest penalty in Wall Street history.

Bond Markets. Long-term bond yields continued the fall that began in 1985. The 30-year U.S. Treasury bonds began the year paying 9.5 per cent interest, then fell sharply, fluctuating between 7.6 per cent and 8 per cent through November. They finished the year at 7.49 per cent.

The big news in the bond markets in 1986 was the increasing use of so-called junk bonds, paying high interest, to finance take-over bids. In 1986, nonfinancial corporations issued new bonds at the rate of $19.5 billion per month. Of these, 25 per cent were junk bonds used to finance a record 3,600 corporate take-overs.   Donald W. Swanton

In WORLD BOOK, see BOND; INVESTMENT; STOCK, CAPITAL.

SUDAN. The military leaders who overthrew President Gaafar Mohamed Nimeiri in 1985 kept their promise to restore civilian rule in 1986. The first multiparty elections since 1968 were held from April 1 to 12, 1986. Some 4.5 million voters cast ballots for a 264-member National People's Assembly. The voters chose from among 1,000 candidates representing 30 political parties. The Assembly has 301 seats, but voting was postponed in 37 southern districts because of civil war there.

The dominant Umma and Democratic Unionist (DUP) parties won 99 and 63 seats respectively and agreed on May 4 to form a broad-based government. The fundamentalist National Islamic Front (formerly the Muslim Brotherhood) emerged as a strong opposition force with 51 Assembly seats.

Umma leader Sadiq el Mahdi was named prime minister, and a five-man Supreme Council was appointed to act as head of state. After much hard bargaining, a coalition Cabinet dominated by the Umma and DUP took office on May 15.

Big Problems. The new government faced awesome political and economic problems. The most critical political problem was the continued civil war in the South, where guerrillas—most of whom are Christian or practice local religions—have been fighting against Muslim domination of the region. The rebel Sudanese People's Liberation

Army (SPLA) demanded the abolition of Islamic law and greater participation in the new national government as the price for reconciliation.

It was SPLA control of much of the South that forced the postponement of the April elections. By May, guerrilla successes and defections from the government forces had limited the government's authority to the region's major towns.

In August, the SPLA surrounded the provincial capital, Juba. The siege and especially the shooting down of a Sudan Airways plane by rebels on August 16, killing all 60 people aboard, created a desperate situation. The rebels said they would not permit flights over their territory, so food supplies could not be delivered to government-held areas and millions of people faced starvation. An October agreement allowed relief agencies to resume food deliveries.

Economic Woes. With foreign debts of $10 billion, agricultural output dropping, cotton sales low, and costs of $400,000 a day for the civil war, it seemed that Sudan might become the first African country to go bankrupt.

Foreign Relations. On March 30, Sudan dissolved the 1982 joint Nile Valley Unity Assembly agreement with Egypt, calling it "an irrelevant legacy" of Nimeiri's regime.   William Spencer

See also AFRICA (Facts in Brief Table); MAHDI, SADIQ EL. In WORLD BOOK, see SUDAN.

SUPREME COURT OF THE UNITED STATES. In its 1986 term, which ended on July 7, the Supreme Court of the United States produced a body of landmark opinions that eluded such easy labels as conservative, liberal, or activist.

There were two changes on the court in 1986. William H. Rehnquist, an associate justice since 1972, became chief justice on Sept. 26, 1986. He succeeded Warren E. Burger, who retired to head the nation's 1987 bicentennial of the Constitution of the United States. Also, on Sept. 26, 1986, Antonin Scalia, a judge on the U.S. Court of Appeals in Washington, D.C., was sworn in as an associate justice to fill the position vacated by Rehnquist.

Rebuffs to Administration. During the year, the court issued three important decisions upholding the concept of *affirmative action*, the preferential treatment of minority groups and women in hirings, layoffs, and promotions. The justices said lower courts are correct to uphold affirmative action programs for employers or unions with a record of discriminatory practices. The rulings were a disappointment to the Administration of President Ronald Reagan, whose view was that affirmative action should be used to help only those individuals who could prove that they themselves had been victims of discrimination.

On another sensitive issue, the court on June 11 struck down a Pennsylvania abortion law that it concluded would "intimidate women" from seeking to end an unwanted pregnancy. The 5 to 4 decision was a major setback for the Administration, which had urged the court to overrule *Roe v. Wade*—the landmark 1973 ruling that lifted most state restrictions on abortion.

Two days earlier, the court handed the Administration another important setback by ruling that "Baby Doe" regulations, which required hospitals to treat and feed severely handicapped infants, exceeded government authority. The 1984 regulations gave the U.S. Department of Health and Human Services access to the hospital records of any handicapped infant whose life or health was at stake, regardless of the wishes of the parents.

Also in June, the court for the first time interpreted the Voting Rights Act, as amended in 1982. In a ruling on a North Carolina case, the justices cleared the way for blacks and other minority groups to contest redistricting plans that weaken their voting strength.

In an Indiana case, the court also held for the first time that *gerrymandering*—the redrawing of election district lines to the advantage of one political party—is unconstitutional. The court, however, made lawsuits challenging such redistricting difficult to win by imposing a heavy burden of proof. A political party must show that the disputed reapportionment destroyed its chances for success in more than one election.

Portion of Deficit Law Rejected. One conspicuous victory for the Administration was the court's 7 to 2 ruling on July 7 that the "automatic" spending-cut provisions of the so-called Gramm-Rudman Act were unconstitutional. The law, passed by Congress in 1985, is aimed at reducing the federal deficit in each fiscal year and achieving a balanced budget by 1991. The court said the statute was flawed because it gave the comptroller general, a congressional official subject to removal by Congress, the power to dictate to the President what budget items must be cut. The justices ruled that such an arrangement violates the separation-of-powers doctrine, which forbids the three branches of government from encroaching on one another's authority.

Individual Rights. One of the court's most controversial rulings in 1986 involved the rights of homosexuals. On June 30, in a 5 to 4 decision, the court upheld a Georgia sodomy law that makes certain sexual practices illegal, even when performed in private by consenting adults. In the majority opinion, Justice Byron R. White said the idea "that any kind of private sexual conduct between consenting adults is constitutionally insulated from state prosecution is unsupportable."

Among the court's other significant rulings on individual rights in 1986 was the unanimous decision on June 19 that the sexual harassment of em-

New U.S. Chief Justice William H. Rehnquist, right, and Associate Justice Antonin
Scalia shake hands after being sworn in on September 26 in Washington, D.C.

ployees violates the federal law prohibiting sex discrimination in the workplace.

On the last day of its 1986 term, the court ruled
that public school students do not enjoy the same
First Amendment rights as adult political speakers. The ruling reversed a lower-court decision
that officials of a Spanaway, Wash., high school
had violated the rights of a 17-year-old student by
suspending him for two days for giving a speech
with sexual overtones at a school assembly.

Black Defendants in criminal trials won a victory
in 1986. On April 30, the court handed down a 7
to 2 decision that made it easier for such defendants to contest the exclusion of blacks from trial
juries. Traditionally, states have allowed attorneys
for both the prosecution and defense to reject a
certain number of prospective jurors without giving any explanation to the judge. But the use of
jury challenges by prosecutors as a tool of racial
discrimination has come under increasing attack
in lower courts and led to state reforms.

Under new rules in the Supreme Court's 1986
decision, black defendants would no longer be required to show that prosecutors repeatedly used
their challenges to exclude blacks from panels of
prospective jurors. The ruling reversed key portions of a controversial 1965 Supreme Court decision, *Swain v. Alabama*. In that ruling, the court
held that the use of challenges to exclude blacks

from juries was unconstitutional only if it was
done repeatedly over a period of years, rather
than in a single case.

Other Important Rulings by the Supreme Court
in 1986 included the following decisions:
■ A 7 to 2 ruling on February 25 that the Constitution allows cities to use zoning restrictions to
prohibit adult theaters near residential neighborhoods, churches, parks, and schools.
■ A 5 to 4 ruling on April 21 that a person bringing a libel suit against a publication for a news
story about a matter of public concern cannot recover damages without showing that the statements about him or her in the story are false.
■ A 7 to 2 ruling on June 30 that the public and
press enjoy a qualified First Amendment right of
access to preliminary proceedings in a criminal
case. Such proceedings cannot be closed to the
public unless there is a "substantial probability"
that the defendant's right to a fair trial will be
jeopardized by publicity.   Glen R. Elsasser

See also COURTS; REHNQUIST, WILLIAM H.;
SCALIA, ANTONIN. In the Special Reports section,
see THE U.S. CONSTITUTION: 200 YEARS OF HIS-
TORY. In WORLD BOOK, see SUPREME COURT OF
THE UNITED STATES.
SURGERY. See MEDICINE.
SURINAME. See LATIN AMERICA.
SWAZILAND. See AFRICA.

SWEDEN was shocked on Feb. 28, 1986, when an unidentified man gunned down its popular prime minister, Olof Palme, on a Stockholm street. Palme had just seen a motion picture with his wife, Lisbet, and one of their sons. The prime minister and his wife were walking along the street when the assailant started to talk to them. The man then pulled a gun and shot Palme at short range. Olof Palme died in the arms of his wife on the snow-covered pavement. A ricocheting bullet injured Lisbet Palme slightly.

No Protection. The government had assigned two bodyguards to Palme, but he used them for official functions only. Political violence is rare in Sweden, and Palme refused protection when at home in Stockholm or on vacation at his villa on the Baltic Island of Gotland. He was a familiar figure in the area near his home, shopping and often stopping to chat with passers-by.

Hunt for Killer. Police arrested several individuals in connection with Palme's murder, but all the suspects were released. The motive behind the killing was unclear, though two extremist political organizations—the Red Army Faction and a West German neo-Nazi group—claimed responsibility.

New Leader. On March 12, the Riksdag (parliament) elected Ingvar Carlsson prime minister. Carlsson, who was acting prime minister and served as minister of the environment since 1985, pledged to continue the policies laid down by Palme. See CARLSSON, INGVAR.

Strikes Averted. A last-minute wage agreement on April 9 prevented strikes that would have brought industry to a standstill. White-collar workers received a raise of 5.5 per cent, effective April 1, 1986, and were scheduled for a 4 per cent hike in 1987. Government mediators settled a dispute in the heavy equipment industry on June 6, only hours before 140,000 workers were due to strike.

Nuclear Disaster. Sweden reacted angrily to the Soviet Union's failure to inform Sweden that a nuclear disaster had occurred at the Soviets' Chernobyl nuclear power station on April 26. Windborne contaminants from Chernobyl boosted radioactivity in Sweden to between 10 and 100 times its normal level. The Swedish government advised citizens not to use rain water. Dairy farmers kept their cows out of the fields for three months after the disaster. See ENERGY SUPPLY (Close-Up).

New Party Leader. Conservative Party leader Ulf Adelsohn resigned on June 4. Political observers said that Adelsohn quit partly because his party fared poorly in national elections in September 1985. The agriculture-based Center Party elected Karin Soder as party leader on June 17. She became the first woman to head a political party in Sweden.   Kenneth Brown

See also EUROPE (Facts in Brief Table). In WORLD BOOK, see SWEDEN.

SWIMMING. Matt Biondi, the world's outstanding swimmer in 1985, was the most successful again in 1986. On July 24 and 26, during the United States world-championship trials in Orlando, Fla., he set world records in both the men's 50-meter (22.33 seconds) and 100-meter (48.74 seconds) freestyle events.

In the World Aquatics championships in Madrid, Spain, from August 13 to 24, Biondi won the men's 100-meter freestyle in 48.94 seconds, finished second in the 100-meter butterfly, and placed third in both the 50-meter and 200-meter freestyle events. In three relay races, he anchored the U.S. teams to a pair of first-place finishes and one third place. His seven medals were a record for a world championship.

Biondi, a 20-year-old from Moraga, Calif., was one of the few successes for the United States in the world championships. The only other American winners were Tom Jager of Collinsville, Ill., in the men's 50-meter freestyle (22.49 seconds); Pablo Morales of Santa Clara, Calif., in the men's 100-meter butterfly (53.54 seconds); Betsy Mitchell of Marietta, Ohio, in the women's 100-meter backstroke (1 minute 1.74 seconds); and Mary T. Meagher of Louisville, Ky., in the women's 200-meter butterfly (2 minutes 8.41 seconds).

East Germany led the United States in total

Carolyn Waldo of Canada gives a victory salute after capturing one of her three gold medals at the world swimming championships in Spain in August.

medals (30-24) and gold medals (14-7). Among the women, East Germany's dominance was overwhelming—13 victories in 16 events.

World Records. In addition to Biondi's performances, two other Americans broke world records in 1986—both during the world-championship trials. Morales swam the 100-meter butterfly in 52.84 seconds, and Mitchell did the women's 200-meter backstroke in 2 minutes 8.60 seconds.

By the end of world-championship competition, five world records were broken and one was equaled. World records were established in 8 of the 17 events for women. Tamara Costache of Romania bettered the record for the women's 50-meter freestyle four times within 10 weeks, finally lowering her time to 25.28 seconds on August 23 during the world championships.

Other world records were established by Vladimir Salnikov of the Soviet Union and by Michael Gross of West Germany. At the Goodwill Games in Moscow on July 4, Salnikov, 26, set his 14th world record, swimming the 800-meter freestyle in 7 minutes 50.64 seconds. Gross established his 11th world record when he swam the 200-meter butterfly in 1 minute 56.24 seconds on June 28 at a meet in Hannover, West Germany.   Frank Litsky

See also SPORTS. In the Special Reports section, see BIG BOOM IN WOMEN'S SPORTS. In WORLD BOOK, see SWIMMING.

Protesters demonstrate at a Swiss chemical warehouse from which poisons flowed into the Rhine River during a fire on November 1.

SWITZERLAND. A coalition of Socialists, pacifists, and youth and religious organizations presented to the Swiss government on Sept. 10, 1986, a petition to abolish the nation's army. Some 120,000 citizens signed the petition.

Switzerland is traditionally a neutral country, but able-bodied males between the ages of 20 and 50 must serve in the army. Most young men spend at least three weeks each year on active duty.

Men who are unfit for military service must join the civil defense forces, and disabled men must pay a special tax. The government also exempts men who refuse to serve for religious reasons, provided a military court accepts their objections. But each year, more than 500 young men who refuse military service go to prison.

To abolish the army, the Swiss must cast ballots against it in a *referendum*, or direct vote. Political observers said that the army-abolition issue was unlikely to appear on the ballot for several years.

Chemical Disaster. On November 1, fire fighters dousing a blaze at a warehouse in Schweizerhalle, about 6 miles (10 kilometers) southeast of Basel, washed an estimated 30 short tons (27 metric tons) of agricultural chemicals, solvents, and mercury into the Rhine River. The plant belonged to Sandoz A.G., one of Switzerland's largest chemical and pharmaceutical firms.

On November 3, dead fish began turning up in the river. The next day, a town in West Germany turned off its water system, which was fed by the Rhine. A number of other towns soon followed suit. (The river flows northward, emptying from the Netherlands into the North Sea.)

By November 12, hundreds of thousands of fish and eels had died in the river. Switzerland, France, West Germany, and the Netherlands shut down all their plants that processed Rhine River water for drinking. Those nations also banned fishing in the river and closed sluice gates and locks to prevent water from seeping out of the Rhine on the way to the sea. Scientists feared that chemicals were destroying not only fish and eels, but also the plants and microscopic organisms that serve as the basis of the river's ecosystem.

On November 12, Switzerland accepted responsibility for the accident and agreed to pay other countries for damage. Switzerland said it would consider tightening its antipollution laws.

No to UN. In a referendum on March 16, 75.7 per cent of the voters opposed a proposal for Switzerland to become a full member of the United Nations (UN). The voter turnout was 50.2 per cent. Switzerland presently has *observer status* in the UN—that is, the right to attend General Assembly sessions but not to take part.   Kenneth Brown

See also EUROPE (Facts in Brief Table). In WORLD BOOK, see SWITZERLAND.

SYRIA. Frequent charges by other countries that the regime of Syria's President Hafiz al-Assad is a major sponsor of international terrorism were given credence in October 1986. During the trial in London of a Jordanian, Nezar Hindawi, on charges of planting a bomb on an Israeli El Al passenger jet at Heathrow Airport on April 17, evidence was presented of direct Syrian involvement in the plot. Great Britain broke diplomatic relations with Syria on October 24. In November, discovery of apparent Syrian involvement in an April bombing in West Berlin, West Germany, led the European Community (EC or Common Market) to impose sanctions on Syria. These included a ban on arms sales and reductions in Syrian diplomatic missions.

A possible motive for Syria's involvement in both plots was anger over the February 4 interception by Israeli jets of a Libyan civilian airliner, which the jets forced to land in Israel. The plane was carrying leaders of Syria's ruling Baath Party back to Damascus from meetings in Tripoli, Libya. Israel claimed that it thought that leaders of the Palestine Liberation Organization (PLO) were aboard. The Syrians were released after questioning, but Assad denounced the interception as an act of international piracy.

Internal Terrorism. A series of bombings of buses and trains in April in Damascus and other cities caused heavy casualties. Assad at first accused Israel of the attacks, which he said were designed to keep Syria off guard. But a May 8 report on the government-run television attributed the attacks to the Muslim Brotherhood, a fundamentalist group opposed to Assad.

National Elections for a new People's Council were held in February. The ruling Baath Party won 129 of the 195 seats in the council. The National Progressive Front, a socialist opposition coalition, won 57 seats, and the Communist Party, which is legal in Syria, won 9.

The Lebanon Problem. Syria's intermittent efforts to end the Lebanese civil war intensified in 1986. In June, a Syrian-sponsored peace plan was accepted by the various Lebanese factions, and 400 Syrian troops were sent to Beirut to enforce it. But they had little success.

The Economy. Mismanagement, heavy foreign debts, and diplomatic isolation confronted Syria with an economic crisis. A 1982 agreement to buy oil inexpensively from Iran expired and was not renewed. Inflation reached 100 per cent, with severe shortages of electricity, water, and basic commodities. Foreign debts totaled $1.5 billion. The one positive note was the start-up of production at the new Thayyem oil field near Dayr az Zawr in October.   William Spencer

See also MIDDLE EAST (Facts in Brief Table). In WORLD BOOK, see SYRIA.

TAIWAN. Amid growing challenges to its political control, the Kuomintang, Taiwan's ruling party, announced on Oct. 15, 1986, that it would end 37 years of martial law and allow the formation of opposition political parties. The government, however, set no date for ending martial law.

Martial law was imposed in 1949, soon after Nationalist leader Chiang Kai-shek and his army retreated to the island from mainland China in the face of advancing Communist forces. The Nationalists continued martial law, claiming it was necessary to preserve stability and thwart any Communist activity. In allowing political opposition, the Kuomintang mandated that all political parties be anti-Communist, renounce violence, and support the unification of China and Taiwan.

The Move toward easing political restrictions began in March when President Chiang Ching-kuo convened a meeting of Kuomintang leaders to discuss a policy of liberalization. Although some government leaders opposed any changes, in May Chiang established a 12-member committee to study reform. Chiang also decided to allow the Public Policy Association, one of two loosely organized opposition groups, to open permanent offices throughout the island on May 10.

On September 28—more than two weeks before the lifting of the ban on opposition political par-

Taiwanese diplomats in May announce arrangements for the return of a hijacked plane after Taiwan's first talks with China since 1949.

ties had been announced—opponents of Kuomintang rule known as the *tangwai* (outside the party) established the Democratic Progressive Party.

In elections on December 6, the new party made a surprisingly strong showing. Its candidates won 12 of 73 seats in the Legislative Yuan, Taiwan's lawmaking body, and 11 of 84 seats in the less powerful National Assembly, which elects the country's president and vice president.

Stalemate Ended. The government ended its ban on official contacts with China in order to negotiate the return of a cargo plane hijacked by its pilot to the mainland. The plane, destined for Hong Kong from Bangkok, Thailand, landed in Guangzhou (Canton), China, on May 3. The pilot announced that he had defected to be reunited with his family. After negotiations between the two countries on May 20, the pilot remained in China, but two other crew members returned.

The Economy. Taiwan's economy grew by 8.1 per cent during the first half of 1986. Engaging in foreign trade with China was still an offense punishable by death. Some such trade occurred, however, and more than $1 billion worth of goods was traded through Hong Kong. More than 48 per cent of Taiwan's exports were shipped to the United States.   Henry S. Bradsher

See also ASIA (Facts in Brief Table). In WORLD BOOK, see TAIWAN.

TANZANIA. In January 1986, President Ali Hassan Mwinyi, who was elected in October 1985, began to deal firmly with Tanzania's declining productivity, shortages of consumer goods, unemployment, and other long-term economic ills. Drought, expenditures on imported oil, and the lingering effects of a 1979 war with Uganda were factors in the crisis. Corruption among government and business leaders and the socialist policies of former President Julius K. Nyerere were also blamed.

IMF Loan. In August 1986, the Mwinyi government received an $800-million loan from the International Monetary Fund (IMF), an agency of the United Nations. The loan enabled Tanzania to pay the interest on its $3-billion foreign debt and to import spare parts and raw materials for the nation's lagging industries. Previous negotiations with the IMF broke down in 1980 when Nyerere objected to its strict conditions for a loan.

Preparing for the 1986 IMF loan, the Mwinyi regime devalued the unit of currency, the shilling; cut subsidies on social services; lowered government workers' salaries; and reduced the bureaucracy. The administration also dismantled several of the 400 government-run corporations.

Mwinyi also tried in 1986 to deal with Tanzania's chronic food shortages and the escalating migration of rural dwellers to the cities. His new economic program emphasized a free-market approach to agriculture. Since taking office, Mwinyi has moved away from a system of collective farms and state direction of the economy toward a policy of giving farmers fairer prices and easier access to seed, fertilizer, equipment, and credit. Mwinyi in January urged Tanzanians to return to traditional methods of cultivation and food storage, rather than relying on mechanization.

To Ease Political Tensions, Mwinyi in April released 14 people accused in a 1983 plot against Nyerere. The former president was to continue until 1987 as head of the leftist Chama Cha Mapinduzi, the dominant political organization. In June, Nyerere, a long-time advocate of one-party politics, made the surprising announcement that single-party systems stifled innovation and permitted leaders to become inflexible and complacent.

Foreign Relations. Although the United States cut its aid to Tanzania in 1986 because Tanzania defaulted on its foreign-debt repayment, the Mwinyi regime increased economic ties with other Western countries. Reversing Nyerere's policies, Mwinyi also opened or expanded transport, trade, and tourism links with Kenya and Malawi. Tanzania, Zambia, and China agreed in April to refinance and reequip the Tazara Railway line between Tanzania and Zambia.   J. Gus Liebenow and Beverly B. Liebenow

See also AFRICA (Facts in Brief Table). In WORLD BOOK, see TANZANIA.

TAXATION. The Tax Reform Act of 1986, signed by President Ronald Reagan on October 22, made the most sweeping changes in the United States income tax code in more than 40 years. Enactment of the historic measure, which had been Reagan's top domestic-policy goal during his second term, ended a two-year bipartisan effort in Congress to reform and simplify the tax code.

The eventual consequences of the new law could only be guessed at. Virtually every American will be touched by the law's provisions, which couple a dramatic reduction in individual and corporate income tax rates with the elimination of many deductions, tax shelters, and other tax breaks.

A Triumph for Reagan. In a 1985 television address, the President called the old tax system "unwise, unwanted, and unfair." He proposed compressing the system's 14 tax brackets for individuals into three, ranging from 15 to 35 per cent. After the Senate Finance Committee on May 7, 1986, proposed a top rate of only 27 per cent, the overhaul movement gathered strong momentum and a compromise bill took shape. In signing the measure, Reagan declared, "This tax bill is less a reform . . . than a revolution."

The law consolidates the 14 individual tax rates, which ranged from 11 per cent to 50 per cent, into just 2 rates of 15 per cent and 28 per cent, starting Jan. 1, 1988. In addition, a surcharge will create a third rate of 33 per cent for a relatively small number of high-income taxpayers. During 1987, a transitional system of five tax rates, ranging from 11 to 38.5 per cent, will be in effect. Analysts predicted that individual taxpayers would reap an average tax cut of 6.1 per cent once the law is fully implemented.

Tax cuts for individuals will be offset by an increase of $120 billion per year in corporate tax collections. The present top corporate tax rate of 46 per cent will be reduced to 34 per cent, but a stiff minimum tax will be imposed on companies that have escaped federal taxation in the past.

Other Provisions. The new law increases the personal tax exemption in three steps from $1,080 to $2,000. It also raises the standard deduction to $3,000 for people filing single returns and to $5,000 for people filing joint returns—up from $2,480 and $3,670, respectively. Because of the restructured tax brackets, some 6 million low-income Americans will no longer have to pay federal income taxes, and an estimated 80 per cent of individual taxpayers will pay only the bottom rate of 15 per cent. The new 28 per cent individual rate will apply to taxable income above $17,850 for single taxpayers, $29,750 for joint filers, and $25,288 for single heads of households. Some taxpayers, however, were expected to face a one-year tax hike under the 1987 interim tax code.

A number of tax breaks—including deductions for sales-tax payments and for interest paid on credit-card debt, car loans, and other nonmortgage debts—were to be eliminated or considerably reduced by 1988. Home-mortgage interest will continue to be deductible, but sharp limits will be placed on deductions for medical and miscellaneous expenses and for contributions to Individual Retirement Accounts (IRA's). Medical deductions will be allowed only when they exceed 7.5 per cent of adjusted gross income, up from 5 per cent. For investors, all *capital gains*—profits from the sale of stocks and other investments—will be taxed as ordinary income.

The law also wipes out many tax shelters, notably in real estate, while allowing certain others, such as oil and gas shelters, to continue. Individuals and corporations whose extensive use of deductions or other tax breaks would otherwise allow them to escape paying taxes will now have to pay a minimum tax of 21 per cent.

Business tax breaks for investment will be limited under the new code, as will tax advantages for particular industries, notably the oil, gas, banking, timber, and defense industries. And in an assault on "expense account living," Congress decreed that deductions for business meals and entertainment would be limited to 80 per cent of cost. Such expenses had been fully deductible.

Representative Dan Rostenkowski (D., Ill.), left, and Senator Bob Packwood (R., Ore.) vow in June to "go to the trenches" in the battle for tax reform.

Pursuing Tax Evaders. In April, an official of the General Accounting Office (GAO), a congressional watchdog agency, told a subcommittee of the House of Representatives that the Internal Revenue Service (IRS) did not have enough money to pursue all the tax cheats identified by its computer system. The GAO official said that, as a result, the IRS had been forced to ignore at least 14 million instances of apparent underreporting of income. Congress voted to provide more money to the IRS to enable the agency to increase its tax-collection efforts.

The IRS had a change of command during the year. Lawrence B. Gibbs, a Dallas lawyer who served as IRS assistant commissioner during the Administrations of Presidents Richard M. Nixon and Gerald R. Ford, succeeded Roscoe L. Egger, Jr., as commissioner.

State and Local Revenues. According to a private study released in January 1986, state and local tax revenues in the 12-month period ending in June 1985 increased by 8 per cent to $345.8 billion. State tax receipts were up 8.8 per cent, and local revenues rose 6.6 per cent. Property taxes, the largest single source of revenue for state and local governments, increased by 5.5 per cent to $103.7 billion. Frank Cormier and Margot Cormier

See also STATE GOVERNMENT. In WORLD BOOK, see INCOME TAX; TAXATION.

TELEVISION

TELEVISION. The year 1986 was a transitional one for all three major television networks—the American Broadcasting Companies (ABC), CBS Inc., and the National Broadcasting Company (NBC)—all of which were under new management. As the "Big Three" faced financial belt-tightening, a new enterprise—Fox Broadcasting Company—attempted to establish itself as "the fourth network."

Corporate Shakeups. CBS Inc., which fought take-over attempts in 1985, underwent a management change in September 1986, when its board of directors ousted Thomas H. Wyman, chairman and chief executive officer. Replacing Wyman as acting chief executive was Laurence A. Tisch, a businessman who had joined CBS's board of directors less than a year before and had become the company's largest shareholder. Along with Tisch, CBS founder and patriarch William S. Paley re-emerged as the company's acting chairman.

NBC Chairman Grant Tinker retired in August, as he said he would when NBC's parent company, the RCA Corporation, announced its agreement in 1985 to merge with the General Electric Company (GE). Tinker was replaced by Robert C. Wright, a GE executive. At ABC, management predicted the network itself would lose $60 million in 1986. But the parent company, Capital Cities Communications, Incorporated, said it would

Top-Rated Television Series

The following were the most-watched television series for the 31-week regular season—Sept. 22, 1985, through April 20, 1986—as determined by the A. C. Nielsen Company.

 1. "The Cosby Show" (NBC)
 2. "Family Ties" (NBC)
 3. "Murder, She Wrote" (CBS)
 4. "60 Minutes" (CBS)
 5. "Cheers" (NBC)
 6. (tie) "Dallas" (CBS)
        "Dynasty" (ABC)
        "The Golden Girls" (NBC)
 9. "Miami Vice" (NBC)
10. "Who's the Boss?" (ABC)
11. "Perfect Strangers" (ABC)
12. "Night Court" (NBC)
13. "CBS Sunday Night Movie" (CBS)
14. (tie) "Highway to Heaven" (NBC)
        "Kate & Allie" (CBS)
16. "NFL Monday Night Football" (ABC)
17. "Newhart" (CBS)
18. (tie) "Knots Landing" (CBS)
        "Growing Pains" (ABC)
20. "227" (NBC)
21. "NBC Sunday Night Movie" (NBC)
22. (tie) "Hotel" (ABC)
        "NBC Monday Night Movies" (NBC)
24. "Falcon Crest" (CBS)
25. "Moonlighting" (ABC)

make a profit from the stations it owned and from other business ventures.

The financial problems at ABC, CBS, and, to a lesser extent, NBC, were caused by rising programming costs and reduced advertising revenues. Adding to these woes was the continued presence of independent television stations throughout the United States and cable television, which, according to the Arbitron ratings service, was available in 38 per cent of all U.S. households in 1986. Cable and independent stations—as well as the use of videocassette recorders (VCR's) to watch rented movies—lured many viewers away from network TV.

The Ratings Game. NBC retained the highest A. C. Nielsen ratings—which measure TV viewership—in the all-important prime-time evening hours, as it did during the 1985-1986 season. At year-end, NBC's ratings had surpassed those of ABC and CBS during every week of the new season that began in September 1986. Based on this midseason dominance, it seemed likely that NBC would be the top-rated network for the 1986-1987 viewing season.

New Network. In October, the three networks faced new competition from the Fox Broadcasting Company. The network, created by media magnate Rupert Murdoch, promised to establish a full schedule of programs within a few years.

Howard Hesseman, right, the star of ABC's "Head of the Class," plays a substitute teacher assigned to a class of gifted high school students.

Cybill Shepherd tells a thing or two to Bruce Willis, her detective partner on "Moonlighting," an ABC comedy that gained a large following in 1986.

Fox premiered the "Late Show with Joan Rivers," a variety-talk show aired by about 80 independent, Fox-affiliated stations opposite NBC's "The Tonight Show Starring Johnny Carson." Carson remained the most-watched late-night talk-show host, but Rivers, a risqué comedienne, stirred controversy. Prior to her show's premiere, Rivers had frequently hosted "The Tonight Show" in Carson's absence and owed much of her success to appearances there. Carson reportedly was angered with Rivers because he was unaware that she was negotiating to host a competing program.

TV Shopping. The most unusual development of the year was the popularity of a cable-television channel, Home Shopping Network (HSN). HSN featured a host or hostess displaying items—ranging from toasters to diamond necklaces—and inviting viewers to call in within a specified time to buy the item, presumably at a discount.

By year's end, HSN, in addition to a cable channel that reached 11.5 million homes, had purchased conventional TV stations in 10 other cities, expanding its market by another 26 million homes. The success of HSN prompted other cable operators and television syndicators to begin similar programming.

The 1986-1987 Season did not produce any runaway hit shows, but a few programs sparked critics' and viewers' interest. NBC's "Crime Story," a 1960's-era police show based in Chicago, won plaudits, as did that network's "L.A. Law," a legal drama. Two offbeat comedies were NBC's "ALF," which served up the misadventures of a wisecracking alien taken in by a suburban family, and ABC's "Perfect Strangers," in which a befuddled European immigrant attempted to adapt to life in the United States. Another ABC hit was "Head of the Class," starring Howard Hesseman as the laid-back teacher of a class of geniuses. Also on ABC, "Moonlighting," a light-hearted detective show starring Cybill Shepherd and Bruce Willis, grew in popularity as it began a second regular season.

Television's most popular program continued to be "The Cosby Show," starring Bill Cosby. The Thursday night comedy, in its third season, was largely responsible for NBC's overall ratings success. The network claimed that, based on the Nielsen ratings, more Americans watched the Cosby show during the 1985-1986 season than any other situation comedy in the history of television.

Television often entertained—and sometimes disappointed—its audience during 1986. One example was the syndicated special *The Mystery of Al Capone's Vaults*. In this live program that aired in April, Geraldo Rivera, a former ABC news correspondent, presided over the opening of a vault in an abandoned Chicago hotel where the infamous gangster of the 1930's had once had his head-

Susan Dey and Harry Hamlin play Los Angeles lawyers in "L.A. Law," NBC's new fall series from the creators of "Hill Street Blues."

quarters. At the end of the show, which set viewership records in some cities, the demolition team found only a discarded bottle.

Another television nonevent was the well-publicized return of actor Patrick Duffy to "Dallas," the CBS prime-time soap opera series. Duffy's character, Bobby Ewing, supposedly died in the last episode of the 1984-1985 season. But Duffy agreed to return to the series, leading viewers to wonder during summer 1986 how scriptwriters would resurrect him. In the first episode of the 1986-1987 season, Ewing's wife, Pamela (played by Victoria Principal), awoke to discover that Bobby's death—and everything that had happened in the previous season—was only a dream.

Some of the best prime-time entertainment occurred in made-for-TV movies and miniseries, though the latter genre appeared to be losing popularity. Noteworthy miniseries included NBC's "Peter the Great," filmed almost entirely in the Soviet Union, and CBS's "Dream West," starring Richard Chamberlain. ABC presented "North and South, Book II," a 12-hour miniseries based on John Jakes's popular novel of the Civil War.

Movies made for TV included NBC's *Deliberate Stranger*, a character study of convicted murderer Ted Bundy; CBS's *Acceptable Risks*, a story concerning a company's cover-up of a deadly chemical spill, and *Promise*, a drama about a bachelor who assumes responsibility for his schizophrenic brother; and ABC's *Under Siege*, a docudrama about terrorism in the United States.

Public Television. Some conservative groups and some TV critics complained that a Public Broadcasting Service (PBS) documentary series, "The Africans," was sympathetic to pro-Communist governments on that continent. The National Endowment for the Humanities, which helped underwrite the British-made production, removed its name from the credits, but the program ran as scheduled without widespread criticism.

Well-received documentary programs included "The Story of English," a nine-part series on the evolution of the English language, and "Planet Earth," a science series. A PBS series called "Wonderworks" adapted for television *Anne of Green Gables* (1908), a classic children's book by Canadian author Lucy Maud Montgomery. And "Masterpiece Theatre" presented "Paradise Postponed," John Mortimer's post-World War II satire.

Golden Anniversary. The British Broadcasting Corporation (BBC) celebrated its 50th anniversary in 1986. Amid widespread skepticism, the BBC began the world's first regularly scheduled television service on Nov. 2, 1936.   P. J. Bednarski

See also AWARDS AND PRIZES. In WORLD BOOK, see TELEVISION.

TENNESSEE. See STATE GOVERNMENT.

TENNIS. The most successful tennis players of 1985 repeated their winning ways during 1986. They were Ivan Lendl of Czechoslovakia and Boris Becker of West Germany among the men and Martina Navratilova of Dallas among the women.

It was a frustrating time for John McEnroe of Douglaston, N.Y., for years the leading American male tennis player. It was a frustrating time in general for the American men, who failed to put anyone into the United States Open semifinals for the first time since 1966.

Men. The 26-year-old Lendl, who lives in Greenwich, Conn., maintained his standing as the world's leading male player. He retained his United States Open championship on September 7 in Flushing Meadow, N.Y., when he routed 16th-seeded Miloslav Mecir of Czechoslovakia, 6-4, 6-2, 6-0. It was the fifth straight United States Open final for Lendl. Finalists in the women's competition were Navratilova and Helena Sukova, making all four finalists Czechoslovak-born.

Earlier, in June, Lendl won the French Open final in Paris from Mikael Pernfors, 22, of Sweden, 6-3, 6-2, 6-4. Lendl was most comfortable on hard and clay courts and was not at his best on grass, the surface for the Wimbledon championships in England. And as it happened, Lendl was to meet Becker, who was ranked sixth but who played his best on grass, in the Wimbledon final.

Lendl advanced to the Wimbledon final after five-set victories over Slobodan Zivojinovic of Yugoslavia and Tim Mayotte of the United States. In the final on July 6, Becker's powerful play produced 15 aces and 13 service winners, and he defeated Lendl, 6-4, 6-3, 7-5.

Women. Navratilova, 29, had her usual yearlong struggles with Chris Evert Lloyd of Amelia Island, Fla., her 31-year-old rival. In the French Open final on June 7 on clay in Paris, Lloyd defeated her, 2-6, 6-3, 6-3, for Lloyd's seventh French title, a record.

In the succeeding major championships, Lloyd lost to Hana Mandlikova of Czechoslovakia in the Wimbledon semifinals, 7-6, 7-5, and to Sukova in the U.S. Open semifinals, 6-2, 6-4. Both winners lost to Navratilova in the finals of those events.

Navratilova on July 5 won her fifth consecutive Wimbledon title and seventh overall title by beating Mandlikova, 7-6, 6-3. On September 7, Navratilova won her third United States Open by routing Sukova, 6-3, 6-2. The best match of the United States Open was the semifinal in which Navratilova eliminated 17-year-old Steffi Graf of West Germany, 6-1, 6-7, 7-6.

Navratilova's most emotional moments came in

Boris Becker, 18, of West Germany dives for a shot by Ivan Lendl and goes on to win the Wimbledon men's singles in July for the second straight year.

Prague, Czechoslovakia, in July when she helped the United States win the Federation Cup, the women's equivalent of the Davis Cup. It marked the first return to her homeland since she defected in 1975. Government officials there ignored her, and newspapers carried only the scores of her matches. The spectators, however, received her warmly, and she cried at the closing ceremonies.

McEnroe. The 27-year-old McEnroe, tired from years of high-pressure competition, left the professional tennis tour in January for six months. In the United States Open, he lost to Paul Annacone in the first round of singles and was disqualified from the doubles after he was delayed in traffic and arrived 20 minutes late for his match.

J. Randolph Gregson, president of the United States Tennis Association (USTA), refused to allow McEnroe to play for the United States Davis Cup team. McEnroe had played Davis Cup for seven years until he withdrew in 1985 after the USTA had assailed his conduct and that of Jimmy Connors during cup matches.

Without McEnroe and Connors, the United States Davis Cup team defeated Ecuador in March 1986 and Mexico in July before losing to Australia in October. Australia defeated Sweden in the final in December in Australia.   Frank Litsky

In WORLD BOOK, see TENNIS.

TEXAS. See HOUSTON; STATE GOVERNMENT.

THAILAND held parliamentary elections on July 27, 1986, and a record 61.4 per cent of eligible voters participated. The coalition of political parties headed by Prime Minister Prem Tinsulanonda won enough seats to remain in power. Prem himself belonged to no party. King Bhumibol Adulyadej on August 4 reappointed Prem as prime minister, a post he has held since 1980.

Early Elections. Prem, who regards himself as politically neutral, called the elections 11 months before parliament's term was scheduled to end. He called early elections because his government was defeated in a May 1 parliamentary vote. Prem's government had called for support of a royal decree to raise taxes on some vehicles.

The army commander, General Arthit Kamlang-ek, was suspected of helping organize the May 1 parliamentary vote against Prem. Prem dismissed Arthit on May 27 and replaced him with General Chaovalit Yongchaiyuth. Arthit was widely believed to have been seeking to take over the post of prime minister.

Chaovalit is credited with masterminding a strategy that drastically reduced the number of Communist guerrillas in Thailand during the late 1970's and early 1980's. He indicated he might retire from the army and enter politics. With Prem expected to retire in 1987, observers thought Chaovalit might be in a position to succeed him.

Fighting occurred during 1986 on three of Thailand's four borders. Vietnamese troops fought Khmer Rouge rebels all year long on the Thai-Kampuchean border. The Vietnamese occupied a hill 1 kilometer (0.6 mile) inside Thailand but were driven back by Thai soldiers on October 1. Laotian troops penetrated 10 kilometers (6 miles) into Thailand on June 14, killing 35 people in an attack on a Laotian refugee camp. Along Thailand's border with Burma, officials reported that local war lords and Burmese Communist rebels fought in October over control of the opium trade.

At least 50,000 demonstrators on the southern resort island of Phuket burned a $46-million chemical plant on June 23. The plant was set up to refine the rare metal tantalum, used in making electronic components. Local residents feared the plant would pollute the water and damage the tourist business there.

Economic Growth was spurred by falling prices of imported oil and increased exports of manufactured goods, food, and raw materials. The government on October 15 announced plans to build Thailand's first deepwater port, at Laem Chabang, to relieve congestion at Bangkok, Thailand's capital, largest city, and chief port.   Henry S. Bradsher

See also ASIA (Facts in Brief Table); KAMPUCHEA; LAOS. In WORLD BOOK, see THAILAND.

THEATER. A charming Cockney lad who comes out of a London slum to become lord of an English manor won the hearts of Broadway theatergoers in 1986. Song-and-dance man Robert Lindsay proved irresistible as the star of *Me and My Girl*, a reconstructed 1937 English musical from London. The 50-year-old crowd-pleaser—composed by Noel Gay, with book and lyrics by L. Arthur Rose and Douglas Furber—was a merry combination of corny jokes and flashy musical numbers, including "The Lambeth Walk."

The show's New York City producers brought over the cheery old-fashioned musical in August 1986 to open a brand-new Broadway theater, the 1,600-seat Marquis Theatre. The new musical house is located in Times Square, New York City, in the $450-million Marriott Marquis Hotel constructed on the site of two theaters, the Helen Hayes and the Morosco, which were torn down in 1982. No other musical that opened on Broadway in 1986 captured audience affection as wholeheartedly as *Me and My Girl*.

Musicals. The biggest disappointment was *Rags*, a period musical by Joseph Stein, Charles Strouse, and Stephen Schwartz about the Jewish immigrants who poured into New York City in the late 1800's and early 1900's. Reviewers dismissed the show as being underwritten and overproduced, but applauded Teresa Stratas, an international op-

John Mahoney plays a fame-hungry zookeeper with Swoosie Kurtz as his demented wife in John Guare's award-winning black comedy, *The House of Blue Leaves.*

era star, who made her theater debut as a Russian immigrant determined to make a good life for her family in the New World.

Another costly failure was *Big Deal*, a musical set in the Great Depression that combined popular songs of the 1930's and Bob Fosse's choreography. The story, about a lovable gang of small-time crooks, was adapted from the 1958 Italian film classic *Big Deal on Madonna Street.*

Another Bob Fosse show, a revival of the 1966 musical *Sweet Charity*, got a better response. Audiences cheered dancer-singer Debbie Allen in the role of Charity, the prostitute with a heart of gold.

By November, Broadway was ready to try out another big musical, *Smile*—a show about an American beauty pageant. Marvin Hamlisch, whose earlier work included *A Chorus Line*, wrote the music. Howard Ashman adapted his story from the 1975 movie that took a more satirical look at the backstage reality of small-town beauty pageants. Audiences seemed to take more pleasure than most critics from the $4-million musical.

One short-lived musical deserving of special mention was *Raggedy Ann*, a children's theater version of the beloved nursery tale. Despite a book by William Gibson, who wrote *The Miracle Worker* (1959), and a score by composer Joe Raposo of television's "Sesame Street," the show lasted only a few nights on Broadway. Earlier in 1986, however,

under the title of *Rag Dolly*, the show became the first American theatrical production to play in Moscow since 1979.

Drama. The most eagerly awaited new play arrived in December. It was *Broadway Bound*, the final play in Neil Simon's autobiographical trilogy that began in 1983 with *Brighton Beach Memoirs* and continued in 1985 with *Biloxi Blues*. In the new comedy-drama, Eugene Jerome—Simon's alter ego, played by Jonathan Silverman—comes home from World War II and begins writing.

Michael Frayn's *Benefactors*, a British import that opened in January, proved to be the most thoughtful drama of the season. The play is about an architect, played by Sam Waterston, who tries to build decent housing for the poor and ends up betraying his own principles.

Benefactors reminded some critics of the work of Russian playwright Anton Chekhov, who was also represented on Broadway in Frayn's adaptation of *Platonov*. Retitled *Wild Honey*, the play starred Ian McKellen as a mild-mannered, much-beloved schoolteacher.

Revivals. There were also some major American revivals on Broadway during the year. Jack Lemmon stirred theatergoers as the blustery actor James Tyrone in a remake of Eugene O'Neill's 1941 masterpiece, *Long Day's Journey into Night*. Jean Stapleton left them laughing in a revival of

Arsenic and Old Lace, Joseph Kesselring's 1941 comedy about two murderous old ladies. And *The House of Blue Leaves*, John Guare's 1970 black comedy about a fame-hungry zookeeper and his bizarre family, proved such a treat for audiences at the Lincoln Center for the Performing Arts that it was transferred to Broadway.

Another popular revival was *The Front Page*, Ben Hecht and Charles MacArthur's 1928 comedy classic about yellow journalism, which arrived at Lincoln Center in late November 1986. John Lithgow played the hard-bitten newspaper editor, and Richard Thomas was his star reporter.

Broadway Stars. Some old and new stars appeared on Broadway in 1986. The distinguished theatrical couple Hume Cronyn and Jessica Tandy appeared in *The Petition*, a new play by Brian Clark about the 50-year marriage of a British Army general and his wife. Marlo Thomas was a hit in the domestic comedy *Social Security*. Film star Robert De Niro made an important debut in *Cuba and His Teddy Bear*, a realistic drama about a drug-dealing Cuban-American and his teen-aged son, played by Ralph Macchio, star of the 1984 motion picture *The Karate Kid*.

Some big-name performers also showed up on smaller theater stages in 1986. Film star Matthew Broderick played a lovesick young man in Horton Foote's *The Widow Claire*. *Lily Dale*, another drama by Foote, starred Molly Ringwald. Kathleen Turner got a lot of attention when she played the title role in a new stage version of *Camille*, based on the novel by Alexandre Dumas *fils*, at the Long Wharf Theatre in New Haven, Conn. And Kevin Kline appeared off-Broadway in the taxing title role of William Shakespeare's *Hamlet*.

Other off-Broadway activity in 1986 included *The Perfect Party*, a comedy of manners by A. R. Gurney, Jr.; *The Common Pursuit*, Simon Gray's drama about college friends who lose their high ideals; and Sam Shepard's *A Lie of the Mind*, a blistering drama about a California family, which opened officially in late 1985. Probably the most interesting off-Broadway show of the year was *Vienna: Lusthaus*, a stunning dance-drama by director-choreographer Martha Clarke that fascinated theatergoers with its erotic scenes and exotic style.

Chicago Theater. During 1986, Chicago hosted an important month-long International Theatre Festival in April and May that showcased significant works from Great Britain, Israel, Italy, Japan, South Africa, and Spain. National attention continued to be drawn, meanwhile, to *off-Loop* (neighborhood) theaters, mainly for their vigorous efforts to discover new plays and playwrights.

Anniversaries. Houston's Alley Theatre, one of the oldest and most respected resident professional theaters in the United States, celebrated its 40th anniversary in 1986. Another milestone was passed in Los Angeles, where the Mark Taper Forum celebrated its 20th season of producing new plays of social significance. Ellen Stewart's La Mama E.T.C. in New York City, the most famous experimental theater company in the United States, observed its 25th birthday. And in Washington, D.C., the landmark National Theatre was 150 years old. Every U.S. President since Andrew Jackson has attended the National.

Regional Debuts. Resident theaters such as Steppenwolf in Chicago and the Mark Taper in Los Angeles—along with such university-affiliated theaters as the Yale Repertory Theatre in New Haven and Harvard University's American Repertory Theatre in Cambridge, Mass.—continued to send their shows into New York City commercial production. The most recent Steppenwolf transfer was a production of Harold Pinter's *The Caretaker* that opened in January. Regional theaters in other areas also have begun to produce shows with commercial expectations.

In April, the Alliance Theater in Atlanta, Ga., sent a show to Broadway. Sandra Deer's *So Long on Lonely Street* did not survive long after its opening, but it represented an important trend in which Broadway draws new plays from regional theater.   Marilyn Stasio

See also AWARDS AND PRIZES. In WORLD BOOK, see DRAMA; THEATER.

THOMAS, DEBI (1967-   ), performed a series of triple jumps during the final freestyle program to win the women's individual title at the World Figure Skating Championships in Geneva, Switzerland, on March 21, 1986. In taking the gold medal, Thomas became the first black to attain world champion status in ice skating. Thomas' performance denied a third consecutive world championship to East German Katarina Witt, who took second place. Thomas' world championship followed her U.S. title, which she won on Feb. 9, 1986, at Uniondale, N.Y. See ICE SKATING.

Thomas was born on March 25, 1967, in Poughkeepsie, N.Y., and grew up in San Jose. She began taking ice-skating lessons at age 5, entering—and winning—her first competition four years later. In 1980, Thomas took second place in the Novice National Championships. From 1983 to the end of 1986, she participated in 16 national and international competitions, winning 8 of them and finishing second in 3.

Despite training up to seven hours a day in preparation for the national and world championships, Thomas attended college full-time. In September 1985, she entered Stanford University in Palo Alto, Calif., as a freshman premedical student.   Kevin J. Hawker

TIMOR. See ASIA.

TOGO. See AFRICA.

TORONTO, Canada's largest metropolitan area and its main financial and manufacturing center, was buoyed by another year of growth and development in 1986. The continuing surge of prosperity prompted some grand schemes for the future, such as a huge new athletic stadium and entertainment complex.

But there were sharp contrasts in the city's development. Although the municipal and provincial governments were able to find $60 million (Canadian dollars; $1 = U.S. 72 cents on Dec. 31, 1986) to supplement private industry financing of the sports stadium, the Toronto area continued to be troubled by a critical shortage of rental housing, particularly for lower-income families. The housing shortage, as well as lower mortgage rates and consumer prosperity, spurred spectacular increases in real estate prices over the year.

There were also marked contrasts in employment. Although the Toronto metropolitan area and the Lake Ontario north shore had the lowest unemployment rate in Canada—less than 6 per cent compared with the national average of nearly 10 per cent—Toronto's welfare rolls increased as unemployed jobseekers flocked to the area.

Property Tax. The central political issue of 1986 was reform of Metropolitan Toronto's property-tax system, which imposes vastly different tax bills on owners of homes of equal market value. For older homes, the system is based on a 1953 assessment that used 1940 values. Newer properties are assessed on their value at the time they were built. Under the new proposal, all properties would be reassessed at their recent market value. Although most people agreed that the new system would be more fair, politicians argued about implementing it, fearing the reaction of voters facing tax increases of as much as 200 per cent.

There was also disagreement among individual municipalities about the amounts they contribute to run the Metropolitan Toronto government. (Metropolitan Toronto is a grouping of five neighboring boroughs and the City of Toronto. Its chief governing body is the Metropolitan Council of the Municipality of Metropolitan Toronto—popularly referred to as "Metro." The local governments collect the taxes and turn over about 75 per cent to finance the Metro authority and education.) Metro finally approved property tax reform in principle, but only on the condition that low-income property owners be protected from staggering tax increases. The council also insisted that the system by which the boroughs contribute to Metro costs would have to be revised. Such requirements were expected to delay tax reform until 1988 or later.

Sports Dome. Promoters of a 58,000-seat athletic stadium with a retractable dome finally got planning approval in September, and the sod-turning ceremony took place on October 3. The $242.6-million project includes a $60-million hotel with some rooms overlooking the stadium playing field and a high-tech entertainment complex featuring robots and electronic games. The stadium was expected to be ready for the opening of the baseball season in 1989.

With this sports facility in the works, the City of Toronto (as distinct from Metro) decided to apply for the right to host the 1996 Summer Olympic Games. Toronto's application faces strong opposition from Athens, Greece. Many people believe that the centennial of the modern Olympics should take place in Greece, the birthplace of the games. Another group of promoters is planning to bid for a world's fair in Toronto in 1990.

The Financial Community of Toronto was jolted by the Canadian government's announcement on Feb. 26, 1986, that it intends to designate Montreal, Que., and Vancouver, B. C., as international banking centers. This action would enable the two cities to provide some financial services—such as foreign exchange—on a tax-free basis, giving them an important advantage over Toronto. The Ontario provincial government has indicated, however, that it will match any such tax concessions, dollar for dollar, to maintain Toronto's preeminence in financial services in Canada. Robert R. Duffy

See also ONTARIO. In WORLD BOOK, see TORONTO.

TOYS AND GAMES. Retail sales of toys in the United States grew slowly in 1986, with an increase of 6 per cent over 1985 sales expected. A dominant, hot-selling new product failed to emerge in 1986. Toy experts predicted that this fact, along with the declining popularity of some best-selling items from previous years, would boost the sales of traditional playthings, such as dolls, stuffed animals, and board games, in 1986. Sales of these toys were also expected to increase because of the growing number of children under the age of 5 and the increasing number of grandparents, many of whom like to buy traditional toys for their grandchildren.

High-Tech Toys. One of 1985's best-selling toys, Teddy Ruxpin, a talking stuffed bear manufactured by Worlds of Wonder, Incorporated, of Fremont, Calif., spawned a new demand for toys that respond to children. In 1986, Lewis Galoob Incorporated of San Francisco unveiled Baby Talk, a doll that talks in response to sound or touch, thanks to a concealed microchip. A Baby Talk doll also has a moving mouth and makes sucking sounds when a bottle is placed in it. Toys such as Baby Talk are different from Teddy Ruxpin because they interact with children in response to the child's voice or touch. Teddy Ruxpin moves its eyes and mouth along with a voice on a prerecorded cassette tape inside the bear.

A Baby Talk doll, introduced in the fall, is more than just huggable—a microchip enables it to talk and move in response to a child's voice.

TRACK AND FIELD. Sergei Bubka of the Soviet Union and Jackie Joyner of the United States set major world records in 1986. Bubka established both indoor and outdoor pole-vault records. Joyner twice bettered the record for the women's heptathlon, a two-day, seven-event competition.

In 1985, Bubka became the first man to vault 6 meters, clearing 19 feet 8¼ inches. On July 8, 1986, at the Goodwill Games in Moscow, he vaulted 19 feet 8¾ inches (6.01 meters) for a new world record.

During 1986 indoor competition, Bubka broke the world record four times in a period of nine weeks; Billy Olson of Abilene, Tex., broke it four times; and Joe Dial of Norman, Okla., once. The final record of the season was Bubka's 19 feet 6¼ inches (5.95 meters) on February 28 at the Mobil/USA championships in New York City.

Joyner, a top U.S. female long jumper and a world-class athlete in the 400-meter hurdles and the triple jump, displayed her dominance in the heptathlon in 1986. On July 6 and 7 at the Goodwill Games, she scored 7,148 points. On August 1 and 2 at the United States Olympic Festival in Houston, she earned 7,161 points. No one had ever scored 7,000 points before.

In Moscow, Joyner achieved personal records in four of the seven events. In Houston, she set hep-

Video Fun. With one-third of all U.S. households owning a videocassette recorder (VCR), toy companies decided the market was ready for VCR games. A number of games, some able to accommodate as many as six players, were introduced in 1986. They included Flash Match, a memory game, and Predicaments, a soap-opera parody, both from Mattel Incorporated of Hawthorne, Calif.; and Candy Land and Chutes and Ladders, new versions of classic board games from Milton Bradley Company of Pawtucket, R.I.

Ugly Craze. American Greetings Corporation of Cleveland introduced Madballs in 1986, a new example of the "ugly toy" trend. Madballs are small rubber balls with distorted faces, including some showing dislodged eyeballs and exposed brains. Another 1986 "ugly" hit was Garbage Pail Kids trading cards from Topps Chewing Gum Company of New York City. The cards feature caricatures of children with names such as Sara Slime and Messy Tessy.

Rubik's Latest. Erno Rubik, the Hungarian professor who gave the world the mind-boggling Rubik's Cube, introduced a new puzzle in 1986. Called Rubik's Magic, it consists of eight squares of plastic printed with three rainbow-colored rings. The trick is to intertwine the rings by moving the squares.   Diane P. Cardinale

In WORLD BOOK, see DOLL; GAME; TOY.

Norway's Ingrid Kristiansen sets a world record in the 5,000 meters in August, giving her world-best times in all three women's long-distance events.

World Track and Field Records Established in 1986

Men

Event	Holder	Country	Where set	Date	Record
Discus throw	Jurgen Schult	E. Germany	Neubrandenburg, E. Germany	June 6	243 ft. (74.08 m)
Hammer throw	Yury Sedykh	Soviet Union	Stuttgart, W. Germany	Aug. 30	284 ft. 7 in. (86.74 m)
Javelin throw (new javelin)	Klaus Tafelmeier	W. Germany	Como, Italy	Sept. 21	281 ft. 3 in. (85.72 m)*
Pole vault	Sergei Bubka	Soviet Union	Moscow	July 8	19 ft. 8¾ in. (6.01 m)
Shot-put	Udo Beyer	E. Germany	East Berlin	Aug. 20	74 ft. 3½ in. (22.64 m)

Women

Event	Holder	Country	Where set	Date	Record
200 meters	Heike Drechsler	E. Germany	Jena, E. Germany	June 29	:21.71†
2,000 meters	Maricica Puica	Romania	London	July 11	5:28.69
5,000 meters	Ingrid Kristiansen	Norway	Stockholm, Sweden	Aug. 5	14:37.33
10,000 meters	Ingrid Kristiansen	Norway	Oslo, Norway	July 5	30:13.74
100-meter hurdles	Yordanka Donkova	Bulgaria	Ljubljana, Yugoslavia	Sept. 7	:12.26
400-meter hurdles	Marina Stepanova	Soviet Union	Tashkent, Soviet Union	Sept. 17	:52.94
High jump	Stefka Kostadinova	Bulgaria	Sofia, Bulgaria	May 31	6 ft. 9¾ in. (2.08 m)
Long jump	Heike Drechsler	E. Germany	Moscow	June 2	24 ft. 5½ in. (7.45 m)
Triple jump	Esmeralda Garcia	Brazil	Indianapolis	June 5	44 ft. 10¾ in. (13.68 m)
Javelin throw	Fatima Whitbread	Great Britain	Stuttgart, W. Germany	Aug. 28	254 ft. 1 in. (77.44 m)
Heptathlon	Jackie Joyner	U.S.A.	Houston	Aug. 1-2	7,161 points

m = meters; *unofficial record; †tied.

tathlon world records of 22.85 seconds for the 200-meter dash and 23 feet ¾ inch (7.03 meters) for the long jump.

Other Stars. In 1986, Ingrid Kristiansen of Norway became the first athlete to hold simultaneous world records for 5,000 meters and 10,000 meters and a world best in the marathon. In July, she set a women's record of 30 minutes 13.74 seconds for the 10,000 meters and in August ran a record time of 14 minutes 37.33 seconds for the 5,000 meters. In the 1985 London Marathon, she finished in 2 hours 21 minutes 6 seconds. Because marathon courses vary in layout, times are not listed as world records.

Heike Drechsler of East Germany raised her world record in the women's long jump to 24 feet 5½ inches (7.45 meters) on June 21 and equaled it 12 days later. She also twice tied the world record of 21.71 seconds for the 200-meter dash.

Edwin Moses of Newport Beach, Calif., was sidelined until June 26 because of knee and back injuries. Then he ran the 400-meter hurdles in 10 meets and won them all, extending his nine-year unbeaten streak in that event to 119 races (102 finals, 17 preliminaries).

From March 29 to April 27, Jud Logan set U.S. records in the hammer throw four times: 254 feet 9 inches (77.66 meters); 256 feet 3 inches (78.10 meters); 263 feet 4 inches (80.26 meters); and 265 feet 4 inches (80.88 meters). From April 12 to 25, Dial improved the American record in the pole vault three times: 19 feet 2¾ inches (5.86 meters); 19 feet 3½ inches (5.88 meters); and 19 feet 4¼ inches (5.90 meters).

On June 20, at the United States outdoor championships in Eugene, Ore., Carl Lewis won the 100-meter dash in 9.90 (wind-aided) seconds and the long jump at 28 feet 5½ inches (8.67 meters, wind-aided). The next night, the 1984 Olympic hero finished fourth in the 200-meter final. He then lost three straight 100-meter races to Ben Johnson of Canada before a strained tendon in the left knee ended his season.

The Soviet Union won 36 medals and East Germany took 29 in the European championships held in Stuttgart, West Germany, from August 26 to 31. Said Aouita of Morocco won the men's overall title and Yordanka Donkova of Bulgaria the women's in the International Amateur Athletic Federation Grand Prix series. An unofficial world record for the new men's javelin, designed for shorter throws—and thus more safety—was established six times during the year, the last time by Klaus Tafelmeier of West Germany with 281 feet 3 inches (85.72 meters). Frank Litsky

In the Special Reports section, see BIG BOOM IN WOMEN'S SPORTS. In WORLD BOOK, see TRACK AND FIELD.

TRANSIT

TRANSIT systems in United States cities suffered ridership declines in 1986 for the first time in four years. According to the American Public Transit Association (APTA), a Washington, D.C.-based trade association that represents public mass-transit systems, ridership from January to May 1986 dipped 2.54 per cent below 1985 levels. Major cities reporting declines included Baltimore, with a 2.5 per cent decrease; Cincinnati, Ohio, a 2.7 per cent decline; and Cleveland, a 2.8 per cent drop.

Some systems posted ridership increases, however. For example, Metra, the system of commuter railroads serving the Chicago area, reported a 3 per cent increase in ridership for the 12 months ending in April 1986. Some transit companies launched promotions to attract new riders. For example, on September 1 the transit system in Louisville, Ky., introduced free rides for senior citizens on Mondays and Fridays from 10 A.M. to 3 P.M. The Tacoma, Wash., transit system saw a 38.5 per cent increase in ridership after it instituted a free-ride program on Wednesdays.

Extensions of Transit Systems were begun or completed in several cities during 1986. On September 8, a 15-mile (24-kilometer), $282-million light-rail passenger line opened in Portland, Ore. Light-rail systems use electrically powered railroad passenger cars that run on street-level tracks.

In Canada in August, the Montreal Urban Community Transit Society opened a 2.1-mile (3.4-kilometer) subway section, adding five new stops to its system. In the Washington, D.C., area, the transit authority opened a 9-mile (14-kilometer) ground-level extension of its Orange Line subway on June 16, serving four new stations in northern Virginia.

In April, the Miami Metromover project opened. The 1.9-mile (3.1-kilometer) system, which has eight stations and connects with the city's existing rapid-transit system, circles the heart of downtown Miami on a pair of monorail tracks. The Metromover represents the first urban mass-transit use of the so-called people-mover technology—a totally automated system of electrically powered cars. People movers are currently in use at several major airports.

New Projects. Ground was broken in September for a 4.4-mile (7.1-kilometer) segment of a proposed 18.6-mile (29.9-kilometer) subway in Los Angeles. The subway will form the first operating link in a planned 150-mile (241-kilometer) rapid transit network serving the entire Los Angeles-Long Beach metropolitan area.

In Canada, the Toronto Transit Commission received approval in August to build a 4.75-mile (7.6-kilometer), $536-million subway line across

The Miami Metromover, a monorail system that uses fully automated "people-mover" cars, opened in April. The system circles the downtown Miami area.

the city's northern tier. The San Francisco Bay Area Rapid Transit Board of Directors approved plans in May for a 24-mile (39-kilometer) extension of its subway system in eastern Alameda County.

In September, the Dallas Rapid Transit Board of Directors adopted a plan for the construction of 93 miles (150 kilometers) of commuter rail lines by the year 2010. The plan calls for the $2.78-billion project to be built without federal assistance. It is to be financed almost entirely by a 1 per cent local sales tax.

Federal Funding. The Surface Transportation Assistance Act, which provided federal funds for both highway and mass transit projects, expired in September. Under that act, 1 cent of the 9-cents-a-gallon (3.8 liters) federal gasoline tax was earmarked for transit projects. The Administration of President Ronald Reagan proposed new legislation establishing a block-grant program, under which states would receive a lump sum of money that they could allocate in any proportion to either highway or mass transit projects. The Reagan Administration proposal ran into strong congressional opposition and eventually was dropped. Congress adjourned for the year without replacing the expired law.   David M. Cawthorne

In WORLD BOOK, see BUS; ELECTRIC RAILROAD; SUBWAY; TRANSPORTATION.

TRANSPORTATION companies in the United States showed mixed results in earnings and traffic during 1986. Net income for the trucking industry for the first six months of the year rose 61 per cent above 1985 levels. Shipping lines, on the other hand, continued to suffer from surplus capacity and lagging demand, and mass transit systems showed their first ridership drop in four years. Railroad freight traffic held steady during the first 10 months of the year.

Frank Smith of Transportation Policy Associates, a consulting firm, estimated U.S. transportation revenue at $281 billion for 1986, up 3.7 per cent from 1985. Intercity freight on the United States mainland, measured in ton-miles, increased 1.5 per cent, with railroad freight up 1 per cent, truck freight up 4 per cent, air freight up 8 per cent, and pipeline volume up 2 per cent.

New Laws. A number of laws affecting the transportation industry were enacted in the United States in 1986. A provision permitting a public sale of the government's interest in Conrail (*Con*solidated *Rail* Corporation) was signed into law in October as part of the federal government deficit reconciliation bill. The federal government holds 85 per cent of the stock in Conrail, which is a major freight carrier in the Northeast and Midwest. Sale of the government's stock would repre-

sent a major gain for President Ronald Reagan's so-called privatization policy of selling government assets to private businesses. Reagan also signed legislation permitting a regional authority to lease the two federally owned airports that serve the Washington, D.C., area—Washington National Airport and Dulles International Airport.

A bill to combat illegal drugs, which was signed into law in October, included an amendment establishing minimum licensing standards for commercial truck and bus drivers. The new law also gave the U.S. Coast Guard—which in peacetime is a branch of the Department of Transportation—more power to deal with drug smugglers.

Reagan also signed a law deregulating the freight-forwarding industry. Freight forwarders combine smaller shipments into larger ones and make their profit on the rate difference.

Congress also approved legislation authorizing $16 billion in water projects, including $5 billion for port and waterway improvements. The bill, which became law in November, required state and local governments to pay a far larger share of the cost of such projects than in the past. The legislation also included money for the construction or improvement of seven lock-and-dam projects.

Highway Funds. Congress adjourned for 1986 without acting on multiyear funding legislation for highway and mass transit systems. The Reagan Administration had originally sought a four-year, $52-billion program that would have given the states block grants to allocate as they saw fit between highway and mass transit projects.

Although both houses of Congress rejected the Administration's block-grant proposal, they failed to resolve bitter disputes over the future of the 55-mile (89-kilometer) per-hour speed limit and the number of highway projects to be paid for entirely by the federal government. Emergency legislation giving the states more freedom to use highway funds earmarked for specific projects also failed to clear Congress, and some experts predicted that half the states would run out of highway money by early 1987.

Insurance. Skyrocketing insurance costs had a drastic impact on all modes of transportation during 1986. Trucking companies and railroads, acting under special procedures adopted by the Interstate Commerce Commission (ICC), imposed special freight surcharges to cover the higher insurance costs. Some trucking companies took advantage of a change in ICC policy that permitted them to act as their own insurers. Mass transit systems in at least 16 states were also considering plans to become self-insured.   David M. Cawthorne

See also AUTOMOBILE; AVIATION; RAILROAD; SHIP AND SHIPPING; TRANSIT; TRUCK AND TRUCKING. In WORLD BOOK, see TRANSPORTATION.

TRINIDAD AND TOBAGO. See LATIN AMERICA.

TRUCK AND TRUCKING. Earnings for the trucking industry in the United States increased in 1986. Net income for the first six months of 1986 was up about 61 per cent from 1985 levels. Revenues climbed about 6.6 per cent, while expenses increased only about 4.5 per cent.

Insurance costs rose about 29 per cent from 1985 levels. But operating expenses dropped about 9 per cent, largely due to reduced fuel costs.

New Owners. Railroad holding companies acquired several trucking companies in the United States during 1986. In September, Union Pacific Corporation, which owns the Union Pacific Rail System, agreed to pay $1.2 billion to purchase Overnite Transportation Company, one of the largest U.S. trucking firms. At year's end, the sale was awaiting approval from the Interstate Commerce Commission (ICC), the federal agency that regulates the trucking and railroad industries. Burlington Northern, Incorporated, which owns the Burlington Northern Railroad, received ICC approval during 1986 to acquire Wingate Trucking Company and Taylor Maid Transportation.

In a move that could have jeopardized most railroad purchases of trucking lines, a federal appeals court in the District of Columbia in September ordered the ICC to reconsider its decision permitting Norfolk Southern Corporation, a railway holding company, to acquire North American Van Lines Incorporated. The court noted that in the past the ICC had required a railroad to use an acquired trucking firm as part of its rail operations. The court ruled that the ICC had applied a less stringent standard to the Norfolk Southern deal and that by so doing it had misinterpreted antitrust law. In October, however, President Ronald Reagan signed legislation instructing the ICC not to consider the Norfolk Southern purchase a violation of antitrust law.

Business Failures. Competitive pressures forced some major U.S. trucking companies to abandon or curtail their operations in 1986. Through the first six months of the year, 841 trucking firms filed for bankruptcy, compared with 740 for the same period in 1985. One of the most dramatic of these bankruptcy actions occurred in January, when McLean Trucking Company, the fifth-largest U.S. carrier, announced it was going out of business and disposing of its assets.

Legislation. The Tax Reform Act of 1986 signed into law by President Reagan on October 22 was expected to help the trucking industry because of improvements in allowances for equipment depreciation and lower overall tax rates. The President also signed a law that established minimum federal licensing standards for commercial truck and bus drivers.

David M. Cawthorne

See also TRANSPORTATION. In WORLD BOOK, see TRUCK.

TRUDEAU, PIERRE ELLIOTT (1919-   ), continued to shun publicity and live a highly private life during 1986. Since his resignation as prime minister of Canada in 1984, Trudeau has worked in a Montreal, Que., law firm. He has turned down every public assignment offered him.

In April 1986, Trudeau attended a four-day conference of former heads of state in Tokyo. He then led a group of Canadian industrialists on a two-week trip to China.

In November, Trudeau made a rare public statement at a conference in Atlanta, Ga., on democracy in Latin America. He denounced United States intervention in Central America, saying that sovereign countries have the right to choose their own political systems. Tackling "poverty, disease, and human dejection" is the top priority in Central America, he added.

During most of the year, however, Trudeau lived quietly at his home on the slopes of Mount Royal in Montreal with his three sons—Justin, 14; Sacha, 12; and Michel, 11. Trudeau received custody of the boys after he and his wife, Margaret, were divorced in 1984. During 1986, the former prime minister was often seen in public with Canadian-born actress Margot Kidder, who played Lois Lane in the *Superman* films.

David M. L. Farr

In WORLD BOOK, see TRUDEAU, PIERRE E.

Canada's former Prime Minister Pierre Trudeau visits the Northwest Territories Pavilion at the Expo 86 world's fair in Vancouver, Canada, in May.

TUNISIA. President Habib Bourguiba tightened his control of the government in 1986, showing few effects of his 83 years or of several illnesses. In a speech to delegates at the 12th congress of the ruling Socialist Destour Party (PSD) in June, he promised he would preside over the next congress, to be held in 1991.

Bourguiba also surprised the PSD congress by personally appointing a 20-member Central Committee, which is normally chosen by balloting. He said his action would "avoid the negative aspects of voting, which often cause conflict."

On July 8, Bourguiba ousted Prime Minister Mohamed Mzali, his designated successor under the Constitution. Bourguiba had become disenchanted with Mzali, blaming him for Tunisia's economic difficulties, the failure of the educational system to produce qualified graduates, and the weakening of the single-party system. In April and May, Bourguiba had begun to replace Mzali's Cabinet appointees with his own favorites. Bourguiba named Rachid Sfar, a former finance minister, to succeed Mzali.

The Bourguiba purge extended to his own family. On January 7, his son, Habib Bourguiba, Jr., was fired as special adviser for criticizing the president's anticorruption drive. In August, the president divorced his wife, Wassila, for "unauthorized" statements urging constitutional changes to democratize the presidential succession.

Political Crackdown. With parliamentary elections scheduled for November, the PSD tightened the screws on the opposition parties. In April, Ahmed Mestiri, leader of the Social Democratic Movement, was jailed for four months for organizing a demonstration protesting the United States April 15 air raid on Libya. The sentence meant that Mestiri, as a convicted criminal, could not run in the elections. Mestiri and 13 associates were jailed again on November 1, and their party was declared illegal.

The November 2 election produced a clean sweep of the 125 parliamentary seats for the PSD. The remaining opposition parties had withdrawn from the race, and voters had only the PSD candidates on the ballot.

The Economic Scene. With the economy hurting from a decline in oil revenues and tourism, and with an expected drop in grain production, the new prime minister announced an austerity program in August. The dinar was devalued 10 per cent, government spending was cut by $82 million, and price increases were set on basic commodities, including a 15 per cent increase in the price of bread. The bread price rise was offset by food grants of from $110 to $200 per family for the country's 80,000 poorest families.   William Spencer

See also AFRICA (Facts in Brief Table). In WORLD BOOK, see TUNISIA.

TURKEY. Continued economic difficulties during 1986, plus the inevitable broadening of the political process following the restoration of civilian rule, brought a decrease in the popularity of the ruling Motherland Party headed by Prime Minister Turgut Ozal.

Motherland candidates received 45 per cent of the popular vote and won 10 of 16 mayor's seats in local elections in May. But on September 28, in special elections for 11 vacancies in the Grand National Assembly, Turkey's parliament, the party's popular vote dropped to 32 per cent and it won only 6 of the seats. Three cabinet ministers were defeated. In October, the cabinet was reshuffled to emphasize party unity.

The decline in public support for Ozal and his party was matched by an increase in the popularity of other parties and their leaders. The Assembly passed a bill in April lifting a ban on public speeches by political leaders active before a 1980 military coup. But these leaders were still prohibited from engaging in political activity. The chief beneficiary of the law was former Prime Minister Suleyman Demirel, toppled in the 1980 coup. His True Path Party won four Assembly seats in the September elections. They were joined by 20 independents in parliament, giving the party a small but influential bloc in the 400-member Assembly.

In another development, the Nationalist Democracy Party dissolved itself in May. A majority of its members formed a new right wing party, the Free Democrats. With 74 Assembly seats, it became Turkey's third-largest party, behind Ozal's Motherland Party and the Social Democratic Populist Party.

Political Violence and Terrorism. Although Turkey remained neutral in regional conflicts, it was affected by the general climate of terrorism and political violence. Turkish jets attacked Kurdish villages in Iraq in August in retaliation for Kurdish guerrilla ambushes of Turkish patrols that resulted in the death of 12 soldiers.

The Arab-Israeli conflict bloodied Turkish soil on September 6 when terrorists disguised as photographers threw hand grenades and fired submachine guns during a Sabbath service in Istanbul's largest synagogue. Twenty-one worshipers and the two terrorists, described as Arabs, died. A number of Arab groups claimed responsibility for the attack.

The Economy. The government was faced with a budget deficit of $1.3 billion. This was caused by lower export and tourism revenues and less money sent back to Turkey by Turkish workers in other countries. In October, the government devalued the lira and raised prices of basic commodities by as much as 64 per cent.   William Spencer

See also MIDDLE EAST (Facts in Brief Table). In WORLD BOOK, see TURKEY.

A guerrilla of the National Resistance Army, Uganda's largest rebel group, guards a captured government soldier after the fall of Kampala in January.

UGANDA. In January 1986, the December 1985 cease-fire arranged in Nairobi, Kenya, among the warring factions in Uganda's civil war collapsed. On January 26, troops of the National Resistance Army, led by Yoweri Museveni, drove forces loyal to Chairman Tito Okello Lutwa from the capital, Kampala, and toppled the government. Government troops continued to hold out in parts of northern Uganda until March, and there was a renewal of fighting in October.

Museveni assumed the title of president in January. He refused to set a target date for the nation's return to civilian rule or indicate the form of government he intended to impose. A Cabinet and National Resistance Council named by Museveni were dominated by Museveni's party, the National Resistance Movement (NRM), but included representatives from all parties except the Uganda National Liberation Front, a group loyal to former dictator Idi Amin Dada. Only the NRM, however, was permitted to function openly as a political party.

Continuing Strife. The public's initial optimism about Museveni's victory was short-lived. By March, Museveni's troops were harassing civilians as well as extorting and looting—the same sorts of abuses that had been committed by previous military regimes in Uganda.

Violations of human rights increased as the year

wore on. In June, the government banned a private newspaper and arrested its editor, and in August the regime announced the existence of a "Baganda plot" against Museveni. Former Vice President Paulo Muwanga, three Cabinet members, and other members of the Ganda, also called the Baganda—the nation's largest and wealthiest ethnic group—were charged with seeking to secede from Uganda and to restore their king, or *Kabaka.*

Ideology and Economic Aid. The victory of Museveni encouraged agencies of the United Nations and other donors to contribute more than $100-million for the rehabilitation of Uganda. To secure greater aid from the West, Museveni deemphasized his previous socialist rhetoric.

Museveni agreed to honor all past Ugandan debts. He also introduced austerity measures aimed at reducing inflation, the black market, and government spending. In his economic program, announced in May, Museveni said the government was doubling prices paid to coffee growers to stimulate production of coffee beans, Uganda's primary export.　　J. Gus Liebenow and Beverly B. Liebenow

See also AFRICA (Facts in Brief Table). In WORLD BOOK, see UGANDA.

UNEMPLOYMENT. See ECONOMICS; LABOR.

UNION OF SOVIET SOCIALIST REPUBLICS (U.S.S.R.). See RUSSIA.

UNITED NATIONS (UN) on Oct. 10, 1986, elected Javier Pérez de Cuéllar of Peru to a second five-year term as secretary-general. On July 24, Pérez de Cuéllar had quadruple by-pass heart surgery, but before long he was back on the job.

Money Problems. In his annual secretary-general's report on September 9, Pérez de Cuéllar said that the UN faced the most severe financial crisis in its history because a number of member countries—mainly for political reasons—had not paid their dues. He said the UN's operations were endangered because its financial reserves were running low, and that the organization faced the likelihood that the principal contributor—the United States—would withhold a substantial part of its dues. The United States, regularly billed for one-quarter of the UN budget, had paid only $48.8-million of its outstanding UN dues, which totaled $295,792,249 for 1986 and prior years.

Pérez de Cuéllar also said that the UN Secretariat, or permanent staff, should be reduced. On October 31, he notified five undersecretaries-general, who earned $141,000 per year, and six $107,000-per-year assistant secretaries-general that he was laying them off at the end of the year. Two were from Syria, and one each from Belgium, China, Japan, Mali, Nigeria, Pakistan, the Soviet Union, Spain, and the United States.

The secretary-general also said that "criticism of the United Nations by relatively small groups" had affected confidence in its effectiveness. He urged UN backers to "speak more boldly and knowledgeably" in its defense.

On December 8, the General Assembly's finance committee approved a $50-million increase in the budget for 1986 and 1987. The United States and the Soviet Union objected to the increase, while developing nations supported it. On December 11, the Assembly approved the budget by a vote of 122 to 13, with 10 abstentions.

Year of Peace. Jan. 1, 1986, marked the start of the International Year of Peace proclaimed in a 1985 resolution of the General Assembly. Pérez de Cuéllar issued a proclamation saying humanity was at a crossroads "with one way leading to peace and the other to self-destruction."

Anti-Israel Resolutions. The United States vetoed several resolutions in the 15-member Security Council in 1986. A "no" vote, or veto, by any of the five permanent members—China, France, Great Britain, the Soviet Union, and the United States—defeats a measure.

Three of these resolutions were directed against Israel. On January 17, the Security Council held its third meeting in seven days on Lebanon's complaint against the presence of Israeli forces in

Vernon A. Walters, chief United States delegate to the United Nations (UN), tells the UN Security Council why U.S. jets bombed Libya in April.

The new president of the UN General Assembly, Humayun Rashid Choudhury of Bangladesh, right, chats with the chief Soviet delegate.

On February 6, the United States vetoed a resolution that would have condemned Israel for the "forcible interception and diversion" of a Libyan plane flying over the Mediterranean Sea on February 4. Israeli warplanes forced the Libyan craft to land in Israel because Israeli officials thought that it was carrying Palestinian terrorist leaders. Actually, the craft was taking a Syrian political delegation home from an official visit to Libya. Australia, Denmark, France, and Britain abstained.

South Africa. The Security Council considered three major resolutions directed against South Africa. The United States and Great Britain abstained from voting on one of the resolutions and vetoed the other two.

Sudan, acting on behalf of a group of African nations, requested a series of Security Council meetings on South Africa in February. The Council responded with nine meetings between February 5 and 13, and adopted a resolution demanding an immediate end to *apartheid* (racial segregation) in South Africa as a step toward "a nonracial democratic society." The vote was 13-0, with Britain and the United States abstaining.

On May 23, after a two-day debate, Britain and the United States each cast a veto to kill a resolution that would have strongly condemned "the racist regime of South Africa for the recent military raids into Botswana, Zambia, and Zimbabwe." France abstained, and the other Council members voted yes. See SOUTH AFRICA.

On June 18, the United States and Great Britain vetoed a resolution that would have condemned South Africa's military presence in Angola, and would have imposed economic sanctions against South Africa as a protest against apartheid. France abstained. See ANGOLA.

Iran-Iraq War. In a case brought by Iraq and six other Arab countries, the council drafted a resolution calling on Iran and Iraq to end their war and seek a peaceful settlement of their differences. The Council voted unanimously in favor of the resolution on February 24.

On March 14, the Council received a report from specialists sent by Pérez de Cuéllar to investigate charges that chemical weapons were being used in the Iran-Iraq war. The report said that Iraq reportedly had used such weapons against Iranian troops and was still using them. On March 21, the Council issued a statement condemning "this continued use of chemical weapons" and cited a 1925 international ban on such weapons.

U.S.-Libya Clash. From March 26 to April 24, the Security Council held 14 meetings on armed conflict between the United States and Libya. On March 23 and 24, the United States had sent naval vessels and planes into the Gulf of Sidra along Libya's Mediterranean coast to challenge Libya's claim that the gulf is Libyan territory. The two

southern Lebanon. The meeting climaxed with a U.S. veto of a Lebanese resolution calling for the withdrawal of Israeli forces. The United States said that the resolution was unbalanced because it did not mention rocket attacks on Israel from inside Lebanon.

Bulgaria, China, Congo, France, Ghana, Madagascar, the Soviet Union, Thailand, Trinidad and Tobago, the United Arab Emirates (U.A.E.), and Venezuela voted for the resolution. Australia, Denmark, and Great Britain abstained.

On January 30, the United States vetoed a resolution that accused Israel of violating the sanctity of Jerusalem's Haram Al-Sharif complex, which Muslims consider holy. The resolution also called for scrapping all laws that had altered the status of Jerusalem, once divided between Israel and Jordan. One such law, adopted by Israel in 1980, declared that all of Jerusalem was Israel's capital.

On January 11, an inspection party from Israel's Knesset (parliament) had entered the complex to see whether Arabs were engaging in unauthorized construction. According to arrangements worked out by Teddy Kolleck, the mayor of Jerusalem, Jews were not allowed to pray there. But two of the Israeli legislators began reciting a prayer as soon as they entered the complex.

Thailand abstained from voting on the resolution. The other 13 members voted in favor of it.

sides had clashed. And on April 15, United States jets bombed Libya because, according to the United States, Libya was behind the April 5 terrorist bombing of a nightclub in West Berlin, West Germany.

On April 21, the Security Council finally voted on a resolution that sought to condemn the April 15 attack. The sponsors of the resolution were Congo, Ghana, Madagascar, Trinidad and Tobago, and the U.A.E.

Nine countries voted for the resolution. Venezuela abstained, and Australia, Denmark, France, Great Britain, and the United States voted against the resolution. Because each of the last three countries has veto power in the Council, the resolution failed.

Contra Struggle. The United States used the veto again on July 31 to kill a resolution—favored by Nicaragua—that would have called on all countries to refrain from promoting any political, economic, or military actions against any Central American country "that might impede the peace objectives of the Contadora Group." This group—Colombia, Mexico, Panama, and Venezuela—sought a settlement of the conflict in Nicaragua between the government and *contra* rebels.

On June 27, the UN-affiliated International Court of Justice (World Court) in The Hague, the Netherlands, ordered the United States to stop arming and training contras and to reimburse Nicaragua for damage the contras had done as a result of U.S. aid. The United States ignored the order.

The General Assembly started its 41st regular fall session on September 16. Foreign Minister Humayun Rashid Choudhury of Bangladesh was elected president for the session.

Speaking on September 22 in the Assembly's general debate, U.S. President Ronald Reagan said the United States was prepared to discuss with the Soviet Union "ways to implement a step-by-step parallel program of limiting and ultimately ending nuclear testing." Soviet Foreign Minister Eduard A. Shevardnadze told the Assembly on September 23 that his country already had a "unilateral moratorium on nuclear explosions." He said that "for more than a year now, the Soviet testing sites have remained silent."

On November 20, the Assembly adopted a resolution condemning the U.S. April 15 attack on Libya. The vote was 79-28 with 33 abstentions. See LIBYA.

Later on November 20, the Assembly removed 10 unfavorable references to the United States and 1 to Israel from two resolutions on independence for Namibia, which is administered as a territory of South Africa. The Assembly then adopted the resolution.   William N. Oatis

In WORLD BOOK, see UNITED NATIONS.

UNITED STATES, GOVERNMENT OF THE. The United States federal budget deficit totaled a record $220.7 billion in the 1986 fiscal year, which ended on Sept. 30, 1986. The huge shortfall occurred despite the enforcement of a landmark 1985 law aimed at reducing deficits in each fiscal year and eliminating them by 1991.

To abide by the so-called Gramm-Rudman law, Congress cut spending in federal programs by $11.7 billion across the board during the year. Still, the government ran up its fourth record deficit in the five full fiscal years of the Administration of President Ronald Reagan, with red ink exceeding the previous record of $212.3 billion a year earlier. But as a percentage of the *gross national product* (GNP)—the nation's total output of goods and services—the deficit declined to 5.3 per cent in fiscal 1986 from a peak of 6.3 per cent in 1983.

Reagan, who took office in 1981 promising a balanced budget, complained in November 1986 about a "budget fiasco." The President blamed Congress for the problem and promised to make budget reform his top legislative priority in 1987.

Congressional Actions in 1986 to restrain spending, sell federal assets, and approve assorted bookkeeping changes brought the fiscal 1987 budget into compliance—of sorts—with the Gramm-Rudman deficit target of $144 billion. But many members of Congress expected the eventual deficit to exceed the target, and few of them thought that the 1988 target of $108 billion could be reached without large tax increases of the type adamantly opposed by the President. There was increasing talk about "solving" the problem by stretching out the six-year schedule for eliminating the deficit.

Congress had built into the Gramm-Rudman law a mechanism requiring large, automatic spending cuts if yearly deficit targets were exceeded—a provision that relieved the lawmakers from the responsibility of having to take politically risky votes on specific budget items. The law stated that if the deficit was expected to exceed target levels by more than $10 billion, the comptroller general, as head of the General Accounting Office, would issue an order imposing mandatory cuts to reach the specified goals. The cuts would take effect automatically unless Congress adopted an alternative deficit-reduction blueprint within six weeks.

On July 7, however, the Supreme Court of the United States ended the congressional dream of painless budget balancing by ruling 7 to 2 that the comptroller general's role was unconstitutional.

Ten days later, Congress reaffirmed, and thus legalized, $11.7 billion in spending cuts the comptroller general had ordered in March. The House margin was 339 to 72, and the Senate gave its ap-

Major Agencies and Bureaus of the U.S. Government*

Executive Office of the President

President, Ronald Reagan
  Vice President, George H. W. Bush
  White House Chief of Staff, Donald T. Regan
  Presidential Press Secretary, James S. Brady
  Assistant to the President for National Security Affairs—Frank C. Carlucci
  Council of Economic Advisers—Beryl W. Sprinkel, Chairman
  Office of Management and Budget—James C. Miller III, Director
  Office of Science and Technology Policy—William R. Graham, Director
  U.S. Trade Representative, Clayton K. Yeutter

Department of Agriculture

Secretary of Agriculture, Richard E. Lyng
  Agricultural Cooperative Service—Randall E. Torgerson, Administrator
  Agricultural Marketing Service—J. Patrick Boyle, Administrator
  Agricultural Research Service—Terry B. Kinney, Jr., Administrator
  Agricultural Stabilization and Conservation Service—Milton J. Hertz, Administrator
  Animal and Plant Health Inspection Service—Bert W. Hawkins, Administrator
  Commodity Credit Corporation—Daniel G. Amstutz, Chairman
  Economic Research Service—John E. Lee, Jr., Administrator
  Extension Service—Myron Johnsrude, Administrator
  Farmers Home Administration—Vance L. Clark, Administrator
  Federal Crop Insurance Corporation—E. Ray Fosse, Manager
  Food and Nutrition Service—Robert E. Leard, Administrator
  Forest Service—R. Max Peterson, Chief
  Soil Conservation Service—Wilson Scaling, Chief

Department of Commerce

Secretary of Commerce, Malcolm Baldrige
  Bureau of Economic Analysis—Allan H. Young, Director
  Bureau of the Census—John G. Keane, Director
  Economic Development Administration—Orson G. Swindle III, Assistant Secretary
  International Trade Administration—Bruce Smart, Undersecretary
  Minority Business Development Agency—James H. Richardson Gonzales, Director
  National Bureau of Standards—Ernest Ambler, Director
  National Oceanic and Atmospheric Administration—Anthony J. Calio, Administrator
  Patent and Trademark Office—Donald J. Quigg, Commissioner

Department of Defense

Secretary of Defense, Caspar W. Weinberger
  Secretary of the Air Force—Edward C. Aldridge, Jr.
  Secretary of the Army—John O. Marsh, Jr.
  Secretary of the Navy—John F. Lehman, Jr.
  Joint Chiefs of Staff—
    Admiral William J. Crowe, Jr., Chairman
    General Larry D. Welch, Chief of Staff, Air Force
    General John A. Wickham, Jr., Chief of Staff, Army
    Admiral Carlisle A. H. Trost, Chief of Naval Operations
    General Paul X. Kelley, Commandant, Marine Corps

Department of Education

Secretary of Education, William J. Bennett
  Office of Bilingual Education and Minority Languages Affairs—Carol Pendas Whitten, Director

Department of Energy

Secretary of Energy, John S. Herrington
  Economic Regulatory Administration—Marshall A. Staunton, Administrator
  Federal Energy Regulatory Commission—Martha O. Hesse, Chairman
  Office of Energy Research—Alvin W. Trivelpiece, Director

Department of Health and Human Services

Secretary of Health and Human Services, Otis R. Bowen
  Family Support Administration—Wayne A. Stanton, Administrator
  Health Care Financing Administration—William L. Roper, Administrator
  Office of Human Development Services—Jean K. Elder, Assistant Secretary

*As of Jan. 1, 1987.

  Public Health Service—Robert E. Windom, Assistant Secretary
  Alcohol, Drug Abuse, and Mental Health Administration—Donald Ian Macdonald, Administrator
  Centers for Disease Control—James O. Mason, Director
  Food and Drug Administration—Frank E. Young, Commissioner
  National Institutes of Health—James B. Wyngaarden, Director
  Surgeon General of the United States, C. Everett Koop
  Social Security Administration—Dorcas R. Hardy, Commissioner

Department of Housing and Urban Development

Secretary of Housing and Urban Development, Samuel R. Pierce, Jr.
  Federal Housing Commissioner—Thomas T. Demery
  Government National Mortgage Association—Glenn R. Wilson, Jr., President

Department of the Interior

Secretary of the Interior, Donald P. Hodel
  Bureau of Indian Affairs—Ross O. Swimmer, Assistant Secretary
  Bureau of Land Management—Robert F. Burford, Director
  Bureau of Mines—Robert C. Horton, Director
  Bureau of Reclamation—C. Dale Duvall, Commissioner
  National Park Service—William Penn Mott, Jr., Director
  U.S. Fish and Wildlife Service—Frank H. Dunkle, Director
  U.S. Geological Survey—Dallas L. Peck, Director

Department of Justice

Attorney General, Edwin Meese III
  Bureau of Prisons—Norman A. Carlson, Director
  Drug Enforcement Administration—John C. Lawn, Administrator
  Federal Bureau of Investigation—William H. Webster, Director
  Immigration and Naturalization Service—Alan C. Nelson, Commissioner
  Solicitor General—Charles Fried
  U.S. Marshals Service—Stanley E. Morris, Director
  U.S. Parole Commission—Benjamin F. Baer, Chairman

Department of Labor

Secretary of Labor, William E. Brock III
  Bureau of Labor Statistics—Janet L. Norwood, Commissioner
  Employment and Training Administration—Roger D. Semerad, Administrator
  Employment Standards Administration—Susan R. Meisinger, Deputy Undersecretary
  Occupational Safety and Health Administration—John A. Pendergrass, Administrator

Department of State

Secretary of State, George P. Shultz
  U.S. Representative to the United Nations, Vernon A. Walters

Department of Transportation

Secretary of Transportation, Elizabeth Hanford Dole
  Federal Aviation Administration—Donald D. Engen, Administrator
  Federal Highway Administration—Ray A. Barnhart, Administrator
  Federal Railroad Administration—John H. Riley, Administrator
  Maritime Administration—John A. Gaughan, Administrator
  National Highway Traffic Safety Administration—Diane K. Steed, Administrator
  Saint Lawrence Seaway Development Corporation—James L. Emery, Administrator
  U.S. Coast Guard—Admiral Paul A. Yost, Jr., Commandant

Department of the Treasury

Secretary of the Treasury, James A. Baker III
  Bureau of Alcohol, Tobacco and Firearms—Stephen E. Higgins, Director
  Bureau of Engraving and Printing—Robert J. Leuver, Director
  Bureau of the Public Debt—William M. Gregg, Commissioner
  Internal Revenue Service—Lawrence B. Gibbs, Commissioner
  Office of the Comptroller of the Currency—Robert L. Clarke, Comptroller
  Treasurer of the United States—Katherine D. Ortega
  U.S. Customs Service—William von Raab, Commissioner
  U.S. Mint—Donna Pope, Director
  U.S. Savings Bond Division—Katherine D. Ortega, National Director
  U.S. Secret Service—John R. Simpson, Director

Supreme Court of the United States

Chief Justice of the United States, William H. Rehnquist

Associate Justices
William J. Brennan, Jr.   Lewis F. Powell, Jr.
Byron R. White   John Paul Stevens
Thurgood Marshall   Sandra Day O'Connor
Harry A. Blackmun   Antonin Scalia

Congressional Officials

President of the Senate pro tempore—John C. Stennis
Senate Majority Leader—Robert C. Byrd
Senate Minority Leader—Robert J. Dole
Speaker of the House—James C. Wright, Jr.
House Minority Leader—Robert H. Michel
Congressional Budget Office—Rudolph G. Penner, Director
General Accounting Office—Charles A. Bowsher, Comptroller
   General of the United States
Library of Congress—Daniel J. Boorstin, Librarian of Congress
Office of Technology Assessment—John H. Gibbons, Director

Independent Agencies

ACTION—Donna M. Alvarado, Director
Agency for International Development—M. Peter McPherson,
   Administrator
Central Intelligence Agency—William J. Casey, Director
Commission on Civil Rights—Clarence M. Pendleton, Jr.,
   Chairman
Commission of Fine Arts—J. Carter Brown, Chairman
Commodity Futures Trading Commission—Susan M. Phillips,
   Chairman
Consumer Product Safety Commission—Terrence M. Scanlon,
   Chairman
Environmental Protection Agency—Lee M. Thomas,
   Administrator
Equal Employment Opportunity Commission—Clarence Thomas,
   Chairman
Export-Import Bank of the United States—John A. Bohn, Jr.,
   President
Farm Credit Administration—Frank W. Naylor, Jr., Chairman
Federal Communications Commission—Mark S. Fowler, Chairman
Federal Deposit Insurance Corporation—L. William Seidman,
   Chairman
Federal Election Commission—Joan D. Aikens, Chairman
Federal Emergency Management Agency—Julius W. Becton, Jr.,
   Director
Federal Home Loan Bank Board—Edwin J. Gray, Chairman
Federal Maritime Commission—Edward V. Hickey, Jr., Chairman
Federal Mediation and Conciliation Service—Kay McMurray,
   Director
Federal Reserve System—Paul A. Volcker, Chairman
Federal Trade Commission—Daniel Oliver, Chairman
General Services Administration—Terence C. Golden,
   Administrator
Interstate Commerce Commission—Heather J. Gradison,
   Chairman
Merit Systems Protection Board—Daniel R. Levinson, Chairman
National Aeronautics and Space Administration—James C.
   Fletcher, Administrator
National Endowment for the Arts—Francis S. M. Hodsoll,
   Chairman
National Endowment for the Humanities—Lynne V. Cheney,
   Chairman
National Labor Relations Board—Donald L. Dotson, Chairman
National Mediation Board—Charles L. Woods, Chairman
National Railroad Passenger Corporation (Amtrak)—W. Graham
   Claytor, Jr., Chairman
National Science Foundation—Erich Bloch, Director
National Transportation Safety Board—James E. Burnett, Jr.,
   Chairman
Nuclear Regulatory Commission—Lando W. Zech, Jr., Chairman
Office of Personnel Management—Constance J. Horner, Director
Peace Corps—Loret Miller Ruppe, Director
Postal Rate Commission—Janet D. Steiger, Chairman
Securities and Exchange Commission—John S. R. Shad, Chairman
Selective Service System—Wilfred L. Ebel, Acting Director
Small Business Administration—James Abdnor†, Administrator
Smithsonian Institution—Robert McC. Adams, Secretary
Tennessee Valley Authority—Charles H. Dean, Jr., Chairman
U.S. Arms Control and Disarmament Agency—Kenneth L.
   Adelman, Director
U.S. Information Agency—Charles Z. Wick, Director
U.S. International Trade Commission—Susan Wittenberg
   Liebeler, Chairman
U.S. Postal Service—Preston R. Tisch, Postmaster General
Veterans Administration—Thomas K. Turnage, Administrator

†Nominated but not yet confirmed.

proval by voice vote. But Congress was unable to agree on ways to get around the Supreme Court's ruling and find an alternative enforcement mechanism for the budget-balancing law.

U.S. Space Program. The explosion of the space shuttle *Challenger* during a launch attempt at Cape Canaveral, Fla., on January 28 shocked Americans. For many, the tragedy was especially heartfelt because the seven-member crew included the shuttle program's first "citizen observer"—Christa McAuliffe, a Concord, N.H., high-school teacher who was to broadcast from space to the nation's classrooms.

A presidential commission headed by William P. Rogers, secretary of state in the Administration of President Richard M. Nixon, investigated the *Challenger* disaster. In its conclusions, the commission faulted the management of the National Aeronautics and Space Administration (NASA). It also criticized NASA's decision to launch the *Challenger* in cold weather over the objections of some engineers who foresaw the potential for disaster in the seals of the shuttle's solid-fuel rocket boosters—the precise cause of the explosion.

On August 15, Reagan ordered NASA to build a replacement for *Challenger*, at a cost of at least $2.4 billion, without specifying how the new spacecraft would be financed. At the same time, he directed the agency to abandon its practice of raising money by launching commercial satellites from its shuttles. On November 5, NASA announced a reorganization of shuttle-program management, with top authority shifted back to its Washington, D.C., headquarters from the Lyndon B. Johnson Space Center in Houston. See SPACE EXPLORATION (Close-Up).

The problems posed by *Challenger*'s destruction, and the subsequent grounding of the three remaining shuttles until 1988, were just the beginning. In later months, five unmanned rockets, some with secret payloads, failed after liftoff. For a time, government and military leaders were concerned that the United States would not be able to keep enough spy satellites in orbit to maintain an adequate check on the Soviet Union's military activities. But the string of failures ended on September 5 with the successful launch from Cape Canaveral of a Delta rocket carrying a classified experiment for the Strategic Defense Initiative (SDI or "Star Wars") antimissile project.

Military Shakeup. Over the objections of the Pentagon, Congress in 1986 approved an overhaul of the military's top command structure. The measure was signed by Reagan on October 1. The law's major objective is to change, by 1990, the decision-making process of the Joint Chiefs of Staff. Under the expiring system, the five chiefs must reach a consensus. That arrangement, critics have charged, leads to fuzzy decisions and the ducking

Federal Spending

United States Budget for Fiscal 1986*

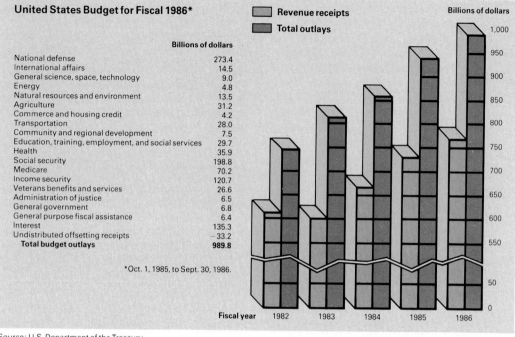

	Billions of dollars
National defense	273.4
International affairs	14.5
General science, space, technology	9.0
Energy	4.8
Natural resources and environment	13.5
Agriculture	31.2
Commerce and housing credit	4.2
Transportation	28.0
Community and regional development	7.5
Education, training, employment, and social services	29.7
Health	35.9
Social security	198.8
Medicare	70.2
Income security	120.7
Veterans benefits and services	26.6
Administration of justice	6.5
General government	6.8
General purpose fiscal assistance	6.4
Interest	135.3
Undistributed offsetting receipts	−33.2
Total budget outlays	**989.8**

*Oct. 1, 1985, to Sept. 30, 1986.

U.S. Income and Outlays

Revenue receipts
Total outlays

Billions of dollars

Fiscal year 1982 1983 1984 1985 1986

Source: U.S. Department of the Treasury.

of responsibility as individual services seek to further their own interests.

The new system makes the chairman of the Joint Chiefs of Staff the principal military adviser to the President, freeing the chairman to offer advice independent of the other chiefs. In addition, the revised command structure greatly expands the powers of field commanders, who in many cases will be authorized to act without seeking approval from the Pentagon bureaucracy.

The U.S. Supreme Court "opened under new management" on October 6 as it began its 1986-1987 term with its 16th chief justice, William H. Rehnquist. Rehnquist, an associate justice since 1972, was sworn in on September 26 to succeed Chief Justice Warren E. Burger, who retired. Sworn in at the same time as the 103rd member of the court was Antonin Scalia, a federal Appeals Court judge who became the first high-court justice of Italian descent. Although some Senate Democrats tried to block Rehnquist's nomination, he was confirmed by a 65 to 33 vote. The Senate confirmed Scalia 98 to 0.

Cabinet. There were two changes in Reagan's Cabinet during the year. In January, the President chose Richard E. Lyng as his new secretary of agriculture. Lyng, a former deputy secretary of agriculture, succeeded John R. Block, who resigned effective February 14.

On November 25, John M. Poindexter, Reagan's national security adviser, resigned. Poindexter was implicated in the Administration's secret sale of arms to Iran and funneling of the profits to Nicaraguan rebels (see PRESIDENT OF THE UNITED STATES). On December 2, Reagan named Frank C. Carlucci to replace Poindexter.

As 1986 ended, two former top assistants to Reagan, Michael K. Deaver and Lyn Nofziger, were being investigated to determine if they had violated federal ethics laws. At issue was whether the former aides had lobbied their old White House associates on behalf of private clients sooner than is legally allowed after leaving government service.

New U.S. Commonwealth. In November, the Northern Mariana Islands in the western Pacific Ocean officially became a United States commonwealth. Frank Cormier and Margot Cormier

See also ARMED FORCES; CONGRESS OF THE UNITED STATES; REAGAN, RONALD WILSON; SUPREME COURT OF THE UNITED STATES. In WORLD BOOK, see UNITED STATES, GOVERNMENT OF THE.

UNITED STATES CONSTITUTION. See CONSTITUTION OF THE UNITED STATES. In the Special Reports section, see THE U.S. CONSTITUTION: 200 YEARS OF HISTORY.

URUGUAY. See LATIN AMERICA.

UTAH. See STATE GOVERNMENT.

VANDER ZALM, WILLIAM NICK (1934-   ), a millionaire businessman, was sworn in as the 27th premier of British Columbia on Aug. 6, 1986. He replaced William R. Bennett, 54, who announced his retirement on May 22, 1986, after 10 years in office. See BRITISH COLUMBIA.

Vander Zalm quit politics in 1983 while serving as the province's minister of education but reentered the political ring to run for premier. A member of the controlling Social Credit Party (Socred), Vander Zalm won twice as many votes as his closest opponent to become Socred leader.

Born on May 29, 1934, in the Netherlands, Vander Zalm immigrated to Canada with his family when he was 13 years old. In 1968, he was elected mayor of Surrey, a Vancouver suburb, and held the position for six years. From 1975 to 1978, he was British Columbia's minister of human resources, and he served as the province's minister of municipal affairs from 1978 to 1982. Aside from his political career, Vander Zalm was owner and president of Art Knapp Nurseries, a chain of garden centers he sold in 1984, and owner of Fantasy Garden World, a theme park outside Vancouver. Vander Zalm and his wife, Lillian, have four children.   Mary A. Krier

VANUATU. See PACIFIC ISLANDS.

VENEZUELA. See LATIN AMERICA.

VERMONT. See STATE GOVERNMENT.

VETERANS. On July 2, 1986, President Ronald Reagan signed legislation establishing the Military Retirement Reform Act. Under the new system, anyone entering the armed forces after Aug. 1, 1986—and retiring after 20 years of service—will receive a pension amounting to 40 per cent of the average of the highest three years of base pay. The previous pension level was 50 per cent.

In April, Thomas K. Turnage replaced Harry N. Walters as Veterans Administration (VA) director. A retired Army major general, Turnage had directed the Selective Service System since 1981.

Physician John W. Ditzler resigned as medical director of the VA on Aug. 8, 1986. Ditzler resigned four days before he was to testify before a House of Representatives subcommittee investigating an increase in medical malpractice awards and high mortality rates at VA medical centers.

During rededication ceremonies held on Memorial Day, May 26, in Washington, D.C., the names of 110 deceased servicemen were added to the 58,022 names of the war dead engraved on the Vietnam Veterans Memorial. The 110 had been omitted originally because they did not die in a Vietnam combat zone. Frank Cormier and Margot Cormier

In WORLD BOOK, see VETERANS ADMINISTRATION; VETERANS' ORGANIZATIONS.

VICE PRESIDENT OF THE UNITED STATES. See BUSH, GEORGE H. W.

An estimated 200,000 people march through downtown Chicago in June in the largest parade of Vietnam War veterans ever held.

VIETNAM made sweeping leadership changes in 1986 after official admission of policy failures. On Dec. 18, 1986, the Vietnamese Communist Party named an economic reformer, Nguyen Van Linh, to the nation's top job, party general secretary.

New Leadership. Linh was the third person to be general secretary during the year. Le Duan, who had held the post since Ho Chi Minh's death in 1969, died on July 10, 1986, at the age of 78. He was succeeded by Truong Chinh, 79 years old.

At the party's Sixth Congress, held in Hanoi from December 15 to 18, Chinh and two other senior leaders, Premier Pham Van Dong and party policymaker Le Duc Tho, retired from active party roles. The announced reason was their "advanced age and failing health," though only Dong was known to have been sick. All three became party advisers.

Linh, who was 73 years old when he became general secretary, was party secretary for Ho Chi Minh City, formerly Saigon, from 1981 to 1985. In that job, he experimented with the use of material incentives to stimulate production, the abolition of rationing, and other economic reforms.

Reform Debates had begun before Le Duan died. An announcement on June 9 said the party's Central Committee had discussed "shortcomings and errors in leadership, supervision, and execution of tasks." It implied that the public lacked "confidence in the party leadership."

With unemployment estimated by foreign observers as up to one-third of Vietnam's workers, Chinh admitted on October 19 failures of economic policies. He called on Communist officials to free themselves from "simplistic concepts of socialism." Chinh's report to the party congress said that trade problems, "inappropriate distribution of commodities, and soaring prices are exerting a negative impact on productivity, the people's life, and society." By stepping down, he gave Linh a chance to try fresh approaches to problems.

Missing Americans. Vietnamese and Americans met four times during 1986 to try to resolve the cases of at least 1,789 U.S. servicemen missing since the Vietnam War. Vietnam denied it held any living Americans, but a former director of the U.S. Defense Intelligence Agency said on September 29 that an investigative panel had concluded that "a large volume of evidence" showed some Americans might be prisoners in Indochina.

In April, the Vietnamese returned the remains of 21 U.S. servicemen. On November 26, Vietnam handed over what it described as the remains of 3 more U.S. soldiers. Vietnam said it had begun investigating reports of other remains. Henry S. Bradsher

See also ASIA (Facts in Brief Table); KAMPUCHEA. In WORLD BOOK, see VIETNAM.

VIRGINIA. See STATE GOVERNMENT.

VITAL STATISTICS. See CENSUS; POPULATION.

WALDHEIM, KURT (1918-   ), was elected president of Austria on June 8, 1986, amid controversy concerning his record as a German Army officer during World War II (1939-1945), when Austria was part of Germany. He had claimed in an autobiography that he was discharged from the army in 1941, but he actually served until 1944. He had denied, then later admitted, knowing about atrocities committed by the army group in which he served. He also was charged with, but continued to deny, taking steps leading to the execution of civilians and war prisoners. See AUSTRIA.

Waldheim was born on Dec. 21, 1918, in St. Andrä-Wördern, near Vienna. He earned a law degree at the University of Vienna. After the war, he joined the Austrian foreign office. He led Austria's first delegation to the United Nations (UN) in 1955 and was appointed ambassador to Canada in 1958.

Waldheim served as Austria's permanent representative to the UN from 1964 to 1968 and in 1970 and 1971, and as Austria's foreign minister from 1968 to 1970. He ran unsuccessfully for president of Austria in 1971. In 1972, Waldheim was elected secretary-general of the UN. He was reelected in 1976; in 1981, he withdrew from the race for a third term to break a voting deadlock.

Waldheim and his wife, Elisabeth, have three children. Jay Myers

WALES. An accident at the Chernobyl nuclear reactor in the Soviet Union in April 1986—which released radioactive material into the air—created problems for farmers in northern Wales. On June 13, the British government prohibited the slaughter of sheep in the area after tests on lambs showed they had higher levels of radioactive cesium than lambs in the rest of the country. The ban was enacted to ensure that the lamb and mutton available in shops was safe to eat.

Although the ban was lifted in large sections of the affected area in succeeding months, it remained in effect until October for some farmers. The Welsh Office, the country's administrative body, launched an economic aid program to help farmers hurt by the ban.

Coal Industry. The decline of the Welsh coal industry was emphasized on October 31 when two more *pits*, or coal mines, were closed. The mines, located in Cwm at Beddau and Nantgarw, two towns near Cardiff, employed a total of 1,300 workers. The National Coal Board said that heavy losses had forced the closures, which reduced the number of employed miners in southern Wales to approximately 11,000, compared with more than 100,000 in the 1950's.

In June 1986, the last coal mine in one of the most famous coal-producing areas in the world—the Rhondda Valley—ended production when

Mardy Colliery closed its doors. At the height of its mining activity in the early 1900's, the Rhondda Valley contained more than 50 pits.

On February 21, Emlyn Williams, one of the best-known Welsh union leaders, retired. For more than 12 years, Williams was president of the southern Wales area of the National Union of Mineworkers. He was succeeded by Des Dutfield.

Miners in the southern Wales coal fields began a ban against overtime work on August 4 in protest over pay and to support the rehiring of miners fired during a 1984-1985 strike. Miners in Durham joined the ban on September 19.

Residents of the village of Aberfan marked the 20th anniversary of a coal disaster that killed 144 people, including 116 children, on Oct. 21, 1966. The disaster occurred when coal from a *coal tip*, a place where coal is dumped, slid and engulfed the village school.

Unemployment. The decline of the coal industry worsened the country's severe unemployment problem in 1986. Almost 174,000 people in Wales were unemployed by September, approximately 14 per cent of the working population.

Arts. The Royal National Eisteddfod of Wales, a festival promoting Welsh culture, was held at Fishguard in western Wales on August 25. The Chair, one of the two chief poetry prizes, was won by Gwynn ap Gwilym, a clergyman. The other prize, the Crown, went to T. James Jones, an author.

The recent flourishing of Welsh-language films and television shows reached new heights in 1986. The film *Coming up Roses*, made in Welsh by Stephen Bayley, was shown at the Cannes Film Festival in May as one of three films representing Great Britain. This was the first time a Welsh-language film was included in the festival.

Rugby Roughness. On September 1, David Bishop, an internationally known Welsh rugby player, was sentenced to one month in prison for punching an opponent during a game between his team, Pontypool, and its opponent, Newbridge. Bishop appealed the decision on September 17. Although the prison sentence was suspended, he was banned from playing rugby for the rest of the season.

In July, Richard Johnson was jailed for six months for biting off part of an opponent's ear. The incident took place in a match between the Cardiff and Newport police departments.

Welsh Bond. On August 6, film producer Albert Broccoli chose Welsh actor Timothy Dalton to portray James Bond in the 16th film about Ian Fleming's secret agent. Dalton, 38, will be the fifth actor to portray 007. His predecessors were actors Sean Connery, David Niven, George Lazenby, and Roger Moore.
Patrick Hannan

See also GREAT BRITAIN. In WORLD BOOK, see WALES.

WARREN, ROBERT PENN (1905-   ), was named the first official poet laureate of the United States on Feb. 26, 1986. The title was added to that of consultant in poetry at the Library of Congress, a post held by Warren in 1944 and 1945.

Warren was born in Guthrie, Ky., on April 24, 1905. He received a B.A. degree from Vanderbilt University in Nashville, Tenn., in 1925, an M.A. from the University of California at Berkeley in 1927, and a B.Litt. degree from Oxford University in England in 1930.

Warren is probably best known for his novel, *All the King's Men*—a story of a ruthless Southern politician closely resembling Governor Huey P. Long of Louisiana—which won the 1947 Pulitzer Prize for fiction. Warren also won the 1958 Pulitzer Prize for poetry for his collection *Promises: Poems 1954-1956* and the 1979 prize for poetry for *Now and Then: Poems 1976-1978*.

New and Selected Poems 1923-1985, a collection of Warren's poetry, appeared in 1985. The work reflects his Southern heritage and his long-standing interest in such themes as the interaction of past and present, the search for personal identity and knowledge, and the nature of evil.

In 1952, Warren married Eleanor Clark, a writer. They have two children.
Joan Stephenson

See also POETRY.

WASHINGTON. See STATE GOVERNMENT.

WASHINGTON, D.C. Democratic Mayor Marion S. Barry, Jr., easily won a third four-year term on Nov. 4, 1986, receiving 61 per cent of the vote. His Republican challenger, City Council member Carol Schwartz, captured 33 per cent of the vote.

The election returns underscored deep divisions between the affluent and primarily white Third Ward in northwest Washington and the rest of the predominantly black city, which is divided into eight wards. Although Barry, a black, carried the city as a whole by an overwhelming majority, Schwartz, a white, won the Third Ward vote by a 5 to 1 margin.

Prison. Congress in 1986 approved another $20-million for the construction of a new prison within district boundaries, bringing total federal funding for the project to $50 million through fiscal year 1988. The lawmakers set a deadline of Oct. 15, 1986, for Mayor Barry to sign a construction contract for the 700-bed medium-security facility. He met that deadline, awarding a joint $49.8-million contract to two construction companies.

For several years, the mayor had been under a court order to reduce crowded conditions at the city's correctional facilities, and he agreed reluctantly in 1985 to the construction of a new prison. The institution, which is to be built in southeast Washington, will be geared to drug-abuse treatment as well as incarceration.

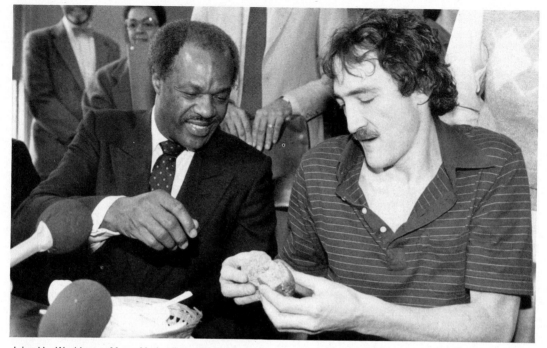

Joined by Washington Mayor Marion Barry, Mitch Snyder, an advocate of the homeless, ends a 32-day fast in March after learning that a shelter he runs will get U.S. funds.

Hundreds of inmates at the district's prison complex in nearby Lorton, Va., rioted on July 10. Twenty-three prisoners and six guards were injured, and fires set by the inmates caused extensive damage. The riot was the second outbreak of violence at the Lorton facility in 1986.

AIDS Insurance. The City Council in May approved legislation prohibiting insurance companies from denying coverage to persons whose blood contains evidence of exposure to the acquired immune deficiency syndrome (AIDS) virus. AIDS destroys the immune system and leaves its victims vulnerable to infections and cancers. The new law, thought to be the broadest of its kind in the United States, also prohibits insurers for five years from charging higher rates to insure persons who may be carrying the AIDS virus. The law does not cover individuals who have AIDS.

After Barry signed the legislation, a number of insurance companies announced they would no longer provide individual life or health insurance policies for district residents. The law became a target of the Moral Majority, a conservative political organization, which unsuccessfully attempted to get it overturned in Congress. (Congress has the power to make laws for the city and to overrule City Council decisions.)

Drinking Age. The City Council in September voted to raise the district's drinking age to 21 for all types of alcohol as of Oct. 1, 1986. The minimum drinking age had been 18 for beer and wine, and 21 for liquor. Individuals who were already 18 by October will still be allowed to purchase and drink beer and wine.

Law School. The City Council in September approved a take-over of the Antioch School of Law, which had lost the financial support of its parent college, Antioch University in Yellow Springs, Ohio. The city planned to turn the institution into a public law school and merge it with the University of the District of Columbia.

Shelter for Homeless. On March 16, the Administration of President Ronald Reagan agreed to provide $5 million for the renovation of a deteriorated building being used as an 800-bed shelter for homeless people. Shelter director Mitch Snyder and 12 other activists ended a 32-day hunger strike after they reached an agreement with the White House. They began the fast on February 12 when the Administration and the activists reached an impasse in negotiations over how the federal government would fulfill an earlier pledge to refurbish the shelter. Snyder held another fast for four days in June, forcing the Administration to release $1 million of the promised funds so renovations could begin.   Sandra Evans

See also CITY. In WORLD BOOK, see WASHINGTON, D.C.

WATER. A major lawsuit involving ground-water contamination was settled out of court on Sept. 22, 1986, with an $8-million payment to the plaintiffs. The lawsuit was filed by eight Woburn, Mass., families who accused three industrial firms—Unifirst Corporation, Beatrice Foods, and W. R. Grace and Company—of contaminating wells in Woburn and causing the subsequent leukemia deaths of at least six people.

Solvents Seep into Wells. In 1979, contamination by industrial solvents, including trichloroethylene and perchloroethylene, or tetrachloroethylene, was discovered in two of the wells that provided water to neighborhoods in Woburn. Residents of this area also appeared to have an abnormally high incidence of leukemia, a form of cancer that disrupts the formation of blood cells. Subsequently, several studies, including one by Harvard University, confirmed the cancer "cluster" and indicated that the drinking water from the polluted wells was a possible cause.

In 1985, Unifirst settled out of court with the plaintiffs for a reported $1 million. The trial of the remaining two defendants, held in the U.S. District Court in Boston, was organized in three parts. In the first phase of the trial, the jury considered who was responsible for contaminating the wells. Depending on this finding, the second part of the trial would determine whether the contamination caused the leukemia. The third phase would determine compensation for the families.

In the first phase of the trial in July 1986, the jury found that W. R. Grace and Company had contaminated the Woburn wells, while Beatrice Foods was not held responsible for any contamination. The presiding judge, however, determined that the jury had been confused by technical issues raised during the court proceedings, and ordered a new trial. Subsequently, the Woburn families decided to settle out of court.

This lawsuit was one of the first in the United States attempting to prove direct cause-and-effect relationships between an illness or death and a specific pollutant. Many similar cases are expected.

Water Veto. On Nov. 6, 1986, President Ronald Reagan vetoed an extension of the Clean Water Act of 1973, saying the proposed $18-billion spending was excessive. See ENVIRONMENTAL POLLUTION.

Great Salt Lake. In June 1986, the Great Salt Lake in Utah reached a record 4,211.85 feet (1,283.77 meters) above sea level. The lake, which had risen rapidly since 1983 because of heavy snowfalls and cool, overcast summers, covered an area of about 2,500 square miles (6,500 square kilometers). The rising waters caused substantial damage to industrial, residential, and recreational sites that border the lake.

The Great Salt Lake, so named because its wa-

The Great Salt Lake Grows Greater

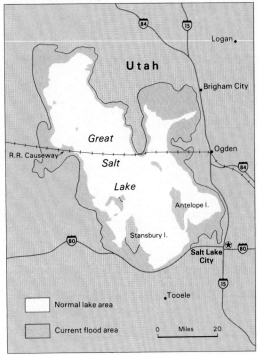

ters are four to seven times saltier than the ocean, forms a basin for the rivers that drain a total area of 23,000 square miles (60,000 square kilometers). The lake has no outflow, and its water volume is controlled solely by evaporation. As a result, water level depends largely on how much water flows into the lake. Its volume changes with the seasons, typically rising in the autumn, winter, and spring, when precipitation and streamflow are high, and falling in the summer, when evaporation is greater than inflow.

The lake waters fell to their lowest level—4,191.35 feet (1,277.52 meters)—in October 1963, following an extended period of minimal rainfall. At that time, the lake covered less than 1,000 square miles (2,600 square kilometers). Since 1982, however, Utah has experienced unusually heavy precipitation.

A further rise in the lake could cause damage exceeding $1 billion. The advancing lake waters threatened Salt Lake City International Airport as well as U.S. interstate highways 15 and 80.

To control the level of the lake, the Utah state legislature in May 1986 approved a $62-million plan to pump lake water into the Great Salt Lake Desert to the west. This project, which will create a new lake to the west of Salt Lake City, was expected to begin in February 1987.   Iris Priestaf

In WORLD BOOK, see WATER.

WEATHER. Warmer than normal temperatures occurred during the first three months of 1986 over most of the United States, including Alaska. The coastal city of Anchorage, Alaska, recorded the fourth warmest January in its history, and temperatures up to 15° F. (8° C) above normal prevailed in the interior of the state. In the lower 48 states of the United States, only Florida had subnormal temperatures. On February 24, Los Angeles had a record high for February of 94° F. (34° C).

Precipitation during the first three months was within normal range nearly everywhere except in the Southeastern states, which received only about 50 per cent of their normal rainfall. Heavy rains fell between February 15 and 20 in California. In San Francisco, 7.48 inches (19 centimeters) fell over a 24-hour period on February 17. Widespread flooding in the Sacramento area, compounded by a broken levee at Yuba City on February 20, drove 50,000 people from their homes. Thirteen deaths resulted.

On February 22 and 23, a heavy snowstorm hit Nova Scotia, Canada. Sydney, N.S., had a two-day snowfall of 29.5 inches (75 centimeters), the heaviest measured there since records began in 1870. On March 17 and 18, an 11-inch (28-centimeter) snowfall in South Dakota forced the closing of Interstate Highway 90.

Spring Snows. April brought more snowstorms to the Midwestern states. A storm moving from the Pacific Coast to Lake Superior in early April dumped 22 inches (56 centimeters) on Snowbird, Utah, near Salt Lake City, and 26 inches (66 centimeters) on Fort Collins, Colo. The storm produced winds of 71 miles per hour (mph) or 114 kilometers per hour (kph) at Pueblo, Colo.

Another storm followed that produced blizzard conditions throughout the Dakotas. Winds at Mitchell, S. Dak., reached 92 mph (148 kph). An April 23 storm brought the latest spring snow ever recorded in Philadelphia and 24 inches (61 centimeters) to Tobyhanna, Pa. An even later storm—from May 13 to 15—paralyzed southern Alberta, Canada, with drifts up to 6 feet (1.8 meters) deep and winds of 50 mph (80 kph).

Heat and Drought. Above-normal temperatures prevailed in most of the United States in June and July. Only Alaska and the Northeast remained near normal. A June hurricane named Bonnie formed in the Gulf of Mexico and crossed eastern Texas on the morning of June 26 with winds of 85 mph (137 kph) and 5-foot (1.5-meter) tides.

By July, the drought in the Southeast reached record proportions. The period from Dec. 5, 1985, to July 31, 1986, was the driest ever recorded in this area. Precipitation was less than 60

Cracked earth and the extremely low water level of a pond near Danville, Ga., bear witness to the long, hot summer that parched the Southeast in 1986.

per cent of normal. Reservoirs and water supplies were severely depleted, and the loss of crops was estimated at more than $1 billion. At the end of July, rainfall returned to nearly normal, but it would be many months before adequate water supplies would be restored.

A record heat wave compounded the effects of the drought. Between July 8 and 18, temperatures reached 104° F. (40° C) at Columbia, S.C.; 105° F. (41° C) at Beaufort, S.C., and 106° F. (41° C) at Macon, Ga. Even higher temperatures developed farther west toward the end of the month, including 110° F. (43° C) at Tulsa, Okla., Wichita, Kans., and Wichita Falls, Tex., on July 30; and at Little Rock, Ark., on July 31. In Atlanta, Ga., a high of 89° F (31.7° C) on August 11 ended a record 38-day string of temperatures above 90° F. (32° C).

Rain and More Rain. August brought welcome rain to the Southeast in the form of thunderstorms. Hurricane Charley formed off the coast of South Carolina on August 15 and added more rain as it traveled northward through eastern North Carolina and the lower Chesapeake Bay on August 18. The storm did little damage, however, before swerving eastward out to sea. Near the end of August, a strong outbreak of cold Canadian air dropped the temperature to 49° F. (9° C) at Washington, D.C., on August 29 and to 25° F. (−4° C) at Bradford, Pa., both records for that day.

Much rain fell during September in the nation's midsection. In central Montana on September 25 and 26, 8 inches (20 centimeters) of rain fell in 18 hours on already wet ground, culminating in the worst flooding in 30 years along the Milk River. Flooding was widespread in Oklahoma, Kansas, Missouri, Michigan, and Illinois, where Governor James R. Thompson called out National Guard troops for help in the disaster. More than 45,000 people were evacuated from their homes, and at least 9 deaths were attributed to the flooding.

Early Winter. Freezing weather hit the Midwest in early November. Butte, Mont., reported a record −32° F. (−36° C) on November 10. Low-temperature records were tied or broken in Iowa, Kansas, Michigan, Minnesota, Missouri, North and South Dakota, and Wisconsin. As the frigid weather moved eastward, Louisville, Ky., set a record low of 16° F. (−9° C) on November 13.

Headed for a Hurricane Disaster? On January 12, the American Meteorological Society published a statement expressing concern that the United States faces a possible hurricane disaster. Studies have shown that it takes at least 20 to 30 hours to evacuate some hurricane-prone areas. But warnings of sufficient certainty to warrant an evacuation cannot generally be made more than 12 hours in advance.   Alfred K. Blackadar

In WORLD BOOK, see METEOROLOGY; WEATHER.
WEIGHT LIFTING. See SPORTS.

WELFARE. The poverty rate in the United States dropped slightly in 1985 for the second straight year, the Bureau of the Census reported on Aug. 26, 1986, and the median family income increased for the third consecutive year. This trend was attributed to a continuation of the economic recovery from the recession of the early 1980's.

Poverty. According to Census Bureau figures, 33,064,000 Americans, or 14 per cent of the population, lived below the government's official poverty line in 1985. The poverty level was defined as an annual cash income of $10,989 or less for a family of four. The poverty rate declined from 14.4 per cent in 1984 and was markedly below the recent peak of 15.2 per cent in 1983. When such statistics were first compiled in 1959, the poverty rate was 22.4 per cent. It dropped to about 11.5 per cent in the 1960's and did not rise sharply until the late 1970's and early 1980's, when inflation and recession took a heavy toll.

Black Americans were the only group to show substantial income gains in 1985. Black median income rose by 5 per cent to $16,786, while the poverty rate among blacks fell to 31.3 per cent in 1985 from 33.8 per cent in 1984.

Welfare. A Census Bureau report in January 1986 stated that 1 out of every 3 American children under 18 in 1984 lived in a household that received some form of government welfare, such as food stamps, Medicaid, or cash benefits. The report revealed that 68 per cent of black children and 52 per cent of Hispanic children lived in households receiving such benefits, which were based on *means tests*. A means test is an examination of an applicant's financial resources to determine eligibility for assistance. The proportion of white children receiving benefits was 25 per cent.

More nonfarm children, 23 per cent, participated in the school-lunch program than any other means-tested government program. The percentages of children participating in other government welfare programs were as follows: food stamps, 14.4 per cent; cash assistance, 13.6 per cent; Medicaid, 12.6 per cent; and subsidized housing and supplemental food assistance, 5.2 per cent.

HHS Reorganized. Secretary of Health and Human Services (HHS) Otis R. Bowen announced on March 17 a major reorganization combining six programs costing more than $11 billion a year and directed at low-income families. The largest of the programs, costing more than $8 billion, was Aid to Families with Dependent Children (AFDC). Two others—community services block grants and the welfare work-incentive program—were among programs President Ronald Reagan has proposed abolishing. Bowen expressed hope that the new Family Support Administration would give greater visibility to the programs and provide better services and policies.

Although such large welfare programs as AFDC, Medicaid, and food stamps are protected against inflation, social welfare programs generally have been cut rather than expanded during Reagan's Administration. In adopting a budget resolution for the 1987 fiscal year, however, Congress called for a three-year, $1.5-billion increase in some relatively small but important programs affecting children. These included added funds for compensatory education for schoolchildren; the Head Start preschool program; immunization services; and infant, maternal, and child health care.

On February 4, in his State of the Union message, President Reagan announced a yearlong study to develop "a strategy for immediate action to meet the financial, educational, social, and safety concerns of poor people." The study was being conducted by the White House Domestic Policy Council headed by Attorney General Edwin Meese III.

Public debate continued in 1986 about whether hunger and homelessness had increased during the Reagan Administration. President Reagan told a high school group on May 21, "I don't believe that there is anyone going hungry in America simply by reason of denial or lack of ability to feed them. It is by people not knowing where or how to get help."   Frank Cormier and Margot Cormier

In WORLD BOOK, see WELFARE.

Jubilant Haitians lift a soldier onto their shoulders in February in celebration of the ouster of President Jean-Claude Duvalier.

WEST INDIES. United States President Ronald Reagan visited Grenada on Feb. 20, 1986, to attend a meeting of Caribbean leaders and to honor the U.S. servicemen who died during the United States invasion of the island in 1983. During his visit, Reagan spoke of his efforts to bolster the economies of Caribbean nations by encouraging U.S. companies to invest in the area. "The climate [in the Caribbean] has become brighter for American business," he told entrepreneurs in Grenada. "It's encouraging to witness what can happen . . . where free enterprise is allowed to flourish."

But many people in the Caribbean felt that Reagan's comments were at odds with the facts. Since he took office, several large U.S. firms have shut down or sold their operations in the West Indies because of political and economic uncertainties. Reagan's own program, the Caribbean Basin Initiative (CBI), has failed to spur U.S. companies to invest in the region, despite the fact that it allows Caribbean-made products to be imported duty-free into the United States. According to figures released by the U.S. Department of Commerce in February 1986, imports from CBI nations had fallen 23 per cent since 1984.

Sugar Quotas. Carlos Morales Troncoso, vice president of the Dominican Republic, attributed the Caribbean's worsening economic troubles to the tightened import quotas for sugar announced by the United States on March 3. According to Troncoso, the U.S. action cut sugar quotas by an estimated 1.7 million short tons (1.5 million metric tons), which translated into a loss of approximately $300 million annually for Caribbean sugar producers.

Dominican Republic. On August 16, Joaquín Balaguer, 78, was inaugurated as president of the Dominican Republic. Balaguer served three previous terms as president during the 1960's and 1970's. See BALAGUER, JOAQUÍN.

Haiti. Following three months of increasingly intense antigovernment protests, Haiti's President Jean-Claude Duvalier fled the island on February 7. His departure ended 29 years of father-son dictatorship.

Grenada. On December 4, 14 people were sentenced to hang for the slaying in 1983 of Prime Minister Maurice Bishop, which touched off the U.S. invasion of the island. Three others were given prison sentences of up to 45 years, and a fourth was acquitted.   Nathan A. Haverstock

See also HAITI; LATIN AMERICA (Facts in Brief Table). In WORLD BOOK, see WEST INDIES.

WEST VIRGINIA. See STATE GOVERNMENT.

WISCONSIN. See STATE GOVERNMENT.

WYOMING. See STATE GOVERNMENT.

YEMEN (ADEN). See MIDDLE EAST.

YEMEN (SANA). See MIDDLE EAST.

YOUTH ORGANIZATIONS. The Boy Scouts of America (BSA) launched two nationwide service projects in 1986. In an effort to help educate Americans about the need to donate tissue and organs for transplants, Scouts distributed information on the subject to family members and neighbors. The BSA also addressed the issue of child sexual abuse by distributing a booklet called *Child Abuse: Let's Talk About It.* The booklet urges parents to discuss this issue with their children and outlines steps to help families deal with suspected cases of sexual abuse.

The BSA expanded Cub Scouting in 1986 by revising membership requirements so that school grade rather than age is the primary requirement for membership and advancement in the program. As a result, all boys in first grade are eligible to join Tiger Cubs. Previously, a boy had to be 7 years old to join. *Boys' Life*, the official magazine of the BSA, celebrated its 75th anniversary in 1986.

Boys Clubs of America (BCA) in 1986 began "Targeted Outreach," a delinquency-prevention program aimed at both delinquent youths and youths in danger of becoming delinquent. The program attempts to channel their energies into more positive pursuits, such as sports. Another new program, "Career Exposure and Exploration," provides information about careers.

In May, BCA began a campaign to collect a million signatures from young people pledging to avoid drugs and encourage their friends to do the same. The organization introduced "Drug Free . . . and Proud to Be," a drug-abuse prevention program that helps young people resist peer and social pressure to take drugs. This program was to be used together with another new program, "Stand Up and Be Counted," designed to encourage teen-agers to avoid drugs and alcohol and to avoid teen-age pregnancy by delaying sexual activity. In September, Shawn Southard of Pittsfield, Mass., was named the 1986-1987 National Youth of the Year.

Camp Fire in 1986 introduced a new uniform for members in club and camping programs. It consists of a white knit shirt with *Camp Fire* printed on the collar in red and blue, and royal-blue pants, shorts, and skirts. A blue cap with the organization's logo completes the uniform.

In June, Camp Fire began a six-month nationwide survey to determine the organization's public image. Camp Fire plans to use the information to help determine its goals and programs for the rest of the 1980's.

4-H Clubs in 1986 expanded their efforts to help young people deal with social and economic problems. Many local 4-H clubs began programs on

President Corazon Aquino of the Philippines receives congratulations after being sworn in as one of that country's newest Girl Scout leaders in April.

drug and alcohol abuse, suicide, teen-age pregnancy, and stress. The organization responded to the financial crisis facing many United States farmers by expanding programs on farm management and marketing and by stepping up efforts to help farm families cope with stress. New programs also helped young people to learn more about economics and to develop work skills.

4-H's Young Agricultural Specialist Exchange Program between the United States and the Soviet Union was reinstated in 1986, with four Soviet agriculture students coming to the United States for study. The program had been discontinued after the 1979 Soviet invasion of Afghanistan. About 1,500 4-H members and supporters attended the 65th National 4-H Congress, held in Chicago from Dec. 6 to 11, 1986.

Future Farmers of America (FFA) held its 59th annual convention in Kansas City, Mo., from November 13 to 15. At the convention, which was attended by nearly 22,000 FFA members and supporters, Chris Thompson, 21, of Midland City, Ala., was named Star Farmer of America. Todd Wilkinson, 20, of White House, Tenn., was named Star Agribusinessman. Also at the convention, Steven McKay of Boonville, Calif., was named the first national winner of the Agri-Science Teacher of the Year award. Established in 1986, the award recognizes agriculture teachers of grades 7 through 12 who stress the applications of agricultural science technology in their curriculums.

Girl Scouts of the United States of America (GSUSA) kicked off a national substance-abuse awareness project in November 1986. The organization also distributed an information booklet called *Tune In to Well-Being: Say No to Drugs*, the first in a series of booklets on contemporary issues for Girl Scout leaders. In July, the GSUSA introduced a second booklet, *Staying Safe*. It discusses actions girls can take to prevent sexual abuse.

In 1986, GSUSA released new handbooks for Brownie and Junior Girl Scouts. The organization also introduced new uniforms for Brownie Girl Scouts. Also in 1986, two Senior Girl Scouts traveled to Antarctica as part of a research expedition. It was the first time the GSUSA had participated in a project sponsored by the National Science Foundation, a federal agency that supports scientific research.

Girls Clubs of America (GCA) launched two new programs in 1986. "Preventing Adolescent Pregnancy," designed for girls ages 12 through 18, includes role-playing to teach girls how to say no to early sexual involvement. "Sporting Chance" encourages girls to become involved in sports as a means of developing their self-esteem and learning leadership and teamwork skills.   Barbara A. Mayes

In WORLD BOOK, see entries on the individual organizations.

YUGOSLAVIA suffered from an economic slump in 1986. In the first nine months of the year, Yugoslavia exported 3.4 per cent less than during the same period of 1985. Exports to the West were 1.1 per cent lower; exports to Communist countries, 6.6 per cent lower. Imports from the West were up 3.4 per cent, while those from the Communist world were down 3.1 per cent.

The government froze prices from July 1 to November 1 to slow down inflation. By the end of the freeze, however, inflation was running at an annual rate of 90.3 per cent.

Business and Labor. On October 29, the Federal Assembly (parliament) passed a law providing for the closure of nonprofitable state-owned businesses. (In Yugoslavia, which is a Communist country, the state owns all large businesses.) The government also announced changes in accounting procedures to enable business managers to determine profitability more easily.

The government issued a decree in June 1986 aimed at rolling back "unjustified" wage increases. Workers responded with strikes. In 1986, Yugoslavia had twice as many strikes as in 1985.

New Leaders. In May 1986, Milka Planinc completed her four-year term as prime minister. Branko Mikulić, an ethnic Croat from the Republic of Bosnia and Hercegovina, succeeded her.

Presidents Daniel Ortega of Nicaragua, left, and Sinan Hasani of Yugoslavia review troops during Ortega's visit to Yugoslavia in August.

Mikulić had a reputation as a good organizer and a hard-line Communist. Sinan Hasani, an ethnic Albanian from Kosovo Province in the Republic of Serbia, became president for one year, succeeding Radovan Vlajković.

Tension in Kosovo between the ethnic Albanian majority and the Serbian minority persisted in 1986. Ethnic Albanians want to upgrade Kosovo to the status of a republic. A law passed in July prohibited ethnic Albanians from buying land in villages occupied mostly by ethnic Serbs.

War Criminal. On February 12, the United States extradited Andrija Artuković to Yugoslavia. Artuković had been minister of the interior in Croatia during World War II, serving under German and Italian occupation forces. He had entered the United States under a false name in 1948. In April 1986, a Yugoslav court tried him as a war criminal. He received a death sentence in May.

Yugoslav Farmers harvested 4.8 million metric tons (5.3 million short tons) of wheat in 1986, 1 per cent less than in 1985. Corn production was 12 million metric tons (13.2 million short tons) in 1986, 23 per cent more than in 1985.

Big Mac Invades. In November, Yugoslavia signed an agreement for the opening of five McDonald's restaurants in Yugoslavia.   Chris Cviic

See also EUROPE (Facts in Brief Table). In WORLD BOOK, see YUGOSLAVIA.

YUKON TERRITORY. A new commissioner for Yukon Territory, J. Kenneth McKinnon, was appointed on March 3, 1986. Although the commissioner holds authority from the federal government to administer the territory, the day-to-day business of government is carried out by the government leader (the head of the political party in power) and his colleagues. McKinnon, who was born in Yukon, had been a minister in the territorial government and later the general manager of a television system.

The political makeup of the territory's Legislative Assembly remained unchanged during the first year in office of the New Democratic Party (NDP) administration elected on May 13, 1985. Of the 16 Assembly seats, the NDP held 8, the Progressive Conservatives 6, and the Liberals 1, with 1 vacancy left after a Liberal member resigned on Oct. 31, 1986.

The reopening of the Cyprus Anvil lead-zinc mine at Faro in January brought an important source of employment and gave new hope to the territory, hard hit by the world fall in ore prices. The mine, closed in 1982, once accounted for 14 per cent of the jobs in the Yukon.   David M. L. Farr

See also CANADA. In WORLD BOOK, see YUKON TERRITORY.

ZAIRE. See AFRICA.

ZAMBIA. See AFRICA.

ZIMBABWE. Foreign-policy initiatives and discussions of a large building program highlighted the eighth conference of the nonaligned movement—a group of 101 Third World nations and organizations—held in September 1986 in Zimbabwe's capital, Harare. Fifty heads of state and other delegates attended the meeting. Zimbabwe's Prime Minister Robert Gabriel Mugabe, the incoming chairman of the nonaligned movement, steered the agenda toward resolutions condemning *apartheid*, South Africa's system of racial segregation.

Relations with South Africa. Despite Zimbabwe's heavy trade, transport, and other links with South Africa, Mugabe vigorously urged the Organization of African Unity; the Commonwealth (Great Britain and its former colonies); the European Community (EC or Common Market); and the United States to impose economic *sanctions* (penalties) on South Africa. Mugabe was critical of the British government's opposition to strong sanctions.

Zimbabwe was angered in May by a South African raid in Harare on suspected sanctuaries of the African National Congress, the main black dissident group opposing apartheid. Mugabe also criticized South African support of rebel groups in Mozambique and Angola.

One-Party State. Progress continued in talks, started in 1985, aimed at merging Mugabe's Zim-

Zimbabwe's Prime Minister Robert Mugabe inspects damage caused in Harare in May by a South African raid on a black nationalist group's headquarters.

babwe African National Union-Patriotic Front (ZANU-PF) and rival Joshua Nkomo's Zimbabwe African People's Union (ZAPU). The two parties held a joint political rally in March in Bulawayo, and the government released some jailed ZAPU leaders.

Mugabe in February reaffirmed his intention to amend the Constitution in 1987. Mugabe hopes to eliminate the upper chamber of the Parliament and strip the white minority of its 20 reserved seats in the lower chamber.

Human Rights. A number of international religious and human-rights groups charged the Mugabe government in 1986 with detention of political dissidents, torture of prisoners, and control of the courts. In August, the government threatened to arrest people if they talked to investigators of Amnesty International, a London-based human-rights organization.

Relations with the United States, already in a bad state, declined further after a diplomatic incident on July 4 at the U.S. Embassy in Harare when former President Jimmy Carter walked out on a Zimbabwean speaker who was criticizing the United States. The U.S. Department of State subsequently said American aid to Zimbabwe would cease.   J. Gus Liebenow and Beverly B. Liebenow

See also AFRICA (Facts in Brief Table). In WORLD BOOK, see ZIMBABWE.

ZOOLOGY. Within the next few decades, between 25 and 50 per cent of the world's species of plants and animals may become extinct. Scientists speaking at a conference in Washington, D.C., sponsored by the National Academy of Sciences and the Smithsonian Institution, in September 1986 issued this warning and urged strong measures to counteract the problem. The major cause of the potential extinction, they said, is the destruction of tropical forests.

Forests Cover only 7 per cent of Earth's surface, but they are home to half of Earth's species. The greatest diversity of species is found in tropical forests. Biologist Edward O. Wilson of Harvard University in Cambridge, Mass., said at the conference that he had found 43 ant species on a single tropical tree, comparable to the total number of ant species found in Great Britain.

Tropical forests are being destroyed at a rate of 92,000 square kilometers (35,500 square miles) per year, according to environmentalist Norman Myers of Oxford, England. Land is being cleared by small-scale slash-and-burn farming, by massive logging operations, and by the collection of firewood. Many biologists believe the world's tropical forests will be destroyed by the end of the century.

In 1986, Congress passed legislation addressing the tropical forest crisis. A sum of $2.5 million was designated from the funds of the Agency for International Development (AID) to save endangered species in the developing countries where most tropical forests are located. AID is a U.S. agency that administers economic and technical foreign aid programs. The legislation also prohibits AID funding to countries engaged in certain tropical deforestation practices. These legislative steps were considered encouraging, but many biologists warned that the problems facing the world's tropical forests require massive funding.

Flying Primates? Animals as distantly related as birds, insects, and the extinct reptiles known as pterosaurs all developed the ability to fly. Among mammals, only bats can truly fly—"flying" squirrels glide, rather than fly.

All bats have traditionally been grouped under the scientific classification Chiroptera. Experts have always realized, however, that the classification includes two very different sorts of bats. One suborder—the small, mouse-sized, insect-eating Microchiroptera, also known as *microbats*—live throughout the world, including the United States. They generally have poor eyesight but find their food and navigate by means of a remarkable *echolocation* system. With echolocation, bats make high-frequency sounds, and by hearing the echoes created when these sounds bounce off objects, they can locate prey and navigate.

The other suborder—the larger, squirrel-sized, fruit- and flower-eating Megachiroptera, also known as *megabats*—live in the tropics. They have excellent eyesight and are able to locate food and navigate largely with vision. These and other differences between microbats and megabats have led biologists to wonder just how closely related the two groups really are.

In March 1986, physiologist John D. Pettigrew of the University of Queensland in Brisbane, Australia, reported finding strong evidence that these two types of bats are only distantly related and may have independently evolved the ability to fly.

Pettigrew studied the nerve connection between the eyes and the brain in several kinds of bats. He examined three species of flying foxes, a type of megabat, and one species of microbat, the Australian ghost bat. By studying their anatomies and the electrical responses between the eyes and brain, Pettigrew found completely different nerve connections in the two types of bats.

The microbats had an eye-brain connection similar to most mammals. But the megabat species had a connection similar to only one other mammalian group—the primates, which include human beings, apes, and monkeys. This finding suggests that megabats may be primates. If Pettigrew's theory is correct, true flight may have evolved twice in mammals.   Clyde Freeman Herreid II

See also PALEONTOLOGY; ZOOS. In WORLD BOOK, see ZOOLOGY.

A rare baby spectacled bear, born on January 14 at the Lincoln Park Zoo in Chicago, sniffs the paw of its mother, Speckles.

ZOOS and aquariums in the United States continued to improve their facilities in 1986 by opening imaginative exhibits devoted to specific *ecosystems*, areas in which animals and plants live together, such as forests or deserts. On February 14, the Arizona-Sonora Desert Museum in Tucson opened a naturalistic mountain habitat for large animals. The habitat provides mountain lions with canyon ledges and a stream. Black bears, white-tailed deer, and endangered Mexican wolves live in ravines, *arroyos* (dry stream beds), and mountains.

The diversity of four regional aquatic ecosystems in the United States is demonstrated at Aquaticus, a 65,000-square-foot (6,000-square-meter) marine-life center that opened on April 6 at the Oklahoma City (Okla.) Zoo. The center contrasts the fish and plant life of the Pacific Northwest, the Gulf of Mexico, the New England and Atlantic states, and the lakes, rivers, swamps, and streams of Oklahoma.

A replica of Australia's Great Barrier Reef opened on June 14 at the San Antonio Zoo. Visitors board a boat that travels along a canal past five aquariums containing a total of 85,000 gallons (322,000 liters) of salt water and a variety of marine life, including lemon sharks, moray eels, and colorful reef fishes.

Savannas on View. The San Diego Zoo took the first step toward creating a large *savanna* (grassland) exhibit when it opened an East African ecosystem habitat on July 4. Visitors follow a path that winds through reproductions of *kopjes* (pronounced *KAHP eez*)—"islands" of rock that were formed by volcanic action millions of years ago and that rise abruptly from the plains. The route offers a variety of angles and levels for viewing such mammals as *klipspringers* (small antelope); *rock hyraxes* (gopherlike animals related to the elephant); and pygmy mongooses.

On September 7, the Toledo (Ohio) Zoo unveiled the first part of a savanna exhibit. Wild grasses, trees, and other plants create an environment for elephants, hippopotamuses, and crocodiles.

Ape World. On June 7, the Philadelphia Zoo opened its World of Primates, outdoor habitats for gorillas, gibbons, orangutans, lemurs, and *drills* (African forest-dwelling baboons). On June 14, the St. Louis (Mo.) Zoo inaugurated Jungle of the Apes, a spacious indoor forest for chimpanzees, gorillas, and orangutans, containing abundant vegetation and waterfalls. A thatched-roof bridge gives visitors a treetop view of the orangutans.

A New Zoo. One of the most notable premieres in 1986 took place August 2 in Syracuse, N.Y., when the city opened Burnet Park Zoo. The new zoo replaces an outdated facility that closed in 1983. The 36-acre (14.5-hectare) park traces the evolution of Earth's inhabitants, using living ani-

Gorillas roam through an indoor forest in the realistic Jungle of the Apes exhibit that opened at the St. Louis (Mo.) Zoo on June 14.

mals to illustrate biological and ecological themes. To explore "antiquity," visitors enter a cave housing such invertebrates as anemones, horseshoe crabs, and starfish, representing the watery origins of life 600 million years ago. The story continues with sharks, which appeared 500 million years ago, and progresses to life today. Subsequent exhibits show how species adapted to different habitats.

Hot and Cold Habitats. In Portland, Ore., the Washington Park Zoo opened new bear grottoes on September 26. Entering through a tunnel, visitors have an underwater view of polar bears in a winter habitat along a rocky, snow-dusted shoreline. The next scene displays the bears in their summer habitat where machine-made waves ripple onto a stony beach. The final scene shifts from polar bears to small sun bears, which are housed in a replica of an Asian tropical forest.

On September 27, New York City's Bronx Zoo opened Himalayan Highlands, a showcase for snow leopards. The new habitat minimizes or hides barriers so that visitors can see the leopards gliding through a spacious, naturalistic forest or bounding down steep rocky slopes as they would in their native Nepal or Tibet. The 2½-acre (1-hectare) exhibit also includes vividly colored pheasants, red pandas, and white-necked cranes.

Rarities. American zoos displayed some unusual species in 1986. The Audubon Park Zoo in New Orleans introduced *Chinese pangolins* (scaly members of the anteater family) on June 12—the only such animals on exhibit in the Western Hemisphere. Several West Coast zoos displayed golden monkeys from China. One of the world's rarest primates, the golden monkey stands up to 4 feet (1.2 meters) tall and has long golden fur, a powder-blue face, and a unique turned-up nose. Among the zoos displaying these monkeys, Portland's Washington Park was the most fortunate—a male golden monkey was born there on July 24. The golden monkeys were also shown at the Woodland Park Zoo in Seattle and at the San Francisco Zoo. The monkeys were returned to China at the end of the summer.

Significant Births. On June 7, the first hatching of a secretary bird in the United States occurred at the Oklahoma City Zoo. The secretary bird is a long-legged predator of the African savanna.

Although Siberian tiger births are relatively common in zoos, an important pair of cubs arrived on April 22 at the Bronx Zoo. Their mother came to New York City from the Soviet Union in 1983 and is a direct descendant of one of the last Siberian tigers removed from the wild. The births of the cubs expanded the gene pool of Siberian tigers in the United States, which is of vital importance in avoiding inbreeding.   Eugene J. Walter, Jr.

In the Special Reports section, see THE NEW LOOK IN ZOOS. In WORLD BOOK, see ZOO.

Answers to the Quiz

1. Moscow.

2. He survived for 620 days with an artificial heart implant, longer than any other human being with the device.

3. U.S. secretary of agriculture.

4. Vladimir Horowitz.

5. A rail tunnel linking the two countries under the English Channel.

6. Cameroon.

7. All the deaths were caused by cyanide-tainted Tylenol capsules.

8. The United States Football League.

9. The Dow Jones Industrial Average.

10. Bolivia.

11. The United States and the Soviet Union.

12. Bicycle racing.

13. *Out of Africa.*

14. Her Royal Highness the Princess Andrew, Duchess of York.

15. Clint Eastwood, who was elected mayor of Carmel-by-the-Sea, Calif.

16. The Statue of Liberty.

17. Jack Nicklaus.

18. Philadelphia and Detroit.

19. Emperor Hirohito of Japan.

20. Chief justice of the United States.

21. The Hands Across America benefit for the homeless.

22. Soccer.

23. *Voyager.*

24. Israel.

25. A series of terrorist bombings.

26. It is being shipped to the drought-stricken Southeast to feed starving livestock.

27. Andrew Wyeth.

28. The World Jewish Congress, several newspapers, and other organizations charged that Waldheim had committed Nazi war crimes.

29. 1, c; 2, d; 3, b; 4, e; 5, a.

30. The rose.

31. U.S. Air Force and Navy jets bombed military and terrorist targets in Libya.

32. South Africa.

33. Alabama Governor George C. Wallace.

34. Switzerland.

35. An imaginary line drawn by Libya across the north end of the Gulf of Sidra. Libya claims the waters south of the line, but the United States and most other governments consider them international territory.

36. Prime Minister Olof Palme of Sweden.

37. The Democratic Party, which gained 8 seats to establish a 55-45 majority.

38. President Jean-Claude Duvalier of Haiti and President Ferdinand E. Marcos of the Philippines.

39. Libya.

40. Civil rights leader Martin Luther King, Jr.

41. An American journalist arrested in Moscow by Soviet KGB police and charged with spying. He was released in September.

42. The Berlin Wall separating East and West Berlin.

43. The Tax Reform Act of 1986.

44. The four finalists for the men's and women's singles titles were all born in Czechoslovakia.

45. Chile's President Augusto Pinochet Ugarte.

46. For the first time in history, both major parties in the state nominated a woman for governor.

47. Halley's Comet.

48. Divorce.

49. The Teamsters Union, which elected Jackie Presser.

50. Iran.

World Book Supplement

To help WORLD BOOK owners keep their encyclopedias up to date, the following new or revised articles are reprinted from the 1987 edition of the encyclopedia.

530   **World War I**
546   **World War II**
578   **AIDS**
578   **Artificial Heart**
579   **Cyclosporine**
579   **Magellanic Clouds**
579   **Milky Way**

See "World War II," p. 561.

Soldiers Headed for the Battlefront at first welcomed the outbreak of World War I. The German soldiers at the left received flowers as they marched off to France. The French cavalrymen at the right confidently rode off to drive the Germans back. Each side expected quick victory.

WORLD WAR I

WORLD WAR I (1914-1918) involved more countries and caused greater destruction than any other war except World War II (1939-1945). An assassin's bullets set off the war, and a system of military *alliances* (agreements) quickly plunged the major European powers into the fight. Each of the warring nations expected quick victory. But the fighting lasted four years and took the lives of nearly 10 million soldiers.

Several developments led to the awful bloodshed of the Great War, as World War I was originally called. War plants kept turning out vast quantities of newly invented weapons capable of extraordinary slaughter. Military drafts raised larger armies than ever before, and extreme patriotism gave many men a cause they were willing to die for. Propaganda whipped up support for the war by making the enemy seem villainous.

On June 28, 1914, an assassin gunned down Archduke Francis Ferdinand of Austria-Hungary in Sarajevo, the capital of Austria-Hungary's province of Bosnia. The killer, Gavrilo Princip, had ties to a terrorist organization in Serbia (now part of Yugoslavia). Austria-Hungary believed that Serbia's government was behind the assassination. It seized the opportunity to declare war on Serbia and settle an old feud.

The assassination of Francis Ferdinand sparked the outbreak of World War I. But historians believe that the war had deeper causes. It resulted chiefly from the growth of extreme national pride among various European peoples, an enormous increase in European armed forces, a race for colonies, and the formation of military alliances. When the fighting began, France, Great Britain, and Russia—who were known as the Allies—supported Serbia. The Allies opposed the Central Powers, made up of Austria-Hungary and Germany. Other

Edward M. Coffman, the contributor of this article, is Professor of History at the University of Wisconsin-Madison and the author of The War to End All Wars: The American Military Experience in World War I.

nations later joined the Allies or the Central Powers.

Germany won early victories in World War I on the main European battlefronts. On the Western Front, France and Britain halted the German advance in September 1914. The opposing armies then fought from trenches that stretched across Belgium and northeastern France. The Western Front hardly moved for $3\frac{1}{2}$ years in spite of fierce combat. On the Eastern Front, Russia battled Germany and Austria-Hungary. The fighting seesawed back and forth until 1917, when a revolution broke out in Russia. Russia soon asked for a truce.

The United States remained neutral in the early years of World War I. But many Americans turned against the Central Powers after German submarines began sinking unarmed ships. In 1917, the United States entered the war on the Allies' side. American troops gave the Allies the manpower they needed to win the war. In the fall of 1918, the Central Powers surrendered.

World War I had results that none of the warring nations had foreseen. The war helped topple emperors in Austria-Hungary, Germany, and Russia. The peace treaties after the war carved new nations out of the defeated powers. The war left Europe exhausted, never to regain the controlling position in world affairs that it had held before the war. The peace settlement also created conditions that helped lead to World War II.

Causes of the War

The assassination of Archduke Francis Ferdinand triggered World War I. But the war had its origins in developments of the 1800's. The chief causes of World War I were (1) the rise of nationalism, (2) a build-up of military might, (3) competition for colonies, and (4) a system of military alliances.

The Rise of Nationalism. Europe avoided major wars in the 100 years before World War I began. Although small wars broke out, they did not involve many countries. But during the 1800's, a force swept across the continent that helped bring about the Great War. The force was *nationalism*—the belief that loyalty to a person's nation and its political and economic goals comes before any other public loyalty. That exaggerated form of pa-

Destruction and Death, instead of quick victory, awaited the warring nations in the long and brutal conflict. After fierce fighting in Belgium, the city of Ypres lay in ruins, *left.* Many men, like the French soldier on the right, met death in a trench along the Western Front.

triotism increased the possibility of war because a nation's goals inevitably came into conflict with the goals of one or more other nations. In addition, nationalistic pride caused nations to magnify small disputes into major issues. A minor complaint could thus quickly lead to the threat of war.

During the 1800's, nationalism took hold among people who shared a common language, history, or culture. Such people began to view themselves as members of a national group, or nation. Nationalism led to the creation of two new powers—Italy and Germany—through the uniting of many small states. War played a major role in achieving national unification in both Italy and Germany.

Nationalist policies gained enthusiastic support as many countries in western Europe granted the vote to more people. The right to vote gave citizens greater in-

The Warring Nations

The table below indicates the date on which each of the Allies and Central Powers entered World War I. More than 20 countries eventually joined the war on the Allied side. However, not all of them sent troops.

The Allies

Belgium (Aug. 4, 1914)	Japan (Aug. 23, 1914)
Brazil (Oct. 26, 1917)	Liberia (Aug. 4, 1917)
British Empire	Montenegro
(Aug. 4, 1914)	(Aug. 5, 1914)
China (Aug. 14, 1917)	Nicaragua (May 8, 1918)
Costa Rica	Panama (April 7, 1917)
(May 23, 1918)	Portugal (March 9, 1916)
Cuba (April 7, 1917)	Romania (Aug. 27, 1916)
France (Aug. 3, 1914)	Russia (Aug. 1, 1914)
Greece (July 2, 1917)	San Marino
Guatemala	(June 3, 1915)
(April 23, 1918)	Serbia (July 28, 1914)
Haiti (July 12, 1918)	Siam (July 22, 1917)
Honduras (July 19, 1918)	United States
Italy (May 23, 1915)	(April 6, 1917)

The Central Powers

Austria-Hungary	Germany (Aug. 1, 1914)
(July 28, 1914)	Ottoman Empire
Bulgaria (Oct. 14, 1915)	(Oct. 31, 1914)

terest and greater pride in national goals. As a result, parliamentary governments grew increasingly powerful.

On the other hand, nationalism weakened the eastern European empires of Austria-Hungary, Russia, and Ottoman Turkey. Those empires ruled many national groups that clamored for independence. Conflicts among national groups were especially explosive in the Balkans—the states on the Balkan Peninsula in southeastern Europe. The peninsula was known as the "Powder Keg of Europe" because tensions there threatened to ignite a major war. Most of the Balkans had once formed part of the Ottoman Empire. First Greece and then Montenegro, Serbia, Romania, Bulgaria, and Albania gained independence in the period from 1821 to 1913. Each state quarreled with its neighbors over national boundaries. Austria-Hungary and Russia also took advantage of the Ottoman Empire's weakness to increase their influence in the Balkans.

Rivalry for control of the Balkans added to the tensions that erupted into World War I. Serbia led a movement to unite the region's Slavs. Russia, the most powerful Slavic country, supported Serbia. But Austria-Hungary feared Slavic nationalism, which stirred unrest in its empire. Millions of Slavs lived under Austria-Hungary's rule. In 1908, Austria-Hungary greatly angered Serbia by adding the Balkan territories of Bosnia and Hercegovina to its empire. Serbia wanted control of those lands because many Serbs lived there.

A Build-up of Military Might occurred among European countries before World War I broke out. Nationalism encouraged public support for military build-ups and for a country's use of force to achieve its goals. By the late 1800's, Germany had the best-trained army in the world. It relied on a military draft of all able-bodied young men to increase the size and strength of its peacetime army. Other European countries followed Germany's lead and expanded their standing armies.

At first, Great Britain remained unconcerned about Germany's military build-up. Britain, an island country, relied on its navy for defense—and it had the world's strongest navy. But in 1898, Germany began to develop a naval force big enough to challenge the British navy.

WORLD WAR I

Important Dates During World War I

1914

June 28 Archduke Francis Ferdinand was assassinated.
July 28 Austria-Hungary declared war on Serbia. Several other declarations of war followed during the next week.
Aug. 4 Germany invaded Belgium and started the fighting.
Aug. 10 Austria-Hungary invaded Russia, opening the fighting on the Eastern Front.
Sept. 6-9 The Allies stopped the Germans in France in the First Battle of the Marne.

1915

Feb. 18 Germany began to blockade Great Britain.
April 25 Allied troops landed on the Gallipoli Peninsula.
May 7 A German submarine sank the liner *Lusitania.*
May 23 Italy declared war on Austria-Hungary, and an Italian Front soon developed.

1916

Feb. 21 The Germans opened the Battle of Verdun.
May 31-June 1 The British fleet fought the German fleet in the Battle of Jutland.
July 1 The Allies launched the Battle of the Somme.

1917

Feb. 1 Germany resumed unrestricted submarine warfare.
April 6 The United States declared war on Germany.
June 24 American troops began landing in France.
Dec. 15 Russia signed an armistice with Germany, ending the fighting on the Eastern Front.

1918

Jan. 8 President Woodrow Wilson announced his Fourteen Points as the basis for peace.
March 3 Russia signed the Treaty of Brest-Litovsk.
March 21 Germany launched the first of its final three offensives on the Western Front.
Sept. 26 The Allies began their final offensive on the Western Front.
Nov. 11 Germany signed an armistice ending World War I.

Germany's decision to become a major seapower made it a bitter enemy of Great Britain. In 1906, the British navy launched the *Dreadnought,* the first modern battleship. The heavily armed *Dreadnought* had greater firepower than any other ship of its time. Germany rushed to construct ships like it.

Advances in *technology*—the tools, materials, and techniques of industrialization—increased the destructive power of military forces. Machine guns and other new arms fired more accurately and more rapidly than earlier weapons. Steamships and railroads could speed the movement of troops and supplies. By the end of the 1800's, modern technology enabled countries to fight longer wars and bear greater losses than ever before. Yet military experts insisted that future wars would be short.

Competition for Colonies. During the late 1800's and early 1900's, European nations carved nearly all of Africa and much of Asia into colonies. The race for colonies was fueled by Europe's ever-increasing industrialization. Colonies supplied European nations with raw materials for factories, markets for manufactured goods, and opportunities for investment. But the competition for colonies and foreign trade strained relations among European countries. Incidents between rival powers flared up almost every year. Several of the clashes nearly developed into war.

A System of Military Alliances gave European powers a sense of security before World War I. A country hoped to discourage an attack from its enemies by entering into a military agreement with one or more other countries. In case of an attack, such an agreement guaranteed that other members of the alliance would come to the country's aid or at least remain neutral.

Although military alliances provided protection for a country, the system created certain dangers. Because of its alliances, a country might take risks in dealings with other nations that it would hesitate to take alone. If war

World War I Battlefronts

The fighting in World War I spread from western Europe to the Middle East. The key battles were fought along the Western Front, which stretched across Belgium and France, and along the Eastern Front, which seesawed across Russia and Austria-Hungary.

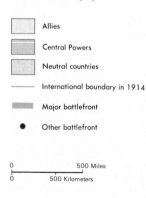

Allies

Central Powers

Neutral countries

International boundary in 1914

Major battlefront

● Other battlefront

0   500 Miles
0   500 Kilometers

WORLD BOOK map

came, the alliance system meant that a number of nations would fight, not only the two involved in a dispute. Alliances could force a country to go to war against a nation it had no quarrel with or over an issue it had no interest in. In addition, the terms of many alliances were kept secret. The secrecy increased the chances that a country might guess wrong about the consequences of its actions.

The Triple Alliance. Germany was at the center of European foreign policy from 1870 until the outbreak of World War I. Chancellor Otto von Bismarck, Germany's prime minister, formed a series of alliances to strengthen his country's security. He first made an ally of Austria-Hungary. In 1879, Germany and Austria-Hungary agreed to go to war if either country were attacked by Russia. Italy joined the agreement in 1882, and it became known as the Triple Alliance. The members of the Triple Alliance agreed to aid one another in the case of an attack by two or more countries.

Bismarck also brought Austria-Hungary and Germany into an alliance with Russia. The agreement, known as the Three Emperors' League, was formed in 1881. The three powers agreed to remain neutral if any of them went to war with another country. Bismarck also persuaded Austria-Hungary and Russia, which were rivals for influence in the Balkans, to recognize each other's zone of authority in the region. He thus reduced the danger of conflict between the two countries.

Germany's relations with other European countries worsened after Bismarck left office in 1890. Bismarck had worked to prevent France, Germany's neighbor on the west, from forming an alliance with either of Germany's two neighbors to the east—Russia and Austria-Hungary. In 1894, France and Russia agreed to *mobilize* (call up troops) if any nation in the Triple Alliance mobilized. France and Russia also agreed to help each other if either were attacked by Germany.

The Triple Entente. During the 1800's, Great Britain had followed a foreign policy that became known as "splendid isolation." But Germany's naval build-up made Britain feel the need for allies. The country therefore ended its isolation. In 1904, Britain and France settled their past disagreements over colonies and signed the Entente Cordiale (Friendly Agreement). Although the agreement contained no pledges of military support, the two countries began to discuss joint military plans. In 1907, Russia joined the Entente Cordiale, and it became known as the Triple Entente.

The Triple Entente did not obligate its members to go to war as the Triple Alliance did. But the alliances left Europe divided into two opposing camps.

Beginning of the War

World War I began in the Balkans, the site of many small wars. In the early 1900's, the Balkan states fought the Ottoman Empire in the First Balkan War (1912-1913) and one another in the Second Balkan War (1913). The major European powers stayed out of both wars. But they did not escape the third Balkan crisis.

The Assassination of an Archduke. Archduke Francis Ferdinand, heir to the throne of Austria-Hungary, hoped that his sympathy for Slavs would ease tensions between Austria-Hungary and the Balkans. He arranged to tour Bosnia with his wife, Sophie. As the couple rode through Sarajevo on June 28, 1914, an assassin

UPI/Bettmann Newsphotos

Archduke Francis Ferdinand of Austria-Hungary, *far right,* was shot to death on June 28, 1914, shortly after this photo was taken. His assassination triggered the outbreak of World War I.

jumped on their automobile and fired two shots. Francis Ferdinand and Sophie died almost instantly. The murderer, Gavrilo Princip, was linked to a Serbian terrorist group called the Black Hand.

The assassination of Francis Ferdinand gave Austria-Hungary an excuse to crush Serbia, its long-time enemy in the Balkans. Austria-Hungary first gained Germany's promise of support for any action it took against Serbia. It then sent a list of humiliating demands to Serbia on July 23. Serbia accepted most of the demands and offered to have the rest settled by an international conference. Austria-Hungary rejected the offer and declared war on Serbia on July 28. It expected a quick victory.

How the Conflict Spread. Within weeks of the archduke's assassination, the chief European powers were drawn into World War I. A few attempts were made to prevent the war. For example, Great Britain proposed an international conference to end the crisis. But Germany rejected the idea, claiming that the dispute involved only Austria-Hungary and Serbia. However, Germany tried to stop the war from spreading. The German *kaiser* (emperor), Wilhelm II, urged Czar Nicholas II of Russia, his cousin, not to mobilize.

Russia had backed down before in supporting its ally Serbia. In 1908, Austria-Hungary had angered Serbia by taking over Bosnia and Hercegovina, and Russia had stepped aside. In 1914, Russia vowed to stand behind Serbia. Russia first gained a promise of support from France. The czar then approved plans to mobilize along Russia's border with Austria-Hungary. But Russia's military leaders persuaded the czar to mobilize along the German border, too. On July 30, 1914, Russia announced it would mobilize fully.

Germany declared war on Russia on Aug. 1, 1914, in response to Russia's mobilization. Two days later, Germany declared war on France. The German army swept into Belgium on its way to France. The invasion of neutral Belgium caused Britain to declare war on Germany on August 4. By the time the war ended in November 1918, few areas of the world had remained neutral.

The Western Front. Germany's war plan had been prepared in 1905 by Alfred von Schlieffen. Schlieffen was chief of the German General Staff, the group of officers who provided advice on military operations. The Schlieffen Plan assumed that Germany would have to fight both France and Russia. It aimed at a quick defeat of France while Russia slowly mobilized. After defeating France, Germany would deal with Russia. The Schlieffen Plan required Germany to strike first if war came. Once the plan was set in motion, the system of military alliances almost assured a general European war.

The Schlieffen Plan called for two wings of the German army to crush the French army in a pincers movement. A small left wing would defend Germany along its frontier with France. A much larger right wing would invade France through Belgium; encircle and capture France's capital, Paris; and then move east. As the right wing moved in, the French forces would be trapped between the pincers. The success of Germany's assault depended on a strong right wing. However, Helmuth von Moltke became chief of the General Staff in 1906 and directed German strategy at the outbreak of World War I. Moltke changed the Schlieffen Plan by weakening the right wing.

Belgium's army fought bravely but held up the Germans for only a short time. By Aug. 16, 1914, the right wing of the German army could begin its pincers motion. It drove back French forces and a small British force in southern Belgium and swept into France. But instead of swinging west around Paris according to plan, one part of the right wing pursued retreating French troops east toward the Marne River. The short cut left the Germans exposed to attacks from the rear.

Meanwhile, General Joseph Joffre, commander in chief of all the French armies, had recognized the danger from the German right wing. Joffre stationed his forces near the Marne River east of Paris and prepared for battle. Fierce fighting, which became known as the First Battle of the Marne, began on September 6. On September 9, German forces started to withdraw.

The First Battle of the Marne was a key victory for the Allies because it ended Germany's hopes to defeat France quickly. Moltke was replaced as chief of the German General Staff by Erich von Falkenhayn.

The German army halted its retreat near the Aisne River. From there, the Germans and the Allies fought a series of battles that became known as the Race to the Sea. Germany sought to seize ports on the English Channel and cut off vital supply lines between France and Britain. But the Allies stopped the German advance to the sea in the First Battle of Ypres in Belgium. The battle lasted from mid-October until mid-November.

By late November 1914, the war reached a *deadlock* along the Western Front as neither side gained much ground. The battlefront extended more than 450 miles (720 kilometers) across Belgium and northeastern France to the border of Switzerland. The deadlock on the Western Front lasted $3\frac{1}{2}$ years.

The Eastern Front. Russia's mobilization on the Eastern Front moved faster than Germany expected. By late August 1914, two Russian armies had thrust deeply into the German territory of East Prussia. The Germans learned that the two armies had become separated, and they prepared a battle plan. By August 31, the Germans had encircled one Russian army in the Battle of Tannenberg. They then chased the other Russian army out of East Prussia in the Battle of the Masurian Lakes. The number of Russian *casualties*—that is, the number of men killed, captured, wounded, or missing—totaled about 250,000 in the two battles. The victories made heroes of the commanders of the German forces in the east—Paul von Hindenburg and Erich Ludendorff.

Austria-Hungary had less success than its German ally on the Eastern Front. By the end of 1914, Austria-Hungary's forces had attacked Serbia three times and

The Western Front: 1914-1917

Fighting began in August 1914, when Germany invaded Belgium and France. The two sides were locked in trench warfare along the Western Front by year's end. The Western Front remained deadlocked for nearly $3\frac{1}{2}$ years.

Allies

Central Powers

Neutral countries

International boundary in 1914

Farthest German advance into France – September 1914

Trench line after November 1914

Allied forces

German forces

✳ Major battle

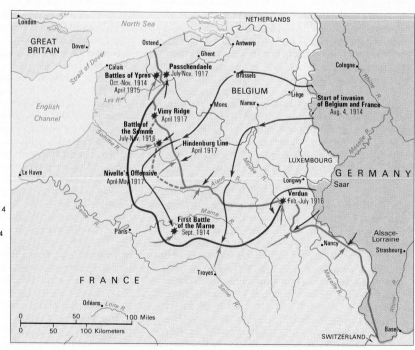

Weapons of World War I

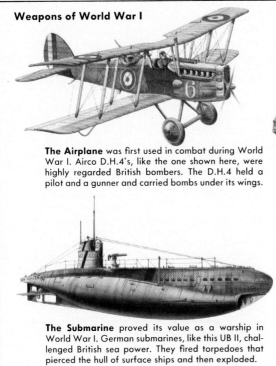

The Airplane was first used in combat during World War I. Airco D.H.4's, like the one shown here, were highly regarded British bombers. The D.H.4 held a pilot and a gunner and carried bombs under its wings.

The Tank was a British invention of World War I. Tanks were designed to rip through barbed wire and crawl across trenches. Crews inside gunned down the enemy. This MK IV tank first saw action in 1917.

The Machine Gun made World War I more deadly than earlier wars. The gun's rapid fire slaughtered attacking infantrymen. The 8-millimeter Hotchkiss gun used by the French army is shown here.

The Submarine proved its value as a warship in World War I. German submarines, like this UB II, challenged British sea power. They fired torpedoes that pierced the hull of surface ships and then exploded.

WORLD BOOK illustrations by Tony Gibbons, Linden Artists Ltd.

been beaten back each time. Meanwhile, Russia had captured much of the Austro-Hungarian province of Galicia (now part of Poland and the Soviet Union). By early October, a humiliated Austro-Hungarian army had retreated into its own territory.

Fighting Elsewhere. The Allies declared war on the Ottoman Empire in November 1914, after Turkish warships bombarded Russian ports on the Black Sea. Turkish troops then invaded southern Russia. Fighting later broke out in the Ottoman territories on the Arabian Peninsula and in Mesopotamia (now mostly Iraq), Palestine, and Syria.

Britain stayed in control of the seas following two naval victories over Germany in 1914. The British then kept Germany's surface fleet bottled up in its home waters during most of the war. As a result, Germany relied on submarine warfare.

World War I quickly spread to Germany's overseas colonies. Japan declared war on Germany in late August 1914 and drove the Germans off several islands in the Pacific Ocean. Troops from Australia and New Zea-

land seized other German colonies in the Pacific. By mid-1915, most of Germany's empire in Africa had fallen to British forces. However, fighting continued in German East Africa (now Tanzania) for two more years.

The Deadlock on the Western Front

By 1915, the opposing sides had dug themselves into a system of trenches that zigzagged along the Western Front. From the trenches, they defended their positions and launched attacks. The Western Front remained deadlocked in trench warfare until 1918.

Trench Warfare. The typical *front-line trench* was about 6 to 8 feet (1.8 to 2.4 meters) deep and wide enough for two men to pass. Dug into the sides of the trenches were holes large enough to protect men during enemy fire. *Support trenches* ran behind the front-line trenches. Off-duty soldiers lived in dugouts in the support trenches. Troops and supplies moved to the battle-front through a network of *communications trenches*. Barbed wire helped protect the front-line trenches from surprise attacks. Field artillery was set up behind the

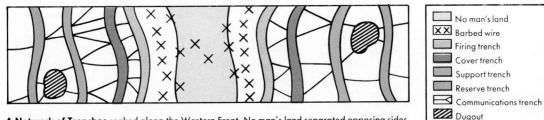

▨	No man's land
XX	Barbed wire
	Firing trench
	Cover trench
	Support trench
	Reserve trench
	Communications trench
▨	Dugout

A Network of Trenches snaked along the Western Front. No man's land separated opposing sides. Firing and cover trenches protected front-line soldiers from enemy fire. Communications trenches linked front lines with support and reserve troops at the rear. Dugouts sheltered off-duty troops.

Gernsheim Collection, Harry Ransom Humanities Research Center, University of Texas

Gas Masks were worn by soldiers on the Western Front for protection against poisonous fumes. Germany was first to use poison gas, in April 1915 during the Second Battle of Ypres.

support trenches. Between the enemy lines lay a stretch of ground called "no man's land." No man's land varied from less than 30 yards (27 meters) wide at some points to more than 1 mile (1.6 kilometers) wide at others. In time, artillery fire tore up the earth, making it very difficult to cross no man's land during an attack.

Soldiers generally served at the front line from a few days to a week and then rotated to the rear for a rest. Life in the trenches was miserable. The smell of dead bodies lingered in the air, and rats were a constant problem. Soldiers had trouble keeping dry, especially in water-logged areas of Belgium. Except during an attack, life fell into a dull routine. Some soldiers stood guard. Others repaired the trenches, kept telephone lines in order, brought food from behind the battle lines, or did other jobs. At night, patrols fixed the barbed wire and tried to get information about the enemy.

Enemy artillery and machine guns kept each side pinned in the trenches. Yet the Allies repeatedly tried to blast a gap in the German lines. Allied *offensives* (assaults) followed a pattern. First, artillery bombarded the enemy front-line trenches. The infantry then attacked as commanders shouted, "Over the top!" Soldiers scrambled out of trenches and began the dash across no man's

land with fixed bayonets. They hurled grenades into enemy trenches and struggled through the barbed wire. But the artillery bombardment seldom wiped out all resistance, and so enemy machine guns slaughtered wave after wave of advancing infantry. Even if the attackers broke through the front line, they ran into a second line of defenses. Thus, the Allies never cracked the enemy's defensive power.

Both the Allies and the Central Powers developed new weapons, which they hoped would break the deadlock. In April 1915, the Germans first released poison gas over Allied lines in the Second Battle of Ypres. The fumes caused vomiting and suffocation. But German commanders had little faith in the gas, and they failed to seize that opportunity to launch a major attack. The Allies also began to use poison gas soon thereafter, and gas masks became necessary equipment in the trenches. Another new weapon was the flame thrower, which shot out a stream of burning fuel.

The Battle of Verdun. As chief of the German General Staff, Falkenhayn decided in early 1916 to concentrate on killing enemy soldiers. He hoped that the Allies would finally lack the troops to continue the war. Falkenhayn chose to attack the French city of Verdun. He believed that France would defend Verdun to the last man. Fierce bombardment began on February 21.

Joffre, commander of the French armies, felt that the loss of Verdun would severely damage French morale. Through spring and summer, the French forces held off the attackers. As Falkenhayn predicted, France kept pouring men into the battle. However, Falkenhayn had not expected the battle to take nearly as many German lives as French lives. He halted the unsuccessful assault in July 1916. The next month, Hindenburg and Ludendorff—the two German heroes of the Eastern Front—replaced Falkenhayn on the Western Front. Hindenburg became chief of the General Staff. Ludendorff, his top aide, planned German strategy.

General Henri Pétain had organized the defense of Verdun and was hailed a hero by France. The Battle of Verdun became a symbol of the terrible destructiveness of modern war. French casualties totaled about 315,000 men, and German casualties about 280,000. The city itself was practically destroyed.

The Battle of the Somme. The Allies planned a major offensive for 1916 near the Somme River in

Imperial War Museum

A Cry of "Over the Top!" signaled the start of an assault. At the command, troops scrambled out of their trenches to begin the dash toward enemy trenches. The Canadian soldiers shown here were following an officer over the top during the Battle of the Somme in France in July 1916.

France. The Battle of Verdun had drained France. Thus, the Somme offensive became mainly the responsibility of the British under General Douglas Haig.

The Allies attacked on July 1, 1916. Within hours, Great Britain had suffered nearly 60,000 casualties. It was Britain's worst loss in one day of battle. Fierce fighting went on into the fall. In September, Britain introduced the first primitive tanks. However, the tanks were too unreliable and too few in number to make a difference in the battle.

Haig finally halted the useless attack in November. At terrible cost, the Allies had pushed the Germans back about 7 miles (11 kilometers). The Battle of the Somme caused more than 1 million casualties—over 600,000 German soldiers, more than 400,000 British, and nearly 200,000 French. In spite of the tragic losses at Verdun and the Somme, the Western Front stood as solid as ever at the end of 1916.

The War on Other Fronts

During 1915 and 1916, World War I spread to Italy and throughout the Balkans, and activity increased on other fronts. Some Allied military leaders believed that the creation of new battlefronts would break the deadlock on the Western Front. But the war's expansion had little effect on the deadlock.

The Italian Front. Italy had stayed out of World War I during 1914, even though it was a member of the Triple Alliance with Austria-Hungary and Germany. Italy claimed that it was under no obligation to honor the agreement because Austria-Hungary had not gone to war in self-defense. In May 1915, Italy entered World War I on the side of the Allies. In a secret treaty, the Allies promised to give Italy some of Austria-Hungary's territory after the war. In return, Italy promised to attack Austria-Hungary.

The Italians, led by General Luigi Cadorna, hammered away at Austria-Hungary for two years in a series of battles along the Isonzo River. The river lay just inside Austria-Hungary's border. Italy suffered enormous casualties but gained very little territory. The Italian Front failed to help the Allies by drawing Austria-Hungary's troops away from the Eastern Front.

The Dardanelles. After World War I began, the Ottoman Empire closed the waterway between the Aegean Sea and the Black Sea. It thereby blocked the sea route

The Italian Front

Italy entered the war against Austria-Hungary in May 1915. In spite of many bitter battles, the Italians gained very little territory. But they wore down the armies of Austria-Hungary.

WORLD BOOK map

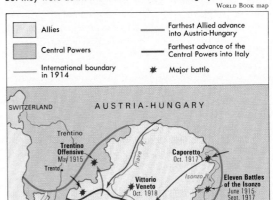

to southern Russia. French and British warships attacked the Strait of the Dardanelles, part of the waterway, in February and March 1915. The Allies hoped to open a supply route to Russia. However, underwater mines halted the assault.

In April 1915, the Allies landed troops on the Gallipoli Peninsula on the west shore of the Dardanelles. Troops from Australia and New Zealand played a key role in the landing. Ottoman and Allied forces soon became locked in trench warfare. A second invasion in August at Suvla Bay to the north failed to end the standstill. In December, the Allies began to evacuate their troops. They had suffered about 250,000 casualties in the Dardanelles.

Eastern Europe. In May 1915, the armies of Germany and Austria-Hungary broke through Russian lines in Galicia, the Austro-Hungarian province Russia

Robert Hunt Library

Robert Hunt Library

Atop a Rocky Peak near Austria-Hungary's border, Italian troops prepared to do battle, *far left.* They first had to hoist artillery into position, *near left.* The rugged Alps hampered Italy's efforts to advance into Austria-Hungary.

had invaded in 1914. The Russians retreated about 300 miles (480 kilometers) before they formed a new line of defense. In spite of the setback, Czar Nicholas II staged two offensives to relieve the pressure on the Allies on the Western Front. The first Russian offensive, in March 1916, failed to pull German troops away from Verdun.

The second Russian offensive began in June 1916 under General Alexei Brusilov. Brusilov's army drove Austria-Hungary's forces back about 50 miles (80 kilometers). Within a few weeks, Russia captured about 200,000 prisoners. To halt the assault, Austria-Hungary had to shift troops from the Italian Front to the Eastern Front. The Russian offensive nearly knocked Austria-Hungary out of the war. But it also exhausted Russia. Each side suffered about a million casualties.

Bulgaria entered World War I in October 1915 to help Austria-Hungary defeat Serbia. Bulgaria hoped to recover land it had lost in the Second Balkan War. In an effort to aid Serbia, the Allies landed troops in Salonika, Greece. But the troops never reached Serbia. By November, the Central Powers had overrun Serbia, and Serbia's army had retreated to Albania.

Romania joined the Allies in August 1916. It hoped to gain some of Austria-Hungary's territory if the Allies won the war. By the end of 1916, Romania had lost most of its army, and Germany controlled the country's valuable wheat fields and oil fields.

The War at Sea. Great Britain's control of the seas during World War I caused serious problems for Germany. The British navy blockaded German waters, preventing supplies from reaching German ports. By 1916,

Germany suffered a shortage of food and other goods. Germany combated British seapower with its submarines, called *U-boats*. In February 1915, Germany declared a submarine blockade of the British Isles and warned that it would attack any ship that tried to get through the blockade. Thereafter, U-boats destroyed great amounts of goods headed for Britain.

On May 7, 1915, a U-boat torpedoed without warning the British passenger liner *Lusitania* off the coast of Ireland. Among the 1,198 passengers who died were 128 Americans. The sinking of the *Lusitania* led U.S. President Woodrow Wilson to urge Germany to give up unrestricted submarine warfare. In September, Germany agreed not to attack neutral or passenger ships.

The warships that Britain and Germany had raced to build before World War I remained in home waters during most of the war. There, they served to discourage an enemy invasion. The only major encounter between the two navies was the Battle of Jutland. It was fought off the coast of Denmark on May 31 and June 1, 1916. Admiral Sir John Jellicoe commanded a British fleet of 150 warships. He faced a German fleet of 99 warships under the command of Admiral Reinhard Scheer. In spite of Britain's superior strength, Jellicoe acted cautiously. He feared that he could lose the entire war in a day because the destruction of Britain's fleet would give Germany control of the seas. Both sides claimed victory in the Battle of Jutland. Although Britain lost more ships than Germany, it still ruled the seas.

The War in the Air. Great advances in aviation were made by the Allies and the Central Powers during World War I. Each side competed to produce better airplanes than the other side. Airplanes were used mainly

The Eastern Front

The Eastern Front swung back and forth until the exhausted Russians agreed to stop fighting late in 1917. Under the Treaty of Brest-Litovsk, Russia gave much territory to Germany. To the south, the Central Powers had crushed Serbia in 1915 and Romania in 1916.

Allies

Central Powers

Neutral countries

International boundary in 1914

Farthest advance westward by Allies

Farthest advance eastward by Central Powers

Allied forces

Forces of the Central Powers

Major battle

0   250 Miles

0   250 Kilometers

WORLD BOOK map

On the Seas, Germany tried to starve Britain into surrender by sinking Allied cargo ships headed for its ports. The ship shown here was torpedoed by the German submarine in the foreground.

Robert Hunt Library

to observe enemy activities. The pilots carried guns to shoot down enemy observation planes. But a pilot risked shooting himself if a bullet bounced off the propeller.

In 1915, Germany developed a machine gun timed to fire between an airplane's revolving propeller blades. The invention made air combat more deadly and led to *dogfights*—clashes between enemy aircraft. A pilot who shot down 5 or more enemy planes was called an *ace*. Many aces became national heroes. Germany's Baron Manfred von Richthofen, who was known as the Red Baron, shot down 80 planes, more than any other ace. Other famous aces included Billy Bishop of Canada, René Fonck of France, Edward Mannock of Great Britain, and Eddie Rickenbacker of the United States.

Aerial bombing remained in its early stages during World War I. In 1915, Germany began to bomb London and other British cities from airships called *zeppelins*. But bombing had little effect on the war.

The Final Stage

Allied Failures. During 1917, French and British military leaders still hoped that a successful offensive could win the war. But German leaders accepted the deadlock on the Western Front and improved German defenses. In March 1917, German troops were moved back to a strongly fortified new battle line in northern France. It was called the Siegfried Line by the Germans and the Hindenburg Line by the Allies. The Siegfried Line shortened the Western Front and placed German artillery and machine guns to best advantage. It also led to the failure of an offensive planned by France.

General Robert Nivelle had replaced Joffre as commander in chief of French forces in December 1916. Nivelle planned a major offensive near the Aisne River and predicted he would smash through the German line within two days. Nivelle's enthusiasm inspired the French troops. Germany's pullback to the Siegfried Line did not shake Nivelle's confidence.

In April 1917, shortly before Nivelle's offensive began, Canadian forces seized a hill called Vimy Ridge. Many Allied troops had fallen in earlier attempts to dislodge the Germans from that height in northern France.

Nivelle's offensive opened on April 16, 1917. By the end of the day, it was clear that the assault had failed. But fighting continued into May. Mutinies broke out among the French forces after Nivelle's offensive collapsed. The troops had had enough of the pointless bloodshed and the horrid conditions on the Western Front. They no longer had faith in their leaders. Men who had fought bravely for almost three years refused to go on fighting. Pétain, the hero of Verdun, replaced Nivelle in May 1917. Pétain improved the soldiers' living conditions and restored order. He promised that France would remain on the defensive until it was ready to fight again. Meanwhile, any further offensives on the Western Front remained Britain's responsibility.

General Haig was hopeful that a British offensive near Ypres would lead to victory. The Third Battle of Ypres, also known as the Battle of Passchendaele, began on July 31, 1917. For more than three months, British troops and a small French force pounded the Germans in an especially terrible campaign. Heavy Allied bombardment before the infantry attack began had destroyed the drainage system around Ypres. Drenching rains then turned the water-logged land into a swamp where thousands of British soldiers drowned. Snow and ice finally halted the disastrous battle on November 10. In late November, Britain used tanks to break through the Siegfried Line. But the failure at Ypres had used up the troops Britain needed to follow up that success.

In 1917, first France and then Britain thus saw their hopes for victory shattered. Austria-Hungary drove the Italians out of its territory in the Battle of Caporetto in the fall. A revolution in Russia made the Allied situation seem even more hopeless.

Bettmann Archive

In the Skies, enemy pilots clashed in *dogfights*. A pilot who shot down five or more planes was an *ace*. This dogfight was between pilots of German planes (cross on wings) and British planes.

Bettmann Archive

War-Weary Russian Soldiers retreated in disorder in the summer of 1917 after learning that the Germans had smashed through their battle line. By year's end, Russia had quit fighting.

The Russian Revolution. The Russian people suffered greatly during World War I. By 1917, many of them were no longer willing to put up with the enormous casualties and the severe shortages of food and fuel. They blamed Czar Nicholas II and his advisers for the country's problems. Early in 1917, an uprising in Petrograd (now Leningrad) forced Nicholas from the throne. The new government continued the war.

To weaken Russia's war effort further, Germany helped V. I. Lenin, a Russian revolutionary then living in Switzerland, return to his homeland in April 1917. Seven months later, Lenin led an uprising that gained control of Russia's government. Lenin immediately called for peace talks with Germany. World War I had ended on the Eastern Front.

Germany dictated harsh peace terms to Russia in a peace treaty signed in Brest-Litovsk, Russia, on March 3, 1918. The Treaty of Brest-Litovsk forced Russia to give up large amounts of territory, including Finland, Poland, the Ukraine, Bessarabia, and the Baltic States— Estonia, Livonia (now Latvia), and Lithuania. The end of the fighting on the Eastern Front freed German troops for use on the Western Front. The only obstacle to a final German victory seemed to be the entry of the United States into the war.

The United States Enters the War. At the start of World War I, President Wilson had declared the neutrality of the United States. Most Americans opposed U.S. involvement in a European war. But the sinking of the *Lusitania* and other German actions against civilians drew American sympathies to the Allies.

Several events early in 1917 persuaded the United States government to enter World War I. In February, Germany returned to unrestricted submarine warfare, which it assumed might bring the United States into the war. But German military leaders believed that they could still win the war by cutting off British supplies. They expected their U-boats to starve Britain into surrendering within a few months, long before the United States had fully prepared for war.

Tension between the United States and Germany increased after the British intercepted and decoded a message from Germany's foreign minister, Arthur Zimmermann, to the German ambassador to Mexico. The message, known as the "Zimmermann note," revealed a German plot to persuade Mexico to go to war against the United States. The British gave the message to Wilson, and it was published in the United States early in March. Americans were further enraged after U-boats sank several U.S. cargo ships.

On April 2, Wilson called for war, stating that "the world must be made safe for democracy." Congress declared war on Germany on April 6. Few people expected that the United States would make much of a contribution toward ending the war.

Mobilization. The United States entered World War I unprepared for battle. Strong antiwar feelings had hampered efforts to prepare for war. After declaring war, the government worked to stir up enthusiasm for the war effort. Government propaganda pictured the war as a battle for liberty and democracy. People who still opposed the war faced increasingly unfriendly public opinion. They could even be brought to trial under wartime laws forbidding statements that might harm the successful progress of the war.

During World War I, U.S. government agencies directed the nation's economy toward the war effort. President Wilson put financier Bernard M. Baruch in charge of the War Industries Board, which turned factories into producers of war materials. The Food Administration, headed by businessman Herbert Hoover, controlled the prices, production, and distribution of food. Americans observed "meatless" and "wheatless" days in order that food could be sent to Europe.

Manpower was the chief contribution of the United States to World War I. The country entered the war with a Regular Army of only about 126,000 men. It soon organized a draft requiring all men from 21 through 30 years old to register for military service. The age range was broadened to 18 through 45 in 1918. A lottery determined who served. Many men enlisted voluntarily, and women signed up as nurses and office

Granger Collection

A Propaganda Poster urged Americans to buy war bonds by showing the enemy as a vicious killer. *Hun* was a scornful term applied to Germans during World War I.

American Gunners crawled through a war-torn area of northeastern France in the fall of 1918 during the last assault of World War I. The area lay between the Meuse River and the Argonne Forest. Almost a million U.S. troops took part in the assault, known as the Meuse-Argonne offensive.

workers. The U.S. armed forces had almost 5 million men and women by the end of the war. Of that number, about $2\frac{3}{4}$ million men had been drafted. The Army hastily built training camps for the recruits. However, few soldiers received much training before going overseas because the Allies urgently needed them.

Before U.S. help could reach the Western Front, the Allies had to overcome the U-boat threat in the Atlantic. In May 1917, Britain began to use a *convoy system*, by which cargo ships went to sea in large groups escorted by warships. The U-boats proved no match for the warships, and Allied shipping losses dropped sharply.

American Troops in Europe. The soldiers sent to Europe by the U.S. Army made up the American Expeditionary Forces (AEF). General John J. Pershing, commander of the AEF, arrived in France in mid-June 1917. The first troops landed later that month. Pershing told U.S. military authorities that he needed 3 million American troops, a third of them within the next year. The American officials were shocked. They had planned to send only 650,000 troops in that time. In the end, about 2 million Americans served in Europe.

Britain, France, and Italy knew well how desperately they needed U.S. manpower by the fall of 1917. In November, the Allies formed the Supreme War Council to plan strategy. They decided to make their strategy defensive until U.S. troops reached the Western Front. The Allies wanted Americans to serve as replacements and fill out their battered ranks. But Pershing was convinced that the AEF would make a greater contribution by fighting as an independent unit. The argument was the major wartime dispute between the Europeans and their American ally. Pershing generally held firm, though at times he lent troops to France and Britain.

The Last Campaigns. The end of the war on the Eastern Front boosted German hopes for victory. By early 1918, German forces outnumbered the Allies on the Western Front. In spring, Germany staged three offensives. Ludendorff counted on delivering a crushing blow to the Allies before large numbers of American troops reached the front. He relied on speed and surprise.

Germany first struck near St.-Quentin, a city in the Somme River Valley, on March 21, 1918. By March 26, British troops had retreated about 30 miles (50 kilometers). In late March, the Germans began to bombard Paris with "Big Berthas." The enormous guns hurled

shells up to 75 miles (120 kilometers). After the disaster at St.-Quentin, Allied leaders met to plan a united defense. In April, they appointed General Ferdinand Foch of France to be the supreme commander of the Allied forces on the Western Front.

A second German offensive began on April 9 along the Lys River in Belgium. British troops fought stubbornly, and Ludendorff called off the attack on April 30. The Allies suffered heavy losses in both assaults, but German casualties were nearly as great.

Germany attacked a third time on May 27 near the Aisne River. By May 30, German troops had reached the Marne River. American soldiers helped France stop the German advance at the town of Château-Thierry, less than 50 miles (80 kilometers) northeast of Paris. During June, U.S. troops drove the Germans out of Belleau Wood, a forested area near the Marne. German forces crossed the Marne on July 15. Foch ordered a counterattack near the town of Soissons on July 18.

The Second Battle of the Marne was fought from July 15 through Aug. 6, 1918. It marked the turning point of World War I. After winning the battle, the Allies advanced steadily. On August 8, Britain and France attacked the Germans near Amiens. By early September, Germany had lost all the territory it had gained since spring. In mid-September, Pershing led U.S. forces to easy victory at St.-Mihiel.

The last offensive of World War I began on Sept. 26, 1918. About 900,000 U.S. troops participated in heavy fighting between the Argonne Forest and the Meuse River. Ludendorff realized that Germany could no longer overcome the superior strength of the Allies.

The Fighting Ends. The Allies won victories on all fronts in the fall of 1918. Bulgaria surrendered on September 29. British forces under the command of General Edmund Allenby triumphed over the Ottoman army in Palestine and Syria. On October 30, the Ottoman Empire signed an armistice. The last major battle between Italy and Austria-Hungary began in late October in northeastern Italy. Italy's army, with support from France and Great Britain, defeated Austria-Hungary near the town of Vittorio Veneto. Austria-Hungary signed an armistice on November 3.

Germany teetered on the edge of collapse as the war continued through October. Britain's naval blockade had nearly starved the German people, and widespread discontent led to riots and rising demands for peace. Kaiser Wilhelm gave up his throne on November 9 and fled to the Netherlands. An Allied delegation headed by Foch met with German representatives in a railroad car in the Compiègne Forest in northern France.

In the early morning on Nov. 11, 1918, the Germans accepted the armistice terms demanded by the Allies. Germany agreed to evacuate the terrorities it had taken during the war; to surrender large numbers of arms, ships, and other war materials; and to allow the Allied powers to occupy German territory along the Rhine River. Foch ordered the fighting to stop on the Western Front at 11 A.M. World War I was over.

Consequences of the War

Destruction and Casualties. World War I caused immeasurable destruction. Nearly 10 million soldiers died as a result of the war—far more than had died in all the wars during the previous 100 years. About 21 million men were wounded. The enormously high casualties resulted partly from the destructive powers of new weapons, especially the machine gun. Military leaders contributed to the slaughter by failing to adjust to the

The Western Front: 1918

Germany staged three assaults from March to June of 1918. With American help, the Allies halted the German advance outside Paris in June. Thereafter, the Allies steadily drove the Germans back. An armistice ended the fighting on Nov. 11, 1918.

WORLD BOOK map

Allies	Farthest German advance in June 1918
Central Powers	Allied forces
Neutral countries	German forces
International boundary in 1914	Major battle

changed conditions of warfare. In staging offensives, they ordered soldiers armed with bayonets into machine-gun fire. Only in the last year of the war did generals successfully use tanks and new tactics.

Germany and Russia each suffered about $1\frac{3}{4}$ million battle deaths during World War I—more than any other country. France had the highest percentage of battle deaths in relation to its total number of servicemen. It lost about $1\frac{1}{3}$ million soldiers, or 16 per cent of those mobilized. No one knows how many civilians died of disease, starvation, and other war-related causes. Some historians believe as many civilians died as soldiers.

Property damage in World War I was greatest in France and Belgium. Armies destroyed farms and villages as they passed through them or, even worse, dug in for battle. The fighting wrecked factories, bridges, and railroad tracks. Artillery shells, trenches, and chemicals made barren the land along the Western Front.

Economic Consequences. World War I cost the fighting nations a total of about $337 billion dollars. By 1918, the war was costing about $10 million an hour. Nations raised part of the money to pay for the war through income taxes and other taxes. But most of the money came from borrowing, which created huge debts. Governments borrowed from citizens by selling war bonds. The Allies also borrowed heavily from the United States. In addition, most governments printed extra money to meet their needs. But the increased money supply caused severe inflation after the war.

The problem of war debts lingered after World War I ended. The Allies tried to reduce their debts by demanding *reparations* (payments for war damages) from the Central Powers, especially Germany. Reparations worsened the economic problems of the defeated countries and did not solve the problems of the victors.

World War I seriously disrupted economies. Some businesses shut down after workers left for military service. Other firms shifted to the production of war materials. To direct production toward the war effort, governments took greater control over the economy than ever before. Most people wanted a return to private enterprise after the war. But some people expected government to continue to solve economic problems.

The countries of Europe had poured their resources into World War I, and they came out of the war exhausted. France had lost nearly one-tenth of its work force. But in most countries, unemployment became a problem as soldiers returned from the war and could not find jobs. In addition, Europe lost many of the markets for its exports while producing war goods. The United States and other countries that had played a smaller role in the war emerged with increased economic power.

Political Consequences. World War I shook the foundations of several governments. Democratic governments in Britain and France withstood the stress of the war. But four monarchies toppled. The first monarch to fall was Czar Nicholas II of Russia in 1917. Kaiser Wilhelm II of Germany and Emperor Charles of Austria-Hungary left their thrones in 1918. The Ottoman sultan, Muhammad VI, fell in 1922.

The collapse of old empires led to the creation of new countries in the years after World War I. The prewar territory of Austria-Hungary formed the independent republics of Austria, Hungary, and Czechoslovakia, as well as parts of Italy, Poland, Romania, and Yugosla-

Cheering the End of World War I, a joyful crowd streamed through the streets of a French town on Nov. 11, 1918. The long, horrible war had taken the lives of nearly 10 million soldiers.

National Archives

via. Russia and Germany also gave up territory to Poland. Finland and the Baltic States—Estonia, Latvia, and Lithuania—gained independence from Russia. Most Arab lands in the Ottoman Empire were placed under the control of France and Britain. What remained of the Ottoman Empire became Turkey. European leaders took national groups into account in redrawing the map of Europe. In so doing, they strengthened the cause of nationalism.

World War I gave the Communists a chance to seize power in Russia. Some people expected Communist revolutions to break out elsewhere in Europe as well. Although revolutionary movements gained strength after the war, Communist governments did not take hold.

Social Consequences. World War I brought enormous changes in society. The death of so many young men affected France more than other countries. During the 1920's, France's population dropped because of a low birth rate. Millions of people were uprooted by the war. Some fled war-torn areas and later found their houses, farms, or villages destroyed. Others became refugees as a result of changes in governments and national borders, especially in central and eastern Europe.

Many people chose not to resume their old way of life after World War I. Urban areas grew as peasants settled in cities instead of returning to farms. Women filled jobs

in offices and factories after men went to war, and they were reluctant to give up their new independence. Many countries granted women the vote after the war.

The distinction between social classes began to blur as a result of World War I, and society became more democratic. The upper classes, which had traditionally governed, lost some of their power and privilege after having led the world into an agonizing war. Men of all classes had faced the same danger and horror in the trenches. Those who had bled and suffered for their country came to demand a say in running it.

Finally, World War I transformed attitudes. Middle- and upper-class Europeans lost the confidence and optimism they had felt before the war. Many people began to question long-held ideas. For example, few Europeans before the war had doubted their right to force European culture on the rest of the world. But the destruction and bloodshed of the war shattered the belief in the superiority of European civilization.

The Peace Settlement

The Fourteen Points. In January 1918, 10 months before World War I ended, Woodrow Wilson proposed a set of war aims called the Fourteen Points. Wilson believed that the Fourteen Points would bring about a just peace settlement, which he termed "peace without victory." In November 1918, Germany agreed to an armistice. Germany expected that the peace settlement would be based on the Fourteen Points.

Eight of Wilson's Fourteen Points dealt with specific political and territorial settlements. The rest of them set forth general principles aimed at preventing future wars. The last point proposed the establishment of an international association—later called the League of Nations—to maintain the peace. For a summary of the Fourteen Points, see WILSON, WOODROW (The Fourteen Points).

The Paris Peace Conference. In January 1919, representatives of the victorious powers gathered in Paris to draw up the peace settlement. They came from 32 nations. Committees worked out specific proposals at the Paris Peace Conference. But the decisions were made by four heads of government called the Big Four. The Big Four consisted of Wilson, Britain's Prime Minister David Lloyd George, France's Premier Georges Clemenceau, and Italy's Premier Vittorio Orlando.

The Paris Peace Conference largely disregarded the lofty principles of the Fourteen Points. The Allies had sacrificed far more than the Americans during the war, and they wanted to be paid back. Wilson focused his efforts on the creation of the League of Nations. He yielded to France and Britain on many other issues.

In May 1919, the peace conference approved the treaty and presented it to Germany. Germany agreed to it only after the Allies threatened to invade. With grave doubts, German representatives signed the treaty in the Palace of Versailles near Paris on June 28, 1919. The date was the fifth anniversary of the assassination of Archduke Francis Ferdinand.

In addition to the Treaty of Versailles with Germany, the peacemakers drew up separate treaties with the other Central Powers. The Treaty of St.-Germain was signed with Austria in September 1919, the Treaty of Neuilly with Bulgaria in November 1919, the Treaty

Military Casualties in World War I (1914-1918)*

	Dead	Wounded
The Allies		
Belgium	14,000	44,700
British Empire	908,400	2,090,200
France	1,385,000 †	4,266,000
Greece	5,000	21,000
Italy	650,000	947,000
Portugal	7,200	13,800
Romania	335,700 †	120,000
Russia	1,700,000	4,950,000
Serbia and Montenegro	48,000	143,000
United States	116,516 ‡	234,428 ‡
The Central Powers		
Austria-Hungary	1,200,000	3,620,000
Bulgaria	87,500	152,400
Germany	1,773,000	4,216,000
Ottoman Empire	325,000	400,000

*Except for the United States, all figures are approximate.
†Includes missing.
‡Official U.S. government figure.
Source: *World War I: An Outline History* by Hanson W. Baldwin. Copyright © 1962 Hanson W. Baldwin. Reprinted by permission of Harper & Row, Publishers, Inc., and Curtis Brown, Ltd.

of Trianon with Hungary in June 1920, and the Treaty of Sèvres with the Ottoman Empire in August 1920.

Provisions of the Treaties that officially ended World War I stripped the Central Powers of territory and arms and required them to pay reparations. Germany was punished especially severely. One clause in the Treaty of Versailles forced Germany to accept responsibility for causing the war.

Under the Treaty of Versailles, Germany gave up territory to Belgium, Czechoslovakia, Denmark, France, and Poland and lost its overseas colonies. France gained control of coal fields in Germany's Saar Valley for 15 years. An Allied military force, paid for by Germany, was to occupy the west bank of the Rhine River for 15 years. Other clauses in the treaty limited Germany's armed forces and required the country to turn over war materials, ships, livestock, and other goods to the Allies. A total sum for reparations was not set until 1921. At that time, Germany received a bill for about $33 billion.

The Treaty of St.-Germain and the Treaty of Trianon reduced Austria and Hungary to less than a third their former area. The treaties recognized the independence of Czechoslovakia, Poland, and a kingdom that later became Yugoslavia. Those new states, along with Italy and Romania, received territory that had belonged to Austria-Hungary. The Treaty of Sèvres took Egypt, Lebanon, Mesopotamia, Palestine, Syria, and Transjordan away from the Ottoman Empire. Bulgaria lost territory to Greece and Romania. Germany's allies also had to reduce their armed forces and pay reparations.

The Postwar World. The peacemakers found it impossible to satisfy the hopes and ambitions of every nation and national group. The settlements they drew up disappointed both the victors and the defeated powers.

In creating new borders, the peacemakers considered the wishes of national groups. However, territorial claims overlapped in many cases. For example, Romania gained a chunk of land with a large Hungarian population, and parts of Czechoslovakia and Poland had many Germans. Such settlements heightened tensions between countries. In addition, some Arab nations were bitter because they had failed to gain independence.

Certain borders created by the peace settlements made little economic sense. For example, the new countries of Austria and Hungary were small and weak and unable to support themselves. They had lost most of their population, resources, and markets. Austria's largely German population had wanted to unite with Germany. But the peace treaties forbade that union. The peacemakers did not want Germany to gain territory from the war.

Among the European Allies, Britain entered the postwar world the most content. The nation had kept its empire and control of the seas. But Britain worried that the balance of power it wanted in Europe could be upset by a severely weakened Germany and a victory by the Communists in a civil war in Russia. France had succeeded in imposing harsh terms on Germany—its traditional foe—but not in safeguarding its borders. France had failed to obtain a guarantee of aid from Britain and the United States in the event of a German invasion. Finally, Italy had gained less territory than it had been promised and felt it deserved.

In the United States, the Senate reflected public opinion and failed to approve the Treaty of Versailles. It thereby rejected President Wilson. The treaty would have made the United States a member of the League of Nations. Many Americans were not yet ready to accept

Europe and the Near East After World War I

World War I led to changes in many borders. Austria-Hungary and the Ottoman Empire split into national states. Russia and Germany gave up territory. Although several states won independence, most Arab lands that had belonged to the Ottoman Empire were placed under French and British rule.

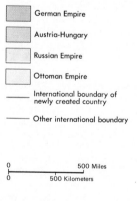

- German Empire
- Austria-Hungary
- Russian Empire
- Ottoman Empire
- ——— International boundary of newly created country
- ——— Other international boundary

0   500 Miles
0   500 Kilometers

WORLD BOOK map

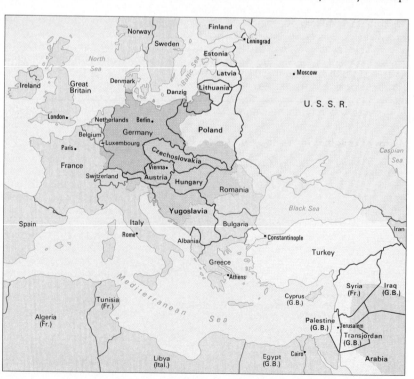

the responsibilities that went along with their country's new power. They feared that the League of Nations would entangle the country in European disputes.

The Treaty of Versailles imposed harsher terms than Germany had expected. The responsibility of having accepted those terms weakened Germany's postwar government. During the 1930's, a strongly nationalist movement led by Adolf Hitler gained power in Germany. Hitler promised to ignore the Treaty of Versailles and to avenge Germany's defeat in World War I. In 1939, Germany invaded Poland. World War II had begun. EDWARD M. COFFMAN

Related Articles in WORLD BOOK. See the HISTORY section of articles on the countries that took part in World War I. See also the following articles:

BATTLE AREAS

Alsace-Lorraine
Balkans
Flanders Field
Jutland, Battle of

Saar
Siegfried Line
Verdun, Battles of
Vimy Ridge, Battle of

ALLIED MILITARY BIOGRAPHIES

Albert I
Allenby, Lord
Bishop, Billy
Byng, Julian H. G.
Foch, Ferdinand
Haig, Earl
Jellicoe, Sir John R.
Joffre, Joseph J. C.

Kitchener, Horatio H.
March, Peyton C.
Mitchell, Billy
Pershing, John J.
Pétain, Henri Philippe
Piłsudski, Jôzef
Rickenbacker, Eddie
York, Alvin C.

ALLIED CIVILIAN BIOGRAPHIES

Asquith, Herbert H.
Baruch, Bernard M.
Borden, Sir Robert L.
Clemenceau, Georges
Hoover, Herbert C.
Lloyd George, David

Nicholas II (of Russia)
Orlando, Vittorio E.
Poincaré, Raymond
Venizelos, Eleutherios
Wilson, Woodrow

CENTRAL POWERS BIOGRAPHIES

Hindenburg, Paul von
Ludendorff, Erich F.W.

Wilhelm (II)
Zeppelin, Count von

OTHER BIOGRAPHIES

Ataturk, Kemal
Cavell, Edith L.
Constantine (I) (of Greece)

Lawrence, T. E.
Lenin, V. I.
Mata Hari

FORCES, MATERIALS, AND WEAPONS

Air Force
Air Force, United States
Aircraft, Military
Airship
Army
Army, United States
Artillery
Automobile (World War I)
Aviation

Camouflage
Chemical-Biological-
  Radiological Warfare
Machine Gun
Navy
Navy, United States
Submarine
Tank

TREATIES

Saint Germain, Treaty of
Sèvres, Treaty of

Trianon, Treaty of
Versailles, Treaty of

OTHER RELATED ARTICLES

American Legion
American Legion Auxiliary
Fourteen Points
League of Nations
Lusitania
Mandated Territory
Neutrality
Refugee
Red Cross

Stars and Stripes
Triple Alliance
Triple Entente
United States, History of the
Unknown Soldier
Veterans Day
War Aces
War Crime
War Debt

Outline

I. Causes of the War
A. The Rise of Nationalism
B. A Build-up of Military Might
C. Competition for Colonies
D. A System of Military Alliances

II. Beginning of the War
A. The Assassination
   of an Archduke
B. How the Conflict Spread
C. The Western Front
D. The Eastern Front
E. Fighting Elsewhere

III. The Deadlock on the Western Front
A. Trench Warfare
B. The Battle of Verdun
C. The Battle of the Somme

IV. The War on Other Fronts
A. The Italian Front
B. The Dardanelles
C. Eastern Europe
D. The War at Sea
E. The War in the Air

V. The Final Stage
A. Allied Failures
B. The Russian Revolution
C. The United States Enters the War
D. The Last Campaigns
E. The Fighting Ends

VI. Consequences of the War
A. Destruction and Casualties
B. Economic Consequences
C. Political Consequences
D. Social Consequences

VII. The Peace Settlement
A. The Fourteen Points
B. The Paris Peace Conference
C. Provisions of the Treaties
D. The Postwar World

Questions

What were the four chief causes of World War I?

What country first used poison gas in World War I? What country first used tanks?

Which World War I heads of government made up the Big Four?

Which countries formed the Triple Entente? The Triple Alliance? How did the two alliances differ?

How did Germany combat British naval power during World War I?

What was the chief contribution made by the United States to World War I?

What was the Schlieffen Plan in World War I?

Why was the First Battle of the Marne so important?

Why did French troops mutiny in 1917?

How did Germany try to weaken Russia's war effort in 1917?

Reading and Study Guide

See *World War I* in the RESEARCH GUIDE INDEX, Volume 22, for a *Reading and Study Guide*.

Additional Resources

BARNETT, CORRELLI. *The Great War.* Putnam, 1980.

COFFMAN, EDWARD M. *The War to End All Wars: The American Military Experience in World War I.* Univ. of Wisconsin Press, 1986. First published in 1968.

KENNEDY, DAVID M. *Over Here: The First World War and American Society.* Oxford, 1980.

The Marshall Cavendish Illustrated Encyclopedia of World War I. Ed. by Peter Young and Mark Dartford. 12 vols. Rev. ed. Cavendish, 1984.

STOKESBURY, JAMES L. *A Short History of World War I.* Morrow, 1981.

TAYLOR, A. J. P. *Illustrated History of the First World War.* Putnam, 1964.

TERRAINE, JOHN. *To Win a War: 1918, The Year of Victory.* Doubleday, 1981.

TUCHMAN, BARBARA W. *The Guns of August.* Macmillan, 1962.

The Fighting Fronts in World War II spread to nearly every part of the globe. In Europe and northern Africa, they included cities and desert wastes. Little remained standing in Tournai, Belgium, *left*, after a German bombing raid. Tank warfare kept armies on the run in Egypt, *right*.

Süddeutscher Verlag

Imperial War Museum

WORLD WAR II

WORLD WAR II (1939-1945) killed more people, destroyed more property, disrupted more lives, and probably had more far-reaching consequences than any other war in history. It brought about the downfall of western Europe as the center of world power and led to the rise of the Soviet Union. The development of the atomic bomb during the war opened the nuclear age.

The exact number of people killed because of World War II will never be known. Military deaths probably totaled about 17 million. Civilian deaths were even greater as a result of starvation, bombing raids, massacres, epidemics, and other war-related causes. The battlegrounds spread to nearly every part of the world. Troops fought in the steaming jungles of Southeast Asia, in the deserts of northern Africa, and on islands in the Pacific Ocean. Battles were waged on frozen fields in the Soviet Union, below the surface of the Atlantic Ocean, and in the streets of many European cities.

World War II began on Sept. 1, 1939, when Germany invaded Poland. Germany's dictator, Adolf Hitler, had built Germany into a powerful war machine. That machine rapidly crushed Poland, Denmark, Luxembourg, the Netherlands, Belgium, Norway, and France. By June 1940, Great Britain stood alone against Hitler. That same month, Italy joined the war on Germany's side. The fighting soon spread to Greece and

northern Africa. In June 1941, Germany invaded the Soviet Union. Japan attacked United States military bases at Pearl Harbor in Hawaii on Dec. 7, 1941, bringing the United States into the war. By mid-1942, Japanese forces had conquered much of Southeast Asia and had swept across many islands in the Pacific.

Germany, Italy, and Japan formed an alliance known as the Axis. Six other nations eventually joined the Axis. The United States, Great Britain, China, and the Soviet Union were the major powers fighting the Axis. They were called the Allies. The Allies totaled 50 nations by the end of the war.

During 1942, the Allies stopped the Axis advance in northern Africa, the Soviet Union, and the Pacific. Allied forces landed in Italy in 1943 and in France in 1944. In 1945, the Allies drove into Germany from the east and the west. A series of bloody battles in the Pacific brought the Allies to Japan's doorstep by the summer of 1945. Germany surrendered on May 7, 1945, and Japan on Sept. 2, 1945.

An uneasy peace took effect as a war-weary world began to rebuild after World War II. Much of Europe and parts of Asia lay in ruins. Millions of people were starving and homeless. Europe's leadership in world affairs had ended. The United States and the Soviet Union had become the world's most powerful nations. But their wartime alliance broke down soon after the war. New threats to peace arose as the Soviet Union sought to spread Communism in Europe and Asia.

WORLD WAR II / Causes of the War

Many historians trace the causes of World War II to problems left unsolved by World War I (1914-1918). World War I and the treaties that ended it also created new political and economic problems. Forceful leaders

in several countries took advantage of those problems to seize power. The desire of dictators in Germany, Italy, and Japan to conquer additional territory brought them into conflict with democratic nations.

The Peace of Paris. After World War I ended, representatives of the victorious nations met in Paris in 1919 to draw up peace treaties for the defeated countries. The treaties, known together as the Peace of Paris, followed a long and bitter war. They were worked out in haste by

James L. Stokesbury, the contributor of this article, is Professor of History at Acadia University and the author of A Short History of World War II.

National Archives   Charles Kerlee from National Archives

Battlegrounds in Asia and the Pacific included tropical jungles and vast ocean spaces. Troops waded across muddy rivers and crawled through thick vegetation, *left,* in Southeast Asia and on Pacific islands. Planes based on aircraft carriers, *right,* did much of the fighting at sea.

countries with opposing goals and failed to satisfy even the victors. Of all the countries on the winning side, Italy and Japan left the peace conference most dissatisfied. Italy gained less territory than it felt it deserved and vowed to take action on its own. Japan gained control of German territories in the Pacific and thereby launched a program of expansion. But Japan was angered by the peacemakers' failure to endorse the principle of the equality of all races.

The countries that lost World War I—Germany, Austria, Hungary, Bulgaria, and Turkey—were especially dissatisfied with the Peace of Paris. They were stripped of territory and arms and were required to make *reparations* (payments for war damages).

The Treaty of Versailles, which was signed with Germany, punished Germany severely. The German government agreed to sign the treaty only after the victorious powers threatened to invade. Many Germans particularly resented a clause that forced Germany to accept responsibility for causing World War I.

Economic Problems. World War I seriously damaged the economies of European countries. Both the winners and the losers came out of the war deeply in debt. The defeated powers had difficulty paying reparations to the victors, and the victors had difficulty repaying loans from the United States. The shift from a wartime economy to a peacetime economy caused further problems. Many soldiers could not find jobs after the war.

Italy and Japan suffered from too many people and too few resources after World War I. They eventually tried to solve their problems by territorial expansion. In Germany, runaway inflation destroyed the value of money and wiped out the savings of millions of people. In 1923, the German economy neared collapse. Loans from the United States helped Germany's government restore order. By the late 1920's, Europe appeared to be entering a period of economic stability.

A worldwide business slump known as the Great Depression began in the United States in 1929. By the early 1930's, it had halted Europe's economic recovery. The Great Depression caused mass unemployment and spread poverty and despair. It weakened democratic

governments and strengthened extreme political movements that promised to end the economic problems. Two movements in particular gained strength. The forces of Communism, known as the Left, called for revolution by the workers. The forces of fascism, called the Right, favored strong national government. Throughout Europe, the forces of the Left clashed with the forces of the Right. The political extremes gained the most support in countries with the greatest economic problems and the deepest resentment of the Peace of Paris.

Nationalism was an extreme form of patriotism that swept across Europe during the 1800's. Supporters of nationalism placed loyalty to the aims of their nation above any other public loyalty. Many nationalists viewed foreigners and members of minority groups as inferior. Such beliefs helped nations justify their conquest of other lands and the poor treatment of minorities within their borders. Nationalism was a chief cause of World War I, and it grew even stronger after that war.

Nationalism went hand in hand with feelings of national discontent. The more people felt deprived of national honor, the more they wished to see their country powerful and able to insist on its rights. Many Germans felt humiliated by their country's defeat in World War I and its harsh treatment under the Treaty of Versailles. During the 1930's, they enthusiastically supported a violently nationalistic organization called the Nazi Party. The Nazi Party declared that Germany had a right to become strong again. Nationalism also gained strength in Italy and Japan.

The Peace of Paris established an international organization called the League of Nations to maintain peace. But nationalism prevented the League from working effectively. Each country backed its own interests at the expense of other countries. Only weak countries agreed to submit their disagreements to the League of Nations for settlement. Strong nations reserved the right to settle their disputes by threats or, if tough talk failed, by force.

The Rise of Dictatorships. The political unrest and poor economic conditions that developed after World War I enabled dictatorships to arise in several countries, especially in those countries that lacked a tradition of democratic government. During the 1920's and 1930's, dictatorships came to power in the Soviet Union, Italy, Germany, and Japan. They held total power and ruled without regard to law. The dictatorships used terror and secret police to crush opposition to their rule. People who objected risked imprisonment or execution.

In the Soviet Union, the Communists, led by V. I. Lenin, had seized power in 1917. Lenin set up a dictatorship that firmly controlled the country by the time he died in 1924. After Lenin's death, Joseph Stalin and other leading Communists struggled for power. Stalin eliminated his rivals one by one and became the Soviet dictator in 1929.

In Italy, economic distress after World War I led to strikes and riots. As a result of the violence, a strongly nationalistic group called the Fascist Party gained many supporters. Benito Mussolini, leader of the Fascists, promised to bring order and prosperity to Italy. He vowed to restore to Italy the glory it had known in the days of the ancient Roman Empire. By 1922, the Fascists had become powerful enough to force the king of Italy to appoint Mussolini premier. Mussolini, who took the title *il Duce* (the Leader), soon began to establish a dictatorship.

In Germany, the Nazi Party made spectacular gains as the Great Depression deepened during the early 1930's. Many Germans blamed all their country's economic woes on the hated Treaty of Versailles, which forced Germany to give up territory and resources and pay large reparations. In 1933, Adolf Hitler, the leader of the Nazis, was appointed chancellor of Germany. Hitler,

who was called *der Führer* (the Leader), soon made Germany a dictatorship. He vowed to ignore the Versailles Treaty and to avenge Germany's defeat in World War I. Hitler preached that Germans were a "superior race" and that such peoples as Jews and Slavs were inferior. He began a campaign of hatred against Jews and Communists and promised to rid the country of them. Hitler's extreme nationalism appealed to many Germans.

In Japan, military officers began to hold political office during the 1930's. By 1936, they had strong control of the government. Japan's military government glorified war and the training of warriors. In 1941, General Hideki Tojo became premier of Japan.

Aggression on the March. Japan, Italy, and Germany followed a policy of aggressive territorial expansion during the 1930's. They invaded weak lands that could be taken over easily. The dictatorships knew what they wanted, and they grabbed it. The democratic countries responded with timidity and indecision to the aggression of the dictatorships.

Japan was the first dictatorship to begin a program of conquest. In 1931, Japanese forces seized control of Manchuria, a region of China rich in natural resources. Some historians consider Japan's conquest of Manchuria as the real start of World War II. Japan made Manchuria a puppet state called Manchukuo. In 1937, Japan launched a major attack against China. It occupied most of eastern China by the end of 1938, though the two countries had not officially declared war. Japan's military leaders began to speak about bringing all of eastern Asia under Japanese control.

The World at War: 1939-1945

Germany, Italy, Japan, and their Axis partners fought Great Britain, the Soviet Union, the United States, and the other Allies in World War II. This map shows the Allies and the lands controlled by the Axis nations at the height of their power. Few countries remained neutral.

WORLD BOOK map

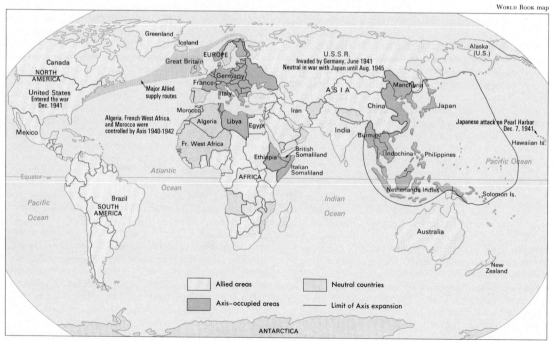

Italy looked to Africa to fulfill its ambitions for an empire. In 1935, Italian troops invaded Ethiopia, one of the few independent countries in Africa. The Italians used machine guns, tanks, and airplanes to overpower Ethiopia's poorly equipped army. They had conquered the country by May 1936.

Soon after Hitler took power, he began to build up Germany's armed forces in violation of the Treaty of Versailles. In 1936, Hitler sent troops into the Rhineland, a region of Germany along the banks of the Rhine River. Under the treaty, the Rhineland was to remain free of troops. In March 1938, German soldiers marched into Austria and united it with Germany. Many people in Germany and Austria welcomed that move.

The acts of aggression were easy victories for the dictatorships. The League of Nations proved incapable of stopping them. It lacked an army and the power to enforce international law. The United States had refused to join the League or become involved in European disputes. Great Britain and France were unwilling to risk another war so soon after World War I. The two powers knew they would bear the burden of any fighting.

The aggressors soon formed an alliance. In 1936, Germany and Italy agreed to support one another's foreign policy. The alliance was known as the Rome-Berlin Axis. Japan joined the alliance in 1940, and it became the Rome-Berlin-Tokyo Axis.

The Spanish Civil War. A civil war tore Spain apart from 1936 to 1939. In 1936, many of Spain's army offi-

The Warring Nations

The Allies

Argentina (March 27, 1945)	India (Sept. 3, 1939)
Australia (Sept. 3, 1939)	Iran (Sept. 9, 1943)
Belgium (May 10, 1940)	Iraq (Jan. 16, 1943)
Bolivia (April 7, 1943)	Lebanon (Feb. 27, 1945)
Brazil (Aug. 22, 1942)	Liberia (Jan. 26, 1944)
Canada (Sept. 10, 1939)	Luxembourg (May 10, 1940)
Chile (Feb. 14, 1945)	Mexico (May 22, 1942)
China (Dec. 9, 1941)	Mongolian People's Republic
Colombia (Nov. 26, 1943)	(Aug. 9, 1945)
Costa Rica (Dec. 8, 1941)	Netherlands (May 10, 1940)
Cuba (Dec. 9, 1941)	New Zealand (Sept. 3, 1939)
Czechoslovakia	Nicaragua (Dec. 8, 1941)
(Dec. 16, 1941)	Norway (April 9, 1940)
Denmark (April 9, 1940)	Panama (Dec. 7, 1941)
Dominican Republic	Paraguay (Feb. 8, 1945)
(Dec. 8, 1941)	Peru (Feb. 11, 1945)
Ecuador (Feb. 2, 1945)	Poland (Sept. 1, 1939)
Egypt (Feb. 24, 1945)	San Marino (Sept 24, 1944)
El Salvador (Dec. 8, 1941)	Saudi Arabia (March 1, 1945)
Ethiopia (Dec. 1, 1942)	South Africa (Sept. 6, 1939)
France (Sept. 3, 1939)	Soviet Union (June 22, 1941)
Great Britain	Syria (Feb. 26, 1945)
(Sept. 3, 1939)	Turkey (Feb. 23, 1945)
Greece (Oct. 28, 1940)	United States (Dec. 8, 1941)
Guatemala (Dec. 9, 1941)	Uruguay (Feb. 22, 1945)
Haiti (Dec. 8, 1941)	Venezuela (Feb. 16, 1945)
Honduras (Dec. 8, 1941)	Yugoslavia (April 6, 1941)

The Axis

Albania (June 15, 1940)	Italy (June 10, 1940)
Bulgaria (April 6, 1941)	Japan (Dec. 7, 1941)
Finland (June 25, 1941)	Romania (June 22, 1941)
Germany (Sept. 1, 1939)	Thailand (Jan. 25, 1942)
Hungary (April 10, 1941)	

Dates are those on which each country entered the war.

AP/Wide World

Members of the Nazi Party marched in a rally in Nuremberg, Germany, in 1938. Their banners bore the Nazi emblem, the *swastika.* The Nazi Party gained control of Germany in 1933.

Lee Lockwood, Black Star

Two European Dictators, Adolf Hitler of Germany, *left,* and Benito Mussolini of Italy, *right,* dreamed of building powerful empires. Their actions plunged much of Europe and Africa into war.

The Glorification of Military Power accompanied the rise of a dictatorship in Japan during the 1930's. This military band was showered with confetti as it marched through Tokyo in 1937.

AP/Wide World

cers revolted against the government. The army rebels chose General Francisco Franco as their leader. Franco's forces were known as Nationalists or Rebels. The forces that supported Spain's elected government were called Loyalists or Republicans. The Spanish Civil War drew worldwide attention. During the war, the dictatorships again displayed their might while the democracies remained helpless.

Hitler and Mussolini sent troops, weapons, aircraft, and advisers to aid the Nationalists. The Soviet Union was the only power to help the Loyalists. France, Britain, and the United States decided not to become involved. However, Loyalist sympathizers from many countries joined the International Brigades that the Communists formed to fight in Spain.

The last Loyalist forces surrendered on April 1, 1939, and Franco set up a dictatorship in Spain. The Spanish Civil War served as a military proving ground for World War II because Germany, Italy, and the Soviet Union

used it to test weapons and tactics. The war in Spain was also a rehearsal for World War II in that it split the world into forces that either supported or opposed Nazism and Fascism.

The Failure of Appeasement. Hitler prepared to strike again soon after Germany absorbed Austria in March 1938. German territory then bordered Czechoslovakia on three sides. Czechoslovakia had become an independent nation after World War I. Its population consisted of many nationalities, including more than 3 million people of German descent. Hitler sought control of the Sudetenland, a region of western Czechoslovakia where most of the Germans lived. Urged on by Hitler, the Sudeten Germans began to clamor for union with Germany.

Czechoslavakia was determined to defend its territory. France and the Soviet Union had pledged their support. As tension mounted, Britain's Prime Minister Neville Chamberlain tried to restore calm. Chamberlain wished to preserve peace at all cost. He believed that war could be prevented by meeting Hitler's demands. That policy became known as *appeasement*.

Chamberlain had several meetings with Hitler during September 1938 as Europe teetered on the edge of war. Hitler raised his demands at each meeting. On September 29, Chamberlain and French Premier Édouard Daladier met with Hitler and Mussolini in Munich, Germany. Chamberlain and Daladier agreed to turn over the Sudetenland to Germany, and they forced Czechoslovakia to accept the agreement. Hitler promised that he had no more territorial demands.

The Munich Agreement marked the height of the policy of appeasement. Chamberlain and Daladier hoped that the agreement would satisfy Hitler and prevent war—or that it would at least prolong the peace until Britain and France were ready for war. The two leaders were mistaken on both counts.

The failure of appeasement soon became clear. Hitler broke the Munich Agreement in March 1939 and seized the rest of Czechoslovakia. He thereby added Czechoslovakia's armed forces and industries to Germany's military might. In the months before World War II began, Germany's preparations for war moved ahead faster than did the military build-up of Britain and France.

WORLD WAR II / Early Stages of the War

During the first year of World War II, Germany won a series of swift victories over Poland, Denmark, Luxembourg, the Netherlands, Belgium, Norway, and France. Germany then attempted to bomb Britain into surrendering, but it failed.

The Invasion of Poland. After Hitler seized Czechoslovakia, he began demanding territory from Poland. Great Britain and France pledged to help Poland if Germany attacked it. Yet the two powers could aid Poland only by invading Germany, a step that neither chose to take. Britain had only a small army. France had prepared to defend its territory, not to attack.

Great Britain and France hoped that the Soviet Union would help defend Poland. But Hitler and Stalin

shocked the world by becoming allies. On Aug. 23, 1939, Germany and the Soviet Union signed a *nonaggression pact*—in which they agreed not to go to war against each other. They secretly decided to divide Poland between themselves.

On Sept. 1, 1939, Germany invaded Poland and began World War II. Poland had a fairly large army but little modern equipment. The Polish army expected to fight along the country's frontiers. However, the Germans introduced a new method of warfare they called *blitzkrieg* (lightning war). The blitzkrieg stressed speed and surprise. Rows of tanks smashed through Poland's defenses and rolled deep into the country before the Polish army had time to react. Swarms of German dive

Germany's *Blitzkrieg* (**Lightning War**) overran Poland at the outbreak of World War II. In Tczew, the people deserted the streets as German armored vehicles rumbled through, *above*.

Ullstein Bilderdienst

bombers and fighter aircraft knocked out communications and pounded battle lines.

The Poles fought bravely. But Germany's blitzkrieg threw their army into confusion. On Sept. 17, 1939, Soviet forces invaded Poland from the east. By late September, the Soviet Union occupied the eastern third of Poland, and Germany had swallowed up the rest.

The Phony War. Great Britain and France declared war on Germany on Sept. 3, 1939, two days after the invasion of Poland. But the two countries stood by while Poland collapsed. France moved troops to the Maginot Line, a belt of steel and concrete fortresses it had built after World War I along its border with Germany. Britain sent a small force into northern France. Germany stationed troops on the Siegfried Line, a strip of defenses Hitler built in the 1930's opposite the Maginot Line. The two sides avoided fighting in late 1939 and early 1940. Journalists called the period the Phony War.

The Conquest of Denmark and Norway. Valuable shipments of iron ore from Sweden reached Germany by way of Norway's port of Narvik. Hitler feared British plans to cut off those shipments by laying explosives in Norway's coastal waters. In April 1940, German forces invaded Norway. They conquered Denmark on the way. Britain tried to help Norway, but Germany's airpower prevented many British ships and troops from reaching the country. Norway fell to the Germans in June 1940. The conquest of Norway secured Germany's shipments of iron ore. Norway also provided bases for German submarines and aircraft.

Chamberlain, the champion of appeasement, resigned after the invasion of Norway. Winston Churchill replaced him as Britain's prime minister on May 10, 1940. Churchill told the British people he had nothing to offer them but "blood, toil, tears, and sweat."

The Invasion of the Low Countries. The low countries—Belgium, Luxembourg, and the Netherlands—hoped to remain neutral after World War II began. However, Germany launched a blitzkrieg against them on May 10, 1940. The Low Countries immediately requested Allied help. But Luxembourg surrendered in one day, and the Netherlands in five days. British and French forces rushed into Belgium and fell into a German trap. As the Allied forces raced northward, the main German invasion cut behind them through the Belgian Ardennes Forest to the south. The Germans reached the English Channel on May 21. They had nearly surrounded Allied forces in Belgium.

King Leopold III of Belgium surrendered on May 28, 1940. His surrender left the Allied forces trapped in Belgium in great danger. They were retreating toward the French seaport of Dunkerque on the English Channel. Britain sent all available craft to rescue the troops. The rescue fleet included destroyers, yachts, ferries, fishing vessels, and motorboats. Under heavy bombardment, the vessels evacuated about 338,000 troops from May 26 to June 4. The evacuation of Dunkerque saved most of Britain's army. But the army left behind all its tanks and equipment. The remaining Allied troops in Dunkerque surrendered on June 4, 1940.

AP/Wide World · Keystone

The Evacuation of Dunkerque rescued about 338,000 Allied soldiers in 1940. While the Germans attacked, every available British vessel, including small craft like those above, ferried the troops to safety. At the right, soldiers waded out to a ship.

World War II in Europe and Northern Africa: 1939-1942

Germany's powerful war machine brought much of Europe under Axis control during the early stages of the war. By November 1942, Axis-controlled territory extended from Norway to northern Africa and from France to the Soviet Union. That month, Allied forces invaded northern Africa.

WORLD BOOK map

The Fall of France. France had expected to fight along a stationary battlefront and had built the Maginot Line for its defense. But German tanks and aircraft went around the Maginot Line. The Germans passed north of the Maginot Line as they swept through Luxembourg and Belgium and into northern France in May 1940. They launched a major assault against France on June 5. The blitzkrieg sent French forces reeling backward. As France neared collapse, Italy declared war on France and Great Britain on June 10.

German troops entered Paris on June 14, 1940. The French government had already fled the capital. Paul

Reynaud had become premier of France in March. Reynaud wanted to fight on. But many of his generals and cabinet officers believed that the battle for France was lost. Reynaud resigned, and a new French government agreed to an *armistice* (truce) on June 22.

Under the terms of the armistice, Germany occupied the northern two-thirds of France and a strip of western France along the Atlantic Ocean. Southern France remained in French control. The town of Vichy became the capital of unoccupied France. Marshal Henri Pétain, a French hero of World War I, headed the Vichy government. He largely cooperated with the Germans.

**Important Dates in Europe
and Northern Africa: 1939-1942**

1939

Sept. 1	Germany invaded Poland, starting World War II.
Sept. 3	Britain and France declared war on Germany.

1940

April 9	Germany invaded Denmark and Norway.
May 10	Germany invaded Belgium and the Netherlands.
June 10	Italy declared war on France and Great Britain.
June 22	France signed an armistice with Germany.
July 10	Battle of Britain began.

1941

April 6	Germany invaded Greece and Yugoslavia.
June 22	Germany invaded the Soviet Union.
Sept. 8	German troops completed the blockade of Leningrad, which lasted until January 1944.

1942

Aug. 25	Hitler ordered his forces to capture Stalingrad.
Oct. 23	Britain attacked the Axis at El Alamein in Egypt.
Nov. 8	Allied troops landed in Algeria and Morocco.

Mauritius, Black Star

After France Fell, victorious German soldiers paraded down the Champs Élysées, the famous Paris boulevard. France's surrender in June 1940 left Britain alone in the fight against Germany.

In November 1942, German troops occupied all France.

One of the French generals, Charles de Gaulle, had escaped to Britain after France fell. In radio broadcasts to France, he urged the people to carry on the fight against Germany. The troops who rallied around de Gaulle became known as the Free French forces.

The Battle of Britain. Hitler believed that Great Britain would seek peace with Germany after the fall of France. But Britain fought on alone. Hitler made preparations to cross the English Channel and invade southern England. Before the Germans could invade, however, they had to defeat Britain's Royal Air Force (RAF). The Battle of Britain, which began in July 1940, was the first battle ever fought to control the air.

In August 1940, the German air force, the Luftwaffe, began to attack RAF bases. Germany's aircraft outnumbered those of the RAF. But radar stations along England's coast provided warning of approaching German planes and helped the RAF intercept them.

Each side greatly overestimated the number of enemy planes it had shot down. By September 1940, the Luftwaffe mistakenly believed it had destroyed the RAF. The Germans then halted their strikes against RAF bases and began to bomb London and other civilian targets. They hoped to weaken civilian morale and force Britain to surrender. Air raids known as the Blitz took place nearly every night through the fall and the winter. In May 1941, Germany finally gave up its attempts to defeat Britain from the air.

Hitler's decision to end the attacks on the RAF enabled Britain to rebuild its air force. Britain's survival was immensely important later in the war because the country served as a base for the Allied *liberation* (freeing) of Europe from Nazi rule.

BBC Hulton from Bettmann Archive

UPI/Bettmann Newsphotos

The Bombing of London, called the Blitz, began in September 1940 and caused much destruction, *left.* Londoners sought safety in subway tunnels during the nightly raids, *above.* In May 1941, Germany stopped trying to bomb Britain into surrendering.

553

World War II had become a global conflict by the end of 1941. Fighting spread to Africa, the Balkan Peninsula of southeastern Europe, and the Soviet Union. The Axis and the Allies also battled each other at sea. In December 1941, the United States entered the war.

Fighting in Africa. The Italians opened battlefronts in Africa at about the time of the Battle of Britain. Mussolini expected easy victories over the small British forces in British Somaliland (now northern Somalia) and Egypt. In August 1940, the Italians pushed eastward from Ethiopia and overran British Somaliland. The following month, Italian forces stationed in Libya invaded Egypt.

For two years, the fighting seesawed back and forth across Libya and Egypt. Britain fought to keep the Axis out of Egypt. Axis control of Egypt would have cut Britain off from oil fields in the Middle East and from the Suez Canal, the shortest sea route to Britain's empire in Asia. Britain struck back at the Italians in December 1940, sweeping them out of Egypt and back into Libya. However, an Italian invasion of Greece then drew part of Britain's force from Africa and ended the advance.

Early in 1941, Hitler sent tank units trained in desert warfare to help the Italians in northern Africa. The tank units, known as the Afrika Korps, were led by General Erwin Rommel. Rommel's clever tactics earned him the nickname "The Desert Fox." During the spring, Rommel recaptured the Libyan territory the Italians had lost and drove into Egypt. The British again pushed the Axis forces back into Libya. In May 1942, Rommel broke through British lines and reached El Alamein, only 200 miles (320 kilometers) from the Suez Canal.

However, the Germans did not save Mussolini's empire in eastern Africa. By May 1941, Britain had defeated the Italians in British Somaliland and Ethiopia.

Fighting in the Balkans. Hitler used threats to force Bulgaria, Hungary, and Romania into joining the Axis. Those countries supplied Germany with food, petroleum, and other goods. Yugoslavia's government signed an agreement with the Axis in March 1941. But Yugoslavia's armed forces rebelled and overthrew the government. An enraged Hitler ordered that Yugoslavia be crushed. German troops began to pour into the country on April 6. Yugoslavia surrendered 11 days later. During that time, Hitler had to rescue Mussolini's troops elsewhere on the Balkan Peninsula.

Mussolini had tired of playing Hitler's junior partner, and he badly wanted a victory to boost his standing. In October 1940, Italian forces based in Albania invaded Greece. They expected to defeat the poorly equipped Greek army easily. The Greeks fought fiercely, though they were greatly outnumbered. By December, they had driven the Italians out of Greece and had overrun part of Albania. Britain sent a small force to help Greece. But in April 1941, a much larger German force came to the aid of the Italians. By the end of April, the Axis controlled Greece.

British troops in Greece withdrew to the island of Crete in the Mediterranean Sea. On May 20, 1941, thousands of German paratroopers descended on Crete and seized an airfield. More German troops then landed. The first airborne invasion in history gave Germany an important base in the Mediterranean by the end of May.

The defeats in the Balkans were serious blows to Britain. However, some historians believe that the detours into Yugoslavia and Greece were costly for Hitler because they delayed his invasion of the Soviet Union. Hitler confidently predicted victory over the Soviet Union within eight weeks, and he had failed to prepare for a winter war.

Süddeutscher Verlag

Ullstein Bilderdienst

In the Battle of the Atlantic, German submarines, called *U-boats,* sank ships headed for Britain. Britain's survival depended on shipments across the Atlantic from North America. At the left, a U-boat surfaced to look for targets. At the right, a U-boat officer prepared to launch a torpedo.

The Invasion of the Soviet Union. Germany and the Soviet Union proved to be uneasy partners. Hitler viewed the Soviet Union as Germany's chief enemy. He feared Soviet ambitions to expand in eastern Europe. Hitler also wanted control of Soviet wheat fields and oil fields. His 1939 nonaggression pact with Stalin served merely to keep the Soviet Union out of the war while Germany overran western Europe.

Stalin distrusted Hitler, and he sought to obtain more naval bases and to strengthen Soviet borders. In November 1939, the Soviet Union invaded Finland. The Finns surrendered in March 1940 after a fierce fight. In the summer, the Soviet Union seized the countries of Estonia, Latvia, and Lithuania along the Baltic Sea.

Germany's invasion of the Soviet Union, which was code-named Operation Barbarossa, began on June 22, 1941. It took the Soviet Union by surprise. German tanks smashed through Soviet battle lines. During the first few weeks of the campaign, the German armies encircled and killed or captured hundreds of thousands of Soviet troops. As the Germans advanced, the Soviet people destroyed factories, dams, railroads, food supplies, and anything else that might be useful to the enemy. The Germans appeared headed for victory by late July. They then began to make mistakes.

Hitler's generals wanted to press on to Moscow. But Hitler overruled them. Instead, he reinforced the German armies heading north toward Leningrad and south toward the Crimean Peninsula on the Black Sea. While the Germans wasted time transferring forces, Stalin brought in fresh troops. The German advance slowed in September, though the Germans took the city of Kiev in the south. Heavy rains fell in October, and German tanks and artillery bogged down in mud.

By November 1941, the Germans had surrounded Leningrad and had begun to encircle Moscow. They reached the suburbs of Moscow by early December. The temperature then plunged to $-40°$ F. $(-40°$ C). An unusually severe Soviet winter had begun early. German troops lacked warm clothing and suffered from frostbite. Their tanks and weapons broke down in the bitter cold. Winter had saved the Soviet Union.

The Battle of the Atlantic. Britain's survival in World War II depended on shipments of food, war materials, and other supplies across the Atlantic Ocean from North America. Throughout the war, Germany tried to destroy such shipments, while Britain struggled to keep its Atlantic shipping lanes open.

Germany's surface fleet was far too weak to challenge Britain's Royal Navy in battle during World War II. But individual German battleships attacked British cargo vessels. The Royal Navy hunted down and sank such raiders one by one. The biggest operation was against the powerful German battleship *Bismarck*. In May 1941, a fleet of British warships chased, trapped, and finally sank the *Bismarck* about 400 miles (640 kilometers) off the coast of France. Afterward, Germany rarely allowed its large warships to leave harbor.

The greatest threat to British shipping came from German submarines, called *Unterseeboote* or *U-boats*. U-boats prowled the Atlantic, torpedoing any Allied cargo ships they spotted. The conquest of Norway and of France gave Germany excellent bases for its U-boats. To combat the U-boats, Britain began to use a *convoy system*. Under that system, cargo ships sailed in large groups escorted by surface warships. But Britain had few such ships available for escort duty.

From 1940 to 1942, Germany appeared to be winning the Battle of the Atlantic. Each month, U-boats sank thousands of tons of Allied shipping. But the Allies gradually overcame the U-boat danger. They used radar and an underwater detection device called *sonar* to locate German submarines. Long-range aircraft bombed U-boats as they surfaced. Shipyards in North America stepped up their production of warships to accompany convoys. By mid-1943, the Allies were sinking U-boats faster than Germany could replace them. The crisis in the Atlantic had passed.

WORLD WAR II / The United States Enters the War

After World War II began in Europe in 1939, President Franklin D. Roosevelt announced the neutrality of the United States. Canada declared war on Germany almost at once. As part of the British Commonwealth of Nations, it entered the war on Sept. 10, 1939, one week after Great Britain did.

The majority of people in the United States thought that their country should stay out of World War II. Yet most Americans hoped for an Allied victory. Roosevelt and other *interventionists* urged all aid "short of war" to nations fighting the Axis. They argued that an Axis victory would endanger democracies everywhere. *Isolationists*, on the other hand, opposed U.S. aid to warring nations. They accused Roosevelt of steering the nation into a war it was not prepared to fight.

All the countries in North and South America eventually declared war on the Axis. But only Brazil, Canada, Mexico, and the United States sent troops. The United States played a key role in the final Allied victory.

The Arsenal of Democracy. Roosevelt hoped to defeat the Axis powers by equipping the nations fighting them with ships, tanks, aircraft, and other war materials. Roosevelt appealed to the United States to become what he called "the arsenal of democracy."

At the start of World War II, U.S. neutrality laws forbade the sale of arms to warring nations. Congress soon changed the laws to help Britain and France. A new law permitted warring nations to buy arms for cash. But by late 1940, Britain had nearly run out of funds for arms. Roosevelt then proposed the Lend-Lease Act, which would permit him to lend or lease raw materials, equipment, and weapons to any nation fighting the Axis. Congress approved the act in March 1941. In all, 38 nations received a total of about $50 billion in aid under Lend-Lease. More than half the aid went to the British Empire and about a fourth to the Soviet Union.

Japan Attacks. Japan, not Germany, finally plunged the United States into World War II. By 1940, Japa-

The Attack on Pearl Harbor by Japanese planes on Dec. 7, 1941, drew the United States into World War II. The air raid crippled the U.S. Pacific Fleet. Within hours, six of the eight battleships moored at Pearl Harbor had gone to the bottom, and about 150 planes had been destroyed.

Bettmann Archive

nese forces were bogged down in China. The Chinese government, led by Chiang Kai-shek, had fled to central China. But China refused to give up. To force China to surrender, Japan decided to cut off supplies reaching China from Southeast Asia. Japan also wanted the rich resources of Southeast Asia for itself. Japan's military leaders spoke of building an empire, which they called the Greater East Asia Co-Prosperity Sphere.

The United States opposed Japan's expansion in Southeast Asia. In 1940, Japanese troops occupied northern Indochina (today part of Laos and Vietnam). In response, the United States cut off important exports to Japan. Japanese industries relied heavily on petroleum, scrap metal, and other raw materials from the United States. Tension rose after Japan seized the rest of Indochina in 1941. Roosevelt then barred the withdrawal of Japanese funds from American banks.

General Hideki Tojo became premier of Japan in October 1941. Tojo and Japan's other military leaders realized that only the United States Navy had the power to block Japan's expansion in Asia. They decided to cripple the U.S. Pacific Fleet with one forceful blow.

On Dec. 7, 1941, Japanese aircraft attacked without warning the U.S. Pacific Fleet at anchor in Pearl Harbor in Hawaii. The bombing of Pearl Harbor was a great success for Japan at first. It disabled much of the Pacific Fleet and destroyed many aircraft. But in the long run, the attack on Pearl Harbor proved disastrous for Japan. It propelled enraged Americans to arms.

The United States, Canada, and Great Britain declared war on Japan on Dec. 8, 1941. The next day, China declared war on the Axis. Germany and Italy declared war on the United States on December 11. World War II had become a global conflict.

WORLD WAR II / The Allies Attack in Europe and Northern Africa

Allied defeats in Europe ended late in 1941. Soviet forces held off the German advance in eastern Europe in 1942 and won a major victory at Stalingrad in 1943. The Allies invaded northern Africa in 1942 and forced Italy to surrender in 1943. Allied troops swarmed ashore in 1944 in northern France in the largest seaborne invasion in history. Allied attacks from the east and the west forced Germany to surrender in 1945.

The Strategy. Churchill, Roosevelt, and Stalin—the leaders of the three major Allied powers—were known during World War II as the Big Three. The Big Three and their military advisers planned the strategy that defeated the Axis. Churchill and Roosevelt conferred frequently on overall strategy. Stalin directed the Soviet war effort but rarely consulted his allies.

Roosevelt relied heavily on his military advisers, the Joint Chiefs of Staff. They consisted of General of the

Army Henry H. Arnold, commanding general of the Army Air Forces; General of the Army George C. Marshall, chief of staff of the Army; Fleet Admiral Ernest J. King, chief of naval operations; and Fleet Admiral William D. Leahy, Roosevelt's chief of staff. Churchill had a similar advisory body.

The main wartime disagreement among the Big Three concerned an Allied invasion of western Europe. Stalin constantly urged Roosevelt and Churchill to open a second fighting front in western Europe and thus draw German troops from the Soviet front. Both Roosevelt and Churchill supported the idea but disagreed on where and when to invade. The Americans wanted to land in northern France as soon as possible. The British argued that an invasion of France before the Allies were fully prepared would be disastrous. Instead, Churchill favored invading Italy first. His view won out.

Roosevelt and Churchill first met in August 1941 aboard ship off the coast of Newfoundland. They issued the Atlantic Charter, a statement of the postwar aims of the United States and Great Britain. After the Japanese attacked Pearl Harbor, Roosevelt and Churchill conferred in Washington, D.C. The two leaders felt that Germany was a nearer and a more dangerous enemy than Japan. They decided to concentrate on defeating Germany first.

In January 1943, Roosevelt and Churchill met in Casablanca, Morocco. They agreed to invade the Mediterranean island of Sicily after driving the Germans and Italians from northern Africa. At the conference, Roosevelt announced that the Allies would accept only *unconditional* (complete) surrender from the Axis powers. Churchill supported him.

Roosevelt and Churchill first met with Stalin in November 1943 in Teheran, Iran. The Big Three discussed plans for a joint British and American invasion of France in the spring of 1944. They did not meet again until Germany neared collapse. In February 1945, Roosevelt, Churchill, and Stalin gathered at Yalta, a Soviet city on the Crimean Peninsula. They agreed that their countries would each occupy a zone of Germany after the war. France was to occupy a fourth zone. At the Yalta Conference, Stalin pledged to permit free elections in Poland and other countries in eastern Europe after the war. He later broke that pledge. Roosevelt died in April 1945, two months after the Yalta Conference.

On the Soviet Front. Soviet forces struck back at the Germans outside Moscow in December 1941. The Soviet troops pushed the invaders back about 100 miles

National Archives

The Big Three set overall Allied strategy. They were Soviet leader Joseph Stalin, *left;* U.S. President Franklin D. Roosevelt, *center;* and British Prime Minister Winston Churchill, *right.*

(160 kilometers) from Moscow during the winter. The Germans never again came so close to Moscow as they had been in December 1941. However, the Soviet recovery was short lived.

In the spring of 1942, the Germans again attacked. They overran the Crimean Peninsula and headed eastward toward Soviet oil fields in the Caucasus region. Hitler ordered General Friedrich von Paulus to press on and to take the city of Stalingrad (now Volgograd). A savage five-month battle for Stalingrad began in late August. By September, German and Soviet soldiers were fighting hand to hand in the heart of the city.

Süddeutscher Verlag   Ullstein Bilderdienst

In the Soviet Union, winter weather and the determination of the army and the people slowed the German advance. German equipment broke down in the cold and had to be pushed through the snow, *left.* In the ruins of Stalingrad, *right,* Soviet soldiers fought the Germans building by building.

With winter approaching, Paulus asked permission to pull back from Stalingrad. Hitler ordered him to hold on and fight. Soviet troops counterattacked in mid-November. Within a week, they had trapped Paulus' army. The Luftwaffe promised to supply the army by air. But few supplies landed. Each day, thousands of German soldiers froze or starved to death. On Feb. 2, 1943, the last German troops in Stalingrad surrendered.

The Battle of Stalingrad marked a turning point in World War II. It halted Germany's eastward advance. About 300,000 German troops were killed or captured. An enormous number of Soviet soldiers also died.

In Northern Africa. The Germans took a beating in northern Africa about the same time as their defeat at Stalingrad. In the summer of 1942, German and Italian forces led by Rommel faced the British at El Alamein, Egypt. General Harold Alexander and Lieutenant General Bernard L. Montgomery commanded the British forces in northern Africa.

Rommel attacked in late August 1942 at Alam el Halfa south of El Alamein. The British halted the attack, partly because they had secretly learned of Rommel's battle plan. Churchill called for an immediate counterattack. But Montgomery refused to rush into

World War II in Europe and Northern Africa: 1943-1945

The Allies attacked the Axis in Europe after defeating it in northern Africa in May 1943. Italy surrendered in September 1943, two months after the invasion of Sicily. In June 1944, the Allies landed in northern France. Attacks from the east and west forced Germany to surrender in May 1945.

WORLD BOOK map

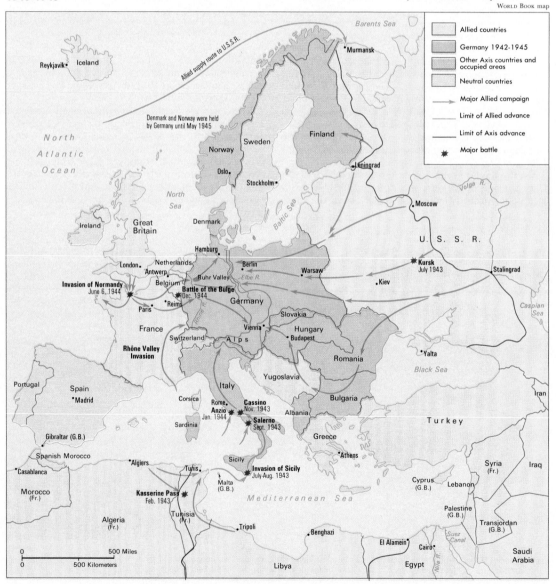

battle before he was fully prepared. On October 23, Montgomery struck at El Alamein. He had broken through the enemy lines by early November. The Axis forces retreated toward Tunisia with the British in hot pursuit. The Battle of El Alamein, like the Battle of Stalingrad, marked a turning point in the war. In both battles, the Allies ended Hitler's string of victories.

Soon after the Battle of El Alamein, the Allies invaded French colonies in northern Africa. Allied troops commanded by Lieutenant General Dwight D. Eisenhower of the United States landed in Algeria and Morocco on Nov. 8, 1942. Vichy French forces in northern Africa fought back for a few days. They then joined the Allied side.

The Allies hoped to advance rapidly into Tunisia and thereby cut off the Axis forces from their home bases in Italy and Sicily. But Axis troops moved faster and seized Tunisia first. There, Rommel prepared for battle. American troops first engaged in combat with the Germans in February 1943 near Kasserine Pass in northern Tunisia. Rommel defeated the inexperienced Americans in hard fighting. But thereafter, the Allies steadily closed in. The last Axis forces in northern Africa surrendered in May. Rommel had already returned to Germany. By clearing the Axis forces from northern Africa, the Allies obtained bases from which to invade southern Europe.

The Air War. Before World War II began, some aviation experts claimed that the long-range bomber was the most advanced weapon in the world. They believed that bombers could wipe out cities and industries and so destroy an enemy's desire and ability to go on fighting. Their theory was tested during World War II.

The first great air battle in history opened in 1940 between Germany's Luftwaffe and Britain's Royal Air Force. During the Battle of Britain, Marshal Hermann Goering, commander of the Luftwaffe, failed to defeat Britain from the air. RAF fighter planes, including Spitfires and Hurricanes, helped win the Battle of Britain by shooting down German bombers. By May 1941, the bombing of Britain had largely stopped. But RAF bombers pounded Germany until the end of the war.

At first, Britain's bombing campaign was costly and

Imperial War Museum

The Air War Against Germany was aimed at destroying its ability to keep on fighting. Bombers like this American B-17 struck factories, railroads, and other industrial targets.

ineffective. The RAF relied on *area bombing* in the hope of hitting a target by plastering the area with bombs. It favored nighttime raids, which were safer than daytime raids. But pilots often missed their targets in the dark. In 1942, Britain turned to *saturation bombing* of German cities. About 900 bombers battered Cologne on May 30, 1942, in the first such massive raid.

The United States joined the air war against Germany in 1942. The American B-17 bomber carried a better bombsight than British planes. B-17's were known as Flying Fortresses because of their heavy armor and many guns, and they could take much punishment. For those reasons, the Americans favored *pinpoint bombing* of specific targets during daytime rather than area bombing at night. From 1943 until the end of the war, bombs rained down on Germany around the clock.

In spite of the massive bombardment, German industries continued to increase production, and German morale failed to crack. The air war achieved its goals only during the last 10 months of World War II. In that time, nearly three times as many bombs fell on Germany as in all the rest of the war. By the end of the war, Germany's cities lay in ruins. Its factories, refineries, railroads, and canals had nearly ceased to operate. Hundreds of thousands of German civilians had been killed. Millions more were homeless. The bomber had finally become the weapon its supporters had foreseen.

Germany's air defenses rapidly improved during World War II. The Germans used radar to spot incoming bombers, and they used fighter aircraft to shoot them down. In 1944, Germany introduced the first jet fighter, the Messerschmitt 262. The speedy plane could easily overtake the propeller-driven fighters of the Allies. But Hitler failed to use jet fighters effectively, which kept Germany from gaining an advantage in the air war.

In 1944, Germany used the first guided missiles against Britain. The V-1 and V-2 missiles caused great

**Important Dates in Europe
and Northern Africa: 1943-1945**

1943

Feb. 2	The last Germans surrendered at Stalingrad.
May 13	Axis forces in northern Africa surrendered.
July 4	Germany opened an assault near the Soviet city of Kursk.
July 10	Allied forces invaded Sicily.
Sept. 3	Italy secretly surrendered to the Allies.
Sept. 9	Allied troops landed at Salerno, Italy.

1944

June 6	Allied troops landed in Normandy in the D-Day invasion of northern France.
July 20	A plot to assassinate Hitler failed.
Dec. 16	The Germans struck back at U.S. troops in the Battle of the Bulge.

1945

April 30	Hitler took his life in Berlin.
May 7	Germany surrendered unconditionally to the Allies in Reims, France, ending World War II in Europe.

The Campaign in Italy was a slow and bitter struggle against strongly defended German positions. The U.S. infantrymen above belonged to the 92nd Division, a black unit that served in Italy.

damage and took many lives. But the Germans introduced the weapons too late to affect the war's outcome.

The Invasion of Italy. The Allies planned to invade Sicily after driving the Axis forces out of northern Africa. Axis planes bombed Allied ships in the Mediterranean Sea from bases in Sicily. The Allies wanted to make the Mediterranean safe for their ships. They also hoped that an invasion of Sicily might knock a war-weary Italy out of the war.

Allied forces under Eisenhower landed along Sicily's south coast on July 10, 1943. For 39 days, they engaged in bitter fighting with German troops over rugged terrain. The last Germans left Sicily on August 17.

Mussolini fell from power on July 25, 1943, after the invasion of Sicily. The Italian government imprisoned Mussolini, but German paratroopers later rescued him. Italy's new premier, Field Marshal Pietro Badoglio, began secret peace talks with the Allies. Badoglio hoped

to prevent Italy from becoming a battleground. Italy surrendered on September 3. However, Field Marshal Albert Kesselring, Germany's commander in the Mediterranean region, was determined to fight the Allies for control of Italy.

Allied forces led by Lieutenant General Mark W. Clark of the United States landed at Salerno, Italy, on Sept. 9, 1943. They fought hard just to stay ashore. Another Allied force had already landed farther south. The Allies slowly struggled up the Italian Peninsula in a series of head-on assaults against well-defended German positions. By early November, the Allies had nearly reached Cassino, about 75 miles (120 kilometers) south of Rome. But they failed to pierce German defenses there. Some of the most brutal fighting of World War II occurred near Cassino.

In January 1944, the Allies landed troops at Anzio, west of Cassino, in an effort to attack the Germans from behind. However, German forces kept the Allies pinned down on the beaches at Anzio for four months. Thousands of Allied soldiers died there.

The Allies finally broke through German defenses in Italy in May 1944. Rome fell on June 4. The Germans held their positions in northern Italy through the fall and winter. But in the spring, the Allies swept toward the Alps. German forces in Italy surrendered on May 2, 1945. Mussolini had been captured and shot by Italian resistance fighters on April 28.

D-Day. Soon after the evacuation of Dunkerque in 1940, Great Britain started to plan a return to France. In 1942, the United States and Britain began to discuss a large-scale invasion across the English Channel. That summer, the Allies raided the French port of Dieppe on the channel. The raiders met strong German defenses and suffered heavy losses. The Dieppe raid convinced the Allies that landing on open beaches had a better chance of success than landing in a port.

Throughout 1943, preparations moved ahead for an

U.S. Coast Guard

Hitting the Beach, Allied infantrymen swarmed ashore along the Normandy coast of northern France on D-Day—June 6, 1944. It was the largest seaborne invasion in history. Hitler had boasted that German defenses along the coast could resist any attack. But he was wrong.

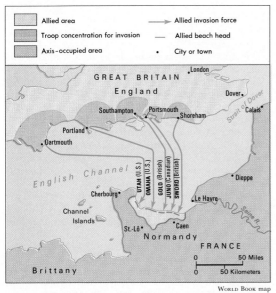

WORLD BOOK map

U.S. Army

The Normandy Invasion on June 6, 1944, brought Allied forces ashore on five beaches, shown with their code names. Within a week, the Allies held the area outlined in blue.

Talking to His Men, General Dwight D. Eisenhower, commander of the Normandy invasion, wished paratroopers luck before they dropped behind German lines in France on D-Day.

invasion of northern France the following year. The invasion plan received the code name Operation Overlord. The Allies assembled huge amounts of equipment and great numbers of troops for Overlord in southern England. General Dwight D. Eisenhower was selected to command the invasion.

The Germans expected an Allied invasion along the north coast of France in 1944. But they were unsure where. A chain of fortifications, which the Germans called the Atlantic Wall, ran along the coast. Hitler placed Rommel in charge of strengthening German defenses along the English Channel. Rommel brought in artillery, mined the water and the beaches, and strung up barbed wire. The Germans concentrated their troops near Calais, at the narrowest part of the English Channel. But the Allies planned to land farther west, in a region of northern France called Normandy.

Eisenhower chose Monday, June 5, 1944, as D-Day—the date of the Normandy invasion. Rough seas forced him to postpone D-Day until June 6. During the night, about 2,700 ships carrying landing craft and 176,000 soldiers crossed the channel. Minesweepers had gone ahead to clear the water. Paratroopers dropped behind German lines to capture bridges and railroad tracks. At dawn, battleships opened fire on the beaches. At 6:30 A.M., troops from the United States, Britain, Canada, and France stormed ashore on a 60-mile (100-kilometer) front in the largest seaborne invasion in history.

D-Day took the Germans by surprise. But they fought back fiercely. At one landing site, code-named Omaha Beach, U.S. troops came under heavy fire and barely managed to stay ashore. Nevertheless, all five Allied landing beaches were secure by the end of D-Day. The Allies soon had an artificial harbor in place for unloading more troops and supplies. A pipeline carried fuel

across the channel. By the end of June 1944, about a million Allied troops had reached France.

The Allied forces advanced slowly at first. The Americans struggled westward to capture the badly needed port of Cherbourg. British and Canadian soldiers fought their way to Caen. The battle for Cherbourg ended on June 27. Caen, which the British hoped to capture on D-Day, fell on July 18. Near the end of July, the Allies finally broke through German lines into open country.

The Drive to the Rhine. On July 25, 1944, Allied bombers blasted a gap in the German front near St.-Lô, about 50 miles (80 kilometers) southeast of Cherbourg. The U.S. Third Army under Lieutenant General George S. Patton plowed through the hole. The battlefield had opened up. During August, the Allies cleared the Germans out of most of northwestern France. Allied bombers hounded the retreating Germans.

Patton's army rolled eastward toward Paris. On Aug. 19, 1944, Parisians rose up against the occupying German forces. Hitler ordered the city destroyed. But his generals delayed carrying out the order. American and Free French forces liberated Paris on August 25.

In mid-August 1944, Allied forces landed in southern France. They moved rapidly up the Rhône River Valley. Meanwhile, Patton raced eastward toward the German border and the Rhine River. In late August, his tanks ran out of fuel. To the north, British forces led by Field Marshal Bernard L. Montgomery swept into Belgium and captured Antwerp on September 4. The Allies planned a daring airborne operation to carry them across the Rhine. On September 17, about 20,000 paratroopers dropped behind German lines to seize bridges in the Netherlands. But bad weather and other problems hampered the operation. It became clear that victory over Germany would have to wait until 1945.

Robert Capa, Magnum

Wild with Joy, Parisians welcomed Allied troops as they rode down the Champs Élysées on Aug. 26, 1944. Paris had been freed the day before, after more than four years of Nazi occupation.

Germany's generals knew they were beaten. But Hitler pulled his failing resources together for another assault. On Dec. 16, 1944, German troops surprised and overwhelmed the Americans in the Ardennes Forest in Belgium and Luxembourg. However, the Germans lacked the troops and fuel to turn their thrust into a breakthrough. Within two weeks, the Americans stopped the German advance near the Meuse River in Belgium. The Ardennes offensive is also known as the Battle of the Bulge because of the bulging shape of the battleground on a map.

The Soviet Advance. The Soviet victory in the Battle of Stalingrad ended Germany's progress in eastern Europe. After January 1943, Soviet soldiers slowly pushed the Germans back. Soviet forces had improved by 1943, and they greatly outnumbered the opposing German armies. Supplies poured into the Soviet Union from Britain and the United States, and Soviet factories had geared up for wartime production.

Nevertheless, the Germans returned to the offensive in July 1943 near the Soviet city of Kursk. They massed about 3,000 tanks for the assault. Soviet forces lay waiting for them. In one of the greatest tank battles in history, Soviet mines, tanks, antitank guns, and aircraft blew apart many German tanks. Hitler finally called off the attack to save his remaining tanks.

Soviet troops moved slowly forward during the summer and fall of 1943. In January 1944, a Soviet offensive ended the siege of Leningrad, which had begun in September 1941. About a million Leningraders died during the siege, mostly from lack of food and heat. But the city never surrendered.

In June 1944, soon after the Normandy invasion, Stalin's armies attacked along a 450-mile (720-kilometer) front. By late July, Soviet troops had reached the outskirts of Warsaw. Poland's Home Army rose up against German forces in Warsaw on August 1. But Soviet troops refused to come to Poland's aid. Stalin permitted the Germans to destroy the Home Army, which might have resisted his plans to set up a Communist govern-

ment in Poland after the war. The Home Army surrendered after two months. More than 200,000 Poles died during the Warsaw uprising. Soviet forces entered Warsaw in January 1945.

Meanwhile, Soviet troops drove into Romania and Bulgaria. The Germans pulled out of Greece and Yugoslavia in the fall of 1944 but held out in Budapest, the capital of Hungary, until February 1945. Vienna, Austria's capital, fell to Soviet soldiers in April. By then, Soviet troops occupied nearly all of eastern Europe.

Victory in Europe. The Allies began their final assault on Germany in early 1945. Soviet soldiers reached the Oder River, about 40 miles (65 kilometers) east of Berlin, in January. Allied forces in the west occupied positions along the Rhine by early March.

British and Canadian forces cleared the Germans out of the Netherlands and swept into northern Germany. American and French forces raced toward the Elbe River in central Germany. Hitler ordered his soldiers to fight to the death. But large numbers of German soldiers surrendered each day.

As they advanced, the Allies discovered horrifying evidence of Nazi brutality. Hitler had ordered the imprisonment and murder of millions of Jews and members of other minority groups in concentration camps. The starving survivors of the death camps gave proof of the terrible suffering of those who had already died.

The capture of Berlin, then Germany's capital, was left to Soviet forces. By April 25, 1945, Soviet troops had surrounded the city. From a *bunker* (shelter) deep underground, Hitler ordered German soldiers to fight on. On April 30, however, Hitler committed suicide. He remained convinced that his cause had been right but that the German people had proven unworthy of his rule.

Grand Admiral Karl Doenitz briefly succeeded Hitler as the leader of Germany. Doenitz arranged for Germany's surrender. On May 7, 1945, Colonel General Alfred Jodl, chief of staff of the German armed forces, signed a statement of unconditional surrender at Eisenhower's headquarters in Reims, France. World War II had ended in Europe. The Allies declared May 8 as V-E Day, or Victory in Europe Day.

Imperial War Museum

Survivors of a Nazi Death Camp—some too weak to stand— provided proof of Nazi savagery. The Nazis imprisoned and murdered millions of Jews, Slavs, and members of other groups.

The Spitfire was an outstanding British fighter plane of World War II. Spitfires were noted for their high speed, ability to make tight turns, and rapid climbing rate. For those reasons, they could outmaneuver most German fighters. In 1940, Spitfires helped defeat Germany in the Battle of Britain. A Spitfire IA is shown at the left.

The B-17 was a widely used U.S. bomber of World War II. B-17's became famous for daytime raids over Germany. They were called Flying Fortresses because of their heavy armor and many guns. The B-17G, *right,* carried 13 machine guns.

The DUKW, nicknamed the "Duck," was an American six-wheeled truck that traveled over water and land. Ducks carried men and supplies from transport ships to enemy shores in *amphibious* (seaborne) landings. They were first used in the Allied invasion of Sicily in July 1943 and later in amphibious operations in the Pacific.

The Tank played a key role in combat in World War II. Germany, in particular, made use of the tank's mobility and firepower. In early victories, Germany massed its tanks and smashed through enemy battle lines in surprise attacks. The German Tiger, *right,* was a type of heavy tank that could outgun almost all Allied tanks.

The Aircraft Carrier was a floating airfield that became the backbone of the U.S. Navy during World War II. Carrier-based planes took part in many battles in the Pacific and helped defeat Japan's navy. The irregular pattern on the U.S.S. *Wasp, below,* made it difficult for enemy submarines to determine the ship's course.

WORLD BOOK illustrations by Tony Gibbons

The attack on Pearl Harbor on Dec. 7, 1941, left the U.S. Pacific Fleet powerless to halt Japan's expansion. During the next six months, Japanese forces swept across Southeast Asia and the western Pacific Ocean. Japan's empire reached its greatest size in August 1942. It stretched northeast to the Aleutian Islands of Alaska, west to Burma, and south to the Netherlands Indies (now Indonesia). The Allies halted Japan's expansion in the summer of 1942. They nibbled away at its empire until Japan agreed to surrender in August 1945.

Early Japanese Victories. On Dec. 8, 1941, within hours of the attack on Pearl Harbor, Japanese bombers struck the British colony of Hong Kong on the south coast of China and two U.S. islands in the Pacific Ocean—Guam and Wake. The Japanese invaded Thailand the same day. Thailand surrendered within hours and joined the Axis. Japanese troops took Hong Kong, Guam, and Wake Island by Christmas.

From Thailand, Japanese forces soon advanced into Malaya (now part of Malaysia) and Burma. Great Britain then ruled that region. The British wrongly believed that soldiers could not penetrate the thick jungles of the Malay Peninsula. They expected an assault by sea instead. But Japanese troops streamed through the jungles and rapidly overran the peninsula.

By late January 1942, the Japanese had pushed British forces back to Singapore, a fortified island off the tip of the Malay Peninsula. The Japanese stormed the island on February 8, and Singapore surrendered a week later. Japan captured about 85,000 soldiers, making the fall of Singapore Britain's worst military defeat ever.

Japan's next target was the petroleum-rich Netherlands Indies, south of Malaya. Allied warships protected those islands. Japan's navy mauled the ships in February 1942 in the Battle of the Java Sea. The Netherlands Indies fell in early March.

Meanwhile, Japanese forces had advanced into southern Burma. China sent troops into Burma to help Britain hold onto the Burma Road. Weapons, food, and other goods traveled over that supply route from India to China. In April 1942, Japan seized and shut down the Burma Road. The Japanese had driven Allied forces from most of Burma by mid-May.

Only the conquest of the Philippines took longer than Japan expected. Japan had begun landing troops in the Philippines on Dec. 10, 1941. American and Philippine forces commanded by U.S. General Douglas MacArthur defended the islands. In late December, MacArthur's forces abandoned Manila, the capital of the Philippines, and withdrew to nearby Bataan Peninsula. Although suffering from malnutrition and disease, they beat back Japanese attacks for three months.

President Roosevelt ordered MacArthur to Australia, and he left the Philippines in March 1942. He promised the Filipinos, "I shall return." On April 9, about 75,000 exhausted troops on Bataan surrendered to the Japanese. Most of them were forced to march about 65 miles (105 kilometers) to prison camps. Many prisoners died of disease and mistreatment during what became known as the Bataan Death March. Some soldiers held out on Corregidor Island, near Bataan, until May 6. By then, the Japanese were victorious everywhere.

Japan's string of quick victories astonished even the Japanese. It terrified the Allies. The fall of the Netherlands Indies left Australia unprotected. The capture of Burma brought the Japanese to India's border. Both Australia and India feared a Japanese invasion. Japanese planes bombed Darwin on Australia's north coast in February 1942.

The Tide Turns. Three events during 1942 helped turn the tide against Japan in World War II. They were (1) the Doolittle raid, (2) the Battle of the Coral Sea, and (3) the Battle of Midway.

The Doolittle Raid. To show that Japan could be beaten, the United States staged a daring bombing raid on the Japanese homeland. On April 18, 1942, Lieutenant Colonel James H. Doolittle led 16 B-25 bombers in a surprise attack on Tokyo and other Japanese cities. The bombers took off from the deck of the *Hornet*, an aircraft carrier more than 600 miles (960 kilometers) east of Japan. The raid did very little damage. But it alarmed Japan's leaders, who had believed that their homeland was safe from Allied bombs. To prevent future raids, the Japanese determined to capture more islands to the south and the east and so extend the country's defenses. They soon found themselves in trouble.

American Soldiers in the Philippines had to march to prison camps after they were captured by the Japanese in April 1942. Many died during what is known as the Bataan Death March.

Important Dates in the Pacific: 1941-1942

	1941
Dec. 7	Japan bombed U.S. military bases at Pearl Harbor in Hawaii.
Dec. 8	The United States, Great Britain, and Canada declared war on Japan.
	1942
Feb. 15	Singapore fell to the Japanese.
Feb. 26-28	Japan defeated an Allied naval force in the Battle of the Java Sea.
April 9	U.S. and Philippine troops on Bataan Peninsula surrendered.
April 18	U.S. bombers hit Tokyo in the Doolittle raid.
May 4-8	The Allies checked a Japanese assault in the Battle of the Coral Sea.
June 4-6	The Allies defeated Japan in the Battle of Midway.
Aug. 7	U.S. marines landed on Guadalcanal.

UPI/Bettmann Newsphotos

The Battle of the Coral Sea. In May 1942, a Japanese invasion force sailed toward Australia's base at Port Moresby on the south coast of the island of New Guinea. Port Moresby lay at Australia's doorstep. American warships met the Japanese force in the Coral Sea, northeast of Australia. The Battle of the Coral Sea, fought from May 4 to 8, was unlike all earlier naval battles. It was the first naval battle in which opposing ships never sighted one another. Planes based on aircraft carriers did all the fighting. Neither side won a clear victory. But the battle halted Japan's assault on Port Moresby and temporarily checked the threat to Australia.

The Battle of Midway. Japan next sent a large fleet to capture Midway Island at the westernmost tip of the Hawaiian chain. The United States had cracked Japan's naval code and thus learned about the coming invasion. Admiral Chester W. Nimitz, commander of the U.S. Pacific Fleet, gathered the ships that had survived the raid on Pearl Harbor and the Battle of the Coral Sea. He prepared to ambush the Japanese.

The Battle of Midway opened on June 4, 1942, with a Japanese bombing raid on Midway. Outdated U.S. bombers flew in low and launched torpedoes against Japanese warships. But Japanese guns downed most of the slow-moving planes. American dive bombers swooped in next. They pounded enemy aircraft carriers while their planes refueled on deck. During the three-day battle, the Japanese lost 4 aircraft carriers and more than 200 planes and skilled pilots. Japan sank 1 U.S. aircraft carrier and shot down about 150 U.S. planes.

The Battle of Midway was the first clear Allied victory over Japan in World War II. Aircraft carriers had become the most important weapon in the war in the Pacific. Japan's naval power was crippled by the loss of 4 of its 9 aircraft carriers.

Although Japan failed to capture Midway, it seized two islands at the tip of Alaska's Aleutian chain on June 7, 1942. The Americans drove the Japanese out of the Aleutians in the spring and summer of 1943.

The South Pacific. After the Battle of Midway, the Allies were determined to stop Japanese expansion in the South Pacific. In the battles that followed, American

World War II in Asia and the Pacific: 1941-1942

After Japan attacked Pearl Harbor on Dec. 7, 1941, its forces rapidly advanced across Southeast Asia and the Western Pacific Ocean. This map shows key battles in that campaign and the greatest extent of Japan's empire. The Allies halted Japan's expansion in the summer of 1942.

WORLD BOOK map

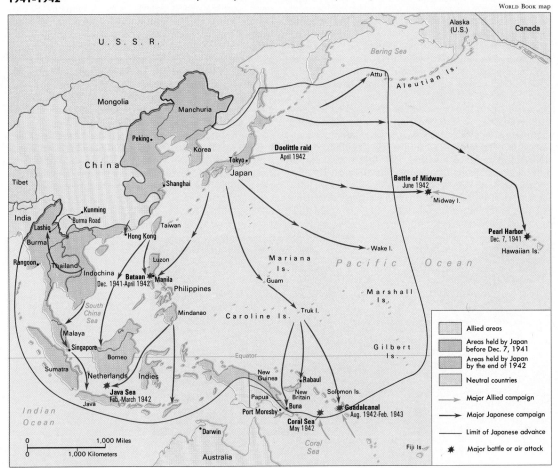

soldiers and marines fought many jungle campaigns on Pacific islands. The jungle itself was a terrifying enemy. Heavy rains drenched the troops and turned the jungle into a foul-smelling swamp. The men had to hack their way through tangled, slimy vegetation and wade through knee-deep mud. The Japanese hid everywhere, waiting to shoot unsuspecting servicemen. Scorpions and snakes were a constant menace. Malaria and other tropical diseases took a heavy toll.

The Americans also encountered Japan's strict military code in the South Pacific. The code required Japanese soldiers to fight to the death. Japanese soldiers believed that surrender meant disgrace, and the Allies rarely captured them alive. When cornered, the Japanese sometimes charged at Allied troops in nighttime suicide attacks. Rather than admit defeat, Japan's military leaders took their lives by stabbing themselves in the abdomen according to the tradition of *hara-kiri*.

The Allies developed two major campaigns against Japan in the South Pacific. One force under MacArthur checked the Japanese on New Guinea. Another force under Nimitz battled the Japanese in the Solomon Islands northeast of Australia. MacArthur and Nimitz aimed at taking the port of Rabaul on New Britain. Rabaul was Japan's chief base in the South Pacific. Japanese aircraft and warships attacked Allied ships from Rabaul, and Japan supplied other islands in the South Pacific from that base.

New Guinea. Japanese troops landed on New Guinea's north coast in the summer of 1942. They then began an overland drive across New Guinea's rugged, jungle-covered mountains to the Australian base of Port Moresby on the south coast. An Allied force made up chiefly of Australians quickly counterattacked. By November, the Japanese had been pushed back across the mountains. MacArthur then attacked Japanese positions along the north coast in a series of brilliant operations that combined air, sea, and land forces. Brutal fighting continued on New Guinea until mid-1944.

Guadalcanal. On Aug. 7, 1942, U.S. marines invaded the island of Guadalcanal in the first stage of a campaign in the Solomon Islands. The Japanese were building an air base on Guadalcanal from which to attack Allied ships. The invasion took the Japanese by surprise. But they fought back, and a fierce battle developed.

The six-month battle for Guadalcanal was one of the most vicious campaigns of World War II. Each side depended on its navy to land supplies and troop reinforcements. In a series of naval battles, the Allies gained control of the waters surrounding Guadalcanal. They then cut off Japanese shipments. Until that time, Allied supplies had been short, and the marines had depended on rice captured from the enemy. By February 1943, the starving Japanese had evacuated Guadalcanal.

After defeating the Japanese on Guadalcanal, American forces led by Admiral William F. Halsey worked their way up the Solomon Islands. In November 1943, they reached Bougainville at the top of the chain.

Rabaul. In the summer of 1943, Allied military leaders canceled the invasion of Rabaul. Instead, American bombers pounded the Japanese base, and aircraft and submarines sank shipments headed for Rabaul. About 100,000 Japanese defenders waited there for an attack that never came. The Allies spared many lives by isolating Rabaul rather than capturing it.

Island Hopping in the Central Pacific. From late 1943 until the fall of 1944, the Allies hopped from island to island across the Central Pacific toward the Philippines. During the island-hopping campaign, the Allies became expert at *amphibious* (seaborne) invasions. Each island they captured provided a base from which to strike the next target. But rather than capture every island, the Allies by-passed Japanese strongholds and invaded islands that were weakly held. That strategy, known as *leapfrogging*, saved time and lives. Leapfrogging carried the Allies across the Gilbert, Marshall, Caroline, and Mariana islands in the Central Pacific.

Admiral Nimitz selected the Gilbert Islands as the first major objective in the island-hopping campaign. American marines invaded Tarawa in the Gilberts in November 1943. The attackers met heavy fire from Japanese troops in concrete bunkers. But they inched forward and captured the tiny island after four days of savage fighting. About 4,500 Japanese soldiers died

Department of Defense

Hugging the Ground to avoid enemy gunfire, U.S. marines crawled over the sandy shores of Tarawa in the Gilbert Islands in November 1943. Lessons learned in the costly battle for Tarawa helped the Allies improve their seaborne landing techniques.

defending the island. Only 17 remained alive. More than 3,000 marines were killed or wounded in the assault. The Allies improved their amphibious operations because of lessons learned at Tarawa. As a result, fewer men died in later landings.

In February 1944, U.S. marines and infantrymen leaped north to the Marshall Islands. They captured Kwajalein and Enewetak in relatively smooth operations. Allied military leaders meanwhile had decided to by-pass Truk, a key Japanese naval base in the Caroline Islands west of the Marshalls. They bombed Truk instead and made it unusable as a base.

The Americans made their next jump to the Mariana Islands, about 1,000 miles (1,600 kilometers) northwest of Enewetak. Bitter fighting for the Marianas began in June 1944. In the Battle of the Philippine Sea on June 19 and 20, Japan's navy once again attempted to destroy the U.S. Pacific Fleet. During the battle, which was fought near the island of Guam, the Allies massacred Japan's navy and destroyed its airpower. Japan lost 3 aircraft carriers and about 480 airplanes, or more than three-fourths of the planes it sent into battle. The loss of so many trained pilots was also a serious blow to Japan.

By August 1944, American forces occupied Guam, Saipan, and Tinian—the three largest islands in the Marianas. The occupation of the Marianas brought Nimitz' forces within bombing distance of Japan. Tojo resigned as Japan's prime minister in July 1944 after the loss of Saipan. In November, American B-29 bombers began using bases in the Marianas to raid Japan.

A final hop before the invasion of the Philippines took U.S. forces to the Palau Islands in September 1944. The islands lie between the Marianas and the Philippines. The attackers met stiff resistance on Peleliu, the chief Japanese base in the Palaus. About 25 per cent of the Americans were killed or injured in a monthlong battle.

The Liberation of the Philippines. The campaigns in New Guinea and the Central Pacific brought the Allies within striking distance of the Philippine Islands. MacArthur and Nimitz combined their forces to liberate the Philippines. Allied leaders decided to invade the island of Leyte in the central Philippines in the fall of 1944.

The Allies expected the Japanese to fight hard to hold the Philippines. They therefore assembled the largest landing force ever used in the Pacific campaigns. About 750 ships participated in the invasion of Leyte, which began on Oct. 20, 1944. It had taken MacArthur more than 2½ years and many brutal battles to keep his pledge to return to the Philippines.

While Allied troops poured ashore on Leyte, Japan's navy tried yet again to crush the Pacific Fleet. The Battle for Leyte Gulf, which was fought from Oct. 23 through 26, 1944, was the the greatest naval battle in history in total tonnage. In all, 282 ships took part. The battle ended in a major victory for the United States. Japan's navy was so badly damaged that it was no longer a serious threat for the rest of the war.

During the Battle for Leyte Gulf, the Japanese unleashed a terrifying new weapon—the *kamikaze* (suicide pilot). Kamikazes crashed planes filled with explosives onto Allied warships and died as a result. Many kamikazes were shot down before they crashed. But others

FPG

An Attack by a Japanese *Kamikaze* (Suicide Pilot) set this aircraft carrier aflame. In a last desperate effort to win the war, kamikazes crashed their planes onto Allied ships.

caused great damage. The kamikaze became one of Japan's major weapons during the rest of the war.

The fight for Leyte continued until the end of 1944. On Jan. 9, 1945, the Allies landed on the island of Luzon and began to work their way toward Manila. The city fell in early March. The remaining Japanese troops on Luzon pulled back to the mountains and went on fighting until the war ended.

About 350,000 Japanese soldiers died during the campaign in the Philippines. American casualties numbered nearly 14,000 dead and about 48,000 wounded or missing. Japan was clearly doomed to defeat after losing the Philippines. But it did not intend to surrender.

The China-Burma-India Theater. While fighting raged in the Pacific, the Allies also battled the Japanese on the Asian mainland. The chief *theater of operations* (area of military activity) involved China, Burma, and India. By mid-1942, Japan held much of eastern and southern China and had conquered nearly all Burma. The Japanese had closed the Burma Road, the overland supply route from India to China. China lacked equipment and trained troops and barely managed to go on fighting. But the Western Allies wanted to keep China in the war because the Chinese tied down hundreds of thousands of Japanese troops. For three years, the Allies flew war supplies over the world's tallest mountain system, the Himalaya, from India to China. The route was known as "the Hump."

China. By 1942, five years after Japan had invaded China, the opposing armies were near exhaustion. Japanese troops staged attacks especially to capture China's food supplies for themselves and to starve the country into surrender. As a result, millions of Chinese people died from lack of food during the war.

A struggle between China's Nationalist government, headed by Chiang Kai-shek, and Chinese Communists further weakened the country's war effort. At first, the Nationalist forces and the Communists had joined in fighting the Japanese invaders. But their cooperation gradually broke down as they prepared to fight each other after the war.

World War II in Asia and the Pacific: 1943-1945

From 1943 to August 1945, the Allies worked their way across the Pacific toward Japan. Allied forces on the Asian mainland recaptured Burma. This map shows the Allied route and gives the dates of key battles in the Pacific campaign. Japan still held much territory when it surrendered.

WORLD BOOK map

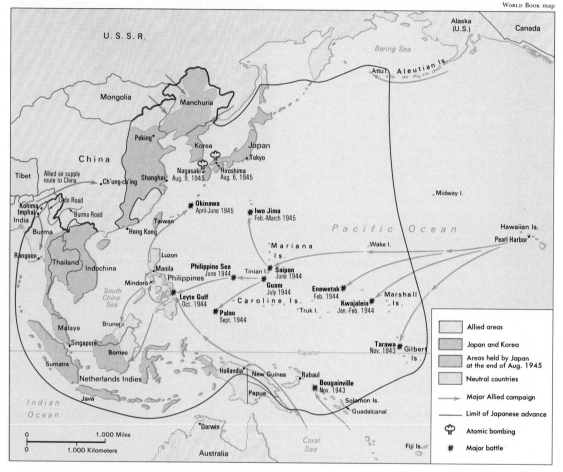

The United States sent military advisers as well as equipment to China. Colonel Claire L. Chennault, for example, trained pilots and established an air force in China. By the end of 1943, his pilots controlled the skies over China. But they could not help exhausted Chinese troops on the ground. Major General Joseph W. Stilwell served as Chiang's chief of staff and trained the Chinese army. Stilwell also commanded the U.S. forces in China and Burma.

Burma. The Allied campaign in Burma was closely linked to the fighting in China. From 1943 until early 1945, the Allies fought to recapture Burma from the Japanese and reopen a land route to China. But rugged jungle, heavy rains, and a shortage of troops and supplies hampered the Allies in Burma.

Admiral Louis Mountbatten of Great Britain became supreme Allied commander in Southeast Asia in August 1943. He directed several successful offensives in Burma in late 1943 and in 1944. By the end of 1944, Allied forces had battled their way through the jungles of northern Burma. They opened a supply route across

northern Burma to China in January 1945. Rangoon, Burma's capital, fell to the Allies in May. The Allies finally regained Burma after a long, horrible campaign.

India. India became an important supply base and training center for Allied forces during World War II. Japan's conquest of Burma in 1942 placed India in great danger. In early 1944, Japanese troops invaded India and encircled the towns of Imphal and Kohima just inside India's border. The British supplied the towns by air. The attackers finally began to withdraw from India late in June. Thousands of Japanese soldiers died of disease and starvation during the retreat.

Closing in on Japan. Superiority at sea and in the air enabled the Allies to close in on Japan in early 1945. By then, Japan had lost much of its empire, most of its aircraft and cargo ships, and nearly all its warships. Hundreds of thousands of Japanese soldiers remained stranded on Pacific islands by-passed by the Allies. American B-29 bombers were pounding Japan's industries, and American submarines were sinking vital supplies headed for Japan.

Important Dates in the Pacific: 1943-1945

1943

Nov. 20	U.S. forces invaded Tarawa.

1944

June 19-20	A U.S. naval force defeated the Japanese in the Battle of the Philippine Sea.
July 18	Japan's Prime Minister Tojo resigned.
Oct. 20	The Allies began landing in the Philippines.
Oct. 23-26	The Allies defeated Japan's navy in the Battle of Leyte Gulf in the Philippines.

1945

March 16	U.S. marines captured Iwo Jima.
June 21	Allied forces captured Okinawa.
Aug. 6	An atomic bomb was dropped on Hiroshima.
Aug. 8	The Soviet Union declared war on Japan.
Aug. 9	An atomic bomb was dropped on Nagasaki.
Aug. 14	Japan agreed to surrender unconditionally.
Sept. 2	Japan signed surrender terms aboard the battleship U.S.S. *Missouri* in Tokyo Bay.

U.S. Air Force

Allied Flights over the Himalaya, the world's tallest mountains, supplied China with war materials from 1942 to 1945. The dangerous air route from India to China was called "the Hump."

In January 1945, Major General Curtis E. LeMay took command of the air war against Japan. LeMay ordered more frequent and more daring raids. American bombers increased their accuracy by flying in low during nighttime raids. They began to drop *incendiary* (fire-producing) bombs that set Japanese cities aflame. A massive incendiary raid in March 1945 destroyed the heart of Tokyo. By the end of the month, about 3 million people in Tokyo were homeless.

Japan's military leaders went on fighting, though they faced certain defeat. The Allies decided they needed more bases to step up the bombing campaign against Japan. They chose the Japanese islands of Iwo Jima and Okinawa.

Iwo Jima lies about 750 miles (1,210 kilometers) south of Japan. About 21,000 Japanese troops were stationed there. They prepared to defend the tiny island from fortified caves and underground tunnels. Allied aircraft began bombarding Iwo Jima seven months before the invasion. American marines landed on Feb. 19, 1945, and made slow progress. The Japanese hung on

desperately until March 16. About 25,000 marines—about 30 per cent of the landing force—were killed or wounded in the campaign for Iwo Jima.

Okinawa, the next stop on the Allied route toward Japan, lies about 350 miles (565 kilometers) southwest of Japan. Allied troops began to pour ashore on Okinawa on April 1, 1945. Japan sent kamikazes to attack the landing force. By the time the battle ended on June 21, kamikazes had sunk at least 30 ships and damaged more than 350 others. The capture of Okinawa cost the Allies about 50,000 casualties. About 110,000 Japanese died, including many civilians who chose to commit suicide rather than be conquered.

By the summer of 1945, some members of Japan's government favored surrender. But others insisted that Japan fight on. The Allies planned to invade Japan in November 1945. American military planners feared that the invasion might cost as many as 1 million U.S. lives. Some Allied leaders believed that Soviet help was

AP/Wide World

Supplies Poured Ashore on Iwo Jima after U.S. marines secured beaches on the Japanese island in February 1945. The battle for Iwo Jima was one of the bloodiest campaigns of World War II.

An Atomic Blast demolished the center of Hiroshima, Japan, *above*, on Aug. 6, 1945. Japan agreed to surrender after a second atomic bomb was dropped on Nagasaki on August 9.

UPI/Bettmann Newsphotos

Japan's Surrender on Sept. 2, 1945, ended World War II. General of the Army Douglas MacArthur, *far left*, signed for the Allies, and General Yoshijiro Umezu, *right*, for the Japanese army.

UPI/Bettmann Newsphotos

needed to defeat Japan, and they had encouraged Stalin to invade Manchuria. However, the Allies found another way to end the war.

The Atomic Bomb. In 1939, the German-born scientist Albert Einstein had informed President Roosevelt about the possibility of creating a superbomb. It would produce an extremely powerful explosion by splitting the atom. Einstein and other scientists feared that Germany might develop such a bomb first. In 1942, the United States set up the Manhattan Project, a top-secret program to develop an atomic bomb. The first test explosion of an atomic bomb occurred in the New Mexico desert in July 1945.

Roosevelt died in April 1945, and Vice President Harry S. Truman became President of the United States. Truman met with Churchill and Stalin in Potsdam, Germany, in July, shortly after Germany's defeat. At the Potsdam Conference, Truman learned of the successful test explosion of the atomic bomb and informed the other leaders of it. The United States, Britain, and China then issued a statement threatening to destroy Japan unless it surrendered unconditionally. In spite of the warning, Japan went on fighting.

On Aug. 6, 1945, an American B-29 bomber called the *Enola Gay* dropped the first atomic bomb used in warfare on the Japanese city of Hiroshima. The explosion killed from 80,000 to 100,000 people and destroyed about 5 square miles (13 square kilometers) of Hiroshima. After Japanese leaders failed to respond to the bombing, the United States dropped a larger bomb on Nagasaki on August 9. It killed about 40,000 people. Later, thousands more died of injuries and radiation from the two bombings. Meanwhile, on August 8, the Soviet Union declared war on Japan and invaded Manchuria. Soviet troops raced south toward Korea.

Victory in the Pacific. Although Japan's emperors had traditionally stayed out of politics, Hirohito urged the government to surrender. On August 14, Japan agreed to end the war. Some of the country's military leaders committed suicide.

On Sept. 2, 1945, representatives of Japan signed the official statement of surrender aboard the U.S. battleship *Missouri*, which lay at anchor in Tokyo Bay. Representatives of all the Allied nations were present. Truman declared September 2 as V-J Day, or Victory over Japan Day. World War II had ended.

WORLD WAR II / *The Secret War*

Throughout World War II, a secret war was fought between the Allies and the Axis to obtain information about each other's activities and to weaken each other's war effort. Codebreakers tried to decipher secret communications, and spies worked behind enemy lines to gather information. Saboteurs tried to disrupt activities on the home front. Many people in Axis-held territories joined undercover *resistance groups* that opposed the occupying forces. All the warring nations used propaganda to influence public opinion.

The Ultra Secret. Soon after the outbreak of World War II, Britain obtained, with the help of Polish spies, one of the machines Germany used to code secret messages. In an outstanding effort, British mathematicians

and codebreakers solved the machine's electronic coding procedures. Britain's ability to read many of Germany's wartime communications was known as the Ultra secret. Ultra helped the Allies defeat Germany.

The Ultra secret played an important role in battle. During the 1940 Battle of Britain, for example, Ultra supplied advance warning of where and when the Luftwaffe planned to attack. Ultra also helped Montgomery defeat the Germans in Egypt in 1942 by providing him with Rommel's battle plan. The British carefully guarded the Ultra secret. They were extremely cautious about using their knowledge so that Germany would not change its coding procedures. The Germans never discovered that Britain had broken their code.

Spies and Saboteurs were specially trained by the warring nations. Spies reported on troop movements, defense build-ups, and other developments behind enemy lines. Spies of Allied nations also worked with resistance groups and supplied them with weapons and explosives. Saboteurs hampered the enemy's war effort in any way they could. For example, they blew up factories and bridges and organized slowdowns in war plants.

Germany had spies in many countries. But its efforts at spying were less successful in general than those of the Allies. The U.S. government set up a wartime agency called the Office of Strategic Services (OSS) to engage in spying and sabotage. The OSS worked closely with a similar British agency, the Special Operations Executive. The Soviet Union operated networks of spies in Allied nations as well as in Germany and Japan.

Resistance Groups sprang up in every Axis-occupied country. Resistance began with individual acts of defiance against the occupiers. Gradually, like-minded people banded together and worked in secret to overthrow the invaders. The activities of resistance groups expanded as the war continued. Their work included publishing and distributing illegal newspapers, rescuing Allied aircrews shot down behind enemy lines, gathering information about the enemy, and sabotage.

In such countries as France, Yugoslavia, and Burma, resistance groups engaged in *guerrilla warfare*. They organized bands of fighters who staged raids, ambushes, and other small attacks against the occupation forces.

All resistance movements suffered many setbacks. But they also achieved outstanding successes. For example, the French resistance interfered with German efforts to turn back the Allied invasion of Normandy in 1944. Norwegian resistance workers destroyed a shipment of *heavy water* headed for Germany. Heavy water is a substance needed in the production of an atomic bomb. Yugoslavia had the most effective resistance movement of all—the Partisans. With Allied help, the Partisans drove the Germans out of Yugoslavia in 1944.

Even in Germany itself, a small underground movement opposed the Nazis. In July 1944, a group of German army officers planted a bomb intended to kill Hitler. However, Hitler escaped the explosion with minor injuries. He ordered the plotters arrested and executed.

The risks of joining the resistance were great. A resistance worker caught by the Nazis faced certain death. The Germans sometimes rounded up and executed hundreds of civilians in revenge for an act of sabotage against their occupation forces.

Propaganda. All the warring nations used propaganda to win support for their policies. Governments aimed propaganda at their own people and at the enemy. Radio broadcasts reached the largest audiences. Motion pictures, posters, and cartoons were also used for propaganda purposes.

The Nazis skillfully used propaganda to spread their beliefs. Joseph Goebbels directed Germany's Ministry of Propaganda and Enlightenment, which controlled publications, radio programs, motion pictures, and the arts in Germany and German-occupied Europe. The ministry worked to persuade people of the superiority of German culture and of Germany's right to rule the world.

...we here highly resolve that these dead shall not have died in vain...

REMEMBER DEC. 7th!

Bettmann Archive

A U.S. Government Poster reminded Americans of the event that plunged them into war—Japan's attack on Pearl Harbor. All warring nations used propaganda techniques to stir patriotism.

After the war began to go badly for the Axis, the Germans claimed that they were saving the world from the evils of Communism.

Mussolini stirred the Italians with dreams of restoring Italy to the glory of ancient Rome. Italy's propaganda also ridiculed the fighting ability of Allied soldiers.

Japan promised conquered peoples a share in the Greater East Asia Co-Prosperity Sphere, which would unite all eastern Asia under Japanese control. Using the slogan "Asia for the Asians," the Japanese claimed that they were freeing Asia from European rule.

Nightly newscasts beamed by the British Broadcasting Corporation (BBC) to the European mainland provided truthful information about the day's fighting. The Nazis made it a crime for people in Germany and German-held lands to listen to BBC broadcasts.

The U.S. government established the Office of War Information (OWI) to encourage American support for the war effort. The agency told Americans that they were fighting for a better world. In 1942, the Voice of America, a government radio service, began broadcasting to Axis-occupied countries.

The warring countries also engaged in *psychological warfare* intended to destroy the enemy's will to fight. American planes dropped leaflets over Germany that told of Nazi defeats. The Axis nations employed a few traitors who broadcast radio programs to weaken the morale of Allied soldiers. For example, Mildred Gillars, an American known as "Axis Sally," made broadcasts for Germany. Another American, Iva D'Aquino, who was called "Tokyo Rose," broadcast for Japan. Such broadcasts merely amused most troops.

National Archives

"Rosie the Riveter" became the humorous yet respectful name for the millions of American women who worked in defense plants during the war. This "Rosie" worked on an airplane assembly line.

World War II affected the civilian populations of all the fighting nations. But the effects were extremely uneven. Much of Europe and large parts of Asia suffered widespread destruction and severe hardship. The United States and Canada, which lay far from the battlefronts, were spared most of the horror of war. North America, in fact, prospered during World War II.

In the United States and Canada, most people fully backed the war effort. Nearly all Americans and Canadians despised Nazism and wished to defeat it. Americans sought also to avenge the bombing of Pearl Harbor.

Producing for the War. Victory in World War II required an enormous amount of war materials, including huge numbers of ships, tanks, aircraft, and weapons. The United States and Canada built many plants to manufacture war goods. They also turned old factories into war plants. For example, automobile factories began to produce tanks and aircraft.

The United States astonished the world with its wartime output. Roosevelt called for the production of 60,000 aircraft during 1942—a goal many industrialists believed was impossible to achieve. Yet U.S. war plants turned out nearly 86,000 planes the following year. Shipbuilding gains were just as impressive. For example, the time needed to build an aircraft carrier dropped from 36 months in 1941 to 15 months in 1945.

Canada also greatly expanded its output during World War II. Wartime expansion made Canada a leading industrial power by the war's end.

Millions of women in the United States and Canada joined the labor force during World War II, after men left for combat. Women worked in shipyards and aircraft factories and filled many jobs previously held only by men. The number of working women in the United States climbed from about 15 million in 1941 to about 19 million in 1945. Canadian women replaced men on farms as well as in factories. They helped raise the crops that fed Allied troops.

New opportunities opened up for American blacks during World War II. In 1941, Roosevelt created the Fair Employment Practices Committee to prevent job discrimination in U.S. defense industries. Large numbers of Southern blacks moved to the North to work in war plants.

Mobilizing for the War. The United States introduced its first peacetime draft in September 1940. Under the draft law, all men aged 21 through 35 were required to register for military service. The draft was later extended to men 18 through 45. More than 15 million American men served in the armed forces during World War II. About 10 million were drafted. The rest volunteered. About 338,000 women served in the U.S. armed forces. They worked as mechanics, drivers, clerks, and cooks and also filled many other noncombat positions.

Canada also expanded its armed forces greatly during World War II. At the outbreak of the war, the Canadian government promised not to draft men for service overseas. Canada relied on volunteers for overseas duty until November 1944. By then, it suffered from a severe shortage of troops and began to send draftees overseas. More than a million Canadians, including about 50,000 women, served in the armed forces during the war.

Financing the War. The U.S. and Canadian governments paid for the costs of World War II in several ways. In one major method, they borrowed from individuals and businesses by selling them war bonds, certificates, notes, and stamps. The United States raised nearly $180 billion from such sales. Canada's government also raised several billion dollars.

Taxes also helped pay for World War II. Income increased tremendously during the war years. As a result, revenue from income taxes soared. In the United States, the tax rate on the highest incomes reached 94 per cent.

AP/Wide World

Government Rationing helped assure the fair distribution of scarce goods in the United States and Canada. Ration books enabled citizens to buy limited amounts of meat and other items.

AP/Wide World

The Wartime Confinement of Japanese Americans in relocation camps was a denial of their rights. It resulted from distrust of
all Japanese after the attack on Pearl Harbor.

The government also taxed entertainment and such luxury goods as cosmetics and jewelry. Corporations paid
extra taxes on higher-than-normal profits. Canadians
also paid increased taxes during the war.

In spite of greater borrowing and higher taxes, the
U.S. and Canadian governments spent more than they
raised to pay for the war. In the United States, the national debt rose from about $49 billion in 1941 to $259
billion in 1945. Canada's national debt rose from $4 bil-
lion in 1939 to $16 billion in 1945.

Government Controls over civilian life in the United
States and Canada expanded during World War II. In
both countries, the national government established
various agencies to direct the war effort on the home
front. The agencies helped prevent skyrocketing prices,
severe shortages, and production foul-ups. The War Production Board, for example, controlled the distribution
of raw materials needed by U.S. industries. The Office of
Price Administration limited price increases in the
United States. It also set up a *rationing program* to dis-
tribute scarce goods fairly. Each family received a book
of ration coupons to use for purchases of such items as
sugar, meat, butter, and gasoline.

Canada's government had even greater wartime powers. For example, the National Selective Service controlled Canada's work force. It forbade men of military
age to hold jobs it termed "nonessential." Such jobs included driving a taxi or selling real estate. Canada's
Wartime Prices and Trade Board determined wages and
prices and set up a rationing program.

Treatment of Enemy Aliens. During World War II, the
U.S. government classified more than a million newly
arrived immigrants from Germany, Italy, and Japan as
enemy aliens. However, only the Japanese were treated
unjustly. After the bombing of Pearl Harbor, some
Americans directed their rage at people of Japanese ancestry. In 1942, anti-Japanese hysteria led the U.S. government to move about 110,000 West Coast residents of
Japanese ancestry to inland relocation camps. They lost
their homes and their jobs as a result. About two-thirds
of them were citizens of the United States. Canada also
relocated about 21,000 people of Japanese ancestry during the war.

In Germany, most of the people greeted the start of
World War II with little enthusiasm. But Germany's
string of easy victories from 1939 to mid-1941 stirred
support for the war. By the summer of 1941, the Germans did not expect the war to last much longer.

Civilian Life. Food, clothing, and other consumer
goods remained plentiful in Germany during the early
years of the war. Imports poured in from Nazi-occupied
countries of Europe. The Allied bombing of Germany
got off to a slow start and did little damage at first.

Germany's situation had changed by late 1942. The
armed forces bogged down in the Soviet Union, and
there were fewer reports of German victories to cheer the
people. Allied bombs rained down day and night on
German cities. Consumer goods became increasingly
scarce. Yet the people continued to work hard for the
war effort.

The Nazi Terror. Hitler's dreaded secret police, the
Gestapo, ruthlessly crushed opposition to the Nazi
Party. The Gestapo arrested anyone suspected of oppos-
ing Nazism in Germany and in German-held territories.

To free German men for combat, the Gestapo recruited workers from occupied countries. Millions of Europeans were eventually forced to work long hours under
terrible conditions in German war plants. Many died of
mistreatment or starvation.

The Nazis brutally persecuted several groups, including Jews, Gypsies, and Slavs. By 1942, Hitler had
started a campaign to murder all European Jews. The
Nazis rounded up Jewish men, women, and children
from occupied Europe and shipped them in boxcars to
concentration camps. About 6 million Jews died in concentration camps during World War II. Many were
mowed down by firing squads or killed in groups in gas
chambers. Others died of lack of food, disease, or torture.
The Nazis also slaughtered many Poles, Gypsies, and
members of other groups.

In Other Countries, conditions on the home front depended on the nearness of the fighting and on the length
of the war effort. Conditions were especially difficult in
the Soviet Union, where fierce fighting went on for
nearly four years. Stalin ordered retreating Soviet soldiers to burn everything in their path that German
troops could use for food or shelter. But that *scorched-
earth policy* also caused great hardships for the Soviet
people. Millions of Soviet civilians died of famine and
other war-related causes. In the Ukraine and areas occupied by the Soviet Union, many of the people at first
welcomed the conquering German troops. They believed that the Germans would deliver them from Stalin's harsh rule. But the cruelty of the Nazi occupation
forces turned the people against them. During World
War II, civilians and soldiers in the Soviet Union fought
the Germans with a hatred and determination seldom
matched elsewhere in Europe.

The civilian population of Great Britain also united
wholeheartedly behind the war effort. The people
worked long hours in war plants and accepted severe
shortages of nearly all goods. Prime Minister Churchill
inspired the British people with his stirring words.

Life was especially hard in the countries under Nazi
rule. Germany looted the conquered lands to feed its

own people and fuel its war effort. Opponents of Nazism lived in constant fear of Gestapo brutality.

Japan came closest to collapse of all the warring nations. As the Allies closed in, they deprived Japan of more and more of the raw materials needed by the coun-try's industries. American bombers pounded Japan's cities, and American submarines sank Japanese cargo ships. By 1945, hunger and malnutrition were widespread in Japan. But the Japanese people remained willing to make enormous sacrifices for the war effort.

WORLD WAR II/Consequences of the War

Deaths and Destruction. World War II took more lives and caused more destruction than any other war. Altogether, about 70 million people served in the armed forces of the Allied and Axis nations. About 17 million of them lost their lives. The Soviet Union suffered about $7\frac{1}{2}$ million battle deaths, more than any other country. The United States and Great Britain had the fewest battle deaths of the major powers. About 400,000 American and about 350,000 British military personnel died in the war. Germany lost about $3\frac{1}{2}$ million servicemen, and Japan about $1\frac{1}{4}$ million.

Aerial bombing during World War II rained destruction on civilian as well as military targets. Many cities lay in ruins by the end of the war, especially in Germany and Japan. Bombs wrecked houses, factories, and transportation and communication systems. Land battles also spread destruction over vast areas. After the war, millions of starving and homeless people wandered among the ruins of Europe and Asia.

No one knows how many civilians died as a direct result of World War II. Bombing raids destroyed many of the records needed to estimate those deaths. In addition, millions of people died in fires, of diseases, and of other causes after such essential services as fire fighting and health care broke down in war-torn areas.

The Soviet Union and China suffered the highest toll of civilian deaths during World War II. As many as 20 million Soviet civilians and as many as 10 million Chinese civilians may have died. Many of the deaths resulted from famine.

Displaced Persons. World War II uprooted millions of people. By the war's end, more than 12 million *displaced persons* remained in Europe. They included orphans, prisoners of war, survivors of Nazi concentration and slave labor camps, and people who had fled invading armies and war-torn areas. Others were displaced by changes in national borders. For example, many Germans moved into Poland, Czechoslovakia, and other lands in eastern Europe that the Nazis took over. After the war, those countries expelled German residents.

To help displaced persons, the Allies established the United Nations Relief and Rehabilitation Administration (UNRRA). UNRRA began operating in 1944 in areas freed by the Allies from Nazi occupation. The organization set up camps for displaced persons and provided them with food, clothing, and medical supplies. By 1947, most of the displaced persons had been resettled. However, about a million people still remained in camps. Many had fled from countries in eastern Europe and refused to return to homelands that had come under Communist rule.

New Power Struggles arose after World War II ended. The war had exhausted the leading prewar powers of Europe and Asia. Germany and Japan ended the war in complete defeat, and Great Britain and France were severely weakened. The United States and the Soviet Union emerged from the war as the world's leading powers. Their wartime alliance soon collapsed as the Soviet Union sought to spread Communism in Europe and Asia. The struggle between the Communist world, led by the Soviet Union, and the non-Communist world, led by the United States, is known as the Cold War.

The United States had fought the Axis to preserve democracy. After the war, Americans found it impossible to return to the policy of isolation their country had followed before the war. Americans realized that they needed strong allies, and they helped the war-torn nations recover.

World War II had united the Soviet people behind a great patriotic effort. The Soviet Union came out of the war stronger than ever before, in spite of the severe destruction it had suffered. Before the war ended, the Soviet Union had absorbed three nations along the Baltic Sea—Estonia, Latvia, and Lithuania. It had also taken parts of Poland, Romania, Finland, and Czechoslova-

Keystone

The Human Suffering caused by World War II was enormous. Cities lay in ruins, and millions of people had to be resettled. These homeless Germans reflected the widespread despair.

kia by mid-1945. At the end of the war, Soviet troops occupied most of eastern Europe. In March 1946, Churchill warned that an "Iron Curtain" had descended across Europe, dividing eastern Europe from western Europe. Behind the Iron Curtain, the Soviet Union helped Communist governments take power in Bulgaria, Czechoslovakia, Hungary, Poland, and Romania.

Communism also gained strength in the Far East. The Soviet Union set up a Communist government in North Korea after the war. In China, Mao Zedong's Communist forces battled Chiang Kai-shek's Nationalist armies. Late in 1949, Chiang fled to the island of Taiwan, and China joined the Communist world.

By 1947, Communists threatened to take control of Greece, and the Soviet Union was demanding military bases in Turkey. That year, President Truman announced that the United States would provide military and economic aid to any country threatened by Communism. American aid helped Greece and Turkey resist Communist aggression.

In 1948, the United States set up the Marshall Plan to help war-torn nations in Europe rebuild their economies. Under the plan, 18 nations received $13 billion in food, machinery, and other goods. The Soviet Union forbade countries in eastern Europe to participate in the Marshall Plan.

The Nuclear Age opened with the development of the atomic bomb during World War II. Many people believed that weapons capable of mass destruction would make war unthinkable in the future. They hoped that the world would learn to live in peace. But a race to develop ever more powerful weapons soon began.

At the end of World War II, only the United States knew how to build an atomic weapon. In 1946, the United States proposed the creation of an international

Military Casualties in World War II (1939-1945)

	Dead	Wounded
The Allies		
Australia	23,365	39,803
Belgium	7,760	14,500
Canada	37,476	53,174
China	2,200,000	1,762,000
France	210,671	390,000
Great Britain*	329,208	348,403
Poland	320,000	530,000
Soviet Union	7,500,000	5,000,000
United States	405,399	671,278
The Axis		
Austria	380,000	350,117
Bulgaria	10,000	21,878
Finland	82,000	50,000
Germany	3,500,000	7,250,000
Hungary	140,000	89,313
Italy	77,494	120,000
Japan	1,219,000	295,247
Romania	300,000	(†)

*Including colonials.
†Figure unavailable.
Source: James L. Stokesbury, author of *A Short History of World War II*.

agency that would control atomic energy and ban the production of nuclear weapons. But the Soviet Union objected to an inspection system, and the proposal was dropped. Stalin ordered Soviet scientists to develop an atomic bomb, and they succeeded in 1949. During the early 1950's, the United States and the Soviet Union each tested an even more destructive weapon, the hydrogen bomb.

People have lived in fear of nuclear war since the nuclear age began. At times, Cold War tensions have threatened to erupt into war between the two superpowers. But the terrifying destructiveness of nuclear weapons may well have kept them from risking a major war.

WORLD WAR II/*Establishing the Peace*

Birth of the United Nations (UN). Out of the horror of World War II came efforts to prevent war from ever again engulfing the world. In 1943, representatives of the United States, Great Britain, the Soviet Union, and China met in Moscow. They agreed to establish an international organization that would work to promote peace. The four Allied powers met again in 1944 at Dumbarton Oaks, an estate in Washington, D.C. The delegates decided to call the new organization the United Nations. In April 1945, representatives from 50 nations gathered in San Francisco, Calif., to draft a charter for the United Nations. They signed the charter in June, and it went into effect on October 24.

Peace with Germany. Before World War II ended, the Allies had decided on a military occupation of Germany after its defeat. They divided Germany into four zones, with the United States, the Soviet Union, Great Britain, and France each occupying a zone. The four powers jointly administered Berlin.

At the Potsdam Conference in July of 1945, the Allies set forth their occupation policy. They agreed to abolish Germany's armed forces and to outlaw the Nazi Party. Germany lost territory east of the Oder and Neisse rivers.

Most of the region went to Poland. The Soviet Union gained the northeastern corner of this territory.

The Allies brought to trial Nazi leaders accused of war crimes. The trials exposed the monstrous evils inflicted by Nazi Germany. Many leading Nazis were sentenced to death. The most important war trials took place in the German city of Nuremberg from 1945 to 1949.

Soon after the occupation began, the Soviet Union stopped cooperating with its Western allies. It blocked all efforts to reunite Germany. The Western allies gradually joined their zones into one economic unit. But the Soviet Union forbade its zone to join.

The city of Berlin lay deep within the Soviet zone of Germany. In June 1948, the Soviet Union sought to drive the Western powers from Berlin by blocking all rail, water, and highway routes to the city. For more than a year, the Western allies flew in food, fuel, and other goods to Berlin. The Soviet Union finally lifted the Berlin blockade in May 1949, and the airlift ended in September.

The Western Allies set up political parties in their zones and held elections. In September 1949, the three Western zones were officially combined as the Federal

Republic of Germany. It is also known as West Germany. In May 1955, the Western Allies signed a treaty ending the occupation of West Germany, and granting the country full independence. But the treaty was not a general peace treaty because the Soviet Union refused to sign it.

The Soviet Union set up a Communist government in its zone. In October 1949, the Soviet zone became the German Democratic Republic, also called East Germany. Soviet control over East Germany remains strong, though the country became officially independent in 1955.

Peace with Japan. The military occupation of Japan began in August 1945. Americans far outnumbered other troops in the occupation forces because of the key role their country had played in defeating Japan. General MacArthur directed the occupation as supreme commander for the Allied nations. He introduced many reforms designed to rid Japan of its military institutions and transform it into a democracy. A Constitution drawn up by MacArthur's staff took effect in 1947. The Constitution transferred all political rights from the emperor to the people, granted voting rights to women, and denied Japan's right to declare war.

The Allied occupation forces brought to trial 25 Japanese war leaders and government officials accused of war crimes. Seven of them were executed. The others received prison sentences.

In September 1951, the United States and most of the other Allied nations signed a peace treaty with Japan. The treaty took away Japan's overseas empire. But it permitted Japan to rearm. The Allied occupation of Japan ended soon after the signing of the treaty. However, a new treaty permitted the United States to keep troops in Japan. China's Nationalist government signed its own peace treaty with Japan in 1952, and the Soviet Union and Japan signed a separate peace treaty in 1956.

Peace with Other Countries. Soon after World War II ended, the Allies began to draw up peace treaties with Italy and four other countries that had fought with the Axis—Bulgaria, Finland, Hungary, and Romania. The treaties limited the armed forces of the defeated countries and required them to pay war damages. The treaties also called for territorial changes. Bulgaria gave up territory to Greece and Yugoslavia. Czechoslovakia gained land from Hungary. Finland lost territory to the Soviet Union. Italy gave up land to France, Yugoslavia, and Greece. The country also lost its empire in Africa. Romania gained territory from Hungary but lost land to Bulgaria and the Soviet Union.   JAMES L. STOKESBURY

WORLD WAR II/Study Aids

Related Articles in WORLD BOOK. See the *History* section of articles on countries that took part in World War II. Additional related articles in WORLD BOOK include:

BATTLES

Bataan Peninsula	Midway Island
Chinese-Japanese Wars	Okinawa
Corregidor	Pearl Harbor Naval Base
Dunkerque	Russo-Finnish Wars
Guam	Saipan
Iwo Jima	Stalingrad, Battle of
Manila Bay	Wake Island

ALLIED MILITARY LEADERS

Alexander of Tunis, Earl	McNaughton, Andrew G. L.
Arnold, Henry H.	Montgomery, Bernard L.
Bradley, Omar N.	Mountbatten, Louis
Chennault, Claire L.	Nimitz, Chester W.
Clark, Mark W.	Patton, George S., Jr.
Clay, Lucius D.	Ridgway, Matthew B.
Doolittle, James H.	Roosevelt, Theodore, Jr.
Eisenhower, Dwight D.	Spaatz, Carl
Halsey, William F., Jr.	Spruance, Raymond A.
Hobby, Oveta C.	Stilwell, Joseph W.
King, Ernest J.	Taylor, Maxwell D.
Leahy, William D.	Wainwright, Jonathan M.
LeMay, Curtis E.	Wavell, Archibald P.
MacArthur, Douglas	Zhukov, Georgi K.
Marshall, George C.	

AXIS MILITARY LEADERS

Doenitz, Karl	Keitel, Wilhelm
Goering, Hermann W.	Rommel, Erwin
Heydrich, Reinhard	Yamamoto, Isoroku
Jodl, Alfred	Yamashita, Tomoyuki

ALLIED POLITICAL FIGURES

Attlee, Clement R.	Chamberlain (Neville)
Beneš, Eduard	Chiang Kai-shek

Churchill, Sir Winston L. S.	Leopold (III)
Daladier, Édouard	Molotov, Vyacheslav M.
De Gaulle, Charles A. J. M.	Roosevelt, Franklin D.
Eden, Anthony	Stalin, Joseph
Haile Selassie I	Stimson, Henry L.
Hull, Cordell	Tito, Josip Broz
Knox, Frank	Truman, Harry S.

AXIS POLITICAL FIGURES

Eichmann, Adolf	Mussolini, Benito
Goebbels, Joseph	Pétain, Henri P.
Hess, Rudolf	Quisling, Vidkun A. L.
Himmler, Heinrich	Ribbentrop, Joachim von
Hirohito	Rosenberg, Alfred
Hitler, Adolf	Speer, Albert
Laval, Pierre	Tojo, Hideki

OTHER BIOGRAPHIES

Bonhoeffer, Dietrich	Mauldin, Bill
Frank, Anne	Miller, Dorie
Kaiser, Henry J.	Pyle, Ernie
Krupp (family)	Wallenberg, Raoul

CONFERENCES AND TREATIES

Munich Agreement	San Francisco Conference
Pan-American Conferences	Teheran Conference
Potsdam Conference	Yalta Conference

FORCES, MATERIALS, AND WEAPONS

Air Force	Army	Coast Guard,
Air Force,	Army, United States	United States
United States	Atomic Bomb	Commando
Aircraft, Military	Aviation	Convoy
Aircraft Carrier	Bazooka	Fifth Column
Airplane	Blitzkrieg	Guided Missile
Ammunition	Bomb	Helmet
Amphibious	Bulldozer	Hostage
Warfare	Camouflage	

Intelligence	Navy	Sniperscope
Service	Navy, United States	Sonar
Jeep	Propaganda	Submarine
Jet Propulsion	PT Boat	Tank
Kamikaze	Radar	Torpedo
Lend-Lease	Radio Control	Walkie-Talkie
Marine	Rationing	War Aces
Mine Warfare	Rocket	War Correspondent
Minesweeper	Savings Bond	Warship

ORGANIZATIONS

American Legion	United Nations
American Legion Auxiliary	United Service
AMVETS	Organizations
Red Cross	Veterans of Foreign Wars
Strategic Services, Office of	of the United States

OTHER RELATED ARTICLES

Alaska Highway	Maquis
Atlantic Charter	Neutrality
Azores	Nuremberg Trials
Bismarck (ship)	Partisan
Burma Road	Polish Corridor
Concentration Camp	Refugee
D-Day	Stars and Stripes
Draft, Military	V-E Day
Four Freedoms	V-J Day
Gestapo	Underground
Graf Spee	United States, History of the
Hiroshima	Unknown Soldier
Holocaust	War Crime
Jews (The Holocaust)	War Debt
Korean War	World War I
Lidice	Yank

Outline

I. Causes of the War
A. The Peace of Paris
B. Economic Problems
C. Nationalism
D. The Rise of Dictatorships
E. Aggression on the March
F. The Spanish Civil War
G. The Failure of Appeasement

II. Early Stages of the War
A. The Invasion of Poland
B. The Phony War
C. The Conquest of Denmark and Norway
D. The Invasion of the Low Countries
E. The Fall of France
F. The Battle of Britain

III. The War Spreads
A. Fighting in Africa
B. Fighting in the Balkans
C. The Invasion of the Soviet Union
D. The Battle of the Atlantic

IV. The United States Enters the War
A. The Arsenal of Democracy
B. Japan Attacks

V. The Allies Attack in Europe and Northern Africa
A. The Strategy
B. On the Soviet Front
C. In Northern Africa
D. The Air War
E. The Invasion of Italy
F. D-Day
G. The Drive to the Rhine
H. The Soviet Advance
I. Victory in Europe

VI. The War in Asia and the Pacific
A. Early Japanese Victories
B. The Tide Turns
C. The South Pacific
D. Island Hopping in the Central Pacific
E. The Liberation of the Philippines
F. The China-Burma-India Theater
G. Closing in on Japan

H. The Atomic Bomb
I. Victory in the Pacific

VII. The Secret War
A. The Ultra Secret
B. Spies and Saboteurs
C. Resistance Groups
D. Propaganda

VIII. On the Home Front
A. In the United States and Canada
B. In Germany
C. In Other Countries

IX. Consequences of the War
A. Deaths and Destruction
B. Displaced Persons
C. New Power Struggles
D. The Nuclear Age

X. Establishing the Peace
A. Birth of the United Nations (UN)
B. Peace with Germany
C. Peace with Japan
D. Peace with Other Countries

Questions

Why did Japan decide to cripple the U.S. Pacific Fleet at anchor in Pearl Harbor?

Which two battles marked a turning point for the Allies in the war against Germany?

What was *appeasement*? When did it become clear that that policy had failed?

What terrifying new weapon did Japan introduce in 1944 during the Battle for Leyte Gulf?

What was the largest seaborne invasion in history?

Which two leaders shocked the world by becoming allies in 1939?

How did the United States help the Allies before it entered World War II?

How was the Battle of the Coral Sea unlike all earlier naval battles?

How did the bombing campaigns against Germany by the United States and Great Britain differ?

What was the Ultra secret? How did it help Great Britain win the Battle of Britain?

Reading and Study Guide

See *World War II* in the RESEARCH GUIDE/INDEX, Volume 22, for a *Reading and Study Guide*.

Additional Resources

ANDERSON, KAREN. *Wartime Women: Sex Roles, Family Relations, and the Status of Women During World War II.* Greenwood, 1981.

ARNOLD-FORSTER, MARK. *The World at War.* Stein & Day, 1973.

BUCHANAN, ALBERT R. *Black Americans in World War II.* ABC-Clio, 1977.

CHURCHILL, WINSTON. *The Second World War.* 6 vols. Houghton, 1948-1953.

DANIELS, ROGER. *Concentration Camps North America: Japanese in the United States and Canada During World War II.* Krieger, 1981. First published in 1971 as *Concentration Camps USA: Japanese Americans and World War II.*

LIDDELL HART, BASIL H. *History of the Second World War.* Putnam, 1979. First published in 1971.

LUKACS, JOHN A. *The Last European War: September 1939-December 1941.* Doubleday, 1976. *1945, Year Zero.* 1978.

The Rand McNally Encyclopedia of World War II. Ed. by John Keegan. Abingdon, 1979. First published in 1977.

SHERWIN, MARTIN J. *A World Destroyed: The Atomic Bomb and the Grand Alliance.* Random House, 1975.

STOKESBURY, JAMES L. *A Short History of World War II.* Morrow, 1980.

TERKEL, STUDS. *"The Good War": An Oral History of World War Two.* Random House, 1984.

World War II. 39 vols. Time-Life Books, 1976-1983. Each of the books in this series focuses on a different aspect of the war, such as *Prelude to War* (1976) and *The War in the Desert* (1977).

AIDS

AIDS is an extremely serious disorder that results from severe damage to the body's defenses against disease. It often leads to death. AIDS stands for *A*cquired *I*mmune *D*eficiency *S*yndrome. The name refers to the fact that the disorder affects the victim's disease-fighting immune system. AIDS was first identified in 1981 in the United States. Since then, cases of AIDS have been diagnosed throughout most of the world.

Cause. AIDS is caused by one of the group of viruses called *retroviruses*. Research teams in France and the United States made independent discoveries of the virus. French researchers discovered a virus that they linked to AIDS in 1983. They named it the *lymphadenopathy-associated virus* (LAV). In 1984, American researchers isolated a virus as the cause of AIDS, calling it the *human T-lymphotropic virus type III* (HTLV-III). These two viruses were later found to be the same virus.

The AIDS virus attacks certain white blood cells that form a key part of the body's immune system. These cells, called *T-helper cells*, are killed by the virus. This destruction of the T-helper cells makes AIDS victims susceptible to certain illnesses that are normally not serious. These illnesses are called *opportunistic* because they take advantage of damage to the immune system.

Symptoms. Infection with the AIDS virus can produce symptoms often associated with other, less serious conditions. With AIDS, however, these symptoms are usually prolonged. They include enlarged lymph glands, tiredness, fever, loss of appetite and weight, diarrhea, and night sweats. The AIDS virus may also infect the brain or central nervous system, resulting in such symptoms as thinking or memory disorders and coordination problems.

People with AIDS also suffer from severe opportunistic illnesses. There are about 12 such illnesses that affect AIDS patients. *Pneumocystis carinii* pneumonia and Kaposi's sarcoma are the most common, afflicting about 85 per cent of people with AIDS. *Pneumocystis carinii* pneumonia, a parasitic infection of the lung, is the leading cause of death among AIDS patients. Kaposi's sarcoma is a form of cancer that usually arises in the skin and looks like a bruise, but grows and spreads.

Some people infected with the AIDS virus never develop any symptoms or only suffer from minor symptoms. Others have many of the AIDS symptoms but none of the opportunistic illnesses. Some of these patients may develop AIDS.

How AIDS Virus Is Transmitted. Researchers have identified three ways in which the AIDS virus is transmitted: (1) intimate sexual contact, (2) exposure to infected blood, and (3) transmission from an infected pregnant woman to her fetus. The most common way of becoming infected is through intimate sexual contact. Sexual transmission of the AIDS virus has occurred mainly among homosexual men, but it has also occurred among bisexual and heterosexual men and women. The AIDS virus also afflicts intravenous drug users, who can be exposed to infected blood by sharing hypodermic needles and syringes. Transfusion recipients and hemophiliacs have contracted the virus from the blood or plasma of infected donors. An infected pregnant woman can transmit the AIDS virus to her child even if she has no symptoms.

Medical authorities stress that the AIDS virus is not highly contagious. No known cases of AIDS have resulted from sharing kitchens, bathrooms, laundries, eating utensils, or living space. Studies of AIDS cases also indicate that the virus is not transmitted in nonsexual social situations, through air, food, or water.

Diagnosis and Treatment. A test for detecting signs of the AIDS virus in the blood became widely available in 1985. The test determines the presence of *antibodies* to the AIDS virus. Antibodies are proteins produced by certain white blood cells to combat specific viruses, bacteria, or foreign substances that enter the body. Thus, the presence of antibodies to the AIDS virus indicates infection with the virus. The use of the AIDS virus antibody test on donated blood has greatly reduced the chances of contracting the virus from transfusions.

Many treatments for AIDS have been tried, both to fight the viral infection and to restore the body's lost immunity. Researchers have discovered several experimental drugs that stop the growth of the AIDS virus in laboratory cultures. Some patients have responded to efforts to strengthen their immune systems. But an effective treatment has yet to be found.

Prevention. To prevent transmission of the AIDS virus, intimate sexual contact with infected partners should be avoided. Drug users should never use, or at least never share, hypodermic needles. Educating the public about AIDS and how it is transmitted is becoming increasingly important in the prevention effort. In addition, researchers are working to develop a safe, effective, and economical vaccine against the infection.

D. PETER DROTMAN

ARTIFICIAL HEART is a device designed to replace the function of the natural heart. Like the natural heart, it has two *ventricles* (chambers) that pump blood through the body. One ventricle pumps blood to the lungs, and the other pumps blood to other organs of the body. Artificial hearts are designed to fit in the space that remains when a diseased natural heart is removed.

Artificial hearts consist of two pumps, each with separate inlet and outlet valves; an external power system to energize the pumps; and a system to regulate the pumping rate. Materials used to construct artificial hearts include plastic, titanium, and carbon.

The artificial heart was invented by scientists led by Willem Kolff, a Dutch-born physician. He first tested the device in an animal in 1957. Artificial hearts were extensively tested in animals, particularly calves, to identify problems. The first use of an artificial heart in a human being occurred in 1969. That year, a team of surgeons headed by Denton Cooley of the Texas Heart Institute used the device to temporarily support blood circulation in a patient until a natural heart became available for transplantation. The artificial heart kept the patient alive for more than 60 hours, until the transplant was performed.

In 1982, a surgical team led by William DeVries of the University of Utah implanted an artificial heart as the first permanent human heart replacement. The device used, an air-powered Jarvik-7 heart, was designed by American physician Robert K. Jarvik. The recipient, Barney B. Clark, survived for 112 days. Since then, other patients have received the Jarvik-7 device as a permanent or temporary heart. Some of the patients have suf-

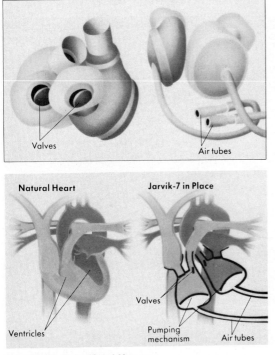

Valves

Air tubes

Natural Heart

Jarvik-7 in Place

Valves

Ventricles

Pumping
mechanism

Air tubes

The Jarvik-7 Artificial Heart

Like a natural heart, the Jarvik-7 artificial heart has two *ventricles* (chambers). Each ventricle has inlet and outlet valves. A disk-shaped pumping mechanism in each ventricle expands and contracts to send blood through the body. Air tubes connect the ventricles with a power system that drives the pumps.

fered from strokes caused by blood clots that form in the pumps and then break off and block brain arteries. This problem, along with the need for a large external power unit and air tubes that pass through the skin, has led some physicians to question the suitability of the air-powered heart for permanent use.

During the 1980's, scientists experimented with electrical artificial hearts. Some of these devices can be powered by a wearable battery or a low-voltage current and do not require any break in the skin.   William S. Pierce

CYCLOSPORINE, *sy kloh SPAWR een,* is a drug that fights the rejection of transplanted body tissues and organs. It is produced from cultures of a fungus, *Tolypocladium inflatum.* Jean Borel, a Swiss immunologist, discovered the medicinal properties of cyclosporine in 1972. The drug has been proven effective in operations in which the heart, liver, pancreas, bone marrow, a kidney, or a lung of one person is transferred to another person. Its use has lowered the frequency of complications and deaths resulting from these operations.

Cyclosporine works by suppressing the functioning of a person's immune system. The drug is believed to block production of a type of white blood cells called *T-helper cells.* These blood cells attack invading substances and thus cause the body to reject transplanted tissues or organs. In addition to its use during and after transplant operations, cyclosporine has shown promise in the treatment of certain diseases involving the immune system.

Patients may take cyclosporine orally by mixing it in orange juice or milk. The drug also may be injected into the bloodstream. Cyclosporine may produce a number of side effects. The most serious of these include high blood pressure, reduced kidney function, liver damage, and abnormal growth of hair.   Bruce A. Reitz

MAGELLANIC CLOUDS, *maj uh LAN ihk,* are two galaxies visible in the Southern Hemisphere as small, hazy patches of light. They are the galaxies closest to the Milky Way, the galaxy that contains the sun, the earth, and the rest of our solar system. The Large Magellanic Cloud is about 160,000 light-years away from the earth, and the Small Magellanic Cloud is about 180,000 light-years away. A light-year is the distance that light travels in one year—about 5.88 trillion miles (9.46 trillion kilometers).

Astronomers classify the Magellanic Clouds as *irregular galaxies* because the distribution of the stars within them does not follow a particular pattern. The Magellanic Clouds contain billions of stars, but individual stars can be distinguished only with the most powerful telescopes. As a result, the galaxies appear cloudy to the naked eye. The Magellanic Clouds also contain a huge quantity of gas. New stars are constantly forming from this gas, which is composed mainly of hydrogen. In addition, much of the light from the Magellanic Clouds comes from young, extremely luminous, hot blue stars that are surrounded by glowing clouds of this gas.

Because they are visible only in the Southern Hemisphere, the Magellanic Clouds were long unknown to astronomers in the Northern Hemisphere. They were first recorded in the early 1500's during the circumglobal voyage of the Portuguese explorer Ferdinand Magellan, after whom they were named. However, it was not until the early 1900's that the clouds were recognized as galaxies outside the Milky Way.   Mark Morris

MILKY WAY is the galaxy that includes the sun, the earth, and the rest of our solar system. The Milky Way Galaxy contains hundreds of billions of stars. Huge clouds of dust particles and gases lie throughout the Galaxy. The name *Milky Way* is also used to refer to the portion of the Milky Way Galaxy that can be seen by the naked eye. On clear, dark nights, it appears as a broad, milky-looking band of starlight stretching across the sky. Dark gaps in the band are formed by dust and gas clouds that block out light from the stars that lie behind them.

Shape of the Galaxy. The Milky Way is shaped like a thin disk with a bulge in the center. Stars, dust, and gases fan out from the central bulge in long, curving arms that form a *spiral* (coiled) pattern. For this reason, astronomers classify the Milky Way as a *spiral galaxy.* To someone far above the Milky Way, the Galaxy would resemble a huge pinwheel. However, because of our location inside the Galaxy, we see only the hazy light from the strip of stars around the earth.

The flat part of the Milky Way disk contains many young stars and small, irregularly shaped groups of stars called *open clusters,* also known as *galactic clusters.* It also has most of the Galaxy's dust and gases. A vast number of older stars are found in the central bulge of the galactic disk. The bulge and the disk are surrounded by a

The Milky Way Galaxy is shaped like a thin disk with a bulge in the center. The Galaxy contains dust, gases, and hundreds of billions of stars, including our sun. The dust, gases, and stars fan out from the galatic center in long, curving arms that form a *spiral* (coiled) pattern. To someone far above it, the Milky Way would look like a huge, rotating pinwheel.

WORLD BOOK illustration by Anne Norcia

sphere of stars known as a *halo*. The halo contains relatively old stars arranged in dense, ball-like groups called *globular clusters*.

Size of the Galaxy. The diameter of the Milky Way is about 100,000 light-years. A light-year is the distance that light travels in one year—about 5.88 trillion miles (9.46 trillion kilometers). The Milky Way is about 10,000 light-years thick at the central bulge and much flatter toward the edges of the disk. Our solar system is located in the outskirts of the Galaxy, about 26,000 light-years away from the center. The distance between the stars in our section of the Milky Way averages about 5 light-years. Stars in the galactic center are about 100 times closer together. Most astronomers estimate that the total mass of the Milky Way is more than 100 billion times that of the sun (see Mass). Much of the mass is concentrated toward the center of the Galaxy.

The Center of the Galaxy. All stars and star clusters in the Milky Way orbit the center of the Galaxy, much as the planets in our solar system orbit the sun. For example, the sun completes an almost circular orbit of the center once about every 250 million years. Almost all the bright stars in the Milky Way orbit in the same di-

rection. For this reason, the entire galactic system appears to rotate about its center.

The clouds of dust and gases in the Milky Way prevent us from seeing very far into the center of the Galaxy. However, astronomers studying radio waves and infrared rays—which can penetrate the clouds—have discovered that the central region gives off enormous amounts of energy. Studies with radio and infrared telescopes have also revealed a powerful gravitational force that seems to come from the exact center of the Galaxy. Some astronomers believe that the Milky Way's center is a massive *black hole*, an invisible object whose gravitational pull is so great that not even light can escape from it (see BLACK HOLE). They think the center's energy is generated when the black hole swallows gas and other matter from the surrounding Galaxy.   MARK MORRIS

See also GALAXY; NEBULA; SOLAR SYSTEM; STAR.

Additional Resources

BOK, BART J. and P. F. *The Milky Way*. 5th ed. Harvard, 1981.
GALLANT, ROY A. *Once Around the Galaxy*. Watts, 1983. Suitable for younger readers.
KÜHN, LUDWIG. *The Milky Way: The Structure and Development of Our Star System*. Wiley, 1982.

Dictionary Supplement

This section lists important words from the 1987 edition of THE WORLD BOOK DICTIONARY. This dictionary, first published in 1963, keeps abreast of our living language with a program of continuous editorial revision. The following supplement has been prepared under the direction of the editors of THE WORLD BOOK ENCYCLOPEDIA and Clarence L. Barnhart, editor in chief of THE WORLD BOOK DICTIONARY. It is presented as a service to owners of the dictionary and as an informative feature to subscribers to THE WORLD BOOK YEAR BOOK.

A a

ag|ro|bac|te|ri|a (ag′rō bak tir′ē ə), *n.pl.* bacteria present in the soil: *The usual procedure for introducing a new gene into plant cells is to insert the gene into agrobacteria and then let the bacteria infect protoplasts* (Daniel L. Hartl).

antigenic determinant, the part of an antigen which causes a reaction in the immune system, especially an epitope: *It should be possible to make vaccines consisting of synthetic antigenic determinants rather than natural whole antigens* (Ben Patrusky).

an|ti|re|jec|tion (an′tē ri jek′shən), *adj.* designed to combat immunological rejection, especially in transplant surgery: *Doctors abandoned the operation because of high rejection rates. But the new antirejection techniques have revived their interest* (Newsweek).

ARC (ärk), *n.* AIDS-related complex, a milder form of AIDS, characterized by swollen glands, loss of weight, and weakness: *While no patient has been known to recover from AIDS, there is new evidence . . . that some ARC patients do get better* (Time).

associative memory or **storage,** a computer memory whose data locations are made accessible by its contents; content-addressable memory: *Associative memories can be rated by their storage density* (Michael F. Deering).

awesome, *adj.* **3** filling with awe; impressive: *"It was awesome when they announced a staff for their Midwest office that was larger than the number of officers we have in our corporate banking department"* (Business Week). **4** *Informal.* tremendous, spectacular: *The party was really awesome.*

B b

bi|o|re|gion (bī′ō rē′jən), *n.* a place or area as defined by the biological systems in it: *The Island's East End is a self-sufficient bioregion that is being damaged by exploitative development* (New York Times). **—bi′o|re′gion|al,** *adj.* **—bi′o|re′gion|al|ly,** *adv.*

bi|o|re|gion|al|ism (bī′ō rē′jə nə liz′əm), *n.* activity in behalf of the preservation of a bioregion: *Bioregionalism has its roots in the ecology and appropriate-technology movements* (Rick Whaley). **— bi′o|re′gion|al|ist,** *n., adj.*

bi|o|tox|in (bī′ō tok′sən), *n.* a biotoxic substance: *Forces in Laos, Cambodia, and possibly Afghanistan have used deadly biotoxins produced by the live fungus fursarium* (Christian Science Monitor).

bronz|er (bron′zər), *n.* a cream or lotion used to give a bronze or tan color to the skin: *Some moisturizers are also bronzers, for example, Braggi's Face Bronzer . . . and Lagerfeld's Moisturizing Bronzer* (which boasts a sunscreen) (Jane Ogle).

bulletin board 2 a computer service that displays information, messages, and news to subscribers and often allows them to communicate directly with each other: *The best way to tap into the free software market is to belong to a user's group or find the local computer bulletin board* (Washington Post).

C c

cam|cord|er (kam′kôr dər), *n.* a videocassette recorder combined with a color camera: *The camcorder has an electronic viewfinder and a power zoom lens. Other features include fast forward and reverse, speeded-up visual search, and high-fidelity sound* (Howard Bierman). [< *cam*(era) + (re)*corder*]

cap|let (kap′lit), *n.* a coated medicinal tablet shaped like a capsule: *The caplet is a solid form of Tylenol pain reliever, which research has proven is the form most preferred by consumers. Unlike tablets, it is specially shaped and coated for easy, comfortable swallowing* (New York Times). [< *cap*(sule) + (tab)*let*]

challenge grant, a sum of money given in proportion to the amount raised by public contribution, a matching grant: *NEA has awarded it a prestigious Challenge Grant* (they receive $1 for every $3 raised) (Time).

comparable worth, the concept that men and women whose jobs are comparable in skills, training, and responsibility should earn the same pay: *Critics of comparable worth say . . . that making such comparisons objectively is virtually impossible. Advocates, however, believe that* [it] *can help to close the gap between men's and women's earnings* (Martha G. Wiseman).

crack, *n.* **13** *U.S.* an extremely potent form of cocaine with a short-term effect: *Crack, a highly addictive form of cocaine, is available from most of the 50 drug dealers doing business in Washington Square Park and on Greenwich Village streets 24 hours a day* (New York Times).

D d

dark matter, *Astronomy.* a hypothetical form of matter that does not emit or absorb electromagnetic radiation: *85 per cent of the matter unaccounted for* [in the universe] *must be in the form of dark matter—mass that is not incorporated in the stars* (David N. Schramm). *This missing matter is unlike ordinary matter that gives off or absorbs light, hence the name—dark matter* (Stephen S. Murray).

da|ta|flow (dā′tə flō′, dat′ə-, dä′tə-), *n.* the flow or transfer of data between computers or within a network of computers: *The units . . . provide all functions necessary to establish, maintain, and monitor the dataflow from and to the branch system* (ABA Banking Journal).

death star, = Nemesis: *The possible mechanism that has stirred the greatest interest and debate . . . is the one involving the Sun's theorized companion star called Nemesis, or the "death star"* (John N. Wilford).

de|mand-driv|en (di mand′driv′ən, -mänd′-), *adj.* caused by increased demand for a product or service: *Rubber has had a demand-driven price rise. The price of rubber depends on the demand for tyres, and thus on the state of the car industry* (Economist).

designer drug, *U.S.* a narcotic made so that it is not a chemically controlled substance: *"Designer drugs"—designed . . . by underground chemists who tinker with the molecular structure of illegal narcotics to produce variants that are not explicitly banned by federal law* (Time).

docu-, *combining form.* a documentary: [He] *calls it a "documusical," with songs and dramatic re-creations about America's railroads* (TV Guide). *The combination is a new kind of historical production— docuhistory* (Manchester Guardian). *Some basic matters are touched on too lightly in this docu-reenactment* (Christian Science Monitor).

E e

ep|i|tope (ep′i tōp), *n.,* the part of an antigen molecule to which a specific antibody molecule becomes attached: *The specific patterns that are recognized by antibody molecules are epitopes* (Scientific American). [< *epi-* into + Greek *tópos* place]

Eu|ro|par|lia|ment (yür′ō pär′lə mənt), *n.* = European Parliament.

Eu|ro|par|lia|men|tar|i|an (yür′ō pär′lə men tär′ē ən), *n.* a member of the European Parliament: [He] *skipped an appointment with Europarliamentarians so that he could stroll about town* (Newsweek).

Eu|ro|par|lia|men|ta|ry (yür′ō pär′lə men′tər ē), *adj.* of or having to do with the European parliament: *. . . the inhibiting effect of the campaign for the Europarliamentary elections* (Financial Times).

F f

fractal geometry, the branch of geometry that deals with fractals: *The increasing popularity of fractal geometry . . . stems from the vast diversity of physical problems that can be viewed as variations on a similar theme* (Science News).

G g

gen|o|gram (jen′ə gram), *n.* a graph that traces the interplay of generations within a family to identify repetitive patterns of behavior: *A genogram of the family of Eugene O'Neill shows a pattern of estrangement between father and children over three generations* (Daniel Goleman). [from Greek *génos* race, stock + English *-gram*[1]]

gimme cap, *U.S.* a visored cap with a clasp for adjusting it to any head size: *You will not see his cowboys fixing a baler or wearing . . . gimme caps. They wear broad-rimmed hats* (Newsweek).

gravitational lens, *Astronomy.* a lens-like effect produced by the strong gravitational field of a massive object, such as a galaxy, causing light reflected from a quasar or other very distant object to bend or intensify as it passes through the field: *The twin quasars go beyond this phenomenon in showing that a massive body can act as a gravitational lens, creating multiple images of an object as an optical lens does* (Scientific American).

grid|lock 2 any complete stoppage of activity due to overcrowding: *Sometimes, the entire city seemed to be jammed in telephone gridlock with everyone on the phone and no one getting through* (New Yorker).

gro|dy (grō′dē), *adj. U.S. Slang.* disgusting; gross: *Mom, like that's . . . grody to the max, just gruesome* (New York Times). [perhaps alteration of *grotesque.* Compare **grotty.**]

gross social product, *Economics.* the total monetary value of all goods produced in a nation during a certain period of time; gross national product minus the value of services: *Investments . . . in Yugoslavia amounted to some 43 per cent of the gross social product (GSP) of the country* (Financial Times). *Abbr:* GSP (no periods).

H h

hard|scape (härd′skāp), *n.* the man-made objects in a designed landscape, such as paving stones, benches, and fountains: *Landscape architect Ben Gary says [about] the material of hardscape: "It's wonderful stuff—you don't have to cut or water it"* (Mike Kenney).

hemorrhage, *n.* 2 *Figurative: The union has since lost 240,000 members. The hemorrhage is not yet over* (Financial Times).

H-ras (āch′ras′), *n.* a human gene of the ras group: *. . . yeast cells contain two genes that are similar to a human cancer gene known as H-ras* (Maynard V. Olson). [< *H*(uman) + *ras*]

I i

im|mu|no|mod|u|la|tor (i myü′nō moj′ù lā′tər), *n.* a drug used to stimulate activity of the body's immune system: *The class of drugs . . . is called immunomodulators, meaning drugs which can modify the body's own defense system* (Financial Times).

im|mu|no|stim|u|lant (i myü′nō stim′yə lənt), *n.* = immunomodulator: *He now takes a variety of "immunostimulants," including . . . the controversial cancer drug laetrile and a lot of vitamins and dietary supplements* (Newsweek).

information technology, the application of computers and techniques of using computers to the handling of masses of data: *The revolutionary impact of information technology has been greatly exaggerated* (New Republic).

in|for|mer|cial (in′fər mėr′shəl), *n. U.S.* a television commercial in the form of a program featuring demonstrations or discussions of various products or services: *A totally new type of commercial, or "informercial" . . . will range in length from 30 minutes to four hours* (Time). [blend of *information* and *commercial*]

J j

jazz tap, tap-dancing to jazz music or rhythms: *Teaching . . . "focuses on the rhythm patterns" of jazz tap, which she values as "both musical and physical expression"* (New York Times).

jet-lag|ging (jet′lag′ing), *adj.* of or having to do with jet lag: *Right from the jet-lagging start, I was knocked out by the place* (Life).

L l

laser card, 1 a small plastic card that has information stored on it to be read by a laser: *Subscribers will receive a laser card on which several hundred pages of A4 text are recorded, in place of the conventional printed paper* (Financial Times). 2 **Laser Card.** a trademark for this card.

laser gyro, a gyroscope having a ring of laser light instead of a wheel to indicate change in direction, used especially in guidance systems for space flight: *Britain claims world-class skills in laser gyros and logic array chips* (U.S. News & World Report).

light piping, *Botany.* the transmission of minute quantities of light down the stem of a plant to its parts underground: *This natural phenomenon, known as light piping, affects the way a seed grows into a plant. Light acts as a trigger that starts or otherwise controls the various life processes of plants* (Frank B. Salisbury).

M m

max (maks), *n., v. U.S. Informal.* —*n.* the greatest possible amount; maximum: *The policemen around the Mall call the overtime limit "the max"* (Blaine Harden). *A . . . new single from southern California has been riding the airways to the max* (Newsweek). —*v.i.* Usually, **max out.** to reach a maximum: *"They're just about maxing out on the covers"—industry jargon meaning that the restaurant is feeding people as fast as it can* (New York Times). —*v.t.* to perform or execute to one's maximum capacity: *[He] has just finished maxing the push-up test at 68* (Washington Post).

mi|cro|burst (mi′krō bėrst′), *n. Meteorology.* an intense downward surge of cool air sometimes occurring during a thunderstorm: *Since microbursts are often accompanied by rapid changes of wind speed and direction, they pose a threat to aircraft during take-off and landing* (W. Lawrence Gates).

mover and shaker, *U.S.* a person of power and influence: *Columbia, like its peers, is unashamedly trying to admit the movers and shakers of tomorrow* (Newsweek).

N n

Nemesis, *n.* 2 *Astronomy.* a hypothetical companion star to the sun that causes showers of comets as it orbits the sun over a period of millions of years, creating disturbances in the earth's atmosphere which may severely alter its climate and result in mass extinctions; death star: *Nemesis is an unseen object with an orbit of a most unusual kind . . . [that] has been invoked to explain a possible pattern in extinction* (Economist). *Nemesis . . . may orbit around our solar system regularly every 26 million years* (John N. Wilford).

network, *n.* 3 a group of people who work together informally to promote common goals: *Thinking women may be rethinking the whole concept of women-only networks* (Training).
—*v.i.* to meet informally with groups of people who share interests or causes: *"If you've networked with people when you were doing a film, you have a natural inter-*

est in seeing their reaction to the film" (Washington Post).

net|work|ing (net′wėr′king), *n.* the promotion of political goals or the exchange of ideas and information among people who share interests or causes: *. . . an interesting political process called networking, whereby the new breed of women in power in government and business make job connections and push the latest causes* (New York Times).

now|cast (nou′kast′, -käst′), *v.i.* **-cast** or **-cast|ed, -cast|ing.** to provide a description of atmospheric conditions as they occur or develop: *Recent advances in meteorology and oceanography provide the basis for accurate and efficient nowcasting, forecasting, and simulating of complex marine systems* (Boston Globe).

O o

oral biography, a biography based on and containing interviews with relatives and acquaintances of the subject: *An oral biography . . . is less a biography than an exercise in gossip, an excuse for people to talk about themselves and settle old scores under the guise of reminiscing about the celebrated figure they have known. One of the salient features of . . . oral biography is an abundance of irrelevant trivia* (New York Times Book Review).

-oriented, *combining form.* geared to; directed toward: *an action-oriented person, land-oriented recreation, a word-oriented computer program. They take obvious pride in their outdoor-oriented life style* (Reader's Digest).

P p

Planet X, *Astronomy.* a hypothetical planet orbiting the sun in a region beyond Pluto and within the Oort Cloud: *Every 28 million years, Planet X's orbit carries it through a disk of comets lying just beyond Neptune, dislodging many of them* (Time). *Since Planet X . . . must be quite dim, astronomers expect their best chance for proving its existence would come from heat emissions detected by infrared telescopes* (John N. Wilford).

pre-AIDS (prē ādz′), *n.* = ARC; AIDS-related complex: *There are many names for signs and symptoms that have been associated with infection by the AIDS virus: AIDS-related complex, AIDS-related conditions, . . . or pre-AIDS* (U.S. News & World Report).

pre|wire (prē wir′), *v.t.* **-wired, -wir|ing.** 1 to install electrical wiring during construction of a building or room. 2 *Figurative: All newborns smile, . . . and all babies tightly clutch objects placed in their palms. Both habits have apparently been prewired into the brain as firmly as the optic nerve* (Newsweek).

Pronunciation Key: hat, āge, cãre, fär; let, ēqual, tėrm; it, īce; hot, ōpen, ôrder; oil, out; cup, pủt, rüle; child; long; thin; ŦHen; zh, measure; ə represents a in about, e in taken, i in pencil, o in lemon, u in circus.

R r

ras[2] (ras), *n.* any one of a group of genes that are normally present in human, animal, and yeast cells but can cause cancer under certain conditions: *Normal non-cancer-forming versions of ras genes play a key role in the cell's production and use of an important substance called cyclic AMP, which has vital functions in almost all aspects of cells' metabolism, including growth and use of energy* (Harold M. Schmeck Jr.). *Mutant yeast strains that lack both ras genes cannot grow* (Maynard V. Olson). [< *ra*(t) + (viru)*s* (because the original gene was found in association with a rat virus)]

S s

satellite dish, a large microwave antenna shaped like a dish that tracks and receives signals from earth satellites: *The brown stucco apartment house, bristling with antennas and a satellite dish, is the home of [the] airwaves monitor for Israel Radio and Television* (Christian Science Monitor).

sexual harassment, harassment of a person because of her or his sex, as by making unwelcome sexual advances or otherwise engaging in sexist practices that cause the victim loss of income, mental anguish, and the like: *We are concerned about the sexual harassment suffered by working women and students* (New York Times).

so|ca (sō′kə), *n.* a combination of soul and calypso music: *His sharp ear for rhythm has enabled him to fuse funk, reggae, West African rhythms, and the soca (soul-calypso) beat of the British West Indies into a rhythmic dialect of his own* (Robert Palmer). [< *so*(ul) + *ca*(lypso)]

social savings, the difference between the cost of a new technology and the cost of the technology it replaces: *What would the additional costs have been of transporting the same quantity of goods by the next best alternative—in this case mostly the canals? The difference, —called the "social savings," would be the true measure of the significance of the railways in the American economy* (Times Literary Supplement).

sonograph, *n.* **2** a two-dimensional image made by ultrasonic waves: *There is a sonograph . . . showing a six-month-old human fetus in utero* (New York Times).

squeak|y-clean (skwē′kē klēn′), *adj. Informal.* **1** spotlessly clean: *. . . the important basic of squeaky-clean skin* (Tuscaloosa News). *Hair is always squeaky-clean* (Manchester Guardian Weekly). **2** *Figurative: . . . a squeaky-clean election financing law* (Maclean's). *The . . . Commission is designed to keep financing squeaky-clean* (New York Times).

su|per|cell (sü′pər sel′), *n. Meteorology.* a massive low-pressure center characterized by a very large cumulonimbus cloud and long-lasting thunderstorm, often producing numerous and violent tornadoes: *A typical cumulonimbus storm lasts about an hour, but a supercell, which expands to cover a vast area, lasts for six hours or longer* (Robert C. Cowen).

surrogate mother, a female who carries until birth the surgically implanted fertilized egg or embryo of another female: *Suppose the surrogate mother who carries another's child to term refuses to give it up? . . . Objection to natural or human incubators, which is what surrogates are, is equaled by objection to artificial gestation* (Joseph Fletcher). *Embryo transplant at the Bronx Zoo allowed a common dairy cow to give birth to a gaur, a rare wild ox, in the first successful use of a domestic animal as a surrogate mother for a vanishing wild species* (Science News).

sword and sorcery, fantasy novels or stories involving knightly quests, magic and witchcraft, mythical creatures, and the like: *The Disney organization co-produced "Dragonslayer," a dark slice of sword and sorcery* (Newsweek).

su|per|chip (sü′pər chip), *n.* a silicon computer chip that has thousands of components on it which can process large amounts of data at very high speed: *There have been two thrusts toward greater speed: the much-discussed supercomputer and the less visible superchip* (New York Times).

T t

tanning booth, a small enclosure with ultraviolet lamps for producing a tan: *A man is much better off using a bronzer instead of a tanning booth during the winter months because of the cancer hazards of ultraviolet radiation* (New York Times Magazine).

tel|e|mar|ket (tel′ə mär′kit), *v.t.* **1** to sell by telephone: *[He] had a great way to telemarket his flowers and the good sense to trademark it* (Inc.). **2** to solicit sales from by telephone: *He has been telemarketed, and . . . he may not like it or buy anything* (American Banker). —**tel′e|mar′ket|er**, *n.*

tel|e|van|gel|ist (tel′i van′jə list), *n. U.S.* a television evangelist; preacher of an electronic church: *His syndicated Sunday morning TV service, The Hour of Power, reaches an audience of almost 3 million, placing him among the nation's top-rated televangelists* (Time). —**tel′e|van′gel|ism**, *n.*

trail mix, a mixture of nuts, seeds, and dried fruits, used as a snack by hikers and campers: *"I carry trail mix the way some people carry chewing tobacco"* (New Yorker).

trans|bound|a|ry (trans boun′dər ē), *adj.* crossing a boundary, especially between two countries: *The Administration [is] negotiating with Canada and Mexico to reduce transboundary air pollution* (New York Times).

two-tier (tü′tir′), *adj.* having two parts: *The new rule is expected to make compa-nies less eager to mount "two-tier" offers, whereby they typically offer cash for part of a company and a lower price, in stock, for the rest* (New York Times).

W w

wafer chip, an electronic silicon wafer provided with a microcircuitry equal to the power of a hundred or more microchips: *Because processing video images takes so much memory and computer power, image processing could be the main near-term market for wafer chips* (Business Week).

wal|ly|ball (wôl′ē bôl′), *n. U.S.* volleyball played in a walled court: *Wallyball is . . . played on a racquetball court. Instead of a white leather ball, the players bang around an electric-blue ball of texturized rubber. Unlike volleyball, they are allowed to use the side walls. Each team is made up of two to four players* (New York Daily News).

wimp|ish (wim′pish), *adj. Slang.* of or resembling a wimp; unassertive: *They . . . played a deliberately wimpish kind of pool to make friends with a succession of macho . . . Brazilian pool players* (Edward Hoagland). —**wimp′ish|ly**, *adv.* —**wimp′ish|ness**, *n.*

wonk (wongk), *n. U.S. Slang.* a person who is too bookish; bookworm: *"Wonk" means grind, and an unattractive one at that, sporting a plastic . . . pack for pens and wearing glasses repaired with adhesive tape* (New York Times).

X x

X-ray laser, a device that amplifies X rays by stimulated emission to produce a beam of greater penetrating power than that of a regular laser beam: *It took longer to develop the technology that could create X-ray lasers because they require a great deal of energy* (Alexander Hallemans).

Z z

zap, *v.t.* **4** Also, **zap out.** *U.S.* to switch off (unwanted parts of a television program or videotape) by zapping: *Viewers can happily zap the commercials they find insulting, irritating, or in poor taste* (Harvard Business Review).

Z particle, an elementary particle with a neutral charge and a mass about 99 times that of the proton, held to be a carrier, or quantum unit, of the weak interaction: *The two scientists were honored for their role in proving the existence of subatomic particles called the W and Z particles. These particles transmit the weak force, one of four fundamental forces in nature* (I.B. Keller).

Index

How to Use the Index

This index covers the contents of the 1985, 1986, and 1987 editions of THE WORLD BOOK YEAR BOOK.

Each index entry is followed by the edition year and the page number, as:

> *"Crocodile" Dundee*: motion pictures, 87-402

This means that information about this film is on page 402 in the 1987 edition of THE YEAR BOOK.

An index entry that is the title of an article appearing in THE YEAR BOOK is printed in capital letters, as: **TAXATION.** An entry that is not an article title, but a subject discussed in an article of some other title, is printed: **Tornado.**

The "See" and "See also" cross-

references are to other entries within the index. Clue words or phrases are used when two or more references to the same subject appear in the same edition of THE YEAR BOOK, as:

> **CONSTITUTION OF THE UNITED STATES,** 87-270, 86-273, 85-265; gardening, 87–329; Special Report, 87-78

The indication "il." means that the reference is to an illustration only. An index entry in capital letters followed by "WBE" refers to a new or revised WORLD BOOK ENCYCLOPEDIA article in the supplement section, as:

> **MAGELLANIC CLOUDS:** WBE, 87-579

A

A Nation Prepared: Teachers for the 21st Century: education, 87–299
Abbas, Muhammad: Italy, 86–362; President, 86–447
ABC (American Broadcasting Companies): radio, 87–453; television, 87–492, 86–491
Abdallah: dancing, 86–280
Abdul-Jabbar, Kareem: basketball, 87–224, 86–224, 85–216
Abortion: Roman Catholic, 86–460, 85–465; Supreme Court, 87–485
Academy of Motion Picture Arts and Sciences: awards, 87–214, 86–214, 85–208
Accidents. See **DISASTERS; SAFETY.**
Achille Lauro: Italy, 86–362; Middle East, 87–396, 86–401
Acid rain: Canada, 87–241, 86–240, 85–233; coal, 87–259; conservation, 87–270; environmental pollution, 86–311, 85–306; national parks, Special Report, 87–111; Norway, 87–422; Sweden, 86–488
Acquired Immune Deficiency Syndrome. See **AIDS.**
Acute congestive glaucoma: vision, Special Report, 86–147
Adams, Sherman: deaths, 87–280
Aden. See **Yemen (Aden).**
Adler, Renata: literature, 87–379
Adolescent: teen-age drinking, Special Report, 87–116
Adventures of Huckleberry Finn, The: theater, 86–496
ADVERTISING, 87–176, 86–176, 85–174; food, Close-Up, 86–325. See also **MAGAZINE.**
Aegyptopithecus zeuxis: anthropology, Close-Up, 85–186
Aerospace industry. See **AVIATION; SPACE EXPLORATION.**
Afars and Issas, Territory of. See **Djibouti.**
Affirmative action: civil rights, 87–256, 86–258, 85–251; Supreme Court, 87–485, 85–492
AFGHANISTAN, 87–177, 86–177, 85–175; Asia, 87–202, 86–200, 85–196; Middle East, 86–402; Pakistan, 85–435
AFRICA, 87–178, 86–178, 85–177; civil rights, 86–258, 85–251; popular music, 86–440; Special Report, 85–31. See also entries for specific countries.
African Methodist Episcopal Church: religion, 87–457, 86–457, 85–463
African Methodist Episcopal Zion Church: religion, 87–457, 86–457, 85–463
African National Congress (ANC): South Africa, 87–470
"Africans, The": television, 87–494
Age-related macular degeneration (AMD): vision, Special Report, 86–154
Agent Orange: health, 87–341; veterans, 86–512, 85–515
Aging: vision, Special Report, 86–147
Agriculture. See **FARM AND FARMING.**
Aherne, Brian: deaths, 87–280
Aid to Families with Dependent Children: city, 87–254; welfare, 87–519
AIDS (Acquired Immune Deficiency Syndrome): armed forces, 86–197; child welfare, 86–248; city, 86–256; civil rights, 87–257; drugs, 87–293; handicapped, 87–340; health, 87–341; 86–343, 85–339; hospital, 87–346; Los Angeles, 86–387; public health, 87–451; Protestantism, 86–449; state govt., 86–479; Washington, D.C., 87–516; WBE, 87–578
Air Force. See **ARMED FORCES.**
Air India jetliner: India, 86–352
Air pollution: coal, 87–259; conservation, 86–272; nuclear energy, Special Report, 86–96; national parks, Special Report, 87–111. See also **ENVIRONMENTAL POLLUTION.**
Air-traffic controllers: aviation, 87–213; safety, 86–465
Airbag: safety, 87–464, 85–473
Aircraft crashes. See **AVIATION; DISASTERS.**
Airline. See **AVIATION.**

Airship: WBE, 86–530
Akhmilovskaya, Elena: chess, 87–246
Alabama: state govt., 87–480, 86–480, 85–488
Alabama (music group): popular music, 87–442
Alaska: conservation, 87–269; state govt., 87–480, 86–480, 85–488
ALBANIA, 87–183, 86–184, 85–182; Alía, Ramiz, 86–187; Europe, 87–314, 86–315, 85–311
ALBERTA, 87–184, 86–185, 85–182; Getty, Donald R., 86–336
Albuquerque: city, 87–252, 86–254, 85–248
Alcoholic beverage: advertising, 86–176; drug abuse, 87–292; teen-age drinking, Special Report, 87–116
Alda, Robert: deaths, 87–280
Alexander, Lincoln MacCauley: Ontario, 86–427
"Alf": television, 87–493
Alfonsín, Raúl Ricardo: Argentina, 87–192, 86–194, 85–190
ALGERIA, 87–185, 86–186, 85–183; Africa, 87–180, 86–182, 85–178; WBE, 86–533
ALÍA, RAMIZ, 86–187; Albania, 87–183, 86–184
Alien. See **IMMIGRATION.**
Aliens: il., 87–402
Alliluyeva, Svetlana: newsmakers, 87–416
All-terrain vehicle (ATV): safety, 86–465
Alpha-interferon: medicine, 87–390
Alpine skiing. See **SKIING.**
Aluminum: labor, 87–367
Alvin: ocean, 87–424
Alzheimer's disease: drugs, 87–293; health, 85–340
Amal militia: Lebanon, 87–375; Middle East, 86–399
American Ballet Theatre: dancing, 87–278, 85–273
American Baptist Association: religion, 87–457, 86–457, 85–463
American Baptist Churches in the U.S.A.: religion, 87–457, 86–457, 85–463
American Craft Museum: art, 87–198
American Federation of Teachers (AFT): education, 87–299, 86–304
American Indian. See **INDIAN, AMERICAN.**
American Kennel Club. See **DOG.**
AMERICAN LIBRARY ASSOCIATION (ALA), 87–185, 86–187, 85–184
American Lutheran Church, The: religion, 87–457, 86–457, 85–463
American Motors Corporation: automobile, 87–210
American Music Awards: awards, 87–214, 86–214, 85–208
America's Cup: boating, 87–228, 86–227, 85–220
AMERIPEX '86: stamp collecting, 87–478
Amphetamines: teen-age drinking, Special Report, 87–122
Amphipithecus: anthropology, 86–189
Amtrak. See **RAILROAD.**
Anabolic steroids: sports, 86–475
Andorra: Europe, 87–314, 86–315, 85–311
ANDREW, PRINCE, 87–186; Ferguson, Sarah, 87–320; Great Britain, Close-Up, 87–336
Andropov, Yuri Vladimirovich: Close-Up, 85–471; Close-Up, 86–463; il., 87–45
Angle-closure glaucoma: vision, Special Report, 86–147
Anglicans. See **Episcopal Church, The.**
Anglo-Irish Agreement: Northern Ireland, 87–421
ANGOLA, 87–186, 86–187, 85–184; Africa, 87–180, 86–182, 85–178; Namibia, 85–412; South Africa, 87–471
Animal: psychology, 86–450. See also **CAT; CONSERVATION; DOG; FARM AND FARMING; ZOOLOGY; ZOOS.**
Anthology program: television, 86–492
Anthropoid: anthropology, 86–189
ANTHROPOLOGY, 87–186, 86–188, 85–185. See also **ARCHAEOLOGY.**
Antibody: biochemistry, 86–226; medicine, 86–395
Antigen: biochemistry, 86–227; gene-splicing, Special Report, 85–68

Antigua and Barbuda: Latin America, 87–371, 86–375, 85–374
Antiochian Orthodox Christian Archdiocese of North America, The: religion, 87–457, 86–457, 85–463
Anti-Semitism: Alberta, 86–185
Anxiety: biochemistry, 86–227; mental illness, 85–392; psychology, 85–457
ANZUS: Australia, 87–208, 86–207, 85–202; New Zealand, 87–410, 85–416
Apartheid: Europe, 87–315; Protestantism, 87–448, 85–457; South Africa, 87–470, 86–471; UN, 86–507
Aquariums. See **ZOOS.**
Aquaticus: zoos, 87–525
Aqueous humor: vision, Special Report, 86–146
Aquino, Benigno S., Jr.: Philippines, 86–436, 85–444
AQUINO, CORAZON, 87–188; Asia, 87–202; il., 87–521; Philippines, 87–434, 86–436
Arabia. See **MIDDLE EAST; SAUDI ARABIA.**
Arabs: Iraq, 87–357; Israel, 86–361; Libya, 86–381; Pakistan, 87–429; Turkey, 87–505. See also **MIDDLE EAST.**
Arafat, Yasir: Jordan, 87–363; Middle East, 87–398, 86–399; United Nations, 86–506
Arbitrage: stocks, 87–484
ARCHAEOLOGY, 87–189, 86–190, 85–187; Monticello, Special Report, 85–102. See also **ANTHROPOLOGY.**
Archaeopteryx: paleontology, 87–429
Archery: sports, 87–476, 86–476, 85–484
Arches National Park: il., 87–106
ARCHITECTURE, 87–191, 86–192, 85–189; Special Report, 86–126. See also **BUILDING AND CONSTRUCTION.**
Architecture (computer): computer, 87–262
Arctic: newsmakers, 87–413
Arctic Dreams: literature, 87–380
Arctic National Wildlife Refuge: conservation, 87–269
ARDITO BARLETTA VALLARINA, NICOLÁS, 85–190; Panama, 86–431
ARGENTINA, 87–192, 86–194, 85–190; Brazil, 87–231; Latin America, 87–371, 86–375, 85–374; soccer, 87–469
Argo: ocean, Close-Up, 86–425
Arguello, Alexis: boxing, 86–231
Ariane (spacecraft): space exploration, Special Report, 86–39; space, 87–473, 85–481
ARIAS SÁNCHEZ, OSCAR, 87–193
Arizona: state govt., 87–480, 86–480, 85–488
Arizona-Sonora Desert Museum: zoo design, Special Report, 87–56; zoos, 87–525
Arkansas: education, 86–303; state govt., 87–480, 86–480, 85–488
Arlen, Harold: deaths, 87–280
ARMED FORCES, 87–194, 86–195, 85–192; building, 86–233; public health, 87–451; space exploration, Special Report, 86–46; U.S. govt., 87–511, 86–508. See also entries for specific continents and countries.
Armenian Apostolic Church of America: religion, 87–457, 86–457
Armenian Church of America, Diocese of the: religion, 87–457, 86–457, 85–463
Arms-control negotiations: Europe, 87–310; President, 87–446, 86–444, 85–453; Russia, 87–461, 86–462, 85–470; United Nations, 86–506, 85–508
Army, United States. See **ARMED FORCES.**
Arnaz, Desi: deaths, 87–280
ART, 87–196, 86–513, 85–516
Art restoration: Special Report, 87–130
Articles of Confederation: Constitution, Special Report, 87–89
Artificial heart: medicine, 87–391, 85–390; WBE, 87–578
Artificial intelligence: computer, 86–265
Artificial sweetener: food, 86–326
Arts: awards, 87–214, 86–214, 85–208. See also **ARCHITECTURE; ART; CLASSICAL MUSIC; DANCING; LITERATURE; MOTION PICTURES; POETRY; POPULAR MUSIC; THEATER.**
Artukovic, Andrija: Yugoslavia, 87–523
Asbestos: environmental pollution, 87–312; safety, 87–465

ASEAN: Asia, 87–204, 86–202, 85–197
Ashford, Evelyn: il., 87–70
ASIA, 87–201, 86–198, 85–194; civil rights, 86–257. See also entries for specific countries.
Asia-Africa Conference: Asia, 86–201
Assad, Hafiz al-: Syria, 87–489, 86–489
Assassination: Chile, 87–248; Sweden, 87–487
Assemblies of God: religion, 87–457, 86–457, 85–463
Association of Southeast Asian Nations. See **ASEAN.**
Asteroid: astronomy, 86–203; extinction, Special Report, 86–100; paleontology, 86–430
Astronaut. See **SPACE EXPLORATION.**
ASTRONOMY, 87–204, 86–202, 85–199
AT&T (American Telephone and Telegraph Company): communications, 87–261, 86–263, 85–254; consumerism, 87–271, 85–265
AT&T Building (New York City): architecture, Special Report, 86–128
Ataturk Dam: building, 87–235
Atherosclerosis: cholesterol, Special Report, 85–134; nutrition, 87–422
Athletics. See **OLYMPIC GAMES; SPORTS;** and names of specific sports.
Atlanta: city, 87–252, 86–254, 85–248
Atlantic Accord: Canada, 86–236
Atlantis (spacecraft): space, 86–473; Special Report, 86–46
Atwood, Margaret: Canadian literature, 86–242, 85–235
Auctions and sales. See **ART; COIN COLLECTING; STAMP COLLECTING.**
Austin: city, 87–252, 86–254, 85–248
Austral Plan: Argentina, 87–193
AUSTRALIA, 87–206, 86–206, 85–201; Asia, 87–202, 86–200, 85–196; forest, 86–330; mining, 87–400, 85–400; Murdoch, Rupert, 85–407; Sinclair, Ian, 85–477; stamps, 85–486
Australia Act 1986: Australia, 87–208
Australopithecus: anthropology, 87–186, 86–188, 85–185
AUSTRIA, 87–208, 86–207, 85–202; Europe, 87–314, 86–315, 85–311; Waldheim, Kurt, 87–514
Autocrine motility factor (AMF): biochemistry, 87–226
Automation: manufacturing, 87–390, 86–393
AUTOMOBILE, 87–209, 86–208, 85–203; building, 86–233; Canada, 86–239; consumerism, 87–271, 86–274, 85–265; Detroit, 87–289, 86–291, 85–285; labor, 86–371, 85–306; newsmakers, 87–416; safety, 87–464, 86–465; teen-age drinking, Special Report, 87–118
AUTOMOBILE RACING, 87–211, 86–211, 85–205; WBE, 86–539
AVIATION, 87–212, 86–212, 85–206; espionage, Special Report, 87–41; Great Britain, 87–335; handicapped, 87–340, 86–342; India, 86–352; Japan, 86–364; safety, 87–464, 86–465. See also **DISASTERS; TRANSPORTATION.**
AWARDS AND PRIZES, 87–214, 86–214, 85–208; Canadian Library Association, 86–242, 85–234; Nobel Prizes, 87–420, 86–421, 85–420. See also entries for specific activities, such as **GARDENING; MEDICINE; POETRY;** also specific awards, such as **Grammy Awards.**
AWACS (Airborne Warning and Control System): Saudi Arabia, 86–466
AZCONA DEL HOYO, JOSÉ, 87–219; Honduras, 87–343, 86–347
Aztec: Mexico, 86–398

B

Babangida, Ibrahim: Nigeria, 87–419, 86–419
"Baby Doe" ruling: child welfare, 85–243; handicapped, 87–340, 85–338; hospital, 87–345, 85–344; Supreme Court, 87–485
Baby Jesse: medicine, 87–391
Baby Talk doll: toys and games, 87–499
BACCHUS (Boost Alcohol Consciousness Concerning the Health of University Stu-

dents): teen-age drinking, Special Report, 87–126
Back to the Future: motion pictures, 86–406
Bacteria: environmental pollution, 86–312; gene-splicing, Special Report, 85–61
Baddeley, Hermione: deaths, 87–280
Badminton: sports, 87–476, 86–476, 85–484
Bahamas: Latin America, 87–371, 86–375, 85–374
Bahrain: Middle East, 87–396, 86–400, 85–398
BAKER, JAMES ADDISON, III, 86–218; economics, 86–299; Latin America, 86–374
BALAGUER, JOAQUIN, 87–219
Ballet. See **DANCING.**
Baltimore: city, 87–252, 86–254, 85–248
Banff National Park: il., 87–108
BANGLADESH, 87–219, 86–218, 85–212; Asia, 87–202, 86–200, 85–196; India, 86–352
BANK, 87–220, 86–219, 85–212; Canada, 86–239; economics, 87–298, 86–299; international trade, 86–356; Latin America, 86–372, 85–375
Bankruptcy: consumerism, 85–266; farm, 87–318
Banks, Willie: track, 86–500
Baptist Bible Fellowship, International: religion, 87–457, 86–457
Baptist Missionary Association of America: religion, 87–457, 86–457, 85–463
Barbados: Latin America, 87–371, 86–375, 85–374
BARCO VARGAS, VIRGILIO, 87–221; Colombia, 87–261
Barnacle: chemistry, 87–245
Barry, Marion S., Jr.: Washington, D.C., 87–515
Bartholdi, Frédéric Auguste: stamps, 86–478; Statue of Liberty, Special Report, 86–52
Base-load power plant: nuclear energy, Special Report, 86–95
BASEBALL, 87–221, 86–221, 85–214; perspective, 85–168; Rose, Pete, 86–461; Toronto, 86–498
BASKETBALL, 87–224, 86–223, 85–216; Ewing, Patrick, 86–317; WBE, 85–540
Bat: zoology, 87–524
Batchelder Award. See **LITERATURE FOR CHILDREN.**
Bauer, Eddie: deaths, 87–280
Bausch, Pina: dancing, 86–281, 85–275
Baxter, Anne: deaths, 86–282
Beagle Channel: Latin America, 86–376
Bears, Chicago: football, 87–324, 86–326
Beattie, Ann: literature, 86–381
Beatrix, Queen: il., 87–407
Beauvoir, Simone de: deaths, 87–280
Beaux-arts tradition: architecture, Special Report, 86–135
Beck, Julian: deaths, 86–282
BECKER, BORIS, 86–225; tennis, 87–495, 86–495
Behavioral immunology: psychology, 86–450
Beirut: Middle East, 85–396; President, 86–447
Belau: Pacific Islands, 86–428
BELGIUM, 87–226, 86–225, 85–218; Europe, 87–314, 86–315, 85–311; soccer, 86–470
Belize: Latin America, 87–371, 86–375, 85–374
Beloff, Leland: Philadelphia, 87–434
Bendjedid, Chadli: Algeria, 87–185, 86–186, 85–183
Benefactors: theater, 87–497
Bengal. See **BANGLADESH.**
Benin: Africa, 87–180, 86–182, 85–178
BENNETT, WILLIAM JOHN, 86–226; education, 86–301; religion, 86–457
Bennett, William R.: British Columbia, 86–232, 85–224; il., 85–224
Benoit, Joan: sports, 87–476
Berlin: Germany, East, 87–331; il., 87–313
Berry, Walter: basketball, 87–225
Berton, Pierre: Canadian literature, 85–235
Beschloss, Michael E.: literature, 87–379
Best sellers. See **LITERATURE.**
Bestall, Alfred: deaths, 87–280
Beta-blocker: psychology, 85–457; vision, Special Report, 86–149

Betancur, Belisario: Colombia, 86–262, 85–254
Bethe, Hans A.: physics, 87–437
Bhopal, India: chemical industry, 85–237; environmental pollution, 86–310, 85–306
Bhutan: Asia, 87–202, 86–200, 85–196
Bhutto, Benazir: Pakistan, 87–428
Bialer, Seweryn: literature, 87–380
Bias, Len: crime, 87–276; sports, 87–476; teen-age drinking, Special Report, 87–122
Biathlon: sports, 87–476, 86–476, 85–484
Bicycle. See **Cycling.**
Big game hunting: hunting, 87–348
Bighorn sheep: hunting, 87–348
Bikini Atoll: Pacific Islands, 86–428
Bilingualism: immigration, Special Report, 86–68; Manitoba, 86–391, 85–387; New Brunswick, 87–407; Quebec, 87–453, 86–453
Bill of Rights: Constitution, Special Report, 87–92
Billiards: sports, 87–476, 86–476, 85–484
Binnig, Gerd: Nobel Prizes, 87–420
BIOCHEMISTRY, 87–226, 86–226, 85–218
Biography. See **CANADIAN LITERATURE; DEATHS; LITERATURE; NEWSMAKERS;** and names of individuals.
Biondi, Matt: swimming, 87–487, 86–488
Bird: hunting, 85–346; paleontology, 87–429
Bird, Larry: basketball, 87–224, 86–224, 85–216
Bird, Rose Elizabeth: courts, 87–273
Birth control: China, Special Report, 86–124; drugs, 86–296; education, 87–300; health, 87–341, 86–344; Roman Catholic Church, 85–468
Births. See **CENSUS; POPULATION.**
Bistoury: art restoration, Special Report, 87–141
Black-footed ferret: conservation, 87–270
Black hole: astronomy, 86–203
Blacks: WBE, 85–552; census, 86–245; civil rights, 86–258, 85–251; Democratic Party, 86–288; elections, 86–305; Philadelphia, 86–434; popular music, 87–440, 86–440, 85–410; Republican Party, 86–459; South Africa, 87–470, 86–471; Supreme Court, 87–486; welfare, 87–519
Blair, Bonnie: ice skating, 87–348
Blessed Assurance: literature, 87–380
Blindness: vision, Special Report, 86–146
Blood: chemistry, 86–246
Blood, Johnny: deaths, 86–282
Blood clot: medicine, 87–392
Bloodletting: archaeology, Close-Up, 87–190
Bloomers: women's sports, Special Report, 87–70
Blue Jays, Toronto: Toronto, 86–498
BOATING, 87–228, 86–227, 85–220
Bobsledding: sports, 87–476, 86–476, 85–484
Body building: il., 87–71
Boeing Company: Japan, 86–364
Boesky, Ivan F.: crime, 87–274; stocks, 87–484
Boff, Leonardo: Roman Catholic Church, 87–460, 86–459, 85–467
Boitano, Brian: ice skating, 87–348
BOLIVIA, 87–229, 86–228; Latin America, 87–371, 86–375, 85–374; Paz Estenssoro, Víctor, 86–431
Bombings: Great Britain, 86–340, 85–332; Middle East, 85–396; Tunisia, 86–504; Washington, D.C., 86–517, 85–519
Bonds. See **STOCKS AND BONDS.**
Bone: biochemistry, 87–227
Bone marrow: medicine, 87–391
Bonner, Yelena G.: civil rights, 86–258, 85–251
Books. See **CANADIAN LITERATURE; LITERATURE; LITERATURE FOR CHILDREN; POETRY; PUBLISHING.**
Booth, Philip: poetry, 87–438
Bophuthatswana: Africa, 86–182, 85–178
Bordallo, Ricardo J.: Pacific Islands, 87–428
Borges, Jorge Luis: Latin America, 87–373
Boston: city, 87–252, 86–254, 85–248
Boston Red Sox: baseball, 87–221
BOTANY, 87–229, 86–228, 85–221. See also **GARDENING.**
Botha, Pieter Willem: Africa, 86–180; Europe,

87–315; South Africa, 87–470, 86–472, 85–479
Botswana: Africa, 87–180, 86–182, 85–178
BOURASSA, ROBERT, 86–229; Canada, 87–239; Montreal, 86–403; Quebec, 86–453
Bourguiba, Habib: Tunisia, 87–505
BOWEN, OTIS RAY, 86–229
BOWLING, 87–230, 86–229, 85–221
BOXING, 87–230, 86–230, 85–222
Boy George: England, 87–309
Boy Scouts of America (BSA). See **YOUTH ORGANIZATIONS.**
Boys Clubs of America (BCA). See **YOUTH ORGANIZATIONS.**
Braddick, Donnie: fishing, 87–321
Bradley, Pat: golf, 87–333
Bradley, Thomas: Los Angeles, 86–387
Braids: il., 87–197
Brain: anthropology, 87–188; psychology, 85–457
Brambilla Barcilon, Pinin: art restoration, Special Report, 87–140
Brautigan, Richard: deaths, 85–276
BRAZIL, 87–231, 86–231, 85–223; archaeology, 87–189; Latin America, 87–371, 86–375, 85–374; Sarney, José, 86–466
Breakfast Club, The: motion pictures, 86–405
Breast cancer: medicine, 86–395
Breeder reactor: nuclear energy, Special Report, 86–94
Breeders' Cup Series. See **HORSE RACING.**
Brezhnev, Leonid Ilich: Russia, Close-Up, 86–463, 85–471
Bridge: building, 87–235
BRIDGE (game), 87–232, 86–232, 85–223
Brisco-Hooks, Valerie: il., 87–70
BRITISH COLUMBIA, 87–232, 86–232, 85–224; Vander Zalm, William Nick, 87–513
British West Indies. See **WEST INDIES.**
Broad construction: Constitution, Special Report, 87–93
Broadway Bound: theater, 87–497
Brock, Lou: baseball, 86–222
BROCK, WILLIAM EMERSON, III, 86–233
Broncos, Denver: football, 87–326
Bronx Zoo: zoo design, Special Report, 87–50; zoos, 87–526, 86–525
Brookfield Zoo: ils, 87–53, 56; zoos, 85–528
Brooklyn Botanic Garden: gardening, 86–333
Brown, Harrison S.: deaths, 87–280
Brown, Jonathan: literature, 87–379
Brown, Michael S.: Nobel Prizes, 86–421
Browning, Edmond Lee: Protestantism, 87–448, 86–450
Bruhn, Erik: dancing, 87–279
BRUNDTLAND, GRO HARLEM, 87–233; Norway, 87–422
Brunei Darussalam: WBE, 85–579; Asia, 87–202, 86–200, 85–196
Bubka, Sergei: track, 87–500, 86–499, 85–502
Buchanan, James McGill: Nobel Prizes, 87–420
Budd, Zola: track, 85–503
Budget, Defense. See **ARMED FORCES.**
Budget, Federal: Congress, 87–268, 86–266, 85–257; Constitution, 87–270; U. S. govt., 87–509, 86–508, 85–510
Buffalo: city, 87–252, 86–254, 85–248
Bug (listening device): espionage, Special Report, 87–42
BUHARI, MUHAMMADU, 85–224; il., 85–43; Nigeria, 86–419, 85–419
BUILDING AND CONSTRUCTION, 87–233, 86–233, 85–224; city, 86–256; Detroit, 86–291; Great Britain, 87–338; safety, 87–465; Toronto, 86–498. See also **ARCHITECTURE; HOUSING.**
BULGARIA, 87–235, 86–234, 85–226; Europe, 87–314, 86–315, 85–311
Burgee, John: architecture, Special Report, 86–128
Burger, Warren E.: courts, 85–267; Supreme Court, Close-Up, 86–485
Burkina Faso: Africa, 87–180, 86–182
Burma: Asia, 87–202, 86–200, 85–196; WBE, 86–546
Burnet Park Zoo: zoos, 87–525
Burundi: Africa, 87–180, 86–182, 85–178
Bus: disasters, 87–290, 86–293, 85–287

BUSH, GEORGE H. W., 87–236, 86–235, 85–227; ils., 87–363, 465, 85–465
Business. See **ECONOMICS; INTERNATIONAL TRADE; LABOR; MANUFACTURING;** also specific industries, such as **MINING.**
Byrd, Robert C.: il., 87–286

C

Cabinet, Canadian: Canada, 87–237, 86–238
CABINET, U.S., 87–236, 86–235, 85–227. See also names of Cabinet members.
Cable television: communications, 87–262, 85–255; Washington, D.C., 86–517. See also **TELEVISION.**
Caesar, Adolph: deaths, 87–280
Cagney, James: deaths, 87–280
Caldecott Medal. See **LITERATURE FOR CHILDREN.**
California: Los Angeles, 87–383, 86–387, 85–384; state govt., 87–480, 86–480, 85–488
Callaghan, Morley: Canadian literature, 86–242
CAMBODIA. See **KAMPUCHEA.**
Camcorder: photography, 86–437
Camera. See **PHOTOGRAPHY.**
CAMEROON, 85–227; Africa, 87–180, 86–182, 85–178; geology, 87–330
Camp Fire. See **YOUTH ORGANIZATIONS.**
CANADA, 87–236, 86–236, 85–228; awards, 87–217, 86–216, 85–210; coal, 87–259; energy supply, 87–309, 86–308; fishing industry, 87–323; football, 86–328, 85–323; handicapped, 86–342; Indian, American, 87–352, 86–354; international trade, 87–355; Mulroney, M. Brian, 87–406, 86–409, 85–407; national parks, Special Report, 87–108; petroleum, 86–434, 85–443; Sauvé, Jeanne M., 87–466, 86–467, 85–475; Trudeau, Pierre E., 87–504, 86–503, 85–507. See also **CANADIAN LIBRARY ASSOCIATION; CANADIAN LITERATURE,** and by province.
Canadian Encyclopedia, The: Canadian literature, 86–242
Canadian Football League: football, 87–327, 86–328, 85–323
CANADIAN LIBRARY ASSOCIATION, 87–241, 86–242, 85–234
CANADIAN LITERATURE, 87–242, 86–242, 85–235
Cancer: biochemistry, 87–226, 86–226; dentistry, 86–290; drugs, 87–293; health, 87–341, 85–340; medicine, 87–390, 86–394; Reagan, Ronald W., 86–455
Candlestick Tower: il., 87–101
Cannes International Film Festival: awards, 87–214, 86–214, 85–208
Cannibalism: anthropology, 87–187
Canoeing: sports, 87–476, 86–476, 85–484
Cape Verde: Africa, 87–180, 86–182, 85–178
Capital investment: manufacturing, 87–389, 86–392, 85–388
Capital punishment: mental illness, 87–392; prison, 87–448, 85–454
Capsules: drugs, 87–294
Captive-breeding programs: conservation, 87–270
Carbon dioxide: geology, 87–330; nuclear energy, Special Report, 86–96
Career ladder plan: education, 86–303
Caribbean. See **WEST INDIES.**
Caribbean Basin Initiative (CBI): Latin America, 85–372; West Indies, 87–520
Carlin, Paul N.: Postal Service, 87–444, 85–450
CARLSSON, INGVAR, 87–243
Carlton, Steve: baseball, 87–223
Carlucci, Frank C.: President, 87–446
Carney, Patricia: Canada, 87–238
Carpio Nicolle, Jorge: Guatemala, 86–341
Carr, Zack: fashion, 87–319
Carson, Johnny: television, 87–493
Cartagena Group: Latin America, 86–373
CARTER, JAMES EARL, JR., 87–243, 86–244, 85–236; Ford, Gerald R., 86–329; il., 85–290
Cartoon: art restoration, Special Report, 87–137
Carver, Raymond: poetry, 86–439

Casey, Albert V.: Postal Service, 87–444
Cash, Norm: deaths, 87–281
Castelo, Anita S.: Reagan, Ronald W., 87–455
Casting: sports, 87–476, 86–476, 85–484
Castro, Fidel: Cuba, 86–278, 85–271; il., 87–276
CAT, 87–244, 86–244, 85–236
Cataract: vision, Special Report, 86–144
Catholics. See **ROMAN CATHOLIC CHURCH.**
CAVACO SILVA, ANÍBAL, 86–244; Portugal, 86–443
Cave art: archaeology, 87–189
CBS Inc.: courts, 85–269; television, 87–492, 86–491, 85–498
CD-ROM (Compact Disk Read-Only Memory): computer, 87–263
Ceausescu, Nicolae: Romania, 87–461, 86–461, 85–468
Celtics, Boston: basketball, 87–224, 85–216
Censorship: American Library Association, 87–185; Canadian Library Association, 86–242, 85–234; civil rights, 85–251
CENSUS, 87–244, 86–245, 85–237. See also **POPULATION.**
Center for Plant Conservation: botany, 86–229
Central African Republic: Africa, 87–180, 86–182, 85–178
Central America. See **LATIN AMERICA.**
Central Ballet of China: dancing, 87–278
CEREZO, VINICIO, 87–244
Certificate of deposit (CD): bank, 87–221
Ceylon. See **SRI LANKA.**
CHAD, 86–245, 85–237; Africa, 87–180, 86–182, 85–178
Challenger: Houston, 87–346; space exploration, Close-Up, 87–474, 86–472, 85–480; U.S. govt., 87–511
Champion Marietta National Acclaim: dog, 87–292
Championship Auto Racing Teams (CART). See **AUTOMOBILE RACING.**
Chaovalit Yongchaiyuth: Thailand, 87–496
Charge-coupled device (CCD): electronics, 86–306
Charles, Prince: architecture, 85–189; Great Britain, 86–340; ils., 85–336
Charlotte: city, 87–252, 86–254, 85–248
Charter of Rights and Freedoms: Canada, 86–236
Chazov, Yevgeny I.: Nobel Prizes, 86–421
Chebrikov, Viktor M.: espionage, Special Report, 87–45
Checks and balances: Constitution, Special Report, 87–92
Cheka: espionage, Special Report, 87–43
CHEMISTRY, 87–245, 86–245, 85–238. See also **NOBEL PRIZES.**
Chemotherapy: drugs, 87–293
CHERNENKO, KONSTANTIN USTINOVICH, 85–239; deaths, 86–282; Russia, 85–468, Close-Up, 86–463
Chernobyl nuclear power station: energy supply, Close-Up, 87–306; Europe, 87–313; Scotland, 87–467; Russia, 87–462; Wales, 87–514
CHESS, 87–246, 86–246, 85–239; WBE, 86–552
Chiang Ching-kuo: Asia, 85–194; Taiwan, 87–489, 85–495
Chiburdanidze, Maya: chess, 87–246, 85–239
CHICAGO, 87–246, 86–247, 85–240; city, 87–254, 86–254, 85–248; ils., 86–137, 139; theater, 87–494; transit, 85–504
Chicago Sun-Times: newspaper, 87–417
Chihuahua (state): Mexico, 87–394
CHILD WELFARE, 87–247, 86–248, 85–241; city, 86–252; crime, 86–277, 85–269; Great Britain, 86–310; mental illness, 86–396; sexual abuse, Close-Up, 85–242; state govt., 86–479, 85–487. See also **EDUCATION; WELFARE.**
Children of the Maya: literature for children, 87–383
Children's books. See **LITERATURE FOR CHILDREN.**
CHILE, 87–248, 86–249, 85–243; archaeology, 86–192; civil rights, 85–251; Latin America, 87–371, 86–375, 85–374
CHINA, 87–248, 86–249, 85–243; anthropol-

ogy, 86–190; Asia, 87–202, 86–200, 85–196; coal, 86–261; dancing, 87–278; farm, 86–319; fishing industry, 86–323; Russia, 87–463, 86–462, 85–470; space exploration, Special Report, 86–42; space, 87–475; Special Report, 86–110; Taiwan, 87–490, 85–495; women's sports, Special Report, 87–75; zoology, 85–527

China syndrome: nuclear energy, Special Report, 86–89

Chinh, Truong: Vietnam, 87–514

CHIRAC, JACQUES, 87–251; France, 87–328

Chissano, Joaquim A.: Mozambique, 87–406

Cholesterol: Nobel Prizes, 86–421; nutrition, 87–422, 86–423, 85–424; Special Report, 85–132

Christian and Missionary Alliance: religion, 87–457, 86–457, 85–463

Christian Church (Disciples of Christ): religion, 87–457, 86–457, 85–463

Christian Churches and Churches of Christ: religion, 87–457, 86–457, 85–463

Christian fundamentalists: Protestantism, 87–450; religion, 87–456

Christian Methodist Episcopal Church: religion, 87–457, 86–457, 85–463

Christian Reformed Church in North America: religion, 87–457, 86–457, 85–463

Christiansen, Jack: deaths, 87–281

Chromatograph: art restoration, Special Report, 87–140

Chrysler Corporation: automobile, 86–209; Detroit, 87–289

Chun Doo Hwan: Japan, 85–360; Korea, South, 87–365, 86–368, 85–365

Church of God (Anderson, Ind.): religion, 87–457, 86–457, 85–463

Church of God (Cleveland, Tenn.): religion, 87–457, 86–457, 85–463

Church of God in Christ: religion, 87–457, 86–457, 85–463

Church of God in Christ, International, The: religion, 87–457, 86–457, 85–463

Church of Jesus Christ of Latter-day Saints: literature, 86–383; Protestantism, 86–450; religion, 87–457, 86–457, 85–463

Church of the Brethren: religion, 87–457, 86–457, 85–463

Church of the Nazarene: religion, 87–457, 86–457, 85–463

Churches. See **EASTERN ORTHODOX CHURCHES; JEWS AND JUDAISM; PROTESTANTISM; RELIGION; ROMAN CATHOLIC CHURCH.**

Churches of Christ: religion, 87–457, 86–457, 85–463

CIA (Central Intelligence Agency): espionage, Special Report, 87–37

Ciardi, John: deaths, 87–281

Cigarettes: advertising, 87–176; consumerism, 86–274; medicine, 86–395

Cincinnati: city, 87–252, 86–254, 85–248; zoos, 86–526

Ciskei: Africa, 86–182, 85–178

Citizen Kane: motion pictures, Close-Up, 86–407

CITY, 87–251, 86–252, 85–246. See also entries for specific cities.

CIVIL RIGHTS, 87–256, 86–257, 85–251; Constitution, Special Report, 87–98

Civil War: Constitution, Special Report, 87–95

Claiborne, Harry E.: Congress, 87–269; courts, 87–273, 85–267

Clark, Joseph: Canada, 86–240

CLASSICAL MUSIC, 87–258, 86–259, 85–407; awards, 87–214, 86–214, 85–208

Claus, Prince: il., 87–407

Clean Coal Technology: coal, 87–259

Clemens, Roger: baseball, 87–223

Cleveland: city, 87–252, 86–254, 85–248

Climate. See **WEATHER.**

Clothing. See **FASHION.**

Clunn, Rickey: fishing, 87–321, 86–322

COAL, 87–259, 86–260, 85–252; energy supply, 86–307; Hungary, 87–347; mining, 87–399; nuclear energy, Special Report, 86–95; Scotland, 86–467; Wales, 87–514, 86–516, 85–518

Coalition on Government Information: library, 87–376

Coatsworth, Elizabeth: deaths, 87–281

Cobalt: mining, 86–403, 85–400

Cobra: motion pictures, 87–404

Coca-Cola Company: advertising, 86–176; food, Close-Up, 86–325

Cocaine: Bolivia, 87–229; child welfare, 87–247; crime, 87–276; drug abuse, 87–292; il., 85–270; sports, 87–476; teen-age drinking, Special Report, 87–122

Cohabitation: France, 87–328

Cohen, Myron: deaths, 87–281

Cohen, Stanley: Nobel Prizes, 87–421

Cohn, Roy M.: deaths, 87–281

COIN COLLECTING, 87–260, 86–262, 85–253

COLA (cost-of-living adjustment): labor, 86–369; social security, 87–470, 86–470

Cold, Common: chemistry, 86–245

Coles, Robert: literature, 87–380

Collecting. See **COIN COLLECTING; STAMP COLLECTING.**

Collective bargaining: education, 86–304; labor, 87–366, 86–369, 85–366

College: The Undergraduate Experience in America: education, 87–301

COLOMBIA, 87–261, 86–262, 85–254; Barco Vargas, Virgilio, 87–221; Latin America, 87–371, 86–375, 85–374

Color of Money, The: motion pictures, 87–402

Colorization process: motion pictures, 87–402

Colorado: state govt., 87–480, 86–480, 85–488

Columbia: space, 87–472; space exploration, Special Report, 86–36

Columbus, Christopher: archaeology, 87–189

Columbus, Ohio: city, 87–252, 86–254, 85–248

Coma (comet): astronomy, Close-Up, 86–205

COMECON (Council for Mutual Economic Assistance): Europe, 86–317, 85–312; Russia, 85–470

Comet: astronomy, 86–202, 85–199; Close-Up, 86–204; extinction, Special Report, 86–100; paleontology, 86–430

Comic books: newsmakers, Close-Up, 87–412

Commerce. See **ECONOMICS; INTERNATIONAL TRADE.**

Common Market. See **European Community.**

Commonwealth Games: sports, 87–476

Commonwealth. See **GREAT BRITAIN;** articles on various countries of the Commonwealth.

COMMUNICATIONS, 87–261, 86–263, 85–254; chemistry, 87–245; consumerism, 86–273, 85–265. See also **LITERATURE; MOTION PICTURES; POSTAL SERVICE, U.S.; PUBLISHING; RADIO; SPACE EXPLORATION; TELEVISION; TRANSPORTATION.**

Communications Workers of America (CWA): labor, 87–367

Communist Party: China, 86–249, Special Report, 86–111; Gorbachev, Mikhail, 86–337; Gromyko, Andrei, 86–341; Philippines, 87–436; Russia, 86–462, Close-Up, 86–463

Comoros: Africa, 87–180, 86–182, 85–178

Compact of Free Association: Pacific Islands, 87–427, 86–429

Comparable worth: civil rights, 87–257, 86–258; labor, 87–368; women, Special Report, 85–128

Competency test: education, 87–299

COMPUTER, 87–262, 86–264, 85–256; chemistry, 85–239; communications, 86–263, 85–254; library, 86–380; stocks, 87–484; vision, Special Report, 86–148

Computer, Personal: WBE, 86–555

Comrades: South Africa, 87–470

Concessionaire: national parks, Special Report, 87–110

Congenital glaucoma: vision, Special Report, 86–148

Congo (Brazzaville): Africa, 87–180, 86–182, 85–178

Congo (Kinshasa). See **Zaire.**

CONGRESS OF THE UNITED STATES, 87–264, 86–265, 85–257; armed forces, 86–197; courts, 85–267; Democratic Party, 85–283; economics, 86–300; energy supply, 86–307; farm, 86–318; lobbying, Special Report, 85–145; social security, 86–470; U.S. govt., 87–509, 86–508; water, 86–517. See also **ELECTIONS.**

Connecticut: state govt., 87–480, 86–480, 85–488

Conquest, Robert: literature, 87–379

Conrail: railroad, 87–453, 86–454, 85–460; transportation, 87–503

CONSERVATION, 87–269, 86–271, 85–263; farm, 86–318; gardening, 85–327; national parks, Special Report, 87–101; water, 86–518. See also **Endangered species; ENERGY SUPPLY; ENVIRONMENTAL POLLUTION.**

Conservative Baptist Association of America: religion, 87–457, 86–457, 85–463

Conservative Party: Great Britain, 86–338, 85–332

Consolidated Rail Corporation. See **Conrail.**

CONSTITUTION OF THE UNITED STATES, 87–270, 86–273, 85–265; gardening, 87–329; Special Report, 87–78

Construction. See **BUILDING AND CONSTRUCTION.**

Consumer Price Index (CPI): bank, 87–220. See also **CONSUMERISM.**

Consumer Product Safety Commission: safety, 86–465, 85–473

CONSUMERISM, 87–271, 86–273, 85–265; safety, 86–465

Contadora Group: Latin America, 85–373; United Nations, 87–509

Contextualism: architecture, Special Report, 86–143

Continental drift. See **Plate tectonics.**

Contraception. See **Birth control.**

Contras: armed forces, 87–195; Colombia, 86–262; Congress, 86–271; courts, 87–272, 86–275; Honduras, 86–347; Latin America, 87–372, 86–376; Nicaragua, 87–417, 86–418; President, 87–444, 85–452; United Nations, 87–509

Control rod: nuclear energy, Special Report, 86–86

Cook, Steve: bowling, 87–230

Cook Islands: Pacific Islands, 86–429, 85–434

Cooney, Jane: Canadian Library Association, 87–241

Cooper, Charlotte: women's sports, Special Report, 87–71

Copper: labor, 87–367; mining, 87–399, 86–403, 85–400

Copyright laws: Canadian Library Association, 87–241, 86–242; publishing, 87–452, 86–452, 85–458

Core (reactor): nuclear energy, Special Report, 86–86

Cornea: vision, Special Report, 86–146

Correa, Johnny Lozada: Latin America, 87–374

Correctional institution. See **PRISON.**

COSBY, BILL, 87–272; ils., 86–380, 85–496; television, 86–492

"Cosby Show, The": television, 87–493

Cosmic string: astronomy, 87–206

Cost-of-living adjustment. See **COLA.**

Costa Rica: Arias Sánchez, Oscar, 87–193; Latin America, 87–371, 86–375, 85–374

Costache, Tamara: swimming, 87–488

Costello, Patty: bowling, 87–230, 86–230

Council for Mutual Economic Assistance. See **COMECON.**

Counterespionage: espionage, Special Report, 87–37

Country music. See **AWARDS AND PRIZES; POPULAR MUSIC.**

Court tennis: sports, 87–476, 86–476

COURTS, 87–272, 86–275, 85–267; civil rights, 87–257; communications, 87–262; drugs, 86–296; handicapped, 86–342; petroleum, 86–433; television, 85–497. See also **CONGRESS OF THE UNITED STATES; STATE GOVERNMENT; SUPREME COURT OF THE UNITED STATES; UNITED STATES, GOVERNMENT OF THE.**

Cousins, Frank: deaths, 87–281

Crack: drug abuse, 87–292; teen-age drinking, Special Report, 87–122

Cram, Steve: track, 86–499

Craxi, Bettino: Italy, 87–359, 86–362, 85–369

Credit: consumerism, 87–271, 86–274; farm, 87–317

Cretaceous Period: extinction, Special Report, 86–101

CRIME, 87–274, 86–276, 85–269; chemistry, 86–246; child welfare, Close-Up, 85–242; city, 87–256, 86–253, 85–247; Detroit, 87–289; mental illness, 86–397; Supreme Court, 86–486. See also **COURTS;** and the articles on various countries and cities.
Crimes of the Heart: motion pictures, 87–402
Critical thinking skills: psychology, 86–451
Criticism. See LITERATURE.
"Crocodile" Dundee: motion pictures, 87–402
Crop plant. See FARM AND FARMING.
Croquet: sports, 87–477
Cross-country: sports, 87–477, 86–476, 85–484
Crossover: television, Close-Up, 86–493
Crothers, Scatman: deaths, 87–281
Crowley, Jim: deaths, 87–281
Cruise, Tom: motion pictures, 87–402
Cruise missile: Canada, 85–233; Europe, 86–317; Netherlands, 85–413
Crystal: chemistry, 87–245; physics, 86–438
CSX Corporation: ship, 87–467
CUBA, 87–276, 86–278, 85–271; immigration, 87–349, 86–352; Latin America, 87–371, 86–375, 85–374; Puerto Rico, 87–452
Cuba and His Teddy Bear: theater, 87–498
Cultural Revolution: China, 87–248, 86–249; Special Report, 86–112
Cunningham, Merce: dancing, 86–280
Cuomo, Mario: Roman Catholic, 85–465; WBE, 86–578
Curling: sports, 87–477, 86–476, 85–484
Curran, Charles E.: Roman Catholic Church, 87–459
Currency. See **BANK; INTERNATIONAL TRADE; Money.**
Custer, George Armstrong: archaeology, Close-Up, 86–191
Cycling: sports, 87–476, 86–476, 85–484; il., 87–477
Cyclosporine: WBE, 87–579
Cyprus: Greece, 86–341, 85–337; Middle East, 87–396, 86–400, 85–398
CZECHOSLOVAKIA, 87–277, 86–279, 85–272; Europe, 87–314, 86–315, 85–311

D

Dalkon Shield: drugs, 86–296
Dallas: building, 87–234; city, 87–252, 86–254, 85–248
"Dallas": television, 87–494
Dalton, Timothy: Wales, 87–515
Dam: building, 87–235, 85–226
DANCING, 87–277, 86–279, 85–272; popular music, 86–441, 85–410
Daniloff, Nicholas S.: Russia, 87–462
Danzig Connection: horse racing, 87–345
Darts: sports, 87–477, 86–475, 85–484
Data processing. See COMPUTER.
D'Aubuisson, Roberto: El Salvador, 86–307, 85–302
Davies, Robertson: Canadian literature, 86–242
Da Vinci, Leonardo: art restoration, Special Report, 87–132
Davis, Patti: il., 85–462; Reagan, Ronald W., 87–455
Davis Cup. See TENNIS.
Daylight-saving time: energy supply, 87–307
Dean, Laura: dancing, 87–278
Death rates. See POPULATION.
DEATHS, 87–280, 86–282, 85–276
Deaver, Michael K.: Cabinet, U.S., 87–236
De Bettignies, Louise: espionage, Special Report, 87–40
Decker, Mary: track, 86–500, 85–503
Decontrol. See Deregulation.
Defense: Canada, 86–240. See also **ARMED FORCES.**
Deficit, Federal: city, 86–252; Congress, 87–268, 86–265, 85–257; economics, 87–297, 86–300, 85–291; international trade, 86–357; U.S. govt., 86–508, 85–510
Defoe, Daniel: espionage, Special Report, 87–40
Delegated powers: Constitution, Special Report, 87–94
De la Madrid Hurtado, Miguel: Mexico, 87–393, 85–393; Special Report, 87–154

Delaware: state govt., 87–480, 86–480, 85–488
Delta rocket: space, 87–472
De Niro, Robert: WBE, 86–578
Democracy: espionage, Special Report, 87–46
Democratic National Committee (DNC): Democratic Party, 86–288
DEMOCRATIC PARTY, 87–286, 86–288, 85–282. See also **CONGRESS; ELECTIONS.**
Democratic Progressive Party: Taiwan, 87–490
Demography. See **CENSUS; POPULATION.**
Dene Indians: Northwest Territories, 86–422
Deng Xiaoping: China, 86–249, 85–244; Special Report, 86–112
Denktas, Rauf R.: Greece, 86–341, 85–337
DENMARK, 87–287, 86–289, 85–283; Europe, 87–314, 86–315, 85–311
DENTISTRY, 87–288, 86–290, 85–284; advertising, 87–176
Denver: city, 87–252, 86–254, 85–248
Depression: psychology, 87–450
Deregulation: petroleum, 86–434; railroad, 85–460; transportation, 86–502; truck, 86–503, 85–506
DETROIT, 87–289, 86–291, 85–285; city, 87–252, 86–254, 85–248; newspaper, 87–417
Devaluation. See **INTERNATIONAL TRADE; Money; Recession.** See also individual countries.
Developing countries: disasters, 85–286; international trade, 87–354, 86–356, 85–352. See also **POPULATION.**
DeVries, William C.: medicine, 86–393, 85–390
Dharsono, Hartono R.: Indonesia, 87–352
Diabetes: medicine, 87–390, 85–390; vision, Special Report, 86–149
Diablo Canyon nuclear power plant: energy supply, 87–307, 86–309
Dial, Joe: track, 87–501
Diana, Princess of Wales: Great Britain, 86–340; il., 85–336
Diatreme: geology, 87–330
Díaz, Porfirio: Mexico, Special Report, 87–150
"Dick Tracy": deaths, Close-Up, 86–285
Dictatorship: espionage, Special Report, 87–46
Dictionary: World Book Dictionary supplement, 87–581, 86–581, 85–581
Didrikson, Babe: women's sports, Special Report, 87–72
Digital electronics: electronics, 87–304
Dine, Jim: WBE, 86–578
Dinosaur: extinction, Special Report, 86–100; paleontology, 87–430, 86–430; Nova Scotia, 87–422
Dioxin: environmental pollution, 86–312; veterans, 85–515
Disarmament. See **Arms-control negotiations.**
DISASTERS, 87–290, 86–292, 85–286
Discovery (spacecraft): space, 86–472; Special Report, 86–46
Discrimination: handicapped, 86–342, 85–338; state govt., 85–487; Supreme Court, 87–485, 85–491. See also **CIVIL RIGHTS; Desegregation.**
Disease. See **DRUGS; HEALTH AND DISEASE; MEDICINE; MENTAL ILLNESS; PUBLIC HEALTH.**
Disinformation: espionage, Special Report, 87–45
District of Columbia. See WASHINGTON, D.C.
Diving. See **SPORTS; SWIMMING.**
Divorce: Ireland, 87–357
Djibouti: Africa, 87–180, 86–182, 85–178
DNA (deoxyribonucleic acid): anthropology, 87–188; gene-splicing, Special Report, 85–62
Doe, Samuel K.: Africa, 85–182; Liberia, 87–375, 86–379
Doerr, Bobby: baseball, 87–223
DOG, 87–292, 86–294, 85–288
Dole, Robert J.: Congress, 86–265; Republican Party, 87–458
Doll. See TOYS AND GAMES.
Dollar: automobile, 87–209; Congress, 86–271; economics, 87–297, 86–299; Europe, 86–314
Dominica: Latin America, 87–371, 86–375, 85–374

Dominican Republic: Balaguer, Joaquín, 87–219; Latin America, 87–371, 86–375, 85–374; West Indies, 87–520, 85–523
Donovan, Raymond James: Cabinet, 85–227; crime, 87–274; labor, 86–371, 85–309
Doré, Jean: Montreal, 87–400
Dos Santos, José Eduardo: Angola, 87–186, 86–187
Dotson, Gary E.: Chicago, 86–247
Double agent: espionage, Special Report, 87–37
Doubleday & Company: publishing, 87–452
Dow Jones Industrial Average: stocks, 87–483, 86–482, 85–490
Drag racing: automobile racing, 87–211
Drama: awards, 87–215, 86–214, 85–208. See also **THEATER.**
Drapeau, Jean: il., 86–404; Montreal, 87–400, 85–401
Drechsler, Heike: track, 87–501
Drinking, Teen-age: Special Report, 87–116
Drought: Africa, 86–178, 85–177; farm, 87–317; New York City, 86–412. See also **WATER; WEATHER.**
DRUG ABUSE, 87–292; baseball, 86–222; Bolivia, 87–229; child welfare, 87–247; Colombia, 87–261, 85–254; Congress, 87–268; crime, 87–276; drugs, Close-Up, 86–295; education, 87–301; health, 86–343; Malaysia, 87–386; Mexico, 87–394; sports, 87–476, 86–475; teen-age drinking, Special Report, 87–116; Washington, D.C., 86–517; youth organizations, 87–521
Drug Enforcement Administration (DEA): drugs, Close-Up, 86–295
Drug testing: civil rights, 87–257; drug abuse, 87–292; football, 87–326; labor, 87–369
DRUGS, 87–293, 86–294, 85–289; chemistry, 87–245, 85–239; Congress, 87–268; consumerism, 86–273; gene-splicing, Special Report, 85–69; mental illness, 87–393; vision, Special Report, 86–148
Drusen: vision, Special Report, 86–154
DUARTE, JOSÉ NAPOLEÓN, 85–290; El Salvador, 87–305, 86–307, 85–302
Duchenne dystrophy: medicine, 87–390
Duffy, Patrick: television, 87–494
Dupras, Claude: Montreal, 87–400
Dutch elm disease: gardening, 87–329
Duvalier, Jean-Claude: Haiti, 87–339; West Indies, 87–520, 86–521
DUVALL, ROBERT, 85–290; il., 85–209
Dylan, Bob: popular music, 86–441
Dynamic random access memory (DRAM): electronics, 87–304

E

Eanes, António: Portugal, 86–443
Earnhardt, Dale: automobile racing, 87–211
Earthquakes: building, 86–234; El Salvador, 87–305; geology, 86–333; Mexico, 86–397. See also **DISASTERS.**
Eastern Airlines: aviation, 87–212; labor, 86–370
EASTERN ORTHODOX CHURCHES, 87–294, 86–296, 85–290
Eastland, James O.: deaths, 87–281
Eastwood, Clint: il., 87–255; newsmakers, 87–410
Ecology: tallgrass prairie, Special Report, 85–47. See also **Endangered species; ENVIRONMENTAL POLLUTION.**
Economic Justice for All: Roman Catholic Church, 87–461
ECONOMICS, 87–295, 86–297, 85–291. See also **NOBEL PRIZES.**
ECONOMY, 87–295, 86–297, 85–291. See also **BANK; Budget, Federal; Inflation; INTERNATIONAL TRADE; LABOR; MANUFACTURING; Money; Prices; Recession;** and specific country, province, and city articles.
Ecosystem habitat: zoos, 87–525
Ecstasy: drugs, Close-Up, 86–295
Ecuador: conservation, 86–272; Febres-Cordero, León, 85–317; Latin America, 87–371, 86–375, 85–374
Ederle, Gertrude C.: women's sports, Special Report, 87–71

EDUCATION, 87–299, 86–301, 85–295; Bennett, William John, 86–226; city, 86–256; college sports, Special Report, 85–88; health, 86–343; Houston, 87–347, 86–349; psychology, 86–450; state gov't., 87–482, 86–479, 85–486. See also **NATIONAL PTA; Universities and colleges.**
Eelam: Sri Lanka, 87–478
EGYPT, 87–301, 86–304, 85–298; Israel, 87–358; Libya, 86–381; Middle East, 87–396, 86–400, 85–398
Egypt, Ancient: WBE, 86–557
Eisenhower: literature, 87–378
Eisteddfod: Wales, 87–515, 86–516, 85–518
ELECTIONS, 87–302, 86–304, 85–298; advertising, 85–174; civil rights, 87–257. See also **DEMOCRATIC PARTY; REPUBLICAN PARTY;** and articles on specific countries, provinces, and cities.
Electric power: coal, 86–260; nuclear energy, Special Report, 86–84; WBE, 86–568. See also **ENERGY SUPPLY.**
Electron-neutrino: physics, 87–437
Electronic novel: publishing, 86–452
ELECTRONICS, 87–304, 86–306, 85–301; Japan, 86–363. See also **MANUFACTURING.**
Electroshock: mental illness, 86–396
Elena, Hurricane: weather, 86–520
Elizabeth II: Great Britain, 87–338; ils., 87–203, 249
Ellis Island: coins, 86–262; Statue of Liberty, Special Report, 86–58
Ellison, Pervis: basketball, 87–225
Elm: gardening, 87–329; newsmakers, 87–413
El Paso: city, 87–252, 86–254, 85–248
EL SALVADOR, 87–305, 86–307, 85–302; armed forces, 85–193; civil rights, 87–256, 86–258; Duarte, José Napoleón, 85–290; Latin America, 87–371, 86–375, 85–374
Emergency core cooling system (ECCS): nuclear energy, Special Report, 86–89
Emigration. See **IMMIGRATION.**
Emmy Awards: awards, 87–214, 86–214, 85–208
Emotional disorders. See **MENTAL ILLNESS.**
Employment. See **ECONOMICS; LABOR; SOCIAL SECURITY; Unemployment; WELFARE.**
Encyclopedia: Canadian literature, 86–242; *World Book Encyclopedia* supplement, 87–528, 86–530, 85–530
Endangered species: botany, 86–228; conservation, 86–271; zoos, 85–528
Endorphins: women's sports, Special Report, 87–70
Energy, Department of (DOE): petroleum, 87–431, 86–433, 85–441. See also **ENERGY SUPPLY.**
ENERGY SUPPLY, 87–307, 86–307, 85–303; Herrington, John, 86–345; nuclear energy, Special Report, 86–82; Romania, 86–461. See also **COAL; CONSERVATION; PETROLEUM AND GAS.**
Engineering. See **BUILDING AND CONSTRUCTION.**
Engineering work station: computer, 87–263
ENGLAND, 87–309, 86–309, 85–305. See also **GREAT BRITAIN.**
English Channel: building, 87–235; Great Britain, 87–338
Enrile, Juan Ponce: Philippines, 87–435
Entertainment. See **CLASSICAL MUSIC; MOTION PICTURES; POPULAR MUSIC; RADIO; RECORDINGS; SPORTS; TELEVISION; THEATER.**
ENVIRONMENTAL POLLUTION, 87–310, 86–310, 85–305; coal, 86–260; Congress, 87–268; water, 87–517, 86–518, 85–520. See also **CONSERVATION.**
Eón, Chevalier d': espionage, Special Report, 87–40
EPA (Environmental Protection Agency): chemical industry, 85–238; environmental pollution, 87–310, 86–310, 85–305
Episcopal Church, The: Protestantism, 87–448, 86–450; religion, 87–457, 86–457, 85–463
Epoxy: zoo design, Special Report, 87–57
Equatorial Guinea: Africa, 87–180, 86–182, 85–178

Equestrian events: sports, 87–477, 86–476, 85–484. See also **OLYMPIC GAMES.**
Erdrich, Louise: literature, 87–378
Eritrea: Africa, 85–177; Ethiopia, 86–313
Ershad, Hussain Muhammad: Bangladesh, 87–219, 86–218, 85–212
Escape from the Glue Factory: Canadian literature, 87–242
Eskimos: il., 85–459; Northwest Territories, 87–421, 86–422
Espionage: armed forces, 87–196, 86–196; courts, 87–274; crime, 86–277; Germany, West, 86–335; Ghana, 86–336; Great Britain, 86–339; Norway, 86–423; Special Report, 87–34
ETHIOPIA, 87–312, 86–312, 85–307; Africa, 87–180, 86–182, 85–178; Jews and Judaism, 86–365; WBE, 86–573
Ethiopian Jews: Ethiopia, 86–313; il., 86–361; Jews and Judaism, 86–365
Ethridge, Kamie: basketball, 87–226
Eurocommunism: Finland, 86–321, 85–317
EUROPE, 87–312, 86–313, 85–308; civil rights, 86–257. See also by name of country.
European Community: international trade, 87–355; Portugal, 85–450; Spain, 86–474, 85–482. See also **EUROPE.**
European Space Agency: space exploration, Special Report, 86–39
Evangelical Lutheran Church in America: Protestantism, 87–448
Evangelical Orthodox Church: Eastern Orthodox Churches, 87–294
Evangelicals: Protestantism, 87–450, 85–455; religion, 87–456
Everglades National Park: il., 87–114
Everly Brothers: il., 87–440
Evert Lloyd, Chris: tennis, 86–495, 85–499
Evolution: anthropology, 87–186, 86–189, 85–187; religion, 87–457
EWING, PATRICK, 86–317; basketball, 87–224; ils., 86–224, 85–216
Executive privilege: Constitution, Special Report, 87–98
Exercise: women's sports, Special Report, 87–70
Exhibitions. See **ART.**
Exploration: newsmakers, 87–413
Explosions: disasters, 87–290, 86–293, 85–287; energy supply, Close-Up, 87–306
Expo 86: British Columbia, 87–233; il., 87–237
Exports: farm, 87–318. See also **ECONOMICS; INTERNATIONAL TRADE.**
Extinctions: botany, 87–229, 86–228; conservation, 87–270, 86–271; gardening, 86–333; paleontology, 87–430, 86–430; Special Report, 86–98; zoology, 87–524, 86–525
Exxon Corporation: China, 85–245; petroleum, 86–433
Eye: vision, Special Report, 86–144

F

FAA (Federal Aviation Administration. See **AVIATION.**
Fabius, Laurent: France, 86–331, 85–325; il., 86–523
Fahd ibn Abd al-Aziz Al Saud: il., 85–474; Saudi Arabia, 86–466
Falashas: Ethiopia, 86–313; il., 86–361; Jews and Judaism, 86–365
Falkland Islands: Argentina, 87–192
Fallout: energy supply, Close-Up, 87–306; environmental pollution, 87–310
Family: census, 86–245; magazine, 87–385
Famine: Africa, 86–178, 85–177; Ethiopia, 86–312, 85–307; Mozambique, 85–407; radio, 86–454
Famine relief: newsmakers, Close-Up, 87–414
Fare, Transportation: See **AVIATION; TRANSIT.**
Farm Aid: il., 86–318; newsmakers, Close-Up, 87–414; popular music, 86–440
FARM AND FARMING, 87–316, 86–317, 85–313; biochemistry, 87–227; census, 87–244; China, Special Report, 86–116; Congress, 86–267; economics, 86–299; Europe, 86–316, 85–310; food, 87–322, food, 87–322; gene-splicing, Special Report, 85–61

Farm Credit System: bank, 86–219; farm, 87–318, 86–319
Farr, Tommy: deaths, 87–281
FASHION, 87–319, 86–320, 85–316
Fats: cholesterol, Special Report, 85–137; nutrition, 87–423
FBI (Federal Bureau of Investigation): courts, 85–269; espionage, Special Report, 87–39
FCC (Federal Communications Commission): communications, 87–262, 86–263, 85–254
FDA (Food and Drug Administration): consumerism, 86–275, 85–265; drugs, 87–293, 86–294, 85–289
FDIC (Federal Deposit Insurance Corporation). See **BANK.**
FEBRES-CORDERO, LEÓN, 85–317
Federal Reserve System (Fed). See **BANK.**
Federal Trade Commission: consumerism, 85–274, 85–265
Feline leukemia virus: cat, 86–244
Fencing: sports, 87–476, 86–475, 85–483
Ferdinand: horse racing, 87–344
FERGUSON, SARAH, 87–320; Andrew, Prince, 87–186; Great Britain, Close-Up, 87–336
Ferraro, Geraldine A.: elections, 85–299; New York City, 87–408; Roman Catholic Church, 85–465
Ferret: conservation, 87–270, 86–271
Fertility: biochemistry, 87–227; census, 87–244
Fetal monitoring: medicine, 87–392
Fiberoptics: chemistry, 87–245
Fiction. See **CANADIAN LITERATURE; LITERATURE; LITERATURE FOR CHILDREN.**
Field hockey: sports, 87–477, 86–476
Figure skating. See **ICE SKATING.**
Fiji: Pacific Islands, 87–427, 86–429, 85–434
Film. See **PHOTOGRAPHY.**
Films. See **MOTION PICTURES.**
FINLAND, 87–320, 86–321, 85–317; Europe, 87–314, 86–315, 85–311
Fires: disasters, 87–290, 86–293, 85–287; Los Angeles, 87–383
First Amendment: Supreme Court, Close-Up, 86–484
First Lessons: A Report on Elementary Education in America: education, 87–300
Fischl, Eric: art, 87–197
Fish and Wildlife Service, U. S. See **CONSERVATION.**
Fisher, Mel: ocean, 86–426
FISHING, 87–321, 86–322, 85–319; Newfoundland, 86–413
FISHING INDUSTRY, 87–322, 86–323, 85–318; Newfoundland, 87–410; Pacific Islands, 87–426, 86–429
Fission: nuclear energy, Special Report, 86–85
FitzGerald, Frances: literature, 87–380
FitzGerald, Garret: Ireland, 87–357, 85–357
Flatterer: horse racing, 87–344
Fletcher, Pam: skiing, 87–468
Floating-point operations: computer, 87–263
Floods: farm, 87–317; water, 85–520. See also **DISASTERS.**
Florida: education, 86–303; forest, 86–330; geology, 86–334; state govt., 87–480, 86–480, 85–488
Flower. See **GARDENING.**
Fluoride: dentistry, 85–284
Flutie, Doug: football, 87–324, 85–323
Follicle-stimulating hormone: biochemistry, 87–227
Fonseca, Rubem: literature, 87–377
FOOD, 87–322, 86–323, 85–319; Asia, 86–198; consumerism, 87–271, 85–266; Europe, 87–315; psychology, 86–450; public health, 86–451. See also **FARM AND FARMING.**
Food stamps: city, 87–254; welfare, 87–519
FOOTBALL, 87–324, 86–326, 85–320; college sports, Special Report, 85–96; television, 85–498. See also **SOCCER.**
Force Field: dancing, 87–278
FORD, GERALD RUDOLPH, 87–327, 86–329, 85–324; publishing, 85–277
Ford Motor Company: automobile, 87–210, 86–209
Foreign Investment Review Agency (FIRA): Canada, 86–236
Forest: zoology, 87–524

FOREST AND BRUSH FIRES, 86–330; Africa, Special Report, 85–33; conservation, 86–272
Forest Service, United States: conservation, 87–269
Formula One car: automobile racing, 87–211, 86–212, 85–205
For-profit hospital: hospital, 87–345
Fort Worth: city, 87–252, 86–254, 85–248
Forward Area Air Defense program: armed forces, 87–195
Fosse, Bob: theater, 87–497
Fossil: anthropology, 86–188, 85–185; Nova Scotia, 87–422. See also **PALEONTOLOGY.**
Foster, Peter: Canadian literature, 87–243
Foster care: child welfare, 87–247
Fountain Place: building, 86–234
4-H Clubs. See **YOUTH ORGANIZATIONS.**
Fox Broadcasting Company: television, 87–492
FRANCE, 87–328, 86–331, 85–325; art, 87–197; Chirac, Jacques, 87–251; dancing, 87–277; Europe, 87–314, 86–315, 85–311; Middle East, 87–395; New Caledonia, 86–411; New Zealand, 87–410; Pacific Islands, 87–428, 86–428, 85–434
Free trade: Canada, 87–240, 86–239; international trade, 86–358
Free Will Baptists: religion, 87–457, 86–457, 85–463
Freight. See **AVIATION; RAILROAD; SHIP AND SHIPPING; TRANSPORTATION; TRUCK AND TRUCKING.**
Fresco: art restoration, Special Report, 87–133
Frisbee: sports, 87–477, 86–476, 85–484
Fuel. See **CONSERVATION; ENERGY SUPPLY; PETROLEUM AND GAS.**
Fuel rod: nuclear energy, Special Report, 86–86
Functional illiteracy: library, 87–376
Fundamentalist Christians: Jews and Judaism, 85–362; Protestantism, 86–450; religion, 87–456
Fur: fashion, 87–320
Fusion energy: energy supply, 87–309; physics, 85–446
Future Farmers of America (FFA). See **YOUTH ORGANIZATIONS.**

G

Gabon: Africa, 87–180, 86–182, 85–178
Gaddis, William: literature, 86–381
Galapagos Islands: conservation, 86–272
Gallant, Mavis: Canadian literature, 87–243
Galtieri, Leopoldo F.: Argentina, 87–192, 85–191
Gambia: Africa, 87–180, 86–182, 85–178
GAMES AND TOYS, 87–499, 86–332, 85–326. See also **BRIDGE; CHESS; SPORTS.**
Gandhi, Indira Priyadarshini: Asia, Close-Up, 85–198; India, 85–348
GANDHI, RAJIV, 85–327; Asia, 85–194; India, 87–350, 86–352, 85–349; Sri Lanka, 86–477
Gannett Company: newspaper, 87–417, 86–417
Garbage Pail Kids: toys and games, 87–500
GARCÍA PÉREZ, ALAN, 86–333; Latin America, 86–374; Peru, 87–430, 86–432
Garden of Eden, The: literature, 87–380
GARDENING, 87–329, 86–333, 85–327; Monticello, Special Report, 85–111
Gas: environmental pollution, 87–310
Gas and gasoline. See **ENERGY SUPPLY; PETROLEUM AND GAS.**
Geagea, Samir: Lebanon, 87–374, 86–378
Geldof, Bob: newsmakers, 87–414; popular music, 86–440
Gemayel, Amin: il., 86–489; Lebanon, 86–378, 85–375; Middle East, 85–395
Gene splicing: Special Report, 85–61
General Agreement on Tariffs and Trade: Latin America, 87–373
General Association of Regular Baptist Churches: religion, 87–457, 86–457, 85–463
General Motors Corporation: automobile, 87–210, 86–209, 85–204; consumerism, 86–274; Ontario, 87–426

Genet, Jean: deaths, 87–281
Genetic engineering: biochemistry, 87–227, 86–227; drugs, 87–293, 86–294; farm, 87–319; gene-splicing, Special Report, 85–62; medicine, 87–390
Genetics: biochemistry, 87–226; nutrition, 87–422
GEOLOGY, 87–330, 86–333, 85–328
George-Brown, Lord: deaths, 86–283
Georgia: geology, 86–334; state govt., 87–480, 86–480, 85–488
GERMANY, EAST, 87–331, 86–334, 85–329; Europe, 87–314, 86–315, 85–311. See also **GERMANY, WEST.**
GERMANY, WEST, 87–332, 86–335, 85–330; dancing, 86–282; Europe, 87–314, 86–315, 85–311. See also **GERMANY, EAST.**
Gerrymandering: Supreme Court, 87–485
GETTY, DONALD ROSS, 86–336; Alberta, 87–184, 86–185
Geyser: ocean, 87–424
GHANA, 87–333, 86–336, 85–331; Africa, 87–180, 86–182, 85–178
GHIZ, JOSEPH A., 87–333; Prince Edward Island, 87–447
Ghosh, Amitav: literature, 87–378
Giants, New York: football, 87–326
Gibbs, Lawrence B.: taxation, 87–491
Gibraltar: Spain, 86–474
Giotto (spacecraft): astronomy, 87–205; Close-Up, 86–205; space, 87–473
Girardelli, Marc: skiing, 87–468, 86–469
Girl Scouts of the United States of America (GSUSA). See **YOUTH ORGANIZATIONS.**
Girls Clubs of America (GCA). See **YOUTH ORGANIZATIONS.**
Glasgow: Scotland, 87–467
Glaucoma: vision, Special Report, 86–144
Glenholmes, Evelyn: Ireland, 87–357
Global Islamic Movement: Iran, 87–355
Glubb, Sir John Bagot: deaths, 87–282
Glue: dentistry, 87–288
GNP (gross national product). See **BANK; ECONOMICS.**
Goetz, Bernhard H.: crime, 86–277; New York City, 86–412
Gold: Brazil, 85–223; Pacific Islands, 87–427. See also **COIN COLLECTING.**
Goldberg, Whoopi: il., 87–215
Golden Gate, The: poetry, 87–438
"Golden Girls, The": television, 86–492
Golden monkey: zoos, 87–526
Golden Temple: il., 87–351; India, 85–348; religion, 85–462
Goldstein, Joseph L.: Nobel Prizes, 86–421
GOLF, 87–333, 86–336, 85–331; Nicklaus, Jack, 87–419
González Márquez, Felipe: il., 86–474; Spain, 87–475
Goodall, Jane: literature, 87–380
Goode, W. Wilson: Philadelphia, 86–434
Gooden, Dwight: baseball, 86–221, 85–215
Goodman, Benny: popular music, Close-Up, 87–441
Goodwill Games: sports, 87–476
GORBACHEV, MIKHAIL SERGEEVICH, 86–337; Asia, 86–203; ils., 87–331, 86–316; President, 86–444; Russia, 87–461, Close-Up, 86–463
Gordievsky, Oleg A.: Europe, 86–313; Great Britain, 86–339
Gordon, Lynne: Canadian literature, 87–242
Gould, Chester: deaths, Close-Up, 86–285
Government. See **CITY; STATE GOVERNMENT; UNITED STATES, GOVERNMENT OF THE;** entries on specific countries.
Governor General's Literary Awards. See **CANADIAN LITERATURE.**
Goya, Francisco: art, 87–197
Grading: coin collecting, 87–261
Gradualism: extinction, Special Report, 86–101
Graham, Martha: dancing, 87–279
Gramm-Rudman Bill: Congress, 87–268, 86–266; Constitution, 87–270; economics, 86–301; Supreme Court, 87–485; U. S. govt., 87–509
Grammy Awards, 87–214, 86–214, 85–208
Grand Canyon: national parks, Special Report, 87–101

Grand Prix. See **AUTOMOBILE RACING.**
Grand Slam: golf, 85–331; tennis, 85–498
Grandy, Fred: il., 87–303
Grant, Cary: deaths, 87–282
Granville, Christine: espionage, Special Report, 87–40
Graves, Michael: architecture, Special Report, 86–137
Gravitational lens: astronomy, 87–206
GREAT BRITAIN, 87–335, 86–338, 85–332; Andrew, Prince, 87–186; coal, 86–261; dancing, 87–278; Europe, 87–314, 86–315, 85–311; Ferguson, Sarah, 87–320; Portugal, 87–443; Russia, 86–462; soccer, 87–469, 85–478; Spain, 86–474; sports, 87–476. See also **ENGLAND; NORTHERN IRELAND; SCOTLAND; WALES.**
Great Depression: Constitution, Special Report, 87–96
Great Lakes: environmental pollution, 86–311
Great Plains coal gasification plant: energy supply, 87–307
Great Salt Lake: water, 87–517
GREECE, 87–338, 86–341, 85–336; Albania, 87–183, 86–185, 85–182; Eastern Orthodox, 85–291; Europe, 87–314, 86–315, 85–311
Greek Orthodox Archdiocese of North and South America: religion, 87–457, 86–457, 85–463
Green Party: Germany, West, 87–332
Greenpeace: France, 86–331; il., 85–183; New Zealand, 86–412
Grenada: Latin America, 87–371, 86–375, 85–374; West Indies, 87–520, 86–521, 85–523
Gretzky, Wayne: hockey, 87–342, 86–345, 85–342
Grocery stores. See **FOOD.**
GROMYKO, ANDREI A., 86–341; Russia, 86–462
Gross, Michael: swimming, 87–488, 86–488
Grosskurth, Phyllis: Canadian literature, 87–242
Ground-water contamination: water, 87–517, 85–520
Grove City College v. Bell: women's sports, Special Report, 87–77
GRU: espionage, Special Report, 87–43
Guadeloupe: West Indies, 86–522, 85–523
Guam: Pacific Islands, 87–428
GUATEMALA, 86–341; Cerezo, Vinicio, 87–244; Latin America, 87–371, 86–375, 85–374; Mexico, 85–393
Guggenheim Museum: visual arts, 86–513
Guilford Transportation Industries: railroad, 87–454
GUINEA, 85–337; Africa, 87–180, 86–182, 85–178; Conté, Lansana, 85–267
Guinea-Bissau: Africa, 87–180, 86–182, 85–178
Gulf Canada Corporation: Northwest Territories, 87–421
Guri Dam: building, 87–235
Guyana: Latin America, 87–371, 86–375, 85–374
Gwilym, Gwynn ap: Wales, 87–515
Gymnastics: il., 87–71; sports, 87–476, 85–483

H

Habré, Hissein: Chad, 86–245
Hagenbeck, Karl: zoo design, Special Report, 87–51
Hagler, Marvin: boxing, 87–230, 86–231
Haida Indians: British Columbia, 87–233, 86–232
Haile-Mariam, Mengistu: Ethiopia, 87–312
Hairy cell leukemia: medicine, 87–390
HAITI, 87–339; Latin America, 87–371, 86–375, 85–374; West Indies, 87–520, 86–521, 85–523
Halberstam, David: literature, 87–380
Hale, Nathan: espionage, Special Report, 87–40
Halley's Comet: astronomy, 87–205; Close-Up, 86–204; newsmakers, 87–410; space, 87–473, 86–474

Hallucinogens: teen-age drinking, Special Report, 87–123
Hamilton, Alexander: Constitution, Special Report, 87–93
Hanauer, Chip: boating, 87–228, 86–227
Handball: sports, 87–477, 86–476, 85–484
HANDICAPPED, 87–340, 86–342, 85–338
Handmaid's Tale, The: Canadian literature, 86–242
Hands Across America: newsmakers, Close-Up, 87–414
Hang gliding: sports, 87–477, 86–476, 85–484
Hannah and Her Sisters: motion pictures, 87–404
Hansen, Rick: il., 87–340
Haram Al-Sharif complex: United Nations, 87–508
Harlem Globetrotters: newsmakers, 86–414
Harness racing. See HORSE RACING.
Harriman, W. Averell: deaths, 87–282
Hasani, Sinan: Yugoslavia, 87–523
Hasenfus, Eugene: Nicaragua, 87–418; President, 87–444
Hassan II: Morocco, 87–401, 86–405, 85–402
Hastings, Alcee L.: courts, 87–273
Hatfield, Richard B.: New Brunswick, 87–407, 86–411, 85–414
Hauptman, Herbert A.: Nobel Prizes, 86–421
Hawaii: state govt., 87–480, 86–480, 85–488
Hawke, Robert James Lee: Australia, 87–206, 86–206, 85–201
Hayden, Sterling: deaths, 87–282
Hazardous wastes: nuclear energy, Special Report, 86–91. See also ENVIRONMENTAL POLLUTION.
"Head of the Class": il., 87–492
HEALTH AND DISEASE, 87–341, 86–343, 85–339; city, 85–246; state govt., 86–479. See also DENTISTRY; DRUGS; HOSPITAL; MEDICINE; MENTAL ILLNESS; PUBLIC HEALTH.
Health and Human Services, Department of: Bowen, Otis R., 86–229; medicine, 87–391
Heart disease: biochemistry, 86–226; cholesterol, Special Report, 85–133; health, 86–344; nutrition, 87–422, 86–423, 85–424
Heart transplant: medicine, 87–391, 86–394, 85–390; nutrition, 86–423
Heartburn: motion pictures, 87–404
Heckler, Margaret Mary: Cabinet, 86–235; ils., 86–343, 452
Heisman Trophy. See FOOTBALL.
Helpmann, Sir Robert: deaths, 87–282
Hemingway, Ernest: literature, 87–378, 86–382
Henie, Sonja: women's sports, Special Report, 87–71
Hepatitis B: drugs, 87–293, 85–289
Herbal medicine: dentistry, 86–291
Herbicide: environmental pollution, 87–311; health, 87–341; Nova Scotia, 85–424
Heredity. See GENETICS.
HERNÁNDEZ COLÓN, RAFAEL, 86–344; Puerto Rico, 86–453, 85–458
Heroin, Synthetic: drugs, Close-Up, 86–295
HERRINGTON, JOHN STEWART, 86–345
Herschbach, Dudley R.: Nobel Prizes, 87–420
Hersey, John: literature, 86–381
Heseltine, Michael: Great Britain, 87–335
Hieroglyphs: archaeology, 87–190
High blood pressure. See Hypertension.
High-technology industry: manufacturing, 86–392
High-temperature gas reactor (HTGR): nuclear energy, Special Report, 86–94
Highway: transportation, 87–503
Hijacking: aviation, 86–213, 85–207; Italy, 86–362; Middle East, 86–399; President, 86–447
Hindawi, Nezar: Great Britain, 87–337
Hindus: Sri Lanka, 87–478
Hippies: England, 87–309
Hirohito: Japan, 87–361
Hispanic Americans: civil rights, 86–258; immigration, 87–349; Latin America, 86–378; Los Angeles, 87–383
History. See CANADIAN LITERATURE; LITERATURE.
Hobbies. See COIN COLLECTING; GAMES; STAMP COLLECTING.

Hobeika, Elie: Lebanon, 87–374, 86–378
Hobson, Laura Z.: deaths, 87–282
HOCKEY, 87–342, 86–345, 85–341
HODEL, DONALD PAUL, 86–346; petroleum, 86–433
Hogan, Paul: motion pictures, 87–402
Holland. See NETHERLANDS.
Holman, Marshall: bowling, 86–229
Holmes, Larry: boxing, 86–230, 85–222
Holy War Islamic group: Lebanon, 85–377; Middle East, 85–399
Home appliance: consumerism, 87–272
Home Shopping Network (HSN): television, 87–493
Homeless persons: city, 87–255, 86–253; Los Angeles, 85–384; mental illness, 87–392; Washington, D.C., 87–516, 86–517, 85–519
Hominid: anthropology, 87–186, 86–188, 85–185; archaeology, 85–187
Homo erectus: anthropology, 86–190, 85–185
Homo habilis: anthropology, 87–187
Homosexuals: health, 86–343; Houston, 86–349, 85–345; Roman Catholic, 86–461; Supreme Court, 87–485, 86–487
HONDURAS, 87–343, 86–347, 85–342; Azcona del Hoyo, José, 87–219; Latin America, 87–371, 86–375, 85–374
Honecker, Erich: Germany, East, 87–331, 86–334, 85–329
HONG KONG, 85–343; architecture, 86–193; Asia, 86–201
Honolulu: city, 87–252, 86–254, 85–248
Hopper, Grace Murray: newsmakers, 87–413
Hoover, J. Edgar: espionage, Special Report, 87–46
Hormone: drugs, 86–294; biochemistry, 85–218; medicine, 86–395
Horowitz, Vladimir: classical music, 87–258
HORSE RACING, 87–344, 86–347, 85–343
Horseshoe pitching: sports, 87–477, 86–476, 85–484
Horticulture. See BOTANY; GARDENING.
HOSPITAL, 87–345, 86–348, 85–344; mental illness, 86–396. See also DRUGS; HEALTH AND DISEASE; MEDICINE; PUBLIC HEALTH.
Hostages: Colombia, 86–262; Middle East, 87–395
House of Blue Leaves, The: theater, 87–498
House of Representatives. See CONGRESS OF THE U.S.; DEMOCRATIC PARTY; ELECTIONS; REPUBLICAN PARTY.
Housing: prison, 87–447; Washington, D.C., 86–517; welfare, 85–522. See also BUILDING AND CONSTRUCTION.
HOUSTON, 87–346, 86–349, 85–345; architecture, 86–193; city, 87–252, 86–254, 85–248
Houston, Whitney: newsmakers, 87–415
Howe, Sir Geoffrey: Europe, 87–315
Hu Yaobang: China, 87–249, 86–251
Huaca: archaeology, 87–191
Hubble Space Telescope: space exploration, Special Report, 86–49
Hughes, Howard: poetry, 85–447; WBE, 86–579
Human growth hormone: drugs, 86–294
Human rights: Argentina, 87–192, 86–194; Chile, 86–249; civil rights, 86–257, 85–251; Guatemala, 86–341; Latin America, 86–377; Russia, 85–468; Uganda, 87–506; Zimbabwe, 87–524
Human sacrifice: archaeology, Close-Up, 87–190
Humana Building (Louisville): architecture, 86–193; il., 86–135
HUNGARY, 87–347, 86–350, 85–345; Europe, 87–314, 86–315, 85–311
Hunger: nutrition, 85–424; welfare, 86–521, 85–522
Hunt, Guy: il., 87–303
Hunthausen, Raymond G.: Roman Catholic Church, 87–459
HUNTING, 87–348, 86–350, 85–346
Hurricanes: disasters, 87–290, 86–293, 85–287; weather, 87–519, 86–519
HURT, WILLIAM, 87–348; il., 87–216
Hussein I: il., 85–399; Jordan, 87–363, 86–366, 85–363; Middle East, 86–399; President, 85–452
Hussein, Saddam: Iraq, 87–357

Hutton, E. F., & Company: crime, 86–277
Hydroelectric power: energy supply, 86–307
Hyman, Flo: deaths, 87–282
Hypertension: biochemistry, 85–219; medicine, 86–394
Hypnosis: mental illness, 87–392

I

I Wear the Morning Star: literature for children, 87–382
Iacocca, Lee: publishing, 86–452; WBE, 86–579
Iakovos, Archbishop: Eastern Orthodox, 86–296, 85–291
IBM (International Business Machines Corporation): communications, 85–254; computer, 86–265
Icahn, Carl C.: labor, 86–371
Ice hockey. See HOCKEY.
ICE SKATING, 87–348, 86–351, 85–347; Olympics, 85–433; Thomas, Debi, 87–498
Iceboating: sports, 87–477, 86–476
Iceland: conservation, 87–270; Europe, 87–314, 86–315, 85–311
Idaho: state govt., 87–480, 86–480, 85–488
Iditarod Trail Sled Dog Race: newsmakers, 86–415
Ignatow, David: poetry, 87–438
Illegal aliens: census, 87–244; Congress, 87–264; il., 86–419; immigration, 87–349, 86–352, 85–348, Special Report, 86–72; Latin America, 87–373, 86–377
Illinois: Chicago, 87–246, 86–247, 85–240; Democratic Party, 87–287; state govt., 87–480, 86–480, 85–488
Illiteracy: American Library Association, 85–184; library, 87–376, 86–380
IMMIGRATION, 87–349, 86–352, 85–348; Australia, 85–202; city, 86–256; Congress, 87–264; Latin America, 87–373, 86–377; Special Report, 86–66
Immigration Reform and Control Act of 1986: Latin America, 87–373
Immunization: public health, 86–452
Implied powers: Constitution, Special Report, 87–93
Imports: farm, 87–318. See also ECONOMICS; INTERNATIONAL TRADE.
Inca: archaeology, 87–191
Income, Personal. See CENSUS.
Income tax: Congress, 87–267, 85–258. See also TAXATION.
INDIA, 87–350, 86–352, 85–348; Asia, 87–202, 86–200, 85–196; Sri Lanka, 86–477
India, Festival of: visual arts, 86–514
INDIAN, AMERICAN, 87–351, 86–354, 85–350; archaeology, Close-Up, 86–191; British Columbia, 87–233, 86–232; Canada, 86–236, 85–230; Northwest Territories, 86–422
Indiana: elections, 86–305; state govt., 87–480, 86–480, 85–488
Indianapolis: city, 87–252, 86–254, 85–248
Indianapolis 500. See AUTOMOBILE RACING.
INDONESIA, 87–352, 86–355, 85–351; Asia, 87–202, 86–200, 85–196
Industrial solvent: water, 87–517
Industry. See also ECONOMICS; INTERNATIONAL TRADE; LABOR; MANUFACTURING; entries on specific industries, countries, and provinces.
Infallibility: Roman Catholic Church, 87–459
Infant mortality: health, 87–342
Infertility: health, 86–344; medicine, 87–391
Inflation: bank, 87–220, 86–219; economics, 87–299, 86–297, 85–291; international trade, 86–356. See also entries on specific countries and cities.
Inherently safe reactor: energy supply, Close-Up, 87–306
Insect: chemistry, 87–245
Insecticide. See Pesticide.
Instant replay. See FOOTBALL.
Institutional Revolutionary Party (PRI): Mexico, 87–394
Insulin pump: medicine, 87–390
INSURANCE, 87–353, 86–355, 85–352; mental illness, 86–397; Mexico, 86–398; state govt., 87–481; transportation, 87–503; truck,

86–503; Washington, D.C., 87–516. See also **SOCIAL SECURITY.**
Integral fast reactor (IFR): nuclear energy, Special Report, 86–94
Integration. See **CIVIL RIGHTS.**
Intelligence: psychology, 87–450
Intelligence (information): espionage, Special Report, 87–36
Intelligence, Artificial: computer, 86–265
Interest rates: bank, 87–220, 86–219, 85–212; consumerism, 87–271; economics, 86–297, 85–291
Intergovernmental Oceanographic Commission (IOC): ocean, 86–426
Internal Revenue Service. See **TAXATION.**
International Church of the Foursquare Gospel: religion, 87–457, 86–457
International Cometary Explorer (ICE): astronomy, 86–202
International Council of Community Churches: religion, 87–457, 86–457
International Court of Justice: courts, 87–272, 86–275, 85–267; President, 85–452
International Longshoremen's Association (ILA): labor, 87–368, 85–308
International Monetary Fund (IMF): international trade, 87–354, 86–356, 85–353
International Olympic Committee (IOC). See **OLYMPIC GAMES.**
International Style: architecture, Special Report, 86–132
INTERNATIONAL TRADE, 87–353, 86–356, 85–352; China, Special Report, 86–119; Europe, 87–316; farm, 87–316, 86–320, 85–313; steel, 86–481, 85–489. See also entries for specific continents and countries.
Interstate Commerce Commission: truck, 86–503
Inuits (Eskimos): il., 85–459; Northwest Territories, 87–421, 86–422
Investments. See **BANK; ECONOMICS; STOCKS AND BONDS.**
Ionization: astronomy, 86–202
Iowa: state govt., 87–480, 86–480, 85–488
IRA (Irish Republican Army): Great Britain, 86–340, 85–332; Ireland, 86–360; Northern Ireland, 85–422
IRAN, 87–355, 86–358, 85–355; Iraq, 87–356, 86–359; Libya, 86–381; Middle East, 87–396, 86–400, 85–398; petroleum, 87–432; President, 87–444; United Nations, 87–508
IRAQ, 87–356, 86–359, 85–356; Iran, 87–356, 86–358; Libya, 86–381; Middle East, 87–396, 86–400, 85–398; petroleum, 87–432; United Nations, 87–508
IRELAND, 87–357, 86–360, 85–357; Europe, 87–314, 86–315; 85–311. See also **NORTHERN IRELAND.**
Irian Jaya: Pacific Islands, 86–428
Iridium: extinction, Special Report, 86–101; paleontology, 87–430
Iris: vision, Special Report, 86–146
Iron and steel. See **STEEL INDUSTRY.**
Irradiation: consumerism, 87–272; food, 86–324
Isamu Noguchi Garden Museum: visual arts, 86–514
Isherwood, Christopher: deaths, 87–282
Islam: Africa, 87–179; Iran, 87–355, 86–358; Malaysia, 86–390. See also **Muslims.**
Islamic Jihad: Middle East, 86–400
ISRAEL, 87–358, 86–361, 85–357; Africa, 87–183; armed forces, 87–196; Egypt, 87–302, 86–304; international trade, 85–354; Jordan, 86–366; Lebanon, 86–378; Middle East, 87–396, 86–400, 85–398; Peres, Shimon, 85–437; Russia, 87–480; Syria, 87–489; Tunisia, 86–504; United Nations, 87–507. See also **JEWS AND JUDAISM.**
ITALY, 87–359, 86–362, 85–359; Europe, 87–314, 86–315, 85–311; Libya, 87–377
IUD (intrauterine device): health, 86–344
Ivory Coast: Africa, 87–180, 86–182, 85–178

J

Jackson, Bo: football, 86–329
Jackson, Jesse Louis: Cuba, 85–271; Demo-
cratic Party, 87–287; il., 85–282; Jews and Judaism, 85–362
JACKSON, MICHAEL, 85–360; ils., 85–77, 210; music, popular, 85–410
Jacksonville, Fla.: city, 87–252, 86–254, 85–248
Jacobs, Marc: fashion, 87–320
Jacobsen, David P.: Middle East, 87–395
Jahn, Helmut: architecture, Special Report, 86–138
Jails. See **PRISON.**
Jamaica: Latin America, 87–371, 86–375, 85–374
JAPAN, 87–360, 86–363, 85–360; Asia, 87–202, 86–200, 85–196; automobile, 87–209, 86–209; fishing industry, 87–322; international trade, 87–354, 85–354; space, 87–475; space exploration, Special Report, 86–42
Japan Air Lines: Japan, 86–364
Jaruzelski, Wojciech: Poland, 87–439, 86–439
Jarvik-7 artificial heart: medicine, 87–391, 86–393
Jarvis, Gregory B.: il., 87–283
Javits, Jacob K.: deaths, 87–282
Javits Convention Center: architecture, 87–191; il., 87–408
Jaw: dentistry, 87–288
Jayewardene, Junius Richard: Sri Lanka, 87–478, 86–477, 85–485
Jazz. See **AWARDS AND PRIZES; POPULAR MUSIC.**
Jefferson, Thomas: Constitution, Special Report, 87–93; Monticello, Special Report, 85–102
Jefferson Awards: awards, 87–217, 86–217, 85–211
Jehovah's Witnesses: religion, 87–457, 86–457, 85–463
Jenco, Lawrence Martin: Middle East, 87–395
Jensen, Ken: Canadian Library Association, 87–241
JEWS AND JUDAISM, 87–362, 86–365, 85–362; Alberta, 86–185; Ethiopia, 86–313; literature, 87–379; religion, 87–457, 86–457, 85–463. See also **ISRAEL.**
Jhabvala, Ruth Prawer: literature, 87–378
Jiang Qing: Special Report, 86–112
Joffrey Ballet: dancing, 87–278
John F. Kennedy Center for the Performing Arts: awards, 87–214, 86–214, 85–208
John Henry: horse racing, 87–345, 86–348
John Paul II: Africa, 86–184; civil rights, 86–257; Eastern Orthodox, 86–296; Jews and Judaism, 87–363; religion, 87–456; Venezuela, 86–511. See also **ROMAN CATHOLIC CHURCH.**
Johnson, Don: television, 86–492
Johnson, Tish: bowling, 87–230
Johnston, Wayne: Canadian literature, 87–242
JOIDES Resolution **(ship):** ocean, 87–424, 86–424
Jolley, Elizabeth: literature, 87–378
JORDAN, 87–363, 86–366, 85–363; Israel, 87–359; Middle East, 87–396, 86–400, 85–398
Jordan, Michael: basketball, 86–224, 85–217; Olympics, 85–427
Jordan, Stanley: popular music, 87–442
Journalism: awards, 87–215, 86–215, 85–209. See also **MAGAZINE; NEWSPAPER.**
Joyner, Jackie: track, 87–500
Juan Carlos I: ils., 87–316, 85–482
Judaism. See **JEWS AND JUDAISM.**
Judicial review: Constitution, Special Report, 87–94
Judiciary. See **COURTS.**
Judo: sports, 87–477, 86–476, 85–484
Junejo, Mohammed Khan: Pakistan, 87–428
JungleWorld: zoo design, Special Report, 87–50; zoos, 86–525
Junior Achievement. See **YOUTH ORGANIZATIONS.**
Junk bonds: stocks, 87–484
Jury system: Supreme Court, 87–486

K

Kahane, Meir: Israel, 86–361
Kahn, Ann: National PTA, 86–410

KAMPUCHEA, 87–364, 86–366, 85–364; Asia, 87–202, 86–200, 85–196
Kansas: state govt., 87–480, 86–480, 85–488
Kansas City, Mo.: city, 87–252, 86–254, 85–248
Kansas City Royals: baseball, 86–221
Karamanlis, Constantine: Greece, 86–341
KARAMI, RASHID, 85–365; Lebanon, 87–375
Karle, Jerome: Nobel Prizes, 86–421
Karmal, Babrak: Afghanistan, 87–177, 85–175
Karpov, Anatoly: chess, 87–246, 85–239
Kasparov, Gary: chess, 87–246, 86–246, 85–239
Keillor, Garrison: literature, 86–381
Kekkonen, Urho K.: deaths, 87–282
Kelly, Gene: newsmakers, 86–414
Keneally, Thomas: literature, 87–378
Kenilorea, Sir Peter: Pacific Islands, 87–428
Kennedy, Caroline: newsmakers, 87–415
Kennedy, Joseph P, II: il., 87–303
Kent, Clark: newsmakers, Close-Up, 87–412
Kentucky: state govt., 87–480, 86–480, 85–488
Kentucky Derby. See **HORSE RACING.**
KENYA, 87–365, 86–367, 85–365; Africa, 87–180, 86–182, 85–178
Kesterson National Wildlife Refuge: water, 86–518
KGB: espionage, Special Report, 87–43
Khamenei, Ali: Iran, 86–358
Kharg Island: Iraq, 87–356
Khieu Samphan: Kampuchea, 87–364
Khmer Rouge: Kampuchea, 87–364, 86–366
Khomeini, Ruhollah: Iran, 87–355, 86–358
Kidney stones: medicine, 87–392
Kim Dae Jung: civil rights, 86–258; Korea, South, 86–368, 85–365
Kim Il-song: Asia, 85–194; Korea, North, 87–365, 86–368, 85–365; Korea, South, 87–366
Kim Young Sam: Korea, South, 86–368, 85–365
King, Billie Jean: women's sports, Special Report, 87–75
King, Edward J.: Republican Party, 86–458
KING, STEPHEN, 86–368
Kinnock, Neil Gordon: Great Britain, 87–337, 86–338, 85–334
Kiribati: Pacific Islands, 87–427, 86–429, 85–434
Kirkwood gaps: astronomy, 86–203
Kirov Ballet: dancing, 87–277
Kiss of the Spider Woman: motion pictures, 86–408
Kizim, Leonid D.: space, 87–473
Klinghoffer, Leon: Middle East, 86–401; President, 86–447
Knight, Ray: baseball, 87–223
Knight, Ted: deaths, 87–282
Knight-Ridder Newspapers: newspaper, 87–417
Koch, Edward I.: New York City, 87–408, 86–411
Kohl, Helmut Michael: Germany, East, 86–334; Germany, West, 87–332, 85–330
Kokoschka, Oskar: art, 87–197
KOREA, NORTH, 87–365, 86–368, 85–365; Asia, 87–202, 86–200, 85–196. See also **KOREA, SOUTH.**
KOREA, SOUTH, 87–365, 86–368, 85–365; Asia, 87–202, 86–200, 85–196; automobile, 87–211; civil rights, 87–256; Japan, 85–360. See also **KOREA, NORTH.**
Kristiansen, Ingrid: il., 87–70; track, 87–501
Kuomintang: Taiwan, 87–489
Kurdish nationalists: Turkey, 87–505, 86–505, 85–507
Kurdistan: Iran, 87–355
Kurosawa, Akira: motion pictures, 86–408
Kuwait: Middle East, 87–396, 86–400, 85–398
Kyprianou, Spyros: Greece, 86–341, 85–337

L

"L.A. Law": il., 87–494
Labeling: food, 87–323
LABOR, 87–366, 86–369, 85–366; aviation, 87–212; Brock, William E., 86–233; census,

86–245; education, 86–304; women, Special Report, 85–119. See also entries for specific countries, provinces, and cities.

Laboulaye, Edouard-René Lefebvre de: Statue of Liberty, Special Report, 86–52

Labour Party: Great Britain, 87–337, 86–338, 85–334

Lacrosse: sports, 87–477, 86–476, 85–484

Ladies Professional Bowlers Tour. See **BOWLING.**

Lady's Secret: horse racing, 87–344

Lakers, Los Angeles: basketball, 86–224, 85–216

Land development: national parks, Special Report, 87–110

Lane, Lois: newsmakers, Close-Up, 87–412

Lang, Fritz: WBE, 86–579

Language: psychology, 86–450

LAOS, 87–369, 86–372, 85–370; Asia, 87–202, 86–200, 85–196

LaRouche, Lyndon H., Jr.: Democratic Party, 87–287

Larson, Mervin: zoo design, Special Report, 87–56

Lartigue, Jacques-Henri: photography, 87–437

Laser, ils., 86–195, 438; vision, Special Report, 86–149

Last Judgment, The: art restoration, Special Report, 87–132

Last Supper, The: art restoration, Special Report, 87–132

LATIN AMERICA, 87–370, 86–372, 85–370; civil rights, 87–256, 86–258, 85–251; economics, 87–298; literature, 87–377; Roman Catholic Church, 87–460. See also by name of country.

Lava rock: ocean, 87–424

Law enforcement. See **Police; PRISON.**

Lawn bowling: sports, 87–477, 86–476, 85–484

Laws. See **COURTS; CRIME; SUPREME COURT OF THE U.S.**

Lawson product: physics, 85–446

Laxalt, Paul: Republican Party, 87–458

Lead poisoning: hunting, 87–348, 86–350, 85–346

Lean, Sir David: WBE, 86–579

LEBANON, 87–374, 86–378, 85–375; Israel, 87–359, 86–361; Middle East, 87–396, 86–400, 85–398; Protestantism, 86–449; Syria, 86–489; United Nations, 87–507

Le Carré, John: literature, 87–378

Le Duan: Vietnam, 86–512, 85–515

Lee, Russell: photography, 87–437

Lee, Yuan T.: Nobel Prizes, 87–424

LeFevour, Richard F.: courts, 86–275

Legislation. See **CONGRESS OF THE UNITED STATES; COURTS; PRESIDENT OF THE UNITED STATES; STATE GOVERNMENT; SUPREME COURT OF THE UNITED STATES; UNITED STATES, GOVERNMENT OF THE;** entries on specific countries.

Lekhanya, Justinus M.: Africa, 87–182

Lemon law: consumerism, 87–272

LeMond, Greg: il., 87–477; newsmakers, 87–411

Lendl, Ivan: tennis, 87–495, 86–495, 85–499

Leonard, Sugar Ray: boxing, 87–230, 85–222

Lerner, Alan Jay: deaths, 87–283

Lesotho: Africa, 87–180, 86–182, 85–178; South Africa, 87–471

Leukemia: medicine, 87–391; water, 87–517

Lévesque, René: Quebec, 86–453, 85–459

Levi, Primo: literature, 87–377

Levi-Montalcini, Rita: Nobel Prizes, 87–420

Levine, James: WBE, 86–580

Lewis, Carl: track, 87–501, 86–500, 85–502

Liability insurance: insurance, 87–353, 86–355; state govt., 87–481

Libby, Leona Marshall: deaths, 87–283

Libel: courts, 86–276, 85–269

Liberal Party: Canada, 87–238, 85–228

Liberation theology: Roman Catholic Church, 87–460, 86–459, 85–467

LIBERIA, 87–375, 86–379; Africa, 87–180, 86–182, 85–178

Liberty, Statue of: Close-Up, 87–409; coins, 87–260, 86–262; Special Report, 86–51; stamps, 86–478

LIBRARY, 87–376, 86–380, 85–377; Los Angeles, 87–383. See also **AMERICAN LIBRARY ASSOCIATION; CANADIAN LIBRARY ASSOCIATION.**

LIBYA, 87–376, 86–380, 85–377; Africa, 87–180, 86–182, 85–178; Algeria, 87–185; armed forces, 87–194; Chad, 85–237; Europe, 87–312; Germany, West, 87–332; Greece, 87–338; Morocco, 86–405, 85–402; petroleum, 87–432; President, 87–447; Syria, 86–489; Tunisia, 86–504; United Nations, 87–508

Lichtenstein, Roy: il., 87–198

Liechtenstein: Europe, 87–314, 86–315, 85–311

Life expectancy. See **POPULATION.**

Lincoln Center (New York City): theater, 86–498

Lindbergh, Pelle: hockey, 86–346

Line of Death: Libya, 87–376

Lingeman, Richard: literature, 87–379

Linh, Nguyen Van: Vietnam, 87–514

Lipoprotein: cholesterol, Special Report, 85–135

Lite Food Labeling Act: food, 87–323

LITERATURE, 87–377, 86–381, 85–378; King, Stephen, 86–368. See also **AWARDS AND PRIZES; CANADIAN LITERATURE; LITERATURE FOR CHILDREN; NOBEL PRIZES.**

LITERATURE FOR CHILDREN, 87–380, 86–384, 85–381

Little Bighorn, Battle of the: archaeology, Close-Up, 86–191

Litvinchuk, John: chess, 87–246

Livaditis, Steven: crime, 87–275

Live Aid: newsmakers, Close-Up, 87–414; popular music, 87–440; radio, 86–454

Livestock: biochemistry, 87–227

Liver cancer: medicine, 87–391

Living will: state govt., 86–479

Lizza, Tommy: fishing, 87–321

Lloyd, Chris Evert. See **Evert Lloyd, Chris.**

Lloyd's building: il., 87–192

Loan rates. See **Credit.**

Lobbying: Special Report, 85–144

Local area network: computer, 86–265

Lochner v. New York: Constitution, Special Report, 87–96

Locusts: Africa, 87–179

Logan, Jud: track, 87–501

Lombardi, Ernie: baseball, 87–223

Lon Nol: Asia, 86–202

London Stock Exchange: stocks, 87–484

Lone Ranger: newsmakers, 86–415

Long Beach: city, 87–252, 86–254, 85–248

Longshoremen: labor, 87–368

Lopez, Nancy: golf, 86–337

López Portillo, José: Mexico, Special Report, 87–146

LOS ANGELES, 87–383, 86–387, 85–384; city, 87–252, 86–254, 85–248; il., 85–384; Latin America, 87–370; visual arts, 85–516

Loss-of-coolant accident: nuclear energy, Special Report, 86–88

Lottery: newsmakers, 86–413; state govt., 87–481

Louganis, Greg: il., 85–426; sports, 86–475; swimming, 85–493

Lougheed, Peter: Alberta, 86–185, 85–182

Louis Vieux (tree): newsmakers, 87–413

Louisiana: state govt., 87–480, 86–480, 85–488

Love Always: literature, 87–381

Lown, Bernard: Nobel Prizes, 86–421

LPGA (Ladies Professional Golfers Association). See **GOLF.**

LTV Corporation: steel industry, 87–483

Lubbers, Ruud: Netherlands, 87–406, 85–413

Lucas, William: Republican Party, 86–458

Luge: sports, 87–477, 86–476, 85–484

Lukas, J. Anthony: literature, 86–383

Lumber industry: British Columbia, 87–233; Canada, 87–240

Lumpectomy: medicine, 86–395

Lunette: il., 87–136

Lung cancer: il., 86–343; medicine, 86–395; public health, 87–451

LUSINCHI, JAIME, 85–385; Venezuela, 85–514

Lutheran Church in America: religion, 87–457, 86–457, 85–463

Lutheran Church-Missouri Synod, The: religion, 87–457, 86–457, 85–463

Lutherans: Protestantism, 87–448, 86–450, 85–457. See also **RELIGION.**

Luxembourg: Europe, 87–314, 86–315, 85–311

Luxembourg reforms: Denmark, 87–287

Lyle, Sandy: golf, 86–336

Lynch, Beverly P.: American Library Assn., 87–185, 86–187

LYNG, RICHARD EDMUND, 87–384

Lyons, Ted: deaths, 87–283

M

M1: bank, 87–220, 86–219, 85–212

M2: bank, 87–220, 86–219, 85–213

Maazel, Lorin: music, classical, 85–408

MacEachen, Allan Joseph: Canada, 85–233

Machel, Samora Moisés: Mozambique, 87–406, 86–409, 85–406; South Africa, 87–471

Macheteros, Los: Puerto Rico, 87–452

Machine. See **MANUFACTURING; Technology.**

Machine tool industry: manufacturing, 87–389, 86–393

Machine vision: manufacturing, 87–390

MacLean, W. J.: Nova Scotia, 87–422

Macmillan, Harold: deaths, 87–283

Macpherson, Wendy: bowling, 87–230

MacRae, Gordon: deaths, 87–283

Macular degeneration: vision, Special Report, 86–154

Madagascar: Africa, 87–181, 86–183, 85–178

Madballs: toys and games, 87–500

MADD (Mothers Against Drunk Driving): teen-age drinking, Special Report, 87–128

MADONNA, 86–388

Mafia: courts, 87–274; crime, 87–275. See also **Organized crime.**

MAGAZINE, 87–385, 86–388, 85–385; awards, 86–215, 85–209. See also **PUBLISHING.**

Magellanic Clouds: WBE, 87–579

Magic Horse, The: literature for children, 87–380

Magnetic field: paleontology, 87–430

Mahathir bin Mohamed: Malaysia, 87–386, 86–390, 85–387

MAHDI, SADIQ EL, 87–386; Africa, 87–182

Mailer, Norman: literature, 87–379

Maine: state govt., 87–480, 86–480, 85–488

Major Indoor Soccer League (MISL): soccer, 87–469, 86–470, 85–478

Malamud, Bernard: deaths, 87–283

Malawi: Africa, 87–181, 86–183, 85–179

MALAYSIA, 87–386, 86–390, 85–387; Asia, 87–202, 86–200, 85–196

Maldives: Asia, 87–202, 86–200, 85–196

Mali: Africa, 87–181, 86–183, 85–179

Malpractice insurance: state govt., 86–479

Malta: Europe, 87–314, 86–315, 85–311

Man with the Golden Helmet, The: visual arts, 86–515

Mandela, Nelson: South Africa, 86–471

MANDELA, WINNIE, 87–387

Mandlikova, Hana: tennis, 86–495

MANITOBA, 87–387, 86–391, 85–387

Mankiller, Wilma P.: Indian, American, 86–354

Mann, Aimee: popular music, 86–442

Manoon Roopkachorn: Thailand, 86–496

Mansell, Nigel: automobile racing, 87–211

MANUFACTURING, 87–388, 86–391, 85–387. See also **LABOR; Technology.**

Manufacturing automation protocol (MAP): manufacturing, 87–390

Mao Zedong: China, 85–243; Special Report, 86–111

Maradona, Diego Armando: soccer, 87–469

Marathon: women's sports, Special Report, 87–66. See also **OLYMPIC GAMES; SPORTS.**

Marcos, Ferdinand C.: Asia, 87–202; Philippines, 87–434, 86–436, 85–444

Marijuana: drug abuse, 87–292; teen-age drinking, Special Report, 87–122

Marine Corps, U.S.. See **ARMED FORCES.**

Marlowe, Christopher: espionage, Special Report, 87–40

Maronite Christians: Lebanon, 87–374

Marquis Theatre: theater, 87–496
Marshall Islands: Pacific Islands, 87–427, 86–428; stamps, 85–486
Martens, Wilfried A. E.: Belgium, 87–226, 86–226, 85–218
Martial law: Taiwan, 87–489
Maryland: bank, 86–220; state govt., 87–480, 86–480, 85–488
Mason, Bobbie Ann: literature, 86–381
Mass transit. See **TRANSIT; TRANSPORTATION.**
Massachusetts: state govt., 87–480, 86–480, 85–488
Masse, Marcel: Canada, 87–238
Masters tournament. See **GOLF.**
Mata Hari: espionage, Special Report, 87–40
Matabele (people): Zimbabwe, 86–524
Mauritania: Africa, 87–181, 86–183, 85–179
Mauritius: Africa, 87–181, 86–183, 85–179
Maxxum electronic camera: photography, 86–437
Maya: archaeology, Close-Up, 87–190, 86–192, 85–187
Mayday: literature, 87–379
Mayors, U.S. Conference of: city, 86–252, 85–246
Mazankowski, Donald Frank: Canada, 87–238
McAuliffe, Christa: education, 87–301; il., 87–283
McAuliffe, Sharon C.: newsmakers, 86–415
McCloskey, Frank: elections, 86–305
McCovey, Willie: baseball, 87–223
McEnroe, John: tennis, 87–496, 85–499
McFarlane, Robert C.: President, 87–444
MCI Communications Corporation: communications, 86–263
McIntyre, Richard D.: elections, 86–305
McKay, Steven: youth organizations, 87–522
McKenna, Siobhan: deaths, 87–283
McKinney, Tamara: skiing, 86–469, 85–477
McKinnon, J. Kenneth: Yukon Territory, 87–523
McNair, Ronald E.: il., 87–283
McPhee, John: literature, 87–380
MDMA: drugs, Close-Up, 86–295
Me and My Girl: theater, 87–496
Medal of Freedom: awards, 87–217, 86–217
Media. See **Arts; COMMUNICATIONS; MAGAZINE; NEWSPAPER; RADIO; TELEVISION.**
Median Trough: El Salvador, 87–305
Medicare: hospital, 86–348, 85–344; medicine, 87–391; social security, 87–470, 85–478
MEDICINE, 87–390, 86–393, 85–390; Houston, 86–349; Ontario, 87–426; vision, Special Report, 86–144. See also **DRUGS; HEALTH AND DISEASE; HOSPITAL; MENTAL ILLNESS; NOBEL PRIZES.**
Medved, Miroslav: Russia, 86–464
MEESE, EDWIN, III, 86–396; Cabinet, 86–235, 85–227; Congress, 85–257; Supreme Court, 86–487, Close-Up, 86–485; U.S. govt., 86–509
Megaevent: newsmakers, Close-Up, 87–414
Meltdown: nuclear energy, Special Report, 86–88
Memory: chemistry, 87–245
Memory (computer): computer, 85–257; electronics, 87–304, 85–302
Memphis: city, 87–252, 86–254, 85–248
MENGELE, JOSEF, 86–396; Latin America, 86–377
Menotti, Gian Carlo: classical music, 87–259
MENTAL ILLNESS, 87–392, 86–396, 85–392; biochemistry, 85–219
Meow That Saved the Kingdom, The: classical music, 87–259
Mergers: advertising, 87–176, 86–177; aviation, 87–212, 86–212; communications, 87–261; hospital, 86–349; newspaper, 86–417; railroad, 87–453, 86–454, 85–460
Merkin, Daphne: literature, 87–378
Metastasis: biochemistry, 87–226
Meteorite: astronomy, 86–203; geology, 86–334; il., 86–102; paleontology, 86–430, 85–436
Meteorology. See **WEATHER.**
Metro Toronto Zoo: zoos, 86–526
Metropolitan Opera Company: classical music, 87–258

Mets, New York: baseball, 87–221
Mexican Revolution: Mexico, Special Report, 87–149
MEXICO, 87–393, 86–397, 85–393; aviation, 87–212; geology, 86–333; Latin America, 87–371, 86–375, 85–374; Special Report, 87–144
Mexico City: Latin America, 86–377; Mexico, Special Report, 87–150
Miami: city, 87–252, 86–254, 85–248; Latin America, 86–375; transit, 87–502
"Miami Vice": television, 86–492
MIA's (missing in action): Laos, 86–372; Vietnam, 87–514, 86–512
Michelangelo: art restoration, Special Report, 87–132
Michigan: Detroit, 87–289, 86–291, 85–285; state govt., 87–480, 86–480, 85–488
Michnik, Adam: literature, 87–378
Microdot: espionage, Special Report, 87–42
Micronesia, Federated States of: Pacific Islands, 87–427, 86–429
Microprocessor: computer 87–263, 86–264, 85–256; games, 86–332
Microwave surgery: vision, Special Report, 86–157
Mid-Atlantic Ridge: ocean, 87–424
MIDDLE EAST, 87–394, 86–399, 85–395; United Nations, 86–506. See also names of specific countries.
Midland nuclear plant: energy supply, 87–309
Mies van der Rohe, Ludwig: architecture, 87–191; architecture, Special Report, 86–132
Mikheyev, S. P.: physics, 87–438
Mikulić, Branko: Yugoslavia, 87–522
Mikulski, Barbara A.: il., 87–303
Military. See **ARMED FORCES.**
Military Retirement Reform Act: veterans, 87–513
Milky Way galaxy: astronomy, 86–203; WBE, 87–579
Millenium Grove: conservation, 87–269
Miller, Cheryl: basketball, 85–218; il., 85–484
Miller, Frank: Ontario, 86–427
Miller, Richard W.: courts, 87–274; crime, 86–277; U.S. govt., 85–513
Miller, Sue: literature, 87–378
Milwaukee: city, 87–252, 86–254, 85–248
MINING, 87–399, 86–403, 85–400; Bolivia, 87–229; disasters, 87–290, 86–293, 85–288; Yukon Territory, 86–524. See also **COAL; PETROLEUM AND GAS.**
Minisupercomputer: computer, 87–263
Minneapolis: city, 87–252, 86–254, 85–248
Minnelli, Vincente: deaths, 87–284
Minnesota: education, 86–301; state govt., 87–480, 86–480, 85–488
Minnesota Zoo: ils., 87–53, 54
Minot, Susan: literature, 87–378
Minudri, Regina U.: American Library Assn., 87–185
Mir: space, 87–473
Miranda: astronomy, 87–204
Missile, Nuclear: Netherlands, 87–407, 86–410, 85–413
Mission specialist: space exploration, Special Report, 86–36
Mississippi: state govt., 87–480, 86–480, 85–488
Missouri: state govt., 87–480, 86–480, 85–488
Mitchell, Betsy: swimming, 87–487
Mitchell, George J.: il., 87–286
Mitterrand, François: France, 87–328, 86–331, 85–325
Mixed-sector company: Iraq, 85–356
Modern pentathlon: sports, 87–477, 86–476, 85–484
Modernism: architecture, Special Report, 86–128
Modigliani, Franco: Nobel Prizes, 86–421
Moi, Daniel T. arap: Kenya, 87–365
Mole (spy): espionage, Special Report, 87–37
Molotov, Vyacheslav M.: deaths, 87–284
Moment of silence: education, 86–302; state govt., 86–485
Monaco: Europe, 87–314, 86–315, 85–311
MONDALE, WALTER FREDERICK, 85–400; Democratic Party, 85–282; elections, 85–298; ils., 85–241

Money: city, 85–247; Europe, 87–316; Japan, 86–363. See also **BANK; COIN COLLECTING; ECONOMICS.**
Mongolia: Asia, 87–202, 86–200, 85–196
Monkees: popular music, 87–442
Monkeys: literature, 87–378
Monoclonal antibodies: biochemistry, 86–226
Montana: forests, 85–324; state govt., 87–480, 86–480, 85–488
Monterey Bay Aquarium: zoo design, Special Report, 87–60
MONTREAL, 87–400, 86–403, 85–401
Montreal Canadiens: hockey, 87–342
"Moonlighting": il., 87–493
Moore, Brian: Canadian literature, 86–242
Moore, Clayton: newsmakers, 86–415
Moore, Henry: deaths, 87–284
Morales, Pablo: swimming, 87–487
Morgan, Dodge: boating, 87–228
MOROCCO, 87–401, 86–405, 85–402; Africa, 87–181, 86–183, 85–179
Mortimer, John: literature, 87–378
Morton Thiokol, Incorporated: space exploration, Close-Up, 87–474
Moses, Edwin: Olympics, 85–427; track, 87–501, 86–500
Motherland Party: Turkey, 87–505
MOTION PICTURES, 87–402, 86–405, 85–402; awards, 87–214, 86–214, 85–208; Field, Sally, 86–321; Hurt, William, 87–348; Page, Geraldine, 87–428
Motorcycle racing: sports, 87–477, 86–476, 85–484
Mott, William Penn, Jr.: conservation, 86–272
Mouthwash: dentistry, 86–290
MOVE: Philadelphia, 87–433, 86–434
Movement for the Restoration of Democracy: Pakistan, 87–428
Movement of April 19: Colombia, 86–262, 85–254
Mowat, Farley: Canadian literature, 86–242; newsmakers, 86–415
MOZAMBIQUE, 87–406, 86–409, 85–406; Africa, 87–181, 86–183, 85–179; South Africa, 87–471
Mozambique National Resistance (MNR): Africa, 86–180; Mozambique, 87–406, 86–409, 85–406
Mozart, Wolfgang Amadeus: classical music, 87–259
Mswati III: il., 87–178; newsmakers, 87–413
Mubarak, Hosni: Egypt, 87–301, 86–304, 85–298; il., 85–399
Mugabe, Robert Gabriel: Africa, 87–183; Zimbabwe, 87–523, 86–524, 85–526
Muhammad, Ali Nasir: Middle East, 87–398
Mujahedeen: Afghanistan, 86–177, 85–175; Middle East, 85–397
Mulliken, Robert S.: deaths, 87–284
MULRONEY, M. BRIAN, 87–406, 86–409, 85–407; Canada, 87–236, 86–236, 85–228; coal, 87–259; WBE, 85–575
Multi-infarct dementia: chemistry, 87–245
Munro, Alice: Canadian literature, 87–242
Muon-neutrino: physics, 87–438
MURDOCH, RUPERT, 85–407; Great Britain, 87–338; newspaper, 87–417; television, 87–492, 86–491
Murphy, Lionel K.: Australia, 87–208
Murray, Lowell: Canada, 87–238
Mururoa Atoll: New Zealand, 86–412; Pacific Islands, 86–428
Musa Hitam: Malaysia, 87–386
Musavi-Khamenei, Hosein: Iran, 87–355, 85–356
Muscular dystrophy: medicine, 87–390
Museum: architecture, 87–192; il., 86–193. See also **ART; VISUAL ARTS.**
Museum of Modern Art (MOMA): architecture, 87–191; art, 87–198
Museveni, Yoweri: Africa, 87–182; Uganda, 87–506
Music, Classical. See **CLASSICAL MUSIC.**
Music, Popular. See **POPULAR MUSIC.**
Music awards: awards, 87–214, 86–214, 85–208
Music videos: popular music, 87–442, 86–442, 85–411; Special Report, 85–74
Musicals: awards, 87–215, 86–214, 85–209; theater, 87–496, 86–496, 85–501

Muslims: Algeria, 86–186, 85–184; Indonesia, 86–355; Lebanon, 87–375; Middle East, 86–400; Sudan, 87–484. See also **Islam.**
Mwinyi, Ali Hassan: Tanzania, 87–490
MX missile: armed forces, 85–192; Congress, 86–267
Myrdal, Alva Reimer: deaths, 87–284
Mystery of Edwin Drood, The: theater, 86–497

N

Najibullah: Afghanistan, 87–177
Nakasone, Yasuhiro: ils., 86–335, 356; Japan, 87–360, 86–363, 85–360
NAMIBIA, 86–410, 85–412; Africa, 87–181, 86–183, 85–179; Angola, 86–188; South Africa, 87–471
Namphy, Henri: Haiti, 87–339
Namu (typhoon): Pacific Islands, 87–428
NASA: geology, 85–328; space exploration, Special Report, 86–36. See also **SPACE EXPLORATION.**
NASCAR: auto racing, 87–211, 86–211, 85–206
Nashville: city, 87–252, 86–254, 85–248
National Academy of Recording Arts and Sciences: awards, 87–214, 86–214, 85–208
National Academy of Television Arts and Sciences: awards, 87–214, 86–214, 85–208
National Aeronautics and Space Administration. See **NASA.**
National bank: Constitution, Special Report, 87–92
National Baptist Convention of America: religion, 87–457, 86–457, 85–463
National Baptist Convention, U.S.A., Inc.: religion, 87–457, 86–457, 85–463
National Coal Association (NCA). See **COAL.**
National Congress of Parents and Teachers. See **NATIONAL PTA.**
National defense. See **ARMED FORCES** and entries on specific countries.
National Education Association (NEA): education, 87–299, 86–304, 85–248
National Endowment for the Arts: dancing, 85–275
National flower: gardening, 87–329
National Football League. See **NFL.**
National Gallery of Art: architecture, Special Report, 86–142; art, 87–199
National Gardening Week: gardening, 87–329
National Hockey League (NHL): hockey, 87–342, 86–345, 85–341
National Institutes of Health (NIH): biochemistry, 87–226
National origins quota system: immigration, Special report, 86–70
National Park System: conservation, 87–269, 86–272; Special Report, 87–100
National Primitive Baptist Convention, Inc.: religion, 87–457, 86–457, 85–463
NATIONAL PTA, 87–406, 86–410, 85–413
National Security Act (1947): espionage, Special Report, 87–37
National Security Agency (NSA): espionage, Special Report, 87–39
National Security Council (NSC): espionage, Special Report, 87–39
NATO: Europe, 87–313, 85–308; Greece, 85–336; Netherlands, 85–413; Spain, 87–475, 86–474, 85–482
Natural gas. See **ENERGY SUPPLY; PETROLEUM AND GAS.**
Nauru: Pacific Islands, 87–427, 86–429, 85–434
Navajo Indians: Indian, American, 87–351
Navistar International Corporation: automobile, 87–211
NAVRATILOVA, MARTINA, 85–413; Czechoslovakia, 87–277; tennis, 87–495, 86–495, 85–498; women's sports, Special Report, 87–75
Navy, U.S. See **ARMED FORCES.**
Nazaré, Maria da Conceição: Brazil, 87–232
Nazca (Peru): archaeology, 87–189
Nazi Doctors, The: literature, 87–379
NBA (National Basketball Association). See **BASKETBALL.**

NBC (National Broadcasting Company): radio, 87–453; television, 87–492, 86–491
NCAA (National Collegiate Athletic Association): basketball, 87–224, 86–223, 85–216; college sports, Special Report, 85–88; sports, 86–475, 85–482
Nebraska: state govt., 87–480, 86–480, 85–488
Nemesis: extinction, Special Report, 86–108
Nepal: Asia, 87–202, 86–200, 85–196
Nerve gas: armed forces, 87–195
Nerve regeneration: chemistry, 86–245
NETHERLANDS, 87–406, 86–410, 85–413; Europe, 87–314, 86–315, 85–311
Netherlands Antilles: West Indies, 86–521
Nevada: state govt., 87–480, 86–480, 85–488
Nevado del Ruiz (volcano): Colombia, 86–262; Latin America, 86–377
NEW BRUNSWICK, 87–407, 86–411, 85–414
NEW CALEDONIA, 86–411; Pacific Islands, 87–428, 85–434
New Christian Right: Protestantism, 87–450
New Deal: Constitution, Special Report, 87–96
New Hampshire: state govt., 87–480, 86–480, 85–488
New Jersey: education, 86–303; state govt., 87–480, 86–480, 85–488
New Korea Democratic Party (NKDP): Korea, South, 87–365, 86–368
New Mexico: state govt., 87–480, 86–480, 85–488
New Orleans: city, 87–252, 86–254, 85–248
New People's Army: Philippines, 87–436, 86–436, 85–445
New York (state): state govt., 87–480, 86–480, 85–488
NEW YORK CITY, 87–408, 86–411, 85–415; architecture, 87–192; city, 87–252, 86–254, 85–248; Northern Ireland, 87–421; theater, 85–502; zoos, 86–525
New York City Public Library: library, 87–376
New York Mets: baseball, 87–221
NEW ZEALAND, 87–410, 86–412, 85–416; Asia, 87–202, 86–200, 85–196; Australia, 86–207; Europe, 86–313; France, 86–331
Newark: city, 87–252, 86–254, 85–248
Newbery Medal. See **LITERATURE FOR CHILDREN.**
NEWFOUNDLAND, 87–410, 86–413, 85–417
Newman, Paul: motion pictures, 87–402
NEWSMAKERS, 87–410, 86–413, 85–437. See also **DEATHS.**
NEWSPAPER, 87–417, 86–417, 85–417; awards, 87–215, 86–215, 85–209; courts, 86–276; Detroit, 85–193; Great Britain, 87–338; Philadelphia, 86–435; Taiwan, 86–490. See also **PUBLISHING.**
NFL (National Football League): sports, 87–476. See also **FOOTBALL.**
NHL (National Hockey League). See **HOCKEY.**
NICARAGUA, 87–417, 86–418, 85–418; armed forces, 87–195, 85–193; civil rights, 87–256; Congress, 86–271; courts, 87–272, 86–275, 85–267; Honduras, 87–343; Latin America, 87–371, 86–375, 85–374; Ortega, Daniel, 86–427; President, 87–444, 85–452; United Nations, 85–509
Nichols, Dandy: deaths, 87–284
Nicholson, Arthur D., Jr.: armed forces, 86–196
NICKLAUS, JACK, 87–419; il., 87–334
Nielsen, Erik H.: Canada, 87–238
Niger: Africa, 87–181, 86–183, 85–179
NIGERIA, 87–419, 86–419, 85–419; Africa, 87–181, 86–183, 85–179; Africa, Special Report, 85–31
Nimeiri, Gaafar Mohamed: Middle East, 86–402; Sudan, 86–483, 85–491
Nios, Lake: geology, 87–330
NIXON, RICHARD MILHOUS, 87–419, 86–420, 85–420
Nixon, Walter L., Jr.: courts, 87–273, 86–276
Nkomo, Joshua: Africa, 87–183; Zimbabwe, 87–524
NOAA (satellite): space, 87–473
NOBEL PRIZES, 87–420, 86–421, 85–420
Nofziger, Lyn: Republican Party, 87–457
Nordic skiing. See **SKIING.**
Noriega, Manuel Antonio: Latin America, 87–372

Norman, Greg: golf, 87–333
North, Andy: golf, 86–336
North, Oliver L.: President, 87–445
North American Soccer League: soccer, 86–470, 85–478
North Atlantic Treaty Organization. See **NATO.**
North Carolina: state govt., 87–480, 86–480, 85–488
North Dakota: state govt., 87–480, 86–480, 85–488
NORTHERN IRELAND, 87–421, 86–422, 85–422. See also **IRELAND.**
Northern Mariana Islands: Pacific Islands, 87–427; U.S. govt., 87–512
Northern Rhodesia. See **Zambia.**
NORTHWEST TERRITORIES, 87–421, 86–422, 85–422
NORWAY, 87–422, 86–423, 85–423; Brundtland, Gro H., 87–233; Europe, 87–314, 86–315, 85–311
NOVA SCOTIA, 87–422, 86–423, 85–424; paleontology, 87–429
NOW account: bank, 87–221
Nuclear energy: Close-Up, 87–306; England, 87–309; Finland, 87–320; Germany, West, 87–332; Special Report, 86–82. See also **ENERGY SUPPLY.**
Nuclear Regulatory Commission (NRC): energy supply, 87–307; nuclear energy, Special Report, 86–91
Nuclear weapons: armed forces, 87–194; Australia, 86–207; Congress, 86–267; Europe, 86–313, 85–310; Netherlands, 86–410, 85–413; New Zealand, 86–412, 85–416; Russia, 87–461
Nucleus (comet): astronomy, 87–205; Close-Up, 86–205
Nureyev, Rudolf: dancing, 87–278
NUTRITION, 87–422, 86–423, 85–424; health, 86–344. See also **FOOD.**
Nyerere, Julius K.: Africa, 87–183; Tanzania, 87–490

O

Oakland: city, 87–252, 86–254, 85–248
Obesity: biochemistry, 87–226; health, 86–343; nutrition, 87–422, 86–424
Obituaries. See **DEATHS.**
OCEAN, 87–424, 86–424, 85–425; mining, 86–403
Ocean Drilling Program: ocean, 87–424, 86–424, 85–425
Office of Strategic Services (OSS): espionage, Special Report, 87–37
Ohio: bank, 86–220; state govt., 87–480, 86–480, 85–488
Oil. See **PETROLEUM AND GAS.**
Oil spill: Latin America, 87–373
Okeechobee, Lake: conservation, 87–270
O'Keeffe, Georgia: deaths, 87–284
Okello, Basilio Olara: Uganda, 86–505
Okello Lutwa, Tito: Uganda, 86–505
Oklahoma: state govt., 87–480, 86–480, 85–488
Oklahoma City: city, 87–252, 86–254, 85–248
Old age. See **SOCIAL SECURITY.**
Old-Age and Survivors Insurance Trust Fund. See **SOCIAL SECURITY.**
Oleic acid: nutrition, 87–423
Oligosaccharides: botany, 86–229
OLYMPIC GAMES, 87–424, 86–427, 85–426; coins, 86–262, 85–253; Korea, North, 87–365; women's sports, Special Report, 87–66
Olympic National Park: il., 87–103
Omaha: city, 87–252, 86–254, 85–248
Oman: Middle East, 87–396, 86–400, 85–398
Omnicom Group: advertising, 87–176
Ondrik, Richard S.: China, 86–252
Onizuka, Ellison S.: il., 87–283
ONTARIO, 87–425, 86–427, 85–433; geology, 86–334; hospital, 87–346; Peterson, David R., 86–432
Oort cloud: extinction, Special Report, 86–108
OPEC (Organization of Petroleum Exporting Countries): Europe, 87–316. See also **PETROLEUM AND GAS.**

Open-angle glaucoma: vision, Special Report, 86–147
Opera. See **CLASSICAL MUSIC.**
Operation Greylord: Chicago, 87–246, 85–240; courts, 86–275
Ophthalmology: vision, Special Report, 86–144
Optic nerve: vision, Special Report, 86–146
Optical disk: computer, 87–263
Optical storage disk: computer, 86–265; electronics, 86–306
Orchestra. See **CLASSICAL MUSIC.**
Oregon: state govt., 87–480, 86–480, 85–488
Organ transplants: medicine, 87–391
Organization of African Unity (OAU): Africa, 87–179, 86–184, 85–180
Organization of Petroleum Exporting Countries. See **OPEC.**
Organization of the Islamic Conference (OIC): Nigeria, 87–419
Organizations. See **YOUTH ORGANIZATIONS;** names of specific organizations.
Organized crime: city, 85–247; crime, 87–275; Philadelphia, 87–434, 85–444
Original intention: Constitution, Special Report, 87–99
ORTEGA, DANIEL, 86–427; ils., 87–522, 86–278; Nicaragua, 86–418, 85–418
Orthodox Church in America: religion, 87–457, 86–457, 85–463
"Oscar" Awards: awards, 87–214, 86–214, 85–208
Osteogenic growth factor: biochemistry, 87–227
Osteoporosis: women's sports, Special Report, 87–70
Oversight powers: espionage, Special Report, 87–39
Overthrust Belt: national parks, Special Report, 87–110
Ozal, Turgut: Turkey, 87–505
Ozone: national parks, Special Report, 87–111

P

PACIFIC ISLANDS, 87–426, 86–428, 85–434
Paddle tennis: sports, 87–477, 86–476, 85–484
PAGE, GERALDINE, 87–428; il., 87–216
Painting: art, 87–196; art restoration, Special Report, 87–132; visual arts, 86–513, 85–516
PAKISTAN, 87–428, 86–430, 85–435; Afghanistan, 87–177; Asia, 87–202, 86–200, 85–196; India, 87–350
Palacios, Tatiana: Latin America, 87–374
Palau: Pacific Islands, 87–426
PALEONTOLOGY, 87–429, 86–430, 85–436. See also **ANTHROPOLOGY; ARCHAEOLOGY; Fossil; GEOLOGY.**
Palestine. See **ISRAEL; JORDAN; MIDDLE EAST.**
Palestinians: Israel, 86–362, 85–359; Jordan, 86–366; Middle East, 86–399
Palme, Olof: Sweden, 87–487, 86–487
Palmer, Lilli: deaths, 87–284
PAN (National Action Party): Mexico, Special Report, 87–156
PANAMA, 86–431, 85–437; Ardito Barletta Vallarina, Nicolás, 85–190; Latin America, 87–371, 86–375, 85–374
Pancasila: Indonesia, 86–355, 85–351
Papandreou, Andreas: Greece, 86–341
Pappas, James: Republican Party, 86–459
Papua New Guinea: Pacific Islands, 87–427, 86–429, 85–434
PARAGUAY, 87–430; Latin America, 87–371, 86–375, 85–374
Parallel processing: computer, 87–262, 86–265
Parents and Teachers, National Congress of. See **NATIONAL PTA.**
Paris Notebooks: Canadian literature, 87–243
Paris Opera Ballet: dancing, 87–277
Park Service, National: national parks, Special Report, 87–102
Parks Canada: national parks, Special Report, 87–108

Parochial schools: state govt., 86–485
Parti Québécois: Montreal, 86–403; Quebec, 87–452, 86–453, 85–459
Pass laws: South Africa, 87–470, 86–471
Pawley, Howard: Manitoba, 87–387, 85–387
Payola: popular music, 87–443
PAZ ESTENSSORO, VÍCTOR, 86–431; Bolivia, 87–229, 86–228
PCB's (polychlorinated biphenyls): environmental pollution, 86–311
Peabody Broadcasting Awards: awards, 87–216, 86–215, 85–209
Pebble-Bed Reactor: nuclear energy, Special Report, 86–94
Pecos Bill: literature for children, 87–380
Peggy Sue Got Married: il., 87–403
Pelotte, Donald E.: il., 87–460
Penguin Encounter: zoo design, Special Report, 87–60
Penkovsky, Oleg: espionage, Special Report, 87–40
Penn State heart: medicine, 86–394
Pennington, Jon: newsmakers, 87–411
Pennsylvania: Philadelphia, 87–433, 86–434, 85–444; state govt., 87–480, 86–480, 85–488
Pennzoil Company: courts, 87–274
Pentagon: newspaper, 85–417; U.S. govt., 86–508. See also **ARMED FORCES.**
Pentax IQZoom: photography, 87–436
People Express: aviation, 87–212, 85–206
People Mover: Detroit, 86–291; transit, 87–502
People's Republic of China. See **CHINA.**
Peptide: biochemistry, 86–227
PERES, SHIMON, 85–437; Israel, 87–358, 86–362, 85–357; Middle East, 86–401
Pérez de Cuéllar, Javier: il., 86–181; United Nations, 87–507
"Perfect Strangers": television, 87–493
Perkins, Marlin: deaths, 87–284; il., 86–416
Perry, William: football, 86–334
Personal computer: WBE, 86–555
PERU, 87–430, 86–432, 85–440; archaeology, 87–189; García Pérez, Alan, 86–333; Latin America, 87–371, 86–375, 85–374
Pesticide: environmental pollution, 87–311, 86–311, 85–306
PETROLEUM AND GAS, 87–431, 86–432, 85–441; Canada, 86–236; consumerism, 87–272; courts, 87–274; Europe, 87–316; labor, 85–366; manufacturing, 87–389; Mexico, Special Report, 87–146; Northwest Territories, 87–421; Scotland, 87–466. See also **ENERGY SUPPLY** and articles on specific countries, provinces, and cities.
Petroleum Exporting Countries, Organization of. See **OPEC.**
PGA (Professional Golfers' Association). See **GOLF.**
Phacoemulsification: vision, Special Report, 86–147
Phelps, Willard: Yukon Territory, 86–524
PHILADELPHIA, 87–433, 86–434, 85–444; architecture, 86–192; city, 87–252, 86–254, 85–248; il., 86–441; zoos, 87–525, 86–526
Philaret, Archbishop: Eastern Orthodox, 86–296
Philately. See **STAMP COLLECTING.**
Philby, Harold: espionage, Special Report, 87–40
PHILIPPINES, 87–434, 86–436, 85–444; Aquino, Corazon, 87–188; Asia, 87–202, 86–200, 85–196
Phoenix: city, 87–252, 86–254, 85–248
Phoenix heart: medicine, 86–394
Phonograph. See **CLASSICAL MUSIC; POPULAR MUSIC; Recordings.**
Photocopying: Canadian Library Association, 87–241
PHOTOGRAPHY, 87–436, 86–437, 85–445; Canadian literature, 86–243; electronics, 86–306; visual arts, 86–514, 85–516
Photovoltaic cell: nuclear energy, Special Report, 86–97
Phoumi Vongvichit: Laos, 87–369
PHYSICS, 87–437, 86–438, 85–446. See also **NOBEL PRIZES.**
Physiology: Nobel Prizes, 87–420, 86–421, 85–421

Picasso, Pablo: visual arts, 86–513
Pictograph: archaeology, 87–189
Pinochet Ugarte, Augusto: Chile, 87–248, 86–249, 85–243
Pittsburgh: city, 87–252, 86–254, 85–248
Planetesimal: astronomy, 87–205
Plant. See **BOTANY; FARM AND FARMING; GARDENING.**
Plaque (dental): advertising, 87–176
Plastics: chemistry, 87–245
Plate tectonics: geology, 86–333, 85–328
Platform tennis: sports, 87–477, 86–476
Platinum: mining, 87–399
Playboy magazine: library, 87–376
Pleistocene Epoch: archaeology, 86–190
PLO (Palestine Liberation Organization): Jews and Judaism, 87–362; Jordan, 87–363, 86–366; Lebanon, 87–374; Middle East, 87–398, 86–399, 85–399; Tunisia, 86–504
Plutonium: New York City, 86–412
POETRY, 87–438, 86–439, 85–447; Warren, Robert Penn, 87–515. See also **CANADIAN LITERATURE; LITERATURE FOR CHILDREN.**
Poindexter, John M.: Cabinet, U.S., 87–236; President, 87–445
Point Defiance Zoo and Aquarium: il., 87–62
Poison gas: disasters, 85–286; environmental pollution, 86–310, 85–306; geology, 87–330
Poisoning: drugs, 87–294
POLAND, 87–439, 86–439, 85–448; Europe, 87–314, 86–315, 85–311; United Nations, 85–510
Polanyi, John C.: Nobel Prizes, 87–420
Polar bear: il., 87–62
Pole vault. See **TRACK AND FIELD.**
Police: mental illness, 87–392; Netherlands, 87–407; Philadelphia, 87–434, 86–435; Supreme Court, 86–486
Polisario Liberation Front: Africa, 87–179, 85–180; Morocco, 87–401, 86–405, 85–402
Polish National Catholic Church of America: religion, 87–457, 86–457, 85–463
Political parties. See **Communist Party; DEMOCRATIC PARTY; REPUBLICAN PARTY;** and names of other parties.
Political prisoners: civil rights, 86–257; Israel, 86–361
Pollard, Jonathan Jay: armed forces, 87–196; crime, 86–277
Pollution: coal, 87–259; national parks, Special Report, 87–101. See also **CONSERVATION; ENERGY SUPPLY; ENVIRONMENTAL POLLUTION; Water pollution.**
Polo: sports, 87–477, 86–476, 85–484
Polysaccharides: botany, 86–229
Pope. See **John Paul II; ROMAN CATHOLIC CHURCH.**
POPULAR MUSIC, 87–440, 86–440, 85–410; awards, 87–214, 86–214, 85–208; Madonna, 86–388; music videos, Special Report, 85–76; Turner, Tina, 86–505
POPULATION, 87–443, 86–442, 85–449. See also specific continents, countries, regions.
Population, U.S. See **CENSUS; CITY.**
Pornography: crime, 87–276
Portland, Ore.: city, 87–252, 86–254, 85–248
PORTUGAL, 87–443, 86–443, 85–450; Cavaco Silva, Aníbal, 86–244; Europe, 87–314, 86–315, 85–311; Spain, 86–474
Post-Modernism: architecture, 86–192; Special Report, 86–128
POSTAL SERVICE, U.S., 87–444, 86–444, 85–450; consumerism, 85–265
Poverty: city, 87–251, 86–252, 85–246; welfare, 87–519, 86–520, 85–522
Powel, Robat: Wales, 86–516
Powerboating. See **BOATING.**
Pregnancy: health, 86–344; medicine, 85–391
Prehistoric people. See **ANTHROPOLOGY; ARCHAEOLOGY.**
Prem Tinsulanonda: Thailand, 87–496, 86–496, 85–500
Preminger, Otto L.: deaths, 87–284
Presbyterian Church (U.S.A.): Protestantism, 86–449, 85–455; religion, 87–457, 86–457, 85–463
Presbyterian Church in America: religion, 87–457, 86–457
PRESIDENT OF THE UNITED STATES, 87–444, 86–444, 85–451; Canada, 86–239;

Congress, 86–265, 85–257; Constitution, Special Report, 87–98; labor, 86–371; social security, 86–470; United Nations, 86–506. See also **CABINET; UNITED STATES;** and the names of the Presidents.
Press: Supreme Court, 86–486. See also **Journalism; MAGAZINE; NEWSPAPER.**
Presser, Jackie: labor, 87–369; truck, 86–503
Pressurized water reactor (PWR): nuclear energy, Special Report, 86–86
PRI (Institutional Revolutionary Party): Mexico, Special Report, 87–149
Price, Reynolds: literature, 87–378
Prices: farm, 85–313; food, 87–322; petroleum, 87–431, 86–432, 85–441. See also **CONSUMERISM; Cost of living; ECONOMICS; FOOD; Inflation;** and various countries and cities.
PRIDE (Parents' Resource Institute for Drug Education): teen-age drinking, Special Report, 87–125
Primaries. See **ELECTIONS.**
Prime interest rate: bank, 87–221
PRINCE EDWARD ISLAND, 87–447, 86–447, 85–454; Ghiz, Joseph A., 87–333
PRISON, 87–447, 86–448, 85–454; Brazil, 86–231; Peru, 87–430; state govt., 86–481; Washington, D.C., 87–515
Prizes. See **AWARDS AND PRIZES.**
Process Inherent Ultimately Safe reactor (PIUS): nuclear energy, Special Report, 86–94
Professional Bowlers Association: bowling, 87–230, 86–229, 85–221
Programmable Implantable Medication System: medicine, 87–390
Progress of Love, The: Canadian literature, 87–242
Progressive Conservative Party: Canada, 87–236, 86–236, 85–228
Progressive National Baptist Convention, Inc.: religion, 87–457, 86–457, 85–463
Project Alpha: automobile, 86–210
Proprietary hospital: hospital, 86–349
Prost, Alain: auto racing, 86–212
Protectionist trade legislation: Democratic Party, 87–287; economics, 87–297, 86–300
Protein: biochemistry, 87–226, 86–226; gene-splicing, Special Report, 85–62
PROTESTANTISM, 87–448, 86–448, 85–455
Protoavis: paleontology, 87–429
Pseudorabies: biochemistry, 87–227
Psoriasis: drugs, 87–293
Psychiatry. See **MEDICINE; MENTAL ILLNESS.**
PSYCHOLOGY, 87–450, 86–450, 85–457
Psychosis: mental illness, 86–397
PTA. See **NATIONAL PTA.**
PUBLIC HEALTH, 87–451, 86–451
Public lands: national parks, Special Report, 87–101
Public service: awards, 87–217, 86–217, 85–211
Public television. See **TELEVISION.**
Public transportation. See **CITY; TRANSIT; TRANSPORTATION.**
PUBLISHING, 87–452, 86–452, 85–458. See also **CANADIAN LITERATURE; LITERATURE; MAGAZINE; NEWSPAPER.**
PUERTO RICO, 87–452, 86–453, 85–458; Hernández Colón, Rafael, 86–344; Latin America, 87–371, 86–375, 85–374
Pulitzer Prizes: awards, 87–217, 86–217, 85–211
Punic War: il., 86–504; newsmakers, 86–414
Punjab state: India, 87–350, 86–352
Pupil: vision, Special Report, 86–146
Purdy, Alfred: Canadian literature, 87–243

Q

Qadhafi, Muammar Muhammad al-: Libya, 87–376, 86–380, 85–377; Middle East, 85–399; President, 87–447
Qatar: Middle East, 87–396, 86–400, 85–398
Quagga: zoology, 86–525
Quarter horse racing. See **HORSE RACING.**
Quasar: astronomy, 87–206
QUEBEC, 87–452, 86–453, 85–459; Bourassa, Robert, 86–229

Queenie Pie: classical music, 87–259
Quiwonkpa, Thomas: Africa, 86–184
Quota system (hiring): civil rights, 86–258
Quota system (immigration): immigration, Special Report, 86–70

R

Racing. See **AUTOMOBILE RACING; BOATING; HORSE RACING; ICE SKATING; OLYMPIC GAMES; SKIING; SPORTS; SWIMMING; TRACK AND FIELD.**
Racquetball: sports, 87–477, 86–476, 85–484
Racquets: sports, 87–477, 86–476, 85–484
Radial keratotomy: vision, Special Report, 86–156
Radiation: consumerism, 85–266; energy supply, Close-Up, 87–306
RADIO, 87–453, 86–454, 85–460; awards, 87–216, 86–215, 85–209; Paraguay, 87–430
Radio Martí: Cuba, 86–278
Radioactive material: environmental pollution, 87–310; nuclear energy, Special Report, 86–85
Radioactive wastes: energy supply, 87–309
Radon: environmental pollution, 87–310; public health, 87–451
Rahal, Bobby: automobile racing, 87–211
RAILROAD, 87–453, 86–454, 85–460; building, 87–235; Russia, 85–469; truck, 87–504. See also **DISASTERS; TRANSPORTATION.**
Rainbow Warrior: Europe, 86–313; France, 87–329, 86–331; il., 86–413; New Zealand, 87–410
Rambo's Rocky Mountain Sunrise: cat, 87–244
Ramos, Fidel V.: Philippines, 87–435
Random access memory (RAM): electronics, 87–304
Rap music: popular music, 87–442, 85–410
Ratzinger, Joseph Cardinal: Roman Catholic Church, 87–459, 86–460
Rawlings, Jerry John: Ghana, 87–333
Raymond, Michael: Chicago, 87–246
Reactor: energy supply, Close-Up, 87–306
Reagan, Maureen: Reagan, Ronald W., 86–456, 85–462; Republican Party, 87–458
Reagan, Nancy: il., 86–455; Reagan, Ronald W., 87–455, 85–462
Reagan, Ronald P.: Reagan, Ronald W., 87–455, 86–456, 85–462
REAGAN, RONALD WILSON, 87–454, 86–455, 85–461; Canada, 87–241; courts, 87–272; ils., 86–186, 297, 356, 474, 85–357, 485. See also **PRESIDENT OF THE UNITED STATES.**
Reckless Disregard: literature, 87–379
Recombinant DNA. See **Genetic engineering.**
Recombivax HB: drugs, 87–293
Recordings: awards, 87–214, 86–214, 85–208; popular music, 87–440, 86–440
Red Sox, Boston: baseball, 87–221
Red wolf: conservation, 87–270
Redl, Alfred: espionage, Special Report, 87–40
Reduced-Instruction-Set Computer (RISC): computer, 86–265
Reed, Charles: fishing, 87–321
Reed, Donna: deaths, 87–284
REEVES, PAUL, 86–456
Reformed Church in America: religion, 87–457, 86–457, 85–463
Refugees: Asia, 87–204, 86–214, 85–197; Ethiopia, 86–312; Germany, East, 87–331; il., 87–182; Pacific Islands, 86–428; Protestantism, 87–449; Vietnam, 85–516
Regan, Donald: Cabinet, 86–235; ils., 86–297, 85–291
Regional holding company (RHC): communications, 87–261
Regular Rolling Noah, A: literature for children, 87–381
Regulation Q: bank, 87–221
Rehabilitation. See **HANDICAPPED.**
Rehabilitation (construction): building, 87–234
REHNQUIST, WILLIAM, 87–456; il., 87–268; Supreme Court, 87–485
Reilly, Sidney: espionage, Special Report, 87–40

RELIGION, 87–456, 86–456, 85–462; education, 87–301; Romania, 86–461; state govt., 86–484. See also **EASTERN ORTHODOX CHURCHES; Islam; JEWS AND JUDAISM; PROTESTANTISM; ROMAN CATHOLIC CHURCH.**
Remineralization: dentistry, 87–288
Rent control: Washington, D.C., 86–517
Reorganized Church of Jesus Christ of Latter Day Saints: Protestantism, 85–456; religion, 87–457, 86–457, 85–463
Replay, Instant: football, 87–326
Repoussé: Statue of Liberty, Special Report, 86–52
Representatives, House of. See **CONGRESS.**
REPUBLICAN PARTY, 87–457, 86–458, 85–464. See also **CONGRESS; ELECTIONS.**
Research and development: manufacturing, 87–390, 86–392, 85–389. See also **SCIENCE AND RESEARCH.**
Resnik, Judith A.: il., 87–283
Resolution (ship): ocean, 87–424
Restaurants. See **FOOD.**
Restoration: art restoration, Special Report, 87–130
Retinopathy: vision, Special Report, 86–149
Reykjavík summit: President, 87–446; Russia, 87–461
Rheumatoid arthritis: drugs, 86–294
Rhine River: environmental pollution, 87–310; Europe, 87–315; Switzerland, 87–488
Rhinovirus: chemistry, 86–246
Rhode Island: state govt., 87–480, 86–480, 85–488
Rhodesia. See **ZIMBABWE.**
Rhondda Valley: coal, 87–260
Rhythmic gymnastics: sports, 87–477, 86–476
Richie, Lionel: popular music, 87–440
Rickover, Hyman George: deaths, 87–284
Right to life: courts, Close-Up, 85–268
Rigid fixation: dentistry, 87–288
Riots: Belgium, 86–225; China, 87–251; Egypt, 87–301; Great Britain, 86–339; Peru, 87–430; prison, 86–448; soccer, 86–470; Washington, D.C., 87–516
Risk arbitrage: stocks, 87–484
Rivabella, Omar: literature, 87–377
Rivera, Diego: art, 87–197
Rivera, Geraldo: television, 87–493
Rivers, Joan: television, 87–493
Roa Bastos, Augusto: literature, 87–377
Robert O. Anderson Building: art, 87–198
Robertson, Marion G. (Pat): Protestantism, 87–450; religion, 87–456; Republican Party, 87–459
Robotics: games, 85–327; manufacturing, 87–390, 86–393
Rock (cocaine): drug abuse, 87–292
Rock music: newsmakers, Close-Up, 87–414; radio, 86–454. See also **POPULAR MUSIC.**
Rockefeller Commission: espionage, Special Report, 87–47
Rodeo: sports, 87–477, 86–476, 85–484
Rogers, Don: deaths, 87–284; sports, 87–476; teen-age drinking, Special Report, 87–122
Rogers, Richard: architecture, 87–191
Rohrer, Heinrich: Nobel Prizes, 87–420
Rojas de Negri, Rodrigo: Chile, 87–248
Roller hockey: sports, 87–477
Roller skating: sports, 87–477, 86–476, 85–484
ROMAN CATHOLIC CHURCH, 87–459, 86–459, 85–465; Brazil, 87–232; Czechoslovakia, 87–277, 86–279, 85–272; Ireland, 86–360; Netherlands, 86–410; Protestantism, 87–448; religion, 87–457, 86–457, 85–463
ROMANIA, 87–461, 86–461, 85–468; Europe, 87–314, 86–315, 85–311
Room with a View, A: motion pictures, 87–405
Roosevelt, Franklin D.: Constitution, Special Report, 87–96
Rosenblatt, Joe: Canadian literature, 87–242
Rosenquist, James Albert: WBE, 86–580
Rostenkowski, Dan: Congress, 86–267
Roth, D. Douglas: Protestantism, 86–450
Round Midnight: popular music, 87–442
Rowing: sports, 87–476, 86–475, 85–483
Roy, Patrick: hockey, 87–343

Royal Society of Canada: awards, 87–218, 86–217, 85–211
Rubber: labor, 86–370. See also **MANUFACTURING.**
Rubik's Magic: toys and games, 87–500
Rudolph, Paul: WBE, 86–580
Rugby: sports, 87–477, 86–476, 85–484; Wales, 87–515
Running: women's sports, Special Report, 87–66
Rural Life, A: Canadian literature, 87–243
Ruschi, Augusto: Brazil, 87–232
Ruska, Ernst: Nobel Prizes, 87–420
RUSSIA, 87–461, 86–462, 85–468; Afghanistan, 86–177, 85–175; armed forces, 87–194; Asia, 87–202, 86–201, 85–195; aviation, 87–213; China, 87–251; energy supply, 86–309; espionage, Special Report, 87–36; Europe, 87–314, 86–315, 85–311; farm, 87–318; Gromyko, Andrei, 86–341; Israel, 87–359; Japan, 87–361; Jews and Judaism, 87–362, 86–365; Korea, North, 86–368; President, 87–446, 86–444, 85–453; space, 87–473, 86–473, 85–481; Special Report, 86–46; women's sports, Special Report, 87–75
Rwanda: Africa, 87–181, 86–183, 85–179
Ryan, Nolan: baseball, 86–221
Ryder Cup: Scotland, 86–468

S

Sacks, Oliver: literature, 87–378
Sacramento: city, 87–252, 86–254
Sacrifice, Human: archaeology, 87–190
SADD (Students Against Driving Drunk): teenage drinking, Special Report, 87–121
Sadler's Wells Ballet: dancing, 87–278
SAFETY, 87–464, 86–465, 85–472; aviation, 87–212, 86–212, 85–207; building, 85–234; energy supply, Close-Up, 87–306; nuclear energy, Special Report, 86–91. See also **DISASTERS.**
Sailing. See **BOATING.**
St. Bartholomew's Church: architecture, 87–192
Saint Christopher and Nevis: WBE, 85–579; Latin America, 87–371, 86–375, 85–374
St. Louis: city, 87–252, 86–254, 85–248
Saint Lucia: Latin America, 87–371, 86–375, 85–374
St. Vincent and the Grenadines: Latin America, 87–371, 86–375, 85–374
Sakharov, Andrei D.: civil rights, 85–251; Russia, 87–463, 85–469
Salary. See **Wages.**
Salle, David: art, 87–197
Salmonella: public health, 86–451
Salnikov, Vladimir: swimming, 87–488
SALT (Strategic Arms Limitation Talks): armed forces, 86–195; President, 87–447
Salvation Army: religion, 87–457, 86–457, 85–463
Salyut: space, 87–473, 86–473, 85–481; space exploration, Special Report, 86–47
Sambo: sports, 87–477
Samrin, Heng: Kampuchea, 86–366
Samuelson, Joan Benoit: sports, 87–476
San Antonio: city, 87–252, 86–254, 85–248; zoos, 87–525
San Diego: city, 87–252, 86–254, 85–248; zoos, 87–525
San Francisco: architecture, 86–192; city, 87–252, 86–254, 85–248; dancing, 86–279; il., 85–505; zoos, 86–526
San Jose: city, 87–252, 86–254, 85–248
San Marino: Europe, 87–314, 86–315, 85–311
San Salvador: El Salvador, 87–305
Sanctions: Canada, 86–241; Europe, 87–315; immigration, Special Report, 86–80; South Africa, 87–470, 86–472
Sanctuary movement: immigration, 86–352; Protestantism, 86–444
Sandinista National Liberation Front: armed forces, 87–195; courts, 87–272, 86–275; Honduras, 87–343; Latin America, 86–376; Nicaragua, 87–417, 86–418, 85–418; United Nations, 87–509

SANGUINETTI, JULIO MARIA, 86–466; il., 86–376; Uruguay, 85–514
Santa Maria delle Grazie: art restoration, Special Report, 87–132
São Tomé and Príncipe: Africa, 87–181, 86–183, 85–179
Sapphire: newsmakers, 87–415
SARNEY, JOSÉ, 86–466; Brazil, 87–231, 86–231; Latin America, 86–374
Sartzetakis, Christos: Greece, 86–341
SASKATCHEWAN, 87–465, 86–466, 85–473
Satellite, Artificial. See **SPACE EXPLORATION.**
Satellite, Communications: communications, 87–262, 86–263; space, 86–472, 85–480
Saturn Corporation: automobile, 86–210
SAUDI ARABIA, 87–465, 86–466, 85–474; Middle East, 87–396, 86–400, 85–398
SAUVÉ, JEANNE M., 87–466, 86–467, 85–475
Savage-Rumbaugh, E. Sue: psychology, 86–450
Savannah: zoos, 87–525
Savimbi, Jonas: Angola, 87–186, 86–187, 85–184; il., 85–180
Savings and loans: bank, 86–220
Scalable computer system: computer, 87–262, 86–264
SCALIA, ANTONIN, 87–466
Scandinavia. See **DENMARK; NORWAY; SWEDEN.**
Scargill, Arthur: Great Britain, 86–338, 85–332
Scatter photocoagulation: vision, Special Report, 86–151
Schlossberg, Edwin A.: newsmakers, 87–415
Schlüter, Poul: Denmark, 87–287, 86–289, 85–283
Schmidt, Mike: baseball, 87–223
School. See **EDUCATION; Universities and colleges.**
School health clinic: education, 87–300
School prayer: education, 86–302; state govt., 86–484; Supreme Court, Close-Up, 86–485
Schroeder, William J.: medicine, 87–391, 86–393, 85–390
Schurke, Paul: newsmakers, 87–413
Schuyler, James: poetry, 86–439
Schuylkill Expressway: Philadelphia, 87–434
Schwarzenegger, Arnold: il., 87–411
Schwitters, Kurt: visual arts, 86–515
Sciascia, Leonardo: literature, 87–377
Science and research: awards, 87–218, 86–217, 85–211. See also **NOBEL PRIZES** and articles on specific sciences.
Scientific creationism: paleontology, 87–430; religion, 87–457
Sclera: vision, Special Report, 86–146
Scobee, Dick: il., 87–283
SCOTLAND, 87–466, 86–467, 85–475
Sea World (San Diego): zoo design, Special Report, 87–60
Seabrook nuclear power plant: state govt., 87–482
Seagram Building: il., 86–129
Seat bag: safety, 87–464
Seat belts: insurance, 85–352; safety, 86–465; state govt., 87–482; transportation, 85–505
Seattle: city, 87–252, 86–254, 85–248
Second Continental Congress: Constitution, Special Report, 87–88
Securities and Exchange Commission (SEC): crime, 87–272
Seirawan, Yasser: chess, 87–246
Seismic tomography: geology, 87–330
Sellafield nuclear plant: England, 87–309
Semenov, Nikolai N.: deaths, 87–285
Semiconductor: electronics, 87–304, 86–306, 85–302
Senate. See **CONGRESS OF THE U. S.; DEMOCRATIC PARTY; ELECTIONS; REPUBLICAN PARTY.**
Senegal: Africa, 87–181, 86–183, 85–179
Septuplets: newsmakers, 86–414
Sepulveda Amor, Bernardo: Latin America, 86–374
Sequoyah nuclear plant: energy supply, 86–309
Seraphim, Archbishop: Eastern Orthodox, 86–296

Sergeant York air defense gun: armed forces, 86–197, 85–194
Serra, Richard: art, 87–198; visual arts, 86–514
Service industries: manufacturing, 87–388, 86–391
Set-aside contract: civil rights, 87–256
Seth, Vikram: poetry, 87–438
Seventh World Bridge Championships: bridge, 87–232
Seventh-day Adventists: religion, 87–457, 86–457, 85–463
Sex discrimination: civil rights, 86–258, 85–251; Supreme Court, 85–492; women, Special Report, 85–129
Sexual abuse of children: crime, 85–269; psychology, 85–457. See also **CHILD WELFARE.**
Sexual harassment: Supreme Court, 87–485
Seychelles: Africa, 87–181, 86–183, 85–179
Shakespeare, William: newsmakers, 86–417
Shamir, Yitzhak: Israel, 87–358, 85–357
"Shamrock Summit": Canada, 86–239
Shanker, Albert: education, 86–304
Shark: fishing, 87–321; il., 86–322
Sharon, Ariel: courts, 86–276; il., 86–389
Shcharansky, Anatoly B.: il., 87–257; Jews and Judaism, 87–362, 86–366; newsmakers, 87–413
Shear growth: chemistry, 87–245
Sheehan, Patty: golf, 85–331
Shehu, Mehmet: Albania, 86–184
Shenouda III, Pope: Eastern Orthodox Churches, 86–296
Shevardnadze, Eduard A.: President, 86–446; Russia, 86–462
Shielding the Flame: literature, 87–379
Shiite Muslims: Israel, 86–361; Lebanon, 87–375, 86–378; Middle East, 86–399
Shin Bet: Israel, 87–358
Shining Path: Peru, 87–430
SHIP AND SHIPPING, 87–467, 86–468, 85–476. See also **DISASTERS; TRANSPORTATION.**
Shippingport Atomic Power Station: nuclear energy, Special Report, 86–82
Shipwreck, Ancient: archaeology, 86–192, 85–188; il., 87–189
Shock radio: radio, 87–453
Shooting: sports, 87–477, 86–476, 85–484. See also **HUNTING.**
Short, Nigel: chess, 86–247
Shriver, Maria: il., 87–411
Siberian tiger: zoos, 87–526
Sidra, Gulf of: President, 87–447
Sierra Leone: Africa, 87–181, 86–183, 85–179
Siggins, Maggie: Canadian literature, 86–243
Sigma Delta Chi: awards, 87–216, 86–215, 85–209
Sihanouk, Samdech Norodom: Kampuchea, 87–364, 86–366, 85–364
Sikhs: India, 87–350, 86–352, 85–348; religion, 86–456, 85–462
Silver. See **COIN COLLECTING.**
Simon, Claude: Nobel Prizes, 86–421
Simon, Mary: Northwest Territories, 87–421
Simpson-Mazzoli bill: immigration, 85–348; Special Report, 86–80
Sims, Zoot: deaths, 86–286
SINCLAIR, IAN McCAHON, 85–477
Singapore: Asia, 87–202, 86–200, 85–196
Singer, Isaac Bashevis: literature, 86–381
Single-lens reflex camera: photography, 87–436, 86–437, 85–445
Sinn Fein: Ireland, 87–357; Northern Ireland, 86–422
Sistine Chapel: art restoration, Special Report, 87–132
Skateboarding: sports, 87–477, 86–476
Skating. See **HOCKEY; ICE SKATING; Roller skating.**
Skidelsky, Robert: literature, 87–379
SKIING, 87–468, 86–469, 85–477
Skyjacking. See **Hijacking.**
Slaney, Mary Decker: track, 86–500
Slavery: Constitution, Special Report, 87–95
Sled-dog racing: sports, 87–477, 86–476, 85–484
Smile: theater, 87–497
Smirnov, A. Y.: physics, 87–438

Smith, Ian: Zimbabwe, 86–524
Smith, Kate: deaths, 87–285
Smith, Michael J.: il., 87–283
Smog: national parks, Special Report, 87–111
Smokeless tobacco: public health, 87–451
Smoking: consumerism, 86–274; health, 86–344, 85–340; medicine, 86–395; public health, 87–451; safety, 85–473
Snake, Reuben: Indian, American, 86–354
Snow Chief: horse racing, 87–344
Snowmobile racing: sports, 87–477, 86–477, 85–484
Snyder, Mitch: Washington, D.C., 87–516, 86–517
Soares, Mário: Portugal, 87–443, 86–443, 85–450
SOCCER, 87–469, 86–470, 85–478; England, 86–309
Social contract: Constitution, Special Report, 87–88
Social sciences. See **ANTHROPOLOGY; AR-CHAEOLOGY; CIVIL RIGHTS; COURTS; CRIME; ECONOMICS; EDUCATION; PSY-CHOLOGY.**
SOCIAL SECURITY, 87–470, 86–470, 85–478; handicapped, 86–342; taxation, 86–470, 85–495
Softball: il., 87–76; sports, 87–477, 86–477, 85–484
Soil conservation: farm, 86–318
Solar energy: energy supply, 86–309
Solar wind: astronomy, 86–202
Soldier bug: gardening, 86–333
Solid-state physics: physics, 86–438
Solidarity: Poland, 87–439, 85–448
Solomon Islands: Pacific Islands, 87–427, 86–429, 85–434
Solovyov, Vladimir: space, 87–473, 85–481
Solvent: art restoration, Special Report, 87–135
Somalia: Africa, 87–181, 86–183, 85–179; Kenya, 85–365
Son Sann: Kampuchea, 87–364
Sorge, Richard: espionage, Special Report, 87–40
Souphanouvong: Laos, 87–369
SOUTH AFRICA, 87–470, 86–471, 85–479; Africa, 87–181, 86–183, 85–179; Angola, 87–186, 86–188, 85–184; Canada, 87–241, 86–241; Europe, 87–315; Japan, 87–361; Mandela, Winnie, 87–387; mining, 87–399; Mozambique, 86–409; Protestantism, 87–448, 86–448; United Nations, 87–508, 86–507; Zimbabwe, 87–523
South America. See **LATIN AMERICA.**
South Asian Association for Regional Coop-eration: Asia, 87–204, 86–202
South Carolina: state govt., 87–480, 86–480, 85–488
South Dakota: state govt., 87–480, 86–480, 85–488
South Lebanon Army (SLA): Lebanon, 86–378
South West Africa. See **NAMIBIA.**
Southern Baptist Convention: Protestantism, 87–448, 86–449, 85–455; religion, 87–457, 86–457, 85–463
Southern Methodist University: sports, 86–475
Southern Ocean Racing Conference. See **BOATING.**
Southern Yemen, People's Republic of. See **Yemen (Aden).**
Sovereignty: Constitution, Special Report, 87–89
Soviet Paradox, The: literature, 87–380
Soviet Union. See **RUSSIA.**
Soyinka, Wole: Nobel Prizes, 87–420
Soyuz: il., 86–43; space, 87–473, 86–473
SPACE EXPLORATION, 87–472, 86–472, 85–480; astronomy, Close-Up, 86–205; news-makers, 87–411; Special Report, 86–34; U.S. govt., 87–511
Space shuttle: Close-Up, 87–474; deaths, 87–283; newsmakers, 86–415; space, 87–472, 86–472, 85–480; space exploration, Special Report, 86–36
Space station: space exploration, Special Re-port, 86–47
Space Transportation System. See **Space shuttle.**

Spacelab: il., 86–40; space, 86–472
Spadafora, Hugo: Panama, 86–431
SPAIN, 87–475, 86–474, 85–482; Europe, 87–314, 86–315, 85–311
Spanish Sahara. See **Western Sahara.**
Spectacled bear: il., 87–525
Speed limit: state govt., 87–482
Speed skating. See **ICE SKATING.**
Speer, Thomas Said: Honduras, 87–344
Sperber, A. M.: literature, 87–379
Spined soldier bug: chemistry, 87–245
Spingarn Medal: awards, 87–217, 86–217, 85–211
Spinks, Michael: boxing, 87–230, 86–230
SPORTS, 87–476, 86–475, 85–482; college sports, Special Report, 85–87; education, 87–301; women's sports, Special Report, 87–64. See also **OLYMPIC GAMES;** entries for specific sports.
Spring of Butterflies, The: literature for chil-dren, 87–382
SPRINGSTEEN, BRUCE, 86–477; il., 86–442; popular music, 87–442, 85–410
Sprint, U.S.: communications, 87–262
Spy. See **Espionage.**
Squash racquets: sports, 87–477, 86–477, 85–484
Squash tennis: sports, 87–477, 86–477, 85–484
SRI LANKA, 87–478, 86–477, 85–485; Asia, 87–202, 86–200, 85–196
SR-71 Blackbird (airplane): il., 87–43
St. Louis Post-Dispatch: newspaper, 87–417
STAMP COLLECTING, 87–478, 86–478, 85–485
Stand by Me: motion pictures, 87–402
Standard & Poor's index: stocks, 87–483, 86–482, 85–490
Stanley, Charles F.: Protestantism, 86–449
Stanley Cup. See **HOCKEY.**
"Star Wars" defense program. See **Strategic Defense Initiative.**
STATE GOVERNMENT, 87–479, 86–478, 85–486. See also **ELECTIONS.**
State of the Parks: national parks, Special Re-port, 87–101
States' rights: Supreme Court, 86–483
Statue of Liberty: Close-Up, 87–409; coin, 87–260, 86–262; Special Report, 86–51; stamps, 86–478
Stay laws: Constitution, Special Report, 87–90
Stealth fighter plane: armed forces, 87–195, 85–192
STEEL INDUSTRY, 87–482, 86–481, 85–489; labor, 87–366, 86–371; Mexico, 87–393
Steeplechasing. See **HORSE RACING.**
Steger, Will R.: newsmakers, 87–413
Steiner, Ralph: photography, 87–437
Steroids: football, 87–327; sports, 86–475
Stevenson, Adlai E., III: Democratic Party, 87–287
Still-video camera: photography, 87–436
Stock car. See **AUTO RACING.**
Stockman, David A.: Cabinet, 86–235; litera-ture, 87–379
STOCKS AND BONDS, 87–483, 86–482, 85–490; courts, 86–276; crime, 87–274; eco-nomics, 87–295, 86–299; Great Britain, 87–338; newspaper, 85–417
Storms. See **DISASTERS; WEATHER.**
Story of Bobby O'Malley, The: Canadian litera-ture, 87–242
Strabismus: vision, Special Report, 86–156
Strange, Curtis: golf, 86–336
Strategic Arms Limitation Talks. See **SALT.**
Strategic Defense Initiative (SDI): armed forces, 87–194, 85–192; Europe, 86–313; President, 86–445, 85–453; space explora-tion, Special Report, 86–46; Russia, 87–461
Street Talk: literature for children, 87–382
Strict construction: Constitution, Special Re-port, 87–94
Strikes: aviation, 86–212; baseball, 86–222; la-bor, 87–367; steel, 87–482, 86–481. See also entries on specific countries and cities.
Stroessner, Alfredo: Paraguay, 87–430
Student aid: education, 86–302
Suazo Córdova, Roberto: Honduras, 86–347
Subatomic particles: physics, 87–437
Subsidies: farm, 87–318

SUDAN, 87–484, 86–483, 85–491; Africa, 87–181, 86–183, 85–179; Jews and Juda-ism, 86–365; Libya, 86–380; Mahdi, Sadiq el, 87–386; Suwar el-Dahab, Abdul, 86–487
Sudbury Igneous Complex: geology, 86–334
Sugar: West Indies, 87–520
Suharto: Indonesia, 86–355, 85–351
Suicide: child welfare, 87–248, 86–248
Sukhanov, Aleksandr V.: Russia, 86–464
Sulfites: consumerism, 86–275; health, 87–341, 86–344
Sullivan, Danny: auto racing, 86–211
Sullivan Award: sports, 87–476, 86–475, 85–483
Sun: physics, 87–437
Sunken treasure: il., 86–414; ocean, 86–426
Sunshine Skyway: building, 87–235
Super Bowl: football, 87–326, 86–326, 85–322
Super NOW account: bank, 87–220
Supercomputer: computer, 87–263, 85–256
Superfund: Congress, 87–268; environmental pollution, 87–310, 86–311
Superman: newsmakers, Close-Up, 87–412
Supermarkets. See **FOOD.**
Supersymmetric theories: physics, 86–439
SUPREME COURT OF THE U.S., 87–485, 86–483, 85–491; Constitution, Special Report, 87–94; Rehnquist, William H., 87–456; reli-gion, 86–457; Scalia, Antonin, 87–466; U.S. govt., 87–512, 86–509. See also **COURTS.**
Surfing: sports, 87–477, 86–477, 85–484
Surgery. See **MEDICINE.**
Suriname: Latin America, 87–371, 86–375, 85–374
Surveillance device: espionage, Special Re-port, 87–42
Susan B. Anthony dollar: coins, 86–262
SUWAR EL-DAHAB, ABDUL RAHMAN, 86–487; Sudan, 86–483
Swan Lake: il., 87–278
Swaziland: Africa, 87–181, 86–183, 85–179; newsmakers, 87–413
SWEDEN, 87–487, 86–487, 85–493; Carls-son, Ingvar, 87–354; Europe, 87–314, 86–315, 85–311; petroleum, 87–433
SWIMMING, 87–487, 86–488, 85–493; wom-en's sports, Special Report, 87–77
Swing music: popular music, Close-Up, 87–441
SWITZERLAND, 87–488, 86–488, 85–494; Eu-rope, 87–314, 86–315, 85–311
Symons, Scott: Canadian literature, 87–242
Synchronized swimming: sports, 87–477, 86–477, 85–484
Synfuels. See **ENERGY SUPPLY.**
SYRIA, 87–489, 86–489, 85–494; Europe, 87–315; Lebanon, 87–375, 86–378; Middle East, 87–396, 86–400, 85–398
Szent-Györgyi, Albert: deaths, 87–285

T

Table tennis: sports, 87–477, 86–477, 85–484
Tae kwon do: sports, 87–477, 86–477, 85–484
TAIWAN, 87–489, 86–490, 85–495; Asia, 87–202, 86–200, 85–196
Tamil Eelam: Sri Lanka, 87–478, 85–485
Tampering: drugs, 87–294; food, 87–323
Tango Argentino: Latin America, 87–373
TANZANIA, 87–490; Africa, 87–181, 86–183, 85–179
Tariff: Canada, 87–240; Democratic Party, 87–287. See also **INTERNATIONAL TRADE.**
Tartar: advertising, 87–176
Taussig, Helen Brooke: deaths, 87–285
Taung child: anthropology, 86–188; Close-Up, 85–186
Tax Reform Act of 1986: Congress, 87–264; state govt., 87–479; taxation, 87–490
TAXATION, 87–490, 86–490, 85–495; Can-ada, 86–239; Congress, 87–264; consumer-ism, 87–272; social security, 86–470, 85–478; U.S. govt., 86–508. See also **CON-GRESS; STATE GOVERNMENT.**
Taylor, Peter: literature, 87–378
Teachers. See **EDUCATION.**

Team handball: sports, 87–477, 86–477, 85–484
Technology: awards, 87–218, 86–217, 85–211. See also **MANUFACTURING.**
Teen-age drinking, Special Report, 87–116
Telephone: communications, 87–261, 86–263, 85–254; consumerism, 87–271, 86–273
Telescope: space exploration, Special Report, 86–49
TELEVISION, 87–492, 86–491, 85–496; advertising, 87–176, 85–174; architecture, 87–191; awards, 86–214, 85–208; communications, 87–262, 85–255; football, 86–326, 85–320; il., 86–306; mental illness, 86–396; Olympics, 86–427
Tempera: art restoration, Special Report, 87–139
Teng Hsiao-p'ing. See Deng Xiaoping.
Tennessee: prison, 86–448; state govt., 87–480, 86–480, 85–488
Tennessee-Tombigbee Waterway: transportation, 86–503
TENNIS, 87–495, 86–495, 85–498; Becker, Boris, 86–225
Tenzing Norgay: deaths, 87–285
Terrace, Herbert S.: psychology, 86–450
Terrorism: armed forces, 86–195; Chile, 85–243; crime, 86–276, 85–269; El Salvador, 86–307; Europe, 86–317; France, 87–329; Germany, West, 87–332; Great Britain, 87–337; India, 87–350; Israel, 86–361, 85–359; Ireland, 87–357; Italy, 87–359; Jews and Judaism, 87–362; Libya, 87–376; Middle East, 87–394, 86–400, 85–396; Pakistan, 87–429; Portugal, 87–443; Spain, 87–475; Sri Lanka, 87–478, 85–485; Syria, 87–489; Turkey, 87–505
Testorf, Helga: art, 87–196
Texaco Incorporated: courts, 87–274
Texas: Houston, 87–346, 86–349, 85–345; ocean, 85–425; state govt., 87–480, 86–480, 85–488
Texas Air Corporation: aviation, 87–212
THAILAND, 87–496, 86–496, 85–500; Asia, 87–202, 86–200, 85–196; Laos, 86–372, 85–370
Thatcher, Margaret Hilda: Great Britain, 87–335, 86–338, 85–332
THEATER, 87–496, 86–496, 85–500; awards, 87–215, 86–214, 85–209
Theology. See RELIGION.
Third World: Roman Catholic Church, 87–460. See also **Developing countries.**
THOMAS, DEBI, 87–498; ice skating, 87–348, 86–351
Thomas, Philip Michael: television, 86–492
Thompson, Chris: youth organizations, 87–522
Three Mile Island Nuclear Power Station: energy supply, 86–308, 85–304; nuclear energy, Special Report, 86–90
Tiedge, Hans Joachim: Germany, West, 86–335
Tierra del Fuego: Argentina, 87–193
Tigerman, Stanley: architecture, Special Report, 86–138
Time for Results: The Governors' 1991 Report on Education: education, 87–300
Times Mirror Company: newspaper, 87–417
Tin: mining, 87–400
Tisch, Laurence A.: television, 87–492
Tisch, Preston R.: Postal Service, U. S., 87–444
Titanic **(ship):** ocean, 87–424, Close-Up, 86–425
Tobacco: biochemistry, 87–227
Tobago. See Trinidad and Tobago.
Togo: Africa, 87–181, 86–183, 85–179
Toledo: city, 87–252, 86–254, 85–248
Tolentino, Arturo M.: Philippines, 87–436, 86–436
Tolmie, Ken: Canadian literature, 87–243
Tomb, Maya: archaeology, 85–187
Tomorrow's Teachers: education, 87–299
Tonga: Pacific Islands, 87–427, 86–429, 85–434
Tongass National Forest: conservation, 87–269
Tony Awards: awards, 87–215, 86–214, 85–209

Tool, Ancient: archaeology, 87–191
Tooth decay: dentistry, 87–288, 86–290
Top Gun: motion pictures, 87–402
Tornado. See DISASTERS; WEATHER.
Torness nuclear plant: Scotland, 87–467
TORONTO, 87–499, 86–498; zoos, 86–526
Tort system: insurance, 87–353
Tour de France: newsmakers, 87–411
Tourism: national parks, Special Report, 87–109
Toxic wastes: Congress, 87–268; conservation, 85–263; state govt., 87–482; water, 85–520. See also **ENVIRONMENTAL POLLUTION.**
Toyota Motor Corporation: automobile, 87–211
TOYS AND GAMES, 87–499, 86–332, 85–326. See also **BRIDGE; CHESS; SPORTS.**
TRACK AND FIELD, 87–500, 86–499, 85–502; women's sports, Special Report, 87–76
Trade. See ECONOMICS; Federal Trade Commission; INTERNATIONAL TRADE.
Trade union. See Union, Labor.
Traffic Alert Collision Avoidance System: aviation, 87–212
Train. See DISASTERS; RAILROAD.
Traitor: espionage, Special Report, 87–36
Tranquilizer: drugs, 87–293
TRANSIT, 87–502, 86–501, 85–504. See also **TRANSPORTATION** and articles on specific cities.
Transplantation surgery: medicine, 87–391
TRANSPORTATION, 87–503, 86–502, 85–505; safety, 87–464, 86–465. See also **AUTOMOBILE; AVIATION; RAILROAD; SHIP; TRANSIT; TRUCK.**
Transportation, Department of: railroad, 86–454; ship, 86–468; transportation, 86–503
Treasure Houses of Britain: visual arts, 86–514
Treasury bill: bank, 87–220
Tree: gardening, 87–329; newsmakers, 87–413. See also **BOTANY.**
Treehouse Zoo: il., 87–57
Treholt, Arne: Norway, 86–423, 85–423
Triathlon: sports, 87–477, 86–477, 85–484
Trinidad and Tobago: Latin America, 87–371, 86–375, 85–374
Triumph of Politics, The: literature, 87–379
Tropic World: ils., 87–53, 56
Tropical Ocean and Global Atmosphere project (TOGA): ocean, 86–426
Tropical rain forest: botany, 87–229; zoology, 87–524
Trost, Carlisle A. H.: armed forces, 87–196
TRUCK AND TRUCKING, 87–504, 86–503, 85–506; disasters, 87–290, 85–286; France, 85–326; labor, 86–369. See also **TRANSPORTATION.**
TRUDEAU, PIERRE ELLIOTT, 87–504, 86–503, 85–507; Close-Up, 85–231
Trump, Donald J.: architecture, 87–192; New York City, 87–408, 86–412
Truong Chinh: Vietnam, 87–514
Tucker, Forrest: deaths, 87–285
Tucker, Kevin M.: Philadelphia, 86–435
Tucson: city, 87–252, 86–254, 85–248
Tulsa: city, 87–252, 86–254, 85–248
Tumor: biochemistry, 86–226
Tuna: fishing industry, 87–322; Pacific Islands, 87–426
TUNISIA, 87–505, 86–504, 85–507; Africa, 87–181, 86–183, 85–179
Tunnel: building, 87–235
TURKEY, 87–505, 86–505, 85–507; Bulgaria, 87–235, 86–235; Europe, 87–314, 86–315, 85–311; Greece, 87–338, 85–336
Turner, J. M. W.: il., 85–517
Turner, Kathleen: il., 87–404
Turner, Ted: sports, 87–476; television, 86–491
TURNER, TINA, 86–505
Tutu, Desmond Mpilo: Nobel Prizes, 85–420; Protestantism, 87–448, 86–448; WBE, 86–580
Tuvalu: Pacific Islands, 87–427, 86–429, 85–434
TWA hijacking: aviation, 86–213, President, 86–447
Tway, Bob: golf, 87–333

Twenty-Fifth Amendment: Constitution, 86–273
Typhoon: Pacific Islands, 87–428

U

U-2 aircraft: espionage, Special Report, 87–41
UGANDA, 87–506, 86–505; Africa, 87–181, 86–183, 85–179
Ulster. See NORTHERN IRELAND.
Unemployment: automobile, 85–203; economics, 87–295, 86–299; geology, 87–330; manufacturing, 85–387. See also **CITY; ECONOMICS; LABOR; SOCIAL SECURITY; STATE GOVERNMENT; WELFARE;** individual cities, provinces, and countries.
Union, Labor: aviation, 86–212; Great Britain, 86–339, 85–332; steel, 86–482; Supreme Court, 86–486; railroad, 87–454. See also **LABOR.**
Union Carbide Corporation: chemical industry, 85–237; environmental pollution, 86–310
Union of Soviet Socialist Republics. See RUSSIA.
UNITA: Africa, 86–180; Angola, 87–186, 86–187, 85–181; il., 85–180
Unitarian Universalist Association: religion, 87–457, 86–457
United Arab Emirates: Middle East, 87–396, 86–400, 85–398
United Church of Christ: religion, 87–457, 86–457, 85–463
UNITED KINGDOM. See GREAT BRITAIN.
United Methodist Church, The: Protestantism, 85–455; religion, 87–457, 86–457, 85–463
UNITED NATIONS, 87–507, 86–506, 85–508; courts, 86–275; Walters, Vernon, 86–516
United Pentecostal Church, International: religion, 87–457, 86–457, 85–463
UNITED STATES, GOVERNMENT OF THE, 87–509, 86–508, 85–510; census, 86–245; Constitution, Special Report, 87–78; library, 86–380. See also names of individual government officials and entries on various government agencies.
United States Constitution. See CONSTITUTION OF THE UNITED STATES.
United States Football League. See FOOTBALL.
United Steelworkers of America: labor, 87–366; steel industry, 87–482
Universities and colleges: college sports, Special Report, 85–87; education, 85–295; sports, 86–475. See also **BASKETBALL; FOOTBALL.**
Upper Volta. See Burkina Faso.
Uranium: energy supply, 86–309; mining, 87–399, 86–403
Uranus: astronomy, 87–204
Urban transportation. See TRANSIT; TRANSPORTATION.
URUGUAY, 85–514; Latin America, 87–371, 86–375, 85–374; Sanguinetti, Julio, 86–466
USA for Africa: popular music, 86–440; radio, 86–454
USFL (United States Football League). See FOOTBALL.
U.S.S.R. See RUSSIA.
USX Corporation: steel industry, 87–482
Utah: state govt., 87–480, 86–480, 85–488; water, 87–517
Utilities. See COMMUNICATIONS; ENERGY SUPPLY; PETROLEUM AND GAS.

V

Vaccine: biochemistry, 87–227, 86–227; drugs, 87–293, 86–294, 85–289
Valium: drugs, 86–294
Vallee, Rudy: deaths, 87–285
Values clarification: teen-age drinking, Special Report, 87–123
Vanden Boeynants, Paul: Belgium, 87–226
VANDER ZALM, WILLIAM NICK, 87–513; British Columbia, 87–232
Vanuatu: Pacific Islands, 87–427, 86–429, 85–434
Vargas Llosa, Mario: il., 86–383; literature, 87–377

Vatican. See **ROMAN CATHOLIC CHURCH.**
Vatican II: Roman Catholic Church, 86–460
VCR (videocassette recorder): electronics, 85–302; music videos, Special Report, 85–83; photography, 85–446; television, 86–494; toys and games, 87–500
Veeck, Bill: deaths, 87–285
Vega **(spacecraft):** astronomy, 87–205; Close-Up, 86–205; space, 87–473, 86–474
Venda: Africa, 86–183, 85–179
VENEZUELA, 86–511, 85–514; Latin America, 87–371, 86–375, 85–374
Venus: astronomy, 85–199; space, 86–474
Vermont: state govt., 87–480, 86–480, 85–488
VETERANS, 87–513, 86–512, 85–515
Vice President of the United States. See **BUSH, GEORGE H. W.**
Videla, Jorge Rafael: Argentina, 85–191; Latin America, 86–377
Vienna: Lusthaus: theater, 87–498
VIETNAM, 87–514, 86–512, 85–515; Asia, 87–202, 86–200, 85–196; Kampuchea, 87–364, 86–367, 85–364; Laos, 86–372; Thailand, 86–496, 85–500
Vietnam veterans: ils., 87–513, 85–519
Vigilantes: South Africa, 87–470
Vinpocetine: chemistry, 87–245
Virginia: elections, 86–304; state govt., 87–480, 86–480, 85–488
Virginia Beach: city, 87–252, 86–254
Virus: cat, 86–244; health and disease, 87–341, 85–339
Vision: Special Report, 86–144
VISUAL ARTS, 86–513, 85–516. See also **ART.**
Vital statistics. See **CENSUS; POPULATION.**
Vitreous humor: vision, Special Report, 86–146
Volcano: astronomy, 85–199; Colombia, 86–262; Latin America, 86–377
Volleyball: sports, 87–477, 86–477, 85–484
Von Bülow, Claus: courts, 86–276
Von Klitzing, Klaus: Nobel Prizes, 86–421
Voss, Peter E.: Postal Service, U.S., 87–444
Voting. See **ELECTIONS.**
Voyager **(spacecraft):** astronomy, 87–204; il. 87–413; space, 87–473
Vranitzky, Frantz: Austria, 87–208
Vrdolyak, Edward R.: Chicago, 86–247, 85–240

W

Waddington, Miriam: Canadian literature, 87–243
Wages: civil rights, 87–257, 85–252; economics, 87–295, 86–299; labor, 87–366, 86–369; Los Angeles, 86–387. See also **ECONOMICS; LABOR; Unemployment;** and various city articles.
Walcott, Derek: poetry, 87–438
WALDHEIM, KURT, 87–514; Austria, 87–208
Waldo, Carolyn: il., 87–487
WALES, 87–514, 86–516, 85–518; coal, 87–260
Walkaway reactor: nuclear energy, Special Report, 86–94
Walker, Arthur J.: armed forces, 86–196
Walker, John A., Jr.: armed forces, 86–196; espionage, Special Report, 87–47
Walker, Michael L.: armed forces, 86–196
Walliser, Maria: skiing, 87–468
WALTERS, VERNON ANTHONY, 86–516
Waltrip, Darrell: auto racing, 86–211
War: Afghanistan, 87–177, 85–175; Africa, 87–179, 86–180, 85–177; Asia, 87–204, 86–199, 85–195; El Salvador, 87–305, 85–302; Iran, 86–358; Iraq, 87–356, 86–359; Lebanon, 86–378; Middle East, 87–397, 86–399, 85–395; Nicaragua, 87–417; Peru, 86–432; United Nations, 87–508
WARREN, ROBERT PENN, 87–515
Warsaw Pact: Europe, 86–317
Washington (state): state govt., 87–480, 86–480, 85–488
WASHINGTON, D.C., 87–515, 86–517, 85–519; city, 87–252, 86–254, 85–248
Washington, Harold: Chicago, 87–246, 86–247, 85–240; city, 85–250; il., 86–256

Washington Park Zoo: zoos, 87–526
Waste disposal: England, 87–309; energy supply, 87–309; nuclear energy, Special Report, 86–91
WATER, 87–517, 86–518, 85–520; Congress, 87–268; Indian, American, 85–350
Water pollution: conservation, 87–270, 86–272; New York City, 86–412; Switzerland, 87–488; water, 86–518. See also **ENVIRONMENTAL POLLUTION.**
Water polo: sports, 87–477, 86–477, 85–484
Water-skiing: sports, 87–477, 86–477, 85–484
Watt, James Gaius: coal, 85–252; national parks, Special Report, 87–107; petroleum, 86–433
Weapons: Congress, 86–267; Saudi Arabia, 87–466. See also **ARMED FORCES; Nuclear weapons.**
"We Are the World": popular music, 86–440; radio, 86–454
WEATHER, 87–518, 86–519, 85–520
Webb, Cathleen Crowell: Chicago, 86–247
Weddeye, Goukouni: Chad, 86–245
Weightlifting: sports, 87–477, 86–477, 85–483. See also **OLYMPIC GAMES.**
Weinberger, Caspar W.: China, 87–251
Weir, Benjamin: Protestantism, 87–449, 86–449
Welch, Larry D.: armed forces, 87–196
WELFARE, 87–519, 86–520, 85–522; city, 85–246; state govt., 86–479. See also **CHILD WELFARE.**
Well water: water, 87–517
Welland Canal: ship, 86–468
Welles, Orson: Close-Up, 86–407; motion pictures, 87–402
Wennerstrom, Stig: espionage, Special Report, 87–40
West Bank: Israel, 87–359, 86–362; Jordan, 87–363; Middle East, 85–398
WEST INDIES, 87–520, 86–521, 85–523
West Virginia: state govt., 87–480, 86–480, 85–488
Western Accord: Canada, 86–236
Western Sahara: Africa, 87–179, 85–180; Morocco, 87–401, 86–405, 85–402
Western Samoa: Pacific Islands, 87–427, 86–429, 85–434
Westland PLC: Great Britain, 87–335
Westminster Kennel Club. See **DOG.**
Westmoreland, William C.: courts, 86–276, 85–269; television, 85–498
Whale: conservation, 87–270; il., 86–206; newsmakers, 86–417
White, Patrick: literature, 87–378
White, Theodore H.: deaths, 87–285
White shark: fishing, 87–321; il., 86–322
Whitmire, Kathryn J.: Houston, 86–349
Whitney Museum: visual arts, 86–513
Whitworth, Jerry A.: courts, 87–274; il., 87–46
Wiesel, Elie: Jews and Judaism, 87–363; Nobel Prizes, 87–420
Wilder, Billy: newsmakers, 87–411
Wilderness areas: conservation, 87–273; environment, 85–307; mining, 86–403; national parks, Special Report, 87–101
Wildlife: conservation, 87–270
Wilhelm, Hoyt: baseball, 86–222
Wilkinson, Todd: youth organizations, 87–522
Williams, Emlyn: Wales, 87–515
Williams, Shirley Anne: literature, 87–378
Williams, Walter Ray, Jr.: bowling, 87–230
Willoch, Kaare: Norway, 87–422, 86–423
Wills, Helen N.: women's sports, Special Report, 87–71
Wilson, Michael Halcombe: Canada, 87–239
Wilson, Teddy: deaths, 87–285; popular music, Close-Up, 87–441
Windsor, Duchess of: deaths, 87–285
Windsor, Treaty of: Portugal, 87–443
Wine: Austria, 86–207; Italy, 87–359
Wisconsin: state govt., 87–480, 86–480, 85–488
Wisconsin Evangelical Lutheran Synod: religion, 87–457, 86–457, 85–463
Wise Men, The: literature, 87–379
Witt, Katarina: ice skating, 87–348, 86–351, 85–347

Wolf: conservation, 87–270
Wollman Memorial Rink: New York City, 87–408
Women: census, 85–237; civil rights, 87–257, 86–258, 85–251; Los Angeles, 86–388; popular music, 87–440, 86–442; prison, 87–447; Special Report, 85–119; United Nations, 86–507; women's sports, Special Report, 87–64. See also **BASKETBALL; BOWLING; GOLF; SKIING; TENNIS.**
Woodland Park Zoo: zoo design, Special Report, 87–58
Workfare program: city, 87–254
World Bank: international trade, 86–356, 85–353
World Book Dictionary: supplement, 87–581, 86–581, 85–581
World Book Encyclopedia: supplement, 87–530, 86–530, 85–530
World Council of Churches: Eastern Orthodox, 85–290; Protestantism, 85–456
World Court. See **International Court of Justice.**
World Cup: soccer, 87–469
World Series. See **BASEBALL.**
World War I: WBE, 87–530
World War II: espionage, Special Report, 87–37; WBE, 87–546
Wrestling: sports, 87–476, 86–476, 85–483; television, Close-Up, 86–493
WT 17000 (hominid): anthropology, 87–186
Wyeth, Andrew: art, 87–196
Wynn, Keenan: deaths, 87–285
Wyoming: state govt., 87–480, 86–480, 85–488

X

X (The Life and Times of Malcolm X): classical music, 87–259

Y

Yachting. See **BOATING.**
Yamani, Ahmed Zaki: il., 86–433; Saudi Arabia, 87–465
Yellowstone National Park: national parks, Special Report, 87–103
Yemen (Aden): Middle East, 87–396, 86–400, 85–398
Yemen (Sana): Middle East, 87–396, 86–400, 85–398
Yen: Japan, 87–360
Yosemite National Park: national parks, Special Report, 87–107
Young, Coleman A.: Detroit, 87–289, 86–291, 85–285
YOUTH ORGANIZATIONS, 87–521, 86–522, 85–524
YUGOSLAVIA, 87–522, 86–523, 85–525; Albania, 87–183, 86–185, 85–182; Europe, 87–314, 86–315, 85–311
YUKON TERRITORY, 87–523, 86–524, 85–526
Yurchenko, Vitaly: President, 86–446; Russia, 86–464

Z

Zaccaro, John A.: Ferraro, Geraldine A., 85–317; New York City, 87–408
Zaire: Africa, 87–181, 86–183, 85–179
Zakharov, Gennadi F.: Russia, 87–462
Zambia: Africa, 87–181, 86–183, 85–179
ZANU-PF (Zimbabwe African National Union-Patriotic Front): Zimbabwe, 87–524, 86–524, 85–526
Zero-age rock: ocean, 87–424
Zhivkov, Todor: Bulgaria, 87–235, 85–226
Zia-ul-Haq, Mohammad: Pakistan, 87–428, 86–430, 85–435
ZIMBABWE, 87–523, 86–524, 85–526; Africa, 87–181, 86–183, 85–179
ZOOLOGY, 87–524, 86–525, 85–527
ZOOS, 87–525, 86–525, 85–528; zoo design, Special Report, 87–48
Zurbriggen, Pirmin: skiing, 87–468, 86–469

Acknowledgments

The publishers acknowledge the following sources for illustrations. Credits read from top to bottom, left to right, on their respective pages. An asterisk (*) denotes illustrations and photographs that are the exclusive property of THE YEAR BOOK. All maps, charts, and diagrams were prepared by THE YEAR BOOK staff unless otherwise noted.

9	Bruce Davidson, Magnum
10	AP/Wide World
12	Gamma/Liaison; Sygma
13	Pamela Price, Picture Group; Peter Turnley, Black Star
14	Andy Hernandez, Sygma; Patrick Durand, Sygma
15	Bruce Davidson, Magnum
16	Allen Tannebaum, Sygma
17	Terry Orban, Sygma; Jerry Bergman, Picture Group
18	Ben Martin, *Time* Magazine; Gamma/Liaison
19	Focus on Sports; Bob Penn; © 1986 Twentieth Century Fox Film Corporation. All rights reserved.
20	Focus on Sports; AP/Wide World
21	AP/Wide World; Robin Moyer, *Time* Magazine; Tass from Sovfoto
22	AP/Wide World; J. L. Atlan, Sygma; Focus on Sports
23	Focus on Sports; Jacques Pavlovsky, Sygma; Novosti Press from Gamma/Liaison
24	P. Martin-Morice, Sygma; *Minneapolis Star and Tribune;* Dennis Brack, Black Star; Tom Ebenhoh, Black Star
25	Koni Nordmann, Contact Press; J. L. Altan, Sygma; Onze, Sygma
26	Christopher Norris, Black Star; Peter Turnley, Black Star
27	Andy Hernandez, Sygma; Terry Orban, Sygma; Francois Duhamel, Sygma
28	Patrick Durand, Sygma; Jacques Pavlovsky, Sygma; R. Gaillarde, Gamma/Liaison
29	Sygma; T. Graham, Sygma; Adam J. Stoltman, Duomo
30	Jacques Gardin, Sygma; Claude Urraca, Sygma
31	A. Nogues, Sygma
33	Robert Frerck*
34	Tom Herzberg*
38	Harold Flecknoe; Central Intelligence Agency
40	Culver; Culver; UPI/Bettmann Newsphotos
41	Central Intelligence Agency; AP/Wide World; © 1961 The New York Times Company. Reprinted by permission.
42	Bob Adelman, *Time* Magazine
43	*Time* Magazine; Stanley Tretick, Sygma
44	Movie Still Archive
45	Wally McNamee, *Newsweek;* Laurent Maous, Gamma/Liaison
46	Doug Menuez, Picture Group
48	Alfred B. Thomas, Animals Animals
52	Sea World; Tim Fuller, Arizona Sonora Desert Museum; Tim Fuller, Arizona Sonora Desert Museum; Robert Frerck*
53	Tom Cajacob, Minnesota Zoo
54	Annie Griffiths
55	Franz Lanting
56	Robert Frerck*; Annie Griffiths
57	New York Zoological Society; Treehouse Zoo, Philadelphia
58	Alice Dole*; Robert Frerck*
59	New York Zoological Society; Harry De Zitter
61	Robert Frerck*
62	Point Defiance Zoo and Aquarium
64	Culver; A. Hubrich, H. Armstrong Roberts
67	Joe Rogers*
68	The Blanchard Collection from Associated Features; The Wimbledon Lawn Tennis Museum; Culver; Culver; UPI/Bettmann Newsphotos; AP/Wide World; Nancy Graham-Stowe, National Ski Hall of Fame
69	AP/Wide World; International Swimming Hall of Fame; UPI/Bettmann Newsphotos; Focus on Sports; Focus on Sports; *Powerlifting USA* Magazine; AP/Wide World
71	A. Hubrich, H. Armstrong Roberts; © Marty Heitner, Taurus
72-74	Joe Rogers*
76	© Michael P. Manheim from Marilyn Gartman; Camerique from H. Armstrong Roberts; © Terry McKoy, Taurus
77	Tony Duffy, All-Sport; Tony Duffy, All-Sport; Michael King, All-Sport
78	National Archives
79	*Signing of the Constitution* (1860's), an oil painting on canvas by Thomas Rossiter; Independence National Historical Park Collection, Philadelphia
86	Bob Addison*
100	Gordon Anderson
103	Thomas Kitchin, Tom Stack & Assoc.
104	Gordon Anderson; Dan Budnick, Woodfin Camp, Inc.
105	Laurance Aiuppy; Dewitt Jones
106	Travelpix from FPG; Dewitt Jones
108	Jerg Kroener, Reflexion
112	Daniel J. Cox; Dewitt Jones; Rick McIntyre, Tom Stack & Assoc.
113	Dan Budnick, Woodfin Camp, Inc.
114	Brian Parker, Tom Stack & Assoc.
116-127	Phill Renaud*
128	Phill Renaud*; © Lee Balterman from Marilyn Gartman
130-131	Vatican Museums
133	Nippon Television Network-Tokyo/Vatican Museums; Buonarroti Archive, Florence, Italy
134-136	Vatican Museums
137	Cathy Miller
138	Soprintendenza ai Monumenti, Milan, Italy
139	Soprintendenza per i beni Artistici e, Storici, Milan, Italy
140	Pinin Brambilla Barcilon
141	Soprintendenza per i beni Artistici e Storici, Milan, Italy; Olivetti, Milan, Italy
142	Soprintendenza per i beni Artistici e Storici, Milan, Italy
144	Sergio Dorantes, Gamma/Liaison
148	© Robert Frerck
151	Tony O'Brien, Picture Group; © Robert Frerck
152	Chuck O'Rear, Woodfin Camp, Inc.; Sergio Dorantes, Gamma/Liaison
155	R. Gaillarde, Gamma/Liaison
156	Robert Frerck, Woodfin Camp, Inc.
160	Alice F. Dole*; Library of Congress
161	Alice F. Dole*; Newberry Library, Chicago; Granger Collection; Newberry Library, Chicago
163	C. S. Fly, Museum of New Mexico
164	Newberry Library, Chicago; George Meany Memorial Archives
165	Sears, Roebuck & Co.
166	Alice F. Dole*; Bradley Smith; Newberry Library, Chicago; Drawing by Reginald B. Birch from *Little Lord Fauntleroy* by Frances Hodgson Burnett © 1894 Frederick Warne and Company; Newberry Library, Chicago
167	U.S. Geological Survey; Provincial Archives of British Columbia, Canada
170	© Edmund Engleman
173	UPI/Bettmann Newsphotos
174	AP/Wide World; © 1986 Chicago Tribune Company. All rights reserved. Used with permission
175	© Leonard Andrews; AP/Wide World
176	Transamerica Corporation
178	Reuters/Bettmann Newsphotos
182	AP/Wide World
184	Greig Reekie, *The Calgary Sun*
187	William Campbell, *Time* Magazine
188	UPI/Bettmann Newsphotos
189	AP/Wide World
190	© Justin Kerr
192	Jonathan Player, NYT Pictures
193	Reuters/Bettmann Newsphotos
194-196	AP/Wide World
197	© Leonard Andrews
198	Jack Manning, NYT Pictures
199	Tass from Sovfoto
200	Chris Morris, Black Star
203	AP/Wide World
205	California Institute of Technology
206	Jet Propulsion Laboratory
207	*Canberra Times*
209	AP/Wide World
210	Rob Nelson, Picture Group
212	Cartoon Features Syndicate
213	AP/Wide World
215	UPI/Bettmann Newsphotos
216-218	AP/Wide World
220-223	UPI/Bettmann Newsphotos
227	Myron Daniels, Massachusetts General Hospital
228	AP/Wide World
232	Jose R. Lopez, NYT Pictures
233	Canapress
234	Ray Stanyard, Figg & Muller Engineers
236	Paul Conklin
240	Trudy Rogers*
242	Jerry Bauer, McClelland and Stewart Ltd.

A Preview of 1987

January

					1	2	3
4	5	6	7	8	9	10
11	12	13	14	15	16	17
18	19	20	21	22	23	24
25	26	27	28	29	30	31

1 **New Year's Day.**

5 **Twelfth Night,** traditional end of Christmas festivities during the Middle Ages.

6 **Epiphany,** 12th day of Christmas, celebrates the visit of the Three Wise Men to the infant Jesus.

19 **Martin Luther King, Jr., Day,** honoring the slain civil rights leader, is celebrated on the third Monday in January, according to law. The actual anniversary of his birth is January 15.

25 **Super Bowl XXI,** the National Football League's championship game, in Pasadena, Calif.

26 **Australia Day** marks Captain Arthur Phillip's landing in 1788 where Sydney now stands.

29 **Chinese New Year** begins year 4685, the Year of the Hare, on the ancient Chinese calendar.

February

1	2	3	4	5	6	7
8	9	10	11	12	13	14
15	16	17	18	19	20	21
22	23	24	25	26	27	28

1 **Black History Month** through February 28.

2 **Ground-Hog Day.** Legend says six weeks of winter weather will follow if the ground hog sees its shadow.
  Candlemas, Roman Catholic holy day, commemorates the presentation of the infant Jesus in the Temple.

8 **Boy Scouts of America Birthday Anniversary** marks the founding of the organization in 1910.

12 **Abraham Lincoln's Birthday,** observed in most states.

13 **Friday the 13th,** widely believed to be an unlucky day. Also March 13 and November 13.

14 **Valentine's Day,** festival of romance and affection.
  Tu B'Shebat, Jewish arbor festival, observed by donating trees to Israel.

16 **George Washington's Birthday,** according to law, is celebrated on the third Monday in February. The actual anniversary is February 22.

March

1	2	3	4	5	6	7
8	9	10	11	12	13	14
15	16	17	18	19	20	21
22	23	24	25	26	27	28
29	30	31				

1-31 **Red Cross Month.**

3 **Mardi Gras,** celebrated in New Orleans and many Roman Catholic countries, is the last merrymaking before Lent.

4 **Ash Wednesday,** first day of Lent for Christians, begins the period of repentance that precedes Easter.

8-14 **Girl Scout Week** marks the group's 75th birthday.

15 **Purim,** Jewish festival commemorating how Esther saved the Jews from the tyrant Haman.

15-22 **Camp Fire Birthday Week** marks the 77th anniversary of the group.

17 **St. Patrick's Day,** honoring the patron saint of Ireland.

19 **St. Joseph's Day,** Roman Catholic feast day honoring the husband of the Virgin Mary.

20 **First Day of Spring,** 10:52 P.M. E.S.T.

30 **Academy Awards Night,** when the Academy of Motion Picture Arts and Sciences presents the Oscars.

April

			1	2	3	4
5	6	7	8	9	10	11
12	13	14	15	16	17	18
19	20	21	22	23	24	25
26	27	28	29	30		

1 **April Fool's Day,** a traditional day for jokes and tricks.

5 **Daylight-Saving Time** begins at 2 A.M.

5-11 **National Library Week.**

12 **Palm Sunday** marks Jesus Christ's last entry into Jerusalem, where people covered His path with palm branches.

14 **Passover,** Jewish festival that celebrates the exodus of the Jews from bondage in Egypt.

15 **Income Tax Day** in the United States.

16 **Maundy Thursday,** Christian celebration of Christ's commandment to love others.

17 **Good Friday** marks the death of Jesus on the cross. It is a public holiday in many countries and several states of the United States.

19 **Easter Sunday,** commemorating the Resurrection of Jesus Christ.

22 **Professional Secretaries Day** acknowledges the contributions of secretaries in business, government, and other fields.

May

					1	2
3	4	5	6	7	8	9
10	11	12	13	14	15	16
17	18	19	20	21	22	23
24	25	26	27	28	29	30
31						

1 **May Day,** observed as a festival of spring in many countries and as a holiday honoring workers in socialist and Communist countries.
  Law Day U.S.A. emphasizes the importance of law in American life.

2 **Kentucky Derby,** thoroughbred horse race at Churchill Downs in Louisville, Ky.

3-9 **National Music Week.**

10 **Mother's Day.**

16 **Armed Forces Day** honors all branches of the armed forces in the United States.

18 **Victoria Day,** in Canada, marks the official birthday of the reigning monarch.

24 **Rogation Sunday,** fifth Sunday after Easter, when Roman Catholics bring their animals to church for a special blessing.

25 **Memorial Day,** by law, is the last Monday in May.

28 **Ascension Day,** or Holy Thursday, 40 days after Easter, celebrates the ascent of Jesus Christ into heaven.

June

	1	2	3	4	5	6
7	8	9	10	11	12	13
14	15	16	17	18	19	20
21	22	23	24	25	26	27
28	29	30				

1 **Stratford Festival** of drama through November 1 in Stratford, Canada.

3 **Shavuot,** Jewish Feast of Weeks, marks the revealing of the Ten Commandments to Moses on Mount Sinai.

6 **D-Day** commemorates the Allied landing in Normandy in 1944, during World War II.

7 **Pentecost,** or Whitsunday, the seventh Sunday after Easter, commemorates the descent of the Holy Spirit upon the 12 disciples.

14 **Trinity Sunday,** the eighth Sunday after Easter, honors the union of the Father, Son, and Holy Spirit.
  Flag Day.

21 **Father's Day.**
  First Day of Summer, 6:11 P.M. E.D.T.

22 **All-England (Wimbledon) Tennis Championship,** through July 5 in Wimbledon, near London.

July

		1	2	3	4	
5	6	7	8	9	10	11
12	13	14	15	16	17	18
19	20	21	22	23	24	25
26	27	28	29	30	31	

1 **Canada Day,** in Canada, celebrates the Confederation of the provinces in 1867.

2 **Halfway Point of 1987,** when the year is half over.

4 **Independence Day,** in the United States, the anniversary of the day on which the Continental Congress adopted the Declaration of Independence in 1776.

14 **Bastille Day,** in France, commemorates the uprising of the people of Paris against King Louis XVI in 1789 and their seizure of the Bastille, a hated Paris prison.
Baseball All-Star Game, Oakland, Calif.

15 **St. Swithin's Day.** According to legend, if it rains on this day, it will rain for 40 more.

25 **Puerto Rico Constitution Day.**

August

						1
2	3	4	5	6	7	8
9	10	11	12	13	14	15
16	17	18	19	20	21	22
23	24	25	26	27	28	29
30	31					

4 **Tishah B'Ab,** Jewish holy day, marks the destruction of the first and second temples in Jerusalem in 587 B.C. and A.D. 70.

6 **Hiroshima Day,** memorial observance for victims of the first atomic bombing in Hiroshima, Japan, in 1945.

6-9 **Professional Golfers' Association of America Championship,** Palm Beach Gardens, Fla.

7-23 **Pan American Games,** competition by amateur athletes from North and South America, in Indianapolis.

10-30 **Edinburgh International Festival** of music, dance, and theater in Edinburgh, Scotland.

11-13 **Perseid Meteor Shower.**

15 **Feast of the Assumption,** Roman Catholic and Eastern Orthodox holy day, celebrates the ascent of the Virgin Mary into heaven.

19 **National Aviation Day** commemorates the birthday of pioneer pilot Orville Wright in 1871.

26 **Women's Equality Day** commemorates the enactment of the 19th Amendment in 1920 giving women the vote.

September

		1	2	3	4	5
6	7	8	9	10	11	12
13	14	15	16	17	18	19
20	21	22	23	24	25	26
27	28	29	30			

7 **Labor Day** in the United States and Canada.

13 **National Grandparents Day** honors grandfathers and grandmothers.

15-16 **Mexico Independence Days.**

17 **Citizenship Day** celebrates the rights and duties of U.S. citizens.

23 **First Day of Fall,** 9:45 A.M. E.D.T.

24 **Rosh Ha-Shanah,** or Jewish New Year, beginning the year 5748 according to the Jewish calendar.

25 **Native American Day** honors American Indians.

27 **Gold Star Mother's Day** honors mothers who lost sons in World Wars I and II, the Korean War, and the Vietnam War.

30 **End of the Fiscal Year** for the United States government.

October

				1	2	3
4	5	6	7	8	9	10
11	12	13	14	15	16	17
18	19	20	21	22	23	24
25	26	27	28	29	30	31

3 **Yom Kippur,** or Day of Atonement, the most solemn day in the Jewish calendar.

4-10 **National 4-H Week.**

5 **Child Health Day.**

8 **Sukkot,** or Feast of Tabernacles, begins—eight-day Jewish festival that originally marked the harvest season.

11 **Pulaski Day** honors Casimir Pulaski, Polish general who fought in the Revolutionary War in America.

12 **Columbus Day** commemorates Christopher Columbus' landing in America in 1492.
Thanksgiving Day in Canada.

13 **Baseball's World Series** begins.

16 **Simhat Torah,** Jewish festival of rejoicing in God's law, end of the annual cycle of Scripture readings.

17 **Sweetest Day,** when sweethearts exchange cards and gifts.

25 **Standard Time Resumes** at 2 A.M.

31 **Halloween.**
United Nations Children's Fund (UNICEF) Day.
Reformation Day, celebrated by Protestants, marks the day in 1517 when Reformation leader Martin Luther posted his Ninety-Five Theses.

November

1	2	3	4	5	6	7
8	9	10	11	12	13	14
15	16	17	18	19	20	21
22	23	24	25	26	27	28
29	30					

1 **All Saints' Day,** observed by the Roman Catholic Church.

5 **Guy Fawkes Day,** in Great Britain, marks the failure of a plot to blow up King James I and Parliament in 1605.

11 **Veterans Day** in the United States. Remembrance Day in Canada.

15-21 **American Education Week.**

16-22 **National Children's Book Week.**

22-29 **National Bible Week,** an interfaith drive to promote reading and study of the Bible.

26 **Thanksgiving Day** in the United States.

29 **Advent** begins, first of the four Sundays in the season before Christmas.

30 **St. Andrew's Day,** feast day of the patron saint of Scotland.

December

		1	2	3	4	5
6	7	8	9	10	11	12
13	14	15	16	17	18	19
20	21	22	23	24	25	26
27	28	29	30	31		

6 **St. Nicholas Day,** when children in many European countries receive gifts.

10 **Nobel Prize Ceremony** in Stockholm, Sweden.
Human Rights Day marks the anniversary of the adoption of the Universal Declaration of Human Rights in 1948.

13 **St. Lucia Day,** in Sweden, celebrates the return of light after the darkest time of the year.

15 **Bill of Rights Day** in the United States marks the ratification of that document in 1791.

16 **Hanukkah,** or Feast of Lights, eight-day Jewish festival that celebrates the defeat of the Syrian tyrant King Antiochus IV in 165 B.C., through December 24.

22 **First Day of Winter,** 4:46 A.M. E.S.T.

24 **Christmas Eve.**

25 **Christmas Day.**

26 **Kwanzaa,** black American holiday based on a traditional African harvest festival, through January 1.
Boxing Day, holiday in Canada and Great Britain when mail carriers and others who perform services receive Christmas boxes.

31 **New Year's Eve.**

World Book Encyclopedia, Inc., offers a line of related products including The Letter People, a reading readiness program for preschoolers, and an attractive wooden bookrack for displaying *The World Book Encyclopedia*. For further information, write WORLD BOOK ENCYCLOPEDIA, INC., P.O. Box 3405, Chicago, Illinois 60654.